STATESMEN WHO
CHANGED THE WORLD

Statesmen Who Changed the World

A BIO-BIBLIOGRAPHICAL DICTIONARY OF DIPLOMACY

Edited by
Frank W. Thackeray
and
John E. Findling

Greenwood Press
Westport, Connecticut • London

Library of Congress Cataloging-in-Publication Data

Statesmen who changed the world : a bio-bibliographical dictionary of
diplomacy / edited by Frank W. Thackeray and John E. Findling.
    p.   cm.
    Includes bibliographical references and index.
    ISBN 0–313–27380–4 (alk. paper)
    1. Statesmen—Biography. 2. Diplomats—Biography. 3. Kings and
rulers—Biography. 4. World politics—Bio-bibliography.
I. Thackeray, Frank W. II. Findling, John E.
D108.S73 1993
909.08′0922—dc20
  [B]   92–14616

British Library Cataloguing in Publication Data is available.

Library of Congress Catalog Card Number: 92–14616
ISBN: 0–313–27380–4

First published in 1993

Greenwood Press, 88 Post Road West, Westport, CT 06881
An imprint of Greenwood Publishing Group, Inc.

Printed in the United States of America

The paper used in this book complies with the
Permanent Paper Standard issued by the National
Information Standards Organization (Z39.48–1984).

10 9 8 7 6 5 4 3 2 1

CONTENTS

PREFACE

This book, which contains bio-bibliographical essays on more than sixty statesmen of the modern Western world, is designed to serve two purposes. First, for
each subject, the author has provided a reasonably thorough and insightful biographical sketch covering the subject's life and career, with particular emphasis
on his or her involvement in international affairs. Second, each author has written
a bibliographical essay for his or her subject, describing the archival materials
available for the individual, works written by and about the individual, and the
most recent scholarship related to the individual and his or her work and influence.
For easy reference, we have also included a bibliography with complete citations
at the end of each essay. Following the essays are five appendixes that provide
additional information useful to the reader. Four of these appendixes are glos-
saries of names and terms mentioned but not fully explained in the essays.
Reference to the brief biographical sketches or explanations of events, organizations, treaties, and diplomatic or political terms will help the reader understand
the main essays more completely. The fifth appendix provides a listing of the
royal houses or other governments of the major European states as well as a
listing of U.S. presidents and their secretaries of state. Throughout the book,
subject cross-referencing is indicated by asterisks.

The subjects included in this volume were selected on the basis of our collective
experience teaching and conducting research in U.S. and European diplomatic
history and suggestions from our colleagues and contributors. Of course, any
pair of editors would arrive at a somewhat different lineup, but we believe that
we have assembled a group of subjects that provides balanced and comprehensive
coverage of the major periods in post-Renaissance Western history.

The reader will note that some of the subjects were heads of state, while others
held ministerial positions in the area of foreign relations. We strove to identify
those individuals, regardless of their title or position, who most influenced or
changed the world in which they lived. Thus some of our statesmen, by virtue
of regnal, dictatorial, or constitutional authority, wrought changes as heads of
state, while others did so in the role of foreign minister or secretary of state. A

few subjects were neither heads of state nor foreign ministers but were persons who significantly influenced the world around them through work in an international organization or by formulating an internationally accepted doctrine that altered the way states behaved.

As editors, we wish to acknowledge the help that many people gave us as we assembled this work. Cynthia Harris, our editor at Greenwood Publishing Group, made the initial suggestion for this work and followed it up with constant encouragement. Our major student research assistant, Kathy Theilen, gave us cheerful help at every stage of the project. Louise Elble was particularly helpful in communicating with various authors. Brigette Colligan always had her computer warmed up to take on any word-processing chore and finish it with exemplary promptness. Other valuable clerical help was provided by Mary Ann Braden, Lesley Schulz, Janlea Lackey, Cora MacNabb, Bob Marshall, and Kimberly Pelle. We are grateful to the reference librarians at Indiana University Southeast, especially Nancy Totten, who good-naturedly answered any question, checked any fact, and located any source that we needed. Indiana University Southeast's stable of computer wizards, particularly chief magician Kirk Klaphaak, applied their talents to the manuscript with both unfailing success and unending patience for the uninitiated. And we are grateful to the university also for providing the funding that enabled us to hire the student assistants. In addition, we wish to thank the authors of the essays that make up the body of this book. The vast majority were cooperative and punctual and presented us with interesting and well-written pieces that usually stayed within the word limit. Without them, there would be no book.

Finally, we wish to express our appreciation to our spouses, Kathy Thackeray and Carol Findling, and to our children, Sasha and Max Thackeray and Jamey Findling, who bravely tolerated the demands that books such as this place on families and put up with the weird things that editors do. For that, we are grateful.

STATESMEN WHO
CHANGED THE WORLD

THE DICTIONARY

Dean Gooderham Acheson (1893–1971).   Born on April 11, 1893, into a prominent Connecticut family, Dean Acheson, like many young men of the "American aristocracy," chose law as a profession and as the path to public service. As the rector of Holy Trinity Church in Middletown, Connecticut, and Episcopal bishop of the state, his father, Edward Acheson, brought to the family a trenchant paternalism embodying a strong sense of social order, intellectual discipline, individualism, and a pervasive stoicism. From his mother, Eleanor, a woman of "striking carriage," Acheson acquired his appreciation for status as well as a rich sense of humor.

Acheson's six years at Groton and four at Yale, from which he graduated in 1915, were unremarkable. It was during his four years at Harvard Law School that Acheson experienced an intellectual awakening. Rigorous training in law brought out his incisive and formidable powers of logical analysis and argument. Fostered by a fortuitous association with Felix Frankfurter, Acheson was named to the law review and upon graduation was asked by Justice William Brandeis to be his law clerk.

After earning his law degree and serving a brief tour in the Naval Auxiliary Reserve, Acheson arrived in Washington a young man possessed of great elegance and ambition, harboring few illusions about the world, certain of his principles and code of personal ethics, and driven to overcome what he considered society's pervasive mediocrity and stupidity. In 1921 he joined the law firm of Covington, Burling and Rublee, with which he was to be associated until his retirement as a senior partner in 1964.

Acheson first entered public service in 1933, when he was appointed undersecretary of the treasury in the *Franklin D. Roosevelt administration. A liberal Democrat, Acheson enthusiastically supported Roosevelt's New Deal and foreign policy. As the administration cautiously prepared the nation for war after September 1939, Acheson argued forcibly for intervention in Europe.

In 1941 Acheson was named assistant secretary of state for congressional relations and international agreements. There he was instrumental in gaining congressional approval of the Lend-Lease program. During the six years between mid–1943 and January 1949, when he became secretary of state in the second Truman cabinet, Acheson served under four men at State: as assistant secretary of state under Cordell Hull and Edward Stettinius; and as under-secretary of state to James F. Byrnes and *George C. Marshall, prompting one historian to quip that Acheson was a career appointee.

During the war Acheson provided leadership variously as chairman of the Office of Far Eastern Coordination, the Board of Economic Operations, the Executive Committee on Economic Foreign Policy, the Policy and Coordinating Committee, and the Committee for Economic Foreign Policy in Liberated Areas. Most important, he headed the American delegation that helped establish the short-lived United Nations Relief and Rehabilitation Agency (UNRRA) in November 1943.

Acheson was a driving force behind the creation of the United Nations Food and Agricultural Administration, and he served as U.S. delegate at the UN monetary and financial conference that convened at Bretton Woods, New Hampshire, in July 1944 and established the International Monetary Fund (IMF) and the Reconstruction and Development Bank (World Bank). Overseeing State Department relations with Congress, Acheson prevailed in winning support from isolationist Republican senator Arthur Vandenberg for U.S. membership in the fledgling United Nations in January 1945.

Acheson, like most of Roosevelt's men, had a down-to-earth appreciation for postwar possibilities. He expected that tenuous U.S.-Soviet relations would be sustained, but only if *Joseph Stalin embraced the principles of the Atlantic Charter, Four Freedoms, and Bretton Woods agreements. Those expectations were quickly shattered. The end of World War II confronted the Truman administration with grave challenges.

One immediate issue, after termination of Lend-Lease, was continued aid to Great Britain. Acheson was adamant that the United States reaffirm its "special relationship" with Britain, and his testimony helped persuade Congress to endorse a loan for Britain that laid the basis for a new American relationship with Europe.

Alarmed by aggressive Soviet policies threatening Greece and Turkey in 1945–1946, the Truman administration determined to resist. Because of Britain's inability to defend Western interests in the region, Acheson believed that it was in America's interest to assume expanded responsibilities. He counseled President Truman that the crisis in the eastern Mediterranean and the growing Soviet menace required nothing less than a historic departure in American foreign policy. Acheson drafted the speech that Truman delivered on March 12, 1946, and helped win congressional support for what became known as the Truman Doctrine, which called for unilateral intervention in the internal affairs of nations threatened by communism as well as creation of anti-Soviet alliances to "contain" communism. The free world could prevail by creating "situations of strength," in Acheson's famous phrase, everywhere communism threatened.

Although bearing Secretary George C. Marshall's name, the European Recovery Program, or Marshall Plan, hammered out at the London Conference during the winter of 1947 and enacted by Congress on March 20, 1948, embodied Acheson's analysis of the crisis in Europe and what America's response should be. He was the first administration official to call publicly for massive economic aid to forestall Communist exploitation of economic chaos. Beyond this extraordinary commitment, however, Acheson was not a proponent of foreign aid. His lukewarm support for Truman's pet project (Point Four) revealed his belief that vague economic assistance programs had little tangible value.

Acheson's concern for the new strategic environment created by the advent of nuclear weapons prompted the Acheson-Lilienthal Report, which called for the internationalization of atomic energy, although he rejected sharing nuclear secrets with the Soviet Union. Indeed, when the Soviet Union tested its first nuclear weapon on September 13, 1949, Acheson led the battle to develop the hydrogen bomb.

As the Cold War developed, Acheson's position vis-à-vis the Soviet Union changed from guarded optimism to resolute pessimism. Believing negotiation futile, he counseled aggressive resistance to Stalin's quest for world domination. While financial assistance to Europe was key in Acheson's thinking, he also believed that remobilization and commitment of U.S. military forces were essential. As chairman of the U.S.-Canadian Permanent Joint Defense Board (1947–1948), Acheson ensured that the close wartime relationship was expanded to provide strategic cooperation for defense of North America.

Acheson's principal concern, however, was the defense of Western Europe, and it was here that he made perhaps his most significant contribution. After becoming secretary of state in January 1949, he moved aggressively to bring the United States and Western Europe into the North Atlantic Treaty Organization, an unprecedented military alliance. The creation of NATO dramatically realized Acheson's strategic-diplomatic design. At home his persuasive skill again overcame objections of isolationist senators in the Vandenberg Resolution, which assured congressional support for the alliance and for the Mutual Defense Assistance Act (September 1949). Abroad he reassured skeptical allies, divided and fearful particularly of a rearmed Germany, and harmonized interests with his British counterparts, Ernest Bevin and Sir Anthony Eden, and French foreign ministers *Robert Schuman and René Pleven. He used his friendship with Canadian Foreign Minister *Lester Pearson to persuade *Winston Churchill to accept a reduced British role in postwar arrangements. Finally, his success in negotiating a peaceful end to the Berlin Blockade in May 1949 without concessions to Stalin further encouraged Allied cooperation.

With Senate ratification of the North Atlantic Treaty, a grateful President Truman acknowledged, ''There would have been no NATO without Dean Acheson.'' However, Acheson did not shrink from challenging the president on occasion. He moderated Truman's personal antipathy for the Franco regime in Spain in the interest of strengthening NATO and argued in hearings before

Congress for a position that was, as always, utilitarian. Likewise, he demonstrated his "realism" by persuading idealogues in Congress and the administration to assist the Communist regime of *Josip Broz Tito in Yugoslavia.

Undoubtedly Acheson's most difficult challenge came in the Far East. In October 1949, Communist forces defeated the Nationalist government of Chiang Kai-shek, declared the People's Republic of China, and precipitated the establishment of a rival Chinese government on Formosa, to which Acheson subsequently pledged U.S. support and protection. Then, in June 1950, North Korean forces crossed the 38th Parallel to begin the Korean War.

In his famous "Press Club" speech in January 1949, Acheson was interpreted to have suggested that Korea lay outside America's defense perimeter, and in August the State Department felt compelled to issue a white paper to explain American policy in China. Acheson's analysis of Far Eastern questions reflected wholly realistic assessments of the limitations of American power. Still, he was condemned for "losing" China by his "do nothing policies," and for having encouraged North Korea.

Acheson's response to these attacks and to the crisis in Korea was the model of diplomatic conduct. Believing the invasion to be Kremlin-inspired and symptomatic of a global Communist movement, he strongly endorsed military intervention, fought for collective UN sanctions, wrote Truman's message to a special session of Congress which secured bipartisan support for the "police action," and worked closely with the Defense Department for the quick deployment of General Douglas MacArthur's forces from Japan. In due course, he supported the decision to attack across the 38th Parallel, rejected the possibility of a Chinese military response, and backed the UN resolution for a unified Korea. Throughout the crisis his deft handling of Congress and his close relationship with Marshall, now secretary of defense, added important stability and cohesion.

Acheson believed that a quick, victorious end to the war in the Far East was critical for preserving NATO in Europe and for lessening the chance of a wider conflict. He firmly backed President Truman's removal of MacArthur from command despite its political repercussions. During the MacArthur hearings in May 1951, Acheson presented a masterful and exhaustive defense of the administration's Far Eastern policy. Although initially skeptical of armistice negotiations, he worked closely with the Defense Department to establish a cease-fire line and to formulate a framework for the repatriation of prisoners of war. The war would be ended by the Eisenhower administration, but Acheson was instrumental in establishing the Armistice Commission and the basis for a negotiated end to hostilities.

Korea fundamentally reordered U.S. foreign policy. Acheson dominated the early years of the National Security Council (NSC), established by Congress in the National Defense Act of 1947 as the executive advisory body to the president. Charged with formulating long-range strategic objectives and short-term policy response, the NSC wrote analyses and recommendations that were to become the blueprint for massive military rearmament and global commitment.

Acheson's other major contributions were the peace treaty with Japan and the dramatic reversal of policy toward Southeast Asia, both precipitated by the Korean War. Although the Japanese treaty was negotiated by *John Foster Dulles as a bipartisan gesture, Acheson was its driving force. The positioning of Japan as an American surrogate in the Pacific was soon complemented by defense treaties with the Philippines and with Australia and New Zealand.

The Korean War also set in motion far-reaching changes for the U.S. role in Southeast Asia. Acheson's "vague" ideas on the region were sharpened, and his previous opposition to French colonialism was tempered. Acheson defined the "fall" of China, Korea, and Vietnamese nationalism in terms of French support for NATO and fear of the "domino effect" a Communist victory would entail. Thus he acquiesced in backing the French war against the Viet Minh after the North Korean invasion, viewing Korea and Indochina as one war. Indeed, he was convinced of explicit linkage among the various issues that now confronted the United States. He cautioned against becoming involved in another ground war in the region—"no more Koreas"—but he was adamant that the United States, in concert with the Allies, must oppose all Communist aggression. As a result, the Truman administration supported the French colonial regime of Bao Dai. Acheson believed that the United States must accept the lesser of two evils in pursuit of larger objectives. Thus he helped create the rationale that guided the administrations of Eisenhower, Kennedy, Johnson, and *Nixon in prosecuting the war in Vietnam.

Acheson left the State Department in January 1953. Until his death in 1971, Acheson remained active in foreign affairs matters as a public speaker, author, and presidential advisor. He remained concerned primarily with Europe and the Soviet Union and largely neglected other areas as he had done while secretary. Indeed, these preoccupations left him vulnerable to criticism that he missed opportunities to set policy direction for Africa, Latin America, and, to a lesser extent, the Middle East.

There his attempts had been to strike a delicate balance between support for the new Jewish state of Israel and its Arab neighbors in the Tripartite Declaration. In this policy he again opposed Truman's pro-Zionist bias and forcefully pressured Britain on the issue of Egyptian nationalism and its colonial interests. As in Indochina, Acheson showed a clear preference for policy in support of colonial powers where American interests outweighed other considerations.

During the second Berlin crisis (1958–1961) Acheson condemned the Eisenhower-Dulles "New Look" strategy, which he believed had left the United States vulnerable to Soviet intimidation. Still, he urged President Kennedy to stand firm whatever the risk of war. This same hard-line advice was offered during the Cuban Missile Crisis of October 1962, when he urged Kennedy to authorize air strikes against the missile sites. Above all he counseled the president that he must convince Nikita Khrushchev that the United States would never accept the presence of missiles in Cuba or such threats to American security.

Vietnam confronted Acheson with particularly difficult dilemmas. Abandoning his earlier reservations about military involvement, he reassured Lyndon Johnson that the war was a ''necessary and inevitable price of America's role in the world.'' However, in the aftermath of the Tet offensive (January 1968), his views changed dramatically. As head of a senior advisory group he confronted Johnson with evidence that the war was unwinnable, that he was being deceived by his civilian and military advisors, and that the United States must withdraw.

Perhaps fittingly, one of his last policy contributions was testimony before Congress that was instrumental in defeating the Mansfield Amendment calling for substantial reductions of American military commitment to NATO. An admiring President Nixon reassured Acheson that he had thus not only been present at the creation but at the ''resurrection.'' Dean Acheson died of a stroke at his beloved Sandy Springs, Maryland, farm on October 12, 1971.

In demeanor and language in dealing with others, Acheson was often abrasive, uncompromising, imperious, and condescending. He had a compulsion for order, ethical certainty, and a logical, rational mastery of any question or negotiation. He especially relished grappling with intractable problems. He was well known for his policy disagreements within the administration and his impatience with mediocrity, ''sloppy'' abstraction, misplaced moralism, and idealism. Because his personality was the antithesis of that expected from a diplomat, Acheson was uniquely suited for complementing the personality and views of his superior, Harry Truman, and for matching obdurate Soviet diplomacy. Above all it was this fortuitous combination that gave Truman era foreign policy such cohesion and unswerving direction.

Acheson's personal views often clashed with his public conduct. Disdainful of imagery and public diplomacy, he had little respect for Congress or its role in foreign policy, did not like the State Department, and did not place much faith in the UN. These contradictions caused Acheson no difficulty and, indeed, he used them to his advantage. He did not shrink from making enemies, provoking respect and animosity in equal measure.

Acheson alone did not introduce new ideas or policies, but he espoused an alluring global view and strategic objectives with unmatched erudition. Only *George Kennan approached (some would claim surpassed) him in this regard. What is undeniable is that his diplomacy inspired psychological and political change in Western Europe without which its postwar recovery would have been impossible.

His greatest success was in formulating the strategic design to meet the challenges of communism in Europe; his securing of Allied support for NATO and the Truman Doctrine were remarkable accomplishments. At home he was extremely successful in compelling support for American initiatives in the UN, in winning backing for his policies in Congress, and in his leadership in the State Department. Failure is more difficult to assess because judgment in part requires speculation about alternative policies and outcomes that cannot be known.

Of less relative importance, but personally most frustrating, was his failure to secure approval of the European Defense Community (EDC) before he left office. Certainly, in Acheson's support of the war in Korea and the decision to attack across the 38th Parallel and advance to the Yalu, he failed to understand or to give credence to China's warning with the same clarity that characterized his decisions in Europe. Moreover, his misperception of the nature of the conflict in Indochina and his decision to support the French was, given America's subsequent experience, a fateful one. These lapses can be attributed in part to the distraction of Europe and his predisposition to view developments there as more important to U.S. interests.

His preoccupation with a monolithic communism led him to elevate peripheral matters to vital interests, which blurred important distinctions and nuances and led to policy errors. Whether a willingness to negotiate with Stalin would have brought the United States closer to its objectives in Europe and made the Cold War a less dangerous confrontation can never be known with certainty. Only Soviet archives might provide such answers. What is incontrovertible is that neither Acheson nor Truman did anything to dissipate the "reciprocal, reinforcing imagery" of fear, suspicion, and uncertainty.

Whether this policy of diplomatic confrontation and hard-line realism unnecessarily deepened and prolonged a half-century of shattered peace and misjudged the forces of history in the wake of communism's internal collapse can only be speculative. Certainly the dangers and possibilities appeared far different in 1946 than forty-five years later. For that half-century humankind avoided a third world war, albeit at incalculable costs in obsessive militarism, squandered human and fiscal resources, and possibilities deferred.

Annotated Bibliography

There are several important archival sources on Acheson. The Truman Library, Independence, Missouri, contains the Dean Acheson Papers (Acheson's official papers and letters as secretary of state) as well as the Dean Acheson Oral History Seminars on the State Department Years (Harriman, Nitze), Princeton University, 1952–1953, microfilm collection; Acheson's personal papers, Sterling Library, Yale University; and Dean Acheson Oral History Collection, 1964, John F. Kennedy Library, Boston, Massachusetts.

During his lifetime Dean Acheson authored eight books, numerous scholarly and popular articles, public addresses, editorials, and lectures. His most highly praised book, *Present at the Creation: My Years in the State Department* (1969), won a Pulitzer Prize and is an extremely important personal and political memoir and perhaps the best account of Truman era foreign policy. Among his other books, *A Democrat Looks at His Party* (1955) and *A Citizen Looks at Congress* (1957) offer insights into Acheson's often acerbic views on political parties, Congress, and public opinion. *Power and Diplomacy* (1958) presents a series of four William L. Clayton lectures Acheson gave at the Fletcher School of Law and Diplomacy, in which he discussed international relations in the nuclear age, the strategy of limited war and flexible response, and the importance of NATO. In *Sketches from Life of Men I Have Known* (1961), Acheson discusses with candor and humor the personalities and views of prominent statesmen with whom he interacted. Among his last books, *Morning and Noon* (1965) is an intimate memoir completed through 1941, while *Fragments of My Fleece* (1971) and, posthumously, *Grapes and Thorns* (1972) are collected essays by Acheson on foreign policy and other subjects. Also of interest are the collected articles and speeches published by David Acheson as *This Vast External Realm* (1973), which is a useful supplement to *Present at the Creation*. The collection of Acheson's public statements by McGeorge Bundy, ed., *The Pattern of Responsibility* (1952), is also enlightening.

There are additional government sources that one must consult in any study of Acheson or the period: U.S., Congress, Senate, Foreign Relations Committee, *Reviews of World Situations: 1949–1950, Historical Series* (1974), 81st Cong., 1st and 2nd sess., 1949–1951; U.S., Congress, Senate, Committee on Foreign Relations and Committee on Armed Services, Hearing: *Military Situation in the Far East*, 81st Cong. 2nd sess., 1951; U.S. Department of State, *The State Department Policy and Planning Staff Papers, 1947–1949*, 3 vols. (1983); U.S. State Department, *Foreign Relations of the United States*, published annually with special supplements; *U.S. Relations with China with Special Reference to the Period 1944–1949* (1951); and Council on Foreign Relations, *The U.S. in World Affairs, Annual Survey for the Years from 1949 to 1953*. Useful as specialized studies are Acheson, Lilienthal, McCloy, et al., *A Report on the International Control of Atomic Energy* (March 17, 1946); Stephen L. Reardon, *History of the Office of the Secretary of Defense: The Formative Years, 1947–1950* (1984); and State, War, Navy Coordinating Committee Subcommittee, "Information Paper on U.S. Aid to Greece" (March 4, 1947), prepared for Dean Acheson.

Anyone interested in Truman-Acheson foreign policy (and the history of American foreign relations generally) must first consult the indispensable reference edited by Richard Dean Burns, *Guide to American Foreign Relations Since 1700* (1983), an exhaustive bibliographical and annotated resource. One should also see "Index to *Diplomatic History*, vols. 1–14," Mark M. Dodge, comp., *Diplomatic History* 15, 1 (Winter 1991): 137–166. Useful discussions of the historiographical debate and the various schools of thought are Charles S. Maier, "Revisionism and the Interpretations of Cold War Origins," *Perspectives in American History* 4 (1970), and Lloyd Gardner, Hans Morganthau, and Arthur Schlesinger, Jr., *Origins of the Cold War* (1970). For additional informative and useful discussions see Douglas Little, "Crackpot Realists and Other Heroes: The Rise and Fall of the Postwar American Diplomatic Elite," *Diplomatic History* 13, 1 (Winter 1989); Geir Lundestad, "Moralism, Presentism, Exceptionalism, Provincialism, and Other Extravagances in the American Interpretations of the Early Cold War Years," *Diplomatic History* 13, 4 (Fall 1989); and Robert J. McMahon, "The Cold War in Asia: Toward a New Synthesis," *Diplomatic History* 12, 3 (Summer 1988).

Among the dozens of books and monographic studies that assess Truman era foreign affairs are Ray Baldwin, *Reminiscences from Middletown* (1969), which discusses Acheson's early life; Coral Bell, *Negotiation from Strength: A Study of the Policy of Power* (1963), an appraisal of Acheson and Dulles that views their policies as identical but equally unfortunate; Norman A. Graeber, ed., *An Uncertain Tradition: America's Secretaries of State in the Twentieth Century* (1961), the first supportive analysis of Acheson; Lloyd C. Gardner, *Architects of Illusion: Men and Ideas in American Foreign Policy, 1941–1949* (1970), a highly critical account of Acheson's hard-line, confrontational tenure; David Halberstam, *The Best and the Brightest* (1972), a much discussed book that offers a scathing indictment of Acheson and other key policy makers; Walter Isaacson and Evan Thomas, *The Wise Men: Six Friends and the World They Made* (1986), an impressionistic but thorough analysis of policy issues and personalities, and the interaction between elites in the foreign policy establishment; E. J. Kahn, *The China Hands: American*

Foreign Service Officers and What Befell Them (1976), good for discussion of Acheson's later years; Joseph Jones, *The Fifteen Weeks* (1955), a personal narrative by a State Department official of policy development; David S. McLellan and David Acheson, eds., *Among Friends: Personal Letters of Dean Acheson* (1980), offering an enlightening selection of correspondence with Acheson's closest associates and friends. David S. McLellan, *Dean Acheson: The State Department Years* (1976), is the most thorough biography and analysis of Acheson's policies and decisions; Robert H. Ferrell and David S. McLellan, "Dean Acheson: Architect of a Manageable World Order," included in Frank J. Merli and Theodore A. Wilson, eds., *Makers of American Diplomacy from Benjamin Franklin to Henry Kissinger* (1974), is an appraisal that confirms Acheson's success as secretary of state during difficult times; Barry Rubin, *Secrets of State: The State Department and the Struggle over U.S. Foreign Policy* (1985), offers a generally sympathetic verdict, particularly emphasizing Acheson's triumph in elevating the State Department for the first time to its modern policy-making role in government; Gaddis Smith, "Dean Acheson," in Robert Ferrell, ed., *American Secretaries of State and Their Diplomacy*, vol. 16 (1972), is perhaps the best critical assessment of Acheson-Truman policies and of Acheson's decisions. Smith argues that Acheson reacted to events in the context of traditional responses to threats to American security and fear of repeating mistakes of the 1930s. Ronald Steel, *Imperialists and Other Heroes* (1971), is a thoroughly revisionist work that is particularly critical of Acheson's advice during the Cuban Missile Crisis; and Ronald J. Stupak, *The Shaping of Foreign Policy: The Role of the Secretary of State as Seen by Dean Acheson* (1969), focuses on Acheson's philosophy and approach to making foreign policy.

Bibliography

Acheson, David. *This Vast External Realm*. New York: Norton, 1973.
Acheson, Dean Gooderham. *A Citizen Looks at Congress*. New York: Norton, 1957.
———. *A Democrat Looks at His Party*. New York: Harper, 1955.
———. *Fragments of My Fleece*. New York: Norton, 1971.
———. *Grapes and Thorns*. New York: Norton, 1972.
———. *Morning and Noon*. Boston: Houghton Mifflin, 1965.
———. *Power and Diplomacy*. Cambridge, Mass.: Harvard University Press, 1958.
———. *Sketches from Life of Men I Have Known*. New York: Harper, 1961.
Baldwin, Ray. *Reminiscences from Middletown*. Boston: Middlesex County Historical Society, 1969.
Bell, Coral. *Negotiation from Strength: A Study of the Policy of Power*. New York: Knopf, 1963.
Bohlen, Charles E. *Witness to History, 1929–1969*. New York: Norton, 1973.
Bundy, McGeorge, ed. *The Pattern of Responsibility*. Boston: Houghton Mifflin, 1951.
Burns, Richard Dean, ed. *Guide to American Foreign Relations Since 1700*. Santa Barbara, Calif.: Society for Historians of American Foreign Relations, 1983.
Dodge, Mark M., comp. "Index to *Diplomatic History*, vols. 1–14." *Diplomatic History* 15, 1 (Winter 1991): 137–166.
Ferrell, Robert H., and David McLellan. "Dean Acheson: Architect of a Manageable World Order." In *Makers of American Diplomacy from Benjamin Franklin to Henry Kissinger*. Edited by Frank J. Merli and Theodore A. Wilson. New York: Scribner's, 1974.

Gardner, Lloyd. *Architects of Illusion: Men and Ideas in American Foreign Policy, 1941–1949*. Chicago: Quadrangle Books, 1972.

Gardner, Lloyd, Hans Morganthau, and Arthur Schlesinger, Jr. *Origins of the Cold War*. Waltham, Mass.: Ginn, 1970.

Graebner, Norman A., ed. *An Uncertain Tradition: American Secretaries of State in the Twentieth Century*. New York: McGraw-Hill, 1961.

Halberstam, David. *The Best and the Brightest*. New York: Random House, 1972.

Isaacson, Walter, and Evan Thomas. *The Wise Men: Six Friends and the World They Made*. New York: Simon and Schuster, 1986.

Jones, Joseph. *The Fifteen Weeks*. New York: Viking, 1955.

Kahn, E. J. *The China Hands: American Foreign Service Officers and What Befell Them*. New York: Viking, 1976.

Maier, Charles S. "Revisionism and the Interpretations of Cold War Origins." *Perspectives in American History* 4 (1970): 313–347.

McLellan, David S. *Dean Acheson: The State Department Years*. New York: Dodd, Mead, 1976.

McLellan, David S., and David Acheson, eds. *Among Friends: Personal Letters of Dean Acheson*. New York: Dodd, Mead, 1980.

Rubin, Barry. *Secrets of State: The State Department and the Struggle over U.S. Foreign Policy*. New York: Oxford University Press, 1985.

Smith, Gaddis. "Dean Acheson." In *American Secretaries of State and Their Diplomacy*, vol. 16. Edited by R. H. Ferrell. New York: Cooper Square, 1972.

Steel, Ronald. *Imperialists and Other Heroes*. New York: Random House, 1971.

Stupak, Ronald J. *The Shaping of Foreign Policy: The Role of the Secretary of State as Seen by Dean Acheson*. New York: Odyssey Press, 1969.

JONATHAN M. NIELSON

John Quincy Adams (1767–1848).   John Quincy Adams, widely regarded as the greatest U.S. secretary of state, was born in Quincy, Massachusetts, on July 11, 1767. Son of Abigail and John Adams, the nation's preeminent revolutionary couple, John Quincy Adams from his earliest days was groomed to be a statesman and a leader of his country. His parents stressed to young John Quincy that public service and private righteousness were essential to the survival and success of the republican revolution.

Adams's early education consisted of Abigail's homeschooling in the Bible and in the classics. Her constant admonitions instilled in him a faith that a loving God exercised His will in ways that could be discerned by a rational, educated, and moral mind. Adams came to believe that the United States was an agent of divine will and that he was destined to play a major role in the nation's divine mission to remake the world in the image of the American republic. A compelling sense of duty and destiny guided Adams's actions throughout his life.

Adams had the ideal training for a statesman. At age twelve he served abroad as his father's personal secretary during the negotiations ending the War of Independence. At age fourteen he served as Francis Dana's French interpreter on a mission to Russia. Adams received preparatory school training in Paris and Amsterdam and later attended the University of Leyden and Harvard University. By his teens, Adams was fluent in five languages.

George Washington, who along with *Thomas Jefferson served as Adams's patron, appointed the aspiring diplomat to his first post in 1794, as minister to the Netherlands. From there Adams went to London in 1795 to assist in the final negotiations for Jay's Treaty. From 1797 to 1801, Adams served as the first U.S. minister to Prussia. In 1809 President *James Madison appointed Adams minister to Russia, a post he held until 1814. While in Russia Adams cultivated a personal relationship with Tsar *Alexander I and gained further insight into the intricacies of European balance of power politics.

In 1814 Adams went to Ghent to take part in the negotiations to end the War of 1812. His critical role in the "Peace of Christmas Eve" earned for Adams the most prestigious position in the American diplomatic corps—minister to Great Britain. While at the Court of St. James, Adams negotiated the Anglo-American Commercial Convention of July 1815 and laid the diplomatic foundation for what would become the Rush-Bagot Agreement of 1817, a landmark pact limiting naval forces on the Great Lakes. James Monroe rewarded Adams's many achievements and long years of service by naming him secretary of state in 1817.

Adams's diplomatic accomplishments during his seven and a half years as secretary of state are unrivaled in American history. As the director of American foreign policy from 1817 to 1825, Adams guided the nation through the uncertainties and divisions of the post–War of 1812 era to the position of hemispheric supremacy implicit in the articulation of the Monroe Doctrine of 1823.

While the Monroe Doctrine has received far more study from scholars, the Transcontinental Treaty of 1819 with Spain was Adams's most significant diplomatic accomplishment and proved an essential precondition to the making of the Monroe Doctrine. Samuel Flagg Bemis correctly termed the Transcontinental Treaty "the greatest single victory ever won by an American statesman." The pact finalized the Louisiana Purchase (whose legitimacy Spain had long contested), acquired for the United States the Floridas, resolved long-standing disputes over spoliation claims, and, most important, extended the nation's first transcontinental boundary claim. Together with the Convention of 1818 with Great Britain, the Transcontinental Treaty established a firm American claim to the Pacific Northwest.

While Adams negotiated the Transcontinental Treaty with Spanish minister Don Luís de Onís, the agreement that was reached was made possible by Adams's artful manipulation of international and domestic politics. At the center of his efforts was a campaign to improve Anglo-American relations in such a way that Britain's interest would be more closely identified with the United States than with the Spanish monarchy. Reconciliation with Great Britain had begun at the close of the War of 1812, yet it was Adams who best understood the terms under which Anglo-American cooperation could take place. It was primarily to avoid angering the British that Adams vehemently opposed the recognition of the various South American independence movements during the years prior to 1822. Adams wished to allay British foreign secretary *Castlereagh's fears that the

United States sought to supplant British commercial influence in the emerging nations of South America. Above all, Adams wanted to prevent the British from leading or even supporting any effort by the European powers to forcibly restore Spanish colonial rule in the Western Hemisphere. From the time of the Congress of Aix-la-Chapelle in 1818, it was clear to Adams that Great Britain had no inclination to take part in any such expedition.

By refraining from recognizing the South American rebels, Adams ensured that Britain would not side with Spain in a showdown over disputed territories. He was then free to apply military pressure on the Spanish borderlands as a means to bring Onís to terms. The most visible aspect of this strategy was Andrew Jackson's invasion of the Floridas in 1818, known today as the First Seminole War. Whether or not Jackson exceeded his orders in conquering the Floridas on a mission ostensibly designed to prevent cross-border attacks by "marauding Indians" is unclear even today. It is clear that Jackson's capture, court-martial, and execution of Alexander Arbuthnot and Robert C. Ambrister, British subjects accused of inciting the Seminoles, certainly was not within the general's jurisdiction. Yet it was Adams, alone among the members of Monroe's cabinet, who defended Jackson's campaign (even while agreeing in principle to return the captured territory to Spain) as a justified response to alleged Indian perfidy and Spanish dereliction. Adams knew that Jackson's actions were essential to extracting the desired concessions from Spain. If those actions were disavowed, Spain would be unlikely to capitulate at the bargaining table. Hence, Adams defended Jackson against attacks both within the administration and in Congress, where a full-scale debate was held in early 1819 on the merits and constitutionality of the invasion of the Floridas. Adams's most significant contribution to this debate was his landmark November 28, 1818, letter to American minister George Erving in Madrid (made public in late December) in which Adams manipulated both the facts of the incident and the very words he used to describe the case in such a way as to legitimize Jackson's campaign. Jefferson described Adams's "Erving letter" as "among the ablest I have ever seen, both as to logic and style"; Bemis claimed that it was the greatest state paper of Adams's career.

Adams's astuteness regarding Anglo-American affairs was emphasized when Castlereagh, despite a public outcry, took no action to avenge the deaths of the executed British subjects. Adams knew that the deaths of the captured Britons, unlike the recognition of South American independence, would not harm tangible British interests and therefore would not elicit a strong response. Adams's keen sense of British statecraft was again demonstrated in 1823 when he argued against accepting Britain's potentially hand-tying joint declaration opposing European intervention in the Western Hemisphere. Why should the United States back a policy that Britain would pursue out of its own interests? He fought to maintain American freedom of action by arguing to the other cabinet members that "it would be more candid, as well as more dignified, to avow our principles explicitly to Russia and France, than to come in as a cock-boat in the wake of the British man-of-war" (Adams, *Memoirs*, 6:179).

A lifelong commitment to the American republican revolution guided Adams's foreign policy outlook. Basic to the republican revolution were the principles of freedom of the seas and equality of commercial access to the world's markets, an idea later known as the Open Door. Adams believed that commerce was "among the natural rights and duties of men." He envisioned international commerce as the foundation of a global community of peoples whose very interdependence would make war a relic of the past. Hence, Adams viewed with suspicion the attempts of the Chinese during the 1830s and 1840s to limit European commercial access: "The cause of the war is the Kowtow! the arrogant and unsupportable pretension of China that she will hold commercial intercourse with the rest of mankind, not upon terms of equal reciprocity, but upon the insulting and degrading forms of the relation between lord and vassal" (Quoted in LaFeber, p. 49).

Continentally, Adams conceived of North America as the natural limit of the United States and devoted much of his energy to territorial expansion. He predicted in 1819 that "the world shall become familiarized with the idea of considering our proper dominion to be the continent of North America. From the time when we became an independent people it was as much a law of nature that this should become our pretension as that the Mississippi should flow to the sea" (Adams, *Memoirs*, 4:438). The Transcontinental Treaty symbolized Adams's tangible contribution to this mystical ambition, as did his earlier support of the Louisiana Purchase. Adams's vigorous advocacy of expansionism was central to his conception of himself as the "man of the whole nation," a leader above party and sectional interests.

Despite his conviction that the United States was destined to lead the regeneration of the world, Adams rejected direct entanglement in foreign controversies as a threat to the mission he envisioned for the United States. In a famous address of July 4, 1821, he warned of the consequences to the nation of overinvolvement in foreign disputes: "The fundamental maxims of her policy would insensibly change from *liberty* to *force*. . . . She might become the dictatress of the world. She would no longer be the ruler of her own spirit" (quoted in LaFeber, p. 48).

Adams's statesmanship casts a long shadow over the subsequent history of American foreign policy. Final ratification of the Transcontinental Treaty in 1821 signaled the end of the first phase of American continental expansion by resolving long-standing uncertainties about the nation's borders. By exchanging a claim to Oregon for an equivalent claim to Texas, the treaty established a dynamic that would influence American political development until the Civil War.

The establishment of a transcontinental boundary claim proved to be America's first official step toward becoming a Pacific power. In this sense Adams's Transcontinental Treaty may be considered to mark the origin of American global empire. The westward thrust of Adams and Monroe built upon the trail first noted by fur magnate John Jacob Astor, blazed by Lewis and Clark, and championed by Jefferson. At the end of the trail lay a foothold on the Pacific and access to the trans-Pacific trade. By acquiring a claim to the Northwest coast,

Adams and Monroe had made the United States a force to be reckoned with in the emerging imperial struggle among Russia, Spain, and Great Britain. Within fifty years the United States would secure clear title to the Oregon country, annex California, and purchase Alaska. By the turn of the twentieth century, Hawaii and the Philippines would be acquired and the Open Door policy firmly established with regard to China. In the twentieth century, the drive into the western Pacific would result in a war with Japan for supremacy in Asia and the creation of a truly global American empire.

The Jeffersonian origins of the transcontinental claim should not obscure Adams's critical role in pushing the nation's boundaries to the Pacific. It was Adams who perceived the nation's long-term imperial interest amid the tangled skein of diplomatic controversies confronting the United States. Adams rightfully saw the transcontinental boundary as his great contribution to the American nation. In pursuit of this end, Adams walked a diplomatic tightrope. He outmaneuvered opponents both at home and abroad, responded shrewdly to contingency, and tempered his diplomacy with the strategic use of force. It was a bravura performance in the tradition of classic European diplomacy. From the perilous circumstances facing the country when Adams took the helm of American foreign policy, the United States emerged poised to conquer a continent. It was this dramatic increase in the nation's relative position internationally that made Adams the most successful statesman in American history, indeed the most successful statesman of his time, a period known as the "golden age" of European diplomacy. The legacy of Adams's statecraft would be seen in the policies of protégé *William Seward and grandson Henry Adams's confidant, John Hay.

The Monroe Doctrine of 1823 was the culmination of Adams's shrewd management of American foreign policy. Its declaration that the Western Hemisphere was henceforth off limits to further European colonization and intervention served as a benchmark for later assertions of hemispheric unilateralism by the United States. Questions of authorship aside, there can be no doubt that Monroe could not have pronounced his famous doctrine without the statesmanship of Adams paving the way.

Another legacy of the Adams term as secretary of state was the substantial enlargement of the presidential war-making power. The de facto military conquest of Florida definitively established that undeclared war would be a foreign policy tool available to the president. Unlike Jefferson and Madison, who both had shied away from using force to acquire Florida, Monroe (at Adams's urging) had defended Jackson's seizure of Florida and then had withstood congressional attacks on the campaign. Jackson's invasion of Florida established a precedent that would often be repeated in the nineteenth and twentieth centuries. The First Seminole War debate was the moment at which the power to make war shifted decisively (and so far irrevocably) in the direction of the executive. While presidents have usually felt it necessary to obtain congressional support before committing troops to combat, the success of presidential war messages and the reluctance of legislators to cut off funds to troops already in the field indicate that Congress's control of the war power has long been more symbolic than real.

In spite of his unparalleled success as an American statesman, John Quincy Adams's public life proved bittersweet. Adams was tormented that his actions as a diplomat compromised his personal integrity. While he was secretary of state, the exigencies of power and expediency clashed repeatedly with the imperatives of reason and morality. Adams realized that his determined efforts to acquire Florida chiefly served a society based on the morally indefensible institution of slavery. He confronted the central dilemma of Western statesmen from the time of Machiavelli: how to reconcile the force, fraud, and hypocrisy of statecraft with the maintenance of personal moral rectitude. More than any other American statesman, Adams wrestled with the moral conundrums implicit in the pursuit of a realist foreign policy by a nation so self-consciously idealist in its orientation. Adams, to his mortification, came to understand that there is no dichotomy between the morality of the statesman and the morality of the state he serves—the two are one.

Given John Quincy Adams's vast accomplishments, it is one of the cruel ironies of American history that he was not the consensus choice for president in 1824. His achievements as secretary of state dwarfed those of his predecessors, Jefferson, Madison, and Monroe. By the old rules Adams had earned the presidency. Unfortunately for him, the era of selecting presidents by consensus was over. In spite of his deep desire to be president, Adams advertised his disinterest in the office and refused to advance his candidacy in any substantive way. He suffered the ignominy of finishing second in the electoral vote to Jackson, the man whose career he had saved in 1818. Adams's trangression of his personal moral code was complete when he schemed to win the House of Representatives' presidential vote (Jackson having won less than a majority of the electoral vote in a four-way race) by making the infamous "corrupt bargain" with third-place finisher and arch-rival Henry Clay. In exchange for swinging his support to Adams, Clay was made secretary of state when Adams was chosen president.

Adams became one of the least successful presidents in American history. The hostility of Jackson's supporters stymied his domestic program, and there were no foreign policy achievements even remotely comparable to either the Transcontinental Treaty or the Monroe Doctrine. His humiliating defeat at the hands of Jackson in 1828 meant that for the second time in two generations the American people had rejected the program, the leadership, and the values of the Adams family. Adams now knew that the destiny of his family was not to lead the nation but rather to serve as a symbol for all that Jacksonian America meant to change.

In the wake of his rejection by the American public and the suicide of his son George in May 1829, Adams underwent a severe personal crisis. A life founded on the proposition that God's purposes on earth could be determined and acted upon by an educated, moral mind had been shattered. He experienced agonizing doubts over the existence of God and the meaning of life. The triumph of Jackson and the greed characteristic of Jacksonian America symbolized to him the destruction of the American experiment in liberty and republican government.

This backdrop of despair and doubt makes Adams's return to Congress seem all the more quixotic. His election to the House of Representatives in 1830 as a member of the Massachusetts delegation marked the beginning of seventeen more years of public service. Adams's second career in the House saw him repudiate many of the achievements of his first career as "the man of the whole nation." He became a staunch opponent of Indian removal, opposed the annexation of Texas, and fought to restrain presidential war-making power.

Adams's resistance to the annexation of Texas naturally led him to oppose vehemently the Mexican War. Despite his age and physical frailty, he was the spiritual leader of the antiwar faction in the House, being one of only fourteen members to vote against a declaration of war. He urged American officers to resign their commissions rather than fight in what he termed an "unrighteous war." He called for the unilateral withdrawal of American forces from Mexico and peace without territorial indemnities. Adams's opposition to the spirit and tactics of Manifest Destiny was intense, which makes his role as secretary of state in generating expansionist fever all the more ironic. Adams, biographer Samuel Flagg Bemis writes, "had all but coined the magic making phrase 'Manifest Destiny.' "

As he neared the end of his life, Adams predicted, even welcomed, the breakup of the Union. To Adams, slavery had so tainted the noble experiment in republican government that he believed disunion desirable. As early as 1820 he was convinced that "the bargain between freedom and slavery contained in the Constitution is morally vicious, inconsistent with the principles upon which alone our revolution can be justified." In 1845 he apocalyptically described the Constitution as "a menstruous rag" and the Union as "sinking into a military monarchy, to be rent asunder like the empire of Alexander or the kingdoms of Ephraim and Judah."

Despite a debilitating stroke in November 1846, Adams kept his House seat, a silent sentinel of the antiwar movement. On February 21, 1848, while voting against a measure recommending the decoration of Mexican War veterans, John Quincy Adams collapsed at his desk. He died in the Capitol two days later, unaware that on February 22 President Polk had submitted to the Senate for ratification the Treaty of Guadalupe Hidalgo, which ended the Mexican War and proved a prelude to disunion. A life that had begun at the birth of independence had ended in the shadow of civil war.

Annotated Bibliography

Researching the life of John Quincy Adams begins with the study of his voluminous and fascinating diary. Adams kept a record of his life beginning in 1785 and continuing almost without missing a day until his death in 1848. The diary (the original of which, along with the rest of the Adams family papers, is at the Massachusetts Historical Society; microfilm copies are available at numerous research libraries across the nation) recounts both the major events and minor details of Adams's life. It reveals his hopes, his fears, and his pervasive sense of persecution at the hands of his enemies, both real and imagined.

Samuel Flagg Bemis described Adams's diary as "a secret tuning fork for his pent-up emotions." The self-conscious tone of many of the entries indicates that Adams thought someone was looking over his shoulder, even if it was only his own conscience. Whatever tendency Adams had consciously to distort the record he compiled, the sheer mass of his diary writings provides a candid view of the subject. The diary's frank observations, comprehensiveness, hostility, self-loathing, and personal, political, and historical reflections make it an unparalleled narrative of the history of the early republic.

John Quincy Adams's diary was excerpted by his grandson, Charles Francis Adams, in *Memoirs of John Quincy Adams, Comprising Portions of His Diary from 1795 to 1848* (1874–1877). For most purposes, this widely available and comprehensive record can be consulted instead of the original. Yet if one truly wants to understand John Quincy Adams, there is no substitute for closely scrutinizing his own writings. A selection of Adams's official and private correspondence is published in Worthington C. Ford. ed., *The Writings of John Quincy Adams* (1913–1917). Again, the source is useful as far as it goes, but the sheer volume of Adams's writings means that the printed record touches only a portion of his life.

Some of Adams's official diplomatic correspondence can be found reprinted in the American State Papers series. The entire record of his official correspondence is at the Records of the Department of State at the National Archives in Washington, D.C. A very useful compendium of Adams's ideas and attitudes concerning foreign affairs is Walter LaFeber's *John Quincy Adams and American Continental Empire* (1965).

The secondary literature on Adams begins with Samuel Flagg Bemis's monumental biography in two volumes, *John Quincy Adams and the Foundations of American Foreign Policy* (1949) and *John Quincy Adams and the Union* (1956). Benefiting from early access to the Adams papers (kept from the public until 1956), Bemis's work is unsurpassed. Volume 1 (awarded the Pulitzer Prize) deals primarily with Adams's diplomatic achievements and is an essential companion to anyone presuming to study the record of his diplomacy. Yet *John Quincy Adams and the Union* is ultimately a more revealing and satisfying work in that it probes Adams's inner life more fully than the one-dimensional Adams-as-hero approach of Volume 1.

Adams's role in the making of the Transcontinental Treaty is described in Philip C. Brooks, *Diplomacy and the Borderlands: The Adams-Onís Treaty of 1819* (1939). Brooks examines in detail the circumstances leading to the treaty. Bemis's discussion of the treaty in *John Quincy Adams and the Foundations of American Foreign Policy* drew heavily on Brooks's work. Adams's role in the making of the Transcontinental Treaty is also discussed in Charles Carroll Griffin's *The United States and the Disruption of the Spanish Empire, 1810–1822: A Study of the Relations of the United States with Spain and the Rebel Spanish Colonies* (1937). A recent reinterpretation of the treaty and of Adams's statecraft is William Earl Weeks, *John Quincy Adams and American Global Empire* (1992). Weeks argues that rapprochement with Great Britain was essential to extracting a favorable treaty from Spain and that the diplomacy surrounding the Transcontinental Treaty paved the way for the Monroe Doctrine. The circumstances surrounding Adams's Erving letter of 1818 are described in William Earl Weeks, "John Quincy Adams's 'Great Gun' and the Rhetoric of American Empire," *Diplomatic History* 14, 1 (1990): 25–42.

Adams's role in the making of the Monroe Doctrine is highlighted in Volume 1 of Bemis's biography. Arthur Preston Whitaker's *The United States and the Independence of Latin America, 1800–1830* (1941) emphasizes Monroe's contribution to the success of American diplomacy. Adams's influence on the deliberations leading to the doctrine is documented in Worthington C. Ford, "John Quincy Adams and the Monroe Doctrine," *American Historical Review* 7, 4 (1902): 676–696. Ernest May, *The Making of the Monroe Doctrine* (1975), argues that Adams's support for a strong statement was motivated by his political ambitions. Russian scholar N. N. Bolkhovitinov, "Russia and the Declaration of the Non-colonization Principle: New Archival Evidence," *Oregon Historical Quarterly* 72, 2 (1971); 101–126, claims that the Russian ukase of 1821 was used as a pretext by Adams to establish a noncolonization principle that was actually aimed at Great Britain. William Appleman Williams, "The Age of Mercantilism: An Interpretation of American Political Economy, 1763–1828," *William and Mary Quarterly* (1958), convincingly contends that the doctrine was the culmination of over fifty years of American foreign policy and that Adams "devoted his energies to building" an American mercantile empire.

The central importance of Adams and Castlereagh to the reconstruction of Anglo-American relations is detailed in Bradford Perkins, *Castlereagh and Adams: England and the United States, 1812–1823* (1964). Perkins is especially useful on the negotiations at Ghent. George Dangerfield's gracefully written *Era of Good Feelings* (1952) remains an insightful examination of Adams's and Monroe's foreign policy. Adams's foreign policy as president is described in Mary W.M. Hargreaves, *The Presidency of John Quincy Adams* (1985). A more recent look at Adams's outlook on foreign affairs during his "second career" as a House member is Leonard Richards, *The Life and Times of Congressman John Quincy Adams* (1986). Adams's evolving attitude toward Native Americans is revealed in Lynn Hudson Parsons, " 'A Perpetual Harrow upon My Feelings': John Quincy Adams and the American Indian," *New England Quarterly* 46 (September 1973): 339–379.

Bibliography

Adams, John Quincy. *Memoirs of John Quincy Adams. Comprising Portions of his Diary from 1795 to 1848.* 12 vols. Edited by C. F. Adams. Philadelphia: Lippincott, 1874–1877.

———. *The Writings of John Quincy Adams.* 7 vols. Edited by Worthington C. Ford. New York: Macmillan, 1913–1917.

Bemis, Samuel Flagg. *John Quincy Adams and the Foundations of American Foreign Policy.* New York: Knopf, 1949.

———. *John Quincy Adams and the Union.* New York: Knopf, 1956.

Bolkhovitinov, N. N. "Russia and the Declaration of the Non-colonization Principle: New Archival Evidence." Translated by Basil Dmytryshyn. *Oregon Historical Quarterly* 72, 2 (1971): 101–126.

Brooks, Philip C. *Diplomacy and the Borderlands: The Adams-Onís Treaty of 1819.* Berkeley: University of California Press, 1939.

Dangerfield, George. *The Era of Good Feelings.* New York: Harcourt, Brace, 1952.

Ford, Worthington C. "John Quincy Adams and the Monroe Doctrine." *American Historical Review* 7, 4 (1902): 676–696.

Griffin, Charles Carroll. *The United States and the Disruption of the Spanish Empire, 1810–1822: A Study of the Relations of the United States with Spain and the Rebel Spanish Colonies.* New York: Columbia University Press, 1937.

Hargreaves, Mary W.M. *The Presidency of John Quincy Adams.* Lawrence: University of Kansas Press, 1985.

LaFeber, Walter. *John Quincy Adams and American Continental Empire*. Chicago: Quadrangle Books, 1965.

May, Ernest. *The Making of the Monroe Doctrine*. Cambridge, Mass.: Harvard University Press, 1975.

Parsons, Lynn Hudson. " 'A Perpetual Harrow upon My Feelings': John Quincy Adams and the American Indian." *New England Quarterly* 46 (September 1973): 339–379.

Perkins, Bradford. *Castlereagh and Adams: England and the United States, 1812–1823*. Berkeley: University of California Press, 1964.

Richards, Leonard. *The Life and Times of Congressman John Quincy Adams*. New York: Oxford University Press, 1986.

———. *John Quincy Adams and American Global Empire*. Lexington: University Press of Kentucky, 1992.

Weeks, William Earl. "John Quincy Adams's 'Great Gun' and the Rhetoric of American Empire." *Diplomatic History* 14, 1 (1990): 25–42.

Whitaker, Arthur Preston. *The United States and the Independence of Latin America, 1800–1830*. Baltimore: Johns Hopkins University Press, 1941.

Williams, William Appleman. "The Age of Mercantilism: An Interpretation of the American Political Economy, 1763–1828." *William and Mary Quarterly* 15, 4 (1958): 419–437.

WILLIAM EARL WEEKS

Konrad Adenauer (1876–1967).   Konrad Adenauer was born on January 5, 1876, in Cologne, Germany, to an upwardly mobile, lower-middle-class, devoutly Roman Catholic household. His father, also named Konrad, a clerk in the law courts, and his mother, the former Helene Scharfenberg, had three other children. Adenauer earned an *Abitur* at the *Apostel-gymnasium* in Cologne in 1894 and studied law and economics from 1894 to 1897 at the universities of Freiburg, Munich, and Bonn. Passing state law examinations, Adenauer went into practice in Cologne. He was elected deputy mayor of the city council in 1906 and 1909, became senior deputy mayor in 1911, and was inaugurated as lord high mayor on October 18, 1917, for a twelve-year term. In 1929 he was reelected to that post.

Family and religious values were at the core of this self-confident, implacable statesman's being, and influenced his political activities. In 1904 he married Emma Weyer, who came from a politically prominent family. She bore him three children: Konrad (1906), Max (1910), and Ria (1912). Emma died in 1916, and in 1919 Adenauer married Auguste Zinsser, by whom he had Paul (1923), Lotte (1925), Libeth (1928), and Georg (1931). Weak lungs and a government position kept Adenauer out of military service during World War I. In 1917 he was injured in an automobile accident, and subsequent plastic surgery froze his features into an enigmatic mask. This proved to be an asset for a diplomat. Although in his national career Adenauer showed himself more astute in foreign than in domestic policy, throughout the 1920s he flourished at the local and provincial levels. From 1917 to 1933 he served on both the Provincial Diet of the Rhine Province and the Prussian State Council.

The Nazis, whom Adenauer opposed on moral and intellectual grounds, forced him to resign all his offices in 1933. Under the Nazis, Adenauer spent his time confined to his home, reading and gardening. He was briefly imprisoned by the Gestapo in 1934 and 1944, the latter time on charges that he was tangentially involved with the plot against *Adolf Hitler. Perhaps due to his instinct for self-preservation, Adenauer had actually rejected a feeler from the plotters. Sent to a camp in Cologne, not far from his home in Rhöndorf, Adenauer faked a heart ailment. His hospitalization saved him from being dispatched to an extermination camp. He escaped from the hospital, was again incarcerated, but was released when his son Max, then in the army, intervened on his behalf.

Adenauer cooperated with the Americans after they captured Cologne in March 1945. They reinstated him as mayor, but British Colonel John Barraclough dismissed him as too intractable when the Allies transferred that area to the British zone of occupation. Ironically, this ouster freed Adenauer for national politics. In 1946, in the new state of North Rhine-Westphalia, he helped to found the Christian Democratic Union (CDU), a party that united Catholic and Protestant middle-class voters. Its "social market" philosophy, combining free market capitalism with state responsibility for the public welfare, helped to provide the basis for West Germany's remarkable economic progress.

A humanist and a pragmatist, Adenauer acutely realized that the Allies had won the war, and he sought to work with them. With time, however, he insisted that West Germany be treated as a partner rather than as a defeated enemy. He accepted German guilt for Nazism and sought to restore his country's moral standing by aligning it against communism and with the West. He had personal as well as practical motivations for his actions. Harboring bitter personal memories of *Bismarck's *Kulturkampf*, he never really wanted Berlin to become Germany's capital again. He had a politician's gift for reducing complex situations to simple choices, sometimes too simple. He essentially saw everything Prussian as disagreeably militaristic, nationalistic, and, in a contradictory fashion, both Marxist and materialistic. The Western Allies conveniently agreed. Since he had developed a dislike for the British during their role in occupying the Rhineland after World War I, he could side more easily with the United States or even with France in inter-Allied disputes, even though his worldview, formed before 1914, took for granted a Eurocentric universe characterized by a historic Franco-German antagonism. His pragmatic sense helped him to adjust this conflicting view to some extent.

Called "der Alte," or "the old man," Adenauer was also known as "the old fox" for his realism in a time of upheaval and change. Always a self-assertive man who loved to be the center of attention, this patriarchal figure assumed the presidency of the German Parliamentary Council charged with writing the Basic Law, which served as the new constitution, on September 1, 1948, by declaring himself to be the senior member of that group. After the promulgation of the Basic Law on May 23, 1949, national elections were held on August 14. Subsequently, on September 15, Adenauer was elected chancellor by a one-vote majority. He helped to get the de facto capital of the Federal Republic located in Bonn, not far from his residence, rather than in Frankfurt. In October 1950 Adenauer was elected as his party's national chairman and was reelected eight more times before reluctantly resigning that post in 1966.

As chancellor, Adenauer set out forcefully to achieve his goals of restoring and stabilizing Germany by aligning it with the West and integrating Germany with Europe. He opted for a democratic West Germany, at least temporarily, rather than a neutral united homeland under conditions of diminished freedom, as the Soviets proposed. His bridge-building to the West had been foreshadowed by his attempt during the 1920s to found a Rhineland separate from Prussia, but within Germany, to counter French desires for annexation.

On December 15, 1949, Adenauer signed an agreement with the United States for Marshall Plan assistance. In retaining the position of foreign minister as well as that of chancellor from March 15, 1951, through June 5, 1955, Adenauer underlined his interest in foreign policy. Yet Adenauer did not speak foreign languages, nor did he travel abroad until he became chancellor. On April 18, 1951, on his first visit to France, he signed the treaty establishing the European Coal and Steel Community. From June 14 to 18, 1951, he went to Italy on his first official state visit to a foreign country. He visited Britain later in 1951 and made his first visit to the United States two years later.

Other visits abroad included his meeting with Nahum Goldmann, president of the World Zionist Organization, in London on December 6, 1951. This first encounter between an official representative of the Jewish people and an official representative of the German nation was secret. Without clearance from his cabinet or parliament, Adenauer agreed to reparations of $1 billion to Israel for "historical and moral reasons." Adenauer had listened uninterruptedly for twenty to twenty-five minutes, saying that he felt "the wings of history in this room." A formal agreement of reparations to Israel was signed in Luxembourg on September 10, 1952. Adenauer forbade police who intercepted a bomb sent to him by misguided Jewish terrorists to reveal their action to the German public, lest the negotiations fail.

On May 21, 1951, the Federal Republic of Germany became a member of the Council of Europe. Treaties signed in Paris on October 21–23, 1954, which went into effect on May 5, 1955, restored sovereignty to West Germany and ended Allied occupation, but allowed some American troops to remain. West Germany also became a member of NATO at that time. The Rome Treaties of 1957, which took effect on January 1, 1958, were arguably the high point of Adenauer's efforts to restore Germany's place in Europe. They created both the European Economic Community and the European Atomic Energy Community. Walter Hallstein of Adenauer's foreign affairs department became the first president of the European Economic Community Commission.

Adenauer made a much heralded journey to Moscow in September 1955. There he sought Soviet help on German reunification, the restoration of diplomatic relations, and the return of German prisoners of war. Adenauer and a large

German delegation were able to achieve the last two objectives but not the first. Approximately ten thousand German POWs returned, and twice that many civilian internees. But Moscow's answer to the reunification question was punctuated by its grant of full sovereignty to the German Democratic Republic (East Germany) on September 20 of that year.

Reconciliation with other countries and recognition of West Germany's normalized international standing continued throughout the 1950s. The Hallstein Doctrine, whereby West Germany threatened to withdraw recognition from any country that recognized East Germany, was a tool used by West German diplomacy until Chancellor *Willy Brandt dropped it in 1970. In 1955 West Germany signed an accord with Denmark on the protection of minorities on both sides of the border. In 1956 West Germany initiated an agreement with Belgium on border and cultural affairs. A June 1956 understanding with France allowed the return of the Saar after a 1955 referendum had indicated where that region's loyalties lay. On January 1, 1957, it became the state of Saarland in the Federal Republic.

In 1956 there were visits to Bonn by Prime Minister Jawaharlal Nehru of India and President Sukarno of Indonesia, while President Dwight D. Eisenhower made the journey in 1959. Adenauer himself made a state visit to Japan in 1960 and traveled several times to the United States. He had become fast friends with *John Foster Dulles, with whom he shared the view that communism threatened Western civilization. Both viewed post-Stalinist Soviet "peace offensives" with extreme skepticism, if not disdain. After Dulles died, Adenauer tilted more toward *Charles de Gaulle and France, especially so that West Germany would not be seen as unduly under America's influence. This was capped by Adenauer's last great diplomatic feat, the Treaty of Friendship between France and West Germany, signed on January 22, 1963, one week after France had vetoed Britain's admission into the Common Market. This treaty, however, did not result in an extended honeymoon between the two countries.

Adenauer's problems at home and abroad began to accumulate in the late 1950s. According to some, he should have responded to the 1956 events in Poland and Hungary. In 1957 he ignored Polish foreign minister Adam Rapacki's proposal to ban atomic weapons from central Europe. In the spring of 1959 Adenauer announced that he would seek the presidency, but changed his mind when Economics Minister Ludwig Erhard emerged as his likely successor as chancellor. This uncovered a hostility that soured much of the rest of Adenauer's tenure in office. The construction of the Berlin Wall on August 13, 1961, was a stark setback to his foreign policy efforts. In general elections held on September 17, 1961, the CDU lost its majority and had to return to a coalition government, reducing its freedom of movement. The coalition partner, the Free Democrats, preferred Erhard to Adenauer. The so-called *Spiegel* affair in the fall of 1962 resulted in a government scandal and the resignations of some cabinet members over attempted restrictions on freedom of the press. To garner support in forming a new cabinet, Adenauer promised to resign within a year of the reshuffling. When he stepped down on October 16, 1963, Erhard was elected in his stead. Adenauer was further rebuffed in March 1966 when he resigned as party leader. The CDU gave this post to Erhard as well, rather than to Adenauer's preferred successor, Rainer Barzel. Admittedly, Adenauer had waited too long to groom likely successors.

Advancing age made Adenauer lessen his activities, but he never retired completely, remaining in the Federal Bundestag until his death on April 19, 1967. He wrote three volumes of his memoirs, but did not complete them, and he continued to travel abroad. A May 1966 trip to Israel was marred by anti-German demonstrations there, which he said he understood, despite the steps he had taken to reconcile the two countries. His last trip abroad was to Spain in February 1967 on behalf of the political unification of Europe. Adenauer continued to criticize Erhard for his compliant, pro-American policies. He preferred Erhard's successor, Kurt Kiesinger, for what he saw as Kiesinger's more evenhanded approach. And yet Adenauer respected America's importance in the world. His fear that continued U.S. involvement in Asia would cause it to neglect Europe prompted him to advocate American withdrawal from Vietnam. He was also anxious about détente between the United States and the Soviet Union.

As always, Adenauer's was a Eurocentric view. He preferred a united Europe, while de Gaulle favored old national entities. Unable immediately to get the first, Adenauer settled for the second, although still striving for greater European unity. Pro-Western, he remained independent; chastened by World War II, he pursued realistic goals of reconciliation. He helped bring together competing European interests as he had helped conciliate competing Catholic and Protestant factions in the CDU. A practitioner of Cold War rhetoric, Adenauer nevertheless journeyed to Moscow in 1955 and was criticized for his tepid responses to the Soviet invasion of Hungary in 1956 and the construction of the Berlin Wall in 1961.

Adenauer was a contradictory but estimable figure at home and abroad. Authoritarian, he was also modest and democratic. Cunning, sometimes ruthless, with a sly, often aggressive sense of humor, he was admired but not really loved. Unapproachable, he had almost no real confidants outside his family circle. He often used friendliness as he used bluff, when it was politically profitable. He was patient in getting what he wanted, and his sense of righteousness seemed to be what Germans emerging from the moral horror of the Nazi years wanted. Often ridiculed for his slow speech and heavy Rhenish accent, he was also invariably given the enviable title of "Dr." even though he had never earned a Ph.D. With a good feeling for the public mood, and relying more on instinct than on analysis, Adenauer really was more skilled in foreign affairs, where he could work with his peers, than in domestic affairs. Adenauer successfully integrated 12 million refugees and expellees from the East into West Germany and integrated the western part of Germany into a neo-Carolingian unit with France, Italy, and the Benelux countries at a time when German unification seemed unattainable.

Annotated Bibliography

Researchers interested in primary source materials on Konrad Adenauer's life and career should begin with two German repositories. The first is the Konrad Adenauer Stiftung, Bundeskanzler Adenauer Haus, located on Konrad Adenauer Strasse in Rhöndorf. The second is the Konrad Adenauer Stiftung, located on Rathausallee in St. Augustin bei Bonn. Information about holdings and restrictions at these repositories as well as a letter of introduction can be obtained by writing to Konrad Adenauer Stiftung, Washington Research Office, 1330 New Hampshire Ave., N.W., Suite 104, Washington, D.C. 20036; or by telephoning (202) 296–9137.

Konrad Adenauer was not a prolific writer. Except for his *Memoirs*, 3 vols. (1966, trans.), written in retirement, one must rely chiefly on his correspondence and collected speeches and pronouncements for a sense of his vision of a post–World War II Germany. Fortunately, much of Adenauer's correspondence has been published. Hans Peter Mensing edited four volumes, *Briefe 1945–1947* (1983), *Briefe 1947–1949* (1984), *Briefe, 1949–1951* (1985), and *Briefe, 1951–1953* (1987). The last volume is particularly good for foreign policy matters. *Bundestagsreden* (1967) contains Adenauer's speeches on German politics and on postwar world politics given before the German parliament.

Adenauer's *World Indivisible, with Liberty and Justice for All* (1955) gives the chancellor's view of postwar European politics. His *Journey to America* (1953) contains much on German-American relations. In *Reden, 1917–1967: Ein Auswahl* (1975), Hans-Peter Schwarz has done a fine job of collecting and editing Adenauer's speeches on twentieth-century Germany. Although most of the speeches focus on domestic issues, some deal with foreign policy questions. A different side of Adenauer can be glimpsed in his Christmas meditations, *Nachdenken und inner Einkehr* (1962) and *Nachdenken über die Werte* (1976?).

There is no definitive biography of Adenauer. The best available studies of the crusty German chancellor include Paul Weymar, *Adenauer: His Authorized Biography* (1957), which is useful but predictably laudatory; Terence Prittie, *Konrad Adenauer, 1876–1967* (1971), by the German bureau chief of the *Manchester Guardian* from 1946 to 1963; *Konrad Adenauer* (1964) by Rudolf Augstein, the publisher of *Der Spiegel*; and Charles Wighton, *Adenauer: A Critical Biography* (1963). In German, two recent biographical studies are Peter Koch, *Konrad Adenauer: Eine Politische Biographie* (1985), and Wilhelm von Sternburg, *Adenauer, Eine Deutsche Legende* (1987). Earlier works include Franz Rodens, *Konrad Adenauer: Der Mensch und Politiker* (1963), Robert Strobel, *Adenauer und der Weg Deutschlands* (1965), and Ulrich Frank-Planitz, *Konrad Adenauer: Eine Biographie in Bild und Wort* (1975).

Some of Adenauer's close associates have written of "der Alte." Rainer Barzel, an Adenauer protégé, focused on the question of German reunification in *Im Streit und Umstritten: Anmerkungen zu Konrad Adenauer, Ludwig Erhard und den Ostvertragen* (1986). Hans Edgar Jahn, who was a personal advisor to Adenauer, wrote *An Adenauers Seite: Sein Berater Erinnert Sich* (1987). The texts of several letters that passed between the chancellor and his foreign minister, Heinrich von Brentano, are found in Arnulf Baring, *Sehr Verehrter Herr Bundeskanzler!: Heinrich von Brentano im Briefwechsel mit Konrad Adenauer, 1949–1964* (1974).

Foreigner observers also commented on Adenauer and his policies. Franz-Rudolph von Weiss, the Swiss consul-general in Cologne in the 1940s, wrote *Kriegsende und Neuanfang am Rhein: Konrad Adenauer in dem Berichten des Schweizer Generalkonsuls Franz-*

Rudolf von Weiss, 1944–1945 (1986). Another important book is George Crews McGhee, *At the Creation of a New Germany: From Adenauer to Brandt. An Ambassador's Account* (1989). McGhee was U.S. ambassador to the German Federal Republic from 1963 to 1968 and was familiar with the chancellor's policies even though the chancellor had retired.

There are a number of good monographs and articles on the many European issues that confronted Adenauer. Werner Weidenfeld has written on the drive for European unity in *Konrad Adenauer und Europe* (1976). The leading figure in the drive for European unity, *Jean Monnet, also wrote on Adenauer's role in the establishment of the European Economic Community in *Le Chancelier Adenauer et la construction de l'Europe* (1966). Adenauer's role in the ill-fated European Defense Community is covered in Arnulf Baring, *Aussenpolitik in Adenauers Kanzlerdemokratie* (1969). In "Die Identität der Europäischen Gemeinschaften," *Aussenpolitik* 23 (1972): 505–512, Berndt von Staden discusses the influence of Charles de Gaulle and Adenauer on the shape of the European Economic Community. In "Adenauer und Europa," *Vierteljahrshefte für Zeitgeschichte* 27 (1979): 471–523, Hans-Peter Schwarz analyzes Adenauer's views on European unity based on the speeches and letters preserved at the Adenauer house in Rhöndorf.

Edgar Alexander, *Adenauer and the New Germany: The Chancellor of the Vanquished* (1957), with an epilogue by Adenauer himself, gives a very positive picture of the chancellor's work during the early 1950s, especially focusing on his goal of German reunification. A more recent examination of the same subject is Josef Foschepoth, ed., *Adenauer und die deutsche Frage* (1988).

A number of works have compared Adenauer the German statesman both to his predecessors and to his successors. Among the more valuable of these works are the well-written *From Bismarck to Adenauer: Aspects of German Statecraft* (1965) by Gordon Craig; Klaus Hildebrand, *German Foreign Policy from Bismarck to Adenauer: The Limits of Statecraft* (1989); and Waldemar Besson, *Die Aussenpolitik der Bundesrepublik: Erfahrungen und Massstäbe* (1970). Helmut Wagner, "The Federal Republic of Germany's Foreign Policy Objectives," *Millennium* 17 (1988): 43–59, compares Adenauer's foreign policy with that of his most famous successor, Willy Brandt. Robert Keyserlingk, *Patriots of Peace* (1972), is a comparative study of Adenauer, Alcide de Gasperi, and *Robert Schuman.

There are several good surveys of West German foreign policy which, of course, devote a good deal of attention to "der Alte." Among the better ones are Peter Merkl, *German Foreign Policies, West and East* (1974), Wolfram Hanrieder, *West German Foreign Policy, 1949–1979* (1980), and F. Roy Willis, *France, Germany, and the New Europe, 1945–1967* (1968).

Bibliography

Abelshauser, Werner. "Die frühen fünfziger Jahre: Ein Briefwechsel zwischen dem hohen Kommissar John McCloy und Bundeskanzler Adenauer." *Vierteljahrhefte für Zeitgeschichte* 30 (1982): 715–756.
Adenauer, Konrad. *Briefe 1945–1947*. Berlin: Siedler, 1983.
———. *Briefe 1947–1949*. Berlin: Siedler, 1984.
———. *Briefe, 1949–1951*. Berlin: Siedler, 1985.
———. *Briefe, 1951–1953*. Berlin: Siedler, 1987.
———. *Bundestagsreden*. Bonn: A-Z Studio, 1967.

———. *Die Heue Regelung unserer Nahrungs Mittelwirtschaft.* Berlin: Concordia Deutsche Verlagsanstalt, 1915.

———. *Journey to America: Collected Speeches, Statements, Press, Radio, and T.V. Interviews.* Washington, D.C.: German Diplomatic Mission, 1953.

———. *Memoirs.* 3 vols. Translated by Beate Ruhm von Oppen. London: Weidenfeld and Nicolson, 1966.

———. *Nachdenken über die Werte.* Buxheim/Allgäu: Martin Verlag Berger, 1976?

———. *Nachdenken und inner Einkerhr: Weihnachtsansprache 1961.* Buxheim/Allgäu: Martin Verlag, 1962.

———. *Reden, 1917–1967: Ein Auswahl.* Edited by Hans-Peter Schwarz. Stuttgart: Deutsche Verlags-Anstalt, 1975.

———. *Redin auf Adenauer.* Munich: Langen/Munchen, 1967.

———. *World Indivisible, with Liberty and Justice for All.* New York: Harper, 1955.

Alexander, Edgar. *Adenauer and the New Germany: The Chancellor of the Vanquished.* With an epilogue by Konrad Adenauer. New York: Farrar, Straus, and Cudahy, 1957.

Augstein, Rudolf. *Konrad Adenauer.* London: Secker and Warburg, 1964.

Baring, Arnulf. *Aussenpolitik in Adenauers Kanzlerdemokratie.* Munich: Oldenbourg, 1969.

———. *Sehr Verehrter Herr Bundeskanzler!: Heinrich von Brentano im Briefwechsel mit Konrad Adenauer, 1949–1964.* Hamburg: Hoffman and Campe, 1974.

Barzel, Rainer. *Im Streit und Umstritten: Anmerkungen zu Konrad Adenauer, Ludwig Erhard und den Ostvertragen.* Frankfurt am Main: Ullstein, 1986.

Besson, Waldemar. *Die Aussenpolitik der Bundesrepublik: Erfahrungen und Massstäbe.* Munich: Piper, 1970.

Bonin, Bogislaw von. *Opposition gegen Adenauers Sicherheits-politik.* Hamburg: Verlag Neue Politik, 1976.

Borner, Rolf. *Die verräterische Politik der Führung der Adenauer—CDU im Spiegel ihrer Parteiprogramme, 1945–1961.* N.p., 1961.

Brehm, Max Martin. *Mit dem Bundeskanzler in U.S.A.* Hochstadt Aisch: Mens-Verlag, 1953.

Buchheim, Hans, ed. *Der Patriotismus Konrad Adenauers.* Bonn: Bouvier, 1960.

Cahn, Jean-Paul. "Réflexions sur l'attitude de l'hebdomadaire allemand 'Der Spiegel' face au problème sarrois (1954–1955)." *Revue Allemagne* 12 (1980): 261–277.

Craig, Gordon Alexander. *From Bismarck to Adenauer: Aspects of German Statecraft.* New York: Harper and Row, 1965.

Dittmann, Knud. *Adenauer und die Deutsche Wiedervereinigung: Die politische Diskussion des Jahres 1952.* Dusseldorf: Droste, 1981.

Dollinger, Hans, ed. *Die Bundersrepublik in der Ära Adenauer, 1949–1963.* Munich: Desch, 1966.

Dreher, Klaus. *Ein Kampf um Bonn.* Munich: List, 1979.

Erdmann, Karl Dietrich. *Adenauer in der Rheinlandpolitik nach dem ersten Weltkrieg.* Stuttgart: E. Klett Verlag, 1966.

———. "Der 'entmythologisierte' Adenauer." *Historische Zeitschrift* 243 (1986): 627–637.

Foschepoth, Josef, ed. *Adenauer und die deutsche Frage.* Göttingen: Vandenhoeck and Ryprecht, 1988.

Frank-Planitz, Ulrich. *Konrad Adenauer: Eine Biographie in Bild und Wort.* Bergisch-Gladbach: Lubbe, 1975.

Gerst, Wilhelm Karl. *Bundesrepublik Deutschland unter Adenauer*. Berlin: Verlag die Wirtschaft, 1957.

Goldmann, Nahum. "Entretiens avec Konrad Adenauer." *Nouvelle Revue des Deux Mondes* (1981): 368–377.

Gotto, Klaus. *Konrad Adenauer*. Stuttgart: Bonn Aktuell, 1988.

Gotto, Klaus, et al. *Konrad Adenauer: Seine Deutschland und Aussenpolitik, 1945–1963*. Munich: Deutscher Taschenbuch-Verlag, 1975.

Hanrieder, Wolfram. *West German Foreign Policy, 1949–1979*. Boulder, Colo.: Westview Press, 1980.

Hildebrand, Klaus. *German Foreign Policy from Bismarck to Adenauer: The Limits of Statecraft*. Translated by Louise Willmot. Boston: Unwin Hyman, 1989.

Hiscocks, Richard. *The Adenauer Era*. Philadelphia: Lippincott, 1966.

Jahn, Hans Edgar. *An Adenauers Seite: Sein Berater Erinnert Sich*. Munich: Langen Muller, 1987.

Joffe, Josef. "Westvertrage, Ostvertrage und die Kontinuität der deutschen Aussenpolitik." *Europa Archiv* 28 (1973): 111–124.

Keyserlingk, Robert Wendelin. *Patriot of Peace*. Gerrards Cross, Eng.: Smythe, 1972.

Koch, Peter. *Konrad Adenauer: Eine Politische Biographie*. Reinbek bei Hamburg: Rowohlt, 1985.

Koerfer, Daniel. *Kampf ums Kanzleramt: Erhard und Adenauer*. Stuttgart: Deutsche Verlags-Anstalt, 1987.

Kusters, Hanns Jurgen. "Adenauers Europapolitik in der Gründungsphase der Europäischen Wirtschaftsgemeinschaft." *Vierteljahrhefte fur Zeitgeschichte* 31 (1983): 646–673.

Legoll, Paul. *Konrad Adenauer et l'idée d'unification européenne, janvier 1948–mai 1950: Un homme politique "européen" et son environment dans le contexte international*. New York: Lang, 1989.

Loch, Theo M. *Adenauer*. [Bonn]: Athenaeum Verlag, 1963.

McGhee, George Crews. *At the Creation of a New Germany: From Adenauer to Brandt. An Ambassador's Account*. New Haven, Conn.: Yale University Press, 1989.

Merkl, Peter. *German Foreign Policies, West and East: On the Threshold of a New European Era*. Santa Barbara, Calif.: ABC-Clio, 1974.

Mischlich, Robert. "Une Mission secrète à Bonn (9 mai 1950)." *Revue d'Allemagne* 19 (1987): 371–378.

Moller, Horst. "Das Haus Konrad Adenauers in Rhöndorf: Museum, Archives, Research Location." *Geschichte in Wissenschaft und Unterricht* 32 (1981): 47–50.

Monnet, Jean. *Le Chancelier Adenauer et la construction de l'Europe*. Lausanne: Centre de recherches européennes, 1966.

Morsey, Rudolf. *Brüning und Adenauer: Zwei deutsche Staatmänner*. Dusseldorf: Droste, 1972.

———, ed. *Konrad Adenauer und die Gründung der Bundesrepublik Deutschland*. Stuttgart: Belser, 1979.

Neumann, Erich Peter. *Umfragen über Adenauer: Ein Porträt in Zählen*. [Allenbach]: Verlag für Demoskopie, 1961.

Osterheld, Horst. *"Ich gehe nicht leichten Herzens": Adenauers letzte Kanzler Jahre: Ein dokumentarischer Bericht*. Mainz: Grunewald, 1986.

———. *Konrad Adenauer: Ein Charakterbild*. Bonn: Eichholz, 1973.

Poidevin, Raymond. "La Question de la Sarre entre la France et la République Fédérale d'Allemagne en 1952." *Revue d'Allemagne* 18 (1986): 63–71.

Pöttering, Hans-Gert. *Adenauers Sicherheitspolitik, 1955–1963: Ein Beitrag zum deutsch-amerikanischen Verhältnis.* Dusseldorf: Droste, 1975.

Prittie, Terence. *Konrad Adenauer, 1876–1967.* [Chicago]: Cowles, 1971.

Rodens, Franz. *Konrad Adenauer: Der Mensch und Politiker.* Munich: Knauer, 1963.

Roth, Reinhold. *Parteisystem und Aussenpolitik: Zur Bedeutung des Parteiensystems für den aussenpolitischen Entscheidungsprozess in der BRD.* Meisenheim am Glan: Verlag Anton Main, 1973.

Schwarz, Hans-Peter. "Adenauer und Europa." *Vierteljahrshefte für Zeitgeschichte* 27 (1979): 471–523.

Staden, Berndt von. "Die Identität der Europäischen Gemeinschaften." *Aussenpolitik* 23 (1972): 505–512.

Sternburg, Wilhelm von. *Adenauer, eine deutsche Legende.* Frankfurt am Main: Athenaum, 1987.

Strobel, Robert. *Adenauer und der Weg Deutschlands.* Lucerne: Bucher, 1965.

Stutzle, Walther. *Kennedy und Adenauer in der Berlin-Krise, 1961–1962.* Bonn–Bad Godesberg: Verlag Neue Gesellschaft, [1973].

Thomas, Siegfried. *Konrad Adenauer und die Entstehung der Bundesrepublik Deutschland.* Berlin: Dietz, 1989.

Uexkull, Gosta von. *Konrad Adenauer in Selbstzeugnissen und Bolddokumenten.* Reinbek bei Hamburg: Rowahlt, 1976.

Wagner, Helmut. "The Federal Republic of Germany's Foreign Policy Objectives." *Millennium* 17 (1988): 43–59.

Weber, Jürgen, ed. *Die Republik der fünfziger Jahre: Adenaurs Deutschlandpolitik auf dem Prufstand.* Munich: Olzog., 1989.

Weidenfeld, Werner. *Konrad Adenauer und Europe: d. Geistigen Grundlagen d. westeurop. Integrationspolitik d. erste Bonner Bundeskanzlers.* Bonn: Europa Union Verlab, 1976.

Weiss, Franz-Rudolph von. *Kriegsende und Neuanfang am Rhein: Konrad Adenauer in dem Berichten des Schweizer Generalskonsuls Franz-Rudolph von Weiss, 1944–1945.* Munich: Oldenbourg, 1986.

Weymar, Paul. *Adenauer: His Authorized Biography.* New York: Dutton, 1957.

Wighton, Charles. *Adenauer: A Critical Biography.* New York: Coward-McCann, 1963.

Willis, F. Roy. *France, Germany, and the New Europe, 1945–1967.* Stanford, Calif. Stanford University Press, 1968.

Winter, Ingelore M. *Der unbekannte Adenauer.* Dusseldorf and Cologne: Diederichs, 1976.

Winzer, Otto. *Der Vaterlandsverrat des Dr. Konrad Adenauer, vom Separatismus zur "Integraton Europas."* Berlin: Dietz, 1952.

Wuermeling, Henri, and Paul Mautner, eds. *Adenauer und die Deutschen: Gedanken und Erinnerungen.* Stüttgart: Bon Aktuell, 1987.

FREDERICK J. AUGUSTYN, JR.

Alexander I (1777–1825).   The determination that Tsar Alexander I demonstrated in his leadership against *Napoleon I and in the reestablishment of Europe has placed him among the truly significant rulers of the nineteenth century. His intelligence and decisiveness distinguished him from his mediocre fellow monarchs, who relied on famous ministers such as *Castlereagh, *Metternich, and

Karl von Hardenberg. In battle he showed heroism and even tactical skill, in diplomacy shrewdness, and in politics a far-seeing awareness of the historical forces that were leading to the replacement of absolutism with representative forms of government. Alexander granted a constitution to newly conquered Finland, resurrected Poland as a constitutional state, agreed that Restoration France was to have a constitution, and encouraged constitutional rule in the minor German principalities.

The tsar made preliminary moves to emancipate the serfs, modernize the bureaucracy, and educate the population. He founded new universities at Kharkov, Kazan, and St. Petersburg, and revitalized older institutions at Moscow, Dorpat, and Vilnius. His reign witnessed the flowering of literature, the opening of libraries, and the publication of studies in criticism, philosophy, and the sciences. Although the government sponsored collections for the poor, the handicapped, and the victims of disaster, Alexander remained an unbending autocrat. He failed to introduce meaningful social and political reforms, he turned education over to repressive obscurantists, he abandoned the cause of European freedom, and he brought about the conditions that after his death led the Decembrists to attempt to overthrow the monarchy.

These incongruities have intrigued his biographers, who speak of his ''Hamlet'' characteristics, ''enigmatic'' qualities, ''mysticism,'' and even ''paranoia.'' His ''failures'' have suggested to some a responsibility for the Polish uprisings later in the century, for the delay and unsatisfactory nature of serf emancipation in 1861, for the inadequate constitution after the 1905 revolution, and even for the extremism of 1917. However, his maintenance of Russian independence, stabilization of the autocracy, beneficent paternalism, and sponsorship of new ideas preserved the empire and contributed in the long run to late nineteenth-century achievements in local self-government, mass education, medical services, the professionalism of the bureaucracy, and the expansion of academic institutions.

Born on December 23, 1777 (N.S.), Alexander was the son of Grand Duke Pavel (Paul) Petrovich, heir to the throne of Russia, and Sophie Dorothy, princess of Wurttemberg, who on converting to Russian Orthodoxy took the name Maria Fedorovna. His grandmother was *Catherine the Great, and the young child soon became a pawn in the long and bitter struggle between Paul and Catherine. Alexander spent most of his youth at Catherine's cosmopolitan and sophisticated court, where his grandmother employed as his chief tutor Frédéric-César de La Harpe. But at the same time, the boy frequently visited the rival, militaristic Gatchina court of his father, where he was exposed to harsh military discipline and learned to be a martinet. It has been argued that the conflict between the two courts and Alexander's perception of the grave weaknesses in both contributed to the future tsar's lifelong skill in dissimulation. Many biographers have supposed that since the conspiracy in 1801 to remove his father from the throne resulted in Paul's murder, the sensitive heir never overcame his guilt. A few authors, on the basis of imaginative use of unsatisfactory evidence, have accepted the fantastic legend that in 1825 Alexander staged his own death at Taganrog on the Azov Sea so that he could abandon the cares of office and spend the rest of his life in atonement as a hermit.

Remarks that Alexander made in his youth about the chaotic nature of administration under his grandmother and then under his father offer slim but unpersuasive material to support the conclusion that his 1825 "death" was a giant conspiracy. He had confided to friends his aversion to power and his wish to grant "freedom" to his people. His religious interests during and after the conflict with Napoleon showed, under a cover of religiosity, a recurrence of the human impulse to withdraw from ugly reality. However, dreams of retirement—hardly a remarkable phenomenon in anyone—did not interfere with the sense of responsibility he felt both for the well-being of his empire and for the peace of Europe. His decisions on domestic and foreign policy were rational and well-intentioned, even if many then and later regarded his actions as ill-considered or even disastrous.

Students of Alexander's foreign policy have shown that despite the suspicion of other powers, the emperor personally was not an expansionist. He resented Catherine II's role in the destruction of Poland and dreamed of restoring that country's independence. Alexander had no intention of continuing his father's policies directed against the French Revolution, nor did he wish to continue Paul's campaign against Great Britain, undertaken out of pique and a misunderstanding of Napoleon's aims. To devote himself to domestic reform, the new emperor in 1801 obtained peace with both Britain and France. The incorporation of Georgia in 1801 was not the result of ambition for new territories, but occurred because earlier rivalry with Persia and alliances with prominent Georgian families had already involved Russia in Georgian affairs. Alexander did, however, contribute to the gradual Russification of Georgian institutions.

Peace allowed the tsar to devote himself to domestic reforms—modification of his father's arbitrary police procedures, clarification of the role of the Senate, creation of ministries, and institution of a public education program. But by 1804 Napoleon's high-handed actions convinced Alexander that the British government had rightly assessed French actions as threatening the balance of power. It was time for another grand coalition to curb France's pretensions. What gave negotiations for this Third Coalition their peculiar character was not the obvious desirability of combining the strength of Britain, Austria, Prussia, and Russia to challenge Napoleon, but Alexander's view that some kind of ideal should replace old hostilities among the powers.

The famous instructions given by the tsar (on the advice of the Pole *Adam Czartoryski) to Nicholas Novosiltsev for his visit to the British government in the autumn of 1804 combined a practical plan of alliance with a far-reaching proposal for a Europe of cooperative powers. Peoples subjected to Napoleon were to enjoy constitutional rule, while a system of arbitration, consultation, and collective security would prevent future wars. However, concessions were to be made to legitimate monarchs. Interestingly, the eventual agreement with England substituted for the lofty aspects of the tsar's plan details of a military arrangement against Napoleon to achieve the old-fashioned balance of power. Prussia's reluctance to join the coalition and lack of coordination between Austria and Russia contributed to Napoleon's decisive victories over the Austrians at Ulm (October 1805) and over the Russians at Austerlitz (December 1805). Alexander's arrogance in directing the Russian forces seriously damaged the allied effort. He had delayed linking his troops with the Austrians and risked battle when experienced commanders advised retreat.

Napoleon's victories forced Austria out of the war, while Britain and Russia negotiated peace. The negotiations were not successful, however, and late in 1806 the war was renewed when Prussia finally moved against the French. The enormity of the Prussian collapse, especially at the Battle of Jena (October 1806), stirred Alexander to another military attempt. Dreadful battles were indecisive until finally at the Battle of Friedland (June 1807) severe Russian casualties persuaded the tsar to make peace. The subsequent Peace of Tilsit brought Russia into the system of Napoleonic alliances that would result in Russia's war with Sweden and the 1809 incorporation of Finland into the Russian Empire, a nominal war against England, and even cooperation—albeit minimal—with Napoleon when in 1809 Austria temporarily broke from France.

Speculation about which monarch charmed and captivated the other at Tilsit may enliven biographies, but it is doubtful that either Napoleon or Alexander regarded their agreement as anything more than a stopgap measure. Certainly the Russian-French alliance had few supporters in Russia. Official proclamations had depicted Napoleon as the Antichrist, while there were severe economic losses in breaking from England. A war with Turkey, begun in 1806 over control of Moldavia and Wallachia, continued without French aid. That war ended in 1812 with the incorporation only of Bessarabia since Russia required all its troops to meet Napoleon's invading forces. In terms of numbers and organization, the French were better prepared to invade in 1812 than were the Russians to resist. An army of French and allied forces of more than half a million men soon swept through western Russia, and though his army suffered huge casualties at the Battle of Borodino, Napoleon occupied Moscow in September. In the early nineteenth century it was not possible to supply such a large army over vast distances; consequently, perhaps but a fifth of the invading force actually entered the old Russian capital.

The ability of the Russians to keep intact the remnants of their army after Borodino and the disintegration of Napoleon's army in the retreat from Moscow gave Alexander the opportunity to make good his pledge that he would not negotiate with the French leader so long as an enemy soldier was in Russia. The retreat encouraged the tsar to pursue the war to "free Europe." Isolationist sentiment in Russia criticized the emperor for squandering Russian resources in western European concerns, but Alexander showed compassionate interest in the welfare of his soldiers and in their disciplined behavior. He had good reason to doubt that Napoleon's humiliation in Russia alone would have restored European equilibrium and assured Russia's security. The Russian ruler's diplomatic skills in bringing Prussia and Austria into the alliance with Britain and Russia, and his heroism at the Battle of Leipzig in 1813, meant the end of French hegemony and the beginning of Europe's post-Napoleonic state system. The Quadruple Alliance of March 1814 produced Napoleon's final defeat. The tsar continued to dominate strategy when he seized Paris, thereby causing French civil and military leaders to abandon Napoleon. Alexander's triumphant parade through Paris was well deserved.

The magnitude of Russian military power and the emperor's glorious role revived western European fears of Russian ambitions. Alexander, who saw himself as the instrument of Providence, was offended when diplomats doubted his humanitarian professions. In the negotiations at the Congress of Vienna in 1814–1815, his plans to recreate the Polish kingdom—with himself as king— evoked a short-lived alliance among Britain, Austria, and the newly restored French monarchy against Russia and Prussia, to whom the tsar had wished to offer Saxony. However, the Great Powers avoided a war they could not afford when Alexander accepted a smaller Poland, and Prussia a smaller part of Saxony. The allies were reconciled by 1815, when Napoleon returned to France from exile and was defeated at Waterloo. The establishment of a constitutional Polish kingdom infuriated Russian nationalist opinion but also disappointed the Poles, who resented Russian overlordship in Polish affairs and especially objected to the Polish army coming under the control of Alexander's brother, Grand Duke Constantine. Polish nationalists also envisioned the addition of Lithuania to their kingdom, a prospect that alarmed many Russians.

Apart from the matter of Poland, the tsar worked amiably enough with the other powers to carve up the Napoleonic empire in a manner that met the security interests of Britain, Austria, and Prussia. He did not much like the Bourbon Louis XVIII of France, but the Russian ruler influenced the king to adhere to constitutional government and to avoid royalist extremism. During these nego- tiations, Alexander confused diplomats with his turn to religion. By September 1815 he persuaded the Prussian king and the Austrian emperor to join with him in issuing a proclamation for a Holy Alliance, whereby the rulers guaranteed that henceforth they would follow Christian principles in their relationships with each other and also with their subjects. The three invited all European rulers to append their signatures; all would, with the exception of the prince regent of England, the pope of Rome, and the sultan of Turkey.

Probably Alexander had in mind little more than to repeat in religious terms the hope for peaceful international relations based on high moral principles that he and Czartoryski had expressed in the 1804 instructions to Novosiltsev. Re- ligious philosophers had been arguing for some time that the excesses of the French Revolution showed the need to rely on religious principles for justice and unity. Nevertheless, it is not surprising that both publicists and statesmen saw in the emperor's religious professions an excuse for Russian interference in the affairs of foreign states or even a justification for a move against Turkey's European provinces—to the possible injury of British and Austrian interests.

Writers later would apply the term "Holy Alliance" to the activity of the Great Powers (apart from Britain) in suppressing liberalism, but in 1815 Alexander still favored liberal political concepts. There is no evidence that he intended anything other than to guarantee that Russia would play a respectable role in the maintenance of peace.

To this end the emperor devoted much time in the final decade of his reign to foreign affairs, attending the great congresses. His initial support of constitutionalism puts him among the "moderate conservatives" or "moderate liberals," but soon he distanced himself from "false liberalism," which he blamed for assassinations, rebellions in the Iberian peninsula and in Italy, and disturbances in the Germanies. He incorrectly attributed these events to an international liberal revolutionary conspiracy, and he supported intervention against liberal revolutionaries. When in 1820 he learned of a riot in a St. Petersburg regiment of the guards, he thought the conspiracy had reached Russia, although officials tried to explain that the cause was the brutality of the regiment's colonel. Alexander's repressive measures in Russia and his support of the old order in western Europe darkened the final years of his rule.

The Greek uprising against Turkey in 1821 was a complication for the Russian government on several levels. The leader of the initial move against the Turks, Alexander Ypsilanti, was an officer in the Russian service who gave the impression that he had his government's support. Any Russian move on behalf of the Greeks would arouse suspicion that the tsar intended to pursue Catherine II's plans for expansion in the Middle East. Both Britain and Austria were apprehensive of Russian expansion in the eastern Mediterranean. Some saw the attempt of the Greeks to attain freedom as part of a general European movement for emancipation, and therefore condemned it as a threat to all established governments. Both conservatives and radicals in Russia sympathized with the Greeks as Orthodox Christians who had been the victims of barbarous acts of vengeance. Under pressure from Russian public opinion, and motivated by his sympathy for the cause of Orthodox Slavs as well as Greeks under Turkish rule, Alexander nevertheless prudently avoided bellicosity in favor of consultation to find some way to end the turmoil. He avoided war and laid the foundations for the measures of cooperation that would subsequently lead to Greek independence.

For radicals—especially from among the more widely read military officers—Alexander's refusal to intervene on behalf of the Greeks was another example of his betrayal of the cause of progressive humanitarianism. They accused him of neglecting national interests, of being under Metternich's thumb, of having abandoned the cause of the peasants, of substituting despotism for constitutionalism, of allowing obscurantists to injure public education and censorship to discourage intellectual advancement. These malcontents, including prominent writers and officials, formed secret societies such as the Union of Salvation (1816), the Union of Welfare (1818), and the Northern and Southern Societies (1821), which planned by 1824, through the assassination of the imperial family and a military dictatorship, to establish conditions for serf emancipation and eventually democratic government. They took no action in Alexander's reign; however, after his death on December 1, 1825, the revolt they precipitated during the period of confusion as to which brother, Constantine or Nicholas, would succeed Alexander went far beyond earlier palace coups. Although the new tsar, Nicholas I, crushed the Decembrists, historians regard the movement as the "first" Russian revolution.

The Decembrists and the many other educated members of the nobility who shared most of their attitudes were reformers who, under the influence of fashionable pietist, Enlightenment, and sentimentalist notions, looked to the transformation of Russian society. It was the tragedy of Alexander's rule that the emperor himself had held similar attitudes but was in part unable and in part unwilling to carry out the modernization necessary to achieve the reformers' aspirations.

Annotated Bibliography

Patricia Kennedy Grimsted, in *Archives and Manuscript Repositories in the USSR. Moscow and Leningrad* (Zug, Switzerland: Inter Documentation Co., 1976), has described manuscript holdings relating to the imperial government. Especially important are the Central State Archives of Ancient Acts, Bol'shaia Pirogovskaia ulitsa, 17, Moscow G–435, and the Central State Historical Archives of the USSR, naberezhnaia Krasnogo flota, 4, St. Petersburg. Because of the recent changes in Russia, some former restrictions on archival materials have been removed, but the situation in the archives is fluid. Many of Alexander's personal letters were destroyed after his death, but the printed collections of letters and documents that survive are listed in the bibliography. Printed primary materials are available also in the great historical journals such as *Chtenie v Imperatorskom obschestve istorii i drevnostei pri Moskovskom universitete* [Readings in the Imperial Society of Russian History and Antiquity at Moscow University] (1846–1918), *Russkii akhiv* [The Russian Archives] (1866–1917), and *Russkaia starina* [The Russian Past] (1870–1917), and in *Sbornik Imperatorskago Ruskago istoricheskago obshchestva* [The Collection of the Imperial Russian Historical Society] (1867–1914). The latter is especially valuable for foreign affairs, where most documents appear in French. Fourteen volumes of sources, mostly in French (with Russian translations), are published in the modern Soviet series, *Vneshniaia politika* [External Politics] and listed in the bibliography.

The great nineteenth-century biographies of Alexander supply a large part of the sources still used by twentieth-century historians. M. I. Bogdanovich's six-volume *Istoriia tsarstvovaniia imperatora Aleksandra I i Rossii v ego vremiia* [The History of the Reign of the Emperor Alexander I and the Russia in His Times] (1869–1871) is especially valuable for its accounts of battles—with large maps—but also has a great deal of material on diplomatic history, domestic policies, the budget, and education. The sources in the appendices include diplomatic records in French. N. K. Shil'der's massive four-volume *Imperator Aleksandr Pervyi, ego zhizn' i tsarstvovanie* [The Emperor Alexander the First, His Life and Reign] (1897–1898) contains additional sources. He concentrates more than Bogdanovich on Alexander's own activities, but the appendices of sources, especially for diplomacy, are more extensive. Soviet authorities tended to regard these two authors as too "official" and as having neglected social change and class tensions, but neither author was uncritical. Both revealed opposition to the emperor's Polish policies, his "mystical reaction," and his military colonies.

Important letters may be found in N. F. Dubrovin's *Pis'ma glavneishikh deiatelei v tsarstvovanie imperatora Aleksandra I (s 1807–1829 god)* [Letters of Leading Figures in the Reign of the Emperor Alexander I (1807–1829)] (1883), while Czartoryski's memoirs and some correspondence appear in *Memoirs of Prince Adam Czartoryski and His correspondence with Alexander I*, edited by Adam Gielgud (1888). Early examples of the publication of diplomatic correspondence are Albert Vandal, *Napoléon et Alexandre Ier. L'alliance russe sous le premier empire*, 3 vols. (1893–1897), and Paul Bailleau, ed., *Briefwechsel könig Friedrich Wilhelm's III und der königen Luise mit kaiser Alexander I* (1900).

Very early in this century Grand Duke Nikolai Mikhailovich published original materials showing views of Alexander as well as the opinions of his immediate advisors in a number of works, especially *Le Comte Paul Stroganov*, 3 vols. (1905). A helpful collection of diplomatic correspondence is the grand duke's *Les Relations diplomatiques de la Russie et de la France d'après les rapports des ambassadeurs d'Alexandre et de Napoléon, 1808–1812*, 6 vols. (1905–1908). The same author's biography of Alexander, *L'Empereur Alexandre Ier, essai d'étude historique*, 2 vols. (1912), is an excellent example of objective scholarship and moreover contains new sources.

The many popular biographies of Alexander wrestle with his complex personality, repeat the familiar stories of his encounters with Napoleon, and assess the influence of his tutor La Harpe and the prophetess Julie von Krüdener. A few of these biographies are K. Waliszewski, *La Russie il y a cent ans; le règne d'Alexandre Ier*, 3 vols. (1923–1925), Maurice Paléologue, *The Enigmatic Czar: The Life of Alexander I of Russia* (1938), Leonid I. Strakhovsky, *Alexander I of Russia: The Man Who Defeated Napoleon* (1947), Constantin de Grunwald, *Alexandre Ier. Le tsar mystique* (1955), E. M. Almedingen, *The Emperor Alexander I* (1964), Alan Palmer, *Alexander I: Tsar of War and Peace* (1974); and Henri Troyat, *Alexander of Russia: Napoleon's Conqueror* (1982). Almedingen and Palmer are the most useful. A wonderfully graphic account of Napoleon's invasion is Curtis Cate's *The War of the Two Emperors. The Duel Between Napoleon and Alexander: Russia, 1812* (1985). The most satisfactory analysis of Alexander's policies is Allen McConnell's *Tsar Alexander I: Paternalistic Reformer* (1970).

Foreign affairs for the whole reign are covered in Patricia Kennedy Grimsted's remarkable scholarly work, *The Foreign Ministers of Alexander I: Political Attitudes and Conduct of Russian Diplomacy, 1801–1825* (1969). Among its many merits is its astonishing survey of archival and other sources. A standard treatment of the Polish question is Marian Kukiel's *Czartoryski and European Unity* (1955), but most pertinent on Alexander and Poland is Frank W. Thackeray's *Antecedents of Revolution: Alexander I and the Polish Kingdom, 1815–1825* (1980). He shows how the Polish administration worked under the constitution and how Alexander dominated that country. The most thorough account of the Decembrist movement is M. V. Nechkina's *Dvizhenie dekabristov* [The Decembrist Movement], 2 vols. (1955).

Bibliography

Almedingen, E. M. *The Emperor Alexander I*. New York: Vanguard, 1964.

Arkhiv kniazia Vorontsova [The Archives of Prince Vorontsov]. 40 vols. Moscow: A I Mamoiatov, 1870–1895.

Bailleau, Paul, ed. *Briefwechsel könig Friedrich Wilhelm's III und der königen Luise mit kaiser Alexander I*. Leipzig: Herzel, 1900.

Bogdanovich, M. I. *Istoriia tsarstvovaniia imperatora Aleksandra I i Rossii v ego vremiia*

[The History of the Reign of the Emperor Alexander I and the Russia of His Times]. 6 vols. St. Petersburg: Sushchinksii, 1869–1871.

Cate, Curtis. *The War of the Two Emperors. The Duel Between Napoleon and Alexander: Russia, 1812.* New York: Random House, 1985.

Czartoryski, Adam Jerzy. *Memoirs of Prince Adam Czartoryski and His correspondence with Alexander I.* Edited by Adam Gielgud. 2nd ed. London: Remington, 1888.

Dubrovin, N. F. *Pis'ma glavneishikh deiatelei v tsarstvovanie imperatora Aleksandra I (s 1807–1829 god)* [Letters of Leading Figures in the Reign of the Emperor Alexander I (1807–1829)]. St. Petersburg: Akademiia nauk, 1883.

Grimsted, Patricia Kennedy. *The Foreign Ministers of Alexander I: Political Attitudes and Conduct of Russian Diplomacy, 1801–1825.* Berkeley: University of California Press, 1969.

Grunwald, Constantin de. *Alexandre Ier. Le Tsar mystique.* Paris: Amiot Dumont, 1955.

Kukiel, Marian. *Czartoryski and European Unity.* Princeton, N.J.: Princeton University Press, 1955.

Ley, Francis. *Alexandre Ier et sa sainte-alliance (1811–1825).* Paris: Librairie Fischbacher, 1975.

Lobanov-Rostovsky, Andrei A. *Russia and Europe, 1789–1825.* Westport, Conn.: Greenwood Press, 1968.

Mazour, Anatole G. *The First Russian Revolution, 1825: The Decembrist Movement, Its Origins, Development, and Significance.* Stanford, Calif.: Stanford University Press, 1967.

McConnell, Allen. *Tsar Alexander I: Paternalistic Reformer.* New York: Crowell, 1970.

Mordvinov, N. S. *Arkhiv grafov Mordvinovykh* [The Archives of the Counts Mordvinov]. 10 vols. Edited by V. A. Bil'basov. St. Petersburg: Skorokhodov, 1901–1903.

Nechkina, M. V. *Dvizhenie dekabristov* [The Decembrist Movement]. 2 vols. Moscow: Akademiia nauk, 1955.

Nesselrode, Karl Robert. *Lettres et papiers du chancelier comte de Nesselrode, 1760–1850.* 11 vols. in 10. Paris: Lahure, 1904–1912?

Nikolai Mikhailovich, Grand Duke. *Le Comte Paul Stroganov.* 3 vols. Paris: Imprimerie nationale, 1905.

———. *Correspondance de l'empereur Alexandre Ier avec sa soeur, la grande-duchesse Catherine, princesse d'Oldenbourg, puis reine de Wurtemberg, 1805–1818.* Paris: Manzi, Joyant, 1910.

———. *L'Empereur Alexandre Ier, essai d'étude historique.* 2 vols. St. Petersburg: Manufacture des papiers de l'état, 1912.

———. *Les Relations diplomatiques de la Russie et de la France d'après les rapports des ambassadeurs d'Alexandre et de Napoléon, 1808–1812.* 6 vols. St. Petersburg: Manufacture des papiers de l'état, 1905–1908.

Paléologue, Maurice. *The Enigmatic Tsar: The Life of Alexander I of Russia.* New York: Harper, 1938.

Palmer, Alan. *Alexander I: Tsar of War and Peace.* London: Weidenfeld and Nicolson, 1974.

Raeff, Marc. *Michael Speransky: Statesman of Imperial Russia, 1772–1839.* 2nd ed. The Hague: Martinus Nijhoff, 1969.

Saul, Norman E. *Russia and the Mediterranean, 1797–1807.* Chicago: University of Chicago Press, 1970.

Shil'der, N. K. *Imperator Aleksandr Pervyi, ego zhizn' i tsarstvovanie* [The Emperor

Alexander the First, His Life and Reign]. 4 vols. St. Petersburg: Suvorin, 1897–
   1898.
Strakhovsky, Leonid I. *Alexander I of Russia: The Man Who Defeated Napoleon*. New
   York: Norton, 1947.
Suny, Ronald Grigor. *The Making of the Georgian Nation*. Bloomington: Indiana Uni-
   versity Press, 1988.
Thackeray, Frank W. *Antecedents of Revolution: Alexander I and the Polish Kingdom,
   1815–1825*. Boulder, Colo.: East European Monographs, 1980.
Troyat, Henri. *Alexander of Russia: Napoleon's Conqueror*. New York: Dutton, 1982.
Vandal, Albert. *Napoléon et Alexandre Ier. L'alliance russe sous le premier empire*. 3
   vols. Paris: Plon-Nourrit, 1893–1897.
Vneshniaia politika Rossii XIX i nachala XX veka [Foreign Policy of Russia in the
   Nineteenth and the Beginning of the Twentieth Centuries]. 14 vols. [1801–1825].
   Moscow: Gosudarstvennoe izdatelstvo politicheskoi literatury, 1960–1985.
Waliszewski, Kazimierz. *La Russie il y a cent ans; le règne d' Alexandre Ier*. 3 vols.
   Paris: Plon-Nourrit, 1923–1925.
Woodhouse, C. M. *Capodistria: The Founder of Greek Independence*. New York: Oxford
   University Press, 1973.

                                                               FRANKLIN A. WALKER

Otto von Bismarck (1815–1898).   Few historical figures have had their contributions immortalized in print and their actions scrutinized with such frequency
and intensity as the German statesman Otto von Bismarck. Since King Wilhelm
I appointed Bismarck Prussian prime minister in 1862 at the height of a constitutional crisis, no year has gone by without the appearance of at least one book
chronicling every aspect of the chancellor's life from his birth in 1815 until his
death in 1898. Reminiscences, compilations of speeches, anecdotes, personal
recollections of former classmates, friends, and government officials, biographies, as well as other Bismarckiana abound, giving the aficionado of history
enough information to become a Bismarck connoisseur. Bismarck's stature as a
national figure—the architect of the German nation, the advocate of national
integration, the statesman of Europe, and the relentless, irascible, but pragmatic
leader—helps explain in part the notoriety the chancellor has attained over the
past century. The fascination with Bismarck stems from his interaction with the
swiftly moving events of the mid- and late nineteenth century, from his ability
(or in some cases, his inability) to direct what he called the "stream of time."
   Napoleonic Europe was nearing its ignominious end as Wilhelmine Luise (née
Mencken) von Bismarck and Ferdinand von Bismarck celebrated the birth of
their second surviving son, Otto, on April 1, 1815, at their Brandenburg estate
of Schönhausen near Magdeburg. Indeed, to some extent Bismarck was a product
of the winds of social change that swept across Europe following the French
Revolution of 1789. Although his father belonged to a fiercely independent
Prussian landed noble family with a pedigree traceable to the fourteenth century,
his mother came from the ranks of the rising bourgeoisie. Her ancestors, unlike
those of her Junker husband, had served the Prussian state as enlightened civil
servants who welcomed a certain degree of reform within society, the church,

and the state. The same tensions that over the course of the nineteenth century evolved between a formidable old aristocracy whose wealth and prestige were derived from land and a confident bourgeoisie buoyed by education, skill, and sheer determination, and that eventually played themselves out in the course of German unification, were detectable in Bismarck's own life.

At the tender age of six young Otto was sent away to a prestigious boarding school, the Plamann Institute in Berlin. The formalities and rigor of school life, the lack of physical contact with his parents on a regular basis, and the general insecurities of a young child, coupled with a zest for the freedom of the countryside, produced in Bismarck a kind of schizophrenia that remained with him throughout his adulthood. He associated his fears and melancholy, which he blamed on the urban environment and the educational system, with his bourgeois mother, and cherished, therefore, the aristocratic bearing of his father and rural society. Bismarck's later disdain of the city, dominating women, intellectuals, and bureaucrats, and his emphasis on authority may be traced in large part to his childhood experiences.

As much as Bismarck may have discounted the influence of his overbearing mother, he could not escape the fact that he inherited her intellect and willful determination. Although Bismarck disliked the trappings of a formal education, his years in the gymnasium and at the University of Göttingen introduced him to new avenues, especially with regard to literature. Even as the "ablest statesman in Europe," as a *Vanity Fair* cartoon of October 15, 1870, described him, Bismarck never lost his interest in the German literary giants Goethe and Schiller, or in their English counterparts, Shakespeare and Lord Byron. Their ideas and written work remained etched upon his memory until his very last days, and he was fond of quoting from them in his memorable speeches to the Reichstag. Of course, Bismarck was equally enamored of dueling, drinking, smoking, and eating, which he often did to excess and which nearly ended his life at an early age. It was not incongruous with his youthful actions that he obtained the epithet "Wild Bismarck."

But even the most disinherited spirits seem to find their way eventually back to the fold, and this was the case for Bismarck. The 1830s and 1840s were transitional periods for the future German statesman. At the University of Göttingen he fell under the influence of the historian Arnold Heeren and his pragmatic approach to the interests of the state and European diplomacy. It has been suggested that Heeren's theories provided the basis for Bismarck's famous Realpolitik. Bismarck's student days coincided with the transformation of Europe's political and social fabric by liberalism and nationalism. Having been unleashed by the French Revolution, both movements threatened to destabilize the traditional balance of power—liberalism by replacing the social, political, and economic fabric of the "old aristocratic order" based on birth, landed wealth, and political power with middle-class talent, business savvy, and what *Metternich called "presumption,"; and nationalism by destroying the geographic foundations upon which the European states and their monarchies had rested. The revolutions of 1848, produced in part by liberal values and economic distress, thrust Bismarck in a new direction.

In the decade following his university studies, Bismarck's life was nearly as tumultuous as the society around him; after a brief engagement in the civil service, he entered into a series of failed love affairs, finally marrying the pietistic Johanna von Puttkamer in 1847. Bismarck, who now claimed to have undergone a religious conversion, entered the provincial Diet as a representative during the initial months of the 1848 revolution. From the "Wild Bismarck" of the 1830s he became the pragmatic Bismarck of the 1850s.

Bismarck's defense of the monarchy during both the revolutions of 1848 (including his role in the founding of the conservative newspaper *Kreuzzeitung*) and the controversy with Austria that ended with the Olmütz Punctation of 1850, led to his appointment as envoy in Frankfurt (1851–1859) and St. Petersburg (1859–1862) and as ambassador in Paris (1862). In these capacities Bismarck observed the intricacies of diplomacy from the inside and formulated his own ideas regarding policymaking, the latter shaped by the social and economic conditions of the 1850s. He came to value the power of public opinion (which he later skillfully exploited on many occasions), understand the significance of industrialization, and appreciate the potential power of German nationalism. Indeed, one might argue that Bismarck's broad appeal as statesman and administrator (especially among the bourgeoisie) lay in his ability to portray himself as a man of the people, as businessman, farmer, dutiful Christian, and observant nationalist. A staunch monarchist and firm believer in the omnipotence of the state, Bismarck envisioned himself as a servant of both the state and the king.

And serve both interests well he did. Bismarck, it seemed, thrived on conflict, and it was appropriate, therefore, that his swift rise to power occurred during what was known as the *Konfliktszeit* (time of conflict). A serious rift between the newly crowned king, Wilhelm I, and the Liberals in the *Landtag*, ostensibly over the expansion of the Prussian army, but in fact over the parliament's constitutional role in financial affairs, brought Bismarck into the fray in 1862. As the *Konfliktsminister*, Bismarck relished the opportunity to bring the recalcitrant Liberals into line; nonetheless, the task proved to be difficult, albeit not insurmountable. Some years later Bismarck compared his dealings with parliamentary representatives to the skill of a circus juggler, adding that in politics there were "no formulae or rules from which the solution may be deduced in advance." Indeed, Bismarck was fond of reiterating that no one, himself included, could steer the currents of history. All he could do was to direct them as best he could. A combination of events—wars against Denmark over Schleswig and Holstein (1864), Austria (1866), and finally France (1870)—enabled Bismarck not only to reestablish the position of the monarch over his Liberal opponents but also to unify Germany in 1871 under the auspices of Prussia.

Bismarck's reward for his hard work was the chancellorship of the new German nation, a position he held until 1890. For two decades the "Iron Chancellor" left his indelible imprint on Germany in both domestic and foreign policy. Unlike the fine red wine he loved, however, the chancellor did not mature gracefully; while in public he demanded the complete obedience of his officials and his citizens that he believed was due an elder statesman, in private all too often he acted like a spoiled child, even occasionally threatening the king with resignation and feigning or exaggerating illness to ensure that others appreciated his indispensability. This portrait of Bismarck is less familiar but no less essential to a balanced view of his personality and policies. Bismarck's ability to pursue his domestic and foreign policies also depended on the good graces of his monarch, Kaiser Wilhelm I. After the death of Wilhelm I in 1888, followed by the untimely demise of the crown prince from throat cancer that same year, Bismarck's maneuverability was severely restricted by their successor, Wilhelm II (*William II). Their different approaches to issues, as well as their conflicting personalities, placed the chancellor and the new kaiser on a collision course. In March 1890, Wilhelm II resolved the conflict by dismissing his veteran minister. Bismarck's era had come to an end. Eight years later, on July 28, 1898, he died at the age of eighty-three.

Accounting for, let alone assessing, all of Bismarck's achievements throughout the three decades he served the German state from 1862 to 1890 is a daunting task for any historian. Bismarck's name, of course, will always be inextricably linked with the wars that resulted in the establishment of a unified Germany in 1871, the Three Emperors' League (initiated in 1873), the Berlin Conference of 1878, and German colonialism, which began in the early 1880s. In little more than two decades Bismarck molded Germany into the most formidable power on the Continent; his accomplishments were no mean feat, despite *Napoleon I's claim that the Germans were ripe for leadership, a destiny the emperor himself believed he would fulfill. Nevertheless, that Bismarck was able to accomplish as much as he did in such a short time is astonishing in itself.

What made Bismarck a great statesman? How was he able to accomplish as much as he did for Germany? Were his acts of diplomacy always successful? Bismarck thought of himself as a "disciplined statesman who subordinates himself to the total needs and requirements of the state in the interests of peace and the welfare of [his] country." Rejection of partisan politics was also a prerequisite for a statesman, since Bismarck believed that political bickering served to divide rather than unify the state. Yet even if a statesman followed Bismarck's definition, he might fail the ultimate test. The Iron Chancellor often emphasized that diplomacy was an art, not a craft that "could be learnt by years and developed by rote on a roller." "Diplomacy is no shoemaker's stool on which one can sit, stretch a kneestrap, and put a patch on a hole." A premium was placed on flexibility and realism. "In politics one certainly has to reckon with given and unknown quantities at one and the same time," Bismarck once said. Some of his contemporaries (such as *Napoleon III), recalling only his earlier excesses or inflexibility, underestimated their man and were taught a painful lesson, but others recognized that Bismarck's pragmatism was now effectively harnessed to a strong sense of purpose and personal ambition. When Great Britain's prime minister, *Benjamin Disraeli, met Bismarck and heard that he intended to unify Germany under Prussian auspices, Disraeli observed that Bismarck was a man worth noting as someone who meant what he said, however improbable.

The swiftness with which German unification was achieved (in less than a decade) and the circumstances under which it occurred (successive Prussian victories over three rivals, Denmark, Austria, and France) lent themselves to myth making. The 1860s were Bismarck's heroic years. Bismarck himself cultivated this image in subsequent speech and actions. "From the very beginning of my career," Bismarck remarked, "I have had only one guiding principle: By what means and in what way can I make Germany a united nation? And when this object has been attained, how can I fortify and encourage this unity, so that it may of its own free will take advantage of all the surrounding circumstances to maintain itself forever?" One is immediately struck by the strength of Bismarck's resolve. But unification was not achieved by will alone; the weakness of his opponents' armies (particularly those of Denmark and Austria), their underestimation of a Prussian military machine aided by new technology (including the needle gun and the railway), and the sudden vacancy on the Spanish throne in 1868, which led to the nomination of a Hohenzollern candidate, presented Bismarck with a series of opportunities for achieving his goal. Of course, the resolution of the domestic crisis that brought Bismarck into power depended on his ability to rally public opinion and divide his Liberal opponents. Certainly, domestic policy in part underpinned Bismarck's realpolitik of the 1860s.

Yet, concerns of foreign policy also influenced Bismarck's decisions about Prussia's role in the process of unification. Since the days of the Holy Roman Empire, Austria and Prussia had been at loggerheads over territorial claims. The Congress of Vienna gave the responsibility for the protection of the German states formerly belonging to the Holy Roman Empire to both Austria and Prussia. When in 1850 Austria and Prussia nearly went to war over a dispute in Hesse-Kassel (culminating in the Olmütz Punctation), Bismarck argued that Prussia should refrain from engaging its rival in what he believed would be a "war of principle" contrary to the interests of the state. What Bismarck meant was that Prussia was not prepared to do battle with Austria in 1850. That a conflict between the two rival powers would eventually occur was clear in his mind. According to Bismarck, Prussia's domestic as well as foreign interests necessitated the removal of Austria as a factor in the process of German unification. The prime minister's distaste for Roman Catholicism, in particular its emphasis on the authority of the pope as opposed to that of the state, also colored his views about the necessity of a *Kleindeutsch* (or Prussian) solution devoid of any Austrian participation or influence.

The war against Denmark over Schleswig and Holstein in 1864, fought by both Austria and Prussia, enabled Bismarck to further isolate his expendable ally. For two years Bismarck played upon Austria's desire to cooperate with Prussia over Schleswig-Holstein, while he promoted the interests of the Prussian state. Bismarck counted on Austria's having to choose between its Italian and

Prussian interests, on increasing nationalistic unrest in Austria to destabilize the domestic sphere, and on France's neutrality should Prussia go to war with Austria. Once the latter was secured, Bismarck pursued his aim of annexing Schleswig and Holstein, forcing Austria into a war in July 1866 that ended seven weeks later in Prussian victory.

With Austria no longer a threat, Bismarck's next target was obviously France. The defeat of Austria had brought some but not all of the German states into the Prussian sphere. Only a war in which France appeared as the aggressor could possibly bring the remaining states into the new union created by Bismarck in 1867 (the North German Confederation). The controversy over the succession to the Spanish throne provided an opportunity; when Bismarck received a telegram confirming that the German candidate for the Spanish throne had withdrawn, he edited the so-called Bad Ems Dispatch to indicate that French sensibilities had been brutally insulted. With French honor at stake, war was now inevitable, and though France resisted longer than had Austria, the Franco-Prussian War (1870–1871) ended in Prussia's triumph. The new German Empire was proclaimed in Versailles, a reminder that the road to unification had been paved with blood and diplomacy.

If the decade of the 1860s can be viewed in terms of Prussia's military prowess and territorial expansion against its neighbors, the decade of the 1870s reflected the Iron Chancellor's desire for peace and stability on the Continent. He insisted that Germany was now a satiated nation and that its neighbors need not live in fear. Bismarck's desire was to promote the progress of national integration within Germany, a process that relied on foreign as well as domestic stability. While on the home front he launched a series of campaigns against the Roman Catholic Church (*Kulturkampf*) and the nascent socialist movement (Anti-Socialist Laws) and parted company with his Liberal allies, in 1873 Bismarck created the Three Emperors' League, a foreign alliance reminiscent of the former Holy Alliance.

The alliance between Austria, Russia, and Germany was a marriage of convenience in that it prevented the parties involved from forming separate antagonistic alliances against each other. For Bismarck, too, it functioned as a shield against a vengeful France. The chancellor's Francophobia, however, was not shared to the same degree by his alliance partners, and even he was fearful that the alliance might drive France into the arms of Britain. The "War-in-Sight" crisis of 1875, provoked by news of the French army's expansion and aggravated by a rumor that the archbishop of Paris (angered by the German chancellor's anti-Catholic programs) had placed a bounty on Bismarck's head, heightened tensions on the Continent. The stability of the chancellor's alliance, however, depended not only on anti-French rhetoric, but also on the cooperation of Austria and Russia over their interests in the Balkans.

The Eastern Question remained a thorn in the side of European peacemakers throughout the nineteenth century. In July 1875 the Balkans once again exploded in a series of ethnic uprisings against the Ottoman Empire, whose demise was anticipated and welcomed. A combination of explosive issues such as nationalism, religion, economics, and government inefficiency was as much to blame as ethnic animosities for the persistent unrest. Russia, Austria, and Britain all claimed interests in the region. Russia sought to enlarge its geographic position in the West and employed the Pan-Slavic movement as a vehicle for its territorial designs; Austria feared both the nationalistic fervor that threatened to destroy its own fragile multinational state and the loss of Austrian business interests in the area; while Britain worried that Russian expansion would endanger British commerce and the jewel of its empire, India. Russia's declaration of war against the Ottoman Empire in April 1877 and its rapid advance across Ottoman territory prompted the British to warn that a Russian seizure of Constantinople, thereby threatening the passageway to India, would result in a declaration of war against Russia. Neither Austria nor Britain was prepared to see the balance of power tilted in favor of the Russians. When events in the Balkans threatened to unleash a full-scale war among Russia, Austria, and England, Bismarck offered his services as a mediator in the dispute. During June and July of 1878, ministers from these countries met with Bismarck in Berlin. By the conclusion of the Congress of Berlin Bismarck had succeeded in arranging a settlement, although the Russians felt betrayed by his professed neutrality and their own inability to secure greater territorial concessions from the Ottoman Empire. One might argue that the Congress of Berlin strengthened the bonds between Austria and Germany, while it placed Germany's long-term relationship with Russia in doubt.

With the Eastern Question temporarily settled, Bismarck turned, somewhat reluctantly at first, to the issue of colonialism. France, Spain, Britain, and even tiny Belgium and the Netherlands already had colonial possessions; but Germany had none. German businessmen's interest in colonialism, however, preceded that of the German state. Although Bismarck entertained doubts about the efficacy of colonial acquisitions in view of the cost of administration and the absence of a viable German navy to protect them, by 1883–1884 a combination of factors led him to reverse his stand. His concern for a weakened German economy and the possible exclusion of German business from overseas markets in a climate of protectionism, coupled with his belief that international stability favored German expansion, resulted in Germany's bid for a colonial empire. Throughout the 1880s Germany secured parts of Africa, including the Cameroons, Southwest Africa, and East Africa. The extension of the German flag abroad certainly improved Germany's international visibility and generally found support among the German bourgeoisie. Nevertheless, as late as 1888, Bismarck's assertion that his map of Africa lay in Europe, with Germany in the middle surrounded by potential enemies (France and Russia), suggested where his true concerns lay.

Annotated Bibliography

That Bismarck's career as a statesman has received as much attention and provoked as much controversy as it has owes in part to the survival of primary and secondary materials about the chancellor. For example, Bismarck's *Nachlass* (including his political correspondence, manuscripts, family history, and other papers) can be found in the

Bismarck-Archiv, Friedrichsruh (Bezirk Hamburg), at the family estate. Other portions of the *Nachlass* are on microfilm at the Bundesarchiv Koblenz, Potsdamer Straße 1, Postfach 320, 5400 Koblenz 1. Bismarck's memoirs, speeches, and correspondence (including that with his wife, leading political figures, and Wilhelm I) are recorded for posterity in Otto von Bismarck, *Erinnerung und Gedanke* (1898), reprinted many times; *Fürst Bismarcks Briefe an seine Braut und Gattin* (1900); and *Die politische Reden des Fürsten Bismarcks* (1892–1905). Available in English translation is Heinrich von Poschinger, ed., *Conversations with Prince Bismarck* (1900).

Since 1862 thousands of scholarly as well as amateur books and articles have been published about Bismarck and his legacy. Historiographically, Bismarck's impact as statesman and architect of the German nation is often viewed from two extremes: in positive terms, as the forceful but pragmatic German administrator who raised Germany's continental and international status, and, in a more negative cast, as the engineer of the locomotive that nearly sixty years later brought Adolf Hitler to power. With regard to the latter view, Bismarck's proclivity for flexing Germany's military muscle and enlarging its geographic borders set a dangerous precedent for future generations. Thus, Bismarck's historical role depends on one's interpretation of the aims of his foreign policy. Was it pursued for purposes of stabilizing domestic politics (*Primat der Innenpolitik*) or for the sake of achieving international prestige (*Primat der Aussenpolitik*)?

A.J.P. Taylor's provocative *Bismarck: The Man and the Statesman* (1955) was one of the first attempts by a historian to portray Bismarck as a fallible human being rather than a titan. Taylor suggests that Bismarck's foreign policies cannot be linked to Hitler and the Third Reich. A more comprehensive and analytical biography of the Iron Chancellor is Lothar Gall's two-volume *Bismarck, the White Revolutionary* (1986) which guides the reader gracefully through the labyrinth of Bismarck's foreign and domestic policy with precision. Gall argues that Bismarck's success in foreign policy lay in his flexibility and suggests that the chancellor belongs to Hegel's category of "world-historical individuals." In 1985 the East German Ernst Engelberg published the first part of what would be a two-volume study in German, *Bismarck. Urpreuße und Reichsgründer*. The second volume appeared in 1990 as *Bismarck, Das Reich in der Mitte Europas*. Engelberg, in contrast to Gall, stresses the importance of principles in Bismarck's decision making, insisting, for example, that from the mid-1850s Bismarck understood that German unification was possible only within the framework of a *Kleindeutsch* solution and by meeting the desires of Germany's liberal bourgeoisie for a national state.

The newest of the comprehensive Bismarck biographies is the long anticipated three-volume study by Otto Pflanze, published in the fall of 1990 under the title *Bismarck and the Development of Germany*. Pflanze refuses to choose between the notions of *Primat der Aussen* and *Primat der Innenpolitik*, arguing that neither of these spheres is fully autonomous since they are interdependent. Moreover, Pflanze insists that the tide of German nationalism alone was insufficient to achieve unification; it occurred primarily as a result of Bismarck's "stimulation." In assessing the direction and aim of Bismarck's foreign policy after 1871, Pflanze concludes that it helped to create an international order that survived until 1914.

West German historian Hans-Ulrich Wehler's classic history of Bismarckian imperialism, *Bismarck und der Imperialismus* (1969), the argument of which is condensed in "Bismarck's Imperialism, 1862–1890," *Past and Present* 48 (1970): 119–155, depicts Bismarck as a social imperialist who manipulated imperialism as a device to integrate a German state riven with social cleavages (*Primat der Innenpolitik*). Wehler suggests that the chancellor's policies of "pragmatic expansion" inaugurated what would develop as a persistent theme in German foreign policy, the resort to aggressively nationalistic measures that in the hands of less "pragmatic" individuals such as Hitler would have the most terrible consequences.

Bibliography

Aretin, Karl Otmar Freiherr von. *Bismarcks Aussenpolitik und der Berliner Konferenz.* Wiesbaden: Steiner, 1978.

Engelberg, Ernst. *Bismarck. Das Reich in der Mitte Europas.* Berlin: Siedler, 1990.

———. *Bismarck. Urpreuße und Reichsgründer.* Berlin: Siedler, 1985.

Eyck, Erich. *Bismarck and the German Empire.* London: Allen and Unwin, 1950.

Förster, Stig, Wolfgang J. Mommsen, and Ronald Robinson, eds. *Bismarck, Europe, and Africa: The Berlin Africa Conference 1884–85 and the Onset of Partition.* Oxford: Oxford University Press, 1988.

Hamerow, Theodore, ed. *Reminiscences and Reflections.* New York: Harper and Row, 1968.

Gall, Lothar. *Bismarck, the White Revolutionary.* 2 vols. Boston: Allen and Unwin, 1986.

———, ed. *Gedanken und Erinnerungen. Bismarck.* Frankfurt: Propyläen, 1990.

Geiss, Imanuel. *German Foreign Policy 1871–1914.* London: Routledge and Kegan Paul, 1976.

Howard, Michael. *The Franco-Prussian War.* London: Hart-Davis, 1961.

Kennedy, Paul M. *The Rise of the Anglo-German Antagonism, 1860–1914.* London: Allen and Unwin, 1980.

Kohl, Horst, ed. *Die politischen Reden des Fürsten Bismarck.* 14 vols. Stuttgart: Cotta, 1892–1905.

Medlicott, W. N. *Bismarck and Modern Germany.* London: Hodder and Stoughton, 1965.

———. *Bismarck, Gladstone, and the Concert of Europe.* Westport, Conn.: Greenwood Press, 1969.

———. *Congress of Berlin and After.* 2nd ed. London: Methuen, 1963.

Mosse, Werner E. *The European Powers and the German Question 1848–1871.* Cambridge: Cambridge University Press, 1958.

Pflanze, Otto. *Bismarck and the Development of Germany.* 3 vols. Princeton, N.J.: Princeton University Press, 1990.

Poschinger, Heinrich Ritter von, ed. *Conversations with Prince Bismarck.* New York: Harper, 1900.

Steefel, Lawrence D. *Bismarck, the Hohenzollern Candidacy, and the Origins of the Franco-German War.* Cambridge, Mass.: Harvard University Press, 1962.

———. *The Schleswig-Holstein Question.* Cambridge, Mass.: Harvard University Press, 1932.

Strandmann, Hartmut Pogge von. "The Domestic Origins of Germany's Colonial Expansion under Bismarck." *Past and Present* 42 (1969): 140–159.

Taylor, A.J.P. *Bismarck: The Man and the Statesman.* London: Hamish Hamilton, 1955.

———. *Germany's First Bid for Colonies 1884–1885.* London: Macmillan, 1938.

Turner, Henry A. "Bismarck's Imperialist Venture: Anti-British in Origin?" In *Britain and Germany in Africa*, pp. 47–82. Edited by P. Gifford and W. R. Lewis. New Haven, Conn.: Yale University Press, 1967.

Waller, Bruce. *Bismarck at the Crossroads.* London: Athlone Press, 1974.

Wehler, Hans-Ulrich. "Bismarck's Imperialism, 1862–1890. *Past and Present* 48 (1970): 119–155.

———. *Bismarck und der Imperialismus.* Cologne: Kiepenheuer und Witsch, 1969.

MARILYN SHEVIN-COETZEE

James G. Blaine (1830–1893).   James Gillespie Blaine was perhaps the most prominent and controversial national political figure ever appointed to the office of U.S. secretary of state, a post he held on two occasions, in 1881 and again from 1889 to 1892. Because of his enormous fame, Blaine, always more of a political figure than a diplomat, was able to create a new public interest in and awareness of foreign policy issues at a time when the inward-looking nation was preoccupied with domestic matters. In the decades preceding the overseas expansion of 1898 and the emergence of the United States as a world power, Blaine was the premiere spokesman urging a greater role for his nation in the Western Hemisphere and the Pacific.

Blaine was born on January 31, 1830, in West Brownsville, Pennsylvania, where his father, a businessman, was active in local politics. He entered Washington College at the age of thirteen and graduated in 1847, tied with two others for highest honors in a class of thirty-three. A gifted speaker possessing an engaging personality and a solid, well-proportioned physique, young Blaine taught briefly at the Western Military Institute in Georgetown, Kentucky, and then at the Pennsylvania Institute for the Education of the Blind from 1852 to 1854. He also read law while residing in Philadelphia, but did not complete his studies, nor did he seek admission to the bar.

In June 1850 Blaine secretly married Harriet Stanwood, a teacher he met while in Kentucky. Her family had roots in New England, and with the assistance of his father-in-law Blaine moved to Augusta, Maine, where he acquired an interest in the Kennebec *Journal* and the Portland *Advertiser*. Early in his journalistic career Blaine, who as a young Whig had admired Henry Clay, demonstrated a keen interest in national politics, particularly the issue of slavery. A founder of the Republican party in his new home state, he was a delegate to the first national Republican convention in 1856 and served as one of its secretaries. In 1859 he became chairman of the Republican state committee and held that post until 1881. He was elected to the state legislature in 1858, won reelection twice, and served there as Speaker of the House in 1861–1862. He was elected to the U.S. House of Representatives in 1862 and began a rapid rise to national prominence.

An enthusiastic supporter of Lincoln and the cause of the Union throughout the Civil War, Blaine approved granting the franchise to black men; however, during the early years of Reconstruction he broke with Republicans advocating radical measures. Allied with "western" leaders in Congress, such as James A. Garfield of Ohio, Blaine was elected Speaker of the House in 1869. He continued to oppose the more extreme reconstruction measures during the Grant administration; however, he rejected a general amnesty for southerners. His positions on most matters, such as currency and tariff issues, were moderate, and Blaine emerged as a leader of the "Half-Breeds," a party faction opposed to Grant and the more conservative Stalwarts.

In 1876 Blaine appeared to be the leading candidate for his party's nomination for the presidency until bitter opposition from political rival Roscoe Conkling of New York and charges of personal corruption diminished his popularity and weakened his support. Blaine defended himself against allegations that, as Speaker of the House, he had unethically helped secure a land grant in 1869 for the Little Rock and Ft. Smith Railroad, a corporation in which he later held a financial interest. He also defended himself against charges that he had accepted a bribe of Union Pacific bonds worth $64,000. While the accusations were not proven, too many questions remained about his acquisition of personal wealth without visible means, and Blaine's candidacy failed. The GOP's nomination went to Governor Rutherford B. Hayes of Ohio. After receiving an appointment to the U.S. Senate in 1876, Blaine was later elected to that body, where he supported the Hayes administration against attacks from Conkling and the Stalwarts. His role in the Senate kept Blaine in the public eye, and in 1880 he again emerged as the most prominent contender for his party's presidential nomination. But once again he was denied. The nomination went instead to Garfield, with Conkling's ally Chester A. Arthur added to the ticket as the vice-presidential candidate.

Following his election victory, Garfield selected Blaine to serve as secretary of state. Now, for the first time in his public career, Blaine turned his attention to the planning and administration of foreign policy. Garfield and his secretary of state enjoyed a close personal relationship. Although Garfield recognized Blaine as overly ambitious, uninterested in political reform, and not entirely trustworthy, the president admired his energetic, persuasive, and politically astute colleague and consulted regularly with him on matters of patronage and strategy. The two also worked closely to develop an ambitious new American foreign policy, although, according to Garfield's most authoritative biographer, Allan Peskin, it is difficult to determine the extent to which either man was responsible for the initiatives, since neither had previously addressed important diplomatic questions.

The Garfield administration took office at a time when U.S. involvement in world affairs was at its nadir. While his immediate predecessors had occupied themselves with relatively routine matters, Blaine, an ardent nationalist, felt strongly that the United States deserved a place among the world's leaders. He refused to limit himself to endless negotiations involving restrictions on the importation of American pork and the condition of Irish prisoners in British jails.

In seeking to advance U.S. interests abroad, the administration turned its attention to Latin America and, to a lesser extent, the Pacific. Blaine saw in the new Pan-American diplomacy an opportunity to turn the principles of the Monroe Doctrine (1823) into a positive force. In addition, he believed that a Pan-American initiative could limit the influence of the British and other European powers in the hemisphere, thereby fulfilling Henry Clay's vision of an American System.

When the administration came into office in 1881, Mexico and Guatemala were near war over a border dispute. Costa Rica and Colombia were also having border problems, as were Chile and Argentina. France was threatening military action against Venezuela to collect a debt, and Chile was engaged in war against both Bolivia and Peru. Meanwhile, the United States and Great Britain were reconsidering the Clayton-Bulwer Treaty of 1850. To address these problems, the administration sought to adopt a comprehensive plan, amounting to a major redirection of American policy to preserve the status quo in the Western Hemisphere under the peaceful and benevolent leadership of the United States. Blaine intended to initiate this new program with a Pan-American Conference in Washington. However, the assassination of Garfield (which reduced Blaine to tears) and the succession to the presidency of Conkling's man, Arthur, ended the Pan-American initiative as well as Blaine's service in the cabinet. He left office December 18, 1881, after having served less than a year.

Blaine learned in February 1882 of Arthur's plans to cancel the Washington conference on Pan-American issues, and he attempted without success to change the president's mind. "Beyond the philanthropic and Christian ends to be obtained by the American Conference," he wrote, "... we might well hope for material advantages as a result of better understanding and closer friendship with the nations of America." But Arthur was determined to chart a different course from his predecessor. Moreover, Blaine's own lack of tact and diplomatic skill had aroused suspicion and resentment at home and abroad, making it easier for Arthur to abandon the bold departure from traditional U.S. policy that Garfield and Blaine had initiated.

Blaine's brief tenure marked new directions in Latin American relations in several controversial matters. He sought unilaterally to void the Clayton-Bulwer Treaty of 1850 (under which the United States and Great Britain had agreed to a joint development of a canal in Panama, then part of Colombia) by inviting other nations to join in a guarantee of neutrality. Recognizing that a canal dominated by the United States and providing unrestricted passage to his nation's naval forces was essential for the new role he envisioned in the Western Hemisphere, Blaine sought to eliminate British involvement in the canal. Blaine claimed that conditions had changed following Colombia's concession to a French company for building a canal. A heated exchange of notes between the United States and Great Britain followed. However, as no realistic or peaceful means of voiding the treaty presented itself, Blaine turned his attention away from further negotiations with Great Britain and focused on negotiating with Nicaragua for a canal to be built and defended by the United States.

Considering the various disputes among the Latin American nations and between Latin American nations and European powers to be a threat to hemispheric stability, Blaine forcefully interceded, claiming for the United States the role of arbitrator or broker. To prevent the French from seizing the Venezuelan customs houses in their dispute over unpaid debts, Blaine insisted that the United States serve as the agent through which the Venezuelans would pay, and threatened that the United States would itself seize the customs houses if payments were not forthcoming within three months. In June 1881 Blaine issued a letter of protest to Spain seeking to have the United States rather than that European nation serve as arbitrator in a boundary dispute between Colombia and Costa Rica. Blaine also put forth the United States as a mediator in disputes between Mexico and Guatemala and between Chile and Peru, where his agent, William H. Trescot, warned the Chileans that their aggression could bring about the intervention of the United States.

Blaine's second opportunity to head the State Department came in 1889 when, after some hesitation, President Benjamin Harrison asked his onetime rival to serve in the cabinet. In the years following his first tenure as secretary of state, Blaine's political ambitions had been frustrated. In 1884, following a bitter campaign, he lost to the Democrat Grover Cleveland in the presidential election. Then, in 1888, Blaine withdrew as a candidate for his party's nomination when it became clear to him that he could not secure it. Nevertheless, Blaine remained a formidable politician with a loyal following. Harrison was cognizant of this; however, he was leery of Blaine and chose to involve himself directly in shaping foreign relations, relying heavily on advice from Secretary of the Navy Benjamin Tracy, senior State Department officials, and former diplomat turned international lawyer John W. Foster. Further, Blaine's frequent and prolonged illnesses and the death of a daughter and two of his sons kept him away from the active role he had enjoyed in the Garfield administration.

Despite their differences in style and personality, Blaine and Harrison shared a belief in the need for greater American involvement in world affairs, particularly in Latin America and the Pacific. Both held that the United States needed greater access to overseas markets, particularly for agricultural products. To achieve this the administration looked to acquire what the president called "stations and points of interest." Blaine described the objective as "annexation of trade," and in 1891 advised the president that "there are only three places that are of value enough to be taken that are not continental. One is Hawaii and the others are Cuba and Puerto Rico. Cuba and Puerto Rico are not now imminent and will not be for a generation. Hawaii may come up for decision at any unexpected hour and I hope we shall be prepared to decide in the affirmative." Blaine's analysis proved prophetic, although Cuba and Puerto Rico became critical issues in less than half a generation. Hawaii did indeed come up, but only after Blaine had left office and been succeeded by John W. Foster. Although Blaine's ambitions for insular expansion were not realized until years later, most scholars credit him with helping develop a foreign policy view that would gain national acceptance by the close of the nineteenth century.

To the extent allowed by his failing health, family tragedies, and lack of rapport with Harrison, Blaine pursued an assertive foreign policy. In October 1889 a Pan-American Congress, provided for by legislation passed in the final year of the Cleveland administration, met in Washington, D.C., and

Blaine presided over lengthy sessions that drafted nonbinding recommendations for arbitration and improved commercial intercourse. The conference's
lasting contribution was the establishment of a Bureau of American Republics in Washington. In an effort to improve trade with Latin America, Blaine
advocated the negotiation of reciprocal trade agreements, and reciprocity
treaties were successfully concluded with Brazil, with Spain for its colonies
of Cuba and Puerto Rico, and with several other nations. However, these
agreements were in place for too short a duration for their effectiveness to
be assessed.

The administration aggressively pursued an end to Germany's prohibition of
the importation of American pork (although Blaine's position on this issue was
far more conciliatory than that of Harrison). Blaine and the president also took
an aggressive stand against Great Britain over the harvesting of fur seals by
Canadian vessels in the Bering Sea. A joint protectorate over Samoa was negotiated with Great Britain and Germany.

Meanwhile, unsuccessful efforts were made to acquire the Danish West
Indies, secure a lease for Samano Bay in Santo Domingo, and arrange for a
concession of the Mole Saint Nicolas in Haiti. Serious consideration was
given to the establishment of a naval base in Chimbote, Peru; and, in the
administration's most aggressive international action, the United States demanded an apology and reparations from Chile following an ugly incident in
1891 in which sailors from the U.S.S. *Baltimore* were attacked by a Chilean
mob.

Beyond his efforts to advance American interests and prestige, Blaine demonstrated an interest in the general improvement of international relations. He
negotiated a treaty on extradition with Great Britain, joined in international efforts
to suppress the African slave trade, and put in effect the nation's first international
copyright treaties.

Blaine's two disconnected terms as secretary of state were characterized by
frustration. The assassination of Garfield ended Blaine's plans for Pan-American
diplomacy in 1881; and his strained relationship with the unfriendly, suspicious,
and insecure Harrison, coupled with his personal troubles, limited his effectiveness during his second tenure. In addition, Blaine lacked experience in foreign
affairs. With no background in diplomacy or international law, he proved un-
skilled as a tactician and strategist. Moreover, his recommendations for overseas
appointments, often made on the basis of political patronage, proved inept with
embarrassing regularity. Also, Blaine was notoriously lacking in administrative
skills, and this weakness became increasingly obvious as his health deteriorated.
Blaine died on January 27, 1893, in Washington, D.C.

Blaine's importance as an international statesman rests largely with his enormous political stature, unique among U.S. secretaries of state before and since.
Blaine clearly brought heightened public attention to foreign affairs. He served
as an important spokesman in two administrations for an expanded United States
presence in the world, a Pan-American policy in which the United States would

assume a leadership role in the hemisphere to the exclusion of the European powers, promotion of American commercial interests in the Far East and the Western Hemisphere, and the acquisition of insular possessions in the Pacific and the Caribbean. Blaine, like his political ideal Henry Clay, argued for an America for Americans and exhibited hostility toward the European powers, particularly Great Britain. Yet for all his public rhetoric, expressed largely for domestic political purposes, Blaine's actions as secretary of state were moderate. In fact, especially during the Harrison administration, Blaine often found himself alone in urging caution and compromise. Indeed, his public expressions often camouflaged his true Anglophile sentiments, for he privately shared the notion of Anglo-Saxon superiority and admired British institutions. Although Blaine holds a place as the most important secretary of state in the three decades between *William H. Seward and John Hay, he remains significant more for his vision than for his actual accomplishments.

Annotated Bibliography

The few Blaine papers that exist are held in the Manuscripts Division of the Library of Congress (about a dozen boxes) and the Georgetown University Archives in Washington, D.C. *The Correspondence between Benjamin Harrison and James G. Blaine*, edited by Albert T. Volwiler (1940), sheds light on Blaine's relationship with the president and the formation of foreign policy. Blaine's own numerous publications, particularly *Twenty Years of Congress: From Lincoln to Garfield*, 2 vols. (1884–1886), and *Political Discussions: Legislative, Diplomatic, and Popular, 1856–1886* (1887), provide his views on many subjects. Also of interest concerning Blaine's domestic life is Harriet (Stanwood) Blaine Bealle, ed., *Letters of Mrs. James G. Blaine*, 2 vols. (1908).

Blaine has proved a difficult subject for biographers to assess, both as a politician and a diplomat. Historian Lester Langley notes that most early biographies, including campaign pieces and those by family intimates Mary Abigail Dodge (Gail Hamilton) and Edward Stanwood, portray Blaine as a righteous Republican and an intellectual. Scholarly evaluations have been less kind, and revisionist historians of the 1960s and 1970s, particularly William A. Williams in *The Roots of the Modern American Empire* (1969) and Walter LaFeber in *The New Empire* (1963), see Blaine as a major figure in the effort to penetrate industrial and agricultural markets, and view reciprocity as a tactic for achieving a position of dominance in trade with Latin America.

Blaine was often the subject of contemporary writers, but much of this material is of limited value. Among the many campaign and popular biographies of Blaine, the most useful are Gail Hamilton (Mary Abigail Dodge), *Biography of James G. Blaine* (1895), and Edward Stanwood, *James Gillespie Blaine* (1905). Also of interest are Edward H. Strobel, *Mr. Blaine and His Foreign Policy* (1884), Thomas H. Talbot, *The Proudest Chapter of His Life* (1884), and William Henry Hurlbert (*sic*), *Meddling and Muddling: Mr. Blaine's Foreign Policy* (1884). Contemporary journalist Theron C. Crawford's life of Blaine is of particular interest. Although Crawford's biography exonerates Blaine from charges of corruption, historian Donald A. Ritchie sees parallels in Crawford's *James G. Blaine: A Study of His Life and Career* (1893)

and his novel *A Man and His Soul: An Occult Romance of Washington Life* (1894),
which depicts the fall of a popular politician and his ambitious wife as a result of financial misdeeds.

Scholarly, book-length biographies providing serious analysis of Blaine as a politician
and cabinet member are limited to the useful but out-of-date studies of Alice Felt Tyler,
The Foreign Policy of James G. Blaine (1927), and David S. Muzzey, *James G. Blaine:
A Political Idol of Other Days* (1935). Tyler views Blaine as a man of vision and as a
transitional figure holding a place between the expansionist policy of William H. Seward
and the insular expansion and economic penetration pursued by later administrations.
Muzzey is sympathetic to his subject and blames the defeat of Blaine's Pan-American
policy in 1881 on political rivals. Muzzey's work provides a good analysis of trade and
tariff issues and portrays Blaine as more moderate in his second tenure as secretary of
state. Also dated but useful is Joseph B. Lockey, "James G. Blaine," in *American
Secretaries of State and Their Diplomacy*, edited by Samuel F. Bemis (1958), vol. 7,
363–397, and vol. 8, 109—184. The need for a new scholarly biography of Blaine should
soon be addressed by Hal Williams in *James G. Blaine: A Biography*, forthcoming in
1993 or 1994.

Important interpretive essays produced in the past two decades reflect new approaches
to the study of American diplomatic history. Lester D. Langley, "James G. Blaine: The
Ideologue as Diplomatist," in Frank J. Merli and Theodore A. Wilson, eds., *Makers of
American Diplomacy: From Benjamin Franklin to Henry Kissinger* (1974), is the best
interpretive essay of Blaine's diplomatic record. Langley portrays Blaine as a creative
ideologist, influential spokesman, and sincere peacemaker. His essay also includes an
excellent discussion of the various interpretations of the controversial statesman. Allan
Peskin's "Blaine, Garfield and Latin American: A New Look," in Robert Frank, ed.,
The Americas (1978), provides insights into the relationship between the amiable president
and the ambitious secretary of state, and gives Garfield credit for much of the Pan-
American initiative. Allan B. Spetter, "Harrison and Blaine: Foreign Policy, 1889–
1893," *Indiana Magazine of History* 65 (September 1969): 214–227, presents a persuasive
argument that Blaine was usually out of sync and often lacking in influence as Harrison's
secretary of state; and Mike Sewell, "Political Rhetoric and Policy Making: James G.
Blaine and Britain," *Journal of American Studies* 24 (1990): 61–84, concludes that
Blaine's policies show him to be a skilled politician especially in his first tenure as
secretary of state. Sewell believes that Blaine, rather than being a demagogue or an
Anglophobe, consciously sought to mold U.S. policies to fit the reality of America's new
status as an emerging power.

Additional studies examining aspects of Blaine's Pan-American diplomacy include
Russell H. Bastert, "Diplomatic Reversal: Frelinghuysin's Opposition to Blaine's Pan
American Policy in 1882," *Mississippi Valley Historical Review* 42 (1956): 653–671,
and "A New Approach to the Origins of Blaine's Pan American Policy," *Hispanic
American Historical Review* 39 (August 1959); 375–412; and A. Curtis Wilgus,
"James G. Blaine and the Pan American Movement," *Hispanic American Historical
Review* 5 (November 1922): 662–708. Michael J. Devine suggests, in *John W. Fos-
ter: Politics and Diplomacy in the Imperial Era, 1873–1917* (1981) and "John W.
Foster and the Spiritual Diplomacy of the 1890s," *Indiana Historical Collections* 53
(1981): 267–288, that Indiana politician and diplomat John W. Foster played an important behind-the-scenes role in the Harrison administration during Blaine's frequent
illnesses and absences.

Still of value is Albert T. Volwiler, "Harrison, Blaine and American Foreign Policy, 1889–1893," *American Philosophical Society Proceedings* 79 (1938). Also see Carl Russell Fisher, "James G. Blaine," *Dictionary of American Biography* (1933): 11; 322–329.

Bibliography

Works by Blaine

Bealle, Harriet S. Blaine. *Letters of Mrs. James G. Blaine.* New York: Duffield, 1908.
Blaine, James G. *Political Discussions: Legislative, Diplomatic, and Popular, 1856–1886* Norwich, Conn.: Henry Bill, 1887.
———. *Twenty Years of Congress: From Lincoln to Garfield.* 2 vols. Norwich, Conn.: Henry Bill, 1884–1886.
Volwiler, A. T., ed. *The Correspondence between Benjamin Harrison and James G. Blaine.* Philadelphia: American Philosophical Society, 1940.

Works about Blaine

Hamilton, Gail [Mary Abigail Dodge]. *Biography of James G. Blaine.* Norwich, Conn.. Henry Bill, 1895.
Muzzey, David S. *James G. Blaine: A Political Idol of Other Days.* New York: Dodd, Mead, 1935.
Tyler, Alice Felt. *The Foreign Policy of James G. Blaine.* Minneapolis: University of Minnesota Press, 1927.

Related Works

Bastert, Russell H. "Diplomatic Reversal: Frelinghuysen's Opposition to Blaine's Pan American Policy in 1882." *Mississippi Valley Historical Review* 42 (1956): 653–671.
———. "A New Approach to the Origins of Blaine's Pan American Policy." *Hispanic American Historical Review* 39 (August 1959): 375–412.
Burnham, Walter Dean. *Critical Elections and the Mainsprings of American Politics.* New York: Norton, 1970.
Calhoun, Charles C. "Benjamin Harrison, Centennial President: A Review Essay." *Indiana Magazine of History* 84 (June 1988): 135–160.
Campbell, Charles S. "The Anglo-American Crisis in the Bering Sea, 1890–1891." *Mississippi Valley Historical Review* 48 (December 1961): 393–414.
———. "The Bering Sea Settlement of 1892." *Pacific Historical Review* 32 (November 1963): 347–367.
———. *The Transformation of American Foreign Relations, 1865–1900.* New York: Harper and Row, 1976.
Crawford, Theron C. *James G. Blaine. A Study of His Life and Career from the Standpoint of a Personal Witness of the Principal Events in His History.* Philadelphia: Winston, 1893.
———. *A Man and His Soul: An Occult Romance of Washington Life.* New York: Reed, 1894.
Devine, Michael J. *John W. Foster: Politics and Diplomacy in the Imperial Era, 1873–1917.* Athens: Ohio University Press, 1981.

———. "John W. Foster and the Spiritual Diplomacy of the 1890s." *Indiana Historical Collections* 53 (1981): 267–288.

Doenecke, Justus. *The Presidencies of James A. Garfield and Chester A. Arthur.* Lawrence: Regents Press of Kansas, 1981.

Dozer, Donald. "Benjamin Harrison and the Presidential Campaign in 1892." *American Historical Review* 54 (October 1948): 49–77.

Fisher, Carl Russell. "James G. Blaine." *Dictionary of American Biography* (1933): 11: 322–329.

Foster, John W. *Diplomatic Memoirs.* 2 vols. Boston: Houghton Mifflin, 1909.

Gignilliat, John L. "Pigs, Politics and Protection: The European Boycott of American Pork, 1879–91." *Agricultural History* 35 (January 1961): 3–12.

Goldberg, Joyce. *The "Baltimore" Affair.* Lincoln: University of Nebraska Press, 1986.

Grenville, John A. S., and George Berkeley Young. *Politics, Strategy and American Diplomacy: Studies in Foreign Policy, 1873–1917.* New Haven, Conn.: Yale University Press, 1966.

Hays, Samuel P. "The Social Analysis of American Political History, 1880–1920." *Political Science Quarterly* 80 (1965): 373–394.

Hurlbert, William H. *Meddling and Muddling: Mr. Blaine's Foreign Policy.* New York: N.p., 1884.

Jordan, David M. *Roscoe Conkling of New York: Voice in the Senate.* Ithaca, N.Y.: Cornell University Press, 1971.

LaFeber, Walter. *The New Empire: An Interpretation of American Expansion, 1860–1898.* Ithaca, N.Y.: Cornell University Press, 1963.

Langley, Lester D. "James G. Blaine: The Ideologue as Diplomatist." In *Makers of American Diplomacy: From Benjamin Franklin to Henry Kissinger.* Edited by Frank J. Merli and Theodore A. Wilson. New York: Scribner's, 1974.

Lockey, Joseph B. "James G. Blaine." In *American Secretaries of State and Their Diplomacy.* Edited by Samuel F. Bemis. New York: Pageant, 1958–1967.

Morgan, H. Wayne. *From Hayes to McKinley: National Party Politics, 1877–1896.* Syracuse, N.Y.: Syracuse University Press, 1969.

Peskin, Allan. "Blaine, Garfield and Latin America: A New Look." In *The Americas.* Edited by Robert Frank. Millerton, N.Y.: Aperture, 1978.

Plesur, Milton. "America Looking Outward: The Years from Hayes to Harrison." *Historian* 22 (May 1960): 280–295.

———. *America's Outward Thrust: Approaches to Foreign Affairs, 1865–1890.* DeKalb: Northern Illinois University Press, 1971.

Pletcher, David. *The Awkward Years: American Foreign Relations under Garfield and Arthur.* Columbia: University of Missouri Press, 1962.

———. "Reciprocity and Latin America in the Early 1890's: A Foretaste of Dollar Diplomacy." *Pacific Historical Review* 47 (February 1978): 53–89.

Sewell, Mike. "Political Rhetoric and Policy Making: James G. Blaine and Britain." *Journal of American Studies* 24 (1990): 61–84.

Spetter, Allan B. "Harrison and Blaine: Foreign Policy, 1889–1893." *Indiana Magazine of History* 65 (September 1969): 214–227.

Stanwood, Edward. *American Tariff Controversies in the Nineteenth Century.* 2 vols. Boston: Houghton Mifflin, 1903.

Strobell, Edward H. *Mr. Blaine and His Foreign Policy.* Boston: Hall, 1884.

Talbot, Thomas H. *The Proudest Chapter of His Life. Mr. Blaine's Administration of the State Department.* Boston: Cupples, Upham, 1884.

Terrill, Tom E. *The Tariff, Politics and American Foreign Policy, 1874–1901*. Westport, Conn.: Greenwood Press, 1973.

Wilgus, A. Curtis. "James G. Blaine and the Pan American Movement." *Hispanic American Historical Review* 5 (November 1922): 662–708.

Williams, R. Hal. *Years of Decision: American Politics in the 1890's*. New York: Wiley, 1978.

Williams, William Appleman. *The Roots of the Modern American Empire*. New York: Random House, 1969.

MICHAEL J. DEVINE

Willy Brandt (Herbert Frahm) (1913–1992).   Willy Brandt, future foreign minister and chancellor of the Federal Republic of Germany, was born on December 18, 1913, as Herbert Ernst Karl Frahm, the illegitimate son of a Lübeck cooperative store clerk. Brandt was raised by his grandfather, a truck driver and socialist, who had a lasting influence on him. Brandt's excellence in school won him a place at Johanneum, Lübeck's prestigious *Realgymnasium*, where he was one of a few working-class students. By the age of fifteen, he was contributing articles to the *Volksbote*, edited by Lübeck's leading socialist, Julius Leber.

Brandt joined the Socialist Democratic party (SPD) in 1930, but left in 1931 to join the Socialist Workers' party (SAP), a revolutionary Marxist party. He attended a secret conference of his outlawed party in Dresden on March 12, 1933, under an alias, Willy Brandt, the first time he had used this name. Traveling under his new name, Brandt was sent to Oslo to set up an SAP office abroad.

Brandt's exile experiences cooled his radicalism and nudged him in the direction of a reformist, social democratic outlook. He directed the SAP Oslo bureau, and until the outbreak of World War II traveled to SAP congresses in exile. In 1936 Brandt entered Germany with a false passport to investigate conditions in Berlin and later went to Spain during the civil war as a reporter for the socialist press. What Brandt observed in Spain and what he heard of the Moscow trials served as an antidote to what he later referred to as his "political dilettantism." His disillusionment with Soviet Russia was capped by the Nazi-Soviet Non-Aggression Pact, after which he believed that any relations with the Soviets had to be conducted with reserve and skeptical realism.

When the Nazis occupied Norway in 1940, Brandt made his way to Sweden, where he was joined by his lover, Carlotta Thorkildsen, a Norwegian socialist intellectual, and their daughter. Later, Brandt married Rut Hansen, a Norwegian refugee, with whom he had three sons.

Brandt's primary political concern was the end of the Third Reich. Beyond that his loyalties were divided. He was committed to both Norway and Germany. He was an active member of the Norwegian Labor party, and at the same time he wished to contribute to the revival of an international socialist organization. He played an instrumental role in the formation of the International Group of Democratic Socialists, the forerunner to the postwar Socialist International, and led the SAP into a merger with the SPD in October 1944.

After the war, Brandt covered the Nuremberg Trials for Norwegian and Swedish newspapers. At a January 1946 SPD meeting at Offenbach, he was introduced to Kurt Schumacher, the head of the postwar SPD. Though he disagreed with Schumacher's nationalism and his unimaginative repetition of a stale Marxism, Brandt decided that it was as a German and in the SPD that he could do the most for the future of Europe and democratic socialism. At Schumacher's request, Brandt took over public relations for the Berlin SPD on January 1, 1948. Four months later, the provincial government in Kiel renewed his German citizenship under the name of Willy Brandt. In Berlin, Brandt found his political career bedeviled by the resentment of some party leaders against his past. However, he found a spirited supporter in Ernst Reuter, the SPD mayor of Berlin, who also challenged Schumacher's rigidity.

In contrast to Schumacher, Reuter and Brandt advocated cooperation with the Western powers. Indeed, Terence Prittie has called them "the foremost German protagonists of integration with the western world." Their expectations were borne out in the successful resistance to the Berlin Blockade and the establishment of the Federal Republic. Brandt and Reuter rejected unification at the cost of neutrality. They believed that social progress was the most effective counter against communism, and that a free Berlin might prevent East Germany from being Bolshevized.

With the formation of the Federal Republic, Brandt went to the Bundestag as an SPD delegate from Berlin. In Bonn, he established a productive and friendly association with the ex-Communist Herbert Wehner and was active in committee work, especially regarding foreign affairs. Brandt believed that an opportunity was lost when the West did not take advantage of *Joseph Stalin's death to push for a peace treaty and the reunification of Germany, and he was appalled by Western inaction during the 1953 rising in East Berlin.

Brandt advanced in Berlin's local politics and in the SPD as a champion of a dogma-free democratic socialism. He became president of the Berlin City Parliament in 1954, mayor of Berlin on October 3, 1957, chairman of the Berlin SPD in early 1958, and a member of the SPD's national executive in May 1958.

All the while Brandt advocated a bipartisan foreign policy that endorsed co-operation with the Western powers. He advocated German participation in the European Coal and Steel Community, did not oppose rearmament in 1955, and supported the establishment of the European Economic Community. These positions were not in harmony with the old SPD leadership, which early in 1959 had drafted a Deutschland-Plan calling for big power disengagement in central Europe and a European security pact as a prelude to a peace treaty and German reunification. Brandt's ideas, however, influenced the party's program. He wished to push the SPD from its status as a party of the working class to a party of the entire nation. Brandt had reservations about the Deutschland-Plan. He did not object to offering the Russians an opportunity to negotiate, but had no hope that they would give up their effort to transform East Germany into a border bastion that was a carbon copy of their own regime.

Brandt saw his efforts to reorient the SPD along pragmatic and pro-Western lines come to fruition at the SPD's 1959 Bad Godesberg conference, where remnants of Marxism were pushed aside in favor of Germany's social market economy. Bad Godesberg also signaled a shift away from the policy of disarmament and neutrality. Despite Brandt's commitment to Western security, he did not envision a military solution to German division. He espoused flexible political action, but in no way advocated capitulation. His German policy at this time rested primarily on the maintenance of a free West Berlin. Brandt believed that as long as it was free, there was hope for the eventual transformation of the whole Eastern bloc. To maintain a free Berlin, West Germany needed the determined support of powerful allies. If Berlin remained, then flexible and imaginative policies might bring reunification nearer. He urged increased social and cultural contacts lest the two Germanies be irreconcilably estranged. While some accused Brandt of concessions and even collaboration, he believed that contacts with the West would undermine the very existence of the East German regime. His position won general approval in the SPD, and after the death of Erich Ollenhauer, who had succeeded Schumacher, Brandt was chosen SPD leader in 1963.

When the Berlin Wall went up on August 13, 1961, Brandt called for quick and strong diplomatic action to reassert the responsibility of the Four Powers for the entire city. He was upset by the acquiescence of both Chancellor *Konrad Adenauer and the Allies. When the Christian Democrats (CDU) lost their absolute majority in the 1961 election, Brandt advocated an all-party coalition to present a united front. Adenauer, with his basic antipathy toward socialism, rejected this notion. Brandt believed that Adenauer's policies were widening the gulf between the two Germanies. In Brandt's opinion, Walter Ulbricht's Communist regime in East Germany throve on isolation and paranoia.

Gerhard Schroeder, the CDU foreign minister from 1961 to 1966, to some extent shared Brandt's outlook. He espoused a pragmatic policy that envisioned pressure for improved conditions for the Germans in the East. Adenauer, however, was unwilling to deal with the Russians. Brandt and his advisor, Egon Bahr, were less inhibited. While maintaining a strong alliance with the United States and full participation in the economic and military system of the West, they wanted to improve relations with the Soviet Union and eastern Europe and negotiate with the German Democratic Republic as long as the right of German self-determination was never forsaken. Here in essence was *Ostpolitik*.

On July 15, 1963, Bahr elaborated the policy labeled *Wandel durch Annäherung* (Change Through Approach), which called for a gradual rapprochement between the East and the West rather than a single momentous agreement to solve the German Question. The Soviet Union had to be convinced that it would be better to be on friendly terms with a Germany of 70 million people than to be on good terms with a few individuals who speciously claimed to represent 17 million. Brandt and Bahr believed that tension made the German Democratic Republic more dependent on the Soviet Union and simultaneously strengthened Ulbricht's hand. They viewed détente as a practical tactical step that could bring benefits to Germany as a whole, not one dictated by weakness or a repudiation of democratic principles.

Schroeder's "policy of movement" laid the groundwork for Brandt's future success. The Hallstein Doctrine, enunciated after the establishment of diplomatic relations between the Federal Republic and the Soviet Union in 1955, stressed the indivisibility of Germany by refusing to have diplomatic relations with any state, other than the Soviet Union, which recognized the German Democratic Republic. The Hallstein Doctrine was gradually shelved, starting in 1963 with the establishment of West German trade missions in Poland, Hungary, and Romania. This flexibility provided an opportunity for SPD and CDU cooperation in foreign policy.

When the Free Democrats (FDP) left the cabinet of Chancellor Ludwig Erhard in October 1966, the new CDU leader, Kurt-George Kiesinger, proposed a grand coalition of the CDU and SPD to deal with the problems of recession and the rise of the right-wing National Democrats and, incidentally, to teach the FDP a lesson. Despite perceived political dangers, Brandt and Wehner believed that the risks were overshadowed by the opportunity to join the government and prove to a larger segment of the middle class that the SPD was a party worthy of confidence.

The opportunity to develop a cohesive *Ostpolitik* was a potent factor in Brandt and Wehner's support for the coalition. Wehner became the minister for All-German Affairs, providing strong support for Brandt, who became foreign minister on December 6, 1966.

Brandt spoke of the "long road" of step by step progress toward needed reconciliation and cooperation with eastern Europe. By increasing contact between Europeans, détente would loosen the Soviet Union's grip on its satellites. He singled out Czechoslovakia and Poland, with whom better relations should be fostered by a repudiation of the Munich Agreement and by agreements between Bonn and Warsaw to regularize Germany's eastern frontier. He stated that no preconditions should be allowed to stand in the way of détente's development. He emphasized that contacts among Germans should be developed to prevent the two parts of "our country" from growing further apart. In Brandt's opinion, a strong NATO was a prerequisite for successful détente. However, stressing the need for nuclear arms control and mutual force reductions in Europe, he added that division would be less painful if peaceful coexistence could be achieved.

On January 31, 1967, the first step in Brandt's *Ostpolitik* came with the establishment of diplomatic relations between the Federal Republic and Romania. The East Germans reacted defensively, trying to shore up their position in the East. Brandt let them know that the Federal Republic was not rejecting realities or attempting to isolate the German Democratic Republic. Brandt believed, although it could not be publicly expressed in West Germany, that reunification was totally unattainable for the time being. Kiesinger, who agreed with Brandt's realistic assessment and his *Ostpolitik*, recognized that West Germany could no longer make German unity a precondition for East-West negotiations and that the first priority for the present was peace in Europe.

In the summer of 1967 a trade agreement was negotiated with Czechoslovakia and in 1968 diplomatic relations (ruptured in 1957) were restored with Yugoslavia. In February, addressing the Soviet Union, Brandt spoke of the two parts of Germany, thus launching his formula of one nation but two states. But the August invasion of Czechoslovakia by the Warsaw Pact, which Brandt condemned, forced him to hold his *Ostpolitik* in abeyance for the next year and led to doubts about the policy among the CDU leadership.

Brandt, as a result of this CDU disenchantment and growing extraparliamentary opposition to the grand coalition, explored other options. The new left-liberal head of the FDP, Walter Scheel, agreed to form a coalition with the SPD if it could muster a sufficiently large parliamentary majority after the September 1969 election. Though the results of the election were disappointing to the SPD, Brandt pushed ahead, and the coalition government was approved by a three-vote margin on October 29.

As chancellor, Brandt was determined to move his foreign initiatives forward. Scheel became foreign minister, with the double task of holding the FDP together and in the new coalition, and of executing Brandt's *Ostpolitik*. With Wehner assuming the leadership of the SPD in the Bundestag, Egon Franke headed the Ministry for All-German Affairs, now renamed the Ministry for Internal German Relations.

On October 30, Brandt restated his readiness to meet with Ulbricht or Willi Stoph, the East German premier, and negotiate with the German Democratic Republic on a basis of equality and without preconditions. He added, however, that his government would not deal with East Germany as a foreign power because special relations should exist between the two German states. He also expressed his willingness to meet with the Soviets and the Poles to put frontier questions on a normal footing. This was his consistently advanced policy of the attainable, to maintain freedom in those parts of Germany that possessed it, to settle problems peacefully, and to nurture human rights for all Germans.

Brandt and Stoph met on March 19, 1970, at Erfurt. Stoph repeated East German demands for recognition of its sovereignty, the establishment of normal diplomatic relations, and the entry of the two German states into the United Nations. Brandt countered that the German nation still existed despite the fact that it had been divided by the war and subsequent Cold War.

Brandt made a six-point proposal, which included the following: that the unity of the German nation be preserved in the form of two states not foreign to one another; that they respect one another's territorial integrity and settle disputes peacefully; that they cooperate as neighbors; that the rights and responsibilities of the Four Powers in Berlin be respected; and that the situation in and around Berlin be improved.

Brandt's visit to the East was returned by Stoph, who came to Kassel in May. Brandt, though he viewed the East Germans with skepticism, believed that the very fact that the talks occurred was positive. He was confident that progress with the Soviet Union and Poland would shake the intransigence of the East Germans, and those countries agreed to negotiate nonaggression pacts with the Federal Republic. Brandt was right. In July Ulbricht admitted that the two Germanies could reach agreement on a basis short of full diplomatic recognition for the German Democratic Republic.

The Soviet-German Treaty was signed on August 12, 1970. The Soviet Union waived its rights as a victor in the Federal Republic; both countries joined in a mutual renunciation of force; they agreed to accept existing boundaries and the territorial integrity of all European states, but the Federal Republic did not recognize East Germany as a sovereign entity under international law. Brandt, although he refrained from making the linkage public, also required that talks between the Four Powers concerning the rights of West Berlin have satisfactory results before the treaty would be ratified. Ultimately the concessions made by the Soviets weakened the East German regime, and Ulbricht had to resign his position as chairman of the Socialist Unity party in May 1971.

A treaty with Poland was signed on December 6, 1970. West Germany accepted the Oder-Neisse line as Poland's de facto western frontier. Though it did not recognize the frontier de jure, West Germany regarded the Polish frontier as inviolable and rejected the use of force to change it. Poland, to the satisfaction of Brandt, dropped its demand for West German recognition of East Germany. On September 3, 1971, a Berlin settlement was achieved that recognized West Berlin's ties to the Federal Republic and guaranteed its status and its access to the West. Brandt regarded this as the supreme test for his government and foreign policy.

Even before the ratification of the treaties on May 17, 1972, Brandt had received the Nobel Prize for Peace on October 20, 1971, for "concrete initiatives leading to the relaxation of tension." The pacts with the Soviet Union and Poland and the ratification of the Nuclear Non-Proliferation Treaty were specifically mentioned as well as Brandt's effort "to secure for the people of West Berlin the fundamental rights of personal security and full freedom of movement." For his efforts Brandt was also named *Time* "Man of the Year."

Before the ratification of the Soviet and Polish treaties, negotiations had begun with the East Germans. In November 1971 a series of discussions were launched between Bahr, who represented Brandt, and Michael Kohl, the East German representative. On May 26, 1972, an agreement was reached on traffic between West and East Germany. On November 8, 1972, Bahr and Kohl completed their work. The Basic Treaty was signed on December 21, 1972, and was ratified in June 1973. The treaty was described as guaranteeing the "status quo plus." The Federal Republic recognized the German Democratic Republic without specifically admitting its sovereignty and agreed to conduct relations with it on the basis of equality. The Federal Republic insisted, despite its recognition of the Democratic Republic, that there was only one German nation and that all Germans had the right of West German citizenship. The treaty guaranteed access between

West Germany and West Berlin and gave West Germans the right to visit East Berlin and the rest of East Germany. The protocol governing the exchange of representatives completed in March 1974 stipulated that West German relations with East Germany were to be conducted not through the Foreign Office and an embassy but through the Ministry of All-German Affairs and a permanent mission in East Berlin. The treaty also provided for simultaneous application by the two German states for membership in the United Nations, which they received in 1973.

Brandt has been judged by some to be Germany's best foreign minister. At the very least it is safe to concur with Herbert Wehner's assessment: "As Foreign Minister he gained moral and political credit for his country." Brandt's achievements were significant. He produced legal recognition of the existence and rights of West Berlin. He established contacts and a degree of interaction between the two German states. He did not give away anything that had not already been lost to Germany, and perhaps in the long run contributed, as he had predicted, not to the strengthening of the East German regime but to its ultimate demise. Brandt's successes resulted in the confirmation of his government by West German voters on November 19, 1972, but political disaster struck on April 24, 1974, when Gunther Guillaume, a personal aide of Brandt, was arrested as an East German spy. Brandt resigned on May 7, 1974.

After his resignation from the chancellorship, Brandt retained the chairmanship of the SPD until 1987; as leader of the Socialist International from 1976 to September 1992, he continued to agitate for peace and justice on a worldwide basis; and in 1977 Brandt became chairman of the North-South Commission, an independent commission on international development issues. Following the reunification of Germany in 1990, Brandt was lauded by many East Germans as a leader who had never forgotten them. When Brandt died of cancer on October 8, 1992, German President Richard von Weizsäcker said that Brandt had "changed the Germans' relationship with the world, as well as the world's to Germany."

Annotated Bibliography

Several archives in Germany house material on Willy Brandt. The Landesarchiv Berlin, Klackreuthstrasse 1–2, W–1000 Berlin 30 (Tel. [030] 21 23–0), contains material on the administration of the city. The records for the Governing Mayor's Office and the Senate from 1951 to 1967 are available to scholars.

The Archiv der sozialen Demokratie, Friedrich-Ebert-Stiftung, Godesberger Allee 149, W–5300 Bonn 2 (Tel. [0228] 88 31), the archive of the Social Democratic party, contains the Brandt Papers as well as party records for the whole Brandt period. In addition to the Brandt Papers, see the Büro Willy Brandt; the SPD Fraktion records from Berlin; the records of the SPD Chair; the records of the SPD Executive; and the records of the SPD Bundestag delegation.

The Foreign Office records are located in the Auswärtiges Amt, Politisches Archiv, Adenaueralle 99–103, W–5300 Bonn (Tel. [0228] 17 21 61). These records can be consulted with permission in writing from the Auswärtiges Amt. A thirty-year rule applies.

Other useful sources are the Forchungsinstitut der Deutschen Gesellschaft für Auswärtige Politik, Bonn; the Bibliothek des Deutschen Bundestages, Bonn; and the Zentrales Dokumentationsystem des Presse- und informationsamtes der Bundesregierung, Bonn.

Brandt wrote extensively about Germany and the Germans, his political career, and his views on diplomacy. In his first important work, *Nach dem Siege* (After Victory; 1944), Brandt argued that a system and its representatives can be hated without directing hatred toward the nation involved. He repudiated German nationalism and called for the rehabilitation and democratization of Germany. In *Verbrecher und andere Deutschen* (Germany and Other Criminals; 1948), Brandt recognized the necessity of the Nuremberg Trials. He asserted that there is a shared responsibility for such crimes even in an authoritarian state, but contended that responsibility is not the same as guilt. *My Road to Berlin* (1960) is an early autobiography.

Written before Brandt assumed the post of foreign minister, *The Ordeal of Coexistence* (1963) expresses his views on foreign policy. *Friedenssicherung in Europa* (The Securing of Peace in Europe; 1968) and *Aussenpolitik, Deutschlandpolitik, Europapolitik* (1968) discuss *Ostpolitik*. *In Exile—Essays, Reflections, and Letters* (1971) uses a selection of Brandt's writing and correspondence to provide a view of his years in exile. *Peace: Writings and Speeches of the Nobel Peace Prize Winner, 1971* (1971) contains selected foreign policy statements made by Brandt between 1963 and 1971. Brandt's reflections on his rise to power, the grand coalition, the beginning of *Ostpolitik*, and his chancellorship can be found in *People and Politics: The Years 1960–1975* (1976). *Willy Brandt. Erinnerungen* (1989) contains Brandt's most recent memoirs. In this work he follows and evaluates his political life from 1948 to the present.

Although much has been written about Brandt, the contemporary nature of his activity leaves any attempt at analysis or interpretation vulnerable to the tides of history. Nevertheless, several good treatments of the German statesman's career are available. Herman Bolesch and Hans Dieter Leicht, *Willy Brandt: A Portrait of the German Chancellor* (1971), though lacking perspective and written even before *Ostpolitik* had come to full fruition, identified Willy Brandt as the best foreign minister Germany ever had. Terence Prittie, *Willy Brandt: Portrait of a Statesman* (1974), sympathetically covers Brandt's political career from 1948. The book includes a credible defense of Brandt's achievements in foreign policy. Robert Spencer's "Legacy of Brandt and Ostpolitik as German Leadership Changes," *International Perspectives* 5 (1974): 13–17, is an excellent analysis of the complex issues involved in Brandt's *Ostpolitik*. Spencer regards Egon Bahr as the father of *Ostpolitik*. However, he adds that "*Ostpolitik* as it has unfolded since 1969 has been particularly Willy Brandt's."

David Binder provides a comprehensive and favorable biography of Brandt in *The Other German: Willy Brandt's Life and Times* (1975). According to Binder, Brandt's nine years as mayor of Berlin, where he had firsthand experience of Cold War confrontation, were a powerful influence on his foreign policy. Binder believed that Brandt's visit to Erfurt helped to unleash a power struggle within the German Democratic Republic that brought down Walter Ulbricht.

According to William Griffith, *The Ostpolitik of the Federal Republic of Germany* (1978), the central aim of Willy Brandt's *Ostpolitik* was to preserve the identity of the German nation. Adenauer's belief that reunification could be accomplished through strength seemed to have been proven erroneous, and Brandt concluded that the achievement of West German goals for East Germany and Berlin depended upon Moscow. Griffith believes that the treaties negotiated by Brandt were prerequisites for the Helsinki Conference on European Security and Cooperation, which formally recognized the territorial status quo in Europe. For Lawrence Whetten, *Germany East and West: Conflicts, Collaboration, and Confrontation* (1980), the construction of the Berlin Wall and the development of détente produced a decisive turning point in the foreign policy of West Germany. Whetten believes that both the Federal Republic and the German Democratic Republic achieved their minimal objectives in 1973. The German Democratic Republic escaped from isolation and gained international recognition. The Federal Republic achieved East German recognition of its relationship with West Berlin and hoped that it was contributing to the improvement of conditions for the Germans in the East.

Bibliography

Binder, David. *The Other German: Willy Brandt's Life and Times.* Washington, D.C.: New Republic, 1975.

Bolesch, Hermann Otto, and Hans Dieter Leicht. *Willy Brandt: A Portrait of the German Chancellor.* Tübingen and Basel: Horst Erdmann Verlag, 1971.

Bracher, Karl Dietrich, Wolfgang Jäger, and Werner Link. *Geschichte der Bundesrepublik Deutschland. Republik im Wandel, 1969–1974: Die Ära Brandt.* Stuttgart: Deutsche Verlags-Anstalt, 1986.

Brandt, Willy. *Aussenpolitik, Deutschlandpolitik, Europapolitik.* Berlin: Berlin Verlag, 1968.

———. *Friedenssicherung in Europa.* Berlin: Berlin Verlag, 1968.

———. *In Exile—Essays, Reflections, and Letters.* London: Oswald Wolf, 1971.

———. *My Road to Berlin.* London: Peter Davies, 1960.

———. *Nach dem Siege.* Stockholm: N.p., 1944.

———. *The Ordeal of Coexistence.* Cambridge, Mass.: Harvard University Press, 1963.

———. *Peace: Writings and Speeches of the Nobel Peace Prize Winner, 1971.* Bonn: Neue Gesellschaft, 1971.

———. *People and Politics: The Years 1960–1975.* Boston: Little, Brown, 1976.

———. *Verbrecher und andere Deutschen.* Oslo: Aschehong, 1948.

———. *Willy Brandt. Erinnerungen.* Frankfurt: Propylaen, 1989.

Drath, Viola Herms. *Willy Brandt: Prisoner of His Past.* Radnor, Pa.: Chilton, 1975.

Freund, Michael. *From Cold War to Ostpolitik: Germany and the New Europe.* London: Oswald Wolff, 1972.

Frey, Eric G. *Division and Detente: The Germanies and Their Alliances.* New York: Praeger, 1987.

Griffith, William E. *The Ostpolitik of the Federal Republic of Germany.* Cambridge, Mass.: MIT Press, 1978.

Hanrieder, Wolfram F. "West German Foreign Policy: 1949–1979: Necessities and Choices." In *West German Foreign Policy: 1949–1979*, pp. 15–36. Edited by Wolfram Hanrieder. Boulder, Colo.: Westview Press, 1980.

Harpprecht, Klaus. *Willy Brandt: Portrait and Self-Portrait.* Translated by Hank Keller. Los Angeles: Nash, 1971.

Hildebrand, Klaus. *Geschichte der Bundesrepublik Deutschland: Von Erhard zur Großen Koalition, 1963–1969.* Stuttgart: Deutsche Verlags-Anstalt, 1985.

Hofmann, Gunter. *Willy Brandt—Porträt eines Aufklärers aus Deutschland.* Hamburg: Rowohlt, 1988.

Homze, Alma, and Edward Homze. *Willy Brandt, a Biography.* Nashville: T. Nelson, 1974.

Jäger, Wolfgang, and Werner Link. *Geschichte der Bundesrepublik Deutschland: Republik im Wandel, 1974–1982: Die Ära Schmidt.* Stuttgart: Deutsche Verlags-Anstalt, 1987.

Koch, Peter. *Willy Brandt: eine politische Biographie.* Berlin: Ullstein, 1988.

Marshall, Barbara. *Willy Brandt*. London: Cardinal, 1990.
Merkl, Peter H. *German Foreign Policies, West and East: On the Threshold of a New European Era*. Santa Barbara, Calif.: ABC-Clio, 1974.
Prittie, Terence. *Willy Brandt: Portrait of a Statesman*. New York: Schocken, 1974.
Spencer, Robert. "Legacy of Brandt and Ostpolitik as German Leadership Changes." *International Perspectives* 5 (1974): 13–17.
Tilford, Roger, ed. *The Ostpolitik and Political Change in Germany*. Lexington, Mass.: Lexington Books Heath, 1975.
Viola, Tom. *Willy Brandt*. New York: Chelsea House, 1988.
Whetten, Lawrence L. *Germany East and West: Conflicts, Collaboration, and Confrontation*. New York: New York University Press, 1980.

BERNARD A. COOK

George Canning (1770–1827).   George Canning played a pivotal role in determining British policy during and after the tumultuous Napoleonic Wars. As foreign minister (twice), president of the Board of Control for India, and, finally, prime minister, Canning helped to thwart the Napoleonic menace, secure India for Great Britain, protect British interests in Latin America, and, eventually, withdraw Great Britain from continental entanglements, thereby launching Britain on its century-long policy of "splendid isolation."

George Canning was born on April 11, 1770, to George Canning, the black sheep of a gentry household from Londonderry, and Mary Ann Costello. His father died in 1771, leaving his mother destitute. She took to the then lowly profession of the stage and remained there until her son arranged for a government pension in 1801. Thanks to the generosity of his father's family, Canning went to Eton, where he distinguished himself as a student and as a contributor to the *Microcosm*, a weekly paper that he and his friends published. In 1787 he entered Christ Church at Oxford. His uncle introduced the young man to leaders of the Whigs, but dislike of the French Revolution led him toward *William Pitt the Younger and the conservative Tories.

Entering Parliament in 1794, Canning held several junior posts in Pitt's government, including undersecretary for foreign affairs from 1796 to 1799. He supported Pitt's policies both in the war against France and in the seeking of peace, even when the foreign secretary, Lord Grenville, opposed the prime minister. When Pitt resigned in 1801 over the question of Irish emancipation, Canning followed him out.

Canning married Joan Scott on July 8, 1800. She brought with her a £100,000 dowry, making him financially independent at a time when members of Parliament were not paid. They had three sons and a daughter. During his years out of office (1801–1804), he attacked the Addington government. When Pitt formed a new government in 1804, Canning returned to office as treasurer of the navy. He felt uncomfortable, however, since the new government contained six ministers who had served in the previous government, which he had spent the last years attacking. He left office when Pitt died in 1806.

In March 1807, Canning took over the Foreign Office. These were bad days for the British; the Napoleonic Wars went badly, and relations with the United States worsened. Canning's position required him to cooperate with officials from the military departments and to be part of Britain's military planning. Simultaneously, he worked to keep the peace with the United States.

His primary concern was to maintain relations with those nations that could be potential allies. This meant keeping on good terms with Russia while not rejecting Austrian peace efforts. Yet this was the height of *Napoleon I's success, and Russia was not only forced out of the war but into alliance with France.

The Treaty of Tilsit (1807), which took Russia out of the war against Napoleon, made life difficult for the Foreign Office. Britain was now alone against France. The Treaty of Tilsit even called for Russia to go to war against Britain if Britain did not make peace with France. Yet Canning worked to avoid a direct conflict and to maintain some form of relations with Russia for the future.

This precarious situation led to the adoption of various stop-gap strategies until Napoleon's grip loosened. There was an effort to secure the seas for Britain. Canning and Robert Stewart, Viscount *Castlereagh, secretary for war and colonies, used naval action in place of diplomacy to secure Denmark's fleet for Britain. The cabinet felt that Denmark's "neutral" fleet could be a threat and had to be kept out of the war. The first British efforts were at negotiation, but when these failed the navy bombarded Copenhagen for three days until the Danes conceded their fleet and naval stores. Less violently, Canning's Foreign Office successfully negotiated the removal of the Portuguese royal family and fleet to Brazil, thereby placing them beyond French grasp.

With respect to the rest of Europe, Canning waited for cracks to develop in Napoleon's common front. One such crack appeared in Spain when Napoleon attempted to place his brother Joseph on the throne. The Spanish rebelled, and Great Britain attempted to exploit this opening by helping the Spanish rebels. The ensuing Peninsular campaign, while unsuccessful during Canning's tenure, would eventually be important in bringing about Napoleon's end.

Canning's work to balance relations with the United States helped prevent war. The *Chesapeake* affair, in which the HMS *Leopard* fired on the USS *Chesapeake* in 1807, began his term. He decided to disavow the action of the *Leopard* in firing on the *Chesapeake*; and the navy recalled, then promoted, Admiral Berkeley. He hoped to settle the matter quickly and concentrate on European affairs. The American desire to tie the affair to the question of freedom of the seas kept it an open sore for a number of years. Canning worked to modify the Orders in Council of 1807 to make them more acceptable to the United States, resulting in the Orders in Council of 1809. His most important effort to maintain relations with the United States ended in the failure of the Erskine mission.

David Erskine was sent to the United States as minister-plenipotentiary with instructions that were to be read to the secretary of state. However, because of his pro-American sympathies, Erskine ignored this directive. He glossed over the two nations' differences and negotiated a treaty. When the treaty reached

London, Canning disavowed it because he considered it too favorable to the United States. The disavowal distressed the United States and strained relations, but Canning worked to draw out the process and allow tempers to cool.

In 1809 Canning worked to have Castlereagh removed from the War Office, and the Duke of Portland, the prime minister, seemed to have agreed. When the plans did not work out, Canning resigned. In 1810, when Castlereagh discovered the plot to have him removed, he challenged Canning to a duel. The duel damaged Canning's reputation, and it was twelve years before he returned to the Foreign Office.

From November 1814 to July 1815, Canning served as ambassador to the Portuguese regency while the Portuguese court continued to reside at Rio de Janeiro. Relations between the two countries had been troubled for some time. Portugal felt that Britain was overbearing, and Britain felt that Portugal had misused its subsidies. Canning was unable to secure a commitment from the Portuguese to help the British in their efforts to deal with Napoleon, who had escaped from Elba and reestablished himself in France.

From June 1816 to January 1821, Canning served as president of the Board of Control for India, a body that gave the government some control over the affairs of India in coordination with the East India Company's court of directors. In this position he interacted with the Foreign Office in matters dealing with Persia and the Middle East. Canning justified the continuing expansion of British colonial power in the region, although this required him to balance the interests of the Anglican evangelicals with the need to protect Hindu sensibilities. He left office over his poor relations with King George IV, and not for reasons of Indian policy.

In 1822 Lord Liverpool offered Canning the governor-generalship of India. Canning accepted, but Castlereagh's suicide later in that year meant that Canning would return to the Foreign Office. From September 1822 to April 1827, Canning served a second term as foreign secretary. His return to the Foreign Office occurred during a period of deterioration in the European alliance system that had defeated Napoleon. Canning's concerns included preventing a French revival on the Continent while maintaining a balance of power, keeping the United States from dominating Latin America, and protecting old allies. These objectives led Great Britain to accept French action against Spanish constitutionalists in order to prevent a general war in Europe.

The absolutist monarchies of Europe were concerned over events in Spain. By midsummer 1822, King Ferdinand VII had lost control of his country to liberals after years of conflict. Tsar *Alexander I wanted to crush the Spanish constitutionalists, while Canning opposed any intervention in Spanish affairs. France chose to go to war with Spain, while Great Britain remained neutral. Canning expressed hope for a Spanish victory, but concluded that avoiding a general war in Europe was a more important objective for Britain. The British position annoyed the other Great Powers, but Britain experienced no negative repercussions.

The Congress of Verona, which had sanctioned French intervention in Spain, was the last such conference Britain would attend. Canning now withdrew Great Britain from the Congress System designed by Castlereagh and *Metternich, the Austrian foreign minister, to maintain European stability after the Napoleonic Wars. As European reactionaries came to employ the Congress System to crush any sign of liberalism on the Continent, the system had become less and less appealing to Castlereagh, and he may have withdrawn Britain had he lived. With Castlereagh's death, however, it was Canning who completed Britain's disengagement from its continental policy and initiated a foreign policy subsequently known as "splendid isolation," adhered to for the next sixty years.

The desire to protect traditional allies focused British attention on Turkey and Portugal. Britain involved itself in the Greek revolution against Turkey to prevent Russian military intervention. Opposing sets of concerns drove Britain's policy in the Balkans. Canning felt that Britain had to protect Turkey's place in the region while gaining limited autonomy for Greece. The Ottoman Empire was an old friend and a counterweight to Russia. On the other hand, the idea of Greek independence was popular with the British public. Russia was also at cross-purposes. Not only did it support the Orthodox Greeks and want to be a major player in the region, it was also committed to preserving the status quo. Anglo-Russian relations were troubled because of differing aims in the Balkans when Alexander I died in 1825. Canning sent the celebrated war hero, the Duke of Wellington, to carry condolences and to talk to the new tsar, Nicholas I. In choosing Wellington, Canning hoped to flatter the tsar. When it appeared that the new tsar had settled on bilateral matters between Turkey and Russia, Canning decided to work with Russia to force Ottoman acceptance of an agreement with the Russians and the Greeks. Canning then hoped to use Anglo-Russian cooperation in the Balkans to place the region on the back burner, but the Greek problem would not be finally resolved until 1830.

Portugal went through a period of constitutional turmoil after the death of King John on March 10, 1826. John's eldest son and successor, Dom Pedro, decided to keep the crown of Brazil and abdicated the Portuguese throne in favor of his eight-year-old daughter, Donna Maria. However, before leaving Portugal he gave the country a constitution. Dom Pedro's brother, Dom Miguel, who had a following in Portugal, believed in absolutist monarchy and allied himself with Ferdinand of Spain, another absolutist. Spain helped Miguel's forces, which finally invaded Portugal on November 22, 1826. On December 9, 1826, Canning decided to intercede to protect Portugal's independence. British intervention led Spain to withdraw support for Dom Miguel and encouraged the Portuguese army to defeat the invaders without the use of British troops. For the time being, the old ally's new constitution had been protected.

Slavery was another major issue. Britain opposed the slave trade, but Canning rejected any attempt to impose its view on others through the use of its navy. He faced the dilemma of negotiating an end to the slave trade with uncooperative nations while placating British public opinion with the appearance of progress in stopping the trade. The French resisted efforts to limit their activity in the slave trade. Even though the Americans had outlawed the trade, the British did not believe them to be effective at stopping it. Canning's Foreign Office negotiated an agreement with the Americans that required the United States to make greater efforts to stop the trade. Despite initial success, efforts to limit the Spanish slave trade collapsed after France returned Ferdinand to the Spanish throne.

Perhaps Canning's most important and successful policy was the recognition of the Latin American republics. Although the king disapproved of this policy, Canning understood its political and economic value. With the French invasion of Spain, it was useful to keep the Spanish colonies that were fighting for independence beyond French control. His effort to coordinate this policy with the United States failed, but it was part of the process leading to the Monroe Doctrine. In summer 1824, the British government decided to open negotiations with the Spanish colony of Buenos Aires, effectively recognizing its independence. Finally, at the end of the year, Canning persuaded the cabinet to recognize the revolutionary governments of Buenos Aires, Mexico, and Colombia.

Upon the death of Lord Liverpool, Canning became prime minister in April 1827. He had only a short tenure, during which he continued to implement his foreign policy. He died on August 8, 1827, after a period of failing health.

Annotated Bibliography

The Public Record Office (Chancery Lane, London, England) maintains the records of the Foreign Office, including those from Canning's terms as foreign minister. The Canning family's (from the Earl of Harewood) collection can be accessed through the Leeds Archives Department, Leeds City Library (Leeds, England). This collection contains a large percentage of Canning's personal papers, including political correspondence, engagement diaries, and papers from his time at the Foreign Office. There are other collections containing letters regarding Canning at the Fitzwilliam Museum (Trumpington Street, Cambridge, England), Gloucestershire Records Office (Shire Hall, Gloucestershire, England), Greater London Record Office (Country Hall, London, England SE1), and the Central Library (St. Peter's Square, Manchester, England, M2 5PD).

In the United States, there are several small repository holdings of Canning's letters or dispatches. One of the larger is at the Pierpont Morgan Library (29 E. 36th St., New York, New York 10016). Its Canning Collection has letters from and to Canning by the Marquess of Wellesley as well as others. The University of Michigan–William L. Clements Library (S. University Ave., Ann Arbor, Michigan 48109) has a British Statesmen series that includes a Canning Collection. A number of other libraries have collections that include letters from Canning. Indiana University–Lilly Library (Bloomington, Indiana 47405) has letters regarding Brazilian independence in its Stuart de Rothesay Collection. The New York Public Library, Research Libraries (5th Ave. & 42nd St., New York, New York 10018) has dispatches from the United States during the Napoleonic Wars. Many American universities have microprint copies of the British Sessional Papers, the official papers of Parliament, as well as papers that were laid before Parliament by government ministries such as the Foreign Office.

Canning wrote very little about foreign policy or politics. Perhaps his most interesting contribution is his *Reasons against national despondency: in refutation of Mr. Erskine's view of the causes and consequences of the present war: with some remarks upon the supposed scarcity of specie* (1797), which defends Tory policies against attack by the Whigs. Canning's *Speeches*, collected by R. Therry and published in a six-volume set (1828), covers several issues that were important to Canning, especially matters of foreign policy. Occasionally individual speeches were published, such as *Substance of Mr. Canning's speech, in the House of Commons, Tuesday, December 11, 1798: on Mr. Tierney's motion respecting continental alliances* (1799), in which he defended Pitt's government from attempts to limit its alliance-making powers and from possible censure by the House of Commons. Canning's contribution to *Poetry of the Anti-Jacobin* (1799) shows his negative attitudes about the French Revolution and republicanism.

Canning's life and foreign policy have inspired a large number of books and articles. Harold Temperley's *The Foreign Policy of Canning, 1822–1827* (1966) focuses primarily on Britain's recognition of the New World and its efforts to deal with the reactionary forces in Europe. This is the most comprehensive work on Canning's foreign policy.

Cedric Collyer's "Canning and the Napoleonic Wars," *History Today* 11 (April 1961): 227–235, is a good overview of Canning's life and policies up to 1812, but it can only be a starting point for any study of the period. Bradford Perkins's "George Canning, Great Britain and the United States, 1807–1809," *American Historical Review* 63 (1957): 1–22, and *Prologue to War: England and the United States, 1805–1812* (1961), discuss Canning's relations with the United States. Perkins argues that while Canning was no friend of the United States, neither was he an enemy. Although Canning tended to speak negatively of the United States, Perkins points out that the British statesman worked to prevent war and tried to keep Anglo-American relations on an even keel. V. N. Vinogradov's "George Canning, Russia and the Emancipation of Greece," *Balkan Studies* 22 (1981): 3–33, effectively examines Great Britain's attitude toward Greek as well as Anglo-Russian relations in post-Napoleonic Europe.

Over the last century and a half, Canning's biographers have reevaluated their subject as his efforts have become better understood in their historical context. With increasing frequency, historians see Canning less as a heroic and innovative character and more as an important diplomat contributing to the success of an evolutionary rather than revolutionary foreign policy. In particular, recent historians see his accession to the Foreign Office in 1822 as signifying a change of style rather than a change of course. Although it lacks details and has been surpassed by later works, Sir Charles Petrie's *George Canning* (1946) is still a good introduction. P.J.V. Rolo's *George Canning: Three Biographical Studies* (1965) looks at Canning from three different perspectives: as a man, a politician, and a statesman. Wendy Hinde's *George Canning* (1973) provides a comprehensive examination of Canning's career with particular emphasis on his work at the Foreign Office. Thomas Kebbel's entry on Canning in the *Dictionary of National Biography* gives a very good overview of Canning's life and policies. Peter Dixon's *George Canning, Politician and Statesman* (1976) focuses more on Canning the politician, but it successfully integrates his work as foreign secretary. Laureen Baillie's *British Biographical Archive*, fiche numbers 195–196, is a series of biographical sketches of Canning indicating how the view of Canning has changed over the last century and a half.

For the events of the Canning era in the Foreign Office see John Clarke, *British Diplomacy and Foreign Policy, 1782–1865* (1989), and Harold Temperley and Lillian Penson, eds., *A Century of Diplomatic Blue Books, 1814–1914* (1938). The former gives a useful overview of British foreign policy and is especially good when dealing with the

British decision to recognize revolutionary Latin American states. The latter is helpful in finding documents in the British Sessional Papers applicable to foreign relations for every foreign secretary from Castlereagh to Grey.

Bibliography

Works by Canning

Augustan Reprint Society. *Parodies of ballad criticism (1711–1781): William Wagstaffe. A comment upon the history of Tom Thumb, 1711: George Canning, The knave of hearts/selected with an introduction by William K. Wimsatt Jr.* New York: Kraus Reprint, 1967.

Canning, George. *Reasons against national despondency: in refutation of Mr. Erskine's view of the causes and consequences of the present war: with some remarks upon the supposed scarcity of specie.* London: Printed for T. Cadell and W. Davis, 1797.

———. *Substance of Mr. Canning's speech, in the House of Commons, Tuesday, December 11, 1798: on Mr. Tierney's motion respecting continental alliances.* London: For J. Wright, 1799.

New Tory Guide. London: Printed by S. Gosnell for J. Ridgway, 1819.

Poetry of the Anti-Jacobin. London: Printed for J. Wright, 1799.

Works about Canning

Baillie, Laureen, ed. *British Biographical Archives.* Fiche numbers 195–196. London: Saur, 1984.

Clarke, John. *British Diplomacy and Foreign Policy, 1782–1865.* London: Unwin Hyman, 1989.

Collyer, Cedric. "Canning and the Napoleonic Wars." *History Today* 11 (April 1961): 227–235.

Davis, R. W. "The Tories, the Whigs and Catholic Emancipation, 1827–1829." *English Historical Review* 97 (1982): 89–98.

Dictionary of National Biography, 1973 ed., s.v. "Canning, George (1770–1827)," by Thomas E. Kebbel.

Dixon, Peter. *George Canning, Politician and Statesman.* New York: Mason Charter, 1976.

Hinde, Wendy. *George Canning.* London: Collins, 1973.

Machin, G.I.T. "Canning, Wellington and the Catholic Question, 1827–1829." *English Historical Review* 99 (1984): 94–100.

Perkins, Bradford. "George Canning, Great Britain and the United States, 1807–1809." *American Historical Review* 63 (1957): 1–22.

———. *Prologue to War: England and the United States, 1805–1812.* Berkeley: University of California Press, 1961.

Petrie, Sir Charles. *George Canning.* London: Eyre and Spottiswoode, 1946.

Rolo, P.J.V. *George Canning: Three Biographical Studies.* London: Macmillan, 1965.

Temperley, Harold. *The Foreign Policy of Canning, 1822–1827; England, the Neo-Holy Alliance and the New World. With a new introduction by Herbert Butterfield.* Hamden, Conn.: Archon, 1966.

Temperley, Harold, and Lillian M. Penson, eds. *A Century of Diplomatic Blue Books, 1814–1914*. Cambridge, Eng.: The University Press, 1938.
Vinogradov, V. N. "George Canning, Russia and the Emancipation of Greece." *Balkan Studies* 22 (1981): 3–33.

DONALD E. HEIDENREICH, JR.

Robert Stewart, Viscount Castlereagh (1769–1822).   Robert Stewart, later Viscount Castlereagh and Lord Londonderry, was born in Dublin on June 18, 1769, to an Ulster landowning family. Castlereagh entered British political life in the 1790s and held several offices, the most important being foreign secretary from 1812 until his death in 1822. He was one of the most important political leaders in Europe during this period and is recognized as the prime architect of Great Britain's and Europe's foreign policy from 1813 to 1820.

Castlereagh was educated at the Royal School in Armagh and at St. John's College, Cambridge. He was elected to the Irish Parliament in 1790 after winning a fiercely contested election at County Down. He entered the Irish Parliament as a critic of the Dublin Castle government, an English-appointed executive supported by Irish landowners. Quickly, however, Castlereagh turned his eyes to Westminster, which he entered in 1794 as a supporter of the Tory *William Pitt the Younger.

The first office Castlereagh held weighed heavily on him throughout his career. He was the Irish secretary during the Rebellion of 1798 and was the official most responsible for suppressing the rebellion and restoring order. While Castlereagh encouraged lenient treatment of the rebels, many Irish still saw him as a traitor. Criticism mounted when he supported Pitt's Act of Union, which abolished the Irish Parliament and brought direct Irish representation to the Parliament in Westminster. He was, however, a consistent supporter of Catholic emancipation.

In 1802 Castlereagh was appointed president of the Board of Control, an office that attempted to exercise control over the powerful East India Company. In 1805 Castlereagh became the secretary of state for war, an office more to his liking. He proved to be an effective war secretary, reforming recruitment for the regular and auxiliary forces and accomplishing the appointment—against strenuous opposition—of Arthur Wellesley, the future Duke of Wellington, as commander in Spain. Castlereagh left office in 1809 as a result of a disintegrating government and an unsuccessful war. Shortly after his resignation, he fought a memorable and often-criticized duel with *George Canning, a fellow Tory and officeholder.

Castlereagh remained out of office until 1812, when he became foreign secretary. He also served at the same time as government leader in the House of Commons. While government colleagues regarded him as one of the ablest managers of the Commons, Castlereagh, because he was often responsible for introducing and defending government measures, came to be identified as the leader of reactionary domestic policies designed to control and repress citizen activities in the post-Napoleonic era. On the whole, this interpretation was incorrect. While Castlereagh did support the existing social order, he was far more moderate in his attitude toward social and political problems than many of his colleagues. The charges against him, however, tainted his image and achievements well into the nineteenth century. Part of Castlereagh's poor public image was due to his shy and aloof manner. Moreover, while his speeches were well reasoned, he was not a particularly effective orator.

When Castlereagh became foreign secretary, British foreign policy was preoccupied with issues involving the Napoleonic Wars. *Napoleon's invasion of Russia in 1812, and the resulting loss of much of his army, helped to change the diplomatic and military scene and gave Castlereagh the opportunity to display his diplomatic skills. Castlereagh's scheme for dealing with European problems was based primarily on William Pitt's memorandum of January 19, 1805, wherein the prime minister detailed a plan to restore political stability to Europe by containing France and providing for an agreement among the Great Powers to ensure long-term stability. The basis for the plan included restoring and maintaining the balance of power.

As the Russian army pursued the remnants of Napoleon's army, other nations gradually raised forces against the French, including Prussia, Sweden, and a reluctant, careful Austria. Negotiations among the nations were at best difficult, and Castlereagh feared that after victories over Napoleon cooperation among nations would cease because of different aims. Beginning in January 1814, Castlereagh personally led negotiations on the Continent to put together a formal alliance against Napoleon. British aims were few but definite: defeating Napoleon, freeing the Low Countries from French control, securing British freedom of action on the high seas, and containing French power in the future. The problems facing Castlereagh—and, indeed, all the other leaders—included the actual defeat of the ever-dangerous Napoleon as well as divisions and mistrust among the allies. Castlereagh's power rested upon British subsidies and a successful military effort, particularly Wellington's victories over French forces in Spain. Ultimately, however, victory over Napoleon depended on the military power of Russia, Prussia, and Austria.

The greatness of Castlereagh was his ability to overcome the differences among the leaders and to marshal all of the available resources against Napoleon, while at the same time protecting British interests. He persuaded the European leaders to concentrate first on defeating Napoleon, postponing to a later date the disposition of eastern Europe. He also reduced the many individual agreements between the various nations to one great alliance. He attained this primarily by personal diplomacy and a shrewd understanding of the character and needs of the others involved. Also, Napoleon's victories in several battles forced the coalition once again to coordinate its resources and arrive at a decisive agreement, the Treaty of Chaumont, on March 1, 1814.

Chaumont was, perhaps, Castlereagh's greatest diplomatic achievement. The treaty provided for an alliance to wage war against Napoleon until he was defeated. Each of the four major allies, including Britain, agreed to contribute

150,000 men, with Britain providing a £5 million subsidy to the others in 1814. France was to be confined to its 1792 boundaries, and, to provide security against France, Spain and an enlarged independent Netherlands were to be restored, and Prussia was to gain territory on the Rhine. The distinctive aspect of the treaty was that the alliance was to continue for a period of twenty years after Napoleon's defeat in order to protect Europe from potential French aggression.

When negotiations with Napoleon failed, the allies marched on Paris, entering the city on March 31, 1814. Napoleon abdicated and, under the initiative of Tsar *Alexander I, was permitted to retain his title and was given power over the island of Elba. Royalist forces in France helped restore the Bourbons to the throne. While Castlereagh was upset with the tsar's mild treatment of Napoleon, he welcomed the Bourbons' restoration. Having restored a ''legitimate'' Bourbon to the throne, Castlereagh and the allies dealt leniently with the French government. In the first Treaty of Paris, signed on May 30, 1814, France was permitted to retain its boundaries as of 1792. It paid no indemnity and retained art treasures confiscated during the wars. Castlereagh helped ensure that France regained fishing rights at Newfoundland, and all the colonies seized by England, with the exceptions of Mauritius, Tobago, and St. Lucia, were returned to France. Castlereagh had thus gained what he so desired for the restoration of a peaceful Europe: a politically and economically stable France.

The Treaty of Paris had settled relations only with France. The Congress of Vienna, which was to grapple with the remaining problems of Europe, opened in October 1814. The host of the conference was the Austrian chancellor, *Clemens von Metternich. While most European nations were present, ultimate authority rested in the representatives from Britain, Austria, Prussia, and Russia. France, represented by its foreign minister, *Talleyrand, played a significant role. Britain had no territorial demands on the Continent to make at Vienna; it did, however, insist on retaining supremacy on the high seas and gaining certain strategic posts overseas. Castlereagh's primary concern was Britain's security, which would be obtained by making certain that the settlement provided for the containment of France and a stable Europe in the future.

Castlereagh's activities at the Congress proceeded from his understanding of the balance of power and a just equilibrium. The balance of power was perceived as making certain that no one state could dominate the others. It was to be applied not only to France, but to any state—particularly Russia—that might pose a threat to Europe's peace. A just equilibrium helped to form a balance of power, and Castlereagh believed that both Austria and Prussia needed strengthening against France and against Russia, which had gained territory toward the end of the war and demanded additional territory in Poland. Castlereagh wished to strengthen France's neighbors. He also believed that while smaller states should be protected, they might at times have to suffer if the balancing mechanism required it.

The final settlement of the congress does not fit into simple categories. Castlereagh was above all a pragmatist, and at times he gained much less than he wanted. In some instances, as in Spain, Portugal, and Naples, monarchs were restored to their former positions. Switzerland was restored as an independent and neutral nation. The German states, having gone through so many changes, were not reconstituted, but formed into a loosely knit confederation. Austria, uninterested in regaining control over the Austrian Netherlands, was compensated with Lombardy and Venetia in northern Italy. The kingdom of Sardinia was strengthened through the addition of Genoa. In all of this Castlereagh helped to create a northern Italy that could act as a barrier to France.

Castlereagh was determined to attach the Austrian Netherlands to another nation, since the area was too small to stand alone, had no separate identity, and would be an easy prey for France. Agreement earlier had been reached for the area, named Belgium, to be attached to the Netherlands. Castlereagh had also restored most of the Dutch colonies to the Netherlands, although Britain had retained the Cape Colony as a naval port. Out of these negotiations Castlereagh gained a strengthened Dutch bulwark against France.

By far the greatest problem facing the negotiators was the realignment of central Europe, and Castlereagh failed to reach an agreement with Tsar Alexander for the establishment of an independent Poland. Alexander was adamant about setting up a large Poland under his protection. This reconstituted Poland would include territory from both Austria and Prussia, which had shared in the dismemberment of Poland in the 1700s. Alexander was able to gain Prussia's agreement by promising it Saxony. Metternich, however, feared both the extension of Russian influence so deeply into central Europe and the addition of so much German territory to Prussia. Castlereagh supported Metternich's objections, because a powerful Russia could pose a threat to peace in central Europe. War over the division of central Europe became a real possibility. Castlereagh helped initiate an alliance (January 3, 1815) among Austria, England, and France against Russia and Prussia. The alliance helped to break the deadlock, and Alexander accepted a somewhat reduced Poland, while Prussia gained about one-half of Saxony. To a great extent Alexander had won, however, for he had gained control over a large Poland.

Historians still dispute the extent to which Pitt's plan of 1805 was carried out in the 1814–1815 negotiations. Many of the broad principles, such as the containment of France and the freeing of several states, as well as the level of subsidy, were indeed adhered to. On the other hand, the shape of Germany was considerably different than what Pitt envisaged. The pragmatic Castlereagh, responding to the conditions of 1814, not those of 1805, would have expected such variations.

As the leaders were concluding their deliberations at Vienna (Wellington having replaced Castlereagh, who had returned to Great Britain), Napoleon escaped from Elba and war broke out anew. After a second and decisive defeat of Napoleon, Castlereagh had to work hard to prevent France's dismemberment. He succeeded on the whole in controlling the talks and achieving his aims, helped as much by the exhaustion of the other powers as by the major role played by Wellington and the British forces at the Battle of Waterloo. The second Treaty of Paris cost France more of its territory, with boundaries roughly those of 1790. France was also required to pay a substantial indemnity. To provide for stronger containment and to appease demands for harsh reprisals against France, Castlereagh agreed to allied occupation of the northeastern part of France. The soldiers, under the Duke of Wellington, were to be paid by France. France, however, was not humiliated, and the Bourbon monarchy was again restored.

The Quadruple Alliance, comprising Russia, Austria, Prussia, and Britain, was signed on November 20, 1815, the same day the second Treaty of Paris was signed. Following the lines of the agreements at Chaumont and Vienna, it called for the continuation of the alliance for twenty years in order to control France and carry out the provisions of the Treaty of Paris and the final settlement of Vienna. The signatories also agreed, under Article VI, to hold periodic meetings to deal with European problems and to help ensure the peace of Europe. Castlereagh provided the impetus for the inclusion of Article VI—he had written it himself—which brought into being the Congress System. This system, also known as the Concert of Europe, was to be particularly useful to both Castlereagh and Metternich. Both not only wished to maintain peace and stability in western Europe, but also looked to the Congress System, with its personal diplomacy, to help contain an aggressive Russia.

The Holy Alliance, Alexander's scheme to base peace on the application of Christian principles, was totally separate from the Quadruple Alliance. Although it was not the reactionary conspiracy that critics later charged, the Holy Alliance was never supported or agreed to by Castlereagh or the British government.

One foreign policy issue that occupied much of Castlereagh's time was the abolition of the slave trade. By 1814 Castlereagh was under enormous pressure from abolitionists to make their cause an integral part of all the proceedings in Europe. Britain had abolished the slave trade in 1807, and the abolitionists argued that all the rest of Europe should follow. Although an early opponent of abolition, Castlereagh had come to recognize the validity of the abolitionists' arguments. A general declaration condemning the slave trade was a part of the final Vienna accord, and several nations with little vested interest in the trade abolished it in 1815. Individual treaties between Britain and Spain and Portugal over the abolition of the trade were not reached until 1817, and enforcement of these treaties proved extremely difficult.

Possibly no aspect of the Congress of Vienna and its aftermath has caused more criticism than the negotiators' apparent failure to accommodate the forces of liberalism and nationalism. Nationalist historians have charged that the negotiators disregarded people's aspirations, ignored the rights of the small states, and created political entities that combined historically hostile elements. Even admirers of Castlereagh's foreign policy have argued that his commitment to the maintenance of the status quo blinded him to reactionary repression. One of the first writers to question this interpretation was Lord Salisbury, later prime minister, who in the 1860s argued that national movements in the early nineteenth century were not sufficiently well developed or identifiable to warrant being taken into consideration in the settlement of Europe. Twentieth-century studies of Castlereagh, Metternich, and others have helped to reshape their image, leading to an appreciation of the great practical difficulties they faced. Moreover, these statesmen came increasingly to be viewed as representatives of their period and of governments which, after the long and bitter wars against France, would naturally and justly view movements that created unrest and change as dangerous to the order of nations and society. John Derry convincingly argues that Castlereagh, as an Irishman, was well aware of the existence and the power of nationalism, but that he also perceived its dangers. Castlereagh knew that change in political entities and institutions would and should come, but without destroying the existing social and political fabric.

Castlereagh's attitude toward nationalism and liberalism can be better appreciated after examining his use of the Congress System and the policy of nonintervention. Several meetings of the Great Powers were held between 1818 and 1822, to a great extent continuing the relationships developed in 1814–1815. Castlereagh believed these meetings to be vital to enforcing treaty terms as applied to France and to maintaining European stability. At the first meeting at Aix-la-Chapelle in 1818, Castlereagh rejected Tsar Alexander's call for a statement empowering the Great Powers to intervene in the affairs of nations in order to maintain the status quo. Revolts in various parts of Europe, including Naples and Spain, appalled many leaders, some of whom called for the Great Powers to intervene.

In May 1820, Castlereagh drew up a major state paper that became the basis for British nonintervention in continental matters. H.W.V. Temperley and Lillian Penson refer to it as "the most famous State Paper in British history and the one of the widest ultimate consequence." Castlereagh argued that the purpose of the Quadruple Alliance was to contain France and put down revolutions there that might cause European complications. It was never designed to allow intervention in the domestic affairs of nations. The Spanish revolt neither posed a danger to European peace nor threatened the Great Powers. In addition, Castlereagh maintained that governments would be unable to agree on concerted action. He also stressed that the British public would not support participation in such intervention. On the other hand, Castlereagh was willing to permit individual states to intervene in affairs within their recognized spheres of interest, thus justifying Austria's intervention in Italy.

The Congress System broke down by the time of Castlereagh's death in 1822. To a great extent it was never a "system," but rather periodic meetings called when necessary. Differences between the Great Powers ultimately proved too great, as the three eastern states went their own way. No permanent organization or set agenda for meetings had ever developed. Castlereagh could never commit his government to intervention, even had he wanted to, because of the power of Parliament and public opinion. The nations continued cooperating only so long as their differences were limited; when the differences became too great, the Congress meetings soon stopped.

For Castlereagh, relations with the Americas were always of secondary importance. As war secretary in 1807, Castlereagh declared that Britain had no desire to add to its territory in Latin America, nor would it become involved in the area's internal politics. This document set the basis for British policy for much of the nineteenth century, although the wars of independence waged by Spain's colonies severely tested British diplomacy.

The Treaty of Ghent, signed in late 1814, marked the end of Britain's war with the United States. Castlereagh, preoccupied with affairs on the Continent, had not been directly involved with the negotiations. He had, however, hoped for the war's end, even if the differences responsible for the conflict between the two nations were not resolved. From 1815 to 1822 Castlereagh worked hard to improve relations with the United States, appreciating the growing power of that nation and believing good relations to be in Britain's self-interest. Bradford Perkins emphasizes that Castlereagh was the first British foreign secretary to treat the United States as an equal. Under Castlereagh, the two nations agreed on disarmament on the Great Lakes, fishing rights, and the Canadian-U.S. boundary. Although United States military action in Spanish Florida produced disagreement between the two, Castlereagh did not permit a break in relations.

Castlereagh committed suicide on August 12, 1822, shortly before he was to represent Britain at a congress meeting at Verona. He had been noticeably distressed in the days shortly before his death, perhaps fearing that political enemies would charge him with homosexual activity. There appears, however, to have been no basis for the charges, and suicide probably came from overwork and stress due to his dual roles of foreign secretary and leader of the House.

Castlereagh was one of the most important shapers of foreign policy in Britain and Europe in the modern period. He was British foreign secretary for a longer consecutive period than any statesman, and held the office during a time of momentous events. Castlereagh played a personal role in these events and exercised a European perspective while protecting the self-interests of his nation. According to Charles Webster, he was "the most European Foreign Minister" in British history. Although Castlereagh was a mediocre orator, in negotiations he was quite equal to his brilliant European contemporaries, Metternich and Talleyrand. He was never comfortable dealing with the role of Parliament, the press, and public opinion in the development of foreign policy.

Castlereagh was the prime architect of the coalition that defeated Napoleon, a major figure at the Congress of Vienna, and the driving force behind the Congress System. Not all of Castlereagh's Vienna settlement lasted, but it did provide for security against France and for cooperation among the powers. The Vienna accord established a balance of power that held for much of the nineteenth century. Castlereagh helped to institute the tradition of European diplomats meeting and discussing outstanding problems. From 1812 to 1913 the Great Powers held twenty-six conferences. The idea that territory should not change hands without the approval of the Great Powers worked for much of the century, breaking down during the period of nation-building from 1856 to 1871. The system generally worked when dealing with smaller powers; it did not work when the Great Powers were directly involved or disagreed. Castlereagh would not have been surprised.

Castlereagh bequeathed to Europe a very personal style of diplomacy. His meetings were not a forerunner of the League of Nations or the United Nations; rather, the congress meetings, which included only the Great Powers, resembled more our present-day meetings of the seven major economic powers. To Castlereagh, the Great Powers had earned the right to make the crucial decisions.

Annotated Bibliography

Castlereagh Papers are deposited at the Northern Ireland Public Record Office, 66 Balmoral Avenue, Belfast BT9 6NY, and the Durham County Record Office, County Hall, Durham DH1 5UL. Records of the Foreign and War offices, and the William Pitt Papers, are located at the Public Record Office, Ruskin Avenue, Kew, Richmond, Surrey TW9 4DU. The British Library, Department of Manuscripts, Great Russell Street, London WC1B 3DG, holds many valuable manuscripts, including the Aberdeen and Liverpool Papers. The bibliography in C. J. Bartlett's *Castlereagh* (1966) has an extensive listing of manuscripts and their locations. The Metternich Papers are located in the Haus-, Hof- und Staatsarchiv at Minoritenplatz 1, Vienna.

Background material on Europe, Britain, Castlereagh, and foreign policy can be found in F. R. Bridge and Roger Bullen's *The Great Powers and the European States System, 1815–1914* (1980), Jacques Droz's *Europe Between Revolutions, 1815–1848* (1967), R. W. Seton-Watson's comprehensive *Britain in Europe, 1789–1914* (1937), L.C.B. Seaman's interesting and provocative *From Vienna to Versailles* (1955), and especially Muriel E. Chamberlain's *"Pax Britannica"? British Foreign Policy, 1789–1914* (1988), whose chapter on Castlereagh and his foreign policy is the best review incorporating recent scholarship. George Rudé's *Debate on Europe* (1972) examines various historians' views on the period, especially on Castlereagh, Metternich, the Concert of Europe, and the Holy Alliance.

An exceptionally handy reference work is David Weigall's *Britain and the World, 1815–1986* (1987). Also very useful is Charles Middleton's *The Administration of British Foreign Policy, 1782–1846* (1977), which includes a chapter on the setting of foreign policy, tying the eighteenth and nineteenth centuries together; there is also a valuable listing, with brief biographical outlines, of the personnel of the Foreign Office. Excellent recent biographies of Castlereagh are C. J. Bartlett's *Castlereagh* (1966), the strongest on foreign policy; John W. Derry's *Castlereagh* (1976), superb at describing his character and his critics in the nineteenth century; and Wendy Hinde's *Castlereagh* (1981).

Castlereagh's important role in foreign policy was not appreciated in the nineteenth century because critics so closely associated him with Britain's repressive domestic policies. His half-brother Charles Stewart, the third Marquess of Londonderry, attempting to defend Castlereagh, published his twelve-volume *Memoirs and Correspondence of Viscount Castlereagh, Second Marquess of Londonderry* (1848–1853). Documents from the Duke of Wellington, with whom Castlereagh had a close and supportive relationship, were published in *The Dispatches of Field Marshal the Duke of Wellington*, compiled by Lieutenant Colonel John Gurwood (1834–1839), and in *Supplementary Despatches*, edited by the second Duke of Wellington (1858–1872). While containing valuable information, these collections were too voluminous to provide on their own for any change in the interpretation of Castlereagh and foreign policy. Lord Salisbury furnished an early favorable reassessment in a sketch first published in the *Quarterly Review* in 1862 and reprinted in his *Biographical Essays* (1905). Archibald Alison's *The Lives of Lord Castlereagh and Sir Charles Stewart* (1861) commented positively on his character and policy. J. W. Fortescue, in a series of lectures published as *British Statesmen of the Great War* (1911), praised Castlereagh as a most effective war secretary and foreign minister. A. W. Ward and others edited *The Cambridge Modern History*, whose pertinent volumes appeared in 1907; W. Alison Phillips stressed the important role Castlereagh played in the congress meetings. A. W. Ward and G. P. Gooch edited *The Cambridge History of British Foreign Policy, 1783–1919* (1922), with several chapters touching on Castlereagh as an effective leader.

Charles Webster's magisterial two-volume study, *The Foreign Policy of Castlereagh* (1925, 1931), provided the most fundamental and favorable reevaluation. All subsequent studies of Castlereagh and British foreign policy of the period have acknowledged their debt to Webster. While working for the War Office at the end of the Great War, he wrote *The Congress of Vienna* (1919) in preparation for the upcoming Paris Peace Conference.

For the balance of power, see eight superb articles edited by Alan Sked in *Europe's Balance of Power, 1815–48* (1979), Edward Gulick's *Europe's Classical Balance of Power* (1955), and S. R. Graubard's "Castlereagh and the Peace of Europe," *Journal of British Studies* 3 (1963): 79–87, stressing that Castlereagh's ideas were closely tied to the eighteenth century. Coalition-building and Vienna are discussed in Harold Nicolson's well-written *The Congress of Vienna* (1946) and Henry Kissinger's *A World Restored* (1957), the latter stressing that Castlereagh was equal to Metternich in negotiations, and in Gulick's chapter in C. W. Crawley's *New Cambridge Modern History*, Vol. 9 (1965). In "Castlereagh, Bernadotte and Norway," *Scandanavian Journal of History* 8 (1983): 193–223, Lars Tangeraas contends that Castlereagh attempted to protect Norway's interest in its forced union with Sweden. G. J. Renier's *Great Britain and the Establishment of the Kingdom of the Netherlands 1813–1815: A Study in British Foreign Policy* (1930) explains his dealing with Belgian nationalism. In *Power and the Pursuit of Peace* (1963), F. H. Hinsley discusses the differences between Castlereagh and Alexander on the Holy Alliance and the Congress System. Carsten Holbraad, *The Concert of Europe* (1970), shows Castlereagh's role in developing the Concert of Europe. D. L. Hafner, in "Castlereagh, the Balance of Power, and Non-'Intervention,' " *Australian Journal of Politics and History* 26 (1980): 71–84, effectively argues that Castlereagh believed that intervention could upset the balance of power. D.C.M. Platt's *Finance, Trade and Politics* (1968) and J. M. Sherwig's *Guineas and Gunpowder* (1969) examine the impact of trade and finance on foreign policy in Europe and overseas. Castlereagh's determination to remain at peace with Russia is explained in John Gleason's *The Genesis of Russophobia in Great Britain* (1950).

For Latin America see C. K. Webster's valuable collection of documents in *Britain and the Independence of Latin America* (1938) and H. S. Ferns's *Britain and Argentina in the Nineteenth Century* (1960), which includes a discussion of Castlereagh's memorandum of May 1807 on South America. For Castlereagh's determination to maintain peace with the United States, see Kenneth Bourne's *Britain and the Balance of Power in North America* (1967) and Bradford Perkins's *Castlereagh and Adams* (1964).

Castlereagh's relations with Metternich are treated most effectively in Paul W. Schroeder's *Metternich's Diplomacy at Its Zenith* (1962) and Alan Palmer's *Metternich* (1972). For other political leaders with whom Castlereagh had important ties, see especially

H.W.V. Temperley's *The Foreign Policy of Canning* (1925), Norman Gash's *Lord Liverpool* (1984), Muriel Chamberlain's *Lord Aberdeen* (1983), and Elizabeth Longford's *Wellington* (1969, 1972).

There are several excellent collections of documents, including Edward Hertslet's exhaustive *The Map of Europe by Treaty* (1875) and Michael Hurst's *Key Treaties for the Great Powers* (1972). Temperley and Penson include three important documents from the Castlereagh period in *Foundations of British Foreign Policy* (1938), while Joel H. Wiener includes many documents, often abridged, in *Great Britain: Foreign Policy and the Span of Empire* (1972). Webster's collection, *British Diplomacy, 1813–1815* (1921), reproduces many of the documents on the building of the coalition, the Treaties of Paris, and the Congress of Vienna. One should also consult the *British and Foreign State Papers* for various treaties, and *Hansard Parliamentary Debates* for Castlereagh's speeches in Parliament. Bartlett's *Castlereagh* has a listing of diplomatic papers and their locations.

Bibliography

Alison, Archibald. *The Lives of Lord Castlereagh and Sir Charles Stewart*. 3 vols. London: William Blackwood, 1861.

Bartlett, C. J. *Castlereagh*. London: Macmillan, 1966.

Bourne, Kenneth. *Britain and the Balance of Power in North America, 1815–1908*. Berkeley: University of California Press, 1967.

Bridge, F. R., and Roger Bullen. *The Great Powers and the European States System, 1815–1914*. London: Longman, 1980.

Chamberlain, Muriel E. *Lord Aberdeen*. London: Longman, 1983.

———. *"Pax Britannica"? British Foreign Policy, 1789–1914*. London: Longman, 1988.

Crawley, C. W., ed. *The New Cambridge Modern History*. Vol. 9. Cambridge: Cambridge University Press, 1965.

Derry, John W. *Castlereagh*. New York: St. Martin's Press, 1976.

Droz, Jacques. *Europe between Revolutions, 1815–1848*. Ithaca, N.Y.: Cornell University Press, 1967.

Ferns, H. S. *Britain and Argentina in the Nineteenth Century*. Oxford: Oxford University Press, 1960. Reprint. New York: Arno Press, 1977.

Fortescue, J. W. *British Statesmen of the Great War, 1793–1814*. Oxford: Clarendon Press, 1911.

Gash, Norman. *Lord Liverpool*. Cambridge, Mass.: Harvard University Press, 1984.

Gleason, John Howes. *The Genesis of Russophobia in Great Britain*. Cambridge, Mass.: Harvard University Press, 1950. Reprint. New York: Octagon Books, 1972.

Graubard, S. R. "Castlereagh and the Peace of Europe." *Journal of British Studies* 3 (1963): 79–87.

Gulick, Edward V. *Europe's Classical Balance of Power*. Ithaca, N.Y.: Cornell University Press, 1955.

Hafner, D. L. "Castlereagh, the Balance of Power, and Non-'Intervention.' " *Australian Journal of Politics and History* 26 (1980): 71–84.

Hertslet, Edward. *The Map of Europe by Treaty*. Vol. 1. London: Butterworths, 1875.

Hinde, Wendy. *Castlereagh*. London: Collins, 1981.

Hinsley, F. H. *Power and the Pursuit of Peace*. Cambridge: Cambridge University Press, 1963.

Holbraad, Carsten. *The Concert of Europe: A Study in German and British International Theory, 1815–1914*. London: Longman, 1970.

Hurst, Michael, ed. *Key Treaties for the Great Powers, 1814–1914*. Vol. 1. New York: St. Martin's Press, 1972.

Kissinger, Henry A. *A World Restored: Metternich, Castlereagh and the Problems of Peace, 1812–22*. Boston: Houghton Mifflin, 1957.

Londonderry, Marquess of, ed. *Memoirs and Correspondence of Viscount Castlereagh, Second Marquess of Londonderry*. 12 vols. London: H. Colburn, 1848–1853.

Longford, Elizabeth. *Wellington*. 2 vols. New York: Harper and Row, 1969, 1972.

Middleton, Charles R. *The Administration of British Foreign Policy, 1782–1846*. Durham, N.C.: Duke University Press, 1977.

Nicolson, Harold. *The Congress of Vienna*. New York: Harcourt Brace Jovanovich, 1946.

Palmer, Alan. *Metternich*. New York: Harper and Row, 1972.

Perkins, Bradford. *Castlereagh and Adams: England and the United States, 1812–1823*. Berkeley: University of California Press, 1964.

Platt, D.C.M. *Finance, Trade and Politics in British Foreign Policy, 1815–1914*. Oxford: Oxford University Press, 1968.

Renier, G. J. *Great Britain and the Establishment of the Kingdom of the Netherlands, 1813–1815: A Study in British Foreign Policy*. The Hague: Martinus Nijhoff, 1930.

Rudé, George. *Debate on Europe, 1815–1850*. New York: Harper and Row, 1972.

Salisbury, Lord. *Biographical Essays*. London: John Murray, 1905.

Schroeder, Paul W. *Metternich's Diplomacy at Its Zenith, 1820–23*. Austin: University of Texas Press, 1962.

Seaman, L.C.B. *From Vienna to Versailles*. 1955. New York: Harper and Row, 1963.

Seton-Watson, R. W. *Britain in Europe, 1789–1914*. New York: Macmillan, 1937.

Sherwig, J. M. *Guineas and Gunpowder: British Foreign Aid in the Wars with France, 1793–1815*. Cambridge, Mass.: Harvard University Press, 1969.

Sked, Alan, ed. *Europe's Balance of Power, 1815–48*. New York: Barnes and Noble, 1979.

Tangeraas, Lars. "Castlereagh, Bernadotte and Norway." *Scandinavian Journal of History* 8 (1983): 193–223.

Temperley, H.W.V. *The Foreign Policy of Canning, 1822–1827*. 1925. 2nd ed. Hamden, Conn.: Frank Cass, 1966.

Temperley, H.W.V., and Lillian M. Penson, eds. *Foundations of British Foreign Policy from Pitt (1792) to Salisbury (1902)*. 1938. London: Frank Cass, 1966.

Ward, A. W., and G. P. Gooch, eds. *The Cambridge History of British Foreign Policy, 1783–1919*. Vols. 1 and 2. 1922. Reprint. New York: Octagon Books, 1970.

Ward, A. W., G. W. Prothero, and Stanley Leathes, eds. *The Cambridge Modern History*. Vols. 9 and 10. Cambridge: Cambridge University Press, 1907.

Webster, C. K., ed. *Britain and the Independence of Latin America, 1812–1830*. 2 vols. 1938. New York: Octagon Books, 1970.

Webster, Charles K. *British Diplomacy 1813–1815. Select Documents Dealing with the Reconstruction of Europe*. London: Bell, 1921.

———. *The Congress of Vienna*. 1919. New York: Barnes and Noble, 1963.

———. *The Foreign Policy of Castlereagh, 1812–1815*. London: Bell, 1931.

———. *The Foreign Policy of Castlereagh, 1815–1822*. London: Bell, 1925.

Weigall, David. *Britain and the World, 1815–1986: A Dictionary of International Relations*. New York: Oxford University Press, 1987.

Wellington, Duke of. *The Dispatches of Field Marshal the Duke of Wellington. 13 vols. in 12.* Compiled by Lieutenant Colonel John Gurwood. London: J. Murray, 1834–1839.

———. *Supplementary Despatches and Memoranda of Field Marshal Arthur, Duke of Wellington.* 15 vols. Edited by the second Duke of Wellington. London: John Murray, 1858–1872.

Wiener, Joel H., ed. *Great Britain: Foreign Policy and the Span of Empire: 1689–1971. A Documentary History.* Vol. 1. New York: McGraw-Hill, 1972.

LOWELL J. SATRE

Fidel Castro (b. 1927).   Perhaps no one in recent United States history has been as despised, vilified, and underestimated as Cuba's Fidel Castro. Certainly, few have received as much attention. For more than thirty years American policy makers and journalists have predicted the imminent downfall of a Castro popularly portrayed as a bearded, khaki-clad, cigar smoking, charismatic caudillo. He has survived unceasing hostility, economic embargo, assassination attempts, sabotage, and even an invasion of Cuba. In the process he has remade Cuba and, more important, has consistently and successfully challenged U.S. hegemony in the Western Hemisphere and the Third World. While few Latin Americans desire to emulate the Cuban Revolution as a model for economic or human rights achievements, Castro is widely admired for his defiance of the United States and his ability to exert a significant impact in the world arena—something virtually without precedent among undeveloped nations. This success makes Fidel Castro the greatest Latin American statesman since Simón Bolivar.

There has always been an aura of greatness around Castro. Even his enemies concede that he is a talented statesman, strategist, and tactician. Castro has the ability to anticipate events and is adroit at manipulating them for short-term gain. Extremely intelligent and a prodigious worker, he is confident that he can master any subject or situation. Castro's energy, physique, extraordinary breadth of knowledge and interests, and gilded tongue combine to project an image of omniscience and omnipotence. Even Castro's supporters would probably concede that he is ruthless and has gradually become more inflexible.

Castro's foreign policies are conditioned by a series of long-held beliefs and assumptions. Perhaps the most important is his hatred of the United States and his belief in the fundamental incompatibility of U.S. and Cuban interests, a belief grounded in history and reinforced by the dialectic of hostility. This belief also reinforces a vision of his destiny to become the new Bolivar and lead a second independence movement against U.S. hegemony, a vision also strengthened by his determinism. Thus, Castro's declaration that "the Andes will become the Sierra Maestra of Latin America" is more than a threat—it is prophesy. This sense of a historic mission, seen as early as 1953 in his "History Will Absolve Me" speech, gives him an extraordinary reservoir of strength, confidence, courage, and willingness to take enormous risks. Castro's fundamental hostility to the United States (and vice versa) makes it difficult to compromise or negotiate differences; his understanding of history has led him to conclude that he can never surrender to the United States on any major point.

Castro's internationalism also results from his assumption of the existence of a capitalistic, imperialistic world system led by the United States. Revolutionary regimes cannot succeed in isolation, but must assist other revolutions in order to survive. This attitude propelled Castro to send troops to Africa, to provide generous economic and technical assistance to the Third World, and to support guerrilla insurgencies. As Castro stated in his Second Declaration of Havana in 1962, "it is the duty of every revolutionary to make revolution." Although experience has taught him to be more pragmatic and patient in his conduct of policy, and circumstances at times force him to moderate his behavior, Castro's diplomacy can best be described as the diplomacy of revolution.

Fidel Castro Ruz, the son of a prosperous Spanish farmer in Cuba's northwest, was born on August 13, 1927. He received a private Jesuit education and excelled in athletics before entering the University of Havana and earning a law degree. His university career coincided with the disillusionment of Cuban society under the corrupt government of Ramón Grau San Martin (1944–1948) and the consequent radicalization of student politics. In 1947 Castro participated with other students in an ill-fated invasion of the Dominican Republic that sought to overthrow strongman Rafael Trujillo. A year later he witnessed the massive uprisings in Bogotá, Colombia, after the assassination of Jorge Eliécer Gaitán, a charismatic left-wing politician.

After graduation, Castro practiced law and politics, married, and became a member of Eddy Chibás's moderately oppositionist Ortodoxo party. Chibás's apparent suicide and Fulgencio Batista's coup d'état in 1952 convinced Castro to take up arms against the government. On July 26, 1953, Castro and 165 followers attacked the Moncada army barracks near the city of Santiago in hopes of fomenting rebellion. The attack was a disaster, and Castro was captured with his brother Raúl and sentenced to fifteen years in prison after making an impassioned "History Will Absolve Me" defense plea.

In 1955, following a general amnesty, Castro traveled to Mexico to organize a new force and met Ernesto "Ché" Guevara, who became the revolution's second-in-command. In November 1956, aboard the yacht *Granma* (the name of Cuba's official newspaper), Castro and eighty-two followers again tried to overthrow the government, with similar results. Castro, his brother, and Guevara barely escaped and fled into the Sierra Maestra to begin a guerrilla war. There, Castro was assisted by peasants, Batista's inept but brutal attempts to repress dissent, and a series of newspaper articles by *New York Times* correspondent Herbert Matthews, which gave him credibility abroad and recruits at home. By mid–1958 Batista began to lose support of key groups, such as the clergy, labor unions, the middle class, and the United States, which terminated arms shipments in March. After a fraudulent election failed to stave off the *barbudos* (bearded ones), Batista fled on January 1, 1959. Castro entered Havana as a hero on January 9 amid pandemonium and euphoria. The successful rebellion allowed Castro to implement the most complete revolution in Latin American history.

From 1959 to 1962 Castro consolidated his power by establishing an author-itarian regime and implementing his program of radical social and economic reform, featuring nationalization of the economy, egalitarian socioeconomic pol-icies such as land and income redistribution, and economic independence from the United States. Such policies placed the revolution on a collision course with the United States. The Eisenhower administration, which had never been en-thusiastic about Castro or his revolution, moved quickly into opposition after a radical Agrarian Reform Law was decreed on May 17, 1959, expropriating all farmlands over 1,000 acres and prohibiting foreign ownership of agricultural land. Meanwhile, at the United Nations Castro extolled neutralism and urged the creation of an anti-U.S. bloc in the Organization of American States (OAS). By the end of 1959, a growing number of Cuban exiles began receiving assistance from the Central Intelligence Agency (CIA) in their efforts to reverse the rev-olution. By that time, the United States had made the removal of Castro its chief goal in Cuba.

The mutual antipathy between Castro and the United States forced him to turn increasingly to the Soviet bloc in order to protect and extend the revolution. In February 1960, the two nations signed a modest trade agreement and resumed diplomatic relations. In June, Castro expropriated petroleum refineries owned by Texaco, Standard Oil, and Royal Dutch Shell after the companies refused to refine Soviet crude. In response, Eisenhower eliminated the Cuban sugar quota, which prompted further Cuban expropriations. In October, Eisenhower an-nounced an embargo of all U.S. exports, which prompted further expropriations. Such actions led the CIA to begin training an exile force in Guatemala for an invasion of the island; this prompted Castro to create the Committees for the Defense of the Revolution, a citizens' civil defense organization. It also provided the rationale to end freedom of the press and autonomy for universities and trade unions, thereby swelling the number of exiles and aiding CIA efforts.

The revolution's radicalization and the progressive deterioration of U.S.-Cuban relations were major issues in the 1960 presidential campaign. John F. Kennedy, the Democratic standard-bearer, attacked the Republicans for losing Cuba and pledged to be more aggressive toward Castro. Kennedy's victory and Eisenhower's subsequent severing of relations on January 3, 1961, assured this ill-fated confrontation. Three months after Kennedy assumed office, a U.S.-backed Cuban expeditionary force landed at the Bay of Pigs.

The Bay of Pigs marked Fidel Castro's greatest victory. Familiar with the terrain and personally leading the revolutionary army, he crushed the invasion and captured virtually the entire brigade. The predicted groundswell of opposition never materialized; instead the people rose to cheer the revolution. Castro's victory was so complete that he was able to increase his prestige and consolidate his position. Within days of the fiasco, Kennedy announced a new and grandiose Alliance for Progress (dubbed the ''Castro Plan'' by Latin American skeptics) to promote development and thereby reduce the appeal of revolution in the region.

In the wake of Castro's victory and subsequent espousal of Marxist-Leninism

(December 1961), the Soviet Union pledged to defend the island. Only a full-scale invasion, which at the time seemed plausible, if not imminent, could succeed in removing Castro. The Soviet decision to install intermediate-range missile bases resulted in the most dangerous confrontation in the Cold War era, the Cuban Missile Crisis of October 1962.

The consequences of the missile crisis were as far-reaching as those of the Bay of Pigs. Throughout the crisis Castro was not consulted and, in fact, made futile efforts to block an agreement between the superpowers. The result was that Latin Americans saw Cuba as a satellite of the Soviet Union, which substantially reduced Castro's appeal in the region. Almost as important, however, was that in return for the Soviet missile withdrawal, the United States pledged not to invade Cuba, which brought a measure of security to Castro, although it did not stop the CIA from trying to sabotage the revolution or assassinate Castro.

The missile crisis occurred after a new phase in the revolution had begun. In February 1962, just a few days after the OAS expelled Cuba, Castro issued the Second Declaration of Havana, a virtual declaration of war against the United States and its Latin American allies. Castro's famous call to revolution and repudiation of the Soviet Union's caution signaled the onset of active support for guerrilla insurgencies, not only in Latin America, but throughout the Third World, and marked a high point in *fidelista* radicalism. Over the next several years, Castro struggled to maintain his independence from Moscow while simultaneously demanding Soviet protection from the United States. Thus, while Cuba participated in the Warsaw Pact's common market (COMECON), Castro refused to take sides in the Sino-Soviet split. As the decade progressed, however, Cuban economic failures (aggravated by the OAS embargo and CIA sabotage) made the island more dependent on the Soviets for subsidies, while events such as the missile crisis exposed Cuba's military impotence. Moreover, although Fidel was able to win endorsement to create "two, three, many Vietnams" at the Tricontinental Conference (January 1966), the death of Ché Guevara in Bolivia proved the futility of such a strategy. By 1968 a bankrupt and isolated Cuba crawled into the Soviet orbit, and a chastened Castro publicly supported the Soviet invasion of Czechoslovakia in August.

Ironically, Cuba's increased dependence on the Soviet Union gave Castro the opportunity to institutionalize his revolution and to play an increasingly important role on the world stage. Guaranteed Soviet assistance allowed Castro to cultivate Latin American governments instead of revolution, particularly Peru's leftist generals and Salvador Allende of Chile. By the late–1970s, Castro had broken out of his diplomatic isolation and had cordial relations with many Western Hemisphere nations, including Mexico, Costa Rica, Panama, Venezuela, and Jamaica. Discussions with the United States also held the promise of improved relations (travel restrictions were lifted; surveillance flights ceased), although such hopes did not materialize.

Perhaps the most surprising aspect of Castro's new prominence in world affairs was his military and development assistance to a variety of Third World nations, especially in Africa. In 1975 and 1976, Cuba sent 30,000 troops to Angola to help the Popular Movement for the Liberation of Angola (MPLA) defeat the U.S. and South African–backed National Union for the Total Independence of Angola (UNITA) in a civil war. Two years later, Castro repeated his triumph by sending 15,000 troops to ensure the survival of Ethiopian strongman Colonel Mengistu Haile Mariam against a Somalian invasion. In the late 1970s Cuba began sending an increasing number of technicians (doctors, teachers, engineers, agronomists) abroad on low-cost, high-impact projects. The effect of these programs was a substantial increase in Cuban prestige, revealed by Castro's election to head the Nonaligned Movement and the selection of Havana as the site of the Sixth Nonaligned Summit (September 1979), which called for the creation of a New International Economic Order. In addition, the successes of the Sandinista Revolution in Nicaragua and of Maurice Bishop's New Jewel Movement in Grenada provided Castro with hemispheric allies. These triumphs strengthened Cuba's image as a world power and made Castro appear to be an important statesman.

The image proved an illusion, and Castro suffered a series of reverses that once again exposed his impotence. His support for the Soviet invasion of Afghanistan cost him Third World and nonaligned supporters and seemed to indicate a greater degree of subservience to the USSR than really existed. The events leading to the Mariel boatlift, where 125,000 Cubans fled Cuba between April and September 1980, revealed a petty tyrant and a dissatisfied population. After Colombian authorities discovered a cache of Cuban arms in 1981, several Latin American nations broke relations, further isolating Cuba. Castro was forced to limit support for the Sandinistas and the Frente Farabundo Martí para la Liberación Nacional (FMLN) guerrillas in El Salvador. Castro also proved incapable of resisting the U.S. invasion of Grenada in 1983.

This does not mean that Castro had no victories in the 1980s. He supported Argentina unequivocally in the 1982 Falklands/Malvinas War. The war provided an ironic twist in that Castro defended the ideas behind the Monroe Doctrine and the Inter-American Treaty of Reciprocal Assistance (Rio Treaty). Cuba's withdrawal from Angola in 1988 was accompanied by a South African withdrawal from Namibia. Castro also proved to be moderate, reasonable, and capable as a statesman in his support for the Contadora process in Central America, détente between the superpowers, and a comprehensive multilateral debt package. In fact, through the 1980s and into the 1990s Castro has increasingly focused on economic issues instead of geopolitical issues, a focus necessitated by the phased withdrawal of Soviet aid. This has made him a leading spokesman for the Third World on North-South issues. By the end of 1991, with the projected end of Soviet economic and military assistance, Castro may be more isolated and vulnerable than at any time since the Bay of Pigs. Despite a severe and worsening economic crisis and increasing domestic discontent, it is probably premature to write any eulogies for the revolution or to place Fidel Castro in his proper historical context.

Annotated Bibliography

Although Castro is a prodigious worker and a voracious reader, he has not yet written his memoirs. Despite this, there is an abundance of primary materials. Castro's speeches have been collected in a number of works. Some of the most relevant are *War and Crisis in the Americas: War and Crisis in the Americas.* (1985); *Atlas Armas* (1963), which covers the 1959–1962 period; and Rolando E. Bonachea and Nelson P. Valdes, eds., *Revolutionary Struggle, 1947–1958: Selected Works of Fidel Castro* (1972). Martin Kenner and James Petras, eds., *Fidel Castro Speaks* (1969), is a compilation of translated speeches from 1960 to 1968. In addition, the appendices of H. Michael Erisman's *Cuba's International Relations: The Anatomy of a Nationalist Foreign Policy* (1985) contain several of Castro's most important speeches and declarations. Castro has also been interviewed extensively, although usually on a broad range of topics and not just on Cuban foreign relations. Two easily obtained interviews that reveal his motives, objectives, and foreign policy are Lee Lockwood, *Castro's Cuba, Cuba's Fidel* (1969), and Frank Mankiewicz and Kirby Jones, *With Fidel: A Portrait of Castro and Cuba* (1975).

Fidel Castro and the Cuban Revolution are so intertwined and so central to recent Cuban history that it is impossible to separate the two. Likewise, it is nearly impossible to distinguish between Cuban foreign relations and Castro's activities as a statesman because Castro makes virtually all important decisions.

There have been several outstanding biographies of Castro. The most comprehensive and balanced is Tad Szulc's *Fidel: A Critical Portrait* (1986). Szulc is able to present an appealing personal portrait even while condemning many of Castro's policies. Szulc also benefits from the extensive cooperation he received from Cuban officials, including Castro himself. Among the better pro-Castro biographies are Peter Bourne's *Fidel: A Biography of Fidel Castro* (1986), which purports to be a psychoanalytical study; Lockwood's *Castro's Cuba*; and Herbert Matthews's seminal *Fidel Castro* (1969). The best anti-Castro works include Theodore Draper, *Castroism: Theory and Practice* (1965); Maurice Halperin, *The Rise and Decline of Fidel Castro: An Essay in Contemporary History* (1972) and *The Taming of Fidel Castro* (1981); Edward Gonzalez, *Cuba under Castro: The Limits of Charisma* (1974); and Manuel Urrutia Lleó, *Fidel Castro and Company, Inc.* (1984).

Literature on Cuban foreign relations since the revolution has tended to be dominated by Cold War considerations. Thus, Cuba's relations with the United States and the Soviet Union have received the greatest amount of attention, with fewer studies focusing on Africa and Latin America. Chronologically, scholars have focused on the period beginning with the triumph of the revolution (January 1959) to the Cuban Missile Crisis (October 1962), although a number of studies deal with Cuban policies in Africa and Central America in the 1970s and 1980s.

There have been many good works on U.S.-Cuban relations during the revolution's early years. Firsthand accounts have been provided by Earl E. T. Smith, *The Fourth Floor: An Account of the Castro Communist Revolution* (1962), which condemns State Department policy as contributing to the triumph of communism; Philip W. Bonsal, *Cuba, Castro and the United States* (1971); E. Howard Hunt, *Give Us This Day* (1973); Bradley Earl Ayers, *The War That Never Was: An Insider's Account of CIA Covert Operations Against Cuba* (1976); and Wayne S. Smith, *The Closest of Enemies: A Personal and Diplomatic Account of U.S.-Cuban Relations Since 1957* (1987), an outstanding overview with a personal touch. Among the best works on the Bay of Pigs are

Peter Wyden, *Bay of Pigs: The Untold Story* (1979), and Trumbull Higgins, *The Perfect Failure: Kennedy, Eisenhower, and the CIA at the Bay of Pigs* (1987). Stephen G. Rabe, *Eisenhower and Latin America: The Foreign Policy of Anticommunism* (1988), places the relationship in its larger context for the Eisenhower administration, as does Thomas G. Peterson, ed., *Kennedy's Quest for Victory: American Foreign Policy, 1961–1963* (1989), for the JFK years.

The American view of the Cuban Missile Crisis is covered by many former officials, including Robert F. Kennedy, *Thirteen Days* (1969). More recent and reasoned accounts can be found in Raymond L. Garthoff, *Reflections on the Cuban Missile Crisis* (1987); James G. Hershberg, "Before 'The Missiles of October': Did Kennedy Plan a Military Strike Against Cuba?," *Diplomatic History* 14, 2 (1990): 163–198; and James G. Blight and David A. Welch, *On the Brink: Americans and Soviets Reexamine the Cuban Missile Crisis* (1989). The revolution's impact on U.S. politics can be seen in Richard E. Welch, Jr., *Response to Revolution: The United States and the Cuban Revolution, 1959–1961* (1985); Kent M. Beck, "Necessary Lies, Hidden Truths: Cuba in the 1960 Campaign," *Diplomatic History* 8, 1 (1984): 37–59; and Richard Ned Lebow, "Domestic Politics and the Cuban Missile Crisis: The Traditional and Revisionist Interpretations Reevaluated," *Diplomatic History* 14, 4 (1990): 471–492. An excellent overview of U.S.-Cuban relations is Morris H. Morley, *Imperial State and Revolution: The U.S. and Cuba, 1952–1986* (1987). David D. Newsom, *The Soviet Brigade in Cuba: A Study in Political Diplomacy* (1987), examines the public relations blunder by the Carter administration over the presence of a Soviet training brigade.

Historians of the early phase of the revolution have speculated on whether or not Castro was a Marxist-Leninist when he first came to power and whether the United States pushed Castro into the Soviet camp. This debate began even before Castro's triumphant entry into Havana on January 9, 1959, and was always framed in Cold War rhetoric. The conventional wisdom is that Castro was not a Communist but was committed to hemispheric revolution and independence from the United States, and that U.S. hostility to those goals forced Castro into making an alliance with the Soviet Union.

A prevalent deficiency in the Cold War-centric studies is the tendency to focus on either the United States or the Soviet Union while ignoring the ostensible subject. This is particularly true of works dealing with the Bay of Pigs and the Cuban Missile Crisis, but can also be seen in fairly recent works, such as Jiri Valenta and Herbert J. Ellison, eds., *Grenada and Soviet/Cuban Policy: Internal Crisis and U.S./OECS Intervention* (1986), and Carla Anne Robbins, *The Cuban Threat* (1985). A major reason for this tendency is the belief that Cuba is a Soviet proxy without separate goals, interests, or policies. Even a sophisticated work such as that of Robbins suffers from the obsession with U.S. Cold War policy. Although there has been a multitude of examples of Soviet-Cuban divergence, this belief persists, in part because it has long been the official view of the United States government. This view of Cuba as a Soviet surrogate has had a devastating effect on both U.S. policy and scholarship.

Despite the surrogate thesis, Castro's undeniable importance as a statesman has resulted in a proliferation of studies on Cuban foreign policy. Perhaps the best is Jorge I. Dominguez, *To Make a World Safe for Revolution: Cuba's Foreign Policy* (1989), a companion to his seminal *Cuba: Order and Revolution*, which focused on domestic, social, political, and economic trends in revolutionary Cuba. As in the earlier work, Dominguez combines exhaustive research and a dispassionate writing style to present a comprehensive overview of the island's foreign relations. Many of his theses support Robbins's *The Cuban Threat* and Erisman's *Cuba's International Relations,* which Dominguez displaces as the most important work. Other useful overviews include Cole Blasier and Carmelo Mesa-Lago, eds., *Cuba in the World* (1979); Martin Weinstein, ed., *Revolutionary Cuba in the World Arena* (1979); Pamela Falk, *Cuban Foreign Policy: Caribbean Tempest* (1986); and Edward Gonzalez and David Ronfeldt, *Castro, Cuba, and the World* (1986).

Cuban-Soviet relations have been examined by a number of authors. W. Raymond Duncan, *The Soviet Union and Cuba: Interests and Influence* (1985), is a well-written argument against Cuba as a Soviet proxy, but depends almost entirely on secondary sources. Jacques Levesque, *The USSR and the Cuban Revolution: Soviet Ideological and Strategic Imperatives, 1959–1977* (1978), gives the Soviet perspective on the relationship.

Castro's policies in Latin America and Africa in the 1970s and early 1980s received much attention from cold warriors and political scientists, especially after the success of the Sandinista Revolution. Barry Levine, ed., *The New Cuban Presence in the Caribbean* (1983), Jorge Domínguez, "Cuba's Relations with Caribbean and Central American Countries," *Cuban Studies/Estudios Cubanos* 13 (Summer 1983): 79–112, and Carlos Montaner, *Cuba, Castro, and the Caribbean: The Cuban Revolution and the Crisis in Western Conscience* (1985), analyze Castro's objectives and the competition between Cuba and the United States. For Cuba's policies in Angola and Ethiopia, see William LeoGrande, *Cuba's Policy in Africa, 1959–1980* (1980), which is extremely useful, and June Belkin and Carmelo Mesa-Lago, eds., *Cuba in Africa* (1982).

Bibliography

Works by Castro

Castro, Fidel. *Atlas Armas.* Havana: Gobierno Municipal Revolucionario, 1963.
———.*War and Crisis in the Americas.* New York: Pathfinder Press, 1985.

Works about Castro

Beck, Kent M. "Necessary Lies, Hidden Truths: Cuba in the 1960 Campaign." *Diplomatic History* 8, 1 (1984): 37–59.
Bonachea, Rolando E., and Nelson P. Valdes, eds. *Revolutionary Struggle, 1947–1958: Selected Works of Fidel Castro.* Cambridge, Mass.: MIT Press, 1972.
Bourne, Peter. *Fidel: A Biography of Fidel Castro.* New York: Dodd, Mead, 1986.
Franqui, Carlos. *Family Portrait with Fidel.* Translated by Alfred MacAdam. New York: Random House, 1984.
Halperin, Maurice. *The Rise and Decline of Fidel Castro: An Essay in Contemporary History.* Berkeley: University of California Press, 1972.
———. *The Taming of Fidel Castro.* Berkeley: University of California Press, 1981.
Kenner, Martin, and James Petras, eds. *Fidel Castro Speaks.* New York: Grove Press, 1969.
Lleó, Manuel Urrutia. *Fidel Castro and Company, Inc.* New York: Praeger, 1984.
Lockwood, Lee. *Castro's Cuba, Cuba's Fidel.* New York: Vintage, 1969.
Mankiewicz, Frank, and Kirby Jones. *With Fidel: A Portrait of Castro and Cuba.* Chicago: Playboy Press, 1975.
Martin, Lionel. *The Early Fidel: Roots of Castro's Communism.* Secaucus, N.J.: Lyle Stuart, 1978.
Matthews, Herbert. *Fidel Castro.* New York: Simon and Schuster, 1969.
Szulc, Tad. *Fidel: A Critical Portrait.* New York: Morrow, 1986.

Related Books

Ayers, Bradley Earl. *The War That Never Was: An Insider's Account of CIA Covert Operations Against Cuba*. Indianapolis: Bobbs-Merrill, 1976.

Belkin, June, and Carmelo Mesa-Lago, eds. *Cuba in Africa*. Pittsburgh: University of Pittsburgh Press, 1982.

Blasier, Cole, and Carmelo Mesa-Lago, eds. *Cuba in the World*. Pittsburgh: University of Pittsburgh Press, 1979.

Blight, James G., and David A. Welch. *On the Brink: Americans and Soviets Reexamine the Cuban Missile Crisis*. New York: Hill and Wang, 1989.

Bonsal, Philip W. *Cuba, Castro, and the United States*. Pittsburgh: University of Pittsburgh Press, 1971.

Domínguez, Jorge I. *Cuba: Order and Revolution*. New York: McGraw-Hill, 1979.

———. *To Make a World Safe for Revolution: Cuba's Foreign Policy*. Cambridge, Mass.: Harvard University Press, 1989.

Draper, Theodore. *Castroism: Theory and Practice*. New York: Praeger, 1965.

Duncan, W. Raymond. *The Soviet Union and Cuba: Interests and Influence*. New York: Praeger, 1985.

Erisman, H. Michael. *Cuba's International Relations: The Anatomy of a Nationalist Foreign Policy*. Boulder, Colo.: Westview Press, 1985.

Falk, Pamela S. *Cuban Foreign Policy: Caribbean Tempest*. Lexington, Mass.: Lexington Books, 1986.

Franqui, Carlos. *Diary of the Cuban Revolution*. New York: Viking, 1980.

Garthoff, Raymond L. *Reflections on the Cuban Missile Crisis*. Washington, D.C.: Brookings Institution, 1987.

Gonzalez, Edward. *Cuba under Castro: The Limits of Charisma*. Boston: Houghton Mifflin, 1974.

Gonzalez, Edward, and David Ronfeldt. *Castro, Cuba, and the World*. Santa Monica, Calif.: Rand, 1986.

Higgins, Trumbull. *The Perfect Failure: Kennedy, Eisenhower, and the CIA at the Bay of Pigs*. New York: Norton, 1987.

Hunt, E. Howard. *Give Us This Day*. New Rochelle, N.Y.: Arlington House, 1973.

Kennedy, Robert F. *Thirteen Days*. New York: Norton, 1969.

LeoGrande, William. *Cuba's Policy in Africa, 1959–1980*. Berkeley: University of California Press, 1980.

Levesque, Jacques. *The USSR and the Cuban Revolution: Soviet Ideological and Strategic Imperatives, 1959–1977*. New York: Praeger, 1978.

Levine, Barry. *The New Cuban Presence in the Caribbean*. Boulder, Colo.: Westview Press, 1983.

Montaner, Carlos. *Cuba, Castro, and the Caribbean: The Cuban Revolution and the Crisis in Western Conscience*. Translated by Nelson Duran. New Brunswick, N.J.: Transaction Books, 1985.

Morley, Morris H. *Imperial State and Revolution: The U.S. and Cuba, 1952–1986*. Cambridge: Cambridge University Press, 1987.

Newsom, David D. *The Soviet Brigade in Cuba: A Study in Political Diplomacy*. Bloomington: Indiana University Press, 1987.

Paterson, Thomas G., ed. *Kennedy's Quest for Victory: American Foreign Policy, 1961–1963*. New York: Oxford University Press, 1989.

Perez, Louis A., Jr. *Cuba: An Annotated Bibliography*. Westport, Conn.: Greenwood Press, 1988.

Rabe, Stephen G. *Eisenhower and Latin America: The Foreign Policy of Anticommunism*. Chapel Hill: University of North Carolina Press, 1988.

Robbins, Carla Anne. *The Cuban Threat*. New York: McGraw-Hill, 1985.

Ruiz, Ramon Eduardo. *Cuba: The Making of a Revolution*. Amherst: University of Massachusetts Press, 1968.

Smith, Earl E.T. *The Fourth Floor: An Account of the Castro Communist Revolution*. Washington, D.C.: Selous Foundation Press, 1962.

Smith, Wayne S. *The Closest of Enemies: A Personal and Diplomatic Account of U.S.-Cuban Relations Since 1957*. New York: Norton, 1987.

Valenta, Jiri, and Herbert J. Ellison, eds. *Grenada and Soviet/Cuban Policy: Internal Crisis and U.S./OECS Intervention*. Boulder, Colo.: Westview Press, 1986.

Weinstein, Martin, ed. *Revolutionary Cuba in the World Arena*. Philadelphia: Institute for the Study of Human Issues, 1979.

Welch, Richard E., Jr. *Response to Revolution: The United States and the Cuban Revolution, 1959–1961*. Chapel Hill: University of North Carolina Press, 1985.

Wyden, Peter. *Bay of Pigs: The Untold Story*. New York: Simon and Schuster, 1979.

Related Articles

Domínguez, Jorge. "Cuba's Relations with Caribbean and Central American Countries." *Cuban Studies/Estudios Cubanos* 13 (1983): 79–112.

Hershberg, James G. "Before 'The Missiles of October': Did Kennedy Plan a Military Strike Against Cuba?" *Diplomatic History* 14, 2 (Spring 1990): 163–198.

Lebow, Richard Ned. "Domestic Politics and the Cuban Missile Crisis: The Traditional and Revisionist Interpretations Reevaluated." *Diplomatic History* 14, 4 (Fall 1990): 471–492.

Smith, Wayne S. "Castro, Latin America, and the United States." In *United States Policy in Latin America*, pp. 288–306. Edited by John Martz. Lincoln: University of Nebraska Press, 1988.

———. "Critical Junctures in U.S.-Cuban Relations: The Diplomatic Record." *Diplomatic History* 12, 4 (Fall 1988): 463–481.

W. MICHAEL WEIS

Catherine the Great (1729–1796).   Catherine II, empress of Russia, apparently never actually accepted the sobriquet "the Great" during her lifetime even though it was officially offered to her several times and was routinely employed by foreign contemporaries. When she died after a long and busy life, the label began to be commonly used everywhere except in the Soviet Union. The matter holds some significance because the sobriquet is frequently interpreted as referring specifically to her role in Russia's emergence as a European Great Power. It is rather ironic that this title was bestowed principally because of her successes in foreign policy and territorial expansion, because she ascended the throne as a peace candidate and disapproved of *Peter the Great's militarism and brutality.

Born Sophia Augusta Fredericka, princess of Anhalt-Zerbst, on April 21/May

2, 1729,* in Stettin, she was the first daughter of a minor German prince in Prussian service and a well-connected princess of Holstein-Gottorp, Johanna Elizabeth. Through her mother she inherited a Russian connection in her first cousin, Karl Peter Ulrich (1728–1762), a grandson of Peter the Great who later became Grand Duke Peter Fedorovich of Russia and eventually Emperor Peter III (1761–1762). With the enthusiastic support of King Frederick II of Prussia, young Sophia was chosen by the childless Empress Elizabeth (1741–1761) to be the bride of her nephew and heir, Peter Fedorovich. With her mother, Sophia went to Russia in February 1744, converted to Orthodoxy with the Russian name of Catherine (Ekaterina Alekseevna), and married Peter Fedorovich on August 21, 1745.

Before going to Russia, Sophia/Catherine had been educated at home by tutors and had traveled extensively with her mother to several courts, including Brunswick and Berlin. Supposedly she was a precocious child and something of a tomboy who liked to rule the roost. Her appointed role in life was to serve as ''brood mare'' of the Romanov dynasty, but this proved to be more than difficult inasmuch as her husband was probably both sterile and impotent. She rapidly made herself at home in her new environment by learning the language, history, and customs of the country, all of which facilitated wide friendships and acquaintances. Grand Duchess Catherine finally produced the required male heir on September 20, 1754, giving birth to Paul (Pavel Petrovich), whose father was probably Sergei Saltykov, a Russian nobleman with important court connections. Her dynastic duties thus acquitted, Catherine entered more vigorously into political matters through a passionate affair with Stanislaus Poniatowski, a Polish aristocrat attached to the staff of British ambassador Sir Charles Hanbury Williams.

The elderly Williams sought to counteract a Franco-Russian rapprochement on the eve of the Seven Years' War by working through Catherine, to whom he advanced large amounts of money. The two corresponded intensively in 1756–1757, and Catherine learned much about European politics even as she educated herself by reading Voltaire, Bayle, Montesquieu, and others. At the same time she became close to Chancellor Aleksei Bestuzhev-Riumin, a walking encyclopedia of Russian and European political lore who despised Prussia, disliked France, and distrusted Grand Duke Peter Fedorovich, whose succession appeared imminent in view of Elizabeth's declining health. In 1757 Bestuzhev and Catherine discussed the possibility of a regency in case of Elizabeth's death, but this prospect was undercut in early 1758 with the disgrace of Bestuzhev and the departure of Poniatowski abroad. Catherine barely survived this debacle, and as a result she acted more circumspectly in the last years of Elizabeth's reign. She continued her self-education and in 1760 began an affair with Lieutenant Grigory

---

*The Old Style, or Julian calendar, which was used in the Russian empire, was eleven days behind the New Style, or Gregorian calendar, in the eighteenth century. Dates are Old Style unless otherwise indicated.

Orlov, a dashing guardsman and military hero. At this time she also drew close to her son's new ober hofmeister, Nikita Panin, a Europeanized Russian aristocrat and former ambassador to Denmark and Sweden in whom she professed to see a future vice-chancellor of foreign affairs.

When Elizabeth died on December 25, 1761, Catherine was almost six months pregnant by Orlov and in no position to contest her husband's succession. His accession automatically gave her the title of empress, but the consorts drifted farther apart during Peter III's six-month reign. Meanwhile, Peter III's about-face in international politics—he withdrew from the Seven Years' War and allied himself with his idol, Frederick II, in a new war to recover Schleswig from Denmark—antagonized Denmark, France, and Austria, all of whom gave Catherine and her partisans funds to block Russia's sudden tilt toward Prussia. Presumably these funds were used to build resistance to Peter III among the guards regiments. Thus the tangled state of Russia's foreign affairs became an important factor in motivating Catherine's coup d'état of June 28–29, 1762, which overthrew her husband.

As empress, Catherine II immediately cancelled the Danish campaign and the alliance with Prussia, but she let the other powers know that she had no intention of rejoining the Seven Years' War, which was winding down in any event. Yet on August 2, 1762, she wrote to Poniatowski promising to support him for Poland's elective kingship. At the same time she supported the restoration of the aged Ernst Johann Biron to the Duchy of Kurland, a fief of the Polish crown which had become a virtual Russian satellite. Both maneuvers aimed at reinforcing Russian control over the ramshackle Polish-Lithuanian Commonwealth, an aristocratic republic headed by an elective monarch.

From the very start of her reign, morever, she showed her desire to manage foreign policy. When asked whether she wished to review ambassadors' despatches in extract, she demanded to see the full reports. For advice she recalled Bestuzhev-Riumin from exile, but she declined to name anybody chancellor and in 1763 appointed Nikita Panin senior member of the College of Foreign Affairs, perhaps as much to remove him from domestic policymaking as to take advantage of his expertise in foreign affairs. Bestuzhev-Riumin was soon eased out of office because of his age, drunkenness, and opposition to Russia's rapprochement with Prussia, which became official in the treaty of March 31/April 11, 1764.

This Russo-Prussian treaty became the fulcrum of Russian foreign policy for the next two decades. Both were rising powers that had demonstrated their military might against each other in the Seven Years' War. Neither wished to repeat the experience, and both had come away alienated from France, Austria, and Britain, and thus dangerously isolated. Their alliance was to last for eight years and called for cooperation in Poland and Sweden. The initial focus was on Poland-Lithuania, where Stanislaus Poniatowski was duly elected king on August 26/September 6, 1764. But Nikita Panin hoped to expand the Russo-Prussian alliance into a Northern Accord that would include Sweden, Denmark, Britain, Poland, and Saxony to counter balance the Bourbon-Habsburg powers to the south. Only part of this scheme materialized, however, in the shape of a treaty with Denmark in March 1765, cooperation with Prussia in Sweden against the pro-French Cap party in 1765–1766, and a trade agreement with Britain in 1766. Britain's refusal of a "Turkish clause" precluded a full-scale Anglo-Russian alliance. Catherine and Panin were beginning to think in European-wide terms and several years ahead.

In these first few years of her reign Catherine and her advisors also gave evidence of their insistence on being treated as equals in negotiations with the other Great Powers. The empress and Panin employed French in all such negotiations, for example, and Catherine answered the British envoy in Russian when he presumed to address her in English. Catherine's conversational skill and fluency in French, German, and Russian were gifts that she constantly employed in all manner of negotiations. She often cultivated foreign diplomats personally and impressed most of them. Russian statesmen also declined pensions from the other powers as a sign of inferior status. In economic policy Catherine sought to strengthen state finances by a favorable balance of trade and stimulated the economy by inviting foreign immigration, especially from central Europe.

Another factor that assisted Russia's emergence as a European Great Power was the weakening of Anglo-French hegemony on the Continent in the aftermath of the Seven Years' War and the simultaneous strengthening of the three eastern empires, Austria, Prussia, and Russia. Their collective power was further exemplified by their three-way partition of Poland in 1772–1773 and Russia's defeat of the Ottoman Empire in 1768–1774.

The Russo-Turkish conflict was a direct outgrowth of Russian intervention in Poland-Lithuania, where civil war broke out in early 1768. The Porte declared war on September 25/October 6, 1768. Russia was ready for the conflict, and Catherine convened a meeting of nine top advisors on November 4, 1768, to frame general strategy; this group was soon institutionalized as the Imperial Council that met twice weekly to consider all matters proposed by the empress, who presided in person when great issues were considered. Initially a temporary advisory body, the council lasted for the rest of the reign as the supreme coordinating committee for diplomatic and military affairs.

Catherine and her council quickly adopted an offensive strategy against the Turks. Their initial war aims were free navigation on the Black Sea, possession of a port and fortress there, and stabilization of defensible borders with Poland. A striking innovation was proposed by Grigory Orlov, namely, to dispatch the Russian Baltic fleet to the Mediterranean to take the Turks from the rear and to support anticipated anti-Ottoman uprisings among the Greeks, in the Balkans, and in the Near East. The venture required British assistance and foreign loans, both of which were soon arranged, and the expedition was placed under the overall command of Aleksei Orlov. The Russian squadrons arrived in the Mediterranean in 1769–1770, by which time the main Russian armies had defeated the Turks and their Crimean Tatar vassals several times and had occupied the Danubian Principalities. Orlov's fleet was victorious at Chesme on June 24–26, 1770—a devastating triumph.

Despite Russian occupation of the Crimea in 1771, the war bogged down in the Balkans and was complicated by a terrible plague epidemic that swept into southeastern Poland, struck Kiev, and devastated Moscow. Austria took advantage of the situation to encroach on Polish territory and to make a secret treaty with the Turks. Russian influence in Stockholm declined abruptly with Gustavus III's restoration of royal absolutism. Some weeks later Catherine and Grigory Orlov experienced what amounted to a divorce, and the empress became much occupied with finding a European bride for her son. This predicament led directly to the three-way partition of Poland in 1772–1773, an arrangement that relieved the Austro-Prussian pressure on Russia to make concessions to the Porte and recouped some of Russia's expenses in Poland and against the Turks. But a new complication arose in the fall of 1773 with the outbreak of the Pugachev rebellion on the southeastern frontier, which threatened to encourage Turkish intransigence and to divert Russian forces from the Danube.

Assisted by Grigory Potemkin, her gifted new favorite, Catherine kept military pressure on the Turks that resulted in the Peace of Kuchuk Kainardji on July 10, 1774, which capped a clear-cut victory over the Turks and tipped the balance of power in the south for decades. The Crimea was declared independent of Ottoman suzerainty except in religious affairs, and Russia obtained three forts ringing the peninsula along with free navigation on the Black Sea, a huge indemnity, and the right to station consuls on Ottoman territory and to make representations on behalf of an Orthodox Church in Constantinople—a provision later twisted to imply Russian mediation on behalf of all the Orthodox population under Ottoman rule. Leaving Russia in a favorable position to encroach further on Tatar and Ottoman territory, this was by far Russia's greatest victory over the Turks.

But the high cost of these successes led to a period of lessened activity abroad after 1775 as Catherine concentrated on domestic reform. She likewise pursued a cautious policy in the "independent" Crimea, while Potemkin supervised Russian settlement of Novorossiia (southern Ukraine) and foundation of a naval base at Kherson on the lower Dnieper. On the European scene her prestige rose higher with the visit of King Gustavus III of Sweden to St. Petersburg in June 1777, the first monarch to meet her at home. Catherine acted coolly during the brief War of the Bavarian Succession in 1778–1779, which Russia jointly mediated with France. The Treaty of Teschen made Russia a guarantor of the constitution of the Holy Roman Empire—impressive testimony of its heightened prestige in Europe. In 1780 Catherine led the formation of the League of Armed Neutrality against British and French maritime might, another novelty in the annals of Russian diplomacy.

A fundamental reorientation of Russian foreign policy took place in 1780–1781 when an alliance was made with Austria replacing the long-term ties with Prussia. Joseph II met Catherine at Mogilev in May 1780 and revisited her in St. Petersburg that summer. They began discussions about the fate of Ottoman possessions in Europe that evolved into the so-called Greek Project: the plan for a Russo-Austrian alliance that would drive the Turks out of Europe, place Catherine's grandson Constantine on the throne of a reconstituted Byzantine Empire, and create a Kingdom of Dacia in the eastern Balkans to be ruled by a Christian prince (presumably Potemkin). The plan was drawn up by Alexander Bezborodko, a young Ukrainian noble who soon displaced Panin as Catherine's principal advisor on foreign affairs. He argued that the international situation was uniquely propitious for the accomplishment of Russia's centuries' old urge to conquer the Crimea and become a Black Sea power. Once Maria Theresa died and Joseph II assumed sole rule, he and Catherine quickly negotiated an alliance.

In practice, Russia's alliance with Prussia had ended, and a tougher stance toward the Crimea was assumed with tacit Austrian backing. The first fruits of the new alliance were Russia's almost bloodless annexation of the Crimea in the summer of 1783 and a protectorate over Georgia. That same year both Nikita Panin and Grigory Orlov died, and the southern strategy associated with Potemkin and Bezborodko proceeded apace with rapid consolidation of Russian possession of the Crimea and its magnificent natural harbor at the newly renamed Sevastopol, scarcely two days' sail from Constantinople itself.

An unreconciled Turkey declared war on Russia in August 1787 in hopes of regaining the Crimea and reasserting its authority in the Danubian Principalities. Though this war ended in Russian victory in 1791, its course proved nerve-wracking and costly, complicated as it was by a short, bloody war with Sweden in 1788–1790, the beginning of the French Revolution, a war scare with Britain and Prussia in the spring of 1791—the so-called Ochakov Crisis—and complications in Poland that led to the Second Partition in 1792–1793.

In contrast to the first Russo-Turkish war, Catherine met this one with misgivings. Yet when Potemkin panicked at the Black Sea fleet's being damaged by storm and threatened by Ottoman attacks on the Crimea, she showed her steadiness and refused her viceroy's pleas to abandon her newest conquests. She was heartened by Austria's quick mobilization to join the conflict and began plans for a new Mediterranean naval expedition. This had to be cancelled when Sweden suddenly declared war on June 22, 1788. She was extremely worried about the Swedish threat until the Russian fleet repulsed the Swedes and Potemkin reported victories in the south. Though Russia steadily defeated both the Turks and the Swedes, the conflicts dragged on interminably as Austria did badly against the Turks, whereas Britain, Poland, and Prussia reacted hostilely to Russian successes. Potemkin and General Alexander Suvorov finally captured Ochakov and other Ottoman fortresses, and the war with Sweden ended suddenly with no loss of territory in the August 3, 1790, Peace of Verela. But the Turks still refused to sue for peace, and Britain and Prussia tried to force Catherine to give up Ochakov in the spring of 1791. She foiled the inept policy of British prime minister *William Pitt the Younger by inciting his parliamentary opposition and deftly deflecting the Anglo-Prussian ultimatum. Potemkin's death in October 1791 stunned the empress, but his successors were able to complete the Treaty of Jassy on December 29, 1791/January 9, 1792, which certified Russia's second great victory over the Ottoman Empire.

In May 1792, Russian forces invaded Poland in concert with a Russian-sponsored confederation of Polish rebels opposed to the reformist constitution of May 3, 1791, a campaign that Catherine proclaimed as her contribution to thwarting the French Revolution abroad. When Polish resistance evaporated, a second partition with Prussia was soon arranged, and a third and final one followed upon the crushing of the Polish revolt of 1794. Poland was expunged from the map as a result, and Stanislaus Poniatowski was interned in Russia. Catherine also authorized an invasion of Persian territory along the Caspian Sea in 1796, led by Valerian Zubov, younger brother of her new favorite, Platon Zubov. The empress compared Zubov's Persian campaign with that of Peter the Great, but its gains proved to be just as temporary as Peter's had been.

In opposing the French Revolution, which she detested from the start, Catherine encouraged Prussia and Austria, Britain and Sweden to fight the French actively and provided some naval forces to assist in the blockade of France and attacks on French commerce. She also assisted the French emigrés and authorized an expeditionary force against France shortly before her death at Petersburg on November 6, 1796. Upon ascending the throne, Tsar Paul I countermanded that undertaking as well as Zubov's Persian campaign.

The balance sheet of Catherine's reign shows impressive territorial gains in the west and south amounting to some 700,000 square miles (185,000 from the destruction of Poland) and an increase in population of about 13 million to a total of some 36 million. The western border was pushed some 250 miles westward, and Russia now shared borders with Prussia and Austria. The Russian army grew to be the largest in Europe, with about 313,000 men under arms. Russia had substantial fleets in the Baltic and the Black seas. New ports such as Odessa were founded in the south, and Russian commerce increased sharply, especially grain exports from the Ukraine and former Polish territories. Russia was well on its way to gaining more territory in the Caucasus and along the Caspian. It was now seen as the major threat to the Ottoman Empire and the Persian state and, some feared, to the balance of power in Europe as a whole.

Catherine has received much credit for these accomplishments and deservedly so. She certainly displayed determination and agility in playing the game of Great Power politics. She showed great skill in selecting diplomats and commanders who could carry out her policies effectively, and she constantly sought advice and listened carefully to her advisors. She was well informed about the traditions of Russian diplomacy and war, well read in history, and attentive to the policies and plans of other powers. She evinced an acute understanding of military and economic methods of exercising power. Though not herself a theorist of international relations, Catherine was knowledgeable about the general notions of international relations—especially the balance of power as practiced in Europe—and closely involved in implementing those notions. Of course, Catherine's gains also brought problems: longer borders, different nationalities, economic complexities, greater fears and antipathies among potential foes. Russo-Polish animosity grew apace, for instance, and as a result of the partitions of Poland a substantial Jewish minority appeared for the first time within the empire's borders. Catherine II became known as "the Great" above all because Russia was recognized as a Great Power during her reign, and because Russia was viewed as an autocracy; she was credited (or blamed) for Russia's emergence as a European Great Power with global aspirations.

Annotated Bibliography

The bulk of Catherine's unpublished papers are preserved in the Central State Archive of Old Documents in Moscow, which houses the former state archives, and in the Archive of Foreign Affairs of the Ministry of Foreign Affairs. Guides to these are discussed in Patricia Kennedy Grimsted, *Archives and Manuscript Repositories in the USSR: Moscow and Leningrad* (1972), which includes addresses and brief descriptions. Recent experience is summarized by Hugh Ragsdale, "A Report on Working in the Arkhiv Vneshnei Politiki Rossii," *Slavic Review* 48 (1989): 269–271.

There is no authoritative large-scale biography of Catherine II because none has been completed in the land she ruled over, and the best studies currently available were done by foreign scholars who had to rely on printed sources above all. Thus the general historiography is strangely lopsided and peculiarly sparse in the USSR, where the scholarly establishment appears to be poorly informed about the considerable scholarship produced abroad.

For general bibliographical guidance to works in English see Philip Clendenning and Roger Bartlett, *Eighteenth Century Russia: A Select Bibliography of Works Published since 1955* (1981); Peter A. Crowther, *A Bibliography of Works in English on Russian History to 1800* (1969); and David R. Eagan and Melinda A. Eagan, *Russian Autocrats from Ivan the Great to the Fall of the Romanov Dynasty: An Annotated Bibliography of English Language Sources to 1985* (1987).

None of Catherine's voluminous writings is specifically addressed to foreign relations, but many of her thousands of letters touch on such topics. A few are available in English, such as *Correspondence of Catherine the Great when Grand-Duchess, with Sir Charles Hanbury-Williams and Letters from Count Poniatowski,* edited and translated by the Earl of Ilchester and Mrs. Langford-Brooke (1928), and *Voltaire and Catherine the Great: Selected Correspondence,* edited and translated by Antony Lentin (1974). A key source is her autobiographical writings, her so-called memoirs, which appeared in some seven different drafts composed over a period of about forty years. The fullest edition is in Russian, *Zapiski imperatritsy Ekateriny Vtoroi* (1907; printed 1989). The best English edition is that by Katherine Anthony, *Memoirs of Catherine the Great* (1927), which does not include the older version first published abroad by Russian radicals, *Memoirs of Catherine the Great, Written by Herself with a Preface by Alexander Herzen* (1859).

Contemporary scholarship must now begin with the huge synthesis by Isabel de Madariaga, *Russia in the Age of Catherine the Great* (1981), which includes a large bibliography and devotes great attention to foreign relations. Though not a biography, it accords much space to Catherine's personal role and sees her foreign policy as generally successful. More condensed treatments by the same author are *Catherine the Great: A Short History* (1990) and "Catherine the Great," in H. M. Scott, ed., *Enlightened Absolutism: Reform and Reformers in Later Eighteenth-Century Europe* (1990), both of which take account of scholarship since 1981. Addressed to a broader audience, more biographical, and more inclined to psychological analysis is John T. Alexander, *Catherine the Great: Life and Legend* (1989), which advances a "crisis" concept of Catherine's life and reign. Two older biographical works are A. G. Brikner/Alexander Brückner, *Istoriia Ekateriny Vtoroi* (1885), also available in German (1883), and V. A. Bil'basov, *Istoriia Ekateriny Vtoroi*, 3rd ed. (1900), the latter only reaching 1764. An astute recent overview with penetrating comments on Russia's role in European politics is H. M. Scott's "Russia as a European Great Power," in Roger Bartlett and Janet Hartley, eds., *Russia in the Age of the Enlightenment: Essays for Isabel de Madariaga* (1990). For background on Elizabeth's reign with a long chapter on foreign policy, see E. V. Anisimov, *Rossiia v seredine XVIII veka: bor'ba za nasledie Petra* (1986), to be issued in English translation by Academic International Press. For a recent Soviet survey of Catherine's life and reign, see A. B. Kamenskii, "Ekaterina II," *Voprosy istorii* 3 (1989): 62–88, an edited version of which will appear in translation in an anthology edited by James Cracraft. Several generalizing essays are included in Marc Raeff, ed., *Catherine the Great: A Profile* (1972).

The rest of the scholarship surveyed here treats more specific topics. For particular crises involving foreign and domestic policies, see John T. Alexander, *Autocratic Politics in a National Crisis: The Imperial Russian Government and Pugachev's Revolt, 1773–1775* (1969), which places the revolt squarely in the context of the Russo-Turkish war and the First Partition of Poland, and the same author's *Bubonic Plague in Early Modern Russia* (1980), which does the same for the epidemic of 1769–1772. Russian expansion in the south is detailed in Muriel Atkin, *Russia and Iran, 1780–1828* (1980), and Alan W. Fisher, *The Russian Annexation of the Crimea, 1772–1783* (1970), the latter emphasizing Catherine's cautious policy. For the court politics behind Russia's switch to a southern orientation, see David M. Griffiths, "The Rise and Fall of the Northern System: Court Politics in the First Half of Catherine II's Reign," *Canadian Slavic Studies* 4 (1970): 547–569. Similar issues receive even greater attention in David L. Ransel, *The Politics of Catherinian Russia: The Panin Party* (1975). Unfortunately, a recent Soviet work, A. V. Gavriushkin, *Graf Nikita Panin: Iz istorii russkoi diplomatii XVIII veka* (1989), suffers from strident nationalism and ignorance of foreign scholarship. Recent revisionist studies of the "Greek Project" include Harvey L. Dyck, "New Serbia and the Origins of the Eastern Question, 1751–55: A Habsburg Perspective," *Russian Review* 40 (1981): 1–19, and the same author's "Pondering the Russian Fact: Kaunitz and the Catherinian Empire in the 1770s," *Canadian Slavonic Papers* 22 (1980): 451–469. These may be supplemented by Karl A. Roider, Jr., *Austria's Eastern Question, 1700–1790* (1982), Hugh Ragsdale, "Evaluating the Traditions of Russian Aggression: Catherine II and the Greek Project," *Slavonic and East European Review* 66 (1988): 91–117, and Stephen K. Batalden, *Catherine's Greek Prelate: Eugenious Voulgaris in Russia, 1771–1806* (1982). Curious Turkish and Russian documents are provided in translation and with commentary by Norman Itzkowitz and Max Mote, eds., *Mubadele: An Ottoman-Russian Exchange of Ambassadors* (1970). Different perspectives are offered by Roger P. Bartlett, *Human Capital: The Settlement of Foreigners in Russia, 1762–1804* (1979), and by Robert E. Jones, "Opposition to War and Expansion in Later Eighteenth Century Russia," *Jahrbücher für Geschichte Osteuropas* 32 (1984): 34–51.

Russo-Polish relations may be approached through Herbert H. Kaplan, *The First Partition of Poland* (1962), Robert H. Lord, *The Second Partition of Poland* (1915), and J. Lojek, "Catherine II's Armed Intervention in Poland," *Canadian Slavic Studies* 3 (1970): 570–593, the last of which makes use of Polish dispatches from Petersburg. Russian reactions to the French Revolution of 1789 may be explored in Charles de Larivière,

Catharine II et la Révolution Française (1895), James W. Marcum, "Catherine II and the French Revolution," *Canadian Slavonic Papers* 16 (1974): 189–202, and two Soviet books, M. M. Shtrange, *Russkoe obshchestvo i frantsuzskaia revoliutsiia 1789–1794 gg.* (1956), and K. E. Dzhedzhula, *Rossiia i velikaia frantsuzskaia burzhuaznaia revoliutsiia kontsa XVIII veka* (1972). See also the recent revisionist article by V. G. Sirotkin, "Absoliutistskaia revstavratsiia ili kompromiss s revoliutsiei? (Ob odnoi malizvestnoi zapiske Ekateriny Velikoi)," in A. L. Narochnitskii et al., eds., *Velikaia frantsuzskaia revoliutsiia i Rossiia* (1989). An earlier phase of Franco-Russian relations is explored by Frank Fox, "Negotiating with the Russians: Ambassador Segur's Mission to Saint-Petersburg, 1784–1789," *French Historical Studies* 7 (1971): 47–71.

Russian relations with other parts of Europe are treated in H. Arnold Barton, *Scandinavia in the Revolutionary Era, 1760–1815* (1986), Michael F. Metcalf, *Russia, England and Swedish Party Politics, 1762–1766* (1977), and Michael Roberts, "Great Britain, Denmark, and Russia, 1763–1770," in Ragnhild Hatton and M. S. Anderson, eds., *Studies in Diplomatic History: Essays in Memory of D. B. Horn* (1970). The Teschen Congress of 1779 is studied by G. A. Nersesov, *Politika Rossii na Teshenskom kongresse (1778–1779)* (1988), and the masterful account by Isabel de Madariaga, *Britain, Russia, and the Armed Neutrality of 1780* (1962). On an earlier phase of Anglo-Russian relations, see Philip Clendenning, "The Background and Negotiations for the Anglo-Russian Commercial Treaty of 1766," in A. G. Cross, ed., *Great Britain and Russia in the Eighteenth Century: Contacts and Comparisons* (1979). Russia's role in Germany is investigated by K. O. Freiherr von Aretin, "Russia as a Guarantor Power of the Imperial Constitution under Catherine II," *Journal of Modern History* 58 (1986): supplement, S141–160.

Naval policies are explored by Andreas Bode, *Die Flottenpolitik Katharinas II. und die Konflikte mit Schweden und der Türkei (1768–92)* (1979), while Russo-American relations receive informed analysis from the Russian side in Nikolai N. Bolkhovitinov, *The Beginnings of Russo-American Relations, 1775–1815*, translated by Elena Levin (1975), and *Russia and the American Revolution*, translated by C. J. Smith (1976), and from the American perspective in Norman E. Saul, *Distant Friends: The United States and Russia, 1763–1867* (1991), and the articles of David M. Griffiths, "An American Contribution to the Armed Neutrality of 1780," *Russian Review* 30 (1971): 164–173; "American Commercial Diplomacy in Russia, 1780–1783," *William and Mary Quarterly*, 3rd series, 27 (1970): 379–410; and "Nikita Panin, Russian Diplomacy, and the American Revolution," *Slavic Review* 28 (1969): 1–24.

Russian policies in the Far East have been studied by Clifford M. Foust, *Muscovite and Mandarin: Russia's Trade with China and Its Setting, 1727–1805* (1969), and Glynn Barratt, *Russia in Pacific Waters, 1715–1825* (1981).

Bibliography

General Bibliographies

Clendenning, Philip, and Roger Bartlett. *Eighteenth Century Russia: A Select Bibliography of Works Published since 1955*. Newtonville, Mass.: Oriental Research Partners, 1981.

Crowther, Peter A. *A Bibliography of Works in English on Russian History to 1800*. Oxford: Blackwell, 1969.

Eagan, David R., and Melinda A. Eagan. *Russian Autocrats from Ivan the Great to the*

Fall of the Romanov Dynasty: An Annotated Bibliography of English Language Sources to 1985. Metuchen, N.J.: Scarecrow, 1987.

Works by Catherine the Great

Correspondence of Catherine the Great when Grand-Duchess, with Sir Charles Hanbury-Williams and Letters from Count Poniatowski. Translated and edited by the Earl of Ilchester and Mrs. Langford-Brooke. London: Butterworth, 1928.

Joseph II und Katharina von Russland: Ihr Briefwechsel. Edited by Alfred Ritter von Arneth. Vienna: Breumuller, 1969.

Memoirs of Catherine the Great. Edited by Dominique Maroger. Translated from the French by Moura Budberg. London: Hamilton, 1955.

Memoirs of Catherine the Great. Translated by Katharine Anthony. New York: Knopf, 1927.

Memoirs of Catherine the Great, Written by Herself with a Preface by Alexander Herzen. New York: Appleton, 1859.

Voltaire and Catherine the Great: Selected Correspondence. Translated and edited by Antony Lentin. Cambridge, Mass.: Oriental Research Partners, 1974.

Zapiski imperatritsy Ekateriny Vtoroi. St. Petersburg: Suvorina, 1907. Reprint. Moscow: Orbita, 1989.

Related Works

Alexander, John T. *Autocratic Politics in a National Crisis: The Imperial Russian Government and Pugachev's Revolt, 1773–1775.* Bloomington: Indiana University Press, 1969.

————. *Bubonic Plague in Early Modern Russia.* Baltimore: Johns Hopkins University Press, 1980.

————. *Catherine the Great: Life and Legend.* New York: Oxford University Press, 1989.

Anisimov, E. V. *Rossiia v seredine XVIII veka: bor'ba za nasledie Petra.* Moscow: Mysl', 1986.

Anthony, Katherine. *Catherine the Great.* New York: Knopf, 1925.

Atkin, Muriel. *Russia and Iran, 1780–1828.* Minneapolis: University of Minnesota Press, 1980.

Barratt, Glynn. *Russia in Pacific Waters, 1715–1825.* Vancouver: University of British Columbia Press, 1981.

Bartlett, Roger P. *Human Capital: The Settlement of Foreigners in Russia, 1762–1804.* Cambridge: Cambridge University Press, 1979.

Barton, H. Arnold. *Scandinavia in the Revolutionary Era, 1760–1815.* Minneapolis: University of Minnesota Press, 1986.

Batalden, Stephen K. *Catherine's Greek Prelate: Eugenious Voulgaris in Russia, 1771–1806.* Boulder, Colo.: East European Monographs, 1982.

Bil'basov, V. A. *Istoriia Ekateriny Vtoroi.* 3rd ed. Berlin: Shtura, 1900.

Bode, Andreas. *Die Flottenpolitik Katharinas II. und die Konflikte mit Schweden und der Türkei (1768–92).* Munich: East European Institute, 1979.

Bolkhovitinov, Nikolai N. *The Beginnings of Russo-American Relations, 1775–1815.* Translated by Elena Levin. Cambridge, Mass.: Harvard University Press, 1975.

————. *Russia and the American Revolution.* Translated by C. J. Smith. Tallahassee, Fla.: Diplomatic Press, 1976.

Brükner, Alexander. *Katharina die Zweite*. Berlin: Grote, 1883.

Clendenning, Philip. "The Background and Negotiations for the Anglo-Russian Commercial Treaty of 1766." In *Great Britain and Russia in the Eighteenth Century: Contacts and Comparisons*, pp. 145–164. Edited by A. G. Cross. Newtonville, Mass.: Oriental Research Partners, 1979.

———. "The Economic Awakening of Russia in the Eighteenth Century." *Journal of European Economic History* 14 (1985): 443–472.

Dyck, Harvey L. "New Serbia and the Origins of the Eastern Question, 1751–55: A Habsburg Perspective." *Russian Review* 40 (1981): 1–19.

———. "Pondering the Russian Fact: Kaunitz and the Catherinian Empire in the 1770s." *Canadian Slavonic Papers* 22 (1980): 451–469.

Dzhedzhula, K. E. *Rossiia i velikaia frantsuzskaia burzhuaznaia revoliutsiia kontsa XVIII veka*. Kiev: Izd-va Kiev un-ta, 1972.

Fisher, Alan W. *The Russian Annexation of the Crimea, 1772–1783*. Cambridge: Cambridge University Press, 1970.

Foust, Clifford M. *Muscovite and Mandarin: Russia's Trade with China and Its Setting, 1727–1805*. Chapel Hill: University of North Carolina Press, 1969.

Fox, Frank. "Negotiating with the Russians: Ambassador Segur's Mission to Saint-Petersburg, 1784–1789." *French Historical Studies* 7 (1971): 47–71.

Freiherr von Aretin, K. O. "Russia as a Guarantor Power of the Imperial Constitution under Catherine II." *Journal of Modern History* 58 (1986): suppl., S141–160.

Gavriushkin, A. V. *Graf Nikita Panin: Iz istorii russkoi diplomatii XVIII veka*. Moscow: Mezhdunarodyne Otnosheniia, 1989.

Golder, Frank. *John Paul Jones in Russia*. Garden City, N.Y.: Doubleday and Page, 1927.

Griffiths, David M. "American Commercial Diplomacy in Russia, 1780–1783." *William and Mary Quarterly*, 3rd series, 27 (1970): 379–410.

———. "An American Contribution to the Armed Neutrality of 1780." *Russian Review* 30 (1971): 164–173.

———. "Nikita Panin, Russian Diplomacy, and the America Revolution." *Slavic Review* 28 (1969): 1–24.

———. "The Rise and Fall of the Northern System: Court Politics in the First Half of Catherine II's Reign." *Canadian Slavic Studies* 4 (1970): 547–569.

Grot, Ia. K. "Ekaterina II i Gustav III." *Sbornik otdeleniia russkogo iazyka i slovesnosti imperatorskoi Akademii nauk* 19 (1877): 1–115.

Itzkowitz, Norman, and Max Mote, eds. *Mubadele: An Ottoman-Russian Exchange of Ambassadors*. Chicago: University of Chicago Press, 1970.

Jones, Robert E. "Opposition to War and Expansion in Later Eighteenth Century Russia." *Jahrbücher für Geschichte Osteuropas* 32 (1984): 34–51.

———. *Provincial Development in Russia: Catherine II and Jacob Sievers*. New Brunswick, N.J.: Rutgers University Press, 1984.

Kamenskii, A. B. "Ekaterina II." *Voprosy istorii* 3 (1989): 62–88.

Kaplan, Herbert H. *The First Partition of Poland*. New York: Columbia University Press, 1962.

———. *Russia and the Outbreak of the Seven Years' War*. Berkeley: University of California Press, 1968.

Larivière, Charles de. *Catharine II et la Révolution Française*. Paris, 1895.

Lojek, J. "Catherine II's Armed Intervention in Poland." *Canadian Slavic Studies* 3 (1970): 570–593.

Lord, Robert H. *The Second Partition of Poland.* Cambridge, Mass.: Harvard University Press, 1915.

Madariaga, Isabel de. *Britain, Russia, and the Armed Neutrality of 1780.* New Haven, Conn.: Yale University Press, 1962.

————. "Catherine the Great." In *Enlightened Absolutism: Reform and Reformers in Later Eighteenth-Century Europe,* pp. 289–311. Edited by H. M. Scott. Ann Arbor: University of Michigan Press, 1990.

————. *Catherine the Great: A Short History.* New Haven, Conn.: Yale University Press, 1990.

————. *Russia in the Age of Catherine the Great.* New Haven, Conn.: Yale University Press, 1981.

————. "The Secret Austro-Russian Treaty of 1781." *Slavonic and East European Review* 38 (1959): 114–145.

Marcum, James W. "Catherine II and the French Revolution." *Canadian Slavonic Papers* 16 (1974): 189–202.

Metcalf, Michael F. *Russia, England and Swedish Party Politics, 1762–1766.* Totowa, N.J.: Rowman and Littlefield, 1977.

Nersesov, G. A. *Politika Rossii na Teshenskom kongresse (1778–1779).* Moscow: Nauka, 1988.

Raeff, Marc, ed. *Catherine the Great: A Profile.* New York: Hill and Wang, 1972.

Ragsdale, Hugh. "Evaluating the Traditions of Russian Aggression: Catherine II and the Greek Project." *Slavonic and East European Review* 66 (1988): 91–117.

————. *Tsar Paul and the Question of Madness: An Essay in History and Psychology.* Westport, Conn.: Greenwood Press, 1988.

Ransel, David L. *The Politics of Catherinian Russia: The Panin Party.* New Haven, Conn.: Yale University Press, 1975.

Rasmussen, Karen. "Catherine II and the Image of Peter I." *Slavic Review* 37 (1978): 51–69.

Roberts, Michael. "Great Britain, Denmark, and Russia, 1763–1770." In *Studies in Diplomatic History: Essays in Memory of D. B. Horn,* pp. 256–268. Edited by R. Hatton and M. S. Anderson. Hamden, Conn.: Archon, 1970.

Roider, Karl A., Jr. *Austria's Eastern Question, 1700–1790.* Princeton, N.J.: Princeton University Press, 1982.

Saul, Norman E. *Distant Friends: The United States and Russia, 1763–1867.* Lawrence: University Press of Kansas, 1991.

Scott, H. M. "Russia as a European Great Power." In *Russia in the Age of Enlightenment: Essays for Isabel de Madariaga,* pp. 7–39. Edited by Roger Bartlett and Janet Hartley. New York: St. Martin's Press, 1990.

Shchepkin, E. N. *Russko-avstriiskii soiuz vo vremia semiletnei voiny 1746–1758.* St. Petersburg: V. S. Balashev, 1902.

Shtrange, M. M. *Russkoe obshchestvo i frantsuzskaia revoliutsiia 1789–1794 gg.* Moscow: Nauk, 1956.

Shumigorskii, E. S. *Imperatritsa Mariia Feodorovna (1759–1828).* St. Petersburg: I. N. Skorokhodor, 1892.

Sirotkin, V. G. "Absoliutistskaia revstavratsiia ili kompromiss s revoliutsiei? (Ob odnoi malizvestnoi zapiske Ekateriny Velikoi)." In *Velikaia frantsuzskaia revoliutsiia i Rossiia*, pp. 273–188. Edited by A. L. Narochnitskii et al. Moscow: Progress, 1990.

Thaden, Edward C. *Russia's Western Borderlands, 1710–1870*. Princeton, N.J.: Princeton University Press, 1984.

JOHN T. ALEXANDER

Count Camillo Benso di Cavour (1810–1861).   Count Camillo di Cavour was born in Turin on August 1, 1810, to an old aristocratic family of Piedmont with ties to both France and Switzerland. As the second son, Cavour was destined for a career in the army and entered the royal military academy in 1821, where he studied mathematics. Cavour also developed a taste for the liberal arts and began to study history and the English language. His political outlook became Liberal and Benthamite, and he became very interested in the English Poor Law reform. Cavour found that his attitudes clashed with the military's support of King Carlo Alberto's absolutist Piedmontese regime, so he resigned his army commission in 1831.

Cavour then devoted his time to traveling, caring for the family estates, and studying agriculture and politics. He turned to writing and produced articles on the preservation of the union between England and Ireland and the repeal of the English Corn Laws. This blend of the literary and the Liberal led him to help found the Turinese newspaper *Il Risorgimento*. With the revolutions of 1848, Cavour supported granting a constitution to Sardinia-Piedmont. On March 23, 1848, Cavour published a very powerful article, "L'ora suprema della monarchia," which helped to convince Carlo Alberto to support the Milanese in their war against Austria. By this time, Cavour had already developed his desire for "Italy" to be free of the foreign domination it had endured for centuries.

In this respect, Cavour was well within the mainstream of nineteenth-century Liberal thought. Cavour's worldview was particularly influenced by English history and political values. The concepts of constitutional monarchy and representative government, however, had made their way into the political vocabulary of the Continent mostly through the ideas of the French Revolution. These concepts, along with the idea of nationalism, which also grew out of the French Revolution, became the new basis for the ideal government. The state was no longer the monarch, as Louis XIV succinctly phrased it, but was, at least for the Italian mind, all those who spoke the same language. This idea of the national state led some people, like Giuseppe Mazzini, to call for a republic—a state of the people. Those with more education and a greater stake in society realized that while the peasants were members of this "nation," they really had no conception of what that meant. These Liberals, like Cavour, preferred a constitution that would adopt a more paternalistic attitude toward the lower classes along with a monarchy to provide the stability of tradition. Liberal ideas faced major opposition from the three autocratic courts of Austria, Russia, and Prussia. Such was the era in which Cavour lived and worked. Cavour's short career in international politics is inextricably linked to the question of Italian unification and his quest to free the Italian "nation" from foreigners and autocrats. It is impossible to understand his foreign policy without also understanding the internal Italian situation. While Cavour's constant ideal was to establish a united Italy free from foreign domination, the meaning of "united Italy" and the method of achieving it were subject to change.

Cavour's political career coincided with Italian unification. First elected to parliament in June 1848 following the beginning of war against Austria, Cavour became minister of agriculture, commerce, and navy in Marquis Massimo d'Azeglio's government in 1851. The following year Cavour was named minister of finance. In 1852, Cavour was forced to resign from the cabinet when he arranged a political compromise, *connubio*, between the center-left and the center-right parties to elect Urbano Rattazzi as speaker of the chamber without informing d'Azeglio. It was not long before King Vittorio Emanuele II, who had succeeded his father in 1848, called upon Cavour to form a ministry. On November 4, 1852, Cavour assumed the premiership and held that post, with two brief interruptions, until his death in 1861. Besides being prime minister, Cavour was also foreign minister.

In his first major foreign policy decision, Cavour accepted the British offer to associate Sardinia with the Anglo-French alliance against Russia during the Crimean War (1854–1856). By supplying 15,000 Sardinian troops to the war effort, Cavour won the right to sit at the Congress of Paris, which wrote the peace treaty ending the Crimean War. One of Cavour's major achievements was to convince the Great Powers to accept Sardinia on an equal footing at the congress. Cavour realized that Sardinia had little right to set the peace terms with Russia, and he remained relatively quiet. However, he persuaded *Napoleon III and the British representative, Lord Clarendon, to bring up the question of Italy at the congress. While nothing concrete was achieved for Sardinia, on April 8, 1856, the congress officially raised the problem of Neapolitan and papal maladministration. Cavour, at least, had persuaded Europe to admit that there was a problem on the Italian peninsula.

In further discussions with Napoleon III and the British government, Cavour realized that real help for Italian freedom was more likely to come from the French than from the British. Cavour was able to use the Italian and revisionist sympathies of Napoleon III to help him gain Italian independence. Meeting at Plombières in July 1858, Cavour and Napoleon planned a war against the Austrian Empire that would result in a federation of four Italian states with the pope as president. While this agreement may not have been completely to Cavour's liking, he was a skillful enough diplomatist to use circumstances to their most effective end. The major goal of the war was to oust Austria from Italy; any other goals would have to wait.

In order for Napoleon to cooperate in a war against Austria, the war would have to be justifiable to the French people and the other European governments. Cavour mustered his cunning and skill to force Austria into declaring war on Sardinia. In calling up the Sardinian army, Cavour also enlisted fugitives from Austrian Lombardy, thereby provoking Austrian anger. Tensions mounted, and the British and the Russians sought a peaceful solution to the crisis through a European congress. When Napoleon supported this peaceful solution, Cavour had no alternative but to give up his plans for war. The Austrians, however, demanded Sardinian disarmament before any meeting. When Cavour balked, Austria issued an ultimatum, which provided Cavour with an acceptable justification for war. Citing the need to defend Sardinia, Cavour successfully called upon the French emperor for assistance when Austria declared war in April 1859.

Cavour now added the ministry of war to his portfolio, while General Alfonso La Marmora took charge of the army in the field. At the battles of Magenta and Solferino, the French and Sardinian armies pushed back the Austrian armies to the Quadrilateral Fortresses in Venetia. While the Franco-Sardinian alliance called for the liberation of Venetia as well as Lombardy, Napoleon broke with his ally and concluded a separate armistice with the Austrians at Villafranca. Outraged that Napoleon had betrayed the alliance and that Vittorio Emanuele refused to continue the war alone, Cavour resigned in protest in July 1859.

During the war, the central Italian states of Parma, Tuscany, Modena, and Romagna revolted against their rulers. There is much historical debate on the role Cavour played in the outbreak of these insurrections. Some historians maintain that Cavour used the National Society and its leader, Guiseppe La Farina, to engineer revolts in the central Italian states. Others argue that the National Society was not a major factor and that the ousting of the various despots was of local origin. Whatever the case, in accordance with the Treaty of Zurich, which was based on the Truce of Villafranca, the deposed rulers were to regain their thrones.

After Cavour's resignation the king appointed La Marmora as prime minister, but Cavour could not be ignored for long. The weak La Marmora government lasted only a few months, and in January 1860 the king called Cavour to form a ministry. Cavour became not only prime minister, but also foreign and interior minister. One of his first actions after returning to power was to hold plebiscites in the central Italian states. The results were overwhelmingly for annexation to Sardinia. The English urged that Italians should be able to decide their own fate, while Cavour had to compensate Napoleon III with the surrender to France of the Sardinian provinces of Savoy and Nice.

Another major historical controversy swirls around Cavour's involvement with Guiseppe Garibaldi's expedition to Sicily in May 1860. Garibaldi, a republican and revolutionary, set sail for southern Italy on May 5 with his Thousand Red Shirts army. Whether Cavour actively supported this expedition or simply allowed it to occur is still in debate. What is certain is that Cavour was able to use Garibaldi's successful conquest of the Neapolitan regime to his advantage. Fearing Garibaldi's republican tendencies, Cavour used the outbreak of a revolt in the Papal States to invade that region and secure it for the monarchy before

Garibaldi's arrival. When the two forces met, Garibaldi obediently surrendered his conquests to Vittorio Emanuele. After another plebiscite, Cavour proclaimed the united Kingdom of Italy on March 17, 1861. Having completed the unification of Italy, with the exception of Rome and Venetia, Cavour died just four months later, on June 6, 1861.

Though he died rather prematurely, Cavour had a profound effect not only on Italy but on the whole course of international relations. First and certainly most important, he was the overseer if not the architect of Italian unification. Whether by grand design or fortunate circumstance, Cavour presided over the unification of Italy. The unitary, as opposed to the federal, nature of the new state left many in Italy wondering whether Italy was now merely an enlarged Sardinia. While unification was a great event, it did not, of necessity, bring Italy into the ranks of the Great Powers. Here lies Cavour's second claim to importance. Because of the Sardinian signature on the 1856 Treaty of Paris, Cavour and later Italian statesmen were able to claim a place for Italy at various European conferences and congresses to which it might not have been invited otherwise. Finally, Cavour's leadership style led to the weakening of the Italian party system. Cavour's successors, imitating his style, severely retarded the growth of clearly defined political parties in nineteenth-century Italy.

Annotated Bibliography

Many archives contain information relative to the life and work of Count Camillo di Cavour, and many of these are mentioned in both Rosario Romeo's *Cavour e il suo tempo* (1984) and Denis Mack Smith's *Victor Emanuel, Cavour and the Risorgimento* (1971). Perhaps the best archival source is the Archivio Cavour. Administered by the Fondazione "Camillo Cavour," the archive is located in the Castello Cavour, 10026 Santena, a short distance from Turin. When this author requested access to archives at the Castello Cavour, the castle was being "renovated." Other historians have also been refused entry, so be sure to have written permission before arriving. Other archives include the Archivio di Stato, Via Santa Chiara 40, 10122 Turin, which contains the archives of the Sardinian kingdom as well as some of Cavour's private papers, and the Archivio Storico del Ministero degli Affari Esteri, Farnesina, 00195 Rome, which contains records of the Sardinian secretary of state and Sardinian diplomatic representatives abroad from 1815 to 1860. A letter of intent is needed from both the college or university of the researcher and from the USIA office at the U.S. Embassy in Rome. The Archivio Centrale dello Stato, Piazzale degli Archivi EUR, 00144 Rome, deals mostly with central government records, but it does have some private papers of notable Italians including Cavour. An often overlooked archive is the old Museo del Risorgimento, now called the Archivio del Instituto per la Storia del Risorgimento Italiano, located on top of the Monument to Vittorio Emanuele II, Piazza Venezia, 00186 Rome. It contains unpublished and published sources on the Risorgimento.

Perhaps the best, if not always complete, source of Cavour's writings is his published letters. The *Carteggi de Camillo Cavour*, edited by La Commissione Editrice (1926–1954), covers much of Cavour's international activity in fifteen topically arranged volumes. An index is included as a sixteenth volume. The first four volumes, *Il Carteggio Cavour-Nigra dal 1858 al 1861*, consist of Cavour's correspondence with Constantino

Nigra, Sardinian minister to Paris. The first volume discusses the agreement of Plombières; the second, the diplomatic and military campaign of 1859; the third, the cession of Nice and Savoy and the annexation of the central Italian states; and the fourth, the liberation of southern Italy. The next two volumes deal with Cavour's handling of the Roman Question in 1860–1861. Volumes 7 and 8, *Cavour e Inghilterra*, contain documents relating to Cavour's relations with Britain at the Congress of Paris and diplomatic problems during 1856–1861. The next volume includes Cavour's correspondence with his friend Count Roger de Salmour. The last five volumes contain some of Cavour's correspondence relating to the liberation of southern Italy and the formation of the Kingdom of Italy from January 1860 to June 1861.

Other published works of Cavour are less closely tied to his international policy. Another valuable published source for Cavour's thoughts is *Discorsi parlamentari*, edited by Adolfo Omodeo, Luigi Russo, and Armando Saitta (1932–1973). These parliamentary speeches, while not exclusively dealing with international relations, present the official justification of Cavour's actions. They also demonstrate Cavour's ability to use popular ideas to his benefit. The major drawback to this compilation is that Cavour's speeches are taken out of the context of their full parliamentary dialogue. The more complete compilation of Cavour's papers, *Epistolario*, edited by C. Pischedda, N. Nada, and R. Roccia (1962–1985), has been completed only up to the early 1850s. Additional letters and writings appear in other publications, but these are either not relevant to international relations or deal with Cavour's early life. Many of these collections can be found in the bibliographies of the works mentioned below.

Even before his death, Cavour was the subject of biographers. One of the first was Luigi Chiala, who wrote a biography as an appendix to Cavour's *Opere politico-economiche* (1860). Chiala's biography was intended to shed light on the man who had represented Italy at the Congress of Paris. Another early biography, written by Ruggero Bonghi in 1860, is found in *Ritratti et profili di contemporanei*, edited by F. Salata (1935). Bonghi represented Cavour as the astute and wise hero who would save Italy from the politicians of the *Sinistra*.

Bonghi's biography, like others written soon after Cavour's death, was generally hagiographical. In writing *Il Conte di Cavour* (1863), N. Bianchi wanted to smooth over the regional divisions that still existed after the proclamation of the Kingdom of Italy. Consequently, he portrayed Cavour as a great hero whose skill and wisdom brought together a national consensus leading to the creation of a united Italy. Another early work that remains valuable is William de La Rive, *Le Comte de Cavour: Récits et souvenirs* (1863), which was also translated into English and Italian. La Rive was Cavour's Swiss cousin, and the book contains many personal reminiscences about Cavour. La Rive wanted to immortalize Cavour as the true beacon of liberalism guiding Italy along the only safe course between absolutism and republicanism. Despite his lack of objectivity, La Rive did not paint Cavour as a demigod but rather as a shrewd diplomatist who took advantage of situations he could not control. La Rive also acknowledged the important role that Vittorio Emanuele and Garibaldi played in the unification of Italy. On the question of Garibaldi's expedition to Sicily, La Rive claims that Cavour could not resist Garibaldi for fear of losing his popularity.

The idea that Cavour was a champion of liberalism and progress is still evident in W. R. Thayer's *The Life and Times of Cavour* (1911). Thayer, a Protestant and an American, saw Cavour as the champion of freedom not only against the authority of the Roman Catholic Church but also against the type of autocracy ˙Otto von Bismarck brought to a united Germany. Thayer portrayed Cavour as being driven by the idea of Italian unity from the beginning of his career. According to Thayer, Cavour manipulated events and people to achieve this one goal. Cavour wanted to keep Garibaldi away from military action because he feared Garibaldi's radical political ideas.

With the end of World War I and the publication of *Il Carteggio Cavour-Nigra*, a more balanced appraisal of Cavour became possible. According to A. J. Whyte, *The Political Life and Letters of Cavour 1848–1861* (1930), Cavour knew that he would have to subordinate the questions of unity and the papacy to the more important question of independence. Whyte stresses Cavour's untiring and skillful work for the expulsion of Austria and cites Cavour's pretended weakness and fears of European repercussions as his reasons for not being more openly supportive of Garibaldi's expedition to Sicily.

Adolfo Omodeo's unfinished biography, *L'opera politica del conte di Cavour. Parte I, 1848–1857* (1941), and his collection of previously published material, *Difesa del Risorgimento* (1951), contribute greatly to the historiography of Cavour. Omodeo wanted to defend the Risorgimento against the fascist doctrine of history and the glorification of the hero. Consequently, he presented Cavour as a human being reacting to events rather than as a larger than life figure achieving some grand design for Italy. Unlike earlier writers, Omodeo also paid greater attention to the democratic movements of Mazzini and Garibaldi as factors producing Italian unification.

Among English-language historians, Denis Mack Smith is a recognized authority on Cavour and the Risorgimento. Like Omodeo, he concludes that Cavour reacted to events and did not follow any grand master plan. Mack Smith's *Cavour and Garibaldi, 1860: A Study in Political Conflict* (1954) discusses diplomacy only incidentally; however, his *Victor Emanuel, Cavour and the Risorgimento* (1971), a collection of essays, is more concerned with Cavour the statesman. Although Mack Smith questions the ability and importance of Cavour as a diplomat, he acknowledges that Cavour had few equals. He states that while both Mazzini and Cavour were necessary for Italian unification, Cavour was the one who set the tone for Italian action. In his latest book, *Cavour* (1985), Mack Smith portrays Cavour as a hot-tempered, undisciplined, overworked statesman who made serious errors in judgment. Mack Smith, viewing Garibaldi and Mazzini favorably, also argues that whereas Cavour's fears about the radicals were unfair and untrue, the radicals' fears about Cavour were certainly justified.

The other major contemporary biographer of Cavour is the Italian historian Rosario Romeo, who in 1984 completed a three-volume work entitled *Cavour e il suo tempo*. The third volume covers the important years of Cavour's diplomatic activity, 1854 to 1861. In stark contrast to Mack Smith, Romeo believes that Cavour actually foresaw the connection between the events of 1856 and those of 1859.

E. Passerin d'Entrèves wrote a lengthy biography of Cavour for *Dizionario biographico degli italiani* (1983). Including an extensive annotated bibliography, d'Entrèves's entry discusses Cavour's entire life and is not interpretive in nature. Charles Delzell, ed., *The Unification of Italy, 1859–1861: Cavour, Mazzini, or Garibaldi?* (1965), brings together all these clashing opinions. A similar work, Enzo Tagliacozzo's *Cento anni di studi su Cavour* (1974), includes a historiographical survey of Cavourian literature. Another historiographical study, Rosario Romeo's "Cavour," in *Nuove questioni di storia del risorgimento e dell'unità d'Italia* (1969), begins with works written before Cavour's death and continues up to Mack Smith's *Cavour and Garibaldi, 1860*.

Bibliography

Bianchi, N. *Il Conte di Cavour*. Turin: Unione Tipographico-editrice, 1863.

Bonghi, Ruggero. *Ritratti et profili di contemporanei*. Edited by F. Salata. Florence: LeMonnier, 1935.

Cavour, Camillo. *Carteggi di Camillo Cavour*. 16 vols. Edited by La Commissione Editrice. Bologna: Zanichelli, 1926–1954.

———. *Discorsi parlamentari*. Edited by A. Omodeo, L. Russo, and A. Saitta. Florence: La Nouva Italia, 1932–1973.

———. *Epistolario*. Edited by C. Pischedda, N. Nada, and R. Roccia. Bologna: Zanichelli, 1962–1985.

———. *Opere politico-economiche*. With a biographical appendix by Luigi Chiala. Naples: Mirelli, 1860.

De La Rive, William. *Le Comte de Cavour: Récits et souvenirs*. Paris: Hetzel, 1863.

Delzell, Charles, ed. *The Unification of Italy, 1859–1861: Cavour, Mazzini or Garibaldi?* New York: Holt, Rinehart and Winston, 1965.

Dizionario biographico degli italiani. S.v. "Cavour, Camillo Benso conte di," by E. Passerin d'Entrèves.

Mack Smith, Denis. *Cavour*. New York: Knopf, 1985.

———. *Cavour and Garibaldi, 1860: A Study in Political Conflict*. London: Cambridge University Press, 1954.

———. *Victor Emanuel, Cavour and the Risorgimento*. London: Oxford University Press, 1971.

Omodeo, Adolpho. *Difesa del Risorgimento*. Turin: Einaudi, 1951.

———. *L'opera politica del conte di Cavour. Parte I, 1848–1857*. Florence: La Nuova Italia, 1941.

Romeo, Rosario. "Cavour." In *Nuove questioni di storia del risorgimento e dell'unità d'Italia*. Vol. 1, pp. 801–835. Milan: Marzorati, 1969.

———. *Cavour e il suo tempo*. 3 vols. Bari: Editori Laterza, 1984.

Tagliacozzo, Enzo, ed. *Cento anni di studi su Cavour*. Messini: D'Anna, 1974.

Thayer, William R. *The Life and Times of Cavour*. Boston: Houghton Mifflin, 1911.

Whyte, A. J. *The Political Life and Letters of Cavour 1848–1861*. London: Oxford University Press, 1930.

LAWRENCE P. ADAMCZYK

Neville Chamberlain (1869–1940).   Arthur Neville Chamberlain was born on March 18, 1869, the youngest member of the Birmingham mini-dynasty of politicians that included his father, Joseph Chamberlain, the most important Victorian statesman not to become prime minister, and his half-brother, Austen Chamberlain, parliamentary leader and Nobel laureate, who refused the prime ministership. The father and two sons, emerging not from the British aristocracy, but from a screw manufacturing factory, formed one of the most important political families in recent British history. In spite of his successful business and political careers, however, Neville Chamberlain's name has become synonymous with the concepts of appeasement and defeatism.

The Chamberlains were hard-working Unitarians who possessed a strong sense of duty. Neville was born in Edgbaston, an affluent section of Birmingham, in an elaborate red brick Victorian mansion, Highbury; one can still enter the home today and sense the feelings of earnestness and dedication such an environment must have inculcated. After completing Rugby school, young Chamberlain studied business at the local trade school his father would later endow as the University of Birmingham. After proving his abilities as an accountant, the twenty-one-year-old Chamberlain was sent to manage a 20,000 acre estate his father had bought in the Bahamas. He labored fruitlessly for several years growing sisal fiber for rope manufacturing, but the soil was too thin for successful harvests. Although the days were filled with discouraging toil, Chamberlain was able to read history, biography, and science during the lonely nights. The experience probably strengthened his character, but he returned home saddened by the thought that he had not succeeded.

Chamberlain returned to Birmingham in 1897 and spent several years in business. His uncle Arthur operated Kynoch's, a munitions firm, where he could have been placed; on the eve of the Boer War, however, local wags were already saying about Colonial Secretary Joseph Chamberlain and his family that "the more the British Empire expands, the more the Chamberlains contract," hence a less sensitive position needed to be found. A metal ship-berth-making company, Hoskins and Son, became available, and the family managed to purchase it for Neville. The firm remained his major concern until the beginning of World War I.

With his economic fortunes secure, Chamberlain was increasingly able to turn his attention to charitable and political concerns. Like his father and brother before him, he was inexorably drawn to public duties. Already one of the outstanding industrial figures in Birmingham, he soon became active in the Chamber of Commerce, the hospital system, and, ultimately, municipal government. In 1911 he married Annie Cole, daughter of a career officer, and fathered a son and a daughter. A respectable husband and parent for the remainder of his life, he also shared his father's interests of growing hothouse orchids and fishing for salmon in Scotland.

In 1911 he first obtained political office on the Birmingham city council. Four years later he was elected to his first term as lord mayor of Birmingham; during his second term he was appointed by *David Lloyd George to the coalition war cabinet as head of the Central Control Board monitoring liquor traffic. A falling out with Lloyd George resulted in toothless authority at his agency, and he resigned after seven months. The unpleasant experience did focus his ambition on a career in national politics, and in 1918 he first stood for Parliament for Birmingham, a seat he was to retain until his death. No other prime minister has begun a parliamentary career at such a late age.

Although Chamberlain entered Parliament as a Conservative, like his brother, he nonetheless maintained some of the concern for social reform he had demonstrated in Birmingham city government. For his first several years in the House of Commons, while Lloyd George served as prime minister, Chamberlain bided his time on the Conservative back benches. When a back bench revolt against the coalition broke out in 1922, Andrew Bonar Law resigned as chancellor of the exchequer and forced Lloyd George to disband the government. King George V then invited Bonar Law to form a government, in which Neville Chamberlain served as postmaster general. His impressive administrative skills led to his elevation in 1923 to minister of health. In the Stanley Baldwin government he continued to serve as health minister from 1924 to 1929. Although his activity never satisfied the Liberal and Labour parties, he did work to improve the conditions of clinics and hospitals and to help solve the housing shortage plaguing the poor. The health ministry was strengthened during Chamberlain's tenure, as was his reputation as a parliamentarian.

From 1929 to 1931 Ramsay MacDonald headed a Labour government. Although Chamberlain was a leading opposition figure, in 1931 MacDonald named him chancellor of the exchequer in the "national" government of the Depression. For more than five years he remained at the exchequer, laboring to manage a national economic recovery. Further, the responsibility of war reparations, debts, and imperial trade fell to him. The British free trade system, initiated with the abolition of the Corn Laws in 1846, came to an end in 1932 when Chamberlain recommended a general tariff. Although Chamberlain served at the exchequer, he spent considerable time involved in foreign affairs. During the Italian invasion of Ethiopia, the Spanish Civil War, the Japanese menace in China, and the beginnings of German aggression, Chamberlain was a frequent and forceful spokesman during cabinet sessions. By 1936 Stanley Baldwin was noticeably tiring as prime minister; there was by then no rival to Chamberlain. After several months' prelude Baldwin retired, and on May 28, 1937, Chamberlain assumed the prime ministership.

With several months to prepare, Chamberlain had been able to contemplate the trials that awaited. At age sixty-eight, fragile in appearance, seeming almost a wraith from his father's era, he now had to manage the problem of national defense. By 1937 German militarism was all too evident, and Britain was by comparison unprepared. France, equally weak, was an unlikely partner to stop German aggression. The events of the Spanish Civil War, including the spectacle of the massive destruction caused by the latest German military technology, were frightening for both countries. But faced with the joint alliance of *Adolf Hitler and *Benito Mussolini, only Anglo-French collaboration offered any prospect of slowing the drift toward war. Chamberlain liked to say that he wanted no part in war, which he considered cruel and senseless, unless he first exhausted every possibility of preventing it.

Chamberlain was not impervious to Hitler's penchant for violence. Owing to the relative weakness of British land and air power, however, it seemed to him that little could be done with Hitler, especially regarding his expansion in eastern Europe. One approach to the problem was to begin a policy of rapid rearmament even while placating the dictators. Having read the strategic theories of Sir Basil Liddell-Hart, Chamberlain was convinced that the next war would be far more devastating than the last one and therefore initiated a three-year defense program that would provide Britain with "an air force of such striking power that no-one will care to run risks with it."

The first act of German aggression with which the Chamberlain government had to deal was the Anschluss, Hitler's annexation of Austria in March 1938. Hitler ignored British protests, and Chamberlain admitted that he found events "all very disheartening and discouraging," concluding that "force is the only language which Germany understands." Threat of force, however, actual or implied, was not forthcoming from the Chamberlain administration. But war fears were somewhat mollified, when the Germans issued a "general understanding" against further aggression. Nevertheless, Sir Anthony Eden, who had been Britain's foreign secretary until February 1938, exclaimed with disgust that Chamberlain's actions only fortified his own opinion that the prime minister was "a man with a mission to come to terms with the dictators." Unfortunately, Eden's opinion of Chamberlain was to be further strengthened before year's end.

After gobbling Austria, Hitler's appetite was only piqued. Czechoslovakia, central Europe's only democracy, with an army of thirty-five divisions and alliances with the Soviet Union and France, became Hitler's next target. Unfortunately for the Czechs, their country encompassed 3.5 million Sudeten Germans. Nazi claims of Czech mistreatment of the Sudeten Germans were accorded almost complete credence in London, while the protestations of Czech president Edward Benes were almost entirely ignored. When Hitler threatened intervention on behalf of the Sudeten Germans, Chamberlain was in no mood to leap to Czechoslovakia's defense. "In the face of such problems," he stated in a cabinet memorandum of March 20, 1938, "to be badgered and pressed to come out and give a clear, decided, bold, and unmistakable lead, to show 'ordinary courage,' and all the rest of the twaddle, is calculated to vex the man who has to take the responsibility for the consequences" (quoted in Feiling, p. 347). But, in a surprise move designed to dispel any German misunderstanding of the British position, Chamberlain suggested a face to face meeting with Hitler in mid-September.

On Thursday, September 15, Neville Chamberlain took his first plane ride to meet Hitler at Berchtesgaden. Such a meeting was important to Chamberlain; heads of state ought to meet personally to prevent mistakes that might otherwise be caused by intermediaries. Chamberlain was initially charmed by a tour of Hitler's art collection, but as serious discussions began, Chamberlain learned that the Führer had further designs on Czechoslovakia. To placate Chamberlain, however, Hitler did propose that the Sudetenland might be ceded to Germany by self-determination. Amenable to this idea, Chamberlain flew back to London to inform his cabinet. Several days later the proposal was related to representatives of the French government, and the way was paved for the Prague government to cede to Germany areas in which 50 percent or more of the population was German. Britain would then guarantee the new frontiers. President Benes and his cabinet initially rejected the proposal, but when the Western allies refused to continue aid to Czechoslovakia if war occurred, the Czechs submitted on September 21.

On September 22, Chamberlain agreed to meet with Hitler at the Dreesen Hotel in Godesberg. Chamberlain's approach as one business executive to another was not fruitful. The prime minister's report to the Führer was rejected; Hitler now claimed that the Sudeten Germans had suffered many injustices that must be addressed immediately. Czech soldiers must be withdrawn at once and a German occupation force allowed in. Chamberlain was shocked at this departure from the previous agreement. Further discussions on September 23 yielded only Hitler's concession that he would wait until October 1 before invading. Hitler did say that this was "the last of his territorial ambitions in Europe, and that he had no wish to include in the Reich people of any other race than the Germans." The Czech government, meanwhile, had refused the Godesberg demands and had mobilized its army. At this point much of Europe felt that war was imminent.

Chamberlain, however, was still hopeful that war could be averted; he made still another appeal to Hitler about an extended timetable. He then delivered the most widely publicized statement of his wavering resolve toward Czechoslovakia in a radio address to the nation on the evening of September 27:

How horrible, fantastic, incredible, it is that we should be digging trenches and trying on gas-masks here because of a quarrel in a far-away country between people of whom we know nothing. . . . However much we may sympathize with a small nation confronted by a big, powerful neighbor, we cannot in all circumstances undertake to involve the whole British Empire in a war simply on her account. If we have to fight, it must be on larger issues than that. (Quoted in Feiling, p. 372)

He sent a note to Hitler the next morning stating that he would be prepared to meet again with him and other interested parties. Hitler responded affirmatively and sent invitations to France, Italy, and Britain to meet at Munich; no invitation was sent to Czechoslovakia.

Hitler's invitation arrived while Chamberlain was addressing a session of the House of Commons on the evening of September 28. He quickly read the note handed to him and then related to the expectant House: "I have now been informed by Herr Hitler that he invites me to meet him at Munich tomorrow morning. He has also invited Signor Mussolini and M. Daladier. Signor Mussolini has accepted and I have no doubt M. Daladier will also accept. I need not say what my answer will be" (quoted in Feiling, p. 374). The House erupted with cheers, with only a handful withholding their approval. Because the cession of the Sudeten districts had already been settled and there was to be no Czech representation at the conference, the results of the meeting were largely foreordained.

The conference began with neither an agenda nor a chairman. Only Mussolini brought a prepared memorandum, which became the basis for discussion. The four leaders focused on the major points of the discussion. The Czech armed forces were to be evacuated from designated areas of Czechoslovakia beginning October 1; they would be replaced by German occupying forces; the particular conditions for the evacuation would be specified by an international commission;

Britain and France were to guarantee the new frontiers yet to be designated; and Czech compliance was to be mandatory. Convinced that he had prevented war, Chamberlain now determined to conclude a private agreement with Hitler. The two men met the following day, and the resulting statement promised that all future international problems would be settled between the two leaders by private meetings. Specifically, they stated, "We regard the agreement signed . . . as symbolic of the desire of our two peoples never to go to war with one another again" (quoted in Feiling, p. 381). As foolish as those words proved to be in light of future events, Chamberlain probably regretted even more the statement he made standing before No. 10 Downing Street upon his return from Munich: "My good friends, this is the second time that there has come back from Germany peace with honor. I believe it is peace for our time" (quoted in Feiling, p. 381). The crowds cheered that evening but not for many more.

A reversal in emotions was not long in coming. Hitler occupied Prague in March 1939, and the Czech government was forced to capitulate. The policy of appeasement was now dead, "wantonly shattered," he said to the House of Commons while requesting support for an Anglo-French guarantee for Poland. Now hoping for a tricky bit of maneuvering that would entice the Soviet Union into an alliance with France and Poland, Great Britain began negotiations with Stalin in May. However, on August 21, the Soviet Union signed a nonaggression pact with Germany. The following day Chamberlain sent Hitler a final letter, hoping to bring him to his senses and warning him that Britain stood resolute in its determination to defend Polish sovereignty.

Early in the morning of September 1, 1939, German armies crossed the Polish border. On Sunday morning, September 3, Chamberlain broadcast to the nation that "this country is at war with Germany. . . . It is the evil things we shall be fighting against—brute force, bad faith, injustice, oppression and persecution—and against them I am certain that right will prevail." He was less confident however, about the effectiveness of his diplomatic policies. "You can imagine," he said in a tone betraying emerging doubt, "what a bitter blow it is to me that all my long struggle to win peace has failed." And later in the day before the House of Commons, he delivered the formal declaration, stating in final cathartic revelation, "Everything that I have worked for, everything that I have believed in during my public life has crashed into ruins." In ruins, likewise, were his career and his life. He moved quickly to construct a war cabinet, which included *Winston Churchill. In the cabinet only Churchill did not agree with his war policy; this resulted in greater tensions at the cabinet table, Churchill's inflammatory letters, and his bellicose speeches. Following Hitler's thrust into Norway in May 1940, Chamberlain's parliamentary hold quickly crumbled. He resigned in favor of Churchill, but graciously remained as part of the war cabinet, helping the Churchill ministry consolidate its command of the country.

Chamberlain's health, however, steady for a septuagenarian, finally began to fail. By July he was saying, "I have lost my spring and my spirits." This was a sign of the cancer that would eventually kill him. He informed Churchill that his health might force his resignation, and by September he was an invalid. On September 29, Churchill accepted his resignation; he died on November 9, 1940, refusing the Order of the Garter offered by Churchill.

Neville Chamberlain fell under the spell of what some scholars have termed the "psychology of appeasement." His forbearance in the face of repeated rebuffs by Hitler, broken promises, and rude behavior is gentlemanly and admirable. It was easy for Chamberlain to continue to treat Hitler as a middle-class German burgher with values similar to his own. His resolve became stubborn, however, if there was criticism of his policy. Very little opposition came from his own inner circle, a group often described as nonentities, exemplified by Sir Horace Wilson. Although Chamberlain feared by the end that there would be a harsh judgment of his role in prewar events, the leavening of time has been at work, and he fares better in more recent scholarly accounts. In retrospect, his zeal to prevent a war, preserve the diminishing resources of the country and the empire, and maintain an international paramountcy appears more foresighted in light of Britain's dramatically abbreviated world position today.

Annotated Bibliography

The major repository of primary sources on all the Chamberlains is the library of the University of Birmingham. Owing to Joseph Chamberlain's endowment of the university, there is a strong Chamberlain presence there, not just in the manuscript room housing the Neville Chamberlain collection. Correspondence between Chamberlain and political colleagues can be found in the papers of Edward Irwin, First Earl of Halifax, in the India Office Library in London; the papers of the Earl of Selborne at the Bodleian Library, Oxford; the Andrew Bonar Law Papers in the House of Lords Record Office; and the Stanley Baldwin Papers at the Cambridge University Library. Permissions for the use of the above sources can be arranged through the National Registry of Archives in London.

Public manuscript sources such as the Cabinet papers (Cab.), Foreign Office papers (F.O.), and Treasury papers (T.O.) can be found in the respective series of the Public Record Office housed in London at either Chancery Lane or Kew Gardens. National records of the Conservative party such as the Executive Committee Reports, Reports of the Central Committee, Annual Reports of Council, Conference Agendas and Minutes, and the Conservative Research Department, can be found in the Conservative Party Archive, the Bodleian Library, Oxford. Permissions for these sources may be obtained by contacting each agency individually.

The major works covering Neville Chamberlain's statesmanship mostly fall into the categories of studies on appeasement, origins of the war, or biographies of Chamberlain himself. In the first category, one of the most widely cited studies, Keith Middlemas, *Diplomacy of Illusion: The British Government and Germany* (1972), has benefited from the early release of government documents and helps clarify the dynamics of the Chamberlain cabinet. Ian Colvin, *The Chamberlain Cabinet* (1971), is a similar study. One of the earliest works on appeasement was Martin Gilbert and Richard Gott, *The Appeasers* (1963). Gilbert then published *The Roots of Appeasement* (1966), which shows that appeasement was an idea founded in Christianity, personal courage, and common sense. A specialized study by A. L. Rowse, *Appeasement: A*

Study in Political Decline (1961), examines the contribution to appeasement of several colleagues at Oxford University's All Souls College. The role of the opponents of appeasement is related in William R. Rock, *Appeasement on Trial: British Foreign Policy and Its Critics, 1938–1939* (1966). Rock provides a broader interpretive essay in *British Appeasement in the 1930's* (1977).

Research on the origins of the war often begins with A. J. P. Taylor's *The Origins of the Second World War* (1961). This gadfly historian and commentator aroused a furor when his book was initially perceived as an apology for Hitler. His later revisions and explanations did not fully quell the storm. Two excellent works, raising no storms of their own, are Keith Eubank, *the Origins of World War II* (1969), and Laurence Lafore, *The End of Glory: An Interpretation of the Origins of World War II* (1970). Excellent document collections augmenting the views contained in these works are Anthony Adamthwaite, *The Making of the Second World War* (1977), and Keith Eubank, *The Road to World War II: A Documentary History* (1973). A version from the French point of view, with Chamberlain appearing headmasterish, is Maurice Baumont, *The Origins of the Second World War* (1978).

The earliest major biography of Chamberlain is Keith Feiling, *The Life of Neville Chamberlain* (1947). Although this study reproduces some interesting documents and letters, it has been superseded by more recent works. One of the revisionist biographical studies, Iain Macleod, *Neville Chamberlain* (1961), stresses the weakness Chamberlain labored under because of the deficiencies of the British military. He was in no position to do anything but stall for time. David Dilks, *Neville Chamberlain: Pioneering and Reform, 1869–1929* (1984), is the first volume of a projected two-volume set. This massive work utilizes with precision the papers of Neville Chamberlain housed at the University of Birmingham and will be the definitive work for years to come. Two recent studies that deserve mention are Richard Cockett, *Twilight of Truth: Chamberlain, Appeasement and the Manipulation of the Press* (1989), and John Charmley, *Chamberlain and the Lost Peace* (1989). Crockett examines the extent that Chamberlain's government was able to control the press coverage of his policies, while Charmley shows a Chamberlain always dealing from weakness.

Bibliography

Adamthwaite, Anthony. *The Making of the Second World War*. London: Allen and Unwin, 1977.

Baumont, Maurice. *The Origins of the Second World War*. New Haven, Conn.: Yale University Press, 1978.

Charmley, John. *Chamberlain and the Lost Peace*. London: Hodder and Stoughton, 1989.

Churchill, Winston. *The Second World War: The Gathering Storm*. London: Houghton Mifflin, 1948.

Coghlan, F. A. "Armaments, Economic Policy and Appeasement: Background to British Foreign Policy 1931–1937." *History* 57 (June 1972): 205–216.

Cockett, Richard. *Twilight of Truth: Chamberlain, Appeasement and the Manipulation of the Press*. New York: St. Martin's Press, 1989.

Colvin, Ian. *The Chamberlain Cabinet* London: Gollancz, 1971.

Dilks, David. *Neville Chamberlain: Pioneering and Reform, 1869–1929*. Cambridge: Cambridge University Press, 1984.

Eubank, Keith. *The Origins of World War II*. New York: Crowell, 1969.

———. *The Road to World War II: A Documentary History*. New York: Crowell, 1973.

Feiling, Keith. *The Life of Neville Chamberlain*. London: Macmillan, 1947.

Gilbert, Martin. *The Roots of Appeasement*. London: Weidenfeld and Nicolson, 1966.

Gilbert, Martin, and Richard Gott. *The Appeasers*. Boston: Houghton Mifflin, 1963.

Lafore, Laurence. *The End of Glory: An Interpretation of the Origins of World War II*. Philadelphia: Lippincott, 1970.

Macleod, Iain. *Neville Chamberlain*. London: Muller, 1961.

Middlemas, Keith. *Diplomacy of Illusion: The British Government and Germany, 1937–1939*. London: Weidenfeld and Nicolson, 1972.

Rock, William R. *Appeasement on Trial: British Foreign Policy and Its Critics, 1938–1939*. Hamden, Conn.: Archon, 1966.

————. *British Appeasement in the 1930's*. New York: Norton, 1977.

Rowse, Alfred L. *Appeasement: A Study in Political Decline*. New York: Norton, 1961.

Schroeder, P. W. "Munich and the British Tradition." *Historical Journal* 19 (March 1976): 223–243.

Taylor, A.J.P. *The Origins of the Second World War*. London: Atheneum, 1961.

Watt, D. C. "Appeasement: The Rise of a Revisionist School?" *Political Quarterly* 36 (April 1965): 191–213.

NEWELL D. BOYD

Charles V (1500–1558).   The sixteenth century found western Europe on the threshold of modernity. The feudal state was giving way to a new form of centralized dynastic state. The monarchies of England, Russia, and France formed the vanguard of this important development; Austria, the Germanies, and Italy lagged behind, preserving the feudalistic competition among local autonomous governments.

Although the Spanish monarchs, Ferdinand of Aragon and Isabella of Castile, each needed the local assent of their nobility in the Cortes for funding, they had united their dynasties in marriage and collaborated to expel the Moslems from Iberia in 1492. Their grandson, Charles of Burgundy, was born in Brussels on February 24, 1500. His mother was their daughter, Joanna the Mad. His father, Philip the Handsome, was descended from the wealthy House of Burgundy through his mother and the House of Habsburg through his father, the reigning Holy Roman Emperor, Maximilian I.

The second of six children, and the eldest son of Philip and Joanna, Charles was modestly called the Baron of Luxembourg at birth. However, that same year Charles's mother, Joanna, became heir to the Spanish throne. The boy was thus next in line for the thrones of Aragon and Castile. In 1506, when Philip the Handsome died, Charles became the Count of Flanders and titular ruler of the Netherlands and Burgundy, and heir to his father's claims to the Habsburg holdings in Austria and Italy.

Joanna lapsed into deep melancholia and schizophrenia at her husband's death. Ferdinand of Spain brought her home for care and safekeeping in the castle of Tordesillas. Six-year-old Charles, together with his sisters Eleanora, Isabella, and Maria, remained in Brussels. Emperor Maximilian named their Habsburg aunt, Margaret, regent of Burgundy during Charles's minority. The younger brother, Ferdinand, and his sister Katharina were reared in Spain.

Margaret of Burgundy carefully supervised Charles's childhood education. His tutor was a Catholic deacon, Adrian, a future pope. (Margaret selected the devout churchman instead of the humanist Erasmus.) Adrian nurtured the deep faith and solemn piety so characteristic of Charles's world view. Often ill, young Charles developed a strong will to prevail, testing himself in athletic contests, tourneys, and shooting. Charles's political mentor was Margaret's machiavellian chancellor, William de Croy, lord of Chievres. Chievres dominated Charles's childhood, instilling in him an appreciation of traditional courtly ritual and dynastic diplomacy. Recognizing that Charles was Europe's most eligible bachelor, Chievres subjected the boy prince to numerous strategic betrothals. Charles was engaged seven times before he finally married Princess Isabella of Portugal in 1526.

As an adult, Charles was of moderate height and somewhat stout, refusing to discipline a notorious love of rich foods. In later years painful attacks of gout made him pay dearly for his indulgence. Light hair framed his high, broad forehead and clear blue eyes. His prominent cheekbones were balanced by a long, crooked nose. He had the long "Habsburg" underlip, accentuated by his habit of keeping his mouth open. "No heart spoke from his features," wrote William Bradford, an editor of Charles's correspondence, ". . . [only] incessant reflection, tendency to depression, Spanish gravity, obstinacy, severity."

In January 1515, Charles assumed his title as Duke of Burgundy, celebrating his coming of age with tourneys and banquets. Ironically, the event coincided with the coming to power of his most infuriating adversary, Francis I of France. Until Francis died in 1547, these two rulers engaged in deadly competition for control of Italy and diplomatic supremacy in Europe.

Charles's maternal grandfather, Ferdinand of Aragon, died in January 1516, leaving the Spanish throne to Joanna the Mad. A regency was clearly necessary. The court at Brussels did not hesitate. After a memorial service for the late king, they proclaimed the joint rule of Charles and Joanna in Spain. The Spanish Cortes did not contest the claim, but demanded that Charles come immediately to receive its formal acknowledgment. But not until eighteen months later, after negotiating Charles's engagement to the infant daughter of Francis I of France, did Chievres permit Charles to travel to Spain to claim his crown.

In September 1517, Charles and his sister Eleanora sailed for Spain. A severe storm blew them off course and further delayed his encounter at Valladolid with the impatient Castilian aristocracy. Nevertheless, Charles respectfully visited his mother first and then consulted with his brother Ferdinand before presenting himself to the Cortes. The Castilian estates proclaimed him, but they deplored his inability to speak Spanish. They also rejected his advisors from the Netherlands. "For in fact the King is our paid master, and for that reason his subjects share with him part of their profits and benefits, and serve with their persons whenever called upon to do so." Undoubtedly this cool reception influenced Charles to send Ferdinand, a favorite of the Cortes, to Burgundy as his deputy.

In May 1518, the nobility in Aragon acknowledged Charles. With that crown came other important territories: the Balearic Islands, Sardinia, Sicily, and Naples, a legacy that was to trouble him throughout his reign. Finally, Charles met the Cortes in Catalonia and the merchant guilds (*gremios*) in Valencia to receive their acknowledgment. Manual Fernandez Alvarez, Charles's Spanish biographer, points out that throughout his reign Charles had constantly to placate his Spanish nobility in exchange for their financial support for his far-flung wars. They wanted a resident monarch, one who would use his income for the benefit of Spain.

In January 1519, Charles's Habsburg grandfather died. Maximilian I had been the Holy Roman Emperor since 1493, titular ruler of the approximately three hundred feudal German states. Charles was determined to add this dignity to his dynastic crowns in Spain, Naples, and Burgundy. That same year he also authorized the expeditions of Hernando Cortéz against the Aztecs in Mexico and of Ferdinand Magellan to the Spice Islands of the Orient.

The election of the Holy Roman Emperor was conducted under regulations established in 1356 by the papal Golden Bull. Four hereditary German electors and three Roman Catholic bishops voted for the emperor. In truth, the election was usually more like an auction, the winner prevailing through a combination of bribery, flattery, diplomacy, and intimidation. Charles found his candidacy contested by two prominent rivals, Francis I of France and Henry VIII of England. Henry's modest assets failed to impress the electors, but Francis and Charles at first seemed fairly evenly matched. Charles, however, obtained substantial loans from the two great German banking houses, Fugger and Welser. With this extra persuasion he gained unanimous election on June 28, 1519, as Charles V, Holy Roman Emperor. He received the crown in a ceremony at Aachen the following fall.

Thus, at the age of nineteen, Charles reigned over more domains than any other European ruler: Spain, the Netherlands, Austria, the Holy Roman Empire, and significant sections of Italy. The conquest of Mexico in 1521 (and subsequently of Peru in 1535) made him the titular ruler of much of the Western world. Charles spent the rest of his career fighting to maintain his inherited domains. He was involved in all of the major problems of Renaissance Europe.

From 1518, when Charles appointed him, until his death in 1530, Mercurino Gattinara served as Charles's grand chancellor. A lawyer, Gattinara practiced for ten years in Italy, then spent the next decade in the service of Margaret of Burgundy. Gattinara strongly influenced Charles's political ambitions. He proclaimed Charles the new Charlemagne, destined to bring harmony and justice to a reinvigorated empire. Charles wholeheartedly concurred: "At last to me empire (imperium) has been conferred by the single consent of Germany with God, as I deem, willing and commanding. . . . I shall link Spain with Germany and add the name of Caesar to Spanish King." He grandiosely styled himself "King of the Romans, future Emperor, eternally august, King of Spain, Sicily, Jerusalem, the Balearics, the Canary and Indian (Caribbean) Islands, as well as the continent on that side of the ocean, Archduke of Austria, Duke of Burgundy,

Brabant, Steier, Carinthia, Krain, Luxemburg, Limburg, Athens and Neopatria, Count of Habsburg, Flanders, Tirol, Count Palatine of Burgundy, Hennegau, and Rousillon, Landgrave in Alsace, Prince in Swabia, Lord in Asia and Africa.''

Throughout his reign, however, he was confronted by equally talented and determined adversaries: Henry VIII of England (reigned 1509–1547), Francis I of France (reigned 1515–1547), Martin Luther (1483–1546), and Suleiman the Magnificent of the Ottoman Empire (reigned 1520–1566). Aggressive and opportunistic, these men reflected the new humanism and statism of the Renaissance. By contrast, Charles's vision of a continental Catholic empire was backward looking. His religious zeal reached well beyond combatting the Lutheran Reformation in Germany. He intended to protect Europe from the aggressive Islam of the Ottoman Empire and to propagate the faith among the heathen Indians in America. Moreover, as the self-perceived guardian of the faith, Charles sought Catholic Church reform as a way to resolve some of its internal conflicts. Thus he encroached upon the prerogatives of the popes, who, as a result, often sided with his political adversaries. H. G. Koenigsberger, who analyzed the period for the *New Cambridge Modern History*, called him ''the last medieval emperor to whom the religious and political unity of Christendom was both the ideal purpose of his life and a practicable object of policy.''

This was obvious in 1521 when he agreed to give Martin Luther a personal hearing at the meeting of the imperial diet at Worms. Luther, already excommunicated by Pope Leo X, had appealed for the right to present his concerns to the diet. Charles granted a safe-conduct to the outspoken monk, but was deeply offended by his doctrines. Honorably extending the safe-conduct so that Luther could seek refuge in Saxony, Charles nevertheless pronounced Luther and his followers outlaws and ordered the destruction of their writings.

In his personal zeal, Charles disregarded the political attractiveness of Lutheranism to the German nobility. The Knights' War (1522), in which the lesser nobility tried to seize Catholic lands, was suppressed, as was the Peasants' War (1525–1526). But these social upheavals reflected how the intense religious controversy reinforced the preexisting political particularism within the empire.

Following his election as Holy Roman Emperor, Charles traveled to England to meet with Henry VIII. Both monarchs were concerned about Francis I of France. Their suspicions were well founded. Francis I launched an anti-Habsburg campaign by encouraging the rebellion of the Spanish towns (*comuneros*) against Charles in 1520, then moved against Navarre. Charles, supported by the pope and the Italian cities of Mantua and Florence, retaliated in 1521 by marching against Milan, a former Spanish territory which Francis had taken in 1515.

This inaugurated the first of four Habsburg-Valois wars over Italy. Charles moved rapidly, driving the French forces from Milan. He then smashed their armies at the Battle of Pavia and took the king prisoner. Francis was escorted to Madrid under guard and forced to sign the Treaty of Madrid (1525), renouncing his Italian claims and ceding French Burgundy to Charles.

Released on his honor (his two sons remained in Spain as hostages), Francis nevertheless renounced the treaty upon his return to France. Through skillful diplomacy he built a coalition with Venice, the Sforza family, and the new pope, Clement II, who did not want Charles becoming too powerful in Italy. Henry VIII, who was seeking to divorce his Spanish-born queen, Catherine of Aragon, saw little hope of future support from Charles and switched his support to Francis in April 1527.

Charles, meanwhile, turned to fight the Muslim Turks threatening Habsburg Austria after their capture of the Hungarian city of Mohacs in August 1526. Charles saw this as a threat to Christianity as well. Thus the defection of Pope Clement to the French cause enraged him. When he initiated the second Habsburg-Valois war (1527–1529), he sent troops to Rome in May 1527. They sacked the city and forced Clement to seek refuge in the Castle of San Angelo. Francis, however, pressed forward, expelling imperial forces from Milan and Genoa.

At that crucial juncture, Charles successfully negotiated the defection of Andrea Doria, admiral of the Genoese fleet. Promising independence for Genoa, he got Doria to blockade the French and weaken their attack on Naples. It was brilliant diplomacy since it gave Spain a powerful Mediterranean fleet to send against the Turks and provided the additional financial support of a prosperous trading city.

But neither side could prevail. By 1529 both Francis and Charles were ready for peace. In the Treaty of Barcelona, Pope Clement agreed to recognize Charles's brother, Ferdinand, as king in Bohemia and Hungary, and to accept the return of the Medici to Florence. In the north, two exceptional women resolved the conflicting claims over the Netherlands and France. Margaret of Burgundy, Charles's erstwhile guardian, and Louise, the queen mother of Francis I, met at Cambrai. There they wrote the treaty by which Francis renounced his claims to Italy and Charles agreed to renounce French Burgundy. This Paix des Dames (Women's Peace) also set the ransom of the French princes and arranged the marriage of Charles's sister Eleanora to Francis I.

At last at peace with France, Charles had Pope Clement crown him Holy Roman Emperor in Bologna (1530). He was the last German emperor crowned by the pope. In 1531, over the objections of some of the German rulers, he had his brother Ferdinand crowned King of the Romans, the title traditionally given to the heir apparent to the Habsburg lands and the imperial dignity.

Preoccupied with France, Italy, and the dynasty, Charles had paid little attention to affairs in Germany. Because the Protestant princes ignored his edict outlawing Luther, in 1530 he went to the Augsburg meeting of the imperial Reichstag. There the Protestant spokesman, Philip Melanchthon, presented the Augsburg Confession, the new Lutheran creed. Charles sharply reprimanded the Protestants, reminding them that he was their sovereign emperor and lord. He vehemently attacked their religious tenets, but at the same time he wrote to the pope urging him to call a church council to resolve the conflict. "Without a council," he told the pontiff, "Germany, this strongest and most warlike state in Christendom, falls into the greatest danger." The Protestants left the Reichstag and met the following year to form a defensive organization, the Schmalkaldic League. Still seeking a diplomatic solution, Charles reluctantly agreed to the Peace of Nürnberg in 1532, temporarily permitting the free exercise of religion in Germany. He had to deal with a greater emergency elsewhere.

Suleiman the Magnificent, the Muslim ruler of Turkey, was intensifying his campaign against the eastern borders of the Habsburg lands in Austria. Charles sent troops from the Netherlands and Italy, as well as Andrea Doria's fleet, against the sultan. Overwhelmed, Suleiman retreated, and Charles marched triumphantly into Vienna in September 1532.

Charles returned to Spain to be with his wife and five-year-old son, Philip. But Suleiman sent his Libyan vassal, Khair-ed-din Barbarossa, to attack Spain's Mediterranean commerce. The eager pirate plundered shipping and the coast of Spain. In 1535 Charles launched a retaliatory armada of 300 Spanish and Portuguese ships from Barcelona toward North Africa. They sacked Barbarossa's stronghold in Carthage and destroyed over eighty of his ships. The invaders moved next to Tunis, where Barbarossa counterattacked with thousands of men. Despite having his horse shot out from under him, Charles led his forces to a brilliant victory in battle, although Barbarossa escaped.

With Charles thus preoccupied, Francis I decided to try once more to regain Milan. Allied with Suleiman, he inaugurated the third Valois-Habsburg war in Italy. Charles again sought help from the papacy, promising the new pope, Paul III (1534–1549), to protect Italy, restore the true faith to Germany, and launch a new crusade against the Turks. But Paul declined, fearing Charles's interference in church affairs. Charles thus attacked the French through southern France and Belgium. After ten months of destructive but inconclusive campaigns, squeezing his dominions for funds, Charles finally agreed to a cease-fire. He returned to Spain in December 1536, physically and financially exhausted.

There followed a brief peaceful but painful interlude in the constant warfare and travel. For three months he agonized with gout, diverting himself by reading new works on astronomy, philosophy, and mathematics. When he recovered, he traveled through Spain, joining his delighted subjects in summer festivals, even appearing in the arena as a bullfighter. Meanwhile, Pope Paul mediated a ten-year truce between Charles and Francis in 1538. At Francis's instigation, the two met at Aigues-Mortes. Francis brought his queen, Charles's sister Eleanora, to underscore his peaceful intentions. The "gentlemen's agreement" that resulted was well short of a peace treaty, but Charles accepted it.

The interlude ended in May 1539, with the death of Charles's beloved queen, Isabella, in childbirth. In grief, Charles left Spain for the Netherlands, where urban protest had broken out in his long absence. He traveled in state through France, welcomed in Paris by Francis and Eleanora. By 1541 he had suppressed the disturbances in the Netherlands and was in Germany to deal again with the rebellious Protestants.

He called conferences in various German cities to bring both sides together. He then convened the Reichstag at Regensburg, hoping to resolve the conflict, which was polarizing the empire. But compromise and unity were impossible. He dissolved the Reichstag in July 1541, cognizant of his failure and resultant loss of authority. To save face he mounted another strike against the Muslims and their pirates. Straining his finances, he led troops and Andrea Doria's flotilla against Algeria in October 1541. The campaign was a disaster: his Italian armies collapsed and he retreated in defeat.

With Charles in disarray, Francis I opportunistically prepared a new attack. He built a coalition including some rebellious Protestants, Scotland, and the Scandinavian states in the north and Suleiman in the south to gain naval support in the Mediterranean. Charles now realized that if he were to retain his *imperium* he had to defeat Francis once and for all. Despite his antipathy toward Henry VIII of England, who in 1534 had divorced his Spanish wife and renounced the papacy, Charles signed a secret alliance with him. Pope Paul chose to remain neutral. The German states gave Charles financial support only in return for renewing his concession of parity between the two religions.

Charles faced the pending conflict grimly. He made his son, Philip, regent in Spain, and wrote his political testament. "It deeply distresses me," he wrote confidentially to Philip, "that I must leave you an empire in such need, and so weakened internally. . . . The expedition I am about to undertake is, for my honor, my reputation, my life and my fortunes, the most dangerous there could be."

With an army of approximately forty thousand, he advanced on Paris in the early summer of 1544. The city's population panicked, and Queen Eleanora interceded with her brother, urging a diplomatic resolution of the conflict. After tortuous negotiations, both sides agreed to the Treaty of Crespy in September. France once again abandoned its claims in Italy and promised to provide Charles with troops for a campaign against the Turks. For his part, Charles consented to the marriage of Francis's son to his daughter, whose dowry was the Netherlands and the Burgundian province of Franche-Comté. (The prospective bridegroom died the following year, however.)

The French threat eliminated, Charles returned to the German crisis. In 1545 he pressured Pope Paul into convening the Council of Trent (which the Protestants boycotted) to reform the Catholic Church. Then in 1546, the year of Luther's death, he set out to crush the Protestants. In the Schmalkaldic War he defeated the rebels and captured their leader, the Elector of Saxony, in 1547. He then convened the Reichstag in Augsburg and submitted a proposal to revise the imperial constitution, strengthening the powers of the emperor. Success seemed almost in hand when, by year's end, death had also taken his two greatest antagonists, Francis I of France and Henry VIII of England.

Suddenly Charles seemed to have fulfilled his self-proclaimed destiny to be supreme in Europe. It was time to secure the unencumbered succession of his son Philip to his dominions. Incredibly, Joanna the Mad, Charles's mother and co-ruler in Castile, still lived. If Charles's death preceded hers, his brother Ferdinand would succeed to the Spanish throne, and Ferdinand's son, Maximilian, after him. In 1550 Charles forced Ferdinand to renounce his rights to the regency in Spain. In return, the younger brother would succeed to the imperial title, although he agreed to ask that the German electors designate Philip, not Maximilian, as the heir apparent, the King of Rome. In return, Charles had to concede the Italian possessions to his brother's family. Charles then made the Netherlands a legacy of the Spanish crown. This family compact began the ultimate division of Habsburg lands into more modern state territories.

But new European leaders permitted Charles neither respite nor victory. In Germany the Protestant rebellion grew. The Saxon militants allied with the new king of France, Henry II, promising him Metz, Toul, and Verdun in exchange for military support against the emperor. In 1552 France seized the three bishoprics while the Protestant armies surprised Charles and forced him to flee across the Alps into Austria. Defeat was compounded by ill-health. Charles was increasingly debilitated by gout, chronic respiratory infections, and melancholy depression. Fixated on military victory, he ignored pressing matters of state. Local rebellions grew in the Netherlands and Italy.

He could no longer ignore the failure of his grand design for a unified Christian Europe. Exhausted by the long years of struggle, he decided to abdicate and retire to Spain. His mother's death in April 1555 simplified his decision, assuring Philip's Spanish inheritance. First, he accepted the will of the German states. The religious Peace of Augsburg, signed on September 25, 1555, granted parity to Lutheranism and Catholicism in the empire on the principle of *cuius regio eius religio* (whoever rules, his religion becomes the state religion). Then, on October 25, 1555, in the great hall of his Brussels palace, Charles tearfully abdicated the Spanish and imperial thrones to Philip and Ferdinand. When all the ceremonies were completed, he traveled with his widowed sister, Eleanora, to Spain. He spent his final days in reading and contemplation at Yuste. Holding fast to an ivory crucifix, Charles died on September 21, 1558; his last word was "Jesus."

Many scholars have identified Charles as the last of the true medieval statesmen. He reigned rather than ruled; he preferred diplomatic and dynastic solutions to the more opportunistic *raison d'état* of his Renaissance contemporaries. Yet for all his costly wars, his successors received domains that were sufficiently modern and efficient to dominate seventeenth-century Europe. He staved off the Turks. Despite his religious intolerance, his German settlement survived the Thirty Years' War as the basis for the postfeudal consolidation of modern Germany. In summary, his impact was more modern than his own political vision.

Annotated Bibliography

The state papers of Charles's empire are in many languages and distributed in archives throughout western Europe. The most significant are the Spanish Archivo General de Simancas for Spain, Italy, diplomatic negotiations, and finance; the Spanish Archivo General de Indias for papers relating to Spanish America; the Vienna Haus-, Hof- und Staatsarchiv for the Austrian Habsburg papers and, in the Belgian section, papers relating to the Netherlands; and the Archive Général du Royaume Belgique in Brussels for the pertinent Habsburg and Burgundian state papers.

Printed primary sources abound. Charles's interactions with the aristocracy of his realms are recorded in collections such as *Actas de las Cortes de Castilla* (1861–1936) and, for imperial affairs, the first two volumes of the *Deutsche Reichstagsakten, Neue Folge* (1962–). William Bradford's three-volume edition of *Correspondence of the Emperor Charles V and His Ambassadors at the Courts of England and France, from the Original Letters in the Imperial Family Archives at Vienna; with a Connecting Narrative and Biographical Notices of the Emperor, and of Some of the Most Distinguished Officers of His Army and Household; Together with the Emperor's Itinerary from 1519–1551* (1850) gives the English-language reader immediate insight into the breadth and complexity of the emperor's personality, interests, and activities. Karl Lanz edited a similar three-volume collection in German, *Correspondenz des Kaisers Karl V* (1844–1846).

The secondary literature on Charles V, his significant contemporaries, and their activities would fill a major library. The most comprehensive bibliography was compiled by Karl Brandi, *Kaiser Karl V: Werden und Schicksal einer Persönlichkeit und eines Weltreiches* (1976). This landmark biography, first published in 1937, is still unsurpassed. An English-language version, under the title *The Emperor Charles V*, has been published. Other, earlier biographies and monographs by an international roster of scholars are listed in Brandi's splendid bibliography. Brandi, who worked mainly in the Habsburg archives in Vienna, emphasizes Charles's German and Burgundian concerns. An excellent complement to Brandi's study, which discusses Charles's Spanish activities in greater detail, is Manuel Fernández Alvarez, *Charles V: Elected Emperor and Hereditary Ruler* (1975). Fernández Alvarez's work provides a comprehensive updated bibliography, as does the more recent study by M. J. Rodríguez-Salgado, *The Changing Face of Empire: Charles V, Philip II and Habsburg Authority, 1551–1559* (1988). This well-researched volume analyzes the adjustment of the realm from Charles's medieval outlook to Renaissance statecraft. The German historian Peter Rassow has presented thoughtful analyses of Charles's political concepts in *Die Kaiseridee Karls V* (1932) and *Die politische Welt Karls V* (1946).

The best introduction to the period is Helmut Koenigsberger's excellent essay, "The Empire of Charles V in Europe," in the second volume of the *New Cambridge Modern History* (1958). Other commendable overviews in English include the 1972 translation of F. Braudel's *The Mediterranean and the Mediterranean World in the Age of Philip II* (1972–1973) and J. H. Elliot's *Imperial Spain* (1964).

Bibliography

Actas de las Cortes de Castilla. Madrid: 1861–1936.

Bradford, William, ed. *Correspondence of the Emperor Charles V and His Ambassadors at the Courts of England and France, from the Original Letters in the Imperial Family Archives at Vienna; with a Connecting Narrative and Biographical Notices of the Emperor, and of Some of the Most Distinguished Officers of His Army and Household; Together with the Emperor's Itinerary from 1519–1551.* 3 vols. New York: AMS Press, 1850.

Brandi, Karl, comp. The Emperor Charles V; *The Growth and Destiny of a Man and of a World-Empire.* Translated by C. V. Wedgewood. New York: Knopf, 1939.

————. *Kaiser Karl V: Werden und Schicksal einer Persönlichkeit und eines Weltreiches.* 6th ed. Frankfurt: Societäts-Verlag, 1976.

Braudel, F. *The Mediterranean and the Mediterranean World in the Age of Philip II.* 2 vols. New York: Harper and Row, 1972–1973.

Deutsche Reichstagsakten, Neue Folge. 8 vols. Göttingen: Vandenhöck and Ruprecht, 1962– .

Elliot, John H. *Imperial Spain, 1469–1716.* New York: St. Martin's Press, 1964.

Fernández Alvarez, Manuel. *Charles V: Elected Emperor and Hereditary Ruler.* London: Thames and Hudson, 1975.

Koenigsberger, Helmut. "The Empire of Charles V in Europe." In *New Cambridge Modern History,* Volume 2, "The Reformation," pp. 301–333. Edited by G.R. Elton. Cambridge: Cambridge University Press, 1958.

Lanz, Karl, ed. *Correspondenz des Kaisers Karl V.* 3 vols. Leipzig: Brockhaus, 1844–1846.

Rassow, Peter. *Die Kaiseridee Karls V.* Berlin: Ebering, 1932.

———. *Die politische Welt Karl V.* Munich: Rinn, 1946.

Rodríquez-Salgado, M. J. *The Changing Face of Empire: Charles V, Philip II and Habsburg Authority, 1551–1559.* Cambridge: Cambridge University Press, 1988.

ELEANOR L. TURK

Winston Leonard Spencer Churchill (1874–1965).   Winston Churchill, British journalist and statesman, the son of the American-born Jennie Jerome and Lord Randolph Churchill, a descendant of John Churchill, the first Duke of Marlborough and hero of the Battle of Blenheim, was born November 24, 1874, at Blenheim Palace, the ancestral home. He revered his parents, and his career was unquestionably shaped by his determination to earn their respect. In 1908 he married Clementine Hozier, with whom he had five children: Diana, Randolph, Sarah, Marigold, and Mary.

As a youngster, he was at best an average student, especially in those disciplines, such as Latin, that were the curricular hallmark for the children of the aristocracy in that day. This proved particularly ironic since he would earn his living as a journalist and his political leadership would be marked by the eloquence of his language. Although he attended the prestigious public (private) school Harrow, where he was known as Spencer-Churchill, his record there was undistinguished. His father decided that Sandhurst, the training ground for Britain's army officers, was the college for Winston, who was admitted on his third attempt at the entrance examination.

After Sandhurst, he took a brief leave to report on the war of Cuban independence, followed by service in India, his reports of which gave his journalism career prominence. He wrote a novel, *Savrola,* before assuming military and journalistic duties in Egypt, where journalism again won him fame. In 1899 he resigned his commission, lost a by-election for the House of Commons at Oldham, and went to South Africa to cover the war, where his dramatic escapades were a prelude to election from Oldham in 1900.

Out of the shadow of his father, who died in 1895, Churchill advanced quickly up the political ladder, particularly after moving from the Conservative party to the Liberal party. Except for a few weeks in 1910 and the period from 1922 to 1924, he was an M.P. until 1964, holding numerous offices: under secretary in the Colonial Office (1904–1908), president of the Board of Trade (1908–1910), secretary of state for the Home Department (1910–1911), first lord of the admiralty (1911–1915, 1939–1940), chancellor of the Duchy of Landcaster (1915), minister of munitions (1917–1919), secretary of state for war and air (1919–1921), secretary of state for air and the Colonial Office (1921), secretary of state for the Colonial Office (1921–1922), chancellor of the exchequer (1924–1929), prime minister (1940–1945, 1951–1955), minister of defense (1940–1945, 1951–1952), and leader of the Loyal Opposition (1945–1951). In addition, he was leader of the Conservative party (1940–1955) and was made a knight of the Garter in 1953, the year he won the Nobel Prize in Literature. CBS Television News named him Man of the Century. In 1963 the U.S. Congress bestowed upon him its first honorary citizenship.

In this century, no one else held high government office as long as he did. After joining the governing Liberal party in 1904, he reversed course in 1924 to remain a Conservative to the end of his life. In a governing system that put a premium on party loyalty, Churchill's actions were remarkable, particularly in that he held major government office with each party, including every principal cabinet post except foreign secretary.

In the decade of 1929–1939, he was a pariah with mainstream Tories for his vociferous critiques of policies either proposed or seconded by Stanley Baldwin and *Neville Chamberlain, each of whom served both as prime minister and leader of the Conservative party immediately before him. Churchill held a key role in the India Defence League, which opposed independence for India, clearly bucking the tide of history. But he proved prophetic in the other primary target of his criticism: Conservative defense policy, which he regarded as insufficient to counter the expanding Nazi military juggernaut.

He attained the apex of his career in May 1940 upon becoming prime minister. With Britain facing seemingly certain defeat, he inspired it to resist and persevere. Although at retirement age, Churchill was indefatigable as warlord, working long hours, making numerous overseas trips, and all the while serving as an eloquent spokesman for freedom, at least as he understood it. Despite occasional ill health he maintained an arduous pace until *Adolf Hitler's Third Reich fell in May 1945.

Churchill was forced from office when his Conservative party suffered a stunning defeat in the July 1945 general election. Now, he devoted himself to writing his history of World War II and painting. He also traveled and gave speeches, including one at Westminster College in Fulton, Missouri, in 1946 when he popularized the phrase ''Iron Curtain'' in reference to the Soviet empire in eastern Europe. As leader of the Loyal Opposition, he saw his Tories narrowly defeated in the 1950 elections before winning a thin victory the next year.

Back at 10 Downing Street, Churchill sought to strengthen Anglo-American ties, especially through his personal friendships with U.S. presidents Harry S. Truman and Dwight D. Eisenhower. Failing health forced him to resign in 1955.

He chose not to stand for reelection to the House of Commons in the 1964 elections, having become Father of the House by virtue of his senior status there.

On January 24, 1965, he died. His funeral was the grandest since that of the Duke of Wellington in the previous century and was followed on television by millions around the world.

In Churchill's first official position at the Colonial Office in 1904, he addressed the aftermath of the Boer War. Churchill advocated a nonpunitive independence for the Transvaal and termination of the labor contracts that put Chinese workers in the mines there. Although only an under secretary, he was spokesman for colonial policy since his superior, Lord Elgin, as a peer was barred from the House of Commons. That and Churchill's personality gave him unusual influence despite his junior status.

As first lord of the admiralty in 1912 and again as colonial secretary in 1922, he backed Irish Home Rule but with Ulster remaining with the United Kingdom. He participated in the direct negotiations with Irish leaders and piloted the Irish Free State Act through the House of Commons. Michael Collins, head of the Irish Republican Army, a guerrilla force, considered Churchill's role as vital to the proceedings. That was particularly remarkable because Churchill had to forego his trademark flamboyance. Bravado was set aside as the tear in the fabric of British politics that had been ragged for a half century was mended. The Irish Free State, which soon became independent, was created while six of the counties in the province of Ulster remained in the United Kingdom as Northern Ireland.

In 1921 Churchill convened a conference in Cairo to address the fate of Palestine and other Middle East issues. The Ottoman Empire, which had dominated that part of the world for centuries, although more in symbol than in fact in recent generations, had been crushed in World War I. The Arabs, under the urging and leadership of T. E. Lawrence, had risen against the Ottoman regime and contributed to its demise, with the hope of gaining independence. But at the Versailles Peace Conference, the Arab emissaries were ignored. France and Britain carved out their respective spheres of influence in the Middle East through mandates, with France dominating Syria and Lebanon, and Britain doing the same for Iran, Iraq, and Palestine. Riots and uprisings by Arabs across the Middle East followed this settlement, necessitating further consideration of the situation. The Balfour Declaration (1917) had committed Britain to support a Jewish homeland in Palestine, a position that Churchill, who had many Jewish constituents and friends, endorsed.

Lawrence accompanied Churchill to Cairo, where in mid-March the conferees agreed that King Faisal would govern Mesopotamia (Iraq); his brother, King Abdullah, despite Zionist opposition, would rule Transjordan (Jordan). They also settled the extent of the British military presence in the Middle East and its funding. These arrangements did not receive universal approval, even in the cabinet.

After a decade on the sidelines, Churchill returned to the cabinet in 1939 and became prime minister a few months later. There he moved quickly to strengthen both the physical and psychological resources of his people and to establish alliances with those nations that would collectively defeat the Nazi war machine.

At sixty-five, Churchill began to travel the globe, stitching together a patch-work of allies to oppose the fascist regimes in Germany and Japan. Within a year of taking office, his entreaties to the United States were rewarded with the Lend-Lease Act, by which the United States provided supplies, arms, and equip-ment, including used ships, to any country whose defense was deemed vital to the United States. Britain was the immediate beneficiary of this law, and at a time when its own resources were nearly exhausted.

His first major diplomatic effort came in August 1941, aboard ship off the eastern coast of Canada, where he informed the U.S. president, *Franklin D. Roosevelt, of Britain's strategy for defeating Germany. As they adjourned, they issued a joint declaration, the Atlantic Charter, whose eight points set out the principles on which the two nations would wage the war. Although the document was not an alliance or a binding treaty, it had great moral force. Both nations denounced territorial or other gains, proclaimed the right of self-determination for nations, endorsed efforts to promote trade and economic well-being as well as freedom from fear for people of all nations, and advocated the disarmament of aggressor nations. These principles, which formed the basis for the United Nations Charter, were quickly adopted by fifteen anti-Nazi nations, including the Soviet Union.

With the charter, the British sought to reassure Roosevelt that they had no ulterior motives in the war, although Churchill later was ambivalent about ap-plying the self-determination principle to the territories of the British Empire.

In December 1941, Churchill went to Washington, D.C., where he was suc-cessful in persuading Roosevelt to seek victory in Europe before Asia, to attack first the Nazi forces in the Mediterranean (North Africa, then Italy), and to postpone a second front in the form of a landing across the English Channel. This latter point was a source of apprehension for the Soviet Union, which wanted a second front to relieve pressure on its own front line.

In January 1943, the British and U.S. leaders, along with their staffs and top military leaders, met in Casablanca, Morocco. A reluctant General *Charles de Gaulle attended, but the Soviet leader, *Joseph Stalin, declined, asserting that his presence at home was essential to the war effort there. The conference did not resolve the conflicting claims of de Gaulle and General Henri Giraud over leadership of the French forces, but it did designate General Eisenhower as commander of the Allied forces in North Africa. Churchill reluctantly assented to Roosevelt's demand for unconditional surrender of all Axis powers. This doctrine was intended to assure Stalin that there would be no separate peace negotiated with Hitler and to avoid a future claim by a defeated Germany that it had not surrendered, a contention that Hitler had used to discredit the Versailles Treaty.

Beginning in November 1943, the U.S. and British heads of state held two conferences in Cairo. The Chinese leader Generalissimo Chiang Kai-shek and Madame Chiang attended the first. The conferees issued the Cairo Declaration on December 1, which restated the demand for Japan's unconditional surrender and forfeiture of all lands gained by force or League of Nations mandate, while renouncing territorial claims for their own governments. The second conference (December 4–6) included Ismet Inonu, the president of Turkey, who affirmed that nation's alliance with Britain and Turkey's friendship with the United States and the Soviet Union. Roosevelt and Churchill announced that Eisenhower would command the invasion of western Europe.

In between the Cairo meetings, a third conference was held in Teheran, Iran, with Stalin joining the two Western leaders. Here, the main issue was the invasion of western Europe, planned to coincide with a Soviet offensive against Germany. Stalin repeated his promise to join in the war against Japan. Plans were also formulated for an international organization to maintain peace once the war was over.

What came to be the most controversial of the Allied conferences was held February 4–11, 1945, at Yalta in the Crimea, attended by Churchill, Roosevelt, and Stalin. In return for entering the war in Asia, the Soviet Union was to obtain the Kurile Islands, the southern part of Sakhalin Island, an occupation zone in Korea, and privileged status in Manchuria and two Chinese ports, Dairen and Port Arthur. In addition, the two Western leaders recognized the autonomy of Outer Mongolia, which was already in the Soviet sphere, and awarded eastern Poland to the Soviet Union. Poland, in return, would receive German territory on its western and northern borders. Churchill was growing increasingly suspicious of Stalin's intentions, but an ailing Roosevelt was convinced that he could effectively work with the Soviet leader. Unless the Soviets backed off or the Western leaders were willing to use force, the arrangements in Poland were fait accompli since the Soviet military was occupying Poland. Less defensible was the decision to grant the Ukraine and Byelorussia full voting rights in the United Nations as though they were independent nations.

That summer Churchill attended his final conference as Britain's wartime leader at Potsdam, a suburb of Berlin, where he was joined by Stalin and the new U.S. president, Harry Truman. The demand for Japan's unconditional surrender was reiterated, but the main issue was the occupation of Germany, which had surrendered on May 8. It was to be partitioned, at least temporarily, denazified, and democratized. Churchill attended this most contentious meeting of the Big Three from July 17 to 28, when he was replaced by Clement Attlee, leaving Stalin to face two relative foreign policy novices.

In Churchill's second tenure as prime minister, it is difficult to delineate precisely his foreign policy contributions. His longtime heir, Sir Anthony Eden, was a major factor, especially during Churchill's illnesses. Eden also suffered a lengthy illness during which the Foreign Office carried out the government's policies. But the term *government's policies* is crucial; the policies were Churchill's.

In this period hostilities in Korea ended, as did those in Indochina, at least for the French, and a coup returned the shah to the Peacock Throne of Iran. Britain had a secondary role in these events. Dissolution of the empire, begun under Attlee, continued, but with different emphases. In divesting itself of African colonies, Britain was of two minds, granting independence in the near future to the Gold Coast (Ghana), Nigeria, and the Sudan, but delaying that status to those areas with significant European populations, that is, eastern and central Africa, where federation was tried briefly.

Diplomatic success was achieved in removing the British military from Suez after the coup there led by Gamal Abdul Nasser, negotiating the Trieste dispute between Italy and Yugoslavia, helping bring West Germany into NATO and the Western European Union, and staying out of the troubles of Southeast Asia, except to end the threat by Communist guerrillas in Malaya.

Churchill supported the momentum for a united Europe, which would crystallize shortly in the creation of the Common Market, but he also wished to retain Britain's role in the Commonwealth and the special Anglo-American relationship. As it turned out, Britain chose not to be a founding member of the Common Market, which put the nation in an awkward position when it did seek membership in the 1960s.

Churchill was a child of the Victorian age, an era that influenced him throughout his life. Despite that background, he was an enthusiastic advocate of modern technology. During World War I, while at the admiralty, he was the most fervent proponent for developing the military tank. He learned to fly in middle age and was a spokesman for expanding Britain's air force. His use of radio to move public opinion was matched only by Roosevelt.

Partly because of Roosevelt's physical infirmities, partly because of Stalin's paranoia about being away from the Soviet Union, partly because of his own preference for personal diplomacy, Churchill, the eldest of the Big Three, made flight after flight to his counterparts in Washington and Moscow and to numerous other sites around the globe. Only the most important of his many overseas missions are mentioned here; he was unflagging in his efforts of personal diplomacy. This aristocratic child of the nineteenth century became the father of summitry and the consummate political consumer of modern technology for the conduct of diplomacy.

As the United States assumed the greater role in the wartime partnership, Churchill realized that Britain was clearly the junior partner. He was also determined to maintain a strong presence for Britain at the Allied conference table. This he did often by the sheer force of his personality.

Personality was crucial to his political philosophy. He saw himself as the bearer of a great tradition of leadership manifested by his ancestor, the first Duke of Marlborough, and his father. He admired *Napoleon I and was convinced that great personalities shape history. The conduct of his own life was a testament to his faith in personal leadership. Of his contemporaries, perhaps only Roosevelt exceeded him in confidence that his direct intervention could resolve a problem.

From his early days in the cabinet, Churchill eagerly encroached on policy areas that were not strictly in his jurisdiction. Whether within his authority or not, his proposals often were controversial: the Dardanelles operation in 1915, which failed and forced his resignation; his active efforts to assist the White Army in Russia after the Bolshevik seizure of power; and the return to the gold standard in 1925, which had international consequences. He readily admitted that economic issues bored him.

Although he was progressive in many policies, he also espoused positions that appeared reactionary, such as maintaining the empire. He was impressed by imperial pomp and glory. But his advocacy of empire was not merely an emotional reaction. He considered imperial relations to be an elevating force for both the mother country and its overseas dependents. The latter were brought to a higher stage of culture and behavior, while the mentoring, paternal role of the former called for a nobility of conduct that was unlikely in other circumstances.

Moreover, with the breakup of empires and a greater emphasis on national self-determination, Europe and the world beyond it were pulled into an expanding vortex of quarrels among the increased number of small nations, whose destructive parochialism had been contained under the imperialism of Britain, France, Austria-Hungary, and others. A single dominating power, such as the Soviet Union after World War II or Napoleonic France before Waterloo, has small nations at its mercy. Britain had long played the role of balancer, a role necessary to maintain peace in Europe.

Strength and negotiation were the cornerstones of Churchill's diplomacy. He was never unwilling to negotiate but insisted on doing so from a position of strength.

More than any other individual, he was responsible for victory in World War II. His warnings and inspirational leadership rallied not only his countrymen but the entire free world. Almost alone his British forces stemmed the Nazi onslaught on the western front until the addition of the U.S. military helped turn the tide.

At the same time, he was almost indifferent to the threat in the Pacific and let the United States take the lead there. The Pacific was only a peripheral element in the three circles in which he placed British foreign policy: close ties with the Commonwealth, the United States, and Europe.

He preferred self-government to self-determination, contending that only those colonial peoples who were qualified to govern should be granted independence. But he could not hold back the movement toward independence, what Harold Macmillan later called the "wind of change." Winston Churchill provided a model of statesmanship so rare that its equal is unlikely to be seen again within the lifetimes of those who shared the twentieth century with him.

Annotated Bibliography

Archival resources on Churchill are primarily located in two places: the Public Record Office, Ruskin Avenue, Kew, Richmond, Surrey, TW9 4DU (Tel. 081–876–344), where the papers for the Prime Minister's Office, the Ministry of Defence, the Foreign Office, the War Office, the Air Ministry, and the Admiralty are especially pertinent; and the Churchill Trust, 15 Queen's Gate Terrace, London SW7 (Tel. 071–584–9315).

Other material may be found in the Royal Archives; contact the Royal Librarian, Buckingham Palace, London SW1. But primary sources about Churchill are nearly inexhaustible; Martin Gilbert, his official biographer, claims to have examined more than 200 personal archives. Gilbert gives a detailed commentary on source material in the preface to his *Winston S. Churchill*, Vol. 7, *Road to Victory, 1941–1945* (1986).

William Manchester's acknowledgments (pp. 885–889) in *The Last Lion: Winston Spencer Churchill*, Vol. 1, *Visions of Glory, 1874–1932* (1983), contain information on several archival and interview sources. Manchester's bibliography lists several dozen articles by Churchill, as well as an extensive number of publications by and about him. One should not be complacent about primary data. For instance, Peter Boyle ("The Special Relationship with Washington," in John W. Young, ed., *The Foreign Policy of Churchill's Peacetime Administration, 1951–1955* [1988]) notes that the Churchill-Eisenhower correspondence in the Eisenhower Library at Abilene, Kansas, is "slightly fuller" than that at the Public Record Office in England.

Frederick Woods edited *The Collected Works of Sir Winston Churchill* (1973–1976) in thirty-four volumes, which encompasses essentially everything Churchill wrote, including speeches and newspaper despatches for 1897–1900. Woods also compiled *A Bibliography of the Works of Sir Winston Churchill*, 2nd rev. ed. (1979). Robert Rhodes James has edited *Winston S. Churchill: His Complete Speeches, 1897–1963*, 8 vols. (1974), also published in a condensed version, *Churchill Speaks: Winston S. Churchill in Peace and War: Collected Speeches* (1980).

Churchill was the most prolific author among statesmen. He published seventeen books, totaling thirty-one volumes, pertinent to his political views, as well as others on his hobbies. His son Randolph collected and edited seven volumes, under separate titles, of his father's speeches. Churchill's political views are spread throughout his writings, but his international perspective is most clearly expressed in *The Second World War*, 6 vols. (1948–1954), and *The World Crisis*, 5 vols. (1923–1931), which is about World War I and its aftermath. As history, these volumes are suspect, reflecting, as Churchill readily admitted, his personal views. Characteristically, he published his autobiography when in middle age: *My Early Life* (1930; published in the United States as *A Roving Commission*). That, along with his early books, *The Story of the Malakand Field Force* (1898, 1990), *London to Ladysmith via Pretoria* and *Ian Hamilton's March* (both 1900; reprinted 1990 together as *The Boer War*), and *My African Journey* (1908, 1990), reveal his views on the world order, particularly imperialism. His many speeches (both in and beyond the Commons) and periodical articles address specific topics. The eight-volume official biography, *Winston S. Churchill*, with thirteen companion volumes, is the starting point for any extended study of Churchill, whose son Randolph wrote the first two volumes before his death. Martin Gilbert then took over to produce a more readable work. The items in the official biography most pertinent to Churchill's views on international matters are Randolph S. Churchill, Vol. 2, *Young Statesman, 1901–1914* (1967); and Martin Gilbert, Vol. 3, *The Challenge of War, 1914–1916* (1971), Vol. 4, *The Stricken World, 1916–1922* (1975), Vol. 5, *The Prophet of Truth, 1922–1939* (1977), Vol. 6, *Finest Hour, 1939–1941* (1983), Vol. 7, *Road to Victory, 1941–1945* (1986), and Vol. 8, *Never Despair, 1945–1965* (1988).

Among the single-volume biographies, Martin Gilbert's *Churchill: A Life* (1991) is the most authoritative, surpassing Henry Pelling, *Winston Churchill* (1974), which includes extensive endnotes and a lengthy bibliography. Also useful is Robert Payne, *The Great Man: Winston Churchill* (1974), with a lengthy chronology of Churchill's life. Payne puts Churchill in both historical and contemporary context. William Manchester's *The Last Lion* ends in 1940 and is somewhat overwritten but is excellent for providing the flavor of the times in which Churchill lived. A brief but insightful work is Manfred Weidhorn, *Sir Winston Churchill* (1979). This examines recurring themes in Churchill's writings, including the art of war, continents and races, the British character and mission, and major world powers. In contrast, a book from the same publisher's Rulers and Statesmen series, Victor L. Albjerg, *Winston Churchill* (1973), is strangely organized and omits key events in Churchill's career. A succinct treatment, describing Churchill's style of decision making and use of aides, is Paul Addison, "Winston Churchill," in John P. Mackintosh, ed., *British Prime Ministers in the Twentieth Century*, Vol. 2 (1978).

For Churchill's initial tour at the Colonial Office, see Ronald Hyam, *Elgin and Churchill at the Colonial Office, 1905–1908: The Watershed of the Empire-Commonwealth* (1968). On the Irish issue, see Mary C. Bromage, *Churchill and Ireland* (1964). On Churchill and the Middle East, see Helmut Mejcher, "British Middle East Policy, 1917–21," *Journal of Contemporary History* 8 (1973), Mejcher's "Iraq's External Relations, 1921–26," *Middle Eastern Studies* 13 (1977), and David Fromkin's *A Peace to End All Peace* (1989). Raymond A. Callahan, *Churchill: Retreat from Empire* (1984), contends that although Churchill curiously ignored the 1921 Cairo Conference in his memoirs, for a quarter of a century it was the framework of Middle East politics, and he was the leading force in crafting that structure. Callahan's book focuses on the pre–1945 years. Michael J. Cohen, *Churchill and the Jews* (1985), traces Churchill's relations with Jewish issues from his early public career until 1948.

On the tripartite conferences (Moscow, Teheran, Cairo), see Keith Sainsbury, *The Turning Point* (1985); on Yalta, Diana S. Clemens, *Yalta* (1970), and Russell D. Buhite, *Decisions at Yalta: An Appraisal of Summit Diplomacy* (1986); on Potsdam, Charles L. Mee, Jr., *Meeting at Potsdam* (1975).

For the 1951–1955 period, see Anthony Seldon, *Churchill's Indian Summer: The Conservative Government, 1951–55* (1981), which details the various personalities and offices in the cabinet and civil service that were influential in commonwealth, colonial, and foreign policies, as well as the policies themselves. For a briefer treatment, set within the overall record of these years, see Anthony Seldon, "The Churchill Administration, 1951–1955," in Peter Hennessy and Anthony Seldon, eds., *Ruling Performance: British Governments from Attlee to Thatcher* (1987). John Young's *Foreign Policy of Churchill's Peacetime Administration*, has chapters on each of the main foreign policy issues. It is a less favorable assessment than found in Seldon. For an overall view of Britain's difficulty in adjusting to its diminished international status after 1945 and Churchill's primary role in shaping its defense policies, see Arthur Cyr, "The Elements of British Security Policy," *Armed Forces and Society* 8 (1982).

For the most thorough analysis of Churchill's approach to world politics, consult Kenneth Thompson, *Winston Churchill's World View* (1983), and his *Foreign Policy and Arms Control* (1990). Kirk Emmert in *Winston S. Churchill on Empire* (1989) and "Winston S. Churchill on Civilizing Empire," in Harry Jaffa, ed., *Statesmanship* (1981), presents an extensive exploration of Churchill's rationale for imperialism.

Bibliography

Addison, Paul. "Winston Churchill." In *British Prime Ministers of the Twentieth Century*, Vol. 2, *Churchill to Callaghan*. Edited by John P. Macintosh. New York: St. Martin's Press, 1978: 1–36.

Albjerg, Victor L. *Winston Churchill*. New York: Twayne, 1973.

Bromage, Mary C. *Churchill and Ireland*. Notre Dame, Ind.: University of Notre Dame Press, 1964.

Buhite, Russell D. *Decisions at Yalta: An Appraisal of Summit Diplomacy*. Wilmington, Del.: Scholarly Resources, 1986.

Callahan, Raymond A. *Churchill: Retreat from Empire*. Wilmington, Del.: Scholarly Resources, 1984.

Churchill, Randolph S. *Winston S. Churchill*. Boston: Houghton Mifflin. Vol. 1, *Youth, 1974–1900* (1966); Vol. 2, *Young Statesman, 1901–1914* (1967). (See also Martin Gilbert below.)

Churchill, Winston S. *The Boer War*. New York: Norton, 1990. Reprint of *London to Ladysmith via Pretoria* and *Ian Hamilton's March*.

———. *Ian Hamilton's March*. London: Longmans, 1900. (See *The Boer War*.)

———. *London to Ladysmith via Pretoria*. London: Longmans, 1900. (See *The Boer War*.)

———. *My African Journey*. London: Hodder and Stoughton, 1908. Reprint. New York: Norton, 1990.

———. *My Early Life*. London: Butterworth, 1930; published in the United States as *A Roving Commission*.

———. *The River War*. 2 vols. London: Longmans, 1899.

———. *A Roving Commission*. (See *My Early Life*.)

———. *Savrola*. London: Longmans, 1900.

———. *The Second World War*. 6 vols. London: Cassell, 1948–1954.

———. *The Story of the Malakand Field Force: An Episode of Frontier War*. London: Longmans, 1898. Reprint. New York: Norton, 1990.

———. *The World Crisis*. 5 vols. New York: Scribner's, 1923–1931.

Clemens, Diana S. *Yalta*. New York: Oxford University Press, 1970.

Cohen, Michael J. "The British White Paper on Palestine, May, 1939." *Historical Journal* 19, 3 (1976): 727–758.

———. *Churchill and the Jews*. London: Frank Cass, 1985.

Cyr, Arthur. "The Elements of British Security Policy." *Armed Forces and Society* 8, 3 (1982): 389–404.

Emmert, Kirk. *Winston S. Churchill on Empire*. Durham, N.C.: Carolina Academic Press, 1989.

———. "Winston S. Churchill on Civilizing Empire." in Harry V. Jaffa, ed., *Statesmanship*. Durham, N.C.: Carolina Academic Press, 1981.

Fowler, Michael. *Winston S. Churchill, Philosopher and Statesman*. Lanham, Md.: University Press of America, 1985.

Fromkin, David. *A Peace to End All Peace: Creating the Middle East: 1914–1922*. New York: Holt, 1989.

Garson, Robert. "Churchill's Spheres of Influence: Rumania and Bulgaria." *Survey* 24, 3 (1979): 143–158.

Gilbert, Martin. *Churchill: A Life*. London: Heinemann, 1991.

———. *Winston S. Churchill*. Boston: Houghton Mifflin. Vol. 3, *The Challenge of War*,

1914–1916 (1971); Vol. 4, *The Stricken World, 1916–1922* (1975); Vol. 5, *The Prophet of Truth, 1922–1939* (1977); Vol. 6, *Finest Hour, 1939–1941* (1983); Vol. 7, *Road to Victory, 1941–1945* (1986); Vol. 8, *Never Despair, 1945–1965* (1988). (See also Randolph Churchill above. 13 ''companion volumes'' supplement this series.)

————. *Winston Churchill: The Wilderness Years*. Boston: Houghton Mifflin, 1982.

Holdich, P.G.H. ''A Policy of Percentages? British Policy and the Balkans after the Moscow Conference of 1944.'' *International History Review* 9, 1 (1987): 28–47.

Hyam, Ronald. *Elgin and Churchill at the Colonial Office, 1905–1908: The Watershed of the Empire-Commonwealth*. New York: St. Martin's Press, 1968.

Kitchen, Martin. ''Winston Churchill and the Soviet Union During the Second World War.'' *Historical Journal* 30, 2 (1987): 415–436.

Manchester, William. *The Last Lion: Winston Spencer Churchill*. Boston: Houghton Mifflin. Vol. 1, *Visions of Glory, 1874–1932* (1983); Vol. 2, *Alone, 1932–1940* (1988).

Mee, Charles L., Jr. *Meeting at Potsdam*. New York: Evans, 1975.

Mejcher, Helmut. ''British Middle East Policy, 1919–21: The Inter-Departmental Level.'' *Journal of Contemporary History* 8, 4 (1973): 81–101.

————. ''Iraq's External Relations, 1921–26.'' *Middle Eastern Studies* 13, 3 (1977): 340–358.

Payne, Robert. *The Great Man: Winston Churchill*. New York: Coward, McCann and Geoghegan, 1974.

Pelling, Henry. *Winston Churchill*. New York: Dutton, 1974.

Rhodes James, Robert, ed. *Churchill Speaks: Winston S. Churchill in Peace and War: Collected Speeches, 1897–1963*. New York: Chelsea House, 1980.

————, ed. *Winston S. Churchill: His Complete Speeches, 1897–1963*. 8 vols. New York: Chelsea House, 1974.

Sainsbury, Keith. *The Turning Point: Roosevelt, Stalin, Churchill and Chiang-Kai-Shek, 1943*. Oxford: Oxford University Press, 1985.

Sbrega, John. ''Determination versus Drift: The Anglo-American Debate over the Trusteeship Issue, 1941–1945.'' *Pacific Historical Review* 55, 2 (1986): 256–280.

Schonfeld, Maxwell Philip. *The War Ministry of Winston Churchill*. Ames: Iowa State University Press, 1972.

Seldon, Anthony. ''The Churchill Administration, 1951–1955.'' In *Ruling Performance: British Governments from Attlee to Thatcher*, pp. 63–97. Edited by Peter Hennessy and Anthony Seldon. New York: Blackwell, 1987.

————. *Churchill's Indian Summer: The Conservative Government, 1951–55*. London: Hodder and Stoughton, 1981.

Thompson, Kenneth W. *Foreign Policy and Arms Control: Churchill's Legacy*. Lanham, Md.: University Press of America, 1990.

————. *Winston Churchill's World View: Statesmanship and Power*. Baton Rouge: Louisiana State University, 1983.

Weidhorn, Manfred. *Sir Winston Churchill*. Boston: Twayne, 1979.

Woods, Frederick, ed. *A Bibliography of the Works of Sir Winston Churchill*. 2nd ed. London: St. Paul's Bibliographies, 1972.

————, ed. *The Collected Works of Sir Winston Churchill*. 34 vols. London: Library of Imperial History, 1973–1976.

Young, John W. "Churchill's 'No' to Europe: The 'Rejection' of European Union by
    Churchill's Postwar Government, 1951–1952." *Historical Journal* 28, 4 (1985):
    923–937.
———, ed. *The Foreign Policy of Churchill's Peacetime Administration, 1951–1955.*
    Leicester: Leicester University Press, 1988.

THOMAS PHILLIP WOLF

Oliver Cromwell (1599–1658).   Oliver Cromwell was born on April 25, 1599,
into a gentry family of modest importance in Huntingdonshire. He was educated
at Sidney Sussex College (1616–1617), one of the most Puritan of the Cambridge
colleges, but had to return home without taking a degree on the death of his
father. Subsequently he attended the Inns of Court in London. In 1620 he married
Elizabeth Bourchier, daughter of a London merchant. They had eight children
who survived infancy. On the death of his uncle in 1636, Cromwell inherited a
substantial estate, which secured his family's economic position.

He participated in local politics in the 1620s, first entering the national political
scene in 1628, when he was elected to that tumultuous Parliament, which clashed
dramatically with the king about the limits of royal power. His sympathies lay
wholly with the critics of royal policy, and his position was reinforced in the
1630s during the "personal rule" of Charles I. In the early 1640s he served in
Parliament again, continuing as a stalwart of John Pym's party in opposing the
king.

On the outbreak of the Civil War, he worked to organize his native East Anglia
militarily in support of Parliament and, though he had no prior military experience, he soon distinguished himself as a cavalry officer in the army of the
Eastern Association. He was one of the moving spirits behind the organization
of the New Model Army, which markedly strengthened parliamentary efforts to
win the war. Rising to the command of the cavalry, he played important parts
in the battles of Marston Moor (1644) and Naseby (1645), which decisively
defeated the king.

In the difficult years between 1646 and 1649, a solution to the problem of the
country's governance eluded the victors. Cromwell and other senior officers
struggled to contain the radical political demands of the army, stopped its virtual
mutiny, suppressed the attempted royalist revival in the second Civil War and,
finally, concluding that a durable peace with the king was not possible, pressed
a divided and reluctant Parliament to set up a special court, which tried and
executed Charles in January 1649. Waverers in Commons had to be excluded,
and the resulting body, "the Rump," attempted to govern the country thereafter
as a republic known as the Commonwealth. The Commonwealth depended heavily on the support of the army to reduce Ireland and Scotland to obedience and
to crush continued royalist resistance, led now by the young Charles II. Cromwell's crowning victories at Dunbar (1650) and Worcester (1651), which secured
the republic, made him the dominant figure in the army and a leader in the
Commonwealth's Council of State.

However, the new government's inability to devise a stable governance in church and state, and to win legitimacy for itself in a deeply divided country, eventually convinced Cromwell, as commander of the army, to intervene. Abandoning his republican friends, he dismissed the Rump in April 1653 and established himself as Lord Protector in December. In this quasi-monarchical arrangement he governed a nominally republican state with considerable vigor until his death in 1658.

Cromwell's general outlook on foreign policy through the early years of the Civil War was typical of the Calvinist squirearchy, which supported John Pym and the other most vigorous opponents of Charles I. Like them, Cromwell feared Catholicism above all else. Domestically, Catholics were seen as a dangerous subversive force, supporters of royal absolutism and enemies of the true faith. Abroad, the predominant Catholic states, the most powerful ones in Europe, threatened in the long, apocalyptic Thirty Years War to extirpate Protestantism. The greatest menace to Britain was the combined strength of the Habsburgs, the Catholic rulers of Spain who, supported by their Austrian cousins, seemed bent on swallowing the world in a "universal monarchy." The other great Catholic state of western Europe, France, traditionally resisted both this vast combination and the pretensions of the papacy to ultimate authority, but French policy seemed equally bent on the destruction of its own Protestant minority, the Huguenots. Typically, Cromwell assumed that England should pursue "a godly foreign policy," supporting European Protestants and offering Catholic states nothing but hostility. Rhetorically, at least, he supported the ideal of a godly foreign policy to the end of his life.

In the 1640s, preoccupied with civil war, matters of foreign policy had a low priority. Cromwell had, however, in November 1644, urged the most vigorous military measures against the king, rather than negotiations, in part because he feared that Charles would successfully seek foreign intervention to rescue his failing cause. This was not merely a theoretical possibility. Virtually all European states were monarchies—oligarchical Venice was an exception, and the Dutch in their United Provinces a more ambiguous case—but the Stuarts could appeal to something beyond a vaguely self-interested monarchical solidarity against rebellion.

The system of foreign relations in the early seventeenth century was as much a matter of advancing and adjusting the interests of each ruling family as of dealing with national interests, as much interdynastic relations as international ones. Dynastic marriages, linking ruling families, sealed alliances and powerfully influenced the orientation of foreign policy. Charles I, with his French queen of the House of Bourbon, was brother-in-law of Louis XIII and then uncle of the child-king *Louis XIV. His daughter Mary was the wife of Prince William of Orange, eldest son of the Dutch stadtholder. Cromwell's concern that these important dynastic ties might lead to intervention in the Civil War never materialized, for the Dutch and French were far too preoccupied with the Thirty Years War. However, the Stuart dynastic connections posed a serious potential threat to the new republic, which remained diplomatically isolated and was regarded by monarchical Europe with hostility because of the regicide. The most realistic hope of Stuart counterrevolution was the possibility of French aid, though France was deeply embroiled in both a continuing war with Spain and, until 1653, a grave domestic revolt, the Fronde. As for the Dutch, the death of the stadtholder in 1650 brought the republican party to power, making that dynastic connection for the moment of little value to Charles II.

The Commonwealth Council of State, of which Cromwell was a key member, seized the opportunity to offer an ideological alliance to the Protestant and republican Dutch against the Catholic powers. This godly foreign policy foundered on the long-standing Anglo-Dutch commercial rivalry dating back more than half a century. The Dutch were also disinclined to make a common cause against Spain when they had just successfully concluded their eighty years' war against Madrid. The Commonwealth's response to this rebuff was first, in October 1651, the passage of the retaliatory Navigation Acts aimed at the Dutch carrying trade and then, in May 1652, war. It has been argued that this course of action demonstrates how little influence Cromwell had on the making of foreign policy during those years, though historians are not agreed about this.

However that controversy is viewed, there is no question that once Cromwell achieved undisputed power after dismissing the Rump in April 1653, it is possible to speak properly of a Cromwellian foreign policy. He had inherited from the Commonwealth the Dutch war, which he disliked, and, more generally, Britain's potential vulnerability to a renewed Stuart assault supported by foreign aid. The end of the Fronde strengthened the French position and, menacingly, France continued to play host, for dynastic reasons, to Charles II and his Stuart court-in-exile. Cromwell moved briskly to make peace with the Dutch, but had no more success than his predecessors at interesting them in his cherished godly alliance. A sticking point in the negotiations was his insistence that the House of Orange be debarred from offices of importance, showing that counterdynastic concerns were as central to his policy as religious ones. After long negotiations, a peace was patched together in May 1654, but there was no reversal of the Commonwealth's aggressive commercial policy and no easing of the Navigation Acts. Cromwell extended another Commonwealth policy when he continued to expand the royal navy, once again making Britain a feared seapower.

The prolongation of the Franco-Spanish war offered a new opportunity. If Cromwell were prepared to abandon the idea of a godly foreign policy, he might have his choice of alliance with either. Instead, he decided in the summer of 1654 to attack Spain in the Caribbean, though he was concurrently engaged in an undeclared privateering war against French commerce. In October 1654, Admiral Robert Blake was sent with a squadron to the Mediterranean, where he might threaten France or Spain and deal with Algerian piracy as needed. In the spring of 1655, after a fumbling attempt on Hispaniola failed, an English squadron under Admiral William Penn succeeded in seizing Jamaica from Spain. The tendency has been to see this "Western Design" as a revival of a rather anachronistic Elizabethan strategy—to make war on a profitable basis by attacking

Spain in the West Indies. The huge cost of sustaining the newly built fleet was a serious problem. Avoiding recourse to additional (and unpopular) taxation at home made the Caribbean strategy attractive, but it was as illusory a hope for Cromwell as it had been for *Elizabeth I.

An important consequence of the attack on Spain was the development of a closer relationship with France, which bore fruit in October 1655 in a treaty ending the undeclared war at sea and forcing the Stuart court to depart from France. The importance of unhinging Charles II's French base and forcing him to rely on a weak and declining Spain has been insufficiently appreciated. For the royalists, cut off from potential French aid, Spanish help was necessary; but after many decades of unceasing propaganda against Spanish cruelties to God-fearing Englishmen, the Stuart cause was badly damaged when it was forced to seek Spanish support.

In March 1656, Spain reluctantly declared war on Britain. The failure of the Western Design apparently convinced Cromwell to abandon his Caribbean strategy and, in consequence, in March 1657, he accepted a long proffered French compact calling for a joint war on Spain in the Low Countries with the promise that Britain should have Dunkirk as its reward. In June 1658, success in the Battle of the Dunes yielded that prize. Its possession strengthened Cromwell's hand against both the Flemish privateeers and potential invaders of Britain. On this note of triumph, Cromwell died a few months later, on September 3, 1658.

Students of Cromwellian foreign policy in the nineteenth and early twentieth century approvingly saw him as a vigorous builder of both empire and a strongly expansionary commercial policy. More recently, it has been emphasized that the overriding concern shaping his foreign policy was the domestic stability and security of his regime. It is undeniable that under Cromwell's leadership Britain was transformed into a power commanding international respect. The contrast to Britain's weakness under the Stuart kings is quite striking.

Nevertheless, despite his success, the conduct of Cromwell's foreign policy, like the rest of his career, has remained a controversial subject from the beginning. There are two basic lines of criticism. Soon after his death it became apparent that Spanish power had declined quite precipitously. Since France had quickly established itself as the most powerful state in western Europe, the case was made that this was due to Cromwell's failure to appreciate the French threat. Cromwell's anti-Spanish policy and the botched Western Design are seen as products of his backward-looking Elizabethan approach, which blinded him to the danger of rising French power. The international scene had been transformed by the decline of Spain, but Cromwell seemed unaware of it. Similarly, Cromwell has been criticized for subordinating the nation's economic interests to his equally old-fashioned and rather obsessive hopes for a godly alliance, treating Britain's principal commercial rival, the Dutch, far too leniently simply because they were coreligionists.

The true measure of Cromwell's success as a manager of foreign policy, however, must be the grudging respect and security he won for his fragile republic. In the longer perspective, if historian Christopher Hill's interpretation is to be accepted, Cromwell's policy broke new ground, for it was designed purposefully to advance national interests unencumbered by the private concerns of a ruling dynasty. The state was to be used as an instrument in the struggle to gain colonies and to support the country's commercial interests. While this may overstate the case and exaggerate the degree to which it was pursued consciously, it was the direction in which all national policymaking would inexorably move. At the very least, it may be said that Cromwell's readiness to restrain his own religious predilections in pursuit of reasons of state showed that his shrewd pragmatism ultimately prevailed over his ideological enthusiasm. In that respect, he did as well or better than many of the statesmen who have succeeded him in the past three and a half centuries.

Annotated Bibliography

The basic repositories of archival material for the study of Cromwell's diplomacy are the Public Record Office (PRO), Chancery Lane, London, where the official records of the British government before 1700 are kept, and the British Library (BL), Great Russell Street, London, whose manuscript collections hold many relevant official and personal papers. The PRO holdings most germane here are the State Papers Foreign. Arranged by country and chronologically, they contain correspondence from ambassadors and agents, some intelligence reports, drafts of instructions, and treaty proposals. Other relevant materials on domestic political, military, and some naval matters are found in the State Papers Domestic. In the seventeenth century, government papers were very frequently carried away by officials on leaving office and ended up among their surviving personal papers. The BL has many such collections, the most important one for the study of Cromwell being John Thurloe's. The BL also possesses the unmatched collection of printed ephemera from the interregnum, the Thomason Tracts, contemporary pamphlets full of the polemical political and religious controversies of the day and much else. The Bodleian Library at Oxford also has an important body of material relevant to the 1650s, including the Tanner and Rawlinson collections and, for the royalists, the Clarendon State Papers. Some of the latter have been published as *State Papers Collected by Edward, Earl of Clarendon, Commencing 1621* (1767–1786). These libraries all require prior arrangement to make use of their collections.

Cromwell wrote no memoirs or autobiography. A substantial body of his correspondence, especially after 1640, has survived, however. Some of it is official, but much of it is private, revealing something of his character and personality. There are also various accounts of his parliamentary speeches. This material was collected by an admiring Thomas Carlyle in *Oliver Cromwell's letters and speeches; with elucidations* (1892). The work was redone in a fuller fashion, without Carlyle's exuberance and literary flair, by W. C. Abbott, *Writings and Speeches of Oliver Cromwell* (1937–1947), with a perspective far more critical than Carlyle's. Ivan Roots, ed., *Speeches of Oliver Cromwell* (1989), includes a helpful introduction. Cromwell could be forceful and pithy in his speeches. He could also be incoherent and unclear. What he said often reveals his strong emotional commitments, to a godly foreign policy, for example, but his speeches are a poor guide to his thinking about the complexities of international relations.

There is neither a comprehensive, modern, scholarly account of Cromwell's foreign policy nor an adequate, up-to-date overview of British foreign policy in the seventeenth century. This is curious since the general literature about Cromwell is vast. In 1929 Abbott listed more than 3,500 items in his bibliography, and much has been written since. While Cromwell has been well supplied with biographies covering his whole career, most deal only briefly with his foreign policy.

The best detailed narrative of the Protectorate remains S. R. Gardiner's *History of the Commonwealth and Protectorate* (1894–1901), continued down to Cromwell's death by C. H. Firth in *The Last Years of the Protectorate* (1909). Despite their age and a drumbeat of criticism for their outdated Whiggish suppositions, these accounts, based on an unmatched study of the sources, continue to be useful. Both pay attention to the details of Cromwell's foreign policy, which is treated respectfully, if critically, as a partial failure. Firth's *Oliver Cromwell and the Rule of the Puritans in England* (1900) provides a judiciously balanced summary with a chapter devoted to foreign policy. Brief overviews of foreign policy are provided in J. R. Jones, *Britain and Europe in the Seventeenth Century* (1966), and G.M.D. Howat, *Stuart and Cromwellian Foreign Policy* (1974), though neither seems fully satisfactory to many scholars. More recently, Jones has written *Britain and the World 1649–1815* (1980), which is largely concerned with developments after 1688 but devotes a section to the Dutch wars. A problem clearly has been the long neglect of the area. Without a sufficient number of careful monographic studies as a basis, an adequate synthesis can hardly be done.

Controversy over Cromwell's foreign policy began with the Stuart Restoration. James Heath's *Flagellum or the Life of Oliver Cromwell* (1663) was unrelentingly hostile and set the tone for unsparing royalist attacks. Slingsby Bethel, *The World's Mistake in Oliver Cromwell* (1669), made the case against Cromwell's religious fanaticism and tried to hold him responsible for allowing the French menace to develop. Edmund Ludlow's *Memoirs* (1698–1699) present an equally hostile republican view. The Earl of Clarendon's royalist appreciation of Cromwell as ''a brave bad man,'' in his *History of the Rebellion and Civil Wars in England* (1702), concedes the effectiveness of Cromwell's foreign policy, a worthy testimonial from an old enemy who had dealt with many of the same foreign policy problems in the 1660s. The principal defense of Cromwell's foreign policy rested on the case made for him by John Thurloe, his chief of intelligence. No contemporary was better informed than Thurloe about Cromwell's plans, and his papers, *A Collection of the State Papers of John Thurloe* (1742), edited by Thomas Birch, have been the principal published primary source for the Protectorate's foreign policy. In the hostile political climate after the Stuart Restoration, Thurloe tended to stress Cromwell's firmness against the Dutch, simplifying and indeed distorting the Protector's concerns to put him in the most favorable light.

The prevailing view of Cromwell until Carlyle's time was critical, though most of the fire was directed at his domestic politics. Thereafter, Cromwell's reputation grew for the next half century, reaching its height at the same time that British imperial and commercial power did. A classic, late Victorian overview of foreign policy is J. R. Seeley, *The Growth of British Policy* (1895), which devotes approving attention to Cromwell as a founder of the colonial empire. J. S. Corbett, *England in the Mediterranean* (1904), details the Protectorate's naval policy and diplomatic strategy in a similar fashion. Scholarly monographs on various aspects of Cromwellian foreign policy from this period include Jacob N. Bowman, *The Protestant Interest in Cromwell's Foreign Relations* (1900), Guernsey Jones, *The Diplomatic Relations Between Cromwell and Charles Gustavus X of Sweden* (1897), and, rather later, Edgar Prestage, *The Diplomatic Relations of Portugal with France, England and Holland from 1640 to 1668* (1925).

By the time Abbott's collection of writings and speeches began to appear in the late 1920s, establishing a convenient and more reliable basis for further investigation of Cromwell's career, scholarly interest in Cromwellian foreign policy was clearly on the decline. In retrospect, Abbott's unsympathetic view of Cromwell's foreign policy and his general interpretation of Cromwell as a proto-fascist dictator came to be seen as overly influenced by the atmosphere of the 1930s, when parliamentary democracy was under siege. Maurice Ashley's *Oliver Cromwell: The Conservative Dictator* (1937) is similar in tone. Ashley's later *The Greatness of Oliver Cromwell* (1957) is better balanced in its judgments and provides some limited comment on foreign policy. It is Ashley's first book, however, *Financial and Commercial Policy under the Cromwellian Protectorate* (1934), which has retained value as a background to the study of Cromwellian foreign policy with its scrutiny of the state's finances. The distinguished Dutch scholar Peter Geyl, in *Orange and Stuart 1641–1672* (1969), has examined the crucial dynastic connection from Dutch materials with the emphasis on the Orange side of the story.

Cromwell's foreign policy remains neglected despite the steady stream of recent biographies. Robert S. Paul's *The Lord Protector: Religion and Politics in the Life of Oliver Cromwell* (1955) centers on Cromwell's Calvinism. Christopher Hill's *God's Englishman: Oliver Cromwell and the English Revolution* (1970) is a sympathetic portrait of the ruler as tolerant radical and offers a balanced defense of his foreign policy, arguing that Cromwell's religious and economic policies did not necessarily conflict. Antonia Fraser's detailed study, *Cromwell the Lord Protector* (1973), is sympathetic as well. Intended for a general rather than a scholarly audience, it is based almost exclusively on printed materials focusing on the man and the interplay of his personal life with his political career. Though it is as full and as thoughtful an account as the scholars have produced, it has little new to say about foreign policy. Of the most recent biographies, Roger Howell's *Oliver Cromwell* (1977) provides some shrewd comment on foreign policy, generally defending Cromwell. Pauline Gregg's *Oliver Cromwell* (1988) virtually ignores the subject, and a collective effort edited by John S. Morrill, *Oliver Cromwell and the English Revolution* (1990), provides an up-to-date scholarly assessment of the whole career but regards Protectorate foreign policy as beyond its brief.

Despite the paucity of original research or scholarly reinterpretation, some serious work has appeared in journals. Menna Prestwich's sharp critique of Cromwellian economic policy, "Diplomacy and Trade in the Protectorate," *Journal of Modern History* 22 (1950): 103–121, revived Bethel's attack, and that of the London merchant community, on Cromwell. This was answered first by Charles Wilson's study of the first and second Dutch wars, *Profit and Power* (1957), which took a more supportive view of Cromwell's economic policies, and then by Michael Roberts's useful essay, "Cromwell and the Baltic," *English Historical Review* 72(1961): 402–446, which focused on the Protectorate's relations with Sweden and Denmark but also reconsidered the literature on Cromwell's foreign policy. Roberts argued that Cromwell's restraint in dealing with the Dutch in the Baltic was practical and prudent, driven by long-term concerns about access to strategic naval stores, for example, and not confused by religious fanaticism.

In a similar vein, Roger Crabtree's essay in Ivan Roots, ed., *Cromwell: A Profile* (1973), effectively defends Cromwell's foreign policy as a reasonable one based on the assumptions prevalent in his day, and not one driven by religious fanaticism or commitment to an anachronistic Elizabethan worldview. The anachronism, Crabtree suggests, lies in the minds of modern historians expecting a seventeenth-century statesman to share their own assumptions about balance of power politics. R. C. Thompson's "Officers,

Merchants and Foreign Policy in the Protectorate of Oliver Cromwell,'' *Historical Studies Australia and New Zealand* 12 (1966): 149–165, explores the role of pressure groups in the formulation of Cromwellian foreign policy.

Charles P. Korr's *Cromwell and the New Model Foreign Policy* (1975) is the only relatively recent book-length treatment of Cromwell's foreign policy. Based on a careful study of the manuscript record of relations with France, it argues that these were pivotal in the making of British policy. The case is persuasively made that the main objective of Cromwell's foreign policy was the security of the regime and the prevention of a Stuart restoration. The bibliography is extensive. Bernard Capp's *Cromwell's Navy* (1989) devotes a substantial section to Cromwellian diplomacy and draws attention to the policy implications of the heavy financial pressure caused by the need to support the huge republican fleet.

For guidance on the vast literature about Cromwell, see W. C. Abbott's *Bibliography of Oliver Cromwell* (1929), which should be supplemented by Paul Hardacre's "Writings on Oliver Cromwell since 1929," *Journal of Modern History* 33 (1961): 1–14, and for more recent work down to 1980, John Morrill's general bibliography, *Seventeenth Century Britain* (1980).

Bibliography

Abbott, W. C. *Bibliography of Oliver Cromwell: A List of Printed Materials*. Cambridge, Mass.: Harvard University Press, 1929.

———. *Writings and Speeches of Oliver Cromwell*. 4 vols. Cambridge, Mass.: Harvard University Press, 1937–1947.

Ashley, Maurice. *Financial and Commercial Policy under the Cromwellian Protectorate*. London: Oxford University Press, 1934.

———. *The Greatness of Oliver Cromwell*. New York: Macmillan, 1957.

———. *Oliver Cromwell: The Conservative Dictator*. London: Cape, 1937.

Bethel, Slingsby. *The World's Mistake in Oliver Cromwell*. 3rd ed. London: N.p., 1669.

Birch, Thomas, ed. *A Collection of the State Papers of John Thurloe*. 7 vols. London: N.p., 1742.

Bowman, Jacob N. *The Protestant Interest in Cromwell's Foreign Relations*. Heidelberg: Winter, 1900.

Capp, Bernard. *Cromwell's Navy*. Oxford: Oxford University Press, 1989.

Carlyle, Thomas, ed. *Oliver Cromwell's letters and speeches; with elucidations*. 3 vols. complete in one. London: Ward, Lock, Bowden, 1892.

Clarendon, Edward, Earl of. *The History of the Rebellion and Civil Wars in England Begun in the Year 1641*. 6 vols. Edited by W. D. McRay. Oxford: Clarendon Press, 1888.

Corbett, Julian S. *England in the Mediterranean: A Study of the Rise and Influence of British Power within the Straits 1603–1712*. 2 vols. London: Longmans, 1904.

Crabtree, Roger. "The Idea of a Protestant Foreign Policy." In *Cromwell: A Profile*, pp. 160–189. Edited by Ivan Roots. London: Macmillan, 1973.

Firth, C. H. *The Last Years of the Protectorate*. 2 vols. New York: Longmans, 1909.

———. *Oliver Cromwell and the Rule of the Puritans in England*. London: Oxford University Press, 1900.

Fraser, Antonia. *Cromwell the Lord Protector*. New York: Knopf, 1973.

Gardiner, S. R. *History of the Commonwealth and Protectorate*. 3 vols. London: Longmans, 1894–1901.

Geyl, Peter. *Orange and Stuart 1641–1672*. London: Weidenfeld and Nicolson, 1969.

Gregg, Pauline. *Oliver Cromwell*. London: Dent, 1988.

Hardacre, Paul. "Writings on Oliver Cromwell Since 1929." *Journal of Modern History* 33 (1961): 1–14.

Heath, James. *Flagellum or the Life of Oliver Cromwell*. London: N.p. 1663.

Hill, Christopher. *God's Englishman: Oliver Cromwell and the English Revolution*. New York: Dial Press, 1970.

Howat, G.M.D. *Stuart and Cromwellian Foreign Policy*. New York: St. Martin's Press, 1974.

Howell, Roger. *Oliver Cromwell*. Boston: Little, Brown, 1977.

Jones, Guernsey. *The Diplomatic Relations Between Cromwell and Charles Gustavus X of Sweden*. Lincoln, Nebr.: State Journal Co., 1897.

Jones, J. R. *Britain and Europe in the Seventeenth Century*. London: Edward Arnold, 1966.

———. *Britain and the World 1649–1815*. Atlantic Highlands, N.J.: Humanities Press, 1980.

Korr, Charles P. *Cromwell and the New Model Foreign Policy*. Berkeley: University of California Press, 1975.

Ludlow, Edmund. *The Memoirs of Edmund Ludlow, lieutenant-general of the horse in the army of the commonwealth of England*. 2 vols. Edited by C. H. Firth. Oxford: Clarendon Press, 1894.

Morrill, John S., ed. *Oliver Cromwell and the English Revolution*. London: Longmans, 1990.

———. *Seventeenth Century Britain 1603–1714*. Hamden, Conn.: Archon, 1980.

Paul, Robert S. *The Lord Protector: Religion and Politics in the Life of Oliver Cromwell*. London: Luttersworth Press, 1955.

Prestage, Edgar. *The Diplomatic Relations of Portugal with France, England and Holland from 1640 to 1668*. Watford: Voss and Michael, 1925.

Prestwich, Menna. "Diplomacy and Trade in the Protectorate." *Journal of Modern History* 22 (1950): 103–121.

Roberts, Michael. "Cromwell and the Baltic." *English Historical Review* 76 (1961): 402–446.

Roots, Ivan, ed. *Cromwell: A Profile*. London: Macmillan, 1973.

———, ed. *Speeches of Oliver Cromwell*. London: Dent, 1989.

Scrope, R., and T. Monkhouse, eds. *State Papers collected by Edward, earl of Clarendon, commencing from the year 1621*. 3 vols. Oxford: Clarendon Press, 1767–1786.

Seeley, J. R. *The Growth of British Policy*. Cambridge: Cambridge University Press, 1895.

Thompson, R. C. "Officers, Merchants and Foreign Policy in the Protectorate of Oliver Cromwell" *Historical Studies Australia and New Zealand* 12 (1966): 149–165.

Wilson, Charles. *Profit and Power: A Study of the Dutch Wars*. New York: Longmans, Green, 1957.

S. J. STEARNS

Adam Czartoryski (1770–1861).   Few public figures experienced as long or varied a career as Prince Adam Czartoryski. In an active political life spanning seven decades, Czartoryski went from personal advisor and foreign minister to Tsar *Alexander I to de facto leader of a Polish government-in-exile and implacable foe of Tsar Nicholas I. His accomplishments included the construction of an anti-Napoleonic coalition, the preservation of the Polish Question during the nineteenth century, and the stimulation of nascent Balkan nationalisms. Yet Czartoryski remains today one of the least known of nineteenth-century statesmen.

Prince Adam, as Czartoryski came to be known, was born into one of Poland's wealthiest and most influential noble families on January 14, 1770, in Warsaw. Educated at the height of the Enlightenment, Czartoryski absorbed the progressive political virtues of the philosophes: personal liberty, constitutionalism, civic action, and the spirit of egalitarianism. His parents instilled in him a deep sense of Polish patriotism and duty. Extensive travel in Prussia, France, and England acquainted him with the diversity of Europe, helped him established the aristocratic contacts that would serve him in the future, and imbued in him a deep appreciation for the British constitutional system. These experiences also gave him an appreciation of the growing force of nationalism.

Czartoryski's diplomatic career clearly demonstrates the underlying goals that motivated him. He sought the restoration of a viable, independent Polish state; he opposed any attempt to gain hegemony over Europe; he believed that Europe should become a federation of independent nations. Within this context, his activities and his achievements become more understandable.

For practical purposes, Czartoryski's political career may be divided into three segments: the Russian, 1795–1815; the Polish, 1815–1831; and the exile, 1831–1861. The Russian phase began as the result of his family's opposition to Russian domination of Poland. When the Czartoryskis opposed Russia during the Second and Third Partitions of Poland, *Catherine the Great required the family to send Prince Adam to St. Petersburg as surety for its good behavior. At first Czartoryski hated all things Russian. His attitude changed when he became the confidant of the future tsar, Alexander I. Somewhat younger than Prince Adam, Alexander also had been exposed to the ideas of the Enlightenment. Sharing youthful idealism and, at least outwardly, the desire to reform Russia, Czartoryski, despite his Polish roots, found himself part of a small circle of like-minded Russian nobles who surrounded Alexander. Including Count Paul Stroganov, Nicholas N. Novosiltsov, and Prince Victor P. Kochubey, this circle worked to strengthen Alexander's reforming proclivities.

Prince Adam soon earned the enmity of Alexander's father, Tsar Paul, as much for his political ideas as for his love affair with Alexander's wife, the Tsarina Elizabeth. For this he was virtually exiled to Sardinia in 1799. Before returning to St. Petersburg after Paul's death, Prince Adam familiarized himself with Italian affairs, thus beginning his education as a diplomat.

Among Alexander's advisors, Czartoryski took the lead in trying to convince him to introduce a modern constitutional form of government. Although Alexander frequently alluded to constitutional change, even at one point instructing Michael Speransky to prepare plans for a constitution, he never implemented any changes.

Alexander appointed Czartoryski deputy foreign minister to the aged Alexander Vorontsov late in 1802. In 1804 Alexander named him foreign minister. Czartoryski simultaneously held other important posts. As curator of the University of Vilna, he was virtually minister of education for the Lithuanian region. Prince Adam sat in both the Senate and the State Council, where, as principal advisor to Alexander, he enjoyed great power. Nevertheless, the autocratic nature of the system and Alexander's personal whims severely circumscribed Czartoryski's abilities.

In his 1803 memorandum, "Political System to be Adopted by Russia," Prince Adam argued for a union of nations, a view he later elaborated in his *Essai sur la diplomatie*. Czartoryski identified three necessary conditions for this union: (1) the progress of civilization among backward nations; (2) a redrawing of frontiers based on nationality and natural boundaries; and (3) adoption of liberal institutions and representative governments.

Prince Adam's diplomacy was part of a dual strategy he pursued after 1803. Internally, he continued his efforts to persuade Alexander to create the liberal institutions that would transform Russia and allow it to take its place among the nations of Europe. Externally, Czartoryski's foreign policy attempted to build a "Grand Design," modeled after his 1803 memorandum, that would restructure Europe along broadly nationalistic lines in opposition to the hegemony pursued by *Napoleon I.

Despite Alexander's habitual vacillation, Prince Adam eventually built a coalition against Napoleon that might have defeated the French during the War of the Third Coalition. However, disregarding Czartoryski's advice, Alexander intervened in Russia's diplomacy with Prussia, reneged on his pledge to the Poles, angered the British, and precipitated military action against the French, which led to the defeat at Austerlitz. In need of an official scapegoat, Alexander dismissed Czartoryski from office on July 1, 1806.

The remainder of the Napoleonic Wars must have frustrated Czartoryski, who saw Alexander rejecting his ideas and ignoring his advice. Yet Napoleon's defeat opened the way for Czartoryski once again to affect the course of European diplomacy. At the Congress of Vienna, Prince Adam once more found himself the trusted advisor of Alexander.

At the end of 1812, the Grand Duchy of Warsaw, one of Napoleon's puppet creations, appealed to Prince Adam to mediate with Alexander to decide its future. Czartoryski began the series of diplomatic maneuvers that convinced the tsar to create an independent Polish state as part of the general European peace settlement. Through months of difficult negotiations, Czartoryski battled against *Talleyrand, *Metternich, Hardenburg, and *Castlereagh, as well as against many of Alexander's other advisors. That he prevailed and secured the recognition of a Polish state, albeit truncated and joined to Russia, is evidence of Prince Adam's abilities.

After the agreement was reached, Alexander sent Czartoryski to Warsaw to establish the new state's institutions. For a brief period he was de facto ruler, a position he fully expected Alexander would confirm by naming him as viceroy. However, Alexander bypassed Czartoryski and gave control of the Polish state, the so-called Congress Kingdom, to his brother, Grand Duke Constantine. This bitter blow brought to an end the Russian phase of Czartoryski's career.

Although appointed to the Senate and to the Administrative Council of the Congress Kingdom, Czartoryski began the second phase of his career quietly. He effectively withdrew from political life and devoted his energies to his duties as curator of the University of Vilna, to writing, and to marriage. His tenure as curator ended unhappily when the rising spirit of Polish nationalism at the university provoked a harsh crackdown, leading to Czartoryski's dismissal and his final break with Alexander in 1823–1824.

Between 1824 and 1827, Prince Adam traveled abroad, using the opportunity to forge new links with European statesmen. He also wrote his political treatise, *Essai sur la diplomatie*, a major, if little known, contribution to the history of diplomatic thought. Imbued with Enlightenment concepts, Czartoryski's work was modeled after the ideas of the Duc de Sully and argued for restructuring Europe along nationalistic lines. He foresaw a series of federations including a Balkan one, a Slavic one, and a German one, whose existence would maintain peace and harmony in Europe. Basically elaborating on ideas he had developed at the time of the Napoleonic Wars, Czartoryski now viewed Russia rather than France as the chief antagonist in Europe.

Prince Adam returned to Poland in 1827, in time to play a significant role in the trial of Poles accused of conspiracy in the Decembrist uprising at the time of Nicholas I's accession to the Russian throne in 1825. The enmity between Nicholas and Czartoryski was strong, a factor that affected many of Prince Adam's subsequent activities. Much to Nicholas's dismay, Czartoryski convinced the court that the Poles had not been directly involved in the conspiracy (as indeed they were not), thus ensuring that they would receive light punishments. This only increased Nicholas's dislike of the Poles and heightened his resolve to break them.

Prince Adam now found himself leading the struggle for Polish rights against Russia. At no time did he advocate revolution; but the outbreak of revolution in Paris in July 1830 stimulated conspiratorial activity among young Poles seeking independence from Russia. Informed of the plots, Czartoryski attempted to dissuade the conspirators and took steps to persuade Grand Duke Constantine not to take any action against the Poles. Reacting against the Paris revolution, Nicholas hoped to send Russian troops to France to restore the old order. Czartoryski understood clearly that any Polish uprising at this time might save the French from Nicholas but would leave his countrymen vulnerable. Despite his efforts, Prince Adam failed to prevent an uprising against Russia on November 29, 1830.

Electing to join with his people and serve his country, Czartoryski took control of the government shortly after the outbreak of revolution. On January 29, 1831, Czartoryski was elected chairman (president) of the newly proclaimed national government. He held this post until August 15, when the government was over-thrown in a protest against the military failures of the Polish army. As president, Czartoryski worked tirelessly for the Polish cause. He suggested the possibility of establishing a dynastic tie with Austria once the Polish throne was declared vacant. Realizing that both negotiations with the Russians and support from friendly governments depended on military success, Czartoryski urged his generals to push for a victory. Throughout the European capitals, his diplomacy sought understanding and friendship for Poland and attempted to pave the way for mediation with Russia. Although Czartoryski met with sympathy in France and Austria, Britain, under *Palmerston, remained cold to Polish initiatives and limited itself to verbal support for the Polish cause. These posturings convinced Czartoryski that the Poles would have to decide their own fate on the battlefields and not count on foreign support, a conviction that influenced his later actions in exile. Faced with a lack of support from outside Poland, a series of relatively incompetent military commanders, and the overwhelming size of Russia's military forces, even Polish valor could not prevail. As Russian troops continued to occupy the country, Prince Adam, fearing for his life, went into permanent exile on September 27 at Cracow.

Entering exile at a time when most men retire from active life, Prince Adam began a third phase of public activity during which he influenced political developments throughout the Continent. Czartoryski established his permanent home in Paris, where he created what effectively became a government-in-exile and founded an organization to pursue diplomatic activities later known as the Hotel Lambert, named after his residence. He now devised a diplomatic program designed to establish a legitimate Polish presence in international relations and to emphasize to the Western powers the threat posed by Russia.

On this basis Czartoryski initiated a broad-based diplomacy, eventually constructing a network of agencies throughout western Europe and the Near East. Although his Hotel Lambert undertook initiatives across Europe, two areas, France and Britain on one hand and the Ottoman Empire on the other, attained special significance. By the early 1840s, Prince Adam had established permanent agencies in Paris, London, Rome, Constantinople, and Belgrade. He also relied on subordinates in the field to perform specific missions. Although his associates had considerable autonomy in their day-to-day activities, there is no question that Prince Adam determined overall policy. Extensive use of diplomatic mail permitted him to maintain close control over his agents.

At first Prince Adam concentrated his efforts in Paris and London, where he created a secondary center under his nephew, Władysław Zamoyski. Czartoryski sought recognition of the Polish military exiles as political refugees, which would enable them to receive subsidies from the British and French governments, and he attempted to establish Polish Legions as separate military units as a way to assure the continued recognition of a Polish state. Prince Adam also argued that Britain and France, as signatories to the Vienna accords that had established the Congress Kingdom, were guarantors of its legal existence.

In both Paris and London, the Hotel Lambert undertook direct negotiations with the respective governments. Czartoryski also employed propaganda to mobilize influential public opinion in support of the Polish cause. Utilizing the contacts he had cultivated earlier, Prince Adam achieved some success. With the support of enthusiastic and influential Polonophiles such as Lord Dudley Stuart and William Fox Strangways in Britain, and Emile Desages and Pierre Cintrat in France, the Hotel Lambert's exile diplomacy kept the Polish Question alive for several decades. Furthermore, Czartoryski vigorously supported the foreign policies of Britain and France in the hope of gaining not only their diplomatic support but also their future military aid to help restore an independent Poland.

The most significant aspect of Czartoryski's diplomatic program was his Balkan policy, which rested on the belief that the Ottoman state must be preserved, at least temporarily, as a counterweight to Russia. Although basically anti-Russian, Czartoryski's policy interested not only Britain and France, both of whom saw this area as vital to their interests, but also the Slavs and other Christians under Ottoman rule as well as the Slavs under Habsburg domination.

Czartoryski initially advocated a thorough modernization of the Ottoman military. Two missions undertaken by General Wojciech Chrzanowski achieved qualified success. However, the experiences of other agents in the Balkans and a reorientation of the Hotel Lambert's diplomacy toward France as a result of the Anglo-Russian détente of 1840 convinced Czartoryski that a more comprehensive approach was necessary. He now viewed the internal instability of the Ottoman Empire as the major problem.

As early as 1839, Prince Adam had held numerous discussions with the Ottoman ambassador, Reshid Pasha. Czartoryski expressed his views on Ottoman reform and presented him with a memorandum outlining several recommendations for the Ottoman government to improve its political situation. Shortly after Reshid returned to Constantinople to take the post of Grand Vizier, the Hatti Sherif of Gulhane, a document considered to be the beginning of the Tanzimat (Reform) period, was promulgated. To at least some extent, Czartoryski helped to initiate the Ottoman reform movement.

Czartoryski also developed new programs for the Balkan peoples. He advised the Porte to grant the Balkan peoples greater autonomy in their internal development. Simultaneously, he sought to influence the national movements which arose in opposition to Ottoman control and which were encouraged by Russia and Austria. Between 1841 and 1845, these programs met with some success. Czartoryski and his chief agent in Constantinople, Michat Czajkowski, persuaded the government to respect the religions and nationalities of its subjects and to allow them more internal autonomy. At the same time, the Hotel Lambert convinced the Slavs that they had less to fear from Ottoman rule than from Russian control. These efforts checked the threat of Russian encroachment for several years.

In Serbia, Czartoryski's policies helped to establish the anti-Russian and anti-

Habsburg prince Alexander Karageorgevic on the throne. Through his agent in Belgrade, František Zach, Prince Adam transmitted his ideas for Serbia's future political development as the focal point of a south Slav federation, a concept that guided Serbia's politicians well into the twentieth century. In Bosnia, the Hotel Lambert weakened Austrian influence and fostered Bosnia's national development. Among the Bulgarians, Czartoryski's diplomacy aided educational progress and supported the monks Neofit Bozveli and Hilarion Makariopolski in their struggle to gain control of the Bulgarian Orthodox Church from the Greek patriarch.

However, by the mid–1840s Czartoryski had little new to offer to the peoples of the Ottoman Empire. Although he and his followers had fostered the growth of Balkan nationalisms, they failed to evoke any greater responses. The Hotel Lambert attempted tasks beyond the capabilities of even larger diplomatic entities. Lacking funds and manpower, Czartoryski tried, almost singlehandedly, to combat Russian and Austrian influence in the Balkans. France and Britain, although utilizing the Hotel Lambert for their own objectives, saw little reason to oppose Russia or Austria for the sake of a state that no longer existed and still less for the sake of national groups in the Balkans that remained almost totally foreign to them. Deeper involvement meant the risk of war with Russia, a step neither Western power was ready to contemplate.

More significant, however, was the attitude of the Balkan peoples themselves. Although Czartoryski's program was anti-Russian and pro-Ottoman, the Balkan peoples followed Polish suggestions only as long as they served to advance their own political and religious independence. Once they had achieved some success, they rejected Prince Adam's program in favor of developing their own nationalism. The Balkan peoples did not share Czartoryski's deep aversion to Russia. Although mistrustful, they believed that they could use Russia as well as Poland to achieve the liberation of their countries from Ottoman domination. Czartoryski had based his diplomatic initiatives on concepts that rejected one country's domination over another and endorsed the full development of peoples in a spirit of equality among nations. In return, he anticipated that those he aided would lend their support to the cause of Polish independence. Instead they turned away.

The year 1848 marked the close of a major phase in Czartoryski's life. Although his Hotel Lambert would continue to function for many years, the most creative phase of its existence ended. In the course of the next decade, the programs Czartoryski and his associates advocated were, with few exceptions, tepid revisions of older policies. Active participation in Balkan politics had a brief, if fruitless, resurgence during the revolutionary activities of 1848–1849. Czartoryski's Italian policy accomplished nothing, while his efforts in the West met with studied indifference as a new generation of diplomats came on the scene.

During the Crimean War, Polish Legions formed in the Ottoman Empire once again brought the Hotel Lambert a degree of prominence. Their military aid was gratefully accepted by France and Britain in the struggle against Russia, but at the time of the peace settlement Polish aspirations were totally ignored. Czartoryski and his organization had overestimated their importance and received nothing for their efforts. Equally important, the new generation of political leaders, who were far removed from the world that had formed Czartoryski's attitudes, now viewed Prince Adam's policies as anachronistic. After 1856 the prestige and activity of the Hotel Lambert declined. In this sense Prince Adam's death on July 15, 1861, was of little significance to European politics. He had outlived his era, and his numerous successes and often prescient concepts had been forgotten along with the man.

Annotated Bibliography

Prince Adam Czartoryski's papers are located in the Czartoryski Library in Cracow, ul. Św. Marka 17. These are the complete papers, covering not only his youth, but also his period as Russian foreign minister as well as all facets of his exile diplomacy. Included are Czartoryski's correspondence, copies of his instructions to his agents, their reports to him, correspondence to his agents from other sources, some newspaper articles, and copies of official documents. These papers alone fill several hundred volumes. The archives are relatively well organized, and the staff is both knowledgeable and helpful to researchers. Although a letter of introduction is useful and should be presented by anyone doing extensive research, personal identification has been sufficient for anyone doing research for brief periods. There are no restrictions on the use of the material. The library is generally open from 9 A.M. to 2 P.M. during the week, with some evening hours also. It has been the practice to close the library during August.

Prince Adam Czartoryski's *Memoirs* (1888) are primarily concerned with his early life up to the Congress of Vienna. They provide a detailed picture of his upbringing as well as his diplomacy during the time when he was Russian foreign minister engaged in building an anti-Napoleonic coalition. The work is invaluable for his views on Russia's development, his insights concerning Tsar Alexander I, and his actions at Vienna leading to the establishment of the Congress Kingdom. Additions by the editor provide sketchy coverage of Prince Adam's post–1831 life.

Czartoryski's *Essai sur la diplomatie* (1830) develops in detail the principles he first propounded in 1803. In this work, originally published anonymously, Czartoryski calls for restructuring Europe along liberal, national lines. It provides the philosophical outlines that guided Prince Adam's diplomacy throughout his lifetime.

The Polish historian Marceli Handelsman provides the most comprehensive early study of Czartoryski's diplomacy. In *La Question d'Orient et la politique yougoslave du prince Czartoryski après 1840* (1929), *Le Prince Czartoryski et la Roumanie 1834–1850* (1933), *Czartoryski, Nicholas I et la question du Proche Orient* (1934), *Rok 1848 we Włoszech i polityka Ks. Adama Czartoryskiego* (1936), and *Ukraińska polityka księcia Adama Czartoryskiego przed wojną krymską* (1937), Handelsman carefully examined the specific aspects of Prince Adam's diplomacy. He developed the romantic-nationalist view that Czartoryski and Nicholas I personified a struggle between Poland and Russia, between the ideas of the Enlightenment and the Old Regime, between good and evil. Handelsman's greatest achievement, *Adam Czartoryski* (1948–1950), further elaborates these ideas. Published posthumously, the work is difficult to read, but it is the most thorough biography extant.

Marian Kukiel's *Czartoryski and European Unity* (1955) presents Prince Adam as an early proponent of continental unity, stressing the concepts Czartoryski developed in his own published works. Having been director of the Czartoryski Archives, Kukiel was thoroughly familiar with the details of Prince Adam's activities. He tends to concentrate on Czartoryski's life as Russian foreign minister and on the Crimean War.

Patricia Kennedy Grimsted's chapter on Adam Czartoryski in her *Foreign Ministers of Alexander I* (1969) provides a balanced picture of this period in his life. A more detailed account of Prince Adam's efforts to create a coalition to combat Napoleon can be found in Jerzy Skowronek's excellent *Antynapoleońskie koncepcje Czartoryskiego* (1969).

Materials especially helpful in examinir.g Czartoryski's post–1831 diplomacy include the relevant volumes of Władysław Zamoyski's *Jenerał Zamoyski* (1910–1930). Zamoyski, Czartoryski's nephew and chief lieutenant in Great Britain, who also traveled extensively on Hotel Lambert business, provides many details about Czartoryski's Balkan policy and his activity during the Crimean War. Hans Henning Hahn, *Aussenpolitik in der Emigration* (1978), approaches Czartoryski's post–1831 diplomacy from the western European point of view. Focusing primarily on legal arguments and British activities, he concludes that Prince Adam's Hotel Lambert was a forerunner of governments-in-exile. Jerzy Skowronek's *Polityka Bałkańska Hotelu Lambert* (1976) provides a thorough examination of Czartoryski's diplomacy in this area through the Crimean War. His survey stresses the development of Balkan nationalisms as an integral part of Prince Adam's policies.

Bibliography

Czartoryski, Adam Jerzy. *Essai sur la diplomatie: manuscrit d'un Philhellène*. Paris-Marseille: N.p., 1830.

————. *Memoirs of Prince Czartoryski and His Correspondence with Alexander I, with Documents Relative to the Prince's Negotiations with Pitt, Fox Brougham and an Account of His Conversations with Lord Palmerston and Other English Statesmen*. 2 vols. Edited by Adam Gielgud. London: N.p., 1888. Reprint. Orono, Me.: Academic International, 1968.

————. *Pamiętniki i Memoriały Polityczne, 1776–1809*. Edited by Jerzy Skowronek. Warsaw: Pax, 1986.

Grimsted, Patricia Kennedy. *The Foreign Ministers of Alexander I: Political Attitudes and the Conduct of Russian Diplomacy, 1801–1825*. Berkeley: University of California Press, 1969.

Hahn, Hans Henning. *Aussenpolitik in der Emigration: Die Exildiplomatie Adam Jerzy Czartoryskis 1830–1840*. Munich: Oldenbourg, 1978.

Handelsman, Marceli. *Adam Czartoryski*. 3 vols. Warsaw: Towarzystwo Naukowe Warszawskie, 1948–1950.

————. *Czartoryski, Nicholas I et la question du Proche Orient*. Paris: Pedone, 1934.

————. *Le Prince Czartoryski et la Roumanie 1834–1850*. Warsaw: Towarzystwo Naukowe Warszawskie, 1933.

————. *La Question d'Orient et la politique yougoslave du prince Czartoryski après 1840*. Paris: Pedone, 1929.

————. *Rok 1848 we Włoszech i polityka Ks. Adama Czartoryskiego*. Cracow: Polskiej Akademji Umiejętności, 1936.

————. *Ukraińska polityka księcia Adama Czartoryskiego przed wojną krymską*. Warsaw: Prace Ukraińskiego Instytutu Naukowego, 1937.

Kukiel, Marian. *Czartoryski and European Unity 1770–1861*. Princeton, N.J.: Princeton University Press, 1955.
Skowronek, Jerzy. *Antynapoleońskie Koncepcje Czartoryskiego*. Warsaw: Państwowe Wydawnictwo Naukowe, 1969.
———. *Polityka bałkańska Hotelu Lambert (1833–1856)*. Warsaw: UW, 1976.
Zamoyski, Władysław. Jenerał Zamoyski. 6 vols. Poznań: Nakład Biblioteki Kórnickiej, 1910–1930.

ROBERT A. BERRY

Charles de Gaulle (1890–1970).   On March 1, 1941, during the German occupation of France in World War II, General Charles de Gaulle declared in
London that "there is a pact of twenty centuries between the grandeur of France
and the liberty of the world." Twenty-three years later he again asserted that
the nature of the French spirit was "human liberation." These two statements,
the first spoken in exile from a country freshly defeated and under hostile occupation, the second as the leader of an independent, powerful, and prosperous
member of the Western community, summarized de Gaulle's vision of an ancient,
proud, and republican French nation as a force for the progressive unfolding of
human liberty. A career military man who arguably influenced twentieth-century
French political life more than any other one person, de Gaulle fled France after
its defeat by Germany in 1940. He assumed the leadership of the Free French
in exile and returned in triumph in 1944 only to resign in 1946, frustrated by
haggling political parties. He was restored to power during the Algerian crisis
of 1958 and presided over the creation of the Fifth Republic and the extrication
of the French from their long and costly war in Algeria. Through the Nazi
occupation of his homeland and the Soviet-U.S. Cold War domination of Europe,
de Gaulle succeeded in maintaining a high French international presence, first
among the World War II Allies, then in the developing Common Market of the
1960s.
     De Gaulle's insistence that he alone represented France during the occupation
years of 1940–1944, his continual efforts to create a republic with a strong
executive authority, which to some hinted of dictatorship, and his attempts to
weaken American influence in Europe and the world in the 1960s made him a
highly controversial figure during his lifetime. In France, opinions of de Gaulle
varied widely during his career, but since his death they have tended toward an
iconic consensus around him as hero of the Resistance, father of the Fifth
Republic, and restorer of French pride and self-confidence in international affairs.
     Charles André Marie Joseph de Gaulle was born on November 22, 1890, in
the northern French city of Lille. His family roots can be traced at least to 1415
to an ancestor who fought in the Battle of Agincourt against the English. By the
nineteenth century, the de Gaulle family had turned to the practice of law.
Charles's father, Henri, was educated for a military career but was wounded
during the Franco-Prussian War in 1870 and subsequently became a teacher. In
1886 Henri de Gaulle married Jeanne Maillot-Delannoy, a second cousin on his
mother's side. Charles, born in 1890, was the second of five children. His family

was steeped in French history, Catholic and traditional values, and a sense of service. From his parents, Charles de Gaulle also learned to appreciate the elegance of the French language.

Young Charles's early years were spent against a background of the unfolding Dreyfus Affair, in which Captain Alfred Dreyfus, the highest ranking Jewish officer in the French army, was convicted of passing military secrets to the Germans. The "Affair," as it came to be known in France, ended with the exoneration of Dreyfus, but split the Republic into two hostile camps—Republicans, liberals, and socialists, who supported Dreyfus and the Republic, on one hand, and military officers, Church leaders, royalists, and anti-Semites, many of whom opposed the Republic, on the other. In the aftermath of the Dreyfus Affair, Charles, who had been studying at a Jesuit school in Paris, was sent by his father to continue his studies at another Jesuit college, in Belgium. Like others of his generation who sought to serve France but were averse to the parliamentary party politics of the Third Republic, de Gaulle looked for an outlet in the army, in which he enlisted in 1909. A year later he was accepted into the Saint-Cyr military academy, the French equivalent of West Point. Two years later he was posted to a regiment under the command of Colonel Henri Philippe Pétain.

De Gaulle shared with Pétain an austere and aloof demeanor, but both won the respect of their men. Both were outsiders, critical of established military strategies in France and, accordingly, repeatedly passed over for promotion. Fighting under Pétain in World War I, de Gaulle was wounded in action three times and taken prisoner by the Germans during the Battle of Verdun in 1916. Pétain went on to organize the successful defense of Verdun in 1916 and quelled military mutinies in a badly mauled French army the next year. With the victory of 1918, Pétain became a national hero. Despite five unsuccessful attempts to escape, de Gaulle ended up a prisoner of war for the duration of hostilities and spent his time learning German and collecting ideas he used in the books he would later write. After the war, he served with the French forces helping Poland to ward off Bolshevik Russia. In 1921 he returned to Paris, where he married Yvonne Vendroux, the daughter of a biscuit maker from Calais. He was named a history lecturer at Saint-Cyr and with Yvonne settled down to a quiet domestic life, raising a family in Paris. In 1922 he began a course of study at the École Supérieure de Guerre, a war college that favored the defensive tactics of the victorious generals of World War I.

As had once been the case with his patron Pétain, now a marshal of France, de Gaulle rebelled against the military doctrines taught by the General Staff; also like Pétain, he watched promotions go to other candidates. During the mid–1920s, the French military leaders, including Pétain, convinced by their successes in World War I that defense was the strategy of the future, ordered the construction of a series of fortifications, the Maginot Line, to protect against renewed German invasion. De Gaulle argued unsuccessfully for a more mobile strike force to ward off future attacks. Between 1927 and 1931, he served with French forces in Germany and Lebanon, and in 1931 he returned to France, where he continued to argue for a more mobile strike force. The outbreak of World War II in September 1939 found him in command of the tanks of the 5th Army, stationed in support of the Maginot Line along the Rhine in Alsace in eastern France.

During the so-called Phony War, known as the *Drôle de guerre* in France, from September 1939 until May 1940, the Franco-German frontier was relatively quiet while German forces cut through Poland, Denmark, and Norway. On May 10, 1940, the Germans attacked in the west. Although de Gaulle's tank forces fought well, the French army was broken within three weeks by coordinated armored attacks of the kind de Gaulle had favored. On June 17 Marshal Pétain, his old patron, then eighty-four years old and a known supporter of a cease-fire, was named premier. De Gaulle, newly promoted to general, refused to accept the finality of defeat. He and his family sought refuge in London. On June 18 he broadcast a call for the French to defend their national honor and resist the German forces then overrunning the country. Few heard the radio appeal, and most of the French welcomed the armistice that the Pétain government signed, according to which the Germans occupied roughly the northern three-fifths of France, including Paris, and allowed Pétain's government to rule directly in the unoccupied southern zone. The new government set up shop in the spa town of Vichy and promoted collaboration with Hitler's Germany in the belief that Germany would soon defeat England, its lone standing adversary, and rapidly win the war. It was in this setting that de Gaulle was sentenced to death in absentia as a traitor.

To de Gaulle, any collaboration with Germany was a dishonor for France and the values of ''liberty, equality, fraternity,'' for which it had stood since the revolution of 1789. Broadcasting radio speeches back to France, he called upon his fellow citizens to resist the Nazis and organized ''Free France,'' his Resistance movement, renamed ''Fighting France'' in 1942. By the time of the liberation in 1944, he had emerged as the undisputed leader of the French Resistance. Austere and even arrogant in his behavior, de Gaulle saw himself as the incarnation of eternal French ideals and national honor at a time of crisis when no one else would speak up. He refused to compromise on what he considered to be essential issues and quarreled continually with both British Prime Minister *Winston Churchill, his host in exile, and U.S. President *Franklin D. Roosevelt, who withheld formal recognition of the Free French until shortly before the liberation. It was de Gaulle who led the victory parade down the Champs-Élysées in Paris when the city was liberated in August 1944. France was nevertheless excluded from the Yalta and Potsdam conferences, which split Europe into Anglo-American and Soviet zones of influence, and de Gaulle would spend the rest of his career, in and out of office, working to dissolve the bipolar world created in 1945. He was named to head a provisional government while a constitution was drawn up for the new Fourth Republic, but his vision of a republic with a strong executive was thwarted by the rebirth of the prewar political parties, whose increasing strength portended the creation of another factionalized parliamentary regime like the Third Republic, which had died in 1940. Frustrated, he resigned in January 1946.

Out of office, de Gaulle watched France begin a costly war to retain its colony of Indochina. In 1947 the Fourth Republic was established, a virtual copy of the Third. With an intensification of the Cold War between the Soviet Union and the West and the deepening Communist insurgency in Indochina, he launched a new political party, the Rassemblement du Peuple Français (Rally of the French People [RPF]), which emphasized anticommunism and the need for a strong French executive. This party failed to bring him back to power, and he disbanded it in 1953. In 1954 French forces in Indochina were defeated at Dienbienphu and the French withdrew from the country. That same year, a revolt began among the Arabs of Algeria, which had been a French colony since 1830. Dissatisfied with the pace of the military repression of the revolt, European settlers in Algiers and other Algerian cities rioted against the Paris government in May 1958. Metropolitan France was gripped with a fear of crisis and impending civil war. The parliament in Paris invited General de Gaulle to form a new cabinet and voted him the powers to write a revised constitution allowing for a stronger executive.

The result was the Fifth Republic, whose constitution gave added powers to the presidency, especially in the domain of foreign affairs. Named president of the new republic, de Gaulle determined that the only way to end the Algerian war was to grant independence to the Arab insurgents. As his policy became increasingly clear, many of his supporters of 1958 turned bitterly against him, arguing that he had betrayed the cause of French Algeria. Some formed the Organisation Armée Secrète (Secret Army Organization, or OAS), which launched a terror campaign to block the independence of Algeria. De Gaulle withstood coup attempts in 1960 and 1961 and survived several assassination attempts. He maintained his policy, and in March 1962 Algeria was offered independence, confirmed by over 90 percent of the French voting in a referendum the next month. With Algeria gone, de Gaulle then presided over the granting of independence to virtually all of the French colonies in black Africa, thereby changing France from a Western colonial power into a friend of the newly independent countries of the Third World.

In addition to his support for decolonization, de Gaulle worked to build up a strong Europe as a counterbalance to the United States. Through the development of a close working relationship with Chancellor *Konrad Adenauer, he helped create a Franco–West German axis in 1963, which dominated the affairs of the developing Common Market (European Economic Community or EEC, founded 1958). To maintain French influence in the Common Market, he twice vetoed British attempts to join the organization, in 1963 and in 1967. He continued the French nuclear weapons program started under the Fourth Republic and in 1966 pulled the French military out of the North Atlantic Treaty Organization (NATO), which he argued was dominated by the United States. During the early 1960s, he began to move France from a pro-Israel to a more balanced position in Middle East affairs, and after the 1967 Arab-Israeli War he shifted dramatically to a pro-Arab position, further enhancing France's image in the Third World. To spread the *grandeur*, or greatness, of France in the world, he traveled extensively, especially to the Third World, and gave France a larger role in world affairs than was justified by its economic and military power. In support of a greater world role for the French language and Francophone communities, while visiting Montreal in 1967 he called for a "free" Québec, causing a furor in Canada and helping to launch a wave of Québecois national sentiment in the 1970s.

In 1968 President de Gaulle faced his most serious crisis since the Algerian war. University students, angered by authoritarian educational structures and outdated curricula, squalid living conditions among the growing number of Third World and other foreign workers in France, and the American war in Vietnam, took over several campuses in and around Paris during the spring of 1968. French workers opposing governmental policies of low wages joined the students and virtually shut the country down by a general strike in May 1968. Caught off guard by these events, de Gaulle struck a deal with the French military leaders, winning their support against the strikers in return for his granting amnesty to the pro–French Algeria military men charged with plotting against him in the early 1960s. Strengthened by the knowledge that the military would support him in the event of violence, he then called for new parliamentary elections. With increasing numbers of people wearying of the strike, the vote resulted in a sweeping victory for the Gaullists. Nonetheless, de Gaulle's image as a decisive leader had been severely tarnished. To recoup his prestige, early in 1969 he proposed several reforms to decentralize the French government. The package was put to the voters in a referendum that April, and de Gaulle staked his personal prestige on the success of the vote, threatening to resign if it went against him. This time it did. De Gaulle promptly resigned and was succeeded as president by Georges Pompidou, who had been his prime minister from 1961 through the crisis of 1968. Retiring with Madame de Gaulle to their country estate at Colombey-les-deux-Églises, the General worked on his memoirs until his death on November 9, 1970.

In retrospect, three main successes stand out in de Gaulle's career. First of all, he organized and led the Free French back to France with the victorious Allies in 1944. This first success was tarnished, however, because although the movement claimed the legitimacy of the French state, de Gaulle would not allow a test of its claim in elections even among the French refugees in England during the occupation years. As a result his credibility was reduced. The Americans recognized Vichy in 1941 and accepted de Gaulle's government only as a last resort in 1944. His second major achievement was his return in triumph in 1958 to extricate France from the Algerian imbroglio and create a Fifth Republic with the strong executive power he wanted. The Fifth Republic has lasted since 1959 and has been accepted by all major sectors of French public opinion from the Communists through the National Front. De Gaulle's third major success, indirect and posthumous, has been the collapse of Soviet communism in the late 1980s and early 1990s and the growing strength of the European Community, enhanced by the creation of a joint Franco-German military force, which has brought his vision of a Europe stretching from the Atlantic to the Urals closer to reality than was commonly thought possible during his lifetime.

Liberty, within the national community, and international balance of a Machiavellian or Metternichian kind merged to inform de Gaulle's view of the world. He combined *Machiavelli's pragmatic approach to statecraft, *Metternich's sense of balance of power, and Nietzsche's critique of rationalism and insistence on the role of will. De Gaulle's 1932 comment that statecraft required "a strong dose of egoism, pride, firmness, and duplicity" has sometimes led to unflattering comparisons with Machiavelli, but both defended specific views of civilization against potentially overwhelming forces: Machiavelli the classical Latin in Renaissance Florence, and de Gaulle the classic equilibrium of European civilization. Because he preferred the moderation and balance that he associated with France, de Gaulle never shared the interwar attraction to Italian fascism or German Nazism manifested by some of his compatriots. He also borrowed heavily from turn-of-the-century French philosopher Henri Bergson, royalist Action Française leader Charles Maurras, and political writers Charles Péguy and Maurice Barrès. With Bergson, de Gaulle believed in an intuitive, creative, and heroic individual leader, but de Gaulle situated this concept within the Republican context. Maurras and de Gaulle shared the concept of the *pays réel* (real country), the eternal France of history, to whom de Gaulle spoke, in contrast to the *pays légal* (legal country), which existed in the political parties and parliamentary institutions of the Third and Fourth republics. Despite his evocation of the heroic kings or Bonapartes of the French past, however, de Gaulle supported the restoration of neither. Instead, he followed Péguy, who had moved from socialism to a form of Christian humanism combined with a strong sense of the nation. Péguy's view of the nation as an entity above the individuals comprising it, taken from the early nineteenth-century historian Jules Michelet, was basic to de Gaulle. Unlike Maurras, Péguy and Maurice Barrès envisioned a heroic France incorporating the Bonapartist and Republican, as well as the royalist, French past into the concept of *la patrie*, a notion critical to de Gaulle. Indeed, de Gaulle believed that France had bestowed upon the rest of the world the concepts of liberty, equality, and fraternity, which he saw betrayed not only by the collaboration of Vichy but also by the weakness of the Fourth Republic and its toleration of the Communists. Even as the French government fled to Bordeaux to accept the armistice of July 1940, he predicted that forces greater than those of Nazi Germany would return to the Continent to crush the enemies of liberty and restore balance to the affairs of Europe.

De Gaulle's sense of equilibrium in international affairs was reflected after 1958 in his support for the United Nations and the Western alliance as well as in his withdrawal from NATO. While criticizing American leadership in the West and opposing the dollar as the international standard of exchange, de Gaulle nonetheless supported Washington during both the U–2 incident in 1960 and the Cuban Missile Crisis of 1962. He emphasized the need for France to increase its birthrate in order to remain strong and to modernize its industry to compete more effectively in the world. Accordingly, industrial reorganization became part of his program for 1944–1945, although he subsequently limited French *sacré égoïsme* by its involvement, not without difficulties, in the Common Market. Perhaps most dramatically during his visit to Québec in 1967, de Gaulle vigorously promoted *la Francophonie*, his vision of an international Francophone community of independent states that would maintain the French culture zone as a viable alternative to that of the Anglo-Americans. With the legacy of Algeria behind him, he opened France to the Third World and sponsored North-South dialogue, which he supported with financial aid and which has been continued by his successors. Ultimately, de Gaulle envisioned a world balanced among the Americans, the Europeans, and the Third World. Because he viewed nations as more permanent than ideologies, he foresaw and worked toward a dissolution of the Yalta settlement, with the Americans going home and a Europe spreading from the Atlantic to the Urals.

Annotated Bibliography

The main repository for information about Charles de Gaulle is the Institut Charles de Gaulle. In 1971 de Gaulle's Paris headquarters were turned into the Institut, a library and documentation center for his career similar to American presidential libraries, but unusual in France. Additional materials are housed at the Archives Nationales in Paris. Certainly one of the most important future sources of information will be the records of the Ministère des Affaires Étrangères. However, because of the rules of confidentiality, documents bearing on de Gaulle's career as an international figure will enter the public domain at a slow pace.

De Gaulle's ideas are best found in his writings, which established him as a trenchant critic of French military policy and a first-rate stylist in the French language. His first book, *La Discorde chez l'ennemi* (Discord among the Enemy), based on his experiences as a prisoner of war in Germany during World War I, was published in 1924. In it he argued that the virtual dictatorship exercised by General Erich von Ludendorff at the end of the war had weakened the authority of the Imperial government and that a Nietzschean spirit of trying to attain the superhuman had brought on the German collapse of 1918. In 1934, a year after the rise of ˙Hitler to power in Germany, de Gaulle published *Vers l'armée de métier* (translated as *The Army of the Future*), which argued for a mobile and professional army that would be able to repel an invasion of France but which could also be used to police the French Empire in Africa and Asia. Although similar arguments for coordinated tank strategies were gaining currency in German military circles at the time, de Gaulle's book went largely unheeded. The war memoirs, *Mémoires de guerre*, published in three volumes between 1954 and 1959, recount his experiences in the Free French and Provisional Government period from 1940 through 1946. His speculations about the need to balance German power in a future Europe are particularly interesting. *Discours et messages*, five volumes published in 1970, contains the collected speeches and addresses he gave from his arrival in London in 1940 through his resignation as president in 1969. When he died, General de Gaulle was writing the second volume of his memoirs, covering the years beginning with his return to power in 1958. Two volumes of these memoirs, entitled *Mémoires d'espoir* (Memoirs of Hope), appeared in 1970 and 1971.

A 1990 bibliography of works about General de Gaulle, published by the Institut Charles de Gaulle, covering all publications around the world dealing with de Gaulle for just the years 1980 through 1990, comes to over 300 pages. Despite this extensive literature, important archival material remains unavailable to historians because it is legally classified in France, is hidden in private collections, or is simply lost. Jean Lacouture, whose *De Gaulle* (1968), was followed by his two-volume *De Gaulle* (1990–1991) (the English translation of a three-volume French edition, 1984–1986), still did not believe in 1986 that he had the historical perspective from which to evaluate his subject's career. Much of the literature about de Gaulle has a personal slant and fails to see him in the context of long-term French and European sociopolitical development. The changes over which he presided from 1958 through 1969 were enormous for France, yet most views of de Gaulle neglect the changing patterns of French demographics and the evolution of his constituency. In addition, most discussions of his involvement in the Common Market focus on his personal view of French national grandeur rather than the institutional development of the Market itself, or on the shifting attitudes of the French as they began to accept the idea of "Europe," as exemplified in the European elections of 1979 and thereafter. Statements by de Gaulle himself, such as his prediction that after his own departure from the political scene France would need to find another de Gaulle, helped create a myth of the heroic leader standing apart from socioeconomic reality. Representative of this type of account of de Gaulle is Léo Hamon's, which described him, in *De Gaulle dans la République* (1958), as "the affirmation of a nation's will to live," or, on this side of the Atlantic, Don Cook's *Charles de Gaulle: A Biography* (1983), which compared de Gaulle to Moses, saying his "tall figure will cast forever its shadow over the land."

Judgments of de Gaulle in the international arena must be especially tentative because of the inaccessibility of important source material. The collapse of the Soviet bloc in 1989–1991 and the as yet uncertain course of the Common Market also caution against hasty assessments. Much of the literature to date depicts de Gaulle as a powerful leader with a strong conception of historic France and its preeminent role in world affairs, combined with a Machiavellian flexibility in shifting policies, alignments, and personnel. He presided over French policies at a time when larger forces—Nazi Germany and the two superpowers, the Soviet Union and the United States—dictated his attempts at balance in Europe and the world. Not surprisingly, most of the discussion of de Gaulle's foreign policy focuses on either the war period or the years after his return to power in 1958.

During World War II, the key issue was the relationship between the Allies and de Gaulle's Free French. A biography of de Gaulle published in 1941 by his supporter Philippe Barrès, for example, emphasized the support given by England and, it was hoped, by vast mechanized forces that would come from America one day to destroy the Nazis. Arthur L. Funk in *Charles de Gaulle: The Crucial Years, 1943–1944* (1959), wrote that although the personal relations between de Gaulle and Roosevelt bordered on the tragic and created significant misunderstandings between the two, de Gaulle's presence served French long-term interests by forcing the United States to recognize a unitary France rather than several disparate groups of resisters. Dorothy Shipley White, in *Seeds of Discord: De Gaulle, Free France and the Allies* (1964), argued that the wartime disagreements between de Gaulle and the other Allied leaders left a legacy of bitterness that influenced the general's policies toward the United States and Britain in the 1960s. Hillary Footitt and John Simmonds in *France 1943–1945* (1988), maintained that de Gaulle had a "massive" influence in the making of French foreign policy immediately after the liberation, but noted that although he was able to get the other Allies to agree to a French occupation zone in Germany, he was unable to win France a seat at Yalta and the other conferences where the major issues for the postwar era were being settled.

With his return to power in 1958, de Gaulle's policies regarding British entry into the Common Market and his attempts to assert French influence at the expense of the United States became paramount issues. In the April 1966 issue of *Foreign Affairs*, the French socialist politician Gaston Defferre criticized de Gaulle for warning of American influence in France, but then failing to prevent the takeover of European economic enterprises by American big business. W. W. Kulski, in *De Gaulle and the World: The Foreign Policy of the Fifth French Republic*, which also appeared in 1966, saw de Gaulle's France as caught in the middle of the East-West split, on the one hand, and the North-South divide, on the other. De Gaulle's basic policies, he wrote, included support of the French nuclear force, opposition to delegating any French prerogatives to international organizations, sympathy for the Third World, and an anti-American bias. Beyond these, "his fertile and flexible mind might in the future take an unexpected direction."

In the years since de Gaulle's death, much of the literature has attempted to assess his contribution to building the Common Market and his efforts to increase French influence in Europe and the rest of the world at the expense of the United States. At a conference in 1980, the proceedings of which were published in Élie Barnavi and Saul Friedländer, eds., *La Politique étrangère du général de Gaulle* (1985), Léo Hamon compared de Gaulle's foreign policy to that of Cardinal ˙Richelieu, who had been willing to make alliances with heretical Protestants or infidel Turks if it strengthened French national interests against its rival, the Catholic Habsburg House of Austria. Both men, according to Hamon, believed in the Christian character of France, but as political realists they also knew how to shift alliances when necessary. At the same meeting, Mikhaël Harsgor argued that de Gaulle's foreign policy was designed to undo the Yalta settlement and that his policy regarding the United States, rather than being the result of remembered resentment of wartime snubs, was the result of a French policy dating back to the kings who had resisted any attempts, notably by the Germanic Holy Roman Empire, to dominate the Continent. The United States, in this view, was but the latest threat at a hegemony that had to be resisted. A particular point of attack for de Gaulle against American hegemony, according to Jean Lacouture, who also participated in the 1980 meeting, was to back Hanoi during the Vietnam War. Lacouture maintained that de Gaulle believed that the United States had failed to support France during its own Indochina war because of a desire to supplant the French in Southeast Asia.

Addressing the issue of Québec, Marc Laurendeau argued at the conference that de Gaulle's 1967 call for a free Québec, rather than being an isolated outburst, was the product of an evolution of his view from the early 1960s when he became aware of the distinct cultural identity of the Francophone Québecois. The bilingual regulations later adopted by the government of Pierre Elliott Trudeau, according to Laurendeau, were at least in part a consequence of de Gaulle's publicizing the question of Québec's cultural identity. Concluding the conference, Saul Friedländer noted that, as of 1980, prominent biographers of de Gaulle outside France, such as Brian Crozier and Inge and Stanley Hoffmann, had focused on his domestic successes and devalued the results of his international policies. They had emphasized his failure to undo the Yalta settlement and construct a Europe from the Atlantic to the Urals. Instead of emphasizing de Gaulle's failures, however, Friedländer focused on the political leadership rooted in tradition, together with pragmatism and charisma, that had made de Gaulle a model for the world. A similar case was argued in 1986 by Lacouture, whose second and more extensive biography of the general maintained that de Gaulle had failed in three basic goals for France: (1) to become allied with but not a protectorate of the United States; (2) to emerge as the leader of a European community with Paris as its center; and (3) to serve as the instigator of an opening to the East, which might have led to the erosion of the two blocs and the emergence of a multipolar system in which the older continental nations could act as mediators. On the other hand, according to Lacouture, if de Gaulle were to be measured as a pedagogue, determined to teach the French pride in themselves and their role in the world, history's judgment would be much more positive.

The end of the Yalta system has brought new assessments of de Gaulle's foreign policy, still tentative because of the unavailability of archival material. At the 1990 meeting organized by the Institut Charles de Gaulle in Paris commemorating the centenary of the general's birth, Maurice Vaisse stated that the end of the Soviet bloc had confirmed twenty years after his death de Gaulle's vision of a Europe from the Atlantic to the Urals. In the United States, the Fall 1990 issue of *French Politics and Society* was devoted to updating the view of de Gaulle's foreign policy. In it Edward A. Kolodziej divides de Gaulle's career into two parts, with the return to power in 1958 as the demarcation. According to Kolodziej, from the beginning of Free France in 1940 until his return to power, de Gaulle was primarily concerned with keeping Germany weak and, if possible, dismembered so that it would not constitute a renewed threat to France. After 1958, when West Germany had become economically strong and rearmed, he shifted to a preoccupation with ending the Yalta settlement and the Cold War in order to restore French *grandeur*, a program for which he saw Franco-German cooperation as a necessity. Britain could not be relied upon for French security, according to de Gaulle, because it had failed to render effective help in 1940. Furthermore, in the 1960s it was oriented toward the Commonwealth and the United States rather than the Continent. "If de Gaulle can be celebrated as a visionary and political realist," Kolodziej wrote, "it is because he had a unique capacity, for a statesman, of being able to repudiate his own ideas when they no longer suited his national (or personal) purposes" (p. 46). As did Lacouture in 1986, Kolodziej concludes that from the perspective of 1969, when de Gaulle left office, his policies had failed. Seen from the perspective of 1990, however, de Gaulle's vision of a Europe without Yalta appeared far more realistic, and Kolodziej suggests that he may well have helped move the world to a better order. John T.S. Keeler makes a similar point, arguing that it was de Gaulle's efforts in the mid-1960s to establish the Common Agricultural Policy, a system by which West Germany and other members of the Common Market subsidized French farmers "for what an idealistic federalist would have considered all the wrong reasons," namely, France's national interest, that "provided the strongest support for the EEC's most ambitious integration project during its formative (1958–1964) era"(p. 72).

Perhaps for now, the final word should be left to Stanley Hoffman, who had warned in 1964 that cursing de Gaulle was not a policy. In the issue of *French Politics and Society* devoted to de Gaulle's foreign policy, Hoffmann writes that "he restored the national pride of the French while he led them toward necessary adaption to the realities of the postwar world" (p. 86). His success can be measured by the fact that his successors, including his political opponent François Mitterrand, have maintained his foreign policy essentially intact. Hoffmann concludes: "This man of conservative, monarchist origins became a formidably non-conformist republican monarch; this intense French nationalist became an apostle of national self-determination. In their plight, both in 1940 and in 1958, the French were lucky—or maybe, for all their faults, they got what the best part of them deserved'' (p. 92).

Bibliography

Barnavi, Élie, and Saul Friedländer, eds. *La Politique étrangère du Général de Gaulle.* Geneva: Institut Universitaire de Hautes Études Internationales, 1985.

Barrès, Philippe. *Charles de Gaulle.* Garden City, N.Y.: Doubleday, Doran, 1941.

Berstein, Serge. *La France de l'expansion: La République gaullienne 1958–1969.* Paris: Seuil, 1989.

Brohm, Jean-Marie, et al. *Le gaullisme, et après? État fort et fascisation.* Paris: François Maspero, 1974.

Cohen, William B. "De Gaulle and Europe Prior to 1958." *French Politics and Society* 8 (1990): 1–12.

Cook, Don. *Charles de Gaulle: A Biography.* New York: Putnam's, 1983.

Couve de Murville, Maurice. *Une Politique étrangère, 1958–1969.* Paris: Plon, 1971.

Crawley, Aidan. *De Gaulle: A Biography.* Indianapolis: Bobbs-Merrill, 1969.

Crozier, Brian. *De Gaulle.* 2 vols. London: Eyre Methuen, 1973.

Deferre, Gaston. "De Gaulle and After." *Foreign Affairs* 44, 3 (April 1966): 434–445.

DePorte, Anton W. "De Gaulle's Europe: Playing the Russian Card." *French Politics and Society* 8 (1990): 25–40.

———. *Europe between the Superpowers.* New Haven, Conn.: Yale University Press, 1985.

De Gaulle, Charles. *The Army of the Future.* Philadelphia: Lippincott, 1941.

———. *Articles et écrits.* Paris: Plon, 1975.

———. *La Discorde chez l'ennemi.* Paris: Berger-Levrault, 1924.

———. *Discours et messages.* 5 vols. Paris: Plon, 1970.

———. *La France et son armée.* Paris: Plon, 1938.

———. *Lettres, notes et carnets.* 12 vols. Paris: Plon, 1980–1988.

———. *Memoirs of Hope, 1958–62.* New York: Simon and Schuster, 1971.

———. *The War Memoirs, 1940–46.* New York: Simon and Schuster, 1964.

de la Gorce, Paul-Marie. *De Gaulle entre deux mondes.* Paris: Fayard, 1964.

———. *La France contre les empires.* Paris: Grasset, 1969.

Dreyfus, François-Georges. *De Gaulle et le Gaullisme.* Paris: Presses Universitaires de France, 1982.

Footitt, Hillary, and John Simmonds. *France 1943–1945.* New York: Holmes and Meier, 1988.

Funk, Arthur L. *Charles de Gaulle: The Crucial Years, 1943–1944.* Norman: University of Oklahoma Press, 1959.

Gordon, Bertram M. "Charles de Gaulle: A Historical Retrospective." In *Proceedings of the Thirteenth Annual Meeting of the Western Society for French History,* pp. 240–250. Flagstaff: Northern Arizona University Press, 1986.

Gozard, Gilles. *De Gaulle face à l'Europe.* Paris: Collection Espoir/Plon, 1976.

Grosser, Alfred. *La Politique extérieure de la Vᵉ République.* Paris: Seuil, 1965.

Hamon, Léo. *De Gaulle dans la République.* Paris: Plon, 1958.

Harrison, Michael M. *The Reluctant Ally: France and Atlantic Security.* Baltimore: Johns Hopkins University Press, 1981.

Hoffmann, Stanley. "De Gaulle as an Innovative Leader." *French Politics and Society* 8 (1990): 78–92.

Hoffmann, Stanley, and Inge Hoffmann. *De Gaulle: artiste de la politique.* Paris: Seuil, 1973.

Institute Charles de Gaulle, ed. *Approches de la philosophie politique du Général de Gaulle.* Paris: Cujas, 1983.

———, ed. *De Gaulle en son siècle.* 4 vols. Paris: Plon/La Documentation française, 1991–1992.

Jouve, Edmond. *Le Général de Gaulle et la construction de l'Europe, 1940–1966.* Paris: Librairie Générale de Droit et de Jurisprudence, 1967.

Keeler, John T.S. "De Gaulle and Europe's Common Agricultural Policy." *French Politics and Society* 8 (1990): 62–77.

Kersaudy, François. *De Gaulle et Churchill.* Paris: Collection Espoir/Plon, 1982.

Kolodziej, Edward A. "De Gaulle, Germany and the Superpowers." *French Politics and Society* 8 (1990): 41–61.

———. *French International Policy under de Gaulle and Pompidou: The Politics of Grandeur.* Ithaca, N.Y.: Cornell University Press, 1974.

Kuisel, Richard F. "De Gaulle's Dilemma: The American Challenge and Europe." *French Politics and Society* 8 (1990): 13–24.

Kulski, W. W. *De Gaulle and the World: The Foreign Policy of the Fifth French Republic.* Syracuse: Syracuse University Press, 1966.

Lacouture, Jean. *De Gaulle.* Translated by Francis K. Price. New York: Discus/Avon, 1968.

———. *De Gaulle.* Translated by Patrick O'Brian. 2 vols. New York: Norton, 1990–1991.

Langer, William L. *Our Vichy Gamble.* New York: Knopf, 1947.

Ledwidge, Bernard. *De Gaulle.* New York: St. Martin's Press, 1982.

Molchanov, Nikolai. *De Gaulle, His Life and Work.* Moscow: Progress, 1980.

Newhouse, John. *De Gaulle and the Anglo-Saxons.* London: Deutsch, 1970.

Schoenbrun, David. *The Three Lives of Charles de Gaulle.* New York: Atheneum, 1968.

Touchard, Jean. *Le Gaullisme, 1940–1969.* Paris: Seuil, 1978.

Viansson-Ponte, Pierre. *Histoire de la République gaullienne.* 2 vols. Paris: Fayard, 1970–1971.

Werth, Alexander. *De Gaulle: A Political Biography.* Baltimore: Penguin, 1965.

White, Dorothy Shipley. *Seeds of Discord: De Gaulle, Free France and the Allies.* Syracuse, N.Y.: Syracuse University Press, 1964.

BERTRAM M. GORDON

Benjamin Disraeli (1804–1881).   At first glance Benjamin Disraeli might seem a curious choice for inclusion among the world's great statesmen. After all, it is the improbability of his ever having risen to the prime ministership, to "the top of the greasy pole" in his telling phrase, for which he is usually remembered, rather than for what he may have achieved once in office. Even a sympathetic member of his own Conservative party, Lord Randolph Churchill, summarized the bulk of Disraeli's career as "failure, failure, failure, partial success, renewed failure." So somber a verdict was hardly belied by Disraeli's destruction during the late 1840s of his party's most constructive politician, Sir Robert Peel, or by his failure to anticipate that the electoral reform he secured in 1867 was to be followed by a crushing Conservative defeat a year later and the most significant series of Liberal legislative measures of the entire century. It was not difficult, therefore, for contemporaries to dismiss him as an inconsequential figure, a man devoid of principles for whom personal ambition and tactical dexterity were poor substitutes for the political vision he lacked.

And yet, there was another side to "Dizzy." Churchill's concluding assessment of Disraeli's achievement was "ultimate and complete victory." Nor would the four-time Liberal prime minister, William E. Gladstone, have expended so much time, energy, and rhetoric if he thought Disraeli inconsequential. Better than most observers, he recognized the power and significance of Disraeli's challenge. For Disraeli was creative, in that he articulated a particular vision of British power resting on an elevated symbolic role for the monarchy, a publicized commitment to social reform, and a more assertive imperial and foreign policy. His legacy merits consideration, then, as more than an instructive exercise in social mobility; despite his sparkle and wit, he deserves to be taken seriously.

There can be no denying, though, that Disraeli's early life had an air of the fantastic about it. The Conservative party stressed the interests of the landed aristocracy and the Anglican Church, yet Disraeli, born on December 21, 1804, was the eldest son of a Jewish literary figure. His father, who was both a Conservative and something of a religious skeptic, had Benjamin baptized into the Church of England, but his son still lacked the conventional attributes of a junior Conservative, such as a steady income or a public school or university education. Disraeli drifted, shunned a legal career, wandered the Mediterranean and, when he did much of anything, either wrote poor literature or cut an awkward figure on the social scene. In the 1830s, however, Disraeli found a measure of emotional and financial stability when he married an older widow, Mary Anne Wyndham Lewis, establishing a companionship that lasted until her death in 1872. Equally important, he secured a political foothold by attracting an influential Tory patron, Lord Lyndhurst. Disraeli's undoubted flamboyance or erratic judgment aside, these developments indicate that the subsequent trajectory of his career was not as unconventional as he later liked to suggest. In 1837 he finally entered Parliament, for the same constituency formerly represented by his wife's first husband.

His first decade in politics was hardly auspicious. In fact, his literary productivity (including the famous trilogy of novels addressing the "condition of England question") seems to have been induced by his sense of political impotence. Of course, his was a literary sensibility, and his writing shed some light on his commitment to uphold what he described as the "aristocratic settlement." His efforts to preserve the role of the landed classes in a government resting on the carefully graded social hierarchy of rural England, though deeply felt, also provided a convenient platform from which to attack his party's leader, Peel, who had alienated many country gentlemen by renouncing agricultural protection in 1846. Disraeli's vituperative rhetoric aggravated his reputation for ambitious insincerity (not a few observers presumed that he still felt aggrieved by Peel's failure to offer him office five years earlier), but also aligned him with an important wing of the party and improved his political prospects by crippling those of Peel.

Despite the Conservative party's lack of talent, Disraeli would not become prime minister until 1868, and then for only a few months (he served in 1868, and from 1874 until 1880). The delay reflected no lack of ability on Disraeli's part, but rather the context within which he had to operate: the difficulty of reconciling the internal divisions of his party and offering the electorate a distinctive alternative to the moderate Whiggism of *Palmerston. It is useful to recall that Disraeli served a long apprenticeship and that when he finally achieved real power in the 1870s he was a seasoned politician, not a charlatan recently emerged from obscurity. He was also, by then, an old man in deteriorating health; those who expected an energetic burst of governmental action from his administration failed to take this into account, as well as the fundamental question of the way in which Disraeli conceived of his task as a Conservative prime minister.

In domestic policy he sought to restore an equilibrium disrupted by the Liberals. This entailed defending the monarchy and the church from the barbs of republicans and nonconformists, and enhancing the credibility of the landed elites as enlightened paternalists by promoting judicious measures of social reform for the benefit of the lower orders. In practice, apart from a few acts of housing or sanitary reform, little was done in this sphere. In part, such inactivity confirmed the prime minister's own predilections, for the arena that now appeared to him to offer the greatest scope for a creative approach was no longer the domestic (as it had been in 1867 when he had masterminded the Second Reform Act, expanding the urban electorate), but rather foreign affairs.

He had already signaled this particular concentration in 1872, in two famous speeches in Manchester and London (at the Crystal Palace) in which he blasted the Liberals for shamefully neglecting Britain's empire and thereby imperiling its status as a great power. It was this sense of grandeur, so reminiscent of Palmerston's evocation of the security of a Roman citizen anywhere within his far-flung empire, that Disraeli aspired to restore. Within a year of assuming power, Disraeli moved quickly and decisively to assure British interests in Egypt, and simultaneously to forestall those of the French, who were considering the acquisition of the financially troubled khedive's shares in the Suez Canal Company. Stealing a march on the French, Disraeli, with the indispensable assistance of Lord Rothschild, purchased the khedive's 44 percent interest for £4 million in 1875. The British government did not, as is sometimes mistakenly stated, then own the Suez Canal, but Disraeli's prompt action had placed it in a far more influential position. As Lord Cairns, Disraeli's lord chancellor, remarked, "We shall now be armed with a leverage we never had before." Moreover, if military action were required, "in our former condition it must have been war to destroy or take possession of the property of others; now it will be war to defend our own property.'' In 1876 Disraeli lent symbolic weight to his desire to consolidate both the monarchy and British ties to India with the proclamation of Queen Victoria as empress of India. In part too, this decision was prompted by the perennial suspicion of Russian encroachment upon British interests in the East. It was this issue that was to dominate the last half of Disraeli's tenure in office until his defeat in 1880.

By looking to Turkey to serve as a counterweight to Russian ambitions, Disraeli was reaffirming a Palmerstonian policy, though without repeating his predecessor's invocation of liberty or the rights of smaller nations. Critics scorned Turkey as militarily ineffectual and morally indefensible, and were appalled by Disraeli's cavalier dismissal of reports of massacres in 1876 of Bulgarian Christians at the hands of (Moslem) Turkish troops as nothing more than ''coffee house babble.'' His great rival Gladstone, who it once seemed had withdrawn from partisan politics, added his personal sense of outrage to what became known as the ''Bulgarian Agitation.'' Privately, Disraeli detested Gladstone, referring to him as ''A.V.'' (for ''arch villain''), and publicly he was undeterred by the Liberals' broadsides, calmly dispatching a British fleet to Constantinople once the Bulgarian uprisings had widened into a Russo-Turkish war and a full-blown Eastern crisis. His strong verbal assurances to Turkey did not extend so far as military intervention, but they probably scotched efforts at compromise by encouraging the intransigent elements within Turkey. Indeed, when Russia achieved a military victory in March 1878, it seized the opportunity to exact harsh terms in the Treaty of San Stefano. Turkish sovereignty within Europe was virtually eliminated, and the considerable extension of Bulgarian territory implied a commensurate extension of Russian influence, the very thing Disraeli had worked to prevent.

Disraeli's reputation for flexibility and cunning was not unmerited, however, and within months he had retrieved the situation. Closing ranks with Austria, he insisted that the San Stefano settlement was so far-reaching as to require consultation with the other European powers. *Bismarck's preference for diplomatic equilibrium inclined him toward the idea as well, and the result in June 1878 was the Congress of Berlin. Disraeli returned in triumph, for the Russians acceded to a smaller Bulgaria, to Austrian occupation of Bosnia, and to British occupation of Cyprus (to balance Russian gains in the Caucasus). Instead of fighting an unpopular and costly war, Disraeli had bearded the Russian bear and secured, in his words (repeated sixty years later by *Neville Chamberlain), ''peace with honor.'' Of course, Disraeli had not done it all himself—his foreign secretary was the gifted Lord Salisbury, while his increasing deafness and refusal to converse in French isolated him at times during the congress. But, having taken the responsibility, he could legitimately take much of the credit.

In retrospect, the Congress of Berlin marked the end of a Palmerstonian emphasis on a European concert in which Britain's counsel carried great weight among a number of cooperative powers. The Bulgarian settlement was revised within a decade, the Austrian presence in Bosnia only invited further trouble, and the British acquisition of Cyprus pointed toward further territorial gains on the basis of naked power as opposed to shared ties of culture or sentiment. Furthermore, by 1879 specific exclusive alliances were beginning to form (such as that between Germany and Austria), and an increasingly isolated British government found itself faced with border wars in Afghanistan and South Africa. These provided further grist to Gladstone's mill, as he thundered against "Beaconsfieldism" (Disraeli in 1876 having become the Earl of Beaconsfield), a foreign policy he characterized as not merely immoral but now demonstrably expensive and unsuccessful. An increasingly frail Disraeli lacked the stamina to counter such charges, and he was defeated in 1880. Retirement, though, suited him little better, and on April 19, 1881, he succumbed to influenza.

Annotated Bibliography

Disraeli's private papers are collected as the Hughenden MSS in the Bodleian Library, Oxford, where they are available for scholarly research. The entire collection is helpfully indexed; much of it is arranged alphabetically by correspondent. Of course, the letters therein are primarily those written to him, but his responses, scattered in other collections, are being published by the University of Toronto Press under the title *Benjamin Disraeli: Letters*, edited by M. G. Wiebe and numerous collaborators. So far four volumes have been produced, covering the period 1815–1847. Another rich manuscript collection for the study of British foreign policy is that of Disraeli's last foreign secretary and his eventual successor as party leader and prime minister, the Third Marquess of Salisbury. Salisbury's papers are preserved at his ancestral home, Hatfield, a short train ride north of London, where they may be consulted upon prior approval by the archivist. The other obvious relevant sources are the official records of the Foreign Office, housed at the Public Record Office, Kew (also just outside London). But anyone doing archival research in the United Kingdom should be sure to consult the National Register of Archives, whose staff can provide a wealth of information and practical advice.

What have historians made of Disraeli's impact, especially in light of the controversy that swirled around him throughout his political and literary career? The first major assessment of his life was a six-volume biography, *The Life of Benjamin Disraeli, Earl of Beaconsfield*, begun by W. F. Monypenny and completed in 1920 by G. E. Buckle, which quoted extensively from his private correspondence and remains the fullest account. Commissioned to balance John Morley's successful study of Gladstone, the Monypenny and Buckle volumes dealt sympathetically with Disraeli's foreign policy and accepted the idea that his frequently enunciated dedication to the empire was both deeply felt and highly influential.

But no sooner was the final volume published than a Canadian scholar, J. L. Morison, launched a scathing attack in an article entitled "The Imperial Ideas of Benjamin Disraeli," *Canadian Historical Review* 1 (1920): 267–280, arguing that he had none. Morison was struck by Disraeli's "ignorance of detail and his failure to grip essential facts," his lack of foresight with regard to the self-governing colonies, and his callous condemnation of them (in 1852) as "a millstone round our necks." Whereas Buckle had described the Crystal Palace speech (1872) as "the famous declaration from which the modern conception of the British Empire largely takes its rise," Morison minimized it as another example of the wily opportunist trimming his sails in the hopes of catching votes. "Epigram is not statesmanship" was Morison's severe verdict.

These contrasting views—of Disraeli as either a prophet of the new imperialism or an inconsequential windbag mouthing a series of platitudes—seemed likely to coexist without the prospect of synthesis. In 1964 a major study of imperialism by R. Koebner and H.D. Schmidt, *Imperialism: The Story and Significance of a Political Word*, concluded that in practical terms Disraeli's imperialism amounted to very little, and that if his actions were unimpressive, his speeches were even more so, containing nothing original or constructive. Even the notion that Disraeli aided his party immeasurably in the long run by associating the empire with conservatism was called into question.

Yet, just when it seemed that Disraeli's reputation was permanently deflated, up he popped again. In "Disraeli and the Millstones," *Journal of British Studies* 5 (1965): 122–139, S. R. Stembridge, on the basis of a careful survey of Disraeli's attitudes toward colonies and the empire, demonstrated that Disraeli was remarkably consistent throughout his career; the remark about the millstones was written in a fit of irritation and had received disproportionate attention. Even as a young man he had stressed the vital role of the empire, and when he picked up the imperial torch in the 1870s, he did so from sincere conviction rather than from a purely cynical calculation of political gain.

Of course, it is important to recognize that Disraeli could simultaneously display both a remarkable tactical agility and a more settled sense of the ends to which power should be used. Robert Blake's magnificent biography, *Disraeli* (1966), confirms Disraeli's disinterest in the mundane realities of colonial administration and his lack of concern over specific territorial gains. He neither foresaw nor desired the scramble to carve up the globe characteristic of the 1880s and 1890s, and he cannot be regarded as the principal architect of Europe's "new imperialism." In terms of the 1870s, Blake judges Disraeli's foreign policy a success; and the evocative nature of his rhetoric is to be reckoned with as well. It was this somewhat more balanced assessment that held the field after the mid–1960s: a Disraeli with shades of gray, instead of stark black or white.

To some people this seemed a shame, given that for Disraeli, so flamboyant and ever a romantic, a shade of gray hardly seems appropriate. Indeed, Blake concludes his monumental study with the observation that "Disraeli was never a grave statesman." A bold attempt to refurbish Disraeli's imperialist credentials was undertaken in 1980 by Freda Harcourt in "Disraeli's Imperialism, 1866–68: A Question of Timing," *Historical Journal* 23 (1980): 87–109. Rather than focusing on the man of words in 1872, she described a man of action in 1866–1868. In her view, Disraeli recognized that an act of risk-free aggression could enhance British prestige abroad and promote national unity at home in the face of a difficult domestic situation (economic recession, agitation for reform, threats to public order). In Harcourt's argument, the punitive expedition to Abyssinia, ostensibly to rescue a handful of British captives, serves as a corollary to Disraeli's espousal of electoral reform (to incorporate the working class) and as a point of departure for the imperialist ventures later in the century and the subsequent efforts to harvest votes from imperialist seeds. Harcourt's thesis is intriguing and even plausible; the problem is to find direct evidence that Disraeli consciously directed policy in this way.

The search for evidence is complicated by the fact that, unlike many statesmen, Disraeli did not leave extensive memoirs revealing the ways he hoped to be perceived by posterity. His reminiscences were spotty, and, composed in the 1860s, shed little light on his subsequent career. His major public speeches do not entirely fill the gap. He disliked addressing large crowds, a fact that gave his 1872 speeches an added emphasis, quite apart from the two bottles of brandy he consumed while delivering them. Unlike Gladstone, for example, he eschewed the habitual diary-keeping so prevalent among his peers. His novels, entertaining if florid, will not yield a specific agenda for foreign affairs.

One of the most promising ways to explore Disraeli's worldview, therefore, is by considering his Jewishness. Downplayed by Blake, and seemingly repressed after Disraeli's baptism and commitment to worshipping in (and protecting) a Christian church, the issue of his cultural origins was important, and was recognized as such by Disraeli himself. He cultivated an air of "Oriental mystery," to be sure, but beyond that his sense of identity rested on a conception of the Jews as a "natural aristocracy" that persuaded him that he, as an outsider, could nonetheless compete on equal terms with the aristocracy and still cling to notions of social hierarchy that would otherwise disqualify him in the struggle for leadership. It may also have influenced his view of the Eastern Question, as Anne Pottinger Saab has argued in "Disraeli, Judaism, and the Eastern Question," *International History Review* 10 (1988): 559–578. Given the frequency and severity of the persecution of the Jews in eastern Europe, Disraeli may well have wondered whether the sudden stigma attached to the "Bulgarian atrocities" against Christians was hypocritical. Furthermore, Saab suggests that he may have been sympathetically disposed toward Turkey for more than purely strategic reasons; perhaps he was intrigued by its survival as a religiously pluralistic state.

If Disraeli was a more complex individual than is often assumed, and was motivated by more than cynical opportunism, how can his legacy best be understood? Anyone who seeks to extract from his career a fulfilled laundry list of specific measures is looking for the wrong thing. The best testimony to his impact comes from his opponents, whose semantic counterattack employed new words such as "imperialism" or "Beaconsfieldism" to discredit his initiatives. Gladstone's famous Midlothian campaign, considered to have been the first nationwide electoral campaign, was a response to Disraeli's challenge to liberalism on the basis of a national conservatism. Disraeli was not interested in particular colonies. His principal concern was power and he recognized that British power rested to a considerable degree on foreign perceptions of British resolve and resources. His insistence that the Liberals squandered resources and lacked resolve would reshape British domestic politics and stand his own Conservative party in good stead in the future. But his vision of a new political culture was no less significant in redefining the acceptable limits within which future British statesmen could grapple with vexed issues of colonial or naval rivalry and national prestige. In that sense, he bequeathed a legacy they could dispute but not ignore.

Bibliography

Blake, Robert. *Disraeli*. London: Eyre and Spottiswoode, 1966; New York: St. Martin's Press, 1967.

Eldridge, C. C. *England's Mission: The Imperial Idea in the Age of Gladstone and Disraeli, 1868–1880*. London: Macmillan, 1973.

Harcourt, Freda. "Disraeli's Imperialism, 1866–68: A Question of Timing." *Historical Journal* 23 (1980): 87–109.

Koebner, R., and H. D. Schmidt. *Imperialism: The Story and Significance of a Political Word*. Cambridge: Cambridge University Press, 1964.

Millman, Richard. *Britain and the Eastern Question, 1875–78*. Oxford: Oxford University Press, 1979.

Monypenny, W. F., and G. E. Buckle. *The Life of Benjamin Disraeli, Earl of Beaconsfield*. 6 vols. London: John Murray, 1910–1920.

Morison, J. L. "The Imperial Ideas of Benjamin Disraeli." *Canadian Historical Review* 1 (1920): 267–280.

Rogers, Nini. "The Abyssinian Expedition of 1867–1868: Disraeli's Imperialism or James Murray's War?" *Historical Journal* 27 (1984): 129–149.

Saab, Anne Pottinger. "Disraeli, Judaism, and the Eastern Question." *International History Review* 10 (1988): 559–578.

Seton-Watson, R. W. *Disraeli, Gladstone and the Eastern Question.* London: Macmillan, 1935.

Smith, Paul. "Disraeli's Politics." *Transactions of the Royal Historical Society* 37 (1987): 65–85.

Stembridge, Stanley. "Disraeli and the Millstones." *Journal of British Studies* 5 (1965): 122–139.

Swartz, Helen, and Marvin Swartz, eds. *Disraeli's Reminiscences.* London: Macmillan, 1975.

Swartz, Marvin. *The Politics of British Foreign Policy in the Era of Disraeli and Gladstone.* London: Macmillan, 1985.

Vincent, John. *Disraeli.* Oxford: Oxford University Press, 1990.

FRANS COETZEE

Luis María Drago (1859–1921).   Luís Maria Drago left as a legacy the Drago Doctrine, which opposes armed intervention to collect public debts. He defended this doctrine as a delegate at the Second Hague Peace Conference in 1907, which led to his appointment as one of five arbitrators for the International Court of Justice and as delegate to the League of Nations. He derived his inspiration for these tasks from his early life as part of the Argentine upper class and his training in law and journalism.

Born on May 6, 1859, in Buenos Aires, to physician Luis María Drago and his wife Estela Sánchez, Drago was the grandson of Argentine president Bartolomé Mitre. As was customary among wealthy Latin American families of the time, Drago was educated by tutors and at private schools. After the death of his father, when Drago was only sixteen, family members arranged for his employment in the newspaper business. He first proofread and then wrote for the newspapers *La Nación* (founded by Mitre and edited by his son, Dr. Luis Mitre) and *La Tribuna Nacional*. Later he became editor-in-chief of *El Diário*, the leading afternoon paper in Buenos Aires. During these years of apprenticeship, he was sensitized to public opinion and the power of words. Drago would retain a lifelong bond with the press, writing and commenting on political, legal, and cultural issues.

Drago's legal work also influenced his writings and editorship. In 1882 he completed his law studies at the University of Buenos Aires with a thesis on marital law, "El poder Marital." His first appointment was in the Buenos Aires provincial civil court, where his work reinforced his desire to combine his legal and political ambitions. Thus, Drago served briefly in the provincial legislature of La Plata before becoming judge of the criminal court in Buenos Aires.

Drago's political moves were infused with legal arguments when, as Argentine financial officer, he pondered the sovereignty of provinces and their protection from the national government in financial questions. These deliberations produced the theory that "the federal states cannot be destrained," published in 1892 as *Los Estados Federales no pueden ser ejecutados*. Drago resigned over a political disagreement, taking a year-long trip to Europe, where he gathered material for newspaper travel articles. Upon his return he entered the National Congress for the first of three terms.

Already an accomplished legal scholar, politician, journalist, and international traveler, speaking English and French besides his native Spanish, Drago joined an illustrious group of Argentines in national politics during General Julio A. Roca's second presidency (1898–1904). In 1902 the dominant Partido Autónomista Nacional, which supported President Roca, sent Drago to the Chamber of Deputies, but almost immediately he was appointed minister of foreign affairs. It was in this post, which he occupied only a year, that he became internationally famous. When British and German forces bombarded Venezuela and sank one of its gunships in an effort to collect financial obligations, Drago wrote a letter to Washington. In this note of December 29, 1902, he asked the United States to recognize the principle now known as the Drago Doctrine: "That the public debt cannot occasion armed intervention nor even the actual occupation of the territory of American nations by a European power." The note catapulted Drago onto the international political scene as American and European jurists began a debate that eventually resulted in the presentation of the Drago Doctrine to the World Court.

Drago left office in July 1903 over a disagreement with Roca on a diplomatic appointment. He continued his forensic work, participated in debates over commercial treaties, translated Thomas Carlyle's biography of the Paraguayan dictator José Gaspar Francia, and edited a book of publications and letters on the Drago Doctrine, *La República Argentina y el caso de Venezuela*. Despite the popularity of his doctrine, Drago declined to represent Argentina at the Third Pan American Conference, held in Rio de Janeiro in 1906, explaining that the doctrine was no more than a policy statement confined to the hemisphere.

Instead, he reentered congress as a member of the National Coalition, joining such illustrious politicians as Carlos Pelligrini and Emilio Mitre. But within a year he again gave up his seat for the world political stage. At the Pan American Conference, the United States had decided to submit Drago's doctrine to the Second International Peace Conference of 1907 at The Hague. Public clamor in Argentina forced President José Figueroa Alcorta to appoint Drago as one of two delegates to The Hague. Prior to the conference, the international legal community called on Drago to elaborate on his doctrine to facilitate debate at the conference. The result was Drago's article, published almost simultaneously in Paris, Washington, and Buenos Aires, "State Loans in Their Relation to International Policy."

At the Hague Conference, Drago defended his doctrine but eventually supported the U.S. submission known as the Porter Convention, which called for limiting instead of prohibiting the use of force in the collection of public debts. Drago's eloquent defense of his doctrine at the Hague Conference gained him worldwide respect. In 1908 Tsar Nicholas II bestowed on him the Order of St. Stanislas, First Class, and in 1909 the United States, Great Britain, and Venezuela all requested his participation in arbitration proceedings. Drago declined the Venezuelan invitation but accepted the challenge to participate in a long-standing fishing dispute between the United States and Great Britain.

From June 1 to August 12, 1910, Drago and four other arbitrators deliberated the North Atlantic coast fisheries question, one of the most notable arbitration cases prior to World War I. Drago summarized the case in a book and also published an article explaining his dissent on Question V of the arbitration, a dissent that led to the definition of a "historic bay."

In December 1911, through the Carnegie Foundation, Drago became the first Latin American to be invited to visit the United States under a new intellectual exchange program. In 1912 Drago was reelected national deputy for the capital, as the only candidate from Unión Civica. Again he was called on to perform an international function, as Argentine ambassador extraordinary, to convey thanks to the United States for its participation in the Argentina centenary celebration. He declined for health reasons and instead traveled to clinics in Berlin and Vienna for treatment of a respiratory ailment.

On April 3, 1916, he retired from political life but continued as professor of civil law at the University of Buenos Aires and as member of a commission to reform the penal code. He lobbied for Argentina to support the Allied cause in World War I and applauded the U.S. entry into the war in 1917.

In 1920 members of the newly established League of Nations, planning to establish an international court, invited Drago to help draft a statute for a Permanent Court of International Justice. Before he could take on this task, he became seriously ill and died of kidney failure on June 9, 1921, in Buenos Aires.

Drago made two distinct and unrelated contributions to international relations: proclaiming, as foreign minister of Argentina, a political doctrine for the Western Hemisphere, and introducing, as arbitrator of the International Court, the concept of historic bays for the benefit of English and American fishermen. Insofar as there is any connection between the two, it is found in Drago's desire to solve disputes peacefully through international arbitration. In both cases Drago demonstrated that he was not afraid to dissent from popular opinion.

In 1902 Argentina, under the leadership of President Roca, experienced a "Golden Age" when the country became increasingly active politically and economically through an influx of European capital and immigrants. The Argentine upper class envisioned a bright national future for the country. As a player in world events and a leader in the maturation of South American politics, Argentina was a natural setting for the emergence of Drago, a member of the politically powerful oligarchy of Buenos Aires. Drago was also keenly aware of the financial obligations and political instability that had made all of Latin America vulnerable to the predatory inclinations of Europe and North America in the late nineteenth century. Thus Drago's doctrine has to be understood first and foremost as the act of a Latin American politician protecting the Western

Hemisphere against European intervention with principles derived both from international law and from the policies of the United States.

Following the colonization of Africa and Asia, European nations turned their attention to the weaker countries of the Western Hemisphere, in which they had already invested heavily. Seeing the bombardment of the Venezuelan coast and the sinking of a Venezuelan gunboat as an overture to the colonization of a sister republic, Drago responded with a diplomatic message warning Europe against conquest "disguised under the mask of financial intervention."

Since his concepts referred specifically to the Western Hemisphere, he refused to support the efforts of other Latin American countries to convert his idea into an internationally accepted law. Declining to participate in the Third Pan American Conference, he wrote in a letter to his foreign minister on May 9, 1906: "We maintained . . . an American thesis by solidarity with the nations of this continent, with scope and purpose purely American. . . . We would not have spoken had the country compelled by force to pay its debts been Greece or Turkey." It is unclear from his writings to what degree Drago wanted to establish Argentina's leadership with this doctrine, but he did mention that it was not designed for the exclusive benefit of Argentina but rather for all of America. To support his doctrine he invoked three accepted political principles: the Monroe Doctrine's prohibition of further colonization of the Western Hemisphere, the ideas of England's Lord *Palmerston concerning prudent investments, and the notions of the Argentine international legal expert Carlos Calvo on the inadmissibility of force on all "international decisions."

Drago intended to emulate *John Quincy Adams, the father of the Monroe Doctrine, in two important ways. First, he hoped to protect a budding country with powerfully stated words because he had no alternatives at his disposal. In his letter he did not specifically request U.S. support or acquiescence in order to avoid entanglements. Second, by praising England, in his message he must have entertained the vain hope that the British fleet, which had essentially guaranteed the success of the Monroe Doctrine, would indulge the Latin American countries in the same way.

Although in his original letter Drago never specifically referred to Carlos Calvo, he did rely on his compatriot's theoretical pronouncements. In 1868 Calvo maintained in his *International Law of Europe and America in Theory and Practice* that foreign creditors must seek recourse through the domestic courts of countries where they had lent money and that it was illegal for one American nation to interfere in the internal affairs of another.

By invoking the Monroe Doctrine, the practices of the British, and the discussions of international jurists, Drago hoped to ground his ideas firmly in established principles; yet it is exactly these connections that entangled his policy statement in a larger web, thus detracting from his doctrine.

From its inception Drago's doctrine received a mixed response. In Washington there was concern over its implications for U.S. leadership. In the Latin American capitals discussion focused on the value of the doctrine for specific situations.

In the international legal community there was debate over the legal validity of Drago's idea.

To many in Latin America the response from the White House was disappointing because it did not applaud the doctrine directly but related it to *Theodore Roosevelt's pronouncements on the collection of debt and taking of territory. Drago had not asked for a U.S. response, and he complained that the United States had mistranslated his letter, making it appear that his doctrine required U.S. approval. According to Drago, his doctrine was simply an Argentine policy that the United States could accept.

Other responses came from the international community through the initiative of Carlos Calvo, at the time working at the French institute of International Law, who invited his colleagues to comment on Drago's note. Letters poured in from Geneva, London, Göttingen, Paris, Naples, Oxford, Turin, and The Hague, creating an international debate. Although most favored the prohibition of force in the collection of debts, they also criticized Drago on a number of points. Some saw Drago's note as an effort to excuse nonpayment of just obligations. Others questioned whether excessive financial obligations could weaken state sovereignty; still others insisted on the legal right of intervention.

In Latin American capitals, political leaders debated whether to support the Drago note and whether or not to make official statements about it. In April 1906, the governing board of the Bureau of the American Republics called it a very delicate subject because debtor nations could be accused of self-interest if they supported the doctrine. These nations were sensitive to criticism that the only reason they supported Drago was because they supported nonpayment. These developments forced the United States to take over the sponsorship of the doctrine.

Drago must have been pleased to hear Secretary of State *Elihu Root agreeing with him on August 17, 1906, when the American stopped in Buenos Aires on his way to the Second Pan American Conference: "We deem the use of force for the collection of ordinary contract debts to be an invitation to abuses in their necessary results far worse, far more baneful to humanity [than] that the debts contracted by any nation should go unpaid." Drago must have felt some unease when he learned that the United States had sponsored a resolution at the Pan American Conference requesting The Hague to consider to what extent the use of force for the collection of public debts is admissible.

It may be construed as a success for Drago that his doctrine was discussed at The Hague and that because of it all Latin American countries had received invitations to attend, for the first time giving them a forum for their concerns. Drago himself participated as an Argentine delegate but found himself fighting an uphill battle against the United States, which introduced the Porter Convention. On June 19, 1907, General Horace Porter presented a proposition for "an agreement to observe restrictions on the subject of the use of force in the collection of ordinary public debts arising from contracts." He then outlined a weakened Drago Doctrine stipulating that signatory powers had recourse to armed force if the debtor state had refused arbitration or had made impossible the establishment of compromise, or after arbitration had failed to comply with the terms of the award. Drago objected to this convention because it did not guarantee absolute exclusion of military intervention from American soil. In the end, Drago was forced to support the Porter Convention because it provided at least some protection for the poorer countries.

Although his policy was weakened, the force of his personality, the eloquence of his arguments, and the persistence of his character brought him recognition. Yet he witnessed with sadness Argentina's and other Latin American countries' retreat from their support of the Monroe Doctrine.

While his first contribution to international relations originated from purely political considerations, his second was solely that of a legal expert. In his capacity as an arbitrator in the North American fisheries dispute, he dealt with a Question V, the definition of a bay, described at the time as "the greatest lawsuit in the world." Debate on the question had filled volumes. Drago, in his dissenting opinion, contended that a ten-mile rule should have been adopted both because historic practice had made it policy and because to award less space to fishermen would be hazardous and of little value.

Annotated Bibliography

Besides his famous letter of December 1902, reprinted in *Papers Relating to the Foreign Relations of the United States*, Drago left two pieces of writing in English. Both articles, published in the *American Journal of International Law*, are further explanations of his contribution to international law. "State Loans in Their Relation to International Policy" (1907) responds to various criticisms his doctrine had elicited, while "Grounds for the Dissent to the Award on Question V of the Hague Fisheries Decision" (1910) summarizes the debate on the arbitration and his departure from the majority on Question V.

"State Loans" is divided into a response to international lawyers and a response to the political developments his doctrine had caused. Drago reiterated that his letter of 1902 was confined specifically to the issue of "forcible collection of interest on bonds of public debts." The reason for such a specific and narrow definition was Drago's understanding that these specific financial obligations were incurred directly by a state in its capacity as a sovereign power, and therefore the collection of such debts might infringe on its sovereignty. He also admitted that sometimes war was justified, but that it ought not be resorted to in cases where the debtor was incapable of payment due to a financial crisis beyond its control.

In the political section of his article, he presented more evidence on the European imperialist agitation that had justified his note. Sensitive to the proponents of Social Darwinism, he countered with the universal principle of international law "that all nations are to be considered equal and deserve [the] same consideration and respect." New in his deliberations was the warning that his doctrine could also be used against U.S. policing of Latin America. Cause for such a view were the events in the Dominican Republic, where the United States, in order to forestall European intervention, intervened to guarantee debt payment. According to Drago, such intervention also violated a nation's sovereignty and would produce estrangement between the United States and Latin America. He closed his article noting that "if the Drago Doctrine were accepted, the Monroe

Doctrine would lose its terror for South America.'' None of Drago's writings reveals whether he simply used the Monroe Doctrine as a political tool or if he truly endorsed it. It is clear, however, that he hoped to imitate its success. By 1902 the world had accepted the Monroe Doctrine; since the Drago Doctrine was based on the same principles, it ought to have received the same acceptance.

Much of the remainder of Drago's writing does not concern international relations and is available only in Spanish. In 1938 Drago's son edited and published much of his writing and some correspondence relating to important issues. In Volume 2 of the three-volume *Discursos y escritos*, Drago's work as foreign minister, delegate to The Hague, and arbitrator at the International Court is highlighted.

Mariano J. Drago's introduction stressed his father's tireless fight for the acceptance of his policy and showed him to be a man of action whose convictions were often stronger than his prudence about political survival. From these volumes, it becomes clear that Drago was not just an international lawyer with the interests of Argentina on his mind, but a man who deeply understood the challenges of cultural diversity and linguistic idiosyncrasies in international relations.

Despite Drago's attempt to assert Latin America's role on the world stage, a fight that had a major worldwide impact, he has not inspired much academic literature in the English-speaking world. No book exists on either his life or his doctrine. The best analysis of Drago's contribution is in Arthur P. Whitaker's *The Western Hemisphere Idea: Its Rise and Decline* (1954). Whitaker hails the Drago Doctrine as a truly multilateral effort to protect the Western Hemisphere from both European imperialism and American policing and as an attempt to improve relations between Latin America and the United States. He sees it as diametrically opposed to the Roosevelt Corollary to the Monroe Doctrine, which assumed U.S. control over the Western Hemisphere.

Thomas F. McGann also devotes a chapter to the Drago Doctrine in his *Argentina, the United States, and the Inter-American System, 1880–1914* (1957). McGann suggests that the Drago Doctrine "might more properly be known" as the Roca Doctrine because the Argentine president sponsored it in response to public "hysteria" over European aggression against Venezuela. McGann sees Argentina's role in the international incident as due to a sharpened awareness of the issues of intervention and leadership in Latin America between Argentina and the United States.

Most historians of American foreign relations mention Drago only in passing. Two widely used textbooks, Robert Ferrell's *American Diplomacy* (1975) and Thomas G. Paterson's *American Foreign Policy* (1991), do not even mention the Drago Doctrine in their discussion of either the Venezuelan incident or the Hague decisions, while Samuel Flagg Bemis's *The Latin American Policy of the United States* (1943) and Walter La-Feber's *The American Age* (1989), at opposite ends of the ideological spectrum, entirely distort the facts. LaFeber implies that Latin Americans "moved to curb" the Roosevelt Corollary, which radically altered the Monroe Doctrine, when they had the Drago Doctrine established as international law. Bemis, on the other hand, sees the United States warmly and generously supporting the Drago Doctrine at the Hague Conference. Dexter Perkins, in *The Monroe Doctrine 1867–1907* (1937), refutes Drago's argument that connecting his own doctrine to the Monroe Doctrine brought the latter into the pantheon of famous international diplomatic pronouncements.

The most recent and best history on the Drago Doctrine is Alberto A. Conil Paz's balanced and well-researched *Historia de la Doctrina Drago* (1975), based on papers from the Argentine Foreign Ministry and some historical literature from the United States;

Conil Paz agrees with Drago's 1902 concern about European imperialism and sees Drago's efforts as valuable in staving it off.

The only other noteworthy study of Drago's doctrine is in French. H. A. Moulin's *La Doctrine de Drago* (1908) contains a variety of writings on the Drago Doctrine, including the deliberations of the Third Pan American Conference at Rio and the Second International Peace Conference at The Hague.

Bibliography

Works by Luis María Drago

Drago, L. M. *El arbitraje de las pesquerías del Atlántico Norte entre la Gran Bretaña y los Estados Unidos de América*. Buenos Aires: Coni hermanos, 1911.
———. *Cobro coercitivo de deudas públicas*. Buenos Aires: Coni hermanos, 1906.
———. *Discursos y escritos*. 3 vols. Compiled by Mariano J. Drago. Buenos Aires: El Ateneo, 1938.
———. "The Drago Doctrine." *Foreign Relations of the United States* (1903): 1–5.
———. *Los Estados Federales no pueden ser ejecutados*. Buenos Aires: Talleres del Museo de La Plata, 1892.
———. "Grounds for the Dissent to the Award on Question V of the Hague Fisheries Decision." *American Journal of International Law* 4 (October 1910): 988–1000.
———. *Los hombres de presa*. Buenos Aires: Lajouane, 1888.
———. *La República Argentina y el caso de Venezuela*. Buenos Aires, 1903. Reprint. Caracas: Oficina Central de Informacion, 1976.
———. "State Loans in Their Relation to International Policy." *American Journal of International Law* 1 (July 1907): 692–726.

Works about Luis María Drago

Barcia Trelles, Camillo. *Doctrina de Monroe y cooperación internacional*. Madrid: El mundo latina, 1931.
Conil Paz, Alberto A. *Historia de la Doctrina Drago*. Buenos Aires: Abeledo-Perrot, 1975.
Iniques, Daniel Guerra. *Homenaje al Doctor Luís M. Drago*. Caracas: Oficina Central de Informacion, 1976.
Moreno Rodríguez, Rogelio. *La Doctrina Drago y sus proyecciones en la vida internacional*. Córdoba: Universidad de Córdoba, 1960.
Moulin, H. A. *La Doctrine de Drago*. Paris: Libraire de la cour d'appel et de l'ordre des avocats, 1908.
Pérez Triana, Santiago. *La Doctrina Drago*. London: Wertheimer, Lea, 1908.
Saavedra Lamas, Carlos. *Luis María Drago: Su obra, proyecciones y trascendencia*. Buenos Aires: Imprenta de la Universidad, 1943.
Vivot, Alfredo N. *La Doctrina Drago*. Buenos Aires: Coni hermanos, 1911.

Related Works

Barclay, Thomas. *Problems of International Practice and Diplomacy*. . . . Boston: Boston Book, 1907.
Beale, Howard K. *Theodore Roosevelt and the Rise of America to World Power*. Baltimore: Johns Hopkins University Press, 1956.

Bemis, Samuel F. *The Latin American Policy of the United States.* New York: Harcourt, Brace, 1943.

Bowen, Herbert W. "The Monroe, Calvo, and Drago Doctrines." *Independent* 62 (April 18, 1907): 902–904.

Calvo, Carlos. *International Law of Europe and America in Theory and Practice.* N.p., 1868.

Dunn, Frederick S. *The Protection of Nationals.* New York: Columbia University Press, 1933.

Fried, Alfred Hermann. *Die Zweite Haager Konferenz.* Leipzig: Elischer, 1916.

Hershey, Edwin M. "The Calvo and Drago Doctrines." *American Journal of International Law* 1 (January 1907): 26–45.

LaFeber, Walter. *The American Age: United States Foreign Policy at Home and Abroad Since 1750.* New York: Norton, 1989.

McGann, Thomas F. *Argentina, the United States, and the Inter-American System, 1880–1914.* Cambridge, Mass.: Harvard University Press, 1957.

Moore, John Bassett. *A Digest of International Law.* 8 vols. Washington, D.C.: U.S. Government Printing Office, 1906.

Nettles, Edward H. "The Drago Doctrine in International Law and Politics." *Hispanic American Historical Review* 8 (1928): 204–223.

Perkins, Dexter. *The Monroe Doctrine, 1867–1907.* Baltimore: Johns Hopkins Press, 1937.

Peterson, Harold F. *Argentina and the United States, 1810–1910.* Albany: State University of New York Press, 1964.

Phillomore, Robert. *Commentaries upon International Law.* 3rd ed. London: Butterworth, 1882.

Scott, George W. "International Law and the Drago Doctrine." *North American Review* 183 (October 5, 1906): 602–610.

Scott, James Brown. "Argentina and Germany: Dr. Drago's Views." *American Journal of International Law* 12 (January 1918): 140–142.

———, ed. *Hague Conventions and Declarations of 1899 and 1907.* New York: Oxford University Press, 1915.

Shea, Donald R. *The Calvo Clause: A Problem of Inter-American and International Law and Diplomacy.* Minneapolis: University of Minnesota Press, 1955.

Tulchin, Joseph S. *Argentina and the United States.* Boston: Twayne, 1990.

Wharton, Christina M. "The Drago Doctrine: Its Origin and Meaning." *Pan American Magazine* 33 (July 1921): 87–92.

Whitaker, Arthur P. *The Western Hemisphere Idea: Its Rise and Decline.* Ithaca, N.Y.: Cornell University Press, 1954.

Woolsey, T. S. "Drago and the Drago Doctrine." *American Journal of International Law* 15 (October 1921): 558–559.

VERENA BOTZENHART-VIEHE

John Foster Dulles (1888–1959).   February 1959 found John Foster Dulles in Walter Reed Hospital fighting the cancer that soon would take his life. Friends and associates the world over sent him words of encouragement. Senator Lyndon Johnson asked the U.S. Senate to stand in silent prayer for Dulles's recovery. The junior senator from Kentucky sent a bottle of bourbon with the following message: "My late father-in-law . . . used to say that the only truly great strengths left in the Free World were John Foster Dulles and good bourbon whiskey. This whiskey will cure anything.'' But neither the bourbon nor the radium treatments could retard the cancer. His declining health rendered him incapable of carrying out the duties of his office. On April 11 he submitted his resignation to the president.

On May 24, 1959, John Foster Dulles died. Heads of state from around the world attended his funeral: the Soviet, German, British, French, and U.S. foreign ministers adjourned their negotiations at Geneva and flew together to pay their respects. Everyone present, supporters and critics alike, could agree that the world would be a different place without John Foster Dulles. He had been praised for his stalwart opposition to the Communist threat, for his tenacity at the bargaining table, and for his bold and direct initiatives in pursuit of victory in the Cold War. He had been criticized for his ideological inflexibility, his narrow worldview, and his utter lack of political finesse. Forever associated with the well-turned phrases that epitomized the Eisenhower years—"massive retaliation,'' "the agonizing reappraisal,'' the "unleashing'' of Nationalist China, "brinkmanship''—Dulles was either the great bulwark of the free world or the dark prince of cold warriors. Regardless of interpretation, there can be little doubt of his centrality in American foreign policy, even less of his qualifications for office. Dulles was born and bred to be secretary of state.

The son of Edith Foster and Allen Macy Dulles, John Foster Dulles was born on February 25, 1888. His grandfather, John Watson Foster, in whose house he was born, was secretary of state under President Benjamin Harrison. Foster, as he was called, grew up in his father's world of the Presbyterian ministry and his grandfather's world of politics, law, and diplomacy. He showed great promise in each realm. In 1904 he entered Princeton. "The major benefit I got from Princeton,'' he recalled years later, "was participating in Woodrow Wilson's courses where I gained my interest in public affairs.'' It was an interest, combined with a Presbyterian belief in the doctrine of good works, that would dominate his life.

Even before graduation he crossed over from student to actor in the world of international relations. John Watson Foster had been appointed China's representative to the Second Hague Peace Conference in 1907 and invited young Dulles to serve as his secretary. This early exposure to the world of international law and diplomacy had a profound effect. While expected to follow his father into the clergy, Dulles chose instead the calling of "Christian lawyer'' as the career through which he could make a greater contribution. After the Hague Conference and an extended visit to France and Spain, he returned to Washington and entered George Washington Law School. Living with his grandparents on Eighteenth Street and working part-time in his grandfather's law firm, Dulles found himself in the midst of the diplomatic and social life of the capital. He completed law school in two years, passed the bar exam in 1911, and married Janet Avery. His grandfather arranged a clerkship for him at Sullivan and Cromwell, one of Wall Street's most prestigious firms. At age twenty-three, John Foster Dulles was on his way.

At Sullivan and Cromwell, Dulles balanced commitments to his profession and public service, the hallmark of his career. While rising through the ranks of his firm, he undertook a wartime mission to Central America for his uncle, Robert Lansing, *Woodrow Wilson's secretary of state, and served Bernard Baruch as counsel for the American delegation to the Reparations Commission at the end of World War I. He was happy to serve the Wilson administration. He identified with President Wilson; they shared Princeton, Presbyterianism, and a belief in diplomacy as an arena of moral and ethical action. Having applauded his wartime policies, the Fourteen Points, and the League of Nations, Dulles witnessed their erosion and collapse. Wilson placed policy above politics and left behind a legacy of failure and frustration.

The Wilson years taught Dulles another crucial lesson as he watched the deterioration of Lansing's relationship to the president. Eclipsed by Colonel Edward M. House, Lansing felt isolated within the administration, his position untenable. If Dulles ever found himself in the government, he would make neither Wilson's nor Lansing's mistakes.

Over the next three decades, Dulles's legal career flourished and he emerged as a national leader in international affairs, a symbol of bipartisan foreign policy. He served as a Republican advisor to several Democratic secretaries of state and participated actively in the formulation and implementation of U.S. foreign policies. He took part in the San Francisco Conference on World Organization, the early assemblies of the United Nations, the first Council of Foreign Ministers meeting in London in 1945, and their subsequent meetings in Moscow, London, and Paris. From the U.S. side of the bargaining table he watched the Grand Alliance disintegrate into cold war with few doubts about Soviet responsibility. He presented his conclusions in a two-part *Life* magazine article in June 1946.

"The most urgent task of American statesmanship," he asserted, "is to find the policies that will avert a serious clash with the Soviet Union." Soviet foreign policy, formulated and implemented in "a rigid, mechanistic and uncompromising way," would pursue its paranoid drive for security through easy expansion into areas which were "largely a vacuum, as far as faith and order are concerned." In moderate tones, Dulles called for a measured military and economic response to contain Communist aggression and demonstrated a firm belief that the ultimate solution lay in the American example of freedom and opportunity. The spiritual faith of his youth never left his understanding of human nature and international affairs.

During these years of bipartisanship, he began his long and close association with Thomas Dewey. As an internationalist and the reigning Republican expert on foreign policy, Dulles was the logical choice for foreign policy advisor when Governor Dewey received the Republican nomination for the presidency in 1948. Had Dewey won the election, Dulles would have been secretary of state. Dulles's commitment to bipartisanship reinforced the GOP decision to leave foreign policy above the political fray. With Truman's upset victory, Dulles agreed with the party leadership that letting Truman off the hook on communism at home and containment abroad had cost them the election. Almost immediately he had an opportunity to put this bitter knowledge into practice.

Since Dewey was unable to give Dulles a cabinet post, he offered him Robert Wagner's vacant New York Senate seat and the opportunity to run in his own right in 1949. In the Senate, Dulles supported the creation of NATO and the enactment of the Marshall Plan; later, as a State Department consultant, he helped the Truman administration negotiate the final treaty of peace with Japan. But Dulles would never again keep foreign policy aloof from the battles of national politics. In 1949 he launched an aggressive campaign against former Democratic governor of New York Herbert Lehman. He lost, as expected, but his strong showing surprised many political pundits. More significant in the long run were his hard-hitting style and his focus on the Communist threat throughout the campaign. Bipartisanship was in eclipse.

In the wake of his political disappointments of 1948 and 1949, Dulles organized his recent experiences and analysis of international affairs into a book, *War or Peace* (1950). The book represented the hardening of Dulles's antipathy toward the "Godless" Soviet system and his increasing willingness to attack the containment policies of Truman and his secretary of state, *Dean Acheson. He attributed Communist successes to "superb organization to conduct indirect aggression" and the absence of any counteroffensive. Containment had had its day. It had kept Western Europe out of Communist hands, it had rescued Greece, Turkey, and Iran; it had led to regional pacts like NATO that guaranteed the security of these areas. But by drawing a line the Western allies had given the Communists a free hand on the other side, "acquiescing in the consolidation of . . . four-fifths [of the world] by hostile, despotic forces." The Soviet system, like any despotism, was deeply fissured within, but only through outside pressure could those cracks be exploited to bring about the ultimate collapse of the Russian Communist machine.

While Dulles called upon America to "mobilize for peace," the precise nature of that mobilization and the direction of the campaign remained unclear. No longer the Republican elder statesman and apostle of bipartisanship, Dulles was emerging as the partisan cold warrior. He criticized the "defeatist" and "appeasing" containment policies of the Democrats and offered in their stead the "liberation" of captive peoples and the "rollback" of the Communist tide. More concerned with politics than policy, he was never specific regarding the means for achieving those goals.

Republicans were optimistic about recapturing the White House in 1952. Concerned about Robert Taft's isolationism and unelectability and the danger of a divided party, Dulles decided to back Eisenhower. At age sixty-four, Dulles knew that this was most certainly his last shot at the long sought cabinet post. Eisenhower, for his part, was happy to have the endorsement of the dean of Republican diplomats and glad to have him attacking Truman and Acheson.

Dulles campaigned as if he were running for office. Eisenhower recalled that after his victory, the choice of Dulles as secretary of state "was an obvious one.'' Once in office Dulles backed away from the hardest lines of the campaign. When Dulles the campaigner became Dulles the secretary, the world heard less of liberation and rollback. To camouflage his retreat and protect himself from the Republican right, he inaugurated a program of positive loyalty within the State Department. Dulles himself had less than pristine anticommunist credentials, given his erstwhile defense of Alger Hiss, association with bipartisan containment, and ties to Dewey and Republican internationalism. His efforts to prove and protect himself precipitated a crisis in the State Department that included the purge of the ''China hands'' and the dismissal of *George Kennan.

But as the nation's chief diplomat, Dulles faced a larger problem. After a campaign of promises to replace containment with ''a policy of boldness,'' the new administration had to act, and Dulles knew that he had promised more than he could deliver. His solution was to describe in the starkest possible terms the new administration's initiatives, to accentuate the differences between Truman's policies and those of Eisenhower. Nowhere is this effort in political drama clearer than in the administration's handling of the so-called New Look national security policies.

The product of more than a year of extensive study, the New Look picked up the thread of asymmetrical response suggested by Dulles years before. In his January 1954 address to the Council on Foreign Relations, the secretary described the twin threats facing the United States: the threat of Communist aggression from without and the possibility of economic and political crises within if the United States spent too lavishly in search of unattainable total security. Dulles and Eisenhower feared that by defending against the first threat too assiduously, the nation might fall prey to the second. The New Look represented a balanced military posture within the asymmetrical strategy Dulles had described before. It called for regional collective security pacts and increased allied responsibility for the common defense. The press corps, however, seemed to hear only ''massive retaliatory power.'' Not one to miss an opportunity for good publicity, Dulles too seized on the notion of ''massive retaliation'' as the linchpin of the bold new approach. When interviewed by *Life* in 1956, Dulles defended the Eisenhower record and attributed its accomplishments to the ''policy of boldness.''

Critics excoriated Dulles for his risk-taking, for the administration's reliance on nuclear weapons, for its willingness to go to the brink, risking global conflagration for nonvital interests. But for Dulles, brinkmanship accomplished its goal. It created an image of bold action that stood in sharp contrast to the plodding policies of his predecessors. Yet beneath the rhetoric and the political calculation was a hard-headed realism and a lawyer's flexibility in pursuing his client's best interests. Dulles's client was the United States, and the issue was how best to pursue the Cold War at a fiscal, political, and spiritual price the nation could afford.

Thus, there were two John Foster Dulleses. The first was Dulles the ideologue—the tough-minded, phrase-mongering cold warrior and master of the State

Department, the narrow and tactless diplomat whom *Winston Churchill described as "the only case of a bull I know who carries his china closet with
him." The second was a Dulles seldom seen in the public eye—Dulles the
attorney, the advocate of the Eisenhower administration who helped define and
pursue the nation's interests with subtlety and skill, who did nothing without
consultation with the president. In public, Dulles divided the world between
"us" and "them," denouncing neutrality and nonalignment as immoral. But
within the councils of government, Dulles told a different story. He recognized
the legacy of colonial exploitation and understood the appeal of revolutionary
communism. He worried that the United States would be identified with the
European imperialist powers and would lose the Third World to the Kremlin's
influence. Alignment with the cause of nationalism was the only way to avert
this disaster, but it was a solution he considered politically impossible in Cold
War America. Diplomacy was politics, and politics was the art of the possible.
Dulles sought to make the world conform to America's vision rather than change
the underlying image.

In Asia the pattern appears much the same. At the Korean truce talks, debates
over Dien Bien Phu, or the crisis over Quemoy and Matsu, Dulles spoke the
part of the implacable foe as he urged caution and moderation upon his colleagues
and his president. He "went to the brink" in his threatened use of nuclear
weapons, but one must doubt seriously if he would have considered invoking
the ultimate sanction of massive retaliation. While brandishing threats might
serve U.S. short-term interests, those interests did not justify the costs of nuclear
war. While he was the one charged with wielding the threat of massive retaliation,
in National Security Council (NSC) debates over the New Look he questioned
the political viability of weapons of mass destruction; he spoke of the concerns
of the Allies, who feared winning a nuclear war as much as losing one.

Despite occasional differences between his own position and that of the president, he never forgot his place. As the lawyer serves his client, he represented
the policies of the administration. Always careful to maintain the closest working
relationship with Eisenhower, he remembered the experiences of Robert Lansing
and made certain that no such problems would befall him. The relationship that
emerged was one agreeable to both men. Eisenhower often preferred the appearance of Dulles running the nation's international affairs. On unpopular issues,
Dulles drew the criticism, while the president enjoyed untainted popularity. In
success, Eisenhower basked in reflected glory.

Dulles and Eisenhower were of the same generation; they had seen two world
wars and witnessed the failures and successes of collective security. They believed deeply in the superiority of the American system, of democracy and
capitalism, in the bankruptcy of communism and its ultimate failure. But the
lawyer and the general were practical men; they saw international politics as an
arena of power and interest where morality and righteousness, important in their
own right, were part of a rhetorical patina that could not obscure fundamental
national interests. Both men took the long view of the Cold War. They had

experienced long campaigns and knew the price of hot wars. Confident of America's final victory, Dulles and Eisenhower sought not to win the Cold War, but to control it, to fight it step by step, at a price the nation could afford.

Annotated Bibliography

John Foster Dulles's personal papers covering his entire career are held at the Seeley G. Mudd Library at Princeton University. His official papers from 1951 to 1959 are deposited at the Dwight D. Eisenhower Library at Abilene, Kansas. Copies are also available at the Mudd Library. The general records of the State Department for the Dulles years are held at the National Archives, Washington, D.C., in Record Group 59. While many of these records are accessible, the declassification process is ongoing. Various record collections in the Eisenhower Library are also useful for Dulles scholars, particularly the Ann Whitman File within Eisenhower's official papers.

Since the 1970s the State Department and the Dwight D. Eisenhower Library have declassified much of the diplomatic record of the Eisenhower years. Scholarly assessment of that record quickly overturned the conventional wisdom concerning the style and the substance of President Eisenhower's leadership. Eisenhower revisionism has since become the new orthodoxy; researchers are no longer surprised when they turn up new evidence of the old soldier's activism and acumen as chief executive. Comparable reevaluation of Secretary of State John Foster Dulles's diplomacy, however, is still in the early stages. The ongoing declassification process underscores the need for such a reexamination. Eisenhower's management style and his broad delegation of authority make it imperative that students of his administration's foreign policy contend with the imposing figure of Dulles. Once regarded as an easy mark by critics and cartoonists, scholars increasingly find the real Dulles to be even more elusive than Eisenhower. Revision of the conventional, commonly disparaging, wisdom about Dulles lags considerably behind that of his president.

While Eisenhower's stock among scholars rose steadily in the 1980s, historians continued to rank Dulles among the five worst secretaries of state. His abrasive personality and ponderous style contributed to his difficulties with contemporary commentators; they contribute to his difficulties with historians today. A penchant for public moralizing and flag-waving combined with what one colleague called the "icy breath of his self-esteem" to alienate both contemporary critics and defenders of the Eisenhower administration's policies. The president's deliberate use of deputies as lightning rods for criticism added to his secretary of state's public relations problems.

Declassification of the secretary's official papers has already yielded considerable evidence of the private Dulles's sagacity and pragmatism, evidence at odds with well-established conceptions of his diplomacy. But the official record is leading scholars to recognize Dulles's depth of intellect, sense of history, and political skills, and to discard stereotypes about his naive patriotism and Manichean inflexibility.

As scholars subsequently gained a fuller picture of the inner workings of the administration and documented the daily consultations between Eisenhower and Dulles, the pendulum of interpretation, having first located the extremes, found a middle ground. The editor of an important collection of essays reevaluating Dulles's tenure, Richard H. Immerman, in *John Foster Dulles and the Diplomacy of the Cold War* (1990), describes what has become the prevailing view of the Eisenhower-Dulles relationship. Dulles, he wrote, was an "integral actor in the sphere of formulation as well as implementation" of policy. "Eisenhower did not dominate any more than we once thought the reverse true.... They were in a real sense a team" (Immerman, p. 9).

The conventional view that Dulles constituted a one-man team, and the resulting critical consensus regarding his leadership, have long and distinguished histories. Contemporary journalists, who often underestimated and sympathized with the avuncular Eisenhower, commonly blamed his secretary of state for the design and direction of unpopular initiatives. The tendency to inflate Dulles's responsibility for discredited policies such as liberation and massive retaliation carried over into memoirs by Emmet Hughes, *The Ordeal of Power* (1963), and Sherman Adams, *Firsthand Report* (1961), and into preliminary studies by such historians as Norman Graebner, *The New Isolationism* (1956), and George F. Kennan, *Realities of American Foreign Policy* (1954). The secretary's authorized biography by John Robison Beal, *John Foster Dulles: A Biography* (1957), did little to redress the critical consensus. In the 1960s and 1970s biographies by Louis Gerson, *John Foster Dulles* (1967), Michael Guhin, *John Foster Dulles: A Statesman and His Times* (1972), and Townsend Hoopes, *The Devil and John Foster Dulles* (1973), broadened the interpretive spectrum, but did not significantly expand the data base from which those interpretations derived.

At a 1988 centennial conference on Dulles, the historian and diplomat George F. Kennan, who had been unceremoniously dismissed from the State Department by Secretary Dulles, remembered his last encounter with the secretary: "I walked away ... largely ignorant of the intellectual qualities of the man I had just encountered." As the declassification process in the 1980s revealed the nature of those qualities, it "surprised" and "puzzled" not only Kennan; it confounded a whole new generation of students of postwar American diplomacy accustomed to the missionary fervor, melodramatic rhetoric, and patriotic platitudes associated with Eisenhower's front man. In retrospect, Kennan credits Dulles with a "highly sophisticated, politically imaginative intelligence" and believes he was "well ahead of anyone else on the political scene of the day" in his understanding of geopolitical and strategic principles. Seldom has the public perception of an American diplomat contrasted so sharply with the private record.

There was little in his public writings to prepare scholars for the declassified Dulles. His first book, *War, Peace and Change* (1939), reflected his philosophical and religious concerns as much as his extensive interwar international experience. The book's abstract prescriptions of "fellowship" and "curative and creative" reforms represented the culmination of his Wilsonian hopes for conservative, evolutionary change.

War or Peace (1950) was in part a call for domestic unity in foreign affairs; it also reflected his increasing involvement in Republican party politics and his alarm at the pervasiveness of the Communist threat. More interesting than its survey of recent international events was the way the book revealed the author's search for a mass audience. In *War or Peace*, Dulles was perfecting the elements of an increasingly melodramatic style—the religious overtones and histrionic rhetoric—that many would soon denounce as simplistic and provocative.

Dulles and Eisenhower had promised Americans bold new directions in foreign policy at a time when international conditions left little room for maneuver. When calls for "liberation" lapsed after the 1952 election campaign, when realism replaced rhetoric as the administration confronted rebellions in East Germany and Hungary, and when the administration pragmatically compromised its goals to resolve crises in Korea, Indochina, and the Taiwan straits, Dulles thought it politically imperative that Americans regard national goals as principled and uncompromising. As biographers Ronald W. Pruessen,

John Foster Dulles: The Road to Power (1982), and Mark Toulouse, *The Transformation of John Foster Dulles* (1985), make clear, Dulles's diplomatic sermons were at once deeply sincere and self-conscious, and meant to reassure Americans that they held the moral high ground in a perilous global struggle.

Revisionism driven by the opening of new primary sources is steadily transforming Dulles the ideologue into Dulles the realist. The first volume of Pruessen's biography is a landmark in this process. His account of Dulles's presecretarial career traces his intellectual development and reveals the sophisticated worldview that would underpin his years in office. Other studies, most notably *Strategies of Containment* (1982) and *The Long Peace* (1987) by John Lewis Gaddis, demonstrate that the secretary was not a prisoner of his own Cold War oratory. Threats of rollback, massive retaliation, and brinkmanship notwithstanding, the decision-making record reflects considerable caution on Dulles's part regarding the strategic and diplomatic utility of nuclear weapons. By the same token, Nancy Bernkopf Tucker, "John Foster Dulles and the Taiwan Roots of the 'Two Chinas' Policy," in R. H. Immerman, ed., *John Foster Dulles and the Diplomacy of the Cold War* (1990), shows how Dulles's facile public allusions to monolithic international communism and Kremlin-originated "conspiracies" often concealed geopolitical calculations of the divisive forces within the Eastern bloc. They also disguised his pains—within the constraints of cosmetic politics—to fashion policies that could exploit those tendencies. A number of articles in Immerman's *John Foster Dulles and the Diplomacy of the Cold War* dispel impressions that the secretary was a clumsy, albeit tenacious negotiator, and afford insights into how he brought his analytical skills and mental dexterity to bear on relations with the Allies and negotiations with adversaries.

Regardless of whether they generally approve or disapprove of Dulles's diplomacy, revisionist scholars are redirecting the debate over the secretary's career. Leaving behind stale arguments over culpability and style, they are focusing their research on the secretary's worldview, his role in the policymaking process, and the domestic and international constraints within which he operated. Their efforts are already yielding a better understanding of John Foster Dulles's contribution to the American diplomatic tradition.

Bibliography

Adams, Sherman. *Firsthand Report: The Story of the Eisenhower Administration*. New York: Harper and Row, 1961.

Anderson, David L. "J. Lawton Collins, John Foster Dulles and the Eisenhower Administration's 'Point of No Return' in Viet-nam." *Diplomatic History* 12, 2 (Spring 1988): 127–147.

Beal, John Robinson. *John Foster Dulles: A Biography*. New York: Harper and Row, 1957.

Berding, Andrew H. *Dulles on Diplomacy*. Princeton, N.J.: Van Nostrand, 1965.

Bowie, Robert R. "Eisenhower, Dulles and the Suez Crisis." In *Suez 1956: The Crisis and Its Consequences*. Edited by W. R. Louis and Roger Owen. New York: Oxford University Press, 1989.

Brands, H. W., Jr. *Cold Warriors: Eisenhower's Generation and American Foreign Policy*. New York: Columbia University Press, 1988.

———. "Testing Massive Retaliation: Credibility and Crisis Management in the Taiwan Strait." *International Security* 12 (Spring 1988): 124–151.

Chang, Gordon. "To the Nuclear Brink: Eisenhower, Dulles and the Quemoy-Matsu Crisis." *International Security* 12 (Spring 1988): 96–123.

Craig, Gordon. "John Foster Dulles and American Statecraft." In *War, Politics, and Diplomacy: Selected Essays.* New York: Praeger, 1962.

Duchin, Brian R. "The 'Agonizing Reappraisal': Eisenhower, Dulles and the European Defense Community." *Diplomatic History* 16, 2 (Spring 1992): 201–221.

Dulles, John Foster. "Challenge and Response in U.S. Foreign Policy." *Foreign Affairs* 36 (October 1957): 25–43.

———. "Thoughts on Soviet Foreign Policy and What to Do About It," *Life* 20 (June 3, 1946): 113–126 and (June 10, 1946): 118–130.

———. *War or Peace.* New York: Macmillan, 1950.

———. *War, Peace and Change.* New York: Harper and Row, 1939.

Finer, Herman. *Dulles over Suez: The Theory and Practice of His Diplomacy.* Chicago: Quadrangle Books, 1964.

Gaddis, John Lewis. *The Long Peace: Inquiries into the History of the Cold War.* New York: Oxford University Press, 1987.

———. *Strategies of Containment: A Critical Appraisal of Postwar American National Security Policy.* New York: Oxford University Press, 1982.

———. "The Unexpected John Foster Dulles: Nuclear Weapons, Communism, and the Russians." In *John Foster Dulles and the Diplomacy of the Cold War.* Edited by Richard H. Immerman. Princeton, N.J.: Princeton University Press, 1990.

Gerson, Louis. *John Foster Dulles.* New York: Cooper Square, 1967.

Graebner, Norman A. *The New Isolationism: A Study in Politics and Foreign Policy Since 1950.* New York: Ronald Press, 1956.

Guhin, Michael. *John Foster Dulles: A Statesman and His Times.* New York: Columbia University Press, 1972.

Herring, George, Gary R. Hess, and Richard S. Immerman. " 'A Good Stout Effort': John Foster Dulles and the Indochina Crisis, 1954–1955." In *John Foster Dulles and the Diplomacy of the Cold War.* Edited by Richard H. Immerman. Princeton, N.J.: Princeton University Press, 1990.

———. "Passage of Empire: The United States, France, and South Vietnam, 1954–1955." In *Dien Bien Phu and the Crisis in Franco-American Relations, 1954–1955.* Edited by Lawrence S. Kaplan, Denise Artaud, and Mark Rubin. Wilmington, Del.: SR Books, 1990.

Herring, George, and Richard Immerman. "Eisenhower, Dulles and Dienbienphu: 'The Day We Didn't Go to War' Revisited." *Journal of American History* 71, 2 (September 1984): 343–363.

Holsti, Ole. "The 'Operational Code' Approach to the Study of Political Leaders: John Foster Dulles' Philosophical and Instrumental Beliefs." *Canadian Journal of Political Science* 3 (March 1970): 123–157.

———. "Will the Real Dulles Please Stand Up?" *International Journal* 30, 1 (Winter 1974–1975): 34–44.

Hoopes, Townsend. *The Devil and John Foster Dulles.* Boston: Little, Brown, 1973.

Hughes, Emmet. *The Ordeal of Power: A Political Memoir of the Eisenhower Years.* New York: Atheneum, 1963.

Immerman, Richard H. *The CIA in Guatemala: The Foreign Policy of Intervention.* Austin: University of Texas Press, 1982.

———. "Eisenhower and Dulles: Who Made the Decisions?" *Political Psychology* 12 (Autumn 1979): 124–179.

———, ed. *John Foster Dulles and the Diplomacy of the Cold War.* Princeton, N.J.: Princeton University Press, 1990.

———. "The United States and the Geneva Conference of 1954: A New Look." *Diplomatic History* 14, 1 (Winter 1990): 43–66.

Kennan, George F. *Memoirs: 1950–1963*. Boston: Little, Brown, 1973.

———. *Realities of American Foreign Policy*. Princeton, N.J.: Princeton University Press, 1954.

Larson, Deborah Welch. "Crisis Prevention and the Austrian State Treaty." *International Organization* 41 (Winter 1987): 27–60.

Lisagor, Nancy, and Frank Lipsius. *A Law unto Itself: The Untold Story of Sullivan and Cromwell*. New York: Morrow, 1988.

Louis, William Rogers. "Dulles, Suez and the British." In *John Foster Dulles and the Diplomacy of the Cold War*. Edited by Richard H. Immerman. Princeton, N.J.: Princeton University Press, 1990.

Mayers, David Allen. *Cracking the Monolith: U.S. Policy Against the Sino-Soviet Alliance, 1949–1955*. Baton Rouge: Louisiana State University Press, 1986.

Miyasato, Seigen. "John Foster Dulles and the Peace Settlement with Japan." In *John Foster Dulles and the Diplomacy of the Cold War*. Edited by Richard H. Immerman. Princeton, N.J.: Princeton University Press, 1990.

Mosely, Leonard. *Dulles: A Biography of Eleanor, Allen, and John Foster Dulles and Their Family Network*. New York: Dial, 1978.

Nelson, Anna Kasten. "John Foster Dulles and the Bipartisan Congress." *Political Science Quarterly* 102 (Spring 1987): 43–64.

Pruessen, Ronald W. "John Foster Dulles and Germany." In *Perceptions of the Federal Republic of Germany*. Edited by Robert Spencer. Toronto: Centre for International Studies, 1986.

———. "John Foster Dulles and the Predicaments of Power." In *John Foster Dulles and the Diplomacy of the Cold War*. Edited by Richard H. Immerman. Princeton, N.J.: Princeton University Press, 1990.

———. *John Foster Dulles: The Road to Power*. New York: Free Press, 1982.

Rabe, Stephen G. "Dulles, Latin America and Cold War Anticommunism." In *John Foster Dulles and the Diplomacy of the Cold War*. Edited by Richard H. Zimmerman. Princeton: N.J. Princeton University Press, 1990.

Steininger, Rolf. "John Foster Dulles, the European Defense Community, and the German Question." In *John Foster Dulles and the Diplomacy of the Cold War*. Edited by Richard H. Immerman. Princeton, N.J.: Princeton University Press, 1990.

Toulouse, Mark. *The Transformation of John Foster Dulles: From Prophet of Realism to Priest of Nationalism*. Macon, Ga.: Macon University Press, 1985.

Tucker, Nancy Bernkopf. "John Foster Dulles and the Taiwan Roots of the 'Two Chinas' Policy." In *John Foster Dulles and the Diplomacy of the Cold War*. Edited by Richard H. Immerman. Princeton: N.J. Princeton University Press, 1990.

Van Deusen, Henry P., ed. *The Spiritual Legacy of John Foster Dulles: Selections from His Articles and Addresses*. Philadelphia: Westminster, 1960.

BRIAN R. DUCHIN AND DANIEL P. O'C. GREENE

Elizabeth I (1533–1603). Elizabeth I, the fifth and last Tudor monarch of England, was born at Greenwich Palace on September 7, 1533. She was the daughter of Henry VIII and his second wife, Anne Boleyn. Elizabeth's childhood was turbulent because of the chaos at court following her mother's execution for treason and her father's four subsequent marriages. While she spent most of her early years at Hatfield House in Hertfordshire, Elizabeth learned early the importance of prudence and the value of ambiguity as instruments for survival.

Elizabeth's education was conducted by a series of tutors. After the deaths of her father (1547) and brother, Edward VI (1553), Elizabeth had to contend with the reign of her Catholic half-sister Mary, who ruled from 1553 to 1558. The Marian policies of reintroducing Catholicism and realigning England with Rome did not survive Mary's reign.

Elizabeth ascended to the throne on November 17, 1558, when Mary died without a direct heir. For the next forty-five years, Elizabeth ruled the nation during an era of substantive change in which England's society, politics, and international position were transformed radically. Although she was embroiled in marital politics and intrigue, Elizabeth I never married. On her deathbed, Elizabeth recognized James VI of Scotland, son of Mary Stuart, as her heir; she died at Richmond Palace, London, on March 23, 1603.

During her long tenure, Elizabeth I was confronted with a revolutionary international situation. In the first half of the sixteenth century, international relations were dominated by dynastic interests and the impact of the Reformation. However, economics and the emergence of nationalism also began to play important roles in international relations. When Elizabeth became queen at the age of twenty-five, she was advised that the two principal foreign policy concerns of England were its historic animosity toward France and its need to maintain a positive relationship with the Burgundian rulers of the Netherlands. By the end of the reign, Elizabeth was engaging in a drawn-out war with the Spanish Habsburgs, supporting a nationalist revolution in the Netherlands, realigning England's trade relations with Europe, sustaining an internal vigilance against externally based Catholic subversion, and reorienting English politics with the imminent succession of a Scottish king, whose mother had been executed by order of Elizabeth I, to the English throne. Elizabeth responded to these challenges by formulating and implementing policies that secured England and enhanced the nation's prestige. She was assisted by her primary advisors, Sir William Cecil (Lord Burghley) and Francis Walsingham.

During the first decade of her reign, Elizabeth I was preoccupied with domestic considerations. The Elizabethan Settlement (1558–1559), aimed at religious discord, stabilized Protestant control over England. Both Protestants and Catholics welcomed the government's position, which endorsed the official Protestant doctrine but at the same time permitted Catholics to practice their religion privately. It was during this same period that Elizabeth's long-term affair (1564–1588) with Lord Robert Dudley, Earl of Leicester, began. The complexities associated with marital politics provided a consistent theme at court; marriage politics continued until 1583 when, at the age of forty-nine, Elizabeth broke off negotiations with the Duc d'Alençon.

While the prospect of a marriage alliance to a foreign leader, such as the declined offer of *Philip II of Spain, who had been Mary's husband, may have been construed as a major international issue, foreign affairs did not constitute the focus of Elizabeth's agenda during the early years of her reign. However, a few developments had to be addressed. In 1559 England joined with Spain in concluding their war with France in the Treaty of Câteau-Cambrésis. Within three years, a civil war developed in France between the Catholics and the French Huguenots. Elizabeth ordered that English forces be used to assist the Huguenots at Le Havre; while the surrender of the English garrison there in 1563 embarrassed Elizabeth, the English continued to provide financial aid to the Huguenots.

Foreign affairs came to the forefront during the late 1560s as a consequence of Counter-Reformation fervor, the outbreak of a revolution in the Netherlands, and mounting hostility toward Spain. During the 1560s resistance to the Elizabethan Settlement increased among orthodox Catholics. The revived Tridentine Roman Church attracted numerous academics and scholars from Oxford and elsewhere. William Allen established a seminary for English Catholics at Douai for the purposes of maintaining an English Catholic tradition and training priests to serve and expand the English Catholic Church. In 1570 Pope Pius V, in *Excelsis Regnans*, stated that English Catholics should not recognize Elizabeth as the English monarch. In response to these actions, Elizabeth enacted penal laws directed primarily against the actions of these foreign-trained priests; Elizabeth approached this anti-Catholic policy reluctantly during the 1570s.

However, in 1580–1581 the Catholic "assault" on England was aggravated by the arrival of a Jesuit mission headed by Edmund Campion and Robert Parsons. Campion's capture and subsequent execution and Parsons's polemical campaign resulted in a series of more severe measures to eliminate the Catholic "menace." Most English Catholics remained loyal to Elizabeth and demonstrated their loyalty during the war with Spain.

Nonetheless, the Catholic issue constituted a serious threat; the nature and scope of the danger were evident with the involvement of extremist recusant Catholics in four plots against Elizabeth. In 1569 the Rising of the Northern Earls was an attempt to overthrow Elizabeth and restore the old nobility to power; the conspiracy specified that the Duke of Norfolk would marry Mary Stuart and they would succeed to the throne. The revolt failed; Norfolk was imprisoned and about 800 rebels were executed. In 1571 the Ridolfi Plot was initiated by Roberto di Ridolfi, an agent of the Roman Catholic Church. With the support of the Duke of Norfolk and Philip II of Spain, Ridolfi planned a marriage between Mary and Norfolk that would signal an uprising of English Catholics and a Spanish invasion. The plot was revealed before it was launched, and Norfolk was executed in 1572. Francis Throckmorton, author of the Throckmorten Plot, developed a plan involving Philip II, the French, and Mary Stuart; the goal was to eliminate Elizabeth and place the Catholic Mary on the throne. Throckmorton was arrested and executed. Finally, the Babington Plot was advanced by Anthony Babington, who planned to kill Elizabeth and place Mary on the throne. Walsingham's spies gathered information directly implicating Mary, and Elizabeth ordered her cousin's execution in 1587.

The problem of the English Catholics plagued Elizabeth's government to the end; however, the regime succeeded in capitalizing on the rift between the traditional native Catholic clerics and laity and the foreign-trained and -financed Tridentine seminarists. During the 1590s the factionalism within English Catholicism was evident in a series of disagreements. In response to the recusant problem, Elizabeth, Burghley, his son Robert Cecil, and Walsingham formulated a policy that effectively muted this threat and, at the same time, sustained the support of most English Catholics. Elizabeth's management of the recusant question enhanced her authority at home and her reputation as a statesman abroad.

In 1562 a French civil war erupted between the Protestant Huguenots and the Catholic Valois dynasty. This struggle was characterized by a series of atrocities including the St. Bartholomew's Day Massacre (1572), which was planned and executed by the queen mother, Catherine de Medici. Later, the struggle degenerated into a bitter dynastic crisis, the so-called War of the Three Henrys, in which the last of the Valois, Henry III, was opposed by Henry, duc d'Guise, and Henry of Navarre, leader of the Huguenots. In 1589 Navarre became Henry IV and a Catholic. Throughout this struggle, with the exception of the Le Havre relief effort of 1562–1563, English involvement was limited to financial assistance to the Huguenots. On the French side, there was some minor involvement in Elizabethan marriage politics.

Much more significant than Anglo-French relations was the mounting crisis in Anglo-Spanish-Burgundian affairs that dominated Elizabeth's diplomacy. In 1558 England was allied with Spain in a war against France. Within a decade the Anglo-Spanish alliance had vanished, replaced with increased suspicion on both sides. This shift in attitude reflected important developments in the Netherlands, the gateway for English trade on the Continent. In 1558 the Netherlands consisted of seventeen northern provinces held by the Duke of Burgundy, who at that time was Philip II of Spain. During the 1560s a rebellion motivated by religious, political, and economic considerations broke out. English access to the Netherlands, especially the port city of Antwerp, remained crucial to the English.

During the same period, relations between London and Madrid had become strained because of the failure of proposed marriage arrangements, the establishment of the Elizabethan religious settlement, and the hardening of Philip II's pro-Catholic religious policy. Elizabeth I's response to this alteration in Anglo-Spanish relations was to adopt a prudent policy based on the requirement that English merchants retain access to European markets. However, the maintenance of even tenuous relations became difficult with the mounting evidence of Philip II's involvement in the plots against Elizabeth and the English support of the rebels in the Netherlands. Growing English interference with Spanish trade also contributed to the tension. During the 1560s English adventurers such as Sir John Hawkins established an English slave trade. In the 1570s Sir Francis Drake began raiding Spanish shipping and colonies, turning over a share of the profits to Elizabeth I.

Relations with Spain continued to deteriorate during the 1580s. Philip II's support of the Throckmorton and Babington plots was evident to Elizabeth and her ministers. After Mary Stuart's execution, Philip II determined to strike at the English. In 1588 Philip sent the famous Spanish Armada under the command of the Duke of Medina Sidonia into the English Channel. Sidonia was to join with a Spanish army under Alessandro Farnese, the Duke of Parma, in the attack on the English. Between July 21 and 28, 1588, the English and Spanish navies fought in the English Channel. The Armada was dispersed and the Spanish plan failed. The English people, including English Catholics, supported Elizabeth and her efforts to defend the nation.

The war with Spain continued to the end of the reign. Hostilities were extended with an English counterattack against Spain, which failed, the deployment of English troops in the Netherlands to assist the rebels, an English attack on Cadiz in 1596, and Philip II's support of the Irish revolt that commenced in 1598. Elizabeth I retained the support of the English nation during this prolonged struggle, although the financial strain on the country was evident before 1600.

Elizabeth's abilities as a leader were challenged with the outbreak of the Irish revolt in 1598. Led by Hugh O'Neill, the Earl of Tyrone, rebellious Irish forces defeated an English unit at the Battle of Blackwater River. In 1599 the English army, led by the Earl of Essex, failed to break the revolt; Essex would be executed for treason in 1601. Finally, Elizabeth ordered to Ireland an English army under Lord Mountjoy, who defeated the Irish and Spanish forces in 1603 and suppressed the revolt.

Elizabeth I succeeded in her goals of defending English sovereignty, maintaining economic access to Europe, and extending English influence in the Atlantic. Her reign witnessed the unity of the English nation and the emergence of a public sense of national identity, which she nurtured and exploited. Throughout her long reign, Elizabeth I exhibited those traits that transform adequate leaders into great national and international figures. She was prudent, thorough in her preparations, wise in seeking the advice of her councillors, and, most important, perspicacious in assessing the aspirations and will of the nation.

Annotated Bibliography

Most of the primary sources associated with Elizabeth I's leadership in international affairs have been published. Nonetheless, archival depositories at the Public Record Office (London), the Bodleian Library (Oxford), the British Museum and Library (London), Hatfield House (Hertfordshire), and the libraries at Cambridge University (Cambridge) are most useful. Among the more significant of the published state papers are the *Calendar of Letters and State Papers, relating to English Affairs, preserved principally in the Archives of Simancas*, edited by Martin A.S. Hume (1892–1899); *Calendar of Letters, Despatches, and State Papers, relating to the Negotiations between England and Spain, preserved in the Archives at Vienna, Simancas, Besançon, and Brussels*, edited by G. A. Bergenroth et al. (1862–1954); *Calendar of State Papers and Manuscripts, Relating to English Affairs, Existing in the Archives and Collections of Venice, and in Other Libraries of Northern Italy*, edited by Rawdon Brown et al. (1864–1947); *Calendar of State Papers, Domestic Series . . .* , edited by Robert Lemon and Mary A.E. Green (1856–

1872); and the *Calendar of State Papers, Foreign Series . . .* , edited by Joseph Stevenson et al. (1863–1950). Extremely important for an understanding of the formulation of Elizabethan foreign policy is *A Collection of State Papers Relating to Affairs in the Reigns of King Henry VIII, King Edward VI, Queen Mary, and Queen Elizabeth . . . left by William Cecil Lord Burghley,* edited by Samuel Hayes and William Murdin (1740–1759). A collection of *The Letters of Queen Elizabeth,* edited by G. B. Harrison (1935; reprinted 1968), provides a glimpse into the personal life and thoughts of Elizabeth I on international issues as well as many other aspects of Tudor life. Other significant primary sources include the *Correspondence of Robert Dudley, earl of Leycester, during his Government of the Low Countries in the Years 1585 and 1586* (1844); Victor von Klarwill, ed., *Queen Elizabeth and Some Foreigners* (1928); *Relations politiques des Pays-Bas et de l'Angleterre, sous le règne de Philippe II,* edited by Joseph M.B.C. Kervyn de Letterhove and L. Gilliodts van Severen (1882–1900); and *Correspondance diplomatique de Bertrand de Salignac de La Mothe Fénélon,* edited by Alexandre Teulet (1838–1840). Contemporary accounts that provide alternative interpretations include William Allen's *An Admonition to the Nobility and People of England and Ireland . . .* (1588), which provides a rationale for the Catholic position; Sieur de Maisse, *A Journal of All That Was Accomplished by Monsieur de Maisse, Ambassador in England from King Henri IV to Queen Elizabeth, Anno Domini 1597,* translated and edited by G. B. Harrison (1931), which provides French insights into English policies during the war with Spain; Sir Robert Nauton's *Fragmenta Regalia, or Observations on Queen Elizabeth's Times and Favourites, with Portraits and Views* (1641), which presents the interpretation of a political survivor and a protégé of the Earl of Essex; and *Elizabeth of England: Certain Observations Concerning the Life and Reign of Queen Elizabeth,* which was written in 1603 by John Clapham, a member of Burghley's household and clerk of the Court of Chancery, but not published until it was edited by E. P. Read and C. Read in 1951.

The most significant contemporary historian of the Elizabethan era was William Camden. In *The History of the Most Renowned and Virtuous Princess Elizabeth, Late Queen of England,* which first appeared in 1630, Camden presented an excessively laudatory account of Elizabeth and her policies. With the exception of histories written by Catholics or their sympathizers, who opposed Elizabeth's religious policies and were uniformly critical of her, Camden's interpretation survived through the Enlightenment. During the nineteenth century, Elizabeth came under mounting criticism by historians such as James Anthony Froude, who, in his *History of England from the Fall of Wolsey to the Death of Elizabeth* (1881), concluded that Elizabeth was not a major leader as argued by Camden, but rather an inane, second-rate, and vain woman who did not understand politics. Froude maintained that Henry VIII was the dominant political figure during the Tudor era and that Sir William Cecil, Lord Burghley, not Elizabeth, was responsible for the achievements of the Elizabethan era.

In the twentieth century the Froude thesis prevailed until a revisionist movement was launched by Sir John Neale during the 1930s. In *Queen Elizabeth I* (1934), *Elizabeth I and Her Parliaments* (1953–1957), and *Essays in Elizabethan History* (1958), Neale established the ''Gloriana'' interpretation of Elizabeth I as the great leader and statesman. Neale was overwhelmed by Elizabeth I's accomplishments and failed to measure the almost romantic aspects of his view against the realities of the human experience. Nonetheless, the Neale thesis became the standard in the historiographical resurrection of the image of Elizabeth I; indeed, in the public mind, Neale's Elizabeth still survives. Of the three works noted, *Elizabeth I and Her Parliaments* is still worthy of attention because of its analysis of Parliament during this period.

Conyers Read, a contemporary of Sir John Neale, advanced a sympathetic though not uncritical portrait of Elizabeth in *Lord Burghley and Queen Elizabeth* (1960) and *Mr. Secretary Cecil and Queen Elizabeth* (1961). In both of these studies Read focused on the principal ministers and argued that the interdependent relationships between the monarch and her ministers resulted in establishing an effective government. Perhaps Read's most lasting contribution to scholars has been his *Bibliography of British History, Tudor Period, 1485–1603* (2nd ed., 1959), which, not surprisingly, excels in the Elizabethan segment.

While the works of Joel Hurstfield (*Elizabeth I and the Unity of England*, 1960; *The Elizabethan Nation*, 1967; *Freedom, Corruption, and Government in Elizabethan England*, 1973; and *The Illusion of Power in Tudor Politics*, 1979), Elizabeth Jenkins (*Elizabeth the Great*, 1958), Carolly Erickson (*The First Elizabeth*, 1983), and Lacey Baldwin Smith (*Elizabeth Tudor: Portrait of a Queen*, 1975) still command the attention of scholars, the modern study of Elizabeth's international efforts is dominated by R. B. Wernham, Wallace T. MacCaffrey, Christopher Haigh, and G. D. Ramsay. In his classic studies of the Elizabethan period, *Before the Armada: The Emergence of the English Nation, 1485–1588* (1966) and *The Making of Elizabethan Foreign Policy, 1558–1603* (1980), R. B. Wernham advanced a series of theses predicated on the interrelationship of policy and politics. He argued that Elizabethan statesmen recognized the armada experience as a defining moment.

Wallace T. MacCaffrey has been studying the Elizabethan era for the last thirty years. In *The Shaping of the Elizabethan Regime* (1968), *Queen Elizabeth and the Making of Policy, 1572–1588* (1981), and *Elizabeth I, War and Politics, 1588–1603* (1992), MacCaffrey portrayed Elizabeth and her advisors as ''power politicians'' in an England rapidly being transformed into an early modern state.

Christopher Haigh has studied the problems and issues related to northwestern England, the English recusants, and the Elizabethan approach to church-state relations. In *The Reign of Elizabeth*, which Haigh edited in 1985, and *Elizabeth I* (1988), he concludes that Elizabethan policies abroad were effective responses to imposed situations; the issue of identifying an Elizabethan ''foreign policy'' may be most difficult.

G. D. Ramsay, in ''The Foreign Policy of Elizabeth I,'' argued that, while religious and dynastic considerations were evident, the economic requirements of the nation directed foreign policy considerations. He emphasized the need to sustain and expand markets through northwestern European ports. Contemporary scholars have tempered the enthusiasm of Neale but have not restored the severe critical interpretation of Froude. Since 1989, most Elizabethan political, diplomatic, and religious historians have expended considerable attention studying the decade of the 1590s.

Bibliography

Allen, William. *An Admonition to the Nobility and People of England and Ireland*....
    1588. Reprint Menston, Yorkshire: Scolar Press, 1971.
Anglicanus, Palaeophilus. *The Conduct of Queen Elizabeth towards the neighboring
    nations, and particularly Spain, compared with that of James I*.... London:
    Robinson, 1729.
Bassnet, Susan. *Elizabeth I: A Feminist Perspective*. New York: Berg, 1988.
Beckingsale, B. W. *Elizabeth I*. London: Batsford, 1963.
Bindoff, Stanley T. ''A Kingdom at Stake, 1553.'' *History Today* 3, 9 (September 1953):
    642–648.

————. *Tudor England*. Pelican History of England, Volume 5. Baltimore: Penguin, 1950.

Black, John B. *The Reign of Elizabeth, 1558–1603*. 2nd ed. *Oxford History of England*, Volume 8. Oxford: Clarendon Press, 1959.

Bryant, Arthur. *The Elizabethan Deliverance*. New York: St. Martin's Press, 1981.

Calendar of Letters and State Papers, relating to English Affairs, preserved principally in the Archives of Simancas. 4 vols. Edited by Martin A.S. Hume. London: H. M. Stationery Office, 1892–1899.

Calendar of Letters, Despatches, and State Papers, relating to the Negotiations between England and Spain, preserved in the Archives at Vienna, Simancas, Besançon, and Brussels. 13 vols. in 17. Edited by G. A. Bergenroth et al. London: Longman, 1862–1954.

Calendar of State Papers and Manuscripts, Relating to English Affairs, Existing in the Archives and Collections of Venice, and in Other Libraries of Northern Italy. 38 vols. in 40. Edited by Rawdon Brown et al. London: Longman, 1864–1947.

Calendar of State Papers, Domestic Series, of the Reigns of Edward VI, Mary, Elizabeth, and James I, preserved in the State Department of Her Majesty's Public Record Office. 12 vols. Edited by Robert Lemon and Mary A.E. Green. London: Longman, 1856–1872.

Calendar of State Papers, Foreign Series, of the Reign of Elizabeth, preserved in the State Paper Department of Her Majesty's Public Record Office. 23 vols. in 26. Edited by Joseph Stevenson et al. London: Longman, 1863–1950.

Camden, William. *The History of the Most Renowned and Virtuous Princess Elizabeth, Late Queen of England*. 4th ed. London: R. Bentley, 1688. Reprint. New York: AMS Press, 1970.

Clapham, John. *Elizabeth of England: Certain Observations Concerning the Life and Reign of Queen Elizabeth*. Edited by E. P. Read and C. Read. Philadelphia: University of Pennsylvania Press, 1951.

Clarke, Samuel. *The History of the Glorious Life, Reign, and Death, of the Illustrious Queen Elizabeth. . . .* London: Printed for H. Rhodes, 1683.

A Collection of State Papers Relating to Affairs in the Reigns of King Henry VIII, King Edward VI, Queen Mary, and Queen Elizabeth . . . left by William Cecil Lord Burghley, and now remaining at Hatfield House. 2 vols. Edited by Samuel Hayes and William Murdin. London: William Boyer, 1740–1759.

Creighton, Mandell. *Queen Elizabeth*. New ed. London: Longmans, Green, 1899. Reprint. New York: Crowell, 1966.

Elton, G. R. *England under the Tudors*. 2nd ed. *A History of England*, Volume 4. London: Methuen, 1974.

Emmison, F. G. *Elizabethan Life: Disorder*. Chelmford, Eng.: Essex County Council, 1970.

Erickson, Carolly. *Bloody Mary*. Garden City, N.Y.: Doubleday, 1978.

————. *The First Elizabeth*. New York: Summit Books, 1983.

Fénélon, Bertrand de Salignac, seigneur de La Mothe. *Correspondance diplomatigue de Bertrand de Salignac de La Mothe Fénélon*. 7 vols. Edited by Alexandre Teulet. Paris and London: N.p., 1838–1840.

Froude, James Anthony. *History of England from the Fall of Wolsey to the Death of Elizabeth*. 4 vols. New York: Scribner's, 1881.

Haigh, Christopher. *Elizabeth I*. London: Longmans, 1988.

————, ed. *The Reign of Elizabeth*. Athens: University of Georgia Press, 1985.

Harrison, G. B., ed. *The Letters of Queen Elizabeth*. London: Cassell, 1935.

Haugaard, William P. *Elizabeth and the English Reformation: The Struggle for a Stable Settlement of Religion*. Cambridge: Cambridge University Press, 1968.

Haydn, Hiram, ed. *The Portable Elizabethan Reader*. New York: Viking/Penguin, 1981.

Heylyn, Peter. *Ecclesia restaurata, or The history of the reformation of the Church of England. . . .* London: Twyford, Place, and Basset, 1674.

Holinshed, Raphael. *Holinshed's Chronicles of England, Scotland, and Ireland*. 6 vols. London: Johnson, 1807–1808.

Hopkins, Lisa. *Elizabeth I and Her Court*. New York: St. Martin's Press, 1990.

Hudson, Winthrop Still. *The Cambridge Connection and the Elizabethan Settlement of 1559*. Durham, N.C.: Duke University Press, 1980.

Hume, Martin Andrew Sharp. *The Courtships of Queen Elizabeth: A History of the Various Negotiations for Her Marriage*. Rev. ed. London: Eveleigh Nash, 1904.

Hurstfield, Joel. *Elizabeth I and the Unity of England*. New York: Macmillan, 1960.

————. *The Elizabethan Nation*. New York: Harper and Row, 1967.

————. *Freedom, Corruption, and Government in Elizabethan England*. London: Cape, 1973.

————. *The Illusion of Power in Tudor Politics*. London: Athlone Press, 1979.

Jenkins, Elizabeth. *Elizabeth and Leicester*. New York: Coward-McCann, 1962.

————. *Elizabeth the Great*. New York: Coward-McCann, 1958.

Johnson, Paul. *Elizabeth I: A Biography*. New York: Holt, Rinehart and Winston, 1974.

Kervyn de Lettenhove, Joseph M.B.C., and L. Gilliodts van Severen, eds. *Relations politiques des Pays-Bas et de l'Angleterre, sous le règne de Philippe II*. 11 vols. Brussels: Hayez, 1882–1900.

Klarwill, Victor von, ed. *Queen Elizabeth and Some Foreigners*. New York: Brentano's, 1928.

Lee, Frederick George. *The Church under Queen Elizabeth; An Historical Sketch*. Rev. ed. London: Allen, 1892.

Leicester, Robert Dudley, Earl of. *Correspondence of Robert Dudley, earl of Leycester, during his Government of the Low Countries, in the Years 1585 and 1586*. Camden Society, Old Series, 27. London: Nichols, 1844.

Levine, Mortimer. *The Early Elizabethan Succession Questions, 1558–1568*. Stanford, Calif.: Stanford University Press, 1966.

Luke, Mary M. *Gloriana: The Years of Elizabeth I*. New York: Coward, McCann, and Geoghegan, 1973.

MacCaffrey, Wallace T. "The Anjou Match and the Making of Elizabethan Foreign Policy." In *The English Commonwealth, 1547–1640: Essays in Politics and Society Presented to Joel Hurstfield*, pp. 59–75. Edited by Peter Clark, Alan G.R. Smith, and Nicholas Tyacke. Leicester: Leicester University Press, 1979.

————. *Elizabeth I, War and Politics, 1588–1603*. Princeton, N.J.: Princeton University Press, 1992.

————. *Queen Elizabeth and the Making of Policy, 1572–1588*. Princeton, N.J.: Princeton University Press, 1981.

————. *The Shaping of the Elizabethan Regime*. Princeton, N.J.: Princeton University Press, 1968.

MacNulty, Arthur S. *Elizabeth Tudor*. New York: Ungar, 1961.

Maisse, Sieur de. *A Journal of All That Was Accomplished by Monsieur de Maisse,*

Ambassador in England from Henri IV to Queen Elizabeth, Anno Domini 1597. Translated and edited by G. B. Harrison. London: Nonesuch Press, 1931.

Mattingly, Garrett. *The Armada.* Boston: Houghton Mifflin, 1962.

McCollum, John, ed. *The Age of Elizabeth: Selected Source Materials in Elizabethan Social and Literary History.* Boston: Houghton Mifflin, 1960.

Morey, Adrian. *The Catholic Subjects of Elizabeth I.* London: Allen and Unwin, 1978.

Naunton, Robert. *Fragmenta Regalia, or Observations on Queen Elizabeth's Times and Favorites, with Portraits and Views.* 1641. Edited by John S. Cerovski. Washington, D.C.: Folger Shakespeare Library, 1985.

Neale, J. E. *Elizabeth I and Her Parliaments.* 2 vols. London: Cape, 1953–1957.

———. "The Elizabethan Political Scene." *Proceedings of the British Academy* 34 (1948): 97–117.

———. *Essays in Elizabethan History.* London: Cape, 1958.

———. *Queen Elizabeth I.* 1934. Reprint. London: Cape, 1952.

Palliser, D. M. *The Age of Elizabeth: England Under the Later Tudors, 1547–1603.* London: Longmans, 1983.

Perry, Maria. *The Word of a Prince: A Life of Elizabeth I from Contemporary Documents.* Rochester, N.Y.: Boydell Press, 1990.

Plowden, Alison. *Elizabeth Tudor and Mary Stewart: Two Queens in One Isle.* Totowa, N.J.: Barnes and Noble, 1984.

———. *Marriage with My Kingdom: The Courtships of Elizabeth I.* New York: Stein and Day, 1977.

Pulman, Michael Barraclough. *The Elizabethan Privy Council in the Fifteen Seventies.* Berkeley: University of California Press, 1971.

Ramsay, G. D. "The Foreign Policy of Elizabeth I." In *The Reign of Elizabeth I,* pp. 147–168. Edited by Christopher Haigh. Athens: University of Georgia Press, 1985.

Read, Conyers. *Bibliography of British History, Tudor Period, 1485–1603.* 2nd ed. Oxford: Clarendon Press, 1959.

———. *Lord Burghley and Queen Elizabeth.* New York: Knopf, 1960.

———. *Mr. Secretary Cecil and Queen Elizabeth.* New York: Knopf, 1961.

———. *The Tudors: Personalities and Practical Politics in Sixteenth Century England.* New York: Holt, Rinehart and Winston, 1936.

Ridley, Jasper Godwin. *Elizabeth I: The Shrewdness of Virtue.* New York: Viking, 1988.

Rowse, A. L. *The England of Elizabeth: The Structure of Society.* London: Macmillan, 1950.

Smith, Alan G.R. *The Government of Elizabethan England.* London: Arnold, 1967.

Smith, Lacey Baldwin, ed. *Elizabeth I.* St. Louis: Forum Press, 1980.

———. *Elizabeth Tudor: Portrait of a Queen.* Boston: Little, Brown, 1975.

Somerset, Anne. *Elizabeth I.* London: Weidenfeld and Nicolson, 1991.

Strong, Roy. *The Cult of Elizabeth: Portraiture and Pageantry.* Berkeley: University of California Press, 1977.

Tillyard, E.M.W. *The Elizabethan World Picture.* London: Chatto and Windus, 1943.

Wernham, R. B. *Before the Armada: The Emergence of the English Nation, 1485–1588.* New York: Harcourt, Brace and World, 1966.

———. *The Making of Elizabethan Foreign Policy, 1558–1603.* Berkeley: University of California Press, 1980.

Williams, Charles. *Queen Elizabeth I.* London: Duckworth, 1936.

Williams, Neville. *Elizabeth the First: Queen of England.* New York: Dutton, 1968.

————. *The Life and Times of Elizabeth I*. Garden City, N.Y.: Doubleday, 1971.

Williams, Penry. *The Tudor Regime*. Oxford: Clarendon Press, 1979.

Wilson, Charles Henry. *Queen Elizabeth and the Revolt of the Netherlands*. Berkeley: University of California Press, 1970.

Wilson, E. K. *England's Eliza*. Cambridge, Mass.: Harvard University Press, 1939.

WILLIAM T. WALKER

Benjamin Franklin (1706–1790).   Ben Franklin's statement that "Virtuous Men ought to league together to strengthen the Interest of Virtue, in the World" reveals much about the fascinating and multifaceted career of this eighteenth-century American enlightener and statesman. As suggested in biographies and monographs, Franklin was foremost a man of the Enlightenment, believing that reason governed the thinking and behavior of virtuous individuals and enabled them to contribute to the liberal arts and experimental science. Major ideologies and doctrines of the Enlightenment, which stimulated many of Franklin's cultural and civic activities, also helped to shape his career as an American revolutionary statesman.

During his early life in Puritan Boston, Franklin developed a sense of incentive and practicality and a thirst for knowledge. Born on January 17, 1706, in Boston, Benjamin was the youngest son of Abiah and Josiah Franklin. As a child, he displayed interest in learning and was able to read prior to his entry into Boston Grammar School at age eight. After leaving that school at age ten, young Franklin first worked in his father's candle making business and became a printer's apprentice for his brother James, which gave him the opportunity to learn about the printing business and to read with great voracity books about various topics. He developed immense intellectual curiosity and began to write. In 1722 Franklin published a collection of essays under the name of "Silence Dogood" concerned with New England life and the doctrines of Puritanism.

As a consequence of frequent quarrels with James, Franklin ran away to Philadelphia in 1723 and helped to implement concepts of enlightened civic boosterism in the Quaker city. Franklin felt at home in Philadelphia, for this city served as an asylum for persecuted groups and individuals and especially offered him opportunities for advancement. He quickly made friends in the city's printing world, first working the "old shatter'd" press of the eccentric Samuel Keimer in 1724 and then opening his own printing business. As business began to increase, Franklin purchased the *Pennsylvania Gazette* from Keimer in 1730 and transformed it into the largest newspaper in the city. His great success in printing stimulated him to publish *Poor Richard's Almanack* in 1731—a widely read publication issued each year until 1758. Adhering to the belief espoused in *Poor Richard*, namely, that "he that hath not got a Wife, is not yet a Compleat Man," Franklin married Deborah Read in September 1730 and probably produced from this marriage a son named William, who later vehemently opposed his father and supported the Tory cause.

Franklin was very active in cultural activities associated with the Enlightenment in Philadelphia. He established the American Philosophical Society in 1744 and developed this cultural institution into the finest learned society in colonial and revolutionary America. This academy, which resembled the Royal Society of London, recruited scientists and gentlemen interested in Enlightenment culture from both the colonies and Europe, and succeeded as a result of Franklin's scientific reputation.

Franklin's position as a colonial agent between 1757 and 1762 and between 1764 and 1775 was significant, because he acquired valuable diplomatic and leadership skills and promoted the transatlantic Enlightenment. As a result of his electrical discoveries, Franklin was elected a fellow of the Royal Society of London and developed friendships with Sir John Pringle, Joseph Priestley, and other British enlighteners. Franklin became involved in London club life, frequently attending the meetings of the Club of Honest Whigs and eating dinner either at the Dog Tavern or at the Pennsylvania Coffee House. However, problems in the American colonies concerned Franklin during his years in London; he represented Pennsylvania, Massachusetts, New Jersey, and Georgia in various matters, becoming a capable propagandist and an adamant lobbyist for the cause of American expansionism. Franklin denounced the Proclamation of 1763, since colonists would be thwarted in their efforts to settle lands west of the Alleghenies and since the Illinois Company, in which he owned shares, would be severely damaged. Franklin also defended the interests of the Vandalia and Grand Ohio land companies, thus supporting American efforts to settle lands between the Ohio and Mississippi rivers. As tensions between Britain and America increased, Franklin in 1766 called for the repeal of the Stamp Act on the floor of the House of Commons and four years later launched a newspaper campaign against the Townshend Acts.

After his return to Philadelphia in 1775, Franklin, the oldest revolutionary, prudently gave direction to the affairs of the patriots. He was elected in 1775 as a member of the Continental Congress. The next year, Franklin served on the committee for the drafting of the Declaration of Independence; he supported the Jeffersonian natural rights philosophy and signed this pertinent document, which explained to the world the position and ideologies of the American revolutionaries. In 1776 Franklin also served on the Committee of Secret Correspondence, whose chief function was to obtain commercial and military aid for the conduct of the American Revolution. As a result of discussions with Achard de Bonvouloir, who indicated in Philadelphia that France was interested in selling America arms and war supplies, Franklin and other members of this committee drafted the model treaty of amity and commerce. Although primarily intended for France, this treaty was also to be offered to Spain and other enemies of the British. The treaty called for assistance to America in its efforts to obtain independence from Britain, for the selling of military supplies to the patriots, and for the negotiation of commercial treaties with European nations. After ratifying the model treaty, the Continental Congress in September 1776 instructed Franklin to go to Paris and to work with Arthur Lee and Silas Deane in negotiating a treaty with France.

After his arrival at Auray on December 3, 1776, Franklin displayed traits important to his career as a statesman in France. By March 1777, the busy Franklin moved into a comfortable estate at Passy, about ten miles from Versailles. Franklin needed the comforts at Passy, for he frequently suffered from gout, kidney stones, or exhaustion. As a diplomatic negotiator, Franklin proved to be shrewd, persistent, serious, reserved, and cautious. He was effective in making compromises and in utilizing traditional channels to secure his diplomatic goals.

During his first year in Paris, Franklin attempted to achieve significant diplomatic objectives, including obtaining commercial, financial, and military assistance for the American cause. Franklin secured the services of Louis Duportail as chief engineer of the Continental Army and of Count Casimir Pulaski and Friedrich Wilhelm von Steuben to positions of leadership in this army. As a result of his meetings with Pierre A.C. Beaumarchais, Franklin convinced this playwright and adventurer to establish Rodrigue Hortalez and Company, a fictitious firm that would collect funds from European businessmen and governments and distribute them in support of the American Revolution. Franklin also negotiated a free trade pact to sell American tobacco to the Farmers General, a consortium of French businessmen and bankers that administered the government's tobacco monopoly and provided America with funds needed to conduct the revolution. Finally, Franklin placated Comte Charles Vergennes about the vexing problem of American warships using French ports.

A major diplomatic triumph of Franklin was negotiating the Franco-American Treaties of 1778. Here his diplomatic bargaining powers were limited, for Vergennes was unwilling to negotiate commercial and military pacts with him until the Americans had won a major battle against the British. Soon after the American victory at Saratoga on October 17, 1777, Vergennes was ready to negotiate with Franklin, and two treaties were consummated between the French and the Americans on February 6, 1778. The first pact, known as the Treaty of Amity and Commerce, embodied both free trade and most-favored-nation clauses. The second, the Franco-American Treaty of Alliance, also contained significant provisions; both nations agreed that if war ensued between Britain and France, America and France would support each other as allies against England. Both nations also agreed that fighting would continue until American "liberty, sovereignty, and independence, absolute and unlimited," were won and that neither France nor America would conclude a "truce or peace" with Britain without the "formal consent of the other first obtained." Consequently, the provisions of these two treaties went beyond those of the 1776 model treaty.

Other developments relating to Franklin's diplomacy arose immediately after the conclusion of these two treaties. Most important, Franklin succeeded in obtaining needed loans and military aid from the French for the conduct of the War of Independence. However, Franklin encountered unfortunate problems at Passy, where as a result of disorderliness and lax security, Edward Bancroft, who had been a friend of Franklin during his years in London, and other members of the British secret service obtained valuable information from their espionage activities. In addition, Silas Deane, accused of giving British spies sensitive information, was recalled as commissioner soon after the negotiating of the 1778 treaties, and was replaced by John Adams. Franklin also quarrelled with Arthur Lee, a man he considered contentious, vain, and vindictive. As a result of his success in negotiating the 1778 treaties, however, Franklin was appointed head of the American mission in Paris in 1779.

There were other significant facets of Franklin's diplomacy. He was a masterful role player and made effective use of the concepts, doctrines, and symbols of the Enlightenment to promote the cause of America. Parisian savants portrayed Franklin, in his plain attire and his liberty cap, both as an American and as a citizen of the world who best exemplified the Enlightenment qualities of reason and virtue; these savants, in short, helped to create a Franklin cult, especially lauding him for his scientific discoveries and his recent diplomatic achievements.

Franklin's involvement with the Parisian Masonic Lodge of the Nine Sisters provided him with his greatest opportunity to secure support for the American cause. Franklin, who had told his mother in 1738 that the Freemasons "have no principles or practices that are inconsistent with religion and good manners," had been named provincial grand master of Pennsylvania Masonry in 1749 and was elected on May 21, 1779, as master of this Parisian lodge and learned society. During his term as master, an Americanophile party quickly developed. A journal at first sponsored by the French Ministry of Foreign Affairs and then funded in part by members of the lodge, *Affaires de l'Angleterre et de l'Amérique*, contained articles by Franklin about significant military and diplomatic accomplishments and consequently became an important propagandistic organ. During meetings of the lodge, Hilliard d'Auberteril, Brissot de Warville, and Jean Demeunier presented select essays from their works about America; these essays portrayed Americans as virtuous enlighteners from the New World, supported their military efforts against the British, defended their republican ideologies and institutions, and praised Franklin for his diplomatic triumphs in Paris. Just before the end of the War of Independence, the Duke of Rochefoucauld, with the support of Franklin, issued a major translation of six state constitutions and other pertinent American republican writings.

Franklin, too, significantly contributed to the diplomatic settlement that ended the American Revolution. Fatigued and sick, Franklin, whose offer to resign his position was refused by Congress in 1781, worked with John Adams and John Jay to draft a treaty for the creation of the new American nation. Events again favored Franklin, for his old friend Lord Shelburne became chief minister and head of the British cabinet on July 1, 1782; Shelburne favored a policy of reconciliation with America and authorized Richard Oswald, a Scottish merchant and an advocate of free trade, to enter into talks with Franklin. On July 10, 1782, the American statesman offered these proposals: the full and complete independence of America, the cession of Canada to the new nation, the guarantee of American fishing off the banks of Newfoundland and elsewhere, and the settlement of borders between Britain and America. During this session, Franklin even intimated that America would compensate Loyalists for damage suffered during the war. Oswald informed Franklin that Britain would not cede Canada to America and that the United States should make payment for damages to the Loyalists. In October, Franklin agreed to the request concerning remuneration for damages and, with the firm support of Jay, proposed that the western borders of the United states extend from the Ohio to the Mississippi rivers and from the Lake of the Woods to the Gulf of Mexico and to the border of Florida. Franklin's skill as a negotiator was embodied in the Anglo-American Treaty of November 30, 1782, for its terms recognized American independence, its vast western borders, its fishing privileges in Newfoundland, and its navigation rights on the Mississippi River. While not including France in the Anglo-American negotiations and thus violating a major provision of the Franco-American Treaty of Alliance, Franklin succeeded in placating Vergennes; the French foreign minister was quite willing to cease hostilities with the British and to sign the Paris Peace Treaty on September 3, 1783. Frail and sad, Franklin departed for Philadelphia from his French estate on July 12, 1785.

Franklin, who served as a delegate from Pennsylvania to the 1787 Constitutional Convention and who died on April 17, 1790, significantly contributed to American diplomacy. His diplomatic successes greatly exceeded his failures. He tended to be somewhat disorganized as an administrator and frequently failed to communicate with Congress. Franklin did little to minimize espionage activities of British agents at Passy and was unable to resolve conflicts arising between Arthur Lee and Silas Deane. While bringing France into the War of Independence, Franklin indirectly contributed to the demise of the French economy and monarchy. However, Franklin was as capable as the best professionally trained statesmen in Europe. He was a superb propagandist, working through both public and private channels to disseminate his ideas and achieve his diplomatic ends. Franklin developed an effective negotiating style, learning how to listen and knowing when to bluff and when to accommodate. Consequently, he emerged as an important contributor to modern statesmanship, becoming one of the first diplomats to be associated with the cause of revolution.

Franklin's diplomacy had a major impact on the course of international relations. During a session of the Constitutional Convention on September 17, 1787, this American sage made a statement about the rising and the setting of the sun; the sun's rising and setting might well be associated with Franklin's major diplomatic achievements, namely, the creation of a nation based on republican ideologies and American expansion into western lands. Like the sun's diffusive rays, republican ideologies would shine, contributing to the institutional and territorial growth of America during the nineteenth and twentieth centuries and enabling it to serve as a paragon for nations in Latin America, Europe, and Asia. Since the creation of the American federal republic, the diplomacy of expansionism has been intimately involved with the acquisition and settlement of lands between the Mississippi River and the Pacific Ocean, with the relationship of the United States to Britain and France, with the provisions and corollaries of the Monroe Doctrine, and with issues concerning the rise of the United States as a world power during the twentieth century. The twin legacies of republican ideologies and expansionism well might suggest why "virtuous men ought to league together" in 1776 and revealed the successful efforts of Franklin to combine the idealism of the Enlightenment with the realism of European power politics to help create the new American nation.

Annotated Bibliography

There are some fine archival collections with manuscripts about the diplomatic activities of Franklin. Three libraries are located in Philadelphia: Primary materials pertinent to Franklin's career as a colonial agent in London are found in the Franklin manuscript collections of the Historical Society of Pennsylvania and of the Library Company of Philadelphia. Scholars utilizing the facilities of these two libraries are charged minimal fees for research. Scholars will find myriad primary sources about the diplomatic and cultural activities of Franklin in Paris in the manuscript holdings of the American Philosophical Society. This society is working conjointly with Yale University Press to fund the publication of the comprehensive volumes of *The Papers of Benjamin Franklin*. The Franklin manuscript collections at Yale University Library in New Haven and those at the Library of Congress in Washington also contain valuable primary materials. The addresses of these major libraries are as follows:

American Philosophical Society
    104 South Fifth Street
    Philadelphia, PA 19106

The Historical Society of Pennsylvania
    1300 Locust Street
    Philadelphia, PA 19107

The Library Company of Philadelphia
    1314 Locust Street
    Philadelphia, PA 19107

Numerous works contain primary materials about the life of Benjamin Franklin and his career as a diplomat. Two major editions of Franklin's papers were published during the nineteenth century. *The Works of Benjamin Franklin*, 10 vols. (1836–1840), edited by Jared Sparks (the first historian to edit the Franklin papers), has fewer than 1,400 items but includes some valuable papers about Franklin's years in Paris. *The Complete Works of Benjamin Franklin*, 10 vols. (1887–1889), edited by John Bigelow, contains about 1,600 items and includes some major primary materials about the Parisian mission of Franklin. *The Writings of Benjamin Franklin*, 10 vols. (1905–1907), edited by Albert Henry Smyth, is the best of the early editions of the Franklin papers and contains about 1,800 items. Volume 7 is especially important for its valuable primary sources relating to the 1778 treaties.

The Yale University edition of the Franklin papers is the most comprehensive collection of primary materials. *The Papers of Benjamin Franklin*, 28 vols. (1959–), edited by William Willcox, Leonard Labaree, and others, is meticulously edited and reveals much about the multifaceted career of Franklin. Volume 25 is especially instructive, containing important letters and documents about the signing of the commercial and political treaties between America and France in 1778.

Other significant works contain primary sources about the cultural and diplomatic roles of Franklin. Franklin's autobiography, written late in life, reveals much about his early life, his involvement in the printing business, and his contributions to Philadelphia and to Newtonian science. This valuable primary source, available in *Benjamin Franklin: The Autobiography and Other Writings* (1961), edited by Jesse L. Lemisch, unfortunately says relatively little about his years as an American diplomat in Paris. While quite old, *The Revolutionary Diplomatic Correspondence of the United States*, 6 vols. (1889), edited by Francis Wharton, is still a valuable source of major papers and letters of Franklin. Robert Morris and John Adams, *Franklin in France*, 2 vols. (1887–1888), edited by Edward E. Hale and Edward E. Hale, Jr., contains letters and other documents of Franklin not available elsewhere.

Affaires de l'Angleterre et de l'Amérique, 15 vols. (1776–1779), was a journal funded by the French Foreign Ministry and later in part by members of the Parisian Lodge of the Nine Sisters. Published about twice a month, it contained lucidly written articles about the military efforts of the American revolutionaries and about their need for military and financial assistance. *Letters and Papers of Benjamin Franklin and Richard Jackson, 1753–1785* (1947), edited by Carl Van Doren, has several letters regarding Franklin's Parisian mission and his diplomatic achievements.

In addition to treating his civic, cultural, and political activities, biographers of Franklin have devoted some attention to his role as a statesman. Carl Van Doren's *Benjamin Franklin* (1938) is the most comprehensive biographical study of Franklin. Van Doren is certainly sympathetic toward Franklin, but still offers prudent assessments about his career. Esmond Wright, in *Franklin of Philadelphia* (1986), has written a somewhat more interpretive study. The best chapters in the Wright study concern Franklin's boosterism in Philadelphia, his role as a colonial agent in London, and his accomplishments as an Enlightenment propagandist and revolutionary diplomat in Paris. Franklin's achievements as America's major diplomat and enlightener are evaluated in Alfred O. Aldridge, *Benjamin Franklin: Philosopher and Man* (1965), and in Ronald W. Clark, *Benjamin Franklin: A Biography* (1983). A biography stressing the importance of the Enlightenment to the diplomacy of Franklin is Bernard Fay, *Franklin: The Apostle of Modern Times* (1929). This work depicts Franklin as an advocate of democratic ideologies, contains minimal discussion about his diplomatic activities, and stresses the conspiracy theory of history. Unfortunately, it suffers from numerous factual inaccuracies.

Several studies examine Franklin's role as a colonial agent and the emergence of an American foreign policy during the colonial era. Michael G. Kammen, *A Rope of Sand: The Colonial Agents, British Politics and the American Revolution* (1968), is a fine work that fills a void about colonial administrators and their policies toward Britain. Kammen discusses the significance of Franklin's activities as a colonial agent in London and demonstrates the importance of this position in the development of his diplomatic skills. Franklin's years in London are also the focus of another valuable work: Cecil Currey, *Road to Revolution: Benjamin Franklin in England, 1765–1775* (1968), explores major activities of Franklin as a colonial agent and as a land speculator.

As a consequence of problems of taxation with England during the 1760s and early 1770s, did some colonists encourage the development of an American foreign policy? Max Savelle, "The Appearance of an American Attitude Toward External Affairs, 1750–1775," *American Historical Review* 52 (1946–1947): 655–666, argues impressively that

Franklin and other American revolutionaries did develop some commercial and even diplomatic ties prior to 1776, especially with the French.

There are numerous monographs and articles about the origins and evolution of American revolutionary diplomacy. In *To the Farewell Address: Ideas of Early American Foreign Policy* (1961), Felix Gilbert argues that the Enlightenment idealism of the philosophes and the realism of European power politics shaped the thinking and behavior of Franklin and other American statesmen in their quest for aid and independence. Imperial problems between America and Britain and the revolutionary diplomatic activities of Franklin are examined by Richard W. Van Alstyne, *Empire and Independence: The International History of the American Revolution* (1965).

Other significant studies focus on Franklin's role in American revolutionary era diplomacy. Samuel Flagg Bemis, *The Diplomacy of the American Revolution* (1957), advances the theses that American independence was closely related to European diplomacy and that Franklin especially knew how to treat Vergennes and to negotiate the commercial and political pacts of 1778; Bemis portrays Franklin as an experienced diplomat and emphasizes his shrewdness in obtaining western lands from Britain in the 1783 Paris Peace Treaty. Jonathan R. Dull, *A Diplomatic History of the American Revolution* (1985), develops the thesis that France by 1778 had completed its naval rearmament program, was fearful of reconciliation between Britain and America, and consequently was willing to negotiate the two pacts with Franklin that year. Dull demonstrates the aggressive yet shrewd role of Franklin in negotiating the Franco-American Alliance and the 1783 Paris Peace Treaty. Lawrence S. Kaplan, *Colonies into Nation: American Diplomacy, 1763–1801* (1972), assesses the role of Franklin as a colonial agent, demonstrates how he used Enlightenment rhetoric to acquire French support for America, and suggests how Franklin, the former Francophile, engaged in separate negotiations with Britain in an effort to obtain independence and lands west of the Ohio River for the new American republic. In "The American Revolution in an International Perspective: Views from Bicentennial Symposia," *International History Review* 1 (1979): 408–426, Kaplan explores the impact of the diplomacy of the American Revolution, stressing that Franklin's diplomacy led to the spread of republican ideologies in France and other European states and thus revealed the transatlantic character of the American Revolution.

Three additional studies focus on Franklin's diplomacy. Gerald Stourzh, *Benjamin Franklin and American Foreign Policy* (1969), maintains that Franklin blended Enlightenment concepts such as natural liberties, free trade, and material progress with diplomatic notions such as the balance of power and national interest to develop an effective foreign policy. The author claims that Franklin's concept of enlightened self-interest is embodied in the Franco-American pacts of 1778. Stourzh also argues that the 1783 Paris Peace Treaty contains provisions that reflect Franklin's thinking about American security, commerce, and expansionism. In "Benjamin Franklin and the Nature of American Diplomacy," *International History Review* 5 (1983): 346–363, Jonathan R. Dull offers views somewhat different from those of Stourzh. Dull stresses the diplomatic qualities of Franklin, claiming that he was sly and evasive and that he effectively operated through formal diplomatic channels to obtain French support in 1778 and to secure American independence in 1783. Dull's *Franklin the Diplomat: The French Mission* (1982) portrays Franklin as a realist in the realm of diplomacy, for he was patient, prudent, and subtle and consequently became an effective negotiator and conciliator. Dull concludes that Franklin's accomplishments in securing financial and military aid and later in obtaining independence and vast western land tracts attest to his efficacy as the major statesman of the newly created American republic.

Numerous studies focus on Franklin's cultural and social activities in Paris and their importance to his diplomacy. Alfred O. Aldridge, *Franklin and His French Contemporaries* (1957), is a valuable study about the image and perceptions of Franklin in Paris. Another fascinating study about the cultural activities of Franklin in Paris is *Mirage in the West: A History of the French Image of American Society to 1815* (1957) by Durand Echeverria. This work has vivid accounts about the connections of Franklin to Voltaire, French Newtonians, and French writers who helped to edit and finance the American propagandistic organ *Affaires de l'Angleterre et de l'Amérique*. Claude-Anne Lopez, *Mon Cher Papa: Franklin and the Ladies of Paris* (1966), wonderfully recounts the social and cultural activities of Franklin in Paris and suggests their importance to his diplomatic negotiations. The explicit connections of Freemasonry to Franklin's diplomacy and the leadership role of Franklin in the Parisian Lodge of the Nine Sisters are assessed by R. William Weisberger, "Benjamin Franklin: A Masonic Enlightener in Paris," *Pennsylvania History* 53 (1986): 165–180.

There are several studies about Franklin's role in negotiating the 1783 Paris Peace Treaty. Richard B. Morris, *The Peacemakers: The Great Powers and American Independence* (1965), is an interesting, detailed study based on archival materials from America and Europe. While displaying sympathy toward John Jay, Morris depicts Franklin as a reserved, adaptable, and sly statesman. The book, however, contains fine sections about the efforts of Franklin to obtain western lands and Canada from England and explains how Franklin adjusted to British and European statesmen to arrange a "good peace." In *The American Revolution Reconsidered* (1967), Morris argues that Franklin placed too much trust in Vergennes and in 1783 failed to recognize the opposition of the French foreign minister to American movement into lands between the Ohio and Mississippi rivers. Lawrence S. Kaplan, "The Treaty of Paris, 1783: A Historiographical Challenge," *International History Review* 5 (1983): 431–442, maintains, among other things, that most studies of this treaty reflect sympathy either for Franklin or for Jay. Kaplan also argues that historians have not assessed the diplomatic and ideological impact of the treaty in light of America's role in the "Atlantic system."

Bibliography

Aldridge, Alfred O. *Benjamin Franklin: Philosopher and Man*. Philadelphia: Lippincott, 1965.

———. *Franklin and His French Contemporaries*. New York: New York University Press, 1957.

Alsop, Susan. *Yankees at Court: The First Americans in Paris*. Garden City, N.Y.: Doubleday, 1982.

Bemis, Samuel Flagg. *The Diplomacy of the American Revolution*. Bloomington: Indiana University Press, 1957.

Bigelow, John, ed. *The Complete Works of Benjamin Franklin*. 10 vols. New York: G. P. Putnam's, 1887–1889.

Burlingame, Roger. *Benjamin Franklin, Envoy Extraordinaire*. New York: Coward-McCann, 1967.

Clark, Ronald W. *Benjamin Franklin: A Biography*. New York: Random House, 1983.

Corwin, Edward S. *French Policy and the American Alliance of 1778*. Princeton, N.J.: Princeton University Press, 1916.

Currey, Cecil. *Road to Revolution: Benjamin Franklin in England, 1765–1775*. Garden City, N.Y.: Anchor, 1968.

Davidson, Phillip. *Propaganda and the American Revolution*. Chapel Hill: University of North Carolina Press, 1941.

Dull, Jonathan R. "Benjamin Franklin and the Nature of American Diplomacy." *International History Review* 5 (1983): 346–363.

―――. *A Diplomatic History of the American Revolution*. New Haven, Conn.: Yale University Press, 1985.

―――. *Franklin the Diplomat: The French Mission*. Philadelphia: American Philosophical Society, 1982.

Echeverria, Durand. *Mirage in the West: A History of the French Image of American Society to 1815*. Princeton, N.J.: Princeton University Press, 1957.

Fay, Bernard. *Franklin: The Apostle of Modern Times*. Boston: Little, Brown, 1929.

Gilbert, Felix. *To the Farewell Address: Ideas of Early American Foreign Policy*. Princeton, N.J.: Princeton University Press, 1961.

Hale, Edward E., and Edward E. Hale, Jr., eds. *Franklin in France*. 2 vols. Boston: Roberts Brothers, 1887–1888.

Kammen, Michael G. *A Rope of Sand: The Colonial Agents, British Politics and the American Revolution*. Ithaca, N.Y.: Cornell University Press, 1968.

Kaplan, Lawrence S. "The American Revolution in an International Perspective: Views from Bicentennial Symposia." *International History Review* 1 (1979): 408–426.

―――. *Colonies into Nation: American Diplomacy, 1763–1801*. New York: Macmillan, 1972.

―――. "The Treaty of Paris, 1783: A Historiographical Challenge." *International History Review* 5 (1983): 431–442.

Labaree, Leonard, and William Willcox, et al. *The Papers of Benjamin Franklin*. 28 vols. New Haven, Conn.: Yale University Press, 1959–1990.

Lemisch, Jesse L., ed. *Benjamin Franklin: The Autobiography and Other Writings*. New York: Signet Classics, 1961.

Lopez, Claude-Anne. *Mon Cher Papa: Franklin and the Ladies of Paris*. New Haven, Conn.: Yale University Press, 1966.

Morris, Richard B. *The American Revolution Reconsidered*. New York: Harper and Row, 1967.

―――. *The Peacemakers: The Great Powers and American Independence*. New York: Harper and Row, 1965.

Murphy, Orvilee T. *Charles Gravier, Comte de Vergennes: French Diplomacy in the Age of Revolution, 1719–1787*. Albany: State University of New York Press, 1982.

Savelle, Max. "The Appearance of an American Attitude Toward External Affairs, 1750–1775." *American Historical Review* 52 (1946–1947): 655–666.

Shoenbrun, David. *Triumph in Paris: The Exploits of Benjamin Franklin*. New York: Harper and Row, 1976.

Smyth, Albert Henry, ed. *The Writings of Benjamin Franklin*. 10 vols. New York: Macmillan, 1905–1907.

Sparks, Jared, ed. *The Works of Benjamin Franklin*. 10 vols. Boston: Hilliard, Gray, 1836–1840.

Stinchcombe, William C. *The American Revolution and the French Alliance*. Syracuse, N.Y.: Syracuse University Press, 1969.

Stourzh, Gerald. *Benjamin Franklin and American Foreign Policy*. 2nd ed. Chicago: University of Chicago Press, 1969.

Van Alstyne, Richard W. *Empire and Independence: The International History of the American Revolution*. New York: Wiley, 1965.

Van Doren, Carl. *Benjamin Franklin*. New York: Viking, 1938.

————, ed. *Letters and Papers of Benjamin Franklin and Richard Jackson, 1753–1785*. Philadelphia: American Philosophical Society, 1947.

Van Tyne, Claude H. "Influence Which Determined the French Government to Make the Treaty with America, 1778." *American Historical Review* 31 (1915–1916): 528–541.

Weisberger, R. William. "Benjamin Franklin: A Masonic Enlightener in Paris." *Pennsylvania History* 53 (1986): 165–180.

Wharton, Francis, ed. *The Revolutionary Diplomatic Correspondence of the United States*. 6 vols. Washington, D.C.: Government Printing Office, 1889.

Wright, Esmond. *Franklin of Philadelphia*. Cambridge, Mass.: Harvard University Press, 1986.

WILLIAM WEISBERGER

Frederick the Great (1712–1786).   The royal infant Frederick was born in Berlin, the capital of Brandenburg-Prussia, on January 24, 1712. His subsequent career belied the etymology of "Frederick," meaning one "rich in peace." His father ascended the Prussian throne in 1713 as Frederick William I. His mother, Sophia Dorothea from Hanover, was the daughter of the new king of England. Frederick was one of fourteen children, of whom ten survived. Since two older brothers had died in infancy, he was heir apparent to the Prussian throne. Using military genius, administrative adeptness, and strains of enlightened absolutism, Frederick as king was to complete the forging of Brandenburg-Prussia, a patchwork creation of separate territories, into a strong centralized state, a development begun by his Hohenzollern great-grandfather, the Great Elector (r. 1640–1688).

"Little Fritz" was educated to become a Prussian officer. Huguenot Jacques Duhan tutored him in modern history, geography, politics, law and natural rights, religion, mathematics, French, and German. Frederick resisted spelling and mathematics, even though geometry is fundamental for military training. Although he read Luther's translation of the Bible, the model for the German language, Frederick never became fluent in German, which he considered a "semi-barbarous tongue." Instead, he preferred French, the language spoken at home, where Parisian culture and the absolutism of *Louis XIV's Versailles were admired. Young Fritz also learned to play the flute and, under his mother's guidance, developed a love of the arts. Military officers taught him that success on the battlefield was the surest way to honor and glory.

Young Frederick was partly responsible for the famous discord with his harsh and bluff father. Fritz provoked him with sneers, diamond rings, long hair, and pranks with his sister Wilhelmine. Fritz's mother, embittered by the austere Berlin court, encouraged her son's rebellion. On the other side, during *Tabagie* (smoking and drinking sessions with advisors) and sometimes in public, Frederick William struck the crown prince or pulled him by his hair.

At sixteen, Frederick gained experience in the seamier side of courtly life when he accompanied his father to the corrupt court of Augustus II in Dresden, Saxony. Possibly Augustus furnished his first mistress, and Frederick contracted an infection, which required radical surgery. This incident may partly explain his later vindictiveness toward Saxony.

At eighteen, Frederick found intolerable both the physical punishment and passing remorse that the king dispensed. He resolved to flee. Assisted by Peter von Keith and Hans von Katte, two young officers, he planned an escape from Brandenburg while on a tour of the Rhine with his father. The plan was discovered and Frederick was sent east to solitary confinement at Cuestrin on the Oder. Katte was arrested and beheaded under the window of Frederick's cell. This was the most sobering event of Frederick's youth. For a fortnight he feared the same fate; the furious king wanted Frederick court-martialed as a military deserter. But military officers claimed that they lacked authority to try the crown prince.

Tempers cooled after Frederick pledged unconditional loyalty to the king and began an apprenticeship in the state bureaucracy in Cuestrin. He returned briefly to Berlin to attend the marriage of Wilhelmine in November 1731. His father determined that he and his son should continue to live separately, but Frederick was named a colonel in the infantry and resumed his military training. Prince Leopold I, the "Old Dessauer," prepared for him a manuscript history of Prussian regiments.

In 1734 Frederick fought against France along the Rhine in the War of the Polish Succession. From the German high commander, the aged Prince Eugene of Savoy, Frederick learned grand strategy and the poor state of the Habsburg Austrian military. In 1735 Frederick was promoted to major general and visited Berlin; his father had seemed to be on his deathbed. Both were upset that Emperor Charles VI of Austria had not consulted Prussia on the disposition of Lorraine. Frederick likely now contemplated the invasion of Silesia.

In 1732 Frederick had been forced to marry Princess Elizabeth Christine of Brunswick to escape Cuestrin. The unwanted marriage was a formality; his sexual interests were shifting more to men. From 1736 to 1740 Frederick resided with his wife at Rheinsberg near Berlin and prepared to become a philosopher-king. At Rheinsberg he had a personal library of over 3,775 volumes and voraciously read classics in French, military history, Montesquieu, John Locke, and Christian Wolff. He played the flute and violin and composed music. In 1739 Frederick began to compile a tract entitled *Refutation du Prince Machiavel*, arguing that ethics must guide princes in statecraft. When Voltaire arrived in Berlin, he helped refine it into the forceful *Anti-Machiavel*.

In May 1740 Frederick succeeded to the throne. As an individual, he initially exemplified the final stage of absolutism that historians label enlightened absolutism or despotism. This controversial concept contains contradictions but suggests that the ruler is partly influenced to make reforms by Enlightenment ideals. At the start of his reign, Frederick II was the ruler philosophes wanted. He abolished judicial torture, restricted press censorship, and recognized religious toleration for all Christians. He recalled philosopher Christian Wolff from exile to his university post in Halle.

Frederick also promoted a cultural renaissance in Berlin, including revitalization of the Berlin Academy of Sciences. Advanced science and technology were understood to be requisites for national greatness. Under physicist Pierre Maupertuis from Paris and Swiss-born mathematician and theoretical physicist Leonhard Euler from St. Petersburg, the Berlin Academy became one of the foremost centers of scientific research in Europe.

Under Frederick II, Brandenburg-Prussia became one of three new powers in eighteenth-century Europe, the other two being Great Britain and Russia. To attain this status, Frederick gave priority to foreign policy, where he was despotic, aggressive, cynical, and without scruples. "Whether the state . . . is tiny or huge," he wrote, "*aggrandisement* [expansion] is the fundamental law of government."

International relations thus did not pose a moral conundrum for Frederick, as the *Anti-Machiavel* might suggest. Agreeing instead with *Machiavelli that human beings are ruthless in their pursuit and use of power, he concluded in "Épître sur la méchanceté des hommmes" that the preservation of the state requires monarchs to match the immorality of their neighbors, even to the extent of breaking treaties.

Frederick II, like his father, saw Habsburg Austria, which dominated central Europe, as thwarting Prussian growth. In 1740 he was eager to seize the rich Austrian duchy of Silesia. It was an ambitious project. Brandenburg-Prussia had a population of 2.25 million compared to Silesia's 1.5 million. Silesia had a linen industry, arable land, timber, and a large Lutheran minority in the north. Strategically, moreover, it was a gateway to Bohemia, making Bohemia and Austria vulnerable to invasion.

The unexpected death of the Habsburg Charles VI in October excited Frederick. Given the death of Anna of Russia and his father that year, the old political system now seemed to be in the "melting pot." Charles VI's death left Austria in crisis, with an empty treasury, famine, and plague, and without a male heir. Only the Pragmatic Sanction supported the succession of the untested Archduchess Maria Theresa. By contrast, Frederick William I, "the father of Prussian militarism," had left Frederick an effective administration (the General Directory), a treasury with 8 million thaler, and a strong 83,000-man army.

Before any other rapacious neighbor could act during the diplomatic confusion over whether the Pragmatic Sanction would be honored, Frederick challenged Habsburg hegemony in the Holy Roman Empire. In pursuit of *aggrandisement* and glory, he quickly moved Prussian troops into Silesia in the winter of 1740, an action justified by contrived legal claims and an offer to support Maria Theresa's succession in exchange. This seizure was the decisive act of his reign. With Silesia, Prussia was a significant power, but Frederick had to fight three wars to keep it from Austria. Its seizure set off a struggle for dominance in central Europe between Prussia and Austria that lasted over a century. Frederick also supported Charles of Bavaria to be Holy Roman Emperor and claimed that his Silesian invasion was in support of Charles.

Frederick II began the two Silesian Wars, from 1740 to 1742 and from 1744 to 1745, with a strong army and no allies. (These are also known as the War of the Austrian Succession, which ended with a truce in 1748.) With meticulous attention to detail, Frederick began to earn his reputation for military genius, but he still had much to learn. At Mollwitz, for example, he fled just before the Prussians' surprising victory. Frederick could not stop the French from becoming involved, but he refused to be subordinated to them and proved a duplicitous partner. In 1741, for example, he secretly agreed to free Austrian forces to march against the French. After a nearly disastrous campaign in Bohemia in 1744, he faced a quadruple alliance of Saxony, Austria, Britain, and the Netherlands in 1745. That year he triumphed at Hohenfriedeberg and Soor. In December, Maria Theresa accepted the verdict of those battles and, for the time, recognized his sovereignty over Silesia, while he supported her consort Francis's election as Holy Roman Emperor.

With the conquest of Silesia, Frederick established for Brandenburg-Prussia the tradition of the primacy of military action in foreign policy. His and his father's reigns mark the beginning of the domination of militarism in political and social life there. Frederick planned the seizure of Silesia as a limited war. His foreign policy focused on moderate, long-term goals that avoided strategic and military overextension.

As the 1750s opened, rivalry between Britain and France over colonial empire in North America, which Frederick wished to avoid, was intensifying. Empress Maria Theresa and her chancellor, *Wenzel Anton Kaunitz, meanwhile were determined to reclaim Silesia. Kaunitz shrewdly abandoned the old hostility between Bourbon and Habsburg and sought a rapprochement with France. Frederick inadvertently pushed France toward Austria when he signed the defensive Treaty of Westminster with Britain in 1756 without consulting his ally, France. Fearing that an Anglo-French colonial war might spread to Europe, where Russia had just concluded a treaty with Britain, Frederick had arranged the Westminster Treaty. He later called this his worst mistake. His duplicitous behavior in foreign affairs from 1740 had threatened to leave him without allies. To 1756, however, Frederick believed that international relations followed quasi-mechanistic laws, so that one of two hostile parties would side with him. Events of 1756 and 1757 caused him to lose faith in a rational, mechanistic world order and to assert in "Épître sur le hasard" (1757) that "his majesty" chance, not reason, was the single most important factor determining fate.

The Westminster Treaty produced a reversal of alliances known as the diplomatic revolution of 1756. Frederick had not expected that France would no longer guarantee Prussia's acquisition of Silesia and even ally itself with its old nemesis, Habsburg Austria. Austria now surprised European statesmen by an agreement to remain neutral in any Anglo-French war, and Prussia joined Britain and the Netherlands. To this point, the diplomatic revolution's new power alignment followed confessional lines. Completing its circle of alliances, Austria also joined with Russia, Saxony, Sweden, and the smaller German states in opposition to Prussia. Maria Theresa wanted to reacquire Silesia and reduce Prussia to its 1740 boundaries. Russia also welcomed a dismembering of Prussia.

Kaunitz's restraint of Tsarina Elizabeth of Russia forestalled an immediate invasion of Prussia, permitting Frederick to take the offensive. His invasion of Saxony in 1756 began the third Silesian War (or Seven Years War). Historians still debate whether this was a preventive strike to break the encircling coalition of Austria, France, and Russia or simple aggression to conquer Saxony. Frederick had a series of spectacular victories in 1757 at Prague, at Rossbach, where he defeated a larger Franco-Austrian force, and at Leuthen. He now confirmed the epithet "the Great."

Even with these triumphs, a quick victory eluded Frederick. Strategically, the Prussians were in a poor position. Frederick faced a long war on several fronts with only minor allies and limited British financial support. Following defeats at Kolin (1757), Hochkirch (1758), and Kunersdorf (1759), his situation grew desperate. In 1760 foreign armies were in Prussia and the Russians burned Berlin. Frederick's mood turned from stoic to almost suicidal on the battlefield. All seemed lost the next year when Britain ended its subsidy; Frederick berated "perfidious Albion."

Disagreements within the coalition and its disorganized operations combined in 1762 with the death of Elizabeth of Russia to produce a dramatic reversal in the military situation. Her successor, Peter III, was an admirer of Frederick. Once Peter removed Russia from the war, Maria Theresa and Kaunitz's plan to retake Silesia collapsed. The Treaty of Hubertusburg (1763), which ended the Seven Years War, left Silesia in Frederick's hands but restored Saxony to its elector. This restoration of the prewar status represented a Prussian defensive victory.

The three Silesian Wars support German historian Leopold von Ranke's later thesis that rivalries among states influence the course of history more than ideology, class conflict, or technological advances. The financial drain from the Seven Years' War on the British and French treasuries, moreover, had important consequences in the coming age of revolutions.

In 1763 Frederick began to rebuild Brandenburg-Prussia after its recent devastation. His *rétablissement*, which gave priority to the army and agriculture and subordinated local loyalties to state sovereignty, reflected his brand of enlightened absolutism. Frederick also changed the style and rhetoric of absolute monarchs by defining the impersonal state as a collectivity above the monarch. The king was simply the "first servant of the state."

Growing instability in eastern Europe and another possible war with Austria troubled Frederick in his last years. To escape the isolation imposed by France and Great Britain, he allied with Russia, despite fears of *Catherine the Great's desire for expansion. As her ally, Frederick participated in the First Partition of Poland in 1772. To maintain Prussia's new power position in German affairs and check Austrian expansion under Joseph II, he fought in the War of the Bavarian Succession, or "Potato War," 1778–1779, and organized the League of German Princes in 1785. After years of illness with gout and asthma, Frederick died in his palace, Sans Souci, on August 17, 1786.

Annotated Bibliography

Substantial collections on Frederick II and his times exist in the United States and Germany. One may consult the libraries of such leading research universities as Chicago, Columbia, Harvard, Illinois, Johns Hopkins, Princeton, Stanford, and Yale to obtain most of the primary sources and subsequent secondary works. One may also contact Chief, Loan Division, Library of Congress, Washington, D.C. 20540. If visiting the Library of Congress, proceed to the Main Reading Room and order the books you wish to use. Important archives in Germany are the Deutsches Zentralarchiv, Abteilung Merseburg, and the Geheimes Staatsarchiv Preussischer Kulturbesitz, Archivstrasse 12–14, D–1000 Berlin 33 (Dahlem), Germany. The latter has Frederick's correspondence with other monarchs, family, cabinet ministers, generals, and friends, as well as his writings—especially his poetry—the Hohenzollern royal house archives, and proceedings of the civil cabinet.

Frederick's historical and political writings, from "Considérations" (1737–1738) through *Die Politischen Testament* (1752 and 1768), are devoted largely to foreign relations. Although some of these writings are theoretical, most refer to the actual European political constellations.

The *Anti-Machiavel ou Essai de critique sur le Prince de Machiavel* (1740) is Frederick's first major work, and his best known. Its title and polemic against the author of *The Prince* notwithstanding, it reasserts Machiavellian principles in politics, as Frederick implicitly admits that politics must follow *raison d'état* and adapt to given situations rather than following moral principles of conduct. Like Machiavelli, Frederick admits exceptions to the rule that treaties must be respected. "Disturbing necessities" may require rulers to break a treaty, but only if allies are informed and the well-being of the people is at stake. Frederick's vagueness on necessary conditions for breaking a treaty permits a wide interpretation.

Similarly, Frederick abandons the traditional just war theory for a flexible, pragmatic approach. According to him, justified wars include wars to secure a monarch's rights or claims, preventive or preemptive offensive wars, wars that fulfill obligations to allies, and wars "to guarantee the liberty of the world." In essence, Frederick says that all wars are justified. To guarantee peace in Europe, Frederick, like most of his contemporaries, favored balance of power. The "united forces of other powers" counterbalance the hegemony of the strongest state.

In the two *Political Testaments*, written in 1752 and 1768, Frederick expounds on politics, the state, and foreign relations. The first testament portrays the major European powers as jealous or secret enemies. Writing soon after the War of the Austrian Succession, Frederick sees France as a natural ally and Austria as an irreconcilable enemy, "which will never forgive the loss of Silesia." State interests thus demand that Prussia cooperate with France and other Habsburg enemies.

Frederick urges a dynamic, flexible foreign policy. Following the Roman maxim *divide et impera*, the shrewd statesman conceals his designs as he sows distrust, makes a separate peace with minor foes, destroys the chief enemy, and finally returns to the others. In foreign policy the rule of thumb is: "One must conceal the project, exploit favorable situations, and when they come, act with vigor."

Wars did not retard Frederick's "chimeric dreams" that his successor should expand
Prussian territory by incorporating Saxony, Polish Prussia, and Swedish Pomerania.
Territorial expansion was more important than titles like Holy Roman Emperor. To achieve
these goals, Prussia must keep a strong army and not rely heavily upon allies. In an
international atmosphere of envy and distrust, the prudent ruler first develops the power
of his state. The army should be preeminent within the state, and financial policy has to
support it.

The second *Political Testament* incorporates conclusions drawn from the Seven Years
War. The army is called even more important for the survival of the state. Frederick
reviews strengths and weaknesses of Russia, Austria, Great Britain, France, Poland, and
the Ottoman Empire. He evaluates their rulers and political systems, favoring autocracy
and expressing contempt for systems where parliaments and ministers rule. Joseph II of
Austria is seen as an imminent threat to Prussia. After the diplomatic revolution of 1756
and the "betrayal" of Britain in 1761, the only ally left for Prussia is Russia. Again
following Machiavelli's "interests of state," Frederick stresses that a statesman must
sacrifice personal morality for the well-being of his people. Acquisition of adjacent
territory, particularly Saxony and parts of Poland, is more important than hereditary
claims in the west.

The two testaments reveal the character of the Frederician Prussian state with its
emphasis on foreign policy, territorial expansion, and the primacy of the army. Subsequently, in "Considérations sur l'état politique de l'Europe" (1782), Frederick worries
that his successor, Frederick William II, is inadequate to the task of maintaining Prussia's
position within the European state system.

Frederick's historical writings present a sweeping account of his rule and age. These
works, notably *Histoire de mon temps* (1743–1746), show him to be a historian of some
stature who carefully assembles documents and is generally honest, except in treating
diplomacy. His histories imitate Voltaire's, and the British historian G. P. Gooch notes
that "he is the only modern sovereign to have written detailed accounts of all his campaigns
and to have discussed with considerable candor the most controversial features of his
policy." Occasionally Frederick tries to convince readers not to blame him for key foreign
policy decisions. In particular, he regards himself as a victim of aggression in the outbreak
of the Seven Years War.

His first published history, *Mémoires pour servir à l'histoire de la maison de Brandebourg* (1751), follows the Hohenzollerns until 1740. Frederick attempts to teach his
first heir, August Wilhelm (d. 1758), the virtues and vices of his predecessors in order
to prepare him for rule. The Great Elector is praised for standing up against foreign
enemies. Despite their conflict, Frederick's account of his father's rule is positive. He is
grateful for the full treasury and the enlarged army. *Histoire de mon temps* (written in
1743 and 1746 and reworked in 1775) is Frederick's chief historical work. The introduction
assesses leading rulers, resources, and nations of Europe around 1740. Frederick argues
on political and personal grounds that the invasion of Silesia was justified.

Frederick wrote two histories late in his career. His "Histoire de la guerre de sept
ans" (1764) reveals that in 1756 he had informants at the Austrian embassy in Berlin
and the Saxon Foreign Office in Dresden. He maintains that his 1756 attack was preventive, criticizes the inability of the Russians and Austrians to exploit victories, especially
Kunersdorf, and calls the death of the Empress Elizabeth in 1762 the "miracle of the
house of Brandenbourg." His shorter *Mémoires depuis la paix de Hubertusbourg jusqu'à
la fin du partage de Pologne* (1775) praises the first partition of Poland as a peaceful

agreement between three powers that averted war and maintained the balance of power. It also ended the isolation of East Prussia.

In the mid-nineteenth century, German scholars began publishing Frederick's writings and correspondence in French and German translation, although his *Politische Correspondenz*, which includes forty-six volumes to date, is still incomplete. This step opened the way for a more critical analysis of his rule. In Germany, Leopold von Ranke incorporated primary sources from these publications and archives in his impressive *Zwölf Bucher preussischer Geschichte* (1874), after Johann Droysen developed the Hegelian doctrine that Prussia's rise was the result of "historical necessity" in his *Geschichte der preussischen Politik* (1855). Reinhold Koser, Droysen's pupil, wrote a well-balanced biography, *Geschichte Friedrichs des Grossen* (1912–1914). To the end of the Hohenzollern rule (1918), the traditional German view of Frederick's rule was favorable. Indeed, in *Die Hohenzollern und ihr Werk* (1915), Otto Hintze approves of all of Frederick's foreign policy decisions, a view restated by Arnold Berney in his unfinished biography, *Friedrich der Grosse: Entwicklung geschichte eines Staatsmans* (1934), and by Gerhard Ritter, *Friedrich der Grosse: Ein Historisches Profil* (1936).

The assessment of Frederick has been sharply divided and has shifted over the generations. Within imperial Germany, not all historians followed the nationalistic Prussian ideology and *Kleindeutsch* party. Onnon Klopp's Austrophile *Der König Friedrich II. Von Preussen und die deutsche Nation* (1860), and Max Lehmann's *Friedrich der Grosse und der Ursprung des Siebenjährigen Krieges* (1894) attacked Frederick's rule. Lehmann rejected the notion that Frederick's war effort in 1756 was preventive, but the historian Albert Naudé strongly disagreed with Lehmann. The outbreak of the Seven Years War remains a favorite topic among historians; more recent works include Willy Andreas, *Friedrich der Grosse und der Siebenjährige Krieg* (1940), and Alice Carter, *The Dutch Republic in the Seven Years War* (1971).

Until 1914 British historiography basically fell into two camps. On the one side, despite documentary evidence of his chicanery, Thomas Carlyle and W. F. Reddaway defended Frederick as "the last real king" in Europe and a hero of world history, a view that mostly disappeared in Britain after World War I. On the other side, liberal Thomas Macaulay found Frederick an autocratic tyrant.

Since World War II, British and American historians have avoided both extremes. G. P. Gooch, *Frederick the Great* (1947), admires Frederick's intellectual and domestic achievements but strongly criticizes his foreign policy, ranking the seizure of Silesia and the First Partition of Poland "among the sensational crimes of modern history." Herbert Butterfield, *Man on His Past* (1955), concluded, however, that the "real culprit" in causing the Seven Years War was Russia. Christopher Duffy, *The Military Life of Frederick the Great* (1986), is a masterful account of Frederick's life as a soldier-king. Among American historians, Peter Paret, in *Frederick the Great: A Profile* (1972), has translated Ritter's biography and edited a profile with sections on Frederick's life; role as an administrator, soldier, and statesman; response to the Enlightenment; and historical reputation.

Among German scholars, the assessment of Frederick's foreign policy has become more negative since World War II. Karl Aretin, *Friedrich der Grosse und Grenzen des Preussenkonigs* (1985), criticizes Frederick's "evil spirit," while Rudolf Augstein, *Preussens Friedrich und die Deutschen* (1968), attempts to come to terms with Germany's militaristic past. Ingrid Mittenzwei, a Marxist, tries to engender moral contempt for Friedrich in *Friedrich II. von Preussen: Eine Biographie* (1980). The most reliable modern study in German is Theodor Schieder's *Friedrich der Grosse* (1983). This comprehensive work, which goes against the dominant trend of specialized studies, examines Prussian foreign policy toward Austria, France, and Russia, and depicts Frederick as an enlightened absolutist torn between contradictions of humanitarian goals and power politics.

Contemporary Frederician scholarship seems to be moving away from its traditional western orientation. It is adding regional balance with substantial attention to Prussia's foreign policy toward Russia, Poland, and Turkey.

Bibliography

Works by Frederick the Great

Frederick the Great. *Acta Borussica Denkmäler der Preussischen Staatsverwaltung im 18. Jahrhundert*. 31 vols. Edited by Preussische Akademie der Wissenschaften. Berlin: Parey, 1892–1936, 1981.

———. *Anti-Machiavel, où Essaide critique sur le Prince de Machiavel*. N.p.: La Haye, 1740.

———. *Frederick the Great on the Art of War*. Edited by Jay Luvaas. New York: Free Press, 1966.

———. *Gespräche Friedrichs des Grossen*. 3rd ed. Edited by Friedrich von Oppeln-Bronikowski and Gustav Berthold Volz. Berlin: Hobbing, 1926.

———. *Histoire de mon temps*. Leipzig: Hirzel, 1879.

———. *Memoires pour servir à l'histoire de la maison de Brandebourg*. Berlin: La Haye, 1751.

———. *Oeuvres de Frédéric le Grand*. 30 vols. Edited by J.D.E. Preuss. Berlin: Rodolphe Decker, 1846–1856.

———. *Politische Correspondenz Friedrichs des Grossen*. 46 vols. Edited by R. A. Koser et al. Berlin: Duncker, 1879–1939.

———. *Die Politischen Testamente*. Translated by Friedrich von Oppeln-Bronikowski. Berlin: Hobbing, 1922.

———. *The Refutation of Machiavelli's Prince: or, Anti-Machiavel*. Translated by Paul Sonnino. Athens: Ohio University Press, 1981.

———. *Die Werke Friedrichs des Grossen, in Deutscher Übersetzung*. 10 vols. Edited by Gustav Berthold Volz. Berlin: Hobbing, 1912–1914.

Works about Frederick the Great

Andreas, Willy. *Friedrich der Grosse und der Siebenjährige Krieg*. Leipzig: Kohler und Aneling, 1940.

Aretin, Karl Otmar Freiherr von. *Friedrich der Grosse und Grenzen des Preussenkönigs*. Vienna: Herder, 1985.

———. *Friedrich der Grosse. Herrscher zwischen Tradition und Fortschritt*. Gütersloh: Bertelsmann, 1985.

Asprey, Robert B. *Frederick the Great: The Magnificent Enemy*. New York: Ticknor and Fields, 1986.

Augstein, Rudolf. *Preussens Friedrich und die Deutschen*. Frankfurt am Main: Fischer, 1981.

Barker, Thomas M., ed. *Frederick the Great and the Making of Prussia*. New York: Holt, Rinehart and Winston, 1972.

Benninghoven, Friedrich, *Friedrich der Grosse*. Berlin: Nicolaische Verlagsbuchhandlung, 1986.

Berney, Arnold. *Friedrich der Grosse: Entwicklung geschichte eines Staatsmans*. Tubingen: Mohr, 1934.

Bussmann, Walter. *Wandel und Kontinuität in Politik und Geschichte*. Boppard am Rhein: Harald Boldt, 1973.

Butterfield, Herbert. *Man on His Past*. Boston: Beacon Press, 1955.

Calinger, Ronald. "Frederick the Great and the Berlin Academy of Sciences (1740–1766)." *Annals of Science* 24 (1968): 239–249.

Carlyle, Thomas. *History of Frederick the Great*. 6 vols. London: Chapman and Hall, 1858–1865. Reprint. John Clive, ed., Chicago: University of Chicago Press, 1969.

Carter, Alice Clare. *The Dutch Republic in the Seven Years War*. London: Macmillan, 1971.

Cegielski, Tadeusz. "Preussische 'Deutschland- und Polenpolitik' in dem Zeitraum 1740–1792." *Jahrbüch für die Geschichte Mittel- und Ostdeutschlands* 30 (1981): 21–27.

Delbruck, Hans. "Friedrich der Grosse und der Ursprung des siebenjährigen Krieges." *Preussische Jahrbücher* 84 (1896): 32–53.

———. *Geschichte der Kriegskunst im Rahmen der Politischen Geschichte*. 4 vols. Berlin: de Gruyter, 1900–1920.

———. "Über den Ursprung des siebenjährigen Krieges." *Preussische Jahrbücher* 86 (1896): 416–427.

———. "Der Ursprung des siebenjährigen Krieges." *Preussische Jahrbücher* 79 (1895): 254–282.

Dippel, Horst. "Prussia's English Policy after the Seven Years War." *Central European History* 4 (1971): 195–214.

Droysen, Johann Gustav. *Geschichte der preussischen Politik*. Berlin: Veit, 1855.

Duffy, Christopher. *The Military Life of Frederick the Great*. New York: Atheneum, 1986.

Duncker, Max. "Preussen und England im siebenjährigen Kriege." *Preussische Jahrbücher* 60 (1885): 125–150.

———. "Der siebenjährige Krieg." *Historische Zeitschrift* 19 (1868): 103–180.

Gaxotte, Pierre. *Frédéric II*. A. Fayard: Paris, 1938.

Gooch, George Peabody. *Frederick the Great*. New York: Knopf, 1947.

Hintze, Otto. *Die Hohenzollern und ihr Werk 1415–1915*. Berlin: Paul Parey, 1915.

Horn, David B. *Frederick the Great and the Rise of Prussia*. New York: Harper and Row, 1969.

Johnson, Hubert C. *Frederick the Great of Prussia: Absolutism and Administration*. London: Thames and Hudson, 1975.

Kaplan, Herbert H. *Russia and the Outbreak of the Seven Years War*. Berkeley: University of California Press, 1968.

Kittredge, Mary. *Frederick the Great*. New York: Chelsea House, 1987.

Klopp, Onnon. *Der König Friedrich II. von Preussen und die deutsche Nation*. Schaffhausen: Verlag der Friedr, 1860.

Koser, Reinhold. *Geschichte Friedrichs des Grossen*. 4 vols. 7th ed. Stuttgart: Cotta, 1921. Reprint. Darmstadt: Wissenschaftliche Buchgesellschaft, 1974.

———. "Neue Veröffentlichen zur Vorgeschichte des siebenjährigen Krieges." *Historische Zeitschrift* 77 (1896): 1–40.

———. "Die preussische Kriegsführung im siebenjährigen Kriege." *Historische Zeitschrift* 92 (1903–1904): 239–273.

————. "Die preussischen Finanzen im siebenjährigen Kriege." *Forschungen zur brandenburgischen und preussischen Geschichte* 13 (1900): 153–217, 329–375.

Kunisch, Johannes, ed. *Analecta Fridericiana. Zeitschrift für Historische Forschung.* Berlin: Duncker and Humblot, 1987.

————. *Das Mirakel des Hauses Brandenburg. Studium zum Verhältnis von Kabinettspolitik und Kriegführung im Zeitalter des Siebenjährigen Krieges.* Munich: Oldenbourg, 1978.

Lehmann, Max. *Friedrich der Grosse und der Ursprung des Siebenjährigen Krieges.* Leipzig: Hirzel, 1894.

Luckwaldt, Friedrich. "Die Westminsterkonvention." *Preussische Jahrbücher* 80 (1895): 230–267.

Macaulay, Thomas Babington. *Critical and Historical Essays.* 2 vols. London: J. Dent, 1864. Reprint. New York: Dutton, 1907.

Mitford, Nancy. *Frederick the Great.* London: Hamish Hamilton, 1970.

Mittenzwei, Ingrid. *Friedrich II. von Preussen: Eine Biographie.* 2nd ed. Cologne: Pahl-Rugenstein, 1980.

Montesquieu, Baron Charles de. *Considérations sur les causes de la grandeur des Romains et de leur décandence; avec commentaires et notes de Frédéric-Le-Grand.* Paris: Vaton, 1879.

Müller, Michael G. *Polen zwischen Preussen und Russland Souveränitätskrise und Reformpolitik 1736–1752.* Berlin: Colloquium, 1983.

————. "Russland und der Siebenjährige Krieg: Beitrag zu einer Kontroverse." *Jahrbücher für die Geschichte Osteuropas* 28 (1980): 198–219.

————. *Die Teilungen Polens 1772, 1793, 1795.* Munich: Beck, 1984.

Nathan, James A. "The Heyday of the Balance of Power: Frederick the Great and the Decline of the Old Regime." *Naval War College Review* 33 (1980): 53–67.

Naudé, Albert. "Aus ungedruckten Memoiren der Brüder Friedrichs des Grossen. Die Enstehung des siebenjährigen Krieges und der General von Winterfeldt." *Forschungen zur brandenburgischen und preussischen Geschichte* 1 (1888): 231–269.

————. "Beiträge zur Enstehungsgeschichte des siebenjährigen Krieges, Teil I." *Forschungen zur brandenburgischen und preussischen Geschichte* 8 (1895): 523–618.

————. "Beiträge zur Enstehungsgeschichte des siebenjährigen Krieges, Teil II." *Forschungen zur brandenburgischen und preussischen Geschichte* 9 (1897): 101–328.

Paret, Peter, ed. *Frederick the Great: A Profile.* London: Macmillan, 1972.

Preuss, Johann David Erdmann. *Friedrich der Grosse: Eine Lebensgeschichte.* 4 vols. Berlin: Nauck, 1832. Reprint. Osnabruck: Biblio Verlag, 1981.

Ranke, Leopold von. *Collected Works.* Vols. 51 and 52: *Friedrich II. König von Preussen.* Leipzig: Kohlhammer, 1940.

————. *Memoirs of the House of Brandenburg and History of Prussia during the Seventeenth and Eighteenth Centuries.* Translated by Sir Alexander and Lady Duff Gordon. 3 vols. London: Murray, 1849. Reprint. New York: Haskell House, 1969.

————. *Der Ursprung des siebenjährigen Krieges.* Leipzig: Kohlhammer, 1871.

————. *Zwölf Bucher preussischer Geschichte.* 5 vols. in 3. Leipzig: Duncker und Humblot, 1874.

Reddaway, W. F. *Frederick the Great and the Rise of Prussia.* New York: Haskell House, 1969.

Ritter, Gerhard. *Frederick the Great: A Historical Profile.* Translated by Peter Paret. Berkeley: University of California Press, 1968.

———. *Friedrich der Grosse: Ein Historisches Profil.* Leipzig: Quelle und Meyer, 1936.
Rothfels, Hans. "Friedrich der Grosse in den Krisen des siebenjährigen Krieges." *Historische Zeitschrift* 134 (1926): 14–30.
Sagave, Pierre Paul. *Berlin und Frankreich 1685–1871.* Berlin: Haude and Spener, 1980.
Salmonowicz, Stanislaw. "Friedrich der Grosse und Polen." *Acta Poloniae Historica* 46 (1982): 73–95.
Schieder, Theodor. *Friedrich der Grosse: Ein Königtum der Widersprüche.* Frankfurt am Main: Verlag Ullstein, 1983.
———. "Friedrich der Grosse und Machiavelli: Das Dilemma von Machtpolitik und Aufklärung." *Historische Zeitschrift* 234 (1982): 265–294.
Scott, H. M. "Frederick II, the Ottoman Empire and the Origins of the Russo-Prussian Alliance of April 1764." *European Studies Review* 7 (1977): 153–175.
Staszewski, Jacek. "Die Polnisch-Sachsische Union und die Hohenzollernmonarchie 1697–1763." *Jahrbüch für die Geschichte Mittel- und Ostdeutschlands* 30 (1981): 28–34.
Stribny, Wolfgang. *Die Russlandpolitik Friedrichs des Grossen 1764–1786.* Würzburg: Holzner, 1986.
Weiss, Joseph. "Der Streit über den Ursprung des siebenjährigen Krieges." *Historisches Jahrbüch* 18 (1897): 311–321, 831–848.
Zernack, Klaus. "Negative Polenpolitik also Grundlage deutschrussischer Diplomatie in der Machtepolitik des 18 Jahrhunderts." In *Russland und Deutschland: Festschrift für Georg v. Rauch*, pp. 144–159. Edited by Uwe Liszkowski. Stuttgart: Klett, 1974.
———. "Das preussische Königtum und die polnische Republik im europaischen Machtesystem des 18. Jahrhunderts (1701–1763)." *Jahrbüch für die Geschichte Mittel- und Ostdeutschlands* 30 (1981): 4–20.

RONALD CALINGER AND GEORG CAVALLAR

James William Fulbright (b. 1905).   Known affectionately as The Senator, J. William Fulbright, former Democratic senator from Arkansas, was the author of the Fulbright Resolution (1943), which pledged United States membership in the future United Nations, and the founder in 1946 of the Fulbright Scholar international educational exchange program for teachers and students from the United States and abroad. He was born April 9, 1905, in Sumner, Missouri, to Jay and Roberta (Waugh) Fulbright. At an early age he moved with his family to Fayetteville, Arkansas, and in 1925 he graduated from the University of Arkansas. A Rhodes Scholar, Fulbright attended Pembroke College, Oxford University, and earned a B.A. in 1928 and an M.A. in 1931.

Upon returning to the United States, Fulbright enrolled in George Washington University Law School and married Elizabeth Kremer Williams. He graduated from law school in 1934, and after admission to the District of Columbia bar served as special attorney in the Anti-Trust Division of the Department of Justice and lectured at George Washington University in 1935–1936. He returned to the University of Arkansas in the fall of 1936 to teach on the law faculty; in 1939 he became president of the university. He was forced to resign from this post in 1941 because the governor did not like the editorial policy of a newspaper that Fulbright's family owned.

After leaving the university, Fulbright spent a short time in private business before his election to the U.S. House of Representatives in 1942. Upon taking his seat, he became a member of the House Foreign Relations Committee. Fulbright firmly believed that future wars should be prevented and that there needed to be at war's end an organization similar to the League of Nations to prevent future aggression and safeguard peace. To this end, he introduced what became known as the Fulbright Resolution; passed by a 360–29 vote in the House on September 21, 1943, it stated: "Resolved by the House of Representatives (the Senate concurring), that the Congress hereby expresses itself as favoring the creation of appropriate international machinery with power adequate to establish and to maintain a just and lasting peace, among the nations of the world, and as favoring participation by the United States therein through its constitutional processes." The resolution cut across party lines, winning the support of Democrats and Republicans alike as well as that of several former isolationists like John Vorys of Ohio and Hamilton Fish of New York. On November 5, the Senate passed the Connally Resolution, similar to the Fulbright declaration, by a vote of 85 to 5. The Fulbright Resolution led directly to the founding of the United Nations and ended forever the idea of American isolationism. The Fulbright Resolution was a significant part of the process that educated Americans to the realization that some form of collective security organization was a natural conclusion to U.S. involvement in the postwar world. Fulbright would remain a passionate supporter of the United Nations throughout his career.

The following year, Fulbright attended a London conference on international education and recommended a four-point program establishing global educational facilities. Shaped by Fulbright, the final conference report became the basis for the establishment of the U.N.'s Economic and Social Council. These expressions of support for an international security organization came as the Truman administration was drafting proposals for specialized agencies to deal with the postwar problems of relief, reconstruction, and currency stabilization.

Because of the popularity of this resolution and the aplomb that he had shown in shepherding it through congressional channels, Fulbright was encouraged to run for the Senate in 1944. He won the election, defeating Governor Homer M. Adkins, who had been responsible for Fulbright's leaving the University of Arkansas.

As a senator, Fulbright was deeply involved in foreign policy matters as an internationalist, voting for a continuation of the Trade Agreements Act, the acceptance of the United Nations Charter, and the bill authorizing U.S. participation in the United Nations. One of his most important contributions was the Fulbright Act of 1946, which provided that monies acquired by the United States through the sale of surplus property abroad be used to endow a program of international educational exchange dedicated to world peace and cross-cultural understanding. The president would appoint a Board of Foreign Scholarships to administer the program. Americans participating in the new program became known as Fulbright Scholars. The bill was signed by President Truman on August 1, 1946.

In 1961 the Fulbright-Hayes Act upgraded the entire Fulbright educational exchange program, broadening the president's authority to finance the costs of sending Americans abroad and bringing foreigners to the United States for a wide variety of educational, scientific, and cultural purposes. The act passed with broad bipartisan support, indicating the wide appeal of the Fulbright program.

With regard to other significant foreign policy issues, Fulbright supported the Greek-Turkish aid bill implementing the Truman Doctrine (1947), appropriations for the European Recovery Program, known as the Marshall Plan (1948), U.S. entry into the North Atlantic Treaty Organization (1949), the foreign military aid bill (1949), Point Four aid (1950), and extension of the draft and universal military training for the Korean War (1951). He adamantly opposed the U–2 spy plane missions (1960), however, giving one of his most memorable speeches on June 29, 1960, after the capture of a U–2 spy plane inside the Soviet Union. He criticized President Eisenhower's "self-righteous attempts to justify the flights in terms which implied their continuation" and believed that U.S. actions had been "unbearably provocative" and had contributed to the intemperance shown by Nikita Khrushchev in Paris.

But the foreign policy issue for which Fulbright was to become best known was the Vietnam War. Beginning in 1961, he spoke out against deepening U.S. involvement in the war in Southeast Asia. When Congress approved the Gulf of Tonkin Resolution on August 7, 1964, authorizing the president "to take all necessary measures to repel armed attack against the forces of the United States and to prevent further aggression" in Southeast Asia, Fulbright supported it, but he soon became increasingly disenchanted with the conduct of the war and regretted his support for the resolution that was the legal basis for its escalation.

In March 1968 the Senate Foreign Relations committee held televised hearings on the Vietnam War, and President Johnson's policies came under heavy attack. The hearings included a review of the North Vietnamese attacks on U.S. naval vessels in the Gulf of Tonkin in August 1964, the incident that had brought about the Gulf of Tonkin Resolution. Secretary of Defense Robert McNamara and Chairman of the Joint Chiefs of Staff Earle Wheeler testified that the attacks were unprovoked, but critics on the committee continued to raise questions about the incident (later it was revealed that one of the U.S. ships involved, the U.S.S. *Maddox*, had been on a spy mission in North Vietnamese waters) and probed for further answers. Fulbright, as committee chairman, attempted to extract a pledge from Secretary of State Dean Rusk that he would consult with members of the committee before more troops were sent to Vietnam, but Rusk refused. The hearings were significant in publicizing congressional skepticism with regard to the administration's Vietnam policy.

President Johnson's Vietnam War policy had also created dissension within the NATO community. A major problem was France's decision in 1966 to withdraw from NATO and to require the removal of alliance troops and installations. France's action coincided with economic difficulties in Britain and Germany and meant that the United States would have to foot more of NATO's bills in Europe at a time when the country was suffering from the costs of the Vietnam War. Fulbright served on a special Senate committee to study the feasibility of removing some U.S. troops from Europe. The committee recommended reducing the number of U.S. troops in Europe, requesting European countries to shoulder more of the burden for their own defense, and expressing the hope that new technology, especially the ability to move troops quickly by air, would justify this reduction.

Fulbright was reelected to the Senate in 1950, 1956, 1962, and 1968, but was defeated in 1974. In March 1975, he joined the law firm of Hogan and Hartson in Washington, D.C.

Annotated Bibliography

The Fulbright Papers are housed in the Special Collections division of the University of Arkansas library in Fayetteville. They consist of family papers as well as correspondence, legislative documents, speeches, and other records pertinent to Fulbright's congressional career. Finding aids are available for most of the collection, but access to some files is limited.

Three other collections at the library contain related materials. The historical collection of the Bureau of Educational and Cultural Affairs includes information related to U.S. international educational and cultural activities, including the Fulbright program. The library also contains the papers of the Council for International Exchange of Scholars and the National Association of Foreign Student Affairs. As of 1991, these collections are fully available to researchers, although restrictions limit access to some files.

J. W. Fulbright's writings deal with the themes of U.S. foreign policy and America's image in the world. In 1963 Fulbright published *Prospects for the West*. Based on a series of lectures given at Tufts University, the book warned that Western ideas had been under serious challenge since 1914 and that in the future they could not be assumed to have universal applicability. The East was on the march; Third World regions of the globe were demanding their place in the sun. Fulbright recommended accommodations that the United States should make in the international forum. The success of Western nations, he wrote, "depends more on the shaping of their own community and on the character and quality of their own free societies than on their confrontations with those who threaten them from outside." It would be neither wise nor possible to impose the American way of life on the Communist world. America should lead by example. If America's way of life should triumph it would be due to "the magnetism of freedom itself." He predicted that communism, as conceived by Marx and Lenin, would not prevail in the world because it was unrealistic and romantic in its notions. He warned against America's having unrealistic notions about its capabilities to remake the world in its own image. In addition, Fulbright advocated granting massive aid through the World Bank and the International Development Association to underdeveloped nations.

Fulbright of Arkansas: The Public Positions of a Private Thinker (1963), a collection of speeches edited by Karl E. Meyer, illustrates Fulbright's conservative nature in his battles against the "radical reactionaries." Concerned about the maintenance of traditional American values, he warned of the decline of American education. In Fulbright's mind education was the most important aspect of the American domestic agenda for the future. It was a problem to be solved at the national level with national resources.

The Arrogance of Power (1966), one of Senator Fulbright's most noteworthy books, dealt with America's foreign policy. He pointed out that many past empires had fallen because of the arrogance of power and warned the United States to use its international power justly and wisely, lest it go the way of the British, French, and German empires. Hoping to save the United States from a tragic fate, he implored its leaders to reestablish contact with the People's Republic of China (PRC). Fulbright feared isolating the Chinese from world politics, believing that through trade and a scholarly exchange the Chinese could and should be wooed into the camp of the capitalist democracies. He spoke of the folly of fighting a preventive war against China and asserted that Chinese communism would not ultimately be committed to America's destruction. He advocated extending the hand of friendship and allowing the PRC to sit on the U.N. Security Council. He warned of the dangers of a "strident and aggressive" American foreign policy—an arrogance of power—that disregarded local customs, attitudes, feelings, and sensitivities. Fulbright's long historical view provided insight, keen judgment, and candor. Using its failings in Vietnam as an analogy, he predicted that the United States would come to grief through overextension of commitments, and he was proved by subsequent history to be correct. He cautioned the United States about pride before a fall and wondered how much of its involvement was due to arrogance rather than commitment to Vietnam's freedom.

Fulbright's next book, *The Role of Congress in Foreign Policy* (1971), was a treatise on why the president should never again be allowed to maneuver the United States into a war without the consent of Congress. Fulbright explained how the last five presidents had usurped various powers properly belonging to the Congress. The president, he wrote, had taken over the Senate's treaty-making power by negotiating executive agreements, and the Congress's advice and consent functions had been relegated to minor situations or dismissed altogether. Fulbright pointed out how and why the Gulf of Tonkin Resolution, empowering the president to escalate the Vietnam War, had been a great mistake, and candidly regretted having supported its passage. Senator Fulbright's central theme was that the war in Vietnam had greatly compromised the checks and balances system, bringing about far greater centralization of executive authority than was justifiable or good. Fulbright took President Richard Nixon and his predecessors to task for conducting "a constitutionally unauthorized presidential war in Indochina."

In 1972 Fulbright's *The Crippled Giant* pursued similar themes, stating that the United States, in launching and administering the war in Vietnam, had compromised its domestic programs and international stature as model for the free world. American leadership, he concluded, had used deceit, subterfuge, secrecy, and mind control in carrying on the Vietnam War. Yet deception was not the model the United States sought to offer the world; only truth should do. Fulbright's remarks were an ardent plea for Americans to fend off an imperial presidency, partially created by war. The president should never again be allowed to totally dominate American foreign policy as in the Vietnam era; checks and balances must be preserved. *The Crippled Giant* was a clarion call for Congress to reassert its constitutional role.

In *The Price of Empire* (1989), Fulbright restated some themes from the past, such as his stand against the war in Vietnam, and contributed insightful messages for the future. He foresaw the rapprochement between the United States and the Soviet Union, but he still feared America's militarized economy and the constitutional problem of the president usurping congressional power in foreign policymaking. This volume also included an analysis of the Middle East situation.

In *Senator Fulbright* (1966), Tristram Coffin portrays Fulbright as "conservative, aristocratic and intellectual," as opposed to Lyndon B. Johnson, whom he describes as highly patriotic and "Populist in the tradition of Southern poor white politics." Coffin focuses on Fulbright's outrage against Johnson after the 1965 landing of U.S. troops in the Dominican Republic and the sharp escalation of the war in Vietnam in 1966; for Fulbright there was no heroism in war, no devil in communism; the United States was adrift under Johnson's leadership of guns, prayers, and exhortations. Fulbright is cast by Coffin as a hero who had the courage to dissent; he is the conscience of America, complaining about its arrogant misuse of power. While Coffin sees Fulbright as believing in the essential goodness of humankind, David Trask's biographical article in *Makers of American Diplomacy* (1974) concludes that Fulbright "acted in terms of a moderately pessimistic evaluation of human nature." Trask uses Fulbright's growing pessimism as one of his central themes, along with Fulbright's devotion to supranational modes of global organization and his corresponding belief that the system of nation-states was obsolete. Trask's essay relies on Haynes Johnson and Bernard M. Gwertzman's views in their book *Fulbright: The Dissenter* (1968).

The most recent biographical account of Senator Fulbright's life and policies is Eugene Brown's *J. W. Fulbright: Advice and Dissent* (1985). Brown characterizes Fulbright as a "leader of foreign policy dissent," and at times a figure of paradox—"a contemplative man of ideas caught up in the turbulent routines of public life." Brown's book is more balanced than earlier writings on Fulbright, concluding that the images of Fulbright in these works were overdrawn due to the passions of the times. Brown argues that Fulbright's dissent was more "conventional" than previously interpreted and that Fulbright shared the "nation's consensual insistence on its own global primacy."

Bibliography

Works by Fulbright

The Arrogance of Power. New York: Random House, 1966.
The Crippled Giant. New York: Random House, 1972.
Old Myths and New Realities. New York: Random House, 1964.
The Pentagon Propaganda Machine. New York: Vintage Press, 1971.
The Press and American Politics. Washington, D.C.: Ethics and Public Policy Center, Georgetown University, 1978.
The Price of Empire. With Seth Tillman. New York: Pantheon, 1989.
Prospects for the West. Cambridge, Mass.: Harvard University Press, 1963.
The Role of Congress in Foreign Policy. With John Stennis. Washington, D.C.: American Enterprise Institute, 1971.

Works about Fulbright

Berman, William C. *William Fulbright and the Vietnam War: The Dissent of a Political Realist*. Kent, Ohio: Kent State University Press, 1988.
Brown, Eugene. *J. W. Fulbright: Advice and Dissent*. Iowa City: University of Iowa Press, 1985.
Coffin, Tristram. *Senator Fulbright*. New York: Dutton, 1966.
Johnson, Haynes, and Bernard M. Gwertzman. *Fulbright: The Dissenter*. New York: Doubleday, 1968.

Lynn, Naomi B. *The Fulbright Premise: Senator J. William Fulbright's View on Presidential Power*. Lewisburg, Pa.: Bucknell University Press, 1973.

Meyer, Karl E., ed. *Fulbright of Arkansas: The Public Positions of a Private Thinker*. Washington, D.C.: Robert B. Luce, 1963.

Powell, Lee Riley. *J. William Fulbright and America's Lost Crusade: Fulbright's Opposition to the Vietnam War*. Little Rock, Ark.: Rose Publishing Co., 1984.

Trask, David. "J. William Fulbright." In *Makers of American Diplomacy*. Edited by Frank J. Merli and Theodore A. Wilson. New York: Scribner's, 1974.

Related Works

Bullert, Gary. "Jackson, Fulbright, and the Senatorial Critique of Detente." *Journal of Social, Political, and Economic Studies* 13 (Spring 1988): 61–86.

Clayton, William L. *Selected Papers of Will Clayton*. Edited by Frederick J. Dobney. Baltimore: Johns Hopkins University Press, 1971.

Halberstam, David. *The Best and the Brightest*. New York: Random House, 1972.

Jeffrey, Harry P. "Legislative Origins of the Fulbright Program." *Annals of the American Academy of Political and Social Science* 491 (May 1987): 36–47.

Patterson, James T. *Mr. Republican: A Biography of Robert A. Taft*. Boston: Houghton Mifflin, 1972.

Schandler, Herbert Y. *Lyndon Johnson and Vietnam: The Unmaking of a President*. Princeton, N.J.: Princeton University Press, 1977.

BARBARA BENNETT PETERSON

Mikhail Gorbachev (b. 1931).   Mikhail Sergeyevich Gorbachev was born into a peasant family on March 2, 1931, in the village of Privolnoye in southern Russia. The village is located in the agricultural region of Stavropol, and Stavropol played an important role in Gorbachev's accession to national prominence. His birth occurred in the second year of *Joseph Stalin's collectivization drive in which peasants were forced from their individual plots of land onto huge collective farms. Gorbachev's grandfather was a chairman of a *kolkhoz*, or a collective farm; his father, Sergei Andreyevich, was a machine operator in the local tractor station. His mother, who still lives in the Stavropol region, was Sergei's second wife. She is apparently a religious believer, and rumors persist that she had her son baptized.

Stavropol was occupied by the German army in August 1942. Following the return of the Soviet army to the region in late January 1943, Stalin ordered the deportation to Central Asia of thousands on trumped-up charges of collaboration with the Germans. According to some sources, Gorbachev's father was briefly held by Soviet authorities. However, these sources report that he was freed, and the family remained untainted by the imputation of collaboration.

Gorbachev entered Moscow State University in 1950 and decided to study law, a decision that gave him access to the works of Rousseau, Montesquieu, and Locke. He joined the Communist Party of the Soviet Union in 1952 and was extremely active in the youth organization (Komsomol) at the university, but after graduation he rejected a career in the KGB. Following Nikita Khrushchev's famous speech denouncing Stalin at the Twentieth Party Congress in

1956, the new Soviet leader tapped the Komsomol as a source of personnel to replace Stalin's henchmen. Some of Gorbachev's Komsomol colleagues were recruited to lead KGB operations.

Gorbachev's roommate at Moscow State University, Zdenek Mlynar, a Czech who later rejected communism and in 1977 emigrated to the West, has written of Gorbachev's intellectual abilities and his relative open-mindedness. Other accounts indicate that Gorbachev possessed considerable talent. He graduated with a law degree in 1955, but like *Lenin never practiced law. Instead, Gorbachev spent his early career from 1955 to 1978 in the Stavropol region, rising from Komsomol chief to regional first secretary. His career was not that different from those of other party bureaucrats, though he gained quick promotion and refused to be trapped in a narrow political position. He also earned a degree in agricultural economics through correspondence courses. In 1978 Gorbachev was transferred to Moscow for work in the Central Committee. Gorbachev's rapid rise indicates that from early on he impressed the party leadership with his administrative skills.

Following the death of Konstantin Chernenko, Gorbachev was selected to be general secretary of the Communist Party of the Soviet Union on March 11, 1985. Gorbachev's accession to power put an end to weak party leadership and policy drift. At fifty-four, he became the youngest man to assume political control of the Soviet Union since Stalin's rise to power in the 1920s. He was also the first of the post-Stalin generation of Soviet leaders. Gorbachev's youth, education, and lively mind set him apart from Leonid Brezhnev, Yuri Andropov, and Chernenko. Within weeks of coming to power he dazzled the world and captured the public imagination of millions of people. He immediately infused the foreign policy of the Soviet Union with a new, fresh image. In stark contrast to the gloomy, aging men of the Brezhnev generation, the dynamic, stylish Gorbachev and his fashion-conscious wife, Raisa, almost instantly became objects of media attention. Before Gorbachev, Westerners seldom knew whether Soviet leaders had spouses or not. Gorbachev's book, *Perestroika*, even made the best-seller list in North America and Europe.

During his tenure in power, Gorbachev accomplished several major breakthroughs in foreign affairs. On taking office he was faced with a disastrous foreign policy legacy. Six years of bloody conflict in Afghanistan had brought Soviet forces no nearer to victory. In eastern Europe economic and political stagnation threatened a new crisis. Relations with the United States were at a twenty-five-year low. Détente had run aground on many issues, including human rights, wars in Third World countries, deployment of new Soviet missiles, imposition of martial law in Poland, and invasion of Afghanistan. Soviet foreign policy prior to 1985 had resulted in the nightmare of encirclement by Western powers. The Soviet Union had sour relations with all of its neighbors, and even its allies were uncooperative. These problems were exacerbated under Andropov and Chernenko as Soviet foreign policy suffered from a lack of direction. Soviet prestige and influence in the world were eroding, and under ill and aging leadership the Soviet Union appeared rudderless and dangerous.

Gorbachev was committed to retrieving the situation. The need for change was clear to all but the staunchest conservatives. The substance of Gorbachev's foreign policy was subsumed under the general rubric of "new political thinking." What exactly did new political thinking entail? It stressed the importance of peaceful relations and cooperation between socialism and capitalism. Gorbachev also talked about the general moral standards of humanity and the future of the world in the shadow of nuclear weapons. He favored a "balance of interests" among nations and the need for peaceful relations among them. His political views on nuclear arms were rapidly evolving. He was becoming a rationalist who understood that the arms race was senseless and that the sooner it was turned around the better. In an elegant speech on new political thinking, he concluded with a wish to rid the world of nuclear weapons. "Humanity must become stronger and overcome the nuclear sickness and then enter the postnuclear age. . . . Today international relations are made soulless by the worship of force and the militarization of conscience." The Soviet Union, Gorbachev said in 1987, wanted to "humanize" international relations.

The crux of Gorbachev's new political thinking was a belief that the issue of nuclear arms was a political problem rather than just a military one. He demonstrated to his own military bureaucracy that he was the chief of Soviet foreign policy by overriding the Central Committee experts and his foreign minister. His mastery of nuclear arms details and the quality of his reflections proved that he was a forceful leader, commanding the respect of the outside world and therefore deserving respect at home for his foreign policy initiatives.

New political thinking was conditioned by a reevaluation of the nuclear threat, which yielded several important conclusions. Gorbachev decided that military and technical means could not be relied upon to safeguard peace. Instead, he concluded that security was mainly a political dilemma and could only be resolved by political means. Furthermore, new weapons themselves changed the rules of the game, since the decision-making time in the event of perceived attack was now reduced to a few minutes. According to Gorbachev, although the United States military-industrial complex remained the driving force behind the arms race, its potency could be offset by the utility of disarmament (especially reduced costs) and by popular public pressure. Finally, Gorbachev concluded that peaceful cooperation and interaction between countries presented the best opportunity for world peace.

From 1985 until the end of the devolution of the Soviet Union on December 8, 1991, Gorbachev completely transformed Soviet foreign policy. He abandoned many of his predecessors' principles. He jettisoned as atavistic existing Soviet positions in several arms control settings, including the Intermediate-Range Nuclear Forces (INF) negotiations and Strategic Arms Reduction Talks (START) with former president Ronald Reagan. He also displayed a willingness to entertain foreign policy outcomes that Brezhnev, Andropov, and Chernenko had consistently rejected as detrimental to Soviet interests.

Gorbachev moved with particular speed to overturn the dire Brezhnev legacy in Europe, where Brezhnev's rigid and shortsighted diplomacy had produced a disastrous record. Gorbachev, however, faced a real dilemma. To continue the present policy appeared certain to prolong the impasse in East-West relations, but to change course by acceding to Western demands in the INF negotiations, for example, was equally unpalatable, since the Warsaw Pact's military posture, including its nuclear dimension, was vital to the Kremlin's European policy. To resolve this dilemma, Gorbachev reversed Soviet priorities in Europe. In other words, he pushed for "normalized" relations with Western countries ahead of what had always been Moscow's primary objective on the Continent—virtually absolute control over the eastern European nations. Gorbachev encouraged a process of indigenous political reform in eastern Europe. It appears he believed that he could control and direct the forces of reform in order to produce a fundamentally new political order in Europe, one characterized by greater cooperation and mutual stability.

The most significant reason for regarding Gorbachev's new political thinking as more than a tactical device was the dramatic revolution he permitted in eastern Europe in 1989. Since World War II eastern Europe had grappled with the political legacy of Stalinism. Attempts to reform the system were hampered by local Communist bureaucracies and by the physical threat of the Soviet military. Gorbachev simply widened the opportunity for change. In a United Nations speech in 1988, he proclaimed freedom of choice for all nations without exception. In 1989 he openly condemned Brezhnev's 1968 invasion of Czechoslovakia and the 1979 intervention in Afghanistan. He also renounced the Brezhnev Doctrine, which had specifically claimed that the Soviet Union had the right to intervene in the internal affairs of other socialist states if the USSR believed that the socialist system was in political or military danger.

By 1989 Gorbachev abandoned the assumption made by Stalin, Khrushchev, Brezhnev, Andropov, and Chernenko: that the security of the Soviet Union depended on political control of eastern Europe. In the course of the 1989 "quiet revolutions" in Poland, East Germany, Czechoslovakia, Hungary, and Bulgaria, the Communist parties were forced by social and political movements to abandon their monopoly of power. Poland, Hungary, and Czechoslovakia held multiparty elections and initiated substantial economic reforms based on the market principles of capitalism. Bulgarians reelected a local Communist government without any Soviet interference. Romania's reverse was more sudden and violent, but apparently no less complete. Since the Soviet Union no longer maintained thousands of troops in eastern Europe (a gradual withdrawal of troops was agreed to and the Warsaw Pact was dissolved in June 1991), the possibility of military intervention to reverse the movement toward democracy in eastern Europe grew more remote. This was not only because Gorbachev approved of the changes, but because the costs of reimposing a Soviet dictatorship in 1989–1990 would have been enormous. Military intervention would have had a devastating effect on Soviet citizens, especially those who had pinned their hopes on the further development of glasnost, Gorbachev's policy of openness or publicity, and perestroika, his plan to overhaul or restructure the Soviet economic and political systems, and had thus constituted Gorbachev's most loyal following. It would have more than likely met fierce resistance, not only from the new governments and people of eastern Europe but also from sections of the eastern European militaries. And finally, it would have destroyed the gains of Gorbachev's revolutionary policies by subverting the effort to remove the image of a Soviet threat.

Gorbachev's argument that security is a mutual concept was closely related to the situation in eastern Europe and the arms control agreements of 1989–1991. Even after the failed coup against him of August 19, 1991, and after the disintegration of the Soviet Union on December 8, 1991, Gorbachev insisted that the security of the new Commonwealth of Independent States could not be enhanced so long as the United States regarded itself as threatened by the commonwealth's nuclear arms. In fact, he warned of the dangers of the proliferation of nuclear weapons and knowledge after the Soviet Union's collapse. Unlike his predecessors, Gorbachev concluded that the arms race could not be won. In his resignation speech on December 25, 1991, as he transferred power to Boris Yeltsin, he warned Yeltsin that the security of Russia and the Commonwealth of Independent States would best be maintained by coming to some kind of political settlement with the United States.

Until the dramatic shift in Soviet policy on eastern Europe, it was in the area of arms control that Gorbachev had the most significant impact. His decision to present initiatives and to take personal political risks led to essential change in Soviet-American relations between 1985 and 1991. This fundamental change in foreign affairs occurred for several reasons. In the first place, the requirements of domestic reform demanded a peaceful foreign policy in order to shift money from military programs to domestic ones. Significant monetary savings could be gained from arms reduction, especially in conventional weaponry. Second, Gorbachev demonstrated that the class-based, traditional, Marxist-Leninist-Stalinist foundation of Soviet foreign policy no longer made sense. Class struggle, he argued, must yield to the demands of the human race, and this precluded the outbreak of nuclear war. Security for the Soviet Union and the United States therefore became mutual, and the protection of world civilization took precedence over the demands of class struggle.

In addition to this new emphasis on security interdependence, Gorbachev also attempted to redirect the focus of Soviet international economic policy. In the past, Soviet economists tried economic autarky to increase productivity but ultimately failed to compete effectively in the international market. Their methods also failed to meet the basic needs of consumers. Instead of arguing for the development of an alternative socialist economy destined to replace the capitalist system, as Khrushchev and Brezhnev did in the 1960s and 1970s, Gorbachev proposed that the Soviet Union join the global economy. According to Gorbachev, working with the international community was the way to ensure up-to-date technical knowledge and survival.

Gorbachev also initiated new policies in the Third World. He withdrew Soviet forces from Afghanistan and other regions where the Soviet Union was over-extended and where prospects for success were limited. Under his leadership, the Soviet Union withdrew much of its previous military, economic, and political support from revolutionary movements in Africa and Latin America. He agreed with those advisors who insisted that in the long run Soviet interests would be better served by establishing ties with market-oriented states than by emphasizing relations with "national liberation movements" in the Third World. The most important evidence of this new orientation emerged in January 1991, when Gorbachev and U.S. president George Bush cooperated on issues related to Iraq's military takeover of Kuwait. Though differences in objectives and national interests divided Gorbachev and Bush in their policies toward the Middle East conflict, the overriding issues resulted in a wide degree of cooperation and even military coordination.

Several internal constituencies remained extremely displeased with Gorbachev's foreign policy. Generals from all armed forces, for example, were infuriated with his decision to give up eastern Europe, the fruit of Russia's victory in World War II. They despised glasnost, which they faulted for the decline of Soviet military morale, and they were suspicious of perestroika. The generals were appalled by the massive draft dodging (especially in the Baltic republics before their independence in 1991, but also in Georgia and Armenia) and by the talk of an all-volunteer army. They felt that the armed forces, the heart of the regime for decades, had been humiliated. This sort of open criticism of the government by men in uniform had no precedent in Russian history; it illustrated that the armed forces had slipped from Gorbachev's control by mid–1991 and had made common cause with the most reactionary elements in the party.

Much as Gorbachev was honored abroad (he won the Nobel Peace Prize in 1990), he increasingly lost popular support at home, and not only with the armed forces. The older Communist apparatchiks filling the privileged party ranks of what the Communist critic Milovan Djilas referred to as the "new class" continued to obstruct Gorbachev's reform program. Many Soviet citizens, angered by insufficient supplies of food and medicine and desperate economic conditions, blamed Gorbachev. Others, especially Russians, feared the breakup of the USSR. On August 19, 1991, the conservatives Gorbachev had brought into the Kremlin put him under house arrest and declared martial law. The coup was a pathetic attempt, terribly organized by men oblivious to the degree to which Soviet society had changed since 1985. Although the coup failed and Gorbachev regained his freedom, it soon became clear that his days in power were numbered. The Soviet Union disintegrated. Its successor, the Commonwealth of Independent States, was formed on December 21, 1991, and it was made clear to Gorbachev that there was no room for him in the new union. He was finally forced to resign on December 25, 1991.

During his tenure as leader of the Soviet Union, Gorbachev established himself as one of the great statesmen of the twentieth century. His resignation marked the end of a period in which the Soviet Union metamorphosed from a proud totalitarian superpower into a fledgling democracy that no longer hid the truth about its hopeless economy and shameful past. Gorbachev functioned as a reformer, and he ushered in significant changes. Like *Peter the Great, Gorbachev achieved monumental reforms; but unlike Peter, he avoided brutal and vindictive methods. Some changes, of course, inflicted considerable economic hardship and pain. His internal reforms brought chaos and confusion, and ultimately the demise of the Soviet Union itself. Yet, the popular uprising that reversed the hard-liners' coup on August 19, 1991, demonstrated that perestroika had put down deep roots.

In foreign policy Gorbachev made an enormous difference. He engineered a change in Soviet foreign policy from confrontation to cooperation that helped to end the Cold War and brought about the collapse of communism around the world with the exception of a handful of diehards like China, North Korea, and Cuba. He greatly improved the international political situation and significantly contributed to world security. He pushed through reforms at home in order to reduce confrontations abroad, and he effectively led the breakthrough in arms control. To a great extent, he was responsible for ending the Cold War. These achievements alone warrant Gorbachev an eminent place in world history, even if his failed domestic reforms caused him to lose political power.

Annotated Bibliography

Works by Mikhail Sergeyevich Gorbachev were issued in Russian and other languages from 1985 to the end of 1991. Gorbachev's foreign policy speeches are available in a number of collections, among them *Selected Speeches and Articles* (1987) and *Socialism, Peace and Democracy: Writings, Speeches and Reports* (1987). Gorbachev's best-seller, *Perestroika: New Thinking for Our Country and the World* (1987), is now available in several editions. *The August Coup: The Truth and the Lessons* (1991) was published within a few weeks after the coup plotters were arrested. This is not only a memoir but a passionate exercise in spin control, combining a narrative of the coup with an argument for maintaining a political and economic union that few republics seem to want anymore. Gorbachev's advisors, in a feverish attempt to restore his political credibility, won an agreement with foreign publishers to publish the manuscript very quickly; but the book was not a huge success. In fact, the story in the *The August Coup* said more about Gorbachev's diminished status than the coup itself.

Works on Gorbachev have multiplied since the collapse of communism in eastern Europe and the Soviet Union. An excellent overall review is found in Richard Sakwa, *Gorbachev and His Reforms* (1990). According to Sakwa, Gorbachev's most significant achievement was setting the Soviet Union and its peoples on the path of reform. The concept of change itself was now restored to social consciousness after eighteen years of stagnation under Brezhnev in which the core values were authoritarianism and controlled development. Thus, Gorbachev is depicted as a man of history, and his reforms represent the recovery of history by the Soviet people and their increased ability to shape their own politics. Sakwa further suggests that Gorbachev's greatest leadership skills were found in foreign policy rather than in domestic affairs. His reformist drive in respect to nationalities, for example, often gave the appearance of crisis management rather than a mastery over events.

Steven White's *Gorbachev and After* (1991) extensively documents and addresses the crises between the central government and the republics. Describing Gorbachev's embrace of the hard-liners in the fall and winter of 1990, White correctly predicted the anarchy that led to the coup of August 1991. Zhores A. Medvedev's *Gorbachev* (1986) analyzes the making of the general secretary and concentrates on Gorbachev's tenure in power. Medvedev primarily addresses Gorbachev's rapid political rise from obscure apparatchik in Stavropol to general secretary of the Communist Party of the Soviet Union in Moscow. Gorbachev's promotions indicate that early on he impressed the party leadership with his administrative results in Stavropol.

John Parker's *Kremlin in Transition* (1991) provides several interesting insights into Gorbachev's program of reform, arguing that Gorbachev was offering his people a set of laws, accounting procedures, and efficiency standards. According to Parker, Gorbachev was also urging the Soviets to demolish their bureaucratic system without providing them with a clear sense of what would replace it. What exactly were glasnost and perestroika? For many Russians, they were reflections of anarchy and of economic uncertainties. These were alien forces in the Soviet Union, where it had been inconceivable to take any action without a theoretical foundation and a hierarchical system of authority.

Not surprisingly, the enigmatic Gorbachev continues to be the subject of new books and articles, especially since his resignation as president of the Soviet Union on December 25, 1991. Often produced in haste, they include several competent accounts; but as one might expect, they provide little of the in-depth analysis that only detailed research and reflection can yield. Dusko Doder and Louise Branson's *Gorbachev: Heretic in the Kremlin* (1991) provides useful insights into Gorbachev's maneuverings in the Kremlin and examines the interplay of his domestic and foreign policies. Doder and Branson stress that when Gorbachev's program of perestroika did not take off in 1989, he apparently came to the conclusion that the only way to succeed was to revert to the classical tactic of "revolution from above." Robert Kaiser's *Why Gorbachev Happened* (1991) portrays Gorbachev in a manner similar to Doder and Branson. Treating a similar range of topics, he analyzes Gorbachev's personality and shows his penchant for luxury and his love of power.

Two excellent and highly ambitious books on relations between Moscow and the republics during Gorbachev's reign have also appeared recently. As its title implies, *Soviet Disunion: A History of the Nationalities Problem in the USSR* (1991) by Bohdan Nahaylo and Victor Swoboda is a systematic history. Nadia Diuk and Adrian Karatnycky, *Hidden Nations: The People Challenge the Soviet Union* (1991), mainly examines the Gorbachev period. Readable and interpretive, these authors examine various nationality issues throughout the former Soviet Union. Gorbachev's political difficulties with the Baltic republics and the state of Georgia are particularly well analyzed in both books.

Bibliography

Bailer, Seweryn, and Michael Mandelbaum, eds. *Gorbachev's Russia and American Foreign Policy*. Boulder, Colo.: Westview Press, 1988.

Balzer, Harley D., ed. *Five Years that Shook the World: Gorbachev's Unfinished Revolution*. Boulder, Colo.: Westview Press, 1991.

Breslauer, George W., ed. *Can Gorbachev's Reforms Succeed?* Berkeley: Berkeley-

Stanford Program in Soviet Studies, Center for Slavic and East European Studies, University of California at Berkeley, 1990.

Campbell, Kurt M., and S. Neil MacFarlane, eds. *Gorbachev's Third World Dilemmas.* London: Routledge, 1989.

Daley, Tad. *Afghanistan and Gorbachev's Global Foreign Policy.* Santa Monica, Calif.: Rand/UCLA Center for Soviet Studies, 1989.

Dawisha, Karen. *Eastern Europe, Gorbachev, and Reform: The Great Challenge.* Cambridge: Cambridge University Press, 1988.

Diuk, Nadia, and Adrian Karatnycky. *Hidden Nations: The People Challenge the Soviet Union.* New York: Morrow, 1991.

Doder, Dusko, and Louise Branson. *Gorbachev: Heretic in the Kremlin.* New York: Viking, 1991.

Freedman, Robert Owen. *Soviet Policy Toward Israel Under Gorbachev.* New York: Praeger, 1991.

Fukuyama, Francis. *Gorbachev and the New Soviet Agenda in the Third World.* Santa Monica: Rand Corporation, 1989.

Gorbachev, Mikhail S. *The August Coup: The Truth and the Lessons.* New York: HarperCollins, 1991.

———. *Perestroika: New Thinking for Our Country and the World.* London: Collins, 1987.

———. *Selected Speeches and Articles.* Moscow: Progress, 1987.

———. *Socialism, Peace and Democracy: Writings, Speeches and Reports.* New York: Pergamon, 1987.

Halliday, Fred. *From Kabul to Managua: Soviet-American Relations in the 1980's.* New York: Pantheon, 1989.

Harle, Vilho, and Jyrki Iivonen, eds. *Gorbachev and Europe.* New York: St. Martin's Press, 1990.

Horelick, Arnold Lawrence. *Soviet Foreign Policy under Gorbachev.* Santa Monica, Calif.: Rand/UCLA Center for the Study of Soviet International Behavior, 1986.

Kaiser, Robert. *Why Gorbachev Happened.* New York: Simon and Schuster, 1991.

Legvold, Robert. *Gorbachev's Foreign Policy: How Should the United States Respond?* New York: Foreign Policy Association, 1988.

Lewin, Moshe. *The Gorbachev Phenomenon: A Historical Interpretation.* Berkeley: University of California Press, 1988.

Lieven, D.C.B. *Gorbachev and the Nationalities.* London: Centre for Security and Conflict Studies, 1988.

Lynch, Allen. *Gorbachev's International Outlook: Intellectual Origins and Political Consequences.* New York: Institute for East-West Security Studies, 1989.

Mandel, Ernest. *Beyond Perestroika: The Future of Gorbachev's USSR.* New York: Verso, 1989.

Medvedev, Zhores A. *Gorbachev.* New York: Norton, 1986.

Miller, Robert F. *Soviet Foreign Policy Today: Gorbachev and the New Political Thinking.* New York: Unwin Hyman, 1991.

Mlynar, Zdenek. *Can Gorbachev Change the Soviet Union? The International Dimensions of Political Reform.* Translated by Marian Sling and Ruth Tosek. Boulder, Colo.: Westview Press, 1990.

Nahaylo, Bohdan, and Victor Swoboda. *Soviet Disunion: A History of the Nationalities Problem in the USSR.* New York: Free Press, 1991.

Parker, John. *Kremlin in Transition*. Boston: Unwin Hyman, 1991.

Sakwa, Richard. *Gorbachev and His Reforms*. New York: Prentice-Hall, 1990.

Solov'ev, Vladimir. *Beyond the High Kremlin Walls*. New York: Dodd, Mead, 1986.

Thakur, Ramesh, and Carlyle A. Thayer, eds. *The Soviet Union as an Asian Pacific Power: Implications of Gorbachev's 1986 Vladivostok Initiative*. Boulder, Colo.: Westview Press, 1987.

White, Steven. *Gorbachev and After*. Cambridge: Cambridge University Press, 1991.

———. *Gorbachev in Power*. Cambridge: Cambridge University Press, 1990.

Zacek, Jane Shapiro, ed. *The Gorbachev Generation: Issues in Soviet Foreign Policy*. New York: Professors World Peace Academy, 1988.

MICHAEL M. LUSTIG

Dag Hammarskjold (1905–1961). Dag Hjalmar Agne Carl Hammarskjold was born July 29, 1905, in Jonkoping, Sweden, the youngest of five boys. Perhaps symbolic of Hammarskjold's later political career, his father was not present— he was in Karlstad as a delegate to the negotiations on the dissolution of the Swedish union with Norway. Hammarskjold's family upbringing, academic training, and government service prior to his becoming secretary-general of the United Nations prepared him well for the challenges he faced and particularly for the yet-undefined economic and social responsibilities of the United Nations.

His father, Hjalmar, was an austere, conservative, and formidable, man who was a stern father. Hjalmar was minister of justice, minister to Denmark, and governor of the district of Uppland at Uppsala prior to serving as prime minister of Sweden during World War I. Politically unpopular due to his declaration of unreserved neutrality for Sweden in the war, which brought accusations of pro-German leanings, his active political life ended in 1917 when his cabinet resigned and he returned to the appointive post of governor at Uppsala until 1930. Hammarskjold later contended that his father's neutrality policy was not only intended to keep Sweden out of the war but also to establish a position from which Sweden and other Scandinavian nations could promote a new postwar order based on international law. Hjalmar was subsequently the chairman of the League of Nations committee for the codification of international law.

Hammarskjold was especially close to his mother, Agnes Almquist, whom he described as having "a radically democratic view of fellow-humans, 'evangelic' if you like, a childlike openness toward life, an anti-rationalism with warm undercurrents of feeling" (quoted in Urquhart, p.19).

Hammarskjold earned degrees in law and economics from the University of Uppsala and received his Ph.D in economics at the University of Stockholm, where in 1933 he became an assistant professor in political economy. He never married.

At the age of thirty, Hammarskjold was named under secretary of the Swedish Ministry of Finance and chairman of the governors of the Bank of Sweden. From 1936 to 1945 he was secretary-general of the Department of Finance; in 1946 he was named specialist in finance in the Swedish Foreign Ministry. In 1947 he became under secretary in the Foreign Office in charge of all economic questions;

in 1949 he was appointed secretary-general of the Foreign Office. He subsequently served as chairman of the executive committee of the Organization for European Economic Cooperation and as Sweden's minister of state in the Foreign Office. His evolution through the Swedish tradition of a nonpolitical civil service formulated his ideas about the appropriate role of the UN Secretariat.

Within the United Nations prior to 1953, Hammarskjold served as vice-chairman of the Swedish delegation to the sixth session (1951) of the UN General Assembly (GA) and as chairman of its delegation to the seventh session (1952).

Hammarskjold's election in 1953 as secretary-general of the United Nations was made possible by the resignation of the first secretary-general, Trygve Lie. Lie had become embroiled in controversies with the United States and the Soviet Union and had lost his effectiveness both as a neutral figure and as a defender of the Secretariat's integrity and neutrality.

Lie's problems with the United States resulted from internal U.S. politics connected with McCarthyism. Conservatives in the United States had charged that the Secretariat was riddled with Communists and fellow travelers. Lie's estrangement from the Soviet Union developed over the Korean War, which began with North Korea's invasion of South Korea on June 25, 1950. Lie supported the U.S. initiative in support of South Korea and the creation of a UN Unified Command in Korea. As a consequence of his support, Lie's renomination as secretary-general was vetoed by the Soviet Union, and he announced his resignation on November 10, 1952.

The UN Security Council (SC) did not seriously undertake a search for Lie's successor until the spring of 1953. After the major powers had rejected several candidates, Hammarskjold was nominated by the United Kingdom. The Security Council on March 31, 1953, decided to offer the position to Hammarskjold, who had not been consulted and who was said to have been completely surprised by the invitation. After appropriate consultations, he accepted the appointment. The General Assembly on April 7 confirmed the Security Council's recommendation of his appointment. The General Assembly officially installed him as the second UN secretary-general on April 10, 1953, and he served in that position until his death on September 17, 1961, in a mysterious airplane crash near Ndola, Northern Rhodesia.

Hammarskjold took office with a Secretariat at odds with both of the superpowers—with the United States over McCarthyism and with the Soviet Union over the Korean venture—but personally with the approval of all five Great Powers. Since he was relatively unknown outside of Sweden, it was expected that he would be primarily an administrator who would refrain from an overt and public political role as secretary-general.

Hammarskjold's initial challenges were to quiet the turmoil within the UN Secretariat and restore its credibility and morale, and to instill a sense of neutrality and professionalism in the UN's international civil service.

His first charge from the General Assembly was a resolution, passed on April 1, 1953, to submit a full report on personnel policy to the fall GA session. Thus, in the wake of the McCarthy witch-hunt that had extended into the Secretariat, Hammarskjold sought to establish guidelines and procedures that ensured the secretary-general's control of the Secretariat staff and his independence from internal political events in member states. Hammarskjold's view of the nature of an international secretariat, based on the principles established by Sir Eric Drummond, the first secretary-general of the League of Nations, was that in order to assure the freedom, independence, and international character of the UN Secretariat, the secretary-general should have exclusive responsibility for appointments and dismissals.

In November 1953, Hammarskjold rescinded permission for FBI officials to operate on UN premises, stating that such activities violated the international character of UN headquarters. Hammarskjold also strengthened the powers of the secretary-general to dismiss employees whose conduct was interpreted as violating the charter's standards of integrity, independence, and impartiality. At the same time he made it clear that the secretary-general would be the final judge of the evidence received from member governments and that he would ignore unsubstantiated charges against staff members. Hammarskjold informed Senator Joseph McCarthy, through U.S. Ambassador Henry Cabot Lodge, that he would disregard the invoking of the Fifth Amendment by a member of the Secretariat before the McCarthy Committee if he was satisfied with the staff member's explanation, and that he would also disregard previous Communist party membership if a U.S. staff member's present record was clean.

The new secretary-general also persuaded the United States to change its intrusive policy of withholding the passports of U.S. Secretariat officials or denying visas to non-U.S. citizens to work at the UN. Although no agreement was formalized, the United States agreed to consult with him on individual cases of concern.

With regard to Secretariat personnel procedures, Hammarskjold clarified regulations concerning the obligations of Secretariat staff members and sought to ensure their commitment to the neutrality of the international civil service by requiring them to abstain from all national political activities except voting. He also claimed for the secretary-general the right to terminate employees for a variety of causes including ''the interest of good administration of the Organization and in accordance with the standards of the Charter.''

Hammarskjold sought to establish and promote the independent position of the Secretariat and asserted that its members must be guided by the organization's common aims and rules and by recognized legal principles rather than by personal preferences or by directives or wishes of their own governments. Hammarskjold's views on the importance of the Secretariat's neutrality and independence were eloquently expressed in a May 30, 1961, lecture at Oxford University on the nature and responsibilities of the international civil servant.

Under Hammarskjold's tutelage, the office of the secretary-general developed its own distinct role and style and became a focal point for multilateral diplomacy and for the establishment and administration of UN-authorized peacekeeping operations. Hammarskjold defined and developed the secretary-general's leadership role. He flexibly and expansively interpreted specific authorizations, resolutions, and mandates from the General Assembly and the Security Council. In those instances where the resolutions were ambiguous or lacked direction or specificity, he asserted an independent role for the secretary-general. He maintained that the charter gave the secretary-general the right and responsibility to interpret his powers broadly, based on the UN's general principles and goals.

Hammarskjold utilized a wide array of diplomatic techniques. In some situations he depended on specific directives from the General Assembly or the Security Council. However, in several instances he relied on the more ambiguous general authority of the secretary-general grounded in Article 99 of the UN Charter. He also employed ''quiet diplomacy'' and mediation and conciliation, rather than more visible and public diplomacy, in executing a negotiating style based on patience, persistence, tact, and impartiality. Hammarskjold told the Security Council in 1956 that the secretary-general had the duty to maintain his usefulness by avoiding public stands on conflicts between member nations unless such actions might help to resolve the conflict. Thus, particularly in his early years, Hammarskjold conducted much of his diplomacy in private and avoided public pronouncements. He saw the office of the secretary-general not primarily as an independent force but as a catalyst; he consulted extensively with all interested parties and sought to establish a common set of principles agreeable to all sides in a dispute.

For instance, when the General Assembly in 1954 requested him to seek the release from China of U.S. pilots downed on UN missions during the Korean War through ''the means most appropriate to his judgement,'' he used his general authority as secretary-general, rather than the GA resolution, as the basis of his mission to Peking. Through a low-key and personal approach to the Chinese, he obtained the release of all the pilots over the next seven months.

In the 1958 Lebanese crisis, he established, under an SC directive, an observer group (UNOGIL) to investigate Lebanese claims of Syrian infiltration. When Soviet vetoes brought SC guidance to a halt, Hammarskjold told the Security Council that he would fill the vacuum by taking such additional measures as he judged appropriate. On his own authority he significantly enlarged the observer group and provided it with aircraft in order to establish a clearly visible UN presence within Lebanon. He also established a consultative group on Lebanon, consisting of personally appointed representatives from the same seven nations who later served on the United Nations Emergency Force Advisory Group. Primarily as a result of this UN presence and Hammarskjold's quiet diplomacy, the situation in Lebanon stabilized and all foreign forces and the observer group were withdrawn from Lebanon by the end of 1958.

On two occasions, in 1958–1960 in a dispute between Cambodia and Thailand, and in 1959–1960 in Laos, Hammarskjold employed personal representatives to extend the good offices of the secretary-general in efforts to resolve the conflicts. While this diplomatic tool was successful in the first instance, the personal representatives only succeeded in delaying outside intervention in the second.

Hammarskjold's most public legacy is his development of the guidelines for organizing, recruiting, deploying, and administering multinational peacekeeping forces under UN authority. In addition, he developed much of the rationale, philosophy, and terminology for peacekeeping operations as a new and distinctive UN tool.

His first opportunity for developing what became known as "preventive diplomacy" and "UN peacekeeping" came in 1956 in the wake of the British-French-Israeli invasion of Egypt, better known as the Suez Crisis. After Security Council consideration of the situation was cut short by British and French vetoes, the General Assembly met in emergency session under the Uniting for Peace Resolution and on November 4, 1956, authorized the secretary-general to negotiate a cease-fire in the crisis and to submit to the General Assembly within forty-eight hours "a plan for the setting up, with the consent of the nations concerned, of an emergency international United Nations Force to secure and supervise the cessation of hostilities." The principles contained in the guidelines developed by Hammarskjold for the creation of this Middle East peacekeeping force became the basis for future UN peacekeeping operations. On November 7, the General Assembly approved Hammarskjold's plan for the United Nations Emergency Force (UNEF) in the Middle East and authorized him to proceed with its establishment. The General Assembly also created an advisory committee for the UN force under his chairmanship and requested all member states to provide assistance to the UN command. The cease-fire and withdrawal of the British, French, and Israeli forces were dependent upon the successful creation and deployment of UNEF.

Hammarskjold based UNEF on five principles:

1. It could exist only with the approval of the country on whose territory it would function (in this case, Egypt).

2. It would not intervene in the internal affairs of that country.

3. It would include no contingents from any of the five permanent members of the Security Council.

4. The cost would be outside the regular UN budget but generally shared.

5. Executive management of the force, within the limits laid out by the General Assembly or the Security Council, would be in the hands of a UN command responsible to the secretary-general.

With the implementation of UNEF, a new concept came into existence that was quite different from the process envisaged in Articles 39–49 of the UN Charter. Peacekeeping by a multinational police-type force drawn from nonmajor powers was substituted for collective-security action dependent upon the might of the five major powers.

Intense negotiations followed, aimed at convincing the Egyptians to accept UNEF troops on their soil while maintaining full respect for Egypt's sovereignty. The agreement between the secretary-general and Egypt established a relationship under which UNEF operated effectively until early 1967. The creation of UNEF as a face-saving operation of an unprecedented kind raised the influence and executive authority of the secretary-general to a level that it had not previously enjoyed.

The lessons learned in the creation of UNEF in 1956 were used in 1960 in response to the situation in the Congo. Hammarskjold employed for the first time the secretary-general's authority under Article 99 to bring a matter to the attention of the Security Council. Subsequently, the Security Council authorized him to create a peacekeeping force to aid the Congo government in restoring order and to supervise the withdrawal of Belgian and mercenary forces. Although he sought direction from the General Assembly when a Soviet veto deadlocked the Security Council, he did not hesitate to use his own judgment when he deemed that guidance inadequate or ambiguous.

Hammarskjold sought to use UN forces in the Congo to maintain civil order and to prevent the breakdown of economic and social order, while remaining out of quarrels among rival Congolese leaders. He sought to remove Belgian forces from the Congo and to prevent other foreign powers from becoming involved. His refusal to use UN troops to unite the Congo by force led to Soviet obstinancy and vetoes and demands for Hammarskjold's resignation.

Soviet leader Nikita Khrushchev, in a lengthy speech before the General Assembly on September 20, 1960, called for the abolition of the post of secretary-general and its replacement by a "collective executive" made up of three persons representing the three major divisions of the world—the so-called troika. Hammarskjold was accused of being partial to the Western nations in implementing Security Council decisions in the Congo.

Hammarskjold, in response to the attacks on the role of the secretary-general, said, "This is a question not of a man but of an institution." He claimed that the attitude of the secretary-general must be characterized by "independence, impartiality, objectivity," even if this creates "an obstacle for those who work for certain political aims." Although Hammarskjold repeatedly received overwhelming votes of confidence in the General Assembly, and the neutralist states rejected representation through the Soviet Union's troika proposal, his effectiveness was, like that of his predecessor, diminished by the Soviet Union's active hostility.

Many of the principles of UN peacekeeping developed by Hammarskjold in 1956 in the Middle East and refined in 1960 in the Congo were subsequently applied after his death: in 1964 in Cyprus, in 1973 in the Sinai, in 1974 in the Golan Heights, and in 1978 in Lebanon. The 1988 Nobel Peace Prize was awarded to the UN peacekeeping forces worldwide. The prize acknowledged Hammarskjold's greatest contribution to the UN: the development of the secretary-general's ability to lead the UN in deterring or resolving armed conflicts through peacekeeping operations.

Dag Hammarskjold's contributions to the international community's second attempt in the twentieth century to create a global organization to maintain international peace and security were (1) the development of a professional, neutral, and credible civil service within the UN Secretariat; (2) the definition and refinement of an expanded and independent leadership role for the secretary-general; and (3) the formulation of guidelines for organizing, deploying, and administering multinational peacekeeping forces under the authority of the United Nations. While subsequent secretaries-general have brought their own perspectives, styles, and personalities to the position, all have so far operated within the model set by Hammarskjold. Similarly, subsequent UN peacekeeping operations have been variations on the concepts developed by Hammarskjold. Hammarskjold's legacy to the planet is a more credible, more forceful, and more effective global organization seeking to maintain international peace and security.

Annotated Bibliography

Hammarskjold's personal papers are located in a two-part collection in the Manuscript Department of the Royal Library in Stockholm, Sweden. One part of the collection includes materials from the secretary-general's office in New York; the other part, more personal, contains materials from his New York apartment and from his years in Sweden prior to his assumption of his UN position in 1953.

The UN part of this collection contains items relating to Secretariat activities, outgoing correspondence, Hammarskjold's personal financial records, subject areas (Suez, UN-OGIL, Laos, the Congo), and speeches and correspondence relating to speaking engagements. The files are apparently maintained in the manner in which they were originally created in Hammarskjold's office. The index to the collection lists subjects on the basis of how they appear in the files, but it does not indicate their size or describe the content of each file.

The UN Archives is a well-organized and well-indexed collection of documents located in New York City. The original materials are in the process of being transferred to microfilm.

Other relevant collections include the papers of Ralph Bunche and Andrew Cordier, two Secretariat officials who worked closely with Hammarskjold on a daily basis during his secretary-generalship, and the official records of the United Nations.

The Ralph Bunche papers are located in the Special Collections Department of the University of California at Los Angeles. Bunche, under-secretary-general for special political affairs, was one of Hammarskjold's most trusted political advisors and confidants. A fifty-two-page finder's aid provides accurate descriptions of the subject contents of folders found in 160 large boxes but no indication of the number of items in each folder. While Bunche's personal papers are relevant because of his close relationship with Hammarskjold, those that relate to Bunche's duties at the United Nations are located not in this collection but in the archives of the office of the under-secretary-general of the United Nations and are under the control of the secretary-general himself.

The papers of Andrew Cordier, executive assistant to both Hammarskjold and Trygve Lie, are located at Columbia University and consist of over 200,000 items housed in 346 document boxes. A three-volume finder's aid and an index of Cordier's correspondence assist the researcher in using this collection. Cordier's UN papers are also available at the UN Archives.

The official records of the United Nations contain documents, reports, and speeches that reflect the evolution of Hammarskjold's thinking. Of particular value are Hammarskjold's ''Annual Report(s) of the Secretary-General on the Work of the Organization,'' his "Introduction(s) to the Annual Reports of the Secretary-General on the Work of the Organization," and his regular reports to the Security Council and the General Assembly on such crises as Suez, the Congo, Hungary, and Lebanon, and the financing of peace-keeping operations.

Other than his personal and official papers, Hammarskjold left no significant works focusing on his eight years as secretary-general. *Markings* (1964), Hammarskjold's post-humously published diary, contains no direct references to his secretary-generalship.

The most thorough and comprehensive work on Hammarskjold and his secretary-generalship is Brian Urquhart's *Hammarskjold* (1972). Urquhart was in the office of the under-secretaries-general for special political affairs during almost the entire period of Hammarskjold's secretary-generalship. He had been asked by a group of international publishers and encouraged by the trustees of Hammarskjold's papers (who gave him sole access to his private papers) to write an account of Hammarskjold's secretary-generalship. The book is, as Urquhart said, "written mainly from Hammarskjold's point of view as secretary-general." Apart from an introductory biographical chapter on Hammarskjold, it is devoted to the eight years of Hammarskjold's secretary-generalship. Urquhart's access to and extensive use of Hammarskjold's personal papers, both published and unpublished, and of UN documents enabled him to recreate in great detail the evolution of Hammarskjold's thinking. The book contains an extensive citation of sources and a comprehensive index.

A detailed account of UN activities in the Congo is found in Rajeshwar Dayal's *Mission for Hammarskjold: The Congo Crisis* (1976). Dayal was head of the UN mission in the Congo and had previously served on the UN observation group in Lebanon.

An excellent, brief, but very substantive overview of Hammarskjold's many roles is *Dag Hammarskjold Revisited* (1983), compiled and edited by Robert S. Jordan. Assembled in commemoration of the twentieth anniversary of Hammarskjold's death, the book consists of seven essays by individuals who either knew and worked with Hammarskjold or who had written authoritatively about him or the office of the secretary-general. A comprehensive bibliographic essay on Hammarskjold by Larry Trachtenberg is also included. The book has an extensive bibliography.

Bibliography

Bailey, Sydney D. *The Secretariat of the United Nations*. New York: Carnegie Endowment for International Peace, 1962.

Barros, James, ed. *The United Nations: Past, Present and Future*. New York: Free Press, 1972.

Beigbeder, Yves. *Threats to the International Civil Service*. New York: Columbia University Press, 1988.

Bennett, A. LeRoy. *International Organizations: Principles and Issues*. 5th ed. Englewood Cliffs, N.J.: Prentice-Hall, 1991.

Cordier, Andrew W., and Wilder Foote, eds. *Public Papers of the Secretaries-General of the United Nations*. Vol. 2, *Dag Hammarskjold, 1953–1956*; Vol. 3, *Dag Hammarskjold, 1956–1957*; Vol. 4, *Dag Hammarskjold, 1958–1960*; Vol. 5, *Dag Hammarskjold, 1960–1961*. New York: Columbia University Press, 1972–1975.
———.*The Quest for Peace: The Dag Hammarskjold Memorial Lectures*. New York: Columbia University Press, 1965.

Cordier, Andrew W., and Kenneth L. Maxwell, eds. *Paths to World Order*. New York: Columbia University Press, 1967.

Dayal, Rajeshwar. *Mission for Hammarskjold: The Congo Crisis*. Princeton, N.J.: Princeton University Press, 1976.

Foote, Wilder, ed. *Servant of Peace: A Selection of the Speeches and Statements of Dag Hammarskjold, Secretary-General of the United Nations, 1953–1961*. New York: Harper and Row, 1962.

Hammarskjold, Dag. *Markings*. Translated by W. H. Auden and L. Sjoberg. New York: Knopf, 1964.

Jordan, Robert S., ed. *Dag Hammarskjold Revisited: The UN Secretary-General as a Force in World Politics*. Durham, N.C.: Carolina Academic Press, 1983.

Kelen, Emery. *Hammarskjold*. New York: Putnam, 1966.

———, ed. *Hammarskjold, the Political Man*. New York: Funk and Wagnalls, 1968.

Lash, Joseph P. *Dag Hammarskjold: Custodian of the Brushfire Peace*. Garden City, N.Y.: Doubleday, 1961.

Longford, Frank Pakenham, Earl of. *The Search for Peace: A Personal View of Contributions to Peace Since 1945*. London: Harrap, 1985.

Miller, Richard I. *Dag Hammarskjold and Crisis Diplomacy*. Dobbs Ferry, N.Y.: Oceana Publications, 1961.

Rovine, Arthur W. *The First Fifty Years: The Secretary-General in World Politics, 1920–1970*. Leiden: Sijthoff, 1970.

Stolpe, Sven. *Dag Hammarskjold, a Spiritual Portrait*. Translated by Naomi Walford. New York: Scribner's, 1966.

Urquhart, Brian. *Hammarskjold*. New York: Knopf, 1972.

Van Dusen, Henry Pitner. *Dag Hammarskjold: The Statesman and His Faith*. New York: Harper and Row, 1967.

Zacher, Mark W. *Dag Hammarskjold's United Nations*. New York: Columbia University Press, 1970.

ALLEN B. MAXWELL

Adolf Hitler (1889–1945). Adolf Hitler, dictator of Germany, was born in Braunau, Austria-Hungary, on April 20, 1889, into a family of humble origin. His father Alois was illegitimate but had risen from shoemaker to customs official; his mother was a peasant. Adolf clashed with his father's insensitive, authoritarian personality, but his mother was overindulgent. He wanted to become an artist or possibly an architect, but lacked both the talent and the perseverance to realize his dreams. His father died in 1903. With the help of a pension Adolf's mother indulged her son, and he idled away his time at home in Linz and on visits to Vienna after dropping out of school in 1905. In 1907 and 1908 the young Hitler suffered several traumas. His mother died while being treated for breast cancer, and twice he failed the entrance examination to the Vienna Fine Arts Academy. For years after, he drifted without permanent employment, first in Vienna and, after 1913, in Munich, where he had moved perhaps to escape the Austrian draft.

Hitler related in *Mein Kampf* that his years in Vienna helped to shape his worldview. He presumably read racist publications that transformed him into a rabid anti-Semite; he developed a deep hatred of international socialism and embraced a pan-German nationalism tinged with anti-Slavic racialism. Imbued with ardent nationalist feelings, he volunteered for the German army at the outbreak of hostilities in 1914 and served bravely as a dispatch runner in a Bavarian regiment throughout the war. He received the Iron Cross, Second Class, in 1914, and in 1918 he was awarded the Iron Cross, First Class (an exceptional decoration for a corporal). He always remembered his frontline experience with emotion, since he had found there comradeship and escape from the aimlessness of civilian life.

At the end of the war and thereafter, Hitler publicly blamed socialists and Jews for instigating revolution and bringing about the defeat of the German fatherland. After the armistice of 1918 he returned to Munich, where he continued to serve in the army and was trained as a political agent. In September 1919, Hitler was sent to investigate the German Workers' party, a small nationalist organization, which invited him to become a member. Here he discovered his oratorical talent, becoming the party's principal propagandist and, in 1921, its leader. Renamed the National Socialist German Workers' party in 1920, its programmatic tenets incorporated many of the ideas that Hitler had embraced in Vienna: vehement racial nationalism including notions of German living space (*Lebensraum*), anti-Semitism, and opposition to liberal democracy and especially Marxism.

Toward the end of 1923 Hitler and his National Socialist associates felt strong enough to stage the Beer Hall Putsch in order to seize power in Bavaria and then to mount a march on Berlin following *Benito Mussolini's example. The failure of this attempt taught Hitler a critical lesson: the National Socialist movement must strive to attain power by legal means. When tried on charges of treason in 1924, he turned the proceedings into a propaganda triumph, charging that the president of the Weimar Republic and those in government were the real traitors in Germany. Though sentenced to five years of confinement, he was released after nine months but was forbidden to speak in public in many parts of Germany until 1928. He used these years to complete *Mein Kampf* and to reconstitute his party, demonstrating considerable organizational talent.

It is doubtful that Hitler's movement would have become a major force in German politics had it not been for the worsening of economic conditions. In the Reichstag election of 1928 the National Socialists polled a modest 810,000 votes (2.6 percent) and obtained twelve seats. By 1930 unemployment reached 3 million. With increased working-class support going to the Communists, who were seen as a threat to the established order, more and more lower-middle-class and middle-class voters flocked to the National Socialists as a bulwark against revolution. In the 1930 Reichstag election the National Socialists received 6.5 million votes, gained 107 seats, and became the second largest party next to the Social Democrats.

When the Depression in Germany peaked in 1932, there were more than 6.5 million unemployed and uncounted numbers of underemployed. Under such severe economic conditions, deep political polarization was almost inevitable. Three national elections gave Hitler a unique opportunity to engage in mass agitation. Using the airplane to reach many cities and audiences in a matter of days, he revolutionized the style of campaigning. His emotional attacks on the traitors of the Weimar Republic and his calls to avenge Versailles and to restore Germany's greatness found resonance among voters of all social classes. After Hitler captured 36.8 percent of the votes in the presidential election against Hindenburg, his party obtained a record 13.7 million votes and 230 seats in the July Reichstag election. In the subsequent November election for the Reichstag, signs of economic improvement and a shortage of campaign funds reduced the Nazi vote by 2 million and the party's seats to 196. Nevertheless, Hitler, as the leader of the largest party, held out for the office of chancellor. Intrigue by conservative nationalist politicians like Franz von Papen and General Kurt von Schleicher as well as Hitler's shrewd calculations brought his appointment as chancellor by a reluctant President von Hindenburg on January 30, 1933.

Once in office Hitler moved quickly to consolidate his dictatorial powers. Using the Reichstag fire of February 27 as a pretext to curtail civil rights, he harassed and had arrested Communists and many Social Democrats. After gaining an increased plurality, though not a majority, in the March Reichstag election, he masterminded the adoption of the Enabling Act, giving him dictatorial powers. Between May and July he dissolved the trade unions and political parties. One year later, in June 1934, he brutally purged the leadership of the *Sturmabteilung* (SA) under Ernst Röhm in order to mollify the army leadership, the only force that might have challenged him on his road to absolute power. When President Hindenburg died in August 1934, army leaders accepted the merger of the offices of president and chancellor, with Hitler taking the titles of Führer and Reich chancellor. He thereby also became the supreme commander of all the Reich's armed forces, and all officers and soldiers had to swear an oath of personal allegiance. By allowing party subordinates like Hermann Goering, Joseph Goebbels, and Heinrich Himmler to carve out their own competing domains of power and by creating offices arbitrarily, he gave himself the role of supreme arbiter.

Hitler exercised considerable leadership in bringing about Germany's economic recovery and a rapid reduction in unemployment. A combination of intensified industrial activity, public works, and rearmament based on deficit spending achieved this result. Increasingly the German economic system blended features of a market economy and a planned economy. All of this was ultimately designed to enable Germany to pursue a vigorous foreign policy, which was Hitler's greatest interest.

Few historians dispute that after 1933 Adolf Hitler made all the major decisions relating to German foreign affairs. Many scholars contend that all of his foreign policy objectives were outlined in *Mein Kampf*. It is important to recognize that principles and goals were formulated there, but tactics and strategies were determined by the circumstances of the time. In pursuing his goal of *Lebensraum*, Hitler was able to capitalize on the German belief that the territorial losses of the Versailles settlement must be regained. He also appealed to the expansionist aspirations of the German power elite and significant segments of society. In launching his foreign policy, Hitler demonstrated singular opportunism in the means and the timing of his actions while pursuing a clear-cut goal. Despite the fact that he had very little firsthand knowledge of countries outside Austria and Germany, he displayed remarkable skill in exploiting the weaknesses of the democracies. As he moved from success to success, his self-confidence grew, as did the boldness of his actions.

During the first year of his rule, Hitler withdrew Germany from the Disarmament Conference and the League of Nations. In January 1934 he surprised Europeans by concluding a nonaggression pact with Poland, a move that signaled a permanent rejection of the close German-Russian relationship of Weimar days. The 1935 plebiscite that returned the Saarland to Germany was greeted with enthusiasm by Germany and accepted by France. However, the introduction of German conscription, contrary to the Treaty of Versailles, temporarily united Britain, France, and Italy in opposition. Yet only a few months later Germany concluded a naval treaty with Britain. Hitler had taken a personal interest in the negotiations, hoping to pave the way for a more permanent friendship with the British. His most daring move, the remilitarization of the Rhineland in 1936, defied the advice of his military leaders. It provoked western protests but brought no military action. During these heady months the Führer exclaimed in a speech, "I go the way that Providence dictates with the assurance of a sleepwalker." The year 1936 brought a diplomatic revolution; Italy became aligned with Germany, forming the Rome-Berlin Axis.

In a secret conference with military leaders in November 1937, Hitler outlined his plans for future conquests, naming Austria and Czechoslovakia as his first objectives. When several army leaders questioned his program of territorial expansion, Hitler found it expedient to restructure the military command. An inappropriate marriage and a spurious morals charge played into his hands and enabled him to oust the two top military leaders, Werner von Blomberg and Werner von Fritsch; Hitler assumed the responsibilities of the abolished war ministry, thereby further strengthening his hold over the army. Austria was annexed in March 1938. In the fall Hitler prepared to use force against Czechoslovakia but was headed off by British and French concessions at the Munich Conference, which compelled Czechoslovakia to surrender the Sudetenland to Germany. In March 1939, Hitler moved again. German troops occupied Prague, and independent Czechoslovakia ceased to exist. Hitler seemed to believe that Britain would not fight, although he concluded a nonaggression pact with the Soviet Union to fend off a potential two-front war. On September 1, 1939, his attack on Poland unleashed World War II.

War provided a convenient vehicle for the pursuit of Hitler's expansionist goals. Though lacking a formal military education, he read extensively on military affairs and commanded an impressive knowledge of military subjects thanks to an exceptional memory. In military matters, as in foreign policy, he assumed full command. At the outset of the war, Hitler's blitzkrieg strategy, the combination of airplanes, fast mobile armor, and infantry, brought unprecedented successes. Poland, Norway, France, and Yugoslavia quickly succumbed between 1939 and 1941. But Britain presented him with his first strategic deadlock, leading him to make the most crucial mistake of his career, namely, launching an assault on the Soviet Union in June 1941. Hitler expected to defeat Russia with a blitzkrieg strike in six weeks, but the inability of his armies to gain a decisive victory before the onset of winter marked the strategic failure that ultimately doomed his chances of winning the war. Though he proved to be an impressive offensive strategist during the blitzkrieg phase of the war, his later military decisions after the German forces were compelled to fight a defensive war brought disaster and ultimate defeat.

Hitler's war objectives were to achieve territorial hegemony in Europe from the Atlantic to the depths of Russia, and to enslave (and, in the case of the Jews, eliminate) "racially inferior" peoples. His New Order in Europe comprised an empire of concentration camps under Heinrich Himmler and, after 1941, extermination camps in Poland as well. After the conquest of Europe, he appears to have contemplated the removal of millions of Jews to the region between the Bug and Vistula rivers or to Madagascar, but soon concluded that that was impractical. Starting in 1941, he helped unleash an unparalleled program of mechanized murder, the Final Solution, that claimed the lives of close to six million Jews. Millions of others perished as victims of Nazi political and racial persecution.

Adolf Hitler was a man of genius and ruthless drive who came to wield enormous power as a statesman, first in Germany and then in conquered Europe. He carried the potential of uniting Europe under a cohesive order based on new principles. But his megalomania and vulgarity, his twisted and savage concept of humanity, defeated the realization of any kind of constructive state or lasting international arrangement. When he committed suicide in his Berlin bunker on April 30, 1945, he left a fractured Germany, a divided Europe, and a world with memories of unprecedented horror.

Annotated Bibliography

Archival documents relating to Hitler are primarily found at several repositories in the Federal Republic of Germany. A few original sources remain in the United States and elsewhere. Very substantial parts of the documentary collections captured by the Allied forces and brought to Britain and the United States after World War II, but later returned to Germany, were microfilmed. It remains to be seen what new materials will become available from the archives of the former German Democratic Republic following German reunification, and where these collections will be permanently located.

Essential guides giving researchers information on German archives, including addresses, inventories, finding aids, and many useful hints, are Christoph M. Kimmich, ed., *German Foreign Policy, 1918–1945: A Guide to Research and Research Materials* (rev. ed., 1991), and Axel Frohn, *Guide to Inventories and Finding Aids of German Archives at the German Historical Institute, Washington, D.C.* (1989). Some of the information in the Kimmich guide concerning archives in the former GDR is now dated. The German Historical Institute (1607 New Hampshire Ave., N.W., Washington, D.C.

20009) is willing to answer inquiries regarding archival research in Germany and to lend copies of its excellent collection of guides and finding aids to researchers unable to visit the institute's library.

The Politisches Archiv, Auswärtiges Amt (Adenauer Allee 99–103, 5300 Bonn 1) is the principal center in Germany that collects records of the foreign ministry and diplomatic missions as well as working files and personal papers of the individual diplomats. The documents of the Nazi period suffered significant losses and are not complete. George O. Kent compiled several volumes of a catalogue of files and microfilms of materials concerning Hitler, for example, assassination attempts, conference reports with important foreign figures, correspondence, speeches, and proclamations. A selection of documents has been published in a multivolume series, *Akten zur deutschen auswärtigen Politik 1918–1945* (1950–   ). Though there is an English edition of this series, *Documents on German Foreign Policy, 1918–1945*, (1949–   ) the German is more complete.

The Bundesarchiv (Potsdamerstrasse 1, 5400 Koblenz 1) is the most important repository of all noncurrent records of the German government (except most of those of the foreign ministry), private institutions, and individuals. It has the surviving records of Hitler's Reich chancellery as well as records of the different ministries and Nazi agencies. Also important for research on Hitler are documents of his personal adjutant and especially of the party chancellery, first under Rudolf Hess, and later under Martin Bormann. Some of Hitler's speeches are preserved here, as is the manuscript of his "second book." Documents concerning Hitler's early life and career can be identified by referring to Grete Heinz and Agnes Peterson, comps., *NSDAP Hauptarchiv: Guide to the Hoover Institution Microfilm Collection* (1964). Military records including war diaries and papers of some of Hitler's immediate associates like Wilhelm Keitel are found at a branch of the Bundesarchiv (Abteilung Militärarchiv, Wiesentalstrasse 10, 7800 Freiburg i. B.).

The most prominent research center on recent German history is the Institut für Zeitgeschichte (Leonrodstrasse 46b, 8000 Munich 20). It has records, papers, and/or notes of a number of Hitler's associates: Heinrich Himmler, Alfred Jodl, his physician Theodor Morrell, and Otto Wagener. The institute is also noted for its collection of oral interviews with persons in public or governmental life, which was begun several years after the war.

Lastly, the National Archives (8th Street and Pennsylvania Avenue, N.W., Washington, D.C. 20408) has various interrogation reports of German officials during the Third Reich including Hitler's foreign ministers Konstantin von Neurath and Joachim von Ribbentrop. This archive also has the most complete collection of German documents on film.

The German dictator's best-known work, *Mein Kampf*, was published in two volumes in 1925 and 1926. It espoused a primitive Social Darwinist racial concept of history and monomaniacal hatred of international Jewry, who, according to Hitler, conspired to destroy the Aryan race and dominate the world. He asserted that once the National Socialists had conquered the German state, they would secure the land and soil to which the Germans were entitled by expanding into eastern Europe and Russia. He elaborated on his foreign policy goals in his "second book," which he dictated in 1928 but forbade to be published. It was discovered in 1958 and published in English as *Hitler's Secret Book* in 1961. Here he reaffirmed his belief that Britain and Italy might become Germany's allies, whereas France remained an implacable foe.

The best source of Hitler's plans and policies during his years in power is Max Domarus, ed., *Hitler: Reden und Proklamationen 1932–1945*, 2 vols. (1965). This collection of public statements, speeches, proclamations, interviews, and letters is richly annotated with a running commentary. Fortunately, an English translation is in progress and should soon be completed. Norman Baynes, ed., *The Speeches of Adolf Hitler, 1922–1939*, 2 vols. (1942), contains excerpts from public statements made before 1932, but reprints only a selection of representative passages grouped according to subject.

Hitler's leadership during the war can be assessed in several documentary collections. Helmut Heiber edited *Hitlers Lagebesprechungen: Die Protokollfragmente seiner militärischen Konferenzen 1942–1945* (1962). These minutes of Hitler's war conferences comprise the only 800 surviving pages of the original 200,000. (The English collection, edited by Felix Gilbert, contains merely excerpts from the surviving minutes.) These top-secret transcripts offer insight into the Führer's approach to the war and his relations with his military advisors. H. R. Trevor-Roper edited the English version of *Blitzkrieg to Defeat: Hitler's War Directives, 1939–1945* (1964). These directives and later orders woven into the text outline the history of the war as envisaged by the Nazi dictator. Hitler's confidential conversations with foreign statesmen and representatives during the years of his triumph can be followed in Andreas Hillgruber, ed., *Staatsmänner und Diplomaten bei Hitler: Vertrauliche Aufzeichnungen über Unterredungen mit Vertretern des Auslandes 1939–1941*, 2 vols. (1967–1970).

Additional glimpses of Hitler's personality and ideas can be gleaned from Eberhard Jäckel and Axel Kuhn, eds., *Hitler: Sämtliche Aufzeichnungen 1905–1924* (1980), which contains notes, letters, and speeches. The editors later declared that poems included in this edition were spurious. Hitler's rambling monologues on every conceivable subject have been published in various editions, not all equally reliable. Hitler's *Secret Conversations, 1941–1944* (1953), with an introductory essay by H. R. Trevor-Roper, is based on Martin Bormann's notes. Hitler's last words before his suicide can be found in François Genoud, ed., *The Testament of Adolf Hitler: The Hitler-Bormann Documents* (1961).

The memoirs and diaries of Hitler's close associates have also become important sources. *Hitler: Memoirs of a Confidant* (1985), edited by H. A. Turner, contains the conversations of the highly placed Otto Wagener (later disgraced) with the Nazi leader between 1929 and 1933. Albert Speer, Hitler's personal architect and later Reich minister for armaments and war production, offered some revealing comments in *Inside the Third Reich: Memoirs of Albert Speer* (1970) and in *Spandau: The Secret Diaries* (1976). The most important recent source is the definitive edition of Goebbels's diaries, *Die Tagebücher von Joseph Goebbels: Sämtliche Fragmente*, 4 vols., edited by Elke Fröhlich (1987). This collection covers the period 1924 to 1941; a sequel for the years 1942 to 1945 is in preparation.

The burgeoning interpretive literature on Adolf Hitler and the Third Reich is daunting. Helen Kehr and Janet Langmaid, comps., *The Nazi Era 1919–1945* (1982), lists over 6,500 titles in English and German on every conceivable subject related to the Nazi era. A good narrative introduction is Norman Stone's *Hitler* (1980), a slightly ironic essay that corrects some misconceptions, though not without adding some exaggerations. It devotes considerable space to foreign policy and the war. Important aspects of Hitler's achievements, successes, mistakes, and crimes are succinctly but convincingly treated by Sebastian Haffner, *The Meaning of Hitler* (1979). William Carr, *Hitler: A Study in Personality and Politics* (1978), concisely analyzes Hitler as politician, dictator, and military leader, and also explores his intellectual world. A helpful guide to dates and events is M. Hauner's *Hitler: A Chronology of His Life and Time* (1983).

The first major biography of Hitler was Konrad Heiden's two-volume *Adolf Hitler: Eine Biographie* (1936–1937). Though limiting coverage to Hitler's early career and portraying him as an unprincipled opportunist, Heiden also emphasized that Hitler's policies followed his ideas in *Mein Kampf* and that he aspired to achieve the Aryan domination of Europe if not the world. Hitler as a Machiavellian dictator was most fully assessed in Alan Bullock's classic biography, *Hitler: A Study in Tyranny* (rev. ed., 1962). It portrayed the Führer as the principal driving force in the realization of National Socialism and carefully analyzed his thought and policies, diplomatic successes, and role in World War II. Though superseded in many details, this work remains the most notable scholarly treatment of the subject. Another standard study that commands similar respect is Joachim Fest's *Hitler* (1974). Whereas Bullock concentrated on Hitler the man and the historical actor, Fest focused on Hitler in the context of his times. A third full-length biography of the Nazi dictator worth mentioning is John Toland's massive *Adolf Hitler* (1976). Based on published and archival sources as well as hundreds of interviews, this popular account views Hitler as a complex, contradictory, and destructive twentieth-century personality.

Over the years an extensive historiography of Hitler has been in the making, showing marked differences in interpretation and perspective. The most exhaustive treatment is Gerhard Schreiber, *Hitler Interpretationen 1923–1983* (1984). A more accessible analysis is Ian Kershaw, *The Nazi Dictatorship* (2nd ed., 1989). A major controversy in recent historical writing has been between so-called intentionalists and functionalists. Intentionalists have argued that Hitler had a program and definite goals, outlined in *Mein Kampf*, which he attempted to implement through his policies. Functionalists, on the other hand, hold that Hitler could not completely control the course of policy and that the anarchic state of the Nazi administration limited his freedom of action.

Traditional biographies of Hitler have been complemented by the work of psycho-historians, among whom Rudolf Binion and Robert G.L. Waite are especially noted. In *Hitler Among the Germans* (1976), Binion attributed Hitler's anti-Semitism and notions of *Lebensraum* to his traumatization by poison gas in World War I, which activated painful memories of his beloved mother's death from iodoform poisoning while being treated for cancer by a Jewish doctor. In a similar speculative manner, Waite's *Psychopathic God: Adolf Hitler* (1977) declared Hitler a borderline personality between neurosis and psychosis who despite his mental illness functioned very effectively in some areas.

Bradley F. Smith, on the other hand, in his careful study *Adolf Hitler: His Family, Childhood and Youth* (1967), ignored psychoanalytical speculations and portrayed young Adolf as lazy, stubborn, and fond of romantic games. The emerging public Hitler who turned from soldiering to politics was convincingly examined by Albrecht Tyrell, *Vom "Trommler" zum "Führer." Der Wandel von Hitlers Selbstverständnis zwischen 1919 und 1924 und die Entwicklung der NSDAP* (1975). Hitler's unsuccessful attempt to seize political power in Bavaria, from which he learned important political lessons, was fully evaluated by Harold J. Gordon, *Hitler and the Beer Hall Putsch* (1972). Anton Joachimsthaler, *Korrektur einer Biographie: Adolf Hitler 1908–1920* (1989), corrected some of the old historical myths in the writings on Hitler's formative period.

When Edward N. Peterson published *The Limits of Hitler's Power* (1969), he raised some new issues. Based on an analysis of Nazi internal affairs, he concluded that Hitler lacked complete control over the German people because he did not get involved in the day-to-day operation of the government and the party. The image of Hitler as a "weak dictator," at least in domestic affairs, was reinforced by Martin Broszat, *The Hitler State: The Foundation and Development of the Internal Structure of the Third Reich* (German 1969; English 1981). Broszat broke away from a personality-based, Hitler-centered model of the Third Reich, and together with Hans Mommsen and Tim Mason helped establish the functional school of thought. Functionalists do not ignore Hitler's anti-Semitism, anti-Bolshevism, and desire for *Lebensraum*, but emphasize their functional role in the operation of political, economic, and social agencies rather than their pursuit as ends in themselves. A blunting of the functionalist and intentionalist dichotomy can be observed in Rainer Zitelmann, *Hitler: Selbstverständnis eines Revolutionärs* (1987), which analyzed Hitler's economic and social conceptions and his aspirations for the transformation of German society.

An overview of the extensive monographic literature on the Third Reich's international relations can be gained from Kimmich's *German Foreign Policy, 1918–1945*, an indispensable annotated handbook. The earlier view that Hitler's foreign policy followed a revisionist course until 1937 and became expansionist only after that is no longer tenable. The great majority of scholars emphasize that Hitler's aims were directed toward German expansion from the very beginning. Eberhard Jäckel, *Hitler's Weltanschauung: A Blueprint for Power* (1972), asserted that the Nazi leader had a consistent worldview which he translated into a foreign policy with two objectives: territorial expansion and the annihilation of the Jews. A masterly and detailed analysis of how the German dictator set the stage for war is contained in Gerhard Weinberg's two volumes, *The Foreign Policy of Hitler's Germany: Diplomatic Revolution in Europe, 1933–1936* (1970) and *The Foreign Policy of Hitler's Germany: Starting World War II, 1937–1939* (1980). He demonstrated that the broad lines of policy were set in all cases by Hitler himself and consistently aimed at territorial expansion in eastern Europe. Other relevant studies that treat select aspects of Hitler's foreign policy during the 1930s and early 1940s include Hans-Adolf Jacobsen, *Nationalsozialistische Aussenpolitik 1933–1938* (1968), several essays in Manfred Funke, ed., *Hitler Deutschland und die Mächte: Materialien zur Aussenpolitik des Dritten Reiches* (1976), and William Carr, *Arms, Autarky and Aggression* (1973).

The polarization between intentionalists and functionalists is less pronounced among foreign policy authorities than among domestic policy experts since only several of the latter carry this controversy into the realm of external affairs. The most lively and long-lived debate was sparked by A.J.P. Taylor, *The Origins of the Second World War* (1961), which portrayed Hitler not as a would-be conqueror but as a traditional statesman who sought to revise the Versailles settlement rather than to engage in war with Britain and France. Taylor claimed that *Mein Kampf* was not a blueprint for war, merely a grand daydream.

Historians on both sides of the Atlantic have rejected Taylor's image of Hitler as the grand improviser of policy. A typical antidote is Klaus Hildebrand, *The Foreign Policy of the Third Reich* (1973), which emphasized the break in German external policy in 1933 and Hitler's programmatic course pointing toward world domination. The theory that Hitler's expansion would not stop with the conquest of living space in the East but would move to another stage entailing the acquisition of African territories and a system of bases in the Atlantic and Indian Oceans (in preparation for a final showdown with the United States) was first outlined in Andreas Hillgruber's voluminous *Hitlers Strategie: Politik und Kriegführung 1940–1941* (1965) and further developed by Klaus Hildebrand, *Vom Reich zum Weltreich: Hitler, NSDAP und koloniale Frage 1919–1945* (1969). Not all authorities on Nazi foreign affairs agree that Hitler's final aims reached beyond the European continent. Eberhard Jäckel and Hugh Trevor-Roper reject the views of "globalists" like Hillgruber, Hildebrand, and others. Similarly, Norman Rich, an American historian, left open the question of Hitler's colonial aims outside of Europe in his lengthy study *Hitler's War Aims*, 2 vols. (1973–1974). He attempted to explain the interaction of Hitler's ideas and policies in the establishment of the New Order in all of occupied Europe.

Most historians recognize that in addition to territorial expansion Hitler had a second goal, the elimination of Jews from Germany and from Europe. In the interpretation of what is known as the Holocaust, the dichotomy of intentionalism and functionalism resurfaces. Intentionalists hold that the extermination of European Jewry was carried out according to an ideologically motivated design and implemented by a Führer order sometime in 1941. Functionalists stress a piecemeal process of improvised displacement of the Jews, which, as result of administrative difficulties, led to the Final Solution.

Probably the most extreme intentionalist position is found in Lucy Dawidowicz, *The War Against the Jews, 1933–1945* (1975). She argued that anti-Semitism was at the core of all Hitler's plans and that he waged World War II in order to kill the Jews. This view is not shared by other historians. The basic problem for all historians is the lack of a written or verbal Führer order to implement the destruction of the Jews. Based on circumstantial evidence, Gerald Fleming, *Hitler and the Final Solution* (German 1982; English 1984), argued that Hitler not only knew of but initiated the destruction of European Jews. On the functionalist side of the interpretive spectrum stand Martin Broszat and a few others. In "Hitler and the Genesis of the 'Final Solution': An Assessment of David Irving's Theses," in H. W. Koch, ed., *Aspects of the Third Reich* (1985), Broszat sharply refuted Irving's claims that Hitler only wanted to exile Jews from Europe and that it was Heinrich Himmler and Reinhard Heydrich who initiated the extermination program without the Nazi dictator's knowledge. Together with other functionalists, Broszat believes that Hitler knew and approved of the destruction of the Jews. He contends that Hitler did not give an order for the Final Solution, but the killing evolved gradually from a series of murderous actions in 1941 and 1942 and from the administrative impossibility of resettling Jews in Europe or elsewhere. A middle way between intentionalists and functionalists that acknowledges Hitler's central role in the persecution and eventual extermination of the Jews without regarding the Final Solution as a programmed goal from the start is outlined by Ian Kershaw, *The Nazi Dictatorship: Problems and Perspectives of Interpretation* (2nd ed., 1989). In 1986 a major controversy erupted among West German historians concerning the place of Nazism and especially the Holocaust in Germany's past. Known as the "Historikerstreit," this dispute spilled over into the pages of the press. A judicious assessment of this episode has been provided by Richard J. Evans, *In Hitler's Shadow: West German Historians and the Attempt to Escape from the Nazi Past* (1989).

Bibliography

Bibliographies and Research Guides

Frohn, Axel. *Guide to Inventories and Finding Aids of German Archives at the German Historical Institute, Washington D.C.* Washington, D.C.: German Historical Institute, 1989.

Heinz, Grete, and Agnes F. Peterson, comps. *NSDAP Hauptarchiv: Guide to the Hoover Institution Microfilm Collection.* Stanford, Calif.: Hoover Institution, 1964.

Kehr, Helen, and Janet Langmaid, comps. *The Nazi Era 1919–1945: A Select Bibliography of Published Works from the Early Roots to 1980.* London: Mansell, 1982.

Kent, George O., ed. *A Catalog of Files and Microfilms of the German Foreign Ministry Archives, 1920–1945.* 4 vols. Stanford, Calif.: Hoover Institution, 1962–1972.
Kimmich, Christoph M., ed. *German Foreign Policy, 1918–1945: A Guide to Research and Research Materials.* Rev. ed. Wilmington, Del.: Scholarly Resources, 1991.

Primary Works

Akten zur deutschen auswärtigen Politik, 1918–1945. Baden-Baden: Impr. nationale, 1950– .
Baynes, Norman, ed. *The Speeches of Adolf Hitler, 1922–1939.* 2 vols. London: Oxford University Press, 1942.
Documents on German Foreign Policy, 1918–1945. Washington, D.C.: U.S. Government Printing Office, 1949– .
Domarus, Max, ed. *Hitler: Reden und Proklamationen 1932–1945.* 2 vols. Munich: Süddeutscher Verlag, 1965.
———, ed. *Hitler: Speeches and Proclamations, 1932–1945.* Translated by Mary Fran Gilbert. 2 vols. Wauconda, Ill.: Bolchazzy-Carducci, 1990–.
Fröhlich, Elke, ed. *Die Tagebücher von Joseph Goebbels: Sämtliche Fragmente.* 4 vols. Munich: Saur, 1987.
Genoud, François, ed. *The Testament of Adolf Hitler: The Hitler-Bormann Documents.* London: Cassell, 1961.
Gilbert, Felix, ed. *Hitler Directs His War: The Secret Record of His Daily Conferences.* New York: Oxford University Press, 1951.
Heiber, Helmut, ed. *Hitlers Lagebesprechungen: Die Protokollfragmente seiner militärischen Konferenzen 1942–1945.* Stuttgart: Deutsche Verlags-Anstalt, 1962.
Hillgruber, Andreas, ed. *Staatsmänner und Diplomaten bei Hitler: Vertrauliche Aufzeichnungen über Unterredungen mit Vertretern des Auslandes 1939–1941.* 2 vols. Frankfurt am Main: Bernard and Graefe, 1967–1970.
Hitler, Adolf. *Hitler's Secret Book.* Introduction by Telford Taylor. New York: Grove Press, 1961.
———. *Mein Kampf.* Translated by Ralph Manheim. Boston: Houghton Mifflin, 1971.
———. *Secret Conversations, 1941–1944.* Translated by Norman Cameron and R. A. Stevens. New York: Farrar, Straus and Young, 1953.
Jäckel, Eberhard, and Axel Kuhn, eds. *Hitler: Sämtliche Aufzeichnungen 1905–1924.* Stuttgart: Deutsche Verlags-Anstalt, 1980.
Speer, Albert. *Inside the Third Reich: Memoirs of Albert Speer.* Translated by Richard and Clara Winston. New York: Macmillan, 1970.
———. *Spandau: The Secret Diaries.* New York: Macmillan, 1976.
Trevor-Roper, H. R., ed. *Blitzkrieg to Defeat: Hitler's War Directives, 1939–1945.* New York: Holt, Rinehart and Winston, 1964.
Turner, Henry A., ed. *Hitler: Memoirs of a Confidant.* New Haven, Conn.: Yale University Press, 1985.

Studies of Hitler

Binion, Rudolf. *Hitler Among the Germans.* New York: Elsevier, 1976.
Broszat, Martin. "Hitler and the Genesis of the 'Final Solution': An Assessment of David Irving's Theses." In *Aspects of the Third Reich.* Edited by H. W. Koch. London: Macmillan, 1985.

———. *The Hitler State: The Foundation and Development of the Internal Structure of the Third Reich*. New York: Longman, 1981.

Bullock, Alan. *Hitler: A Study in Tyranny*. Rev. ed. New York: Harper and Row, 1962.

Carr, William. *Arms, Autarky and Aggression: A Study in German Foreign Policy, 1933–1939*. New York: Norton, 1973.

———. *Hitler: A Study in Personality and Politics*. Baltimore: Edward Arnold, 1978.

Dawidowicz, Lucy S. *The War Against the Jews, 1933–1945*. New York: Holt, Rinehart and Winston, 1975.

Evans, Richard J. *In Hitler's Shadow: West German Historians and the Attempt to Escape from the Nazi Past*. New York: Pantheon, 1989.

Fest, Joachim C. *Hitler*. Translated by Richard and Clara Winston. New York: Harcourt Brace Jovanovich, 1974.

Fleming, Gerald. *Hitler and the Final Solution*. Berkeley: University of California Press, 1984.

Funke, Manfred, ed. *Hitler Deutschland und die Mächte: Materialien zur Aussenpolitik des Dritten Reiches*. Düsseldorf: Droste, 1976.

Gordon, Harold J. *Hitler and the Beer Hall Putsch*. Princeton, N.J.: Princeton University Press, 1972.

Haffner, Sebastian. *The Meaning of Hitler*. London: Weidenfeld and Nicolson, 1979.

Hauner, Milan. *Hitler: A Chronology of His Life and Time*. New York: St. Martin's Press, 1983.

Heiden, Konrad. *Adolf Hitler: Eine Biographie*. 2 vols. Zurich: Europa Verlag, 1936–1937.

Hildebrand, Klaus. *The Foreign Policy of the Third Reich*. Berkeley: University of California Press, 1973.

———. *Vom Reich zum Weltreich: Hitler, NSDAP und koloniale Frage 1919–1945*. Munich: Wilhelm Fink Verlag, 1969.

Hillgruber, Andreas. *Hitlers Strategie: Politik und Kriegführung 1940–1941*. Frankfurt am Main: Bernard und Graefe, 1965.

Jäckel, Eberhard. *Hitler's Weltanschauung: A Blueprint for Power*. Middletown, Conn.: Wesleyan University Press, 1972.

Jacobsen, Hans-Adolf. *Nationalsozialistische Aussenpolitik 1933–1938*. Frankfurt am Main: Metzner, 1968.

Joachimsthaler, Anton. *Korrektur einer Biographie: Adolf Hitler 1908–1920*. Munich: Herbig, 1989.

Kershaw, Ian. *The Nazi Dictatorship: Problems and Perspectives of Interpretation*. 2nd ed. New York: Edward Arnold, 1989.

Peterson, E. N. *The Limits of Hitler's Power*. Princeton, N.J.: Princeton University Press, 1969.

Rich, Norman. *Hitler's War Aims*. 2 vols. New York: Norton, 1973–1974.

Schreiber, Gerhard. *Hitler Interpretationen 1923–1983*. Darmstadt: Wissenschaftliche Buchgesellschaft, 1984.

Smith, Bradley F. *Adolf Hitler: His Family, Childhood and Youth*. Stanford, Calif.: Hoover Institution, 1967.

Stone, Norman. *Hitler*. Boston: Little, Brown, 1980.

Taylor, A.J.P. *The Origins of the Second World War*. London: Hamish Hamilton, 1961.

Toland, John. *Adolf Hitler*. Garden City, N.Y.: Doubleday, 1976.

Tyrell, Albrecht. *Vom "Trommler" zum "Führer." Der Wandel von Hitlers Selbstver-*

ständnis zwischen 1919 und 1924 und die Entwicklung der NSDAP. Munich: Fink, 1975.

Waite, Robert G.L. *The Psychopathic God: Adolf Hitler*. New York: Basic Books, 1977.

Weinberg, Gerhard. *The Foreign Policy of Hitler's Germany: Diplomatic Revolution in Europe, 1933–36*. Chicago: University of Chicago Press, 1970.

——. *The Foreign Policy of Hitler's Germany: Starting World War II, 1937–1939*. Chicago: University of Chicago Press, 1980.

Zitelmann, Rainer. *Hitler: Selbstverständnis eines Revolutionärs*. New York: Berg, 1987.

GEORGE P. BLUM

Thomas Jefferson (1743–1826).   Thomas Jefferson was born on April 13, 1743, at Shadwell in Goochland (now Albemarle) County, Virginia. As a result of his family's connections with the prominent and influential Randolph family, Jefferson gained entry into Virginia's power structure. After attending the College of William and Mary, he studied law and was admitted to the bar in 1767. On January 1, 1772, he married Martha (Wayles) Skelton; they lived in the new home, Monticello, that Jefferson would continue to remodel for the next forty years. During ten years of marriage, Jefferson's wife gave birth to six children, but three died in infancy or childhood. Martha failed to regain her health after the birth of her last child and died five months later. Jefferson never remarried.

Elected to the House of Burgesses in 1769, Jefferson continued in this position until the House ceased to meet in 1775. From the outset he was a member of the most outspoken group opposed to the British government's new colonial policies. His *Summary View of the Rights of British America* (1774) forcefully asserted that due to the natural right of emigration Parliament had no inherent authority over the American colonies and that the only connection between Great Britain and the settlements in America was through the crown. In 1775 the Virginia convention elected him to serve in the Continental Congress. On June 11, 1776, Congress appointed him to a five-man committee to draft a declaration of independence that was partly meant to gain foreign support for the revolutionary movement. His reputation as an outstanding writer led to his selection as the principal author of the declaration.

Jefferson left the Continental Congress in September 1776 and the next month entered the House of Delegates in Virginia, serving there until his election as governor in June 1779. The Articles of Confederation Congress appointed him a peace commissioner in November 1782, but the Treaty of Paris ending the Revolutionary War was concluded before his departure for Europe.

Elected to the Confederation Congress in June 1783, Jefferson became involved in establishing the nation's new monetary system and in proposing a plan for the organization of the Northwest Territory. In addition, Congress adopted his report on the definitive treaty of peace, and he drafted a report that formed the basis of procedure for negotiating treaties of commerce. In 1784 he was appointed to assist *Benjamin Franklin and John Adams in securing such treaties. The following year the Confederation Congress appointed him to succeed Franklin as minister to France. Overshadowed by Franklin's great reputation, Jefferson nevertheless proved a talented diplomat.

In 1785 Jefferson and his colleagues successfully negotiated a treaty of commerce with Prussia. He joined Adams in London early the following year, but they failed to negotiate a treaty with the British government. The French, however, did accept Jefferson's proposed consular convention, resulting in some lowering of French duties on American products. Earlier Jefferson had endorsed a treaty negotiated with Morocco, but he believed that only the use of force would restrain the Barbary pirates. Toward that end, he convinced Congress to consider an alliance with European nations, an idea that found no interest in Europe.

In October 1789 Jefferson left Europe believing that the United States should maintain its friendship with France. More than simply demonstrating America's gratitude, this course would provide the United States with the means for counteracting British hostility. If war should occur in Europe, Jefferson incorrectly believed that Britain would pay dearly to guarantee America's neutrality.

Soon after Jefferson's return to Monticello in December 1789, President George Washington appointed him the first secretary of state under the Constitution. Almost immediately Jefferson found himself in the middle of a political conflict with Secretary of the Treasury Alexander Hamilton over different interpretations of republican ideology, especially the proper relationship of liberty and power. One element in this difference of opinion between the two secretaries concerned foreign policy. Jefferson favored economic discrimination as a means to force the British to remove their troops from the Northwest Territory and to grant commercial privileges. Fearing a loss in revenue from British imports, Hamilton successfully blocked the passage of any substantial commercial sanctions.

Then, in May 1792, Jefferson submitted to Washington a lengthy report that completely refuted the British case for not upholding certain parts of the Paris peace treaty. Hamilton, however, unofficially and quite secretly informed the British that Jefferson's report did not represent the position of the U.S. government. As a consequence, the British government ignored Jefferson's position.

By this time Hamilton had proposed his extensive fiscal program to establish a commercial empire supported by the leading capitalists and informally allied with Britain. Jefferson opposed the secretary of the treasury's goal of a more commercial and industrialized republic populated with an increasing number of dependent workers. The secretary of state deprecated Hamilton's plan to create bounties for manufacturers and a Bank of the United States. Instead, Jefferson wanted an agrarian republic filled with independent, land-owning farmers who had the means to oppose successfully an increase in economic stratification and political dependence. Only in a nation with a predominantly agrarian lifestyle could republican liberty be protected. Jefferson warned that the national government's powers were expanding dangerously and that commerce was increasing at the expense of agriculture. Nevertheless, Washington endorsed Hamilton's fiscal programs.

Faced with this situation, Jefferson decided to resign his position. Yielding to Washington's request, however, he agreed to remain in office until the end of 1793. This was a time of critical importance in America's foreign affairs. The French Revolution had resulted in war between Britain and France, and this led to a number of problems for the Washington administration. Each belligerent nation wanted America's raw materials for itself but not for its enemy. International law stated that during war neutral nations could trade with belligerent countries if the goods were not directly related to the war effort. But England and France were unwilling to abide by these regulations. Instead, each attempted to control American trade for its own benefit. Britain's practice of impressing American seamen further complicated the situation.

In the United States the effect of the Anglo-French war was to further exacerbate the differences between those who endorsed and those who opposed Hamilton's fiscal program. Despite the French Revolution's excesses, Jefferson believed that the United States government should not openly oppose the principles of the revolution. Although he deplored the deaths of innocent people, he knew this to be part of the process for securing true liberty in France. Nevertheless, he supported the position of Washington and Hamilton that the United States should remain neutral.

Soon after the Anglo-French war began in February 1793, the French government sent Edmond Charles Genêt as its minister to the United States. Jefferson urged the president to avoid the issue of U.S. adherence to the Franco-American alliance of 1778, and he supported the president's proclamation of U.S. neutrality toward the belligerent powers. But the secretary of state also convinced Washington to receive Genêt without qualification. Jefferson warmly welcomed the French minister and came close to supporting unofficial Franco-American military actions against Canada and Spanish Louisiana. When, however, Genêt continued to embarrass the Washington administration by outfitting privateers to prey on British shipping, Jefferson joined with his colleagues to request Genêt's recall.

Jefferson unsuccessfully attempted to change Britain's policy of disregarding American neutral rights. In addition, he failed to gain Spanish recognition of America's right to transport goods on the Mississippi River and deposit them at New Orleans, although the negotiations initiated by Jefferson led to the Pinckney Treaty of 1795, which secured these rights. Overall, as secretary of state, Jefferson convincingly argued in support of American neutrality and the need to keep European markets open for America's raw materials. Jefferson asserted that only in this way could the United States remain a virtuous and respected republic where liberty would be widespread and sustained.

Leaving the cabinet at the end of 1793, Jefferson returned to Monticello, but he could not escape the continuing political controversies. In 1795 he opposed the Jay Treaty, believing it to be a sellout of American rights and a pro-British document. Four years earlier Jefferson had become convinced of the need for an organized opposition against Hamilton's financial program and the pro-British sympathies within the Washington administration. Forming a political alliance with dissatisfied leaders in New York, Jefferson and *James Madison helped create the Democratic-Republican party. In the election of 1796 the Republicans, as they were commonly known, selected Jefferson as their candidate for the presidency. In a close vote, however, the Federalist candidate, John Adams, was elected. Jefferson, winning the second largest number of electoral votes, became the vice president. For the only time in American history, the president and vice president were from different parties.

In 1797 President Adams presented documents to Congress demonstrating that the French government had demanded loans and bribes before beginning negotiations to resolve differences stemming from the Jay Treaty. This XYZ affair led to a widespread reaction against the Republicans, who were viewed by many as pro-French. In 1798 the Federalist-dominated Congress passed four bills aimed at controlling domestic dissent and conspiracy. But the four acts, commonly referred to as the Alien and Sedition Acts, actually revived the Republican party. Denouncing what they called the "Federalist Reign of Terror," the Republicans charged the Adams administration with abusing the Constitution and destroying the principles of liberty. Jefferson and Madison wrote the Kentucky and Virginia resolutions, respectively, advancing the theory that a state may nullify a federal act on constitutional grounds.

The controversy created by the Alien and Sedition Acts, conflict within the Federalist party, and Republican control of New York led to Jefferson's election to the presidency in 1800. Jefferson proudly declared that his election resulted from "the revolution of 1800," which he believed was "as real a revolution in the principles of our government as that of 1776 was in its form." Actually, however, too little changed to justify using the word "revolution."

Nevertheless, from the beginning of his administration Jefferson insisted that new policies were required to return the country to its republican foundations. He worked to reverse numerous Federalist initiatives such as excise taxes and federal expenditures. Most important, Jefferson wanted to implement his own vision of an expanding agrarian republic. Believing that an increase in power threatened liberty, the Virginian wanted to maintain an open and roughly equal society. But economic and social development threatened to destroy the social bases of republicanism. Jefferson felt that human nature could not be altered. The economic and social environment, however, might be changed to limit concentrations of wealth, promote agriculture over manufacturing, and thereby defend republican liberty.

In particular, the Jeffersonians emphasized territorial expansion. They believed that available space in conjunction with access to foreign markets would assure that for generations to come America would be dominated by independent, land-owning farmers. This would prevent the problems associated with urban centers and would also preserve social equality and civic responsibility. In short, the expansion of the United States across the North American continent would delay, if not prevent, the cyclical process of social and economic decay that all past societies had experienced. Furthermore, westward expansion would help reduce the threat from foreign powers by securing America's borders. And Jefferson felt that all new states carved out of the West would be Republican and thus ensure the continued political dominance of an agricultural Republican majority.

Hoping to expand the size of the republic, Jefferson was very disturbed to learn in 1801 that Spain had ceded much of its trans-Mississippi region to France. A year later the Spanish closed the Mississippi River to American commerce, jeopardizing access to the export markets by America's western farmers. When Spain transferred New Orleans to the more powerful French government, Jefferson's consternation grew.

Initially, Jefferson wanted to purchase New Orleans and West Florida from the French, but the French offered to sell all of Louisiana. Expecting a renewal of war with England and reeling from a successful black rebellion in Haiti, *Napoleon I decided to get what he could for France's remaining North American lands. As a consequence, in April 1803 the United States purchased all of the Louisiana Territory, nearly 830,000 square miles, for $15 million. Believing that the end justified the means, Jefferson agreed to the purchase although he did not feel that the Constitution gave the federal government the authority to buy additional territory. In one stroke Jefferson had doubled the size of the nation, and he believed he had guaranteed that the United States would remain overwhelmingly agrarian for many generations to come.

But Jefferson felt that the United States had much more to do to promote its security and prosperity. Beyond increasing military efforts against the Barbary pirates, Jefferson and Secretary of State Madison were somewhat interested in Cuba and even more interested in the rivers and ports of east and west Florida. They believed that the latter were especially important for securing needed outlets to foreign markets. The Jefferson administration, however, failed to persuade the Spanish government to sell the Floridas. As a consequence, Jefferson became increasingly frustrated. Indeed, during the summer and fall of 1805 he even considered seeking an alliance with Spain's enemy, Great Britain. Soon the administration became involved in more urgent foreign policy problems, but the interest in Cuba and especially the Floridas did not disappear. The Florida question became even more complicated during Madison's presidency and was not resolved until the United States finally acquired the territory in 1819 in the Adams-Onís Treaty.

Scarcely two weeks after he had signed away his Louisiana liability, Napoleon reopened hostilities with England. The conflict was of major importance to the United States, since it drained the resources of the European nations and greatly limited their activities in North America. In addition, from 1803 to 1812 the United States was the most important neutral carrier. American farmers and shippers exploited markets that had been closed to them. But British shippers deplored the enrichment of America's merchant marine and the loss of once-profitable markets. Moreover, since much of the American trade strengthened France, the English often looked on the Americans as assisting their arch-enemy. The French, for their part, opposed trade between the United States and England.

By 1805 British and French cruisers were seizing scores of American merchantmen. Furthermore, the British, often short of sailors, continued to impress American seamen into His Majesty's service.

James Monroe and William Pinckney in 1806 signed a treaty with the British that dealt with several of the American grievances. President Jefferson, however, dissatisfied with the treaty since the British would not formally renounce impressment, refused to send the pact to the Senate. By 1807 the violations of America's neutral rights had become serious enough to threaten war between the United States and either Britain or France. In June the captain of a British frigate, the *Leopard*, demanded permission to board an American vessel, the *Chesapeake*, to look for alleged deserters. When permission was denied, the *Leopard* opened fire, killing three and wounding eighteen. Reports of the incident brought demands for immediate war against Great Britain. Jefferson, however, only issued a proclamation prohibiting British ships from entering U.S. ports to obtain supplies. To further ease tensions Britain offered to pay reparations to the families of those killed or wounded, and two impressed sailors were released. Nevertheless, the British government refused to end the practice of impressment. Thus, tensions further increased. To prevent war and to punish both the French and British by denying them America's raw materials, Jefferson in December 1807 signed into law the Embargo Act, which prohibited the export of any goods from the United States by sea or land.

The immediate results were not those that the president had envisioned. Within a year exports fell by more than 75 percent and economic stagnation struck the ports and much of agrarian America. Ironically, in trying to protect an agrarian lifestyle by keeping open European markets, Jefferson seemed to be undermining it, as capital, unable to find any other outlets, began flowing into manufacturing.

In addition, though he had long insisted on minimal government interference in everyday life, Jefferson's embargo encroached on more citizens' lives than any previous governmental action. The embargo's disruption of established patterns of life alarmed Republicans and helped revive the Federalist party. Open talk of secession was heard in New England. The embargo was also a diplomatic failure since the British and French still refused to respect America's neutral rights. Finally, on March 1, 1809, three days before leaving office, Jefferson ended the fourteen-month-old embargo.

The basic purpose of economic coercion had been to liberate American commerce from foreign restrictions, and thus to secure the prosperity of the United States as an agrarian republic. But Jefferson's administration had failed to end foreign restrictions on the republic's commerce. Much was left to be done. Indeed, to the Jeffersonians the continuing American need to export its agricultural surplus to foreign markets remained a matter of the utmost concern. Continued British violations of American neutrality, which placed restrictions on access to foreign markets and created political divisions within the Republican party, ultimately led to the decision in June 1812 by President Madison, Jefferson's hand-picked successor, to request a declaration of war against Great Britain.

Refusing the nomination for a third term in 1808, Jefferson returned to Monticello. There he spent his remaining years planning and building the University of Virginia at Charlottesville. Jefferson died on July 4, 1826, the fiftieth anniversary of the Declaration of Independence.

Annotated Bibliography

The major collection of Jefferson's manuscripts is in the Library of Congress. It has been reproduced on microfilm in the presidential papers series. There are also significant collections of Jefferson's manuscripts at the University of Virginia, the Massachusetts Historical Society, and the Missouri Historical Society.

Printed editions of Jefferson's papers are widely available. An incomplete but important early edition of Jefferson's writings is Paul L. Ford, ed., *The Writings of Thomas Jefferson*, 12 vols. (1904). The definitive edition is Julian P. Boyd et al., eds., *The Papers of Thomas Jefferson* (1950–), projected to include sixty volumes when finished. The first twenty-three volumes cover Jefferson's correspondence to May 31, 1792.

Throughout most of the nineteenth century, the majority of historians analyzed Jefferson's diplomatic efforts within the context of the Hamiltonian-Jeffersonian split. A Federalist-Whig-Republican point of view dominated. For example, at mid-century, Richard Hildreth, a Massachusetts Whig and historian, praised Hamilton's practical approach to issues and denounced Jefferson's application of untried theories to foreign affairs in *The History of the United States of America*, 6 vols. (1854–1856).

The Civil War and its aftermath simply reinforced the anti-Jefferson point of view. To many historians, like Hermann E. Von Holst, in *The Constitutional and Political History of the United States*, 8 vols. (1876–1892), and John Morse, in *Thomas Jefferson* (1883), the war seemed to demonstrate that Hamilton had been correct in his promotion of the development and use of national power. Henry Adams, in his brilliant *History of the United States During the Administrations of Jefferson and Madison*, 9 vols. (1889–1891), provided a more balanced view of the Jefferson administration, but he too condemned the Virginian's foreign policy. Adams especially criticized Jefferson for reducing military expenditures and unwisely developing a foreign policy based on commercial coercion.

The rise of the Progressive movement in the early 1900s did little to change this view. Many Progressives considered Jefferson a symbol of defeat since he had believed that the American republic would endure only as long as most Americans remained independent farmers. This did not fit in with the Progressives' efforts to democratize an increasingly urbanized and industrialized America. Furthermore, Charles A. Beard, a leading Progressive historian, in his important study, *Economic Origins of Jeffersonian Democracy* (1915), condemned Jefferson's foreign policy as a doctrinaire effort to promote agrarian radicalism.

Post–World War I isolationism led several scholars, especially Louis M. Sears, *Jefferson and the Embargo* (1927), to praise Jefferson's use of economic retaliation to avoid war. But when the military conflict began in Europe in 1939, this view began to change once again. Reinhold Niebuhr, in *Christianity and Power Politics* (1940), asserted that Jefferson held a moralistic illusion that generosity toward dictators would stop their desire for more expansionism. To Niebuhr, such a position actually encouraged dictators.

World War II and the Cold War led to a more sympathetic treatment of the British side of Anglo-American relations since the Revolutionary era. An increasing number of diplomatic historians began to analyze how idealism throughout American history had hindered the implementation of a realistic approach to foreign affairs. One consequence was that many historians in this period did not believe that Jefferson had taken a decidedly realistic approach to America's foreign affairs. In *Prologue to War* (1961), Bradford Perkins declared that Jefferson, unlike Washington and Adams, did not keep objective and means in harmony with one another.

Somewhat less critical were Lawrence Kaplan, Reginald Stuart, Paul Varg, and J.C.A. Stagg, who all noted a certain degree of realism on Jefferson's part. But Kaplan, in *Jefferson and France* (1967), thought that this was checked by Jefferson's extreme partisan distrust of alleged Federalist monarchism, his idealistic promotion of pure agrarianism, and his excessive fear of England. In addition, Reginald Stuart, *The Half-Way Pacifist* (1978), and Paul Varg, *Foreign Policies of the Founding Fathers* (1964), declared that Jefferson's idealism led him to misunderstand Europe's political machinations. The embargo thus failed and eventually war came because he did not have the power to achieve his ambitious goals. Emphasizing a different issue, J.C.A. Stagg, *Mr. Madison's War* (1983), contended that before 1807 the coercive potential of American commercial policy was subordinated to other considerations. In particular, American territorial ambitions in the South involved difficulties with Spain that required Jefferson to maintain reasonably good relations with Britain. After 1807 the Jefferson administration seriously miscalculated the unpopularity of the embargo in the northern states and the problems of enforcing it.

In a recent study, *Empire of Liberty* (1990), Robert Tucker and David Hendrickson have generally supported the view that Jefferson allowed his idealism to prevent a realistic approach to the Anglo-American controversy over neutral rights. They have noted that Jefferson could be as manipulative as his European counterparts. Yet, seeing the United States as morally correct, Jefferson refused to accept any compromise with Great Britain. Thus, self-interest was not served in the best way.

In *The Contours of American History* (1961), William Appleman Williams foreshadowed the emergence of the New Left. In his evaluation of the third president, Williams argues that Jefferson was too attached to the concept of private property to violate it in order to ensure economic equality. The Virginian mistakenly emphasized territorial expansion and foreign markets as the necessary means of providing economic growth and thus equality and democracy for agricultural America. Williams's position has never been widely accepted, but it did gain more adherents after 1965 as disillusionment grew over U.S. involvement in Vietnam and U.S. expansionism in general.

Since the mid–1970s, Drew McCoy, *The Elusive Republic* (1980), Lance Banning, *The Jeffersonian Persuasion* (1978), and Forrest McDonald, *The Presidency of Thomas Jefferson* (1976), have placed some of the realist and New Left criticisms within a broader ideological context. They have concluded that the Jeffersonians were greatly influenced by the English Whig (or republican) ideology, which asserted that increased governmental power endangered liberty and that only civic virtue in a predominantly agrarian society could preserve the proper balance of power. This great adherence to agrarianism necessitated foreign markets to preserve an agrarian society. The eventual failure to coerce the removal of foreign restrictions on American commerce led to war with Britain in 1812. Military action, however, was no more successful than economic coercion. In short, under the pressure of the Napoleonic Wars, the Republican alternative had failed.

But the post–World War II period did not witness the end of all sympathetic views of Jefferson's diplomacy. Dumas Malone, *Jefferson and the Ordeal of Liberty* (1962) and *Jefferson the President* (1974), Merrill Peterson, *Thomas Jefferson and the New Nation*

(1970), Alexander DeConde, *Entangling Alliance* (1958), and others, although acknowledging the negative consequences of the embargo, have defended his general approach to foreign affairs. For example, Alexander DeConde concluded that Jefferson and the Republicans had been at least as realistic as the Federalists and were certainly motivated by higher ideals than those espoused by Hamilton.

As this brief overview indicates, every generation of American historians has rewritten the history of Jefferson's diplomacy in terms of its own age. Thus, like all major historiographical debates, the controversy over Jefferson's approach to foreign affairs will continue to enhance our understanding of the past in a variety of ways.

Bibliography

Adams, Henry. *The History of the United States During the Administrations of Jefferson and Madison.* 9 vols. New York: Scribner's, 1889–1891.

Appleby, Joyce O. *Capitalism and a New Social Order: The Republican Vision of the 1790s.* New York: New York University Press, 1984.

Banning, Lance. *The Jeffersonian Persuasion: Evolution of a Party Ideology.* Ithaca, N.Y.: Cornell University Press, 1978.

Beard, Charles A. *Economic Origins of Jeffersonian Democracy.* New York: Macmillan, 1915.

Boyd, Julian P. *Number 7: Alexander Hamilton's Attempts to Control American Foreign Policy.* Princeton, N.J.: Princeton University Press, 1964.

———, ed. *The Papers of Thomas Jefferson.* 23 vols. to date. Princeton, N.J.: Princeton University Press, 1950– .

Brant, Irving. *James Madison: Secretary of State, 1801–1809.* Indianapolis: Bobbs-Merrill, 1953.

Brown, Roger H. *The Republic in Peril: 1812.* New York: Columbia University Press, 1964.

Cunningham, Noble E., Jr. *In Pursuit of Reason: The Life of Thomas Jefferson.* Baton Rouge: Louisiana State University Press, 1987.

DeConde, Alexander. *Entangling Alliance: Politics and Diplomacy Under George Washington.* Durham, N.C.: Duke University Press, 1958.

Ford, Paul L., ed. *The Writings of Thomas Jefferson.* 12 vols. New York: Putnam's, 1904–1905.

Hildreth, Richard. *The History of the United States of America.* 6 vols. Rev. ed. New York: Harper and Bros., 1854–1856.

Kaplan, Lawrence S. *Jefferson and France: An Essay on Politics and Political Ideas.* New Haven, Conn.: Yale University Press, 1967.

McCoy, Drew R. *The Elusive Republic: Political Economy in Jeffersonian America.* Chapel Hill: University of North Carolina Press, 1980.

McDonald, Forrest. *The Presidency of Thomas Jefferson.* Lawrence: University Press of Kansas, 1976.

Malone, Dumas. *Jefferson and the Ordeal of Liberty.* Boston: Little, Brown, 1962.

———. *Jefferson the President: Second Term, 1805–1809.* Boston: Little, Brown, 1974.

Morse, John T. *Thomas Jefferson.* Boston: Houghton Mifflin, 1883.

Nelson, John R., Jr. *Liberty and Property: Political Economy and Policymaking in the New Nation, 1789–1812.* Baltimore: Johns Hopkins University Press, 1987.

Niebuhr, Reinhold. *Christianity and Power Politics: Discerning the Signs of the Times.* New York: Scribner's, 1940.

Perkins, Bradford. *Prologue to War: England and the United States, 1805–1812*. Berkeley: University of California Press, 1961.

Peterson, Merrill D. *Thomas Jefferson and the New Nation*. New York: Oxford University Press, 1970.

Sears, Louis. *Jefferson and the Embargo*. Durham, N.C.: Duke University Press, 1927.

Smelser, Marshall. *The Democratic Republic, 1801–1815*. New York: Harper and Row, 1968.

Spivak, Burton. *Jefferson's English Crisis: Commerce, Embargo, and the Republican Revolution*. Charlottesville: University Press of Virginia, 1979.

Stagg, J.C.A. *Mr. Madison's War: Politics, Diplomacy, and Warfare in the Early American Republic, 1783–1830*. Princeton, N.J.: Princeton University Press, 1983.

Stuart, Reginald. *The Half-Way Pacifist: Thomas Jefferson's View of War*. Toronto: University of Toronto Press, 1978.

Tucker, Robert, and David Hendrickson. *Empire of Liberty: The Statecraft of Thomas Jefferson*. Oxford: Oxford University Press, 1990.

Varg, Paul A. *Foreign Policies of the Founding Fathers*. East Lansing: Michigan State University Press, 1964.

Von Volst, Hermann E. *The Constitutional and Political History of the United States*. 8 vols. Chicago: Callaghan, 1876–1892.

Watts, Steven A. *The Republic Reborn: War and the Making of Liberal America, 1790–1820*. Baltimore: Johns Hopkins University Press, 1987.

Williams, William Appleman. *The Contours of American History*. Cleveland: J Cape, 1961.

STEVEN E. SIRY

Prince Wenzel Kaunitz (1711–1794).   Wenzel Anton Kaunitz-Rietberg was foreign minister of the Habsburg monarchy from 1753 to 1792. He held office for a longer period than any other Habsburg foreign minister or any other minister of a major European power in the modern era. He was born in Vienna on February 2, 1711, to the governor of Moravia, scion of the old Czech nobility of the Kingdom of Bohemia, Count Maximilian Ulrich Kaunitz, and Countess Maria Ernestine Franziska Rietberg, the heiress of the north German free county of Rietberg.

From early on Kaunitz's father intended that his son should follow in the footsteps of his own father, Dominik Andreas Kaunitz, vice-chancellor of the Holy Roman Empire from 1698 to 1705, a post that gave him the dominant voice in Habsburg foreign policy councils. Kaunitz received an unusually thorough education for a man of his class, initially from a private tutor, Johann Friedrich Schwanau, and eventually culminating in several strenuous semesters at the University of Leipzig, where he was imbued with the spirit of the early German Enlightenment tradition of Christian Thomasius and Christian Wolff. After a cavalier tour through the Low Countries, Germany, Italy, and France, he returned to Vienna and received a councillorship in the Imperial Aulic Council (*Reischshofrat*), the traditional springboard to higher office in the Habsburg monarchy. During this time he also met and married Countess Maria Ernestine

Stahremberg, with whom he was to have six sons and a daughter before her premature death in 1749. Kaunitz never remarried.

Although Kaunitz was anxious to pursue a diplomatic career, this proved difficult in an age when diplomats had to finance substantial expenses from private funds. His family's finances had been in a sorry state since the late seventeenth century, and as a result he was forced to decline successive offers to be Habsburg ambassador to Denmark, Savoy, and England. In March 1741 he accepted the modest but affordable position of roving ambassador to Italian courts, with the mission of announcing the birth of an heir to the Habsburg throne, while at the same time testing the diplomatic waters during the growing Austrian succession crisis. Then, with the aid of a mortgage on the family estates, Kaunitz was finally able to take up an ambassadorial position in Turin from June 1742 to April 1744. His reports made such a strong impression on the young queen and future empress, Maria Theresa, that he was promoted to the rank of actual privy councillor (*wirklicher Hofrat*) and appointed minister for the Austrian Netherlands. In this position he was forced to witness the French conquest of Belgium and to sign the capitulation of Brussels in February 1746. During these years Kaunitz began to show the first symptoms of a debilitating viral disease that was to affect him at various times over the next thirty years. His resignation for health reasons was accepted in June 1746, but by the end of the year he was ready to resume his career. Briefly considered for the post of governor of Austrian Lombardy, Kaunitz instead became chief Habsburg delegate to the 1748 peace conference at Aachen (Aix-la-Chapelle), which formally ended the War of the Austrian Succession.

After his return to Vienna, he was admitted to the Order of the Golden Fleece, the highest honor of the Habsburg monarchy, and was appointed to the Privy Conference (*Geheime Konferenz*), the monarchy's top foreign policy decision-making body. Here, in a series of conferences in the spring of 1749, Kaunitz soon distinguished himself with his novel ideas, which posited a revised foreign policy focused on the newly emerged Prussian threat and on a reversal of the traditional enmity to France. In line with these new policy guidelines, Kaunitz served as ambassador to France from the fall of 1750 to the spring of 1753. When vacancies in top honorific court positions provided the opportunity gracefully to retire the nominal foreign minister of the monarchy, Count Corfiz Uhlfeld, Kaunitz returned to Vienna and was formally named to this position on May 13, 1753, with the title of chancellor of state (*Haus-, Hof- und Staatskanzler*).

He retained this post for the balance of Empress Maria Theresa's reign (1740–1780) and throughout the reigns of emperors Joseph II (1780–1790) and Leopold II (1790–1792). Through this ministry, Kaunitz was also charged with administering the peripheral lands of the Habsburg monarchy: Belgium, Lombardy, and, briefly, Galicia (1772–1773). During these years he was awarded numerous other positions and honors, including chancellor of the military Maria Theresa Order in 1757, minister of state in the monarchy's top domestic advisory council (*Staatsrat*) in 1760, and protector of the Academy of Fine Arts in 1766. In 1766 he also received the Grand Cross of the Order of St. Stephen. He was raised to the rank of prince of the Holy Roman Empire in 1764 and to that of prince of the Habsburg hereditary lands in 1776. On August 19, 1792, early in the reign of Emperor Francis II (1792–1835), Kaunitz resigned his positions in protest over Austria's collusion in the Second Partition of Poland, which his foreign ministry subordinates had negotiated behind his back. He died at the age of eighty-three in his summer palace in the Viennese suburb of Mariahilf on June 27, 1794.

Throughout his long career, Kaunitz's foreign policy ideas were dominated by the experience of the Prussian rape of Silesia in 1740. Coming out of a tradition stemming from the so-called Bohemian party of advisors to Emperor Leopold I, Kaunitz wished foreign policy priorities to be ordered in accordance with what was in the best interest of the Austro-Bohemian core of the Habsburg monarchy. In his view the interests of the peripheral territories in the Balkans, Italy, the Low Countries, or along the Rhine had to be subordinated to the interests of the core; indeed, these peripheral territories were even expendable if this would strengthen the center. Traditional Habsburg enmity with the French or Spanish Bourbons or with the Ottoman Turks (after 1699) involved conflicts on the periphery to which the resources and interests of the center were frequently sacrificed. *Frederick the Great's attack on Silesia, however, dealt a blow to the very heart of the monarchy, and as a result of this, Kaunitz argued, Prussia now had to be seen as the greatest and most dangerous enemy. All peripheral interests hence had to be subordinated to the new priority of recouping this loss. In this context, Russia could be seen as a ''natural ally'' in the sense that its engagement with the common Turkish enemy made an Ottoman distraction on the Balkan periphery less likely. However, Austria's traditional ally, Britain, seeing in the Habsburgs mainly a continental counterbalance to the Bourbons, was naturally more interested in Austria's defense of that periphery, which engaged it in conflict with the Bourbons, than with its defense of the center, which did not. From this Kaunitz concluded that, under the new circumstances, Britain was by no means a natural ally of the Habsburgs any more than the Bourbons were natural enemies. What mattered most was the focus on Prussia; all other diplomatic options were flexible.

This was the essential logic behind the dramatic reversal of alliances constituting the Diplomatic Revolution of 1756. There is little doubt that the apparently overwhelming Austro-French-Russian coalition that emerged in the course of the subsequent Seven Years War owed as much to Frederick's errors as to Kaunitz's initiatives. Nevertheless, that war did offer the unique opportunity of reversing the verdict of the War of the Austrian Succession and reducing Prussia to the level of a second-rate German principality. Though the reformed Austrian army was every bit a match for the Prussian, timid and incompetent Habsburg field commanders frittered away golden opportunities. At the same time, the conflicting priorities of the coalition partners made it virtually impossible to focus any coordinated military effort against Frederick. As a result, Prussia survived as a Great Power, and Germany entered the age of dualism, which would produce no decisive verdict until 1866.

The lessons of this war served Kaunitz as guidelines for the rest of his life. France had not proved militarily effective against Prussia and could clearly not be counted on for energetic support of any German initiatives the Habsburgs might take. On the other hand, the French alliance had kept the Italian, Rhenish, and Belgian peripheries tranquil and had permitted the stronger focus on Prussia. Since Prussia remained a Great Power and German policies had to remain the first priority, Bourbon friendship was a guarantor of peace elsewhere, and thus continued to serve Habsburg interests. The rapprochement with the Bourbon courts therefore remained a centerpiece of Kaunitz's foreign policy and was strengthened by a series of marriages between Habsburg archdukes and arch-duchesses and Spanish and French Bourbon princes and princesses. Thereafter, Kaunitz was satisfied to play second fiddle to the Bourbons on the Italian peninsula, contenting himself with "influence" rather than overt territorial aggrandizement.

The second lesson of the Seven Years War was that Russian friendship was a mixed blessing. Kaunitz came to realize during the war that the Russian drift westward constituted a new threat, and he became increasingly reluctant to accommodate Russian territorial ambitions against Prussia, even if these would lead to the much-desired destruction of Prussia as a Great Power. The postwar Russo-Prussian understanding, which gave Russia virtually complete control of the vast Polish-Lithuanian Commonwealth, moreover, made it all the more necessary to keep a wary eye on the north and east, where the best that could be made of a bad situation was to preserve the status quo. The Russo-Turkish War of 1768–1774 made that impossible, and found Kaunitz drawn into the famous partition of Poland as the least destabilizing of the options available to the Habsburg monarchy. On the whole, however, Kaunitz was not in favor of the principle of territorial compensation—ostensibly to preserve the balance of power—that underlay the partition of Poland. Unless the Habsburgs could peacefully reacquire Silesia, or some suitable German equivalent such as Bavaria, other "compensations" only added to Austria's periphery, and consequently would strengthen compensated rivals much more. Kaunitz concluded that it was best to avoid such arrangements altogether if possible. Hence, while he prepared plans that would have exchanged Belgium and other peripheral territories for Bavaria, he was not prepared to make such an exchange if it involved war or the compensation of Prussia with equivalent territories.

At the heart of this vision lay the third great conclusion drawn from the Seven Years War. Despite its lack of success in the war, the Habsburg monarchy in many ways was the state with the greatest economic and social potential of the three eastern powers. All Austria had to do was develop and exploit this potential. The resulting prosperity and power would render all further territorial conquests superfluous. The preservation of the diplomatic status quo was therefore linked in Kaunitz's mind with the enlightened political, social, and economic reform of the Habsburg monarchy. This not only made him one of the principal advocates of "enlightened absolutism," but involved him in virtually every domestic reform of any consequence in the generation between the Seven Years War and the French Revolution. But this meant conducting as pacifistic a foreign policy as possible and eschewing territorial aggression. While this was not always possible when serving the bellicose and aggressive Joseph II, it was the essential point behind Kaunitz's support of Leopold II's reluctance to get involved in the French revolutionary crisis, and behind his resignation in protest over the Second Partition of Poland.

Kaunitz's diplomatic legacy was as poorly understood by his successors as by subsequent historians, who have generally been blinded by the manipulative dexterity behind the Diplomatic Revolution and have failed to focus on the broader vision. Such a vision would, in any case, have been difficult to pursue in the Revolutionary and Napoleonic Wars. But there is little doubt that the absence of this vision contributed to the decline and isolation of the Habsburg monarchy in the international arena during the nineteenth century, and to its defeat on the day of reckoning with Prussia that Kaunitz had always predicted was unavoidable.

Annotated Bibliography

Kaunitz created the modern Habsburg Foreign Office and the modern Habsburg diplomatic corps. Among his innovations in this process was the systematic reorganization of the Habsburg diplomatic and family archives. This was marked by new filing, recording, and indexing procedures and by a thorough centralization of materials. As a result, most of the important archival sources on Kaunitz's foreign policy are well organized and easily accessible at a single location, the *Haus-, Hof- und Staatsarchiv* section of the Austrian State Archives at Minoritenplatz 1, in Vienna, Austria.

The single most important sources are the frequent reports Kaunitz prepared for his sovereigns, called *Vorträge*. During times of crisis these reports were submitted virtually every day, and at other times about three or four times a week for the entire period from 1753 to 1792. These were originally bound in smaller bundles known as fascicles but have been consolidated into eighty larger *Kartons* since World War II, each containing 300–500 folio sheets (or 600–1,000 folio pages) of materials; they are currently indexed as *Staatskanzlei: Vorträge, Kartons 72–151.* These reports, in turn, are based on extensive diplomatic correspondence, organized by country. Ambassadors and other diplomatic agents in each country received instructions (*Weisungen*) and submitted reports (*Berichte*) on a regular basis. Related relevant materials and supporting documents are assembled under the heading *Varia* and are interspersed with these reports and instructions.

Diverse personal correspondence with the monarchs, frequently on diplomatic matters, is to be found in the *Familienarchiv* section of the archive, and personal correspondence with other prominent individuals in the *Grosse Korrespondenz* portion of the so-called *Sonstige Sammlungen* section. This latter collection also contains correspondence with various generals, attachés, and other agents during the Seven Years War under the heading *Kriegsakten*. Both the *Familienarchiv* and *Kabinettsarchiv* sections also contain Kaunitz *Nachläße*. In addition there is a twelve-carton Kaunitz *Nachlaβ*, which was kept on the family estate in Moravia and which is now housed in the Moravian Provincial Archive at Zerotinovo námiesti 3–5, in Brno, Czechoslovakia.

Kaunitz left no autobiography, memoirs, or any other personal publications. On the other hand, he was the author of thousands of extensive memoranda, large-scale reports, and a copious private and official correspondence from which many key documents have been published over the last 200 years. The most significant contribution to this literature is the recent publication by Reiner Pommerin and Lothar Schilling of Kaunitz's seminal memorandum for the Privy Conference of March 1749, which became the springboard for the reversal of alliances and the Diplomatic Revolution of 1756, in Johannes Kunisch, ed., *Expansion und Gleichgewicht* (1986). The failure of the first attempt to implement this new policy during Kaunitz's French embassy is detailed in his secret correspondence with Maria Theresa's private secretary in Hanns Schlitter, ed., *Correspondance secrète* (1899), while many of his briefs and reports during the crisis leading up to the Diplomatic Revolution and the Seven Years War were published by Gustav Berthold Volz and Georg Küntzel in *Preußische und Österreichische Acten zur Vorgeschichte des Siebenjährigen Krieges* (1899), as well as in the extensive endnotes of the fourth volume of the published diary of the Habsburg grand master of the household, Prince Johann Joseph Khevenhüller-Metsch, *Aus der Zeit Maria Theresias* (1907). The other seven volumes of this series also contain important Kaunitz reports and memoranda.

Several of Kaunitz's major position papers dating from 1755 to 1777 were published by Adolf Beer in "Denkschriften des Fürsten Kaunitz," *Archiv für österreichische Geschichte* 48 (1872): 1–158. Beer has also appended larger Kaunitz briefs to his "Die Zusammenkünfte Joseph II. und Friedrich II. zu Neiße und Neustadt," *Archiv für österreichische Geschichte* 47 (1871): 383–527, and in his volume of documents accompanying *Die Erste Teilung Polens*, 3 vols. (1873). Kaunitz's partition priorities in the Polish crisis were published by Gustav Volz in "Die Massinischen Vorschläge: Ein Beitrag Zur Vorgeschichte der ersten Teilung Polens," *Historische Vierteljahrschrift* 10 (1907): 367–373, and the memorandum placing these in the larger context of Habsburg policies by Saul K. Padover in "Prince Kaunitz' Résumé of His Eastern Policy, 1763–71," *Journal of Modern History*, 5 (1933): 352–365. Materials focusing on policies toward the Holy Roman Empire from the War of the Bavarian Succession to the French Revolution appear in the volume of documents accompanying Karl Otmar Aretin's *Heiliges Römisches Reich* (1967). Relations with Rome, which have as much domestic as foreign policy significance, were amply documented in the massive collection by Ferdinand Maass, ed., *Der Josephinismus*, 5 vols. (1951–1961), the first two volumes of which focus almost monomaniacally on Kaunitz's reports. While Alfred Arneth's ten-volume *Geschichte Maria Theresias* (1863–1879) is not strictly a primary source, it contains lengthy citations of Kaunitz in both the text and the endnotes on every diplomatic issue of significance in the empress's reign.

Kaunitz's diplomatic reports and letters during the reigns of Joseph II and Leopold II were published in Sebastian Brunner, ed., *Correspondances intimes* (1871) and *Der Humor in der Diplomatie* (1872); Beer, ed., *Joseph II., Leopold II. und Kaunitz* (1873); Alfred Arneth and M. J. Flammermont, eds., *Correspondence secrète du Comte Mercy-Argenteau*, 2 vols. (1889–1891); and Hanns Schlitter, ed., *Kaunitz, Philipp Cobenzl und Spielmann* (1899). Kaunitz memoranda on the French Revolution and the outbreak of the Revolutionary Wars are published generously in the first two volumes of Alfred Vivenot, ed., *Quellen zur Geschichte der Deutschen Kaiserpolitik Oesterreichs* (1873–1874), which also contains his formal resignation from office. A rare philosophical rumination on the balance of power, also by the aging Kaunitz, is Franz A.J. Szabo, "Prince Kaunitz and the Balance of Power," *International History Review* 1 (1979): 399–408. Finally, documents pertaining to Kaunitz's organization and administration of the Habsburg Foreign Office have been published in the documents volumes of the *Österreichische Zentralverwaltung* series.

The secondary literature is at once voluminous and wanting. No major, full-scale biography of Kaunitz based on extensive research in archival sources exists. The two biographies that have been published are both unsatisfactory and are based only on published sources: the brief, Prussophile, and often inaccurate Georg Küntzel, *Fürst Kaunitz-Rittberg als Staatsman* (1923), and the superficial and journalistic Tibor Simányi, *Kaunitz: Staatskanzler Maria Theresias* (1984). Alexander Novotny, *Staatskanzler Kaunitz als Geistige Persönlichkeit* (1947), contains some materials relevant to diplomatic history, but is, as the title indicates, mainly a study in intellectual history. In contrast, the more concise summaries in biographical dictionaries and the like have generally been of high quality. These include entries on Kaunitz by Friedrich Schlichtegroll in *Nekrolog auf das Jahr 1794* (1796), Joseph Hormayr in *Österreichischer Plutarch* (1807), Constantin Wurzbach in *Biographisches Lexikon* (1864), Arneth in *Allgemeine Deutsche Biographie* (1882), Alfred Dove in *Ausgewählte Schriften* (1898), Heinrich Kretschmayr in *Menschen die Geschichte Machen* (1933), Peter Richard Rohden in *Die klassische Diplomatie* (1939), Friedrich Walter in *Männer um Maria Theresia* (1951), Alexander Novotny in *Gestalter der Geschicke Österreichs* (1962), Aretin in *Neue Deutsche Biographie* (1977), and Szabo in *Maria Theresia und Ihre Zeit* (1979).

Kaunitz's family background and early diplomatic career before 1753, on the other hand, have been extremely well served. The most outstanding work in this respect is Grete Klingenstein, *Der Aufstieg des Hauses Kaunitz* (1975). The earlier Arneth, "Biographie des Fürsten Kaunitz: Ein Fragment," *Archiv für österreichische Geschichte* 88 (1900): 1–201, contains a number of errors and should be read in conjunction with Klingenstein. Kaunitz's early diplomatic career has also been treated in a series of perceptive articles by William J. McGill, who published "The Roots of Policy: Kaunitz in Italy and the Netherlands, 1742–1746," *Central European History* 1 (1968): 131–149; "Wenzel Anton von Kaunitz-Rittberg and the Conference of Aix-la-Chapelle, 1748," *Duquesne Review* 14 (1969); 154–167; and "The Roots of Policy: Kaunitz in Vienna and Versailles, 1749–1753," *Journal of Modern History* 43 (1971): 228–244. The background and pedigree of the policies Kaunitz developed during this time are made clear by Max Braubach, *Versailles und Wien von Ludwig XIV. bis Kaunitz* (1952). Kaunitz's nearly forty-year term as foreign minister, however, has received no concomitant focused attention. There are a few articles with a specialized focus on Kaunitz, such as those by Paul Bernard, "Kaunitz and Austria's Secret Fund," *East European Quarterly* 16 (1982): 129–136, and "Kaunitz and the Cost of Diplomacy," *East European Quarterly* 17 (1983): 1–14; and by Karl A. Roider, "Kaunitz, Joseph II and the Turkish War," *Slavonic and East European Review* 54 (1976): 538–556; and an excellent discussion of Kaunitz's general diplomatic worldview in Harm Klueting, *Die Lehre von der Macht der Staaten* (1986); but there is no systematic survey of his foreign policy. Naturally, given Kaunitz's role in the foreign policy of a European Great Power for half a century, it is not surprising that he would be discussed or mentioned in many of the memoirs, reminiscences, and letters of his contemporaries, and that an analysis of one aspect or another of his policies can be found in virtually every article and monograph dealing with the history of the Habsburg monarchy or the diplomacy of the European powers in the second half of the eighteenth century. This literature is so enormous that it cannot be discussed in detail, though a start may be made by consulting the bibliographies of such recent general surveys as Derek McKay and H. M. Scott, *The Rise of the Great Powers, 1648–1815* (1983).

Bibliography

Aretin, Karl Otmar Freiherr von. *Heiliges Römisches Reich, 1776–1806: Reichsverfassung und Staatssouveränität.* 2 vols. Wiesbaden: Steiner, 1967.

―――. "Kaunitz, Wenzel Anton." *Neue Deutsche Biographie* 11 (1977): 363–369.

Arneth, Alfred Ritter von. "Biographie des Fürsten Kaunitz: Ein Fragment." *Archiv für österreichische Geschichte* 88 (1900): 1–201.

―――. *Geschichte Maria Theresias.* 10 vols. Vienna: Braumüller, 1863–1879.

―――. "Kaunitz." *Allgemeine Deutsche Biographie* 15 (1882): 487–507.

Arneth, Alfred Ritter von, and M. J. Flammermont, eds. *Correspondance secrète du Comte de Mercy-Argenteau avec l'Empereur Joseph II et le Prince de Kaunitz.* 2 vols. Paris: Imprimerie Nationale, 1889–1891.

Beales, D.E.D., and T.C.W. Blanning. "Prince Kaunitz and 'The Primacy of Domestic Policy'," *International History Review* 2 (1980): 619–624.

Beer, Adolf. *Die Erste Teilung Polens.* 3 vols. Vienna: C. Gerold's Sohn, 1873.

―――. "Die Zusammenkünfte Joseph II. und Friedrich II. zu Neiße und Neustadt." *Archiv für österreichische Geschichte* 47 (1871): 383–527.

―――, ed. "Denkschriften des Fürsten Kaunitz." *Archiv für österreichische Geschichte* 48 (1872): 1–158.

―――, ed. *Joseph II., Leopold II. und Kaunitz: Ihr Briefwechsel.* Vienna: Braumüller, 1873.

Bernard, Paul P. "Kaunitz and Austria's Secret Fund." *East European Quarterly* 16 (1982): 129–136.

―――. "Kaunitz and the Cost of Diplomacy." *East European Quarterly* 17 (1983): 1–14.

Braubach, Max. *Versailles und Wien von Ludwig XIV. bis Kaunitz: Die Vorstadien der diplomatischen Revolution im 18. Jahrhundert.* Bonn: Röhrscheid, 1952.

Brunner, Sebastian, ed. *Correspondances intimes de l'Empereur Joseph II avec son ami le Comte de Cobenzl et son Premier Ministre le Prince de Kaunitz.* Mayence: Kirchheim, 1871.

―――, ed. *Der Humor in der Diplomatie und Regierungskunde des 18. Jahrhundert.* 2 vols. Vienna: Braumüller, 1872.

Dove, Alfred. "Kaunitz." In *Ausgewählte Schriften, vornehmlich historischen Inhalts.* Leipzig: Duncker and Humblot, 1898.

Hormayr, Joseph Freiherr von. "Fürst Kaunitz." In *Österreichischer Plutarch.* Vienna: Anton Doll, 1807–1814.

Khevenhüller-Metsch, Rudolf, and Hanns Schlitter, eds. *Aus der Zeit Maria Theresias: Tagebuch des Fürsten Johann Joseph Khevenhüller-Metsch, Kaiserlichen Oberst-hofmeisters. 1742–1776.* 8 vols. Vienna: A. Holzhausen, 1907–1972 .

Klingenstein, Grete. *Der Aufstieg des Hauses Kaunitz: Studien zur Herkunft und Bildung des Staatskanzlers Wenzel Anton.* Göttingen: Vandenhoeck and Ruprecht, 1975.

―――. "Instiutionelle Aspekte der österreichischen Außenpolitik im 18. Jahrhundert." In *Diplomatie und Außenpolitik Österreichs: Elf Beiträge zu ihrer Geschichte,* pp. 74–93. Edited by Erich Zöllner. Vienna: Österreichischer Bundesverlag, 1977.

─────. "Kaunitz kontra Bartenstein: Zur Geschichte der Staatskanzlei in den Jahren 1749–1753." In *Beiträge zur neueren Geschichte Österreichs*, pp. 243–263. Edited by Heinrich Fichtenau and Erich Zöllner. Vienna: Böhlau, 1974.

Klueting, Harm. *Die Lehre von der Macht der Staaten: Das außenpolitische Machtproblem in der "politischen Wissenschaft" und in der praktischen Politik im 18. Jahrhundert.* Berlin: Duncker and Humblot, 1986.

Kretschmayr, Heinrich. "Kaunitz." In *Menschen die Geschichte Machten: Viertausend Jahre Weltgeschichte in Zeit- und Lebensbildern*, 2nd ed., 2: 251–256. Edited by Peter Richard Rohden. Vienna: Seidel, 1933.

Küntzel, Georg. *Fürst Kaunitz-Rittberg als Staatsman.* Frankfurt am Main: Diesterweg, 1923.

Maass, Ferdinand, ed. *Der Josephinismus: Quellen zur seiner Geschichte in Oesterreich, 1760–1790.* 5 vols. Vienna: Verlag Herold, 1951–1961.

McGill, William J. "The Roots of Policy: Kaunitz in Italy and the Netherlands, 1742–1746." *Central European History* 1 (1968): 131–149.

─────. "The Roots of Policy: Kaunitz in Vienna and Versailles, 1749–1753." *Journal of Modern History* 43 (1971): 228–244.

─────. "Wenzel Anton von Kaunitz-Rittberg and the Conference of Aix-la-Chapelle, 1748." *Duquesne Review* 14 (1969): 154–167.

McKay, Derek, and H. M. Scott. *The Rise of the Great Powers, 1648–1815.* New York: Longman, 1983.

Novotny, Alexander. "Staatskanzler Fürst Kaunitz (1711–1794)." In *Gestalter der Geschicke Österreichs*, pp. 253–261. Edited by Hugo Hantsch. Innsbruck and Vienna: Tyrolia-Verlag, 1962.

─────. *Staatskanzler Kaunitz als Geistige Persönlichkeit.* Vienna: Brüder Hollinek, 1947.

Padover, Saul K., ed. "Prince Kaunitz' Résumé of His Eastern Policy, 1763–71." *Journal of Modern History* 5 (1933): 352–365.

Pillich, Walter. "Staatskanzler Kaunitz und die Archivforschung (1762–1794)." In *Festschrift zur Feier des zweihundertjährigen Bestandes des Haus-, Hof- und Staatsarchivs*, 2 vols., 2: 95–118. Edited by Leo Santifaller. Vienna: Druck und Kommissions-Verlag der Österreichischen Staatsdruckerei, 1949–1951.

Pommerin, Reiner, and Lothar Schilling, eds. "Denkschrift des Grafen Kaunitz zur mächtepolitischen Konstellation nach dem Aachener Frieden von 1748." In *Expansion und Gleichgewicht: Studien zur europäischen Mächtepolitik des ancien régime*, pp. 165–239. Edited by Johannes Kunisch. Berlin: Duncker and Humblot, 1986.

Rohden, Peter Richard. *Die klassische Diplomatie von Kaunitz bis Metternich.* Leipzig: Koehler and Amelang, 1939.

Roider, Karl A. "Kaunitz, Joseph II and the Turkish War." *Slavonic and East European Review* 54 (1976): 538–556.

Schlichtegroll, Friedrich. "Wenzel Anton, d.h.R.R. Fürst von Kaunitz." In *Nekrolog auf das Jahr 1794*, 2 vols., 1: 129–162. Gotha: J. Perthes, 1796.

Schlitter, Hanns, ed. *Correspondance secrète entre le Comte A. W. Kaunitz-Rietberg, Ambassadeur impérial à Paris, et le Baron Ignaz de Koch, Secrétaire de l'Impératrice Marie-Thérèse, 1750–1752.* Paris: Plon-Nourrit, 1899.

─────, ed. *Kaunitz, Philipp Cobenzl und Spielman: Ihr Briefwechsel, 1779–1792.* Vienna: A. Holzhausen, 1899.

Simányi, Tibor. *Kaunitz: Staatskanzler Maria Theresias*. Vienna and Munich: Amalthea, 1984.

Szabo, Franz A.J. "Prince Kaunitz and the Balance of Power." *International History Review* 1 (1979): 399–408.

———. "Prince Kaunitz and the Primacy of Domestic Policy: A Response." *International History Review* 2 (1980): 625–635.

———. "Staatskanzler Fürst Kaunitz und die Aufklärungspolitik Österreichs." In *Maria Theresia und Ihre Zeit*, pp. 40–45. Edited by Walter Koschatzky. Salzburg and Vienna: Residenz Verlag, 1979.

Vivenot, Alfred Ritter von, ed. *Quellen zur Geschichte der Deutschen Kaiserpolitik Oesterreichs während der französischen Revolutionskriege, 1790–1801*. 5 vols. Vienna: Braumüller 1873–1890.

Volz, Gustav Berthold. "Die Massinischen Vorschläge: Ein Beitrag zur Vorgeschichte der ersten Teilung Polens." *Historische Vierteljahrschrift* 10 (1907): 367–373.

Volz, Gustav Berthold, and Georg Küntzel, eds. *Preußische und Österreichische Acten zur Vorgeschichte des Siebenjährigen Krieges*. Leipzig: Hirzel, 1899.

Walter, Friedrich. *Männer um Maria Theresia*. Vienna: A. Holzhausens, 1951.

Wurzbach, Constant von. "Kaunitz." *Biographisches Lexikon des Kaiserthums Oesterreich* 11 (1864): 70–86.

FRANZ A.J. SZABO

George F. Kennan (b. 1904). George Frost Kennan has pursued a varied and distinguished career as diplomat, policy maker, historian, and critic of modern international affairs. Few of his compatriots better exemplify the public man who has helped shape the world and influenced how people think about it. In the appreciative view of *Henry Kissinger, "George Kennan came as close to authoring the diplomatic doctrine of his era as any diplomat in our history" (Kissinger, *White House Years* [1979], p. 135).

Kennan was born on February 16, 1904, in Milwaukee, Wisconsin, into a middle-class family. His father, a lawyer and self-made man, was the first of his line to acquire a college education and follow a professional career. Soon after young George was born, his mother died. His father remarried, but Kennan was not close to his stepmother, and some scholars have attributed his "burning desire" to be accepted by authority figures in the State Department to the emotional austerity of his early life. At thirteen, he was dispatched to St. John's Military Academy in Delafield, Wisconsin. Though discipline was strict, the academy was not scholastically rigorous. It was only with considerable difficulty that Kennan passed the entrance exams required for admission to Princeton University. While a student at Princeton (from which he graduated in 1925), Kennan displayed little of that intellectual curiosity and keenness of mind that marked his life in government.

These qualities were developed in the Foreign Service, to which Kennan was appointed in 1926. He performed well during his early overseas assignments in Geneva, Hamburg, Berlin, and Tallinn. In 1929 he was selected as one of a handful of Foreign Service officers to receive specialized education in Soviet history, politics, and economics and in the Russian language. His most important training as a Soviet expert took place at the University of Berlin's Oriental Seminary. While there, he met and married Annelise Soerensen of Norway, with whom he had four children. After Berlin, Kennan joined the American legation in Riga, which in the early 1930s functioned as the principal U.S. government "listening post," monitoring events inside the Soviet Union.

Shortly after the formal establishment of Soviet-U.S. relations in 1933, the American ambassador, William Bullitt, asked Kennan to serve with him as an aide and interpreter. From then until August 1937 (except for a brief interruption caused by illness) Kennan lived in Moscow. He and his colleagues, most notably Charles Bohlen, watched closely the drama of the Great Purges and the efforts to modernize the Soviet Union's industry and agriculture. They also studied *Joseph Stalin's foreign policy and sought to understand the implications for U.S. diplomacy. The overall experience was a formative one for Kennan, and from it he concluded that there was no basis for intimate Soviet-U.S. relations.

In the years immediately preceding U.S. involvement in World War II, Kennan performed additional duties in Washington (where he directed the State Department's Soviet desk), Prague, and Berlin. During the war years, he was assigned to a succession of posts. In Lisbon, where he was chargé d'affaires, he played a role in wartime espionage and counterespionage. In 1943 he went to London as a junior member of the U.S. delegation to the European Advisory Commission, where he helped draw up plans arranging for Germany's surrender and determining the exact zones of Allied occupation. Kennan again served in Moscow from mid-1944 to mid-1946, this time under Ambassador W. Averell Harriman.

Although he readily acknowledged the necessity of Anglo-American cooperation with the Soviet Union to defeat Nazi Germany, Kennan was skeptical that President *Franklin Roosevelt would succeed in preserving the Grand Alliance into the postwar era. He was especially critical of the substance and tone of the Yalta accords and thought that the British and the Americans had gone too far in placating Stalin's regime. Not until after the war, however, was there an occasion for Kennan to register clearly his concerns with Washington officials.

By February 1946, the Grand Alliance was weakening, as the victors bickered over the spoils of war, and ideological suspicions, suppressed during the anti-German struggle, resurfaced. The Soviet Union's failure to budge from its sector in northern Iran caused concern in Washington. At the same time the Soviets were pressing Turkey for easy access through the Black Sea Straits. Throughout eastern Europe, the Soviets began the process that eventually resulted in the sealing off of Soviet-aligned Communist regimes from Western influence and values. In February 1946, responding to a Treasury Department inquiry about Soviet reluctance to join the World Bank and the International Monetary Fund, Kennan wrote an 8,000-word cable that analyzed Soviet attitudes toward the world and Stalin's foreign objectives. In this "Long Telegram," Kennan portrayed a Soviet Union that sought to aggrandize its power in Europe and elsewhere through subversive, semilegal, and ruthless means. He advised that if the United

States failed to check Soviet ambitions, the European balance of power would shift to the disadvantage of the United States; over the long term, Western Hemisphere security would be jeopardized.

The telegram was well received in Washington, especially by the influential navy secretary James Forrestal, and buttressed those in the Truman administration who advocated a firm policy against the Soviet Union. The telegram was also a professional boon to Kennan, whom Forrestal recruited to serve as deputy commandant for foreign affairs at the recently organized National War College in Washington. While at the college, Kennan published his most famous essay, the so-called X-Article, which appeared in the July 1947 *Foreign Affairs*.

In this seminal Cold War document, Kennan elaborated on themes from the Long Telegram and advocated measures to check Soviet ambitions; in aggregate these ideas became known as the containment policy. The most controversial passage from the X-Article, and one whose meaning scholars have long disputed, was ambiguous even by Kennan's own later admission. He had asserted: "The Soviet pressure against the free institutions of the Western world is something that can be contained by the adroit and vigilant application of counter-force at a series of constantly shifting geographical and political points, corresponding to the shifts and maneuvers of Soviet policy." Several analysts at the time and others since (of whom Walter Lippmann was the most prominent) believed that the essence of Kennan's idea was the curtailment of Soviet power by military means. Government papers that Kennan wrote at the time indicate, however, that he intended containment to rely primarily on economic and political programs and only secondarily on military strategies. The militarization of containment, epitomized in the founding of the North Atlantic Treaty Organization (NATO) and the acceleration of the nuclear arms race, seemed excessive and dangerous to him.

As director of the State Department's Policy Planning Staff (1947–1949), Kennan was able to campaign for his version of U.S. policy through work on the Marshall Plan and attempts to rehabilitate postwar Japan. He also contributed to that line of thinking in the State Department that sought through economic, psychological, and political means to drive a wedge between the Soviet Union and its erstwhile allies in Asia (i.e., Mao's China) and Europe (i.e., *Tito's Yugoslavia). Kennan's dissatisfaction, though, with the increasingly military orientation of U.S. foreign policy under secretaries of state *Dean Acheson and *John Foster Dulles helped lead to his resignation from the Foreign Service in 1953.

Kennan twice held ambassadorships: in 1952 to the Soviet Union, which ended unceremoniously when Stalin's government declared him *persona non grata*, and in 1961–1963 to Yugoslavia. The Soviet regime rejected Kennan after he made careless remarks to a reporter likening life in the Soviet Union to that in *Hitler's Germany. Kennan's tenure in Belgrade also met an ignominious end. He resigned in the summer of 1963 after Congress passed legislation denying future financial aid to Yugoslavia and revoking its most-favored-nation status.

This action was taken despite Kennan's insistence that the United States should demonstrate to members of the Warsaw Pact that fruitful collaboration was possible between the capitalist West and those Communist countries operating independently of the Soviet Union.

Kennan's scholarly career began in 1953, when he joined the history faculty at the Institute for Advanced Study at Princeton. While there, he wrote a number of acclaimed books on early Soviet-U.S. relations, twentieth-century American diplomacy, and the origins of World War I. Notwithstanding the meticulousness of his research and the judiciousness of his evaluations, Kennan's labors in historical scholarship have been intended to serve more than conventional academic ends. His histories are also exercises in political edification that resonate with lessons for American readers about the dangers to foreign policy of militancy, philosophical shallowness, and dilettantism.

That Kennan has never let his attention stray far from the current scene of political and diplomatic events, even when preoccupied with exacting research and writing, is also apparent from his many pronouncements since the mid–1950s on international subjects. Indeed, he has won the attention of many statesmen and members of the politically literate public as a commentator on contemporary issues. His written statements, lectures, and expert testimony at congressional hearings have touched on Soviet-U.S. disengagement from Europe, the folly of American involvement in Vietnam, the dangers of an unbridled arms race, the need for accommodation with the Soviet Union, and the desirability of multilateral cooperation to solve global environmental problems.

Despite his intellectual accomplishments, Kennan has never attempted to create a theory of international relations or of U.S. foreign policy. He has dismissed most theorizing as too constricting and irrelevant to the affairs of state. Still, implicit in his writings is a set of underlying assumptions that, taken together, constitute a theory of politics. This blends elements of realpolitik with ideas ultimately traceable to the conservative eighteenth-century thinker Edmund Burke and the modern theologian Reinhold Niebuhr.

For Kennan, the United States must recognize that international problems are properly understood when viewed in historical context and that successful foreign policy requires taking the long view of both problems and solutions. To cultivate a world environment that will contain or prevent large-scale warfare, Americans must also appreciate that their adversaries do not have a monopoly on evil but have a role to play within a vast scheme of history and ultimate purpose. Certainly, Kennan's emphasis on patience to allow the forces of reform adequate time to begin operating in Soviet internal and foreign policies seems vindicated; *Mikhail Gorbachev's innovations represented that very mellowing of Soviet paranoia and police power for which Kennan hoped.

In the final analysis, it is as a diagnostician of U.S. and international problems and as a prescriber of remedies, rather than as an implementer, that Kennan must be judged. And here the record is strong. However near he may have come to it, Kennan has never completely despaired of the United States. As a consequence, he once entertained hopes for a third political party (oriented toward environmental issues); he has tried teaching his compatriots to distinguish between the appearance of morality and its real substance in foreign policy; and he has reminded them that ultimate international success for a wealthy, diverse, continental-sized state will be decided in the domestic sphere. This last point is especially important for Americans, who traditionally have held a narrow understanding of national power and prestige. After all, as Kennan has repeatedly reminded audiences over the years, military might is only one feature of a country's strength; by emphasizing it and neglecting other aspects of power— economic, social, environmental—the United States could damage its overall security and world standing. Kennan's other contributions to understanding foreign policy have also been astute. He has wisely counseled that to be effective the United States must recognize the political limits of military power, acknowledge some hierarchy of interests abroad, and pursue moderate balance of power policies in Europe and East Asia. As for the promotion of human rights, Kennan has taught that the United States is more effective when it uses discreet means than when it publicly bludgeons another regime. Yet Kennan has always retained a belief in ultimate justice. Contemplating a World War II memorial, he wrote: "May all those who sent these men to their death, on whatever side, someday be compelled to account for their action to the God who caused these victims to come into this world, at one time, as sweet innocent children, needful of love, and normally surrounded by it, only to leave it, unfulfilled, in circumstances of such pain, bewilderment, and misery" (Kennan, *Sketches from a Life* [1989], p. 312).

At the core of Kennan's conception of politics is a preoccupation with the continuity and intrinsic value of human cultures and history. As the supreme object is the preservation of civilization, and as the overriding challenge to world leaders is to avoid nuclear war, this understanding of Kennan's shall have to prevail.

Annotated Bibliography

George Kennan's papers are on deposit at the Seeley Mudd Library, Princeton University (Princeton, New Jersey). The collection includes more than thirty manuscript boxes containing personal correspondence, government memoranda, diaries, and photographs. The only restriction that applies to researchers is that they not make photographic copies of any of the materials.

The C. Ben Wright Papers on deposit at the George Marshall Library, Virginia Military Institute (Lexington, Virginia), contain a very large number of Kennan's papers, plus transcripts of interviews with his colleagues and friends. There are some restrictions on the interviews.

Records (Group 59) of the State Department's Policy Planning Staff and Decimal Files are readily available at the National Archives in Washington, D.C.

George Kennan has published three autobiographical volumes: *Memoirs: 1925–1950* (1967), for which he was awarded the Pulitzer Prize; *Memoirs: 1950–1963* (1972); and *Sketches from a Life* (1989). The literary value of these works is extremely high. As such, they belong in the same category of excellent autobiography as Henry Adams's *Education*. Students of the Cold War will find Kennan's first volume especially useful for its analysis of problems posed by the Soviet Union in the late 1940s, the evolution of the Marshall Plan, and portraits of American and Soviet policy makers. The second volume contains information about the Korean War, the impact of McCarthyism on domestic politics and foreign policy, and the emergence of polycentrism in the Communist world. The third volume concentrates on the private side of Kennan's life, but it does include sections of interest to students of the Soviet Union, World War II, and Europe's post–1945 reconstruction.

Kennan's published historical scholarship and political analysis are also important to students of international relations. His first intensive research project dealt with the early phase, 1917–1920, of Soviet-U.S. relations and resulted in a two-volume study, *Russia Leaves the War* (1956), which was awarded the Pulitzer Prize, and *The Decision to Intervene* (1958). These volumes remain the most elegant and definitive treatment of their kind. His investigations into the origins of World War I have also resulted in the publication of *The Decline of Bismarck's European Order* (1979) and *The Fateful Alliance* (1984), both of which analyze the underlying forces and personalities that produced the divided continent and competing alliance systems that eventually gave rise to Europe's war in 1914.

Students of Soviet diplomatic history and of Russian intellectual-political history should consult Kennan's *Soviet Foreign Policy, 1917–1941* (1960) and *The Marquis de Custine and His "Russia in 1839"* (1971). The former is a slender volume that provides thoughtful commentary by Kennan and reproduces excerpts from thirty-four Soviet documents relating to foreign policy from the 1917 Decree on Peace to Soviet-German relations in 1939–1940. His *Marquis de Custine* examines the visit in 1839 by the French aristocrat to Russia and the treatise he subsequently published on the subject. Kennan's treatment is a useful reminder of the continuities in Russian political life before and since the 1917 Bolshevik Revolution.

Most of Kennan's remaining books are compilations of lectures—on topical and historical subjects—delivered since 1950. There are, however, three significant exceptions. His *From Prague after Munich: Diplomatic Papers, 1938–1940* (1968) includes the reports he sent to State Department superiors about conditions in Czechoslovakia during the first period of Nazi administration. *The Cloud of Danger: Current Realities of American Foreign Policy* (1977) surveys the challenges and opportunities that confronted U.S. foreign policy at the beginning of President Jimmy Carter's administration. Among other things, Kennan calls for a relaxed and rather aloof U.S. attitude toward problems in the Third World. Finally, his *The Nuclear Delusion: Soviet-American Relations in the Atomic Age* (1983) brings under one cover his various writings, some of them previously not published, about the nuclear arms race and the need to halt it.

As for his published lectures, *American Diplomacy: 1900–1950* (1951) amounts to a sustained criticism of what he has deplored as the moralistic-legalistic approach in U.S. foreign policy. The book was widely admired as a succinct statement of the realist position and became a primer for generations of U.S. college students interested in foreign affairs. Its appendix includes the entire X-Article. Realist themes are also developed in the following books, which additionally include analyses of political dynamics in the Soviet bloc, potential points of cooperation and rivalry between East and West, and practical suggestions for U.S. foreign policy: *Realities of American Foreign Policy* (1954), *Russia, the Atom and the West* (1957), and *On Dealing with the Communist World* (1964). Of the three, the most significant is *Russia, the Atom and the West*, in which Kennan proposed two controversial schemes: a joint Soviet-U.S. withdrawal from central Europe, and a militia-type defense for the continental NATO states. Neither idea advanced very far in the councils of NATO governments, but each stirred a lively public debate about Europe's political and security future.

Kennan's *Russia and the West under Lenin and Stalin* (1960), based on his Chichele Lectures, is a scholarly assessment of Soviet-Western relations from 1918 to 1953. His *Democracy and the Student Left* (1968), based on a talk delivered at Swarthmore College, was published at the height of student activism in the United States. The book contains an uncompromising critique of the role of civil disobedience in American society.

He has also published numerous articles, book reviews, and editorials. Interviews and congressional testimony have appeared in published form as well. Those of major interest to students of U.S. foreign policy are listed chronologically in David Mayers, *George Kennan and the Dilemmas of US Foreign Policy* (1988). Also see Kennan et al., *Encounters with Kennan: The Great Debate* (1979).

As of 1991, four books have been published about Kennan and at least one more is in progress. Barton Gellman's *Contending with Kennan: Toward a Philosophy of American Power* (1984) and Anders Stephanson's *Kennan and the Art of Foreign Policy* (1989) review the thought and literary qualities of Kennan's written work. They treat his career in government but mainly as it affected his evolving public philosophy. Mayers's *George Kennan and the Dilemmas of US Foreign Policy* and Walter Hixson's *George Kennan: Cold War Iconoclast* (1989) also examine Kennan's political theory. But in contrast with the above, they place greater emphasis on assessing his career in the government apparatus and his part in formulating and executing foreign policy.

Virtually every student of twentieth-century U.S. foreign policy tries to come to grips with Kennan's intellectual and practical position in policymaking. The following are especially worthwhile: John Gaddis's *The Strategies of Containment: A Critical Appraisal of Postwar American National Security Policy* (1982) describes Kennan's version of containment and uses it as a point of reference in explaining U.S. Cold War policy. Lloyd Gardner's *Architects of Illusion: Men and Ideas in American Foreign Policy* (1970) includes a critique of Kennan from the standpoint of Cold War revisionism. Martin Herz, ed., *Decline of the West? George Kennan and His Critics* (1978), includes transcripts of conversations with Kennan and remarks by a number of academic observers. Walter Isaacson and Thomas Evan's *The Wise Men: Six Friends and the World They Made* (1986) includes colorful anecdotal information about Kennan. Anna Kasten Nelson, ed., *The State Department Policy Planning Staff Papers*, 3 vols. (1983), reproduces all of the final recommendations made by the Policy Planning Staff during Kennan's tenure as director. Michael Joseph Smith's *Realist Thought from Weber to Kissinger* (1986) compares Kennan's realism with five other representatives of that school. Kenneth Thompson's *Masters of International Thought* (1980) includes a chapter on Kennan's formative experiences and the development of his ideas. Daniel Yergin's *Shattered Peace: The Origins of the Cold War and the National Security State* (1977) looks at Kennan's contribution to forming the American hard-line position against the Soviet Union.

There are hundreds of articles in scholarly and other journals and newspapers about Kennan. Many of these are listed in Mayers's *George Kennan and the Dilemmas of US Foreign Policy.*

Bibliography

Works by Kennan

Kennan, George F. *American Diplomacy: 1900–1950*. Chicago: University of Chicago Press, 1951.

———. *The Cloud of Danger: Current Realities of American Foreign Policy*. Boston: Little, Brown, 1977.

———. *The Decline of Bismarck's European Order*. Princeton, N.J.: Princeton University Press, 1979.

———. *Democracy and the Student Left*. Boston: Little, Brown, 1968.

———. *The Fateful Alliance*. New York: Pantheon, 1984.

———. *From Prague after Munich: Diplomatic Papers, 1938–1940*. Princeton N.J.: Princeton University Press, 1968.

———. *The Marquis de Custine and His "Russia in 1839."* Princeton, N.J.: Princeton University Press, 1971.

———. *Memoirs: 1925–1950*. Boston: Little, Brown, 1967.

———. *Memoirs: 1950–1963*. Boston: Little, Brown, 1972.

———. *The Nuclear Delusion: Soviet-American Relations in the Atomic Age*. New York: Pantheon, 1983.

———. *On Dealing with the Communist World*. New York: Harper and Row, 1964.

———. *Realities of American Foreign Policy*. Princeton, N.J.: Princeton University Press, 1954.

———. *Russia and the West under Lenin and Stalin*. Boston: Little, Brown, 1960.

———. *Russia, the Atom and the West*. New York: Harper, 1957.

———. *Sketches from a Life*. New York: Pantheon, 1989.

———. *Soviet-American Relations, 1917–1920*. Vol. 1, *Russia Leaves the War*. Princeton, N.J.: Princeton University Press, 1956. Vol. 2, *The Decision to Intervene*. Princeton N.J.: Princeton University Press, 1958.

———. *Soviet Foreign Policy, 1917–1941*. Princeton, N.J.: Van Nostrand, 1960.

———, et al. *Encounters with Kennan: The Great Debate*. London: Frank Cass, 1979.

Books about Kennan

Gellman, Barton. *Contending with Kennan: Toward a Philosophy of American Power*. New York: Praeger, 1984.

Hixson, Walter. *George Kennan: Cold War Iconoclast*. New York: Columbia University Press, 1989.

Mayers, David. *George Kennan and the Dilemmas of US Foreign Policy*. New York: Oxford University Press, 1988.

Stephanson, Anders. *Kennan and the Art of Foreign Policy*. Cambridge, Mass.: Harvard University Press, 1989.

Related Works

Gaddis, John. *The Strategies of Containment: A Critical Appraisal of Postwar American National Security*. New York: Oxford University Press, 1982.

Gardner, Lloyd. *Architects of Illusion: Men and Ideas in American Foreign Policy*. Chicago: Quadrangle Books, 1970.

Herz, Martin, ed. *Decline of the West? George Kennan and His Critics*. Washington, D.C.: Ethics and Public Policy Center, Georgetown University, 1978.

Isaacson, Walter, and Thomas Evan. *The Wise Men: Six Friends and the World They Made*. New York: Simon and Schuster, 1986.

Nelson, Anna Kasten, ed. *The State Department Policy Planning Staff Papers*. 3 vols. New York: Garland, 1983.

Smith, Michael Joseph. *Realist Thought from Weber to Kissinger*. Baton Rouge: Louisiana State University Press, 1986.

Thompson, Kenneth. *Masters of International Thought*. Baton Rouge: Louisiana State University Press, 1980.

Yergin, Daniel. *Shattered Peace: The Origins of the Cold War and the National Security State*. Boston: Houghton Mifflin, 1977.

DAVID MAYERS

Vladimir Ilyich (Ulyanov) Lenin (1870–1924). The second son of Ilya and Maria Ulyanov, Vladimir Ilyich Ulyanov was born on April 10, 1870, in the town of Simbirsk, on the Volga River. He did not use the name Lenin, after the Lena River, until 1901, when he settled on it as a kind of pen name. His father, a man of non-Russian, Kalmyk descent, was a former science teacher who became a provincial director of schools and was granted a rank of nobility for services rendered to the tsarist regime. His mother was of German (and possibly Jewish) ancestry, the daughter of a doctor who bequeathed her a handsome estate where Lenin spent much time as a boy. From their parents, Lenin and his siblings, all of whom became revolutionaries, learned traits of discipline and diligence, a feel for foreign languages, and a love of novels, especially those of Ivan Turgenev.

The Volga River region of Russia, where Lenin grew up, is in the center of the country, where Europe and Asia meet, intermingle, and compete. After the sixteenth century, the non-Slavic, Asian population of the area became increasingly colonized and dominated by the Russians. The fact that Lenin inherited from his father certain Mongolian facial features and lived among Asian minorities helps account for his later denunciations of "Great Russian chauvinism" and his sympathy for Asian struggles against Western imperialism.

Lenin's roots also help explain how Marx's writings, which refer rather contemptuously to the "idiocy of rural life," came to be revised and applied to rural areas around the world. Additionally, the Volga region had been the site of titanic peasant wars in the past, and these, according to Leon Trotsky in *Young Lenin*, came to constitute "the authentic peasant-revolutionary tradition of old Russia."

Lenin's formal education witnessed a string of gold medals for excellence in elementary and secondary school. His entry into the University of Kazan in 1887 was facilitated by the father of Alexander Kerensky, a Simbirsk school official whose son's government Lenin would overthrow thirty years later. Lenin's stay at the university was short; he was expelled for taking part in a student demonstration and returned to his mother's estate. There he began a serious study of Karl Marx's *Das Kapital*, translated into Russian by the famous anarchist Michael Bakunin.

In 1887 Lenin's brother, Alexander, was hanged for his involvement in an amateurish regicide plot. The fact that Alexander Ulyanov had toward the end of his life shifted his interests from science (he had studied the sex lives of worms) to political and social theory, especially Marxism, deeply influenced young Lenin. Observers who saw him studying Marx's writings noted that for young Vladimir "Marxism was not a conviction but a religion," and may indeed have filled a void left by his rejection of organized religion. At the same time, Lenin developed an arrogance, an insolence, and a tendency to mock his enemies that would mark his political behavior in later life.

Lenin acquired an "external" (nonresidential) law degree from St. Petersburg University, passing his examinations in record time. A sympathetic biographer, Christopher Hill, argues that Lenin pledged himself to become a "professional revolutionary" as early as December 1887 and that his law studies "may have proved to be of more use in his subsequent career than is often the case." Indeed, Lenin's study of such topics as the history of Russian slavery, the village commune, wage questions, and the rights of neutrals in international law found its way into his most "scientific" writings, *The Development of Capitalism in Russia* (1899) and *Imperialism, the Highest Stage of Capitalism* (1916).

Lenin may have turned to revolutionary activities and writing because of his failure as a lawyer. He practiced for only a year, in the town of Samara, defending those accused of "petty crimes of poverty." After securing only one acquittal among the dozen cases he handled, he moved to St. Petersburg, ostensibly to practice law but in reality to join fellow Marxists. He was arrested and exiled to Siberia but later continued his vocation in Germany, publishing the party newspaper *Iskra* (The Spark).

In Germany, Lenin was influenced by Karl Kautsky, the leading theoretician of the German Social Democrats. Though Lenin denounced Kautsky in 1918 as a "renegade," the German's book, *Social Revolution*, taught Lenin that armed struggle, and even civil war, would be necessary to topple governments that embarked upon "imperialist wars." From Kautsky, Lenin derived his controversial position of "revolutionary defeatism," where defeat in wartime could become an "accelerator of revolutionary development." The Paris Commune of 1871 had proven the truth of that observation, and the 1905 revolution in Russia, precipitated by the Russian loss in the Russo-Japanese War, drove the point home again.

The 1905 revolution taught Lenin a number of important lessons. It witnessed the birth of a new form of struggle, the general strike, organized by recently formed "soviets" of workers elected in factories. Lenin, who later saw this as a "dress rehearsal," rhapsodized over revolts that were "the greatest movements of the proletariat since the Commune," and later assured his comrades that "1905 will come again. That is how the workers look at things. For them that year of struggle provided a model of what has to be done."

Another lesson Lenin learned in 1905 was that troops of the enemy could be won over to the side of the revolution. As early as July 1906 he urged his comrades to "look at the unrest in the armed forces, at the demands the soldiers are making. Try to regard soldiers who risk being shot for insubordination as . . . part of the people." Later, in 1917, Lenin's Bolsheviks were more successful than any other party in enlisting the troops in Petrograd to their cause.

The violence that accompanied the 1905 revolution also taught Lenin to expect, and even embrace, civil and guerrilla warfare. Any moral condemnation of civil war would be incompatible with Marxism. While the terrorism of his brother's day was the work of intellectual conspirators, Lenin believed that guerrilla warfare was something now waged by the working class. These views not only helped Lenin obtain and hold on to state power, they also sanctioned the civil and guerrilla wars that brought Marxist movements into power elsewhere in later years.

The 1905 revolution had a ripple effect in Asia and the Middle East, sparking nationalist, anti-imperialist upheavals in such places as China, India, and Turkey. Lenin noticed this and in 1908 wrote that a future Russian revolution would have a "great international ally both in Europe and in Asia." Russia, as a Eurasian nation, was particularly qualified to coordinate struggles on both continents, and Lenin would later engage in demographic demagoguery by pointing to the oppressed masses in the colonial world and claiming them as allies; privately, however, he had little faith in the fidelity of these allies, saying that they would support him in the same way a rope supports a hanged man.

Lenin's concern with the struggles of ethnic groups and nationalities, though sharpened by events in the wake of the 1905 revolution, had been with him since his youth along the Volga River. Lenin saw Russia as a "prisonhouse of nationalities." Armed revolts in Poland, the Baltic states, and the Caucasus region had accompanied the 1905 uprising, and Lenin hoped to exploit popular hatred of Russification policies in the border states. In 1914 he tried to reconcile internationalism with support for nationalist struggles by asserting that the task of "proletarian parties . . . must be two-fold: to recognize the right of all nations to self determination [and to] maintain a close, unbreakable alliance in the class struggle of proletarians of all nations." But since the leaders of nationalist struggles for independence were not usually proletarian, Lenin often confronted contradictions not easily reconciled. After coming to power, he eventually recognized the non-Marxist governments of Poland and the Baltic states in 1920, but he also sent the Red Army into Georgia to crush a republic led by the Mensheviks—fellow Marxist socialists.

The Bolsheviks came to power largely on the strength of their opposition to World War I and Lenin's ability to implement his view that "imperialist wars" could be used for revolutionary purposes. In 1907, at a conference of the Second International in Stuttgart, Germany, he joined others in sponsoring a resolution that called on member parties to "utilize the crisis created by war to rouse the masses and . . . hasten the downfall of capitalist class rule." Wars, like other disasters, helped fulfill his cynical motto: *khuzhe, liuche*—"the worse, the better." His view of war was not unlike a notion he expressed about a famine that killed a million or more Russians in 1891: "The famine threatens to create serious disturbances and possibly the destruction of the entire bourgeois order." Efforts to feed the hungry amounted to "saccharine sweet sentimentality so characteristic of our intelligentsia," a statement one scholar has termed "the authentic voice of Lenin." Whereas most Russian intellectuals felt a duty to suffer for the poor, Lenin saw the suffering of the people as grist for the revolutionary mills.

In exile in Switzerland at the beginning of World War I, Lenin attended the Zimmerwald conference of the Second International in 1915, where he developed a plan to end World War I by converting the imperialist war into class (or civil) war within each country. While this idea appalled many socialist intellectuals in Russia and in the West, it apparently appealed to a large number of peasant-soldiers.

In 1917 Lenin returned to Russia from exile, demanding, among other things, that his party encourage peasants to leave the army, seize the estates of their landlords, and "carry the class war to the village[s]." After coming to power, he insisted on making peace with the Central Powers. Although Lenin never relinquished his belief in the successful global proletarian revolution that Marx had predicted, he denounced and mocked the majority within his own Central Committee, saying that their desire to continue the war against Germany made them "romantic knights" who only hoped to die nobly. Lenin claimed to speak for the peasants, who wanted peace at any price.

Consequently, one of Lenin's first actions as premier in November 1917 was to issue a Decree on Peace, calling for a just and democratic peace on behalf of the "war-exhausted toilers . . . of all belligerent nations." The decree called for a general peace without annexations or indemnities, a formula supported by socialists and liberals such as *Woodrow Wilson. It denounced secret diplomacy and called for a peace that would be just for all nationalities. Shortly thereafter, the newly established People's Commissariat of Foreign Affairs (Narkomindel) published and repudiated the secret treaties that Nicholas II had signed with the Allies—pacts that would have given Russia Constantinople, control of the straits connecting the Black Sea with the Mediterranean, and parts of Persia. Small wonder, then, that the new regime would have friendly relations with anti-imperialist nationalists such as Mustafa Kemal of Turkey.

Soviet scholars have argued that Lenin's decree ushered in a new era of international relations, and they are partly correct. But Woodrow Wilson was also championing a new style of diplomacy. Wilson called for peace without victory, and in his famous Fourteen Points asserted the necessity of national self-determination and an end to secret diplomacy. Wilson, then, vied with Lenin for the hearts and minds of a war-weary world, and each made unprecedented use of propaganda to promote his political agenda, appealing to the people over the heads (or behind the backs) of the European leaders who sought a vindictive, self-serving peace.

Some scholars argue that Lenin was too realistic to believe in the "myth of world revolution'' that he appeared to advocate, and suggest that he actually pursued a narrow, nationalistic policy for the new Soviet Union. The naive attitude toward international relations which Lenin purportedly rejected was perhaps best reflected by Soviet Russia's first commissar for foreign affairs, Leon Trotsky, who felt that his duties would require him to do nothing more than issue a few revolutionary declarations and "shut up shop.''

In early December 1917, Lenin agreed to an armistice with the Central Powers, and when the Germans launched a new offensive against Soviet Russia in early 1918, Lenin was able to convince other members of the Central Committee that peace at almost any price was needed. During the negotiations leading up to the Treaty of Brest-Litovsk, Lenin overcame the objections of some, like Trotsky, who felt that Germany's demands were too excessive, and pushed for the peace, not wanting to endanger the "baby of the revolution." The treaty, signed in March 1918, gave Germany much of western Russia (at least for the duration of the war).

Certainly the negotiations at Brest-Litovsk disabused Lenin and his followers of the belief that either their proletarian slogans and declarations or their anti-bourgeois dress and behavior could easily bring about revolution in the industrialized world. In fact, their plunge into European power politics at Brest-Litovsk revealed to the Bolsheviks both the power inherent in a strong military force and the precarious nature of their very existence. A new sobriety now replaced their rather frivolous attitude toward traditional diplomacy.

The debacle at Brest-Litovsk was followed by the failure of the Spartakist uprising in Berlin (January 1919) and the overthrow of Bolshevik-style regimes in Bavaria (May 1919) and Hungary (August 1919). In the wake of these defeats, Lenin initiated a dual course for Soviet foreign policy. He now sought normal relations with the capitalist world for Soviet Russia, while at the same time calling to life an allegedly independent organization dedicated to the defense of the Soviet regime and the spread of Marxist revolution.

In 1918 Lenin revitalized Narkomindel, replacing Trotsky with the experienced and urbane Georgii Chicherin and instructing Soviet diplomats to seek normal relations with the capitalist states. If the promised workers' revolution was to be delayed, it was imperative for the survival of the socialist regime in Russia to reach an acceptable *modus vivendi* with the capitalist states that surrounded and threatened it. In 1920 and 1921, Soviet Russia signed peace treaties with Lithuania, Latvia, Estonia, Poland, and Finland, and reached trade agreements with Austria, Italy, Norway, and Great Britain. The agreement with Britain was of particular importance given that country's international status.

This policy of "normalcy" paid significant dividends for the Soviets on April 16, 1922, when they signed the Rapallo Treaty with Germany, another pariah state. The Rapallo Treaty, which restored diplomatic relations between the countries, ended Soviet Russia's diplomatic isolation and paired it with an important European state. In the wake of Rapallo, the Soviet Union (the Union of Soviet Socialist Republics was proclaimed on December 30, 1922) established formal diplomatic relations with Great Britain in 1924. Later the same year, the USSR gained diplomatic recognition from France, Italy, Austria, Sweden, Norway, Denmark, Greece, Mexico, and China. Japan followed suit in 1925.

While pursuing normal relations with his capitalist neighbors, Lenin did not abandon the goal of global revolution. In March 1919 he formed the Communist International (Comintern), consisting of representatives from left-wing or Communist movements drawn from throughout the world. Lenin urged his fellow leftists to "smash the state" through armed uprisings. In its first proclamation, "To the Workers of All Countries," the Comintern called upon the proletariat to follow the Bolshevik model in toppling capitalist governments and replacing them with workers' power.

Lenin, however, recognized the need to temper reckless advocacy of revolution with a more pragmatic approach when circumstances called for it. In 1920 he wrote *Left-Wing Communism—An Infantile Disorder*, in which he advocated flexibility and attacked those Communists who refused to participate in trade unions or parliamentary life. Lenin argued that under certain conditions such participation could significantly advance the cause of Marxism.

Although the Soviet government denied any connection to the Comintern, the Bolsheviks in fact controlled it. Lenin's ally, Gregorii Zinoviev, was chairman of the Comintern's executive committee, while another Lenin associate, Karl Radek, was its secretary. Headquartered in Moscow, the Comintern took its marching orders from the Kremlin.

In addition to fomenting revolution, the Comintern also served as a vehicle by which the Russian Communists gained control over Communist movements elsewhere. At the Second Congress of the Comintern, held in Moscow in July 1920, conditions were set down for gaining admission to the organization. Modeled after Lenin's restrictive requirements for admission to and participation in the Bolshevik party, these had the effect of "Bolshevizing" any number of national Communist parties.

Lenin's excursion into the world of post–World War I realpolitik showed him to be an adroit, imaginative, and preeminently practical statesman. The dual nature of Lenin's foreign policy—represented by the Narkomindel and the Comintern—served to both advance Soviet interests and confuse his opponents. In the final year of his life, Lenin struggled with the physical effects of a stroke and was preoccupied with domestic issues and party divisions. He tried in vain to oust *Joseph Stalin from his position as general secretary of the party. When Lenin died on January 21, 1924, Stalin succeeded him and felt safe in making an icon of the founder of the Soviet Union. Stalin's rise to power witnessed the victory of the doctrine known as "socialism in one country" over Trotsky's strategy of permanent revolution, based on the hope that communism would spread westward. Lenin's concept of seeking normal relations with capitalism supplanted strategies of revolutionary war and laid the basis for Stalin's more nationalistic policies.

Lenin, as premier, guiding force behind the Comintern and chairman of the

Council of Defense and Labor, increasingly tried to return Soviet Russia to "normality." He invited foreign capital to invest in his country and sought to attract "bourgeois" specialists to aid in reconstruction. His government played on the conflicts between Germany and the West, and he gave specific (and often cynical) advice on how best to exploit the division that the Treaty of Versailles had created. Lenin viewed that treaty as the "best form of agitation," because it forced a humiliated Germany to turn toward Moscow for trade and aid, both military and economic. Such strategies as denouncing the treaty publicly while welcoming it privately, because it suited Russia's national interests, demonstrate Lenin's Machiavellian duplicity. But they also reflect the dilemma Lenin and his successors faced in trying to defend national interests through diplomacy while posing as revolutionary leaders dedicated to overthrowing the status quo.

Annotated Bibliography

The most important primary sources for evaluating Lenin as a statesman, aside from his own works and words, are to be found in *Documenty Vneshnei Politiki SSSR*, which the archives of the Soviet foreign ministry began publishing in 1958 under the editorship of G. Fokina and others. The strategies of the Red Army need to be analyzed by students of foreign policy, and archival sources began to appear in 1969, edited by A. V. Golubev and others, under the title *Direktivy Glavnogo Komandovaniia Krasnoi Armii*. Beginning in 1971, directives of the front commanders, as well as of the central command, began to be published. More recently, foreign scholars have been given direct access to archives, although access to party archives, especially the proceedings of the Politburo and Secretariat, is more difficult. An important source in English is Robert H. McNeal, *Guide to the Decisions of the Communist Party of the Soviet Union, 1917–1967* (1972).

A large number of important documents that Leon Trotsky brought with him when he was expelled from the Soviet Union are in the Houghton Library at Harvard University. These have been translated by Jan Meijer and published as *The Trotsky Papers*, 2 vols. (1964–1971). Other sources of Soviet documents outside of the Soviet Union are the Hoover Library at Stanford University and the Beaverbrook Library in London, where the Lloyd George Papers contain invaluable intercepts of Soviet diplomatic communications.

Among the statesmen who changed the world, Lenin was probably the most prolific writer, with the possible exception of ˙Winston Churchill. The fifth edition of his *Polnoe Sobranie Sochinenii* (Complete Collection of Works) comes to fifty-five volumes. The publication of this edition began in 1958, supplanting *Leninskii Sbornik* (Leninist Collection) and an earlier third edition that was translated into English as *Collected Works* (in forty-five volumes). The serious student of Lenin should learn Russian and consult the latest edition, which contains important materials, such as telegrams, not included in earlier editions.

Lenin's most important work is no doubt *Imperialism, the Highest Stage of Capitalism* (1916). Some argue that it is one of the most significant books of the twentieth century, although in it Lenin relied heavily on the works of others, such as John Hobson and Rudolf Hilferding. It became popular after Lenin's rise to power and appeals today to those seeking a single explanation for both war and the mass misery that exists in Third World countries. Another significant work of Lenin on foreign policy issues is *Left-Wing*

Communism—An Infantile Disorder (1920), in which he justifies the Treaty of Brest-Litovsk and denounces leftists within and outside his own party who opposed signing the so-called annexationist peace.

Until recently, most Soviet writing on Lenin has been hagiographical, while in the West most non-Marxist writers have engaged in what might be called "demonography." Those interested in surveying the immense literature on Lenin in English or English translation should see David and Melinda Egan, *V. I. Lenin: An Annotated Bibliography of English-Language Sources to 1980* (1982). Consisting of almost three thousand books and articles, some from Soviet works in translation, it rightly claims to be "nearly a balance of critical, non-critical, and hagiographical entries." Scholars can benefit from the labors of Soviet archivists who published a twelve-volume *Biograficheskaya Khronika* (1970–1982), which chronicles almost every day of Lenin's adult life, sometimes on an hourly basis, and cites sources.

An overwhelming number of Lenin biographies exist. Perhaps the best single-volume biography of Lenin in English is Ronald W. Clark, *Lenin: The Man Behind the Mask* (1988). Other important biographies include David Shub, *Lenin* (1948), Bertram D. Wolfe, *Three Who Made a Revolution*, (1964), Adam B. Ulam, *The Bolsheviks* (1965), Harold Shukman, *Lenin and the Russian Revolution* (1967), and Robert Conquest, *V.I. Lenin* (1972).

The official view of Soviet policies during and after Lenin's premiership is found in A. Gromyko and B. Ponomaryov, eds., *Istoriia vneshnei politiki SSSR: 1917–1985* (1986). Other compilations include volumes detailing everything Lenin ever wrote about specific topics ranging from Azerbaijan to library organization.

Louis Fischer, *The Soviets in World Affairs, 1917–1929*, 2 vols. (1951), and *Russia's Road from Peace to War: Soviet Foreign Relations, 1917–1941* (1969), provide a good overview of Soviet foreign policy in the years after the revolution. So too does Adam B. Ulam, *Expansion and Coexistence: Soviet Foreign Policy, 1917–1973* (1974). Another valuable source is Thomas T. Hammond, *Soviet Foreign Relations and World Communism: An Annotated Bibliography of 7,000 Books in 30 Languages* (1965).

As with Woodrow Wilson, scholars debate the question of idealism versus realism in Lenin's foreign policy. Arno J. Mayer, *Wilson vs. Lenin: Political Origins of the New Diplomacy, 1917–1918* (1963), compares Lenin's plan for ending the war to those of the idealistic American president. But Piero Melograni, *Lenin and the Myth of World Revolution: Ideology and Reasons of State, 1917–1920* (1989), concludes that Lenin was too realistic seriously to advocate world revolution at the expense of Soviet national interests in 1917 and 1918. Christopher Hill, *Lenin and the Russian Revolution* (1971), and Richard Debo, *Revolution and Survival: The Foreign Policy of Soviet Russia, 1917–1918* (1979), applaud Lenin for signing the Treaty of Brest-Litovsk as necessary for Soviet survival, but Rolf H.W. Theen, *Lenin: Genesis and Development of a Revolutionary* (1973), characterizes Lenin as a failed statesman, while Stefan T. Possony, *Lenin: The Compulsive Revolutionary* (1964), argues that he was a traitor for dealing with hostile powers.

Lenin's willingness to compromise his principles has also generated historical controversy. Robert Conquest describes Lenin as a "detester of compromise," comparable to Woodrow Wilson in the fight for the ratification of the Treaty of Versailles. On the other hand, Ronald W. Clark praises Lenin for his ability to bend with the wind. Perhaps the best insight into Lenin's thought processes is found in Edmund Wilson, *To the Finland Station* (1953).

The Comintern is dealt with in James W. Hulse, *The Forming of the Communist International* (1964), Franz Borkenau, *World Communism: A History of the Communist*

International (1962), Branko Lazitch and Milorad M. Drachkovitch, *Lenin and the Comintern* (1972), and Albert S. Lindeman, *The "Red Years": European Socialism Versus Bolshevism, 1919–1921* (1974).

For Soviet relations with specific countries in the post-revolutionary years, see E. H. Carr, *German-Soviet Relations Between the Two World Wars, 1919–1939* (1951), Werner T. Angress, *Still-Born Revolution: The Communist Bid for Power in Germany, 1921–1923* (1963), Gerald Freund, *Unholy Alliance: Russo-German Relations from the Treaty of Brest-Litovsk to the Treaty of Berlin* (1957), Richard H. Ullman, *Anglo-Soviet Relations, 1917–1921*, 3 vols. (1961–1973), Ronald Tiersky, *French Communism, 1920– 1927* (1974), and Allen S. Whiting, *Soviet Policies in China, 1917–1924* (1954). Special mention should be made of the erudite and perceptive study by ˙George F. Kennan, *Russia and the West under Lenin and Stalin* (1961).

Bibliography

Adams, Arthur E., ed. *Readings in Soviet Foreign Policy: Theory and Practice*. Boston: Heath, 1961.

Angress, Werner T. *Still-Born Revolution: The Communist Bid for Power in Germany, 1921–1923*. Princeton, N.J.: Princeton University Press, 1963.

Balabanoff, Angelica. *Impressions of Lenin*. Ann Arbor: University of Michigan Press, 1968.

Borkenau, Franz. *World Communism: A History of the Communist International*. Ann Arbor: University of Michigan Press, 1962.

Carr, E. H. *German-Soviet Relations Between the Two World Wars, 1919–1939*. Baltimore: Johns Hopkins University Press, 1951.

Clark, Ronald W. *Lenin: The Man Behind the Mask*. London: Faber, 1988.

Conquest, Robert. *V. I. Lenin*. New York: Viking, 1972.

Debo, Richard. *Revolution and Survival: The Foreign Policy of Soviet Russia, 1917– 1918*. Toronto: University of Toronto Press, 1979.

Egan, David, and Melinda Egan. *V. I. Lenin: An Annotated Bibliography of English-Language Sources to 1980*. Metuchen, N.J.: Scarecrow, 1982.

Fiddick, Thomas C. *Russia's Retreat from Poland, 1920: From Permanent Revolution to Peaceful Coexistence*. New York: St. Martin's Press, 1990.

Fischer, Louis. *The Life of Lenin*. New York: Harper and Row, 1964.

————. *Russia's Road from Peace to War: Soviet Foreign Relations, 1917–1941*. New York: Harper and Row, 1969.

————. *The Soviets in World Affairs, 1917–1929*. 2 vols. 2nd ed. Princeton, N.J.: Princeton University Press, 1951.

Freund, Gerald. *Unholy Alliance: Russo-German Relations from the Treaty of Brest-Litovsk to the Treaty of Berlin*. New York: Harcourt, Brace, 1957.

Gromyko, A., and B. Ponomaryov, eds. *Istoriia vneshnei politiki SSSR: 1917–1985*. 2 vols. Moscow: Nauka, 1986.

Hammond, Thomas T. *Soviet Foreign Relations and World Communism: An Annotated Bibliography of 7,000 Books in 30 Languages*. Princeton, N.J.: Princeton University Press, 1965.

Hill, Christopher. *Lenin and the Russian Revolution*. New York: Penguin, 1971.

Hulse, James W. *The Forming of the Communist International*. Stanford, Calif.: Stanford University Press, 1964.

Kennan, George F. *Russia and the West under Lenin and Stalin*. Boston: Little, Brown, 1961.

Lazitch, B., and M. Drachkovitch. *Lenin and the Comintern*. Stanford, Calif.: Hoover Institution Press, 1972.

Lindemann, Albert S. *The "Red Years": European Socialism Versus Bolshevism, 1919–1921*. Berkeley: University of California Press, 1974.

Mayer, Arno J. *Wilson vs. Lenin: Political Origins of the New Diplomacy, 1917–1918*. Cleveland and New York: World Publishing, 1963.

McNeal, Robert H. *Guide to the Decisions of the Communist Party of the Soviet Union, 1917–1967*. Toronto: University of Toronto Press, 1972.

Melograni, Piero. *Lenin and the Myth of World Revolution: Ideology and Reasons of State, 1917–1920*. Translated by Julie Lerro. Atlantic Highlands, N.J.: Humanities Press International, 1989.

Page, Stanley W. *Lenin and World Revolution*. New York: New York University Press, 1959.

Possony, Stefan T. *Lenin: The Compulsive Revolutionary*. Chicago: Henry Regnery, 1964.

Schapiro, L., and P. Reddaway, eds. *Lenin: The Man, the Theorist, the Leader—A Reappraisal*. New York: Praeger, 1967.

Shub, David. *Lenin: A Biography*. Garden City, N.Y.: Doubleday, 1948.

Shukman, Harold. *Lenin and the Russian Revolution*. New York: Putnam, 1967.

Theen, Rolf H.W. *Lenin: Genesis and Development of a Revolutionary*. Princeton, N.J.: Princeton University Press, 1973.

Tiersky, Ronald. *French Communism, 1920–1927*. New York: Columbia University Press, 1974.

Trotsky, Leon. *The Trotsky Papers*. 2 vols. Translated by Jan Meijer. The Hague: Mouton, 1964–1971.

———. *The Young Lenin*. Edited by Maurice Fiedberg. Translated by Max Eastman. Garden City, N.Y.: Doubleday, 1972.

Trush, M. *Soviet Foreign Policy: Early Years*. Moscow: Novosti Press Agency Publishing House, 1973.

Tucker, Robert C. *Political Culture and Leadership in Soviet Russia: From Lenin to Gorbachev*. New York: Norton, 1987.

Tumarkin, Nina. *Lenin Lives! The Lenin Cult in Soviet Russia*. Cambridge, Mass.: Harvard University Press, 1983.

Ulam, Adam B. *The Bolsheviks*. New York: Macmillan, 1965.

———. *Expansion and Coexistence: Soviet Foreign Policy, 1917–1973*. 2nd ed. New York: Praeger, 1974.

Uldricks, Teddy J. *Diplomacy and Ideology: The Origins of Soviet Foreign Relations, 1917–1930*. Beverly Hills: Sage, 1979.

Ullman, Richard H. *Anglo-Soviet Relations, 1917–1921*. 3 vols. Princeton, N.J.: Princeton University Press, 1961–1973.

Valentinov, N. [N. V. Volski]. *The Early Years of Lenin*. Translated and edited by Rolf H.W. Theen. Ann Arbor: University of Michigan Press, 1969.

Wheeler-Bennett, John W. *Brest-Litovsk: The Forgotten Peace, March, 1918*. New York: Norton, 1971.

Whiting, Allen S. *Soviet Policies in China, 1917–1924*. New York: Columbia University Press, 1954.

Wilson, Edmund. *To the Finland Station*. New York: Doubleday, 1953.
Wolfe, Bertram D. *Three Who Made a Revolution*. Rev. ed. New York: Time, 1964.
Wolfenstein, E. Victor. *The Revolutionary Personality: Lenin, Trotsky, Gandhi*. Princeton, N.J.: Princeton University Press, 1967.
Zetkin, Klara. *Reminiscences of Lenin*. London: Modern Books, 1929.

THOMAS C. FIDDICK

David Lloyd George (1863–1945).   David Lloyd George, later first Earl Lloyd-George of Dwyfor, was born on January 17, 1863, in Manchester, England, but raised by an uncle in the North Wales communities of Llanystumdwy and Criccieth. Bilingual in Welsh and English, Lloyd George was trained as a solicitor and practiced law in North Wales and, after 1897, in London. Following election to the House of Commons as a Liberal in 1890, he concentrated on Welsh local issues until 1900, when he became nationally known as a critic of the Boer War. Although stigmatized by Conservatives and some Liberals as "pro-Boer," Lloyd George strengthened his reputation within his party by leading the resistance to the Conservative government's unpopular Education Act of 1902. In 1905 he was included in Sir Henry Campbell-Bannerman's Liberal ministry.

Lloyd George distinguished himself as the Liberal minister for trade (1905–1908) and finance (1908–1915) under prime ministers Campbell-Bannerman and Herbert H. Asquith. Legislation helpful to business and a commitment to improving national efficiency mitigated Lloyd George's previous reputation as a radical populist. His sponsorship of the People's Budget of 1909—with its provisions for taxing the wealthy and land revaluation—and the National Insurance Act of 1911 made his reputation as a constructive social reformer. Historians credit Lloyd George with being one of the founders of the British welfare state. In 1910 he proposed a national coalition government to solve long-standing issues such as Irish government and free trade versus protectionism, but neither the leaders of his own party nor those of the Conservative opposition were receptive.

Before World War I, Lloyd George's interest in international affairs was limited but not insignificant. He was a frequent visitor to the European continent, and in contact with politicians and journalists who kept him well informed of current developments. He had also visited Canada, Argentina, Lebanon, and North Africa, and was much more widely traveled than the Liberal foreign minister, Sir Edward Grey. Lloyd George's antipathy to the Boer War for its aggression against small nations inspired the mistaken belief that he was a pacifist and an anti-imperialist. He was in fact a patriotic, and occasionally bellicose, nationalist. His budgets as finance minister included generous appropriations for military and naval defense, and universal military training was one of the schemes of his abortive coalition. In 1911, in his outspoken Mansion House speech during the second Moroccan crisis, Lloyd George warned Germany against provoking Britain. Subsequently he urged Anglo-German détente so that defense costs could be reduced and the funds saved for domestic programs. Nevertheless, Lloyd

George was well aware of—and approved of—his government's strategic plans for fighting Germany should there be a European war.

Lloyd George was a key figure in the July-August 1914 cabinet crisis over intervention in the war. His solid credentials as a worker for peace enabled him to help Prime Minister Asquith lead a united cabinet and party into the conflict, using defense of Belgian neutrality under a treaty commitment as a convenient rationalization. When it became clear late in 1914 that there would be no quick victory on the western European front, Lloyd George was among the ministers urging consideration of alternative strategies, including the opening of a new theater in the Balkans or the Middle East. He also censured the government's "business as usual" attitude, its unwillingness to recognize the war's magnitude, and its inefficiency in supplying the troops with munitions.

In May 1915, Lloyd George at last got his national coalition, which Asquith accepted to avoid a political crisis. The finance minister gave up his prestigious office to take on a newly created munitions ministry (1915–1916) and then the War Department (1916). In these posts and in the cabinet, Lloyd George became known as the driving force behind the war effort but still was unable significantly to influence strategic policies. To do so—and particularly to commit the government to total defeat of Germany and its allies—he needed to be prime minister. A long-developing conspiracy by Conservatives, dissident Liberals, and powerful newspapermen brought Asquith down in December 1916 and elevated Lloyd George to the premiership.

The year 1917 was frustrating for the new prime minister. Establishment of a five-member war cabinet, a cabinet secretariat, a brain trust of confidential aides, and an imperial war conference of dominion ministers produced a more efficient war, but less was accomplished than he had hoped. Military and naval professionals, whom Lloyd George viewed as stodgy and unimaginative, resisted his blandishments. Hard-won success in persuading the navy to adopt a convoy system to protect shipping from German submarines (possibly saving Britain from famine) was not paralleled by much progress manipulating the generals. Backed by the king, Conservative magnates, and the press, Sir Douglas Haig, Sir William Robertson, and fellow officers overruled Lloyd George's attempts to halt the Passchendaele offensive, which yielded some 400,000 casualties. This disaster, followed by the Caporetto rout in Italy, gave Lloyd George the evidence he needed to persuade British and allied generals to accept a Supreme War Council coordinating strategy—still far short of what he wanted: unity of command.

In the same year, 1917, Russia, following revolution, dropped out of the war against Germany, to be replaced by the United States, and major British gains were made in the Middle East against Germany's Turkish ally. The territory acquired by conquest from Turkey would be added to Britain's sphere of influence, creating many postwar headaches for the nation's policymakers. Not least of these was the Jewish national home established in Palestine by the Balfour Declaration. No less troublesome would be Britain's mixed signals to France,

Italy, Greece, and Turkey's Arab rebels over the disposition of conquered Middle Eastern lands.

Russia's defection enabled Germany to move troops from east to west and launch a great offensive in spring 1918 that came uncomfortably close to smashing through British and French lines. This crisis enabled Lloyd George at last to achieve his unity of command objective. The recalcitrant Haig assented to strategic direction from a French general, Ferdinand Foch. Failure of the spring offensive ended Germany's last hope of winning. Impressive numbers of American troops restored a war of movement in the west for the first time since 1914, and in November Germany acknowledged that it had lost by seeking an armistice. The American intervention had ended the stalemate in the west, and President *Woodrow Wilson's idealistic peace plan—the Fourteen Points—was the basis for Germany's armistice plea.

Lloyd George was esteemed in Britain as "the man who won the war," and his coalition won an overwhelming electoral victory in December 1918. His postwar aims were comparatively modest—essentially a return to the territorial status quo ante bellum, except in the Middle East and Africa where British forces had conquered enemy possessions. They were upstaged by President Wilson's grandiose projects for national self-determination and an international peace-keeping body, not to mention the vengeful claims of Britain's allies. As one of the Big Four national leaders dominating the 1919 Paris Peace Conference, Lloyd George espoused a policy of realism and moderation aimed at reviving European stability and prosperity. He warned that a Germany severely weakened by annexations and indemnities might fall victim to communism and would assuredly seek revenge. Lloyd George effectively prevented hard-liners—notably France's Georges Clemenceau—from imposing a Carthaginian peace. However, the imperfect, compromise treaties that emerged left both winners and losers dissatisfied and bitter, Europe fragmented (especially because of the disappearance of the Austro-Hungarian Empire), and the Middle East a tinderbox. Although Lloyd George could see some merit to Wilson's panacea, the League of Nations, he had little confidence in it.

When he left Paris in June 1919, Lloyd George knew that much work remained if the peace settlement was to last and the shattered international economy be restored. He also had grave domestic problems to confront: recession, unemployment, strikes, a housing shortage, and an Irish revolution. For the next three years, Lloyd George raced back and forth between London—where he tried to keep the lid on his British and Irish troubles—and a series of international conferences in Europe. When not engrossed in foreign affairs, Lloyd George recorded some notable successes on the home front, including smooth demobilization of the wartime army, reconversion of war industries, extension of welfare benefits, house building, conciliation of major labor disputes, and—especially—settlement of the Irish imbroglio.

The new style of conference diplomacy, largely invented by Lloyd George, overshadowed the "old diplomacy" of foreign ministries and ambassadors, and was deplored by Britain's own diplomatic professionals led by Lord Curzon, foreign minister after 1919. As the only major European politician to hold office continuously through the war and the immediate postwar period, Lloyd George was the key figure at these conferences of government heads and ministers. Commanding them with his experience, assertiveness, and mental agility, and aided by his brain trust, the Welsh statesman attempted with mixed success to reconstruct international relations. Among the positive results of the postwar conferences were the paring down of German reparations, early withdrawal of occupation troops, and measures to restore trade. There were also failures, especially the collapse at Genoa in 1922 of Lloyd George's ambitious plan for stabilizing major currencies, settling pre-Soviet Russian debts, readmitting Soviet Russia to the European community, and creating new markets in central and eastern Europe.

Improving relations with Russia's new regime was one of Lloyd George's major preoccupations, pursued against opposition within his government by *Winston Churchill and other anti-Communist zealots. British troops dispatched to Russia during the war to prevent German encroachment were used (against Lloyd George's better judgment) during 1919 to support Whites against Reds in the civil war, but were evacuated in 1920 once Communist hegemony was certain. An Anglo-Russian trade treaty restored normal commerce in 1921, and ministers favoring assistance to the Poles in their war with Russia were rebuffed. The failure of the Genoa plan, however, ruined Lloyd George's project to restore full diplomatic relations with Russia.

More successful were Lloyd George's negotiations with the United States to avoid a naval rivalry that might bankrupt Britain. The Americans, now the world's second naval power, were threatening to challenge Britain for first place. The Anglo-American parity in large warships agreed to at the Washington Conference of 1921–1922 prevented repetition of the costly prewar naval race with Germany. To obtain these favorable terms, the British delegation at Washington (Lloyd George was too busy in London to come) had to accept American demands for nonrenewal of the Anglo-Japanese Alliance of 1902, which Lloyd George wanted to save. In effect, this meant abandoning Japanese friendship to keep American. Britain's dissociation from Japan had a major effect on the policies of both countries during the 1930s and 1940s. The Washington Naval Treaty, or Five-Power Treaty, along with adoption of a ten-year holiday on naval construction, enabled Lloyd George's government to cut defense costs by 80 percent between 1919 and 1922.

Wartime financial costs coupled with postwar hard times necessitated retrenchment for both defense and imperial administration. Lloyd George, although far from a rampant imperialist, was proud of British trusteeship of people unready to govern themselves—such as the Africans acquired by conquest from Germany in the war. He also appreciated the geopolitical significance of a worldwide empire. Regretting the diminished role circumstances forced upon Britain in its new Middle Eastern dependencies, he reluctantly allowed colonial minister Winston Churchill to cut back military commitments from Egypt to Iraq. Although Lloyd George sympathized with Indian nationalism, he did not think the Indians ready for self-government, let alone independence. He found his pro-nationalist minister for India, Edwin Montagu, a difficult colleague, but supported the latter's imaginative Government of India Act of 1919—forerunner of the 1935 law establishing responsible government for Indian provinces.

Lloyd George also crossed swords with both Montagu and Curzon over Turkish policy—an issue that would be fatal to his government. These ministers saw the 1920 Treaty of Sèvres, which ceded Turkey's Smyrna region to Greece, as eroding British influence in the Muslim world, including India. Lloyd George's loathing of Turks and partiality for Greeks—dating from his Gladstonian youth— put him on a collision course with Turkish nationalists led by Mustapha Kemal (later Ataturk). Collapse of the Greek military front in Turkey, and Kemal's invasion of the zone occupied by Britain and France, created a war threat that Lloyd George wanted to meet with force. Lacking the support of France, Italy, and even the self-governing British dominions, however, Lloyd George suffered a political setback when the cabinet resisted his militant policy. Soon after, Conservatives rejected continuation of the coalition, forcing the government's resignation in October 1922.

Although he lived another twenty-two years, Lloyd George never again held office. In 1926 he became leader of the Liberal party after outmaneuvering Asquith's followers, but the party had lost most of its voters to Labour. Lloyd George remained deeply interested in international problems, refought old battles in controversial memoirs in the 1930s, and in the late 1930s was active in the fight against appeasement of Italy and Germany, although he admired *Adolf Hitler. After World War II began in 1939, Lloyd George favored a negotiated peace with Germany. Following the defeat of France in 1940, he argued that Britain alone was not strong enough to win. Lloyd George's defeatist views dissuaded Winston Churchill from giving him a ministerial or ambassadorial appointment. In his last years, Lloyd George was a strong advocate of cooperation with Soviet Russia. He died on March 26, 1945, soon after accepting a peerage, while planning to take part in postwar policy debates in the House of Lords.

Annotated Bibliography

There are important collections of Lloyd George Papers at the House of Lords Record Office, London, and the National Library of Wales, Aberystwyth. The latter, containing mainly family correspondence, has little material relevant to Lloyd George's career as an international statesman.

The documents at the House of Lords Record Office, Houses of Parliament, London SW1A OPW, cover the years 1890 to 1945, but are richest for the war and postwar years, 1914 to 1922. For this period there are over 300 boxes of official and semi-official correspondence, copies of cabinet and departmental papers, notes for speeches, memo-randa by Lloyd George's secretaries and assistants, and press releases and cuttings. Fourteen of these boxes contain diplomatic correspondence, while others include material from the Paris Peace Conference and later international conferences. Many papers were abstracted from official files by Lloyd George, were never returned, and are the only copies. There are detailed finding aids for researchers (H.L.R.O. *Memorandum No. 54* and *Lists No. 117–8*) and no restriction on the use of the papers.

Lloyd George was the author of two multivolume sets of memoirs: *War Memoirs of David Lloyd George* (1933–1936) and *The Truth about the Peace Treaties* (1938). Composed while he was in semi-retirement, they draw heavily upon—and contain many extracts from—official documents, are lucidly written, and are only moderately biased. The long gestation of these memoirs and their controversial use of documents are discussed in Peter Fraser, "Cabinet Secrecy and War Memoirs," *History* 70 (1985): 397–409. More tendentious are the speeches and articles in *Slings and Arrows*, edited by Philip Guedalla, (1929), and the polemical *Truth about Reparations and War Debts* (1932). The ex-premier's highly paid journalism for the Beaverbrook and Hearst newspaper chains in the twenties and thirties, much of it about foreign policy, is scattered through these papers. Lloyd George picked the brains of many experts, including cabinet secretary Sir Maurice Hankey, military analyst Basil Liddell Hart, and members of his former brain trust. The sophistication and comparative restraint of Lloyd George's foreign policy writings owe much to these advisors.

Three diaries furnish significant information and insights about Lloyd George's international statesmanship. The unabridged jottings of Sir George (later Lord) Riddell, Lloyd George's confidant for many years, in *The Riddell Diaries 1908–1923*, edited by John M. McEwen (1986), contain many references to international affairs before, during, and after the Great War. *The Political Diaries of C. P. Scott 1911–1928*, edited by Trevor Wilson (1970), by the *Manchester Guardian* editor known as "Lloyd George's conscience," begins shortly before the second Moroccan crisis. Frances Stevenson, his secretary-mistress, was responsible for *Lloyd George: A Diary* (1971), edited by A.J.P. Taylor, which is especially valuable for the World War I years.

Other published diaries and collections of letters highlight Lloyd George's contributions to war strategy and international politics, including *The Leo Amery Diaries, 1896–1929* (1980), by a Tory politician and wartime advisor; *The Diary of Lord Bertie of Thame* (1924), by a wartime ambassador to France; Lord D'Abernon, *An Ambassador of Peace* (1920–1930), by a financier and diplomat; *The Private Papers of Douglas Haig* (1952), by the British Expeditionary Force commander; Sir James Headlam-Morley, *A Memoir of the Paris Peace Conference 1919* (1972), by a Paris Peace Conference delegate; Thomas Jones, *Whitehall Diary* (1969–1971), by an assistant cabinet secretary; Charles a' Court Repington, *The First World War, 1914–1918: Personal Experiences* (1920), by a military correspondent; Charles Seymour, *Letters from the Paris Peace Conference* (1965), by an American peace conference delegate; Jan Christian Smuts, *Selections from the Smuts Papers, 1886–1950* (1966–1973), by a war cabinet minister; and Sir Charles E. Callwell, *Field-Marshal Sir Henry Wilson: His Life and Diaries* (1927), about Lloyd George's chief wartime military advisor. Also of interest is *Off the Record: Political Interviews 1933–1943* (1973), by W. P. Crozier, Scott's successor at the *Guardian*. It contains transcripts of interviews with Lloyd George as well as observations about him by other interviewees. Randolph S. Churchill and Martin Gilbert, *Winston S. Churchill* (1966–1988), the eight-volume official biography, includes much primary material about Lloyd George, especially in the numerous documentary companion volumes.

Recollections of Lloyd George by his contemporaries abound. Topping the list of those to be consulted respecting his international statesmanship are Lord (formerly Sir Maurice) Hankey, *The Supreme Command 1914–1918* (1961) and *The Supreme Control at the*

Paris Peace Conference, 1919 (1963). These memoirs are based on, and publish extended selections from, the diaries and memoranda of the man who more than any other influenced Lloyd George's strategic thinking during the war and the peace conference. Stephen Roskill, *Hankey: Man of Secrets*, 3 vols. (1970–1974), an exhaustive biography, includes many additional extracts from Hankey's papers. Other germane autobiographical writings are those of L. S. Amery, *My Political Life* (1953–1955); Sir Robert Laird Borden, *Robert Laird Borden: His Memoirs* (1938), wartime Canadian prime minister; Winston Churchill, *The World Crisis, 1911–1918* (1923), cabinet colleague; Georges Clemenceau, *Grandeur and Misery of Victory* (1930), French premier; Ferdinand Foch, *Memoirs* (1931), French general; Lord Hardinge of Penshurst, *Old Diplomacy* (1947), foreign office official; Robert Lansing, *The Big Four and Others of the Peace Conference* (1921), U.S. secretary of state; Basil Liddell Hart, *The Liddell Hart Memoirs* (1965), military advisor to Lloyd George in the 1930s; David Hunter Miller, *My Diary at the Conference of Paris* (1928), U.S. peace conference delegate; and Sir William Robertson, *Soldiers and Statesmen* (1926), wartime general staff chief.

Lloyd George's numerous biographies treat the international aspects of his career in more or less detail, usually emphasizing his World War I leadership. They include Don M. Cregier, *Bounder from Wales* (1976); W. Watkin Davies, *Lloyd George: 1863–1914* (1939); Bentley B. Gilbert, *David Lloyd George: A Political Life* (1987), which ends before August 1914; John Grigg, *Lloyd George*, 3 vols. (1973–1985), which takes the story to 1916; Thomas Jones, *Lloyd George* (1951), still the best short life; Donald McCormick, *The Mask of Merlin* (1963), extremely hostile; Kenneth O. Morgan, *Lloyd George* (1974), lucid and sympathetic; Martin Pugh, *Lloyd George* (1988), readable and brief; and Peter Rowland, *Lloyd George* (1975), rather bogged down in minutiae.

To these general works must be added Michael G. Fry's *Lloyd George and Foreign Policy: The Education of a Statesman, 1890–1916* (1977), the only biographical study to focus exclusively on Lloyd George's role in the making of external policy. A projected sequel to this thoroughly researched work is awaited. W. Watkin Davies, "The Foreign Policy of Lloyd George," *Fortnightly Review*, n.s. 158 (1945): 268–275, links his wartime and postwar initiatives in Europe and the Middle East to his prewar attitudes, which generally stood closer to the Liberal imperialists than to his party's radical internationalists and pacifists. A historiographical article by Kenneth O. Morgan, "Lloyd George and the Historians," *Transactions, Honourable Society of Cymmrodorion*, pt. 1 (1971): 65–85, stresses domestic politics but gives some attention to writings on Lloyd George's postwar diplomacy and opposition to appeasement.

Lloyd George's earliest significant incursion into external affairs—his opposition to the Boer War—is treated in Arthur Davey, *The British Pro-Boers* (1978). Michael L. Dockrill, "David Lloyd George and Foreign Policy Before 1914," in A.J.P. Taylor, ed., *Lloyd George: Twelve Essays* (1971), is a good overview of the subject from 1896. Dockrill views Lloyd George's early concern with foreign affairs as "spasmodic" but intelligent.

Babil M. Kaylani, "Liberal Politics and the British Foreign Office, 1906–1912," *International Review of History and Political Science* 12 (1975): 17–48, calls attention to the fiscal stress between domestic social reform and Great Power politics that worried Lloyd George before the war. Howard S. Weinroth, "The British Radicals and the Balance of Power, 1902–1914," *Historical Journal* 13 (1970): 653–682, and A. J. Anthony Morris, *Radicalism Against War, 1906–1914* (1972), make clear that Lloyd George did not identify with any of the peace groups in Parliament and did not share their criticism of Sir Edward Grey's policies. John W. Coogan and Peter F. Coogan, "The British Cabinet and the Anglo-French Staff Talks, 1905–1914: Who Knew What and When Did He Know It?," *Journal of British Studies* 24 (1985): 110–131, leaves no doubt of Lloyd George's inside knowledge.

The Welshman's connection with the second Moroccan crisis of 1911 is analyzed in Ima C. Barlow, *The Agadir Crisis* (1940), Oron J. Hale, *Publicity and Diplomacy* (1940), and articles by Richard A. Cosgrove (1969), Keith Wilson (1972), and Timothy Boyle (1980). Friedrich W. Wiemann, "Lloyd George and the Struggle for the Navy Estimates of 1914," in Taylor, *Lloyd George: Twelve Essays*, demonstrates the clearsightedness with which he viewed German intentions toward Britain.

The standard work on the July–August 1914 cabinet crises over British intervention in the war is Cameron Hazlehurst, *Politicians at War, July 1914 to May 1915* (1971). Bentley B. Gilbert, "Pacifist to Interventionist: David Lloyd George in 1911 and 1914," *Historical Journal* 28 (1985): 863–885, argues that he viewed Belgium's neutrality as an irrelevancy in the first crisis but skillfully exploited its domestic political value in the second. J. M. Bourne, *Britain and the Great War* (1989), is the best short account of the British war experience, including Lloyd George's part in it. His contributions to foreign policy, before and during his premiership, can be traced in C. J. Lowe and M. L. Dockrill, *The Mirage of Power: British Foreign Policy 1914–1922* (1972), which has an accompanying volume of documents.

Lloyd George's running battle with politicians and brass hats over wartime strategy is featured in Paul Guinn, *British Strategy and Politics 1914 to 1918* (1965), and David French, *British Strategy and War Aims 1914–1916* (1986). David R. Woodward, *Lloyd George and the Generals* (1983), chronicles their invariably stormy relationship. C. J. Lowe, "The Failure of British Diplomacy in the Balkans, 1914–1916," *Canadian Journal of History* 4 (1969): 73–100, discusses Lloyd George's differences with Asquith and Grey over setting Europe's powder keg ablaze, while Aaron S. Klieman does the same for Ottoman Turkey in "British War Aims in the Middle East in 1915," *Journal of Contemporary History* 3 (1968): 237–251. For Lloyd George's involvement in financial diplomacy, see John Milton Cooper, Jr., "The Command of Gold Reversed: American Loans to Britain, 1915–1917," *Pacific Historical Review* 45 (1976): 209–230, and Kathleen Burk, "The Diplomacy of Finance: British Financial Missions to the United States 1914–1918," *Historical Journal* 22 (1979): 351–372.

Hankey's contribution to the cabinet secretariat is examined by John F. Naylor, *A Man and an Institution* (1984), and the notorious brain trust is canvassed in John Turner, *Lloyd George's Secretariat* (1980). The political use of the imperial war conferences is one of the themes of George L. Cook, "Sir Robert Borden, Lloyd George and British Military Policy, 1917–1918," *Historical Journal* 14 (1971): 371–395. "The Erosion of Foreign Office Influence in the Making of Foreign Policy, 1916–1918," *Historical Journal* 15 (1972): 133–159, is the subject of Roberta M. Warman's article.

John Ehrmann, "Lloyd George and Churchill as War Ministers," *Transactions of the Royal Historical Society* 11 (1961): 101–115, compares their different leadership styles. John Terraine examines the problems facing the new prime minister in 1917 in "Lloyd George's Dilemma," *History Today* 11 (1961): 351–359, and "Lloyd George's Expedients," *History Today* 13 (1963): 219–229, 321–330. His difficulties with the navy are treated in Stephen Roskill, "The Dismissal of Admiral Jellicoe," *Journal of Contemporary History* 1 (1966): 69–93. Those with the United States are discussed in Charles Seymour, "War-time Relations of America and Great Britain," *Atlantic Monthly* 133

(1924): 669–677, W. B. Fowler, *British-American Relations 1917–1918* (1969), and Sterling J. Kernek, *Distractions of Peace during War* (1975). Arno J. Mayer, *Political Origins of the New Diplomacy, 1917–1918* (1970), analyzes, from a Marxist perspective, the complications for British policy arising from the Russian Revolution. The long-term effects of the critical year 1917 are the subject of F. S. Northedge, "1917–1919: The Implications for Britain," *Journal of Contemporary History* 3 (1968): 191–210. D. Z. Gillon, "The Antecedents of the Balfour Declaration," *Middle Eastern Studies* 5 (1969): 131–150, and Mayir Vereté, "The Balfour Declaration and Its Makers," *Middle Eastern Studies* 6 (1970): 48–76, consider this vexing subject. Lloyd George's war aims and peace strategies are scrutinized from various perspectives in articles by George Peabody Gooch (1943), David R. Woodward (1971), Artin H. Arslanian (1978), and John S. Galbraith (1984). Richard Lewinsohn, *The Man Behind the Scenes: The Career of Sir Basil Zaharoff* (1929), narrates the activities of one of Lloyd George's intermediaries in the secret world of wartime diplomacy.

The best monograph on Lloyd George's peacemaking role in 1919 is Anthony Lentin, *Lloyd George, Woodrow Wilson and the Guilt of Germany* (1984). Lentin sees the war-guilt clause of the Versailles Treaty—the source of infinite future trouble—as Lloyd George's escape route from his election promise to punish Germany for the war. Other treatments of Lloyd George's Paris experiences include J. M. Keynes's classic, *The Economic Consequences of the Peace* (1919); Harold Nicolson, *Peacemaking 1919* (1939); Arno J. Mayer, *The Politics and Diplomacy of Peacemaking* (1967); Howard Elcock, *Portrait of a Decision* (1973); Charles L. Mee, *The End of Order* (1980); and Marc Trachtenberg, "Versailles after Sixty Years," *Contemporary History* 17 (1982): 487–506. H.W.V. Temperley, ed., *A History of the Peace Conference of Paris*, 6 vols. (1920–1924), is still indispensable for details.

Michael L. Dockrill and J. Douglas Goold, *Peace without Promise* (1981), is illuminating about the central European and Middle Eastern peace settlements. George W. Egerton, "The Lloyd George Government and the Creation of the League of Nations," *American Historical Review* 79 (1974): 419–444, complements Henry R. Winkler, "The Development of the League of Nations Idea in Great Britain, 1914–1919," *Journal of Modern History* 20 (1948): 95–112. Aubrey L. Kennedy, *Old Diplomacy and New* (1922), Gordon A. Craig, "The British Foreign Office from Grey to Austen Chamberlain," in Gordon A. Craig and Felix Gilbert, *The Diplomats* (1953), and Alan J. Sharp, "The Foreign Office in Eclipse, 1919–22," *History* 61 (1976): 198–218, are good introductions to Lloyd George's summit diplomacy. Hines Hall III, "Lloyd George, Briand and the Failure of the Anglo-French Entente," *Journal of Modern History* 50 (1978): D1121–1138, focuses on the 1922 Cannes Conference. Carol Fink, *The Genoa Conference* (1984), is definitive on that catastrophe.

The literature on early Anglo-Soviet relations is legion. Lloyd George's strategy is closely analyzed in Richard H. Ullman, *Anglo-Soviet Relations, 1917–1921*, 3 vols. (1968–1973), a masterly survey. L. J. Macfarlane, "Hands Off Russia," *Past and Present* 38 (1967): 126–152, explains how British labor strengthened Lloyd George's hand against ministers favoring intervention in the Russo-Polish War of 1919–1920. Stephen White, *Britain and the Bolshevik Revolution* (1980), is good for the 1921 trade treaty negotiations. W. P. Coates and Zelda K. Coates, *A History of Anglo-Soviet Relations*, 2 vols. (1943), looks at the whole subject from a Communist perspective.

The Washington Naval Conference of 1921 and the termination of the Anglo-Japanese Alliance are discussed in Stephen Roskill, *Naval Policy Between the Wars* (1968), and

Ira Klein, "Whitehall, Washington, and the Anglo-Japanese Alliance, 1919–1921, *Pacific Historical Review* 41 (1972): 460–483. Sir Algernon Rumbold, *Watershed in India, 1914–1922* (1979), puts into context Lloyd George's disagreements with Edwin Montagu over India policy. His clashes with Montagu, Curzon, and others over the appropriate reaction to Turkish nationalism and Greek imperialism are treated in A. E. Montgomery, "Lloyd George and the Greek Question, 1918–22," in Taylor, *Lloyd George: Twelve Essays*, Michael Llewellyn Smith, *Ionian Vision* (1973), and Dorothy Boyd Rush, "Lord Curzon and Kemalism," *Social Science* 55 (1980): 77–88. David Walder, *The Chanak Affair* (1969), deals with Lloyd George's mishandling of the crisis with Kemalist Turkey. Elizabeth Monroe, *Britain's Moment in the Middle East* (1981), and David Fromkin, *A Peace to End All Peace* (1989), take up his policies toward the Arab Middle East. Max Beloff, *Britain's Liberal Empire, 1897–1921* (1969), traces the Lloyd George government's contribution to the transition from empire to commonwealth.

The interconnection of the Lloyd George coalition's external and domestic policies is analyzed in Kenneth O. Morgan, *Consensus and Disunity* (1979), and continuity with the programs of subsequent governments is examined in Anne Orde, *Great Britain and International Security, 1920–1926* (1977). Herbert A.L. Fisher, "Mr. Lloyd George's Foreign Policy," *Foreign Affairs* 1 (1923): 69–84, and Sir Valentine Chirol, "Four Years of Lloyd-Georgian Foreign Policy," *Edinburgh Review* 237 (1923): 1–20, are insightful contemporary critiques, the first sympathetic, the second hostile. *Documents on British Foreign Policy 1919–1939*, edited by E. L. Woodward et al., 3 ser. (1947–1973), is an essential source.

John Campbell, *Lloyd George: The Goat in the Wilderness 1922–1931* (1977), has only scattered references to external affairs. Maurice Cowling, *The Impact of Hitler* (1975), spotlights Lloyd George's diminishing influence on policy formation in the 1930s. There is more information about Lloyd George's interwar years in Martin Gilbert, *The Roots of Appeasement* (1966), which includes in an appendix notes by T. P. Conwell-Evans of Lloyd George's 1936 interview with Hitler. Two essays in Taylor, *Lloyd George: Twelve Essays*, analyze Lloyd George's last foreign policy demarches: Sidney Aster, "Ivan Maisky and Parliamentary Anti-Appeasement, 1938–39" and Paul Addison, "Lloyd George and Compromise Peace in the Second World War." In *The Napoleonists: A Study in Political Disaffection, 1760–1960* (1970), E. Tangye Lean argues convincingly that Lloyd George showed a "bias in favour of the have-nots in foreign affairs."

Bibliography

Addison, Paul. "Lloyd George and Compromise Peace in the Second World War." In *Lloyd George: Twelve Essays*, edited by A.J.P. Taylor, q.v.

Amery, Leopold S. *The Leo Amery Diaries, 1896–1929.* Edited by John Barnes and David Nicholson. London: Hutchinson, 1980.

———. *My Political Life.* 3 vols. London: Hutchinson, 1953–1955.

Arslanian, Artin H. "British Wartime Pledges: The Armenian Case." *Journal of Contemporary History* 13 (1978): 517–530.

Aster, Sidney. "Ivan Maisky and Parliamentary Anti-Appeasement, 1938–39." In *Lloyd George: Twelve Essays*, edited by A.J.P. Taylor, q.v.

Barlow, Ima C. *The Agadir Crisis.* 1940. Reprint. Hamden, Conn.: Archon, 1971.

Beloff, Max. *Britain's Liberal Empire, 1897–1921.* London: Methuen, 1969.

Bertie of Thame, Viscount. *The Diary of Lord Bertie of Thame.* 2 vols. Edited by Lady Algernon Gordon Lennox. London: Hodder and Stoughton, 1924.

Borden, Sir Robert Laird. *Robert Laird Borden: His Memoirs*. Edited by Henry Borden. Toronto: Macmillan, 1938.

Bourne, J. M. *Britain and the Great War, 1914–1918*. London: Edward Arnold, 1989.

Boyle, Timothy. "New Light on Lloyd George's Mansion House Speech." *Historical Journal* 23 (1980): 431–433.

Burk, Kathleen. "The Diplomacy of Finance: British Financial Missions to the United States 1914–1918." *Historical Journal* 22 (1979): 351–372.

Callwell, Sir Charles E. *Field-Marshal Sir Henry Wilson: His Life and Diaries*. 2 vols. London: Cassell, 1927.

Campbell, John. *Lloyd George: The Goat in the Wilderness 1922–1931*. London: Cape, 1977.

Chirol, Sir Valentine. "Four Years of Lloyd-Georgian Foreign Policy." *Edinburgh Review* 237 (1923): 1–20.

Churchill, Randolph S., and Martin Gilbert. *Winston S. Churchill*. 8 vols. and companion vols. London: Heinemann, 1966–1988.

Churchill, Winston. *The World Crisis, 1911–1918*. 4 vols. London: Butterworth, 1923.

Clemenceau, Georges. *Grandeur and Misery of Victory*. Translated by F. M. Atkinson. New York: Harcourt, Brace, 1930.

Coates, W. P., and Zelda K. Coates. *A History of Anglo-Soviet Relations*. 2 vols. London: Lawrence and Wishart, 1943.

Coogan, John W., and Peter F. Coogan. "The British Cabinet and the Anglo-French Staff Talks, 1905–1914: Who Knew What and When Did He Know It?" *Journal of British Studies* 24 (1985): 110–131.

Cook, George L. "Sir Robert Borden, Lloyd George and British Military Policy, 1917–1918." *Historical Journal* 14 (1971): 371–395.

Cooper, John Milton, Jr. "The Command of Gold Reversed: American Loans to Britain, 1915–1917." *Pacific Historical Review* 45 (1976): 209–230.

Cosgrove, Richard A. "A Note on Lloyd George's Speech at the Mansion House, 21 July 1911." *Historical Journal* 12 (1969): 698–701.

Cowling, Maurice. *The Impact of Hitler: British Politics and British Policy, 1933–1940*. Cambridge: Cambridge University Press, 1975.

Craig, Gordon A. "The British Foreign Office from Grey to Austen Chamberlain." In Gordon A. Craig and Felix Gilbert, *The Diplomats*. Princeton, N.J.: Princeton University Press, 1963.

Cregier, Don M. *Bounder from Wales: Lloyd George's Career Before the First World War*. Columbia: University of Missouri Press, 1976.

Crozier, William P. *Off the Record: Political Interviews, 1933–1943*. Edited by A.J.P. Taylor. London: Hutchinson, 1973.

D'Abernon, Viscount. *An Ambassador of Peace: Pages from the Diary of Viscount D'Abernon*. 3 vols. London: Hodder and Stoughton, 1920–1930.

Davey, Arthur. *The British Pro-Boers, 1877–1902*. Cape Town: Tafelberg, 1978.

Davies, W. Watkin. "The Foreign Policy of Lloyd George." *Fortnightly Review*, n.s. 158 (1945): 268–275.

———. *Lloyd George: 1863–1914*. London: Constable, 1939.

Dockrill, Michael L. "David Lloyd George and Foreign Policy Before 1914." In *Lloyd George: Twelve Essays*, edited by A.J.P. Taylor, q.v.

Dockrill, Michael L., and J. Douglas Goold. *Peace without Promise: Britain and the Peace Conferences 1919–23*. London: Batsford, 1981.

Documents on British Foreign Policy, 1919–1939. Edited by E. L. Woodward et al. 3 ser. London: H. M. Stationery Office, 1947–1973.

Egerton, George W. "The Lloyd George Government and the Creation of the League of Nations." *American Historical Review* 79 (1974): 419–444.

Ehrmann, John. "Lloyd George and Churchill as War Ministers." *Transactions of the Royal Historical Society* 11 (1961): 101–115.

Elcock, Howard. *Portrait of a Decision.* London: Eyre Methuen, 1973.

Fink, Carole. *The Genoa Conference: European Diplomacy 1921–1922.* Chapel Hill: University of North Carolina Press, 1984.

Fisher, Herbert A.L. "Mr. Lloyd George's Foreign Policy." *Foreign Affairs* 1 (1923): 69–84.

Foch, Ferdinand. *Memoirs of Ferdinand Foch.* Translated by T. Bentley Mott. Garden City, N.Y.: Doubleday, Doran, 1931.

Fowler, W. B. *British-American Relations 1917–1918: The Role of Sir William Wiseman.* Princeton, N.J.: Princeton University Press, 1969.

Fraser, Peter. "Cabinet Secrecy and War Memoirs." *History* 70 (1985): 397–409.

French, David. *British Strategy and War Aims 1914–1916.* Winchester, Mass.: Allen and Unwin, 1986.

Fromkin, David. *A Peace to End All Peace: Creating the Modern Middle East, 1914–1922.* New York: Holt, 1989.

Fry, Michael G. *Lloyd George and Foreign Policy: The Education of a Statesman, 1890–1916.* Montreal: McGill-Queen's University Press, 1977.

Galbraith, John S. "British War Aims in World War I: A Commentary on 'Statesmanship.' " *Journal of Imperial and Commonwealth History* 13 (1984): 25–45.

Gilbert, Bentley B. *David Lloyd George: A Political Life. The Architect of Change, 1863–1912.* London: Batsford, 1987.

———. "Pacifist to Interventionist: David Lloyd George in 1911 and 1914. Was Belgium an Issue?" *Historical Journal* 28 (1985): 863–885.

Gilbert, Martin. *The Roots of Appeasement.* London: Weidenfeld and Nicolson, 1966.

Gillon, D. Z. "The Antecedents of the Balfour Declaration." *Middle Eastern Studies* 5 (1969): 131–150.

Gooch, George Peabody. "British War Aims, 1914–19." *Quarterly Review* 280 (1943): 168–179.

Grigg, John. *Lloyd George.* 3 vols. London: Methuen, 1973–1985.

Guinn, Paul. *British Strategy and Politics 1914 to 1918.* Oxford: Clarendon Press, 1965.

Haig, Sir Douglas, Earl Haig. *The Private Papers of Douglas Haig.* Edited by Robert Blake. London: Eyre and Spottiswoode, 1952.

Hale, Oron J. *Publicity and Diplomacy: With Special Reference to England and Germany, 1890–1914.* Charlottesville: University of Virginia Institute for Research in the Social Sciences, 1940.

Hall, Hines, III. "Lloyd George, Briand and the Failure of the Anglo-French Entente." *Journal of Modern History* 50 (1978, on-demand supplement): D1121–1138.

Hankey, Sir Maurice, Baron Hankey. *The Supreme Control at the Paris Peace Conference, 1919.* London: Allen and Unwin, 1963.

———. *The Supreme Command 1914–1918.* 2 vols. London: Allen and Unwin, 1961.

Hardinge of Penshurst, Viscount. *Old Diplomacy.* London: John Murray, 1947.

Hazlehurst, Cameron. *Politicians at War, July 1914 to May 1915: A Prologue to the Triumph of Lloyd George.* London: Cape, 1971.

Headlam-Morley, Sir James. *A Memoir of the Paris Peace Conference 1919*. Edited by Agnes Headlam-Morley. London: Methuen, 1972.

Jones, Thomas. *Lloyd George*. Cambridge, Mass.: Harvard University Press, 1951.

————. *Whitehall Diary*. 3 vols. Edited by Keith Middlemas. London: Oxford University Press, 1969–1971.

Kaylani, Babil M. "Liberal Politics and the British Foreign Office, 1906–1912." *International Review of History and Political Science* 12 (1975): 17–48.

Kennedy, Aubrey L. *Old Diplomacy and New, 1876–1922: From Salisbury to Lloyd George*. London: John Murray, 1922.

Kernek, Sterling J. *Distractions of Peace during War: The Lloyd George Government's Reactions to Woodrow Wilson, December 1916–November 1918*. Philadelphia: American Philosophical Society, 1975.

Keynes, John Maynard. *The Economic Consequences of the Peace*. London: Macmillan, 1919.

Klein, Ira. "Whitehall, Washington, and the Anglo-Japanese Alliance, 1919–1921." *Pacific Historical Review* 41 (1972): 460–483.

Klieman, Aaron S. "British War Aims in the Middle East in 1915." *Journal of Contemporary History* 3 (1968): 237–251.

Lansing, Robert. *The Big Four and Others of the Peace Conference*. Boston: Houghton Mifflin, 1921.

Lean, E. Tangye. *The Napoleonists: A Study in Political Disaffection, 1760–1960*. London: Oxford University Press, 1970.

Lentin, Anthony. *Lloyd George, Woodrow Wilson and the Guilt of Germany*. Leicester: Leicester University Press, 1984.

Lewinsohn, Richard. *The Man Behind the Scenes: The Career of Sir Basil Zaharoff*. London: Gollancz, 1929.

Liddell Hart, Sir Basil. *The Liddell Hart Memoirs*. 2 vols. New York: Putnam, 1965.

Lloyd George, David. *Slings and Arrows*. Edited by Philip Guedalla. London: Cassell, 1929.

————. *The Truth about Reparations and War Debts*. London: Heinemann, 1932.

————. *The Truth about the Peace Treaties*. 2 vols. London: Gollancz, 1938.

————. *War Memoirs of David Lloyd George*. 6 vols. London: Nicholson and Watson, 1933–1936.

Lowe, C. J. "The Failure of British Diplomacy in the Balkans, 1914–1916." *Canadian Journal of History* 4 (1969): 73–100.

Lowe, C. J., and M. L. Dockrill. *The Mirage of Power: British Foreign Policy 1914–1922*. London: Routledge and Kegan Paul, 1972.

————. *The Mirage of Power: The Documents*. London: Routledge and Kegan Paul, 1972.

McCormick, Donald. *The Mask of Merlin: A Critical Study of David Lloyd George*. London: Macdonald, 1963.

Macfarlane, L. J. "Hands Off Russia: British Labour and the Russo-Polish War, 1920." *Past and Present* 38 (1967): 126–152.

Maisky, Ivan. *Memoirs of a Soviet Ambassador*. Translated by Andrew Rothstein. New York: Scribner's, 1968.

Mayer, Arno J. *Political Origins of the New Diplomacy, 1917–1918*. New York: Knopf, 1970.

————. *The Politics and Diplomacy of Peacemaking: Containment and Counterrevolution at Versailles, 1918–1919*. New York: Knopf, 1967.

Mee, Charles L. *The End of Order: Versailles, 1919*. New York: Dutton, 1980.

Miller, David Hunter. *My Diary at the Conference of Paris*. 2 vols. New York: Putnam, 1928.

Monroe, Elizabeth. *Britain's Moment in the Middle East 1914–71*. 2nd ed. London: Chatto and Windus, 1981.

Montgomery, A. E. "Lloyd George and the Greek Question, 1918–22." In *Lloyd George: Twelve Essays*, edited by A.J.P. Taylor, q.v.

Morgan, Kenneth O. *Consensus and Disunity: The Lloyd George Coalition Government 1918–1922*. New York: Oxford University Press, 1979.

———. *Lloyd George*. London: Weidenfeld and Nicolson, 1974.

———. "Lloyd George and the Historians." *Transactions, Honourable Society of Cymmrodorion* (1971): pt. 1. 65–85.

Morris, A. J. Anthony. *Radicalism Against War, 1906–1914: The Advocacy of Peace and Retrenchment*. Totowa, N.J.: Rowman and Littlefield, 1972.

Naylor, John F. *A Man and an Institution: Sir Maurice Hankey, the Cabinet Secretariat and the Custody of Cabinet Secrecy*. Cambridge: Cambridge University Press, 1984.

Nicolson, Harold. *Peacemaking 1919*. New York: Harcourt, Brace, 1939.

Northedge, F. S. "1917–1919: The Implications for Britain." *Journal of Contemporary History* 3 (1968): 191–210.

Orde, Anne. *Great Britain and International Security, 1920–1926*. London: Royal Historical Society, 1977.

Pugh, Martin. *Lloyd George*. London: Longman, 1988.

Repington, Charles a' Court. *The First World War, 1914–1918: Personal Experiences*. 2 vols. London: Constable, 1920.

Riddell, Sir George, Baron Riddell. *The Riddell Diaries 1908–1923*. Edited by John M. McEwen. London: Athlone Press, 1986.

Robertson, Sir William. *Soldiers and Statesmen*. 2 vols. London: Cassell, 1926.

Roskill, Stephen. "The Dismissal of Admiral Jellicoe." *Journal of Contemporary History* 1 (1966): 69–93.

———. *Hankey: Man of Secrets*. 3 vols. London: Collins, 1970–1974.

———. *Naval Policy Between the Wars: The Period of Anglo-American Antagonism, 1919–1929*. London: Collins, 1968.

Rowland, Peter. *Lloyd George*. London: Barrie and Jenkins, 1975.

Rumbold, Sir Algernon. *Watershed in India, 1914–1922*. London: Athlone Press, 1979.

Rush, Dorothy Boyd. "Lord Curzon and Kemalism: The Old World and the New." *Social Science* 55 (1980): 77–88.

Scott, Charles P. *The Political Diaries of C. P. Scott 1911–1928*. Edited by Trevor Wilson. Ithaca, N.Y.: Cornell University Press, 1970.

Seymour, Charles. *Letters from the Paris Peace Conference*. New Haven, Conn.: Yale University Press, 1965.

———. "War-time Relations of America and Great Britain." *Atlantic Monthly* 133 (1924): 669–677.

Sharp, Alan J. "The Foreign Office in Eclipse, 1919–22." *History* 61 (1976): 198–218.

Smith, Michael Llewellyn. *Ionian Vision: Greece in Asia Minor, 1919–1922*. London: Allen Lane, 1973.

Smuts, Jan Christian. *Selections from the Smuts Papers, 1886–1950*. 7 vols. Edited by W. K. Hancock and Jean Van der Poel. Cambridge: Cambridge University Press, 1966–1973.

Stevenson, Frances. *Lloyd George: A Diary*. Edited by A.J.P. Taylor. London: Hutchinson, 1971.

Taylor, A.J.P., ed. *Lloyd George: Twelve Essays*. London: Hamish Hamilton, 1971.

Temperley, H.M.V., ed. *A History of the Peace Conference of Paris*. 6 vols. London: Hodder and Stoughton, 1920–1924.

Terraine, John. "Lloyd George's Dilemma." *History Today* 11 (1961): 350–359.

———. "Lloyd George's Expedients." *History Today* 13 (1963): 219–229, 321–330.

Trachtenberg, Marc. "Versailles after Sixty Years." *Journal of Contemporary History* 17 (1982): 487–506.

Turner, John. *Lloyd George's Secretariat*. Cambridge: Cambridge University Press, 1980.

Ullman, Richard H. *Anglo-Soviet Relations, 1917–1921*. 3 vols. Princeton, N.J.: Princeton University Press, 1968–1973.

Vereté, Mayir. "The Balfour Declaration and Its Makers." *Middle Eastern Studies* 6 (1970): 48–76.

Walder, David. *The Chanak Affair*. London: Hutchinson, 1969.

Warman, Roberta M. "The Erosion of Foreign Office Influence in the Making of Foreign Policy, 1916–1918." *Historical Journal* 15 (1972): 133–159.

Weinroth, Howard S. "The British Radicals and the Balance of Power, 1902–1914." *Historical Journal* 13 (1970): 653–682.

White, Stephen. *Britain and the Bolshevik Revolution: A Study of the Politics of Diplomacy, 1920–1924*. London: Macmillan, 1980.

Wiemann, Friedrich W. "Lloyd George and the Struggle for the Navy Estimates of 1914." In *Lloyd George: Twelve Essays*, edited by A.J.P. Taylor, q.v.

Wilson, Sir Henry. *See* Callwell, Sir Charles E.

Wilson, Keith. "The Agadir Crisis, the Mansion House Speech, and the Double-Edgedness of Agreements." *Historical Journal* 15 (1972): 513–532.

Winkler, Henry R. "The Development of the League of Nations Idea in Great Britain, 1914–1919." *Journal of Modern History* 20 (1948): 95–112.

Woodward, David R. "David Lloyd George, a Negotiated Peace with Germany, and the Kuhlmann Peace Kite of September, 1917." *Canadian Journal of History* 6 (1971): 75–93.

———. *Lloyd George and the Generals*. Newark: University of Delaware Press, 1983.

DON M. CREGIER

Louis XIV (1638–1715). Louis XIV's reign (1643–1715) began and ended amid conflict over the fate of the Spanish Empire. At Louis's accession, France was at war with a once powerful Iberian monarchy now visibly in decline. At the end of his reign, Louis fought the War of the Spanish Succession (1702–1713) in an effort to place a member of his family, the Bourbons, on a throne occupied for the past two centuries by Habsburgs. If any one question dominated French diplomacy in Louis XIV's reign, it was, Who would fall heir to Spain and its worldwide possessions?

Born September 5, 1638, Louis XIV was still a child when his father, Louis XIII, died. His mother, Anne of Austria, assumed the regency; foreign policy remained largely in the hands of the chief minister, Jules Cardinal Mazarin, for the next eighteen years. Mazarin faced a coalition of foreign enemies—among them the Holy Roman Emperor, most prestigious of the German princes, and the chief adversary, Spain. Peace with the emperor came in 1648, when the Treaties of Westphalia conceded to France vaguely defined territories in Alsace while also confirming Dutch independence of Spain. That same year a civil war known as the Fronde (1648–1653) broke out. Even after the rebels had been largely subdued, it took a half-dozen more years and an alliance with *Oliver Cromwell to defeat Spain. The Peace of the Pyrenees (1659) awarded to France some lands along the Spanish Netherlands (modern Belgian) border and in the Pyrenees and stipulated a marriage of Louis and Marie-Thérèse, daughter of the Spanish king, Philip IV (1621–1665).

Although Louis XIV had the highest regard for Mazarin, at the minister's death he chose not to replace him but to fill that role himself. Foreign ministers came and went, but it was Louis XIV who took full responsibility for foreign policy. Mazarin had bequeathed him a peaceful, secure kingdom no longer vulnerable to Spanish pressure. As European predominance was passing from Spain to France, the Dutch response was to insist that Spain, not France, control Belgium; a French presence too close to Holland seemed threatening. Fearful of offending Dutch sensibilities, Mazarin had not sought the entire Spanish Netherlands in the Pyrenees treaty negotiations. In 1662 Louis renewed an alliance with the Dutch, partly to prevent a rapprochement between England and Holland—a formidable combination of wealth and power—and partly in the vain hope that a friendly Holland would permit French encroachment in the Spanish Netherlands. As a result, in 1666 he found himself waging a war as reluctant ally of the Dutch against the English. But it seemed pointless, for Louis's ally was likely to refuse him a foothold in Belgium anyway.

The recent death of Philip IV presented opportunities too good to resist. The Bourbon-Habsburg nuptial settlement had specified that Philip's daughter renounce all claim to Spanish lands—contingent, however, on payment of a dowry, which was out of the question for an empty Spanish treasury. Nonpayment rendered the renunciation invalid, the French argued; moreover, local laws in the Spanish Netherlands allowed certain lands to "devolve" to Marie-Thérèse. Moreover, Louis had an army ready to invade the Spanish Lowlands and precipitate the War of Devolution (1667–1668).

Meanwhile, the Anglo-Dutch War wound down as both belligerents quickly concluded that France was the greater menace. They signed a peace at Breda (1667) and joined Sweden in the Triple Alliance of 1668 to demand that Louis allow them to mediate between himself and Spain; should France refuse, it would face a hostile coalition. The French king gave way, and the Peace of Aachen in 1668 cost Spain a handful of fortified towns—hardly enough to satisfy Louis XIV's ultimate ambition: to conquer the Spanish Netherlands. To silence Dutch opposition to that bold stroke, Louis planned an invasion of Holland in alliance with his Stuart cousin, Charles II of England. In the Treaty of Dover (1670), Charles agreed to join in the raid in return for a French subsidy designed to liberate him from tight parliamentary control. For England the pact meant renewal of the Anglo-Dutch wars of the 1650s and 1660s; the French hoped to turn the war into a conquest of Belgium.

In 1672 French troops launched an invasion of the Dutch Netherlands, anticipating a short war. Initial skirmishes were so successful that Dutch diplomats soon were considering trading land for peace. Louis refused. But since the Dutch had opened the dikes, the rising waters barred French troops from Amsterdam or The Hague. And a coup d'état in the republic ousted the more conciliatory Jan de Witt and installed William III of Orange, who would make it his lifelong business to oppose the French monarch.

As 1673 opened, Louis was undecided where to turn next. Ending the war would spoil a delightful excursion. Amsterdam was out of his reach, but Maastricht was there to be besieged—as much a personal display of arms for Louis as a strategic move. Its capitulation came easily by midsummer, releasing the French to seek new adventures on German soil. There Mazarin had carefully nurtured a friendly League of the Rhine, a collection of states allied to resist the emperor. Louis let the league fall into abeyance, indifferent as he was to German public opinion. So in 1673 what had been a local campaign was allowed to overflow into Germany and became a more general, even aimless, war of attrition. Coalition diplomacy resulted in an alliance among the Dutch, the Spanish, and the emperor. Several more years of campaigning failed to secure for Louis the advantageous peace the Dutch were prepared to grant in 1672.

Across the English Channel, anti-French sentiment was growing. As the war broadened, Charles II wanted no part in a quarrel with Spain or the German princes. Parliament and the king were glad to withdraw from the conflict in 1674. An English threat to reenter the war on the Dutch side encouraged Louis to accept a settlement at Nijmegen (1678–1679). Although Louis XIV emerged with a more defensible frontier in the north, the treaty still denied him Belgium. Annexing Franche-Comté (Free County of Burgundy) from Spain seems small compensation for six years of struggle, especially since de Witt had repeatedly offered Louis terms similar to those of Nijmegen before the Dutch War even commenced. All this is apart from the economic cost of the conflict to France, part of it reflected in deficit finance and ruined trade. Louis, too, must have had doubts about his "triumph"; he dismissed Arnauld de Pomponne, the foreign minister who negotiated the peace.

Twice Louis had seen coalition diplomacy take effect once he threatened his neighbors. In the years after Nijmegen he failed to grasp the fact that his own aggressiveness had prompted these hostile alliances. Louis remained aware, however, that German armies had invaded Alsace during the recent war, and he was determined to lock up that eastern frontier. French acquisitions stipulated by the Westphalia treaties remained unclear, so Louis resorted to a "reunions" policy in the years 1679–1684, directing his own law courts to award to him disputed lands, some in Alsace. A spectacular result of the reunions policy was the occupation of Strasbourg, the major city in Alsace, in 1681. Farther north, Louis seized Luxembourg in a brief war with Spain (1683–1684).

For the moment Louis could call the shots in western Europe because of events in the east, where Turkish (Ottoman) armies marched on Vienna to besiege it in 1683. Preoccupied in the east, the emperor in the Truce of Regensburg (1684) conceded to Louis XIV twenty years' possession of his recent gains in Alsace and elsewhere. But Leopold refused to make that agreement permanent.

Thus far Louis's foreign policy had enjoyed a modicum of success. After the mid–1680s, however, the balance of power gradually tipped against him. The most obvious reasons include a decline in French military resources, a strengthened Habsburg monarchy in eastern Europe, and William III's addition of the English crown in 1688 to his Dutch power base. French aggression provoked various German princes to join the Spanish king and rally around the emperor in the League of Augsburg (1686). Compounding Louis's problems were confusion in his own mind and lack of clear goals.

Nowhere are confusion and cross-purposes more apparent than in the king's ecclesiastical policy. He rarely missed an opportunity to offend Pope Innocent XI (1676–1689) and, by so doing, various Catholic clergy in Germany, a region where Louis desperately needed friends. Louis let a quarrel over appointments and revenues in vacant bishoprics degenerate into the unilateral proclamation of the Gallican Articles of 1682—tantamount to nullifying the pope's authority over the Catholic Church in France. Moreover, the king's tacit support for the Turks against the emperor offended Innocent.

Louis's 1685 revocation of the Edict of Nantes, which had guaranteed religious liberty to French Calvinists since 1598, was a diplomatic disaster. It is difficult to connect the revocation directly to a significant reorientation of French foreign policy then in process—that is, a renewed interest in the Spanish succession—but collateral effects of the revocation are clear. As Protestant exiles left France for England or Holland or Brandenburg, they repeated stories of French barbarism. Louis's action drove thousands out of his own armed forces. Moreover, the revocation jeopardized the position of the new Roman Catholic king of England, James II, by suggesting (erroneously) that James was planning a similar coup. At a time when piecemeal aggression was alarming foreigners, Louis could ill afford the damage the revocation did to his standing in Protestant states. If he thought his action would appeal to Roman Catholic rulers, he miscalculated. The Habsburgs were unenthusiastic; the pope observed sourly that Christ had not armed the Apostles.

As Louis's conflict with the Germans was heating up, so was his quarrel with Rome. To prevent crime, the Vatican had asked foreign states to relinquish diplomatic immunity in districts adjacent to their embassies. Most had complied, but Louis was holding out for concessions. To make the point, his ambassador entered Rome with armed forces in 1687. It hardly seems surprising that in 1688 the pope excommunicated Louis XIV (albeit in secret). Moreover, by mid–1688 the Franco-Vatican feud had merged with a dispute over the electorate of Cologne—a small but strategically important gateway into the Dutch Netherlands and northern Germany. When the pro-French elector-archbishop died, Louis attempted to install his client, William-Egon von Fürstenberg. The emperor's candidate was Joseph-Clement, younger brother of Maximilian Emmanuel, elector of Bavaria, whose family (Wittelsbach) had held the Cologne see since 1580. Emperor Leopold's concern is traceable in part, at least, to the fact that Cologne had one of the eight votes in the electoral college that would choose the next emperor. Louis's lack of understanding of other rulers' sensibilities is clear: while he was trying to bar one Wittelsbach from Cologne, he was seeking a diplomatic accord with another, Maximilian Emmanuel.

Things went badly for Louis XIV. When the Cologne Cathedral chapter voted, neither candidate got the required number of ballots. The matter went directly to Rome for decision. The French talked of war should Fürstenberg be refused; William III, the emperor's partisan, gathered troops not far from Cologne. Louis planned (but later canceled) an amphibious expedition to the Papal States. In September 1688, the king denounced Innocent as pro-Austrian, condemned his refusal to install Fürstenberg, and threatened to invade the papal territory of Avignon (which he in fact did).

Meanwhile Louis XIV learned that the Turks were about to conclude peace with the Habsburgs, in effect leaving Leopold free to challenge the French if he wished. To close a fissure in the eastern frontier and block any German assault, Louis decided to seize the fortress of Philippsburg. His war proclamation demanded that the emperor convert the twenty-year truce of 1684 into a permanent settlement, ensuring Louis's gains in Strasbourg, Luxembourg, and the rest. He blamed the war on the emperor, the Protestants, and the pope! Actually the attack launched in late September 1688 was meant as a minor preemptive strike with limited objectives. Unprepared militarily, Louis had no idea that he was initiating the Nine Years' War, or War of the League of Augsburg, destined to last until 1697 and to involve the emperor, various other German rulers, the Dutch, the Spanish, and even the English.

The historian Andrew Lossky sees the thrust at Philippsburg as part of a larger plan for disengagement on Louis's eastern frontier—to be facilitated by a permanent truce of Regensburg—and for shifting France's attention to the south in anticipation of the Spanish succession. The French navy was already in the Mediterranean area. Thus it behooved the king to avoid border entanglements in the east or quarrels with the Spanish monarchy. If a Bourbon was to be acceptable to the Spanish court, Louis would have to call off his conflict with the pope, and this he delayed doing till 1693. The diplomacy Louis pursued in the late 1680s was self-defeating, but so was the conduct of the war: vandalizing the Palatinate, a nearby German electorate, earned the French a bad reputation indeed.

Once Louis had engaged his army in western Germany, there was little to prevent William from sailing for England in November 1688 to depose his father-in-law, James II, at the invitation of leading opposition politicians. Louis, to whom James had demonstrated little more than friendly neutrality, had no fleet in the Channel to forestall William's move. England yielded William more than a crown; he succeeded in his ambition to bring the island power into the alliance against France (1689).

For France, renewal of war meant stretching meager tax resources thin and borrowing heavily. Economic troubles in 1691–1693 and food shortages debilitated the French people and the war effort; after 1693 peace on Louis's terms was unattainable. In the Treaty of Turin (1696) the French acknowledged failure in Italy. As Louis reduced his terms, the allies agreed to a final settlement at Ryswick in 1697, constituting "a severe check upon French ambitions and pretensions." Apart from Italy, Louis XIV gave up some reunions gains as well as Luxembourg and Philippsburg. In contrast to a friendly League of the Rhine of an earlier day, Louis now faced a cluster of disaffected German states. Moreover, the treaty allowed the Dutch to maintain troops within "barrier" forts in the Spanish Netherlands. Other signs of a shift in the European balance of power were evident: the Anglo-Dutch navy had demonstrated during the war clear superiority; England had proved it could borrow its way through a world war; the Treaty of Karlowitz in 1699 sealed Leopold I's victory over the Turks.

Conclusion of the Nine Years' War was urgent on another count. For years diplomats had anticipated that Charles II, the Spanish king, would soon die without heirs. As early as 1668, Leopold I and Louis XIV had agreed on a partition of the Spanish inheritance, a pact soon to be discarded. If Louis was now to maintain influence at Madrid, far better for him to be at peace with Spain. It was out of the question, though, for the French king to seek the entire inheritance for himself. Spaniards would never tolerate union of two crowns under one ruler, for Spain might then become simply a viceroyalty governed from Versailles. If a Bourbon were to inherit the Spanish throne, it would have to be a relative such as Louis's grandson, Philip of Anjou. But it was no foregone conclusion that Louis would seek the whole inheritance for any Bourbon prince. Some advisors argued that this would offer France no direct territorial gain; what was more, a Bourbon king was apt to become more Spanish than French, or he might draw the French into his quarrels. Others saw advantages to be gained from a Bourbon succession.

There was another option: to agree with William III of England and Holland on a partition of the Spanish legacy. The solution the two kings adopted in 1698 was to award the throne of Spain to a Bavarian prince who stood in the line of succession along with Bourbons and Habsburgs, but who came from a minor dynasty and posed little threat to the European balance of power. William and Louis agreed to compensate France and Austria with Italian lands. But this first partition treaty misfired when the Bavarian candidate died the following year.

William III and Louis XIV negotiated a new agreement in 1700, this one bestowing Spain, Belgium, and Spanish America upon Archduke Charles, younger son of Leopold I and therefore not directly in line to inherit Austria or become emperor himself. In compensation France could push forth its boundaries by acquiring Lorraine and Savoy, whose rulers would be compensated in Italy. To the French it was imperative that Italy, a pathway from a Habsburg Spain to central Europe, not be dominated by that same family.

But the courts of Vienna and Madrid flatly rejected the partition treaty of 1700. Publicly, at least, Leopold claimed the entire inheritance for Habsburgs; in no event would he allow his family's exclusion from Italy. That same year the Spanish king died, leaving a will bound to cause no end of trouble. Perhaps because he thought the Bourbons could best defend it, Charles left the entire inheritance to Philip of Anjou (Philip V); should Louis refuse it, the empire would go to Archduke Charles. Some observers saw the inheritance as a liability for France, one French diplomat predicting that it would cause a long war. That proved to be true; ignoring both the treaty and the will, Leopold invaded Italy in 1701, after Louis had accepted Charles's legacy. While the emperor's preemptive strike reflected a nonnegotiable demand for Spanish Italy, it may well have been meant to compel Louis to strike a deal for a partition of the Spanish legacy. A major war was hardly inevitable.

Over the long term the English would not forgive Louis for failing to uphold the partition treaty of 1700. The immediate issue that brought William into the war, though, was the barrier forts in the Spanish Netherlands manned by the Dutch to restrain France. Ostensibly to hold these strongholds for his grandson, Louis sent troops to oust the Dutch. Unfortunately there was no organization or concert of Europe among rulers to insist upon peaceful partition of the Spanish inheritance. Moreover, Louis clouded the succession issue unnecessarily by failing to explain his refusal to guarantee that Philip would never be king of France; evidently he intended no union of the two crowns but simply wished to ensure that a king of Spain falling heir to the French throne might accept it after abdicating Spain.

Louis XIV's intentions were too clear, however, when it came to the Dutch barrier forts and the trade concessions he sought in the Spanish Empire. In 1701 the maritime powers, England and Holland, reacted by forming the Grand Alliance. Although content to recognize Philip V as long as the Bourbon crowns were not united, they stipulated that Spanish Italy and Belgium go to Archduke Charles. The supreme irony is that several European states would fight the twelve-year War of the Spanish Succession only to settle for terms similar to those outlined by the Grand Alliance of 1701. Before the English actually declared war in 1702, Louis provoked them further by being true to his own monarchical principles: at James II's death, he recognized the latter's son as King James III.

If war is the failure of diplomacy, diplomacy failed again. Moreover, diplomacy was to flounder until 1710. England's war aims expanded in 1703 to include placing Archduke Charles on the Spanish throne and by 1710 came close to unconditional surrender—a rarity in that era, as was the ferocity and human cost of the war, the most expensive of Louis's personal reign.

At the war's inception, the position of the two Bourbon crowns looked formidable on paper. In the Nine Years' War Louis had had almost no allies; now the list included Spain, Savoy, Portugal, and Bavaria. The Bourbons occupied most of the disputed territory, too. But before long the Austrians established a presence in Italy—the land that concerned them most, as it connected Austria with Spain. Meanwhile John Churchill, duke of Marlborough, leader of the Anglo-Dutch forces, and his opposite number in Austria, Prince Eugene of Savoy, in 1704 defeated a Franco-Bavarian force in central Europe at Blenheim. At sea, the French fleet lost control of the Mediterranean and the English took Gibraltar. The year 1706 was also bad for Louis, the French suffering defeat at Ramillies and relinquishing Italy. By 1707 the king was ready to accept terms much the same as those the Grand Alliance had presented in 1701: Italy and Belgium to the archduke, Spain and its colonies to Philip. But the allies were in no mood to settle. The year 1709 saw a terrible winter and food shortages in Paris, an army sapped by desertion, and royal finances in chaos. But when the French asked for terms, they got only unrealistic demands. Although Louis was considering relinquishing post–1648 gains, even Alsace, allied diplomats insisted that he use his army to chase his own grandson out of Spain.

The year 1710 was pivotal. Signs of flexibility appeared in England when a parliamentary election that year ousted the Whigs in favor of the Tories, who were more disposed to give to a public weary of war, taxes, and casualties the peace it wanted. By December, military victory in Spain showed that there was no dislodging Philip. By that time French and English diplomats had already begun secret peace talks. In 1711 news of the death of Emperor Joseph I, Leopold's son, only reiterated the futility of a war to proclaim Archduke Charles king of Spain; now that the latter was Emperor Charles VI, he would possess two crowns if allied policy succeeded.

The terms the Tories offered Louis were far more realistic than the demands put forth earlier. The eventual result in 1713 was the Peace of Utrecht, leaving Louis a border quite similar to that of the 1697 treaty but requiring him to relinquish Newfoundland and Nova Scotia to England. Spain's inheritance was partitioned, of course, its Netherlands going to the emperor along with Milan and Sardinia. The English retained trading privileges in the Spanish colonial empire and a foothold in the Mediterranean, notably Gibraltar. Charles VI finally abandoned hopes of Madrid and consented to peace at Rastadt in 1714.

If Louis XIV during his personal reign acquired a few territories and a string of fortifications and put his grandson on the Spanish throne, the cost was high. The king must have realized that himself, for shortly before his death on September 1, 1715, he advised his heir: "Do not imitate me in war; try always to maintain peace with your neighbors."

Annotated Bibliography

The historian searching for unpublished sources for Louis XIV's foreign policy will probably have to consult several collections—in particular, Ministère des relations extérieures: Bibliothèque (formerly called Archives des affaires étrangères), 37 quai d'Orsay, 75007 Paris. There typical headings include Correspondance Politique: Angleterre (for

Louis's English policy) and Mémoires et Documents: Hollande. Archival citations abound in bibliographies and notes in some of the secondary works to follow. As for printed primary sources, the multivolume *Recueil des instructions données aux ambassadeurs et ministres de France depuis les traités de Westphalie jusqu'à la Révolution française* (Paris, 1884–   ) is often cited. Apart from official documents, Louis's writings are most accessible in Paul Sonnino's translation of *Mémoires for the Instruction of the Dauphin* (1970).

Among biographies, John B. Wolf's *Louis XIV* (1968) is considered best. John C. Rule, "Louis XIV, Roi-Bureaucrate," in his edited volume, *Louis XIV and the Craft of Kingship* (1969), provides a good introduction to the reign. See also his "Bibliographical Introduction" in the same volume. Wolf's summary of diplomatic history, *Toward a European Balance of Power, 1620–1715* (1970), offers a comprehensive overview. S. H. Steinberg, *The Thirty Years War and the Conflict for European Hegemony, 1600–1660* (1967), gives a succinct introduction.

A number of authors throw light on the 1660s. Jean Bérenger, "An Attempted *Rapprochement* Between France and the Emperor: The Secret Treaty for the Partition of the Spanish Succession of 19 January 1668," in *Louis XIV and Europe*, edited by Ragnhild Hatton (1976), argues that this agreement was the main reason Louis accepted the Aachen treaty. Hatton's collection also includes her "Louis XIV and His Fellow Monarchs" and Victor-L. Tapié's "Louis XIV's Methods in Foreign Policy." The Franco-Dutch alliance and its aftermath are the subject of Herbert H. Rowen's "The Origins of the Guerre de Hollande: France and the Netherlands, 1660–1672," in the Western Society for French History's *Proceedings* (hereafter cited as *WSFHP*) 2 (1975). Literature on the Dutch War has grown; see, for example, Rowen's "The Peace of Nijmegen: De Witt's Revenge," in *The Peace of Nijmegen 1676–1678/79: International Congress of the Tricentennial, Nijmegen 14–16 September 1978*, edited by J.A.H. Bots (1980). Other significant works are Rowen's *The Ambassador Prepares for War: The Dutch Embassy of Arnauld de Pomponne, 1669–1671* (1957); Paul Sonnino, *Louis XIV and the Origins of the Dutch War* (1988); and Carl Ekberg, *The Failure of Louis XIV's Dutch War* (1979). For reunions in Alsace, see Franklin Ford, *Strasbourg in Transition, 1648–1789* (1958).

Andrew Lossky's view of Louis's confusion and bungling in the 1680s is developed in "The Intellectual Development of Louis XIV from 1661 to 1715," in *Louis XIV and Absolutism*, ed. Ragnhild Hatton (1976); "The General European Crisis of the 1680s," *European Studies Review* 10 (1980); and "Vicissitudes of Louis XIV's 'Crusade' of the 1680s (Abstract)," *WSFHP* 16 (1989). More about Louis's simulated crusading is found in Paul W. Bamford, *Fighting Ships and Prisons: The Mediterranean Galleys of France in the Age of Louis XIV* (1973). Geoffrey Symcox, "Louis XIV and the Outbreak of the Nine Years War," in *Louis XIV and Europe*, is excellent. John T. O'Connor's "Louis XIV's 'Cold War' with the Papacy," *WSFHP* 2 (1975), and *Negotiator out of Season: The Career of Wilhelm Egon von Fürstenberg, 1629 to 1704* (1978), are valuable.

According to Richard Place, "The Self-Deception of the Strong: France on the Eve of the War of the League of Augsburg," *French Historical Studies* 6 (1970), the French underestimated Leopold's army. Gaston Zeller has scuttled the notion that Louis XIV was pursuing "natural" frontiers—Rhine, Alps, Pyrenees. Rather, he was seeking *strategic* frontiers that were not simply defensive but would permit him to advance beyond France's borders. See Zeller, "Saluces, Pignerol et Strasbourg: la politique des frontières au temps de la prépondérance espagnole,'' *Revue historique* 193 (1942). In "Louis XIV's Strategic Frontier in the Holy Roman Empire,'' *WSFHP* 3 (1976), John T. O'Connor describes the loss of much of that frontier in 1697.

Mark A. Thomson, "Louis XIV and the Origins of the War of the Spanish Succession,'' "Louis XIV and the Grand Alliance, 1705–10,'' and "Self-Determination and Collective Security as Factors in English and French Foreign Policy, 1689– 1718,'' in *William III and Louis XIV: Essays 1680–1720 by and for Mark A. Thomson*, edited by Ragnhild Hatton and J. S. Bromley (1968), are authoritative for the Spanish succession question. G. M. Trevelyan, *England under Queen Anne*, 3 vols. (1930–1934), tells the story from the other side of the Channel. For an Austrian perspective see John P. Spielman, *Leopold I of Austria* (1977). Jean Meuvret, "Fiscalism and Public Opinion under Louis XIV,'' in *Louis XIV and Absolutism*, closely ties public finance to diplomacy and war.

Louis's last foreign minister is the subject of John C. Rule, "Colbert de Torcy, an Emergent Bureaucracy, and the Formulation of French Foreign Policy, 1698–1715,'' in *Louis XIV and Europe*. William J. Roosen, *The Age of Louis XIV: The Rise of Modern Diplomacy* (1976), describes how diplomacy was practiced. The paucity of French-language diplomatic history titles from the last forty years is striking, although a considerable number of Americans have contributed to the field. German-language entries are easily found in citations in the literature above. John B. Wolf, "The Reign of Louis XIV: A Selected Bibliography of Writings since the War of 1914–1918,'' *Journal of Modern History* 36 (1964), is instructive. Finally, a one-volume *Bibliographie annuelle de l'histoire de France* (Paris, 1953/54–) has been appearing yearly.

Bibliography

Bamford, Paul W. *Fighting Ships and Prisons: The Mediterranean Galleys of France in the Age of Louis XIV*. Minneapolis: University of Minnesota Press, 1973.

Bérenger, Jean. "An Attempted *Rapprochement* Between France and the Emperor: The Secret Treaty for the Partition of the Spanish Succession of 19 January 1668.'' In *Louis XIV and Europe*, pp. 133–152. Edited by Ragnhild Hatton. Columbus: Ohio State University Press, 1976.

Bibliographie annuelle de l'histoire de France du cinquième siècle à 1945. Paris: Editions du Centre national de la recherche scientifique, 1953/54– .

Ekberg, Carl. *The Failure of Louis XIV's Dutch War*. Chapel Hill: University of North Carolina Press, 1979.

Ford, Franklin. *Strasbourg in Transition, 1648–1789*. Cambridge, Mass.: Harvard University Press, 1958.

Hatton, Ragnhild. "Louis XIV and His Fellow Monarchs.'' In *Louis XIV and Europe*, pp. 16–59. Edited by Ragnhild Hatton. Columbus: Ohio State University Press, 1976.

Lossky, Andrew. "The General European Crisis of the 1680s.'' *European Studies Review* 10 (1980): 177–198.

———. "The Intellectual Development of Louis XIV from 1661 to 1715.'' In *Louis XIV and Absolutism*, pp. 101–129. Edited by Ragnhild Hatton. Columbus: Ohio State University Press, 1976.

Louis XIV. *Mémoires for the Instruction of the Dauphin*. Translated by Paul Sonnino. New York: Free Press, 1970.

Meuvret, Jean. "Fiscalism and Public Opinion under Louis XIV." In *Louis XIV and Absolutism*, pp. 199–225. Edited by Ragnhild Hatton. Columbus: Ohio State University Press, 1976.

O'Connor, John T. "Louis XIV's 'Cold War' with the Papacy." In *Proceedings of the Second Meeting of the Western Society for French History*, pp. 127–136. Edited by Brison D. Gooch. N.p.: n.p., 1975.

———. "Louis XIV's Strategic Frontier in the Holy Roman Empire." In *Proceedings of the Third Annual Meeting of the Western Society for French History*, pp. 108–117. Edited by Brison D. Gooch. N.p.: n.p., 1976.

———. *Negotiator out of Season: The Career of Wilhelm Egon von Fürstenberg, 1629 to 1704*. Athens: University of Georgia Press, 1978.

Place, Richard. "The Self-Deception of the Strong: France on the Eve of the War of the League of Augsburg." *French Historical Studies* 6 (1970): 459–473.

Roosen, William J. *The Age of Louis XIV: The Rise of Modern Diplomacy*. Cambridge, Mass.: Schenkman, 1976.

Rowen, Herbert H. *The Ambassador Prepares for War: The Dutch Embassy of Arnauld de Pomponne 1669–1671*. The Hague: Martinus-Nijhoff, 1957.

———. "The Origins of the Guerre de Hollande: France and the Netherlands, 1660–1672." In *Proceedings of the Second Meeting of the Western Society for French History*, pp. 120–126. Edited by Brison D. Gooch. N.p.: n.p., 1975.

———. "The Peace of Nijmegen: De Witt's Revenge." In *The Peace of Nijmegen 1676–1678/79: International Congress of the Tricentennial, Nijmegen 14–16 September 1978*, pp. 275–283. Edited by J.A.H. Bots. Amsterdam: Holland Universiteits Pers, 1980.

Rule, John C. "Colbert de Torcy, an Emergent Bureaucracy, and the Formulation of French Foreign Policy, 1698–1715." In *Louis XIV and Europe*, pp. 261–288. Edited by Ragnhild Hatton. Columbus: Ohio State University Press, 1976.

———, ed. *Louis XIV and the Craft of Kingship*. Columbus: Ohio State University Press, 1969.

Sonnino, Paul. *Louis XIV and the Origins of the Dutch War*. Cambridge: Cambridge University Press, 1988.

Spielman, John P. *Leopold I of Austria*. New Brunswick, N.J.: Rutgers University Press, 1977.

Steinberg, S. H. *The Thirty Years War and the Conflict for European Hegemony, 1600–1660*. New York: Norton, 1967.

Symcox, Geoffrey. "Louis XIV and the Outbreak of the Nine Years War." In *Louis XIV and Europe*, pp. 179–212. Edited by Ragnhild Hatton. Columbus: Ohio State University Press, 1976.

Tapié, Victor-L. "Louis XIV's Methods in Foreign Policy." In *Louis XIV and Europe*, pp. 3–15. Edited by Ragnhild Hatton. Columbus: Ohio State University Press, 1976.

Thomson, Mark A. *William III and Louis XIV: Essays 1680–1720 by and for Mark A. Thomson*. Edited by Ragnhild Hatton and J. S. Bromley. Liverpool: Liverpool University Press, 1968.

Trevelyan, G. M. *England under Queen Anne*. 3 vols. London: Longmans, Green, 1930–1934.

Wolf, John B. *Louis XIV*. New York: W.W. Norton, 1968.
————. "The Reign of Louis XIV: A Selected Bibliography of Writings since the War of 1914–1918." *Journal of Modern History* 36 (1964): 127–144.
————. *Toward a European Balance of Power, 1620–1715*. Chicago: Rand McNally, 1970.
Zeller, Gaston. "Saluces, Pignerol et Strasbourg: la politique des frontières au temps de la prépondérance espagnole." *Revue historique* 193 (1942): 97–110.

ANDREW P. TROUT

Niccolò Machiavelli (1469–1527).   Niccolò di Bernardo Machiavelli, the third of four children born to Bernardo di Niccolò di Buoninsegna and Bartolomea de' Nelli, was born on the family estate at Val di Pesa outside Florence on May 3, 1469. Because Machiavelli's well-to-do and politically active family derived its income from the land and rents, and not from the more typical Florentine commercial pursuits, Machiavelli acquired no business skills. His father, schooled in the law, encouraged both humanist learning and ambition, while his mother inspired through her poetry.

Niccolò's Latin instructor was a member of the lawyers' guild to which his father belonged. Significantly, his teacher was connected to both the Florentine government and Renaissance literary circles. Young Niccolò was introduced to a variety of classical sources including Cicero, Ptolemy, Tacitus, Polybius, Plutarch, and Justinian's code of laws. His favorite Italian authors, Dante and Petrarch, influenced his concept of and attachment to *patria*.

Several historical events impressed the young Machiavelli. The Pazzi conspiracy against the ruling Medici family in 1478 illustrated not only debilitating Florentine rivalries but also Florence's role in the fourteenth and fifteenth centuries as both an obstacle to would-be unifiers of the Italian peninsula and as champion of republican liberties. Although typically Florentine in their idealization of civic humanism, Machiavelli's vision and philosophy extended beyond Florence to Italy. Thus, as Machiavelli's education and political experience expanded, he realized that the primary threat to Florence and Italy resided in the "new barbarians" from beyond Italy.

The death of Lorenzo de' Medici in 1492 made a deep impression. Niccolò admired great men who demonstrated ability as well as self-assurance. He did not view the Medici through rose-colored glasses, but he saw that they took action on behalf of their country. Machiavelli realized that an age was passing not just for Florence but for Italy as well.

In particular, the French invasion of Italy initiated a grave crisis. Even though the Sforza of Milan invited Charles VIII of France to lay claim to the throne of Naples and invade Italy, Machiavelli recognized that the occasion was not merely the continuation of factional Italian feuding. It represented a challenge to freedom and independence for all Italy. In the case of Florence, Piero de' Medici attempted to appease the French and was overthrown by a patriotic movement led by a Dominican friar, Girolamo Savonarola. For the next four years Florence endured a puritanical purging of the Medici era's decadent elements. However, the Florentines eventually tired of Savonarola's increasing self-righteousness, and he was removed in 1498. Machiavelli agreed with some of Savonarola's reform aims and gained from him a sharper sense of national crisis as well as a clearer understanding of the new political era.

Although he had been moving toward either a legal or literary career, within a month of Savonarola's demise Machiavelli was elected chancellor of the Second Chancery and later secretary to the Ten of Liberty and Peace, a republican committee handling foreign policy. Thus, quite suddenly, Machiavelli attained prominence in the Florentine government. Although responsible for management of both internal and external affairs, the twenty-nine-year-old bureaucrat was attracted more to diplomacy. As a diplomat, Machiavelli was a quick study, and his journeys within and without Italy broadened his perspective and, even more important, deepened his understanding of Italy's historical position and dilemma. Machiavelli's diplomatic missions also nurtured his ego and stoked his ambition to play a part, if not the major one, in government decisions. His initial missions in 1499 to minor functionaries involved in Florence's conflict with Pisa gave him a taste for, and experience in, diplomacy. During Machiavelli's first non-Italian mission to France in 1500, he learned the difficulty of persuading leaders such as Louis XII that France's interests coincided with those of its ally Florence.

Between his diplomatic missions for the Ten, Machiavelli carried on his domestic chores as chancellor of the Second Chancery. A tireless laborer, he managed the two posts adroitly. Further, Machiavelli maintained an active private life. After his father's death, he married Marietta Corsini in 1501. They had six children.

In 1502 the Florentine Signoria appointed Piero Soderini as permanent gonfalonier. Quickly, the gonfalonier showed respect for Machiavelli's ability by entrusting him with key diplomatic assignments to deal with threats to Florence's security. A mission to the aggressive duke of Romagna, Caesar Borgia, in 1502–1503 gave Machiavelli his most penetrating perspective yet on the Italian political predicament. As he observed Borgia, Machiavelli was struck by a characteristic boldness and, by comparison, with a vacillating Florentine government. While Borgia symbolized strength and industry, Florence's insouciance in the face of threats frustrated Machiavelli. Although Machiavelli admired Borgia's political realism, he also recognized his limitations and dependence upon fortune.

During his mission to the papacy in 1503, Machiavelli witnessed the death of Pope Alexander VI (Caesar Borgia's father) and the political maneuvering that led to the selection of Cardinal della Rovere as Pope Julius II. Julius II's reckless tendencies eventually belied Machiavelli's initial impression that the new pope would continue stable relations with Florence. Upon his return to France for further negotiations with Louis XII in 1504, Machiavelli found time to begin the first contemplative writing of his career, the *First Decennial*, which chronicled Italian events from 1494 to 1504.

After his government decided to move against Pisa in 1505, Machiavelli recruited and trained a citizen army for Florence. Careful observation taught him that reliance on mercenary forces in Italy caused more problems than it solved. Mercenaries usually failed when fighting troops recruited from the native population. Even if successful in war, mercenaries often undermined the liberty of the state. In 1506, at the urging of Machiavelli, Florence's Signoria agreed to establish a new committee, the Nine of Ordnance and Militia, to manage military affairs. Not surprisingly, Machiavelli was named secretary of the Nine.

Meanwhile, Machiavelli continued his diplomatic junkets, attending the papal court of Julius II in 1506 and the Holy Roman Emperor Maximilian in 1508. His initial experiences with the Germans led him to compose a "Report on Germany," which showed much less regard for Maximilian's indecisiveness than either Louis XII or Julius II. Between his German mission and a third trip to France in 1510, Machiavelli raised and commanded troops in the siege of Pisa and negotiated the surrender of the city to Florence in 1509. During a lull in diplomatic activity in late 1509, Machiavelli apparently began the *Second Decennial*, intended to chronicle the decade after 1505.

In 1509 Venice faced the League of Cambrai, composed of France, the Holy Roman Empire, Spain, and the papacy. A minor party to the league, Florence was more concerned with protecting its own interests than with supporting sometimes fickle associates such as France and the papacy. While Venice held its own, an estrangement between allies Louis XII of France and Pope Julius II caused considerable unease in Florence. Thus, Soderini once more sent Machiavelli to France in 1510 to placate Louis XII. He promised France that Florence would respect its treaty obligations, but made no commitments in the event of war between the papacy and France. Because a conflict seemed inevitable, upon Machiavelli's return to Florence he persuaded the Ten to allow him to raise a cavalry force to strengthen Florentine defenses. In fact, Machiavelli virtually took over the inspection and maintenance of fortifications in Florence and Pisa.

Nor did Machiavelli's diplomacy falter. He tried unsuccessfully to convince Louis XII to negotiate with the pope. When the impetuous papacy forged an alliance with Spain in 1511, it was only a matter of time before Florence capitulated. Upon the fall of the pro-French Florentine government in 1512, the Medici returned and soon regained power over the republic. Because of his close association with exiled Gonfalonier Soderini, archenemy of the Medici, Machiavelli was relieved of his governmental positions.

Machiavelli's loss of political office was followed by his arrest and imprisonment four months later, falsely charged in an anti-Medici plot. Machiavelli soon gained his release when Giovanni de' Medici, elected Pope Leo X in 1513, granted amnesty to various prisoners as a goodwill gesture. Despite his imprisonment and torture, Machiavelli felt no animosity toward the Medici. Indeed, he composed some prison sonnets dedicated to the new Florentine ruler, Giuliano de' Medici, a cousin of Pope Leo X. Only a few months after his release, Machiavelli completed *The Prince*, first addressed to Giuliano and later to a Medici nephew, Lorenzo, who succeeded Giuliano in Florence. Undoubtedly, Machiavelli was motivated in part by a desire to regain a post in the Medici government. Yet, the text reflected thought deeper and more politically substantive than the author's personal plight suggested.

Between 1513 and 1517, Machiavelli resided at his family villa at Sant' Andrea, separated from the real political world that fascinated him. His writings were quite varied during this period. In addition to his most famous treatise, *The Prince*, Machiavelli virtually completed his detailed *Discourses on the First Decade of Titus Livy*, which tied the history of ancient Rome to elements of modern republics such as Florence. He also penned *A Dialogue on Language*, the fable *Belfagor*, subtitled *The Devil Who Took a Wife*, and a poetic fantasy, left unfinished, entitled *The Golden Ass*.

Machiavelli's friends persuaded him to leave his rural isolation and venture into the city of Florence in 1517. These young patricians, reflecting interests more literary than political, convened in the gardens of one of their number, Cosimo Rucellai. The participants stimulated Machiavelli's thought, and he accepted their challenge to prepare a history of Florence. In 1519 the deaths of Cosimo Rucellai and Florence's Medici ruler, Lorenzo, again forced Machiavelli to contemplate his own and Florence's future. The new Medici suzerain, Cardinal Giulio, selected by Pope Leo X, requested certain personages to submit views on the governance of Florence. One of those who responded was Niccolò Machiavelli, and his message to the Medici ruler, entitled *Discourse on Florentine Public Affairs*, was simple: Florence was suited only for a republican form of government. In the text, Machiavelli also revealed the essence of his belief that the greatest good that one can accomplish is for one's country.

In 1518 Machiavelli produced his best play, the *Mandragola*, a satire on the sexes. During 1519–1520 Machiavelli completed work on *The Art of War*, which combined personal experience with some detailed study of classical writings. This was the most straightforward of Machiavelli's works, subject to no interpretative entanglements. While on some business for Cardinal Giulio in Lucca, Machiavelli became fascinated by fourteenth-century *condottiere*. The result was a fictionalized biography, *The Life of Castruccio Castracani of Lucca*.

In 1520 Machiavelli accepted a commission to compose a history of Florence. By the 1520s a new and fiercer contest had begun for Italian territory between the Valois and the Habsburgs. French and Spanish armies roamed Italian soil, causing grief for its city-states. The Florentine *Studio* (university), headed by Cardinal Giulio de' Medici, hired Machiavelli to write the history of Florence. Finally having regained the trust of the Medici, and having acquired a reputation as a military theorist and playwright, Machiavelli turned to his lengthiest writing project. The *History of Florence* is not the best example of historical research, and it pales by comparison to the history of Italy by Machiavelli's friend, Francesco Guicciardini. Machiavelli selected his material to suit his own theories. Completed through the rule of Lorenzo the Magnificent, Machiavelli presented the history in 1525 to his patron Giulio, by then Pope Clement VII.

Although plagued by age and infirmities, Machiavelli was thrilled to undertake some diplomatic missions for the Medici pope as well as Florence. Though his political and diplomatic efforts were less significant than earlier in his career, they allowed Machiavelli once more to fret over the future of Italy. He wrote his last major work in 1525, a play called *Clizia*, similar in theme but not quality to the *Mandragola*. Machiavelli died on June 21, 1527, and was buried in the Florentine church of Santa Croce.

The various influences on Niccolò Machiavelli should be neither ignored nor overstated. Machiavelli's family significantly shaped his attitudes toward himself and Italy. He recognized the role of the family in maintaining value systems for the individual and society. Machiavelli was also a man of his times, a Renaissance humanist influenced by contemporary Italian writing styles and themes found in authors such as Petrarch and Dante. His intellectual friendships, from his acquaintances in the Rucellai gardens to his relationships with a diplomatic colleague, Francesco Vettori, and the meticulous historian, Francesco Guicciardini, underscore this humanist tendency. Machiavelli mined from the history of ancient Rome tenets that he found to be timeless, and he used historical events and personalities to buttress and illustrate his political and moral philosophy.

Next, Machiavelli was an Italian patriot, although not in the romantic sense of the Risorgimento, because he could not envisage the nature of the modern state. Rather, as both pragmatist and realist, Machiavelli desired a powerful Italian state or prince, on the Renaissance model, to resist the foreign "barbarians." Like any patriot witnessing the collapse of one's country, Machiavelli hoped for a savior even though he saw the chances as slender. Machiavelli's political and diplomatic experience with the Florentine government allowed him to let practice flow into theory. Thus, his political philosophy synchronized with the actual conditions of the times. Finally, Machiavelli strongly believed that fear of God disciplined society and thus complemented political aims. Not known for his piety, and willing to critique the corruption of the Roman Catholic Church, Machiavelli was neither an atheist nor a pagan. Rather, he formulated a pragmatic application of belief in God and Christian conduct to politics similar to that of St. Augustine.

That Niccolò Machiavelli contributed to the transition from medieval to modern concepts of government and society is undeniable. Generally, the contributions may be divided into the literary and political, although many scholars argue that Machiavelli invoked literary skills to extend and define his political and moral philosophy. The use of history is perhaps the most striking example of the linkage. When Machiavelli was employed to write the history of Florence, he joined a growing body of official historians of Renaissance states. The official history, less concerned with facts than with forms, was used as much for propaganda as for the preservation of a heritage. Nonetheless, Machiavelli found the official history to be an excellent vehicle to demonstrate axiomatically that history, cyclical by nature, teaches political truisms by example. Machiavelli's uncritical use of sources should not detract from his ability to champion a political technique. Machiavelli concentrated more on Florentine foreign than domestic affairs to show that selfish, egotistical leaders without either a vision of, or commitment to, the common good were dangerous to any state. Likewise, he emphasized that strong, wise leaders directed their policies to secure or establish a state. Thus, while Machiavelli's history of Florence bears little resemblance to a dispassionate, well-researched work such as Guicciardini's history of Italy, Machiavelli used his simple literary style and the historical framework to reiterate political views found more explicitly in *The Prince* and the *Discourses*.

Many scholars have argued persuasively that the best understanding of Machiavelli's philosophy comprehends his writing in its entirety rather than piecemeal. The greatest problems with such an approach occur when comparing *The Prince* and the *Discourses*. The former focuses on an essentially authoritarian rule, while the latter features a republican form of government. There is less dispute that Machiavelli preferred a republican system over princely rule. His purposes in writing *The Prince* were twofold: to persuade the Medici to reemploy him in some political post and to encourage a strong prince—Giulio de' Medici may be the best candidate—to rally Italy against foreign invaders. Machiavelli may have seen a strong prince as the only means to repel the foreign threat. Thus, the form or style of government outlined in *The Prince* was necessary in the circumstances, though less preferable than the more ideal form—a republic—detailed in the *Discourses*.

Several key words are crucial to understanding the meaning of Machiavelli's political and moral philosophy. Machiavelli used the word *virtù* to represent the unique ability of the prince/leader to establish and maintain appropriate policies. He believed that there was only a certain amount of *virtù* available, so that only a few rulers were likely to possess these crucial qualities. The virtuous leader would be able to determine the common good for the state and pursue it through the application of arms, religion, and laws. Based on his own methods for discovering what works best, Machiavelli recommended that the prince study history and use practical reason. He was most fascinated by the notion of the "new prince" who arrived like a messiah to deliver his people from chaos or threats. Machiavelli's favorite historical examples were Moses in ancient Israel, Romulus in ancient Rome, Cyrus the Persian, and Theseus the Greek. Thus, the understanding of *occasione*, or the opportunity to act, was also crucial to the role of the "new prince."

Another key word in Machiavelli's lexicon, *fortuna*, was also familiar to Renaissance writers. Machiavelli suggested that perhaps half of all human events were determined by *fortuna*. He wrote that Caesar Borgia had experienced good fortune in his rise to power and bad fortune in his fall. However, Machiavelli did not believe that the prince/leader was necessarily completely at the mercy of *fortuna*. By using *virtù* and experience, the prince/leader might be able to mitigate some of the ill effects of *fortuna*. Some Machiavelli scholars argue that he may have felt that divine intervention affected *fortuna*, but he does not make clear how great a role God may play. At the least, even a capable prince may not be able to control events or circumstances when *fortuna* intervenes.

One of the most debated and controversial aspects of Machiavelli's philosophy is his apparent approval of "immoral" actions by the prince in certain circumstances. Whether known as realpolitik or power politics, the references in *The Prince* have been dissected over the centuries. Machiavelli certainly did not approve of an immoral or treacherous ruler. In his writings he stressed the importance and near necessity that, in addition to competence, the prince be regarded as "good" by his subjects. Yet, he firmly believed that if the state's very life was threatened, acts, not a policy, of cruelty or treachery could be condoned. He recognized that those special circumstances would be rare. Indeed, if such acts became an integral feature of a prince's governance, the ruler would fail. A recent biographer argued that Machiavelli felt that God would excuse the extraordinary acts of the prince if they were conducted for the common good or the security of the state. In short, as long as the prince was motivated by love of country his acts would be morally acceptable.

Machiavelli's diplomatic and military experience, combined with his larger interest in outlining the elements of successful political governance, were the reasons for his subsequent influence. He reflected views from both the past and the future when he emphasized military preparedness and citizen armies as means to protect the state's interests. The importance of nurturing esprit de corps and excellence of training among the military were also time-honored principles. He learned quickly in the negotiations with France that successful diplomacy must be supported by national strength and resolve. Lessons derived from Machiavelli's diplomatic endeavors included the need for resolute, decisive actions in the national interest. He was convinced that political leaders must demonstrate flexible responses to the ebb and flow of events. Machiavelli recognized that a diplomat's informed perspective, based on careful research, was usually more persuasive than personal opinions. While his views on war and diplomacy were not entirely novel, because of Machiavelli's political realism his influence on political and military leaders over the centuries has been profound.

Annotated Bibliography

The original manuscripts of Machiavelli's literary and historical writings as well as diplomatic documents, notes, and correspondence are located in two repositories in Florence, Italy:

Archivio di Stato di Firenze
  Loggiato degli Uffizi
  50100 Florence, Italy   (telephone 055/211–629)

Biblioteca Nazionale Centrale
  Piazza Cavalleggeri, 1–B
  50122 Florence, Italy   (telephone 055/244–441)

The Archivio di Stato is open weekdays and closed on holidays. The Biblioteca Nazionale Centrale, also open on weekdays and closed on holidays, is closed during August as well. American scholars should bring a letter of introduction and their passport to the director's office for permission to use the archives.

Several bibliographical essays in English survey and comment on the vast Machiavelli literature: Eric Cochrane, "Machiavelli: 1940–1960," *Journal of Modern History* 33 (1961): 113–136; Cecil H. Clough, *Machiavelli Researches* (1967); Richard Clark, "Machiavelli: Bibliographical Spectrum," *Review of National Literatures* 1 (1970): 93–135; Felix Gilbert, "Machiavelli in Modern Historical Scholarship," *Italian Quarterly* 14 (1970): 9–26; Isaiah Berlin, "The Originality of Machiavelli," in Myron P. Gilmore, ed., *Studies on Machiavelli* (1972), pp. 147–206; and J. H. Geerken, "Machiavelli Studies since 1969," *Journal of the History of Ideas* 37 (1976): 351–368. Many biographies and monographs also contain excellent bibliographies.

The printed, edited writings of Machiavelli do not exist in a single collection. The most complete English edition of the major works and some lesser ones is Allan Gilbert, *Machiavelli: The Chief Works and Others*, 3 vols. (1965). The most recent, though incomplete, Italian collection is F. Flora and C. Cordie, eds., *Tutte le opere*, 2 vols. (1949–1950). Thousands of Machiavelli's documents and letters are as yet unpublished.

There are few genuine biographies of Machiavelli. The older, unsatisfactory Italian works are Oreste Tommasini, *La vita e gli scritti di N. Machiavelli*, 2 vols. (1883–1911), which prints generous segments of Machiavelli's writings, and Pasquale Villari, *The Life and Times of Niccolò Machiavelli*, 2 vols. (1891). The best Italian biography for its completeness and accuracy is Roberto Ridolfi, *The Life of Niccolò Machiavelli*, (1963), which is especially thorough on Machiavelli's diplomatic career. Two recent, brief life and work treatments are Quentin Skinner, *Machiavelli* (1981), which is judicious and reliable, and Silvia Ruffo-Fiore, *Niccolò Machiavelli* (1982), written from a literary slant. An even briefer treatment can be found in Franco Fido, "Machiavelli in His Times and Ours," *Italian Quarterly* 13 (1970): 3–21. Surely the most provocative yet satisfying biography is Sebastian de Grazia, *Machiavelli in Hell* (1989), because it offers the best analysis of the relationship of the man to his thought. Special sources for Machiavelli's diplomatic career are Nicolai Rubenstein, "The Beginnings of Niccolò Machiavelli's Career in the Florentine Chancery," *Italian Studies* 11 (1956): 72–91; Fredi Chiapelli, "Machiavelli as Secretary," *Italian Quarterly* 13 (1970): 27–44; and Eugenio D. Theseider, *Niccolò Machiavelli diplomatico* (1945).

Monographs on Machiavelli's thought would fill many libraries. A convenient, if arbitrary, method of condensation is to group major works by similarity of interpretation. The most common view, and one of the earliest interpretations outside Italy, was the "power politics school." To these writers, Machiavelli condoned political treachery and immorality rationalized by the ends justifying the means. For the expression of this view in Tudor England, see Felix Raab, *The English Face of Machiavelli* (1964). Condemnation of Machiavelli was not partisan, for both Protestants such as the Huguenot Innocent Gentillet and Catholics such as Cardinal Pole attacked Machiavelli in the sixteenth century. In the eighteenth century, ˙Frederick the Great castigated the Italian in his *Anti-Machiavel*. The twentieth-century equivalents can be found in an article by the Catholic scholar Jacques Maritain, "The End of Machiavellism," *Review of Politics* 4 (1942): 1–32; Leo Strauss's highly controversial *Thoughts on Machiavelli* (1958); and the unconvincing Mark Huilling, *Citizen Machiavelli* (1983).

A second school of interpretation, which might be called the "patriotic school," focuses on Machiavelli's love of country and desire for its salvation. He becomes the champion of republican virtues in the *Discourses* and warns against tyranny in *The Prince*. Some portray him as the progenitor of the Risorgimento. Italian authors expressing this view include Gennaro Sasso, *Niccolò Machiavelli: Storia del suo pensiero politico* (1958); Federico Chabod, *Machiavelli and the Renaissance* (1958); and biographers Tommasini and Villari. For criticism of this school, see Felix Gilbert, "The Concept of Nationalism in Machiavelli's *Prince*," *Studies in the Renaissance* 1 (1954): 38–48.

The "scientific school" sees Machiavelli as the first thinker to break with medieval political traditions and dissect politics with the logical precision of a laboratory scientist. This school argues that Machiavelli objectively separated morals and politics. For these authors, Machiavelli becomes the prototype of the modern political scientist and, some suggest, the founder of *raison d'état*. Italian authors from this school include Benedetto Croce, *Politics and Morals* (1946); Giuseppe Prezzolini, *Machiavelli* (1967) and *The Legacy of Italy* (1948); and the biographer Ridolfi. Other exponents are Herbert Butterfield, *The Statecraft of Machiavelli* (1940); Leonard Olschi, *Machiavelli the Scientist* (1945); Ernst Cassirer, *The Myth of the State* (1946); J. H. Whitfield, *Machiavelli* (1947) and *Discourses on Machiavelli* (1969); Neal Wood, "Machiavelli's Concept of *Virtù* Reconsidered," *Political Studies* 15 (1967): 159–172; and Bruce James Smith, *Politics and Remembrance: Republican Themes in Machiavelli, Burke and Tocqueville* (1985), A critique of the scientific school can be found in J. H. Hexter, *The Vision of Politics on the Eve of the Reformation: More, Machiavelli, and Seyssel* (1973).

A fourth division, which may be deemed the "aesthetic school," is determinedly opposed to the scientific school. This group claims that Machiavelli sees the state as a work of art rather than of science. The new prince molds and shapes men, laws, and institutions like an artist creating a masterpiece. The earliest proponent of this view was the nineteenth-century Swiss historian Jacob Burckhardt in his masterful account of the Italian Renaissance. More recent approaches can be found in Joseph Kraft, "Truth and Poetry in Machiavelli," *Journal of Modern History* 23 (1951): 109–121; Joseph Anthony Mazzeo, *Renaissance and Revolution: The Remaking of European Thought* (1965); Peter E. Bondanella, *Machiavelli and the Art of Renaissance History* (1973); Sydney Anglo's balanced *Machiavelli: A Dissection* (1969); and John Plamenatz's concise "Machiavelli," in his *Man and Society: Political and Social Theory, Machiavelli through Rousseau*, vol. 1 (1963).

Another novel approach features Machiavelli's special influence on early modern political ideas and emerging republics in the English-speaking world. The best sources are Zera Fink, *The Classical Republicans* (1962), and J.G.A. Pocock, *The Machiavellian Moment: Florentine Political Thought and the Atlantic Republican Tradition* (1975).

Finally, several collections of essays on Machiavelli include important insights and information. Among these are Felix Gilbert's sensible *Machiavelli and Guicciardini* (1965) and his collection of journal articles, *History: Choice and Commitment* (1977); Anthony Parel, ed., *The Political Calculus: Essays on Machiavelli's Philosophy* (1972); Martin Fleisher, ed., *Machiavelli and the Nature of Political Thought* (1972); Myron P. Gilmore, ed., *Studies on Machiavelli* (1972); and volume 13 (1970) of the *Italian Quarterly*.

Bibliography

Anglo, Sydney. *Machiavelli: A Dissection.* New York: Harcourt, Brace and World, 1969.
Berlin, Isaiah. "The Originality of Machiavelli." In *Studies on Machiavelli*, pp. 147–206. Edited by Myron P. Gilmore. Florence: Sansoni, 1972.
Bondanella, Peter E. *Machiavelli and the Art of Renaissance History.* Detroit: Wayne State University Press, 1973.
Butterfield, Herbert. *The Statecraft of Machiavelli.* London: Bell, 1940.
Cassirer, Ernst. *The Myth of the State.* New Haven, Conn.: Yale University Press, 1946.

Chabod, Federico. *Machiavelli and the Renaissance*. Translated by David Moore. London: Bowes and Bowes, 1958.

Chiapelli, Fredi. "Machiavelli as Secretary." *Italian Quarterly* 13 (1970): 27–44.

Clark, Richard. "Machiavelli: Bibliographical Spectrum." *Review of National Literatures* 1 (1970): 93–135.

Clough, Cecil H. *Machiavelli Researches*. Naples: Istituto Universitatio Orientale, 1967.

Cochrane, Eric. "Machiavelli, 1940–1960." *Journal of Modern History* 33 (1961): 113–136.

Croce, Benedetto. *Politics and Morals*. New York: Allen and Unwin, 1946.

De Grazia, Sebastian. *Machiavelli in Hell*. Princeton, N.J.: Princeton University Press, 1989.

Fido, Franco. "Machiavelli in His Times and Ours." *Italian Quarterly* 13 (1970): 3–21.

Fink, Zera S. *The Classical Republicans: An Essay in the Recovery of a Pattern of Thought in Seventeenth-Century England*. Evanston, Ill.: Northwestern University Press, 1962.

Fleischer, Martin, ed. *Machiavelli and the Nature of Political Thought*. New York: Atheneum, 1972.

Flora, Francesco, and Carlo Cordie, eds. *Tutte le opere di Niccolò Machiavelli*. 2 vols. Milan: Arnoldo Mondado, 1949–1950.

Geerken, J. H. "Machiavelli Studies Since 1969." *Journal of the History of Ideas* 37 (1976): 351–368.

Gilbert, Allan, ed. *Machiavelli: The Chief Works and Others*. 3 vols. Durham, N.C.: Duke University Press, 1965.

Gilbert, Felix. "The Concept of Nationalism in Machiavelli's *Prince*." *Studies in the Renaissance* 1 (1954): 38–48.

———. *History: Choice and Commitment*. Cambridge, Mass.: Harvard University Press, 1977.

———. *Machiavelli and Guicciardini: Politics and History in Sixteenth Century Florence*. Princeton, N.J.: Princeton University Press, 1965.

———. "Machiavelli in Modern Historical Scholarship." *Italian Quarterly* 14 (1970): 9–26.

Gilmore, Myron P., ed. *Studies on Machiavelli*. Florence: Sansoni, 1972.

Hexter, J. H. *The Vision of Politics on the Eve of the Reformation: More, Machiavelli, and Seyssel*. New York: Basic Books, 1973.

Huilling, Mark. *Citizen Machiavelli*. Princeton, N.J.: Princeton University Press, 1983.

Kraft, Joseph. "Truth and Poetry in Machiavelli." *Journal of Modern History* 23 (1951): 109–121.

Maritain, Jacques. "The End of Machiavellism." *Review of Politics* 4 (1942): 1–32.

Mazzeo, Joseph Anthony. *Renaissance and Revolution: The Remaking of European Thought*. New York: Pantheon, 1965.

Olschi, C., ed. *Libro di Ricordi de Bernardo Machiavelli*. Florence: LeMonnier, 1954.

Olschi, Leonard. *Machiavelli the Scientist*. Berkeley, Calif.: Gillick Press, 1945.

Parel, Anthony, ed. *The Political Calculus: Essays on Machiavelli's Philosophy*. Toronto: University of Toronto Press, 1972.

Plamenatz, John. *Man and Society: Political and Social Theory, Machiavelli Through Rousseau*. Vol. 1. New York: McGraw-Hill, 1963.

Pocock, J.G.A. *The Machiavellian Moment: Florentine Political Thought and the Atlantic Republican Tradition*. Princeton, N.J.: Princeton University Press, 1975.

Prezzolini, Giuseppe. *The Legacy of Italy*. New York: Vann, 1948.

———. *Machiavelli*. Translated by Gioconda Savini. New York: Farrar, Straus and Giroux, 1967.

Raab, Felix. *The English Face of Machiavelli: A Changing Interpretation, 1500–1700*. London: Routledge and Kegan Paul, 1964.

Ridolfi, Roberto. *The Life of Niccolò Machiavelli*. 3rd ed. Translated by Cecil Grayson. Chicago: University of Chicago Press, 1963.

Rubenstein, Nicolai. "The Beginnings of Niccolò Machiavelli's Career in the Florentine Chancery." *Italian Studies* 11 (1956): 72–91.

Ruffo-Fiore, Silvia. *Niccolò Machiavelli*. Boston: Twayne, 1982.

Sasso, Gennaro. *Niccolò Machiavelli: Storia del suo pensiero politico*. Naples: Istituto Italiano, 1958.

Skinner, Quentin. *Machiavelli*. New York: Hill and Wang, 1981.

Smith, Bruce James. *Politics and Remembrance: Republican Themes in Machiavelli, Burke, and Tocqueville*. Princeton, N.J.: Princeton University Press, 1985.

Strauss, Leo. *Thoughts on Machiavelli*. Glencoe, Ill.: Free Press, 1958.

Theseider, Eugenio D. *Niccolò Machiavelli diplomatico*. Milan: Marzorati, 1945.

Tommasini, Oreste. *La vita e gli scritti di N. Machiavelli*. 2 vols. Rome: Loescher, 1883–1911.

Villari, Pasquale. *The Life and Times of Niccolò Machiavelli*. 2 vols. Translated by Linda Villari. New York: Scribner's, 1891.

Whitfield, J. H. *Discourses on Machiavelli*. Cambridge, Eng.: Heffer, 1969.

———. *Machiavelli*. Oxford: Blackwell, 1947.

Wood, Neal. "Machiavelli's Concept of *Virtù* Reconsidered." *Political Studies* 15 (1967): 159–172.

DANIEL W. HOLLIS III

James Madison (1751–1836).   Commonly called the "Father of the U.S. Constitution," James Madison made contributions in the field of international relations that are less frequently recognized but no less important. Born on March 16, 1751, to James Madison and Eleanor "Nelly" Rose Conway Madison, Madison had a childhood similar to that of most aristocratic young men of the mid-eighteenth century. As the eldest son and one of ten children produced by a marriage between elite Virginia planter families, Madison was privately tutored until he reached age eighteen, after which he studied at the College of New Jersey (now Princeton). After completing his course work in two years, Madison returned to the family plantation, Montpelier. His formal studies now finished, he studied law intermittently and continued to read voraciously, maintaining his lifelong love of Latin and Greek.

After his return to Virginia, Madison entered public service as a member of his county's Committee of Safety in 1774. Elected to the Virginia Convention in 1776, he helped draft a plan for the new Virginia state government, then served in the state's House of Delegates and Council of State during the next three years, directing the state's war effort against the British. From 1780 to 1783, he served in the Continental Congress and supported an import duty that would increase federal revenue. Madison returned to the Virginia House of

Delegates for two more years (1784–1786), where he fought to regulate commerce and foreign trade by limiting Virginia to only two ports. Virginia sent Madison to the Annapolis Convention in 1786, a gathering ostensibly called to consider disputes about interstate commerce but which eventually led to the call for a constitutional convention in 1787.

As a delegate to the Constitutional Convention, Madison helped draft portions of the U.S. Constitution, kept extensive daily notes on the debates, and later led the campaign for ratification. Along with Alexander Hamilton and John Jay, Madison wrote *The Federalist*, eighty-five essays designed to sway public opinion in favor of adopting the new constitution with its strong central government. After ratification, Madison began eight years of service in the U.S. House of Representatives (1789–1797), where he authored and helped pass the Bill of Rights, the first ten amendments to the Constitution, comprised mainly of protections of individual rights from abuses by the powerful new national government.

While serving in the House of Representatives, Madison became increasingly opposed to many of the new government's fiscal policies and moved away from his Federalist leanings to become a leader of the opposition Jeffersonian party. Madison also opposed Hamilton's pro-British tendencies and attacked President Washington's neutrality proclamation. After the election of another Federalist president, John Adams, Madison retired from active public service to enjoy farming and married life. He would later return to serve as *Thomas Jefferson's secretary of state (1801–1809) and as president in his own right (1809–1817) before returning to his Virginia estate with his wife Dolly, whom he had married in 1794.

As Jefferson's secretary of state, Madison enjoyed the president's complete confidence, in large part because of their similar political views. Although he had written occasionally about foreign affairs in *The Federalist*, Madison arrived at the post with little prior experience in foreign relations and personal diplomacy. In the Continental Congress, he had sent instructions to diplomats and argued about western land claims and navigation of the Mississippi, but he had never served in a formal diplomatic post or represented the United States in treaty negotiations. Under Madison, ideals of the American Revolution continued to influence the course of foreign relations: republics should be free from conflict, and should prosper from the natural, unrestricted commercial relations among nations. If the nation were challenged, war might be avoided; commerce could be used as a weapon to achieve American objectives.

During Madison's tenure in office, his greatest challenges stemmed from the ongoing war between France and Great Britain and the United States' role as a neutral in that war. The rising tide of American commerce placed its ships and sailors at risk, but shipping in wartime was extremely lucrative. Both nations proclaimed blockades and forbade neutrals to trade war materials or contraband (broadly defined) with the enemy, and seized ships that were doing so. The British policy, clearly aimed at the growing American shipping industry, was based on the "doctrine of continuous voyage," a principle enunciated in the 1805 *Essex* case. Britain also maintained the right to impress British subjects into its navy, even if they were serving on American ships. In their desperation for able-bodied men, British cruisers stopped American ships and virtually kidnapped American sailors, claiming that they were British subjects.

At first, Madison's duties as secretary of state seemed uncomplicated, since the conflict between the warring parties ceased with the Peace of Amiens in 1801. But war resumed in 1803, and American ships and sailors once again became vulnerable to seizure or impressment. Madison protested both the ship seizures and the impressments and asserted the absolute sovereignty of a ship's flag—persons on any ship flying the American flag were protected from seizure, even British citizens. Except for military personnel of the enemy, "the United States can never acknowledge a right in any other nation to take from their vessels on the high seas any persons whatever," wrote Madison. The British never intended to stop impressments, although they hinted that they might— desertions from their own ships would only escalate if they did.

In 1806 Madison anonymously wrote a treatise on the doctrine of neutral trade in which he attacked the British practice of seizing ships of neutral countries that traded with colonies of the enemy but allowing the ships of its own country to trade freely there. In effect, the British were willing to trade with the enemy, but made war on neutrals that might be trading noncontraband items. Madison's research showed that no other country maintained such a law except Great Britain, which enforced the law only through naval supremacy. His protests were to no avail; America's military weakness allowed Britain to continue its depredations.

In 1807, having failed to change British and French policies through diplomatic channels, Madison and Jefferson resorted to a trade embargo that closed American ports and forbade American ships to go to sea. To avoid war with either belligerent, the United States attempted to employ a policy of economic coercion. The embargo failed miserably, severely damaged the U.S. economy, and generated public hostility toward Jefferson's administration. As one of the last acts of his administration, Jefferson repealed the embargo in 1809, but replaced it with the Non-Intercourse Act, which permitted U.S. trade with all nations except Britain and France and promised to allow trade with either nation if it agreed to respect the neutrality of American shipping. After Madison assumed the presidency in March 1809, it slowly became clear that this policy was also ineffective. The Non-Intercourse Act was repealed in 1810 and replaced with Macon's Bill No. 2, which returned to the policy of open trade with all nations, but provided that if either Britain or France agreed to recognize the neutrality of American ships, America would cease trading with the nation that did not recognize those rights. After the French apparently agreed to change their policy and respect the neutrality of American ships, Madison issued a proclamation of nonintercourse with Britain.

With the growing influence of congressional "War Hawks" like John C. Calhoun and Henry Clay, who pressed for a war with Britain in order to seize

Canada and subdue the restless Indians along America's western border, Madison finally requested Congress to declare war on Great Britain in June 1812. Justifying the war because of continued British impressment, Madison claimed that "thousands of American citizens . . . have been torn from their country and from everything dear to them; have been dragged on board ships of war of a foreign nation" and made to fight in battle and risk their lives for a country to which they did not belong. The war lasted two years, and both war-weary nations agreed to peace in the Treaty of Ghent (December 1814), which left the issue of impressment unresolved.

The weakness of the young nation, which lacked a real military force and the necessary infrastructure to support it economically and industrially, had become apparent to Madison. His old republican fears of overly centralized power faded somewhat, to be replaced with a cautious nationalism, built upon moderate tariffs and the Second Bank of the United States. After Madison's departure from the presidency, he turned his attention to issues of slavery, agriculture, higher education, and nullification, leaving the work of foreign affairs to others. He lived in retirement at his Virginia estate until his death on June 28, 1836.

If one looks beyond the continuing popularity of the U.S. Constitution and Bill of Rights, it is astonishing to consider the influence that Madison's vision of neutrality has had on the international law of the sea. The term *neutrality* first appeared as early as the seventeenth century, but theories of neutrality really came to be developed fully in the nineteenth century, in part because of the U.S. role during the Napoleonic Wars. Although not formally banned by the Treaty of Ghent, the impressment of citizens was dropped by the British and has not been used since. More important, the principle that Madison used to oppose impressment—the absolute sovereignty of a ship's flag—has been adopted and universally employed. The Convention on the High Seas of 1958 and the Law of the Seas Convention of 1982 agree that ships under the flag of a given nation are under that nation's exclusive jurisdiction on the high seas. A ship from nation A may not board the ship of nation B without the consent of B's ship master. It does not matter what strength either nation's navy may have; all ships have territorial integrity, similar to that of a nation's embassy, which is considered to be on foreign soil lying within the host country.

Blockades can no longer be as weak and insubstantial as the British "paper blockades" used during the Napoleonic Wars to justify seizing neutral shipping. In the Declaration of Paris (1856), nations agreed not to recognize paper blockades; only a force sufficient to prevent access to the coasts of the enemy is considered an active blockade. A ship that violates an active blockade is still liable to seizure and forfeit. Blockades in their traditional form, however, have gone out of favor with changes in military technology. Belligerent nations now more often rely on the doctrine of continuous voyage, which Madison also protested.

The doctrine of continuous voyage was actually turned against British shipping during the American Civil War. British goods to be transshipped through the

Caribbean, destined for southern ports, were vulnerable to seizure by northern ships before their arrival in the West Indies. In a matter of possible seizure, the trend in the twentieth century has been to consider the ultimate destination of goods that might be contained within the ships, or passing through the territory, of a neutral party—thus supporting the doctrine of continuous voyage. The acceptance of this doctrine may have come about as a result of the nature of modern warfare. The extension of war to a nation's entire population means that essentially all goods supporting them become contraband, and thus legitimate prey for belligerent nations. Although some nations experimented with the licensing of neutral trade during World War II, the freedom of neutral trade exists at the sufferance of warring nations, as in Madison's day.

The influence of Madison's views has waxed and waned with the shifting relations between weak and neutral nations (such as the United States in Madison's time) and strong belligerent ones. From a position of relative weakness in the eighteenth century, neutral nations gained recognition and safety under several of the principles that Madison supported. America's usual role of neutral commercial trader was well served by requirements for active blockades, recognition of the sovereignty of a ship's flag, and the abandonment of impressment. With the increased strength of the United States and its entrance into global conflicts, as well as the changing nature of modern war, the "traditional" areas of freedom accorded to neutrals (and advocated by Madison) have slowly decreased in the twentieth century. Now, of all the policies he supported in the realm of neutrality, only the concept of a ship's flag sovereignty remains fully intact.

Annotated Bibliography

The largest collection of Madison's papers is in the Library of Congress, Washington, D.C., which received the bulk of his manuscripts after his death. The library has approximately 11,500 manuscripts written to or by Madison, journals, and some printed matter. There are eighty-six volumes, eighteen containing material by Madison and sixty-eight containing material sent to him by others. There is a published index, and a calendar of the whole collection is available for use at the library. Much of this collection is available on microfilm.

The holdings of the National Archives, Washington, D.C., include many of Madison's official documents, such as papers from his period of service in the Continental Congress, the House of Representatives, and the Department of State. Much of this collection is also available on microfilm.

Madison did not write extensively on the subject of foreign affairs, but like almost all political figures of the eighteenth century and early nineteenth century, his letters contain much of what he thought and believed. As early as the 1780s, he began saving correspondence that came to him. After his retirement from the presidency in 1817, Madison often kept drafts of letters he sent and made efforts to recover those he had sent earlier in his career. This body of correspondence remained intact only a short time after his death in 1836; but despite the pilfering of his stepson, who sold Madison's letters to raise money, and the editorial efforts of early biographers, who sometimes misplaced documents, there remained a collection of nearly 10,000 papers that the Library of Congress acquired in 1848.

Various editions of Madison's papers have been printed. Between 1900 and 1910, Gallard Hunt published a nine-volume series that briefly addressed Madison's foreign policy, *The Writings of James Madison* (1900–1910). Only volumes 6 through 9 covered the period from 1801 to 1815, and much was omitted, yet Hunt's work remained unsurpassed until recently.

Under the editorship of William T. Hutchinson, Robert Rutland, and others, Madison's collected papers have been published on a regular basis since the 1960s. The first series, and the largest known body of Madison's writings, *The Papers of James Madison*, edited by William T. Hutchinson et al. (1962), together with later additions, consists of his papers before he became secretary of state. The second series, *The Papers of James Madison: Secretary of State Series*, edited by Robert J. Brugger et al. (1986), covers Madison's tenure as Jefferson's secretary of state. The third series, *The Papers of James Madison: Presidential Series*, edited by Robert Rutland et al. (1984), includes Madison's presidential writings, beginning in March 1809. When completed, these three series will comprise a full record of Madison's public career. However, for printed sources, the scholar must still resort to Hunt's volumes for the periods not yet covered by these incomplete series.

Madison's one text on the subject of neutral trade was published anonymously as *An examination of the British doctrine, which subjects to capture a neutral trade . . .* (1806). This might profitably be read in conjunction with another pamphlet written by James Stephens, who argued an opposing view on many of the same questions in *War in Disguise, or the Frauds of the Neutral Flag* (1805). A full discussion of these pamphlets can be found in Irving Brant's biography of Madison.

James Madison has been the subject of several biographers, none more devoted than Brant, author of a six-volume work, *James Madison* (1941–1961). For twenty years Brant, a professional newspaperman, chronicled Madison's life. Of his six-volume series, he devoted three volumes to Madison's service as secretary of state and president. A one-volume abridgment, *The Fourth President*, appeared in 1970. Composed with an eye for detail, well written, and wide ranging in its research, Brant's work still stands as the definitive study of Madison, although historians have taken exception to his narrow focus. Brant became enamored of his subject, praising Madison excessively while attacking his opponents.

Responding to earlier criticisms of Madison, particularly the claim that Madison was merely a pale reflection of Jefferson, Brant assessed Madison's influence in politics and foreign affairs. Later biographers of Madison such as Adrienne Koch, *Jefferson and Madison: The Great Collaboration* (1950), Ralph Ketcham, *James Madison: A Biography* (1971), and Robert Rutland, *The Presidency of James Madison* (1990), have largely agreed with Brant's view, while sometimes disputing the details. Rutland's book contains an extensive bibliography as well.

Other writers have agreed that Madison played a larger role than previously thought, but they differ on what motivated Madison's decisions. J.C.A. Stagg, in *Mr. Madison's War: Politics, Diplomacy, and Warfare in the Early American Republic, 1783–1830* (1983), concluded that Madison's diplomatic choices were often made as a result of domestic politics and international economics. In "James Madison and the Coercion of Great Britain," *William and Mary Quarterly*, 3rd ser. 38, 1 (1981): 3–34, Stagg argues that Madison supported the attack on Canada in an effort to deprive Britain of American goods transported through Canada; otherwise his economic strategies to alter British policy would fail. Stagg has also suggested that challenges brought by other Republican leaders prompted Madison to seek war in an effort to retain political control. Attempting to draw these various strands together, Drew McCoy has found the roots of both Madison's domestic economic views and his policy of discrimination against Great Britain in the fertile soil of Republican ideology and describes them in "Republicanism and American Foreign Policy," *William and Mary Quarterly*, 3rd ser. 31 (1974): 633–646.

Bibliography

Works by Madison

An examination of the British doctrine, which subjects to capture a neutral trade, not open in time of peace. Philadelphia(?): N.p., 1806(?).
The Federalist. Edited by Jacob E. Cooke. Reprint. Middletown, Conn.: Wesleyan University Press, 1967.
The Papers of James Madison. Edited by William T. Hutchinson, William M. Rachal, et al. 17 vols. to date. Chicago: University of Chicago Press, 1962– .
The Papers of James Madison: Presidential Series. Edited by Robert Rutland et al. 1 vol. to date. Charlottesville: University Press of Virginia, 1984– .
The Papers of James Madison: Secretary of State Series. Edited by Robert J. Brugger et al. 1 vol. to date. Charlottesville: University Press of Virginia, 1986– .
The Writings of James Madison: Comprising His Public Papers and His Private Correspondence, including numerous letters and documents now for the first time printed. Edited by Gaillard Hunt. 9 vols. New York: Putnam's, 1900–1910. Microfilm reprint, 1973.

Works about Madison

Brant, Irving. *The Fourth President.* Indianapolis: Bobbs-Merrill, 1970.
———. *James Madison.* 6 vols. Indianapolis: Bobbs-Merrill, 1941–1961.
Kaplan, Lawrence S. "France and Madison's Decision for War." *Mississippi Valley Historical Review* 50, no. 4 (1964): 652–671.
Ketcham, Ralph. *James Madison: A Biography.* New York: Macmillan, 1971.
Koch, Adrienne. *Jefferson and Madison: The Great Collaboration.* New York: Oxford University Press, 1950.
McCoy, Drew. "Republicanism and American Foreign Policy: James Madison and the Political Economy of Commercial Discrimination, 1789–1794." *William and Mary Quarterly*, 3rd ser. 31 (1974): 633–646.
Rutland, Robert A. *The Presidency of James Madison.* Lawrence: University Press of Kansas, 1990.
Smith, Abbot. "Mr. Madison's War: An Unsuccessful Experiment in the Conduct of National Policy." *Political Science Quarterly* 57, no. 2 (1942): 229–246.
Stagg, J.C.A. "James Madison and the Coercion of Great Britain: Canada, the West Indies, and the War of 1812." *William and Mary Quarterly*, 3rd ser. 38, no. 1 (1981): 3–34.
———. "James Madison and the 'Malcontents': The Political Origins of the War of 1812." *William and Mary Quarterly*, 3rd ser. 33, no. 4 (1976): 558–585.
———. *Mr. Madison's War: Politics, Diplomacy, and Warfare in the Early American Republic, 1783–1830.* Princeton, N.J.: Princeton University Press, 1983.

Related Works

Burt, A. L. *The United States, Great Britain, and British North America*. 1940. Reprint. New Haven, Conn.: Yale University Press, 1961.

Horsman, Reginald. *The Causes of the War of 1812*. Philadelphia: University of Pennsylvania Press, 1962.

Perkins, Bradford. *Castlereagh and Adams: England and the United States, 1812–1823*. Berkeley: University of California Press, 1964.

———. *Prologue to War: England and the United States, 1805–1812*. Berkeley: University of California Press, 1961.

Pratt, Julius. *The Expansionists of 1812*. New York: Macmillan, 1925.

Rutland, Robert A. *Madison's Alternatives: The Jeffersonian Republicans and the Coming of War, 1805–1812*. Philadelphia: Lippincott, 1975.

SALLY E. HADDEN

George Catlett Marshall (1880–1959).   George Marshall's career spanned the transformation of the United States from an interested observer of the international order to a superpower responsible for preserving it. When he was born in 1880, his country was a continental power not yet in full control of its own territory. As a junior officer of the United States Army he participated in the first stages of American overseas expansion. And as a general and a cabinet secretary he helped make the United States the leader of the Western world. His balanced judgment, strategic vision, and spotless personal integrity served him and his country well. He was never an inspirational leader or a bold adventurer, but always a steady hand and sober judge on whom others relied in a crisis.

Marshall was born in Uniontown, Pennsylvania, on December 31, 1880, the son of a coke and furnace company president. He attended the Virginia Military Institute, at first motivated more by rivalry with his brother than by any particular interest in the military, and accepted a commission in the army in 1902. His initial assignment was in the Philippines, where he first displayed the quiet competence and steadiness under pressure that would be his hallmark.

When the United States entered World War I, Marshall's horizons broadened to include Europe. As a member of General John J. Pershing's staff, Marshall acquired experience in handling large military organizations and in dealing with fractious allies, which would serve him well later in his career. He also earned the enduring suspicion of Douglas MacArthur, who felt ill-treated by Pershing's headquarters.

During the 1920s Marshall commanded an infantry regiment in volatile China, handling delicate political situations with professionalism and aplomb. Ironically, that regiment was the largest operational unit he ever commanded personally, though he rose to the highest rank in the army. Back home in the 1930s, Marshall's career languished while MacArthur was chief of staff. Despite his reputation as one of the army's brightest officers, Marshall was relegated to training national guard units and running Civilian Conservation Corps programs. However, loyal and efficient service in these posts won him the appreciation of President *Franklin Roosevelt, and once MacArthur left for the Philippines Marshall's career advanced quickly, culminating in his appointment as army chief of staff on September 1, 1939.

Taking office the very day World War II began in Europe, Marshall followed events there with keen interest as he worked to prepare his service for war. His skillful testimony before congressional committees smoothed the path of rearmament, and his organizational genius was instrumental in preparing the peacetime U.S. Army for war in two short years. In addition, his decentralized management style allowed talented subordinates to prove themselves, many of whom (notably Col. Dwight D. Eisenhower) did sterling work in higher positions later on. Unfortunately, this same trust in subordinates led him wrongly to assume that army forces in Hawaii had taken his warnings seriously and were more alert in December 1941 than proved to be the case.

Once the United States entered the war, Marshall's steady hand enabled the Combined Chiefs of Staff to overcome a variety of inter-Allied and interservice tensions and work together successfully for victory in Europe and the Pacific. In particular, Marshall enforced the decision to concentrate first on the defeat of Germany, despite the emotions aroused by Pearl Harbor and the insistent pleas of MacArthur and the navy. Marshall also pressed for a cross-Channel assault at the earliest possible date, over the persistent objections of the British. He was able to get along with such difficult personalities as U.S. Chief of Naval Operations Ernest King, who repeatedly demanded more resources for the Pacific, and British Chief of the Imperial General Staff Alan Brooke, who stubbornly resisted invading Europe. When fundamental principles were at stake, Marshall could be fierce, as when he rejected British Prime Minister *Winston Churchill's Mediterranean sideshows with a vehemence bordering on insubordination, but his real genius was for persuading his opponents while retaining their respect and affection.

The postwar division of Europe was not his doing, though his reluctance to question the political decisions of his superiors or the military decisions of his subordinates made him guilty of sins of omission. He acquiesced in Roosevelt's idealistic plan for a postwar order guaranteed by the United Nations, and failed to press his doubts about the reliability of Soviet friendship. And when Eisenhower decided not to capture Berlin although U.S. forces had the opportunity, Marshall supported him on the grounds that the judgment of the commander on the scene should prevail.

At the end of 1945, as Marshall looked forward to a well-earned retirement, President Harry Truman asked him to go to China to mediate between the Communists and Nationalists. Marshall's profound sense of duty compelled him to accept despite his reluctance, and his second career as a diplomat began. His first taste of civilian diplomacy was not a happy one. Marshall sought to play the role of honest broker, for which his balanced temperament was admirably suited, but he lacked any leverage with which to force concessions, or even sincere effort, from either party. After a full year of hard work, he was unable to make any progress in reconciling the two irreconcilable foes and came home.

Nevertheless, Truman recognized Marshall's value in the high councils of government and appointed him secretary of state in January 1947.

Marshall barely had moved into his office when the British announced that they were no longer able to support Greece and Turkey against internal and external Soviet pressures. After hearing the views of his State Department staff and the secretaries of war and the navy, Marshall recommended to Truman that the United States take on that burden. This became known as the Truman Doctrine, by which the United States accepted responsibility for aiding free nations under threat from foreign or domestic enemies. Marshall's authoritative briefing of a congressional delegation and the nearly unanimous respect he commanded from both political parties were crucial in persuading Congress to approve this substantial new commitment.

Marshall saw the U.S. role as resisting aggression, not crusading against communism. He was no ideologue, and he also felt that the United States lacked the military power for a full-scale confrontation. In fact, the dramatic rhetoric with which the White House chose to justify the Truman Doctrine disturbed Marshall deeply. However, World War II had taught him that the United States could no longer stand aside from international affairs. By supporting free nations without directly confronting the Soviets, he hoped that Western security could be preserved while avoiding a major war.

The Truman Doctrine was not yet announced when Marshall traveled to Moscow for a foreign ministers' conference. This was a watershed event for two reasons. First, the recalcitrant Soviet tone at this conference finally convinced Marshall that the wartime regime of friendly cooperation with the Soviets was no longer possible. And even more important, his tour of western Europe en route to Moscow persuaded Marshall that the stability of Europe hung by a thread and required urgent measures to produce an economic recovery before it was too late.

Marshall concluded that a large infusion of American economic aid was needed, and quickly. This economic commitment to complement the military security provided by the Truman Doctrine became known as the Marshall Plan, a terminological egotism Marshall tolerated with distaste in order to promote the program. As soon as he returned to Washington from Moscow, Marshall obtained recommendations from his State Department staff regarding the nature and amount of aid required. He determined that a multibillion-dollar, multiyear commitment was necessary, that it must finance a recovery program planned by the Europeans themselves and not dictated by the United States, and that it must be available to any European nation willing to participate, including the Soviets.

Marshall announced the plan in a commencement speech at Harvard University in June 1947. For a historic speech, it was not particularly stirring and did not arouse great audience enthusiasm, but the governments of western Europe seized the offer instantly. The Soviet bloc, suspicious of U.S. motives and potential strings attached, refused to participate, freeing the United States from the embarrassment of rebuilding an increasingly obvious enemy. Congress and the

American public were almost as suspicious as the Soviets at first, wondering how much it would cost and why they should rebuild Europe. But once again, Marshall's political skill, persuasiveness in congressional testimony, and reputation for balanced judgment were vital in securing the approval of a reluctant Congress. As a result, Congress passed the first European Recovery Plan appropriation of more than $5 billion in April 1948, and over the next four years over $12 billion financed what the Europeans now call their "economic miracle." In recognition of his efforts Marshall received the Nobel Peace Prize in 1953.

Marshall's (and America's) motives have remained the subject of fierce debate. Hostility to communism, hunger for export markets to avoid a U.S. recession, a desire to make Europe permanently dependent upon the United States, as well as sincere humanitarianism have their advocates. The reality is that all these motives played a part. Marshall employed every argument he could muster in his congressional and public campaigns for the plan. To humanitarian audiences he emphasized the altruistic angle; to businessmen he emphasized the economic argument; and to conservative audiences he emphasized the Communist menace. In his own mind, sincere concern for Allied peoples as well as fear for the stability of Europe were important.

The future of Europe could not be secured, however, until the status of Germany was settled. Marshall had fought two world wars against Germany in thirty years, and thus knew as well as anyone the perils of German militarism, but he also realized that unless Germany recovered economically and politically it would be a permanent drain on American resources and a continuing opportunity for Soviet subversion. He attempted to include the Soviets in four-power rehabilitation efforts, but when Moscow proved interested only in pillage, Marshall endorsed the plan of Lucius Clay, the American military governor, to reform the western occupation zones without Soviet participation.

The Soviets responded with the Berlin blockade in 1948. Marshall insisted that the Allies would remain in Berlin, by force if necessary, but he resisted the military governor's proposal to break the blockade by force immediately. Marshall felt that the blockade could be broken by means short of open warfare, using a military airlift and diplomacy backed by the threat of force. To this end the United States dispatched two B–29 bomber groups to Britain, concentrated American cargo planes in Germany, and waited for the Soviets to blink, as they eventually did. Here Marshall's military background served him well; his thorough knowledge of military logistics enabled him to see the possibilities of airlift, and his knowledge of warfare enabled him to see the risks in a prematurely belligerent response.

The formation of NATO crowned Marshall's role in the rescue of Europe. He had encouraged the Europeans' own efforts to unite for their common defense, but avoided committing the United States until the European Recovery Plan was established. By 1948, however, U.S. association with the European defense pacts was timely, and Marshall entered negotiations for what became the North Atlantic Treaty of 1949. He had never doubted the need for a U.S. role in defense of the Atlantic community, but his patient approach to that step ensured that it had broad public support in the United States.

Of necessity, Europe was the focus of Marshall's tenure as secretary of state, but the Middle East also required his attention when Britain announced that it was surrendering its Palestine mandate and handing the problem over to the United Nations. Marshall sought a realistic settlement acceptable to both Jews and Arabs without war—an impossible goal. He hoped to avoid alienating either side or giving the Soviets an opportunity for mischief in a strategic part of the world. Intransigence on both sides precluded a stable settlement in any case, but Marshall was disturbed to see U.S. policy distorted by White House concern for the 1948 presidential election.

Asian affairs were never a priority for the Marshall State Department. In Japan, Marshall was content to give MacArthur a free hand, recognizing his Asian expertise, and reluctant as always to interfere with a successful man on the scene. And after his 1946 experience, Marshall largely gave up trying to influence events in China. Moreover, he feared that a policy of intervening in every conflict around the world would stretch American resources too thin and allow adversaries the advantage of striking wherever the United States was weakest. U.S. policy focused more on a graceful exit than on helping the Nationalists, and in any case, it is highly unlikely any U.S. action could have prevented the Communist victory.

In January 1949, with Europe on the way to recovery and other global crises for the moment under control, Marshall felt able to retire from government service at last. He handed the State Department over to *Dean Acheson, who had been his undersecretary in 1947. Marshall had been popular in the State Department, an organization not known for admiring soldiers. He gave his subordinates clear guidance and wide responsibility, and unlike the stereotypical general he invariably sought political rather than military solutions. His political skill and towering personal reputation also gave his department an unaccustomed amount of authority.

Marshall had already been brought out of retirement to head the American Red Cross when the Korean War erupted, and Truman called on him in September 1950 to be secretary of defense. As in 1945, Marshall's forbearance allowed superiors and subordinates to pursue muddled policies unchallenged. He failed to control MacArthur, and he failed to demand consistent goals and guidelines from Truman. When Truman and MacArthur finally came to a showdown in April 1951, Marshall was largely an unhappy bystander, urging Truman to be patient but supporting his insistence on the principle of civilian supremacy over the military.

For his strenuous effort to avoid politics (admittedly, a staggeringly naive hope for a cabinet official), Marshall's reward was to be treated by the Republican Congress with a roughness usually reserved for partisan political figures. Senator Joseph McCarthy and his followers accused him of everything from sacrificing China to aiding and abetting ''Acheson's Reds'' in the State Department to tolerating Communists in the Pentagon. Marshall maintained his dignity and integrity throughout, and ultimately his accusers managed only to embarrass themselves. Nevertheless, the experience made him all the more happy to escape public office. In September 1951, with the Korean situation stabilized and his health failing, Marshall once again retired, this time for good. He died in Washington, D.C., on October 16, 1959, a revered hero of war and peace, untainted by politics.

Marshall's diplomatic career marked the last gasp of bipartisanship in U.S. foreign policy. Thereafter, foreign policy would be an ideological and electoral football. But he left an enduring legacy in his example of modest, calm, responsible public service and his foundation of a permanent American partnership with a secure and prosperous Europe.

Annotated Bibliography

The George C. Marshall Research Library on the grounds of the Virginia Military Institute, Lexington, Virginia, is the essential source of archival holdings relating to Marshall. All of his personal papers are stored there, along with transcripts of Marshall biographer Forrest C. Pogue's interviews of Marshall and numerous Marshall associates, as well as copies of all other relevant documents consulted by Pogue in other archives. These others include the National Archives and the Library of Congress in Washington, D.C.; the Eisenhower Library in Abilene, Kansas; the Truman Library in Independence, Missouri; the Franklin D. Roosevelt Library in Hyde Park, New York; and the U.S. Army Military History Institute, Carlisle Barracks, Pennsylvania.

Marshall's regrettable diffidence has deprived history of what would certainly have been one of the most interesting autobiographies of the century. He refused all invitations to write a memoir, and even destroyed his World War II diary. His only written recollection is a short account of his World War I experiences, *Memories of My Services in the World War* (1976), which he unsuccessfully sought to publish in the 1920s and then forgot. For his own view of his life we have only the series of interviews conducted by Forrest C. Pogue. Even there, Marshall's characteristic discretion has left numerous gaps in the topics covered.

Fortunately, in the absence of an autobiography there exists an authoritative and comprehensive four-volume biography by Pogue, *George C. Marshall* (1963–1987). Pogue was a combat historian in Europe in World War II and wrote a volume on the Supreme Command for the official army history of World War II before beginning work on his Marshall study in the 1950s. Pogue interviewed Marshall at length, as well as an army of Marshall associates. He also had full access to Marshall's personal and official correspondence, and obtained copies of all relevant documents stored elsewhere. He covers the full breadth of an exceptionally broad career and is the definitive guide to the documentary evidence concerning Marshall. His regard for Marshall is obvious, but he also discusses Marshall's failures candidly and thoroughly.

There is also a useful one-volume biography by Leonard Mosley, *Marshall: Hero for Our Times* (1983). Necessarily brief and selective in its coverage, and unreliable in some minor details, it nevertheless gives the reader a concise look at the highlights of Marshall's career. Mosley had access to all the evidence gathered by Pogue and did some supplementary interviews of his own. Robert Ferrell's *George C. Marshall 1947–1949* (1966), in the American Secretaries of State and Their Diplomacy series, is a more specialized study of his diplomatic career by a distinguished American diplomatic historian. For the personal side, there is Katherine Marshall, *Together: Annals of an Army Wife* (1946), an anecdotal account by his second wife of their life together from their 1930 marriage to his retirement from the army in 1945. Marshall saw some but not all of the manuscript before publication, so it bears some of his imprint as well. Unfortunately, it concludes before the start of his diplomatic career.

The memoirs of Marshall's associates are also valuable. Dwight Eisenhower, *Crusade in Europe* (1948), and Clay Blair and Omar Bradley, *A General's Life* (1983), both describe admiringly Marshall's leadership in World War II, and the Bradley memoir deals with the postwar period as well. Winston Churchill, *History of the Second World War*, 6 vols. (1948–1953); Arthur Bryant, *The Turn of the Tide* (1957) and *Triumph in the West* (1959), based on the diaries and autobiographical notes of Field Marshal the Viscount Alanbrooke; and Andrew Cunningham, *A Sailor's Odyssey* (1951), give the sometimes different but invariably respectful view from the British side of the wartime conference table.

For Marshall's postwar career there is the colorful and opinionated Harry Truman, *Memoirs*, 2 vols. (1955–1956); Defense Secretary James Forrestal, *The Forrestal Diaries* (1951); Lucius D. Clay, *Decision in Germany* (1950); Ambassador Walter Bedell Smith, *My Three Years in Moscow* (1950); Albert C. Wedemeyer, *Wedemeyer Reports!* (1958), by a fellow general and friend who clashed with Marshall over Asian policy; career diplomat Charles Bohlen, *Witness to History* (1973); postwar British prime minister Clement Attlee, *Twilight of Empire* (1962); and especially Dean Acheson's well-written and informative *Present at the Creation* (1969).

Various collections of personal papers of Marshall associates offer less polished viewpoints, notably Robert H. Ferrell, *Off the Record: The Private Papers of Harry S. Truman* (1980) and *The Eisenhower Diaries* (1981), as well as Arthur H. Vandenberg, Jr., *The Private Papers of Senator Vandenberg* (1952). Biographies of men whose lives were intertwined with Marshall's are also important, particularly Stephen Ambrose, *Eisenhower*, 2 vols. (1983–1984), D. Clayton James, *The Years of MacArthur*, 3 vols. (1970– 1985), and John Backer, *The Winds of History: The German Years of Lucius D. Clay* (1983).

Works on Marshall-related subjects include Pogue's *The Supreme Command* (1954). On the China mission there is John R. Beal, *Marshall in China* (1970), by a journalist who was one of Marshall's assistants during the mission. On the Marshall Plan there is John Gimbel, *The Origins of the Marshall Plan* (1976); an eyewitness account by Joseph M. Jones, *The Fifteen Weeks* (1955); and the official history by Harry B. Price, *The Marshall Plan and Its Meaning* (1955).

For Germany and NATO see John H. Backer, *Priming the German Economy: American Occupational Policies 1945–1948* (1971) and *The Decision to Divide Germany: American Foreign Policy in Transition* (1978); Ernest H. van der Beugel, *From Marshall Aid to Atlantic Partnership* (1966); Timothy P. Ireland, *Creating the Entangling Alliance: The Origins of the North Atlantic Treaty Organization* (1981); Escott Reid, *Time of Fear and Hope: The Making of the North Atlantic Treaty 1947–1949* (1977); Walter F. Davison, *The Berlin Blockade* (1958); and a popular account of the Berlin blockade and airlift by Richard Collier, *Bridge Across the Sky* (1978). On the Korean War see the official history volumes by James F. Schnabel, *Policy and Direction: The First Year* (1972), and Roy E. Appleman, *South to the Naktong, North to the Yalu* (1961), and an excellent study by David Rees, *Korea: The Limited War* (1964).

Bibliography

Acheson, Dean. *Present at the Creation*. New York: Norton, 1969.

Ambrose, Stephen. *Eisenhower*. 2 vols. New York: Simon and Schuster, 1983–1984.

Appleman, Roy E. *South to the Naktong, North to the Yalu*. Washington, D.C.: Department of the Army, 1961.

Attlee, Clement. *Twilight of Empire*. New York: Barnes, 1962.

Backer, John. *The Decision to Divide Germany: American Foreign Policy in Transition*. Durham, N.C.: Duke University Press, 1978.

———. *Priming the German Economy: American Occupational Policies 1945–1948*. Durham, N.C.: Duke University Press, 1971.

———. *The Winds of History: The German Years of Lucius D. Clay*. New York: Van Nostrand, 1983.

Beal, John R. *Marshall in China*. Garden City, N.Y.: Doubleday, 1970.

Blair, Clay, and Omar Bradley. *A General's Life*. New York: Simon and Schuster, 1983.

Bohlen, Charles. *Witness to History*. New York: Norton, 1973.

Bryant, Arthur. *Triumph in the West*. London: Collins, 1959.

———. *The Turn of the Tide*. New York: Doubleday, 1957.

Churchill, Winston. *History of the Second World War*. 6 vols. Boston: Houghton Mifflin, 1948–1953.

Clay, Lucius D. *Decision in Germany*. Garden City, N.Y.: Doubleday, 1950.

Collier, Richard. *Bridge Across the Sky*. New York: McGraw-Hill, 1978.

Cunningham, Andrew. *A Sailor's Odyssey*. London: Hutchinson, 1951.

Davison, Walter F. *The Berlin Blockade*. Princeton, N.J.: Princeton University Press, 1958.

Eisenhower, Dwight D. *Crusade in Europe*. Garden City, N.Y.: Doubleday, 1948.

Ferrell, Robert. *The Eisenhower Diaries*. New York: Norton, 1981.

———. *George C. Marshall 1947–1949*. American Secretaries of State and Their Diplomacy Series. New York: Cooper Square, 1966.

———, ed. *Off the Record: The Private Papers of Harry S. Truman*. New York: Harper and Row, 1980.

Forrestal, James. *The Forrestal Diaries*. New York: Viking, 1951.

Gimbel, John. *The Origins of the Marshall Plan*. Stanford, Calif.: Stanford University Press, 1976.

Ireland, Timothy P. *Creating the Entangling Alliance: The Origins of the North Atlantic Treaty Organization*. Westport, Conn.: Greenwood Press, 1981.

James, D. Clayton. *The Years of MacArthur*. 3 vols. Boston: Houghton Mifflin, 1970–1985.

Jones, Joseph M. *The Fifteen Weeks*. New York: Viking, 1955.

Marshall, George. *Memories of My Services in the World War*. Boston: Houghton Mifflin, 1976.

Marshall, Katherine. *Together: Annals of an Army Wife*. Atlanta: Tupper and Love, 1946.

Mosely, Leonard. *Marshall: Hero for Our Times*. New York: Hearst, 1983.

Pogue, Forrest C. *George C. Marshall*. 4 vols. New York: Viking, 1963–1987.

———. *The Supreme Command*. Washington, D.C.: Department of the Army, 1954.

Price, Harry B. *The Marshall Plan and Its Meaning*. Ithaca, N.Y.: Cornell University Press, 1955.

Rees, David. *Korea: The Limited War*. New York: St. Martin's Press, 1964.

Reid, Escott. *Time of Fear and Hope: The Making of the North Atlantic Treaty 1947– 1949*. Toronto: McClelland and Stewart, 1977.

Schnabel, James F. *Policy and Direction: The First Year*. Washington, D.C.: Department of the Army, 1972.

Smith, Walter Bedell. *My Three Years in Moscow*. Philadelphia: Lippincott, 1950.

Truman, Harry S. *Memoirs*. 2 vols. New York: Doubleday, 1955–1956.

Vandenberg, Arthur H., Jr. *The Private Papers of Senator Vandenberg*. Boston: Houghton Mifflin, 1952.

Van der Beugel, Ernest H. *From Marshall Aid to Atlantic Partnership*. New York: Elsevier, 1966.

Wedemeyer, Albert C. *Wedemeyer Reports!* New York: Holt, 1958.

DAVID MACGREGOR

Prince Clemens Metternich (1773–1859). Clemens von Metternich, the "Coachman of Europe" and the founder of the "Metternich System," has long been considered a key figure in Europe during the time he was foreign minister of Austria, between 1809 and 1848. Like his great adversary, *Napoleon I, Metternich has given his name to a whole era of European history. This Metternich era, between 1815 and 1848, has traditionally been stereotyped as a period of extreme repression and reaction.

The stereotype, developed by German and Italian nationalist writers of the nineteenth century, was perpetuated in the twentieth century by Anglo-American historians until at least the 1960s. In historical studies of recent years, the interpretation of the Metternich era has begun to change. Increasingly the post-Napoleonic era is seen as a time, not of restoration to prerevolutionary society, but of significant change. Reforms of the years of revolution and war were not repealed, but rather accepted as the new building blocks of the modern era. Post-Napoleonic boundaries of France and the former French satellite states remained largely unchanged. New dynasties that had emerged continued to reign, and wartime allies and enemies became fellow negotiators for settlements that were "legitimate" only in terms of general acceptability, not in terms of historicity or tradition.

No longer the prince of darkest reaction and the archfiend of liberals and nationalists, the Austrian foreign minister increasingly has become the man of moderation. Metternich, an imperial count of the defunct Holy Roman Empire, can be seen as a traitor to his class, one of the fathers of modern federal Germany, and a man who urged reactionary popes to undertake enlightened administrative reforms in Italy. Metternich, the opponent of Napoleon, emerges more as Napoleon's admirer and a fellow advocate of enlightened absolutism. The ally of tsars *Alexander I and Nicholas of Russia is seen as the man who sought to restrict their extremes of both euphoric reformism and blind reaction.

To understand Clemens von Metternich one must remember that he began life as the son of a German imperial count in the Rhineland far from the Habsburg court in Vienna. He was born in Coblenz on May 15, 1773, the son of Count Franz George von Metternich. His father, a diplomat of the old Holy Roman

Empire, received his income from the seigniorial revenues of his estates, Winne-burg and Beilstein. Clemens, the eldest son of four children, was a typical product of the old regime. Preparation to be an imperial count and a future functionary of the Holy Roman Empire came through exposure to the grand society of the age and to a finishing school experience at the University of Strasbourg. Wit, charm, and facility with French were the hallmarks of *ancien régime* society, and young Clemens mastered them at an early age. These abilities, along with his flirtations with the ladies, were to mark his life. They won him both friends and enemies among contemporaries. Historians have often misjudged the man because of his sometimes superficial and supercilious manners.

Yet the young man who attended the coronations of Leopold II and Francis II, the last Holy Roman emperors, and married Eleanor von Kaunitz, the grand-daughter of Prince *Wenzel Anton von Kaunitz, the great Austrian chancellor, proved a traitor to his class. This became obvious when, after flight from the revolutionary Rhineland, the Metternichs took up residence in Vienna and Cle-mens served in the Austrian diplomatic corps in Dresden, Berlin, and finally Paris in 1806. In Paris, as Austrian ambassador, Clemens became an admirer of Napoleon Bonaparte, the century's parvenu par excellence. What he admired about Napoleon was obviously not his traditional lineage, but his cleverness, daring, and enlightened despotism. In Napoleon, Metternich found a worthy adversary in the art of diplomacy and survival in a changing world. He would continue to admire Napoleon throughout his time as Austrian foreign minister, a post he received in 1809 when Austrian fortunes against France seemed at their lowest.

It was Metternich the pragmatist who in 1810 advocated the marriage of Napoleon to Marie-Louise, the daughter of Emperor Francis I of Austria. This was a way to link Austria to the parvenu in the interest of Habsburg survival at a time when, as the enemy of Napoleon, the House of Habsburg was defeated and faced the loss of empire. Metternich, a man of the Enlightenment rather than a reactionary, used reason to convince both himself and his Habsburg master that an alliance with Napoleon was the path to the future.

Later, it was Metternich again who attempted to save the stability of Europe by offering Napoleon a negotiated settlement in 1813 that would have kept the foundering French emperor in power and prevented the creation of a power vacuum in central Europe. This attempted settlement on the basis of the status quo in the wake of Napoleon's defeat in Russia has been seen too often by historians, as by Napoleon himself, as Metternich's cynical attempt to find in the Frenchman's intransigence an excuse for Austria to abandon him and join his adversaries. The opposite is true.

Metternich was disappointed that Napoleon rejected the admonition to quit while he and Europe were still ahead. Napoleon's rejection of Metternich's offer of mediation was not a triumph for Austria. It was a defeat for which Metternich would spend the rest of his life trying to compensate. With the end of Napoleon's supremacy, Metternich and Austria were faced with a power vacuum in central

Europe. Prussians and Russians were willing to fill it. There were Prussian statesmen like Baron Heinrich von Stein and Prince Karl von Hardenberg who dreamed such dreams. Stein imagined a restored and reformed Holy Roman Empire run by the traditional nobility. Hardenberg envisioned a Prussian-dominated German empire with limited Austrian influence. The realization of either dream would have been disastrous for Habsburg influence in Europe. Both too inspired the hopes of contemporary and later German liberals and nationalists who mistakenly saw in each plan a lost opportunity for the creation of a united German nation. Neither plan, however, was very attractive to the German princes who as part of Napoleon's Confederation of the Rhine had gained new titles, territories, and independence. It was to these princes that Metternich, like Napoleon before him, appealed.

For Metternich, the admirer of Napoleon as the rationalizer of Europe, neither Stein's backward-looking empire nor Hardenberg's ideas of Prussian dominance seemed an adequate answer to the German Question. Nor did Metternich find attractive the answers suggested by Tsar Alexander of Russia. The tsar was the self-proclaimed savior of Europe, a volatile man whose passion for action and adulation led him to extremes of reformism and reaction. Metternich felt that this made him potentially more dangerous than Napoleon and certainly more threatening than mere Prussian statesmen. The struggle with Tsar Alexander was a main theme of Metternich's foreign policy between 1815 and the tsar's death in 1825.

Alexander I was an unpredictable character at best. He saw himself as the liberator of Europe and during the Vienna Conference proposed a Holy Alliance in which all the Christian rulers of Europe would cooperate for their common good and that of their subjects. The Holy Alliance has often been confused with the Quadruple Alliance and seen as a reactionary conspiracy against popular reform movements. However, the tsar's goals were open-ended. He and his diplomats encouraged constitutionalism within the German states and in Italy. At the same time they urged repression of revolutionaries, even volunteering Russian troops for service as far away from Russia as Italy and Spain. This could hardly be reassuring to an Austrian statesman who was interested in both stability and the balance of power in Europe. Metternich was unwilling to exchange the European hegemony of Napoleon for that of Tsar Alexander.

In this light, Metternich's interest in the preservation of the existing governments in Germany and Italy, though some were of very recent vintage in terms of territories acquired during the Napoleonic period, is more understandable. Far from wishing to restore the prerevolutionary chaos of a central Europe divided among a myriad of contentious principalities, Metternich followed a policy similar to that which he had attempted unsuccessfully with Napoleon in 1813: conservation of the status quo, though old elites might consider that status quo the work of usurpers. At the Congress of Vienna and in the years thereafter, Metternich advocated stability over traditional authority for both Germany and Italy. For him what existed needed to be legitimized; any turning back of the clock on existing reforms would lead to chaos. In France, this meant for Metternich the establishment of a constitutional monarchy after the fall of Napoleon. In Italy, after initially being willing to leave Joachim Murat as king of Naples, Metternich was forced by the return of Napoleon to support a Bourbon restoration. The restoration of the Papal States in central Italy had more to do with Austria's need for an ally in central Europe than with any allegiance to the union of throne and altar. In Germany, Metternich worked for the creation of a German confederation of thirty-nine states, an extension of Napoleon's Confederation of the Rhine with the inclusion of Prussia and Austria. The status quo was to be preserved where possible and European stability achieved at all costs.

Metternich offered protection of German states' rights in return for the exclusion of both French and Russian influences whether those influences might be spread by support for or suppression of popular movements. Though historians often focus on Metternich's manipulation of the fears of the German princes to organize the repression of liberal and nationalist movements inspired by French models, it must be remembered that Metternich was also concerned that antirevolutionary efforts be orchestrated by Germans for Germany and not imposed by the tsar of Russia.

Tsar Alexander, normally considered an ally of Metternich for repression of revolutionary movements, cannot be so easily categorized. Metternich saw him as a most unstable personality, one whose exuberance led to rapid swings of policy. During the period immediately after the Congress of Vienna, Alexander supported, or at least allowed his foreign office under Count Ioannes Capodistria to support, constitutional developments among Alexander's south German relatives. Related to the monarchs of Baden and Württemberg by marriage, Alexander allowed these German princes to appeal for Russian support as they angled for independence from Prussian and Austrian dominance within the German Confederation. Alternately supporting and discouraging these princes, Alexander sought his own vision for Europe and Germany, a vague vision that called for more Russian influence in central Europe than Metternich and Emperor Francis of Austria could tolerate. Metternich was appalled when in response to Russian encouragement the south German states introduced constitutional governments.

Metternich was equally concerned when, in 1818, at the Congress of Aix-la-Chapelle, Alexander advocated German governmental action against student liberals and nationalists. The Carlsbad Decrees of 1819 and the Vienna Final Act of 1820 can be seen as Metternich's response to both Russian initiatives. These products of the Austrian's often criticized secret cabinet diplomacy were efforts to encourage the German princes to cooperate within the German Confederation for the repression of revolutionary movements and for the maintenance of the monarchic principle without benefit of Russian interference in Germany. Metternich, though damned by German nationalists then and now for his efforts to prevent the unification of Germany, in fact encouraged German princes to find German solutions for German problems. With the German Confederation, Metternich offered the German princes the protection of their states' rights through their mutual adherence to federal responsibilities which specified mutual help for endangered princes. While Metternich was hardly a German nationalist in the liberal or *kleindeutsch* mold, he was a German nationalist in the sense that he sought a more united, though not unified, Germany.

But Metternich was first and foremost a European statesman, not a German one. During the congresses of Troppau, Laibach, and Verona between 1820 and 1823, in the period when Metternich's system was said to be at its zenith, he involved the German Confederation not at all in European affairs. Austria and her erstwhile ally and sometime rival, Prussia, cooperated with the other Great Powers to find solutions to revolutions in Italy, Spain, and Greece. Much to the irritation of the particularistic German princes of Württemberg, Bavaria, and Baden, Metternich neither consulted with nor sought to represent their German voices.

Instead, the agreements made at Troppau, Laibach, and Verona were Great Power decisions and pronouncements about intervention to repress revolutions that left no room for participation or consent by the lesser German or European powers. Metternich, the European diplomat, took the lesser powers for granted in his efforts to secure Great Power agreement for the principle of intervention. But Great Power intervention was carefully channeled by Metternich. Such intervention involved only Austrian troops in Italy and later French troops in Spain. Russia was excluded from the military participation that Tsar Alexander offered for both Italy and Spain. And, of course, Metternich also dissuaded Alexander from intervention on behalf of the Greek revolt of the same period. Metternich wisely saw Tsar Alexander's desire for military involvement with revolutions, whether against them in Italy and Spain or for them in Greece, as destabilizing for Europe. Here again, Metternich proved not the reactionary interventionist but the ever cautious conservative, more interested in maintaining the status quo than in upsetting it, whether in the name of revolution or reaction.

This can be seen in Metternich's policies in regard to both the 1830 July Revolution in France and the nationalistic exuberance of France in 1840. In both cases it was Metternich who sought to avoid a European war through international settlements which, if they could not prevent change, would regulate it into forms of mutually agreed upon legitimacy.

In the wake of the July Revolution, it was Austria that joined with Britain and Prussia to recognize the new Orleanist monarchy over the objections of Tsar Nicholas of Russia. This act secured stability for France that might have been endangered had the revolution evolved further. Similarly, with regard to the Belgian revolution of the same year, Metternich, much to the chagrin of Prussia, was willing to have an international conference in London settle the matter and avoid the possibility of war. Only regarding neighboring Italy did Metternich agree with Emperor Francis that Austria needed to take a unilateral military stand against revolution. Only in Italy, where administrative reforms recommended by Metternich had not been carried out and where both the papacy and adjoining states were threatened, did Metternich risk the ire of Louis Philippe's France and the danger of transgressing against the new French doctrine of nonintervention.

But even then, it was Metternich who in diplomatic and military talks in Germany urged a nonprovocative attitude toward France. Metternich wanted neither a war with France nor the disruption of the German Confederation that such a war might cause. It might encourage revolutions in southern Germany or split south Germany and Prussia from Austria in fulfillment of ill-advised Prussian–south German neutrality plans. Instead of dividing Germany by provoking a war with France, Metternich sought to unite the German princes against their common domestic enemies: overzealous liberal diets and the mixture of student and street rebels. Thus the Six Articles and Ten Acts passed by the German Confederation of 1832, and the secret ministerial meetings in 1834 that expanded on the monarchic provisions of the Final Act of 1820, were part of Metternich's policy to unite the German princes in their own interests and in the interest of European stability.

In retrospect, of course, such efforts are seen as reactionary. Yet in the context of the nineteenth century one can hardly have expected any statesman to encourage political movements that would destabilize the existing system. Therein lay Metternich's strength and persuasiveness. German princes and European statesmen alike were captivated by Metternich's diplomacy, not because of his persuasive genius, but because he spoke to their own most immediate fears and concerns. Though Britain and France might protest what they perceived as the increased influence of Austria in a Germany bound to fight revolution through the mutual efforts of the members of the German Confederation, neither state really had much grounds for complaint. The British and French governments of the time were equally concerned by threats of domestic revolution: the English had their Chartists and the French their insurrectionaries in Lyon. Metternich's *Weltanschauung* was not different from that of most of his contemporaries; his success came from the fact that what seemed good for Austria was perceived by fellow statesmen to be good for their rulers as well.

Metternich's policies of the thirties and forties were essentially continuations of those of the previous twenty years. But except for his efforts to thwart the advance of the Prussian Zollverein (tariff union), to avoid the breakup of Germany over the Hanoverian constitutional question of 1837, and to avoid a German war with France in 1840 over the Eastern Question, the highlights of Metternich's career were in the past. Increasingly, as memories of the wars of the French Revolution faded, both liberals and reactionaries were emboldened to pursue their own policies with little thought to their consequences for Europe. While "liberal" reformers in Prussia increasingly pushed the expansion of the Prussian tariff union with the political purpose of alienating Austria from the rest of Germany, a reactionary Hanoverian king, Ernst August, abandoned his constitution. Metternich tried unobtrusively to thwart the political purposes of the Zollverein with no success. Against his better judgment, he found himself forced in the name of the monarchic principle to defend diplomatically Ernst August of Hanover despite the fact that it was always against Metternich's basic principles to try to reverse constitutional developments once they had become part of the status quo.

Metternich's last success before the Revolutions of 1848 swept away the remnants of his system was to avert a European war in 1840. The French government of Prime Minister Adolphe Thiers sought to rally Frenchmen by resurrecting the symbols of the Napoleonic Age, including the completion of the Arch of Triumph and the return of Napoleon's body from St. Helena to France. In this supercharged atmosphere of French nationalism, the Thiers government suffered a severe diplomatic defeat. The Great Powers cooperated militarily and diplomatically to constrain an ally of France, Mehemet Ali, Pasha of Egypt, who was attempting to overthrow Ottoman rule in the Middle East. An embittered French government responded with furious nationalistic rhetoric that threatened an attack on the Rhine in retaliation against Europe. Such an attack might indeed have been unleashed if Metternich had not done everything in his power to warn both the French and Prussian governments against the danger of revolutions in the wake of wars.

King Frederick William IV of Prussia, a romantic nationalist inspired to pugnacity by his advisor, Colonel Joseph Maria von Radowitz, sought to use the war scare to strengthen the role of Prussia in German military affairs. For Metternich war or the emergence of Prussian power within the German Confederation would be destabilizing for Austria, Germany, and all of Europe. In retrospect, historians can see that Metternich was not far off in his assessment both of the potentially revolutionary effect of a European war and the dangers of a Germany united under the banner of Prussian militarism.

Metternich remained consistent until the end of his career in seeking to preserve the status quo against both reactionaries and reformers. Changes, once they were legitimized by acceptance, were to be neither reversed nor advanced further. Such a policy was not a very creative one, but it did seek to give Austria, Germany, and Europe a period of quiescence and stability after twenty-six years of wars and revolutions. Metternich's fall and the failure of his policies after the Revolutions of 1848 came largely because Europe had changed: the wars of forty years before and the dangers of precipitous change were largely forgotten. The men who had been Metternich's allies and erstwhile adversaries, Napoleon, Tsar Alexander I of Russia, and King Frederick William III of Prussia, were all dead.

Metternich stood alone, the observer in the loge; the audience as well as the play had changed. The old man of seventy-five who fled to England from a revolutionary Vienna never admitted to error in his policies. From England, and later after his return to Vienna and until his death at age eighty-six on June 11, 1859, Metternich continued to warn of the dangers of extremism of all kinds. As he did throughout his life, he preached in vain, and perhaps a bit too vainly, that the principles of enlightened absolutism and balance of power were the basis of all sound policy.

Annotated Bibliography

Metternich's diplomatic correspondence and reports to the emperor are found in Vienna in the Haus-, Hof- und Staatsarchiv, still located at this writing in the Chancellory building (Minoritenplatz 1, 1010 Vienna, Austria). Materials are readily accessible to serious scholars. There has been talk of eventually moving these materials, along with those from other Austrian archives, to a recently completed new Staatsarchiv (Nottendorfergasse 2, 1030 Vienna). By 1992, such a move had not occurred.

Less easy to see in the past, because of the nature of the Communist regime, were the many personal letters to Metternich as well as Metternich's copies of his own personal correspondence, which are with the Metternich family papers. These are in the Státní Ústředný Archiv, Prague (Karmelitská 2, Prague 1, Czechoslovakia), in the Rodinný archiv Metternišsky: Acta Clementina holdings. The Metternich estate, along with all other large private holdings, was confiscated during the Communist era, and papers are held by the department responsible for the confiscation, the Department of Agriculture. How easy it will be to visit this collection after the liberalization of eastern Europe remains to be seen.

Works on Metternich have followed the pattern alluded to in the biographical section above. A good overall review of the evolution of the literature is found in Enno E. Kraehe, ed., *The Metternich Controversy* (1971).

Metternich, in the autobiographical sections of his memoirs, *Aus Metternichs nachgelassenen Papieren*, edited by Richard von Metternich (1880–1884), pleads the rationality and principle-based characteristics of his policies from his dealings with Napoleon down until the end of his career. Liberal and nationalist historians of the nineteenth and twentieth centuries have tended to denounce Metternich's policies as pragmatically reactionary. Thus, in Heinrich von Treitschke, *Deutsche Geschichte im neunzehnten Jahrhundert* (1879–1894), Metternich is portrayed as the archfiend of reaction who defended a laughably inept and narrow-minded Austrian government that delayed the "inevitable" unification of Germany under Prussia.

This line of argument, typical of the history written by victors about the losers in politics and wars, continued up until the publication of Heinrich von Srbik, *Metternich: Der Staatsmann und der Mensch* (1925–1954). Srbik, an Austrian and a *grossdeutsch* (greater German) nationalist, portrayed his subject as the man of principle that Metternich claimed himself to be. Though that view was attacked by *kleindeutsch* (smaller German) nationalists, it did find some support in Peter Viereck, *Conservatism Revisited* (1949). Viereck, writing in the wake of World War II, defended Metternich as a contender against nationalist ruffians like those who would later make Nazi Germany the scourge of twentieth-century Europe.

In the Cold War period, Metternich became the preserver of the European balance against the "revolutionary statesman," Tsar Alexander, in Henry Kissinger, *A World Restored* (1957). But it was as pragmatic protector of Austrian interests rather than as preserver of Europe that Metternich was portrayed in an influential book by Paul Schroeder, *Metternich's Policy at Its Zenith, 1820–1823* (1962).

More on target, at least in their attempts to see Metternich within the context of his own age, an age when reactionaries as well as modernizing reformers were a threat, are the volumes by Enno Kraehe, *Metternich's German Policy* (1963–1983), Alan Reinerman, *Austria and the Papacy in the Age of Metternich* (1979–1989), and Robert D. Billinger,

Jr., *Metternich and the German Question* (1991). The authors of these volumes portray Metternich not within post facto developed categories like "reactionary" and "liberal," but within the categories of Metternich's own period. In that context, Metternich appears as an enlightened conservative who resisted rapid and destabilizing change of both the liberal and reactionary kind.

In the same category of revisionism are the award-winning articles by Roy A. Austensen. In "Austria and the 'Struggle for Supremacy in Germany,' 1848–1864," *Journal of Modern History* 52 (1980): 195–225, and "Einheit oder Einigkeit? Another Look at Metternich's View of the German Dilemma," *German Studies Review* 6 (1983): 41–57, Austensen calls for a reassessment of Metternich's German policy and that of his disciples up until 1864. He stresses Metternich's interest in unity rather than unification in Germany and his struggle to keep Prussia in his camp rather than to gain supremacy over Prussia in Germany. Austensen also reminds us that Metternich's German policy was only one part of his European policy and that his European policies always took precedence over purely German matters.

Though primarily narrative rather than interpretative, readable general biographies of Metternich include Alan Palmer, *Metternich* (1972), and Guillaume de Bertier de Sauvigny's *Metternich* (1986), in French. The latter has a section that contains excellent evaluations of the primary sources and selected secondary sources. Bertier de Sauvigny's earlier insights about Metternich, along with excerpts from Metternich's own writings, can also be found in English translation in *Metternich and His Times* (1962).

Bibliography

Austensen, Roy A. "Austria and the 'Struggle for Supremacy in Germany,' 1848–1864." *Journal of Modern History* 52 (June (1980): 195–225.

———. "Einheit oder Einigkeit? Another Look at Metternich's View of the German Dilemma," *German Studies Review* 6 (February 1983): 41–57.

Bertier de Sauvigny, Guillaume de. *Metternich.* Paris: Fayard, 1986

———. *Metternich and His Times.* London: Humanities Press, 1962.

Billinger, Robert D., Jr. *Metternich and the German Question: States' Rights and Federal Duties, 1820–1834.* Newark: University of Delaware Press, 1991.

Kissinger, Henry A. *A World Restored: Metternich, Castlereagh and the Problems of Peace, 1812–1822.* Boston: Houghton Mifflin, 1957.

Kraehe, Enno E. *Metternich's German Policy.* 2 vols. Princeton, N.J.: Princeton University Press, 1963–1983.

———, ed. *The Metternich Controversy.* New York: Holt, Rinehart and Winston, 1971.

Metternich-Winneburg, Clemens Lothar Wenzel Fürst von. *Aus Metternichs nachgelassenen Papieren.* 8 vols. Edited by Prince Richard von Metternich. Vienna: Braumüller, 1880–1884.

Palmer, Alan. *Metternich.* New York: Harper and Row, 1972.

Reinerman, Alan J. *Austria and the Papacy in the Age of Metternich.* 2 vols. Washington, D.C.: Catholic University of America Press, 1979–1989.

Schroeder, Paul W. *Metternich's Policy at Its Zenith, 1820–1823.* Austin: University of Texas Press, 1962.

Srbik, Heinrich von. *Metternich: Der Staatsmann und der Mensch.* 3 vols. Munich: Bruckmann, 1925–1954.

Treitschke, Heinrich von. *Deutsche Geschichte im neunzehnten Jahrhundert*. 5 vols. Leipzig: Hirzel, 1879–1894.

Viereck, Peter. *Conservatism Revisited*. New York: Scribner's, 1949.

ROBERT D. BILLINGER, JR.

Jean Monnet (1888–1979).   Since the time of Charlemagne, the word "Europe" has been little more than an expression of geography. The notion that all Europeans belonged to a single community, united by the Christian faith and Roman law, ultimately succumbed to the competition of religions and nation-states. Countless kings, popes, emperors, and dictators have sought to impose unity on the continent. The most recent such attempt, by *Adolf Hitler, resulted in widespread devastation and the removal of Europe from the locus of world power. Yet today Europe stands on the verge of political and economic integration, as national governments willingly set aside their differences for the common good. Oddly, the architect of this union could claim no hereditary birthright. He held no title and received no mandate from the people. He was a traveling salesman with a vision that would transform Europe. That man was Jean Monnet.

The Charente is a quiet section of rural France. Here, in the town of Cognac, Jean Monnet was born on November 9, 1888. Appropriately, he was descended from a long line of wine grape growers. His father managed a cooperative of small vintners and soon turned it into a business with an international distribution. Monnet's home was continually open to foreign business guests, including visitors from Germany, Great Britain, and North America. Apparently impressed by his father's business travels, Monnet never took well to schooling. "Why take the roundabout route of studying law," he wrote in his memoirs, "when I could go to the school of life and see the world?" Indeed, even though his father had a college education, the young Monnet did not complete his *baccalauréat* (university entrance exams). Instead, his father took him into the business, and at the age of sixteen Monnet began training to become a salesman.

His first years with the firm were spent living with business acquaintances in Britain, where he gained invaluable experience not only with the language but also in dealing with the British business mentality. This experience proved indispensable, since his first major assignment was to consolidate the North American market for Monnet brandy. His many trips to Canada and his dealings with the Hudson's Bay Company were among the most formative experiences of his life. The Canadian frontier stood in sharp contrast to his native Charente, one expanding and bustling with activity, the other a traditional, static society. He found the people unusually trusting and industrious and believed that this resulted from the spontaneity of frontier expansion. Most important, Monnet was struck by the ease and efficiency of trade over the vast distances of the frontier, unhindered by borders and the artificial restraints of tolls and tariffs. This dynamism stood in sharp contrast to his later business travels to Egypt and Greece, where patience was the key to business success.

As World War I broke out, Monnet resolved to help the Allied effort despite a medical deferment that kept him from active duty. He seized upon a logistical problem, namely, the lack of coordination between English and French purchasing and shipping efforts. With youthful naïveté, Monnet asked a family friend to arrange a meeting with French prime minister René Viviani. At this meeting, Monnet suggested pooling Allied resources in an effort to defeat the common enemy. Logically, each ally should contribute that which it could best afford. For the British, untouched by German troop landings, that meant shipping and industrial productivity. France would provide the bulk of the ground forces fighting at the front.

Monnet's ideas, combined with his working knowledge of the English language and customs, convinced the French war department to send him to London as part of the French delegation of the International Supply Committee. Here Monnet spent many months watching French and British agencies compete with each other in the purchase of food and war commodities. Thanks to Monnet's persuasion, the Allied governments formed an executive board in 1916 to negotiate wheat purchases for the combined Allied needs. Reflecting on this achievement, Monnet later wrote, "Suddenly, . . . the notion of national interests took second place to that of the common interest." That revelation became the guiding principle of his life.

Although Monnet's persistence certainly was a factor in the creation of this inter-Allied agency, he knew that more production had to be brought under joint control. Notions of a short conflict had long since disappeared, and partial solutions were insufficient for the needs of total war. As shipping became more vital to the war effort, Monnet's role in the committee continued to grow. Along with Sir Arthur Salter, Monnet helped to convince the Allies to pool all naval tonnage in November 1917.

Much to Monnet's chagrin, the inter-Allied agencies he had made possible crumbled after the armistice, as world traders reverted to the capitalistic notions of supply and demand. Any hope for an international order now rested in the newly created League of Nations. Because of Monnet's experience on the inter-Allied control committees, he was appointed deputy secretary. For three years he helped settle a number of disputes left unresolved by the Treaty of Versailles. He had a hand in finding solutions to the German-Polish border dispute (including the establishment of Danzig as a free city), the 1921 plebiscite leading to the partition of Silesia between Germany and Poland, and the Saar settlement of 1922. In 1921 Monnet engineered the guarantee of Austria from Great Britain, France, Italy, and Czechoslovakia, and their pledge of loans to help secure its government's finances. In his most interesting idea, Monnet suggested that the Allies fix a sum for German reparations. Then, to raise that sum, an international loan could be floated on which Germany would be forced to make interest payments. The French government did not approve.

Monnet resigned from the League in 1923. In his memoirs, he claimed to have been aware of the League's weaknesses, but insisted that they did not influence his decision to leave. The postwar economic slump had brought trouble to the family business, and he was needed in Cognac. For the next decade, he was mostly concerned with private business and banking affairs, although he took part in the stabilization of the Polish and Romanian currencies and helped set up a development bank in China to finance the reconstruction of railroads and other segments of the Chinese infrastructure.

The rise of Nazism again thrust Monnet into world politics. In 1938, as the Anschluss appeared imminent, Monnet met with Edouard Daladier, France's defense minister and later prime minister. Citing the superiority of the German air force, Monnet suggested creating an overseas aircraft industry to supply France if war should come. His suggestion fell on deaf ears until Daladier, returning home from the humiliation of the Munich conference, recalled Monnet for further advice. Convinced of France's vulnerability to air attack, Daladier sent Monnet to the United States to meet with President *Franklin D. Roosevelt in an effort to secure contracts for aircraft. In Roosevelt, Monnet found a man of similar mind regarding the threat posed by Nazism. Along with U.S. treasury secretary Henry Morgenthau and U.S. ambassador to France William Bullitt, Monnet found ways to produce and finance the manufacture of planes for shipment to France. Despite opposition from certain military circles, Monnet succeeded in ordering 600 aircraft and obtained an option to buy 1,500 more in early 1940. He was on another such procurement trip when German troops invaded Poland to start World War II. Monnet returned to France to urge the creation of joint Anglo-French war commissions. The lessons from World War I were not lost. This time his words were heeded, and Monnet was named head of the Anglo-French Coordinating Committee.

The newly purchased American planes did not reach France in time to save it from the German blitzkrieg of 1940. As British troops were being evacuated from the Continent, Monnet, Lord Salter, and René Pleven pleaded with *Winston Churchill to evacuate French forces as well, enabling 26,000 French soldiers to escape capture. In these hours of desperation, Monnet produced his most ambitious and innovative idea: a union of French and British sovereignty, complete with joint citizenship, a common currency, and shared resources. Although many Britons were surprisingly in favor of such a union, events in France precluded its adoption. Shortly after the plan was accepted, Premier Paul Reynaud's government fell and was replaced by one headed by Marshal Henri Pétain.

The fall of the French government and the ensuing armistice ended the need for the Anglo-French committees of cooperation. Monnet returned to London and, freed from his national commitment, asked Churchill for a position in the British war effort. Churchill happily obliged, assigning him to the British Purchasing Commission. Monnet could now continue his efforts to persuade Roosevelt that supplying Britain was in America's best interests. As Monnet put it one evening to a group of friends, "The United States must become a great arsenal, the arsenal of democracy." The phrase found its way into one of Roosevelt's fireside chats and helped explain why the United States, wary of foreign entanglements, should support Britain's war effort. The result was the Lend-Lease program of 1941 and the commitment to build 50,000 more warplanes.

Monnet's reputation as conciliator became established with his efforts to mediate between the Free French movement of *Charles de Gaulle and General Henri Giraud in North Africa in 1943. Monnet flew to Algiers, where he worked his way into Giraud's confidence. Slowly, he managed to wean Giraud from his Vichy sympathies and convinced him to accept de Gaulle's Free French movement as a partner. Monnet also played a critical role in obtaining the United States' acceptance of the de Gaulle–Giraud merger. Thus, a de facto French provisional government was born, and Monnet became its minister of supplies.

Monnet's work with supplies made him the logical choice to head France's economic recovery program after the conclusion of the war. Monnet was busy for the next five years with the reconstruction of France, preventing him from active participation in international affairs. During those years, Europe took major steps toward recovery. The Marshall Plan was announced on June 5, 1947, and in 1948 the Organization for European Economic Cooperation (OEEC) was formed to administer the plan. Although the OEEC functioned well, Monnet knew that it would not lead to the kind of Europe he envisaged. The organization conducted business by majority vote, and its decisions were enforced only with the cooperation and goodwill of the members. If Europe was ever to unite, he concluded, all nations would have to join a supranational governing body and accept common regulations, laws, and institutions. That goal was still distant.

The main obstacle to be overcome was reluctance to surrender national sovereignty. As early as 1949, Monnet began informal discussions with British officials on the possibility of an economic union similar to the one already concluded among the Benelux countries. Unfortunately, British officials seemed more interested in reestablishing Great Britain's prewar economic position than entering into such a union. Reluctantly, Monnet began to contemplate a Europe at least temporarily without Great Britain.

A possible partner did emerge from an unlikely source. *Konrad Adenauer, chancellor of the newly formed Federal Republic of Germany, eagerly grasped at the idea. At a time when the two countries were again arguing over possession of the Saar basin, Monnet struck upon an idea that would change Europe. Turning aside Adenauer's request for a Franco-German union, Monnet proposed that the two countries pool their coal and steel resources. Along with Paul Reuter, Pierre Uri, and Étienne Hirsch, Monnet drafted a proposal to place all German and French coal and steel resources under an international authority open to all European countries. The document, known as the French Declaration of May 9, 1950, led to Europe's first supranational institution.

A coal and steel pool seemed a step backward from the notion of total economic union. However, Monnet was after a larger prize than just a Franco-German agreement. He had come to the conclusion that the coal and steel pool would not only eliminate a source of friction between Germany and France, but could also be the nucleus of wider European cooperation in the future. ''Peace can be founded only on equality,'' he told *Robert Schuman, the French foreign minister. This equality could be achieved through the creation of a High Authority, that is, a committee of administrators to oversee conditions of production and neutralize competition. The revolutionary and controversial part of the plan was that the Authority would be free of national restraints and could issue decisions binding on its members. Further, it would be financed by levies placed on coal and steel production, making it self-supporting and capable of making loans and encouraging investments without ties to national governments.

Monnet made no pretense about the purpose of his revolutionary plan. It was the beginning of the European Community, Monnet's dream of a federation of nations from which no participant could withdraw without permission of the other members. When the proposal was prepared for deliberation, Monnet felt that it would command more attention if someone in governmental circles sponsored it. That is why this proposal, which became known as the Schuman Plan, does not bear Monnet's name. On May 27, 1952, after two years of negotiations, the treaty establishing the European Coal and Steel Community (ECSC) was signed. With its birth, Monnet believed Europe's future to have changed from national confrontation to supranational cooperation.

Monnet accepted the position of president of the High Authority. He must have been pleased by the fact that Great Britain and the United States quickly recognized its independent sovereignty. When the Authority met for the first time in Luxembourg, it could not have foreseen the success the ECSC would enjoy over the next five years. Certainly the increased levels of production were proof enough, but its true success lay in the fact that the ECSC proved that Monnet's vision of a Europe without boundaries was, at least in this one economic sector, quite possible.

That optimism was not universally shared, however. The invasion of South Korea reintroduced the specter of war to world politics. During the Schuman Plan negotiations, Monnet explored ways to integrate the armed forces of Europe into a supranational army. The idea was an attractive way to provide for Europe's defense and confront the problem of German rearmament in a single stroke. From their discussions emerged the Pleven plan, a scheme to create a European defense community under the command of the governmental institutions of united Europe. Again, Monnet acted as mediator between the diplomats on both sides of the Atlantic, but despite his efforts the French government refused to ratify the treaty. The plan was never realized.

With the High Authority well established, Monnet decided not to run for a second term as president and resigned the remainder of his term as delegate. His resignation was not the result of defeat or disillusionment. Monnet felt the need to be free to pursue his ultimate goal, the United States of Europe, and the administrative demands of the ECSC executive did not allow much latitude of action. Freed of his ECSC duties, Monnet formed the Action Committee for the United States of Europe, an organization he headed for the next twenty years. The membership he recruited included labor leaders and politicians of all persuasions and from various nations. This lobby was successful in rallying support for the treaty establishing Euratom, Europe's integrated authority to control the use of atomic energy, and the Treaty of Rome in 1957, which established the European Economic Community.

In the early 1960s, Monnet secured improved diplomatic ties with the United States, a country he saw as a separate but equal partner in a new world order. Much of the remainder of the decade was spent with the Action Committee, preparing for Great Britain's entry into the community. This effort put Monnet at loggerheads with President Charles de Gaulle's vision of a federated Europe of sovereign nations. De Gaulle's persistent vetoes and the withdrawal of French participation in many of the community's activities made the mid-sixties a period of frustration and stagnation. Monnet worked constantly to convince Europe's statesmen that despite the setbacks unity was still possible and indeed necessary. It took de Gaulle's retirement from politics in 1969 before national prejudices could be expunged.

Thanks to the Action Committee, the groundwork for Great Britain's admission to the community was well laid. Approval finally came in 1972. Monnet felt that Europe was now ready to move toward union, and he called for the creation of a provisional European government. After the Middle East crisis of 1973 had passed, the leaders of Germany (Helmut Schmidt), France (Valéry Giscard d'Estaing), and Great Britain (Harold Wilson) agreed to act on Monnet's suggestion. They and their counterparts from the other Common Market countries created the European Council. What made this council different from its predecessor, the Council of Europe, was that its members agreed to be bound by majority decisions. Europe took its first steps toward unity.

In February 1975 Monnet fell ill. With the goals of his Action Committee essentially achieved, he retired on May 9, 1975, the twenty-fifth anniversary of the proposal to create the ECSC High Authority. Much still remained to be accomplished, however. A monetary union was still not in place, nor was there a complete unification of Europe's decision-making process. Monnet would not see these final advancements. He died at his country estate near Montfort l'Amaury outside of Paris on March 16, 1979.

How is it that a traveling salesman could effect such deep changes in the nature of European politics? A large part of the answer may be precisely because Monnet was not a politician. His personality was such that he never sought publicity, preferring to influence events from behind the scenes. Jean Monnet never held public office and rarely let his electoral preferences be known. His disinterest in politics was so pronounced that he supposedly never felt at ease with being called "Mr. President" in the ECSC High Authority. But what better individual to lead a movement for supranational government than one who was not bound by partisan national politics? According to Pierre Uri, Monnet often remarked that the reason politicians would talk to him was because they knew he was not after their jobs. Monnet had no special reverence for politicians. He treated them as equals, and they in turn accepted him into their confidence.

Monnet's approach to diplomacy was equally apolitical. He drew his style from the business world he knew so well. He wrote that concrete action does not proceed from vague principles and generalities; one must simplify the issues and concentrate on a single precise point. To do that, Monnet composed "balance sheets" to compare the assets and liabilities inherent in the problem. Then, much as an accountant uses double-entry bookkeeping, Monnet used the balance sheets to determine the "bottom line," that is, that which must be accomplished. And just as the vintner knows that the best wines need time to ferment, Monnet understood that great changes would not happen overnight. He displayed a willingness to be patient, even though undue delay displeased him. He found that persistence can overcome setbacks; hence he was willing to explore even the most circuitous route if it could lead to success.

Yet, by themselves, patience and persistence were insufficient to achieve the magnitude of change Monnet desired. It was Monnet's sense of purpose, deeply rooted in a philosophy of egalitarianism, that guided his actions throughout life. Simply put, his motivation was peace. European civilization, he believed, would be destroyed in another major war. That is not to say that Monnet saw no value in conflict. He accepted it as a part of reality and felt that "people only accept change when they are faced with necessity, and only recognize necessity when a crisis is upon them." The key was to find a constructive purpose within adversity. The European Community was born of many crises—the disposition of the Saar, the rearmament of Germany, and the threat of communism, to name a few. Monnet's goal was not simply to arbitrate disputes; he searched for ways to eliminate the conditions that cause conflicts. By doing so, he hoped that cooperation would replace competition as the standard of coexistence.

Monnet's approach to institutions reflected his firm belief in the equality of all men. To him, the root of all disagreement was inequality. Two world wars had proven that cooperation between unequal partners was an ineffective safe-guard of the peace. A lasting peace could be achieved only if all the nations of Europe had an equal say in supranational institutions. Those institutions are his legacy.

The balance sheet of Monnet's life shows many assets. The prime ministers and presidents, politicians and labor leaders who knew and trusted him did not forget his accomplishments. He was awarded the United States Presidential Medal of Freedom in 1963 and the Grenville Clark Award in 1975. In 1976 he was named Honorary Citizen of Europe by the European Council. He was awarded honorary doctorates from many universities including Oxford, Yale, Cambridge, and Princeton. However, the awards and degrees are not the most lasting tribute to Jean Monnet. The strength and vitality of the European Community today is a monument to Monnet's vision of a peaceful, united Europe. Monnet believed that although individuals die, their wisdom survives in the institutions they create. If that is so, Jean Monnet's memory is secure.

Annotated Bibliography

Students of Monnet's diplomatic career should begin their investigation at the Centre de recherches européennes in Lausanne, Switzerland, which has published many volumes about Monnet. Its sister organization, the Fondation Jean Monnet (Ferme de Dorigny, CH 1075, Lausanne), is the official repository of Monnet's personal papers. The documentation housed there is open to all researchers. Although the collection covers every period of Monnet's life, its contents are incomplete primarily because many documents were destroyed to prevent capture by the Nazis. Fortunately, a wealth of records since 1940 has survived largely intact. The most readily accessible of these materials cover French postwar reconstruction and the Schuman Plan, the ECSC negotiations and Monnet's tenure as its president, and the ill-fated European Defense Community. The documents in these collections are numbered and abstracted and can be located with finding aids. The organization and microfilming of papers from World War II and those of the Action Committee was completed in 1992.

There is a discouraging lack of published material in English about Monnet's life and work, leaving the statesman as something of an unknown to British and American readers. Until 1978 there was but one full-length monograph on Monnet. Merry and Serge Bromberger's *Jean Monnet and the United States of Europe* (1969) will make interesting reading for the uninitiated, but for serious scholars it falls far short. The work suffers from style and mechanical problems, not the least of which is the lack of notes and bibliography. It aims to combine a biography of Monnet with the history of the European Community, but it is fully successful at neither.

The 1988 centennial of Monnet's birth has led to an increased interest in his career, and some new secondary works have appeared. *Jean Monnet: The Path to European Unity* (1991), edited by Douglas Brinkley and Clifford Hackett, is a useful compendium of historical and personality pieces written by Monnet's closest associates, including Richard Mayne, Jacques van Helmont, and François Duchene. In a similar vein, *Jean Monnet* (1989) relates the proceedings of a symposium organized by the Commission of the European Communities in which Pascal Fontaine, Pierre Uri, Jacques Delors, François Duchene, and many others participated. Their discussions of Monnet's diplomacy are particularly valuable. English-language monographs dealing with specific aspects of Monnet's career are still rare. There are signs, however, that this too is only temporary. John Gillingham's fine book, *Coal, Steel, and the Rebirth of Europe* (1991), is a perfect first step to entice more historians to explore Monnet's impact on modern Europe.

Jean Monnet did not publish a great deal. *Les États-Unis d'Europe ont commencé* (1955) is his only monograph of note. Fortunately, scholars have access to Monnet's thoughts in his *Memoirs* (1978). Monnet's autobiography does not gloat about past accomplishments, nor does it indulge in nostalgia. He presents his life in the same orderly and businesslike manner in which he lived. Nevertheless, the insights he gives on the critical issues confronting the movement for European unity are important. His observations and opinions of the key diplomats he met make this book a lasting contribution to the historiography of twentieth-century Europe.

Far more information is available for those scholars comfortable with the French language. The Centre de recherches européennes has published a great many works by or about Monnet. These are generally excerpts of documents and speeches, and consequently are usually polemical in nature. Although the topics are quite specific, these volumes can be valuable as a source of Monnet's views on the issues of his day. In addition, a number of biographies have been written, but the most promising are Pascal Fontaine's *Jean Monnet: L'Inspirateur* (1988) and Valéry Giscard d'Estaing's *Jean Monnet* (1989).

A number of other volumes provide interesting material on specific incidents in Monnet's career. Researchers will especially want to consult Monnet and Schuman's *Jean Monnet, Robert Schuman: Correspondance, 1947–1953* (1986), which covers the correspondence between them during the ECSC's formative years. For an account of Monnet's role in the formation of the French Committee of National Liberation, see André Kaspi, *La Mission de Jean Monnet à Alger, mars-octobre 1943* (1971). Also, Monnet's part in the creation of the European Council is discussed in Pascal Fontaine's "Le Role de Jean Monnet dans la genèse du Conseil européen," *Revue du Marche Commun* 229 (1979): 357–365.

Bibliography

Books

Binoux, Paul. *Les Pionniers de l'Europe*. Paris: Klincksieck, 1972.

Brinkley, Douglas, and Clifford Hackett, eds. *Jean Monnet: The Path to European Unity*. New York: St. Martin's Press, 1991.

Bromberger, Merry, and Serge Bromberger. *Jean Monnet and the United States of Europe*. New York: Coward-McCann, 1969.

Duroselle, Jean Baptiste. *Deux Types de grands hommes: Le Général de Gaulle et Jean Monnet*. Geneva: Institute universitaire de hautes études internationales, 1977.

Fontaine, François. *Jean Monnet*. Lausanne: Centre de recherches européennes, 1963.

———. *Plus Loin avec Jean Monnet*. Lausanne: Foundation Jean Monnet pour l'Europe, Centre de recherches européennes, 1983.

Fontaine, Pascal. *Le Comité d'Action pour les Étas-Unis d'Europe de Jean Monnet*. Lausanne: Centre de recherches européennes, 1974.

———. *Jean Monnet: A Grand Design for Europe*. Luxembourg: Office for Official Publications of the European Communities, 1988.

———. *Jean Monnet: L'Inspirateur*. Paris: Jacques Grancher, 1988.

Gillingham, John. *Coal, Steel, and the Rebirth of Europe, 1918–1955*. New York: Cambridge University Press, 1991.

Giscard d'Estaing, Valéry. *Jean Monnet*. Lausanne: Fondation Jean Monnet pour l'Europe, Centre de recherches européennes, 1989.

Hermann, Lutz. *Jean Monnet*. Paris: Dalloz, 1968.

Kaspi, André. *La Mission de Jean Monnet à Alger, mars-octobre 1943*. Paris: Editions Richelieu, 1971.

Kenworthy, Leonard Stout. *Twelve Trailblazers of World Community*. Kennett Square, Pa.: Friendly Press, 1988.

Kohnstamm, Max. *Jean Monnet: The Power of the Imagination*. Florence: European University Institute, 1988.

Jean Monnet. Luxembourg: Office for Official Publications of the European Communities, 1989.

Monnet, Jean. *Batir l'Europe*. Lausanne: Fondation Jean Monnet pour l'Europe, Centre de recherches européennes, 1987.

———. *Le Chancelier Adenauer et la construction de l'Europe*. Lausanne: Centre de recherches européennes, 1966.

————. *La Communauté européenne et la Grande-Bretagne.* Lausanne: Centre de re-
cherches européennes, 1958.
————. *La Communauté européenne et l'unité de l'Occident.* Lausanne: Centre de re-
cherches européennes, 1961.
————. *Les États-Unis d'Europe ont commencé.* Paris: Laffont, 1955.
————. *Europe-Amérique. Relations de partenaires nécessaires à la paix.* Lausanne:
Centre de recherches européennes, 1963.
————. *L'Europe et l'organization de la paix.* Lausanne: Centre de recherches euro-
péennes, 1964.
————. *Memoirs.* Translated by Richard Mayne. New York: Doubleday, 1978.
Monnet, Jean, and Robert Schuman. *Jean Monnet, Robert Schuman: Correspondance,
1947–1953.* Lausanne: Foundation Jean Monnet pour l'Europe, Centre de re-
cherches européennes, 1986.
Poos, Jacques F. *Jean Monnet et le Luxembourg dans la construction de l'Europe.*
Lausanne: Centre de recherches européennes, 1989.
Rieben, Henri, Jean Monnet, and Georges Chavallaz. *Jean Monnet.* Lausanne: Centre
de recherches européennes, 1971.
Van Helmont, Jacques. *Jean Monnet comme il etait.* Lausanne: Foundation Jean Monnet
pour l'Europe, Centre de recherches européennes, 1981.

Articles

Beloff, Max. "Jean Monnet's Europe and After: Of Dreams and Realities." *Encounter*
48 (1977): 29–35.
Duchene, François. "First Statesman of Interdependence?" *Encounter* 73 (1989): 32–
41.
Fontaine, Pascal. "Le Role de Jean Monnet dans la genèse du Conseil européen." *Revue
du Marche Commun* 229 (1979): 357–365.
Mayne, Richard. "Gray Eminence." *American Scholar* 53 (1984): 533–540.
Montet, Michel-Pierre. "Europe's Spiritual Origins." *International Management* 44
(1989): 38–39.
"Z" (pseud.). "What Jean Monnet Wrought." *Foreign Affairs* 55 (1977): 630–635.

                                                    RICHARD A. LEIBY

Benito Amilcare Andrea Mussolini (1883–1945).   Benito Mussolini, the future Italian dictator, was born in humble circumstances on July 29, 1883, in the
Romagna, a barren and impoverished region of east central Italy. His father,
Alessandro, a convinced socialist, tutored him in the principles of Marxism and
revolution. Rosa, his mother, a grammar school teacher of bourgeois stock,
supported the family.

    After working in Switzerland as a labor organizer and gaining something of
an international reputation, Mussolini entered the top ranks of the Italian Socialist
party in 1912 when he became editor of *Avanti!* (Forward!), the socialist newspaper published in Milan. A skilled journalist, Mussolini added style to the
stodgy *Avanti!*, and both its circulation and its reputation soared. Barely two
years later, however, Mussolini was removed as editor and expelled from the
party when he advocated Italy's intervention in World War I on the Allied side.
Shortly thereafter he began to publish his own newspaper, *Il Popolo d'Italia*

(Italy's People), which proclaimed irredentist views and championed Italian expansion in the Mediterranean basin. *Il Popolo* later became the official organ of the Fascist party, founded by Mussolini in Milan, on March 23, 1919, at a time of widespread domestic unrest. The movement's name recalled the Roman *fascis*, a symbol of authority. Mussolini was known from the first as *il Duce* (Leader, Commander, Boss).

Early fascism emphasized action over doctrine. Mussolini, in fact, declared that fascism was not a system of beliefs but a revolutionary path to power. He and his followers agreed on the virtues of authority, violence, discipline, imperialism, and war. In May 1921, Mussolini and other fascists were elected to parliament as part of a government-engineered coalition of liberals, conservatives, and fascists designed to thwart the socialists. Mussolini's election as a deputy clearly marked him as a national political figure.

Mussolini had already declared that only a dictator could solve Italy's problems; now he made no secret of his availability for the job. Late in October 1922, Mussolini and the fascists prepared a coup d'état featuring a well-publicized march on Rome by thousands of armed supporters. However, before the march could start King Victor Emmanuel III asked Mussolini to form a government, and on October 30, 1922, Mussolini became the youngest prime minister in the history of Italy. He also took for himself the ministries of foreign affairs and interior. On November 16, 1922, parliament granted Mussolini the unlimited authority he said he needed to bring the country back to order. That step launched a legal, totalitarian dictatorship that lasted until July 25, 1943.

Mussolini married Rachele Guidi, the youngest daughter of his brother's second wife, in 1925. Except for his daughter Edda, who later married the dashing Count Galeazzo Ciano, the future foreign minister, neither Rachele nor their five children played a major role in his life. Mussolini's longtime mistress, Clara Petacci, was more important to him. At the end of April 1945, as Allied units rolled across northern Italy, Mussolini and Petacci fled toward Switzerland until they were apprehended by Communist partisans who executed them on April 28, 1945.

The Benito Mussolini who became the prime minister of Italy in 1922 was a rude, pugnacious rabble-rouser. Paolo Monelli, onetime foreign correspondent for *Il corriere della sera* (The Evening Mail) and Mussolini's biographer, tells how, almost immediately upon Mussolini's arrival in Rome, a junior diplomat was assigned to tutor him in everything from table manners, personal hygiene, and appropriate dress to personal and official protocol.

Although Mussolini told his foreign ministry professionals that he would introduce nothing "original," a fascist foreign policy eventually emerged. Though he followed traditional policy for more than a decade, he soon showed himself to be temperamentally unable to leave diplomacy to the diplomats.

Within weeks of his arrival in Rome, the unprepared Mussolini headed delegations to two diplomatic conferences. His erratic, egocentric behavior led members of both Italian delegations to urge that Mussolini not attend further meetings abroad. Surprisingly, he agreed, admitting that he had been ill at ease in the formal diplomatic environment. Yet he never relinquished control over his delegations to conferences abroad; rather, he bombarded them with detailed instructions. On occasion, unknown to his ambassadors, he sent personal emissaries—including his daughter, Edda—on sensitive missions to key foreign leaders.

After 1924 Mussolini often invited world leaders to Rome, a device that he believed confirmed Rome as the center of European power. He spied on embassies in Rome and he took great delight in revealing bits of gossip he obtained. Despite this unorthodox approach to affairs of state, Mussolini matured in office and became something like a senior European statesman.

Mussolini saw treaties as devices to rebuild Italy's prestige. Like many Italians, he was outraged by the shabby treatment accorded Italy at the postwar peace conferences. Thus, he sent delegations everywhere a treaty was being negotiated. If nothing was going on, he staged conferences in Rome or elsewhere in Italy to which he invited Europe's leaders.

His earlier gauche behavior smoothed a bit, Mussolini played an important personal role in the making of many treaties. He was particularly proud to be among the first to recognize the Soviet Union, in 1924. The Locarno Treaty (1925) addressed broad issues of collective security in the Rhineland and in eastern Europe; along with Britain, Italy undertook to provide troops to enforce the treaty. The Lateran Pact (1929) settled a long-standing dispute with the Vatican and earned Mussolini great personal acclaim. The Pact of Rome (1933) held out the prospect of collaboration among Italy, Germany, France, and Britain. In July 1934, he was praised for his stout defense of Austria in the face of an attempted German coup. As late as 1938, Mussolini was hailed for his role as mediator of the Munich settlement, though his compromise later proved to be a ruse.

Any attempt to summarize Mussolini's philosophical orientation invites endless debate. In his own time the closest he came to a systematic exposition of his views was in a thesis submitted to the University of Rome, in 1924, for an honorary law degree; his subject: "Introduction to Machiavelli." Mussolini's private utterances and personal scribblings offer more concrete guidance. They echo ideas gleaned not only from Machiavelli's *Prince* but also from the works of Friedrich Nietzsche, Georges Sorel, Robert Michels, and Vilfredo Pareto. He gives an occasional nod in the direction of Social Darwinism and Jamesian pragmatism. If there was a system of thought, it was by 1922 eclectic and elastic but rooted in Machiavelli's political amorality.

Mussolini venerated the state as the supreme achievement of man and the source of all civilization. The perpetuation of the state demanded will, discipline, the capacity to endure pain as well as to inflict it, and a hierarchical society. Atop the hierarchy was the wise and heroic leader. Mussolini regarded force, violence, and war as legitimate tools of power, reserved, of course, to the state. Perhaps much as nineteenth-century Americans did, he saw imperialism as manifest destiny. In Mussolini's schema, a strong state was an essential prerequisite to natural and inevitable imperialism. Finally, Mussolini professed always to have had premonitions of greatness. Once asked if he thought of himself as another *Napoleon, he replied, "No. Greater than Napoleon!" In this context, he came to believe that he was infallible—an ultimately fatal conceit.

Well into the 1930s, many of Mussolini's policies followed those of the post-Risorgimento era, from 1861 onward. These included the expansion of Italian power into the Mediterranean basin and the consolidation of early colonial conquests.

*Woodrow Wilson had greatly annoyed the Italians in 1919 when he repudiated the secret Treaty of London (1915) by which the Allies had spelled out the spoils of war due Italy for joining them. The few satisfied war aims were included in the Treaty of St. Germain with Austria (1919), which ceded to Italy the South Tyrol, Trieste, and the Istrian Peninsula—less the city of Fiume (now Rijecka, in Croatia). After 1922 Italy used diplomacy to achieve some other unrealized war objectives. The Treaty of Lausanne (1923) confirmed Italy's claim to the Dodecanese Islands, seized from the Ottoman Turks in 1912. Fiume was acquired by the Pact of Rome (1924), and Italy succeeded in gaining a virtual protectorate over Albania by the Treaty of Tirana (1926).

Modern Italy had turned to Africa as early as 1872. Italian protectorates were established over Eritrea (1882) and Somaliland (1889), but disaster struck in 1869 when Ethiopia repulsed the advancing Italians at Adowa at the cost of 6,000 Italian dead. In 1911–1912 the Italo-Turkish War enabled Italy to acquire a substantial part of what is now Libya. The consolidation of Italian sovereignty over Libya, Eritrea, and Italian Somaliland began soon after Mussolini took office. Later, Mussolini and most other Italians saw the outcome of the Ethiopian war in 1936 as revenge for Italy's disgrace at Adowa, although Italy's African empire proved to be a financial drain.

What was new after 1922 was also largely a result of World War I. Mussolini pursued a revisionist policy toward the Treaty of Versailles. He first opposed the League of Nations, then attempted to control it, and finally left it in 1937 after the Ethiopian war. He pursued active policies among the new Balkan states. He had announced that fascism was not for export, but his agents were soon at work in Italian colonies in North Africa and the Middle East, while he subsidized pro-fascist movements on the Continent as well as in Ireland, the United Kingdom, and the Americas. In 1935 he launched a comprehensive program of international propaganda designed to support his foreign policy.

From the first, much of Mussolini's effort went into making Italy respectable, even feared. Recent foreign policy had supported Britain; now the principal objective became to create a new balance of power in Europe with Italy as the fulcrum. His efforts generated great interest, and he came close to his goal with the Pact of Rome.

But Mussolini had reckoned without *Adolf Hitler, whom he had dismissed as a funny little man of no consequence after the two first met at Venice in May

1934. In July 1934, following the assassination of Austrian chancellor Engelbert Dollfuss, Mussolini's client, Mussolini sent troops to the Brenner Pass to fend off a German putsch; Hitler backed down, but Mussolini was furious because neither Britain nor France lifted a finger to help Austria.

Ironically, the Austrian incident marked a turning point in Italy's relations with Germany. The sequence of events is complex, but it was triggered by the collapse of the united front Mussolini had engineered in May 1935 at Stresa, whereby Italy, France, and Britain guaranteed Austria's independence. After Italy invaded Ethiopia, France and Britain both supported the League of Nations' sanctions against Italy. Meanwhile, they flagrantly appeased Germany. When, in 1936, neither government took action as Germany remilitarized the Rhineland, Mussolini became convinced that his two allies had lost their will to stand up to Hitler.

Consequently, Mussolini moved closer to Hitler. A new policy phase began in 1936 and lasted until 1943 as Mussolini merged his policy with Hitler's by means of the Rome-Berlin Axis (1936), the Anti-Comintern Pact (1937), and, finally, the Pact of Steel (1939), by which he agreed to join Germany whenever war broke out, no matter who attacked whom. Mussolini's motives were mixed: in part, he seemed to believe until almost the last hour that he could influence Hitler against war; in part, he wanted to be on the winning side if war did break out in Europe.

In 1936, also, the appointment of Galeazzo Ciano, Mussolini's son-in-law, as foreign minister hastened the fascistization of the ministry of foreign affairs that Mussolini had begun. The new foreign minister promptly took control of Italy's intervention in the Spanish Civil War. Ciano was also deeply involved in the negotiations with the Germans that eventually led to the Pact of Steel.

In February 1939, Mussolini announced a "new" fascist foreign policy, which included the view that Italy was a prisoner in the Mediterranean, encircled by Great Britain, and that Italy should prepare to "march to the ocean" and assert fascist authority at Gibraltar and Suez. This meant displacing the British and French from the Mediterranean and, possibly, taking British and French territories in West Africa. To achieve this, Mussolini said, Italy must adhere to the Pact of Steel with Germany.

The foundations for this proposed policy had already been laid. Italy's navy and air force had probed British defenses at Gibraltar and Malta and in the Red Sea. Both Mussolini's propaganda and his agents were active in Egypt and Palestine. Other agents were stirring up unrest in Yemen, adjacent to the British naval base at Aden, and in Greece. Staunch fascists were clamoring for action against Corsica, Malta, and Nice in a new outburst of irredentist zeal.

Mussolini also boasted that his policy assured the world several years of peace, enough time for Italy to rearm, build an invincible submarine fleet, and train the native African army that he had proposed some years before. However, Mussolini miscalculated. Hitler had destroyed any semblance of concerted European resistance to Germany by taking Italy out of the equation. Now Hitler's timetable was about to control Italy. By the time Mussolini and Ciano discovered Hitler's real intentions, it was too late to back down. In September 1939, when Britain and France declared war on Germany, somehow both men knew that they had condemned Italy to defeat. The events of World War II confirmed that apprehension with one humiliating loss after another, in the mountains of Albania and Greece, in the deserts of North Africa, and on the frozen steppes of the Soviet Union.

It seems clear that Mussolini was an intuitive Italian politician with a Machiavellian bent. Before 1936, when he allowed himself to be seduced by Hitler's flattery, Mussolini held the attention of his people, if not their affection, and he had the respect of many world leaders. Some tried to deter him from the disasters they saw ahead, but by then he was too isolated and certain of his own infallibility.

In the short run, Mussolini demonstrated an uncanny ability to resolve disputes without recourse to the warfare that he so often advocated. In the long run, his genius, perhaps, was to mount and sustain risky diplomacy without any real backup force. His most effective weapons were those of bluster and bluff and well-orchestrated propaganda. Only too late did Hitler, *Neville Chamberlain, Pierre Laval, and the others realize that Mussolini's strident militancy was a ploy to deceive others about Italy's lamentable lack of military preparedness.

The Lateran Pact of 1929 was probably the most lasting contribution to modern statesmanship that Mussolini made. It took the pope out of captivity and normalized the Vatican's relations with Italy. As expected, Mussolini made good use of the occasion for propaganda purposes, cultivating the goodwill of Catholics all over the world.

Mussolini's legacy to the world is fascism. His vision of the ideal state and its role lives on. Anthony James Joes is among contemporary scholars who claim that fascism has made substantial contributions to international politics, especially in the developing world. Fascism has no monopoly on the following concepts, but taken together they help clarify Mussolini's contribution to the modern state: national mobilization, centralized control, an autarchic economy that emphasizes production rather than redistribution of wealth, massive infrastructure development (roads, railroads, communications, power), land management, scientific agriculture, adequate housing, and universal education.

In any event, Renzo de Felice, Italy's foremost authority on the fascist era, has suggested that Italian historians have been overly moralistic in their evaluations of Mussolini. For most of his regime, Mussolini followed in the tradition of Risorgimento and late nineteenth-century leaders who had made Italy an authoritarian, centrist monarchy dominated by an anticlerical, rightist oligarchy. In the last quarter of the 1800s, Italy's dictatorial, Machiavellian leaders launched the state on an imperialist course. Fifty years later, Mussolini appeared as the historic hero to maintain the same direction.

Finally, Benito Mussolini bequeathed to the world what is now known as "public diplomacy," the full-scale exploitation of media techniques and educational and cultural exchanges to project and enhance the image of any given country in pursuit of foreign policy objectives.

Annotated Bibliography

Important archival holdings relating to Mussolini are located in Italy, the United Kingdom, and the United States. In Rome the Archivo Storico del Ministero degli Affari Esteri and the Archivo Centrale dello Stato hold the private papers of Dino Grandi, the papers of the Segretario Particulare del Duce, and the papers of the President of the Council of Ministers. The Federzoni Archives, also in Rome, has a private collection of documents relating to Mussolini. The Public Record Office in London holds documents dealing with Mussolini in its Foreign Office and Cabinet Office files. Other documents relating to Mussolini, carefully catalogued by F. W. Deakin, comprise the St. Antony's Collection at St. Antony's College, Oxford. The National Archives in Washington, D.C., holds Mussolini's private papers and the Lisbon Papers from Ciano's Secretariat in the Foreign Office. German translations of miscellaneous papers from Ciano's office, Ciano Papers: Rose Garden, are also found at the National Archives.

The literature on Mussolini and his foreign policy is vast and confusing. Readers who wish to explore aspects of Mussolini's life and times are fortunate indeed to have available a comprehensive bibliographical study by Charles F. Delzell, *Italy in the Twentieth Century* (1980).

Those who first published their views of Mussolini's Italy tended to be either Italian socialists and ultraliberals who languished in exile abroad, their followers, or entirely uncritical American sycophants. These early works were all too often poorly documented, if documented at all. Regrettably, much of the later literature reflects their biases.

The extensive and effective use of propaganda by fascist Italy makes unravelling Mussolini's era a challenge. Due to the nature of Mussolini's regime, the Italian press, speeches, and personal interviews are often poor sources for researchers. Moreover, many documentary sources have only recently become available. Howard McGaw Smyth has documented the recovery, evaluation, and classification of several sets of purloined Italian records, now available in the archives of the United States, in *Secrets of the Fascist Era: How Uncle Sam Obtained Some of the Top Level Documents of Mussolini's Period* (1975).

Since Mussolini was a prolific writer, it should come as no surprise that his collected works total thirty-six volumes: *Opera omnia di Benito Mussolini* (1951–1963). Mussolini is associated with three volumes of reputed autobiography. All must be read with the knowledge that Mussolini liked to help history along from time to time. The first of these works, *My Diary, 1915–1917* (1925), relates his experiences during World War I. *My Autobiography* (1928) was actually ghostwritten by Mussolini's brother Arnaldo in collaboration with Richard Washburn Child, former U.S. ambassador to Italy. *The Fall of Mussolini: His Own Story* (1948) relates the events of 1942–1943 that led to his arrest and imprisonment.

Several members of Mussolini's family have written memoirs of uneven quality. Rachele Mussolini, his wife, wrote *La mia vita con Benito* (1948) and *Mussolini: An Intimate Biography* (1974). The latter appends a useful chronology of important events. Edda Mussolini Ciano published *My Truth* (1977), which focuses on her life with her husband, Count Galeazzo Ciano.

More important are Ciano's diaries: *Ciano's Hidden Diary, 1937–1938* (1953) and *The Ciano Diaries, 1939–1943* (1946). The latter has an interesting introduction in which Sumner Welles alleges that Ciano had from the first opposed Mussolini's swing to Hitler, a claim not borne out by later research. A chronology of events provides access to the appropriate diary entries; a section entitled "Dramatis Personae" briefly identifies several hundred people named in the diary. Several sets of memoirs by key figures of the fascist regime, all in the original Italian, supplement Ciano's diaries.

Among English-language biographies, Denis Mack Smith's *Mussolini* (1982) stands out as a scholarly work, though he tends to accept Gaetano Salvamini's much disputed conclusion that Mussolini was a poseur and a victim of his own propaganda. Sir Ivone Kirkpatrick's *Mussolini: A Study in Power* (1964) draws on his personal experience as a member of the British embassy in Rome from 1930 to 1933. James Anthony Joes has written a well-documented, carefully argued revisionist biography, *Mussolini* (1982). Gaudens Megaro's *Mussolini in the Making* (1938) is based on research in Italy, Austria, and Switzerland covering Mussolini's early career to 1914. Paolo Monelli's *Mussolini: An Intimate Life* (1953) survives as the standard work on Mussolini the man.

Giorgio Pini and Duilio Susmel, two Italian journalists with fascist backgrounds, collaborated to produce the four-volume *Mussolini, l'uomo e l'opera* (1953–1955). The real magnum opus is that of Renzo de Felice, Italy's leading specialist on fascism. Four volumes had appeared by 1974: *Mussolini il revoluzionario, 1883–1920*; *Mussolini il fascista: La conquista del potere, 1921–1925*; *Mussolini il fascista: L'organizzazione dello stato fascista 1925–1929*; and *Mussolini il duce: Gli anni del consenso, 1929–1936*. Two more volumes were reported to be in preparation: *Mussolini il duce: Lo stato totalitario* and *L'Alleato, 1939–1945*. Based on archival sources, the works contain many documents.

Regarding Mussolini's diplomacy, Alan Cassels' *Mussolini's Early Diplomacy* (1970) supersedes Maxwell Macartney and Paul Cremona's prewar classic, *Italy's Foreign and Colonial Policy, 1914–1937* (reprinted 1972). Cassels includes a useful bibliography. Gordon Craig and Felix Gilbert's *The Diplomats* (1953) includes chapters entitled "The Early Diplomacy of Italian Fascism" and "Ciano and His Ambassadors." In *The Brutal Friendship* (1962), F. W. Deakin plumbs the depths of German-Italian relations that led to the fall of Mussolini's regime; useful notes on archival sources are appended.

Samuel Halperin includes a number of documents in the appendix to *Mussolini and Italian Fascism* (1964); among others, the texts of the Lateran Pact Accords and the Pact of Steel and Ciano's statement on the 1936 Rome-Berlin Axis are of particular interest. In a well-documented study, *The Pope and the Duce* (1981), Peter Kent contends that Mussolini was much more than an opportunistic buffoon seeking propaganda victories. On the other hand, Denis Mack Smith's *Mussolini's Roman Empire* (1976) focuses on the effects of propaganda and concludes that Mussolini became a victim of his own lies. Meir Michaelis dissects the Jewish question in a definitive work, *Mussolini and the Jews: German-Italian Relations and the Jewish Question in Italy, 1922–1945* (1978). Esmonde M. Robertson's *Mussolini as Empire Builder* (1977) is another recent work supporting the view that Mussolini had a method behind his apparent madness. The pioneering study by Elizabeth Wiskeman, *The Rome-Berlin Axis: A History of the Relations between Hitler and Mussolini* (1949), is somewhat outdated but sound.

Bibliography

Published Documents

Ciano, Galeazzo. *Ciano's Diplomatic Papers*. Edited by Malcolm Muggeridge. London: Odhams Press, 1948.

———. *L'Europa verso la catastrofe*. (184 conversations with Mussolini, Hitler, Franco, Chamberlain, Welles, and others.) Milan: Mondadori, 1948.

France, Ministère des Affaires Étrangères. *Documents diplomatiques français*. Paris: Imprimerie Nationale. (Series.)

Germany. *Documents on German Foreign Policy.* Translations of *Akten zur Deutschen Auswärtigen Politik, 1918–1945.* Washington, D.C.: U.S. Government Printing Office. (Series.)
Hitler, Adolf. *Hitler e Mussolini: Lettere e documenti.* Milan: Rizzoli, 1946.
Italy, Ministero degli Affari Esteri. *I documenti diplomatici Italiani.* (1861–1943.) Rome: Libreria dello Stato, 1952– .
League of Nations. *Official Journal.* Geneva, 1920–1940.
———. *Treaty Series* Geneva, 1920–1946.
United Kingdom. Foreign Office. *Documents on British Foreign Policy.* London: H.M.S.O. (Series.)
———. Royal Institute of International Affairs. Documents. (Series.)
United States. Department of State. *Foreign Relations of the United States.* Washington, D.C.: U.S. Government Printing Office. (Series.)

Works by and about Mussolini

Alfieri, Dino. *Due dittatori di fronte.* Milan: Rizzoli, 1948.
Badoglio, Pietro. *L'Italia nella seconda guerra mondiale: Memorie e documenti.* Milan: Mondadori, 1946.
Bottai, Giuseppe. *Vent'anni e un giorno (24 luglio 1943).* Milan: Garzanti, 1949.
Cassels, Alan. *Mussolini's Early Diplomacy.* Princeton, N.J.: Princeton University Press, 1970.
Ciano, Edda Mussolini. *My Truth.* Translated by Eileen Finletter. New York: Morrow, 1977.
Ciano, Galeazzo. *The Ciano Diaries, 1939–1943.* Edited by Hugh Gibson. Garden City, N.Y.: Doubleday, 1946.
———. *Ciano's Hidden Diary, 1937–1938.* Translated by Andreas Mayor. New York: Dutton, 1953.
Craig, Gordon, and Felix Gilbert, eds. *The Diplomats.* 2 vols. Princeton, N.J.: Princeton University Press, 1953.
Deakin, F. W. *The Brutal Friendship: Mussolini, Hitler, and the Fall of Italian Fascism.* New York: Harper and Row, 1962.
de Felice, Renzo. *Mussolini il duce: Gli anni del consenso, 1929–1936.* Turin: Giulio Einaudi, 1974.
———. *Mussolini il fascista: La conquista del potere, 1921–1925.* Turin: Giulio Einaudi, 1966.
———. *Mussolini il fascista: L'organizzazione dello stato fascista, 1925–1929.* Turin: Giulio Einaudi, 1968.
———. *Mussolini il revoluzionario, 1883–1920.* Turin: Giulio Einaudi, 1965.
De Grand, Alexander J. *The Italian Nationalist Association and the Rise of Fascisim in Italy, 1903–1923.* Lincoln: University of Nebraska Press, 1978.
Delzell, Charles F. *Italy in the Twentieth Century.* Washington, D.C.: American Historical Society, 1980.
Federzoni, Luigi. *L'Italia di ieri per la storia di domani.* Milan: Mondadori, 1967.
Gallo, Max. *Mussolini's Italy: Twenty Years of the Fascist Era.* Translated by Charles Markmann. New York: Macmillan, 1973.
Grandi, Dino. *Dino Grandi racconta.* Venice: N.p., 1945.
Gregor, A. James. *Young Mussolini and the Intellectual Origins of Fascism.* Berkeley: University of California Press, 1979.

Guariglia, Raffaele. *Riccordi, 1922–1946*. Naples: Edizioni Scientifici Italiani, 1950.

Graziani, Rodolfo. *Ho difesa la patria*. Milan: Garzanti, 1948.

Halperin, Samuel W. *Mussolini and Italian Fascism*. Princeton, N.J.: Van Nostrand, 1964.

———. *The Separation of Church and State in Italian Thought from Cavour to Mussolini*. New York: Octagon Books, 1971.

Joes, Anthony James. *Mussolini*. New York: Franklin Watts, 1982.

Kent, Peter C. *The Pope and the Duce: The International Impact of the Lateran Agreements*. New York: St. Martin's Press, 1981.

Kirkpatrick, Sir Ivone. *Mussolini: A Study in Power*. New York: Hawthorne Books, 1964.

Macartney, Maxwell, and Paul Cremona. *Italy's Foreign and Colonial Policy, 1914–1937*. New York: Oxford University Press, 1938. Reprint. New York: Howard Fertig, 1972.

Mack Smith, Denis. *Mussolini*. New York: Knopf, 1982.

———. *Mussolini's Roman Empire*. New York: Viking, 1976.

Megaro, Gaudens. *Mussolini in the Making*. Boston: Houghton Mifflin, 1938.

Michaelis, Meir. *Mussolini and the Jews: German-Italian Relations and the Jewish Question in Italy, 1922–1945*. Oxford: Clarendon Press, 1978.

Monelli, Paolo. *Mussolini: An Intimate Life*. London: Thames and Hudson, 1953.

Mussolini, Benito. *The Fall of Mussolini: His Own Story*. Edited by Max Ascoli. New York: Farrar, Straus, 1948. Reprint. Westport, Conn.: Greenwood Press, 1975.

———. *My Autobiography*. Foreword by Richard Washburn Child. New York: Scribner's, 1928.

———. *My Diary, 1915–1917*. Boston: Small, Maynard, 1925.

———. *Opera omnia di Benito Mussolini*. 36 vols. Edited by Eduardo and Duilio Susmel. Florence: La Fenice, 1951–1963.

Mussolini, Rachele. *La mia vita con Benito*. Milan: Mondadori, 1948.

———. *Mussolini: An Intimate Biography*. New York: Morrow, 1974.

Pini, Giorgio, and Duilio Susmel. *Mussolini, l'uomo e l'opera*. 4 vols. Florence: La Fenice, 1953–1955.

Plehwe, Friedrich Karl. *The End of an Alliance: Rome's Defection from the Axis in 1943*. New York: Oxford University Press, 1971.

Pollard, John F. *The Vatican and Italian Fascism, 1929–32*. Cambridge: Cambridge University Press, 1985.

Robertson, Esmonde M. *Mussolini as Empire Builder: Europe and Africa, 1932–36*. London: Macmillan, 1977.

Smyth, Howard McGaw. *Secrets of the Fascist Era: How Uncle Sam Obtained Some of the Top Level Documents of Mussolini's Period*. Carbondale: Southern Illinois University Press, 1975.

Wiskeman, Elizabeth. *The Rome-Berlin Axis: A History of the Relations between Hitler and Mussolini*. London: N.p., 1949.

ROBERT W. MACDONALD

Napoleon I (1769–1821).   Napoleon Bonaparte was born in Ajaccio, Corsica, on August 15, 1769, shortly after the island had become a French possession. From the minor nobility, the future emperor was the second of eight children. His father decided on a military career for Napoleon and sent him to military schools, first at Brienne and afterwards at the École Militaire. A sublieutenant of artillery upon graduation, Napoleon became a lieutenant colonel in the Corsican National Guard soon after the beginning of the French Revolution.

The Bonaparte family fled to France after becoming embroiled in Corsica's turbulent politics. Napoleon was soon ordered as captain to the army besieging Toulon, a royalist port supported by the royal navy in its uprising against the revolution. When his commander was wounded, Napoleon assumed leadership of the artillery, and his guns drove out the enemy fleet, permitting the conquest of the city. Promoted to general of brigade, he was in Paris in 1795 when a royalist demonstration took place, which Bonaparte dispersed with a "whiff of grapeshot," saving the revolutionary government. Napoleon married Josephine de Beauharnais in 1796 and almost simultaneously was given command of the Army of Italy. In his Italian campaign of 1796–1797, Napoleon defeated larger Austrian armies and forced France's enemies on the Continent to sue for a peace granted at Campo Formio on October 17, 1797. The peace, which complied with Bonaparte's wishes, dissolved the First Coalition, composed of Austria, Great Britain, and Prussia.

Like earlier French revolutionary generals, Napoleon was not content with military victory but set about reorganizing the conquered territories by establishing a Cisalpine republic composed of Habsburg and papal possessions, and by running his own foreign policy. In the peace treaty, Austria recognized the French annexation of Belgium and the Rhine's left bank as well as the establishment of the Cisalpine Republic. Austria was permitted to annex Venice and most of Venetia, while the Ionian Islands, a Venetian possession, went to France. The German princes who lost their territories on the left bank of the Rhine were compensated with church possessions elsewhere in the German lands. In order to secure the best possible positions for themselves in these territories, the German princes competed for the favors of France. The Holy Roman Empire lost most of its ecclesiastical states and free cities in the ensuing reconstruction of the German states, which was ratified in February 1803 by one of the last imperial diets.

In order to defeat Great Britain, France's only remaining enemy, Bonaparte invaded Egypt. He conquered the country, but the destruction of the French fleet at the Battle of the Nile (1798) left the French stranded. The French general busied himself with restructuring Egyptian government and law; however, with Napoleon marooned in the Middle East, France's former enemies took courage. Austria was dissatisfied with French power in the German states, and Napoleon's activities in Egypt frightened Russia. An alliance, known as the Second Coalition and comprising Great Britain, Austria, and Russia, soon formed and engaged France in war. By 1799 the Russian marshal Alexander Suvorov was able to operate freely in Switzerland and northern Italy. In order to extricate himself from a hopeless position, Napoleon abandoned his army in Egypt, returned to Paris, overthrew the Directory through a coup d'état, established a new government called the Consulate, made himself First Consul, and defeated Austria at the Battle of Marengo in 1800. Napoleon then signed a peace treaty with Austria at Lunéville in 1800, initialed a concordat with the pope in 1801, and negotiated peace with Britain at Amiens in 1802. Bonaparte was made Consul for Life in 1802 and Emperor of the French in 1804.

Napoleon was a man of the Enlightenment as well as of the French Revolution, and his enormous belief in himself meant that the principles in which he believed were to be institutionalized wherever he ruled. If he asserted the sovereignty of the people, he assured himself a monopoly of power. A believer in the rule of law, he made certain that the code which bore his name was spread throughout Europe. As consul and emperor, Napoleon established a new order in France as he had in Italy and Egypt. A new constitution, a new law code, an established but subordinate Roman Catholic Church, a social order based on the French bourgeoisie's revolutionary principles but with an aristocracy based not only on blood but also on merit, Napoleonic France proved as great a challenge to the Ancien Régime existing elsewhere on the Continent as had the French revolutionary governments. Although the imperial coronation ceremony employed the crown and sword of Charlemagne as links to the last emperor in France, Napoleon's goals were as far-reaching and as bloody as those of his Jacobin predecessors.

Napoleon can fairly be viewed as the founder of the modern state, with all power exercised by paid agents of government and all citizens subject equally to the authority of that government. The new civil code, often called the Code Napoleon, ensured legal equality to all adult male residents of France. Reason was the foundation of the new legal system, not custom or tradition. Napoleon believed that it was imperative not only to establish the power of France throughout Europe and eventually the world, but also to remold conquered territories in the image of the new France. France could therefore never truly be at peace with the other European powers because they regarded its foundations as an insult and its principles as a threat to their ruling traditions.

While overseas ambitions in Haiti and Louisiana were thwarted and abandoned, Elba and Piedmont in the Italian peninsula were annexed; Napoleon became president of the newly established Italian Republic and mediator of the reorganized Confederation of Switzerland. Interference with British trade brought renewed war with Great Britain. When Napoleon made himself king of Italy, Austria and Russia joined Britain in 1805 in the Third Coalition. Although the British fleet commanded by Lord Nelson destroyed the French and Spanish navies off Cape Trafalgar in October 1805, the Grande Armée soon defeated the Austro-Russian armies at the Battle of Austerlitz (1805) in Bohemia. In the subsequent Treaty of Pressburg, Napoleon annexed Venetia to the Kingdom of Italy. He also dissolved the Holy Roman Empire and replaced it with the Confederation of the Rhine, a federation of German states under Napoleon's dominion. However, British control of the seas and French rule on the Continent led to a long stalemate which permitted neither power to make peace with the other: each side aimed to annihilate the other. The Napoleonic Wars were the last of the worldwide wars fought by Great Britain and France, but they may be considered the first of the "total wars" as modern states mobilized all of their resources to destroy their rival.

Having defeated the two most powerful imperial families, the Habsburgs and Romanovs, Napoleon set about establishing his own family on the thrones of Europe. In 1806 his elder brother Joseph became king of Naples and his brother Louis became king of Holland. Threatened by French domination in the German lands, Prussia and Russia declared war in 1806, but the Prussian armies were quickly defeated at the twin battles of Jena and Auerstädt in October 1806, while Russia met its defeat at the Battle of Friedland in June 1807. The Third Coalition was smashed.

The Franco-Russian negotiations at Tilsit in July 1807 recognized Napoleonic hegemony over Europe and looked to a division of the Eastern Hemisphere. Prussia was crushed and hemmed in by two new states, the Kingdom of West-phalia, ruled by Napoleon's brother Jérôme, and the Duchy of Warsaw, reigned over by Napoleon's ally, Frederick August, the newly minted king of Saxony. In all of the satellite states, Napoleon insisted that the Code Napoleon become the law of the land regardless of local legal traditions. Each of these states had a constitution, legislature, administration, and judiciary modeled on that of France, but taxes, levies, and military conscription meant that the benefits of French rule were generally recognized only after Napoleon's fall.

With only Britain still at war with France, and the French fleet unable to defeat the British navy, Napoleon decided to use trade as his chief weapon. In November 1806, the Continental System was instituted, excluding British and colonial goods from Europe. However, Napoleon had to control the entire European coastline for his scheme to succeed. Consequently, in order to enforce the blockade, Napoleon was inexorably drawn into conquest and annexation. In 1807 Portugal was occupied; in 1808 Spain was deprived of its royal family, the Bourbons, and given Joseph Bonaparte as king. (Naples was given to Napoleon's brother-in-law, Marshal Joseph Murat.) Spanish rebellion developed into the Peninsular War, which lasted for five years, with the British backing the Spanish guerrillas with money, supplies, and eventually armies. Believing Napoleon to be tied down in Spain, and assured of Russia's disinterest, Austria declared war in 1809 but was defeated at Wagram in July. The Treaty of Schön-brunn, signed in October, extended direct French rule into the Balkans, with the annexation of the Illyrian provinces, composed of much of Slovenia and Croatia, to the French Empire. Napoleon's satellite, the Duchy of Warsaw, was given part of Austria's Polish-inhabited provinces in Galicia. The Papal States were annexed and divided between the empire and the Kingdom of Italy, both ruled by Napoleon.

Intent on establishing a legitimate dynasty, Napoleon divorced Josephine in December 1809 and married the Habsburg Archduchess Marie-Louise, daughter of Austria's emperor. The French emperor hoped that his son, born in 1811 and proclaimed king of Rome, would be accepted by Europe's ruling families, but the father's ambitions made the son's future reign no more than a mirage. Intent on enforcing the Continental System, he annexed more territories to the empire: Bremen, Lübeck, and even the Kingdom of Holland, after Napoleon had insisted on the abdication of his brother Louis. When Rome was annexed and the pope protested, Pius VII was interned in France.

Napoleon's authority reached its fullest extent by 1811, when he controlled all of Europe except the Balkan peninsula. French-dominated Europe included the empire itself, which consisted of 130 departments extending up the North Sea and down the Tyrrhenian and the Adriatic; the dependent states, such as Italy, Switzerland, Westphalia, and the Duchy of Warsaw, most of which had French laws, administrators, and even rulers; and the allied states of Prussia, Austria, Russia, Denmark, and Sweden, at war with Great Britain and participating in the Continental System.

Russia, however, was drifting from Napoleon's orbit. Disturbed by French support of Polish interests at Schönbrunn and angered by Napoleon's annexation of the Illyrian provinces, Russia clearly could no longer be considered an ally, nor its emperor, *Alexander I, a friend. When Alexander renounced the Continental System in December 1810, Napoleon prepared to invade Russia, doing so on June 22, 1812, with the largest army ever assembled. While the French armies achieved numerous victories, crowned by the Battle of Borodino (1812), the subsequent occupation of Moscow did not force Alexander I to sue for peace as Napoleon had hoped. Ill prepared for a long winter campaign far from his base, Napoleon retreated. The retreat has entered history as one of the greatest military fiascos. The Russian emperor pursued the French armies beyond his borders, viewing Napoleon not only as a threat to his dominions but also as a menace to Western civilization.

Seeing France so weak, England, Austria, Prussia, and Russia united for the first time against Napoleon. After his defeat at Leipzig in October 1813, Napoleon withdrew his armies from the German territories and continued the war with the allies on French soil. Finally, Napoleon abdicated on April 6, 1814, and was exiled to Elba by the allies, who restored the Bourbons to the French throne. Unrest in France and dissension among the allies meeting in Vienna led Napoleon to believe that he could succeed in winning back the French throne. He escaped from Elba in March 1815 and marched on Paris, winning over the populace. While rebuilding his armies, he hoped for peace from the allies. However, they regarded him as a mortal enemy, and he felt impelled to use arms to ensure his power. Meeting the allied armies at the Battle of Waterloo on June 18, 1815, the French emperor was defeated, and on June 22 he abdicated in favor of his son. Taking refuge on a British warship, he was exiled to St. Helena, an isolated British crown colony in the South Atlantic.

While in exile, Napoleon ensured that his legend would survive him by dictating his memoirs and by engaging in long conversations with his companions. He emphasized the most favorable elements of his reign and remarked that ''the Imperial Guard always marched to the Marseillaise.'' He maintained that his greatest hope was to establish a federation of free peoples in Europe.

No ruler has come closer to establishing political unity in Europe than Napoleon. He can be compared only to the Roman emperors, Charlemagne, and *Adolf Hitler in the scope of his ambitions and his conquests. Certainly, the French emperor consciously cultivated the Roman example, from the Empire style in furniture to the neoclassical canvasses of David and the Arch of Triumph, begun in 1806. Like these other conquerors, he employed bloody methods, and his aims were not limited to conquest alone but extended to reshaping nations and indeed civilization. He was able to couple with or battle against the other European states, depending on circumstances, but his eyes were always set on more than military control. Like all Enlightenment thinkers, he believed in the fundamental unity of European civilization and sought to guarantee that unity through military conquest, constitutional restructuring, and legal uniformity. While he encouraged nationalism in Italy and Poland, he saw it as a tool: the nation-state was not an end in itself. However, the Grand Empire was never uniform. Rather, Napoleon adapted his instruments and goals to his needs and ends. As a result Warsaw ended up with a proportionately greater electorate and a more vocal legislature than France.

Despite his martial means, Napoleon was a builder as well as a destroyer. While his empire perished long before his life ended, the civil code, the hierarchical system of administration, and a more open social structure became the roots of modern France and, through his conquests, of modern Europe. His instruments were more extensive and his aims more ambitious than any conqueror before him. Europe had never seen a greater army than the 700,000 soldiers assembled for the conquest of Russia in 1812. The Continental System was pursued along the entire European coastline, alienating his allies and proving impossible to enforce. The French culture of the Enlightenment and the revolution, which he viewed as universal and a necessary component of his rule, were considered alien impositions in Prussia and the Tyrol, and stimulated the beginnings of German nationalism.

The Napoleonic legend is built on more than the myth Napoleon spun on St. Helena; it is grounded in accomplishments now seen as essential elements of government. While Napoleon died on May 5, 1821, his legend survived him; in 1840 his remains were returned to France and interred in the Invalides, which has become a national shrine.

Annotated Bibliography

Archival holdings pertaining to Napoleon and his foreign policy are numerous. In France, the most important repositories include the Archives Nationales at 60, rue des Francs-Bourgeois, 75003 Paris; the Ministère des Affaires Étrangères at 37, Quai d'Orsay, 75700 Paris; and the Archives de la Guerre, located at the Château de Vincennes outside of Paris.

In Great Britain, the researcher should consult the manuscript section of the British Museum and the Public Record Office. In Austria, the state archives at Vienna—the Haus-, Hof- und Staatsarchiv—holds valuable documents on the career of the French emperor.

The source from which all Napoleonic scholarship must begin is the magisterial *Correspondance de l'empereur Napoléon Ier*, 32 vols. (1858–1870). While this work must be supplemented by subsequent collections, it contains much material relating to Napoleon's international relations, diplomatic concerns, and military plans. Additional important collections of correspondence are Léon Lecestre, *Lettres inédites de Napoléon Ier, 1799–1815* (1897–1898); Leonce de Brotonne, *Lettres inédites de Napoléon Ier* (1898) and *Dernières Lettres inédites de Napoléon Ier* (1903); Arthur Chuquet, *Ordres et apostilles de Napoléon*, 4 vols. (1911–1912), and *Inédits napoléoniens*, 2 vols. (1913–1919); and Maximilien Vox, *Correspondance de Napoléon: Six cents lettres du travail (1806–1810)* (1943). The last four volumes of the *Correspondance* contain Napoleon's writings from his exile in St. Helena. They are a conscious attempt to recast his reputation in European historiography and must be used with caution.

Napoleon has attracted more biographies than any other political figure. The most reliable recollections of Napoleon's contemporaries include Antoine C. Thibaudeau, *Mémoires sur le Consulat*, 2 vols. (1827); André Massena, *Mémoires de Massena* (1848–1850); Achille Broglie, *Souvenirs, 1795–1870* (1886); Amable Barante, *Souvenirs du baron de Barante*, 8 vols. (1890–1891); Jean A. Chaptal, *Mes Souvenirs sur Napoléon* (1893); Claude F. de Ménevel, *Mémoires pour servir à l'histoire de Napoléon Ier depuis 1802 jusqu'à 1815*, 3 vols. (1894); and Agathon J.F. Fain, *Mémoirs* (1908). The most important biographies include Henri Jomini, *Vie politique et militaire de Napoléon, racontée par lui-même*, 4 vols. (1827); August Fournier, *Napoleon I: Eine Biographie*, 3 vols. (1886–1889); J. Holland Rose, *The Life of Napoleon I*, 2 vols. (1901); Pierre Lanfrey, *Histoire de Napoléon Ier*, 5 vols. (1868–1875); Edouard Driault, *L'Immortelle épopée du drapeau tricolore: Napoléon le Grand*, 3 vols. (1930); Jacques Bainville, *Napoléon* (1931); Friedrich M. Kircheisen, *Napoleon I: Sein Leben und seine Zeit*, 9 vols. (1911–1934); Evgenii Tarlé, *Napoleon* (1939); J. M. Thompson, *Napoleon: His Rise and Fall* (1952); Georges Lefebvre, *Napoléon* (1935); J. Christopher Herold, *The Mind of Napoleon* (1955); Albert Manfred, *Napoleon Bonapart* (1971); and Jean Tulard, *Napoléon: ou, le mythe du sauveur* (1977). Lanfrey and Tarlé are most severe in their view of Napoleon and his accomplishments, while, at the opposite extreme, Driault's judgment can be blinded by the grand reach of the emperor.

For Napoleonic diplomacy, the most important works are Louis Bignon, *Histoire de France depuis le 18 brumaire (novembre 1799) jusqu'à la paix de Tilsitt* (juillet 1807), 14 vols. (1829–1850); A. Thiers, *Histoire du Consulat et de l'Empire*, 21 vols. (1845–1874); Albert Vandal, *Napoléon Ier et Alexandre Ier*, 3 vols. (1891–1896); A. A. Sorel, *L'Europe et la Révolution française*, vols. 6–8 (1903–1904); Émile Bourgeois, *Manuel historique de politique étrangère*, vol. 2 (1900); Édouard Driault, *Napoléon et l'Europe*, 5 vols. (1910–1927); Robert Mowat, *The Diplomacy of Napoleon* (1924); Louis Villat, *La Révolution et l'Empire*, 2 vols. (1936); Geoffrey Bruun, *Europe and the French Imperium* (1938); André Fugier, *La Révolution française et l'Empire napoléonien* (1954); Jacques Godechot, *La Grande Nation. L'Expansion révolutionnaire de la France dans le monde, 1789–1804*, 2 vols. (1956). Bignon was a Napoleonic diplomat, and his large-scale work contains much firsthand knowledge of international relations during the period. Thiers's grand treatment of the period's international relations considers Napoleonic aims as focused on overthrowing England's worldwide domain, while Bourgeois places greater emphasis on imperial ambitions in the Near East. Driault agreed with Napoleon's own opinion of himself: that the imperial conquests were essential elements to reunify Europe. Sorel sees continuity between the French Revolution's diplomatic aims and Napoleon's goals: the establishment of France's "natural boundary" on the Rhine, which led to the conquest of ever greater buffer zones for France.

Napoleonic rule in the Grand Empire is dealt with by Owen Connelly, *Napoleon's Satellite Kingdoms* (1965). Also see Paul Pisani, *La Dalmatie de 1797 à 1815* (1893); Herbert Fisher, *Studies in Napoleonic Statesmanship: Germany* (1903); and John Stanley, "The Adaptation of the Napoleonic Political Structure in the Duchy of Warsaw (1807–1813)," *Canadian Slavonic Papers* 31 (1989): 128–145. The finest history of Napoleon's invasion of Russia is Marian Kukiel, *Wojna 1812 roku* (1937), although it is worth perusing Evgenii Tarlé, *Nashestvie Napoleona na Rossiiu: 1812 god* (1938).

The Napoleonic legend began with Napoleon's own writings on St. Helena but was reinforced by the memoirs of his companions in exile: Emmanuel de Las Cases, *Mémorial de Sainte-Hélène*, 8 vols. (1822–1823), and Gaspard Gourgaud, *St. Hélène: Journal inédit de 1815 à 1818* (1899). For treatments of the legend, see Philippe Gonnard, *Les origines de la légende napoléonienne* (1906); Jules Dechamps, *Sur la légende napoléonienne* (1931); Jean Lucas-Dubreton, *Le Culte de Napoléon, 1814–1848* (1960); L. Salvatorelli, *Leggenda e realtà di Napoleone* (1960); and Andrzej Zahorski, *Spór o Napoleona we Francji i w Polsce* (1974).

Bibliography

Bainville, Jacques. *Napoléon*. Paris: Fayard, 1931.

Barante, Amable. *Souvenirs du baron de Barante*. 8 vols. Paris: Calmann Lévy, 1901.

Bignon, Louis. *Histoire de France depuis le 18 brumaire (novembre 1799) jusqu'à la paix de Tilsitt (juillet 1807)*. 14 vols. Paris: Mme ve C. Béchet Firmin Didot frères, 1829–1850.

Bonaparte, Napoléon. *Correspondance de l'empereur Napoléon Ier*. 32 vols. Paris: Plon, 1858–1870.

Bourgeois, Émile. *Manuel historique de politique étrangère*. 4 vols. Paris: Belin, 1900.

Broglie, Achille. *Souvenirs, 1795–1870*. Paris: Calmann Lévy, 1886.

Brotonne, Léonce de. *Dernières lettres inédites de Napoléon Ier*. Paris: Champion, 1903.

———. *Lettres inédites de Napoléon Ier*. Paris: Champion, 1898.

Bruun, Geoffrey. *Europe and the French Imperium*. New York: Harper, 1938.

Chaptal, Jean A. *Mes Souvenirs sur Napoléon*. Paris: Plon, 1893.

Chuquet, Arthur. *Inédits napoléoniens*. 2 vols. Paris: Fontmoing, 1913–1919.

———. *Ordres et apostilles de Napoléon*. 4 vols. Paris: Champion, 1911–1912.

Connelly, Owen. *Napoleon's Satellite Kingdoms*. New York: Free Press, 1965.

Dechamps, Jules. *Sur la légende napoléonienne*. Paris: Champion, 1931.

Driault, Édouard. *L'Immortelle épopée du drapeau tricolore: Napoléon le Grand*. 3 vols. Paris: Rousseaux, 1930.

———. *Napoléon et l'Europe*. 5 vols. Paris: Alcan, 1910–1927.

Fain, Agathon J.F. *Mémoires du baron Fain*. Paris: Plon-Nourrit, 1908.

Fisher, Herbert. *Studies in Napoleonic Statesmanship: Germany*. Oxford: Clarendon Press, 1903.

Fournier, August. *Napoleon I: Eine Biographie*. 3 vols. Leipzig: G. Freytag, 1886–1889.

Fugier, André. *La Révolution française et l'Empire napoléonien*. Paris: Hachette, 1954.

Godechot, Jacques L. *La Grande Nation. L'Expansion révolutionnaire de la France dans le monde, 1789–1804*. 2 vols. Paris: Aubier, 1956.

Gonnard, Philippe. *Les origines de la légende napoléonienne*. Paris: Calmann Lévy, 1906.

Gourgaud, Gaspard. *St. Hélène: Journal inédit de 1815 à 1818*. Paris: Flammarion, 1899.

Herold, J. Christopher. *The Mind of Napoleon: A Selection from His Written and Spoken Words*. New York: Columbia University Press, 1955.

Jomini, Henri. *Vie politique et militaire de Napoléon, racontée par lui-même*. 4 vols. Paris: Anselin, 1827.

Kircheisen, Friedrich M. *Napoleon I: Sein Leben und seine Zeit*. 9 vols. Munich: Müller, 1911–1934.

Kukiel, Marian. *Wojna 1812 roku*. Cracow: Polska Akademia Umiejętności, 1937.

Lanfrey, Pierre. *Histoire de Napoléon Ier*. 5 vols. Paris: Charpentier, 1868–1875.

Las Cases, Emmanuel, Comte de. *Mémorial de Sainte-Hélène*. 8 vols. Brussels: Remy, 1822–1823.

Lecestre, Léon. *Lettres inédites de Napoléon Ier, 1799–1815*. 2 vols. Paris: Plon, 1897–1898.

Lefebvre, Georges. *Napoléon*. Paris: Alcan, 1935.

Lucas-Dubreton, Jean. *Le Culte de Napoléon, 1814–1848*. Paris: Michel, 1960.

Manfred, Albert Z. *Napoleon Bonapart*. Moscow, 1971.

Massena, André. *Mémoires de Massena*. 7 vols. Paris: Paulin et Lechevalier, 1848–1850.

Méneval, Claude F. de. *Mémoires pour servir à l'histoire de Napoléon Ier depuis 1802 jusqu'à 1815*. 3 vols. Paris: Dentu, 1893–1894.

Mowat, Robert. *The Diplomacy of Napoleon*. London: Arnold, 1924.

Pisani, Paul. *La Dalmatie de 1797 à 1815*. Paris: Picard, 1893.

Rose, J. Holland. *The Life of Napoleon I*. 2 vols. New York: Macmillan, 1901.

Salvatorelli, Luigi. *Leggenda e realtà di Napoleone*. Turin: Einaudi, 1960.

Sorel, Albert A. *L'Europe et la Révolution française*. Paris: Plon, 1903–1904.

Stanley, John D. ''The Adaptation of the Napoleonic Political Structure in the Duchy of Warsaw (1807–1813).'' *Canadian Slavonic Papers* 31 (1989): 128–145.

Tarlé, Evgenii. *Napoleon*. Moscow, 1939.

———. *Nashestvie Napoleona na Rossiiu: 1812 god*. Moscow, 1938.

Thibaudeau, Antoine C. *Mémoires sur le Consulat*. 2 vols. Paris: Ponthieu, 1827.

Thiers, Adolph. *Histoire du Consulat et de l'Empire*. 21 vols. Paris: Paulin, 1845–1874.

Thompson, J. M. *Napoleon: His Rise and Fall*. Oxford: Oxford University Press, 1952.

Tulard, Jean. *Napoléon: ou, le mythe du sauveur*. Paris: Fayard, 1977.

Vandal, Albert. *Napoléon Ier et Alexandre Ier*. 3 vols. Paris: Plon, 1891–1896.

Villat, Louis. *La Révolution et l'Empire*. Paris: Les Presses universitaires de France, 1936.

Vox, Maximilien. *Correspondance de Napoléon: Six cents lettres du travail (1806–1810)*. Paris: Gallimard, 1943.

Zahorski, Andrzej. *Spór o Napoleona we Francji i w Polsce*. Warsaw: Państwowe Instytut Wydawnictwo, Naukowe, 1974.

JOHN D. STANLEY

Napoleon III (1808–1873).   Born in Paris on April 20, 1808, the future Emperor of the French was baptized Charles Louis Napoleon Bonaparte, although the name Charles was dropped and the boy entered history as Louis Napoleon. Louis Napoleon was the second surviving son of Louis Bonaparte, *Napoleon I's younger brother, and Hortense de Beauharnais Bonaparte, daughter of the emperor's consort, Josephine. At the moment of his birth, his parents were king and queen of Holland. The marriage of Louis and Hortense Bonaparte had been a purely political arrangement designed by Napoleon to provide Bonaparte heirs, and the couple had never been compatible. Consequently, they separated as soon as they had lost their Dutch crowns, and Louis Napoleon grew to manhood scarcely knowing his father.

For Louis Napoleon, his uncle's exile to St. Helena marked the beginning of years of wandering, harassed by the victorious allies who trusted no Bonapartes. Sojourns at Aix-les-Bains and Geneva as well as in Bavaria finally brought Hortense to a pleasant chateau at Arenenberg, Switzerland, where Louis Napoleon was allowed to reach young manhood in relatively peaceful obscurity. In 1830–1831, when France again gave the example of revolution to Europe, the two sons of Louis and Hortense Bonaparte joined the Italian revolution and saw military action against the papal and Austrian armies during which the older Bonaparte prince died of fever. In July 1832, the Duke de Reichstadt, Napoleon I's only legitimate son, died, thrusting Louis Napoleon to the fore as heir to Bonapartist claims. He passed the next four years living the life of a country gentleman, serving in the Swiss artillery during the summer months. The prince also dabbled in writing, publishing *Considérations politiques et militaires sur la Suisse* in 1835, and a carefully researched *Manuel d'artillerie* in the same year.

On October 30, 1836, Louis Napoleon made his first attempt to restore a Napoleonic empire. Having first subverted a few army officers, he attempted to seize Strasbourg. However, the coup d'état ended in failure. The royal government made the decision to treat Bonapartism with contempt, pardoning the prince unconditionally and thereby avoiding a trial, which would have given Louis Napoleon the publicity he sought. Instead, he was placed aboard the naval cruiser *Andromède* and carried to the United States by way of South America. It was not until March 1837 that he walked ashore in Norfolk, Virginia, a free man again. He then made his way to New York, where he enjoyed being lionized by high society until he returned to Switzerland.

In 1838 the French royal government, which had displayed good sense in minimizing the importance of Bonapartism, now made the error of seeming to persecute it. France began to threaten Switzerland because it had given refuge to Louis Napoleon. The Swiss stood fast in their defense of the right of asylum. The massing of Louis Philippe's army on the Swiss border gave Louis Napoleon the opportunity to play a magnanimous role by voluntarily moving to London, thereby sparing Switzerland embarrassment. The Orleanist government had handed Bonapartism an important public relations triumph.

In London, Louis Napoleon was warmly received and found himself the center of a modest imperial court. In the summer of 1839 the prince published *Des Idées Napoléoniennes*, undoubtedly the most important of his nine major books. It created a Bonapartist philosophy drawn allegedly from the life's work of Napoleon I. According to Louis Napoleon, the Bonapartist ideal was the inheritance of the French Revolution of 1789, committed to the idea of popular sovereignty but grounded in governmental authority and order. The First Empire was described as a happy time when Roman Catholicism enjoyed imperial protection but all religious opinions were equally free, and a benignly generous regime offered protection to the poor from the vicissitudes of laissez-faire capitalism. Napoleon I failed to fulfill his program completely only because war was forced on him by a jealous and illiberal coalition of despots. The promise was held out that the opportunity destroyed at Waterloo would reemerge with a Second Empire.

Ironically, Louis Philippe's government gave Louis Napoleon the opening he sought for an imperial restoration. The royal government determined to repair its dull and unromantic image by wrapping itself in the glories of a cherished Napoleonic legend. In July 1840 a French naval cruiser was dispatched to St. Helena to bring the body of Napoleon I back to France. In attempting to merge the dreary Orleanist aura with the glorious imperial memory, the royal government quite unintentionally created a viable Bonapartist cause.

Louis Napoleon seized the occasion to land at Boulogne on August 6, 1840, with fifty-five followers, most of them his domestic servants, dressed in secondhand French military uniforms. The attempted overthrow of the royal government lasted only five hours, and Louis Napoleon found himself a prisoner en route to confinement at the Conciergerie in Paris. Louis Philippe then made what proved to be a tactical blunder by trying Louis Napoleon in the Chamber of Peers. The prisoner profited handsomely from the drama of a trial in the upper house of the legislature and proved to be fully capable of creating theatrical effects. The relative freedom of the French press made it possible for the rebel to become a martyr whose idealized version of Napoleonic ideas sounded a sympathetic chord with literate Frenchmen.

Louis Napoleon was jailed at the fortress of Ham from 1840 to 1846. Allowed generous visiting privileges including the companionship of a laundress, he was in touch with the legation of Nicaragua and seriously considered obtaining his freedom by becoming president of that republic. He drew up elaborate plans for a canal across that Central American state, anticipating Ferdinand de Lesseps's Panama Canal by thirty years. In 1844 he published *Sur l'extinction du paupérisme*, which called for massive government public works programs. The prince was making excellent use of his time in prison to create an image of the new Bonapartism as a philosophy congenial to all who wanted an orderly yet popularly based society sensitive to the needs of the poor, yet supportive of capitalist enterprise. On May 25, 1846, the prince escaped from Ham and once again took up his English exile.

In February 1848, the French opened a year of European revolution by overthrowing the royal government and creating the Second French Republic. In June 1848, Louis Napoleon was elected to the legislature. When the government declined to admit him to France, riots ensued. Whether through prescient wisdom or simple luck, Louis Napoleon refused to be the cause of civil disorder and declined his seat. His enforced absence in London proved very fortunate for his cause, as he was spared all responsibility for the bloody suppression of the working class's June rebellion against the bourgeois republic. With a conservative republic securely seated at Paris, the legislature filled its empty seats with by-elections. On September 17, 1848, Louis Napoleon Bonaparte was elected and eight days later took his seat at Paris, swearing allegiance to the republic. This time no difficulty was made about his return to France.

A presidential election by universal male suffrage was scheduled for December 10, 1848, and Napoleon threw himself into an expensive campaign featuring torchlight parades, mass rallies, and catchy couplets touting his candidacy. Of more than 7 million votes cast, Louis Napoleon received over 4 million. Until December 1851, Louis Napoleon felt his way carefully, building a consensus that would win him the sincere support of an overwhelming majority of the French. When Joseph Mazzini and Giuseppe Garibaldi drove Pope Pius IX into exile, it was Louis Napoleon's republican France that overthrew the Roman Republic and restored the pope in 1849. Furthermore, French public schools were opened to instruction in the Catholic catechism. At the same time, Louis Napoleon began several public works projects to reduce unemployment. It was this process, later completed by Baron Eugene Haussmann, that resulted in the renewal and beautification of Paris. Such moves, designed to ensure public order and personal prosperity, caused the historian Albert Guérard to describe Louis Napoleon as a forerunner of both *Benito Mussolini and *Franklin Delano Roosevelt. In frequent journeys around the country, the prince-president spoke increasingly of the "Empire" as he responded to the cheers of uniformed veterans of the Napoleonic First Empire shouting "Vive l'empereur."

On December 2, 1851, the prince-president forced a revision of the republican constitution, awarding himself an additional ten-year term as president and the virtual powers of a dictator. Although hundreds of Frenchmen died resisting the power grab and thousands were arrested, the French masses accepted Louis Napoleon's seizure of power as inevitable and indeed desirable. On December 20, 7 million voters supported the new regime in what was to become a model for future totalitarian plebiscites.

It was generally anticipated that President Bonaparte would declare himself Emperor Napoleon, and on December 2, 1852, he took that step. This time force was not needed, as the Senate had petitioned for the restoration of the empire on November 21. A second plebiscite approved the enthronement of "Napoleon III, by the Grace of God and the will of the people." Seven and a half million voters out of eight million approved the change.

Once elevated to imperial dignity, Napoleon III sought a suitable empress. Although he would have preferred an authentic princess, none of the respectable dynasties was prepared to sacrifice one of its daughters to a parvenu adventurer. Thus, in 1853 Napoleon took as his bride Eugénie de Montijo y Teba, twenty-six years old and connected by birth to the most aristocratic families of Spain and Great Britain. Empress Eugénie was a devout Catholic who shared with her husband a belief in France's mission to serve as the keystone of a great alliance of Catholic and Latin nations.

The foreign policy of the Second Empire suffered from the essential schizophrenia of *les idées Napoléoniennes*. Napoleon III's sincere belief that nationalism was a benign force and that France ought to be the liberator and ally of suppressed and divided peoples led him to intervene in the affairs of Italy, Poland, Romania, Hungary, Mexico, Jefferson Davis's Confederate States, and Germany. At the same time, Bonapartism represented social order, protection for religion, and material prosperity. The ideals were in such conflict that they spelled ruin for the regime.

Napoleon III's first great foreign adventure began as an attempt to establish France as the protector of Roman Catholic interests in the Holy Land, countering the rival claims of Russia. That the Crimean War (1853–1856), which grew out of the quarrel, was fought far from Jerusalem was almost incidental. France's victory over Russia satisfied French national pride, which still smarted from the Russian defeat of Napoleon I in 1812. The Treaty of Paris ending the conflict created a cordial and more trusting relationship between France and its old enemy Britain, and permitted Napoleon to present himself as a sponsor for Italian and Romanian national aspirations. At the same time, Napoleon managed to extend a conciliatory hand to the defeated Russians, which made France seem to be a possible future ally.

On January 14, 1858, Napoleon and Eugénie barely escaped assassination at the hands of Italian revolutionaries who felt that Napoleon had betrayed his earlier nationalist commitments. Far from alienating Napoleon, Count Felice Orsini's attempt to murder him spurred the emperor ''to do something for Italy.'' The result was a conspiracy hatched during a secret conference at Plombières in July 1858 between Napoleon and Count *Camillo Benso di Cavour, prime minister of Sardinia-Piedmont. The conspirators would create a situation in which Austria would attack Sardinia and France would fly to the rescue of her little Italian neighbor. That war was indeed fought between April and July 1859, but the results were far different than either Napoleon or Cavour had foreseen. The conspirators had planned a medium-sized Italian state occupying the north of Italy, from which Austria would be expelled. Instead, by February 1861, Italy achieved unification and became Europe's sixth major power. In compensation France received Savoy and Nice, carrying its borders to the Alpine ridges. Nevertheless, a French army remained at Rome guarding the pope and what remained of independent papal territory. Austria still held Venetia, a promise of trouble for the future.

Napoleon also looked beyond the Continent. In 1859–1860 France used the murder of a Catholic missionary as an excuse to begin the conquest of what became French Indochina. In 1860 an international conference gave its blessing to the dispatch of 6,000 French troops to Lebanon and Syria to end the endemic slaughter of Christians there.

In 1861, a French, British, and Spanish joint expedition to Mexico to force the Mexicans to pay their debts was transformed by 1862 into a unilateral French venture to create a Mexican monarchy under Ferdinand Maximilian von Habsburg, who reigned from 1863 to 1867 as emperor of Mexico. Napoleon's original scheme envisioned that Emperor Francis Joseph of Austria would regard a Mexican crown for his brother as a quid pro quo for his abandonment of Venetia to Italy, with Austria free to compensate itself in the Balkans at the expense of Turkey. Francis Joseph, however, declined to regard his brother's Mexican adventure as any favor to Austria and confined himself to allowing Austrian soldiers to enlist as volunteers for service in Mexico. Napoleon's dream of French aggrandizement in Mexico died when Maximilian, even before setting foot in Mexico, declined to cede monopoly mining rights in Mexican Sonora to France. Worst of all, both Napoleon and Maximilian favored a liberal settlement of the dispute between church and state in Mexico, while Maximilian's only Mexican supporters were solidly conservative and clericalist.

Simultaneously, the United States, split asunder by the Civil War (1861–1865), forced Napoleon to weigh that struggle in his diplomatic equation. Although he would have been glad to see the United States permanently divided and was instrumental in encouraging the Confederacy, Napoleon pursued caution and did nothing with respect to the Civil War except as Britain's partner. He persuaded Maximilian to avoid recognition of the Confederacy. At the end, however, when a triumphant United States had crushed the Confederacy, Yankee troops massed on the Rio Grande were sufficient to force French retreat from Mexico in 1866. Maximilian was abandoned to his fate before a Mexican firing squad. For France, the ruin of its Mexican scheme was only one of a series of disasters marking the decade of the sixties.

From January to December 1863, Poland rose in rebellion against Russia. Once again allowing his romantic nationalism to overrule his penchant for legitimate order, Napoleon did everything possible short of war to liberate Poland. The only result was to alienate Russia, even while *Otto von Bismarck, heading the government of Prussia, won Russian gratitude through his pledge to cooperate with Russia on all aspects of the Polish Question. Bismarck's Russo-Prussian rapprochement permitted Prussia to fight both Austria and France in the next seven years without worrying about its eastern flank.

In 1864, when all the German states attacked Denmark to deprive the Danes of the duchies of Schleswig and Holstein, France repeated its mistake of the previous year, encouraging the underdog but doing nothing to save the Danes from defeat. France was thus driven even further into isolation, as the thirty-eight German states resented French opposition to what was popularly regarded there as a war to save German Holstein from foreign rule.

In October 1865, Bismarck entered secret negotiations with Napoleon. Bismarck asked French assistance in getting Italy to support Prussia against Austria in what he foresaw as the inevitable struggle for control of Germany. Napoleon imagined Italy getting Venetia while France received compensation on the Rhine, and perhaps in Belgium and Luxembourg, in exchange for Prussian hegemony in northern Germany and the expulsion of Austria from German affairs. Napoleon did indeed encourage the Italians to sign an alliance with Prussia. The Seven

Weeks' War of June–August 1866 crushed Austria. Nevertheless, Napoleon's peculiarly passive stance at the crucial hour in July 1866 cost him the opportunity to win compensation for France on the Rhine, even though the Prussians achieved hegemony in the North German Confederation and indirect control over the four south German states. Italy received Venetia but saw no need to feel grateful to France.

In 1867 Napoleon's incredibly clumsy attempt to win Prussian support for a French seizure of Belgium handed Bismarck incriminating evidence of France's aggressive designs, which he used in 1870 to persuade Britain that France was an outlaw state. During 1867 Bismarck engineered yet another crisis when France attempted to purchase Luxembourg from the king of the Netherlands. British mediation quieted the resultant war scare, but war between France and Germany was merely delayed.

In 1867 French troops fought Garibaldi once again to save the pope from Italian revolution. The Roman Question in its final form trapped a French army at Rome because clericalist French public opinion would not tolerate abandonment of Pope Pius IX. So long as the French barred Italy from annexing its natural capital city, no Italian government would ally with France. France's only other potential ally against Prussia was Austria, and Austria could not help France unless the Italians were also in the French camp. Thus France approached war with Germany in complete isolation.

The actual *casus belli* is too absurd to be entertained as the work of thoughtful diplomats. In 1867 Queen Isabella II of Spain was overthrown, and a search was begun for a replacement among the liberal Roman Catholic princes of Europe. The choice of the Spanish junta was Leopold of Hohenzollern-Sigmaringen, a German prince with family ties closer to Napoleon III than to King William I of Prussia, the titular head of the house of Hohenzollern. Nevertheless, the popular press whipped up fears of a Hohenzollern encirclement of France if that family occupied thrones in Berlin and Madrid. The newspaper brouhaha was exacerbated by the fact that in 1869 Napoleon III had created a liberal, constitutional democracy to buttress his sagging popularity. France offered the full range of civil rights to its citizens, and the Hohenzollern candidacy became a matter for public excitement. In July 1870, Prince Leopold, not wishing to make his personal ambitions a cause for war, withdrew his candidacy. Nevertheless, to snatch one more newspaper victory in the absence of any genuine diplomatic successes, the French attempted to force King William of Prussia to renounce forever any Hohenzollern claim to the Spanish throne. The king, vacationing at Ems, repulsed the importunate demands of the French ambassador, Count Vincente Benedetti, but sent a telegram describing the affair to Bismarck at Berlin. Bismarck edited the Ems dispatch in such a way that when published it was equally provocative to both Germans and French. With mobs in the streets of both countries demanding war, France declared war on July 15, 1870.

France was woefully unprepared. Napoleon III personally took command, though in agony from gallstones. Two weeks after war began, the German armies won their first significant victory. By late summer the Germans had split the French army in two, trapping the Northern Command under Marshal Patrice MacMahon and the emperor at Sedan. For Napoleon the choice was to break out of Sedan and regain free maneuver or to retreat into neutral Belgium, there to be interned for the war's duration. The French made desperate attempts to break the German ring at Sedan but failed. On September 3, the emperor and all of MacMahon's army surrendered. On September 4, revolution in Paris forced Empress Eugénie to flee to exile in England. The Third French Republic was proclaimed.

After six months of captivity during which the Germans treated him as an imperial guest, Napoleon III was allowed to rejoin his wife and son in England. Increasingly bedeviled by his physical ailments but determined to remain head of the Bonapartist party, the emperor died during surgery on January 7, 1873.

Annotated Bibliography

Because Napoleon III took great care to supervise foreign policy, official diplomatic correspondence is revealing. For a guide to the diplomatic collections of the countries most concerned with France, see Daniel H. Thomas and Lynn M. Case, eds., *Guide to the Diplomatic Archives of Western Europe* (1959, 1976). The Bonaparte family papers are at Prangins, Switzerland, and are open to scholars with the consent of the present head of that dynasty. Dozens of the diplomats stationed at Paris who knew Napoleon and Eugénie well have published their memoirs. A few are exceptionally valuable. See Lord Cowley's *Secrets of the Second Empire* (1929), Baron Hubner's *Neuf ans de souvenirs d'un ambassadeur d'Autriche à Paris sous le second empire, 1851–1859* (1905–1908) and Prince Clemens Metternich's *Mémoires, documents et écrits divers laissés* (1881–1831). From 1852 to 1870, the French Senate published annually the texts of Napoleon's reports to his legislature, titled *Exposé de la situation de l'Empire*. After 1863 the French Ministry of Foreign Affairs published selected diplomatic documents in what came to be officially called the *Livre Jaune* series. Between 1910 and 1925, the French Ministry of Foreign Affairs published twenty-nine volumes intended to clear France of the charge of having been primarily responsible for the Franco-Prussian War. Available on microfilm, this massive publication is titled *Les Origines diplomatiques de la Guerre de 1870–1871*. The huge collection of papers belonging to the Mexican Empire was sent to Austria when Emperor Maximilian fell. The originals are at the Haus-, Hof- und Staatsarchiv at Vienna, but the greater part of that material is available in photocopy and/or microfilm at the Manuscripts Division of the U.S. Library of Congress in Washington.

In addition to the books by Napoleon himself cited in the biography, it is worth noting that in 1865–1866 the emperor published a two-volume *Histoire de Jules César*, evidently intended to identify Caesar with Napoleon I.

The earliest studies of Napoleon III were almost uniformly hostile, dismissing the emperor as a flashy pretender who ruined his country. The best examples of that genre are Rene Arnaud's *The Second Republic and Napoleon III* (1930), a republican analysis, and Sir Lewis Namier's *Vanished Supremacies* (1958), which is contemptuous of Napoleon. In *Napoleon III and the Rhine: The Origin of the War of 1870* (1928), the great German nationalist historian Hermann Oncken, although critical of French policy, endeavored to be balanced and is still worth reading.

Over the last fifty years Napoleon III has been treated more kindly. The most una-bashedly sentimental defense is Albert Guérard's *Napoleon III* (1943). Robert Sencourt's *Napoleon III: The Modern Emperor* (1933) expresses admiration for the emperor as a man ahead of his time. Octave Aubry's *The Second Empire* (1952) categorizes Napoleon as a farsighted European. Frederick Simpson's *Louis Napoleon and the Recovery of France, 1848–1856* (1923) is the oldest of the sympathetic studies. Objective analysis of the Second Empire has reached its finest form in J.P.T. Bury, *Napoleon III and the Second Empire* (1964), Brison D. Gooch, *The Reign of Napoleon III* (1969), and George Peabody Gooch, *The Second Empire* (1961).

Many serious studies exist on the diplomacy of the Second Empire. Derek Beales's *The Risorgimento and the Unification of Italy* (1971) suggests that Britain may have played a greater part in the creation of united Italy than did France. Arnold Blumberg has explored Napoleon's complex relations with Count Cavour in *A Carefully Planned Accident: The Italian War of 1859* (1990) and Napoleon's tragic adventure in the Americas in *The Diplomacy of the Mexican Empire, 1863–1867* (1987). John W. Bush's *Venetia Redeemed: Franco-Italian Relations, 1864–1866* (1967) demonstrates how France en-gineered Italian acquisition of Venetia but gained neither an alliance nor gratitude for its efforts. Lynn M. Case's *Franco-Italian Relations, 1860–1865: The Roman Question and the Convention of September* (1970) is the definitive study of Napoleon's attempt to disentangle himself from his military commitment to protect the pope. Case and Warren F. Spencer coauthored *The United States and France: Civil War Diplomacy* (1970), which describes the extremely cautious policy pursued by Napoleon at a time when he was preoccupied with pressing dangers in Mexico, Poland, and Denmark. William E. Echard's *Napoleon III and the Concert of Europe* (1983) is a solid study of the emperor's en-couragement of summit conferences in order to minimize European suspicions of his policy. Willard A. Fletcher's *The Mission of Vincent Benedetti to Berlin, 1864–1870* (1965) describes the unhappy career of the French ambassador to Prussia. Charles W. Hallberg's *Franz-Josef and Napoleon III, 1852–1864* (1955) describes France's failure to effect a close entente with Austria. Robert H. Lord's classic study, *The Origins of the War of 1870* (1924), is still current and dependable. Werner E. Mosse's *The European Powers and the German Question, 1849–1871* (1985) traces Napoleon's sympathy for all nationalisms, including German nationalism, and describes how that Bonapartist prin-ciple ultimately ruined him. E. Ann Pottinger's *Napoleon III and the German Crisis, 1865–1866* (1966) includes some speculative detective work on Bismarck's private con-versations with Napoleon at Biarritz and St. Cloud in 1865.

Specialized works touching narrow areas of Second Empire studies have begun to make valuable contributions. Lynn M. Case's innovative use of the reports of the procurers-general and departmental prefects to describe imperial sensitivity to public opinion has resulted in a number of studies, including *French Opinion on War and Diplomacy during the Second Empire* (1954). Nancy Nichols Barker's *Distaff Diplomacy: The Empress Eugenie and the Foreign Policy of the Second Empire* (1967) offers a penetrating view of the role played by Napoleon's unhappy consort. Rondo E. Cameron's *France and the Economic Development of Europe, 1800–1914* (1961) pays deserved tribute to Napoleon III's role in his country's economic expansion, especially in the areas of telegraph and railroad construction. Arthur Lewis Dunham's *The Anglo-French Treaty of Commerce of 1860 and the Progress of the Industrial Revolution in France* (1930) spotlights France's only nineteenth-century experiment with free trade.

Alain Plessis, *The Rise and Fall of the Second Empire, 1852–1871* (1985), sums up and reconciles these conflicting analyses in a solid examination of the regime's accomplishments, institutions, and failures.

Bibliography

Arnaud, Rene. *The Second Republic and Napoleon III*. New York: Putnam's, 1930.

Aubry, Octave. *The Second Empire*. Philadelphia: Lippincott, 1952.

Barker, Nancy N. *Distaff Diplomacy: The Empress Eugenie and the Foreign Policy of the Second Empire*. Austin: University of Texas Press, 1967.

Beales, Derek. *The Risorgimento and the Unification of Italy*. New York: Barnes and Noble, 1971.

Blumberg, Arnold. *A Carefully Planned Accident: The Italian War of 1859*. Cranbury, N.J.: Associated University Presses, 1990.

———. *The Diplomacy of the Mexican Empire, 1863–1867*. Malabar, Fla.: Krieger, 1987.

Bury, J.P.T. *Napoleon III and the Second Empire*. London: English Universities Press, 1964.

Bush, John W. *Venetia Redeemed: Franco-Italian Relations, 1864–1866*. Syracuse, N.Y.: Syracuse University Press, 1967.

Cameron, Rondo E. *France and the Economic Development of Europe, 1800–1914*. Princeton, N.J.: Princeton University Press, 1961.

Case, Lynn M. *Franco-Italian Relations, 1860–1865: The Roman Question and the Convention of September*. New York: AMS Press, 1970.

———. *French Opinion on War and Diplomacy During the Second Empire*. Philadelphia: University of Pennsylvania Press, 1954.

Case, Lynn M., and Warren F. Spencer. *The United States and France: Civil War Diplomacy*. Philadelphia: University of Pennsylvania Press, 1970.

Cowley, Henry R. *Secrets of the Second Empire: Private Letters from the Paris Embassy*. New York: Harper, 1929.

Dunham, Arthur Louis. *The Anglo-French Treaty of Commerce of 1860 and the Progress of the Industrial Revolution in France*. Ann Arbor: University of Michigan Press, 1930.

Echard, William E. *Napoleon III and the Concert of Europe*. Baton Rouge: Louisiana State University Press, 1983.

Fletcher, Willard A. *The Mission of Vincent Benedetti to Berlin, 1864–1870*. The Hague: Martinus Nijhoff, 1965.

Gooch, Brison D. *The Reign of Napoleon III*. Chicago: Rand McNally, 1969.

Gooch, George Peabody. *The Second Empire*. London: Longmans, 1961.

Guérard, Albert. *Napoleon III*. Cambridge, Mass.: Harvard University Press, 1943.

Hallberg, Charles W. *Franz-Josef and Napoleon III, 1852–1864*. New York: Bookman Associates, 1955.

Hubner, Joseph A. *Neuf ans de souvenirs d'un ambassadeur d'Autriche à Paris sousle second empire, 1851–1859*. 2 vols. Paris: Plon-Nourrit, 1905–1908.

Isser, Natalie. *The Second Empire and the Press*. The Hague: Martinus Nijhoff, 1974.

Lord, Robert H. *The Origins of the War of 1870*. Cambridge, Mass.: Harvard University Press, 1924.

Metternich, Clemens. *Mémoires, documents et écrits divers laissés*. 8 vols. Paris: Plon, 1881–1931.

Mosse, Werner E. *The European Powers and the German Question, 1848–1871*. Cambridge: Cambridge University Press, 1985.

———. *The Rise and Fall of the Crimean System, 1855–1871: The Fate of a Peace Settlement*. New York: St. Martin's Press, 1963.

Namier, Sir Lewis. *Vanished Supremacies*. London: Hamish Hamilton, 1958.

Oncken, Hermann. *Napoleon III and the Rhine: The Origin of the War of 1870*. New York: Knopf, 1928.

Payne, Howard C. *The Police State of Louis Napoleon Bonaparte, 1851–1860*. Seattle: University of Washington Press, 1966.

Plessis, Alain. *The Rise and Fall of the Second Empire, 1852–1871*. New York: Cambridge University Press, 1985.

Pottinger, E. Ann. *Napoleon III and the German Crisis, 1865–1866*. Cambridge, Mass.: Harvard University Press, 1966.

Sencourt, Robert. *Napoleon III: The Modern Emperor*. New York: Appleton-Century, 1933.

Simpson, Frederick. *Louis Napoleon and the Recovery of France, 1848–1856*. London: Longmans, Green, 1923.

Williams, Roger L. *The Mortal Napoleon III*. Princeton, N.J.: Princeton University Press, 1971.

ARNOLD BLUMBERG

Richard Milhous Nixon (b. 1913) and **Henry Kissinger** (b. 1923). Richard Milhous Nixon was born in Yorba Linda, California, on January 9, 1913, the son of Francis A. and Hannah (Milhous) Nixon. His father, known as Frank, was a ranch foreman. His mother's family, the Milhouses, were Quakers and owned citrus orchards. Richard did well in high school and at Whittier College, where he had excellent grades and was on the debating team. He attended law school at Duke University and worked for a New Deal relief program, the National Youth Administration. As a young lawyer, he returned to Whittier and in 1942, before receiving a commission in the navy and going to the Pacific as a transportation officer, he worked in the Office of Price Administration. After the war he returned to civilian life and politics. President *Franklin D. Roosevelt, he believed, had made the federal government too powerful. The New Deal, he said, desired to ''skewer'' big business. He ran successfully for the U.S. House of Representatives in 1946 as a foe of the New Deal, accusing his opponent, Jerry Voorhis, of helping the Communists. In Congress he was placed on the House Un-American Activities Committee and gained national prominence in the case of former State Department official Alger Hiss. Nixon was elected to the Senate in 1950, and two years later the Republican presidential candidate, Dwight D. Eisenhower, named him his running mate.

As vice president, Nixon presided at meetings of the National Security Council (NSC) in the president's absence, traveled as a special envoy to Latin America, and engaged the Soviet leader, Nikita Khrushchev, in the so-called kitchen debate during a U.S. trade exposition in Moscow. Eisenhower overcame early skepticism and supported his youthful vice president's presidential ambitions in 1960. Although Nixon was defeated by John F. Kennedy that year, he continued to be active in politics, running unsuccessfully for governor of California in 1962, giving speeches at party fundraisers, and supporting other Republican candidates.

In 1968 he again won his party's presidential nomination and defeated Vice President Hubert Humphrey, the Democratic candidate, in a close election.

Henry Kissinger was born on May 27, 1923, in Fuerth, Germany, the son of Louis and Paula (Stern) Kissinger. His father, a teacher in a girls' secondary school, was Jewish. In 1938, to escape Nazi persecution, Louis Kissinger took his family to the United States and settled in New York City. There, Henry graduated from high school and entered the army, becoming a naturalized citizen. He served in a counterintelligence unit and later in the occupation government of Germany. He performed well, and one of his superiors urged Kissinger to apply for admission to Harvard. He did and graduated summa cum laude in 1950. Four years later he earned a Ph.D., writing his dissertation on the diplomacy of the Congress of Vienna at the end of the Napoleonic era in Europe.

From 1954 to 1956 Kissinger directed a study of U.S. defense strategy for the Council on Foreign Relations; the results were published as *Nuclear Weapons and Foreign Policy* (1957). In place of "massive retaliation," the book recommended "flexible response" by which the North Atlantic Treaty forces would have the capacity to respond directly to a Soviet attack with tactical nuclear weapons. In 1957 he returned to Harvard as a lecturer at the Center for International Affairs, and from 1958 to 1960 he served as associate director of the center. In 1959 he became an associate professor of government at Harvard and director of the defense studies program, a post he held until 1969.

Kissinger also served in various government positions during these years. He was an advisor to the National Security Council, the Weapons Systems Evaluation Group of the Joint Chiefs of Staff, the Arms Control and Disarmament Agency, and the State Department at different times between 1955 and 1967. Soon after the United States began to bomb North Vietnam in 1965, Kissinger visited South Vietnam; two years later he facilitated an exchange of messages that eventually led to peace talks. When Richard Nixon was nominated for president in 1968, he asked Kissinger to be his advisor on national security matters; President Nixon named him special assistant for national security affairs. In 1973 Kissinger became secretary of state.

After Nixon resigned the presidency in 1974, his successor, Gerald Ford, asked Kissinger to remain as secretary of state. In 1977 Kissinger left government and joined the faculty of Georgetown University's School of Foreign Service. He became a consultant and guest commentator for ABC News, a senior fellow at the Aspen Institute, and founder of an international relations consulting firm, Kissinger Associates, Inc. He served as an informal advisor to President Ronald Reagan, and in 1983 he was appointed chairman of the National Bipartisan Commission on Central America.

The presidency of Richard Nixon followed a decade of turmoil. During the 1960s Americans had been confident that their nation, the most powerful and prosperous in history, could eliminate poverty at home and prevent aggression abroad. As it turned out, this was a flawed vision, for by 1968 a series of crises had occurred. In quick succession came a failed invasion of Cuba, construction by East Germany of a wall dividing Berlin, a war scare after installation of Soviet nuclear missiles in Cuba, war in the Middle East, and U.S. military intervention in South Vietnam, which divided the nation. The United States refused to recognize the government of mainland China, the world's most populous nation, now with nuclear weapons and cosponsor with the Soviet Union of North Vietnam's efforts to take over South Vietnam. Fearing intimidation, the United States had adopted a strategy known as Mutual Assured Destruction (MAD), calling for a missile and bomber force so numerous and invulnerable that it could absorb a Soviet attack and still destroy much of the enemy's society. Despite the danger and cost of tens of thousands of nuclear weapons, the United States was seeking even more sophisticated delivery vehicles, including bombers, antimissile systems, multiple warhead missiles, and low-flying cruise missiles. The only respites in this stockpiling came in 1963, when the superpowers agreed to stop nuclear testing in the atmosphere, and in 1968, when they signed an international nuclear nonproliferation treaty.

Such were the circumstances under which Nixon and Kissinger began their collaboration. Together, in wide-ranging discussions, they formulated a policy based on *Metternich's nineteenth-century worldview, which sought stability and peace through a balance of power. As Kissinger put it, "Absolute security for one country was absolute insecurity for another." Not the capacity to produce a retaliatory rain of missiles on one's enemy, but rather relative strength—in this case missiles in numbers or concealment sufficient to prevent their loss in a preemptive attack—was what counted. Since both sides could benefit from slowing the arms race, Kissinger called for negotiations that linked arms limitation to mutual assistance in other areas—Soviet pressure on the North Vietnamese, for example, or U.S. overtures to the People's Republic of China that would reduce the threat along the Soviet southern border. Such a process, the two men hoped, might bring a settlement in Vietnam and with it assurance of Nixon's reelection. At the same time, it would lessen the danger and expense of superpower competition, the long-term goal. Such a complicated undertaking required secrecy and therefore a personal approach to the conduct of foreign policy. Accordingly, Kissinger, now special assistant for national security affairs, became chief presidential envoy and negotiator. As chairman of the National Security Council and later as secretary of state, Kissinger was able to shape U.S. foreign policy.

The reduction of Cold War tensions through agreement by the nuclear superpowers to compete peacefully during the early 1970s became known as détente. Working together, Nixon and Kissinger charted new directions in U.S. foreign policy that significantly altered assumptions that had prevailed since the end of World War II. After sending Kissinger to make the arrangements, Nixon, in February 1972, became the first president to travel to the People's Republic of China. He shook hands with Chairman Mao Tse-Tung, walked on the Great Wall, and announced that it was time to "grasp the moment." At a huge banquet the two adversaries toasted each other's nation and agreed to seek better relations, establishing liaison offices to coordinate cultural exchanges and trade. Then in July 1972, Nixon once again astounded the world, becoming the first president to visit the Kremlin. As guest of Soviet premier Leonid Brezhnev, he signed the first treaty for limitation of strategic arms (SALT I), along with agreements to sell grain to the Soviet Union and to cooperate in other areas, including outer space.

U.S. foreign relations, Nixon and Kissinger had decided, needed to reflect the realities of American power, including the diminution of American economic influence. Faced with a large imbalance of foreign payments, Nixon in 1971 abandoned the economic order (and American dominance) established at the Bretton Woods conference in 1944 by freeing the dollar from the gold standard and imposing a 10 percent surcharge on imports. In East Asia the president declared the Nixon Doctrine, by which the United States would remain a Pacific naval power and send assistance only to those countries who were themselves resisting subjugation or aggression. That assistance would be economic and political, with military assistance provided only if the people involved were fighting effectively. In Vietnam this meant stepped-up bombing and ground campaigns, gradual withdrawal of U.S. troops, and increased aid to the army of South Vietnam—a policy called Vietnamization. Among the most notable of Kissinger's many activities were secret trips to Paris for meetings with North Vietnamese representatives and, later, public sessions with North Vietnamese negotiator Le Duc Tho, which culminated in a cease-fire agreement on January 27, 1973. The last U.S. troops departed on March 29, 1973, American prisoners of war were repatriated, and Kissinger, along with Le Duc Tho, received the Nobel Peace Prize.

Elsewhere, Nixon-Kissinger foreign policy entailed both interventions and negotiations. In Africa and Latin America covert CIA activities attempted to overthrow Marxist regimes—such as that of Salvador Allende in Chile—and to keep pro-American ones in power. In the Middle East, Nixon-Kissinger diplomacy (which became known as shuttle diplomacy, for the laborious process of almost continuous round-trip airplane flights Kissinger used) sought to establish a regional balance. Egypt and Syria had attacked Israel during its Yom Kippur holiday in 1973. As an expression of sympathy with their Arab brothers in the ensuing war, the Organization of Petroleum Exporting Countries (OPEC) had stopped oil shipments to American allies in western Europe and the Far East, leading to quadrupled oil prices. At one point in the crisis the Soviet general secretary said he would send troops to the region, but Nixon warned him against this by putting U.S. forces on nuclear alert. Kissinger's subsequent mediation of a cease-fire and withdrawal of Israeli troops from Egypt brought resumption of the oil flow, reduced Soviet influence in the region, and movement toward disengagement and rapprochement. Kissinger's efforts contributed to the success of the Camp David talks in 1978, during the Jimmy Carter administration, which resulted in Egyptian recognition of Israel and the latter's withdrawal from the Sinai peninsula.

During the Nixon presidency the United States accepted measures that reduced tensions in Germany and eastern Europe, ending the disputes that had initiated the Cold War. Following the lead of West Germany, the United States in 1971 signed a treaty recognizing the occupation zones of Berlin and a divided Germany. Two years later it participated in the Conference on Security and Cooperation in Europe (CSCE) of NATO and Warsaw Pact nations at Helsinki, Finland. The conference lowered barriers to the flow of people and information in eastern Europe and sought to guarantee human rights. In return, the West recognized for the first time de facto postwar boundaries in Poland and other eastern European nations.

By the time Nixon left office in 1974 the United States had modified the containment policy, accepting ends more in keeping with its means. Instead of a bipolar world, a handful of powers existed, with the Soviet Union and its southern neighbor, the People's Republic of China, antagonistic toward one another. Loci of world power also included industrial western Europe, Japan, and the petroleum-producing nations of the Persian Gulf. The United States had established relations with the People's Republic of China, signed a treaty that placed limits on the number of nuclear weapons in U.S. and Soviet arsenals, and, under pressure from its allies and protest movements at home, negotiated an armistice in Vietnam. The United States had stopped demanding a free and unified Germany and noncommunist regimes in eastern Europe, accepting the postwar status quo in central Europe. No longer was the United States dominant in the global economy, having lost its lead in industrial innovation and productivity to West Germany and Japan. It had recognized certain dependence on oil-producing Arab nations.

The critics, of course, were numerous. Skeptics on the right said that Nixon and Kissinger had appeased Communists in both Europe and Southeast Asia. The president had acted too quickly, they said, in assuming limits on American power and in trusting Brezhnev and Mao, both enemies of democracy. The president and his secretary of state had betrayed the lives and treasure the United States had expended in Southeast Asia. Critics on the left, on the other hand, questioned a policy that put expediency and concern with military force ahead of human dignity and prosperity through liberty and free enterprise. The Nixon-Kissinger approach, they pointed out, winked at domestic oppression by the army or the secret police in both Communist countries and such places as the Philippines, Taiwan, Iran, South Korea, and Chile. The Helsinki Accords provided inadequate assurances of human rights in eastern Europe. Vietnamization, they said, needlessly prolonged and expanded the war in Southeast Asia. Balance-of-power diplomacy and covert intervention in places such as Chile and the former Portuguese colony of Angola compromised American ideals.

Certainly, Richard Nixon's resignation stemmed in large part from his preoccupation with foreign policy and methods of carrying it out. He was willing to consider himself above the law. The secrecy of his diplomacy seemed to become an obsession, and his determination not just to leave Vietnam but to preserve an independent, noncommunist South Vietnam meant that the struggle would continue. The war widened in 1969 when Nixon, without telling Congress, began bombing Cambodia; the following year he sent troops into enemy sanctuaries there. Before it was over, the United States had bombed Hanoi and Haiphong (sinking four Soviet vessels in the process) and mined the harbors. Hundreds of thousands of Vietnamese died, along with 20,000 more Americans. National Guard troops killed four students participating in an antiwar rally at Kent State University in Ohio, and the *New York Times* published secret information from government sources about the bombing of Cambodia.

Feeling himself under siege, and scornful of journalists and critics generally, Nixon used money from a campaign slush fund to authorize privately hired investigators, called "the plumbers," to stop leaks of classified information. After illegally tapping the telephones of members of his own National Security Council staff (apparently with Kissinger's acquiescence) and those of selected journalists, he sent the plumbers to obtain information to discredit Daniel Ellsberg, the former official who had released to the *New York Times* a secret Defense Department study—the so-called Pentagon Papers—on the origins of U.S. involvement in Vietnam. During the campaign of 1972, these same individuals broke into the Democratic party offices at the Watergate Apartments in Washington to install listening devices on the telephones. Nixon's efforts to thwart the criminal investigation and his subsequent concealment of his own involvement from courts, special prosecutors, and a Senate committee forced his resignation.

The effect of the Watergate affair, as it was called, was to end an era during which the executive branch of the U.S. government had come to dominate foreign policy—what historian Arthur Schlesinger, Jr., dubbed the "imperial presidency." Paradoxically, a president whose power had transformed foreign policy, discovered that his methods had brought diminution of that power. By 1975 Congress reasserted its authority by denying appropriations, insisting on intelligence oversight, and adopting the War Powers Act, requiring automatic removal of U.S. troops from another country after a specified time unless Congress approved.

Henry Kissinger emerged from the Watergate affair and the demise of the Nixon presidency damaged politically. In the last year of the Nixon presidency the two men, never close friends, became distant. The president, insecure psychologically, increasingly believed it necessary to portray himself rather than his charming, globe-trotting secretary of state as the originator of his policy. And during the Watergate crisis, he also sought to draw upon Kissinger's reputation for integrity.

During the Ford presidency Congress rejected the advice of the secretary of state and in 1975 cut off U.S. aid to Cambodia and South Vietnam, precipitating the collapse of friendly regimes in both countries. It also terminated clandestine CIA and NSC operations in Angola, and later, in Nicaragua. The Watergate investigation of wiretaps of the NSC, expansion of the Vietnam War, and the coup against Chilean president Salvador Allende had tarnished Kissinger's earlier image of diplomatic genius.

It is difficult, nevertheless, to find major fault with Nixon-Kissinger foreign policy. The Soviet Union had achieved parity in nuclear weapons by 1968, and continuation of the arms race would have been both costly and dangerous. Lyndon Johnson's political demise had revealed the necessity of finding a way (honorably if possible) to leave Vietnam. Refusal to acknowledge the Sino-Soviet split or to recognize the government of mainland China would have perpetuated an unrealistic isolation from Far Eastern politics. Failure to emphasize human rights compromised American ideals, but President Jimmy Carter's inability to deal constructively with the Soviet Union or with a militant Cuba revealed the futility of that approach in the late 1970s. Movement away from the policy of containment, on the other hand, while an apparent mistake considering the aforementioned problems with the Soviets and Cubans, appeared not so mistaken with the ascendancy of *Mikhail Gorbachev in 1985. The signing of treaties on intermediate-range nuclear forces in Europe (INF) and strategic arms reduction (START), the unification of Germany, and (with help from the Helsinki Accords) the breakup in 1989–1991 of the Soviet Union demonstrated that the Nixon-Kissinger approach, if not prophetic, at least set a precedent for a new era in Soviet-U.S. relations. By and large, one can see in retrospect that the Republican politician and the Harvard professor, in the face of enormous difficulties, had moved U.S. foreign policy in an imaginative and constructive direction.

Annotated Bibliography

The Nixon papers are located at the Nixon Presidential Materials Project in Alexandria, Virginia. They include handwritten notes by White House staff members concerning their daily activities. The National Archives and Nixon have not agreed about the release of other materials created during his administration. The Archives, nevertheless, has been able to open to scholars large numbers of documents that constitute, in the words of Nixon biographer Stephen Ambrose, "significant sections of the basic record." The latter include the tape recordings made in the Oval Office, the cabinet room, and over the telephone.

Other Nixon papers are located in the collections at the Lyndon B. Johnson Library, Austin, Texas; the John Fitzgerald Kennedy Library, Boston; the Dwight David Eisenhower Library, Abilene, Kansas; in the Dean Acheson papers at Princeton and Yale universities; and in the Nixon Vice Presidential Papers in Laguna Niguel, California. In the future, some papers will also be located at the Richard M. Nixon Library and Birthplace, Yorba Linda, California.

In addition to those in the Nixon Presidential Materials Project, Henry Kissinger's papers are located at the Gerald R. Ford Library, Ann Arbor, Michigan.

Richard Nixon's own account of his policies and accomplishments is *RN: The Memoirs of Richard Nixon* (1978). In addition, he has published several books dealing mainly with foreign policy topics: *The Real War* (1980), *Leaders* (1982), *The Real Peace* (1984), *No More Vietnams* (1985), *1999: Victory Without War* (1988), and *In the Arena: A Memoir of Victory, Defeat, and Renewal* (1990). An autobiographical account of Nixon's pre-presidential years is *Six Crises* (1962).

Excellent general interpretations of Nixon and his foreign policy include Raymond Garthoff, *Detente and Confrontation: American-Soviet Relations from Nixon to Reagan* (1985), an extensive and well-researched volume; William G. Hyland, *Mortal Rivals: Superpower Relations from Nixon to Reagan* (1987); John Lewis Gaddis, *Strategies of Containment: A Critical Appraisal of Postwar American National Security Policy* (1982); Robert Litwak, *Detente and the Nixon Doctrine* (1984); C. L. Sulzberger, *The World and Richard Nixon* (1987); Stephen E. Ambrose, *Nixon: The Education of a Politician, 1913–1962* (1987) and *Nixon: The Triumph of a Politician, 1962–1972* (1989).

More interpretive and critical are Tad Szulc, *The Illusion of Peace: Foreign Policy in the Nixon-Kissinger Years* (1979); Jonathan Schell, *Time of Illusion* (1976); Gary Wills, *Nixon Agonistes* (1979); and especially Lloyd Gardner, *The Great Nixon Turnaround* (1973). William E. Leuchtenberg's chapter on Nixon in *In the Shadow of FDR: From Harry Truman to Ronald Reagan* (1985) discusses the influence of Roosevelt and the New Deal on Nixon's thinking.

Accounts of Soviet strategy and nuclear weapons policy during the Nixon years appear in Harry Gelman, *The Brezhnev Politburo and the Decline of Detente* (1984); Adam B. Ulam, *Dangerous Relations: The Soviet Union in World Politics* (1983); Michael Mandelbaum, *The Nuclear Question: The United States and Nuclear Weapons, 1946–1976* (1979); and David Holloway, *The Soviet Union and the Arms Race* (1983).

U.S. foreign policy in various regions of the world during the Nixon-Kissinger era is described in James Bill, *The Eagle and the Lion: The Tragedy of American-Iranian Relations* (1988); Arnold R. Isaacs, *Without Honor: Defeat in Vietnam and Cambodia* (1983); William Shawcross, *Sideshow: Kissinger, Nixon and the Destruction of Cambodia* (1979); Robert G. Sutter, *China Watch: Toward Sino-American Reconciliation* (1978); and Robert J. Alexander, *The Tragedy of Chile* (1978).

Henry Kissinger's memoirs are in two volumes: *The White House Years* (1979) and *The Years of Upheaval* (1982). *A World Restored: Metternich, Castlereagh, and the Problems of Peace, 1812–1822* (1957) is based on Kissinger's doctoral dissertation. See also "The White Revolutionary: Reflections of Bismarck," *Daedalus* 97 (Summer 1968): 888–924, for another example of Kissinger's historical work. His criticism of Eisenhower's defense policy appears in *Nuclear Weapons and Foreign Policy* (1957) and *The Necessity for Choice: Prospects for American Foreign Policy* (1961). His call for a review of U.S. policy toward the North Atlantic Treaty Organization was *The Troubled Partnership: A Re-Appraisal of the Atlantic Alliance* (1965). His view of the Vietnam problem appeared in "The Vietnam Negotiations," *Foreign Affairs* 47 (January 1969): 211–234. Later writings include *For the Record: Selected Statements* (1981); *Observations: Selected Speeches and Essays* (1985); and, with Cyrus Vance, "Bipartisan Objectives for American Foreign Policy," *Foreign Affairs* 66 (Summer 1988): 899–921.

Excellent and favorable accounts on Kissinger and his foreign policy are Bernard and Marvin Kalb, *Kissinger* (1974); John G. Stoessinger, *Henry Kissinger: The Anguish of Power* (1976); Robert Schulzinger, *The Doctor of Diplomacy* (1989); and Seyom Brown, *The Crises of Power: An Interpretation of U.S. Foreign Policy in the Kissinger Years* (1979).

More critical in their treatment of Kissinger are Roger Morris, *Uncertain Greatness: Henry Kissinger and American Foreign Policy* (1977), and especially Seymour M. Hersch, *The Price of Power: Kissinger in the Nixon White House* (1983). See also Robert L. Beisner, "History and Henry Kissinger," *Diplomatic History* 14 (Fall 1990): 511–527. Oriana Fallaci, an Italian journalist, published her lively interviews with Kissinger in

Interview with History (1976), and Gerald R. Ford's memoir, *A Time to Heal* (1979), discusses his relationship with his secretary of state.

Kissinger's ideas and their origins are the themes of books by Stephen Graubard, *Kissinger: Portrait of a Mind* (1973); Harvey Starr, *Henry Kissinger: Perceptions of World Politics* (1983); David Landau, *Kissinger: Uses of Power* (1972); Peter Dickson, *Kissinger and the Meaning of History* (1979); and Joseph M. Smith, *Realist Thought from Weber to Kissinger* (1986).

The best books on the negotiations leading to SALT I are John Newhouse, *Cold Dawn: The Story of SALT* (1973), and Strobe Talbott, *End Game: The Inside Story of SALT II* (1979). Gerard C. Smith, U.S. SALT negotiator, is critical of Kissinger in *Doubletalk: The Story of SALT I* (1980). See also Douglas Hallett, "Kissinger Dolossus: The Domestic Politics of SALT," *Yale Review* 65 (Winter 1976): 161–174, and Stanley Hoffman, "The Doctor of Foreign Policy," *New York Review of Books* (December 5, 1979).

The events leading to the American withdrawal from and eventual fall of South Vietnam are recounted in Larry Berman, *Planning a Tragedy: The Americanization of the War in Vietnam* (1982); A. E. Goodman, *The Lost Peace: America's Search for a Negotiated Settlement of the Vietnam War* (1978); Gregory Tien Hung Nguyen and Jerrold Schecter, *The Palace File* (1986); Leslie Gelb and Richard K. Belts, *The Irony of Vietnam* (1979); and Frank Snepp, *Decent Interval* (1977). See also Dorothy C. Donnelly, "A Settlement of Sorts: Henry Kissinger's Negotiations and America's Extrication from the War in Vietnam," *Peace and Change* 9 (Summer 1983): 127–139.

An excellent overview of U.S. policy in the Middle East, one that reflects the Arab view, is Robert W. Stookey, *America and the Arab States: An Uneasy Encounter* (1975). Kissinger's Middle East activities are described in Edward R.F. Sheehan, *The Arabs, Israelis, and Kissinger* (1976); William Quant, *Decade of Decisions, 1967–1976* (1977); and Matti Golan, *The Secret Conversations of Henry Kissinger: Step by Step Diplomacy in the Middle East* (1976). A critical view is presented in G. Warren Nutter, *Kissinger's Grand Design* (1975).

Specific aspects of Kissinger's diplomacy appear in John King Fairbank, *The Great Chinese Revolution, 1800–1985* (1986); John J. Moresca, *To Helsinki: The Conference on Security and Cooperation in Europe* (1985); and Mohammed A. El-Khawas and Barry Cohen, *The Kissinger Study of Southern Africa* (1976). An account from the chief of the Angola task force is John Stockwell, *In Search of Enemies: A CIA Story* (1978). See also Nathaniel Davis, "The Angola Decision of 1975: A Personal Memoir," *Foreign Affairs* 57 (Fall 1978): 109–124.

Bibliography

Works by Richard Nixon

Nixon, Richard M. *In the Arena: A Memoir of Victory, Defeat, and Renewal.* New York: Simon and Schuster, 1990.
———. *Leaders.* New York: Warner, 1982.
———. *1999: Victory Without War.* New York: Simon and Schuster, 1988.
———. *No More Vietnams.* New York: Arbor House, 1985.
———. *The Real Peace.* Boston: Little, Brown, 1984.
———. *The Real War.* New York: Warner, 1980.
———. *RN: The Memoirs of Richard Nixon.* New York: Grosset and Dunlap, 1978.
———. *Six Crises.* New York: Doubleday, 1962.

Works by Henry Kissinger

Kissinger, Henry. *For the Record: Selected Statements*. Boston: Little, Brown, 1981.
————. *The Necessity for Choice: Prospects for American Foreign Policy*. New York: Harper and Row, 1961.
————. *Nuclear Weapons and Foreign Policy*. New York: Harper and Row, 1957.
————. *Observations: Selected Speeches and Essays*. Boston: Little, Brown, 1985.
————. *The Troubled Partnership: A Re-Appraisal of the Atlantic Alliance*. New York: Harper and Row, 1965.
————. "The Vietnam Negotiations." *Foreign Affairs* 47 (January 1969): 211–234.
————. *The White House Years*. Boston: Little, Brown, 1979.
————. "The White Revolutionary: Reflections of Bismarck." *Daedalus* 97 (1968): 888–924.
————. *A World Restored: Metternich, Castlereagh, and the Problems of Peace, 1812–1822*. Boston: Houghton Mifflin, 1957.
————. *The Years of Upheaval*. Boston: Little, Brown, 1982.
Kissinger, Henry, and Cyrus Vance. "Bipartisan Objectives for American Foreign Policy." *Foreign Affairs* 66 (Summer 1988): 899–921.

Related Works

Alexander, Robert J. *The Tragedy of Chile*. Westport, Conn.: Greenwood Press, 1978.
Ambrose, Stephen E. *Nixon: The Education of a Politician, 1913–1962*. New York: Simon and Schuster, 1987.
————. *Nixon: The Triumph of a Politician, 1962–1972*. New York: Simon and Schuster, 1989.
Beisner, Robert L. "History and Henry Kissinger." *Diplomatic History* 14 (Fall 1990): 511–527.
Berman, Larry. *Planning a Tragedy: The Americanization of the War in Vietnam*. New York: Norton, 1982.
Bill, James. *The Eagle and the Lion: The Tragedy of American-Iranian Relations*. New Haven, Conn.: Yale University Press, 1988.
Brown, Seyom. *The Crises of Power: An Interpretation of U.S. Foreign Policy in the Kissinger Years*. New York: Columbia University Press, 1979.
Dickson, Peter. *Kissinger and the Meaning of History*. New York: Cambridge University Press, 1979.
Donnelly, Dorothy C. "A Settlement of Sorts: Henry Kissinger's Negotiations and America's Extrication from the War in Vietnam." *Peace and Change* 9 (Summer 1983): 127–139.
Fallaci, Oriana. *Interview with History*. New York: Liverwright, 1976.
Ford, Gerald R. *A Time to Heal*. New York: Harper and Row, 1979.
Gaddis, John Lewis. *Strategies of Containment: A Critical Appraisal of Postwar American National Security Policy*. New York: Oxford University Press, 1982.
Gardner, Lloyd. *The Great Nixon Turnaround*. New York: New Viewpoints, 1973.
Garthoff, Raymond. *Detente and Confrontation: American-Soviet Relations from Nixon to Reagan*. Washington: Brookings Institution, 1985.
Gelb, Leslie, and Richard K. Belts. *The Irony of Vietnam: The System Worked*. Washington, D.C.: Brookings Institution, 1979.
Gelman, Harry. *The Brezhnev Politburo and the Decline of Detente*. Ithaca, N.Y.: Cornell University Press, 1984.

Goodman, Allan E. *The Lost Peace: America's Search for a Negotiated Settlement of the Vietnam War*. Stanford, Calif.: Hoover Institution Press, 1978.

Graubard, Stephen. *Kissinger: Portrait of a Mind*. New York: Norton, 1973.

Hallett, Douglas. "Kissinger Dolossus: The Domestic Politics of SALT." *Yale Review* 65 (Winter 1976): 161–74.

Hersch, Seymour M. *The Price of Power: Kissinger in the Nixon White House*. New York: Summit, 1983.

Hoffman, Stanley. "The Doctor of Foreign Policy." *New York Review of Books* (December 5, 1979).

Holloway, David. *The Soviet Union and the Arms Race*. New Haven, Conn.: Yale University Press, 1983.

Hyland, William G. *Mortal Rivals: Superpower Relations from Nixon to Reagan*. New York: Random House, 1987.

Isaacs, Arnold R. *Without Honor: Defeat in Vietnam and Cambodia*. Baltimore: Johns Hopkins University Press, 1983.

Kalb, Bernard, and Marvin Kalb. *Kissinger*. Boston: Little, Brown, 1974.

Landau, David. *Kissinger: Uses of Power*. Boston: Houghton Mifflin, 1972.

Leuchtenberg, William E. *In the Shadow of FDR: From Harry Truman to Ronald Reagan*. Ithaca, N.Y.: Cornell University Press, 1985.

Litwak, Robert. *Detente and the Nixon Doctrine*. New York: Cambridge University Press, 1984.

Mandelbaum, Michael. *The Nuclear Question: The United States and Nuclear Weapons, 1946–1976*. Cambridge, Mass.: Harvard University Press, 1979.

Morris, Roger. *Uncertain Greatness: Henry Kissinger and American Foreign Policy*. New York: Harper and Row, 1977.

Newhouse, John. *Cold Dawn: The Story of SALT*. New York: Holt, Rinehart and Winston, 1973.

Nguyen, Gregory Tien Hung, and Jerrold Schecter. *The Palace File*. New York: Harper and Row, 1986.

Schell, Jonathan. *Time of Illusion*. New York: Knopf, 1976.

Schulzinger, Robert. *The Doctor of Diplomacy*. New York: Columbia University Press, 1989.

Shawcross, William. *Sideshow: Kissinger, Nixon and the Destruction of Cambodia*. New York: Simon and Schuster, 1979.

Smith, Gerard C. *Doubletalk: The Story of SALT I*. New York: Doubleday, 1980.

Smith, Joseph M. *Realist Thought from Weber to Kissinger*. Baton Rouge: Louisiana State University Press, 1986.

Snepp, Frank. *Decent Interval: The American Debacle in Vietnam and the Fall of Saigon*. New York: Random House, 1977.

Starr, Harvey. *Henry Kissinger: Perceptions of World Politics*. Lexington: University of Kentucky Press, 1983.

Stoessinger, John G. *Henry Kissinger: The Anguish of Power*. New York: Norton, 1976.

Sulzberger, C. L. *The World and Richard Nixon*. Englewood Cliffs, N.J.: Prentice-Hall, 1987.

Sutter, Robert G. *China Watch: Toward Sino-American Reconciliation*. Baltimore: Johns Hopkins University Press, 1978.

Szulc, Tad. *The Illusion of Peace: Foreign Policy in the Nixon-Kissinger Years*. New York: Viking, 1979.

Talbott, Strobe. *End Game: The Inside Story of SALT II*. New York: Harper and Row, 1979.
Ulam, Adam B. *Dangerous Relations: The Soviet Union in World Politics*. New York: Oxford University Press, 1983.
Wills, Gary. *Nixon Agonistes*. New York: NAL, 1979.

WILLIAM B. PICKETT

Henry John Temple, Viscount Palmerston (1784–1865).   The third Viscount Palmerston is one of the most controversial figures of nineteenth-century Britain. His name brings to mind gunboat diplomacy and national self-confidence, manifestations of British arrogance at the pinnacle of the country's power. A closer investigation, however, reveals a complex personality who, during his nearly twenty-five-year tenure as foreign secretary and prime minister, attempted to guide his nation through the uncertain international order that followed the upheavals of the French Revolution and the Napoleonic Wars. Caution, as much as recklessness, characterized Palmerston's career, which revealed an equal awareness of Britain's might and of its vulnerability.

Palmerston was a product of Britain's Enlightenment and Regency periods. He was born in London on October 20, 1784, into a family of the Anglo-Irish aristocracy and was christened Henry John Temple. Because the Palmerston title was Irish, its holder could not sit in the House of Lords. Nevertheless, the Temples were socially active members of London's privileged classes, and the second viscount was a member of Parliament. If Henry's father was an English gentleman of the Enlightenment, his mother, Mary Mee, the daughter of a London merchant, was a product of Britain's growing commercial and industrial might. Henry Temple's lineage, therefore, embraced the ancient values of England's landed gentry and the modern acumen of Britain's business class.

Henry's education reinforced the breadth of experience embodied in his family and endowed him with perspectives peculiarly suited to the career that would make him famous. He attended Harrow from 1795 to 1800, where he studied the classics and oratory, and formed important personal ties with his social equals, including two future prime ministers. But even as he acquired the skills necessary for a member of Britain's ruling class, he also gained a knowledge, unusual for an aristocrat in his time, of the forces that governed international relations. Before attending Harrow, Henry Temple became fluent in French and competent in Italian and Spanish while accompanying his parents on an extended tour of Europe. From 1800 to 1803 he studied in Edinburgh under Dugald Stewart, an "advanced Whig" and a disciple of Adam Smith. Stewart instructed Henry in the functions of political economy, national wealth, and free trade. The third viscount Palmerston thus reached maturity with an appreciation not only of other European cultures and languages, but also of the economic forces that drove these societies.

The final years of Henry's education merged into the beginning of his long political apprenticeship. The second Viscount Palmerston died in 1802, leaving Henry, his eldest son, to assume the title. From 1803 to 1806 Henry attended

Cambridge University, where he took part in a debating society. It was therefore natural that in 1806 the third Viscount Palmerston contested the Cambridge seat vacated by the death of the prime minister, *William Pitt the Younger. Although his first attempt to enter Parliament failed, Palmerston secured a pocket borough the following year from one of his father's political allies. Palmerston's father had been a supporter of Pitt, so the Pittite faction (soon to be the Tory party) ruling Britain quickly offered the new member of Parliament positions in the government. From 1807 to 1809 Palmerston served in the admiralty. In 1809 he passed up the opportunity to become chancellor of the exchequer. Although this position was not so prestigious in the early nineteenth century as it is today, Palmerston feared that too speedy a promotion might reveal his inexperience and damage his career. He opted instead for the lesser post of secretary at war, a position he found so comfortable that it threatened to hinder his further promotion.

The secretary *of* war supervised the army's activities in the field. The duties of the secretary *at* war were, by contrast, financial and administrative. Palmerston attended to these duties diligently. In his zeal to improve the army's efficiency, he so angered many officers and civil servants that he became the target of a would-be assassin in 1818. Palmerston remained in this post for nineteen years, turning down various positions outside Britain, including the lord lieutenancy of Ireland and the governor-generalship of India. Had Palmerston died in his early forties, his life would have been that of a relatively obscure bureaucrat.

Only a significant shift in the political spectrum enabled the viscount to embark on a more influential career. Palmerston belonged to a Tory faction led by *George Canning, the foreign secretary, which supported Roman Catholic emancipation. Although Canning was prime minister for only a few months before his death in 1827, his faction survived him and gradually found itself supporting the Whigs over emancipation and reform. Amid these domestic upheavals Palmerston emerged as a defender of Canning's foreign policy. He left office when the Canningites formally split with the Duke of Wellington's government in 1828, but as a member of the opposition he criticized Tory policy toward Portugal and the Ottoman Empire. Dom Miguel and his niece, Donna Maria da Gloria, were rivals for the Portuguese throne. Wellington supported the former, who identified with the country's aristocratic forces. Canning, on the other hand, favored Maria, because her self-proclaimed constitutionalist faction was less likely to allow the Holy Alliance of Austria, Prussia, and Russia to interfere in the policy of one of Britain's oldest allies. Canning supported Maria in order to maintain the balance of power in Britain's favor. Palmerston probably had similar motives, but transformed Canning's approach by publicly portraying his cause as a crusade for liberal constitutional values. He applied these values with equal vigor to the eastern Mediterranean. Greek independence was the first issue to come to Palmerston's attention when he briefly sat in Canning's cabinet. As a member of the opposition, he adopted a romantic, philhellenic attitude almost worthy of

Lord Byron. Greek independence fit perfectly into the constitutional image that Palmerston projected during much of his career. Following the Tory split, however, Palmerston may have added a liberal, ideological slant to Canning's practical approach to the balance of power on the assumption that Whig reformers would succeed domestically. If so, he combined pragmatic career goals with idealistic political aims in a manner he would often repeat. Palmerston seized the opportunity to advance both when the Canningites joined the new Whig government in 1830. He became foreign secretary, a position he held almost continuously until 1841, and then again from 1846 to 1851.

Revolution in France dominated the news from abroad in 1830. Palmerston welcomed the accession of Louis Philippe as the country's constitutional monarch, and even hoped that such moderate revolutionary fervor would spread to the autocratic members of the Holy Alliance. Nevertheless, the new foreign secretary did not wish to see the resurgence of France as a military crusader. Palmerston's support of liberalism soon came into conflict with his resolve to maintain British interests when Belgium declared its independence of the Dutch crown. The Concert of Europe had united the two countries in 1815 in order to create a powerful buffer against France. When Dutch troops attempted to suppress the independence movement in August 1831, Belgian nationalists received military assistance from Louis Philippe. Palmerston could not persuade the French king to withdraw. Rather than deliver a provocative ultimatum, the foreign secretary informed his ambassador in Paris of the inevitability of war if France remained. He shrewdly chose to send this message through the regular mail rather than the diplomatic pouch, knowing that French authorities would intercept it. They did, and France quickly complied with Britain's wishes. This circumvention of a public rift enabled Palmerston to ally Britain with France in order to force the Netherlands to withdraw. He thus used French troops to secure liberal ideological aims, while maintaining the balance of power by limiting Louis Philippe's activities and depriving him of a reason to remain in Belgium. The new kingdom emerged from the crisis with a British guarantee to defend its borders.

The British public now considered Palmerston a champion of liberalism abroad. The foreign secretary strengthened this image in 1834 by extending the alliance with France to the supposedly constitutional regimes in Spain and Portugal. The Quadruple Alliance of western nations reflected British and French desires to prevent *Metternich's Austria from dominating European diplomacy, but Palmerston portrayed it publicly as a "constitutional" rival to the autocratic Holy Alliance. In spite of his successes during these years, the lukewarm condition of Anglo-French relations meant that the alliance was more imaginary than real. When, in 1839, Paris and London disagreed over the Middle East, the French ruined Palmerston's attempt to secure the agreement of all the Great Powers to coordinate their efforts to end the slave trade.

Palmerston's tactless preaching to the leaders of other countries often earned him enmity abroad. During a disagreement in 1839 over the right of British naval officers to inspect suspected slavers, his reference to the Stars and Stripes as "a piece of bunting" outraged Americans. The viscount's comments were particularly dangerous because they came amid a dispute between Britain and the United States over the western boundaries of their territories in North America and over American aid to Canadian rebels. Palmerston rankled Austria in 1848 with his condemnation of its suppression of Milan and his praise of Italian nationalism. He antagonized European Catholics with his support for Protestant liberals in Switzerland. The Spanish government even evicted Britain's ambassador when the latter suggested, with Palmerston's blessing, that the former conduct its domestic policy according to London's wishes because it owed its existence to Whitehall's goodwill.

The victims of these verbal harangues were quick to point out Palmerston's inconsistencies. The viscount appeared to espouse "liberal" movements only if they served British interests. Polish nationalism fit this criterion, but Irish nationalism did not. Constitutional struggles in Spain and Portugal enhanced Whitehall's influence, but Chartist agitation in England did not. Palmerston's reluctance to advocate reform at home with the same vigor that he did abroad eventually lost him the loyalty of many Whig colleagues. His support of moderate liberal and nationalist struggles across the Channel was probably sincere, but he was always willing to subordinate ideology to Britain's practical interests.

Nowhere were Palmerston's priorities more apparent than on the fringes of Europe and in Asia. Twice under his direction Britain went to war against China in order to defend its trading rights. The first instance was the notorious Opium War (1839–1842). Chinese authorities traditionally offered little objection to the opium trade so long as the merchants were not foreigners. Nevertheless, Whitehall placed the rights of its merchants above its desire to suppress illegal drug traffic. It refused Chinese authorities the right to inspect British vessels. Palmerston's frustration over the importance of "a piece of bunting" apparently did not extend to the Union Jack in Asia. Hostilities erupted between London and Beijing after Chinese authorities arrested the crew of a British vessel transporting opium, confiscated its cargo, and refused to provide compensation. British forces ultimately prevailed, and received several trading *entrepôts*, including Hong Kong. The decision to fight was not Palmerston's alone, but he supported it. China's government embodied almost the antithesis of the foreign secretary's liberal, free-trading principles. Although he objected to the opium trade, the viscount argued that a greater cause was at stake. The second Sino-British war demonstrated his assertion. When, in 1856, Palmerston, as prime minister, ordered the royal navy to bombard Canton, opium was not an issue, but China's attempts to limit Western trade by arresting British smugglers and pirates were.

Palmerston did not limit the use of force to Asia. Although the viscount prefaced his career in the foreign office with a veritable ode to Greek nationalism, he eventually resented Athens's failure to pay the charges it owed on British loans. He vented his anger publicly in the Don Pacifico incident. An anti-Semitic attack destroyed the Greek home of Don Pacifico, a Portuguese Jew, in 1847. The Greek government refused to provide adequate compensation. But the victim was fortunate enough to have been born in Gibraltar, which entitled him to claim British citizenship and Whitehall's assistance. Palmerston had the admiralty dispatch part of its Mediterranean fleet to Piraeus. Athens was to settle not only Don Pacifico's claims, but also Britain's, or face the royal navy's wrath. British ships arrived off the coast of Greece in January 1850, and the two countries soon reached a compromise. The Tory opposition was furious. William E. Gladstone denounced the viscount in the House of Commons for failing to heed "the general sentiment of the civilized world."

The foreign secretary's defense of his positions over the previous two decades revealed how his conduct of external affairs reflected his philosophy of the political and social order. He identified British interests with the spread of liberty. Britain had demonstrated this liberty through "the example of a nation, in which every class of society accepts with cheerfulness the lot which Providence has assigned to it; while at the same time every individual of each class is constantly striving to raise himself [peacefully] in the social scale." Palmerston's justification of his policy toward Greece focused not on the loan charges owed to Whitehall, but on the rights of a British subject, Don Pacifico. In perhaps the most memorable defense of the *Pax Britannica*, he argued for a world where "as the Roman, in days of old, held himself free from indignity, when he could say *Civis Romanus sum* [I am a Roman citizen], so also a British subject in whatever land he may be, shall feel confident that the watchful eye and the strong arm of England will protect him against injustice and wrong." Although the viscount survived a vote of no confidence, he resigned the following year during a dispute over his public approval of the coup d'état by Louis Napoleon (*Napoleon III).

Palmerston's support of Turkey matched his anger toward Greece. The Ottoman government was no more "constitutional" than the Chinese, but the collapse of the sultan's authority threatened to create a vacuum into which Britain's rivals would drift. The Eastern Question became a crucial factor in the Eurasian balance of power that Britain and Russia were creating through their territorial acquisitions. The Ottoman Empire was an essential bulwark against St. Petersburg's interests in both the Balkans and the Middle East. Palmerston discovered Turkey's importance in 1833 when the sultan granted the Russian navy the right of passage through the straits separating the Black Sea and the Mediterranean. Through the Straits Convention of 1841, Palmerston restricted Russia's access to the Mediterranean and ensured the continued existence of the Ottoman Empire in exchange for Egyptian independence. Nevertheless, when in 1853 St. Petersburg failed to secure extraterritorial jurisdiction over the sultan's Eastern Orthodox subjects, it invaded Ottoman territories north of the Danube. Britain now faced the specter of Russian troops in Constantinople. Palmerston held no office in March 1854 when the cabinet discussed St. Petersburg's refusal to withdraw from the Balkans, but he submitted a memorandum arguing for intervention. The cabinet heeded the viscount's advice and embarked on a costly and eventually unpopular war in the Crimea that cost the Earl of Aberdeen the premiership the following year.

In 1851 Palmerston alienated almost all important parliamentary factions: Tory, Whig, and Radical. But his public image as a patriotic crusader enabled him to retain a broad base of popular support, and his presence became essential to any Whig-led coalition. From 1852 to 1853 Aberdeen kept Palmerston in the Home Office, far from foreign intrigues. When criticism over Crimea forced the prime minister's resignation, the former foreign secretary was the obvious successor.

The war ended in March 1856 in triumph for Britain. Russia withdrew from its recently acquired Danubian territories and disbanded its Black Sea fleet. The new prime minister soon contended with the Crimea's aftershocks further east. In 1857 he ordered British forces to occupy Bushire in the Persian Gulf in order to force the withdrawal of Persian troops from Afghanistan. The same year saw the Sepoy rebellion in Indian. Palmerston sent reinforcements but initiated legislation to bring the raj under Whitehall's administration. He refused foreign offers of assistance, insisting that Britain could handle this greatest challenge to its Asian empire alone. Nevertheless, the prime minister's sensitivity to foreign criticism brought a temporary personal setback. In January 1858 an Italian nationalist attempted to assassinate the French emperor, Napoleon III. When an investigation revealed that the bomb originated in England, Palmerston introduced a bill to suppress foreign revolutionaries in Britain. This apparent desertion of "constitutional" movements abroad alienated Radicals and forced Palmerston out of office.

The unnatural coalition of Tories and Radicals soon fell apart, and Palmerston resumed his post the following year as the head of the coalition that became the Liberal party. Palmerston's growing reluctance to support individual liberties abroad only added to the disappointment of Radicals over his unwillingness to sanction reforms at home. The prime minister's sympathy toward the gentry of the American South brought Britain to the brink of war with the United States in 1861 when a Union captain removed two Confederate representatives from a British ship sailing from Cuba to England. Only Prince Albert's intervention prevented the foreign office from delivering a provocative letter to the Lincoln administration. Palmerston regarded the Confederacy as a secession movement rather than an institution for the perpetuation of slavery. The South was a major source of cotton, and only its military weakness dissuaded the prime minister from recognizing the rebel government. Palmerston was more cautious regarding the disputed succession of Schleswig-Holstein. He realized the limits of British military power in Europe when Prussia and Austria declared war on Denmark in 1864. The royal navy could enter Danish waters, but Britain could not dislodge the coalition's armies without French assistance. Palmerston, who had recently ordered the construction of coastal fortifications against a possible French invasion of England, could not tolerate Napoleon III's army east of the Rhine. His divided cabinet reluctantly accepted Prussia's expansion.

Palmerston died in office on October 18, 1865. His eighty-year life spanned events from the French Revolution to the American Civil War. The third viscount was a child of the eighteenth century. His career at the foreign office began, appropriately, in the footsteps of Canning. Palmerston never completely abandoned the pragmatism embodied in his political mentor. He crusaded tirelessly for British economic interests abroad and always paid attention to Whitehall's traditional concern over the European balance of power. But unlike his predecessors, Palmerston chose to identify British interests with those of "liberty" as he understood it. That the two were sometimes incompatible helps to explain the apparent inconsistencies of the viscount's policies. Nevertheless, Palmerston transformed Britain's approach to foreign affairs perhaps more than he would have wished. Moral crusades fit well into the framework of Victorian ethics, and the popular association of Britain's welfare with political freedoms abroad would continue well into the twentieth century.

Annotated Bibliography

Most of Palmerston's personal papers are held by the Broadlands Archives Trust at Southampton University Library. Researchers must obtain prior permission from the Archivist, University of Southampton, Archives and Manuscript Collection, Southampton, Hampshire SO9 5NH, England. Palmerston's official correspondence as foreign secretary and prime minister is available at the Public Record Office in Kew, Surrey. Researchers must show identification, such as a passport, in order to receive a reader's card. Address correspondence to the Keeper, Public Record Office, Ruskin Avenue, Kew, Richmond, Surrey TW9 4DU, England.

Other sources for Palmerston's career are available in the collections of individuals with whom he corresponded. Queen Victoria's papers are held in the Royal Archives at Windsor Castle. Collections are not open to students studying for degrees. Other researchers must apply in writing to the Registrar, Royal Archives, Windsor Castle, Windsor, Berkshire, England. The papers of the fourth Earl of Clarendon and Sir J.R.J. Graham, both of whom served under Palmerston, are at the Bodleian Library in Oxford. A reader's card is required. Send inquiries to the Keeper, Oxford University Archives, Bodleian Library, Broad Street, Oxford OX1 3BG, England. The papers of the fourth Earl of Aberdeen, under whom Palmerston served, are at the British Library in London. Researchers must apply for a reader's card to the Manuscripts Librarian, British Library, Department of Manuscripts, Great Russell Street, London WC1B 3DG, England. The first Earl Russell's papers are at the Public Record Office. The Keeper may require special, advanced permission for access. In each case researchers should write to the respective libraries well ahead of their proposed visit.

Although Palmerston published no autobiography or reflections on foreign policy, scholars have compiled various collections of his correspondence. G.H. Francis edited the earliest shortly after the viscount left the foreign office, at least partly to defend his actions. The most recent, compiled by the Royal Commission on Historical Manuscripts, is being released as part of HMSO's Prime Ministers' Papers Series.

For a century after Palmerston's death biographers portrayed him as a man who dominated Britain and the forces that it confronted. Henry Lytton Bulwer's five-volume *Life of Viscount Palmerston* (1871–1876), completed posthumously by Evelyn Ashley, is the official biography. It reflects the sympathies of a man who served under the third viscount. Anthony Trollope's *Lord Palmerston* (1882) describes an honest, practical leader who fought for liberal ideals through his foreign policy. This image of the third viscount has long been the most popular. If Trollope's biography exaggerates the Victorian qualities of its subject, then Philip Guedalla's *Palmerston, 1784–1865* (1927) overemphasizes his debt to the eighteenth century. The viscount emerges as an anachronism who nevertheless steered Britain on a course of his choosing. Both authors' portraits are highly subjective. H. C. Bell's *Lord Palmerston* (1936), on the other hand, employs a wealth of foreign office documents to demonstrate that the viscount was a nineteenth-century nationalist. Bell's emphasis was understandable in the 1930s as Europe's balance of power collapsed under the weight of extreme foreign nationalist movements. He reconciles Palmerston's pragmatism with his public idealism by almost suggesting that Britain's interests were an ideal in themselves.

Recent biographers have asked different questions. Jasper Ridley's *Lord Palmerston* (1970) challenges the long held notion that in the mid-nineteenth century Britain was a world power, superior to its continental neighbors. Far from shaping events abroad, Palmerston responded to them. Ridley shows both Britain and its foreign secretary struggling among diplomatic equals, and sometimes failing. Kenneth Bourne provides the most recent detailed survey of Palmerston's life (to the age of fifty-six) in *Palmerston: The Formative Years, 1784–1841* (1982). Because he had access to Palmerston's private papers, Bourne chose to emphasize the viscount's private life rather than cover detail that Bell and Ridley had already examined. Bourne's Palmerston is a product of the Regency period whose power as foreign secretary is limited and whose motives are not always lofty. Muriel Chamberlain's short biography, *Lord Palmerston* (1987), combines the ideas of Ridley and Bourne with her own work on British foreign policy.

So much of Palmerston's career focused on foreign affairs that some analyses of British diplomacy between 1830 and 1865 almost serve as biographies of the viscount. Scholars have pointed to the tension between Palmerston's publicly stated ideals and his apparently pragmatic motives. Did the statesman manipulate public opinion or follow it? In *The Foreign Policy of Palmerston, 1830–1841* (1969) C. K. Webster provides a detailed analysis of the viscount's first term in the foreign office. Like many of his predecessors, Webster thinks that Palmerston guided, rather than followed, his country's destiny. Although Donald Southgate is sometimes critical of his subject, he arrives at similar conclusions. In *"The Most English Minister . . ."': The Policies and Politics of Palmerston* (1966) Southgate covers the viscount's career from 1828 to his death. He acknowledges that the viscount browbeat his opponents and charmed public opinion, but these qualities only indicated Palmerston's control of foreign policy.

Studies of the foreign office during the early to mid-nineteenth century tend to reinforce the impression that Palmerston tightly controlled his country's diplomatic corps. In *Britain and the Eastern Question* (1971) G. D. Clayton stresses how few decision makers shaped Britain's foreign policy and how much power they had. John Derden's paper, "The British Foreign Office and Policy Formation: The 1840s," *Proceedings and Papers of the Georgia Association of History* (1981): 64–79, discusses Palmerston's iron grip over the foreign office. In *The Foreign Office, 1782–1982* (1984), edited by Roger Bullen, Kenneth Bourne shows how the viscount used private correspondence to exercise personal control over the foreign office and prevent the cabinet from closely examining his diplomatic efforts.

Other scholars emphasize the limits of Palmerston's control over British diplomacy. In "Palmerston, Ponsonby and Mehemet Ali," *East European Quarterly* 15 (1981): 409–424, Charles Middleton discusses the restrictions that slow communications placed on

Palmerston's ability to direct his representatives in the Middle East in the late 1830s. Raymond Jones's *The British Diplomatic Service, 1815–1914* (1983) examines the effects that changes in communications and the British constitution had on the class composition and function of the British diplomatic service.

Many historians fit Palmerston's pragmatism into the context of the challenges that Britain faced. In his contribution to Peter Jagger's *Gladstone, Politics and Religion* (1985), David Steele claims that Palmerston's view of human nature was Hobbesian. The world was a brutal place in which the viscount had to fight for Britain's interests. Steele's position fits Bourne's assertion in his *Foreign Policy of Victorian England, 1830–1902* (1970) that Palmerston placed pragmatism before idealism. How then should one account for the foreign secretary's support of revolutions when he entered office? In "Palmerston and the Revolutions of 1830–1833," *Consortium on Revolutionary Europe 1750–1850* 14 (1984): 406–413, John Rooney maintains that the viscount championed revolution in France only because it was in Britain's best commercial interests. Keith Wilson more than questions the foreign secretary's ideological motives in supporting revolutions in Europe. In *British Foreign Secretaries and Foreign Policy* (1987) he argues that from 1855 onwards the prime minister's liberalism abroad distracted critics from his conservatism at home.

If some scholars regard Palmerston as a pragmatist, others regard him as an opportunist and a manipulator. Karl Marx's polemic treatise, *The Story of the Life of Lord Palmerston*, originally published in 1856, accuses the viscount of helping to perpetuate the interests of his class under the guise of championing liberty. Palmerston's relation to public opinion on the eve of the Crimean War is the subject of two studies. Kingsley Martin's *The Triumph of Lord Palmerston* (1963) has the viscount keeping on the right side of public opinion as it led Britain into conflict with Russia. David Krein's article, "War and Reform: Russell, Palmerston and the Struggle for Power in the Aberdeen Cabinet, 1853–54," *Maryland Historian* (1976): 67–84, argues that Palmerston used public opinion to support his attempt to involve Britain in the Crimean War primarily in order to further his own political career. Angus Hawkins examines similar motives after the war. In "British Parliamentary Party Alignment and the Indian Issue, 1857–1858," *Journal of British Studies* 23 (1984): 79–105, Hawkins shows that considerations of political advancement determined the viscount's reaction to the Sepoy rebellion.

Perhaps the greatest challenge to traditional perceptions of Palmerston's role in history has come from those scholars who question basic assumptions about Britain's position among the Great Powers in the nineteenth century. Historians of the interwar period explained Palmerston's policy in the eastern Mediterranean in terms of the "Great Game in Asia." Both J.A.R. Marriott's *The Eastern Question* (1925) and Harold Temperley's *England and the Near East: The Crimea* (1936) had Britain defending the Ottoman Empire in order to preserve its lines of communication to India. In *British Foreign Policy in the Age of Palmerston* (1980), however, Muriel Chamberlain pays special attention to the long neglected Baltic theater in the Crimean War and maintains that the conflict was really over the balance of power in Europe rather than a western extension of imperial rivalry. Chamberlain further develops this theme in *'Pax Britannica'?* (1988). She suggests that Palmerston and succeeding British statesmen employed the concept of a world peace enforced by Britain in order to disguise the country's ineffectiveness in Europe. In a similar vein, Andrew Lambert's *The Crimean War* (1990) attributes Britain's imperial isolation to its weakness as a European land power.

In this context, studies of Palmerston's policies reveal his awareness of Britain's limitations. Edward Ellsworth's "Anglo-American Affairs in October of 1862," *Lincoln Herald* 66 (1964): 89–96, demonstrates the viscount's sense of vulnerability when dealing with the United States. This insecurity was even more acute concerning France. Ragnhild Hatton's "Palmerston and the Scandinavian Union," *Studies in International History: Essays Presented to W. Norton Medlicott* (1967): 119–144, discusses the prime minister's reluctance to oppose Prussia's bid for Schleswig-Holstein because it would encourage French military involvement east of the Rhine. In "Lord Palmerston: Panic Monger or Naval Peacemaker?" *Social Science* 47 (1972): 203–211, Colin Baxter argues that the French navy posed a real threat to Britain. Palmerston thus emerges from recent historical analysis not as the architect of a new Victorian balance of power, but as the defender of Britain's surprisingly vulnerable place in the world.

Bibliography

Books

Albrecht-Carrie, Rene. *Britain and France: Adaptations to a Changing Context of Power.* New York: Doubleday, 1970.
Anderson, M. S. *The Eastern Question, 1774–1923.* New York: St. Martin's Press, 1966.
Anderson, Olive. *A Liberal State at War: English Politics and Economics During the Crimean War.* New York: St. Martin's Press, 1967.
Baumgart, Winfried. *The Peace of Paris, 1856: Studies in War, Diplomacy, and Peacemaking.* Oxford: ABC-Clio, 1981.
Beales, Derek. *England and Italy, 1859–60.* London: Thomas Nelson, 1961.
Bell, Herbert C.F. *Lord Palmerston.* 2 vols. London: Longmans, Green, 1936.
Bishop, Donald G. *The Administration of British Foreign Relations.* Westport, Conn.: Greenwood Press, 1961.
Bourne, Kenneth. *The Foreign Policy of Victorian England, 1830–1902.* Oxford: Clarendon Press, 1970.
———. *Palmerston: The Formative Years, 1784–1841.* New York: Macmillan, 1982.
Bridge, F. R., and Roger Bullen. *The Great Powers and the European States System, 1815–1914.* London: Longman, 1980.
Bullen, Roger, ed. *The Foreign Office, 1782–1982.* Frederick, Md.: University Publications of America, 1984.
———. *Palmerston, Guizot and the Collapse of the Entente Cordiale.* London: Athlone Press, 1974.
Bulwer, H. L., and E. Ashley. *Life of Viscount Palmerston.* 5 vols. London: Bentley, 1871–1876.
Chamberlain, Muriel E. *British Foreign Policy in the Age of Palmerston.* Harlow, Eng.: Longman, 1980.
———. *Lord Palmerston.* Washington, D.C.: Catholic University Press of America, 1987.
———. *'Pax Britannica'? British Foreign Policy 1789–1914.* London: Longman, 1988.
Clarke, John. *British Diplomacy and Foreign Policy, 1782–1865: The National Interest.* London: Unwin Hyman, 1989.
Clayton, G. D. *Britain and the Eastern Question: Missolonghi to Gallipoli.* London: University of London Press, 1971.
Connell, Brian. *Portrait of a Golden Age: Intimate Papers of the Second Viscount Palmerston, Courtier under George III.* Boston: Houghton Mifflin, 1958.

――――. *Portrait of a Whig Peer: Compiled from the Papers of the Second Viscount Palmerston, 1739–1802*. London: Andre Deutsch, 1957.

――――. *Regina vs. Palmerston: The Correspondence between Queen Victoria and Her Foreign and Prime Minister, 1837–1865*. Garden City, N.Y.: Doubleday, 1961.

Francis, George Henry, ed. *Opinions and Policy of the Right Honourable Viscount Palmerston, as Minister, Diplomatist, and Statesman, During More than Forty Years of Public Life*. London: Colburn, 1852. Reprint. New York: Kraus, 1972.

Gillard, David. *The Struggle for Asia, 1828–1914: A Study in British and Russian Imperialism*. London: Methuen, 1977.

Guedalla, Philip. *Palmerston, 1784–1865*. New York: Putnam's, 1927.

Howard, Christopher. *Britain and the Casus Belli, 1822–1902: A Study of Britain's International Position from Canning to Salisbury*. London: Athlone Press, 1974.

Jagger, Peter J., ed. *Gladstone, Politics and Religion: A Collection of Founder's Day Lectures Delivered at St. Deiniol's Library, Hawarden, 1967–83*. New York: St. Martin's Press, 1985.

Jones, Raymond A. *The British Diplomatic Service, 1815–1914*. Gerrards Cross, Eng.: Colin Smythe, 1983.

Krein, David F. *The Last Palmerston Government: Foreign Policy, Domestic Politics, and the Genesis of "Splendid Isolation."* Ames: Iowa State University Press, 1978.

Lambert, Andrew D. *The Crimean War: British Grand Strategy, 1853–56*. Manchester: Manchester University Press, 1990.

Marriott, J.A.R. *The Eastern Question: An Historical Study in European Diplomacy*. Oxford: Clarendon Press, 1925.

Martin, Kingsley. *The Triumph of Lord Palmerston: A Study of Public Opinion in England Before the Crimean War*. London: Hutchinson, 1963.

Marx, Karl. *Secret Diplomatic History* and *The Story of the Life of Lord Palmerston*. Edited by Lester Hutchinson. New York: International Publishers, 1969.

Middleton, Charles Ronald. *The Administration of British Foreign Policy, 1782–1846*. Durham, N.C.: Duke University Press, 1977.

Palmerston, Henry Temple, Viscount. *Private Correspondence with Sir George Villiers (Afterwards Fourth Earl of Clarendon) as Minister to Spain, 1833–1837*. Edited by Roger Bullen and Felicity Strong. London: H. M. Stationery Office, 1985.

Rich, Norman. *Why the Crimean War? A Cautionary Tale*. London: University Press of New England, 1985.

Ridley, Jasper. *Lord Palmerston*. London: Constable, 1970.

Saab, Ann Pottinger. *The Origins of the Crimean Alliance*. Charlottesville: University Press of Virginia, 1977.

Schroeder, Paul W. *Austria, Great Britain, and the Crimean War: The Destruction of the European Concert*. Ithaca, N.Y.: Cornell University Press, 1972.

Southgate, Donald. *"The Most English Minister . . .": The Policies and Politics of Palmerston*. London: Macmillan, 1966.

――――. *The Passing of the Whigs 1832–1886*. London: Macmillan, 1962.

Temperley, Harold. *England and the Near East: The Crimea*. London: Longmans, Green, 1936.

Trollope, Anthony. *Lord Palmerston*. London: W. Isbister, 1882. Reprint. New York: Arno Press, 1981.

Vincent, John. *The Formation of the British Liberal Party*. New York: Scribner's, 1966.

Webster, C. K. *The Foreign Policy of Palmerston, 1830–1841: Britain, the Liberal Movement and the Eastern Question.* 2 vols. New York: Humanities Press, 1969.

————. *Raleigh Lecture on History: Palmerston, Metternich, and the European System 1830–1841.* New York: Haskell House, 1975.

Wetzel, David. *The Crimean War: A Diplomatic History.* New York: Columbia University Press, 1985.

Wilson, Keith M. *British Foreign Secretaries and Foreign Policy: From Crimean War to First World War.* London: Croom Helm, 1987.

Articles

Andrews, James R. "The Ethos of Pacifism: The Problem of Image in the Early British Peace Movement." *Quarterly Journal of Speech* 53 (1967): 28–33.

Baxter, Colin F. "Lord Palmerston: Panic Monger or Naval Peacemaker?" *Social Science* 47 (1972): 203–211.

Bethell, L. M. "Britain, Portugal and the Suppression of the Brazilian Slave Trade: The Origin of the Palmerston Act of 1839." *English History Review* 80 (1965): 761–784.

Derden, John K. "The British Foreign Office and Policy Formation: The 1840s." *Proceedings and Papers of the Georgia Association of History* (1981): 64–79.

Eldridge, C. C. "Newcastle and the Ashanti War of 1863–64: A Failure of the Policy of 'Anti-Imperialism.' " *Renaissance and Modern Studies* 12 (1968): 68–90.

Ellsworth, Edward W. "Anglo-American Affairs in October of 1862." *Lincoln Herald* 66 (1964): 89–96.

Friedman, Isaiah. "Lord Palmerston and the Protection of Jews in Palestine 1839–1851." *Jewish Social Studies* 30 (1968): 23–41.

Hatton, Ragnhild. "Palmerston and the Scandinavian Union." In *Studies in International History: Essays Presented to W. Norton Medlicott* (1967): 119–144.

Hawkins, Angus. "British Parliamentary Party Alignment and the Indian Issue, 1857–1858." *Journal of British Studies* 23 (1984): 79–105.

Homan, Gerlof D. "Sir Edward C. Disbrowe and the Prelude to Constitutional Reform in the Netherlands in 1848." *Tijdschrift voor Geschiedenis* 79 (1966): 64–69.

Krein, David F. "War and Reform: Russell, Palmerston and the Struggle for Power in the Aberdeen Cabinet, 1853–54." *Maryland Historian* 7 (1976): 67–84.

Lefèvre, André. "La Chute de Palmerston (1851). La Part de responsabilité française." *Revue d'Histoire Diplomatique* 84 (1970): 80–96.

————. "La Reconnaissance de la Seconde République par L'Angleterre." *Revue d'Histoire Diplomatique* 82 (1968): 213–231.

————. "Les Rétombées Londoniennes de l'attentat d'Orsini (1858). Deux Victimes inattendues: Lord Palmerston et le Comte de Persigny." *Revue d'Histoire Diplomatique* 86 (1972): 174–205.

Luxenburg, Norman. "England und die Ursprunge der Tscherkessenkriege." *Jahrbücher für Geschichte* 13 (1965): 183–191.

Middleton, Charles R. "Palmerston, Ponsonby and Mehemet Ali: Some Observations on Ambassadorial Independence in the East, 1838–40." *East European Quarterly* 15 (1981): 409–424.

Reinerman, Alan J. "An Unnatural 'Natural Alliance': Metternich, Palmerston, and the Reform of the Papal States, 1831–1832." *International History Review* 10 (1988): 541–558.

Rodrígues Alonso, Manuel. "Tratado de Comercio Hispano-Britanico, Firado por Medizábal y Villiers en 1835." *Hispania* 39 (1979): 639–648.

Rooney, John W., and Irby C. Nichols, Jr., eds. "Palmerston and the Revolutions of 1830–1833." *Consortium on Revolutionary Europe 1750–1850* 14 (1984): 406–413.

Verete, M. "Why Was a British Consulate Established in Jerusalem?" *English History Review* 85 (1970): 316–345.

Welborn, Robert H. "The Fortifications Controversy of the Last Palmerston Administration." *Army Quarterly and Defence Journal* 112 (1982): 50–61.

Woodall, Robert. "Lord Palmerston and Don Pacifico." *British Heritage* 3 (1982): 48–58.

———. "Orsini and the Fall of Palmerston." *History Today* 26 (1976): 636–643.

A. MARTIN WAINWRIGHT

Lester Pearson (1897–1972).   Lester Pearson, the son of a Methodist parson, was born on April 23, 1897, in the small community of Newtonbrook, Ontario. The era of his birth was one of high expectation, and the nation's newly elected prime minister, Sir Wilfrid Laurier, heralded the next century as belonging to Canada and Canadians. Within the space of a few decades, the nation flung its doors open to peoples from every corner of the world and embarked on the difficult task of developing its resources and defining its identity.

Lester Pearson had the good fortune to be born into a nurturing family that valued education and encouraged his literary interests, which he expressed at the age of eleven in the form of a school essay entitled "Why We Should Abolish the Bar." Pearson enrolled in Victoria College, at the University of Toronto, in 1913 to pursue a literary career. Despite winning the Regent's Prize for English prose in his second year, he had not yet defined his career goals. Like others of his generation, he was excited and alarmed by the news from the French front, and in March 1915 he began to drill with the Officers' Training Corps in the university; within a month he had enlisted while still in the midst of his examinations.

After the war he reenrolled at the University of Toronto, and upon graduation in June 1919, he set out to define a career. Having abandoned his literary pursuits, he attempted law but found it unsatisfactory; he turned to business and similarly found it unrewarding. He turned to academics and successfully secured a place at Oxford University, graduating with a high second-class degree in history in 1922. The students and lecturers at Oxford had vivid memories of the trenches of France; only 300 undergraduates of a community of 3,000 had returned from the war, and Pearson's interaction with the survivors convinced him that the world needed mechanisms to prevent war. His studies had also revealed the forces that compelled nations to undertake war, and he set out to convince others, by participating in the Oxford debating societies and other philosophical and religious clubs, that new approaches were necessary to reduce international conflicts. He confidently urged that political leaders adopt a "high-minded and Christian" approach to political and social issues and was convinced that people, regardless of political orientation, race, or creed, desired peace and could be swayed by rational debate. Pearson had finally defined his political and internationalist philosophy.

After returning to Canada, Pearson took a teaching position in the department of history at the University of Toronto, but soon found the work unchallenging and committed himself to a bureaucratic career in Canada's newly founded Department of External Affairs. After serving his apprenticeship as a junior diplomat in Washington, London, and Geneva, he came to the conclusion that "we [humanity] live in a lunatic asylum." The highly impressionable Pearson realized that people of high moral principles were a rarity in the international environment. Nevertheless, he persevered and emerged as one of the most important figures in Canadian diplomacy. On the eve of World War II, he was the first secretary to Vincent Massey at the Canadian High Commission in London. In January 1941, Pearson was recalled to Ottawa and appointed secretary to Norman Robertson, undersecretary of state for external affairs. In the following year, he was appointed to the Canadian embassy in Washington. By the end of the war he had become ambassador to the United States and in 1947 moved to the post of deputy minister. He was elected to Parliament in 1948 and was sworn in as minister of external affairs on January 26, 1949.

Pearson was nearly fifty years old when he entered political life, and he set out on this new course with much reservation. Lacking eloquence and confidence, he admitted that he "was clearly not a born politician," but neither quality was necessary for holding the seat for Algoma East, a sparsely populated 20,000-square-mile constituency in northwestern Ontario. Throughout his parliamentary career he stressed that Canada must take the "high road" in solving international problems. He encouraged his colleagues in Parliament to debate international issues, but most showed little interest because of the noncontroversial nature of Canadian foreign policy, which could be summarized as (1) maintenance of Canadian national unity, (2) promotion of political liberty, (3) acceptance of the rule of law in national and international affairs, (4) acceptance of Christian principles as a guide in international relations, and (5) acceptance of international responsibilities.

As a result of Cold War tensions, Canada, like the other nations of the Atlantic community, sought security in the North Atlantic Treaty Organization (NATO). Pearson admitted that NATO was born of fear, but he also had high expectations of transforming the defense treaty into something more. His principal contribution is evident in Article Two, which reflected Canada's fear that Quebec would reject the treaty if it was presented as an exclusively military agreement; Pearson believed that the treaty should become the basis of an Atlantic community with social and economic components. Despite initial opposition, the Europeans and the Americans agreed to its inclusion. In subsequent years, Pearson lobbied for the implementation of Article Two, but further cooperation and unity proved impossible. He would write that he "remained on the side of the angels, however remote they were," and he would later admit that the "spirit to implement the economic aspects of Article 2 was *never* there."

By 1952 Lester Pearson was well known in the international community. He had friends in Washington, London, and the other capitals of the world, and his unceasing support for international cooperation would eventually lead to his election as president of the United Nations General Assembly in 1952. He assumed the presidency at a very difficult time in the UN's history; it was still at war in Korea, and assembly debates had degenerated into point-of-order polemics. Pearson was determined to end the interminable wrangling over procedure, and he successfully restored order to the assembly. His accomplishment would prompt some to promote him for the post of secretary general, but it was unattainable because of Soviet opposition. Political squabbling did not end at the United Nations, and Pearson heatedly supported Canada's role in the UN and in the Korean War whenever either former prime minister Mackenzie King or other members of the Liberal party questioned it. He asserted that Canada's participation in the League of Nations and later in the United Nations reflected the nation's political and national orientation at the time. He reminded Mackenzie King that the League of Nations and the United Nations were different creatures, and bolstered his point by adding:

At that time [referring to Canada's participation in the League], many people in Canada thought that we could remain aloof from the approaching struggle [World War II], and that our participation arose in part, through our membership in the Commonwealth. Now the pressures were all from Washington, not London, and it would be extremely difficult for us to isolate ourselves from United States policies because of continental considerations. On the other hand, as the enemy this time would be Russian Communism, feeling in Canada would be united in opposition to that enemy. (Quoted in English, *Shadow of Heaven*, p. 329)

This argument clearly indicates Pearson's inherent pragmatism and general approach to Canadian external relations—Canada was a small nation, and it had to play its role in the context of the prevailing international situation.

Throughout the Korean crisis, Pearson argued, "Our defence in this conflict must mean increasing and then maintaining our strength, while always keeping open the channels of negotiations and diplomacy" (Pearson, *Words and Occasions*, p. 102). He encouraged Canadians to "accept without reservation the view that the Canadian who fires his rifle in Korea or on the Elbe is defending his home as surely as if he were firing it on his own soil" (Pearson, *Words and Occasions*, p. 103). Similarly, he recognized that Canada's relationship with the United States was bound to get closer, and he expressed the hope that Canadians and Americans would continue to exhibit evidence of "mutual understanding and fundamental friendliness."

The real test of Pearson's mettle was the Suez crisis. He was one of the few in the United Nations who had faith in the ability of the organization to settle international conflicts. The Canadian government regarded the Suez crisis as a direct challenge to Anglo-American cooperation and the existence of the Commonwealth. With the support of Prime Minister Louis St. Laurent and the Canadian cabinet, Pearson urged the creation of a UN force to police the Suez.

Despite resistance from Britain, France, and the United States, he introduced the Canadian resolution on November 2, 1956, calling for an immediate cease-fire, military withdrawal, and the creation of a United Nations Emergency Force to police the disputed area. The resolution passed handily; the UN Command was organized, and in November 1956 advance units of the United Nations Emergency Force were in the Suez area. His perseverance and commitment to international peace were rewarded with the Nobel Peace Prize for 1957.

In his acceptance speech at Aula University in Oslo, Pearson reiterated his faith in international cooperation:

The stark and inescapable fact is that today we cannot defend our society by war, since total war is total destruction, and if war is used as an instrument of policy, eventually we will have total war. Therefore, the best defence of peace is not power, but the removal of the causes of war, and international agreements which will put peace on a stronger foundation than the terror of destruction. (Pearson, *Mike*, vol. 2, p. 313)

The Nobel Peace Prize crowned three decades of diplomatic service. During that time he had prevailed on diplomats and heads of state to see the world as a community. He urged peace and order, and held true to his Methodist principles to improve Canadian society and the international community.

Pearson's international record had not gone unnoticed in the Liberal party of Canada, which during the late 1950s was facing a renewed challenge from the Conservatives. The debate on the trans-Canada pipeline and Canadian defense policy had taken its toll, and in June 1957 the Liberals were ousted by the conservative populist John Diefenbaker. Pearson turned over the Department of External Affairs to Diefenbaker and for the first time in his life had little to occupy himself with.

After Louis St. Laurent's resignation in the fall of 1957, Pearson was drawn into the Liberal party leadership race. To many in the party, his international and domestic prestige made him the ideal candidate to beat Diefenbaker in the next general election. In January 1958 the party confirmed Pearson as its new leader. Although the party had high expectations, Pearson failed to match Diefenbaker's forceful debating style. Diefenbaker's minority government eventually fell in February 1963 because of its ill-defined defense policy. The following April Pearson formed a minority government. But the Pearson years marked a difficult time in Canada's history because of national unity and social security problems.

In 1963 French-Canadian nationalists foreswore graffiti for explosives. As the bombs of the Front de Libération du Québec (FLQ) punctuated Canadian politics, Pearson hastily developed a solution in the form of bilingualism. Although the measure was unpopular in certain quarters, it set the tone for future French-English relations while also paving the way for Pierre Trudeau's policy of multiculturalism. Bilingualism, to a long-experienced diplomat who had personally participated in conflict resolution, seemed the obvious solution to a sticky political question. English-Canadians had dominated Canadian national affairs. They had set the pattern of national development and constantly reminded French-Canadians of their limited role in the Canadian union. Pearson's contribution to social peace and Canadian unity was to draw French Canada into the administrative process. In his opening address at the Federal-Provincial Conference in Charlottetown on September 1, 1964, Pearson challenged the provincial premiers to demonstrate "a sense of political realism, a passion for justice, and a gift for compromise." He reminded the premiers that "first among our national goals, the prerequisite to all others, economic, social, or cultural[,] is national unity." He added: "This does not mean and cannot mean uniformity. It does mean Canadian identity, with the symbols and even more the spirit and the pride to foster such identity," (Pearson, *Words and Occasions*, p. 235).

The separatist threat had convinced Pearson that a nation needed national symbols, and the most important for Canada was a flag symbolizing the Canadian experience rather than the British past. The flag debate, which the *Montreal Gazette* described as "an emotional donnybrook of parliamentary and national debate," revealed the distress caused by a dearth of national symbols. As the new flag was officially unfurled on February 15, 1965, Pearson spoke to the nation and expressed his respect for past traditions and the creation of a new future. "As the symbol of a new chapter in our national story," he emphasized, "our Maple Leaf Flag will become a symbol of that unity in our country without which one cannot grow in strength and purpose; the unity that encourages the equal partnership of two peoples on which this Confederation was founded; the unity also that recognizes the contributions and the cultures of many other races" (Matheson, p. 184).

The raising of a new flag was certainly a milestone in Canada's national progress and in Lester Pearson's career. He had devoted his life to resolving disputes, searching for agreement, and avoiding controversy. His most difficult crisis as prime minister came on July 24, 1967, when *Charles de Gaulle addressed Quebeckers with the slogan of Quebec separatists, "Vive le Québec libre!" De Gaulle's affront to Canadians and the federal government of Canada marked a low point in Franco-Canadian relations. Yet the real challenge to Canadian unity came from the provincial government of Quebec, led by Premier Daniel Johnson. Johnson, speaking for many French-Canadians, demanded "equality or independence," and the Pearson government responded by hosting a constitutional conference in February 1968. While the conference failed to resolve the issue, it did reveal that diplomacy could successfully diffuse emotions and avoid a confrontation. This conference was Pearson's last major public activity. On April 6, 1968, he resigned as the leader of the Liberal party of Canada.

Over the course of the next few months, Pearson settled his retirement plans. After having pondered several offers from Canadian and American universities, he finally accepted an appointment to the Commission on International Development for the World Bank. The commission's work was hardly nonpolitical, and Pearson's skill as a negotiator and arbitrator was challenged. His contribution is reflected in the first chapter of the commission's report, *Partners in Development*, published in October 1969. After serving on the commission, Pearson accepted an appointment as professor at Carleton University in Ottawa. Between seminars he turned his attention to his memoirs and sports, the latter having been a longtime fascination. During the last years of his life he struggled with cancer and threw himself into completing his memoirs. On December 27, 1972, Pearson died.

To a large extent, Lester Pearson represented the essential dichotomy of Canada. He combined the best qualities of the Canadian character; his informality and congeniality attracted warm praise from diplomats and world leaders, but his reserve and lack of emotionalism, valuable qualities on the international stage, puzzled a nation that was struggling to define itself. His leadership attributes aside, Pearson established national and philosophical guideposts for Canadians to follow.

Annotated Bibliography

Pearson's private papers are held by the Public Archives of Canada, Ottawa, but as of this writing they are not yet open to public examination. Other primary material is easily accessible, and the reader's attention is drawn to Lester Pearson's Scrapbook (Public Archives of Canada, MG26 N12); the files of prime ministers Mackenzie King and Louis St. Laurent (Public Archives of Canada, MG26); the files of the Department of External Affairs and Norman Robertson; and *Hansard* of the Canadian House of Commons and Senate. The University of Toronto Archives, Toronto, holds the papers of the department of history. Some material is available in non-Canadian archives, and the reader is directed to the college records of St. John's College, Oxford, for personal information on Pearson's term at Oxford University. Additional material is found in the Public Records Office in Britain, but the material is scattered in the files of a number of departments; the most valuable material can be found in the records of the Foreign Office.

The most useful sources of information on Lester Pearson are undoubtedly his speeches and the first volume of his autobiography, entitled *Mike: The Memoirs of the Rt. Hon. Lester B. Pearson* (1973). Volume 1 of this three-volume set provides insight into Pearson's character and intellectual position on international and domestic issues. The second and third volumes were compiled by Pearson's literary executors, Alex Inglis and John Munro, who drew upon his drafts and secondary works. These last two volumes provide an episodic account of Pearson's career after 1948, but the editors fail to match the simple and revealing style of the first volume. Pearson's writings succinctly summarize the major points in his career while revealing the development of ideas on subjects as diverse as religion and international diplomacy. The reader is directed to his published books: *Democracy in World Politics* (1955), *Diplomacy in the Nuclear Age* (1959), *Peace in the Family of Man: The Reith Lectures 1968* (1969), and *Words and Occasions* (1970).

A number of biographical works were published during his lifetime that are satisfactory in the general sense only, the earliest being John Beals's *The Pearson Phenomenon* (1964), which brings Pearson's story to 1963. A complementary volume, *Mr Pearson and Canada's Revolution by Diplomacy* (1966) by W. Burton Ayre, takes the reader as far as the first few years of Pearson's involvement in Canadian politics. Both works provide useful background information, but their general tone is laudatory. Pearson's political colleagues have contributed critical firsthand accounts of his management of Canadian domestic politics. Judy LaMarsh's *Memoirs of a Bird in a Gilded Cage* (1968) is an impressionistic assessment of Pearson's political style and weaknesses. Walter Gordon, another cabinet colleague, was similarly dissatisfied with Pearson's political management; his reflections are explored in *A Political Memoir* (1977) and in Denis Smith's *Gentle Patriot: A Political Biography of Walter Gordon* (1973). The latest Pearson biography is by John English, *Shadow of Heaven: The Life of Lester Pearson*, 2 vols. (1989). Pearson's Protestant roots, general cultural orientation in Victorian and Edwardian Canada, and Oxford experience shaped his philosophy and outlook on international affairs.

Pearson's diplomatic record is adequately covered in the multivolume *Canada in World Affairs* (1941–1973). The first four volumes review the period 1919 to 1946 and trace the various stages of Canadian international awareness. Volumes 5 through 8 cover the period between 1946 and 1955 and are especially useful since they describe Pearson's years as secretary of state for external affairs and the campaign he waged for world peace through international organizations like the United Nations, the North Atlantic Treaty Organization, and the Commonwealth. This series is complemented by Vincent Massey's *What's Past Is Prologue* (1963) and by R. A. Mackay's *Canadian Foreign Policy, 1945–54* (1971). The former provides information on Pearson's role in the Canadian High Commission in London. The latter, more useful from the viewpoint of Pearson's contribution to the evolution of postwar international affairs, reprints Pearson's major policy statements and speeches on the United Nations, the North Atlantic Treaty Organization, the Korean War, and Canadian foreign policy. His contribution to the settlement of the Suez crisis is revealed in a Canadian government publication, *The Crisis in the Middle East: October-December, 1956, January-March 1957* (1957), and reviewed in three major works: Robert W. Reford, *Canada and Three Crises* (1968); Mortimer Lipsky, *Quest for Peace: The Story of the Nobel Award* (1966); and J. L. Granatstein, ed., *Canadian Foreign Policy Since 1945: Middle Power or Satellite?* (1969). All three of these works give the Canadian perspective of the crisis, but Lipsky and Granatstein describe the crisis in the context of international relations and Canadian foreign policy during the 1950s. E.L.M. Burns, the commander of the United Nations Emergency Force, in a chapter entitled "Pearson and the Gaza Strip, 1957" in *Freedom and Change: Essays in Honour of Lester B. Pearson* (1975), also puts the crisis in perspective and confirms that Pearson's solution reflected his religious values and lifelong quest for international peace. The American perspective on the Korean War and the Suez crisis and Pearson's involvement is found in Dean Acheson's *Present at the Creation: My Years in the State Department* (1969). Acheson acknowledges that he and Pearson disagreed sharply on methods for resolving these crises and reveals that Pearson strove to keep open the channels of negotiation while asserting Canadian independence on questions of international importance.

Bibliography

Government Publications

Canada and Post-war Organizations. Ottawa: Canadian Information Bureau, 1945.
The Crisis in the Middle East: October-December, 1956, January-March 1957. Ottawa: Queen's Printer, 1957.

Series

Canada in World Affairs. 17 vols. New York: Oxford University Press, 1941–1973.

Works by Lester Pearson

Pearson, Lester. *Democracy in World Politics*. Toronto: Saunders, 1955.
————. *Diplomacy in the Nuclear Age*. Toronto: Saunders, 1959.
————. *Four Faces of Peace and the International Outlook*. Toronto: McClelland and Stewart, 1964.
————. *The Free Press: A Reflection of Democracy*. Williamsburg, Va.: Colonial Williamsburg, 1958.
————. *Mike: The Memoirs of the Rt. Hon. Lester B. Pearson*. 3 vols. Edited by John A. Munro and Alex I. Inglis. Toronto: University of Toronto, 1973. Reprint. Scarborough, Ont.: New American Library of Canada, 1975.
————. *Partners in Development: Report of the Commission on International Development*. New York: Praeger, 1969.
————. *Peace in the Family of Man: The Reith Lectures 1968*. London: BBC, 1969.
————. *Where Do We Go from Here? A Lecture*. Minneapolis: University of Minnesota Press, 1957.
————. *Words and Occasions: An Anthology of Speeches and Articles Selected from His Papers by the Right Honourable L. B. Pearson*. Toronto: University of Toronto Press, 1970.

Secondary Sources

Acheson, Dean. *Present at the Creation: My Years in the State Department*. New York: Norton, 1969.
Ayre, W. Burton. *Mr Pearson and Canada's Revolution by Diplomacy*. Montreal: N.p., 1966.
Beals, John. *The Pearson Phenomenon*. Toronto: Longmans, 1964.
Bothwell, Robert. *Pearson: His Life and World*. Edited by W. Kaye Lamb. Toronto: McGraw-Hill Ryerson, 1978.
Burns, E.L.M. "Pearson and the Gaza Strip, 1957." In *Freedom and Change: Essays in Honour of Lester B. Pearson*. Edited by Michael G. Fry. Toronto: McClelland and Stewart, 1975.
English, John. *Shadow of Heaven: The Life of Lester Pearson*. 2 vols. Toronto: Lester and Opren Dennys, 1989.
Fry, Michael G., ed. *Freedom and Change: Essays in Honour of Lester B. Pearson*. Toronto: McClelland and Stewart, 1975.
Gordon, Walter. *A Political Memoir*. Toronto: McClelland and Stewart, 1977.
Granatstein, J. L., ed. *Canadian Foreign Policy Since 1945: Middle Power or Satellite?* Toronto: Copp Clark, 1969.
LaMarsh, Judy. *Memoirs of a Bird in a Gilded Cage*. Toronto: McClelland and Stewart, 1968.
Lipsky, Mortimer. *Quest for Peace: The Story of the Nobel Award*. South Brunswick, N.J.: Barnes, 1966.
Mackay, R. A. *Canadian Foreign Policy, 1945–54*. Toronto: McClelland and Stewart, 1971.
Massey, Vincent. *What's Past Is Prologue: The Memoirs of the Right Honourable Vincent Massey*. New York: Macmillan, 1963.
Matheson, John Ross. *Canada's Flag: A Search for a Country*. Boston: Hall, 1980.
Reford, Robert W. *Canada and Three Crises*. Toronto: Canadian Institute of International Affairs, 1968.

Smith, Denis. *Gentle Patriot: A Political Biography of Walter Gordon.* Edmonton: Hurtig, 1973.
Stursberg, Peter. *Lester Pearson and the American Dilemma.* Toronto: Doubleday Canada, 1980.
———. *Lester Pearson and the Dream of Unity.* Toronto: Doubleday Canada, 1978.
Thordarson, Bruce. *Lester Pearson: Diplomat and Politician.* Toronto: Oxford University Press, 1974.

MARIJAN SALOPEK

Peter the Great (1672–1725). In the long line of Russian rulers, Peter the Great occupies a unique position. When he came to power, Russia, as compared to western Europe, was still a medieval and backward nation. Occupied by the Mongols at a time when the Renaissance was changing the European outlook and laying the foundations of the great scientific achievements of the sixteenth and seventeenth centuries, Russia was still set in its old ways. Although the Muscovite rulers had overthrown the Mongol yoke and unified the country, Russia did not count for much in European affairs. The long and savage Thirty Years' War (1618–1648) had left a continent dominated by two great powers, France and Sweden. Peter's lasting achievement would be not only to modernize Russia but also to transform it into a great European power.

Peter was born on May 30, 1672 (O.S.), the first child of Tsar Alexis's second wife, Natalia Naryshkin. With his first wife, Maria Miloslavskii, Alexis had several daughters, the eldest of whom was Sophia, and two sons, Fedor and Ivan. Inevitably, even while Peter's father was still alive, the court factions centering on the Miloslavskii and Naryshkin families contended for power and influence. On Alexis's death in 1676, the eldest son, Fedor, though physically weak, became the tsar. But he died in 1682 without leaving an heir.

Thus Peter was only ten years old when the Kremlin saw an open and violent power struggle between the Naryshkins and Miloslavskiis, who were now supported by the *streltsy*, the special regiments created in the sixteenth century by Ivan IV. The young Peter witnessed the brutal killings of several of the Naryshkin faction, including his mother's former guardian, Artamon Matveev. Although the struggle ended in making Peter and his mentally handicapped half-brother Ivan co-tsars, these unnecessary and savage killings created a deep and lasting impression on him. In the words of Vasili Kliuchevskii, the most respected Russian historian, "he had seen medieval Russia at her worst." The bloody events of 1682, in fact, developed in him a deep hatred toward the *streltsy* and a strong revulsion against the Kremlin and its politics.

During the next seven years, when Peter's half-sister Sophia acted as regent, Peter spent most of his time in the nearby village of Preobrazhenskoe. Because of neglect, he had failed to get a good education even before the 1682 events; this continued to be the case. But Peter used his own devices to acquaint himself with military matters and Western technology. While in Preobrazhenskoe, he amused himself with live "toy" soldiers and later organized them in two well-trained battalions. He gained a rudimentary knowledge of Western science, military technology, and shipbuilding from foreigners, mainly German and Dutch, who lived in the nearby German settlement.

In organizing his battalions at Preobrazhenskoe, Peter showed another important characteristic: his belief in hard work and merit as a measuring stick of one's usefulness. Promotion in the army had to be earned, not awarded on the basis of one's birth. In order to set an example for Russia's noblemen, he worked with his hands, ate common food, and lived in a tent like any other soldier. In addition, he started at the lowest grade as a drummer boy and only later promoted himself. In a society in which the old system of *mestnichestvo* awarded high offices on the basis of noble birth, Peter's emphasis on training and merit had far-reaching consequences.

In 1689 a number of events affected Peter. In January he married Eudoxia Lopukhina, a court official's daughter, with whom he had a son, Alexis, a year later. In August 1689, while at Preobrazhenskoe, he was awakened and told that the *streltsy*, at the orders of Sophia, were on their way to kill him. He took shelter at the Monastery of the Trinity in the northeast, where he was joined by his "toy" regiments, his mother, and the Patriarch. Sophia quickly lost support and was imprisoned in the Novodevichy Convent in Moscow. Peter's mother now served as regent. Her death in 1694, and that of Ivan in 1696, left Peter as the sole ruler of Russia.

Eager to acquire Western knowledge and to seek European allies against Turkey, Peter undertook a long journey to the West in 1697–1698. Traveling with a large Russian delegation as an ordinary member under the assumed name of Peter Mikhailov, he spent several months in Holland learning shipbuilding. He also attended lectures on anatomy, saw operations performed, visited factories and schools, and showed unending curiosity in the Dutch military establishment. He went to England, where he studied naval architecture and the manufacture of ordnance. Peter then journeyed to Austria and Prussia and was about to go to Italy when he learned of a revolt by the *streltsy*. Although the revolt had already been crushed, he hurried home to destroy the *streltsy* forever; but the way he accomplished this showed clearly the savage side of his character as well as the fact that he was ready to deal with anyone who opposed him or his policies in a brutal and merciless manner. Even Patriarch Adrian's intercession could not stop him from publicly beheading the condemned members of the *streltsy*. Eventually, about two thousand fell victim to his ferocity. The act of punishment had turned into a massacre. Not finding any strong evidence for Sophia's complicity, Peter forced her to become a nun. He now enjoyed unchallenged power.

A very important part of Peter's work consisted of acquiring territories on the Black Sea in the south and on the Baltic in the north in order to establish direct links with central and western Europe. Just before he left for his European journey in 1697, he captured Azov on the Black Sea from the Turks. This acquisition was formalized in a treaty the two countries signed in July 1700.

Although Peter had failed to acquire allies against Turkey during his stay in Europe, he did enter into an alliance with Augustus II, King of Poland and elector of Saxony, and with Denmark against the youthful Swedish ruler, Charles XII. But while Augustus and the Danes entered the Great Northern War in early 1700, Peter waited until after the signing of his treaty with Turkey to join the fray. Charles XII, however, proved a tough adversary. He forced Denmark out of the war and then, piercing through a fierce snowstorm, inflicted a humiliating defeat on the Russian army at Narva. It is hard to predict what the outcome would have been had he decided to continue his march toward Moscow, but he suddenly turned toward Poland in order to deal with it first. One of the reasons for the Swedish ruler's decision was the low esteem in which he held the Russians, who appeared to him "something between incendiaries and vermin"; therefore, there was no glory in pursuing such a "wretched force."

Charles XII's decision to turn against Poland was a blessing for Peter, which he exploited to the fullest with great determination, inexhaustible energy, and imagination. From the melting of church bells to replace lost artillery to insisting that individuals of noble background rise in rank only after proper training (as well as enabling commoners to become officers), Peter soon succeeded in recruiting and training a large and efficient army.

As Charles XII became bogged down in his struggle against Poland, Peter used his new army to make inroads into Livonia and Estonia and to defeat the Swedes and establish his predominance over the Gulf of Finland. In 1703 he founded the city of St. Petersburg on the Neva River as his future capital and, in order to protect it, constructed a fortress on Kronstadt Island. He also rapidly built a navy in the Baltic Sea.

Finally defeating Poland in 1706, Charles turned toward Moscow. Rather than attack from the north, he decided to go to the south into the Ukraine, hoping to get the support of the Cossacks and the Ukrainians. But the Russians succeeded in destroying some of his supplies at Lesnaia in September 1708, and though the Cossack leader Hetman Ivan Mazepa supported Charles, the majority of the Ukrainians still remained loyal to Peter. The two armies finally faced each other at Poltava in the Ukraine in July 1709.

Long before the idea of nationalism took root in the European consciousness, Peter exhorted his soldiers at Poltava to fight not for him but for "the fate of the whole fatherland," emphasizing that "either Russia will perish or she will be reborn in nobler shape." In this historic battle, Peter's larger force decisively defeated a depleted Swedish army. The Russian ruler was ecstatic. Many of the reforms he had undertaken since his disastrous defeat at Narva, as well as the indefatigable courage and determination he now showed, brought about this great victory. He showed his debt to the Swedes as "his teachers in the art of war" by proposing a toast to them at a victory feast. The rest of Europe could hardly believe that the Russians had inflicted such a humiliating defeat on Sweden.

Peter's great victory at Poltava was complicated by Turkey's entry into the war. Rather than make peace with the Turks at a time when he was still at war with Sweden, an overconfident Peter sought to enter the Balkans, hoping to incite Turkey's Christian subjects. In appeals such as his "Proclamation to the

Montenegrin People'' and ''Proclamation to the Christian Peoples under Turkish Rule,'' Peter called for armed rebellion against the Islamic authorities. He not only miscalculated the possibility of such revolts taking place, he also encountered problems such as supplying his army. In July 1711 he found himself facing a larger Turkish force on the Pruth River. A short but bitter fight threatened total Russian defeat and surrender. In a mood of desperation, he tried to extricate himself by offering peace to the Turks on their terms. Although he had instructed his emissary to ''agree to all they demand, apart from slavery,'' his main loss, as agreed to in the Treaty of Pruth (1711), was Azov, the Black Sea fortress that he had taken from them earlier. Other terms of the treaty included his promise of safe passage home for Charles XII, who after Poltava had taken refuge with the Porte. In questions of war and peace, the choice is not always between victory and defeat but often between the lesser of two evils. Peter wisely chose a humiliating treaty in order to escape an impossible situation and concentrate on his more important objectives in the north.

The Russian army, in fact, was already acquiring new territories on the Baltic. In 1710 it had captured Viborg, Riga, and Reval. In 1713 Peter's forces conquered southern Finland, and in 1714 his Baltic fleet won a major naval victory over the Swedes at Hangö. But the war still dragged on despite more territorial gains by Russia. Charles's death in 1718 could have led to peace, but the Swedes, now assisted by the British, continued the struggle. When Peter finally decided to invade Sweden proper, the Swedes were ready to end the long conflict. In the Treaty of Nystadt (1721) Peter obtained more than he had aspired to when he first entered the Great Northern War in 1700. In addition to Livonia and Estonia, Russia got Ingria and part of Karelia including Viborg. Russia now enjoyed virtual domination over the Gulf of Finland.

Characterized by Voltaire as Peter's noblest triumph, the Treaty of Nystadt marked a new era in Russian history in another respect. The Russian Senate named him emperor of all the Russias, a title that other European emperors, like the Habsburgs, came to accept only grudgingly. This also marked the beginning of the imperial period in Russian history. The Senate also conferred the appellation ''Great'' upon Peter at this time.

Peter's success in foreign affairs was not confined to his acquisitions from Sweden. His efforts to establish links with China resulted in the Treaty of Kiakhta in 1727, establishing important trade links with Beijing. He encouraged further exploration of Siberia and obtained from Persia territory along the Caspian Sea, including the important port of Baku.

The steps Peter undertook to create a modern and efficient army were directly related to his war efforts. No doubt Russia had large armies before, but they were normally recruited for specific campaigns and disbanded after those campaigns were over. Peter introduced the modern system of conscription, eventually drafting one soldier from every seventy-five serf households. The service-gentry class, which was already obligated to serve the state, now fell under more stringent regulations. Furthermore, members of this privileged class, like the serfs, had to start from the bottom and then rise in rank according to their merit. Peter set an example by accepting the rank of general only after the victory at Poltava and of admiral only after the Treaty of Nystadt.

In the case of the Russian navy, it was truly Peter's own creation. Inheriting only one obsolete vessel, he left to his successors a relatively powerful navy consisting of more than 800 major warships and minor craft. Although Russian seamanship was not yet of the highest quality and many ships built at this time were defective, the navy contributed its share to Russia's victory in the Great Northern War.

Ravaged by syphilis, Peter had been in declining health for several years. His health was further undermined by a severe cold contracted while attempting to rescue soldiers whose boat had capsized in the Gulf of Finland, and he died on January 28, 1725 (O.S.).

A man of inexhaustible energy and determination, Peter succeeded, in a span of only a quarter century, in fulfilling all his ambitions on the Baltic. Russia now came to replace Sweden as a great European power. Theophan Prokopovich, Peter's advisor on church affairs, was not off the mark when he said in his eulogy that Peter had "found but little strength" in Russia but succeeded in making its "power strong like a rock and diamond." On the territory he won from Sweden, he built his new capital as a living symbol of his orientation toward the West. Symbolizing Peter's vision, determination, and an enduring legacy to his country, St. Petersburg stands even today as one of the most beautiful cities of Europe.

While there is hardly any dispute regarding the significance of his accomplishment in creating a modern army and navy, and the remarkable military victories that they made possible, the nature and impact of his reforms aroused a great deal of controversy in his own time. Burdened with ever increasing demands for money and men for his wars, the peasantry suffered immeasurably. A budget that was largely devoted to the war effort had no resources left for improving the lives of the common people. Peter did nothing to change the oppressive institution of serfdom, and his emphasis on shaving beards and giving up old Muscovite clothing, both of which had deep religious significance for the people, led to widespread hostility against him. For many he had become a "bloodsucker" and Antichrist.

Moreover, Peter's reforms touched only the elite of Russian society. Members of this elite were the ones that imbibed some Western cultural traits. This in itself was not insignificant, as it allowed the ideas of the Enlightenment to penetrate into Russia. But, as a whole, Peter's policies created a wide chasm between the elite and the common people.

Although Peter was attempting to break with Russia's Muscovite past, in one respect he followed the old Russian tradition. He did not hesitate to use maximum force, as was the case in his treatment of the rebellious *streltsy*, in order to suppress opposition. Even his reforms, in the Muscovite tradition, were imposed on the people. He also tortured and eventually caused the death of his only son, Alexis, for alleged acts of treason against him.

Peter was both admired and hated not only in his own time but by later generations of Russians as well. His attempt to reform Russia by importing European ideas and technology raised the fundamental question of the concept of Russia itself—whether it was a part of Europe or a world of its own, quite distinct from Europe or Asia. In the nineteenth century Peter became a focus of debate between the Westernizers and the Slavophiles at a time when the Russian intelligentsia fiercely argued about the path the country must take for its salvation—should it turn to the West or look to its own heritage and traditions?

Peter himself was no blind admirer of Europe. He was attracted most by its large and well-built ships, its powerful guns, its advances in medicine, its great scientific achievements, and several fascinating aspects of its culture, but not by such institutions as the English Parliament. Selectively borrowing what he found useful in order to overcome his country's backwardness, he tried to create a new Russia. Although he did not fully succeed, he still left a rich and enduring legacy. In his total dedication to his country's welfare, he also remains one of the earlier examples of an enlightened despot whose policies truly changed the course of Russian history.

Annotated Bibliography

Unpublished archival materials dealing with Peter the Great are located almost exclusively in the former Soviet Union. Undoubtedly the most important repository is Tsentral'nyi Gosudarstvennyi Arkhiv Drevnikh Aktov (Central State Archive of Ancient Acts, or TsGADA), located in Moscow at 17 Bol'shaia Pirogovskaia Street. Within TsGADA there are two major collections. The first is the State Archives of the Russian Empire, or Gosarkhiv, which holds a variety of papers; the second is the Moscow Main Archive of the Ministry of Foreign Affairs, which focuses on foreign policy papers.

Additional papers dealing with international matters can be found in Arkhiv Vneshnei Politki Rossii (Archive of Russian Foreign Policy, or AVPR). This repository is located in Moscow at 15 Bol'shaia Serpukhovskaia Street. Some important sources concerning Peter's military policy are found at Tsentral'nyi Gosudarstvennyi Voenno-Istoricheskii Arkhiv SSSR (Central State Military History Archive of the USSR, or TsGVIA SSSR), which is now located in the prerevolutionary Lefort Palace.

Of the published primary sources on the Petrine period, perhaps the most important is Peter's *Pisma i bumagi Imperatora Petra Velikogo* (1887–1977), which unfortunately covers events only until 1712. Another valuable source is M. M. Bogoslovskii, *Petr I, Materialy dlia biografii*, 5 vols. (1940–1948). The 148-volume collection published by the Imperial Russian Historical Society, *Sbornik Imperatorskogo Russkogo Istoricheskogo Obshchestva* (1867–1916), is indispensable for the study of Peter's foreign policy. N. A. Voskresenskii, ed., *Zakonodatelnye akty Petra I* (1945), and V. I. Lebedev, ed., *Reformy Petra I: Sbornik dokumentov* (1937), contain useful collections of legislative acts and important documentary material on the period. An excellent English translation of Peter's work that became the basis of his church reform is *The Spiritual Regulation of Peter the Great*, edited and translated by Alexander V. Muller (1972). A collection of Peter's army regulations can be found in N. L. Rubinshtein and P. P. Epifanov, eds., *Voennie ustavy Petra Velikogo* (1946). Also significant is a work written by I. T. Pososhkov, a government official during Peter's rule, that discusses the inefficiency and corruption in the administration and is highly critical of the clergy. His *Kniga o skudosti i bogatstve i drugei sochineniia* (1951) also suggests reforms to overcome these deficiencies.

Although accounts by foreigners living in or visiting Russia at this time must be used with caution, they nevertheless provide important sources of information. Peter Putnam, ed., *Seven Britons in Imperial Russia* (1952), and Johann Georg Korb, *Diary of an Austrian Secretary of Legation at the Court of Czar Peter the Great* (1968), are good examples of such sources. The sections dealing with the Petrine period in Francesca Wilson, *Muscovy: Russia Through Foreign Eyes, 1553–1900* (1970), are also valuable.

Because of the importance of this period in Russian history, as well as the fact that Peter's reforms aroused both admiration and criticism among the Russians, there is a vast amount of literature available. One of the best biographies is Alex de Jonge's *Fire and Water: A Life of Peter the Great* (1979), which places Peter and his work in the context of Russian historical traditions. M. S. Anderson's *Peter the Great* (1978) points to both Peter's failures and successes and makes liberal use of the observations of foreign visitors to Russia and of the dispatches sent by foreign diplomats in the Russian capital. L. Jay Oliva in his short but excellent study, *Russia in the Era of Peter the Great* (1969), avoids the temptation to link Petrine Russia to later periods, including the Soviet era. A recent popular biography is Robert K. Massie's *Peter the Great: His Life and World* (1980). Although the study presents a rather admiring and uncritical portrait of Peter, it gives a useful picture of the European world and places Peter's accomplishments in that context.

Among the biographies published in Russia, *Peter the Great* (1958) by V. O. Kliuchevskii is an outstanding work. Written by one of Russia's greatest historians and rich in detail, it is highly critical of Peter's excessive reliance on the use of force. Soviet historian N. Pavlenko's *Petr Pervyi* (1976) is written from a Marxist perspective. A more recent Soviet work is V. I. Buganov's *Petr Velikii i ego vremia* (1989).

On Peter's image among Russian historians and writers from 1700 to the Soviet period, the best study is Nicholas V. Riasanovsky, *The Image of Peter the Great in Russian History and Thought* (1985). Xenia Gasiorowska's *The Image of Peter the Great in Russian Fiction* (1979) confines itself to Russian fiction.

More specialized works on the period include B. H. Sumner's *Peter the Great and the Ottoman Empire* (1965); Sir J.A.R. Marriott's *Anglo-Russian Relations: 1689–1943* (1944); *History of the Russian Fleet During the Reign of Peter the Great, by a Contemporary Englishman*, edited by Vice Admiral Cyprian A.G. Bridge (1899); James Cracraft's authoritative works, *The Church Reform of Peter the Great* (1971) and *The Petrine Revolution in Russian Architecture* (1988); E. V. Tarle's *Severnaia Voina* (1958); and V. E. Vozgrin's *Rossiia i evropeiskie strany v gody Severnoi voiny: Istoriia diplomaticheskikh otnosheniia v 1697–1710 gg.* (1986). Two important articles by Max J. Okenfuss, "The Jesuit Origins of Petrine Education" and "Russian Students in Europe in the Age of Peter the Great," in *The Eighteenth Century in Russia*, edited by J. G. Garrard (1973), discuss a vital aspect of Peter's work. A Soviet writer of the glasnost era, Evgenii Anisimov, takes a dim view of Peter's accomplishments in his essay, "Progress Through Violence: From Peter the Great to Lenin and Stalin," *Russian History* 17 (1990): 409–418, pointing to the fact that Peter's role in Russian history will continue to be looked at differently by different generations of Russians.

Bibliography

Anderson, M. S. *Peter the Great*. London: Thames and Hudson, 1978.

Anisimov, Evgenii V. "Progress Through Violence: From Peter the Great to Lenin and Stalin." *Russian History* 17 (1990): 409–418.

———. *Vremia petrovskikh reform*. Leningrad: Leninzdat, 1989.

Barany, George. *The Anglo-Russian Entente Cordiale of 1697–1698: Peter I and William III at Utrecht*. Boulder, Colo.: East European Monographs, 1986.

Bengtsson, Frans G. *The Life of Charles XII*. Translated by Naomi Walford. London: Macmillan, 1960.

Bogoslovskii, M. M. *Petr I, Materialy dlia biografii*. 5 vols. Moscow: Sotsial'no-ekon, 1940–1948.

Bridge, Cyprian A.G., ed. *History of the Russian Fleet During the Reign of Peter the Great, by a Contemporary Englishman*. London: Navy Records Society, 1899.

Bromley, J. S., ed. *The Rise of Great Britain and Russia, 1688–1725. The New Cambridge Modern History*, vol. 6. Cambridge: Cambridge University Press, 1970.

Buganov, V. I. *Petr Velikii i ego vremia*. Moscow: Nauka, 1989.

Cracraft, James. *The Church Reform of Peter the Great*. Stanford, Calif.: Stanford University Press, 1971.

———. *The Petrine Revolution in Russian Architecture*. Chicago: University of Chicago Press, 1988.

De Grunwald, Constantin. *Peter the Great*. London: Saunders, MacGibbon and Kee, 1956.

De Jonge, Alex. *Fire and Water: A Life of Peter the Great*. New York: Coward, McCann and Geoghegan, 1979.

Gasiorowska, Xenia. *The Image of Peter the Great in Russian Fiction*. Madison: University of Wisconsin Press, 1979.

Kliuchevskii, Vasilii. *Peter the Great*. Translated by Liliana Archibald. New York: St. Martin's Press, 1958.

Korb, Johann Georg. *Diary of an Austrian Secretary of Legation at the Court of Czar Peter the Great*. Translated and edited by Count MacDonnel. 2 vols. in 1. London: Frank Cass, 1968.

Lebedev, V. I., ed. *Reformy Petra I: Sbornik dokumentov*. Moscow: Sotsial'no-ekon, 1937.

Marriott, J.A.R. *Anglo-Russian Relations: 1689–1943*. London: Methuen, 1944.

Massie, Robert K. *Peter the Great: His Life and World*. New York: Knopf, 1980.

Okenfuss, Max J. "The Jesuit Origins of Petrine Education." In *The Eighteenth Century in Russia*, pp. 106–130. Edited by J. G. Garrard. Oxford: Clarendon Press, 1973.

———. "Russian Students in Europe in the Age of Peter the Great." In *The Eighteenth Century in Russia*, pp. 131–145. Edited by J. G. Garrard. Oxford: Clarendon Press, 1973.

Oliva, L. Jay. *Russia in the Era of Peter the Great*. Englewood Cliffs, N.J.: Prentice-Hall, 1969.

Pavlenko, N. *Petr Pervyi*. 2nd rev. ed. Moscow: Molodaia Gvardiia, 1976.

Peter I. *Pisma i bumagi Imperatora Petra Velikogo*. 12 vols. in 19. Moscow: Nauka, 1887–1977.

———. *The Spiritual Regulation of Peter the Great*. Edited and translated by Alexander V. Muller. Seattle: University of Washington Press, 1972.

Pososhkov, I. T. *Kniga o skudosti i bogatstve i drugei sochineniia*. Moscow: Nauka, 1951.
Putnam, Peter, ed. *Seven Britons in Imperial Russia*. Princeton, N.J.: Princeton University Press, 1952.
Riasanovsky, Nicholas V. *The Image of Peter the Great in Russian History and Thought*. New York: Oxford University Press, 1985.
Rubinshtein, N. L., and P. P. Epifanov, eds. *Voennie ustavy Petra Velikogo*. Moscow: Biblioteka Lenina, 1946.
Sumner, B. H. *Peter the Great and the Emergence of Russia*. New York: Collier, 1965.
Sumner, B. H. *Peter the Great and the Ottoman Empire*. Hamden, Conn.: Archon, 1965.
Tarle, E. V. *Severnaia Voina i Shvedskoe Nashestvie na Rossiiu*. Moscow: Sotsial'no-ekon, 1958.
Voskresenskii, N. A., ed. *Zakonodatelnye akty Petra I*. Moscow: Nauka, 1945.
Vozgrin, V. E. *Rossiia i evropeiskie strany v gody Severnoi voiny: Istoriia diplomaticheskikh otnosheniia v 1697–1710 gg*. Leningrad: Nauka, 1986.
Wilson, Francesca. *Muscovy: Russia Through Foreign Eyes, 1553–1900*. London: Allen and Unwin, 1970.

SURENDRA K. GUPTA

Philip II (1527–1598).   Philip II of Spain was the first sovereign in world history to rule an empire on which the sun never set, with dominions in Europe, Africa, Asia, and the Americas. He consolidated during his long reign what diplomatic historians call "the Spanish hegemony" in European affairs.

Philip was born on May 21, 1527, in Valladolid, and died on September 13, 1598, at the Escorial. His father was Holy Roman Emperor *Charles V, his mother, Isabel of Portugal. His parents supervised his education by learned tutors and themselves played significant roles. Because Charles was often absent, Isabel had much to do with the formation of Philip's character, which was dignified, courteous, and reserved. In matters of statecraft, Charles's influence was paramount.

Philip was married four times, first in 1543 to Maria Manuela of Portugal, who died in 1545 after giving birth to the unfortunate Don Carlos (d. 1568). His second wife was Queen Mary Tudor of England (1516–1558); they had no children. His third was Elisabeth de Valois (1546–1568); they had two daughters, Isabel Clara Eugenia (1566–1633) and Catalina (1567–1597), to whom he wrote letters that reveal him as a loving father. His fourth wife, Ana of Austria (1549–1580), bore five children, but only the future Philip III (1578–1621) lived long.

The statecraft of both Charles and Philip was determined first and foremost by Charles's vast and widespread inheritance, of which Philip received the Burgundian Netherlands, where Charles was born; the Franche-Comté; Castile and its possessions in the New World; Aragon; Sicily; Naples; and Sardinia. In addition Philip received Milan, which Charles acquired in 1535. In 1580 he annexed Portugal and its empire to his holdings.

Charles V had also inherited the Habsburg Austrian duchies, but assigned them in 1522 to his brother Ferdinand, who in 1526 added to them Bohemia and what remained of Hungary after it was overrun by the Ottoman Turks. Philip and his Spanish Habsburg successors worked closely with the Austrian Habsburgs descended from Ferdinand to preserve and advance the family interests.

While contemporaries referred to the congeries of states that Philip ruled as the Spanish Monarchy, he held them strictly in dynastic union. Each dominion had its own government, laws, and interests, which he swore to respect. Neither Charles nor Philip sought to unify the institutions of their dominions, although their opponents frequently imputed that their goal was to Castilianize their empire at the cost of local liberties. Because the sovereign could not be physically present in each of his many dominions, he was represented by a viceroy or governor general. While ideally the viceroy or governor was to be a member of the dynasty or a local magnate, during Philip's reign most were Castilian nobles, the persons the king knew best and trusted most fully.

Philip experienced this system as prince, when he served as Charles's regent in Spain on two occasions, the last of which ended in 1554 when Charles arranged for his marriage to Mary Tudor, who as queen had restored England to the Catholic faith. Philip was soon deeply involved in affairs of state in London and Brussels. He and his advisors feared that Charles, whom they saw as prematurely aged, had neglected Italian interests in favor of the Netherlands. Between October 1555 and April 1556, Charles abdicated his dominions to Philip and retired to Spain, whence he continued to shower advice on his son. His imperial crown passed by election to his brother Ferdinand and remained with the Austrian Habsburgs.

When Philip succeeded Charles, his closest advisor was Ruy Gómez de Silva, Prince of Eboli. Portuguese by birth, Eboli had come to Spain with Empress Isabel and long served Philip. Suave in manner, he tended to favor diplomatic solutions to problems. Through patronage he built a faction at court that survived him under the direction of Antonio Pérez.

From Charles, Philip inherited several senior councillors; most important was Fernando Álvarez de Toledo, Duke of Alba, who moved into Philip's circle before Charles's abdication. A skilled military commander and diplomat, Alba became a rival to Eboli. A Venetian ambassador described them as the twin pillars on which rested the fate of half the world.

The four years Philip ruled from Brussels are seen as a period during which the issues that dominated the last years of Charles's reign were settled. Charles unloaded the German problems on Ferdinand. Meanwhile, the Habsburg-Valois conflict, rooted in the Italian Wars that began in 1494, entered its last phase in 1556 when Pope Paul IV invaded Naples. Though the pope was quickly subdued by Alba, France joined the war. Philip's army invaded France and on August 10, 1557, defeated the French at St. Quentin; in January 1558, however, the French surprised Calais, England's last continental possession. In November 1558 Mary Tudor died and *Elizabeth I became queen of England.

All parties were ready for peace. Philip and King Henry II of France were in financial straits and concerned about the spread of Calvinism in France and the Netherlands. Elizabeth feared that France would invade England to put the dauphine, Mary Queen of Scots, on the throne, a course of action that Philip also opposed. He feared an England allied to France more than Elizabeth's Protestant tendencies. In April 1559 representatives of the three sovereigns signed a set of peace treaties at Câteau Cambrésis.

Philip persuaded France to renounce claims to Milan and Naples and to restore most of Savoy to his ally Duke Emmanuel Philibert. The two kings agreed to guarantee peace with the bonds of matrimony, and Philip married Henry's daughter Elisabeth de Valois. Celebrating the treaty, Henry was fatally wounded in a joust, and the crown of France passed to his sixteen-year-old son, Francis II. For the next thirty years, France, the only state in western Europe that could match Philip's power, endured weak kings, factional struggles among the nobility, and religious civil wars.

Philip returned in 1559 to Spain and two years later seated his court in Madrid. The principal institutions for the business of war and peace were the Council of State and the Council of War, over which the king himself presided. In fact he seldom met with either, because he believed that their debates were freer without his presence.

The Council of State discussed foreign policy in the broadest sense. Its members were most often of the high nobility and had held significant government, diplomatic, or military offices. After 1566 it had two secretaries, one for northern European affairs and another for Italian and Mediterranean matters. The secretaries handled the relevant correspondence and kept minutes of the debates, called *consultas*, for the king's review. The king might also consult individually with councillors in person or, more likely, through exchanges of memoranda. Decisions were Philip's.

The potential for intrigue was great, and in 1578 Antonio Pérez was arrested in a case shrouded in mystery. Because Eboli and most other senior councillors of the early reign had died, and Alba was at the time disgraced, Philip established a new team of ministers. He brought from Rome two veteran statesmen, Cardinal Granvelle and Ambassador Juan de Zúñiga. By the time they died in 1586, a younger team of career diplomats had been groomed; Juan de Idiáquez and Cristóbal de Moura worked together in advising Philip on policy for the rest of the reign.

Because of the nature and extent of the monarchy, viceroys and governors general also had councils of state, and often a relatively free hand in regional concerns. The governor general of the Netherlands might negotiate with England; the governor general of Milan, with Savoy; or the viceroy of Naples, with Venice or the pope. Philip saw that their instructions were carefully drafted and that they were fully briefed about his intentions before assuming their offices.

The Council of War in Madrid had Castilian roots and did not get separate secretaries for land and sea until 1586. Its members were veteran commanders and technical experts. To deal with imperial defense, whether in Europe, the Mediterranean, or the New World, special *juntas* were often established to include members of relevant regional councils (Castile, the Indies, Aragon, Italy, Portugal, and Flanders) with the statesmen and military and naval experts.

Viceroys and governors general, unless clerics or women, acted as regional captains general. The professional soldiery were mercenaries, recruited in Spain, Italy, the Netherlands, and Germany; every province also had its militia, commanded by local authorities and generally ragtag.

Naval forces in the Mediterranean were well organized, with Spain, Naples, and Sicily each funding galley squadrons, which were augmented by hired galleys, chiefly from allied Genoa. A captain general of the sea coordinated the squadrons, though he often had to haggle with the concerned viceroys. In the Atlantic, developments were slower and armadas occasional. In the 1560s Spain established a permanent Armada de la Guarda de la Carerra de las Indias (Guard of the Indies Route) to convoy treasure fleets. In the 1580s, with the annexation of Portugal and its empire, a permanent Armada of the Ocean-Sea with the necessary command and support systems appeared.

Philip's diplomatic corps, with traditions dating back to Ferdinand the Catholic, was excellent. The most important post was that of ambassador to the pope in Rome, on whom Philip depended for moral influence in Catholic Europe and, more crassly, for the financial support given him by the Church in his dominions, conceded with papal blessing, which amounted to perhaps a fourth of his revenues.

The embassy to Vienna maintained the bonds of Habsburg solidarity and reported on the affairs of eastern Europe. The embassies to the sovereigns of western Europe were also important, but each proved difficult in its own way. Religious differences, exacerbated by the Counter-Reformation, affected French and English policies toward the rebellious Netherlands, impaired relations, and in time led to rupture and war. In an ideologically charged atmosphere, Philip's diplomats not only dealt with the governments to whom they were accredited, but also with forces bent on overthrowing those very governments. Ambassador Bernardino de Mendoza was expelled from England in 1584 for joining plots against Queen Elizabeth and from France in 1590 for helping to organize Parisian resistance to Henry IV.

Philip did not maintain relations with the Ottoman sultan, though he sent agents to Constantinople to arrange the truces of 1578 and afterwards. He accredited envoys to the sharifs of Morocco and supported their efforts to remain independent of the Ottomans, who threatened them from Algiers. The invasion of Morocco in 1578 by his nephew King Sebastian of Portugal, whom he could not dissuade, put him in an awkward position. He reluctantly provided Sebastian with a contingent of men, who conveniently had not yet joined him when he fell at Alcazarquivir. When Philip gained the Portuguese crown in 1580, he added Tangier, Ceuta, and some smaller North African *presidios* (forts) to Spain's surviving possessions of Oran and Melilla.

With the Portuguese crown also came African way stations, such as Luanda and Mozambique, that marked the long sea route round the Cape of Good Hope to Portugal's Asian possessions. Already the stations on the west coast had become sources for slaves shipped to the New World, a traffic Philip accepted for reasons of economic necessity despite qualms of conscience. He left it in Portuguese hands.

The Portuguese succession vastly enlarged Philip's interests in Asia. Already in 1565 a military and commercial colony had been planted in the Philippines (named after Philip), which was linked to Spain through Mexico. The Portuguese Asian possessions (Goa, Bombay, the Malabar Coast, Ceylon, Malacca, Amboina, and Macao), as well as the African outposts and Brazil in the New World, continued to be administered through Lisbon.

Although the causes of the wars of Philip's reign were many, one must begin with a mentality that possessed a strong sense of rights and a willingness to fight for them. The warrior king was a standard model: it broke Charles and disturbed Philip, who hated war but nevertheless waged it constantly in defense of what he thought right.

Philip thought it right to defend through diplomacy and war both Catholic Christendom and his inheritance. The latter included Portugal, although making good his claim required its conquest. Overseas, Spanish conquistadores extended his holdings in the New World and the Philippines.

During Philip's reign, traditional European dynastic defensive alignments were frequently confounded by what he would call "innovations in religion" spawned in the Protestant Reformation. With lines clearly drawn by 1559, and Philip II and Henry II determined to crush Calvinism, Calvinists became increasingly militant. To Philip, the godly republics established by Calvinists when they had the opportunity seemed proof of his worst fears. He believed in and insisted upon Catholic uniformity in his dominions.

Given this situation, militant Calvinists tried to form Protestant unions within states and promote solidarity across boundaries. Arms were widely available, and generations of warfare meant that many were handy with them. Great nobles kept bands of armed retainers. Self-defense against intolerant authorities or neighbors could lead quickly to civil war, in which sympathetic or interested foreign parties routinely intervened without respect to borders.

To the conflicts of Catholic and Protestant must be added the conflict of Christian and Muslim. From Philip's perspective, Spain and Italy, bonded by a common Roman Catholicism, stood in the forefront. The battleground was the Mediterranean and its littoral. In central Europe, his Austrian kinsmen defended the barricade, for which he sent them aid when he could.

In dealing with the events of the reign following the Peace of Câteau Cambrésis, historians tend to separate the Mediterranean struggle with the Ottoman Empire from events in northwestern Europe, including the revolt of the Netherlands and the closely related Wars of Religion in France, and war with England. It should be remembered, however, that for Philip much occurred simultaneously, giving him understandable migraines and leading to temporary fits of indecision.

Fernand Braudel, in the third part of his magisterial *The Mediterranean and the Mediterranean World in the Age of Philip II*, treats the relation of the two main themes brilliantly, though he takes religious differences for granted and gives little sense of their intensity. Braudel argues that the truces between Spain and the Turks after 1578 mark a shift of "universal history" from the Mediterranean to the Atlantic world. Unable to afford war in two separate theaters, Philip gave priority to the Netherlands. In the course of the shift he acquired Portugal, but he had not anticipated this when he first sought a truce.

The chronological sequence of events in the Mediterranean begins with setbacks late in Charles's reign that led to the disaster at Jerba (1560), which cost Philip and his Italian allies heavily in men and ships. He scrambled to repair the damage, and in 1565 his forces successfully relieved Malta, which the Turks had besieged. After a lull following the death in 1566 of Suleiman the Magnificent, the Turks in 1570 invaded the Venetian island of Cyprus, prompting Pope Pius V to call for a Holy League. Though Philip was advised that he had problems enough in the Netherlands, he could not deny the summons to the crusade. Spain and Italy clamored for it, and Pius, with his spiritual as well as financial clout, expected no less. The league, which included Philip, the pope, and Venice, was shaky, as the interests of each differed, and the great victory of Philip's half-brother, Don John of Austria, at Lepanto (1571) could not hold it together. In 1574 the Turks took Spain's outpost at Tunis; in 1578 Philip obtained a truce, and the scale of violence subsided. There were far fewer forays by war fleets, though piracy remained endemic.

In 1579–1580 Philip concentrated his Mediterranean forces against Portugal; in 1580, after the death of King-Cardinal Henry, King Sebastian's great-uncle, Philip annexed the kingdom and its empire.

With Portugal in hand, Philip gave full attention to the revolt of the Netherlands, which had become his prime concern. Its roots are many. Chief were differences about the distribution of power, the place of the Catholic Church, and the problem of religious toleration. Riots erupted in 1566; Philip sent the Duke of Alba with an army to restore order in 1567. In 1568, which the modern Dutch mark as the beginning of the Eighty Years' War of Independence, Alba executed opposition leaders counts Lamoral Egmont and Philip Horn and repelled an attempt by the Prince of Orange to drive him from the provinces. Conflict continued virtually unabated until the Twelve Years' Truce of 1609, which admitted a division of the Netherlands between the northern United Provinces, which abjured Philip in 1580, and the "obedient" Spanish Netherlands, the germ of modern Belgium.

Because Philip feared that France, as a result of the Wars of Religion or, after 1589, the succession of Henry IV, might turn Protestant and imperil the Netherlands, he repeatedly intervened in French affairs. The war with England that erupted in 1585 grew from direct English intervention in the Netherlands on the rebel side; piracy was a secondary issue. The defeat of the Spanish Armada in 1588 tends to obscure a long and grim war that did not end until 1604 with the Treaty of London.

War and diplomacy beyond Europe and the Mediterranean world, in Asia and the New World, though important, remained peripheral to Philip because distance prevented timely response. He could only trust in the abilities of the men he appointed to distant posts.

Philip died on September 13, 1598. In May he had ended his war with France by the Peace of Vervins, which recognized the succession of Henry IV, who had become Catholic, and reaffirmed the Peace of Câteau Cambrésis. To end the revolt of the Netherlands he had offered them independence under his daughter Isabel Clara Eugenia, who would prove the most adept of his children in statecraft and government, and her husband, Archduke Albert, whom he had carefully groomed. He could not know that his offer would prove unsuccessful.

Though Philip died with his treasury depleted and debts mounting, he had maintained his inheritance, save for the rebellious United Provinces, which he hoped would be recovered. Moreover, he had added to his inheritance both Portugal and its empire. His chief shortcoming, and the principal reason for his loss of the northern Netherlands, was his determination to maintain religious uniformity and his intolerance of religious dissent.

Were it not for his intolerance, characteristic of an age that stressed "one faith, one law, one king" as indispensable to a prosperous and orderly state, Philip II would seem a model enlightened ruler. Though he favored the royal prerogative, confident that a king had a clearer picture of the well-being of his kingdom than any subject, he nonetheless accepted and worked with existing institutions, including representative bodies. He promoted reforms when he believed them to be needed, refined the routines of government, and saw to the codification of laws. Philip was also a patron of the arts and learning.

The reign of his son, Philip III, saw peace with England and the Twelve Years' Truce with the Dutch, and allowed time for recuperation, if not revitalization. During the reign of Philip IV, another generation of wars proved more than Spain and its empire could sustain. In 1640 Portugal broke free, and at the Peace of the Pyrenees in 1659 *Louis XIV of France enjoyed the upper hand that his great-grandfather Philip II held at Câteau Cambrésis.

Annotated Bibliography

To follow the products of Philip's pen and documents bearing his signature would lead the scholar through most of the state and many of the private archives of Spain, the rest of Europe, and the Americas. Certainly the most important repository is the Archivo General de Simancas, the royal archives of Spain. In Seville, the Archivo General de Indias holds huge amounts of documentation about Philip's policy in the New World. There are three additional archives in Madrid that researchers should not ignore: Archivo Historico Nacional de Madrid, Biblioteca Nacional de Madrid, and Academia de la Historia. Also in Madrid, the Archivo de la Casa de las Duques de Alba is an important source of information about Philip and his reign. For Philip's relations with France, the Bibliothèque Nationale, 58 rue Richelieu, Paris, and the Ministère des Affaires Étrangères. 37 quai d'Orsay, 75700 Paris, contain much important information.

Philip's great difficulties in the Low Countries generated reams of orders, letters, and official documents. In Belgium, the Archives Générales du Royaume at Brussels is most important; in the Netherlands, the Algemeen Rijksarchief at The Hague holds valuable materials.

Papers relating to Philip's dealings with his Austrian cousins are found in Vienna at the Haus-, Hof-, und Staatsarchiv (Minoritenplatz 1, 1010 Vienna). For his relations with Great Britain, important materials can be found at the manuscript section of the British Museum and the Public Record Office.

Philip's Mediterranean policy was a focal point of his regime. Accordingly, important documents pertaining to that aspect of his reign can be found in Genoa at the Archivo di Stato, in Florence at the Biblioteca Nazionale, in Rome at the Vatican Archives, and at Venice at the Archivo di Stato.

Louis XIV, most Catholic statesmen of the seventeenth century, and independent observers of Philip's own times, such as the Venetian ambassadors, admired Philip's statesmanship. Protestant, Enlightenment, and Romantic historians, apart from Spaniards, let his religious intolerance or their own national sentiments obscure their view and find his statesmanship despotic and marred by dissimulation and bigotry. Spaniards tend to be apologetic.

Of the contemporary histories of the reign, the best is an extraordinary work by a court undersecretary, Luís Cabrera de Córdoba, *Felipe II, Rey de España* (1876–1877). Protestant hostility is enshrined in *The Apologie of Prince William of Orange Against the King of Spaine*, edited by H. Wansink (1969).

Regarding modern accounts, though much merit can be found in the unfinished biography by William H. Prescott, *History of the Reign of Philip the Second, King of Spain* (1855–1858), and the four-volume *Philippe II* by Henri Forneron (1881–1882), they remain flawed by today's standards. But Leopold von Ranke, *Die Osmanen und die spanische Monarchie im sechszehnten und siebzehnten Jahrhundert* (1827; rev. eds. 1857, 1887), which focuses on government and diplomacy, provides a fair portrait. Carl Bratli, *Philippe II, Roi d'Espagne* (1912), is usually regarded as the first acceptable modern biography.

For an extended list of source materials, the most recent is the bibliographical essay and notes in Peter Pierson, *Philip II of Spain* (1975). For much of the older material Pierson must be augmented by the classic Roger B. Merriman, *Rise of the Spanish Empire in the Old World and the New*, volume 4, *Philip the Prudent* (1934). The scope of the vast bibliography in Fernand Braudel, *La Méditerranée et le monde méditerranéen à l'époque de Philippe II*, 2 vols. (1966), gives a good idea of what serious study of the reign requires. All three bibliographies provide information about the vast archival sources.

Philip II and his statesmanship, perhaps excessively extolled in the Franco era, has not received much attention from recent Spanish scholars, who have rushed into the fields of social, economic, and demographic history. Even Manuel Fernández Alvarez, who began with the excellent *Tres embajadores de Felipe II en Inglaterra* (1951) and argued in *Política Mundial de Carlos V y Felipe II* that the dynasty collected a handful of testaments that summarized the political ideas of Charles and Philip, has plunged into social history while continuing his diplomatic studies.

Since the publication of Pierson's *Philip II of Spain*, Geoffrey Parker's splendid intimate biography, *Philip II* (1978), has appeared, with what is arguably the best portrait of Philip's personality and treatment of the Antonio Pérez case.

The diplomacy of the early reign has received new attention in the important M. J. Rodríguez-Salgado, *The Changing Face of Empire: Charles V, Philip II and Habsburg*

Authority (1988), and in Joycelyne G. Russell, *Peacemaking in the Renaissance* (1986), which offers a detailed account of Câteau Cambrésis. I.A.A. Thompson, *War and Government in Habsburg Spain, 1560–1620* (1976), is a seminal work on an extremely important topic.

Two recent, well-received biographies of men who served Philip II in statecraft are William S. Maltby, *Alba: A Biography of Fernando Alvarez de Toledo, Third Duke of Alba* (1983), and Peter Pierson, *Commander of the Armada* (1989), with new material on the armada campaign of 1588.

The 1988 quatercentenary of the defeat of the Spanish Armada saw a spate of studies, of which Colin Martin and Geoffrey Parker, *Spanish Armada* (1988), is by far the best. It surpasses in important ways the classic Garrett Mattingly, *Armada* (1959). Both Felipe Fernández Armesto, *Spanish Armada* (1988), and Peter Padfield, *Armada* (1988), are useful. Apart from Magdalena de Pazzis Pi Corrales, *Felípe II y la lucha por el dominio del mar* (1989), the best recent Spanish work on the armada has focused on administrative and technical matters.

A curious dimension of Philip's statecraft—the effect of prophecy and revelation on its conduct—is explored by Richard Kagan, *Lucrezia's Dream* (1990). Kagan's *Spanish Cities of the Golden Age* (1989) provides a remarkable pictorial look at Philip's Spain. David C. Goodman explores a modern interest in *Power and Penury: Government, Technology and Science in Philip II's Spain* (1988).

Bibliography

Bratli, Carl. *Philippe II, Roi d'Espagne*. Paris: Champion, 1912.

Braudel, Fernand. *La Méditerranée et le monde méditerranéen à l'époque de Philippe II*. 2 vols. 2nd ed. Paris: Armand Colin, 1966.

Cabrera de Córdoba, Luís. *Felipe II, Rey de España*. 4 vols. Madrid: Aribau, 1876–1877.

Fernández Alvarez, Manuel. *Política Mundial de Carlos V y Felipe II*. Madrid: Consejo Superior de Investigaciones Cientificas, 1966.

———. *Tres embajadores de Felipe II en Inglaterra*. Madrid: Consejo Superior de Investigaciones Cientificas, 1951.

Fernández Armesto, Felipe. *Spanish Armada*. Oxford: Oxford University Press, 1988.

Forneron, Henri. *Philippe II*. 2nd ed. Madrid: Ediciones y Reproduciones Internationales, 1981.

Goodman, David C. *Power and Penury: Government, Technology and Science in Philip II's Spain*. Cambridge: Cambridge University Press, 1988.

Kagan, Richard. *Lucrezia's Dream*. Berkeley: University of California Press, 1990.

———. *Spanish Cities of the Golden Age*. Berkeley: University of California Press, 1989.

Maltby, William S. *Alba: A Biography of Fernando Alvarez de Toledo, Third Duke of Alba*. Berkeley: University of California Press, 1983.

Martin, Colin, and Geoffrey Parker. *Spanish Armada*. London: Hamish Hamilton, 1988.

Mattingly, Garrett. *Armada*. Boston: Houghton Mifflin, 1959.

Merriman, Roger B. *Rise of the Spanish Empire in the Old World and the New*. 4 vols. New York: Macmillan, 1918–1934.

Padfield, Peter. *Armada*. Annapolis: Naval Institute Press, 1988.

Parker, Geoffrey. *Philip II*. Boston: Little, Brown, 1978.

Pazzis Pi Corrales, Magdalena de. *Felípe II y la lucha por el dominio del mar*. Madrid: Editorial San Martin, 1989.

Pierson, Peter. *Commander of the Armada*. New Haven, Conn.: Yale University Press, 1989.

———. *Philip II of Spain*. London: Thames and Hudson, 1975.

Prescott, William H. *History of the Reign of Philip the Second, King of Spain*. Boston: Phillips, Sampson, 1855–1858.

Ranke, Leopold von. *Die Osmanen und die spanische Monarchie im sechszehnten und siebzehnten Jahrhundert*. New York: AMS Press, 1975.

Rodríguez-Salgado, M. J. *The Changing Face of Empire: Charles V, Philip II and Habsburg Authority*. Cambridge: Cambridge University Press, 1988.

Russell, Joycelyne G. *Peacemaking in the Renaissance*. Philadelphia: University of Pennsylvania Press, 1986.

Thompson, I.A.A. *War and Government in Habsburg Spain, 1560–1620*. London: Athlone Press, 1976.

Wansink, H., ed. *The Apologie of Prince William of Orange Against the King of Spain*. Leiden: Brill, 1969.

                                                                          PETER PIERSON

William Pitt the Elder, Earl of Chatham (1708–1778).   William Pitt the Elder was born in Westminster, England, on November 15, 1708, the second son of Robert Pitt, M.P., and the favorite grandson of Thomas "Diamond" Pitt, the East Indies merchant and governor of Madras who had made the family fortune. He received his education at Eton and attended Trinity College, Oxford, but did not receive a degree. He also spent several months studying law at the University of Utrecht in the Netherlands. At an early age he fell victim to gout, an affliction that tormented him the rest of his life.

   His public career began in 1735, when he entered Parliament as member for Old Sarum, the family pocket borough. He quickly emerged as a strong promoter of maritime and colonial warfare, but his hostility to Hanover, which he called a "despicable electorate," earned him the enmity of George II, who finally was forced to make Pitt paymaster general in 1746 because of his growing political stature. He held this post until 1755, not enriching himself like his predecessors, but taking no more than the official salary of £4,000 a year. In 1754, his political career at a standstill, Pitt became ill and retired to Bath. At this point in his life Pitt, age forty-six, looked like a spent politician who could only contemplate a future of declining health and aging bachelorhood. Then suddenly he fell in love with Lady Hester Grenville, thirteen years his junior and totally taken with the aloof and acerbic Pitt. They married in November 1754. She supplied him with the comfort and security of home and family, especially important in his last years when gout, chronic insomnia, and his bouts of manic depression became totally debilitating.

   In 1755 Pitt had been dismissed as paymaster general on the eve of the Seven Years War (1756–1763) because he had opposed new German subsidies designed to secure Hanover. But in fact William Pitt could be an impossible colleague. Trained in the classical tradition, he orated with the commanding presence of Cicero, overwhelming all who dared oppose him. Pitt revealed a character that

was arrogant, condescending, at times mentally deranged, and verging on megalomania—qualities that served him well as a wartime minister.

His career as a statesman began when he found himself returned to office as
secretary of state in 1756. Dismissed shortly thereafter by the king, Pitt and the
duke of Newcastle joined forces to form a ministry in 1757, with Pitt concen-
trating on the war while Newcastle handled the domestic side. Pitt appeared to
be a master of statesmanship, military strategy, and logistic detail. The war had
begun badly for the British, and many wanted to believe Pitt when he boldly
declared, "I am sure I can save this country, and nobody else can." He seemed
to create a consistent and coherent war strategy that concentrated on North
America and India. Pitt demonstrated a good eye for selecting able generals and
admirals, a talent that finally bore fruit in 1759, the "year of victories," when
the capture of Guadaloupe and Quebec, together with the defeat of French fleets
off Lagos and Quiberon Bay, guaranteed victory. But war weariness, Pitt's
haughty manner, and the desire of the new king, George III, to rule personally
led to Pitt's resignation in 1761. The Treaty of Paris (1763) capped Pitt's career
as a stateman, as Britain acquired Canada and territories in the West Indies and
west Africa. Pitt, however, a steadfast enemy of Bourbon France and a passionate
advocate of an ever vaster British Empire, vigorously denounced the concessions
made to France in the treaty.

The remaining years of Pitt's career as a statesman were a sad, downhill slide
into bitterness, failure, and mental instability. When the king called him back
in 1766 to form a ministry, he also accepted the office of Privy Seal, a physically
undemanding sinecure, and entered the peerage as the Earl of Chatham. His
ministry was a complete failure. As gout and mental illness set in, Pitt withdrew
completely, spending the final six months of his doomed ministry at his home,
leaving the business of government to others. His later attempt to direct policy
from the House of Lords without party or cabinet support also ended in failure,
as Pitt found himself increasingly isolated politically and cut off from reality
mentally.

In periods of lucidity, Pitt spoke eloquently against the policies pursued by
the British government against the American colonists. Indeed, when Parliament
passed the Stamp Act in 1765, Pitt was absent due to an attack of gout. When
he returned to Parliament, he managed to have the act repealed. But Pitt soon
suffered another attack, and during his absence a large tax was placed on tea to
raise needed revenue. The Boston Tea Party of 1773 followed, which in turn
led to the disastrous British policy of punishing the colonists. However, Pitt
remained committed to the concept of the British Empire, and in his last speech
in Parliament he argued against any peace that would recognize American independence. He died in Kent on May 11, 1778, as *William Pitt the Younger,
his son and a future prime minister, read to him the passage in Homer's *Iliad*
on Hector's farewell.

Any assessment of William Pitt the Elder as a statesman has to be a mixed
one. His diplomacy seemed to be motivated by three overarching principles: a

dislike of Bourbon France, a desire to expand the British Empire, and a commitment to preserve the territorial and commercial integrity "of this ancient and most noble monarchy." Pitt clearly equated British greatness with domination of world trade. His one concrete legacy was the conquest of Canada. Peter Douglas Brown, one of his biographers, concluded that Pitt was not responsible for any major legislation and remained blissfully unaware of the financial cost of war. Pitt possessed inspirational and visionary leadership, yet lacked the practical finesse and political flexibility to build successful coalitions. At times capable of energetic administration and brilliant strategy, Pitt became a symbol for a nation to rally around, and he fixed in the British national consciousness the patriotic idea that the British Empire should become the epitome of commercial aggrandizement, even at the price of colonial and maritime warfare.

Annotated Bibliography

The Chatham manuscripts are available from the Public Record Office, Chancery Lane, London WC2 1LR, and Ruskin Avenue, Kew, Richmond, Surrey TW9 4DU. The papers covering the Seven Years War are of special importance, and of the private letters those from Addington, Bute, the Grenvilles, Hoods, Lytteltons, Thomas Coutts, and Lord Shelburne are of particular interest. The records of the Foreign Office, Admiralty, War Office, and Colonial Office are also available from the Public Record Office. The Anson Correspondence, the Hardwicke Papers, and the important Newcastle Papers are housed at the British Library, Great Russell Street, London WC1B 3DG. The latter two collections contain a number of letters written by Pitt in addition to providing a vast store of information about eighteenth century. The George Grenville Papers are available at the Huntington Library, San Marino, California 91108.

"Not merely is the complete life of Chatham difficult to write, but impossible. It is safe, indeed, to assert that it never has been written and never can be written. . . . he deliberately enveloped himself in an opaque fog of mystery." Thus wrote Lord Rosebery in his introduction to *Chatham, His Early Life and Connections* (1910). Indeed, Pitt left a relatively small written record, especially with regard to personal correspondence, yet that "opaque fog of mystery" has been lifted since Rosebery's work. Historians now understand fully that William Pitt the Elder suffered from manic-depressive insanity, which led to periods of intense agitation, where he would appear arrogant and restless, followed by periods of deep depression. While Pitt's mental condition is an important consideration, relying on it to explain his behavior can be overdone, as in J. H. Plumb's short, readable biography, *Chatham* (1965). One can never deny the importance of Pitt's mental illness as a factor in his statesmanship, but other, perhaps more satisfactory, explanations should not be ignored.

Pitt's later years were clearly dominated by bitterness, disappointment, increased physical pain, and insanity. So if one wants to judge fairly Pitt's statesmanship, one needs to look at what came to be regarded as his greatest triumph, his leadership during the Seven Years War. And in the words of Richard Middleton, author of *The Bells of Victory: The Pitt-Newcastle Ministry and the Conduct of the Seven Years' War, 1757–1762* (1985), "a persistent feature of historical writing on the war has been the adulation of Pitt. . . . The historiography of Pitt marks the growth of a legend." In a particularly useful appendix, Middleton examines Pitt's legend as propagated by successive generations of writers. He shows that many contemporaries and participants in the war were not as taken with Pitt's genius and leadership as were later historians. Accounts of Pitt in the early nineteenth century frequently portrayed him as at best an intense patriot, and at worst a malingering, erratic politician. But with the publication of Francis Thackeray's *A History of the Right Honourable William Pitt, Earl of Chatham* (1827), Pitt assumed the role of "great strategist and master planner." The work remains sycophantic and uncritical, yet the Pitt legend continued to grow with the help of T. B. Macaulay in "William Pitt, Earl of Chatham," *Edinburgh Review* 58 (1834): 508–544.

At the turn of the century, with Europe at the high-water mark of imperialism, the elder Pitt again received attention with the publication of Albert von Ruville's turgid three-volume biography, *William Pitt, Earl of Chatham* (1907). Still a good source for continental affairs and the diplomacy of Frederick the Great, von Ruville's work was criticized by English reviewers at the time as suffering "from a misunderstanding of many fundamental characteristics of English life." Julian Corbett's *England in the Seven Years' War* (1907) viewed the conflict as "Pitt's war," with "Pitt's system" winning the war. Basil Williams's definitive two-volume biography, *The Life of William Pitt, Earl of Chatham* (1913), complete with tables of Chatham's speeches, took a very uncritical view of Pitt. Following Corbett, Williams portrayed Pitt as a master strategist who handled every detail himself. Although Brian Tunstall's *William Pitt, Earl of Chatham* (1938) did not go beyond Williams in sources or interpretation, it does contain a useful annotated bibliography.

By the 1970s, Pitt and the old-style diplomatic and political histories associated with his life appeared stodgy and dated. Stanley Ayling sensed this change and wrote *The Elder Pitt, Earl of Chatham* (1976), a modern biography revealing Pitt as a man of many contradictions. Ayling differs from the earlier tradition in that he is more humane and less interested in political failings, and he finds only two resounding successes in Pitt's life: the conduct of the Seven Years War and his marriage. Ayling avoids the reverential path, but he is not ready for the completely unheroic, clinical, debunking modern biographical style, sometimes humorously called the "slob" biography. Peter Douglas Brown's study, *William Pitt, Earl of Chatham* (1978), provides a lively account of Pitt's leadership, again showing no doubt as to his military and strategic genius. But the biography is not as balanced as Ayling's book. Brown at times seems unable to place in the proper relationship Pitt's psychological turmoil and his erratic political actions.

Full-blown revisionism arrived in 1985 with Richard Middleton's *The Bells of Victory*. Middleton states his thesis simply: Britain emerged victorious in the Seven Years War because of luck, basic competence, and persistence rather than because of any grand design or Pitt's overbearing personality and genius. Middleton draws on an impressive array of primary sources and frankly admits that his study is "necessarily the product of its environment." In fact, a debunking, revisionist study of Pitt was long overdue. However, in a review of Middleton's work, historian Linda Colley asks an important question: "What is interesting and what Middleton does not really explain is why so many contemporaries—at all social levels—believed that the Seven Years War was pre-eminently Pitt's war." Still, the work remains important because it generated some new discussion about Pitt and his statesmanship, a subject that seemed closed and of little historical interest. Several other studies deserve mention also. O. A. Sherrard's trilogy, *Lord Chatham: A War Minister in the Making* (1952), *Lord Chatham: Pitt and the Seven Years' War* (1955), and *Lord Chatham and America* (1958), constitutes a complete account of the life and times of William Pitt. But Sherrard provides so much detail that Pitt seems to disappear. Sherrard covers party politics and intrigues thoroughly, but he adopts the conventional approach to Pitt's statesmanship, seeing him as the great architect of overseas empire. J. C. Long, *Mr. Pitt and America's Birthright: A Biography of William Pitt, the Earl of Chatham, 1708–1778* (1940), gives a breezy, popular, and historically suspect version of Pitt's life.

Short accounts of Pitt's life are available in W. D. Green's *William Pitt, Earl of Chatham* (1901), from the Heroes of the Nations series, which speaks volumes about popular historical attitudes prior to World War I, and Sir Charles Grant Robertson's *Chatham and the British Empire* (1946), from the optimistic and morally uplifting Teach Yourself History series. John Brooke's *The Chatham Administration, 1766–1768* (1956) does not really deal with international relations but rather focuses on party politics and Chatham's disastrous last ministry. Erich Eyck's *Pitt versus Fox, Father and Son, 1735–1806* (1950) is a collection of loose biographical information with little mention of foreign affairs. The dying art of narrative history receives no resuscitation in this volume. Marie Peters's *Pitt and Popularity: The Patriot Minister and London Opinion during the Seven Years' War* (1980) is designed for specialists, but the general reader can enjoy the excellent introduction and conclusion. Acknowledging that war and society have to be studied together, Peters suggests that Pitt conducted the Seven Years War with an eye toward popularity. If such was the case, then Peters's work offers a vision of future research into Pitt, international relations, and eighteenth-century society.

Bibliography

Ayling, Stanley. *The Elder Pitt, Earl of Chatham*. London: Collins, 1976.

Brooke, John. *The Chatham Administration, 1766–1768*. London: Macmillan, 1956.

Brown, Peter Douglas. *William Pitt, Earl of Chatham*. London: Allen and Unwin, 1978.

Colby, Charles. "Chatham, 1708–1908." *American Historical Review* 14 (1909): 723–730.

Corbett, J. S. *England in the Seven Years' War: A Study in Combined Strategy*. 2 vols. London: Longmans, Green, 1907.

Eyck, Erich. *Pitt Versus Fox, Father and Son, 1735–1806*. London: Bell, 1950.

Green, W. D. *William Pitt, Earl of Chatham*. New York: Knickerbocker Press, 1901.

Hotblack, Kate. *Chatham's Colonial Policy: A Study in the Fiscal and Economic Implications of the Colonial Policy of the Elder Pitt*. 1917. Reprint. Philadelphia: Porcupine Press, 1980.

Kimball, Gertrude Selwyn. *Correspondence of William Pitt When Secretary of State with Colonial Governors and Military Naval Commanders in America*. 2 vols. New York: Macmillan, 1906.

Langford, P. "William Pitt and Public Opinion." *English Historical Review* 88 (1973): 54–59.

Long, J. C. *Mr. Pitt and America's Birthright: A Biography of William Pitt, the Earl of Chatham, 1708–1778*. New York: Frederick A. Stokes, 1940.

Macauley, T. B. "William Pitt, Earl of Chatham." *Edinburgh Review* 58 (1834): 508–544.

McDermott, E. "The Elder Pitt and His Admirals and Generals." *Military Affairs* 20 (1956): 65–77.

Middleton, Richard. *The Bells of Victory: The Pitt-Newcastle Ministry and the Conduct of the Seven Years' War, 1757–1762*. New York: Cambridge University Press, 1985.

Pargellis. S. M. *Military Affairs in North America, 1748–1765: Selected Documents from the Cumberland Papers in Windsor Castle*. New York: Archon, 1936.

Peters, Marie. *Pitt and Popularity: The Patriot Minister and London Opinion during the Seven Years' War*. Oxford: Clarendon Press, 1980.

Plumb, J. H. *Chatham*. Hamden, Conn.: Archon, 1965.

Ritcheson, Charles R. "The Elder Pitt and an American Department." *American Historical Review* 57 (1952): 376–383.

Robertson, Sir Charles Grant. *Chatham and the British Empire*. London: English University Press, 1946.

Rosebery, Lord. *Chatham, His Early Life and Connections*. London: Arthur Humphreys, 1910.

Ruville, A. von. *William Pitt, Earl of Chatham*. 3 vols. Translated by H. J. Chaytor and Mary Morison. New York: Heinemann, 1907.

Sherrard, O. A. *Lord Chatham and America*. Fair Lawn, N.J.: Essential Books, 1958.

———. *Lord Chatham: A War Minister in the Making*. 1952. Reprint. Westport, Conn.: Greenwood Press, 1974.

———. *Lord Chatham: Pitt and the Seven Years' War*. 1955. Reprint. Westport, Conn.: Greenwood Press, 1975.

Taylor, W. S., and J. H. Pringle, eds. *The Correspondence of William Pitt, Earl of Chatham*. 4 vols. London: John Murray, 1838–1840.

Thackeray, F. *A History of the Right Honourable William Pitt, Earl of Chatham*. 2 vols. London: C. and J. Riverton, 1827.

Tunstall, Brian. *William Pitt, Earl of Chatham*. London: Hodder and Stoughton, 1938.

Turberville, H. S. *English Men and Manners in the Eighteenth Century*. Oxford: Clarendon Press, 1926.

Williams, Basil. *The Life of William Pitt, Earl of Chatham*. 2 vols. London: Frank Cass, 1913. Reprint. New York: Octagon, 1966.

Winstanley, D. A. *Lord Chatham and the Whig Opposition*. London: Frank Cass, 1912.

RICHARD A. VOELTZ

William Pitt the Younger (1759–1806).   The second son and fourth child of *William Pitt the Elder (later Earl of Chatham), George II's secretary of state for the Southern Department, and of Hester Grenville was born at Hayes, Kent, on May 28, 1759, the year of his father's most notable military and administrative triumphs during the Seven Years War. As Thomas Babington Macaulay, the great nineteenth-century British historian, put it, "The child inherited a name which, at the time of his birth, was the most illustrious in the civilised world, and was pronounced by every Englishman with pride, and by every enemy of England with mingled admiration and terror." The importance of being the Great Commoner's son to Pitt's subsequent career can scarcely be exaggerated. Not only did it ease his path in the 1780s to the youngest prime ministership in British history, but it also encouraged expectations of success in war and coalition-building after 1793 that never materialized. Those who heralded Pitt in the 1780s not as a chip off the old block but as the old block himself lived to see the inexactitude of their metaphor. And if Pitt was born in the year of his father's greatest triumphs in Germany, Canada, and India, he died in the year of *Napoleon I's smashing victories at Ulm and Austerlitz. Contemporaries were not slow to see the unflattering symmetry.

Because of childhood illness, Pitt was not educated, as were his contemporaries, at a great English public school but at home. In 1773, at fourteen, the precocious lad matriculated at Pembroke Hall at Cambridge University, where he remained until 1779. Two years later he was a member of Parliament; three years later, chancellor of the exchequer; and four years later, six months shy of his twenty-fifth birthday, in the midst of the greatest domestic political crisis since the accession of the House of Hanover, prime minister.

William Pitt served as George III's chief minister from December 1783 until February 1801, slightly over seventeen years, and again from May 1804 until his death in January 1806, or a further twenty months. His tenure in the highest office was longer than that of any prime minister in British history with the one exception of Sir Robert Walpole (1721–1742). He won more general elections (1784, 1790, 1796) than any prime minister between Walpole in the 1730s and Lord Liverpool in the 1820s. Beyond the ephemeral fact of distinguished parentage, the sources of Pitt's power were threefold. First, and probably most important, through peace and war, prosperity and depression, he enjoyed the support of George III. When that support was withdrawn in 1801, over Pitt's plan to place England's and Ireland's Roman Catholics on an equal political footing with the Protestants, Pitt's government quickly fell. Second, in an age when an unparalleled group of orators (William Wilberforce, Charles James Fox, Edmund Burke, William Windham, and Richard Brinsley Sheridan) shone in Parliament, Pitt, with his silver-toned voice, his logical, factual, reasoned speeches, and his supreme ability to isolate the weaknesses in his opponents' arguments, dominated the House of Commons. And third, through his virtuous reputation, his proven ability to manage the nation's financial establishment, and his restoration of Britain's prestige in the European system, Pitt appealed beyond the House of Commons to the public opinion, largely middle class, of an increasingly urbanized and capitalistic-oriented kingdom.

As has often been observed, Pitt's premiership can be neatly separated into two sections, with 1792, the year when the wars of the French revolution commenced in Europe, as the dividing point. The years from 1783 to 1792 were ones of nearly unalloyed triumph. Even those instances where Pitt failed to gain immediate political or statutory success, for example, moderate parliamentary reform and the abolition of the slave trade, have been generally credited as moral and spiritual accomplishments.

Before 1792, in regard to Pitt's role as a world statesman, it is difficult to separate the recovery of Britain's financial equilibrium from its revival as a leading European power. When Pitt became prime minister, Britain's financial and strategic situation had rarely been bleaker. The national debt, which had stood at £128 million at the start of the American war, was £243 million, and the yearly cost of debt redemption alone approached £9 million. Through a specific system of sinking funds and a general rationalization of the entire financial establishment, Pitt oversaw a revival in creditor confidence as great as did William III a hundred years before. Ian R. Christie in fact views Pitt's tenure as the watershed between medieval and modern fiscal administration. In what was perhaps the most important work on the French Revolution prepared for the bicentennial year of 1989, *Citizens*, Simon Schama has argued that even though the British per capita tax burden of the 1780s was three times heavier than that of the French, the investing classes had such confidence in Pitt that he could raise revenue from new taxes without a political crisis ensuing. Similar attempts in France led to the overthrow of the Bourbon monarchy.

Before 1792, Pitt was as successful diplomatically as he was on fiscal matters. The year Pitt became prime minister, Joseph II, Holy Roman Emperor and King of Hungary, thought that Great Britain had fallen to the rank of a second-class power. Its strategic position was probably weaker than at any previous time in the eighteenth century and comparable to her later isolation in 1797. France was allied with Spain and Austria and dominant politically in the Netherlands. Pitt's aims in the 1780s, beyond restoring his country's economy, always a crucial component of any rational foreign policy, were to keep his country at peace, to prevent French domination of the Netherlands, and, in a general sense, to resuscitate British prestige in Europe.

Although never a slavish follower of the laissez-faire doctrines of Adam Smith, Pitt had read *Wealth of Nations* and where practicable attempted to implement Smithian policies. The most noted example was the 1786 free-trade treaty between Great Britain and France. Moderate duties of 10 to 15 percent were established on most items, and British and French ships enjoyed most-favored-nation status in each other's ports. The treaty remained in force until abrogated by the French revolutionary leadership in 1792. Even though the treaty greatly benefited the French wine industry, overall it was a British triumph. Yet, the Anglo-French détente obviously had its limitations. In 1787, when Pitt suggested to the French a mutual reduction in naval manpower, he met with a negative response.

The British commercial advantages flowing from the 1786 free-trade treaty, coupled with the boom in the British economy in general, facilitated Britain's diplomatic recovery from the disaster of the American war. In fact, the reasons for this restoration may have had less to do with Pitt's acumen or Britain's proto-industrial condition than with France's increasing inability to play an economic or political role commensurate with its size, resources, or population. In 1787 the somewhat amateurish attempt by the pro-French Patriots to establish French condominium over the Netherlands ended in a diplomatic victory for the two powers most inclined from dynastic and economic motives to abhor such an outcome, Prussia and Great Britain. The Triple Alliance (1788) between Prussia, Britain, and the Netherlands ended British diplomatic isolation stemming from the pro-American European coalition of the last years of the American war. Equally advantageous to Britain was the settlement of the Nootka Sound dispute in 1790 with Spain. When Spanish ships broke up a British trade settlement on Vancouver Island in the eastern Pacific, Pitt threatened war. Spain backed down and renounced its claim to the ownership of the area around the island. France in 1790 was much too weak to come to the aid of Spain.

Pitt's ill-conceived and poorly executed policy during the last days of the 1791 Russo-Turkish war was an exception to his generally successful diplomacy before 1792. Pitt, partially repaying Prussia for its support over Nootka Sound the previous year, seconded Berlin in its desire to see Russia return Ochakov, a fortress on the Black Sea near Odessa, to the Turks. Ultimatums were issued to *Catherine the Great. British naval forces prepared for the arduous trek to the Black Sea. Yet, the pro-Russian, Foxite wing of the Whig opposition stirred up parliamentary and public opinion against British military action in support of the hated Turk. And despite losing his anti-Russian foreign secretary, the Duke of Leeds, over the matter, Pitt thought better of his stance and gave Catherine II carte blanche over Ochakov. Berlin may have blanched and the Foxites jeered, but Pitt, upon reflection, was not prepared for the sake of the Triple Alliance or for political consistency to involve his country in an eastern European war.

Indeed, Pitt, during his first decade in power, and arguably beyond, showed a marked reluctance to involve his nation in any war. He told the House of Commons in 1787 that to regard France as Britain's natural enemy was "weak and childish." He made no observable attempt to take military or naval advantage of France's obvious weakness after 1788. Even eight months after the flight to Varennes, Pitt was still predicting in the House of Commons fifteen years of European peace. What Pitt really thought of the French Revolution is difficult to gauge. He was not a man, however playful and affectionate he may have been in private, who wrote down his innermost political or philosophical thoughts. However, when the great crisis of 1792–1793 occurred, Pitt's most important modern biographer suspects that, far more than George III, the cabinet, or even the conservative circles of the Whig opposition, Pitt preferred to maintain a policy of neutrality. If John Ehrman is correct, the French revolutionary leadership and army gave Pitt little room for maneuver.

The European war, pitting the conservative monarchies of central and eastern Europe against the new French revolutionary government, commenced in April 1792. After an initial series of monarchical victories against the ill-organized French, the tide turned, and by November the French had crossed the Rhine and were in control of most of the Austrian Netherlands (modern Belgium). Fair or not, one of the foundation stones upon which the European balance rested was articles XIV and XV of the Peace of Westphalia, which closed the Scheldt to oceangoing vessels and—in the interest of the Netherlands—destroyed the prosperity of the Belgian city of Antwerp. The French, on November 16, 1792, decreed freedom of navigation on the Scheldt. Not only Westphalia but also Pitt's Triple Alliance seemed threatened by French action. War was hence probably inevitable even before the execution of Louis XVI in January. In any event, on February 1, 1793, the French Republic declared war on Great Britain.

Between the outbreak of the war and his death in January 1806, William Pitt, more than any other European figure, presided over and subsidized the three coalitions formed to thwart and, if possible, overthrow Jacobin, Directory, and Napoleonic France. All three coalitions, from a European standpoint, were total failures. The First Coalition, comprising almost all the anti-French powers, ended disastrously with the capture of Amsterdam (1795) and the treaties of Basel in 1795, which ended Prussian participation in the war for over a decade, and Campo-Formio in 1797, which drove Austria from the war. The Second Coalition of Britain, Austria, and Russia saw the fiasco of the Anglo-Russian attack on the Netherlands in 1799 and the crushing allied defeats the following year at Marengo and Hohenlinden. In 1801 and 1802, the Second Coalition terminated in the rather shameful peace treaties of Lunéville and Amiens. The Third Coalition of Britain, Naples, Russia, and Austria witnessed in the last year of Pitt's life the even greater catastrophes of Ulm and Austerlitz, and the solidification of Napoleon's control over Europe.

The British, and more specifically Pitt's, role in these successive debacles has been excused and explained, condemned and ridiculed. On the one hand, it is true, Britain's coalition partners before 1812 or 1813 were rarely steadfast. Both Austria and Prussia during the First Coalition appeared more interested in partitioning Poland than in defeating France. The Second Coalition was rent by Austrian and Russian quarrels over the disposition of territory in northern Italy or of armies in Switzerland. The Third Coalition was even more divided over the perennial Prussian desire for Hanover and Austrian suspicions of Russian aims in the Turkish Empire. Nonetheless, Pitt himself was no decisive war leader. Neither a Chatham nor a Churchill, he had little background or apparent interest in military or naval affairs. He admitted in 1794 that he distrusted "extremely" his feel for such matters. Nineteenth and twentieth-century historians have more than echoed Pitt's own doubts. Most have wondered why no British equivalent of the successful French *levée en masse* was attempted. Macaulay, in a seminal, if short, biographical account of Pitt's life, proclaimed his military administration "the laughing stock of all Europe." Modern commentators such as Edward Ingram, Richard Glover, Piers Mackesy, and even his generally sympathetic biographer John Ehrman have emphasized Pitt's naïveté, amateurism, indecisiveness, and weakness.

Generally, Pitt did follow a frustrating war strategy, often too ambitious for his resources, and often accompanied by remarkably poor intelligence. His own indecisiveness was reflected in the lack of coordination and agreement within his talented cabinet. Men such as Lord Grenville, the foreign secretary, Henry Dundas, secretary of war, and William Windham, secretary at war, had strong and often contradictory views on the proper war aims and strategy. Grenville was the European warrior par excellence, determined to defeat French atheism, republicanism, and aggression on the Rhine and on the Elbe, in Switzerland and in the Netherlands, in Savoy and in Naples. Dundas exemplified the old "blue water" school, favoring naval and military expeditions to the West Indies, Spanish South America, or French-held Egypt. Windham, sometimes supported by Grenville, made the restoration of French royalism, with its concomitant necessity for landings on the French coast, his fixation. It was up to Pitt to mediate among these strongly held opinions. Few would argue that he did so convincingly. Too often he dithered and wrung his hands. The leading English historian of the Second Coalition, Piers Mackesy, believes indeed that the weak prime minister ended up accepting the views of the last cabinet minister he consulted.

Oddly, Pitt's own generation was more charitable about the martial accomplishments of "The Pilot That Weathered the Storm" than were subsequent ones. After all, in the long run Britain did win the generation-long war with France. Hence, after Waterloo, Pitt's activities, unlike, for example, Lord North's after Yorktown, might have seemed more the building blocks to ultimate victory than, as Macaulay thought, the exercises of "a driveller." Pitt clubs and Pitt statues dotted the landscape of the United Kingdom after 1815. *Castlereagh and *George Canning regarded themselves as Pittites more than as Tories.

William Pitt also was not a lucky war leader, as perhaps his father and Lord Liverpool and *David Lloyd George were. His war administration had to contend not only with the French revolutionary threat but also with unusually bad harvests in 1795 and 1800, the worst Irish rebellion since 1689, and the debilitating naval mutinies of 1797. Nonetheless, looked at from a purely naval standpoint, his two administrations claimed many of the great victories of British history. From Richard Howe's defeat of the French Brest fleet on the "Glorious First of June" (1794) to the rout of the Spanish fleet at Cape St. Vincent (1797) and of the Dutch fleet at Camperdown (1797) to Nelson's destruction of Napoleon's Toulon fleet at Aboukir Bay (1798) and finally to Trafalgar (1805) itself, St. Paul's Cathedral witnessed many thanksgiving services for naval successes.

From a colonial perspective too, Pitt's wartime achievements were such as to rival his father's as a creator of the modern British Empire. Few aspects of the Younger Pitt's life have been more controversial than his West Indian war strategy. By the time of Pitt's death, rival European powers had been practically swept from the area; however, in the process Britain lost approximately fifty thousand troops, largely to yellow fever. John Holland Rose, Pitt's early twentieth-century biographer and a professor of naval and imperial history at Cambridge, and Sir John W. Fortescue, the historian of the British army, were unsparing in their criticism of Pitt's sending expensive fleets and armies from the primary conflict in Europe to conquer relatively unimportant West Indian islands. Recently, however, historians such as Michael Duffy have reexamined Pitt's West Indian assumptions. The profits of the sugar, coffee, cocoa, ginger, cotton, and indigo industries in all the West Indian islands were massive, more so in fact for France than for Britain. In the 1780s the foreign trade of Santo Domingo alone was as great as that of the entire United States. Britain's own trade with the West Indies was larger than with any other area of the globe except northern Europe. For Henry Dundas and William Pitt, to deprive France of such riches was more important for British interests than for them to aid French royalists at Quiberon Bay. Between the French Revolution and Pitt's death in 1806, the value of British imports and exports (much of it West Indian–oriented) almost doubled, and British reexports almost tripled. Insofar as the nineteenth-century Pax Britannica involved British naval and mercantile domination of the sea lanes, Pitt's administrations played a major part in its realization.

Equally important in the foundation of nineteenth-century British greatness was the enlargement of the British imperium over the Indian subcontinent. Here again, the Pitt administrations played a crucial role. It was Pitt who in 1797 sent his (and Grenville's) protégé, the Earl of Mornington (later Marquess Wellesley), to India as governor general. While the Second Coalition failed ignominiously in Europe, Wellesley in essence created the British raj in India and Britain succeeded the Mogul Empire as the paramount power. This might have happened under any circumstances, but the centrality of 1798 as the decisive year in the history of British India is compelling. Bonaparte and a French army invaded Egypt with the ultimate goal of aligning with Britain's enemy, Tipu, sultan of Mysore. Dundas worried that this might lead to a grand alliance with other anti-British Indian states. The defeat of these French designs and the victories of Wellesley in the Fourth Mysore War might well have been in the long run the most significant British operations of the entire 1793–1815 war. As Edward Ingram has pointed out, the events of 1798 transformed Great Britain from a peripheral state, an island with no borders to defend, into a continental state with vast, if ever shifting, frontiers; into a dual monarchy, in many respects ruled as much from Calcutta as from London.

As the woes of the European wars fell upon him, Pitt, a bachelor, increasingly sought solace in drink. How much alcohol contributed to his increasingly poor health is difficult to say. He had never possessed an iron constitution, and some of his recent biographers suspect that by the early nineteenth century cancer was a probable diagnosis for his maladies. In any case, Pitt's drinking was prodigious. His successor, Henry Addington (later Lord Sidmouth), once remarked that if there was one thing Pitt liked better than a glass of port it was a bottle. And Macaulay, no admirer of Pitt, thought that "two bottles of port were little more to him than two dishes of tea." Like his distant successor during World War I, H. H. Asquith, Pitt not infrequently appeared drunk in public as well as on occasion in the House of Commons. He died at his leased home, Bowling Green House, on Putney Heath, on January 23, 1806. He was forty-six.

Annotated Bibliography

While minor collections of William Pitt's correspondence are scattered about the world in places as diverse as San Marino, California, Ann Arbor, Michigan, and Durham, North Carolina, the major depositories are in Great Britain. The Public Record Office (Kew Gardens) in London contains the chief collections of Pitt's papers, most notably in the voluminous Chatham Papers proper and in the correspondence collection of Pitt's secretary, William Dacres Adams. Other important sources for evaluating Pitt's activities are included in the correspondence of his foreign secretary, Lord Grenville (Dropmore Papers), in the British Library (London), and of his secretary for war, Henry Dundas

(Viscount Melville), at the British Library, the National Library of Scotland (Edinburgh), and the Scottish Record Office (Edinburgh). The papers of Pitt's tutor, confidant, and biographer, George Pretyman Tomline, may be found at Pembroke College (Cambridge) and at the East Suffolk Record Office (Ipswich).

Pitt's official biography, in three volumes, *Memoirs of the Life of the Right Honorable William Pitt* (1821), by his old tutor at Cambridge, George Pretyman Tomline, the bishop of Winchester, is an ill-constructed digest of his speeches and administrative jottings. There is no reason to dissent from Macaulay's view that it is the "worst biographical work of its size in the world." If any defense can be offered of Tomline's literary product, however, it would be that Pitt, unlike *Disraeli or Gladstone, Asquith or *Churchill, was not a statesman who opened his heart in letters. This, plus the almost complete lack of any observable family or sexual life, leaves Pitt's biographies more oriented toward his times than his life. Hence, more than is normally the case in the genre, most of Pitt's biographers have focused on his foreign policy views and activities. This is true of the four-volume *Life of the Right Honourable William Pitt* (1861–1862) by Earl Stanhope; of the rather critical two-volume assessment by John Holland Rose, *William Pitt and the National Revival* (1911) and *William Pitt and the Great War* (1911), and of the magisterial and as yet uncompleted life by John Ehrman, *The Younger Pitt: The Years of Acclaim* (1969) and *The Younger Pitt: The Reluctant Transition* (1983).

The best single-volume study of Pitt's life, *William Pitt the Younger* (1978), is by Robin Reilly. The best essay-length account of Pitt's life, written for the *Encyclopedia Britannica*, is by Thomas Babington Macaulay (1859). General histories of late eighteenth- and early nineteenth-century Britain that provide a skillful weaving together of domestic and foreign policy issues include Ian R. Christie, *Wars and Revolutions: Britain, 1760–1815* (1982), A. D. Harvey, *Britain in the Early Nineteenth Century* (1978), and part of the Oxford History of England, J. Steven Watson, *The Reign of George III* (1960).

Specialized studies of some aspect of Pitt's role in world affairs are plentiful. As a starting point, a good current account of the state of the foreign policy debate is found in John Clarke, *British Diplomacy and Foreign Policy, 1782–1865* (1989). The bulk of this specialized literature has tended to adopt an extremely critical stance on Pitt's foreign policy performance. Sir John Fortescue, in the fourth volume of *A History of the British Army* (1906), set the tone for much of the subsequent negative evaluation of Pitt's post–1793 activities. Fortescue was, like his hero Lord Grenville, a "Europe man," and he regarded the blue water strategy so often pursued by Pitt and Dundas as shortsighted and fundamentally flawed. Most disputants since have echoed such criticism.

Piers Mackesy in two stimulating works on the Second Coalition, *Statesmen at War: The Strategy of Overthrow, 1798–1799* (1974) and *War Without Victory: The Downfall of Pitt, 1799–1802* (1984), regards the prime minister as a ditherer and comparable to Lord North as a war leader. Even more anti-Pittite is Richard Glover's analysis of Pitt's second administration in *Britain at Bay: Defense against Bonaparte, 1803–14* (1973). Glover considers Pitt's war efforts during the Third Coalition as "despicable," though he does give the wider administration credit for a sophisticated coastal defense against a projected French invasion.

Edward Ingram's two arousing if eccentric books on Britain's Far Eastern empire in the late eighteenth and early nineteenth centuries, *The Beginning of the Great Game in Asia, 1828–1834* (1979) and *Commitment to Empire: Prophecies of the Great Game in Asia, 1797–1800* (1981), find Pitt's continuing reputation as a statesman virtually "inexplicable." Given the weakness of British foreign policy during the war of the Second

Coalition, Ingram portrays a Pitt who, far from deserving the appellation "The Pilot That Weathered the Storm," cravenly resigned his office in 1801 "at the height of the hurricane."

Of the nonbiographical, specialized, Pittite literature, only Michael Duffy, in *Soldiers, Sugar, and Seapower* (1987), has produced a major (if not always uncritical) apologia for Pitt's conduct during the wars of both the First and the Second Coalitions. Duffy depicts Pitt's West Indian policy, so despised by Rose, Fortescue, and others, as rational, strategically far-sighted, and of great economic benefit for Great Britain.

Bibliography

Christie, Ian R. *Wars and Revolutions: Britain, 1760–1815*. Cambridge, Mass.: Harvard University Press, 1982.

Clarke, John. *British Diplomacy and Foreign Policy, 1782–1865*. London: Unwin Hyman, 1989.

Duffy, Michael. *Soldiers, Sugar, and Seapower*. Oxford: Clarendon Press, 1987.

Ehrman, John. *The Younger Pitt: The Reluctant Transition*. Stanford, Calif.: Stanford University Press, 1983.

———. *The Younger Pitt: The Years of Acclaim*. New York: Dutton, 1969.

Fortescue, Sir John. *A History of the British Army*. Vol. 4. London: Macmillan, 1906.

Glover, Richard. *Britain at Bay: Defense against Bonaparte, 1803–14*. London: Allen and Unwin, 1973.

Harvey, A. D. *Britain in the Early Nineteenth Century*. London: St. Martin's Press, 1978.

Ingram, Edward. *The Beginning of the Great Game in Asia, 1828–1834*. Oxford: Oxford University Press, 1979.

———. *Commitment to Empire: Prophecies of the Great Game in Asia, 1797–1800*. Oxford: Oxford University Press, 1981.

Mackesy, Piers. *Statesmen at War: The Strategy of Overthrow, 1798–1799*, London: Longman, 1974.

———. *War Without Victory: The Downfall of Pitt, 1799–1802*, Oxford: Clarendon Press, 1984.

Reilly, Robin. *William Pitt the Younger*. New York: Putnam's, 1978.

Rose, John Holland. *William Pitt and the Great War*. London: Bell, 1911.

———. *William Pitt and the National Revival*. London: Bell, 1911.

Stanhope, Earl. *Life of the Right Honourable William Pitt*. 4 vols. London: Murray, 1861–1862.

Tomline, George Pretyman. *Memoirs of the Life of the Right Honorable William Pitt*. 3 vols. London: Murray, 1821.

Watson, J. Steven. *The Reign of George III*. Oxford: Clarendon Press, 1960.

JAMES J. SACK

James Knox Polk (1795–1849).   "Who is James K. Polk?" cried Whig partisans in 1844 when the Democratic party chose the forty-eight-year-old Southerner as the first "dark horse" presidential candidate in U.S. history. Over the next five years, the Whigs would receive a resounding answer to their query as Polk employed diplomacy and war to add approximately 1.2 million square miles to the United States and helped to turn the executive office into the dominant shaper of foreign policy. But who indeed was this tentative choice of the Democrats destined to become America's eleventh president?

Born in 1795 to Samuel and Jane Polk in Mecklenburg County, North Carolina, young James was reared in the agrarian tradition of Jeffersonian democracy—a tradition that he observed in both his father's and grandfather's community leadership. In 1805 the Polk family took James, the influence of "Old Mecklenburg," and their Jeffersonian ideals and relocated in middle Tennessee south of Nashville. There Polk's formal education began at the feet of Presbyterian teachers who nurtured in him a desire for scholarship and a respect for Calvinist discipline. At twenty-one Polk returned to North Carolina to study at the university at Chapel Hill, where he proved to be a diligent student and an active campus leader.

After graduation in 1818 he returned to Tennessee to study law with Felix Grundy in Nashville. The following year he entered Tennessee politics in Murfreesboro with an appointment to a senate clerk's position. In 1820 he established his own law practice in Columbia, Tennessee, and continued to maneuver his way into politics. By 1824 he had married Sarah Childress, secured a seat in the Tennessee legislature, and attached himself to the coattails of the rapidly ascending Andrew Jackson.

In 1825 Polk won the first of seven victories that would place him in the U.S. House of Representatives for fourteen years. While in Washington, he followed the natural course to Jacksonian democracy and was not only mentored by Jackson but became an indispensable tool for President Jackson's domestic policies while chairman of the House Ways and Means Committee. Reaching the post of Speaker of the House in 1835, Polk found himself frustrated with the struggling administration of Jackson's successor, Martin Van Buren. In 1839 Polk relinquished his House seat and returned to Tennessee, where he reentered state politics with a successful gubernatorial bid.

After a disappointing rejection by the national Democratic party as Van Buren's vice presidential running mate in 1840, Polk sought a second term as governor. But this time he was defeated by the same strong Whig momentum that carried William Henry Harrison to the White House. Despite a vigorous campaign, a second attempt to regain the governorship in 1843 failed. Thus Polk, having honed a successful political career from clerk in the Tennessee legislature to Speaker of the U.S. House of Representatives, found himself reeling from two consecutive political defeats when the Democratic party selected him as its 1844 presidential hopeful.

Polk's presidential nomination was neither happenstance nor coincidence. When the political conventions for the 1844 campaign approached, the obvious candidates for both the Whig and the Democratic parties failed to recognize the strong national sentiment for territorial expansion. Whig Henry Clay and Democrat Martin Van Buren both prematurely announced their opposition to the annexation of Texas. Unlike the Whig convention, which accepted Clay as predicted, powerful expansionists in the Democratic party created such a stalemate that a dark horse proved necessary. As a southern advocate of expansion and a protégé of Jackson, Polk was a natural alternative. Campaigning on the promise to "reannex Texas" and to "reoccupy Oregon," Polk won a narrow victory over Clay in November.

The determined and steadfast Polk believed that he had captured the White House on the strength of an expansionist America seeking to fulfill what would shortly be termed "manifest destiny." This national mood and Polk's campaign promises thrust the new president immediately into foreign affairs. Although Polk had no diplomatic training and a perception of international relations dangerously clouded by Jacksonian contempt and suspicion for all foreign governments, the new president took up the task boldly. He reaffirmed his expansionist intentions at his inauguration by describing America's claim to the Oregon Territory as "clear and unquestionable" and by indicating his aim to bring Texas into the Union with a controversial southern boundary at the Rio Grande.

Polk's position on Oregon and Texas, as well as his personal desire for California and his Anglophobic concern that the British also had designs on that land, placed the United States at odds with both Great Britain and Mexico. To keep the expansionist promise to satisfy America's destiny would require the acquisition of all territories contiguous to the United States. This would compel the new president to face down both Great Britain and Mexico.

The contest over Texas awaited Polk when he took office. Three days before Polk delivered his inaugural address, President John Tyler signed a joint congressional resolution for the annexation of Texas. The day following Polk's address the Mexican minister to Washington broke diplomatic relations with the United States and returned to Mexico City. Thus Polk was quickly faced with his first foreign policy decision. He could either tacitly accept Tyler's resolution and fulfill his campaign promise to "reannex" Texas or ignore the resolution and struggle with a divided Senate to get a treaty to annex Texas—risky at best. He chose the former but pressed for the extreme and questionable boundary at the Rio Grande. This decision would not only perpetuate the tension with Mexico but would eventually provoke war.

Polk wasted little time forcing the issue with Mexico. In the summer of 1845 he sent a special emissary to urge Texans to seize the controversial territory between the Nueces River and the Rio Grande. At the same time he deployed U.S. forces to preempt any Mexican response and to hold a position that would permit the United States to secure California should hostilities break out.

Meanwhile the British, provoked by Polk's "clear and unquestionable" assertion to the Oregon Territory, reacted indignantly and exposed the crisis potential surrounding the Oregon Question. Lord Aberdeen, the generally passive British foreign secretary, announced to Parliament his determination to hold the territory in defense of British national honor and, rather sarcastically, proclaimed Her Majesty's title to the territory to be equally "clear and unquestionable."

In July, however, the usually obstinate Polk made a surprising diplomatic move. After having Secretary of State James Buchanan present an exhaustive discourse on the strength of America's claim to the entire Oregon Territory up to Russian America at 54 degrees, 40 minutes, he offered a compromise boundary at the 49th parallel. Polk justified his apparent retreat from an "All Oregon" campaign promise by stating that he was bound by the compromise offers of his predecessors. If indeed Polk had only grudgingly proposed the compromise, he was quickly relieved of this obligation when the British minister in Washington, Richard Pakenham, abruptly rejected the offer. An angry Polk reacted by withdrawing the compromise offer. Polk's unorthodox action created a dangerous stalemate between the two countries in which escalating rhetoric of superior claims and national honor pushed the United States and Great Britain toward confrontation.

With the Oregon Question unresolved, Polk attempted a diplomatic solution to the Mexican problem. In fall 1845 he sent John Slidell to Mexico City with instructions not only to reopen relations, sort out American claims against Mexico, and settle the Texas boundary dispute, but also to offer Mexico up to $40 million for California and New Mexico. While Slidell was en route to Mexico City, Polk sent word to U.S. Consul Thomas Larkin in Monterey, California, and to John C. Frémont's military expedition in northern California to steer California toward annexation and heightened resistance to the British.

Slidell's mission failed, and Polk reacted by deploying General Zachary Taylor's forces to the Rio Grande. Polk probably hoped to pressure the Mexicans into negotiations, but instead pushed them toward war. Although Polk did not want a conflict, he was determined to obtain California and the Rio Grande boundary for the recently admitted state of Texas.

While events were moving toward war with Mexico, Polk attempted to bring the Oregon problem to a head. In his December message to Congress, he called upon the legislators to abrogate the existing agreement with England, which had left the entire territory open to both British subjects and U.S. citizens since 1818. To punctuate his message and make clear America's position not only on Oregon but the entire continent, he announced his determination to exclude all Europeans from further adventure in North America through the so-called Polk Corollary to the Monroe Doctrine. The president both narrowed and expanded the Monroe Doctrine. He narrowed it by specifying North America and yet expanded its meaning by declaring that the United States would oppose even diplomatic interference by Europeans. Polk confided to his diary that America would be willing to resist any such encroachment "at any and all hazard."

The president expected the Democratic majority in Congress to promptly implement his directive to end the existing convention with the British concerning Oregon. But he was disappointed when a coalition of Democrats and Whigs led by Senator John C. Calhoun debated for five months as to whether such a move would lead to war with Great Britain over a territory of questionable value.

Actually, the British were ready to compromise and would have viewed the American abrogation of the agreement as a welcome invitation to reopen negotiations. The sole beneficiary of the territory, the Hudson's Bay Company, had relocated its headquarters to Vancouver Island, and a change in the political environment in England would permit Aberdeen to forfeit British claims without substantial political fallout. Aberdeen had already instructed Pakenham to offer to submit the issue to arbitration in which the British would accept the loss of the entire territory if so ruled by the arbiter.

Polk, however, was not as willing to risk the territory to the discretion of an arbiter. He stubbornly insisted that Her Majesty's government reopen direct negotiations by submitting a proposal. This was most difficult for Aberdeen because of the impasse created when Polk withdrew the U.S. offer. The foreign secretary would need a face-saving pretext for reopening negotiations as well as some indication as to how a proposal would be received.

Not until the U.S. minister to London, Louis McLane, communicated that the British were becoming more militant in their approach to the dispute did Polk become more flexible. Despite the oft-quoted statement of his determination to "look John Bull straight in the eye," Polk softened his position enough to agree to submit a British proposal to the Senate for consideration—an innovative method that would allow the president to dilute responsibility for compromise.

News of Polk's decision, combined with a congressional resolution to abrogate the Convention of 1818 that included an invitation to negotiate the dispute, provided Aberdeen with the pretext he needed. He had Pakenham propose a division of the territory at the 49th parallel with British retention of all Vancouver Island and navigation of the Columbia River for the Hudson's Bay Company.

In June 1846 Polk signed a treaty settling the long-standing Oregon dispute. In the Oregon Treaty of 1846 the United States gained the disputed territory lying between the Columbia River and the 49th parallel and unquestioned supremacy over the extensive area west of the Rocky Mountains between Mexico on the south and the 49th parallel on the north. This gave the United States control of the Columbia River as well as the harbors of the Strait of Juan de Fuca.

The timing was crucial for the Polk administration. Almost simultaneous with the resolution of the Oregon dispute, word came to Washington that the Mexican army had engaged Taylor's forces at the Rio Grande. On May 13, 1846, Polk delivered his war message to Congress. Buchanan insisted that Polk inform the British and French that the United States had no territorial aspirations in the war with Mexico, but an indignant Polk stated that he would make no such disclaimer and would accept responsibility for any consequences. The expansionist Polk had his unwavering gaze set on California and New Mexico.

Throughout the war Polk continued to seek a diplomatic solution. He assisted in the return of the exiled Mexican general, Santa Anna, to Mexico City on the promise that the general would negotiate with the United States for the desired territory. This was a mistake. Santa Anna accepted the assistance but immediately took control of the war effort and moved against Taylor's forces. Polk even resorted to extremely unconventional modes of diplomacy such as his acceptance of an offer from journalists Moses Beach and Jane McManus to negotiate with the Mexican government. Although this proved to be a fiasco, it illustrates the president's desire for a diplomatic solution.

Finally, in spring 1847, Polk sent the chief clerk of the State Department, Nicholas Trist, to join U.S. forces under Winfield Scott in Vera Cruz to serve as official negotiator. The Trist mission began badly. Although it was, like most of Polk's diplomatic ventures, to be secret, the press exposed it immediately. But even more troublesome was the inability of Trist and Scott to get along. The Whig general felt that the president was undercutting his war-making ability by deploying an independent peace-making agent. Trist and Scott would not talk to one another for two months and did not begin to coordinate efforts until July. By then Scott was preparing to march on Mexico City, seize the capital, and end the war.

When Trist sent a Mexican treaty proposal to Washington that offered the Nueces boundary, a frustrated Polk recalled him. Trist, however, ignored his orders because a new Mexican regime intimated a willingness to negotiate. In February 1848 the insubordinate envoy signed the Treaty of Guadalupe Hidalgo. The treaty satisfied Polk's original instructions precisely—giving to the United States California, New Mexico, and the Rio Grande boundary. Compensation to the Mexicans consisted of a $15 million payment and the assumption of American claims against Mexico amounting to approximately $3.25 million. The president grudgingly submitted the treaty to the Senate, knowing that he could not easily reject a treaty that reflected so exactly his own terms. Polk also realized that a delay could allow either of two groups to jeopardize a peace settlement— those who wanted no territory at all and a group of legislators who were pressing for the acquisition of all Mexico. The Senate, with the active behind-the-scenes support of the president, approved the treaty on March 10, 1848.

With the Treaty of Guadalupe Hidalgo, Polk realized the remainder of his foreign policy objectives. He secured California, New Mexico, and the Rio Grande boundary. Before leaving office the president would also sign a postal treaty with Great Britain that reflected British acceptance of the United States on equal terms with European powers.

It should be added that Polk, despite evidence to the contrary, was capable of restraint. In 1848 he declined an invitation by the government of Yucatán to extend American hegemony over the peninsula. At the same time, however, he reaffirmed the noncolonization principle by announcing that the United States would not tolerate the acceptance of Yucatán's invitation by any other nation. Further evidence of Polk's caution can be found in his objection to the acquisition of Cuba by any means other than legitimate purchase from Spain. When Spain declined such an offer, Polk dropped the matter.

Polk had entered the White House with clear-cut foreign policy objectives. When those were satisfied by the Oregon Treaty and the Treaty of Guadalupe Hidalgo, so was Polk. A contented president therefore retired from office at the end of one term. But unfortunately his contentment was short-lived. At the end of an exhaustive celebratory tour toward his home in Nashville, the overworked executive fell ill and died on June 15, 1849.

Annotated Bibliography

Primary sources of use in evaluating the foreign policy of James K. Polk begin with the James K. Polk Papers in the Library of Congress. The collection not only provides pertinent information on Polk's diplomacy, but illuminates the man behind the diplomacy. The published volumes of *The Correspondence of James K. Polk* have not yet reached his presidential years. When they become available, they should provide a convenient source. Meanwhile students of Polk will find his published *Diary* indispensable. The selective version edited by Allan Nevins provides the most concise reflections concerning Polk's foreign policy.

Polk's public pronouncements are recorded in James D. Richardson, ed., *A Compilation of the Messages and Papers of the Presidents*. Information concerning Polk's instructions to his envoys can be found in William R. Manning, ed., *Diplomatic Correspondence of the United States* (1932–1939). For more details diligent students of Polk's foreign policy may consult the State Department documents from Record Group 59 for the appropriate years and countries. Fortunately, most of these documents are available on microfilm from the National Archives in Washington as well as its regional branches.

Few American presidents have undergone more reassessment than James K. Polk. The earliest historians to deal with his foreign policy were Whigs who accused the Southerner of provoking the Mexican War as a coconspirator with a "slavocracy" determined to secure Mexican territory for the extension of slavery. Only after the passion of partisan jealousies diminished and the memory of the Civil War faded did a more accurate view of Polk emerge. Drawing upon Milo Quaife's 1910 publication of Polk's diary, Eugene I. McCormac published the first balanced biography, *James K. Polk: A Political Biography*, in 1922. The frankness of the president's private reflections allowed McCormac to produce an account that not only accepted the significance of Polk's accomplishments but also tempered his critics. McCormac pointed out that shortly after taking office Polk presented to his secretary of the navy, George Bancroft, an agenda that stated as foreign policy objectives the resolution of the Oregon problem and the acquisition of California. In a single term as president he accomplished both. Polk, McCormac contends, was not a puppet of the slaveholders but rather a hardworking and determined leader whose forthright manner should have revealed to any observer that the policies he pursued were his own—right or wrong.

After the publication of McCormac's book, historians' opinions of the eleventh president generally continued to improve. Although the weight of his accomplishments was appreciated, his methods drew criticism. The "plot thesis," for example, which argued that Polk manipulated the Mexicans into a war for which they could be assessed responsibility, has made occasional appearances over the years. Richard R. Stenberg's article, "The Failure of Polk's Mexican War Intrigue of 1845," *Pacific Historical Review* 4, 1 (1935): 39–68, broached the notion, and again in 1967 the notion surfaced in Glenn Price's book, *Origins of the War with Mexico: The Polk-Stockdon Intrigue*. Price argued that Polk had provoked a war with Mexico while using the annexation of Texas as camouflage.

It is true that, as a diplomat, Polk lacked every obvious quality. Resolute to the point of obstinacy, he frequently avoided compromise and relied instead on stubborn perseverance. Although a man of modest ability, Polk was extremely hardworking and mastered the functions of all of his cabinet departments. But since he followed the Jacksonian assumption that only the president truly represented the people, he used his knowledge of the State Department to justify ignoring the advice of his secretary of state. In fact, Polk was slow to take advice from anyone. Once he had determined his own mind, he assumed it to be the mind of the people and pursued his course as though it was predestined. Only when circumstances dictated a compromise did he accept advice. And on those occasions he did so primarily to spread responsibility.

He was convinced that only a forceful approach to foreign policy issues was acceptable. Hence, in the Oregon crisis he took a hard line with Britain, heightening the tension between the two countries. Lord Aberdeen had determined to release the territory but could not in the face of such blustering. Of course Polk's forceful hand was most costly with Mexico, as it led, unintentionally, to war. Had Polk been willing to accept that America's claim to the Rio Grande boundary was without foundation and had he awaited more accurate information about the probable course of the California settlers, he could have avoided a war.

It is on this issue of style and method more than any other that historians of Polk's administration have continued to debate. In 1943 Julius Pratt challenged the opinion that Polk's bold stand on the Oregon dispute caused Aberdeen to offer a partition line at the 49th parallel. His article, "James K. Polk and John Bull," argues that information from the American minister in London that the British were becoming more impatient and militant actually intimidated Polk into forfeiting the territory above 49 degrees. On the other hand, the second of Charles G. Sellers's volumes on Polk, *James K. Polk, Continentalist: 1843–1846* (1966), attempts to justify Polk's direct approach as necessary for forcing issues to resolution.

David Pletcher's indispensable 1973 work, *The Diplomacy of Annexation: Texas, Oregon, and the Mexican War*, argues that Polk's blustering unnecessarily provoked both Great Britain and Mexico and that the president was fortunate that circumstances made success possible. For example, had the British not been preoccupied with rising tension with France, the potato famine in Ireland, and the desire to avoid a fight with an increasingly important trading partner, the Oregon dispute could have ended with the loss of the entire territory or an alliance between Mexico and Great Britain that could have played out a number of scenarios, all bad. Pletcher contends that a little diplomatic finesse and patient information gathering could have won for the United States the same rewards without the cost of crisis with Great Britain and war with Mexico.

Frederick Merk's several publications covering the period are also useful in developing an image of Polk's diplomacy. In *Manifest Destiny and Mission in American History: A Reinterpretation* (1963), Merk adeptly shows how Polk was forced to deal with the alternating pressures of Mexico and Great Britain. Merk's *The Monroe Doctrine and American Expansionism, 1843–1849* (1966) defends Polk's diplomacy, suggesting that, whether real or imagined, the president believed that American security was at stake in Texas, Oregon, and California. In his 1967 collection, *The Oregon Question: Essays in Anglo-American Diplomacy and Politics*, he suggests that Polk, who believed that a division of the Oregon Territory at 49 degrees would retain for the United States the essential part of the territory, utilized his political expertise to ensure Senate passage of the Oregon Treaty.

Norman Graebner would agree that Polk's goals were satisfied below the 49th Parallel. Wrapping the president's expansionism in the commercial potential of Pacific ports, Graebner contends that ocean frontage was the motivation for securing California and enough of Oregon to access the natural harbors on the Strait of Juan de Fuca. Graebner's most thorough exposition on this aspect of expansionism is his 1955 monograph, *Empire on the Pacific: A Study in American Continental Expansion.* His 1978 article, "Lessons of the Mexican War," *Pacific Historical Review* 47, 3 (1978): 325–342, ably discusses the anxiety Polk experienced late in the Mexican War when he found himself pressed by Whigs who opposed the war and wanted no territorial acquisition and by the growing all-Mexico movement.

For Polk's impact on the office of the presidency there remains nothing better than Charles A. McCoy's 1960 work, *Polk and the Presidency.* McCoy devotes an informative chapter to Polk's foreign policy, lauding the president for managing to clear away all major diplomatic problems in just four years. Most significantly, he credits Polk with shifting the authority to declare war from the legislative to the executive branch, bequeathing to all subsequent presidents a considerable amount of diplomatic latitude. The most recent work on Polk's administration, Paul H. Bergeron's *The Presidency of James K. Polk* (1987), also provides a useful and concise analysis of his foreign policy. Bergeron's work completes the transformation of Polk from alleged dupe of a southern slavocracy to astute national leader. The book offers only token criticism and leaves the reader satisfied with the value of Polk's accomplishments and his deserved position among America's most significant statesmen.

Regardless of how one perceives James K. Polk as statesman, there is one factor beyond challenge. His accomplishments were among the most significant of any administration in U.S. history and meant for the world the development of a truly continental power to dominate the Western Hemisphere and, from that base, eventually the international community. For the executive office he set a precedent for nearly total control of diplomacy via the pen and the sword that future presidents ranging from Abraham Lincoln to Theodore Roosevelt would draw upon. And by actually coordinating the war strategy, he took the title commander-in-chief from theory to reality.

Polk's reputation has ascended this century, and the once criticized executive now ranks among the outstanding U.S. presidents. Many historians have seen in his actions the genesis of the powerful and self-confident presidencies of the twentieth century. "Who is James K. Polk?" A self-assertive chief executive who rose steadily through the political ranks, overcoming intellectual mediocrity through hard work and determination, assuring for himself a place among the world's most significant leaders.

Bibliography

Primary Sources

Polk, James K. *The Diary of James K. Polk During His Presidency, 1845–1849.* 4 vols. Edited by Milo Milton Quaife. Chicago: McClurg, 1910.
———. *Polk: The Diary of a President.* Edited by Allan Nevins. New York: Longmans, Green, 1929.

Official Papers

Manning, William R., ed. *Diplomatic Correspondence of the United States: Canadian Relations, 1785–1860.* 4 vols. Washington, D.C.: Carnegie Endowment for International Peace, 1940–1945.
———, ed. *Diplomatic Correspondence of the United States: Inter-American Affairs, 1831–1860.* 12 vols. Washington, D.C.: Carnegie Endowment for International Peace, 1932–1939.

Richardson, James D., ed. *A Compilation of the Messages and Papers of the Presidents.* 11 vols. Washington, D.C.: Bureau of National Literature, 1896–1910.

Books

Bergeron, Paul H. *The Presidency of James K. Polk.* Lawrence: University Press of Kansas, 1987.

Bourne, Kenneth. *Britain and the Balance of Power in North America, 1815–1908.* Berkeley: University of California Press, 1967.

Brown, Charles H. *Agents of Manifest Destiny: The Lives and Times of the Filibusters.* Chapel Hill: University of North Carolina Press, 1980.

Fuller, John D.P. *The Movement for the Acquisition of All Mexico, 1846–1848.* Baltimore: Johns Hopkins University Press, 1936.

Goetzmann, William H. *When the Eagle Screamed: The Romantic Horizon in American Diplomacy, 1800–1860.* New York: Wiley, 1966.

Graebner, Norman A. *Empire on the Pacific: A Study in American Continental Expansion.* New York: Ronald Press, 1955.

Hietala, Thomas R. *Manifest Destiny: Anxious Aggrandizement in Late Jacksonian America.* Ithaca, N.Y.: Cornell University Press, 1985.

Jones, Wilbur D. *The American Problem in British Diplomacy: 1841–1861.* London: Macmillan, 1974.

Kohl, Clayton C. *Claims as a Cause of the Mexican War.* New York: New York University Press, 1914.

Marti, Werner H. *Messenger of Destiny: The California Adventures, 1846–1847, of Archibald Gillespie, U.S. Marine Corps.* San Francisco: Howell, 1960.

McCormac, Eugene I. *James K. Polk: A Political Biography.* Berkeley: University of California Press, 1922.

McCoy, Charles A. *Polk and the Presidency.* Austin: University of Texas Press, 1960.

Merk, Frederick. *The Oregon Question: Essays in Anglo-American Diplomacy and Politics.* Cambridge, Mass.: Harvard University Press, 1967.

Merk, Frederick. *Manifest Destiny and Mission in American History: A Reinterpretation.* New York: Knopf, 1963.

———. *The Monroe Doctrine and American Expansionism, 1843–1849.* New York: Knopf, 1966.

Merli, Frank, and Theodore A. Wilson, eds. *Makers of American Diplomacy.* New York: Scribner's, 1974.

Nelson, Anne K. *Secret Agents: President Polk and the Search for Peace with Mexico.* New York: Garland, 1988.

Pletcher, David M. *The Diplomacy of Annexation: Texas, Oregon, and the Mexican War.* Columbia: University of Missouri Press, 1973.

Price, Glenn W. *Origins of the War with Mexico: The Polk-Stockdon Intrigue.* Austin: University of Texas Press, 1967.

Reeves, Jesse S. *American Diplomacy Under Tyler and Polk.* Baltimore: Johns Hopkins University Press, 1907.

Schroeder, John H. *Mr. Polk's War: American Opposition and Dissent, 1846–1848.* Madison: University of Wisconsin Press, 1973.

Sellers, Charles G. *James K. Polk, Continentalist: 1843–1846.* Princeton, N.J.: Princeton University Press, 1966.

Smith, Justin H. *The War with Mexico*. 2 vols. New York: Macmillan, 1919.

Van Alstyne, Richard W. *The Rising American Empire*. New York: Oxford University Press, 1960.

Varg, Paul A. *United States Foreign Relations, 1820–1860*. East Lansing: Michigan State University Press, 1979.

Weinberg, Albert K. *Manifest Destiny: A Study of Nationalist Expansionism in American History*. Baltimore: Johns Hopkins University Press, 1935.

Articles

Conner, Seymour V. "Attitude and Opinions about the Mexican War, 1846–1970." *Journal of the West* 11, 2 (1972): 361–366.

Farnham, Thomas J. "Nicholas Trist and James Freaner and the Mission to Mexico." *Arizona and the West* 11, 3 (1969): 247–260.

Graebner, Norman A. "How Wars Begin: The Mexican War." In *Proceedings of the Citadel Conference on War and Diplomacy*, pp. 15–25. Edited by David H. White and John W. Gordon. Charleston, S.C.: Citadel Development Foundation, 1979.

———. "Lessons of the Mexican War." *Pacific Historical Review* 47, 3 (1978): 325–342.

———. "Maritime Factors in the Oregon Compromise." *Pacific Historical Review* 20, 4 (1951): 331–345.

———. "Polk, Politics, and Oregon." *East Tennessee Historical Society's Publications*, no. 24 (1952): 11–25.

Harstad, Peter T., and Richard W. Resh. "The Causes of the Mexican War: A Note on Changing Interpretations." *Arizona and the West* 6, 4 (1964): 289–302.

Hussey, John A. "The Origin of the Gillespie Mission." *California Historical Society Quarterly* 19, 1 (1940): 43–58.

Lambert, Paul F. "The Movement for the Acquisition of All Mexico." *Journal of the West* 11, 2 (1972): 317–327.

Merk, Frederick. "Presidential Fevers." *Mississippi Valley Historical Review* 47, 1 (1960): 3–33.

Middleton, Annie. "Donelson's Mission to Texas in Behalf of Annexation." *Southwestern Historical Quarterly* 24, 4 (1921): 247–291.

Northup, Jack. "Nicholas Trist's Mission to Mexico: A Reinterpretation." *Southwestern Historical Quarterly* 71, 3 (1968): 321–346.

Pratt, Julius W. "James K. Polk and John Bull." *Canadian Historical Review* 24, 4 (1943): 341–349.

Sage, Walter N. "The Oregon Treaty of 1846." *Canadian Historical Review* 27, 4 (1946): 349–367.

Schuyler, Robert L. "Polk and the Oregon Compromise of 1846." *Political Science Quarterly* 26, 3 (1911): 443–461.

Sears, Louis M. "Nicholas P. Trist: A Diplomat with Ideals." *Mississippi Valley Historical Review* 11, 1 (1924): 85–98.

Soward, F. H. "President Polk and the Canadian Frontier." *Canadian Historical Association Annual Report* (1930): 71–80.

Stenberg, Richard R. "The Failure of Polk's Mexican War Intrigue of 1845." *Pacific Historical Review* 4, 1 (1935): 39–68.

Van Horn, James. "Trends in Historical Interpretation: James K. Polk." *North Carolina Historical Review* 42, 4 (1965): 454–464.

Vevier, Charles. "American Continentalism: An American Idea of Expansion, 1845–1910." *American Historical Review* 65 (1960): 323–335.

DONALD A. RAKESTRAW

Armand Jean du Plessis de Richelieu (1585–1642).   Born in Paris on September 9, 1585, Armand Jean du Plessis de Richelieu was the third son of a minor nobleman from Poitou who had carved out a successful career for himself in royal service. His father's death when the child was just five forced the family to leave Paris and return to Poitou. There, as the youngest of three sons, Armand was raised with the idea that he would be forced to make his own way in life as a soldier and courtier. However, when he was seventeen his deeply religious brother Alphonse shocked the family by entering a monastery instead of waiting to take up the bishopric of Luçon, which the family had secured for him. Luçon was far too rich a prize to waste, so Armand was instructed by his mother to prepare himself for an ecclesiastical career. Not only did the young man obey, he threw himself wholeheartedly into the study of theology as well as into a life more suited to a future bishop than to a soldier. Indeed, when he was consecrated as bishop in 1606, at the age of twenty-one, he actually went to his diocese to work as the shepherd of his new flock, whereas most young men in his situation would have continued to lurk about the royal court seeking patronage.

The willingness with which Richelieu had accepted his new life and the seriousness with which he took its moral, intellectual, and spiritual dimensions can give us some valuable indications of his character and personality. While ambitious for himself, he had a strong belief in discipline and order. He recognized that his family, his church, and his king all had legitimate claims upon him, and that meaningful success could only be achieved through service to them, rather than through willful egotism. Though hampered by frail health, he also demonstrated as bishop the remarkable energy, intellect, and power of concentration that would mark his entire career. His gentle birth, graceful manners, intellectual gifts, and hard work soon brought him recognition and an opportunity to serve the crown.

The assassination in 1610 of Henry IV, France's first Bourbon monarch, had threatened to return the country to the chaos of the recently ended Wars of Religion. The new king, Louis XIII, was still a child. For all practical purposes, royal authority rested in the anxious hands of the Queen Mother, Marie de Medici. She was confronted by a fractious and turbulent nobility; a strong Protestant minority, the Huguenots, which had acquired enough political and even military privileges under Henry IV to constitute a dangerously independent "state within a state"; and cities and provinces clinging jealously to their medieval exemptions from royal authority. In the face of their stubborn resentment of royal power, Marie could do little more than watch helplessly as the crown became an object of derision.

In 1615 Marie took on the able young bishop of Luçon as an advisor; by the end of the following year Richelieu was sitting on the royal council as secretary of state. This first taste of power was infuriatingly brief, for in 1617 the sixteen-year-old Louis XIII rebelled against his mother's domination. As one of her creatures, Richelieu lost his office and his influence. The next several years were spent patiently working to heal the breach between the young king and his mother, hoping to be returned to favor. Though in 1622 Louis recognized Richelieu's services by getting the pope to make him a cardinal, it was not until 1624 that he was restored to his place on the royal council. There his brilliance and energy quickly made him the dominant figure. Throughout the remaining eighteen years of his life, Richelieu would continue to be the true head of the French government and the director of its policies. Louis XIII, in fact, emerges as a lesser figure than his famous minister. Louis's greatest claim to historical notice is the fact that while he was not intelligent enough to guide France successfully himself, he at least had the honesty to realize this and the shrewdness to recognize the potential for true greatness in Richelieu.

The view from the top of the French government in 1624 could hardly have been encouraging. The internal threats to royal authority with which Marie de Medici and her successors had wrestled since 1610 had lost neither their truculence nor their power. Even more grave, from Richelieu's perspective, was the fact that French confusion and impotence had created the specter of a Europe dominated totally by France's historic enemies, the Habsburgs. The eastern branch of that family ruled the Austrian lands, Bohemia, and parts of Hungary. Its head, Ferdinand II, was also Holy Roman Emperor. With the beginning of the Thirty Years War in 1618, he had embarked on a crusade to endow that largely honorific title with some real authority, crushing the independence of state after state within Germany. It was the western branch, though, that Richelieu perceived to be the more dangerous. Its head, Philip IV of Spain, was also the ruler of Portugal and much of Italy. In addition, vast holdings in America provided a seemingly limitless supply of silver with which to finance his diplomatic and military initiatives. He also ruled the southern Netherlands (roughly modern Belgium), which pressed against France's northeast frontiers. Nor had Philip forgotten his claims to the Dutch republic. Spain had been forced to recognize Dutch independence temporarily in 1609, but that truce had expired in 1621, signaling a renewed Spanish effort to reduce the wealthy and powerful Dutch to submission.

Richelieu was determined to restore France to its status as a great and respected force in European politics. To accomplish this he would have to break the power of the Habsburg—ending their domination of Italy, preventing the reconquest of the Dutch, thwarting their drive to unify and rule Germany, and ending or at least weakening the threat they posed to France's own frontiers. Finding the resources to carry on the great struggle against the Habsburgs entailed subjecting the French people to the authority of the royal government to an unprecedented degree. Richelieu's ceaseless demands for ever more money, men, and obedience inevitably provoked a great deal of resentment and numerous rebellions. Indeed, at several points in the 1620s even the faithful Louis XIII wavered in his support for his remarkable but widely despised minister. In 1630 Richelieu's enemies at court, led by his old patron Marie de Medici, boasted that they had turned Louis against him. The drama ended, though, with the monarch confounding them by signaling that he would remain loyal to the cardinal and his policies. This "day of the dupes" sent many of Richelieu's foes fleeing in panic and secured his position for the next decade.

To obtain the resources and support he needed for his struggle against the Habsburgs, Richelieu broke the political power of the Huguenots (though he left their freedom to worship intact), humbled the great nobles, and eroded many of the local liberties that various French provinces had long enjoyed. He subjected the *parlements* to royal control and extended the crown's authority over the bureaucracy by employing able, loyal officials known as *intendants*. In addition, he vastly increased the size and strength of the royal army and managed to bully enough tax revenues out of the constantly complaining French to pay for his ambitious policies. Many have credited him with being the real architect of the absolute monarchy that was to dazzle Europe in the second half of the seventeenth century under *Louis XIV before crashing so ruinously in 1789. The brutal period of civil strife known as the Fronde, however, which burst out in 1648 and continued for five terrible years, indicates that even after Richelieu's work had been completed, the French still had both the capacity and the will to resist the authority of the crown. Indeed, it appears that for Richelieu, reforming the cumbersome government of France was always subordinate to his true interest, which was fighting the Habsburgs.

Richelieu recognized that this struggle required France to seek alliances among the enemies of the Habsburgs all across Europe. The religious issue, though, freighted this diplomatic quest with serious complications. The Habsburgs proudly draped themselves in the pious robes of Catholic orthodoxy, justifying their wars as crusades against the heretic Protestants. Thus, most of those whom Richelieu could expect to enlist as allies—the Dutch, the Danes, the Swedes, the German and Swiss Protestants—were also the sworn enemies of the Church he served as bishop and cardinal.

With the Habsburgs thundering disapproval, and even many devout Catholics within France horrified by his actions, Richelieu, with supple diplomatic skill, set about building anti-Habsburg coalitions that included powers of both Protestant and Catholic faiths. Many have concluded from this that his foes were essentially correct in their accusations that he was a complete cynic to whom religion meant little or nothing, but the truth appears to be more complex. Richelieu was actually a highly religious man; he was serenely confident that there was not and indeed could not be any true conflict between his duties toward his royal master and the loyalty and service he owed to God and His Church.

Throughout his career Richelieu insisted vehemently that the indispensable precondition for any true and lasting peace in Europe, and for the security of the Roman Catholic Church, was that a stable balance be established in which all states could feel secure against encroachment and none was so overweeningly powerful as to disturb their peace with equanimity. That God desired such a balance was beyond question. The great threat to it, he was convinced, was the limitless ambitions of the Habsburgs, particularly those of Spain. Since the French monarchy was the only power capable of thwarting those ambitions, God's obvious intent was that France do everything in its power to thwart them. If this holy mission entailed alliances with Protestants, then this must also be God's intent.

Thus, it was with a clear conscience that Richelieu in 1625 not only sent French support to Catholic Venice and Savoy in an effort to break the Habsburg hold on northern Italy, but also began to funnel aid to the Protestant Grisons in Switzerland as well. Richelieu's goal in Switzerland was to deny Spain access to the strategic Alpine passes. Spain's effort to reconquer the Dutch depended on its ability to transport men and supplies along the "Spanish Road," which wound sinuously from Spain's possessions in northern Italy, through the Swiss passes, and down the Rhine to the Spanish Netherlands.

It was Richelieu's determination to block this Spanish Road, as well as his antipathy to the Habsburg attempt to unify Germany, which led him to intervene increasingly on the Protestant side in the Thirty Years War. In the late 1620s and early 1630s this intervention was limited to subsidies to various German princes, the Danes, the Dutch, and the Swedes. However, the death of Sweden's Gustavus Adolphus in 1632 and the emperor's crushing of the Protestant forces at the Battle of Nördlingen in 1634 raised anew the specter of a total Habsburg triumph in Germany. In 1635 Richelieu formally declared war on Spain and began to send French troops, as well as French money, into Germany.

Now fully joined, the struggle between France and the Habsburgs would continue unabated until Richelieu's death in 1642, and indeed well beyond. The Thirty Years War would not end in Germany until the Treaty of Westphalia in 1648, while the direct Franco-Spanish war dragged on until the Treaty of the Pyrenees in 1659. By the cardinal's death, though, it had become obvious, perhaps even inevitable, that France was going to emerge triumphant. Spain was by then well into a process of collapse under the crushing burdens imposed by the struggle and the rebellions Richelieu had helped foment in Portugal and Catalonia. Its power in Italy and Switzerland had been irrevocably smashed. The Dutch were secure, and their independence would be formally recognized at Westphalia in 1648. That treaty would also ratify the Habsburgs' failure to unify and dominate Germany, leaving it a fertile field for French intrigue. By Richelieu's death France had also secured its border with Spain by capturing Perpignan, the last Spanish fortress north of the Pyrenees. More dramatic expansion of French frontiers had been achieved in the north and the east, where a number of important lands and fortresses had come under French control. The most significant of these acquisitions was the duchy of Alsace, formally ceded to France at Westphalia.

France, which had been weak and on the defensive when Richelieu took the reins in 1624, had emerged as Europe's greatest single power by the time of his departure eighteen years later. This status, which owed so much to Richelieu's diplomatic finesse and indomitable will, would last for more than two centuries. His success has made him one of the most admired statesmen in European history.

Annotated Bibliography

Papers relating to Richelieu's far-flung diplomatic activities can be found in the archives of every capital in Europe, though the most important collections, of course, are those in Paris. The Archives Nationales, 60 rue des Francs-Bourgeois, 75003 Paris, and the manuscripts section of the Bibliothèque Nationale, 58 rue Richelieu, Paris, contain much significant material. The most important single repository is the archive of the Ministère des Affaires Étrangères, 37 quai d'Orsay, 75700 Paris, which contains the bulk of Richelieu's diplomatic correspondence. Interested scholars can inquire about access to these repositories by writing to the cultural attaché at the French embassy or to any French consulate.

A great deal of scholarly work has been done in publishing Richelieu's letters and other papers. Denis L.M. Avenel's eight-volume collection, *Lettres, instructions diplomatiques et papiers d'état du Cardinal de Richelieu* (1853–1857), is now being updated and vastly expanded in a new series edited by Pierre Grillon. Six of its seven volumes published before 1990 carry domestic affairs through 1631: *Les papiers de Richelieu: Section politique intérieure, correspondance et papiers d'État* (1975–1985). The seventh, edited by Adolf Wild, contains diplomatic correspondence dealing with Richelieu's relations with Germany between 1616 and 1629 under the title *Les papiers de Richelieu: Section politique extérieure, correspondance et papiers d'État* (1982).

The narrative *Mémoires du Cardinal de Richelieu* was published in a well-edited ten volumes between 1907 and 1931. Though probably compiled for the most part by Richelieu's staff under his direction, the *Mémoires* gives a vivid and reliable picture of the cardinal's maneuverings through 1629.

Ever since the eighteenth century, a scholarly debate has raged over the authenticity of Richelieu's *Political Testament*. The controversy over whether this work truly represents the cardinal's final thoughts about his role and his accomplishments or was actually written by his aides after his death is ably summarized in William F. Church's article, "Publications on Cardinal Richelieu since 1945: A Bibliographical Study," *Journal of Modern History* 37 (1965): 421–444. The most complete version of the testament is *Testament politique*, edited by Louis André (1947). Much of the work, though without the "succinct narration" in which Richelieu's foreign policy is discussed, has been translated into English by Henry Hill under the title *The Political Testament of Cardinal Richelieu: The Significant Chapters and Supporting Selections* (1961).

The French have traditionally seen Richelieu as one of the major architects of their nation's status as a great power. As such, French historians have given him a great deal of respectful attention. Massive, multivolume biographies include the four-volume study by George Avenel, *Richelieu et la monarchie absolue* (1884–1890), which concentrates on domestic political development; and Gabriel Hanotaux's six volumes, which were concluded by the Duc de la Force, *Histoire du Cardinal de Richelieu* (1893–1947). The latter, as much a history of the age as a narrowly focused biography, is clearly the more useful work. The authors admired Richelieu's accomplishments enormously and are particularly strong on his ideas and cultural influences. A Swiss diplomat, Carl Burckhardt, has more recently published a three-volume life of Richelieu containing a much more thorough treatment of diplomacy and war. It has the added advantage of being available in English translation as *Richelieu and His Age* (1940–1971).

Several excellent one-volume studies of Richelieu and his age are also available. Those by C. V. Wedgwood, *Richelieu and the French Monarchy* (1962), and Victor-Louis Tapié, *France in the Age of Louis XIII and Richelieu* (1974), are especially vivid and readable. The works of G.R.R. Treasure, *Cardinal Richelieu and the Development of Absolutism* (1972), and D. P. O'Connell, *Richelieu* (1968), are longer and more thorough. Treasure's work is particularly strong on social and economic developments, while O'Connell concentrates on a narrative description of Richelieu's foreign policy.

Even within France, Richelieu has always been a controversial figure. The debate over whether he was an ambitious, self-seeking cynic or truly believed that his policies were not only necessary but justifiable in legal and religious terms shows no signs of ending. Though the latter interpretation appears to have won general scholarly support in recent decades, Richelieu is treated roughly in the works of several respected modern scholars. These include Dieter Albrecht, *Richelieu, Gustaf Adolf und das Reich* (1959); Georges Mongrédien, *10 Novembre 1630: La Journée des Dupes* (1961); Kurt von Raumer, "Westfälischer Friede," *Historische Zeitschrift* 195 (1962): 596–613; and Etienne Thuau, *Raison d'Etat et pensée politique à l'époque de Richelieu* (1966).

Works generally sympathetic to Richelieu, defending his sincerity and sense of morality, include those already cited by Burckhardt and Tapié and an important article by Georges Pagès, "Autour du 'grand orage.' Richelieu et Marillac: deux politiques," *Revue Historique* 179 (1937): 63–97. In addition, William Church, *Richelieu and Reason of State* (1972), gives a reasoned and judicious response to Thuau's arguments about Richelieu's Machiavellianism, while Fritz Dickmann, "Rechtsgedanke und Machtpolitik bei Richelieu," *Historische Zeitschrift* 196 (1963): 265–319, and Hermann Weber, "Richelieu et le Rhin," *Revue Historique* 239 (1968): 265–280, critically evaluate the conclusions of Albrecht and Raumer.

John Elliott, in a highly stimulating comparison of Richelieu and his great Spanish rival, *Richelieu and Olivares* (1984), provocatively raises another question. Should Richelieu, regardless of his goals and motivations, be seen as a success, given the terrible costs of his policies to the suffering peoples of Europe and the French inheritors of his absolutism and ambition?

Several recent works have explored Richelieu's efforts to enhance France's economic and naval power. A listing of relevant works can be found in the bibliographical study by Philip Boucher, *The Shaping of the French Colonial Empire: A Bio-Bibliography of the Careers of Richelieu, Fouquet, and Colbert* (1985). Particularly valuable in this area are the books by David Parker, *La Rochelle and the French Monarchy* (1980), and Henri Hauser, *La pensée et l'action économique du Cardinal Richelieu* (1944). Hauser's study, though not available in English translation, remains more trustworthy than Franklin Palm's attempt to supersede it, *The Economic Policies of Richelieu* (1972).

Bibliography

Albrecht, Dieter. *Richelieu, Gustaf Adolf und das Reich*. Munich and Vienna: Oldenbourg, 1959.

Avenel, George, Vicomte D'. *Richelieu et la monarchie absolue*. 4 vols. Paris: Plon, 1884–1890.

Boucher, Philip R. *The Shaping of the French Colonial Empire: A Bio-Bibliography of the Careers of Richelieu, Fouquet, and Colbert*. New York: Garland Press, 1985.

Burckhardt, Carl J. *Richelieu and His Age*. 3 vols. London: Allen and Unwin, 1940–1971.

Church, William Farr. "Publications on Cardinal Richelieu since 1945: A Bibliographical Study." *Journal of Modern History* 37 (1965): 421–444.

———. *Richelieu and Reason of State*. Princeton, N.J.: Princeton University Press, 1972.

Dickmann, Fritz. "Rechtsgedanke und Machtpolitik bei Richelieu." *Historische Zeitschrift* 196 (1963): 265–319.

Elliott, J. H. *Richelieu and Olivares*. Cambridge: Cambridge University Press, 1984.

Hanotaux, Gabriel, and A. de Caumont, Duc de la Force. *Histoire du Cardinal de Richelieu*. 6 vols. Paris: Société de l'histoire nationale, 1893–1947.

Hauser, Henri. *La pensée et l'action économique du Cardinal Richelieu*. Paris: Presses universitaires de France, 1944.

Mongrédien, Georges. *10 Novembre 1630: La Journée des Dupes*. Paris: Gallimard, 1961.

O'Connell, D. P. *Richelieu*. London: Weidenfeld and Nicolson, 1968.

Pagès, Georges. "Autour du 'grand orage.' Richelieu et Marillac: deux politiques." *Revue Historique* 179 (1937): 63–97.

Palm, Franklin C. *The Economic Policies of Richelieu*. Urbana: University of Illinois Press, 1972.

Parker, David. *La Rochelle and the French Monarchy*. London: Royal Historical Society, 1980.

Raumer, Kurt von. "Westfälischer Friede." *Historische Zeitschrift* 195 (1962): 596–613.

Richelieu, Armand du Plessis, Cardinal Duc de. *Lettres, instructions diplomatiques et papiers d'état du Cardinal de Richelieu*. 8 vols. Edited by Denis L.M. Avenel. Paris: Imprimerie Imperiale, 1853–1857.

———. *Mémoires du Cardinal de Richelieu*. 10 vols. Edited by the Société de l'Histoire de France. Paris: Renouard, 1907–1931.

———. *Les papiers de Richelieu: Section politique extérieure, correspondance et papiers d'État*. Edited by Adolf Wild. Paris: Pedone, 1982.

———. *Les papiers de Richelieu: Section politique intérieure, correspondance et papiers d'État*. 6 vols. Edited by Pierre Grillon. Paris: Pedone, 1975–1985.

———. *The Political Testament of Cardinal Richelieu: The Significant Chapters and Supporting Selections*. Edited by Henry B. Hill. Madison: University of Wisconsin Press, 1961.

———. *Testament politique*. Edited by Louis André. Paris: Laffont, 1947.

Tapié, Victor-Louis. *France in the Age of Louis XIII and Richelieu*. London: Macmillan, 1974.

Thuau, Etienne. *Raison d'Etat et pensée politique à l'époque de Richelieu*. Paris: Armand Colin, 1966.

Treasure, G.R.R. *Cardinal Richelieu and the Development of Absolutism*. London: Adam and Charles Black, 1972.

Weber, Hermann. "Richelieu et le Rhin." *Revue Historique* 239 (1968): 265–280.
Wedgwood, Cicely Veronica. *Richelieu and the French Monarchy.* New York: Collier, 1962.

GARRETT L. McAINSH

Franklin D. Roosevelt (1882–1945). Franklin Delano Roosevelt, thirty-second president of the United States, was born on January 30, 1882, at Hyde Park, New York. He was the son of James Roosevelt, vice president of the Delaware and Hudson Railroad, and Sara Delano, the strong-willed daughter of a wealthy entrepreneur. Roosevelt journeyed several times to Europe with his aristocratic parents and attended Groton Academy. After graduating from Harvard University in 1904, he studied law at Columbia University and was admitted to the New York State bar in 1907. He married Anna Eleanor Roosevelt, niece of President *Theodore Roosevelt, on March 17, 1905. Their five children were Anna Eleanor, James, Elliott, Franklin Delano, Jr., and John.

Stints as a New York state senator from 1909 to 1911 and as assistant secretary of the navy from 1913 to 1921 followed. During World War I, Roosevelt persuaded President *Woodrow Wilson to construct numerous small coastal patrol boats and lay North Sea mines between Norway and Scotland. Roosevelt's 1918 visit to Europe included inspecting navy bases, conferring with Allied leaders, and touring the battlefront in France. Following World War I, the Wilsonian ardently supported American membership in the League of Nations. Roosevelt was defeated as the Democratic party vice presidential candidate in the 1920 elections and contracted polio in 1921 while vacationing at Campobello, Newfoundland. Although permanently crippled, Roosevelt bravely continued his law and political activities and served two terms as governor of New York from 1929 to 1933. He wrote significant articles for *Asia* (July 1923) favoring improved relations with Japan, and for *Foreign Affairs* (July 1928) denouncing the foreign policies of Republican presidents Warren Harding and Calvin Coolidge. Other articles or speeches supported the Five Power Naval Disarmament Treaty of 1922, the adjustment of war debts, and U.S. membership in the World Court, and opposed high protective tariffs.

The 1932 Chicago convention saw the Democrats nominate Roosevelt for the presidency. Roosevelt subordinated international issues during his campaign, stressing the national economic crisis and pledging a new deal. He defeated incumbent Herbert Hoover easily in November and was reelected president in 1936, 1940, and 1944.

From 1932 to 1944, the internationalist Roosevelt stressed nationalism. Roosevelt believed that the United States should play a dynamic role in world affairs, but he sought primarily to build national economic stability. He preferred that the United States seek economic recovery through domestic programs rather than economic cooperation abroad. At the 1933 London Economic Conference, Roosevelt announced that the United States would not join international currency stabilization plans. The United States left the gold standard, required repayment of war debts, and downplayed the Geneva Disarmament Conference. Roosevelt recognized the Communist government in the Soviet Union in November 1933 and finished the development of the Good Neighbor diplomatic policy toward Latin America. Under a reciprocal trade program, the United States negotiated numerous trade agreements with foreign nations. The Senate rejection of U.S. membership in the World Court in 1935 disappointed Roosevelt.

Roosevelt largely functioned as an isolationist from 1933 to 1938. Isolationism prevailed both nationally and in Congress, limiting Roosevelt's maneuverability. Although deploring German, Italian, and Japanese aggression, Roosevelt maintained U.S. neutrality and opposed active involvement in war. "I shall pass unnumbered hours," the president pledged in 1936, "thinking and planning how war may be kept from this nation." The Senate Nye Committee solidified national isolationist sentiment, accusing profiteering bankers and munitions makers of having led the United States into World War I. Congress enacted neutrality legislation in response to the Italian invasion of Ethiopia in 1935 and the Nazi remilitarization of the Rhineland in 1936. The Neutrality Act of 1935 denied arms shipments to all belligerents when the president proclaimed a state of war. Americans could travel on belligerent vessels at their own risk. Congress extended the Neutrality Act in 1936 to cover the Spanish Civil War, but denied the chief executive authority to determine aggressors. Roosevelt preferred to impose an embargo only on arms shipments to aggressors and permit munitions sales to nations under attack. Under the Neutrality Act of 1937, the United States could ship nonmilitary goods to belligerent nations on a cash and carry basis.

Roosevelt favored reducing nonmilitary shipments to Japan. When Japan invaded China in 1937, he refused to invoke the neutrality legislation because China would be penalized. Roosevelt urged quarantining aggressor nations in a speech in Chicago in October 1937 and privately preferred applying economic sanctions against Japan. His quarantine speech infuriated American isolationists, dissuading him from pledging American cooperative action against Japan during the 1937 Brussels Conference. After Japanese aviators sank a U.S. gunboat, the *Panay*, in China, Roosevelt quickly accepted an apology and indemnity.

*Adolf Hitler's expansionist activity personally alarmed Roosevelt, but he still did not intervene in Europe because of prevailing isolationist opinion. When Hitler seized Austria in March 1938, the Roosevelt administration remained silent. The president played a limited role in the Munich Pact six months later, but he welcomed Hitler's pledge to stop further aggression in exchange for acquiring the Sudetenland. The Nazi persecution of German Jews unfortunately did not prod the Roosevelt administration to arouse the national conscience. The United States could have accepted Jewish refugee immigrants, but American public opinion resisted easing immigration barriers because of widespread unemployment. Roosevelt, meanwhile, favored strengthening the U.S. Navy on both the Atlantic and Pacific oceans and constructing factories to increase arms production for victims of aggression. At the president's request in November 1938, annual aircraft production was increased to 10,000 combat planes.

Hitler violated the Munich Pact in March 1939, seizing Prague and bringing the remainder of Czechoslovakia under German control. Roosevelt urged Congress to revise the neutrality legislation, permitting arms shipments to victims of German and Italian aggression. The isolationist-minded Congress, however, refused to alter the neutrality law, letting cash and carry shipment of nonmilitary goods expire in May 1939. Roosevelt summoned legislative leaders to the White House in July 1939 in a futile attempt to break the impasse.

From September 1939 to December 1941, the Roosevelt administration aided Great Britain and France militarily and economically. World War II started in September 1939 when Germany invaded Poland. Great Britain and France declared war on Germany, while Roosevelt proclaimed American neutrality. To deter German aggression, Roosevelt wanted the United States to give substantial economic and military help to Great Britain and France. Most Americans, however, still opposed direct U.S. military intervention. Roosevelt summoned Congress into special session in September to remove the arms embargo. Congress complied, enabling Great Britain and France to purchase American armaments and transport them in their own vessels. When the Soviet Union attacked Finland in November 1939, the Roosevelt administration gave limited economic assistance to Finland while maintaining diplomatic relations with the Soviet Union.

The Nazi blitzkrieg of western Europe in 1940 enhanced Roosevelt's desire to help the Allies short of war. That spring, Germany occupied Denmark and Norway and conquered the Benelux countries and France. Roosevelt dramatically increased American economic and military assistance to Great Britain while withholding the United States from combat. Congress funded at least 50,000 additional planes at the president's request and approved the nation's first peacetime draft in the late summer. In September Roosevelt announced that the United States had negotiated a secret destroyer-base deal with British prime minister *Winston Churchill. Fifty overage American destroyers were exchanged for long-term leases to British bases from Newfoundland to the Caribbean. Because of the worsening European situation, a majority of Americans now favored giving military and economic assistance to Great Britain. Roosevelt decided to seek an unprecedented third term. He and Republican presidential candidate Wendell Willkie both endorsed helping the Allies, but pledged to avoid direct military intervention if possible. "Your boys," Roosevelt vowed, "are not going to be sent into any foreign wars." In November Roosevelt defeated Willkie easily.

Roosevelt's inaugural address in January 1941 outlined his long-range aspirations. The president envisioned a postwar world based on freedom of speech and religion, and freedom from want and fear. Roosevelt, who deemed the defeat of the Nazis essential to accomplish the Four Freedoms, increasingly realized that direct U.S. participation in the war would be required to achieve an Allied victory. Since Americans still rejected direct combat, however, Roosevelt claimed publicly that the United States could aid the Allies without becoming an active belligerent. The president still relied heavily on public opinion and did not provide sufficient dynamic leadership. Preferring to react to public opinion rather than try to change it, he waited for overseas developments to rally Americans behind an all-out war effort.

By December 1940, the British acutely needed American war supplies. Roosevelt persuaded Congress in early 1941 to authorize him to lend war supplies to Great Britain and other nations fighting the Nazis, provided that they repay in kind after the war. The president refrained from lending money because the Johnson Act of 1934 prohibited making cash loans to those nations still owing World War I debts. Lend-Lease, Roosevelt boasted, made the United States "the great arsenal of democracy," providing $48 billion in munitions, aircraft, and other military supplies to Great Britain, France, China, and other allies. U.S. warships escorted Lend-Lease convoys across the Atlantic Ocean. To ensure the safe arrival of these goods, Roosevelt ordered U.S. planes and ships to patrol the North Atlantic for German submarines and stationed U.S. troops in Greenland and Iceland.

In August 1941 Roosevelt conferred with Churchill for the first time at Placentia Bay, Newfoundland. Although no important strategic decisions were made, the conference demonstrated Anglo-American cooperation. Churchill implored the United States to ally fully with Great Britain and declare war on Germany, but Roosevelt preferred that American participation be restricted to sea and air warfare. Roosevelt and Churchill issued the Atlantic Charter, containing idealistic war aims and a general framework for the postwar world. The charter principles included the Four Freedoms, equal trade access, freedom of the seas, stable international peace, and arms reduction. Roosevelt and Churchill, disavowing territorial ambitions, agreed that any territorial changes should get the consent of the parties involved and that self-government should be guaranteed.

The Roosevelt administration, meanwhile, sanctioned combat against German submarines in the North Atlantic. The German submarine attack on the U.S. destroyer *Greer* in September 1941 enabled Roosevelt to expand U.S. military efforts against the Nazis. Roosevelt directed U.S. ships to protect the western half of the Atlantic and U.S. naval commanders to shoot on sight at German or Italian warships entering the North Atlantic region, freeing British vessels to patrol the eastern half of the Atlantic. After German submarines clashed with the USS *Kearney* in October 1941, Roosevelt persuaded Congress to permit American ships to transport arms, ammunition, and implements of war directly to the Allies. When the Germans attacked Russia in June 1941, Roosevelt made the Soviet Union eligible for Lend-Lease assistance. Although disliking communism, the president realized that any nation battling Hitler merited American support.

Japan had conquered much of China and Indochina by 1941, forcing the Roosevelt administration to terminate the 1911 trade treaty, reduce the shipment of scrap iron and aviation gasoline, and freeze all Japanese assets. Diplomatic negotiations reached an impasse because the Japanese military rejected Roosevelt's demand to withdraw from China. On December 7, Japan attacked Pearl Harbor, the primary U.S. naval base in the Pacific. In an address to Congress the next day, Roosevelt denounced Japan's "dastardly attack" on the "date which will live in infamy" and urged a declaration of war against Japan. The Japanese attack silenced remaining isolationist resistance in Congress and across the nation. Congress quickly declared war on Japan, with only one representative dissenting. Three days later, Germany and Italy declared war on the United States.

After Pearl Harbor, Roosevelt's role changed dramatically to that of direct interventionist and commander-in-chief. As direct interventionist, Roosevelt sought complete military victory in the quickest possible time with the lowest possible number of casualties. He gave priority to the defeat of Germany on the Atlantic front while allocating enough manpower and resources to restrain the Japanese on the Pacific front. The United States and Great Britain differed significantly with the Soviet Union but needed *Joseph Stalin's cooperation to defeat Germany and build a stable, peaceful world based on Roosevelt's Four Freedoms. As commander-in-chief, Roosevelt made the ultimate decisions concerning U.S. military conduct of the war. Military procurement and the production of munitions, aircraft, and ships were placed under civilian control. Roosevelt depended heavily on military leaders for determining battlefront strategy. Germany and Japan remained on the offensive during the first few months of direct U.S. military involvement. German troops still controlled the European front, although unable to defeat the Soviet Union or mount another invasion of Great Britain. Japanese forces, meanwhile, conquered Guam, Hong Kong, the Philippines, and Singapore in the western Pacific.

Roosevelt initially favored launching an Allied invasion across the English Channel into France by the spring of 1943. Stalin urged the United States and Great Britain to open a second front to draw some German troops from Russia, but Churchill claimed that the Allies lacked sufficient military power to attack across the English Channel. Churchill warned that the Germans were planning to conquer Egypt and convinced Roosevelt to approve Operation Torch, a joint invasion of French North Africa, in November 1942.

In January 1943 Roosevelt conferred with Churchill at Casablanca, Morocco, becoming the first U.S. president to travel overseas in wartime. Churchill persuaded Roosevelt to postpone the French campaign, substituting an invasion of Sicily and Italy. Roosevelt announced there that the Allies would battle until Germany, Italy, and Japan surrendered unconditionally. Unconditional surrender became official Allied policy, although it probably intensified German and Japanese resistance and deterred German military leaders from overthrowing Hitler.

The Allies, however, remained divided. Roosevelt insisted that the United States, Great Britain, and the Soviet Union collaborate effectively on both military and postwar strategy. Until November 1943, however, Stalin declined Roosevelt's invitation to confer with British and U.S. leaders. Stalin resisted traveling very far from the Russian battlefront and protested Allied delays in launching a cross-Channel invasion. Colonialism, meanwhile, caused disagreement between Churchill and Roosevelt. Churchill favored preserving the British

Empire and dividing the postwar world into spheres of influence among the three major powers, while Roosevelt deplored colonialism and supported an international organization for building collective security. Roosevelt, who comprehended the rising tide of Asian and African nationalism, advocated applying Atlantic Charter principles to colonial possessions. He especially disapproved of the French regaining control of Indochina and urged Great Britain to grant India freedom.

Roosevelt, Churchill, and Stalin conferred jointly for the first time at Teheran, Iran, in November 1943. Churchill proposed additional Anglo-American campaigns in the Balkans, but Roosevelt and Stalin rejected his pleas. Churchill reluctantly consented to Operation Overlord, an Anglo-American invasion of German-held France for the spring of 1944. The Allied desire for a speedy victory prevailed over Churchill's long-range strategic postwar designs. The D-Day invasion of the Normandy beaches seven months later marked a turning point. Anglo-American forces marched through France and western Germany and ousted Hitler within a year, while Russian troops seized Poland and eastern Germany. American voters still backed Roosevelt's handling of war diplomacy and strategy, giving him an unprecedented fourth presidential term in November 1944.

The final meeting between Roosevelt, Churchill, and Stalin came at Yalta in February 1945. Historians have claimed that Roosevelt's declining health impaired his decisions on Poland, eastern Europe, and the Far East but have overlooked how existing conditions limited his maneuverability. Russian forces already occupied most of Poland and eastern Europe. Stalin insisted on retaining a pro-Soviet Communist government at Lublin, Poland, to assure a loyal neighbor to his west. Roosevelt, who hoped to establish a democratic government in Poland, encouraged Stalin to loosen Soviet army control and broaden the existing government. Stalin pledged to assist the eastern European nations in forming democratic governments through free elections, but interpreted those concepts differently than Roosevelt and Churchill. Roosevelt accepted Stalin's pledges because only armed force could have driven the Soviet armies from Poland and the rest of eastern Europe. Churchill persuaded Roosevelt to give France an occupation zone in Germany, but Stalin insisted that the land be carved from the British and U.S. territory. Although setting no final reparations amount, the conferees allowed one-half of Germany's payments to go to the Russians.

At Roosevelt's request, Stalin secretly promised that the Soviet Union would declare war on Japan within three months following Germany's surrender. Roosevelt claimed that Soviet intervention would shorten the Pacific war and save many American lives. Military analysts had warned Roosevelt that the battle against Japan could last two years and cost 500,000 American lives. The Soviet Union did not declare war against Japan until U.S. troops had driven Japan close to surrender, but received Asian territory as compensation. The controversial secret agreement was not published until February 1946. Roosevelt overestimated his ability to win Stalin's cooperation and approved too many vague agreements at Yalta, but he firmly believed that the United States, Great Britain, and the Soviet Union could preserve world peace within the United Nations framework.

At Yalta, plans were finalized for establishing the United Nations as a peace-keeping organization. To protect American interests, Roosevelt proposed that the five permanent Security Council members possess a veto power over substantive UN action, but not over discussion. Stalin preferred extending the veto power to discussion of an item and insisted that all sixteen Soviet republics have votes in the General Assembly. The United States won its version of the veto, while the Soviet Union received three General Assembly seats. Roosevelt planned to address the San Francisco Conference on the United Nations in late April 1945, but died on April 12 of a massive cerebral hemorrhage at Warm Springs, Georgia.

Roosevelt ranks among those statesmen who truly changed the world. He directed the United States through the World War II crisis and strengthened the presidential office internationally, exhibiting charisma, confidence, dedication, idealism, humanitarianism, realism, and pragmatism. U.S. foreign and military policy changed under Roosevelt, shifting from isolationism to interventionism. Roosevelt's idealistic goals, based on the Four Freedoms, spearheaded his quest for a collective security system. Too often, however, he compromised his idealistic goals and followed public opinion. His administration also failed to lower immigration barriers to help beleaguered German Jews and transgressed the civil liberties of Japanese-Americans. Nevertheless, Roosevelt gave the United States and the free world the courage and vision necessary to survive the greatest challenge to democracy in modern world history and enabled the United States to emerge as the strongest nation on the planet.

Annotated Bibliography

The Franklin D. Roosevelt Library at Hyde Park, New York, is indispensable for examining the president's foreign and military policies. Although various documentaries have published much of Roosevelt's significant foreign policy correspondence and many of his oral statements, the Roosevelt Library houses a large collection of important unpublished manuscripts. The four main sections of Roosevelt's papers are the Official File, the President's Personal File, the President's Secretary's File, and the Map Room Papers, valuable for the 1942–1945 period. An extensive alphabetical file has pertinent correspondence from the American public to Roosevelt. At the Roosevelt Library, other appropriate collections include the Eleanor Roosevelt Manuscripts, Adolf A. Berle Manuscript Diary and Manuscripts, Harry Hopkins Manuscripts, John L. McCrea Manuscripts, R. Walton Moore Manuscripts, Henry Morgenthau, Jr., Farm Credit Administration Manuscript Diary, Henry Morgenthau, Jr., Manuscript Diary, Henry Morgenthau, Jr., Presidential Manuscript Diary, Harold D. Smith Manuscript Diary, Charles W. Taussig Manuscripts, and Rexford G. Tugwell Manuscript Diary.

Libraries and repositories elsewhere have pertinent correspondence. These include the Thomas C. Hart, Emory S. Land, Frances Perkins, Samuel I. Rosenman, and Henry A. Wallace Oral Histories at the Columbia University Oral History Collection in New York City; the J. Pierrepont Moffat Manuscript Diary and Manuscripts and William Phillips

Manuscript Diary at Harvard University in Cambridge, Massachusetts; the Henry H. Arnold Manuscripts, Robert W. Bingham Manuscript Diary, Joseph Davies Manuscript Diary, James Farley Manuscripts, Herbert Feis Manuscripts, Cordell Hull Manuscripts, Harold Ickes Manuscript Diary, Frank Knox Manuscripts, William D. Leahy Manuscript Diary, and Breckinridge Long Manuscript Diary at the Library of Congress in Washington, D.C.; the Senate Foreign Relations Committee Manuscripts, U.S. State Department Manuscripts, and U.S. Army Manuscripts at the National Archives in Washington, D.C.; the Edward R. Stettinius, Jr., Manuscript Diary and Manuscripts and Edwin Watson Manuscripts at the University of Virginia in Charlottesville; and the Henry L. Stimson Manuscript Diary and Manuscripts at Yale University in New Haven, Connecticut. The British Public Record Office in London, England, has the Winston Churchill Papers. The pertinent Premier Files contain the Prime Minister's Operational Files and the Prime Minister's Confidential Files.

The Franklin D. Roosevelt Library at Hyde Park, New York, houses Roosevelt's voluminous unpublished foreign policy correspondence. Roosevelt wrote several articles on foreign policy issues from 1915 to 1928, most notably "Shall We Trust Japan?" *Asia* 23 (July 1923): 475–478, 526, 528, and "Our Foreign Policy: A Democratic View," *Foreign Affairs* 6 (July 1928): 573–586. Although Roosevelt never wrote personal memoirs, editor Samuel Rosenman's massive thirteen-volume *Public Papers and Addresses of Franklin D. Roosevelt* (1939–1950) covers the president's notable speeches, proclamations, executive orders, correspondence, and press conferences with explanatory notes. Some Roosevelt foreign policy correspondence appears in Elliott Roosevelt, ed., *F.D.R.: His Personal Letters*, vols. 3–4 (1950). Edgar B. Nixon, ed., *Franklin D. Roosevelt and Foreign Affairs* (1969), contains numerous official documents and ambassadorial reports from Roosevelt's first presidential term. The U.S. Department of State's invaluable *Foreign Relations of the United States* series (1943–1972) has vital World War II correspondence and important volumes on Roosevelt's major diplomatic conferences. Warren F. Kimball, ed., *Churchill and Roosevelt: The Complete Correspondence* (1984), discloses their personal, military, diplomatic, and political views.

The most provocative biography of Roosevelt remains the two-volume work by James MacGregor Burns. His *Roosevelt: The Lion and the Fox* (1956) treats Roosevelt's foreign policy sparingly through Pearl Harbor. *Roosevelt: The Soldier of Freedom* (1970) shows the president's complex character and inability to coordinate his announced foreign policy principles and actions. Other classic works concentrate mainly on Roosevelt's New Deal policies. Frank Freidel's indispensable four-volume biography, *Franklin D. Roosevelt* (1952–1973), describes Roosevelt's life through the middle of 1933, while Arthur M. Schlesinger, Jr., *The Age of Roosevelt*, 3 vols. (1957–1960), brilliantly places Roosevelt in the context of his era through the 1936 presidential elections. In *Franklin D. Roosevelt and the New Deal, 1932–1940* (1963), William E. Leuchtenberg perceptively summarizes Roosevelt's first two presidential terms.

The classic study of Roosevelt's approach to international issues remains Robert Dallek's sympathetic, analytical book, *Franklin D. Roosevelt and American Foreign Policy, 1933–1945* (1979). According to Dallek, the internationalist Roosevelt was a nationalist from 1932 to 1934, an isolationist from 1935 to 1938, a politician from 1939 to 1941, and an idealist as realist from 1942 to 1945. In *Roosevelt and World War II* (1969), Robert A. Divine criticizes Roosevelt's leadership and portrays him variously as an isolationist, interventionist, realist, and pragmatist. Willard Range's *Franklin D. Roosevelt's World Order* (1959) objectively weaves Roosevelt's complex shifting foreign policy views into a coherent pattern. *Roosevelt and the Isolationists, 1932–45* (1983) by Wayne Cole traces the president's often strained relations with the isolationists in Congress and nationally.

Several useful studies treat Roosevelt's foreign policies in the 1930s. Manfred Jonas, *Isolationism in America, 1935–1941* (1966), ably shows the isolationist restraints on Roosevelt. According to Robert A. Divine, *The Illusion of Neutrality* (1962), the neutrality legislation stemmed from vocal isolationist public opinion and Roosevelt's inconsistent leadership. In *American Appeasement: U.S. Foreign Policy and Germany, 1933–1938* (1969), Arnold A. Offner assails the Roosevelt administration's failure to oppose Nazi Germany more vigorously. Roosevelt's efforts to preserve peace with the Soviet Union are described in Edward M. Bennett, *Franklin D. Roosevelt and the Search for Security* (1985). Dorothy Borg, *The U.S. and the Far Eastern Crisis of 1933–1938* (1964), stresses that Roosevelt encouraged China while hoping to avoid war with Japan. For Roosevelt's Latin American views, see Bryce Wood, *The Making of the Good Neighbor Policy* (1961), and Irwin F. Gellman, *Good Neighbor Policy* (1979).

Roosevelt's policy from 1939 to 1941 has intrigued historians. S. Everett Gleason and William L. Langer's *The Challenge to Isolation, 1937–1940* (1950) and *The Undeclared War, 1940–1941* (1953) remain the most comprehensive description of how Roosevelt effectively guided the nation to increased involvement on the international scene. According to Robert A. Divine, *The Reluctant Belligerent* (1979), Roosevelt provided timid, irresolute leadership in moving Congress and the nation slowly from isolationism to internationalism. The best synthesis of U.S. diplomacy toward Germany and Japan from March to December 1941 is Waldo Heinrichs, *Threshold of War* (1988). Richard M. Ketchum, *The Borrowed Years, 1938–1941* (1989), provides a lively, anecdotal portrait of the crucial years leading to Pearl Harbor.

Several books feature Roosevelt's policies toward European nations from 1939 to 1941. David Reynolds, *The Creation of the Anglo-American Alliance, 1937–1941* (1982), brilliantly traces how the close yet cautious and often strained relationship emerged between Roosevelt and Great Britain and how power shifted from Great Britain to the United States. According to James R. Leutze, *Bargaining for Supremacy: Anglo-American Naval Collaboration, 1937–1941* (1977), Roosevelt was determined to make the U.S. fleet the dominant world naval power. Warren F. Kimball, *The Most Unsordid Act: Lend Lease, 1939–1941* (1969), recounts Roosevelt's vast political and diplomatic maneuvering in arranging the most important legislative step toward war. Roosevelt's quasi-naval war with Germany on the Atlantic front in 1941 is detailed in Thomas A. Bailey and Paul B. Ryan, *Hitler Versus Roosevelt* (1979). Henry Feingold, *The Politics of Rescue* (1970), and David S. Wyman, *Paper Walls* (1968), portray the Roosevelt administration's indifference toward the plight of the Jewish refugees. In *The Decision to Aid Russia, 1941* (1959), Raymond H. Dawson relates how Roosevelt secured domestic support for Lend-Lease assistance to the Soviet Union. Julian G. Hurstfield's *America and the French Nation, 1939–1945* (1986) details Roosevelt's policy toward France.

The best description of Roosevelt's policies toward Japan through 1941 still may be Herbert Feis's sympathetic *The Road to Pearl Harbor* (1950). Paul W. Schroeder, *The Axis Alliance and Japanese-American Relations, 1941* (1958), assails Roosevelt's policy toward Japan as too inflexible and making war inevitable. In *Pearl Harbor: Warning and Decision* (1962), Roberta Wohlstetter claims that scant intelligence information indicated a possible Japanese attack on Pearl Harbor. Bruce Russett's *No Clear and Present Danger* (1972) questions Roosevelt's entry into World War II.

Roosevelt's wartime diplomacy and plans for the postwar world are delineated in several works. Herbert Feis, *Churchill, Roosevelt, Stalin* (1957), William H. McNeill, *America, Britain, and Russia, 1941–1946* (1953), and Robert Beitzell, *The Uneasy Alliance* (1972), reveal the clashing aims and objectives of the Big Three and how their goals were compromised. In *American Diplomacy During the Second World War* (1985), Gaddis Smith modifies his earlier criticism of Roosevelt and argues that his leadership helped bring victory over the Axis nations. *After Victory* (1967) by William L. Neumann reveals Roosevelt's struggle with Churchill and Stalin to achieve common postwar goals.

Other books handle Roosevelt's military strategy. An excellent introductory survey is A. Russell Buchanan, *The United States and World War II* (1964). Kent R. Greenfield, *American Strategy in World War II* (1963), and Samuel Eliot Morison, *Strategy and Compromise* (1958), analyze Roosevelt's critical strategic decisions and his differences with the Allies. For Roosevelt's relations with his military staff, see Eric Larrabee, *Commander in Chief* (1987). Raymond G. O'Connor's *Diplomacy for Victory: FDR and Unconditional Surrender* (1971) argues that Roosevelt's policy united the Allies and helped achieve the Allied victory, but Anne Armstrong's *Unconditional Surrender* (1961) claims that the president's Casablanca Conference strategy prolonged the war. According to Richard W. Steele, *The First Offensive, 1942* (1973), politics dictated the North African campaign. Anglo-American differences from 1941 to 1943 are examined in Mark A. Stoler, *The Politics of the Second Front* (1977). *A Changing of the Guard* (1990) by Randall Bennett Woods details the power shift from Great Britain to the United States.

Roosevelt's diplomatic conferences have stirred particular interest. Theodore A. Wilson, *The First Summit: Roosevelt and Churchill at Placentia Bay, 1941* (1969), recounts the Atlantic Conference and the drafting of the Atlantic Charter. The Moscow, Cairo, and Teheran conferences in 1943 are reviewed in Keith Sainsbury's *The Turning Point* (1985), with Keith Eubank's *Summit at Teheran* (1985) probing the final meeting. Roosevelt's role at the Yalta Conference is described variously in Diane Shaver Clemens, *Yalta* (1970), Lisle Rose, *After Yalta* (1973), Athan Theoharis, *The Yalta Myths* (1970), and Russell D. Buhite, *Decisions at Yalta* (1986).

Numerous works illuminate Roosevelt's policy toward the Soviet Union. In *Franklin D. Roosevelt and the Search for Victory* (1990), Edward M. Bennett maintains that Roosevelt applied a pragmatic, flexible approach in shaping Soviet policy from 1939 to 1945. According to George C. Herring, Jr., *Aid to Russia, 1941–1946* (1973), Roosevelt provided American assistance to assure Stalin of Allied cooperation. Robert H. Jones, *The Roads to Russia* (1969), argues that Roosevelt attached no political or economic strings to the massive lend-lease shipments. *The Politics of War* (1968) by Gabriel Kolko assails U.S. economic policies for declining relations with the Soviet Union from 1943 to 1945. Roosevelt's policies caused some problems with the Russians, according to John Lewis Gaddis in *The United States and the Origins of the Cold War* (1972), but the Soviets mainly started the verbal war. Roosevelt's Asian policies also have sparked enormous interest among historians. Christopher Thorne's *Allies of a Kind* (1978) and William Roger Louis's *Imperialism at Bay* (1977) analyze Anglo-American differences over the war against Japan and over the future of colonialism, respectively. In *Power and Culture: The Japanese-American War, 1941–1945* (1981), Akira Iriye argues that Roosevelt and the Japanese foresaw restoring the economic and political cooperation rampant during the 1920s. Roosevelt's China policy is treated in Herbert Feis, *The China Tangle* (1953), Michael Schaller, *The U.S. Crusade in China, 1938–1945* (1978), and Tang Tsou, *America's Failure in China, 1941–1950* (1963).

Historians have examined other Roosevelt policies. Allied problems concerning international organization are reviewed in Thomas Campbell's *Masquerade Peace: America's UN Policy, 1944–1945* (1973). In *The Abandonment of the Jews* (1984), David Wyman deplores the Roosevelt administration's failure to help rescue persecuted Jews.

Bibliography

Armstrong, Anne. *Unconditional Surrender*. New Brunswick, N.J.: Rutgers University Press, 1961.

Bailey, Thomas A., and Paul B. Ryan. *Hitler Versus Roosevelt*. New York: Free Press, 1979.

Beitzell, Robert. *The Uneasy Alliance*. New York: Knopf, 1972.

Bennett, Edward M. *Franklin D. Roosevelt and the Search for Security*. Wilmington, Del.: Scholarly Resources, 1985.

———. *Franklin D. Roosevelt and the Search for Victory*. Wilmington, Del.: Scholarly Resources, 1990.

Borg, Dorothy. *The U.S. and the Far Eastern Crisis of 1933–1938*. Cambridge, Mass.: Harvard University Press, 1964.

Buchanan, A. Russell. *The United States and World War II*. 2 vols. New York: Harper and Row, 1964.

Buhite, Russell D. *Decisions at Yalta*. Wilmington, Del.: Scholarly Resources, 1986.

Burns, James MacGregor. *Roosevelt: The Lion and the Fox*. New York: Harcourt Brace, 1956.

———. *Roosevelt: The Soldier of Freedom*. New York: Harcourt Brace Jovanovich, 1970.

Campbell, Thomas. *Masquerade Peace: America's UN Policy, 1944–1945*. Tallahassee: Florida State University Press, 1973.

Clemens, Diane Shaver. *Yalta*. New York: Oxford University Press, 1970.

Cole, Wayne. *Roosevelt and the Isolationists, 1932–45*. Lincoln: University of Nebraska Press, 1983.

Dallek, Robert. *Franklin D. Roosevelt and American Foreign Policy, 1933–1945*. Oxford: Oxford University Press, 1979.

Dawson, Raymond H. *The Decision to Aid Russia, 1941*. Chapel Hill: University of North Carolina Press, 1959.

Divine, Robert A. *The Illusion of Neutrality*. Chicago: University of Chicago Press, 1962.

———. *The Reluctant Belligerent*. 2nd ed. New York: Knopf, 1979.

———. *Roosevelt and World War II*. Baltimore: Johns Hopkins University Press, 1969.

Eubank, Keith. *Summit at Teheran*. New York: Morrow, 1985.

Feingold, Henry L. *The Politics of Rescue*. New Brunswick, N.J.: Rutgers University Press, 1970.

Feis, Herbert. *The China Tangle*. Princeton, N.J.: Princeton University Press, 1953.

———. *Churchill, Roosevelt, Stalin*. Princeton, N.J.: Princeton University Press, 1957.

———. *The Road to Pearl Harbor*. Princeton, N.J.: Princeton University Press, 1950.

Foreign Relations of the United States. Washington, D.C.: United States Department of State, 1943–1972.

Freidel, Frank. *Franklin D. Roosevelt*. 4 vols. Boston: Little, Brown, 1952–1973.

Gaddis, John Lewis. *The United States and the Origins of the Cold War*. New York: Columbia University Press, 1972.

Gellman, Irwin. *Good Neighbor Policy*. Baltimore: Johns Hopkins University Press, 1979.

Gleason, S. Everett, and William L. Langer. *The Challenge to Isolation, 1937–1940*. 2 vols. New York: Harper and Row, 1950.

————. *The Undeclared War, 1940–1941*. New York: Harper and Row, 1953.

Greenfield, Kent R. *American Strategy in World War II*. Baltimore: Johns Hopkins University Press, 1963.

Heinrichs, Waldo. *Threshold of War*. New York: Oxford University Press, 1988.

Herring, George C., Jr. *Aid to Russia, 1941–1946*. New York: Columbia University Press, 1973.

Hurstfield, Julian G. *America and the French Nation, 1939–1945*. Chapel Hill: University of North Carolina Press, 1986.

Iriye, Akira. *Power and Culture: The Japanese-American War, 1941–1945*. Cambridge, Mass.: Harvard University Press, 1981.

Jonas, Manfred. *Isolationism in America, 1935–1941*. Ithaca, N.Y.: Cornell University Press, 1966.

Jones, Robert H. *The Roads to Russia*. Norman: University of Oklahoma Press, 1969.

Ketchum, Richard M. *The Borrowed Years, 1938–1941: America on the Way to War*. New York: Random House, 1989.

Kimball, Warren F. *The Most Unsordid Act: Lend Lease, 1939–1941*. Baltimore: Johns Hopkins University Press, 1969.

————, ed. *Churchill and Roosevelt: The Complete Correspondence*. 3 vols. Princeton: Princeton University Press, 1984.

Kolko, Gabriel. *The Politics of War*. New York: Random House, 1968.

Larrabee, Eric. *Commander in Chief*. New York: Harper and Row, 1987.

Leuchtenberg, William E. *Franklin D. Roosevelt and the New Deal, 1932–1940*. New York: Harper and Row, 1963.

Leutze, James R. *Bargaining for Supremacy: Anglo-American Naval Collaboration, 1937–1941*. Chapel Hill: University of North Carolina Press, 1977.

Louis, William Roger. *Imperialism at Bay*. Oxford: Clarendon Press, 1977.

McNeill, William H. *America, Britain, and Russia, 1941–1946*. 1953. Reprint. New York: Johnson, 1970.

Morison, Samuel Eliot. *Strategy and Compromise*. Boston: Little, Brown, 1958.

Neumann, William L. *After Victory*. New York: Harper and Row, 1967.

Nixon, Edgar B., ed. *Franklin D. Roosevelt and Foreign Affairs*. 3 vols. Cambridge, Mass.: Belknap Press, 1969.

O'Connor, Raymond G. *Diplomacy for Victory: FDR and Unconditional Surrender*. New York: Norton, 1971.

Offner, Arnold A. *American Appeasement: U.S. Foreign Policy and Germany, 1933–1938*. Cambridge, Mass.: Belknap Press, 1969.

Range, Willard. *Franklin D. Roosevelt's World Order*. Athens: University of Georgia Press, 1959.

Reynolds, David. *The Creation of the Anglo-American Alliance, 1937–1941*. Chapel Hill: University of North Carolina Press, 1982.

Roosevelt, Elliott, ed. *F.D.R.: His Personal Letters*. New York: Duell, Sloan and Pearce, 1950.

Roosevelt, Franklin D. "Our Foreign Policy: A Democratic View." *Foreign Affairs* 6 (July 1928): 573–586.

————. "Shall We Trust Japan?" *Asia* 23 (July 1923): 475–478, 526, 528.

Rose, Lisle. *After Yalta*. New York: Scribner's, 1973.

Rosenman, Samuel, ed. *Public Papers and Addresses of Franklin D. Roosevelt*. 13 vols. New York: Macmillan, 1939–1950.

Russett, Bruce. *No Clear and Present Danger*. New York: Harper and Row, 1972.

Sainsbury, Keith. *The Turning Point*. Oxford: Oxford University Press, 1985.

Schaller, Michael. *The U.S. Crusade in China, 1938–1945*. New York: Columbia University Press, 1978.

Schlesinger, Arthur M., Jr. *The Age of Roosevelt*. 3 vols. New York: Houghton Mifflin, 1957–1960.

Schroeder, Paul W. *The Axis Alliance and Japanese-American Relations, 1941*. Ithaca, N.Y.: Cornell University Press, 1958.

Smith, Gaddis. *American Diplomacy During the Second World War*. 2nd ed. New York: Wiley, 1985.

Steele, Richard W. *The First Offensive, 1942*. Bloomington: Indiana University Press, 1973.

Stoler, Mark A. *The Politics of the Second Front*. Westport, Conn.: Greenwood Press, 1977.

Theoharis, Athan. *The Yalta Myths*. Columbia: University of Missouri Press, 1970.

Thorne, Christopher. *Allies of a Kind*. New York: Oxford University Press, 1978.

Tsou, Tang. *America's Failure in China, 1941–1950*. Chicago: University of Chicago Press, 1963.

Wilson, Theodore A. *The First Summit: Roosevelt and Churchill at Placentia Bay, 1941*. Boston: Houghton Mifflin, 1969.

Wohlstetter, Roberta. *Pearl Harbor: Warning and Decision*. Stanford, Calif.: Stanford University Press, 1962.

Wood, Bryce. *The Making of the Good Neighbor Policy*. New York: Columbia University Press, 1961.

Woods, Randall Bennett. *A Changing of the Guard*. Chapel Hill: University of North Carolina Press, 1990.

Wyman, David S. *The Abandonment of the Jews*. New York: Pantheon, 1984.

———. *Paper Walls*. Amherst: University of Massachusetts Press, 1968.

DAVID L. PORTER

Theodore Roosevelt (1858–1919).   Theodore Roosevelt, Jr., the second of four children and the older of two sons, was born into wealth and comfort in New York City on October 27, 1858. His father was a businessman and a philanthropist whose family's Dutch roots in the area were over two centuries deep; his mother, the former Martha Bulloch, had grown up on a prosperous plantation in antebellum Georgia. The Roosevelts were an extremely close-knit family.

Theodore was educated at home by private tutors. Extended sojourns abroad in 1869–1870 and 1872–1873, which took him to Great Britain, continental Europe, and the Near East, and frequent visits to the countryside helped develop a cosmopolitan spirit and a passionate, lifelong interest in nature. (As an adult, Theodore Roosevelt, though an amateur, would be among the nation's foremost natural scientists.) In 1880 Roosevelt graduated Phi Beta Kappa from Harvard.

In his early adult years Roosevelt's family life was marked by tragedy. He lost his father in 1878. He married Alice Lee in 1880, but on February 14, 1884—two days after the birth of a baby girl, Alice—both his wife and his mother suddenly died. In 1886 Roosevelt married Edith Carow, a close childhood friend, and took up permanent residence in Oyster Bay, New York, in the spacious, comfortable new house that they called Sagamore Hill. By 1897 five children, four sons and a daughter, had joined daughter Alice in the Roosevelt family.

Roosevelt's career over the two decades after Harvard was a varied and interesting one. Beginning in politics as a Republican reformer in the New York State Assembly, Roosevelt then spent time as a rancher and hunter in the Dakota Badlands. Following a defeat in the New York mayoralty race in 1886, Roosevelt returned to politics in 1889 by accepting an appointment to the U.S. Civil Service Commission. Six years later, he became president of New York City's Board of Police Commissioners. From 1897 to 1901, he served as assistant secretary of the navy, colonel of the Rough Riders fighting Spanish forces in Cuba, governor of New York, and vice president of the United States.

Throughout these twenty years, Roosevelt wrote prolifically on a wide range of subjects, including United States history and life in the American West. *The Winning of the West*, a four-volume history of the frontier from 1769 to 1807, was his most significant scholarly endeavor.

The assassination of William McKinley brought Theodore Roosevelt to the presidency on September 14, 1901. A charismatic and politically adept progressive Republican and a "practical idealist," Roosevelt retained the presidency for seven and a half years, decisively winning the election of 1904. He almost certainly would have been reelected had he decided to seek another term in 1908.

Ex-President Roosevelt never really "retired." Continually he wrote about his experiences and his perspectives on contemporary issues. In 1909 he embarked on a long African safari and a tour of England and continental Europe. In 1912 Roosevelt dramatically broke with the Republicans to lead his new Progressive ("Bull Moose") party to a second-place finish in the presidential election. A year later he headed an expedition into previously unexplored areas of Brazil, irretrievably impairing his health. As an outspoken proponent of preparedness and a pro-Allied policy during World War I and a detractor of President *Woodrow Wilson, Roosevelt eventually drifted back into the Republican party. He was considered a prime contender for its 1920 presidential nomination at the time of his death on January 6, 1919.

Well before assuming the presidency, Theodore Roosevelt had become a prominent figure among leading American expansionists. These influential men were big navy advocates who believed strongly in American political and cultural superiority and American beneficence. Very attentive to the foreign relations of the United States, they met and corresponded frequently.

As assistant secretary of the navy during 1897–1898, Roosevelt took full advantage of opportunities to express his views and to affect naval and diplomatic decisions. He regularly outmaneuvered his lethargic superior, John D. Long, most memorably in February 1898 when he sent off his famous telegram to Admiral George Dewey concerning operations in the Philippines in the event of a war with Spain.

The well-traveled Roosevelt came into the presidency, notes Howard K. Beale, with "a direct knowledge of the world and its people that no previous president save the Adamses, Jefferson, and Monroe had possessed." Roosevelt had come to know personally many British intellectuals and members of the ruling elite and, not surprisingly, had thought at great length about Anglo-American relations. As president he counted numerous Britons—especially the professional diplomat Cecil Spring Rice, the Conservative parliamentarian Arthur Lee, the newspaper editor John St. Loe Strachey, the historian-politician George Otto Trevelyan, and the Liberal foreign minister Edward Grey—among his most intimate correspondents.

The *Weltanschauung* of President Theodore Roosevelt had at its foundation a complex mixture of theory, historical perspective, and practical experience. While the president occasionally adjusted this worldview in response to events, he saw most events as reaffirming his outlook, which in its essence did not change.

Roosevelt believed in the superiority of Western, and particularly Anglo-American, civilization. An American nationalist yet also in important respects an internationalist, he viewed imperialism, at least its U.S. and British varieties, primarily as a force for the advance of this superior civilization and the betterment of humankind, and not as a vehicle for economic aggrandizement. As president he closely monitored the United States' experience in the Philippines, finding in it unambiguous evidence of the high-minded benevolence of American imperialism.

Roosevelt looked upon arbitration as a useful device for resolving international disagreements, but only those that did not involve questions of vital interests, territorial integrity, or national honor. Ultimately, he understood clearly, it was power more than any other factor that determined the course of international affairs.

Consistent with this perspective, Theodore Roosevelt adhered to the doctrine of peace through strength: the "righteous" nations should always be well armed and should take particular care to build up and preserve a preponderance of naval power in order to be able to deter aggression and defend their interests. He considered the United States and Great Britain (in that order) to be the two most righteous nations. Moreover, he realized, the two countries' interests tended to coincide. Britain, therefore, was an essential friend for America. Conversely, Roosevelt perceived Japan, Germany, and Russia as potential enemies of the United States. Not only did their interests often clash with those of the United States, but they had not yet attained America's level of civilization.

This dichotomy was reflected in President Roosevelt's thinking about the balance of power. It would be inaccurate to assert that he saw "balance" as the key to stabilizing all areas of possible Great Power conflict. He did indeed desire such balance where the contenders for advantage were Germany and Russia, or Germany and Japan, or, as in Manchuria, Russia and Japan. But when Great Britain or the United States was a party to a dispute with another power, "balance'' was the president's minimum objective. A better guarantee of peace, Roosevelt believed, was an imbalance decidedly favorable to Britain or the United States or the two of them combined. As the world's most civilized countries, Britain and the United States would not abuse a position of military supremacy, and such supremacy would ensure against miscalculation or adventurism on the part of a more selfish, less civilized, less mature power. Thus a preponderance of British or American strength in any region of the globe constituted a safeguard, not a danger. And in the Western Hemisphere specifically the United States was to be the dominant power.

Theodore Roosevelt viewed himself as an idealist who set realistic goals in foreign as well as domestic affairs. He was not one to attempt the impossible. The greater the stakes, however, the more likely he was to take political, diplomatic, and military risks to gain his objective.

Roosevelt's diplomatic style also sheds light on his outlook on international affairs. The president excelled at maneuvering behind the scenes; and he believed that quiet, personal diplomacy—conducted through trusted envoys such as *Elihu Root, Henry White, and Henry Cabot Lodge, or directly by himself—was the most effective way for him to operate in most circumstances. Such an approach provided a means to prevent both public humiliation and misunderstandings. Contrary to the caricature, one of the guiding principles of Roosevelt's ''Big Stick'' diplomacy was to enable an honorable adversary to save face in defeat. Similarly, Roosevelt would not rail publicly, despite the intensity of sentiment often apparent in his private letters, against international (or internal foreign) injustices that he felt powerless to correct. To him, foreign policy was a very serious business and an inappropriate arena for bluster. Two additional principles of Big Stick diplomacy to which he unfailingly adhered were never to bluff and to strike only if prepared to strike hard. His credibility in foreign capitals was exceedingly high.

The first decade of the twentieth century was a busy time in American foreign relations. The most important foreign policy developments of Theodore Roosevelt's presidency centered on the Venezuelan crisis of 1902–1903, the American acquisition of the Panama Canal Zone in 1903, the issuance in 1904 and implementation afterwards of the Roosevelt Corollary to the Monroe Doctrine, the resolution in 1903 of the Alaskan boundary dispute, the Russo-Japanese War of 1904–1905, the Moroccan crisis of 1905–1906, and the tension in U.S.-Japanese relations provoked in 1906 by anti-Japanese Californians.

The Venezuelan crisis was Roosevelt's first major diplomatic foray into Latin America. In December 1902, Germany and Britain embarked on a heavy-handed joint debt collection adventure. They seized Venezuela's navy, bombarded Venezuelan forts, and instituted a blockade of the country. An alarmed Roosevelt quietly ordered the navy to prepare to confront Germany, and privately issued a stern ultimatum to Germany demanding that it agree to submit its claims against Venezuela to arbitration. Germany yielded. Britain, already regretting its actions, posed no obstacle to a peaceful settlement. While Roosevelt assessed British conduct as merely foolish, he considered Germany's behavior to be truly threatening. An enlargement of the Monroe Doctrine was now on the president's agenda.

A primary objective of Roosevelt's first term was to win possession for the United States of a canal route across the isthmus of Panama. Soon after Colombia (which had long ruled Panama) rejected the Hay-Herrán Treaty in August 1903, an angry Roosevelt directed U.S. naval units to prevent Colombia from landing troops to suppress an uprising in Panama. On November 18, 1903, the United States and the government of newly independent Panama signed the Hay-Bunau-Varilla Treaty, which granted the United States sovereignty "in perpetuity" over a ten-mile-wide canal zone and made Panama a virtual protectorate of the United States.

Concerned about the security of the canal, whose construction the United States would now undertake, and determined in any case to prevent a recurrence of the Venezuelan incident, the president issued the Roosevelt Corollary to the Monroe Doctrine in 1904. Under Roosevelt U.S. hegemony in and around the Caribbean had become an established fact. Forcible debt collecting by foreign powers in this region would no longer be either necessary or permissible. The United States, Roosevelt proclaimed, was assuming the responsibility of keeping order in the Western Hemisphere. The president was reserving the right to call to account Latin American countries guilty of "flagrant wrongdoing." In practice, however, Roosevelt proved reluctant to utilize the sweeping new powers he had conferred upon his nation. He employed his corollary only twice—in the Dominican Republic beginning in 1905 and in Cuba from 1906 to 1909—and both interventions were requested by indigenous authorities, smoothly implemented, and remarkably bloodless.

The matter later accurately described by Roosevelt as "the last serious trouble between the British Empire and ourselves" was the disputed boundary between Alaska and Canada. In Roosevelt's eyes Canada had "no case whatever," and the resolution therefore had to be in line with the American position. By making this requirement unmistakably clear to British decision makers, by involving himself intimately in the proceedings, and by offering Britain face-saving concessions on secondary aspects of the boundary quarrel, Roosevelt engineered a mutually acceptable settlement in October 1903. The Anglo-American rapprochement had surmounted a formidable barrier.

In the Venezuelan, Panamanian, and Alaskan situations, Theodore Roosevelt had demonstrated that he would uphold vital U.S. interests when he perceived them to be threatened, whether by friend or by foe. In his handling of the Russo-Japanese War and the Moroccan crisis, he displayed another major element in his repertoire as a diplomatist: the ability to mediate sensitively and effectively between hostile powers, and to keep larger issues in focus as he attended to the specific problems of a particular conflict.

As he viewed the Russo-Japanese War, President Roosevelt understood the complex international context of the hostilities. While far more sympathetic to

Japan than to Russia, he believed that it would be destabilizing for either combatant to be pushed entirely out of the Asian competition. Since France was allied with Russia and Britain was allied with Japan, Roosevelt also perceived a danger to the new Anglo-French entente cordiale, which he strongly supported. As he had expected, an ambitious Germany made every effort to use the war to undermine these alliances and to escape its own isolation. From the outset, Roosevelt was determined to do all he could to bring the war to a conclusion that would restore an Asian balance of power and preserve the existing balance in Europe. When the opportunity to mediate presented itself, Roosevelt readily accepted the challenge. The Treaty of Portsmouth of September 1905—a testament to his tenacity and diplomatic agility—essentially accomplished the president's main objectives. It earned him the Nobel Peace Prize for 1906 and may have been his greatest foreign policy triumph.

The Moroccan crisis began in the spring of 1905 when Germany belligerently defied the Anglo-French agreement on French control in Morocco by calling for an independent Morocco with an open door and for an international conference on the Moroccan question. This crisis, which conceivably could have brought on World War I nine years before it actually began, unfolded in two stages. During the first and more dangerous stage, lasting until July 1905, Roosevelt, operating completely out of the public eye, was instrumental in preventing war by arranging for a conference to be held in Algeciras, Spain. France was assured privately that Roosevelt would sustain its most fundamental Moroccan interests at the coming conference, while a trusting Germany pledged to defer to Roosevelt's judgment should a deadlock arise. Inevitably Germany learned of the president's pro-French outlook during the second stage of the crisis, the Algeciras Conference of January-April 1906. But even as Roosevelt deftly engineered Germany's defeat, he characteristically did his utmost to disguise the reality of the outcome and thereby soften the blow. In the wake of the German capitulation, Roosevelt was generous with encomiums for Germany and its leadership.

The San Francisco school board's passage in October 1906 of a resolution segregating Asian school children sparked the U.S.-Japanese crisis of 1906–1908. President Roosevelt's well-conceived, multifaceted approach entailed pressuring the Californians to end the blatant discrimination while emphasizing to Japan his disapproval of Californian behavior (which he termed ''purely local''); working with Japanese officials to find an amicable way to halt the flow of Japanese laborers to the American mainland; and moving to strengthen the navy both to deter Japan and to prepare for war should it prove unavoidable. The fourteen-month world cruise of the Great White Fleet, dispatched with great enthusiasm by Roosevelt in December 1907, signaled to Japan indirectly but unmistakably that the United States was strong and ready. But there would be no war. A ''Gentlemen's Agreement'' brought the immigration problem under control by the spring of 1908. Then, that November, the Root-Takahira Agreement demonstrated to the world Roosevelt's achievement of respectful and friendly relations between the United States and Japan.

President Theodore Roosevelt was a consummate diplomatist. He was almost uniformly successful both in dealing with specific foreign policy challenges and in advancing his broader objectives. He kept his country at peace while consistently upholding what he defined as its vital interests, and was directly responsible for restoring or preserving peace between other powers. Moreover, his statesmanship significantly enhanced the United States' image in the world. Indeed, it is difficult to escape the conclusion that in the foreign policy arena Roosevelt was probably the greatest of all U.S. presidents.

Roosevelt's only important foreign policy failure—and it is hard to see how he might have avoided it—was that his way of thinking about foreign affairs hardly outlasted his presidency and would not be revived until the 1940s. First of all, some specific policies quickly fell into disuse (or misuse). Under William Howard Taft, America's relationship with Japan deteriorated badly, and it remained unfriendly until after World War II. Taft, Woodrow Wilson, Warren Harding, and Calvin Coolidge employed the Roosevelt Corollary too readily, engendering the Yankeephobia in Latin America that has tended to be blamed on Roosevelt. Wilson and his successors devalued the Anglo-American partnership, which effectively ceased to function in the 1930s. Second, those who followed Roosevelt into the presidency simply did not share his comprehension of the uses of power and the nature of world politics. But again, it would certainly be unfair to fault Roosevelt for possessing a degree of perspicacity that transcended his era.

This is not to suggest that Theodore Roosevelt left no meaningful foreign policy legacy, for quite the contrary is true. One might speculate that if he had been around during the 1930s, the United States would have had its counterpart to *Winston Churchill. As it turned out, the revival in 1939 of close Anglo-American cooperation ultimately extricated the world from the clutches of the most unimaginable tyranny. And the 1980s and early 1990s have witnessed a renewed affirmation of Anglo-American unity, manifested most sharply in a common approach to North Atlantic Treaty Organization missile deployments and in solidarity during the Falklands War of 1982, the bombing of Libya in 1986, and, most impressively, the Persian Gulf conflict of 1990–1991.

More broadly, in the wake of the upheaval of two terrible world wars, U.S. foreign policy makers at last came to realize what Roosevelt had known decades earlier. Although Harry Truman and those who followed him were neither as discerning in thought nor as artful in action as Theodore Roosevelt had been, they all (with the possible exception of Jimmy Carter) understood the need to resist aggression and the crucial role played by military strength in determining the course of international affairs. In a partisan context, one can view Roosevelt as the father and wellspring of legitimacy for the twentieth-century Republican internationalism that waged an uphill struggle against the party's prevailing isolationist tendency from the 1910s through the 1930s; that began to gain the upper hand in the 1940s; and that became the party's dominant strain under Dwight Eisenhower in the 1950s. The bipartisan policy of nuclear and conventional deterrence that ultimately brought victory over the Soviet Union in the Cold War was thoroughly Rooseveltian. And with George Bush, who claims Roosevelt as his hero and model, boldly striking a blow for global security by decimating the war-making capacity of Saddam Hussein's Iraq, it is legitimate to assert that the legacy of Theodore Roosevelt has never been more influential than it is today.

Annotated Bibliography

For students of Theodore Roosevelt's diplomacy, the most important primary resource is the Theodore Roosevelt Papers. This enormous collection is available to researchers on 485 well-indexed reels of microfilm, most of which contain letters written to or by Roosevelt. These papers can be found at the Library of Congress in Washington, D.C. (their original repository), and at Harvard University's Widener Library, which houses the large and rich (particularly with regard to Roosevelt's family life) Theodore Roosevelt Collection.

Theodore Roosevelt wrote voluminously. Many of his books and innumerable essays and published speeches shed light on his foreign policy thinking. The greater part of his writings were gathered together shortly after his death in *The Works of Theodore Roosevelt,* Memorial Edition, 24 vols. (1923–1926), and National Edition, 20 vols. (1926), both edited by Hermann Hagedorn. Particularly useful to analysts of Roosevelt's statesmanship are *The Naval War of 1812* (1882), which offers revealing previews of his naval policies, and *Theodore Roosevelt: An Autobiography* (1913), which provides interesting information and prideful reflections on many facets of Roosevelt's diplomacy and includes a vigorous defense of the manner in which the United States acquired the Panama Canal Zone.

Two other published primary sources must be mentioned. The bulky *Theodore Roosevelt Cyclopedia*, edited by Albert Bushnell Hart and Herbert Ronald Ferleger, which first appeared in 1941 and was reissued in 1989 with an excellent introduction by John Allen Gable, presents well-chosen excerpts from Roosevelt's speeches and writings on a wide variety of topics, many of which relate to his statesmanship. Even more valuable are the eight volumes of *The Letters of Theodore Roosevelt* (1950–1954), masterfully selected and annotated by Elting E. Morison, John M. Blum, and Alfred D. Chandler, Jr. Roosevelt's private thoughts about all major and most minor aspects of his foreign policy are brightly illuminated in *The Letters*, an essential tool for Roosevelt researchers.

Since the 1950s, and especially since the late 1970s, the historical reputation of President Theodore Roosevelt's diplomacy has risen markedly. There appear to be two principal explanations. The first has to do with historians themselves, most prominently Henry F. Pringle, Elting E. Morison, and Howard K. Beale. Pringle's superficial yet well-written and popular *Theodore Roosevelt: A Biography* (1931), which basically caricatured Roosevelt as a "violently adolescent person," cast a long shadow over the field. The nature of the accessible historical record is such that wholesale revision of the Pringle portrait was inevitable. But the sheer bulk of Roosevelt's correspondence—he wrote well over 100,000 letters during his lifetime—posed a formidable obstacle to correction until the publication of *The Letters of Theodore Roosevelt*, of which Morison, as noted, was the chief editor. And in 1956, Beale, who worked without benefit of *The Letters*, published his lengthy and wide-ranging *Theodore Roosevelt and the Rise of America to World Power*, a judicious and rather favorable interpretation that laid the groundwork for a new generation of work on Roosevelt's diplomacy.

The second explanation concerns contemporary developments. Appeasement's disastrous failure created an intellectual climate conducive to a sympathetic reexamination of Roosevelt's statesmanship. Then the apparent soundness throughout the long decades of Cold War of the doctrine of deterrence reminded historians of Roosevelt's emphasis on preparedness and of the relative stability and peace that prevailed among the powers during his presidency. Undoubtedly, too, the ill-fated American venture in Vietnam caused some historians to think more highly of a president who perceptively distinguished vital interests from secondary ones, who undertook foreign policy initiatives only after thoughtfully considering their likely consequences, and who, once he had decided to act, did so decisively.

The trend toward an increasingly positive appraisal of Theodore Roosevelt's diplomacy is evident in leading biographical studies. When comparing John Morton Blum, *The Republican Roosevelt* (1954), William H. Harbaugh, *Power and Responsibility: The Life and Times of Theodore Roosevelt* (1961), and John Milton Cooper, Jr., *The Warrior and the Priest: Woodrow Wilson and Theodore Roosevelt* (1983), each of which is sympathetic to Roosevelt, one finds Harbaugh's assessment of the twenty-sixth president's statesmanship more favorable than Blum's, and Cooper's the most laudatory of the three.

Major studies with a primary focus on Roosevelt's presidential diplomacy present a similar pattern. Almost all of the most important work on the subject since the 1950s has been less critical of Roosevelt the diplomatist than was Beale's *Theodore Roosevelt and the Rise of America to World Power*, and the most enthusiastic interpretations have been published most recently. These major studies include Charles E. Neu, *An Uncertain Friendship: Theodore Roosevelt and Japan, 1906–1909* (1967), David H. Burton, *Theodore Roosevelt: Confident Imperialist* (1968), Raymond A. Esthus, *Theodore Roosevelt and the International Rivalries* (1970), Frederick W. Marks III, *Velvet on Iron: The Diplomacy of Theodore Roosevelt* (1979), William C. Widenor, *Henry Cabot Lodge and the Search for an American Foreign Policy* (1980), and Richard H. Collin, *Theodore Roosevelt, Culture, Diplomacy, and Expansion: A New View of American Imperialism* (1985) and *Theodore Roosevelt's Caribbean: The Panama Canal, the Monroe Doctrine, and the Latin American Context* (1990).

Neu's monograph offers an insightful analysis of his topic and a revealing microcosmic look at the operation of Roosevelt's foreign policy. Neu finds Roosevelt to have been "shrewd, skillful, and responsible" in his dealings with Japan. Burton's very useful intellectual history spans Roosevelt's lifetime and considers the development, maturation, and decline of what the author calls Roosevelt's "confident imperialism." Roosevelt's outlook on the American colonial experiment in the Philippines receives a great deal of attention. Esthus's well-executed study looks closely at Roosevelt's handling of the Russo-Japanese War and the Moroccan crisis—and at the president's thinking and activities prior to and following these crises—and finds Roosevelt to have grown, with good reason, increasingly suspicious of Germany. Esthus demonstrates particularly well the relationships among Roosevelt's various foreign policies.

Marks's largely thematic monograph vigorously puts forward an adulatory assessment of Roosevelt's statesmanship. Among many contributions, Marks establishes beyond a reasonable doubt that Roosevelt did indeed issue Germany an ultimatum during the Venezuelan crisis of 1902–1903 (a finding expertly sustained by Edmund Morris in " 'A Few Pregnant Days': Theodore Roosevelt and the Venezuelan Crisis of 1902," *Theodore Roosevelt Association Journal* 15, 1 [Winter 1989]: 2–13), and ably defends Roosevelt's Panama Canal Zone policy. Historians of Roosevelt's diplomacy need to take seriously the controversial arguments proffered by Marks.

Widenor's fine intellectual biography of Lodge analyzes at length what Widenor terms the "Rooseveltian solution" to the challenge of conducting an effective foreign policy in democratic America. The main components of this solution, the author contends, were "practical idealism," political astuteness, and top-caliber presidential leadership.

Collin's first book lauds Roosevelt's achievements as a diplomatist, attributing them to a combination of the president's extraordinary diplomatic talents and dramatic refinements, in which Roosevelt participated prominently, in American cultural life. While this monograph is at times unconvincing and is not particularly well integrated, it is suggestive and worth reading. It concludes with a superb bibliographical essay. Collin's longer and better second book is equally enthusiastic about Roosevelt's statesmanship. *Theodore Roosevelt's Caribbean* closely examines Roosevelt's dealings with Venezuela, Colombia, Panama, the Dominican Republic, and Cuba in the multiple context of American and international politics and the diverse cultures and political turbulence of Latin America.

To one degree or another, nearly all of the diplomatic historians who have focused on Roosevelt in recent decades can be identified with the "realist" school of the history of U.S. foreign relations. (The realist school accepts power politics and international strife as normal in a world of self-interested, sovereign nations, and often sees merit in balance of power diplomacy.) The one ambitious attempt by a historian of the New Left mold to deal with Roosevelt's foreign policy, Serge Ricard, *Théodore Roosevelt et la justification de l'impérialisme* (1986), is a misguided and faulty study offering little of value to the field.

Most of the aforementioned books are reviewed in far greater depth in William Tilchin, "The Rising Star of Theodore Roosevelt's Diplomacy: Major Studies from Beale to the Present," *Theodore Roosevelt Association Journal* 15, 3 (Summer 1989): 2–24. It might be added that the quarterly *Theodore Roosevelt Association Journal* frequently contains articles pertaining to Roosevelt's statesmanship and can be counted on to keep its readers up to date regarding significant new literature on the subject.

Bibliography

Beale, Howard K. *Theodore Roosevelt and the Rise of America to World Power*. 1956. Reprint. Baltimore: Johns Hopkins University Press, 1984.

Blum, John Morton. *The Republican Roosevelt*. 1954. 2nd ed. Cambridge, Mass.: Harvard University Press, 1954.

Burton, David H. "Theodore Roosevelt and His English Correspondents: A Special Relationship of Friends." *Transactions of the American Philosophical Society* 63, 2 (1973): 3–70.

———. *Theodore Roosevelt: Confident Imperialist*. Philadelphia: University of Pennsylvania Press, 1968.

Chessman, G. Wallace. *Theodore Roosevelt and the Politics of Power*. Boston: Little, Brown, 1969.

Collin, Richard H. "Henry Pringle's Theodore Roosevelt: A Study in Historical Revisionism." *New York History* 52 (1971): 151–168.

———. *Theodore Roosevelt, Culture, Diplomacy, and Expansion: A New View of American Imperialism*. Baton Rouge: Louisiana State University Press, 1985.

———. *Theodore Roosevelt's Caribbean: The Panama Canal, the Monroe Doctrine, and the Latin American Context*. Baton Rouge: Louisiana State University Press, 1990.

Cooper, John Milton, Jr. *The Warrior and the Priest: Woodrow Wilson and Theodore Roosevelt*. Cambridge, Mass.: Belknap Press, 1983.

Dyer, Thomas G. *Theodore Roosevelt and the Idea of Race*. Baton Rouge: Louisiana State University Press, 1980.

Esthus, Raymond A. *Theodore Roosevelt and Japan*. Seattle: University of Washington Press, 1967.

―――. *Theodore Roosevelt and the International Rivalries*. 1970. Reprint. Claremont, Calif.: Regina, 1982.

Friedlander, Robert A. "A Reassessment of Roosevelt's Role in the Panamanian Revolution of 1903." *Western Political Quarterly* 14 (1961): 535–543.

Gable, John Allen. "Theodore Roosevelt: The Renaissance Man as President." In *The Rating Game in American Politics: An Interdisciplinary Approach*, pp. 336–355. Edited by William Pederson and Ann McLaurin. New York: Irvington, 1987.

Grantham, Dewey W., Jr. "Theodore Roosevelt in American Historical Writing." *Mid-America* 43 (1961): 3–35.

Harbaugh, William H. *Power and Responsibility: The Life and Times of Theodore Roosevelt*. 1961. Rev. ed. New York: Oxford University Press, 1975.

Karsten, Peter. "The Nature of 'Influence': Roosevelt, Mahan and the Concept of Sea Power." *American Quarterly* 23 (1971): 585–600.

Marks, Frederick W., III. *Velvet on Iron: The Diplomacy of Theodore Roosevelt*. Lincoln: University of Nebraska Press, 1979.

McCullough, David. *The Path Between the Seas: The Creation of the Panama Canal, 1870–1914*. New York: Simon and Schuster, 1977.

Morris, Edmund. " 'A Few Pregnant Days': Theodore Roosevelt and the Venezuelan Crisis of 1902." *Theodore Roosevelt Association Journal* 15, 1 (1989): 2–13.

Mowry, George E. *The Era of Theodore Roosevelt and the Birth of Modern America*. 1958. Reprint. New York: Harper/Torchbooks, 1962.

Neu, Charles E. *An Uncertain Friendship: Theodore Roosevelt and Japan, 1906–1909*. Cambridge, Mass.: Harvard University Press, 1967.

Osgood, Robert Endicott. *Ideals and Self-Interest in America's Foreign Relations*. Chicago: University of Chicago Press, 1953.

Pringle, Henry F. *Theodore Roosevelt: A Biography*. New York: Harcourt, Brace, 1931.

Reckner, James R. *Teddy Roosevelt's Great White Fleet*. Annapolis: Naval Institute Press, 1988.

Ricard, Serge. *Théodore Roosevelt et la justification de l'impérialisme*. Aix-en-Provence: Université de Provence, 1986.

Roosevelt, Theodore. *The Letters of Theodore Roosevelt*. 8 vols. Edited by Elting E. Morison, John M. Blum, and Alfred D. Chandler, Jr. Cambridge, Mass.: Harvard University Press, 1950–1954.

―――. *Theodore Roosevelt Cyclopedia*. 1941. 2nd ed. Edited by Albert Bushnell Hart and Herbert Ronald Ferleger. Oyster Bay, N.Y., and Westport, Conn.: Theodore Roosevelt Association and Meckler, 1989.

―――. *The Works of Theodore Roosevelt*. Memorial ed. 24 vols. Edited by Hermann Hagedorn. New York: Scribner's, 1923–1926.

―――. *The Works of Theodore Roosevelt*. National ed. 20 vols. Edited by Hermann Hagedorn. New York: Scribner's, 1926.

Tilchin, William. "The Rising Star of Theodore Roosevelt's Diplomacy: Major Studies from Beale to the Present." *Theodore Roosevelt Association Journal* 15, 3 (1989): 2–24.

————. "Theodore Roosevelt, Harry Truman, and the Uneven Course of American Foreign Policy in the First Half of the Twentieth Century." *Theodore Roosevelt Association Journal* 10, 4 (1984): 2–10.

Trani, Eugene P. *The Treaty of Portsmouth: An Adventure in American Diplomacy.* Lexington: University of Kentucky Press, 1969.

Tuchman, Barbara W. "Perdicaris Alive or Raisuli Dead." *American Heritage* 10, 5 (1959): 18–21, 98–101.

Wagenknecht, Edward C. *The Seven Worlds of Theodore Roosevelt.* New York: Longmans, Green, 1958.

Widenor, William C. *Henry Cabot Lodge and the Search for an American Foreign Policy.* Berkeley: University of California Press, 1980.

WILLIAM N. TILCHIN

Elihu Root (1845–1937).   Elihu Root, U.S. secretary of war from 1899 to 1904 and secretary of state from 1905 to 1909, had an unusually long career unusually full of honors. He entered the legal profession shortly after the Civil War, served in the cabinet following the Spanish-American War, sat in the Senate during World War I, and made his last public appearance (speaking briefly at the Carnegie mansion in New York) not long before World War II. In those nearly seven decades, Root registered a remarkable record: Aside from holding two cabinet positions, under presidents William McKinley and *Theodore Roosevelt, he also earned an outstanding reputation as an attorney, won the Nobel Peace Prize, served as a delegate to international conferences, long presided over the Carnegie Endowment for International Peace, and filled exalted positions in the Republican party. Prestigious career citations could be continued; he compiled an impressive resume indeed. While far more conservative on domestic issues than most Americans (he opposed a constitutional amendment prohibiting child labor, for example), in the years before his death in 1937, Root enjoyed an unsurpassed reputation in international affairs.

Slight in stature, unprepossessing in appearance, not noted for personal charisma or oratorical flair, Root made his reputation on uncommon intellectual capacity and hard work. He was blessed with both a lack of ambition for high elective office and an irreverent sense of humor. (In a famous if perhaps apocryphal story, once when Roosevelt vigorously defended his Panama policy and inquired of cabinet members if he had made his point, Root replied that the president had shown he was accused of seduction but had conclusively proved he was guilty of rape.) He had a judicious nature; patient, idealistic, a model of integrity, he gave sound, measured advice to his clients, whether individuals, corporations, or presidents. In 1909 Roosevelt termed Root the ablest man he had ever met. James Bryce, British ambassador in Washington, adjudged him the greatest American secretary of state. Upon Root's death at almost ninety-two, Secretary of State Cordell Hull praised his services to the country as of "inestimable value." His friend Nicholas Murray Butler, president of Columbia University, lauded him as "the most brilliant intellect since Alexander Hamilton." The *New York Times* editorialized only slightly less effusively that he had "an intellect not, perhaps, surpassed in power and lucidity by any American of his time or ours."

Elihu Root began his long, productive life on February 15, 1845, at Clinton, New York, the son of a Hamilton College mathematics professor. From an English heritage long rooted in America, his family boasted education and achievement but only modest financial means. Root finished at Hamilton in 1864. He missed Civil War service due, ironically in view of his longevity, to physical frailty. After teaching school briefly, he studied law at New York University and was admitted to the bar in 1867. His law practice in Manhattan soon succeeded, and in 1878 he married Clara Wales, daughter of a wealthy New York publisher. Specializing in corporate law and wills, Root gained a measure of notoriety (which he never managed to shed) in the early 1870s by participating in the defense of Tammany leader William M. Tweed against charges of corruption. Appointed by President Chester A. Arthur, a sometime legal client, from 1883 to 1885 he held the post of district attorney in New York. As a noted member of the bar, he gained influence in New York Republican circles and became an advisor to rising political star Theodore Roosevelt. In 1898 Root convinced the state Republican convention that Roosevelt legally resided in New York despite Roosevelt's own earlier affidavit, executed for tax purposes, that he lived in Washington D.C. This lawyerly feat made possible the Rough Rider's successful run for the governorship that year.

In 1899, after declining nomination as minister in Madrid, he accepted a surprise appointment as secretary of war. McKinley wanted a lawyer, not a military expert, to take charge of an inefficient, corrupt War Department faced with consolidating the United States' newly won overseas possessions. In Root, he got a first-rate administrator who was able to cooperate effectively with Congress. Root articulated a colonial policy and reorganized his department and the army high command. His range of responsibilities included drafting the Platt Amendment establishing an informal protectorate over Cuba. In 1900, directing foreign affairs briefly in the absence of ailing Secretary of State John Hay, he handled America's response to the Boxer Rebellion in China. In that episode, he not only dispatched U.S. troops to the relief of beseiged legations in Beijing, a considerable logistical achievement, but also orchestrated diplomacy in the swirl of conflicting European and Japanese interests in China. It was his initiation into international politics.

Root returned to private life in 1904 after more than four years as secretary of war, largely at the insistence of his retiring wife. William Howard Taft succeeded him. That year Root declined to run for governor of New York, an office he likely would have won. In 1905, however, he responded to Roosevelt's call following the death of Hay. Clara Root's dislike of social demands notwithstanding, on July 19 he became secretary of state.

Roosevelt dominated foreign policy while Root was in office. Nevertheless, several policy areas marked the new secretary's tenure: making overtures toward Latin America, resolving issues outstanding with Japan and Canada, overseeing the United States' participation in the Hague Peace and Algeciras conferences, encouraging careerism in the consular service, and furthering international arbitration.

Although personally paternalistic toward Latin America, he was not tarred with the brush of Roosevelt's Panama Canal policies, and in 1906 undertook a well-received goodwill tour of seven Latin American nations. In Brazil he addressed a Pan American conference: "We neither claim nor desire any rights, or privileges, or powers that we do not freely concede to every American republic" (quoted in Jessup, 1, p. 481), thereby signaling a new policy direction. He was the first secretary of state to tour Latin America, and the following year he made official visits to Mexico and Canada. He also promoted international arbitration agreements; in 1908 and 1909 he negotiated twenty-four such bilateral treaties with major powers (although the pacts excluded most important issues). Root, who had served on the Alaskan Boundary Tribunal of 1903, additionally reached accords with Canada and Britain on arcane fishing rights. In late 1905, he testified before Congress for a consular reform bill, something no previous secretary of state had done, and helped assure adoption of the measure. He guided U.S. delegates the 1907 Hague Peace Conference, and following the lead of Roosevelt, he instructed the delegates to the 1906 Algeciras Conference on French-German rivalries in Morocco. He had reservations about the latter meeting's policy implications, but Algeciras nevertheless foretold the active world role the United States henceforth expected to play.

Root's tenure as secretary is perhaps best recalled for his resolution of a controversy over immigration with emerging power Japan. In 1907 and early 1908, following initiatives dating back several years, he negotiated a "Gentlemen's Agreement" by which the Japanese government would bar laborers from emigrating via Hawaii to California, where San Francisco authorities had adopted troublesome discriminatory measures. Later in 1908, following the signing of a U.S.-Japanese arbitration treaty, another exchange of carefully worded notes, the Root-Takahira Agreement, addressed broader questions. Each country agreed to respect the other's Pacific possessions, to preserve the political status quo, to support Chinese "independence and integrity," and to maintain the Open Door to foreign commerce in China. These understandings calmed U.S.-Japanese relations and defused the immigration issue until the 1920s.

Root resigned early in 1909 and entered the Senate. The next six years in Washington brought Root, as a senator, few notable accomplishments in foreign affairs, but he continued his tireless, idealistic pursuit of peace through arbitral systems. In 1910 he served as counsel for North Atlantic fisheries negotiations. The same year, President Taft appointed him to the Permanent Court of International Arbitration, an outgrowth of the 1899 Hague Peace Conference. Later he worked diligently for American membership in the Permanent Court of International Justice, or World Court. The award in 1912 of the Nobel Peace Prize recognized his encouragement of international tribunals; his efforts to promote Western Hemisphere peace, including his design of the Central American Court of Justice, the first of its kind; and his role in the "pacification"—a word then not necessarily pejorative—of Cuba and the Philippines. He was only the second American, after Roosevelt, so honored. One of Root's few contentious decisions was a stand in favor of requiring U.S. shipping to pay Panama Canal tolls. He declined a second Senate term and in 1915, at the age of seventy, assumed the role of elder statesman.

Root's participation in foreign affairs was not yet over, however. He advocated American preparedness when World War I began, and President *Woodrow Wilson sent him to Russia in 1917 as head of a mission charged with trying to keep the provisional government in the war against Germany. The group accomplished nothing, and the Democratic administration's lack of attention to its few recommendations soured Root's relations with the president. When the Versailles Treaty came before the country for debate in 1919, Root spoke in favor of the League of Nations in principle, calling it "a great opportunity" for peace. But he advocated reservations to preserve American freedom of action. Among his six proposed amendments to the League covenant was one to have controversial Article Ten, which called for a system of collective security, remain in force only for a limited period. In 1921, during the Warren G. Harding administration, he served as one of the delegates to the naval disarmament conference in Washington. There he led the formulation of an agreement on the use of submarines and of the Nine-Power Treaty on China, the latter yet another statement of the Open Door policy. In 1929 Root made his last trip abroad; he helped to revise World Court rules in the hope—futile, as it developed—that the United States would join. In January 1931, by then almost eighty-six years old, he testified before a Senate committee in favor of his plan.

Pneumonia brought the end for the aged statesman at his upper Fifth Avenue apartment on February 7, 1937. Widower Root—his wife had died nine years earlier—left two sons, Elihu and Edward W., and a daughter, Edith, married to Ulysses S. Grant III.

Root remarked once that "our forefathers are not to be judged by the standards of today." Neither should scholars with the benefit of the historical record judge him or his positions on international issues by standards or values current at a later time. For instance, his comments in 1899 on a colonial policy for the United States sound condescending and highminded to the modern reader. Referring to the transfer of Spanish possessions to the United States, he cited legal principles that gave the nation sovereignty over those teritories, and he held that the people of the ceded territories had no right to statehood or even to protection under the Constitution. Nonetheless, he continued, the United States had obligations: "The people of the ceded islands have acquired a moral right to be treated by the United States in accordance with the underlying principles of justice and freedom which we have declared in our Constitution. . . . [O]ur nation has declared these to be rights belonging to all men" (quoted in Jessup, 1, p. 347). Root went on to emphasize, however, that that freedom did not extend to the principle of self-government, for which he firmly believed the people of the "ceded islands" were unprepared.

Root consistently defended the legality of the acquisition of the Panama Canal Zone and stressed the importance of the Monroe Doctrine, calling it the only American foreign policy tenet sufficiently central to the national interest to raise the possibility of war. Restating the Roosevelt Corollary to the Monroe Doctrine, he proclaimed that "we arrogate to ourselves, not sovereignty over the American continent, but only the right to protect. . . . The obligation of civilization to see that right and justice are done by these republics . . . is an obligation that always must go with the right that we assert" (quoted in Jessup, 1, p. 470).

An "Eastern Establishment" cosmopolite in foreign affairs, Root represented an elite type familiar in American policy-making circles. Confident proponents of a vigorous policy abroad, they were white males, ethnic Anglo-Americans, Protestants, from good families, with good educations and good contacts, and frequently from northeastern cities. Some practiced corporate law until they entered public life in a Republican administration, usually by appointment. Men similar in background and outlook to Root included Hay, Taft, Henry Cabot Lodge, Whitelaw Reid, Robert Bacon, Philander C. Knox, Frank B. Kellogg, and Henry L. Stimson. They, like Root, viewed the world as a stage on which the United States had to assert itself to operate as the great power it had become. The peoples of what decades later came to be called Third World countries counted for little in this early twentieth-century formulation.

Root did not originate or even popularize ideas of overseas empire; that was the task of intellectuals such as Alfred T. Mahan and Brooks Adams and politicians such as Roosevelt and Lodge. Rather, Root pleaded the case for expansion, colonies, his vision of world peace, and such precepts as the Monroe Doctrine and the Open Door, before the bar of American opinion leadership; he was an advisor, advocate, and administrator, not a strategist.

Annotated Bibliography

Department of State files for the period of Root's incumbency as secretary, held in the National Archives, Washington, D.C., provide a basis for assessing his record in office. Record Group (RG) 59, General Records of the Department of State, contains the bulk of the relevant materials. Limited information can also be found in RG 76, Records of Boundary and Claims Commissions and Arbitrations, on North Atlantic fisheries arbitration and international boundary negotiations. RG 43, Records of International Conferences, Commissions and Expositions, includes files relating to the 1906 Conference of American States and the 1921–1922 Washington Disarmament Conference. For Root's tenure as secretary of war, see especially Department of Army RG 165, Records of the War Department General and Special Staffs, 1903–1919. The Archives makes available many of these series on microfilm; the scholar may consult National Archives and Records Administration, *Microfilm Resources for Research* (1986), for listings.

Despite the scholarly interest of these official sources, the Elihu Root papers in the Manuscript Division of the Library of Congress in Washington, D.C., constitute the outstanding primary source on the former secretary of state. Measuring sixty-seven linear feet with about 66,000 items—from correspondence to reports, from appointment books to maps and photographs—the Root collection covers the period 1863 to 1915. Correspondence and letterbooks dominate the collection.

The Library of Congress papers also include items related to Root. As examples, the McKinley papers contain 500 letters to and from Root; the Roosevelt papers, more than 1,100; the Taft papers, more than 1,000; even the Wilson collection includes twenty-nine items of Root correspondence, despite the fact that the two statesmen were far from close. The Hay collection, although not listed in the Root entry to the Manuscript Division's "Dictionary Catalogue of Collections," contains important information, as do the papers of Knox, Philip C. Jessup, publisher and ambassador Whitelaw Reid, and longtime assistant secretary of state Alvey A. Adee. A study of Root's career, therefore, would continue with these various manuscript collections held at the same location.

Scholars will find significant Root materials in few other collections. Root's scrapbooks, which relate mainly to the years he was out of office, are at the New York Public Library. The papers of Lodge are at the Massachusetts Society, Boston, Massachusetts; those of Stimson, at Yale University, New Haven, Connecticut; those of Department of State official Francis M. Huntington Wilson, at Ursinus College Library, Collegeville, Pennsylvania; those of Charles G. Dawes at Northwestern University, Evanston, Illinois. Lord Bryce's papers are at the Bodleian Library, Oxford, England.

If Root did not initiate policy, neither did he write books or publish his memoirs. He prepared few articles written as such. Nonetheless, his public views on international issues are well documented; they are available in the texts of his letters, his formal lectures, and his many speeches and in official reports bearing his personal stamp. His former Carnegie and Department of State colleagues Robert Bacon (who succeeded him briefly as secretary) and James Brown Scott collected and edited eight volumes of these documents between 1916 and 1925. The volumes incorporate his comments on such widely diverse subjects as military education, U.S.-Canadian relations, business and politics, and poison gas. Many of the collected speeches pay tribute to public figures and have little lasting value. But the Bacon-Scott compendiums also present Root's ideas on weightier topics. *The Military and Colonial Policy of the United States* (1916) and *Latin America and the United States* (1917) are particularly informative. *Men and Policies* (1924) contains nearly two dozen documents of World War I issues, the League, and diplomacy in the postwar world. One volume concerns his mission to Russia; another, fisheries arbitration at The Hague. *Miscellaneous Addresses* (1917) includes his comments on the Monroe Doctrine. These collections, six of which have been reprinted, provide hundreds of pages of material pertaining to Root's policies and beliefs. Another publication pulls together his Yale Lectures of 1907 and Princeton Lectures of 1913 on citizenship and the Constitution. In 1906 he had issued a collection of speeches he made in Latin America. One significant pamphlet by Root is *The Ethics of the Panama Question* (1904), thirty-six pages taken from an address in Chicago; a Panamanian journal reprinted the article as late as 1986.

Root published many magazine and journal articles drawn from his speeches. A favorite forum was the *American Journal of International Law*; most of his fourteen *Journal* articles concern legal questions, but several address foreign policy. In 1913 he wrote on the Constitution in the *North American Review*, and about Theodore Roosevelt in the same publication upon the former president's death. In 1922 he published an article on popular democracy in the inaugural issue of *Foreign Affairs*, another on preserving the peace in 1925, and another on public opinion and foreign policy in 1931.

Elihu Root spoke and wrote clearly, if occasionally with a flowery style. Speaking of Alexander Hamilton in dedication ceremonies at his alma mater, Hamilton College, he intoned, "This granite may crumble, this bronze may corrode, this College may be dissolved; but the monument of [Hamilton's] work will remain." His more substantive documents provide valuable accounts of events and policies, even though frequently designed to serve the administration's political interests, and they often demonstrate Root's innate optimism. Extracts from the secretary of war's reports for 1899 through 1902, for example, recount in useful detail the administration's view of events in Cuba. In an address in 1909, Secretary of State Root listed several causes of the war and noted that the least of these was an actual wrong committed by one country against another. His suggested remedies provide insight into his inclination to seek legal solutions to diplomatic problems. Root's voluminous collected works thus repay reading by the student of the man and the period. Unhappy to say, one searches in vain for his famed wit in these publications; in written form, that seems to have been reserved for his private correspondence.

Scholars perhaps owe Root a fresh interpretation. Only two book-length studies are available, the more recent dated 1954. Philip C. Jessup, who knew the statesman in later years, published his two-volume *Elihu Root* in 1938. In this comprehensive, massively documented work, Jessup drew on his personal contact and on papers not then generally available. He viewed Root with great respect, expressing the belief that Root restrained Roosevelt's more extreme policies and actions. But he accorded Root faint praise on some few points, such as his stand on the League. Jessup included an extensive listing of Root's principal speeches and publications. Richard W. Leopold's *Elihu Root and the Conservative Tradition* (1954) is a readable, slightly less admiring study. Taking an analytical approach rather than writing a standard biography, Leopold depicts Root as within the mainstream of antiprogressive, orthodox American conservatism, shown by his reservations on the League. The author presents as well a brief essay on sources. About half of each of these works deals with Root's international affairs career. James Brown Scott assessed that career with unstinted praise in Samuel Flagg Bemis, ed., *The American Secretaries of State and Their Diplomacy* (1929). An excellent though comparatively brief overview of Root's foreign policy stewardship is that of Charles W. Toth in *An Uncertain Tradition: American Secretaries of State in the Twentieth Century* (1961), edited by Norman A. Graebner.

A few authors did not praise Root. Among them were anti-imperialists Moorfield Storey and Julian Codman, who published an indictment of his Philippines policies in *Secretary Root's Record* (1902); Ruhl J. Bartlett in *The League to Enforce Peace* (1944); and Alpheus T. Mason in *Bureaucracy Convicts Itself* (1941).

Seeking secondary sources indirectly concerned with Root's career brings the reader to studies of his contemporaries, the periods during which he was active, or specific issues. It is not feasible to cite here the many sources touching on Root and his policies, but a few that are helpful in understanding him or provide useful background deserve mention. Root's protégé, Henry L. Stimson, secretary of state from 1929 to 1933, with McGeorge Bundy, published a particularly interesting memoir in 1948. An important source on Roosevelt is Howard K. Beale, *Theodore Roosevelt and the Rise of America to World Power* (1956). Two volumes of Roosevelt-Lodge correspondence, *Selections from the Correspondence of Theodore Roosevelt and Henry Cabot Lodge* (1925), edited by H. C. Lodge, are replete with references to Root. Among older studies are A. Whitney Griswold's *The Far Eastern Policy of the United States* (1938) and Thomas A. Bailey on Japanese-American relations, *Theodore Roosevelt and the Japanese-American Crises* (1934).

The body of diplomatic history published in the 1960s and 1970s reopening scholarly debate on the United States' turn-of-the-century expansionism, following William Appleman Williams's lead, has paid only passing attention to Root's policy role. Williams, for example, in *America Confronts a Revolutionary World* (1976), limited himself to quoting Root at length on the Open Door and to describing him as an "intelligent conservative" opposed to Wilson; Lloyd C. Gardner, *Imperial America: American Foreign Policy Since 1898* (1976), and Ernest R. May, *Imperial Democracy: The Emergence of America as a Great Power* (1961), in studies from different perspectives of the period, similarly give only scant mention to Root. Recent diplomatic historians seem almost to have passed over Elihu Root, one of the more accomplished, successful American secretaries of state.

Bibliography

Works by Root

Addresses on Government and Citizenship. Edited by Robert Bacon and James Brown Scott. 1915. Reprint. Cambridge, Mass.: Harvard University Press, 1969.

Addresses on International Subjects. Edited by Robert Bacon and James Brown Scott. 1916. Reprint. Cambridge, Mass.: Harvard University Press, 1969, 1989.

American Ideals During the Past Half-Century. Worcester, Mass.: Carnegie Endowment for International Peace, 1925.

America's Message to the Russian People: Addresses by Members of the Special Diplomatic Mission. Boston: Jones, 1918.

Latin America and the United States: Addresses by Elihu Root. Edited by Robert Bacon and James Brown Scott. Cambridge, Mass.: Harvard University Press, 1917.

Letters of the Hon. Elihu Root Relative to the League of Nations. Washington, D.C.: Government Printing Office, 1919.

Men and Policies: Addresses by Elihu Root. Edited by Robert Bacon and James Brown Scott. 1924. Reprint. Cambridge, Mass.: Harvard University Press, 1968.

The Military and Colonial Policy of the United States. Edited by Robert Bacon and James Brown Scott. 1916. Reprint. Cambridge, Mass.: Harvard University Press, 1970.

Miscellaneous Addresses. Edited by Robert Bacon and James Brown Scott. 1917. Reprint. Cambridge, Mass.: Harvard University Press, 1966.

North Atlantic Coast Fisheries Arbitration at The Hague: Argument on Behalf of the United States. Edited by Robert Bacon and James Brown Scott. 1917. Reprint. Cambridge, Mass.: Harvard University Press, 1982.

The Obligations of the United States as to Panama Canal Tolls. Washington, D.C.: Government Printing Office, 1913. Also published as *Panama Canal Tolls: The Obligations of the United States.* Boston: World Peace Foundation, 1913.

"The Permanent Court of International Justice." *National Institute of Social Sciences Journal* 8 (1923): 21–37.

Speeches Incident to the Visit of Secretary Root to South America. Washington, D.C.: Government Printing Office, 1906.

"Theodore Roosevelt." *North American Review* 210 (December 1919): 171–184.

Related Works

Bailey, Thomas A. "The Root-Takahira Agreement of 1908." *Pacific Historical Review* 9 (March 1940): 19–35.

———. *Theodore Roosevelt and the Japanese-American Crises.* 1934. Reprint. Stanford, Calif.: Stanford University Press, 1964.

Bartlett, Ruhl J. *The League to Enforce Peace*. Chapel Hill: University of North Carolina Press, 1944.

Beale, Howard K. *Theodore Roosevelt and the Rise of America to World Power*. 1956. Reprint. Baltimore: Johns Hopkins University Press, 1984.

Biskupski, M. B. "The Poles, the Root Mission, and the Russian Provisional Government, 1917." *Slavonic and East European Review* 63, 1 (1985): 56–68.

Bowers, Claude G. "Elihu Root." *Current History* 33 (1931): 498–502.

Burns, E. Bradford. *The Unwritten Alliance: Rio-Branco and Brazilian-American Relations*. New York: Columbia University Press, 1966.

Cummins, Lejeune. "The Formulation of the 'Platt' Amendment." *The Americas* 23, 4 (1967): 370–389.

Davis, Calvin DeArmond. *The United States and the Second Hague Peace Conference: American Diplomacy and International Organization, 1899–1914*, Durham, N.C.: Duke University Press, 1976.

Dubin, Martin D. "The Carnegie Endowment for International Peace and the Advocacy of a League of Nations, 1914–1918." *Proceedings of the American Philosophical Society* 123, 6 (1979): 344–368.

———. "Elihu Root and the Advocacy of a League of Nations, 1914–1917." *Western Political Quarterly* 19, 3 (1966): 439–455.

Durrell, Harold Clarke. "Hon. Elihu Root." *New England Historical and Genealogical Register* 91 (1937): 99–103.

Esthus, Raymond A. "The Changing Concept of the Open Door, 1899–1910." *Mississippi Valley Historical Review* 46, 3 (1959/60): 435–454.

———. *Theodore Roosevelt and the International Rivalries*. Claremont, Calif.: Regina Books, 1970.

Griswold, A. Whitney. *The Far Eastern Policy of the United States*. New York: Harcourt, Brace, 1938.

Hendrickson, Embert J. "Root's Watchful Waiting and the Venezuelan Controversy." *The Americas* 23, 2 (1967): 115–129.

Hepworth, Janice C. "A Policy of 'Practical Altruisms,' " *Journal of Inter-American Studies* 33, 3 (1961): 411–418.

Hopkins, C. Howard, and John W. Long. "American Jews and the Root Mission to Russia in 1917: Some New Evidence." *American Jewish History* 69, 3 (1980): 342–354.

Hunt, Gaillard. "Elihu Root as Secretary of State." *Putnam's* (July 1909): 471–479.

Jessup, Philip C. *Elihu Root*. 1938. Reprint. 2 vols. New York: Dodd, Mead, 1964.

Leopold, Richard W. *Elihu Root and the Conservative Tradition*. Boston: Little, Brown, 1954.

Lodge, Henry Cabot, ed. *Selections from the Correspondence of Theodore Roosevelt and Henry Cabot Lodge*. 2 vols. New York: Scribner's, 1925.

Marchand, C. Roland. *The American Peace Movement and Social Reform*. Princeton, N.J.: Princeton University Press, 1972.

Mason, Alpheus T. *Bureaucracy Convicts Itself: The Ballinger-Pinchot Controversy of 1910*. New York: Viking, 1941.

Merritt, Frank W. "Elihu Root's Theory and Practice of Public Speaking." *Bucknell University Studies* 3 (May 1952): 124–138.

Morison, Elting E., ed. *The Letters of Theodore Roosevelt*. 8 vols. Cambridge, Mass.: Harvard University Press, 1951–1954.

Nelson, Otto L. *National Security and the General Staff.* Washington, D.C.: Infantry Journal Press, 1946.

Neu, Charles E. *An Uncertain Friendship: Theodore Roosevelt and Japan, 1906–1909.* Cambridge, Mass.: Harvard University Press, 1967.

Patterson, David S. *Toward a Warless World: The Travail of the American Peace Movement, 1887–1914.* Bloomington: Indiana University Press, 1976.

Pratt, Julius W. *America's Colonial Experiment.* New York: Prentice-Hall, 1950.

Scott, James Brown. "Elihu Root (1845–1937)." In *The American Secretaries of State and Their Diplomacy.* Edited by Samuel Flagg Bemis. 1929. Reprint. New York: Knopf, 1958.

Semsch, Philip L. "Elihu Root and the General Staff." *Military Affairs* 27, 1 (1963): 16–27.

Stimson, Henry L., and McGeorge Bundy. *On Active Service in Peace and War.* New York: Harper, 1948.

Storey, Moorfield, and Julian Codman. *Secretary Root's Record, "Marked Severities" in Philippine Warfare.* Boston: Ellis, 1902.

Toth, Charles W. "Elihu Root (1905–1909)." In *An Uncertain Tradition: American Secretaries of State in the Twentieth Century.* Edited by Norman Graebner. New York: McGraw-Hill, 1961.

Wilgus, A. Curtis. "The Third International American Conference at Rio de Janeiro, 1906." *Hispanic American Historical Review* 12, 4 (1932): 420–456.

Williams, William A. *America Confronts a Revolutionary World.* New York: Morrow, 1976.

HENRY E. MATTOX

Robert Schuman (1886–1963).   Robert Schuman was born on June 28, 1886, in the Grand Duchy of Luxembourg. He grew up in Lorraine, the home of his father. Lorraine had been annexed by Germany in 1871, following the Franco-Prussian War. He received his elementary and secondary education in German-language schools and studied at the universities of Bonn, Berlin, Munich, and Strasbourg. From the latter, he was awarded a doctorate of law. Schuman practiced law in Metz prior to World War I. Although he had served in the Prussian army, he was prevented by poor health from taking up arms against France during the war.

Perhaps like many who lived in the area of medieval Lotharingia, Schuman's national identity was influenced by both Germany and France. All of his life he was a Frenchman, but a Frenchman who always spoke French with a strong German accent. It is tempting to see some special prophetic significance in Schuman's roots in the area that once was the Kingdom of Lothair. Since the ninth century, the area had been the focal point of Franco-German rivalry, the primary obstacle to European unity. In the spring of 1950, when *Jean Monnet and his associates began laying the basis for an economic unification of Europe, they self-consciously referred to their actions as an attempt to reconstitute an "economic Lotharingia." Knowing that Schuman was an ardent believer in European reconciliation, they turned to him for support for their plan.

There was much that Schuman could contribute to a serious effort at achieving

European-wide cooperation. He had a distinguished political career. A devout Roman Catholic who once considered the priesthood but turned to politics instead, he served briefly as deputy mayor of Metz in 1918. In 1919, just six months after Lorraine was returned to France, Schuman was elected to the French Chamber of Deputies. Except for the years when he worked with the French underground during World War II, he was reelected every year until 1962.

Schuman's early political career prepared him for his role in post–World War II European integration. After the return of Alsace-Lorraine to France, Schuman worked at the task of integrating the provinces' legal systems with that of France. In doing so, he was able to retain for Alsace-Lorraine the advanced German social legislation. On the eve of the fall of France in 1940, Schuman assumed the chairmanship of the Chamber of Deputies' Finance Commission, on which he had served for the previous seventeen years.

Schuman served as under secretary of state for refugees in the government of Paul Reynaud, which lasted from March to June 1940. He was arrested by the Gestapo in September 1940 and imprisoned briefly in Metz. From 1942 until the liberation of France, he served in the French underground. He was also instrumental in the founding of the Mouvement Républicain Populaire (MRP), a Catholic political party. Between 1945 and 1962 he served in the French Assembly as an MRP deputy from Metz.

Schuman served a number of governments under the postwar Fourth Republic, twice in the capacity of prime minister. He was appointed chairman of the Finance Committee of the Constituent Assembly in 1945. He served as finance minister under Leon Blum from June to December 1946, and again headed up the Finance Ministry under Paul Ramadier in 1947. The Ramadier government was committed to the ''Monnet Plan'' for rebuilding French industry. Its policies worked so well that within five years France surpassed its prewar industrial level.

The year 1947 was an important one for Schuman. He established close contact with Jean Monnet, whose plan for European economic integration would later bear Schuman's name. Schuman represented France at various international monetary and trade conferences. In November, after strikes called by the Communist-dominated Confédération Générale du Travail (CGT) forced the fall of the Ramadier government, President Vincent Auriol called upon Schuman to form a new government.

Schuman's tenure as prime minister was short, from November 1947 to July 1948. He was succeeded by André Marie of the Radical Socialist party, who appointed Schuman minister of foreign affairs. The Marie government lasted only five weeks, followed by Schuman's return as prime minister for less than one week. Schuman then returned to the Foreign Ministry, where he served ten successive governments between 1948 and 1952.

It was in his capacity as foreign minister that Robert Schuman earned recognition as a statesman. He was an ardent supporter of European reconciliation, but one who, like many Frenchmen, did not trust the Germans. Nevertheless, he saw the need for a Franco-German reconciliation as a basis for the future economic and political integration of Europe. He was the right man in the right place at the right time, for the developing Cold War confrontation between the two superpowers necessitated the rebuilding of West Germany, and that was only possible within the framework of European integration.

Europe stood on the brink of economic collapse in 1947 when *George C. Marshall, then secretary of state under President Harry S. Truman, formulated a plan for the United States to aid in the recovery of Europe. Jean Monnet saw in the proposal the opportunity, with U.S. urging, to establish the first European organization. Thus he urged that such aid be given contingent upon the governments themselves, whether former allies or enemies, taking steps toward formal cooperation. The Marshall Plan was announced on June 5, 1947. On April 16, 1948, the Organization for European Economic Cooperation (OEEC) was established for the distribution of Marshall aid funds. It was a first step along the path that would lead to the European Economic Community, or Common Market.

A formidable obstacle to European unity in the late 1940s remained French distrust and fear of Germany. As late as the summer of 1949, in Jean Monnet's opinion, the French government was still seeking a Versailles-style peace. Meanwhile the realities of a deepening Cold War led to increased pressure on France from the United States, supported by Great Britain, to reach an accommodation with the Germans. The Berlin blockade was in force during the winter of 1948–1949. The Soviet Union exploded its first atomic bomb in 1949. Korea was on the verge of erupting into armed conflict. In light of such developments, the United States was intent on strengthening the free world's defenses by restoring self-government to West Germany and integrating it into the defense of Europe.

French opposition to the restoration of Germany was perceived by Monnet and those close to him as a threat to peace. In August 1949, *Konrad Adenauer announced that the Federal Republic of Germany, proclaimed on September 8, would join not only the Council of Europe but also the Atlantic Alliance. Monnet saw in the events unfolding the opportunity to find the solution to the German problem in a united Europe.

Robert Schuman journeyed to Washington, D.C., in September to meet with *Dean Acheson, George C. Marshall's successor as secretary of state, and British foreign minister Ernest Bevin. It became apparent from that meeting that France's continued opposition to the rebuilding and rearming of Germany was a dead-end policy. But Schuman was hindered by the intransigence of the bureaucrats at the Quai d'Orsay, who were still demanding internationalization of the Ruhr, reparations in coal from Germany, a Franco-Saar union, and no German rearmament. Such demands were clearly unrealistic and were recognized as such by both Monnet and Schuman. Schuman feared that the United States would end the occupation of Germany, resulting in a rearmed and independent Germany without any guarantees of French security.

Schuman tried unsuccessfully during 1949 to forge an economic union with France's closest neighbors, the Netherlands, Belgium, and Luxembourg. When that failed due to conflicts between the Dutch and Belgians, he then opened negotiations with Italy. The French parliament refused to ratify the ensuing treaty. Schuman then began planning a customs union that would embrace France, Italy, and the Benelux union of Belgium, the Netherlands, and Luxembourg. It likewise did not get off the ground.

Progress was to come in 1950 due to a happy coincidence. For the first time "birds of a feather" were in control of foreign policy in France, Germany, and Italy. Robert Schuman, Konrad Adenauer, and Alcide de Gasperi were all devout Roman Catholics and men of high ideals. Each had grown up near foreign borders in territories historically disputed by powerful neighbors. Each had been hunted by the Nazis during World War II. Also, Pope Pius XII, who held strong political opinions, proclaimed a Holy Year dedicated to striving for peace. The Christian Democratic political parties saw an opportunity for a renewed "Christian" Europe. The atmosphere was right for a new initiative aimed at reconciliation between former enemies. That new initiative came from Jean Monnet.

Monnet and his circle had been working on a plan for the economic union of Europe. It was not a new idea. During the 1920s Adenauer, then mayor of Cologne, predicted that only by creating a "community of economic interest" could a lasting peace be achieved between Germany and France. Leon Trotsky had voiced a similar sentiment. In 1949 and 1950, the idea was being reborn on both sides of the border.

Robert Schuman was not part of the group that drafted the proposal that came to be know as the Schuman Plan. Monnet initially sent the proposal to Prime Minister Georges Bidault in April 1950. When he did not receive a response, Monnet appealed to Schuman to present the plan for a European coal and steel community. It was Monnet's opinion that only if presented by Schuman would the plan be given serious attention by the United States and Germany.

The plan harmonized well with Schuman's own dream for the future of Europe. On April 30, 1950, he offered his support to Monnet. From that moment the "Monnet Plan" became the "Schuman Plan." During the following week Schuman and Monnet collaborated on a final draft, which Schuman presented to the French cabinet on May 9. He also informed Secretary of State Dean Acheson of the plan and dispatched a colleague to Bonn to consult with Adenauer. That evening, after receiving a favorable response from Adenauer, Schuman read the proposal at a press conference held at the French Foreign Office. The "Schuman Declaration," as it was referred to, proposed in effect the European Coal and Steel Community (ECSC), the first real step on the road to the European Economic Community (EEC) or Common Market.

In a joint communiqué issued on June 3, the governments of France, the Federal Republic of Germany, Italy, and the three Benelux countries announced their acceptance of the Schuman Plan as a basis for negotiation. On the same day, Great Britain formally rejected the proposal. Konrad Adenauer praised the bold initiative before the Bundestag and gave credit to Jean Monnet as the moving spirit behind the plan. Monnet later commented that through the Schuman Plan, Germany was offered equality in an international organization of basic industries.

From the beginning, he noted, it was expected to bring about reconciliation between old enemies and European unification.

In April 1951, the treaty establishing the European Coal and Steel Community was signed in Paris. But for Schuman, Monnet, Adenauer, and others of like mind, the ECSC, or "Montan Union," was not an end in itself, but a prelude to the political unification of Europe.

On September 12, 1950, Secretary of State Dean Acheson proposed rearming West Germany. In response, Monnet sent a memo to Robert Schuman and French Prime Minister René Pleven proposing a solution to Europe's defense and the problem of German rearmament on a collective basis similar to the Schuman Plan. This proposal for a European Defense Community (EDC) was stillborn. Great Britain refused to participate, and its refusal undermined French support. The French feared being outweighed by Germany in any political union of Europe without British participation. The death of *Joseph Stalin and subsequent easing of East-West tensions also undermined support for the EDC. On August 30, 1954, the French National Assembly rejected the EDC treaty, thus effectively dooming it.

Schuman and the other advocates of European union continued to make progress toward economic union, while their hopes for political union were repeatedly frustrated. On March 25, 1957, France, West Germany, Italy, and the Benelux countries, the six member governments of the ECSC, signed the Treaty of Rome, committing themselves to the founding of a European Economic Community. The Common Market was formally established on January 18, 1958. Robert Schuman served as the first president of its consultative body, the European Parliamentary Assembly, from 1958 to 1960. He remained a member of the assembly until February 1963, when declining health forced him to retire. He died on September 4, 1963, at his home near Metz.

It may be argued that much of what was achieved along the unfinished road to European unity was the work of Jean Monnet and Konrad Adenauer. But no one would dispute that Robert Schuman was a key member of the exclusive club of visionaries who, although patriots of their homelands, saw beyond and became "the Europeans." Schuman's contributions were recognized in 1958, when he was awarded the Charlemagne Prize by the city of Aachen (Aix-la-Chapelle), and in 1959, when the European Cultural Foundation awarded him the Erasmus Prize.

Annotated Bibliography

Robert Schuman's papers are found in several French archives. Perhaps the most important repository is the Archives du Ministère des Affaires Étrangères (37 quai d'Orsay, 75007 Paris), which houses the Papiers Robert Schuman. Especially valuable are the papers found in Series Z, "Europe 1944–1949, 1949–1954"; Series Y, "1944–1949 et années suivantes"; and "Direction des Affaires économiques." Additional archives holding important material on Schuman include Archives de l'Assemblée nationale (Paris), Archives du Sénat (Paris), and Archives départementales (Metz).

Sidney Keller, writing in the New York *Herald Tribune* (November 23, 1947), observed that in his twenty-eight years as a member of the French National Assembly prior to World War II Robert Schuman made fewer speeches than most delegates did during a single month. He was apparently a man of even fewer words in print. From his own pen we have a brief twenty-four page pamphlet, *French Policy Towards Germany Since the War* (1954), as well as *Quelle Europe?* (1958) and *Pour l'Europe* (1963). The latter is his account of his review of Jean Monnet's proposal for a European coal and steel community and his decision to endorse Monnet's request for support of the plan.

Schuman's role as a statesman and one of the architects of European unity must be gleaned from the published memoirs of the statesmen, both within and outside France, who shared his vision for European integration. The Schuman Plan was, of course, Schuman's major achievement, in that it opened the door to all that followed. For that era we have, from among Schuman's associates in France, several important memoirs. Jean Monnet was the actual author of the Schuman Plan. His story is found in *Memoirs* (1978). Georges Bidault, whose support Monnet sought before turning to Schuman, has left a political autobiography, *Resistance* (1965). President Vincent Auriol published a journal, *Journal du septennat, 1947–1954* (1970).

In a very real sense, it was the need to rebuild and rearm West Germany, necessitated in turn by the deepening Cold War confrontation between the United States and the Soviet Union, that made European integration possible. The *Memoirs* of Konrad Adenauer, especially the first volume, covering the years 1945–1953 (1966), are important for the crucial relationship between Schuman and the father of the Federal Republic of Germany. Likewise, on the American side, the memoirs of Secretary of State Dean Acheson, *Present at the Creation* (1969) and *Sketches from Life* (1961), are indispensable. Anthony Eden's *Memoirs* (1960) and Hugh Dalton's *High Tide and After* (1962) give a British view of Schuman while also explaining why Great Britain did not join the European Coal and Steel Community.

Several sources survey Schuman's foreign policy with respect to European integration during the years critical to the implementation of the Schuman Plan. Charles Ledré provides a sympathetic treatment of the years 1945–1954 in *Robert Schuman: Pèlerin de l'Europe* (1954). Raymond Poidevin argues in "Der Faktor Europa in der Deutschland-Politik Robert Schumans," *Vierteljahrshefte für Zeitgeschichte* 30, 3 (1985): 406–419, that Schuman led the French foreign policy planners to begin pursuing a policy of European unity during the summer of 1948 through the spring of 1949. He uses materials from the French Foreign Ministry to show that the new policy direction was necessitated by France's failure to impose a Versailles-like peace on Germany.

Another interpretation is provided by John Gillingham in "Die Französishe Ruhrpolitik und die Ursprünge des Schumanplans," *Vierteljahrshefte für Zeitgeschichte* 35, 1 (1987): 1–24. Gillingham, who made use of the Georges Bidault papers at the Archives Nationales de France, the Archives Jean Monnet, the Bundesarchiv, and French and American printed foreign policy documents, argues that the Schuman Plan arose out of a broad consensus among French foreign policy makers in 1945. One of their objectives was to gain control of key German economic assets through international control.

That Schuman's foreign policy objectives with respect to European integration harmonized well with similar foreign policy objectives of Konrad Adenauer or Alcide de Gasperi is treated in Robert Binoux, *Les pionniers de l'Europe* (1972); Raymond Poidevin, "La Question de la Sarre entre la France et la République Fédérale d'Allemagne en 1952," *Revue d'Allemagne* 18, 1 (1986): 63–71; Giorgio Campanini, "I Fondamenti

Culturali dei Protagonisti dell'Unità Europea," *Civitas* 31, 5 (1980): 35–45; and David Watt, "The Community," *Daedalus* 108, 1 (1979): 75–85.

Two general surveys of French politics during the Fourth Republic provide important background on Schuman: Alexander Werth's *France, 1940–1955* (1956) and Herbert Luethy's *France Against Herself* (1955). Richard Mayne's *The Recovery of Europe* (1970) is an indispensable survey of the history of European integration.

Bibliography

Books

Acheson, Dean. *Present at the Creation.* New York: Norton, 1969.

———. *Sketches from Life.* London: Hamish Hamilton, 1961.

Adenauer, Konrad. *Memoirs.* Vol. 1: *1945–53.* Chicago: Regnery, 1966.

L'Année Politique. Paris, various years.

Anouil, Gilles. *La Grande-Bretagne et la Communauté européenne du Charbon et de l'Acier.* Issoudun [France]: Laboureur, 1960.

Auriol, Vincent. *Journal du septennat, 1947–1954.* Version intégrale établie, introduite et annotée par Pierre Nora. Paris: Colin, 1970.

Bidault, Georges. *Resistance: The Political Autobiography of Georges Bidault.* New York: Praeger, 1965.

Binoux, Robert. *Les pionniers de l'Europe: l'Europe et le rapprochement France-allemand.* Paris: Klincksieck, 1972.

Bromberger, Merry, and Serge Bromberger. *Jean Monnet and the United States of Europe.* New York: Coward-McCann, 1969.

Carmoy, Guy de. *The Foreign Policies of France, 1944–1968.* Chicago: University of Chicago Press, 1970.

Clay, Lucius D. *Decision in Germany.* Garden City, N.Y.: Doubleday, 1950.

Cook, Don. *Floodtide in Europe.* New York: Putnam, 1965.

Dalton, Hugh. *High Tide and After: Memoirs, 1945–1960.* London: Muller, 1962.

Diebold, William, Jr. *The Schuman Plan: A Study in Economic Cooperation, 1950–59.* New York: Praeger, 1959.

Eden, Anthony. *Memoirs: Full Circle.* London: Cassell, 1960.

Elgey, Georgette. *Histoire de la IVᵉ République.* 2 vols. Paris: Fayard, 1965, 1968.

Fontaine, François. *La Nation frein.* Paris: Julliard, 1956.

Graubard, Stephen R., ed. *A New Europe?* Boston: Houghton Mifflin, 1964.

Hallstein, Walter. *United Europe: Challenge and Opportunity.* Cambridge, Mass.: Harvard University Press, 1962.

Hallstein, Walter, and Hans-Jurgen Schlochauer, eds. *Zur Integration Europas: Festschrift für Carl-Friedrich Ophüls.* Karlsruhe: Müller, 1965.

Hanrieder, Wolfram, and Auton Graeme. *The Foreign Policies of West Germany, France, and Britain.* Englewood Cliffs, N.J.: Prentice-Hall, 1980.

Hiscocks, Richard. *The Adenauer Era.* Philadelphia: Lippincott, 1966.

Ledré, Charles. *Robert Schuman: Pèlerin de L'Europe.* Paris: Spes, 1954.

Luethy, Herbert. *France Against Herself: A Perceptive Study of France's Past, Her Politics, and Her Unending Crises.* New York: Praeger, 1955.

Mayne, Richard. *The Community of Europe.* London: Gollancz, 1962.

———. *The Recovery of Europe: From Devastation to Unity.* New York: Harper and Row, 1970.

Monnet, Jean. *Memoirs*. Garden City, N.Y.: Doubleday, 1978.

Nutting, Anthony. *Europe Will Not Wait*. London: Hollis and Carter, 1960.

Racine, Raymond. *Vers une Europe nouvelle par le Plan Schuman*. Neuchâtel: La Baconnière, 1954.

Royal Institute of International Affairs. *Surveys of International Affairs*. London, various years.

Schuman, Robert. *French Policy Towards Germany Since the War*. London: Oxford University Press, 1954.

————. *Pour l'Europe*. Paris: Editions Negel, 1963.

————. *Quelle Europe?* Paris: Fayard, 1958.

Werth, Alexander. *France, 1940–1955*. New York: Holt, 1956.

Willis, F. Roy. *France, Germany and the New Europe, 1945–67*. London: Oxford University Press, 1968.

————. *The French in Germany, 1945–1949*. Stanford, Calif.: Stanford University Press, 1962.

Zurcher, Arnold J. *The Struggle to Unite Europe, 1940–1958*. New York: New York University Press, 1958.

Articles

Cahn, Jean-Paul. "Le SPD et la fin de la Communauté européenne de la Défense (CED): Quelques Aspects du problème." *Revue d'Allemagne* 19, 4 (n.d.): 379–398.

Campanini, Giorgio. "I Fondamenti Culturali dei Protagonisti dell'Unità Europea." *Civitas* 31, 5 (1980): 35–45.

Delmas, Claude. "De l'Europe de Robert Schuman à l'Europe d'aujourd'hui." *Défense Nationale* 31, 5 (1975): 37–50.

Gerbet, Pierre. "La Genèse du Plan Schuman." *Revue Française de Science Politique* 6, 3 (1956): 525–553.

Gillingham, John. "Die Französische Ruhrpolitik und die Ursprünge des Schumanplans. Eine Neubewertung." *Vierteljahrshefte für Zeitgeschichte* 35, 1 (1987): 1–24.

Guillen, Pierre. "La France et la question de la défense de l'Europe occidentale, du Pacte de Bruxelles (Mars 1948) au Plan Pleven (October 1950)." *Storia delle Relazioni Internazionali* 2, 2 (1986): 305–327.

Herbst, Ludolf. "Die Zeitgenössische Integrationstheorie und die Anfänge der Europäischen Einigung, 1947–1980." *Vierteljahrshefte für Zeitgeschichte* 34, 2 (1986): 161–205.

Kohnstamm, Max. "The European Tide." In *A New Europe?* Edited by Stephen R. Graubard. Boston: Houghton Mifflin, 1964.

Lavergne, Bernard. "Les Déclarations de M. Robert Schuman et de M. Jean Monnet." *L'Année Politique et Économique* 43, 215/216 (1970): 186–190.

Mischlich, Robert. "Une mission secrète à Bonn (9 Mai 1950)." *Revue d'Allemagne* 19, 4 (1987): 371–378.

Peeters, Carl. "Robert Schuman et la proposition de créer un pool carbon-acier le 9 mai 1950 ou l'acte de naissance de l'Europe intégrée." *Annals of International Studies* 15 (1986): 7–25.

Poidevin, Raymond. "Der Faktor Europa in der Deutschland-Politik Robert Schumans (Sommer 1948 bis Frühjahr 1949)." *Vierteljahrshefte für Zeitgeschichte* 30, 3 (1985): 406–419.

———. "La Question de la Sarre entre la France et la République Fédérale d'Allemagne en 1952." *Revue d'Allemagne* 18, 1 (1986): 63–71.

Sanchez Gijon, Antonio. "Las Limitaciones de Soberania por la Integración en la Comunidad Económica Europea." *Revista de Estudios Políticos* (1972): 279–290.

Watt, David. "The Community: Performance and Prospects." *Daedalus* 108, 1 (1979): 75–85.

PAUL R. WAIBEL

William Seward (1801–1872). What is the difference between a statesman and a politician? Is a statesman merely a politician who shows wisdom and skill when it comes to conducting national concerns? Although wisdom and skill are necessary prerequisites, so are tenacity and political longevity. To be a successful statesman, an individual cannot move too far ahead of his constituency. A statesman is one who accomplishes what the nation asks. As Daniel Webster's biographer G.S. Hillard wrote, "A statesman makes the occasion, but the occasion makes the politician."

Using Hillard's criteria, William H. Seward was an American statesman. He conducted the business of the nation skillfully. He compromised when necessary and fought whenever he thought it required. His political career embodied foresight and tenacity of purpose. Rarely did he jump too far ahead of the northern electorate. His public career lasted nearly forty years and was filled with triumphs and disappointments. Throughout his career he maintained a consistent vision of what he thought necessary for America's future. In his actions, as both senator and secretary of state, he molded American political developments and shaped how Americans viewed themselves.

Seward was born on May 16, 1801, in Florida, New York. Educated at Union College, he was admitted to the bar in 1822. In 1824 he married Frances Adeline Miller, the daughter of his law partner. In 1830 he entered state politics and ran successfully for the New York Senate as an Anti-Mason. In 1838 he was elected governor as a Whig. Reelected in 1840, Seward declined to run again in 1842. Elected to the U.S. Senate in 1848, he remained a Whig stalwart until 1855, when he joined the new Republican party.

Seward's political philosophy remained constant throughout his career. He believed that the nation's greatness depended on domestic tranquility and a democratic form of government and advocated both territorial and economic growth. As Seward saw it, domestic tranquility fostered economic expansion, which in turn led to territorial acquisitions. However, this expansion could not be achieved unless the nation was morally upright. Seward's commitment to a moral America helps explain his opposition to the extension of slavery.

Seward's reputation as an antislavery advocate often overshadowed his commitment to American expansion in the 1850s. His notion of expansionism differed from that of many of his friends in that he emphasized economic growth rather than territorial acquisitions. In Seward's mind any new territory had to be "strategically located."

When territorial expansion occurred, Seward expected it to occur peacefully.

For this reason he consciously tried to separate the issue of U.S. territorial enlargement from the question of slavery. For example, he supported California's admission to the Union but opposed the Compromise of 1850.

On March 11, 1850, the freshman senator from New York rose to speak on California. In a voice "harsh and unpleasant," Seward touched upon the admission of California and tackled such questions as a fugitive slave law, the Texas boundary, the problems of compromise, Union, secession, and slavery. He argued that a "higher law than the Constitution" applied to the nation when it came to slavery and territorial expansion. The phrase "higher law" caught the nation's attention.

Seward's vision for America rested on the assumption that it would always be a single entity. He repeatedly rebuked Southerners in the 1840s and 1850s for raising the specter of secession. Because he believed in the idea of "nation" so strongly, Seward never understood southern secessionists. He convinced himself that disunionism was a minority view in the South. He could not fathom how any section of the nation could consider leaving the Union. The New York senator maintained that economic prosperity demanded a unified nation.

President Abraham Lincoln took office on March 3, 1861, and Seward became secretary of state. Seward brought strong credentials to his new position. Since 1857 he had sat on the Senate Foreign Affairs Committee, and he had traveled abroad periodically. Equally important, he brought with him a set of beliefs designed to prevent civil war. Throughout the spring of 1861, he sought to provoke Britain to war in the belief that an attack against the Union by a foreign nation would quickly bring Southerners back into the Union. It did not work out this way. After the first battle of Bull Run on July 21, 1861, the secretary of state dropped his proposal for a foreign war.

The Union's relations with European nations during the Civil War were fraught with difficulties. The most important dispute between England and the United States during Seward's tenure as secretary of state occurred in November 1861. The incident that created the international fiasco was the removal by Union naval captain Charles Wilkes of two Confederate envoys, James Mason and John Slidell, from a British ship, the *Trent*. The Trent Affair outraged the British and was averted only by Seward's decision to tone down his rhetoric and release Mason and Slidell.

Lincoln and Seward worried about how the nation would respond to their decision to release the two Confederate diplomats. They could have chosen the easy path to popularity and not released them, though it was dubious if a war with England would result in an American victory. Instead, Seward and Lincoln chose to acquiesce to England's demands. In this instance, Seward, a man who earlier had wanted war with England, convinced Lincoln of the necessity of peace. When the order came to release the Confederate envoys, Seward issued a prepared statement. The secretary's declaration flattered northern opinion yet acknowledged the correctness of Britain's position.

Throughout the remaining years of the Civil War, the secretary of state worked to prevent a foreign war from becoming a reality. Resolving the Trent Affair allowed Seward to pursue other areas of disagreement with England, such as the blockade of southern ports. English officials objected to the blockade because the United States had failed to abide by the Declaration of Paris (1856). Recognizing this fact, the secretary instructed U.S. envoys to inform European governments of the Union's desire to adhere to the Declaration of Paris. By committing the Union, Seward hoped that European nations would shut their ports to Confederate privateering. It also made it more difficult for European governments to recognize the Confederacy's legitimacy. In this instance Seward's action served a dual purpose: it was a sound policy during a time of war, and it brought the United States into the international mainstream.

Mexico presented another problem during the Civil War. The secretary feared that supplies passing through Mexico and then to the Confederacy might break the blockade. Exacerbating this problem was Mexico's economic obligation to England and France. To address these concerns, Seward, working through the U.S. minister to Mexico, tried to buy portions of northern Mexico. Although a treaty concerning these issues was negotiated, the Senate failed to ratify it. Even during America's bloodiest conflict, Seward continued to work for the peaceful extension of U.S. territory.

Mexico again drew the secretary's attention when *Napoleon III sent 30,000 French troops there in 1863. Napoleon hoped to create a dependent Mexican monarchy led by Maximilian I, brother of Austrian emperor Francis Joseph. The French action placed Seward and the Union in a difficult position. If the Union condemned the French, Napoleon might recognize the Confederacy. To avoid this, Seward ordered the U.S. minister to France not to protest, since the Union hoped to avoid a "dispute with any foreign power."

Once the Civil War was over, however, Seward pushed the French government to evacuate Mexico, and the United States massed troops along the Mexican border. Finally, the French government gave a definitive departure date, and the United States watched as Maximilian's regime fell. The secretary had secured both his objectives, preventing French recognition of the Confederacy and eliminating the French threat in Mexico.

In his dealings with Napoleon III, Seward alluded to the Monroe Doctrine without mentioning it by name. However, in disputes with Spain, the secretary specifically raised the doctrine. The first dispute involved the Dominican Republic. In March 1861, responding to the request of the Dominican president, Spain reannexed the country. Seward informed Spain of the Union's displeasure and made reference to the Monroe Doctrine. Spain claimed that the Monroe Doctrine had no bearing on this particular case because the Dominicans had asked Spain for reannexation. Eventually, the Dominicans found Spanish rule unsatisfactory and revolted. The revolt, when coupled with Spanish losses due to disease, led to the Spanish withdrawal from the Dominican Republic. Spain ignored Seward's references to the Monroe Doctrine; Americans, however, believed that the doctrine had influenced Spanish actions.

Spain accepted the Monroe Doctrine when it came to the Chincha Islands, located off the Peruvian coast. The Spanish navy seized the Chincha Islands in 1864. Seward responded by invoking the Monroe Doctrine, and the Spanish government quickly disavowed the seizure of these islands, which offered them little commercial or strategic advantage.

Seward's willingness to resort to the doctrine set a precedent for future secretaries of state. The French decision to leave Mexico and Spain's acceptance of the doctrine regarding the Chincha Islands gave Americans a sense that the United States could now enforce the doctrine. Under Seward's direction, the Monroe Doctrine had become an integral part of U.S. foreign policy.

Seward's success with Spain came at a fortuitous time. On the same evening that Lincoln was assassinated, an accomplice of John Wilkes Booth entered the secretary's Washington, D.C., home intent on killing Seward. The assailant was discovered before he could kill Seward, but the secretary was severely wounded. Despite his injuries, Seward remained secretary of state and a member of President Andrew Johnson's administration.

It was during the political tensions of Reconstruction that Seward renewed negotiations with Russia over Alaska, suspended since the beginning of the Civil War. Seward was not the first American to express interest in the territory. While a senator, he had introduced legislation to survey the Bering Sea and the North Pacific. He wanted to know what the region's economic potential was. Now, with relations between Congress and the president strained, the acquisition of Alaska might prove a tonic to the nation.

Russian officials decided to sell the territory in December 1866, and in March 1867 secret negotiations began. On March 30, 1867, Seward and Baron Edouard de Stoeckl, the Russian minister to the United States, worked out the final details. Only after they reached an agreement did Seward inform Senator Charles Sumner, chairman of the Foreign Relations Committee, of the purchase.

With Sumner's help, the Senate ratified the Alaska purchase. Unfortunately, political factionalism delayed the release of funds to pay for the territory. Finally, on October 18, 1867, the Russian flag over Sitka came down for the last time, and U.S. troops raised their nation's standard in its place.

Republican distrust of President Johnson spilled over to other cabinet members. Seward's other territorial endeavors involved the struggle between the president and Congress. To embarrass the president, Congress rejected the purchase of the Danish West Indies which Seward had negotiated in October 1867. Stymied territorially, Seward renewed his efforts to secure commercial advantages for the nation, looking to Asia as a potential market.

In his dealings with Asia, Seward aimed at one objective: American commercial success. Seward's behavior toward China and Japan illustrates the methods he employed in trying to achieve his policy. His behavior also shows how he shaped his policy around his perceptions of Asian attitudes toward American commerce.

Seward believed that China appreciated his commercial efforts. Therefore, his policy toward China was one of patience and generosity. The Burlingame Treaty of 1868 showed Seward's hope for cordial U.S.-Chinese relations. It replaced the Treaty of Tientsin (1858) and reaffirmed American privileges in China. In return, the United States granted China most-favored-nation status. In China, Seward became a proponent of "free trade" and cooperated with the other nations interested in the country. His acceptance of "free trade" may be said to mark the beginning of America's Open Door policy toward China. Moreover, Seward's cooperative endeavors in China brought the United States into closer contact with the major European powers of the day.

Seward dealt differently with Japan than with China. Since Japan resisted American commercial overtures, Seward believed that Japan could not go unpunished. Seward accepted the European position that only force would change Japan's attitude. Following a naval demonstration, the United States participated in the Convention of 1866, which made Japan an economic ward of the West. In agreeing to the Convention of 1866, Seward had again moved the United States into a cooperative relationship with European countries. Under Seward's leadership, the United States was slowly moving away from its isolationism.

Seward's foreign policy committed the United States to an economically oriented empire. Although his Asian policy anticipated the direction of future American growth, Seward also tried to secure territorial possessions in the Pacific. He attempted to annex Hawaii, but Reconstruction politics prevented him from doing so.

Ulysses S. Grant's election in 1868 marked the end of Seward's political career. When he left office in 1869, he must have had mixed feelings. He had guided the nation's foreign policy through one of its most difficult periods. As secretary of state, Seward worked to use geographic and economic expansion to heal some of the nation's wounds. However, he knew that some of his plans had foundered, such as his exploration of the possibility of a canal through Central America. Following Grant's inauguration, Seward returned to Auburn, New York. In his retirement he traveled to Alaska, Hong Kong, and Mexico. He died on October 10, 1872.

Looking back on a political career of nearly forty years, it is easy to see Seward's importance to American politics. He was never the ideologue his opponents claimed. As a governor, senator, and secretary of state, Seward emphasized the need for national unity and economic expansion. He was one of the first politicians to use the press to shape political opinion. He understood the relationship between foreign and domestic policy. Success in one often facilitates success in the other. Seward's importance cannot be calculated on his accomplishments alone. He anticipated the future direction of U.S. foreign policy and laid the foundation subsequent politicians built on to bring the United States into the twentieth century.

Annotated Bibliography

The Rhees Library at the University of Rochester houses many of Seward's letters and speeches. The Seward collection contains about 150,000 items. What makes the Rhees

Library such an important repository for the Seward collection is that it also contains the papers of Thurlow Weed. Other repositories containing Seward letters and speeches are the New York Historical Society, the Minnesota Historical Society, and the Clements Library at the University of Michigan. The Huntington Library has a surprising number of Seward speeches and many out-of-print monographs on the New Yorker. For printed sources one can consult *The Works of William H. Seward* edited by George E. Baker (1853–1884).

Seward's autobiography concerned his life and political career until 1834. It comprises Volume 1 of a three-volume biography of Seward by his son, Frederick, *William H. Seward: An Autobiography from 1801 to 1834. With a Memoir of His Life and Selections from His Letters* (1891). According to a recent Seward biographer, this account contains numerous factual inaccuracies and a rather "selective" editing of William's letters. For a brief general overview of Seward's life see Dexter Perkins, "William Seward," *Dictionary of American Biography* 16 (1928).

Historiographically speaking, interest in William Seward fluctuates. Politicians, historians, and the public found the New Yorker a fascinating figure in the late nineteenth century and the mid-twentieth century. In the nineteenth century much of the attention focused on Seward's role in saving the Union. This is the thrust of Donn Piatt's chapter on Seward in *Memories of the Men Who Saved the Nation* (1887) and Henry Cabot Lodge's chapter on Seward in *Historical and Political Essays* (1892). Piatt, who knew Seward personally, details private conversations with the senator that give the reader a better understanding of Seward's political philosophy. Henry Cabot Lodge viewed Seward as Lincoln's right hand throughout the Civil War. Lodge argued that Seward masterminded the president's foreign policy and summarized Seward's career as secretary of state as "bold and aggressive," yet prudent.

Two full-length biographies of Seward appeared shortly after the publication of Lodge's work: Thorton Kirkland Lothrop's *William Henry Seward* (1899) and Frederic Bancroft's *The Life of William H. Seward* (1900). Bancroft's work was reissued by Peter Smith Press in 1967. Lothrop's work shows how Seward applied political philosophies developed as governor and senator to his work as secretary of state, while Bancroft's work thoroughly details Seward's career as secretary of state.

A more recent biography of William Seward is Glyndon Van Deusen, *William Henry Seward* (1967). Van Deusen not only places Seward in historical context but also brings the New Yorker to life. The author also provides the reader with an understanding of Thurlow Weed's relationship with Seward that earlier writers misunderstood.

Many books deal with various aspects of Seward's career as secretary of state. Norman B. Ferris, *Desperate Diplomacy: William H. Seward's Foreign Policy, 1861* (1976), places Seward's actions during the first months of the war in perspective. Ferris looks at not only the American factors contributing to the fiasco, but also the English causes. Another work dealing with Seward's career as secretary of state is Ernest N. Paolino, *The Foundations of the American Empire: William Henry Seward and U.S. Foreign Policy* (1973). Paolino argues that Seward's decisions as secretary of state set the stage for later American diplomacy, particularly in the area of Asian-American relations. Under Seward's leadership, the United States worked out an informal alliance system with England and France concerning China and Japan that set the stage for the Open Door policy.

Few of Seward's actions have received as much attention as his decision to purchase Alaska. Thomas A. Bailey, "Why the United States Purchased Alaska," *Pacific His-*

torical Review 3, 1 (1934), argues that the American people wanted Alaska because of its economic potential. Another interpretation of how the American public influenced the Alaska decision is Richard E. Welch, Jr., "American Public Opinion and the Purchase of Russian America," *American Slavic and East European Review* 17, 4 (1958). Paul S. Holbo, *Tarnished Expansion: The Alaska Scandal, the Press, and Congress, 1867–1871* (1983), concludes that the Alaska purchase led to an unintended backlash against territorial expansion in general and argues that it helped fix the patterns of politics that came to characterize the Gilded Age. In many ways, Holbo's work picks up where Donald M. Dozer's article, "Anti-Expansionism During the Johnson Administration," *Pacific Historical Review* 12, 3 (1943), leaves off. Dozer asserted that domestic crises during the Johnson administration shaped attitudes toward expansionism in general. According to Dozer, anti-expansionism became a means of attacking President Johnson, and Seward, as Johnson's secretary of state, became a pawn in a larger political game of chess.

Bibliography

Bailey, Thomas A. "Why the United States Purchased Alaska." *Pacific Historical Review* 3, 1 (1934): 39–49.
Bancroft, Frederic. *The Life of William H. Seward.* New York: Harper, 1900.
Dozer, Donald Marquand. "Anti-expansionism During the Johnson Administration." *Pacific Historical Review* 12, 3 (1943): 253–275.
Farrar, Victor J. *The Purchase of Alaska.* Washington, D.C.: Roberts, 1935.
Ferris, Norman B. *Desperate Diplomacy: William H. Seward's Foreign Policy, 1861.* Knoxville: University of Tennessee Press, 1976.
Foner, Eric. *Free Soil, Free Labor, Free Men: The Ideology of the Republican Party Before the Civil War.* London: Oxford University Press, 1970.
Holbo, Paul S. *Tarnished Expansion: The Alaska Scandal, the Press, and Congress, 1867–1871.* Knoxville: University of Tennessee Press, 1983.
Jensen, Ronald J. *The Alaska Purchase and Russian-American Relations.* Seattle: University of Washington Press, 1975.
Lodge, Henry Cabot. "William H. Seward." In *Historical and Political Essays.* Boston: Houghton Mifflin, 1892.
Lothrop, Thorton Kirkland. *William Henry Seward.* Boston: Houghton Mifflin, 1899.
Paolino, Ernest N. *The Foundations of the American Empire: William Henry Seward and U.S. Foreign Policy.* Ithaca, N.Y.: Cornell University Press, 1973.
Perkins, Dexter. "William Seward." In *Dictionary of American Biography.* Edited by Dumas Malone, vol. 16. New York: Scribner's, 1928.
Piatt, Donn. "William H. Seward." In *Memories of the Men Who Saved the Nation.* New York: Belford, Clarke, 1887.
Seward, Frederick W. *William H. Seward: An Autobiography from 1801 to 1834. With a Memoir of His Life and Selections from His Letters.* New York: Derby and Miller, 1891.
Seward, William H. *Speech of Hon. William H. Seward, at the Cooper Institute, New York.* N.p., 1866.
———. *Speech of William H. Seward, Delivered at Rochester.* N.p., 1858.
———. *Speech of William H. Seward, on the Central American Question.* Washington, D.C.: Buell and Blanchard, 1856.
———. *The Works of William H. Seward.* 5 vols. Edited by G. E. Baker. New York: Refield, 1853–1884.

Van Deusen, Glyndon Garlock. *William Henry Seward*. New York: Oxford University Press, 1967.
Welch, Richard E., Jr. "American Public Opinion and the Purchase of Russian America." *American Slavic and East European Review* 17, 4 (1958): 481–494.

MICHAEL J. MULLIN

Joseph (Djugashvili) Stalin (1879–1953).   Joseph Stalin dominated the Soviet Union for three decades as the successor to *Vladimir Lenin. He continued to implement Communist power and shaped the foreign policies of the USSR. Under his leadership, the Soviet Union became a world power with nuclear weapons. Soviet influence, so vastly expanded during his tenure, remained strong until 1989, when the collapse of Communist regimes in central and eastern Europe shattered the Communist party monopoly and Soviet control of that region.

Born Joseph Vissarionovich Djugashvili on December 9 (Old Style)/December 21 (New Style), 1879, Stalin, the son of a shoemaker, came from a poor background. He was born in the town of Gori, Georgia, and studied in a theological seminary in Tiflis (Tbilisi), Georgia, until authorities dismissed him in 1899 for disruptive behavior. He took part in political activities among Georgian workers and became a revolutionary by 1900. He became a supporter of the Bolshevik party by 1904 and met Lenin for the first time in 1905. Djugashvili used many aliases to avoid the tsarist authorities and adopted "Stalin" as his revolutionary name by 1913. He was elected to the party's Central Committee in 1912 and the Politburo in 1917.

In March 1917, following the collapse of tsarist Russia, Stalin assisted the Bolshevik movement in Petrograd. After Lenin and the Bolsheviks seized power in the capital in November 1917, Stalin entered the new government as commissar of nationalities. From 1920 to 1922 he served as head of the Workers' and Peasants' Inspectorate. Stalin was appointed general secretary of the Bolshevik (Communist) party in April 1922, and was responsible for coordinating all party administrative activities. He held this position until his death on March 5, 1953, at the age of seventy-three. Other major posts in his lifetime include those of chairman of the Council of Ministers (1941 to 1953) and chairman of the Supreme Defense Council.

His three decades in power saw massive industrialization, forced collectivization of agriculture, the destructive purges in the 1930s, and the traumatic German invasion of the Soviet Union during the Great Patriotic War (1941–1945) in which more than 20 million Soviet citizens died. Aside from domestic events affecting the Soviet Union, Stalin set the course for Soviet foreign affairs from the 1920s to the 1950s. This included the development of nuclear weapons, the annexation of territory to the USSR, and the extension of Soviet power among its neighbors. Confrontation and competition with the Western democracies also created the Cold War in the post–World War II period.

Stalin played a minimal role in Soviet foreign policy in the period before Lenin's death in early 1924. Lenin dictated foreign affairs, assisted by Leon Trotsky (commissar of foreign affairs, 1917–1918, and commissar of war, 1918–

1925) and Georgii V. Chicherin (commissar of foreign affairs, 1918–1930). Lenin's foreign policy was a combination of "carrot and stick." He created the Comintern (Communist International) in 1919 to support Communist efforts throughout the world. Lenin also began the New Economic Policy (NEP) in 1921, which included a more cooperative foreign policy with other nations. This led to Western investment, loans, and trade with the Soviet Union, plus the development of diplomatic relations with many nations in the 1920s.

Stalin continued the Comintern and Lenin's accommodating policies after he assumed power in the mid–1920s. He eventually forced Trotsky out of his positions in the government and party, and expelled him from the party in 1927. One of the points of disagreement between the two was whether to promote world revolution energetically or first strengthen the Communist system in the Soviet Union. Trotsky favored the former view, while Stalin called for "socialism in one country." Their differences were more over timing and tactics rather than disagreement over the ultimate objective of the victory of the Communist movement.

China became the prominent focus of their disagreement on this foreign policy issue. In China this was a period of internal strife between warring factions, marked by the rise of Chiang Kai-shek, who eventually opposed the small but growing Chinese Communist party (CCP). The Soviet Union alternated among assistance to the CCP, support for Chiang, and a hands-off policy. By 1928 Chiang had effectively suppressed the CCP, and Moscow's influence waned for the time being.

Relations with the West were uneven, although Moscow generally followed a policy of moderation and cooperation. By the latter part of the decade many countries had recognized the Soviet Union, including all the major nations except the United States.

By the start of the global depression in 1929–1930, Stalin's priorities were to implement his plans for industrialization and the collectivization of agriculture. However, Soviet foreign policy by the mid–1930s intensified in the face of rising international tensions. In 1931 Japanese forces invaded Manchuria, a Chinese territory contiguous to the Soviet Union. Japanese territorial ambitions grew through the 1930s, especially with regard to China. Stalin decided to improve relations with the United States to counter potential further Japanese expansion in the western Pacific. This decision contributed to the establishment of diplomatic relations with the United States in November 1933.

European political conditions gradually deteriorated in the early depression period. Stalin reassessed Soviet foreign policy after *Adolf Hitler's rise to power in early 1933, compounded by *Benito Mussolini's fascist dictatorship in Italy and totalitarian regimes in central and eastern Europe. Consequently, the Soviet Union adopted a new policy toward the League of Nations and became a member in 1934. In addition, Stalin supported the creation of the antifascist "Popular Front" movement, which drew the Soviet Union closer to the League and the Western democracies. An important policy statement can be seen, for example, in Stalin's 1934 report to the Seventeenth Congress of the Communist Party of the USSR, in which he warned of the danger of war unless a broad coalition isolated potential warmongers.

Between 1934 and 1939, Soviet foreign policy revealed a strong commitment to international cooperation and a lessening of Comintern efforts to bring Communist regimes to power. Maxim Litvinov, commissar of foreign affairs from 1930 to 1939, represented this new Soviet orientation. The Soviet Union, under Stalin's direction, also signed agreements with its European neighbors. Several contained military provisions in case of impending or actual war, including alliances with France and Czechoslovakia in 1935.

Events from 1935 onward were portents of the breakdown of peace in Europe, Asia, and even Africa. Italy began its invasion of African territories in 1935. Germany undertook massive military rearmament the same year. The Spanish Civil War began in 1936, with Germany and Italy supporting the effort by the rebels under General Francisco Franco to oust the constitutional government. The Soviet Union provided support for the Spanish Republicans, with both supplies and military personnel, but failed to prevent Franco's victory in 1939. Meanwhile, in 1937, the Japanese embarked on a full-scale invasion of China proper.

The Soviet Union found it difficult to assert itself more effectively in foreign policy due to Stalin's domestic purges, which reached deeply into the military. Four of five marshals, including Chief of the General Staff Michael N. Tukhachevsky, were arrested and shot. Many of the officer corps were removed, arrested, and sentenced to prison or death. Stalin's justification for these purges, especially in 1937–1938, was the allegation that the Soviet military leadership intended to assist the Nazis in an effort to overthrow the Communist party and bring the nation under German control or partition it into weak satellite states. Some of the "evidence" may have been provided by the Nazis themselves to discredit the Soviet military.

A crowning blow to Soviet relations with the West and the League occurred in fall 1938 with Western efforts to negotiate with Hitler over the disputed Sudetenland region of western Czechoslovakia. At the famous Munich conference in late September, the policy of "appeasement" granted Hitler his territorial objectives. Neither Czechoslovakia nor the Soviet Union, two nations with clear interests in the implications of the regional dispute, were invited to attend. Nor did the Soviet alliances with France or Czechoslovakia come into play, and the USSR blamed others for not fulfilling the procedures required for those agreements to be implemented. Stalin concluded that the Western democracies intended to turn Nazi Germany toward the East for future expansion and conquest. The "Popular Front" concept collapsed with the Soviet decision to shift its foreign policy significantly in 1939.

Stalin outlined the new course of Soviet policy in a major speech on March 10, 1939, to the Eighteenth Congress of the Communist Party. Declaring that the foreign policy of the Soviet Union was still peaceful accommodation with other states, he also stated his determination to do whatever would best protect the national interests of the Soviet Union. This indicated a willingness to consider alternative policies in the hope of obtaining the "best deal" from those seeking Soviet help or support. In May 1939 Stalin dismissed Litvinov, replacing him with Viacheslav Molotov, who favored accommodation with Hitler and took a cooler view toward the Western democracies and the League.

Other nations recognized the signals emanating from Moscow, and the "bidding" continued through the summer of 1939 in negotiations with Britain, France, Germany, and Poland. Germany offered the most attractive arrangement, codified in the famous agreement in late August 1939 known as the Nazi-Soviet Pact, calling for a ten-year nonaggression agreement and expanded economic ties. Germany and the USSR also concluded a secret accord providing for a common attack on Poland and its division between them. Hitler also granted the Soviet Union a free hand in the Baltic Sea region. Stalin did not participate in the formal German-Soviet negotiations, but he authorized his negotiators to proceed. He did attend the signing of the major agreements and afterward sent Hitler a congratulatory note.

World War II began in early September 1939 as German forces attacked Poland. The Soviet Union's invasion followed, and Poland soon surrendered. Soviet forces attacked Finland in the fall, beginning the "Winter War" (November 1939–March 1940), which provided strategic territory for the Soviet Union. In 1940 the three independent states of Estonia, Latvia, and Lithuania were annexed to the USSR, along with the region of Bessarabia from Romania.

Economic exchanges with Germany reflected substantial Soviet satisfaction with the Nazi-Soviet Pact, but relations gradually deteriorated throughout 1940 despite Soviet efforts at continued cooperation. Stalin sent Molotov to Berlin in November 1940, but the next month Hitler ordered his military leaders to prepare for an invasion of the Soviet Union in the late spring of 1941. Although delayed for several weeks, the invasion began on June 22, 1941.

During this grim and devastating period, Stalin acted as commander-in-chief and chairman of the Defense Council. The month before the invasion he assumed the position of chairman of the Council of Ministers. Despite later attacks on his wartime leadership, notably by Nikita Khrushchev in his famous "secret speech" at the Twentieth Party Congress (February 1956), Stalin did participate actively in the overall supervision of the war. He fired or transferred many high officials and military officers, making way for able younger generals such as Georgii Zhukov, Constantine Rokossovsky, Vasily Chuikov, Ivan Konev, and others. Major criticisms of Stalin's wartime record include his unwillingness to heed warnings of the intended German invasion, his refusal to permit Soviet forces to withdraw, which led to high casualties and massive numbers of prisoners, plus periods of inattentiveness to war issues alternating with interference with plans once developed.

A high priority during the war involved Stalin's relations with his allies. Following the German invasion in mid–1941, a "Grand Alliance" was created among the Soviet Union, Britain, the United States (after December 1941), plus smaller nations and governments-in-exile. Stalin's correspondence and meetings with foreign diplomats and leaders usually reveal him as a confident and substantial negotiator. He met Allied officials in Moscow during the war, including *Winston Churchill, but his major negotiating role took place in three wartime summit meetings with the top U.S. and British leaders: Teheran (November-December 1943) with *Franklin D. Roosevelt and Churchill; Yalta (February 1945) with Roosevelt and Churchill; and Potsdam (July-August 1945) with Harry Truman, Churchill, and Clement Attlee.

These conferences dealt with many issues affecting wartime strategy and postwar planning. A constant component of Soviet diplomacy was the desire to gain Allied approval for territories absorbed before entering the war, plus the acquisition of new lands on the Soviet Union's frontier and the creation of "spheres of influence" in both eastern Europe and East Asia. Western leaders generally acquiesced in these demands. Other issues discussed at these summit meetings included a second front in Europe, Soviet entry into the war against Japan, treatment of Germany after the war, reparations for Soviet economic reconstruction, and the role of the superpowers in a postwar United Nations.

Memoirs of participants in these meetings and later scholarly accounts based on primary sources consistently reveal Stalin as a determined leader who rarely altered the Soviet position. Promises of Soviet cooperation tended to be vague and general, such as on the issue of democratic elections in Poland after its liberation by Soviet forces. On the other hand, Western leaders believed that they could persuade Stalin to accept their views. These meetings also showed Stalin's tendency to expect extensive help with supplies and military operations. His counterparts frequently found his demands excessive or unrealistic. This helps explain the problems related to Lend-Lease aid and the formation of a second front in Western Europe. He could at times be gracious and cooperative, but at other moments he was petulant, stubborn, and grasping.

The Soviet Union participated at the very end of the war in the Pacific, declaring war on Japan on August 8, 1945, two days after the U.S. atomic bomb attack on Hiroshima and one day before the atomic attack on Nagasaki. Japan surrendered on August 14, with the formal surrender ceremony on September 2. One week of participation in the war gave the Soviet Union added opportunities in the western Pacific.

From 1945 to Stalin's death in 1953, the Soviet Union sought to extend its influence. Military forces liberated the nations of eastern Europe from Nazi domination, and Communist governments took power in these regions. In China, a civil war between the Nationalists under Chiang Kai-shek and the CCP under Mao Tse-tung culminated in Communist victory in October 1949.

After an initial postwar reduction of Soviet forces, increases in military budgets became a high priority during the early Cold War period. Soviet foreign policy was further strengthened by the development of its atomic bomb, first tested in 1949. Stalin's anti-Western perspective and his efforts to extend Soviet power can be clearly traced in this period. The new United Nations also became a diplomatic battleground of sparring power blocs, and the USSR used its veto in the Security Council on many occasions.

A variety of regional disputes and controversies created serious tensions in the immediate postwar era. They included Soviet policies toward Iran and Germany, and formation of the Cominform (Communist Information Bureau) in 1947. The Cold War in Europe became a "hot" war in Asia with the outbreak of the Korean War in 1950, in which the Soviet Union and Communist China supported North Korea against South Korea, the United Nations, and the United States.

Stalin's view of foreign policy after the war can be seen clearly in a major policy speech he delivered in February 1946. He predicted the inevitability of another major war, this time between Communist and Western nations. World War II, he noted, defeated one category of opponent, but hostile capitalism still encircled the Soviet Union and had to be confronted to achieve a future decisive Communist victory in world affairs.

Scholars in recent years have concluded that the Soviet Union had limited resources and hence limited foreign policy objectives, and did not intend to take over the world, as many in the West believed at the time. Soviet weakness, especially related to wartime losses and destruction, would not permit a serious, substantial, and sustained Communist effort to expand. The Soviet Union looked for power vacuums where it could move with a minimum of challenge or opposition. When confronted diplomatically or by potential military response, Stalin usually backed down and tried to hold on to what he had achieved.

Following World War II, Soviet foreign relations with the United States and other Western nations deteriorated quickly, but Stalin's influence with eastern European and Asian Communist movements grew as the Soviet Union's military and economic power increased. Moscow encouraged purges among the Communist party leadership in many eastern European states to enhance Soviet dominance, and in January 1949 it created the Council on Mutual Economic Assistance (COMECON or CMEA) to serve Soviet interests in its economic relations with its eastern European partners. A major military alliance, the Warsaw Pact, was not created until 1955.

One notable problem within the Communist orbit in the postwar era was Soviet relations with *Tito, the Communist leader of Yugoslavia, whose independent policies resisted Soviet efforts at hegemony. This dispute was not resolved until 1955, when Stalin's successors reached an accommodation with Tito. During the interim, from 1948 to 1955, Yugoslavia remained beyond the reach of the Soviet Union, both within the Cominform and in other bilateral relations. Correspondence between Tito and Stalin reveals their disagreements.

A summary of the Soviet Union's foreign policy achievements by the time of Stalin's death can be made. An equilibrium now existed in Europe, divided by what Winston Churchill in 1946 referred to by the picturesque and accurate metaphor of the "iron curtain." In Europe the Soviet Union would make no further territorial gains or experience any substantial increase in influence after

1953. In Asia, a Communist regime had come to power in China and was receiving Soviet ideological support and economic aid by 1953. The Korean War (1950–1953) had stabilized with a virtual draw, and an armistice was signed a few months after Stalin's death. Although the Soviet Union sought to gain credibility and influence with the peoples of Africa, Southeast Asia, South Asia, the Middle East, and Latin America, the results by the time of Stalin's death must have been disappointing to the leadership in Moscow.

The Soviet expansion of the late 1940s had shifted to a relatively balanced and stable equilibrium by the early 1950s. Both the Soviet Union and its partners could take satisfaction in the advancement of the Communist movement, even though its full agenda had not been completed. Stalin's leadership played a crucial role in the achievement of these important and dramatic gains. The last decade of his life had brought about major changes in territorial arrangements and the influence of the USSR. Only in rare cases (as in Iran in 1945–1946) had the introduction of Soviet influence been reversed, although in several other areas (as in Greece and Turkey in 1947–1948, or in Japan during the Allied occupation of 1945–1951) the Soviets failed to gain their objective.

During Stalin's era, the Soviet Union undertook major world responsibilities as a superpower and acquired nuclear weapons. Although not expert in foreign policy skills, training, or experience, Stalin nonetheless can and should be credited with a major revision of the world map after 1945. His skilled associates in diplomacy helped make these advances, but the architect of the effort was primarily Stalin. The world leaders who dealt with him never doubted that they were facing a dominant personality and a daunting opponent. Only decades later, in the late 1980s and early 1990s, is the world finally seeing the fragmentation and disintegration of the edifice he created.

Annotated Bibliography

The most extensive collection of official and private papers relating to Stalin and the Stalin era is located in Moscow. This includes archives of the Central Committee of the Communist party. Party files have not in the past, so far as can be determined, been open to Western scholars. In the aftermath of the failed coup of August 1991, Russian authorities expelled personnel from all Communist party facilities in major cities, sealed these buildings, and placed their contents under police protection. Archival materials thus were preserved, but little definitive indication was given at the time of their future disposition other than the creation of a multi-national commission to study the matter. Access was promised at some unspecified time in the future.

By spring 1992 arrangements had been made between Russian archival personnel and several Western research archives (such as the Hoover Institution). This began the process of developing procedures for utilizing files of the Communist party, the foreign and defense ministries, and several security agencies. Classified or otherwise unknown documents, some going back as early as the Lenin and Stalin periods, began to appear in the press and in the work of research scholars.

Future utilization of these materials now appears very likely, although decisions on sensitive or controversial sources may create uneven access. The sheer volume of materials also will create delays. Nonetheless, compared to the previous conditions, major break-throughs have been achieved in preserving, cataloging, and utilizing these previously inaccessible materials.

Walter Laquer in *Stalin: The Glasnost Revelations* (1990) believed that Stalin's private papers were destroyed in 1953. However, information provided by Russian archivists in March 1992 confirms that approximately 17,000 files of Stalin's documents do exist, referred to as "Stalin's personal papers." The person responsible for these files has announced they will be housed primarily in the Russian Center for the Preservation and Study of Contemporary Historical Documents.

One source estimates that cataloging and classifying these newly available archival collections will take as long as fifteen years to complete before they all are made public. Even so, research on Stalin and the Soviet Union seems destined to provide extensive study and re-assessment as a result.

Winston Churchill, in the early weeks of World War II, said that Russian foreign policy was "a riddle, wrapped in a mystery, inside an enigma." The task of uncovering Stalin's views and motivations at times can be similarly challenging.

Robert H. McNeal's important reference guide, *Stalin's Works: An Annotated Bibliography* (1967), provides the most thorough coverage of his writings, but also notes that "the greatest years in Stalin's career remain extremely ill-documented with materials in his own hand" (p. 159). Stalin's collected *Works* (thirteen volumes in English) covers the period only to 1934. Shorter works, anthologies, and pamphlets help fill gaps for later years. We are left for the most part with studies of Soviet foreign policy through which to attempt to discern Stalin's guiding hand. The most comprehensive bibliographical guide to the subject is Thomas T. Hammond, *Soviet Foreign Relations and World Communism* (1965).

Published foreign policy documentary works for the Stalin period include R. J. Sontag and J. S. Beddie, eds., *Nazi-Soviet Relations, 1939–1941* (1948); Jane Degras, ed., *Soviet Documents on Foreign Policy* (1951–1953); X. J. Eudin and R. C. North, *Soviet Russia and the East, 1920–1927* (1957); X. J. Eudin and H. H. Fisher, *Soviet Russia and the West, 1920–1927* (1957); Jane Degras, ed., *The Communist International, 1919–1943* (1956–1965); and X. J. Eudin and R. M. Slusser, *Soviet Foreign Policy, 1928–1934* (1967). Collections of speeches and documents include those of leading diplomats: Maxim Litvinov, *Against Aggression* (1939), V. M. Molotov, *Problems of Foreign Policy* (1949), and Andrei Vyshinsky, *The U.S.S.R. and World Peace* (1949). Memoirs by key personnel include Andrei Gromyko, *Memoirs* (1989), and Ivan Maisky, *Memoirs of a Soviet Ambassador* (1968).

Interpretations of Stalin tend to follow the widely held view of his determination to expand Soviet territory and influence even if it meant temporary deals with Hitler, followed by the Cold War confrontation in the post–1945 period. Max Beloff, *The Foreign Policy of Soviet Russia* (1947–1949) and *Soviet Policy in the Far East* (1953), and David J. Dallin, *Soviet Russia and the Far East* (1948) and *Soviet Russia's Foreign Policy* (1942), are of this type, as is George F. Kennan, *American Diplomacy* (1951). Herbert Feis makes similar comments on Stalin's relations with the West in *Churchill, Roosevelt, Stalin* (1957), *Between War and Peace* (1960), and *From Trust to Terror* (1970). Louis Fischer, *The Soviets in World Affairs* (1951), shares this critical interpretation. John Snell, ed., *The Meaning of Yalta* (1956), is more generous to the Soviet leader.

Philip E. Mosley, *The Kremlin and World Politics* (1960), interprets Stalin as negotiating from a position of strength and an understanding of power politics. A long-term advance was the goal, even if short-term reverses intervened. Hugh Seton-Watson, *From Lenin to Khrushchev* (1960), describes the steady advance of Soviet hegemony over Eastern Europe, and Kennan, *Russia and the West under Lenin and Stalin* (1961), agrees. Anthony T. Bouscaren, *Soviet Foreign Policy* (1962), stresses Stalin's ideological motivation, balanced by a strong desire for territorial expansion. Marshall D. Shulman, *Stalin's Foreign Policy Reappraised* (1963), offers a divergent view, suggesting that between 1949 and 1953 Stalin significantly moderated his objectives and tactics. Richard F. Rosser, *An Introduction to Soviet Foreign Policy* (1969), interprets the Cold War as due to Stalin's appetite, but notes his occasional tactical caution.

In the 1970s, scholars began to offer more diverse interpretations. Thomas W. Wolfe, *Soviet Power and Europe* (1970), is more traditional, seeing the gradual spread of Soviet power, while Diane S. Clemens, *Yalta* (1970), points to Stalin's cooperative efforts at Yalta. Fischer, *The Road to Yalta* (1972), however, emphasizes Stalin's demands, which were certainly not hidden from Western contemporaries and represent traditional Russian imperialism. Adam B. Ulam, *Expansion and Coexistence* (1974), explains how Stalin's expansionist and ideological motivations shaped Soviet policy, although William O. McCagg, Jr., *Stalin Embattled* (1978), raises the question of domestic factions and problems that hindered Stalin's ability to act decisively in foreign affairs. Vojtech Mastny, *Russia's Road to the Cold War* (1979), calls for a more nuanced assessment of Soviet intentions and policies, seeing no master plan for expansion but testing power vacuums to expand Soviet influence. Robert C. Tucker's "The Emergence of Stalin's Foreign Policy," *Slavic Review* 36 (1977): 563–589, offers an important interpretation of the motivations behind Stalin's foreign policy between 1925 and 1934, especially toward Germany.

William Taubman, *Stalin's American Policy* (1982), portrays Stalin as often cautious and conservative in his foreign policy undertakings, while John L. Gaddis, *The Long Peace* (1987), sees Stalin as naive to believe he could trust Hitler in 1939 but then determined to gain territory following World War II. Jonathan Haslam, *The Soviet Union and the Struggle for Collective Security* (1984), and Jiri Hochman, *The Soviet Union and the Failure of Collective Security* (1984), disagree on Stalin's motives in the 1930s, either cynically seeking an accommodation with Hitler to gain territory or conversely hoping to use the League and the Popular Front to limit Hitler's expansionist goals. Geoffrey Roberts, *The Unholy Alliance* (1989), looks at Stalin's decision in mid-August 1939 to break off talks with the British and French and turn toward Germany. He emphasizes Stalin's control of the situation. Anthony Read and David Fisher, *The Deadly Embrace* (1988), point to Stalin's less than total control in 1939.

Steven M. Miner, *Between Churchill and Stalin* (1988), emphasizes ideological factors behind Stalin's energetic and expansionist foreign policy, while Daniel Rancour-Laferriere, *The Mind of Stalin* (1988), suggests that Stalin's alleged latent homosexuality resulted in a hidden affection for Hitler and a desire to please an aggressor, which culminated in the Nazi-Soviet Pact of 1939. Walter Laquer, *Stalin: The Glasnost Revelations* (1990), describes Stalin's lack of understanding of other nations and their intentions, which hampered his ability to effectively shape and direct Soviet policy toward the West. Gaddis, *Russia, the Soviet Union and the United States* (1990), succinctly lists Stalin's operating assumptions: the hostile world surrounding the Soviet Union, the search for soft spots for spheres of influence, and the primary goal of gaining territory to provide security.

Scholarship on this subject shows some variation over the decades since 1945, but interpretations generally stay within a common range of views. Until Soviet archives are opened to provide additional material for research, it seems likely that few new documents or details can be expected. Also, the current focus on the post-Stalin period hampers the continuation of ground-breaking research on Stalin's foreign policy as that topic gradually recedes in importance in Soviet studies.

Bibliography

Beloff, Max. *The Foreign Policy of Soviet Russia, 1929–1941*. 2 vols. New York: Oxford University Press, 1947–1949.

———. *Soviet Policy in the Far East, 1944–1951*. New York: Oxford University Press, 1953.

Bouscaren, Anthony T. *Soviet Foreign Policy: A Pattern of Persistence*. New York: Fordham University Press, 1962.

Clemens, Diane S. *Yalta*. New York: Oxford University Press, 1970.

Dallin, David J. *Soviet Russia and the Far East: A Survey of the Russian Struggle for Control, 1931–1947*. New Haven, Conn.: Yale University Press, 1948.

———. *Soviet Russia's Foreign Policy, 1939–1942*. New Haven, Conn.: Yale University Press, 1942.

Degras, Jane, ed. *The Communist International, 1919–1943*. 3 vols. New York: Oxford University Press, 1956–1965.

———, ed. *Soviet Documents on Foreign Policy*. 3 vols. New York: Oxford University Press, 1951–1953.

Eudin, X. J., and H. H. Fisher. *Soviet Russia and the West, 1920–1927: A Documentary Survey*. Stanford, Calif.: Stanford University Press, 1957.

Eudin, X. J., and R. C. North. *Soviet Russia and the East, 1920–1927: A Documentary Survey*. Stanford, Calif.: Stanford University Press, 1957.

Eudin, X. J., and R. M. Slusser. *Soviet Foreign Policy, 1928–1934: Documents and Materials*. 2 vols. University Park: Pennsylvania State University Press, 1967.

Feis, Herbert. *Between War and Peace: The Potsdam Conference*. Princeton, N.J.: Princeton University Press, 1960.

———. *Churchill, Roosevelt, Stalin: The War They Waged and the Peace They Sought*. Princeton, N.J.: Princeton University Press, 1957.

———. *From Trust to Terror: The Onset of the Cold War, 1945–1950*. New York: Norton, 1970.

Fischer, Louis. *The Road to Yalta: Soviet Foreign Relations, 1941–1945*. New York: Harper and Row, 1972.

———. *The Soviets in World Affairs: A History of Relations Between the Soviet Union and the Rest of the World, 1917–1929*. Princeton, N.J.: Princeton University Press, 1951.

Gaddis, John L. *The Long Peace: Inquiries into the History of the Cold War*. New York: Oxford University Press, 1987.

———. *Russia, the Soviet Union and the United States: An Interpretive History*. New York: McGraw-Hill, 1990.

Gromyko, Andrei. *Memoirs*. New York: Doubleday, 1989.

Hammond, Thomas T. *Soviet Foreign Relations and World Communism: A Selected Annotated Bibliography of 7,000 Books in 30 Languages*. Princeton, N.J.: Princeton University Press, 1965.

Haslam, Jonathan. *The Soviet Union and the Struggle for Collective Security in Europe, 1933–1939*. New York: St. Martin's Press, 1984.

Hochman, Jiri. *The Soviet Union and the Failure of Collective Security, 1934–1938*. Ithaca, N.Y.: Cornell University Press, 1984.

Kennan, George F. *American Diplomacy, 1900–1950*. Chicago: University of Chicago Press, 1951.

———. *Russia and the West under Lenin and Stalin*. Boston: Little, Brown, 1961.

Laquer, Walter. *Stalin: The Glasnost Revelations*. New York: Scribner's, 1990.

Litvinov, Maxim. *Against Aggression: Speeches by Maxim Litvinov, Together with Texts of Treaties and of the Covenant of the League of Nations*. New York: International Publishers, 1939.

McCagg, William O., Jr. *Stalin Embattled, 1943–1948*. Detroit: Wayne State University Press, 1978.

McNeal, Robert H. *Stalin's Works: An Annotated Bibliography*. Stanford, Calif.: Hoover Institution on War, Revolution and Peace, 1967.

Maisky, Ivan. *Memoirs of a Soviet Ambassador: The War, 1939–1943*. New York: Scribner's, 1968.

Mastny, Vojtech. *Russia's Road to the Cold War: Diplomacy, Warfare and the Politics of Communism, 1941–1945*. New York: Columbia University Press, 1979.

Miner, Steven M. *Between Churchill and Stalin: The U.S.S.R., Great Britain and the Origins of the Grand Alliance*. Chapel Hill: University of North Carolina Press, 1988.

Molotov, V. M. *Problems of Foreign Policy: Speeches and Statements, April 1945–November 1948*. Moscow: Foreign Languages Publishing House, 1949.

Mosley, Philip E. *The Kremlin and World Politics: Studies in Soviet Policy and Action*. New York: Vintage Books, 1960.

Rancour-Laferriere, Daniel. *The Mind of Stalin: A Psychoanalytical Study*. Ann Arbor: Ardis Press, 1988.

Read, Anthony, and David Fisher. *The Deadly Embrace: Hitler, Stalin and the Nazi-Soviet Pact, 1939–1941*. New York: Norton, 1988.

Roberts, Geoffrey. *The Unholy Alliance: Stalin's Pact with Hitler*. Bloomington: Indiana University Press, 1989.

Rosser, Richard F. *An Introduction to Soviet Foreign Policy*. Englewood Cliffs, N.J.: Prentice-Hall, 1969.

Seton-Watson, Hugh. *From Lenin to Khrushchev: The History of World Communism*. New York: Praeger, 1960.

Shulman, Marshall D. *Stalin's Foreign Policy Reappraised*. Cambridge, Mass.: Harvard University Press, 1963.

Snell, John L., ed. *The Meaning of Yalta: Big Three Diplomacy and the Balance of Power*. Baton Rouge: Louisiana State University Press, 1956.

Sontag, R. J., and J. S. Beddie, eds. *Nazi-Soviet Relations, 1939–1941: Documents from the Archives of the German Foreign Office*. Washington, D.C.: Department of State, 1948.

Stalin, Joseph. *Correspondence between the Chairman of the Council of Ministers and the Presidents of the U.S.A. and the Prime Ministers of Great Britain, during the Great Patriotic War of 1941–1945*. 2 vols. in 1. Moscow: Foreign Languages Publishing House, 1957.

———. *For Peaceful Coexistence: Postwar Interviews*. New York: International Publishers, 1951.

———. *From Socialism to Communism in the Soviet Union: Report on the Work of the Central Committee to the 18th Congress of the CPSU (B), Delivered March 10, 1939*. New York: International Publishers, 1939.

———. *The Great Patriotic War of the Soviet Union*. New York: International Publishers, 1945.

———. *Problems of Leninism*. Moscow: Foreign Languages Publishing House, 1947.

———. *The War of National Liberation*. New York: International Publishers, 1943.

———. *Works*. 13 vols. Moscow: Foreign Languages Publishing House, 1952–1955.

Taubman, William. *Stalin's American Policy: From Entente to Detente to Cold War*. New York: Norton, 1982.

Tucker, Robert C. "The Emergence of Stalin's Foreign Policy." *Slavic Review* 36 (December 1977): 563–589.

Ulam, Adam B. *Expansion and Coexistence: Soviet Foreign Policy, 1917–1973*. New York: Praeger, 1974.

Vyshinsky, Andrei Y. *The U.S.S.R. and World Peace: Speeches*. New York: International Publishers, 1949.

Wolfe, Thomas W. *Soviet Power and Europe, 1945–1970*. Baltimore: Johns Hopkins University Press, 1970.

TAYLOR STULTS

Charles-Maurice de Talleyrand (1754–1838). Charles Maurice de Talleyrand-Périgord, indisputably one of history's most brilliant and perceptive diplomats, achieved fame for not only surviving but thriving during the turbulence of the French Revolution, the Napoleonic era, and the "Age of Reaction" after 1815. Because of his impact for nearly four decades on major international events, Talleyrand helped to shape his contemporary world as well as the world of the future.

Talleyrand was born in Paris on February 12 or 13, 1754, to an undistinguished aristocratic family. He effectively exploited the privileges deriving from his social status, combining them with his own considerable abilities to attain great heights. However, a childhood accident left Talleyrand permanently crippled, requiring him to forfeit his rights of primogeniture and disqualifying him for military command.

Talleyrand's parents decided to prepare him for a career in the Roman Catholic Church. Seldom has a person been more ill-suited for the priesthood, and Talleyrand would later ignore his spiritual obligations. Nevertheless, he also praised his theological education for preparing him for a career in diplomacy.

It is imperative for the success of the diplomat that he possess a good understanding of the social, economic, political, and cultural forces driving the events of his world. Talleyrand gained this knowledge during the decade between his ordination as abbé in 1779 and the beginning of the French Revolution in 1789. Residing in Paris, the most important urban center of the Western world, Talleyrand was perfectly located for absorbing the major currents of the age. His association with a heterogenous group of friends from all classes of society, especially businessmen and professionals, was significant. In particular, he acquired a keen awareness of the social and economic changes wrought by commercial capitalism and became an enthusiast of laissez-faire theories. Indeed, Talleyrand began in these years a lifetime of profitable speculation in stock markets and investment projects.

This was also the Age of Enlightenment, and Talleyrand embraced many of its values. He became a follower of the early Enlightenment of Voltaire and Montesquieu, with its emphasis on rational thought, usefulness of learning, confidence in science, tolerance, religious skepticism or deism, and a comprehension of human nature as well as the realistic complexities of the world. He rejected as dangerous and counterproductive, however, the values of the late Enlightenment, with its glorification of abstract ideas, simplistic view of world problems, naive optimism, and belief in human perfectibility and unmitigated progress.

The attributes making for Talleyrand's diplomatic greatness were developed in the Parisian upper-class milieu of salon, boudoir, stock exchange, university, and church. He became adept at winning others over with politeness, amiability, charm, and sensitivity. His remarkable qualities of self-control and grace under pressure matured during these years. Talleyrand conditioned himself to reserve comment until the moment and subject were propitious. Whatever could not be experienced directly he learned vicariously from voracious reading. In general, his work ethic was one of focused intensity, although he occasionally feigned laziness as a means of deception. Toward everything in his life he manifested a calculating open-mindedness.

To these acquired characteristics Talleyrand brought a superior intellect, a capacity for concentration, and an unquenchable curiosity, permitting him to dissect with precision the predictability of human affairs and the frailties of human nature. This extraordinary blend of brilliance, discipline, insight, and knowledge perpetuated his political importance throughout uncertain times. It was true that political superiors frequently found him personally loathsome and untrustworthy, yet they also found his wisdom and talents indispensable, and they ignored or alienated him at their political peril.

Talleyrand gained administrative experience with his appointment as general-agent of the French clergy in 1780. Budgetary affairs, gift payments, and liaison matters between the clerical corporation and secular government came under his jurisdiction. In January 1789 Talleyrand was named bishop of Autun.

The French Revolution found Talleyrand supporting the new order and abandoning the interests of his class and his institutional employer. In all probability, his decision to do so proceeded partly from a sincere desire to create a better world and partly from his shrewd recognition that the Old Regime was dying and that he ought to be on the victorious side. As a member of the National Assembly, he became the principal architect of its most controversial piece of legislation, the Civil Constitution of the Clergy, which permanently alienated the papacy from the revolutionary governments, divided French society, split the French clergy, and provoked Talleyrand's excommunication in 1791. In early 1792 Talleyrand was sent on a mission to London. Although he accomplished nothing, his abilities favorably impressed Prime Minister *William Pitt the Younger. However, a more radical phase of the revolution commenced, and by late September Talleyrand had taken refuge in England. Four years of exile ensued, two in England, where he formed generally positive opinions of its institutions and ruling classes, and two in the United States, where he traveled extensively, speculated in various financial schemes, scandalized Philadelphia society by promenading with his black mistress, and concluded that most Americans were crude, money-hungry, and anti-French. His unpleasant experiences and low appraisal of America later influenced some of his policies as foreign minister.

An end to the Reign of Terror in 1794 made possible Talleyrand's return to Paris in September 1796. Less than a year later, he secured an appointment as foreign minister under the Directory, a position he would hold until July 1799. An assessment of Talleyrand's accomplishments as foreign minister under the Directory and, soon after, under *Napoleon I is exceedingly difficult. The relationship between foreign minister and ruler was generally one of servant and master, with Talleyrand frequently obliged to implement policies contradictory to his own judgment. What he occasionally succeeded in achieving, however, was either a modification of certain decisions or the adoption of his own opinions. Meanwhile, service in high office, especially during the notoriously corrupt Directory, provided Talleyrand with excellent opportunities for financial remuneration.

The Directory (1795–1799) pursued a foreign policy of expansion, which Talleyrand executed while endeavoring to restrain the executive with cautionary admonitions. By October 1797, French armies had emerged victorious against all enemies except England and had established satellite republics in neighboring states. This period also marked the beginning of Talleyrand's volatile relationship with Napoleon. Talleyrand became one of the first officials to recognize genius in the young General Bonaparte, and he cultivated a friendship with Napoleon and encouraged his ambitions.

The most renowned and risky project launched during the Talleyrand ministry was Bonaparte's ill-fated expedition to Egypt in 1798–1799. Talleyrand had advocated the French conquest of Egypt as a means of pressuring England into peace negotiations by threatening its colonial empire in India. Thus Talleyrand emerged as one of the earliest statesmen to understand that whoever controlled Egypt could construct a canal at Suez that would be essential to commerce and colonies in the East. French armies in Egypt might force concessions and eventually an alliance with England; however, the English naval triumph at the Battle of Aboukir Bay destroyed the French fleet, stranding the French army and prompting Napoleon to abandon his forces and return to France in October 1799.

Talleyrand always had an uncanny instinct for discerning the drift of developments. Consequently, by July 1799 he had resigned from the government. Not only were his recommendations usually ignored, the unpopular and unstable Directory was deteriorating and a military coup d'état was growing more likely.

In fact, Talleyrand supported the early conspiratorial negotiations leading to Napoleon's seizure of power on November 9, 1799, although he did not actively participate in the event. Less than two weeks later, Bonaparte offered the foreign ministry again to Talleyrand, who presided there for nearly seven years.

The relationship between Talleyrand and Napoleon over a span of twelve years (1797–1809) deteriorated from mild friendship to opposition and bitter hostility. Actually, both men always shared the highest admiration for each other's exceptional gifts. In his memoirs Talleyrand later described Bonaparte as a "great genius" and "the most extraordinary man that has lived for many centuries." Yet the foreign minister would resign over the French emperor's imperial conquests, which disrupted the balance of power in Europe, overextended the state's capacity to sustain them, and created a dangerous array of powers vowing vengeance on France.

For his part, Napoleon once excoriated Talleyrand in a celebrated public display as "a lot of excrement in a silk stocking" and, after his downfall, declared that he would have survived on the French throne if only he had hanged Talleyrand and his minister of police, Joseph Fouché, for treason. Nonetheless, when the emperor was beleaguered in 1814 and near the end of his reign, he supposedly exclaimed, "If only I had Talleyrand! He could fix things up for me even now." Other observers have noted that Talleyrand was almost alone in the empire as a figure not completely overawed by Napoleon.

So great was Talleyrand's expertise that Bonaparte consulted often with him during the early 1800s on most important matters of state, and in a few instances the foreign minister received authority to act on behalf of his master. One such example was his prominent role in negotiating a compromise with the papacy known as the Concordat of 1801. This agreement largely placed the clergy under state control; however, it was on the advice of Talleyrand that Napoleon insisted that Catholicism be recognized only as "the religion of the great majority of the citizens" of France rather than the sole official faith of the nation, thus guaranteeing religious freedom. Furthermore, Talleyrand presided over the consolidation of the more than 360 German states into fewer than 30 by 1803, most of them organized into the Confederation of the Rhine, a French dependency.

Talleyrand aspired to preserve a balance of power in Europe while channeling the aggressive energy and expansionist tendencies unleashed by the French Revolution toward overseas conquests. For a short while Napoleon adopted these policies. Peace with England was achieved in 1802, the Louisiana Territory was reacquired from Spain, and efforts were made to subdue the former island possession of San Domingo in the Caribbean. However, all of these ventures resulted in failure.

The turning point for Talleyrand came in 1805 when Napoleon ignored his advice to treat a defeated Austria with leniency in anticipation of a future alliance against the more reckless powers of Russia and Prussia; instead, the ensuing humiliation of Austria, the devastation of Prussia in 1806, and the French triumphs in 1806–1807 over Russia left Napoleon with an undeniable yet fragile hegemony over most of the Continent. Nevertheless, it also created a multitude of potential allies for England in a coalition devoted to taming an imperialist and revolutionary France. By this stage, the disruption of the balance of power was so great that the downfall of Napoleon was almost inevitable. Talleyrand resigned the foreign ministry in August 1807.

In spite of Talleyrand's absence from government, Napoleon invited him to attend the Erfurt Conference in the autumn of 1808. There Talleyrand, anticipating the demise of Napoleon, met privately with Tsar *Alexander I and revealed the emperor's vulnerabilities and true intentions. Similar information had already been communicated to the Austrian ambassador in Paris. Convinced that Napoleonic megalomania would be disastrous for all, Talleyrand exhorted the leaders of Austria, Russia, and England to organize a grand alliance to defeat the French emperor.

Several months after Erfurt, while Napoleon campaigned in Spain, Talleyrand intrigued with Fouché to place a manipulable relative of Bonaparte on the French throne in the event that the emperor failed to return. This intrigue enraged Napoleon and resulted in Talleyrand's public disgrace.

Thereafter, Talleyrand retreated to private life while maintaining secret contacts with Napoleon's enemies. Napoleon's fall in the spring of 1814 found Talleyrand communicating with the armies invading France and preparing for a future constitutional monarchy with the restoration of Louis XVIII. Because the Bourbons had been exiled from France for over two decades and popular support was precarious, they understood the necessity of rewarding Talleyrand for his efforts. They also wished to employ his services at the decisive upcoming international conference to reorder Europe. Thus Talleyrand was returned to the foreign ministry on May 13, 1814.

In spite of complaints that his policies were guided by unprincipled opportunism or by desire for personal profit and power, scholars have discerned in Talleyrand's diplomacy at least five constants from which he often deviated as foreign minister, but only under pressure from higher authorities.

The first was his patriotic devotion to France. Talleyrand promoted the interests of his native country out of sentiments of loyalty and pride in his heritage. Ever the cosmopolitan figure, Talleyrand found creativity, worth, and dignity in all peoples and cultures. Nonetheless, his attachment to the mother country was strong; indeed, the essence of the Bonaparte-Talleyrand conflict derived from the general's conviction that Talleyrand was harmful to the best interests of the Napoleonic empire, and from the diplomat's belief that Bonaparte was injurious to the best interests of France.

A second uniformity of his diplomacy was his belief in the long-term ineffectiveness of war. While supporting the necessity for nations to maintain strong armed forces and to employ them periodically for state purposes, Talleyrand nonetheless held views similar to Voltaire, who had judged warfare to be essentially ridiculous and uncivilized. Ambitious expansionism and aggressive militarism, in Talleyrand's opinion, almost invariably brought adversity and potential disaster. Generally speaking, Talleyrand thought that coercive action should be utilized judiciously yet resolutely toward clearly defined objectives.

The third uniformity of his career was his advocacy of the balance of power among European nations and the avoidance of extremism in international affairs. Serious disruptions, he believed, accomplished little in the long term while causing economic chaos and social disorder in the short term.

A fourth uniformity was his practice of the "politics of the possible." Talleyrand possessed a deep understanding of the fundamental nature of human beings. He appreciated the necessity of compromise and flexibility in a world where everything was relative. A realism and objectivity tinged with pessimism always motivated his actions and decisions.

A fifth uniformity of his diplomacy was his desire for France to establish close ties with England. He believed that both nations benefited most when they worked together. Furthermore, the two nations shared progressive political systems, capitalistic economies, overseas colonial aspirations, great cultural traditions, and (after Napoleon) support for European equilibrium.

Talleyrand attained his greatest fame at the Congress of Vienna (1814–1815), the peace conference established after the Napoleonic Wars to restore order and stability to Europe. Although representatives of many small and insignificant states appeared in Vienna, the rulers and statesmen of the four Great Powers in the victorious coalition over Napoleon—England, Austria, Prussia, and Russia— had determined to settle all major questions by themselves.

This was the impediment that Talleyrand, leader of the French delegation, resolved to overcome. He mobilized the delegates of the lesser nations into a united front with France at their head, uncharacteristically posing as protector of the powerless. Private talks ensued with the four major powers that soon brought Talleyrand into the inner circle as an equal partner. At this point the French foreign minister cynically abandoned the smaller states. What he had accomplished for a defeated France was to make it a participant in the decisions that shaped the world's future.

Thereafter, Talleyrand enhanced his leverage at Vienna by exploiting a dispute pitting England and Austria against Russia and Prussia over desires by the latter two nations for territorial aggrandizement in eastern Europe. Consequently, an alliance was negotiated by Talleyrand with England and Austria against the other two nations. Talleyrand had exploited conflict to make France the decisive factor in maintaining a balance of power.

Meanwhile, Talleyrand promoted a principle that could guide the entire settlement at Vienna while concurrently increasing his influence. That principle he termed "legitimacy," meaning the restoration wherever feasible of prerevolutionary ruling dynasties and territorial boundaries. Legitimacy was readily adopted by the Congress, and the principle was applied in so many situations that it emerged as the most identifiable of the settlement's basic concepts. Moreover, Talleyrand argued that to deny France its traditionally conspicuous role in international issues would weaken the new legitimist regime in France, which the Great Powers wished to stabilize. Talleyrand's arguments won converts among the other statesmen and carried the day. The final Vienna settlement proved to be one of the most enduring in history.

Louis XVIII rewarded Talleyrand for his brilliant and devoted efforts at Vienna by dismissing him from office less than four months later and relegating the grand diplomat to a fifteen-year retirement. Talleyrand secured his revenge by supporting the Revolution of 1830, which displaced the Bourbons and elevated to the throne as constitutional monarch the duc d'Orleans, Louis Phillipe, for whom the retired diplomat had clandestinely campaigned. With the inexperienced and unstable new government desperately needing international credibility, the king offered Talleyrand the office of foreign minister. Talleyrand declined, accepting instead the position of ambassador to England.

In London, Talleyrand realized an opportunity to fulfill his lifetime goal of laying the foundation for an Anglo-French rapprochement. He used his English social connections as well as his diplomatic talents to achieve enormous personal popularity in London. The new French government was accepted, and England promised support for France against possible foreign intervention. Convocation of the London Conference in 1830–1831 saw Talleyrand contribute vital recommendations that led to an independent constitutional government in Belgium pledged to neutrality.

In retirement during the last four years of his life, Talleyrand remained active, mentally alert, and happy. His last female companion was his nephew's wife, Dorothée de Dino, a very sophisticated, intelligent, and cultured woman by whom he had fathered a daughter in 1820. He died on May 17, 1838, defying more than one of his detractors who had judged him too evil to die.

Annotated Bibliography

Archives containing bits and pieces by or about Talleyrand are scattered throughout the Western world. The most comprehensive collection of documents relating to Talleyrand in his official capacity is housed at the Archives du Ministère des affaires étrangères, located on the Quai d'Orsay in Paris. Many of the great French statesman's reports and opinions are preserved in the Archives parlementaires, also in Paris, where they are indexed under his name.

There is no comprehensive collection of Talleyrand's extensive correspondence, although the aristocratic Lansdowne family maintains an important collection of Talleyrand's papers at the family estate of Bowood.

A bibliographical study of the works by and about Talleyrand must necessarily commence with a reference to his *Mémoires du prince de Talleyrand*, which were originally composed in 1816, collected and possibly embellished by a comrade after his death, and finally edited with a preface and notes by the Duc de Broglie for publication in five volumes in 1891–1892. Regarded by scholars as accurately reflecting Talleyrand's views, these memoirs provide the background of his life as he would have it believed. The first two volumes, while containing many deletions, carry the narrative to 1814. The last three volumes contain official correspondence emphasizing his diplomatic performance at the Congress of Vienna and the London Conference. As is true of any controversial public figure, his interpretations sometimes sharply conflict with those of other contemporaries and later scholars; however, Talleyrand almost invariably infused his discourse with the clarity, conciseness, and rationality one expects from the best of the Enlightenment.

Several volumes of Talleyrand's letters, edited by M. G. Pallain and predating the publication of his memoirs, are also of great value. *Correspondance du prince de Talleyrand et du roi Louis XVIII* (1888) contains detailed information about the Congress of Vienna; *La mission de Talleyrand à Londres, en 1792* (1889) includes his letters pertaining to his first diplomatic mission; *Le ministère de Talleyrand sous le directoire* (1891) embraces his correspondence as foreign minister from 1797 to 1799; and *L'ambassade de Talleyrand à Londres, 1830–1834* (1891) incorporates his dispatches during the London Conference. One all-inclusive edition of his correspondence published in 1889 also has his letters from America to Lord Lansdowne in England during his two years of exile.

A particularly revealing work by Talleyrand was a small essay presented in 1838 to the French Academy of Moral and Political Sciences. His speech, *Éloge de M. le comte Reinhard*, discussed in an urbane and reasoned manner the qualities of the perfect diplomatist. Furthermore, he analyzed the benefits provided by a theological education in preparation for a career in diplomacy.

Another short work of interest was a speech to the French Institute in 1797. The *Mémoire sur les relations commerciales des États-Unis avec l'Angleterre*, published in London in 1805, outlined Talleyrand's aspirations for reviving French interests in a colonial empire in the New World. Talleyrand argued that it would be better for the future wealth and power of France to conquer territories in America rather than in Europe and to press for a less confrontational rivalry with England by seeking conquests overseas rather than by seeking domination of the Continent.

This memoir also included Talleyrand's brilliant assessment of the American situation. While the United States had won political independence, it remained economically dependent on England and was likely to continue to do so for a long time to come; moreover, although much anti-English sentiment prevailed in the United States, Americans were still very English in their culture, language, institutions, and emotional ties. Thus, although some Americans were supportive of the French Revolution and expressed appreciation for massive assistance during the Revolutionary War, Talleyrand believed that an essential Anglophilia would persist for a considerable period.

Yet another brief essay initially presented as a speech at the Institute in July 1797 was the *Essai sur les avantages à retirer de colonies nouvelles dans les circonstances présentes*, in which Talleyrand set forth the purposes for the expedition to Egypt, including the novel justification of liberating slave laborers.

Many volumes and articles incorporate portions of Talleyrand's correspondence. One of the more important, edited by Pierre Bertrand, is *Lettres inédites de Talleyrand à Napoléon* (1889), which includes more than 300 dispatches from Talleyrand to Napoleon during 1800–1809 and reaffirms the subordination of the foreign minister to the general. Finally, Americans will find *Talleyrand in America as a Financial Promoter: Unpublished Letters and Memoirs* (1942), edited by Hans Huth and Wilma J. Pugh, of particular interest.

A treatment of the most important secondary works on Talleyrand must commence with an explanation of why he has been condemned so vehemently. This interpretation derives less from the fact that he was a highly successful practitioner of Machiavellian means than from the fact that his principal adversary was Napoleon, a Promethean figure whose feats have mesmerized generations of scholars and nonscholars and inspired them to hero worship.

Of all the biographies of Talleyrand, the most detailed is the three-volume *Talleyrand, 1754–1838* (1930–1931) by Georges Lacour-Gayet. While grudgingly acknowledging some of the great diplomat's abilities, the author sees Talleyrand in a thoroughly negative light. The most recent biography in French, by Jean Orieux, *Talleyrand; ou Le sphinx incompris* (1970), is much more balanced, yet it too heaps sarcasm on Talleyrand's more worldly attributes while downplaying the numerous consistencies in his policies.

Probably the best English-language biography of Talleyrand is Crane Brinton's *The Lives of Talleyrand* (1936). Emphasizing an interpretative approach, Brinton presents a favorable and powerfully persuasive analysis of the great diplomat's career. In *Talleyrand, 1754–1838* (1932), Duff Cooper, a British diplomat, presents a more straightforward biography, but one highly sympathetic to Talleyrand. Émile Dard, *Napoleon et Talleyrand* (1935), argues that the two great men had a more equal working relationship and that the foreign minister had much more independence than previously believed.

There are several useful books on the Congress of Vienna. The most reputable is by British diplomat and historian Harold Nicolson, *The Congress of Vienna: A Study in Allied Unity, 1812–1822* (1946), which praises Talleyrand's diplomatic skills. Similar in interpretation is Guglielmo Ferrero, *The Reconstruction of Europe* (1941). A solid yet stodgy study that lauds Talleyrand's role at Vienna is Charles Webster, *The Congress of Vienna, 1814-1815* (1934), written for the British Foreign Office in anticipation of the Versailles Conference. Finally, there is a very thoughtful work by Henry A. Kissinger entitled *A World Restored: Metternich, Castlereagh and the Problems of Peace, 1812–1822* (1957). While recognizing Talleyrand's great gifts, Kissinger sees the French foreign minister's effectiveness as being diminished by shifting allegiances, cynical opportunism, and pursuit of money and power. Ironically, some of these criticisms were later leveled at Kissinger during his service as U.S. secretary of state.

Bibliography

Bernard, Jack F. *Talleyrand: A Biography*. New York: Putnam, 1973.

Brinton, Crane. *The Lives of Talleyrand*. New York: Norton, 1936.

Cooper, Duff. *Talleyrand, 1754–1838*. London: Cape, 1932.

Dard, Émile. *Napoleon and Talleyrand*. Translated by Christopher R. Turner. New York: Appleton-Century, 1937.

Dodd, Anna Bowman. *Talleyrand: The Training of a Statesman, 1754–1838*. New York: Putnam's, 1927.

Ferrero, Guglielmo. *The Reconstruction of Europe: Talleyrand and the Congress of Vienna, 1814–1815*. Translated by Theodore R. Jaeckel. New York: Putnam, 1941.

Greenbaum, Louis S. *Talleyrand, Statesman-Priest: The Agent-General of the Clergy and the Church of France at the End of the Old Regime*. Washington, D.C.: Catholic University of America Press, 1970.

Kissinger, Henry Alfred. *A World Restored: Metternich, Castlereagh and the Problems of Peace, 1812–1822*. Boston: Houghton Mifflin, 1957.

Lacour-Gayet, Georges. *Talleyrand, 1754–1838*. 3 vols. Paris: Payot, 1930–1931.

Loliee, Frederic. *Prince Talleyrand and His Times*. New York: Brentano's, 1912.

Madelin, Louis. *Talleyrand: A Vivid Biography of the Amoral, Unscrupulous and Fascinating French Statesman*. New York: Roy, 1948.

Makanowitzky, Barbara Norman. *Napoleon and Talleyrand: The Last Two Weeks.* New York: Stein and Day, 1976.

Nicolson, Harold George. *The Congress of Vienna: A Study in Allied Unity, 1812–1822.* New York: Viking, 1946.

Noel, Leon. *Énigmatique Tallyrand.* Paris: Fayard, 1975.

Orieux, Jean. *Talleyrand; ou Le sphinx incompris.* Paris: Flammarion, 1970.

Palewski, Gaston. *Le Miroir de Tallyrand: Letters inédites à la Duchesse de Courlande pendant le Congrès de Vienne.* Paris: Perrin, 1976.

Poniatowski, Michel. *Talleyrand aux États-Unis, 1794–1796.* Paris: Librairie Académique Perrin, 1976.

———. *Talleyrand et l'ancienne France: 1754–1789* ::%is: *Librairie Académique Perrin, 1988.*

———. *Talleyrand et le Consulat.* Paris: Librairie Académique Perrin, 1986.

———. *Talleyrand et le Directoire: 1796–1800.* Paris: Librairie Académique Perrin, 1982.

Schumann, Maurice. *Talleyrand: Prophet of the Entente Cordiale.* Oxford: Clarendon Press, 1977.

Talleyrand-Périgord, Charles-Maurice de, prince de Bénévent. *Correspondance diplomatique de Talleyrand: La mission de Talleyrand à Londres, en 1792; correspondance inédite de Talleyrand avec le Département des affaires étrangères, le général Biron, etc.; ses lettres d'Amérique à lord Lansdowne.* With an introduction by G. Pallain. Paris: Plon-Nourrit, 1889.

———. *The Correspondence of Prince Talleyrand and King Louis XVIII during the Congress of Vienna.* Preface by M. G. Pallain. New York: Scribner's, 1881.

———. *Éloge de M. le comte Reinhard.* Paris: Institut royal de France, 1838.

———. *Essai sur les avantages à retirer de colonies nouvelles dans les circonstances présentes.* Paris: Mémoires de l'Institut national des sciences et arts. Sciences morales et politiques, 1798.

———. *Lettres inédites de Talleyrand à Napoléon, 1800–1809. Publiées d'après les originaux conservés aux Archives des affaires étrangères.* Introduction by Pierre Bertrand. Paris: Perrin, 1889.

———. *Mémoire sur les relations commerciales des États-Unis avec l'Angleterre.* New York: Putnam, 1805.

———. *Memoirs of the Prince de Talleyrand.* 5 vols. With a preface and notes by the Duc De Broglie. Translated by Raphael Ledos de Beaufort. Paris: Napoleon Society, 1895.

———. *Talleyrand in America as a Financial Promoter: Unpublished Letters and Memoirs.* Translated and edited by Hans Huth and Wilma J. Pugh. New York: Da Capo Press, 1942.

Webster, Charles Kingsley. *The Congress of Vienna, 1814–1815.* London: Bell, 1934.

DONALD H. BARRY

Tito (Josip Broz) (1892–1980).   Josip Broz, known widely as Tito, was the most significant figure in twentieth-century Yugoslav history. As a revolutionist, resistance leader, politician, and head of state, Broz presided over the construction and development of socialist Yugoslavia during and after World War II.

Born on May 7, 1892, Broz enjoyed a fairly secure, if poor, childhood in

Kumrovec, Croatia, then a part of the Austro-Hungarian Empire. His father, a Croatian peasant, owned a modest homestead. Broz's mother came from a slightly more well-to-do Slovene family. Broz seems to have been a vigorous and healthy youth. He learned Slovene as well as Croatian and did well in school, although he quit after four years to work for the family.

Like many young men of his day, Broz left his native region of Zagorje in search of economic opportunity. Before joining the army in 1913, he worked as a waiter, an apprentice in a locksmithery, and a journeyman with membership in a metalworkers' union. He visited Habsburg and German industrial cities. Broz's political activity seems to have been quite limited. He was proud, though, of his union card and good clothes as emblems of newly won status.

During and after World War I, Broz lived through turbulent times. The rise of Bolshevism, the collapse of the Habsburg Empire, and the birth of a troubled Yugoslavia, followed by world depression and the growth of fascism, shook European society. His radicalization likely began during his army service, perhaps with his brief first imprisonment in Novi Sad for unpatriotic grumbling. In 1915 Broz was wounded and captured by the Russians. He then spent over five years in Russia, much of the time in prison or on the run. Before his return to Croatia, now a part of Yugoslavia, Broz witnessed the two Russian revolutions of 1917, worked for the International Red Guard, and joined the Communist party. He also lived for several months with Kirghiz nomads near Omsk, and married the first of his three wives.

Newly formed Yugoslavia was in a state of near siege when Broz arrived. Even the destitution of the working class, incomplete land reform, and the threats of neighboring states were overshadowed by vitriolic nationalist conflicts over federal structure. The Yugoslav Communist party (KPJ), formed in 1919, took third place in the elections of 1920. The next year, however, King Alexander barred the KPJ from legal political activity. At this time the party had an estimated sixty thousand members, of whom Broz was one. Six months later, King Alexander rammed the Vidovdan Constitution through the *Skupstina* (Parliament), institutionalizing an unpopular parliamentary system.

In the 1920s Broz worked in various mills and a shipyard. As the KPJ built up a network of clandestine cells and publications, Broz grew more active. He published his first article in 1927. The KPJ survived bitter internal feuds, Comintern manipulation, and police repression, but Broz was arrested twice. In prison he read extensively on philosophy, economics, and military science; through the Communist network he also befriended his future comrade-in-arms, Mose Pijade, a Jewish intellectual from Belgrade.

In the 1930s Broz, now using the pseudonym Tito more frequently, visited Moscow three times. These trips were mileposts by which his rise in the Yugoslav party may be measured. During his first stay of twenty months in 1935 and 1936, Tito studied, distanced himself from political squabbles, met another future lieutenant, Edvard Kardelj, and became acquainted with such prominent Communists as Georgi Dimitrov, Dmitri Manuilsky, Walter Ulbricht, Klement Gottwald, and Palmiro Togliatti. Most important, he served as secretary of his country's delegation to the Comintern's Seventh World Congress. It was here that the Soviet-run body publicly adopted the "popular front" policy, which allowed for Communist-bourgeois cooperation against fascism. In October 1936 he was appointed organizational secretary of the KPJ and was sent to Paris, Vienna, and Yugoslavia to shore up the failing organization of General Secretary Milan Gorkic and to organize the illegal flow of Yugoslav volunteers for the Spanish Civil War. Stalin's purges claimed the lives of over 100 Yugoslav Communists, while at home the Yugoslav royal police were suppressing KPJ activity. Nonetheless, under Tito KPJ membership increased slowly from 1,500 (1937) to perhaps 12,000 (1941). Tito began to work with men like Milovan Djilas, Alexander Rankovic, Ivo Lola Ribar, Boris Kidric, and the famous author Miroslav Krleza for the first time; in 1937 he became general secretary of the party.

In August 1938 Tito went back to Moscow for six months, where he helped translate *Joseph Stalin's *History of the Bolshevik Party* into Serbo-Croatian. Even as head of the KPJ, Tito likely felt threatened in the Moscow of the late 1930s. Personal rivalry and political intrigue combined to make his life quite insecure.

In late 1939 Tito made a final, brief visit to Moscow. Europe was ominously close to war and Yugoslavia's King Peter tried to steer a peaceful course. Finally the Axis invaded Yugoslavia in April 1941 and conquered the country in less than two weeks. Tito and the KPJ remained underground. The Soviet directive at this point was to avoid involvement in what Stalin termed an intrabourgeois war.

With the Nazi invasion of the USSR, however, Tito's instructions changed. On July 4, 1941, the party was ordered to initiate a guerrilla war against the occupiers. By the end of the war, Tito commanded a force of over 500,000 men and women. He received a fair amount of Allied material aid, mostly in the form of rifles, artillery, tanks, and air support. He received somewhat less from the Soviets, but he did cooperate with their forces in the liberation of northeastern Yugoslavia in late 1944.

Estimates vary, but in the bloody turmoil of World War II perhaps up to 11 percent of the Yugoslav population (that is, 1.7 million people) died. Many were killed in internecine conflicts. Tito emerged as the undisputed political leader of the new, socialist Yugoslavia. Although popular with many, he assumed power without a fair election. He inaugurated a close relationship with the USSR while playing an important role in the sovietization of eastern Europe. Yugoslavia promulgated a Stalin-style constitution, refused to join the Marshall Plan, and played host to the Cominform. It shot down two American planes in overflight in 1946 and sent aid to the Greek Communist guerrillas. Tito's government evinced open distrust of Britain and hostility over irredenta such as Trieste.

In 1948 Tito was propelled into the final stage of his political career, that of diplomat and head of state. The famed Tito-Stalin rupture evolved from issues of political and economic sovereignty. It led to a public split that was both unwanted and unexpected in Belgrade. When Yugoslavia found itself a pariah among Communist states, subjected to a blockade and threats of attack, Tito took the opportunity to cement his grasp on power. He purged the KPJ, struck up an aid relationship with the United States, and launched Yugoslavia on its "separate road to socialism."

Relations with the USSR improved with Khrushchev's 1955 visit to Belgrade. Tito had subsequent rows with Moscow, but he steered his country clear of Soviet domination. Although Tito refused to join Western alliances, he did show interest in Balkan regional cooperation. By 1961 he was ensconced as a pioneer of national communism. Yugoslavia's "third path" consisted of the economic doctrine of workers' self-management, a new ethnic federal system, and a non-aligned foreign policy. He engaged in a great deal of shuttle diplomacy and vigorously cultivated what one may call *Suedpolitik*, or a policy of solidarity with the developing countries. With the assistance of lieutenants such as Kardelj, Tito fleshed out his *Suedpolitik* with a program of active neutralism and peaceful coexistence in world affairs.

After several months of ill health, Tito died on May 4, 1980, from complications following surgery.

The extent to which Tito's personality and surroundings shaped his worldview does not lend itself to precise measurement. Glimpses into his youth, however, show Tito to have been practical, intelligent, and ambitious. His background was steeped in patriarchalism and poverty, but he was literate and aware of the opportunities in the bigger world around him. As a young man he gradually became adept at husbanding his resources and managing to improve his circumstances; like many villagers, he had a keen desire to improve his social status.

Perhaps his radicalization was influenced as well by the charged atmosphere of Croatian politics, in which the social mobilization of the peasantry and elements of national extremism were at work. Anticlericalism may have touched young Tito early, while the social dislocation accompanying Zagorje's population growth and the breakdown of the old extended family communes affected most families. The region was also home to long memories of foreign domination and peasant unrest.

Tito was the last of the major World War II leaders to die. Having succeeded in mobilizing broad, newly politicized segments of society—peasants, youth, women, and disaffected federalists—Tito capitalized on foreign aid and the mistakes of his many enemies to emerge victorious from the war. Under his guidance Yugoslavia pushed the USSR toward fitful acceptance of polycentrism in the world Communist movement; Hungary, China, Albania, Romania, and Czechoslovakia all contributed later to this same process of challenging Soviet hegemony.

Tito's record boasts many domestic achievements, such as steady economic development and what many saw as an ethnically balanced, if autocratic, federal system. As a Communist he had stitched the ragged party together in the 1930s and prepared it to carry out a social revolution as well as a war of national liberation. Vigorous and intense personal involvement also characterized Tito's long diplomatic career. Expelled from the Soviet camp, he managed to defend Yugoslavia's independence. He enjoyed good relations with most neighboring states and obtained aid from the United States and later the USSR.

In an ideological program that combined attempts at workers' self-management and national self-determination with the *Suedpolitik* of nonalignment, Tito set Yugoslavia's unique course of communism. He supported decolonization and world disarmament, usually voting with the USSR on such issues in the United Nations. Because of his belief that capitalism might be transformed by inner conflicts, Tito did not consider war between the superpower blocs inevitable. He maintained that his policies of active neutrality and peaceful coexistence were aimed at securing justice and harmony in international relations. Tito gained great prestige and many supporters by dint of his diplomacy.

It is probably easier to find fault with Tito's domestic policy than with his foreign policy. Much of the violent turmoil that has gripped the former Yugoslav state since 1991 can be attributed to Tito's shortcomings. Critics note his failure to appoint a strong successor to guide the state. Thirty-five years of undemocratic rule might also have so paralyzed the Yugoslav polity that real solutions to pressing ethnic and economic problems have proven to be unobtainable. Certainly with its disintegration, Yugoslavia is unable to conduct a stable and energetic foreign policy. Furthermore, with the accelerated decay of the nonaligned movement and the collapse of the Soviet Union, Tito's familiar diplomatic formulas are passé. Tito's (and Yugoslavia's) unique position as Communist maverick and European leader of the nonaligned world is in danger of becoming little more than a historical footnote.

Annotated Bibliography

All major archival materials relating to Josip Broz Tito are located in Belgrade. His personal papers, the Kabinet Marsala Jugoslavije, are found in the Arhiv Josipa Broza Tita at the Memorijalni Centar "Josip Broz Tito," Bulevar Oktobarske Revolucije 92. The Arhiv Centralnog Komiteta Saveza Komunista Jugoslavije, Odeljenje za istoriju SKJ, arhiv i dokumentaciju, Trg Marksa i Engelsa 15, houses party documents from the period under study. Military and partisan documents are located at the Vojno-istorijski Institut Jugoslovenske Narodne Armije Arhiv, Bircaninova 5. The Arhiv Jugoslavije, Vase Pelagica 33, holds the papers of the Yugoslav federal government.

All investigators of Tito's diplomacy can benefit from consulting several fine bibliographies. Marija Sentic's exhaustive *Josip Broz Tito, Bibliografije* (1984) includes over 2,800 books and brochures by or about Broz published in Yugoslavia. Two general bibliographies on Yugoslavia are John J. Horton, ed., *Yugoslavia* (1990), and Michael Boro Petrovich, *Yugoslavia: A Bibliographic Guide* (1974). A bibliography specifically on Yugoslav foreign affairs is Brian Hunter, *Soviet-Yugoslav Relations, 1948–1972: A Bibliography of Soviet, Western, and Yugoslav Comment and Analysis* (1976).

Because the KPJ came into existence espousing solidarity with the USSR, nearly every early speech or article in Tito's name makes some reference to foreign policy. Henry

Christman, ed., *The Essential Tito* (1970), includes such postwar policy statements as his August 1945 "Address at the Third Session of the Anti-Fascist Council for the National Liberation of Yugoslavia"; his 1948 "Report to the Fifth Congress of the Communist Party of Yugoslavia"; his 1960 address to the Fifteenth Session of the UN; and his 1961 speech to the First Conference of Heads of State or Government of Nonaligned Countries. A collection of Tito's speeches and articles, *Selected Speeches and Articles, 1941–1961* (1963), contains a detailed selection of writings, ranging from reports on active neutralism and peaceful coexistence to speeches of solidarity delivered in developing countries.

Tito left no memoirs, but his collected works appear in two series: *Govori i clanci*, 21 vols. (1959–1972), and *Sabrana Djela*, 20 vols. (1977–1984). Additional volumes of the latter set are still in production. Wartime pronouncements and telegrams, discussions on Balkan Communist cooperation, press conferences with foreign journalists, and many postwar letters and speeches on behalf of nonaligned and leftist causes are included.

Zdravko Zidovec's compilation, *Josip Broz Tito. Intervjui* (1980), reprints interviews given between 1944 and 1979. Tito's wide-ranging comments touch on Yugoslav relations with socialists in Western countries, on ties to the developing world, and on specific meetings of the nonaligned movement such as the controversial sixth summit in Havana in 1979.

Addresses from party and other organizational gatherings appear in the two volumes of Stanislav Stojanovic, ed., *Nezavisnost i savremeni svijet* (1982). This work is dedicated to Tito's foreign policy statements and begins with a 1936 article in support of the Republicans in the Spanish Civil War. The first volume contains much wartime correspondence, while the second includes statements to the press and governments of developing countries such as Egypt, Mongolia, Algeria, Cambodia, Zambia, and Sri Lanka. Addresses on foreign relations to a number of Yugoslav fora, from Zagreb to Skopje, are also reprinted.

Slobodan Nesovic and Branko Petranovic, eds., *AVNOJ i revolucija. Tematska zbirka dokumenata, 1941–1945* (1983), includes representative samples of Tito's foreign policy documents. Specimens range from the guerrilla call to arms in 1941 through cooperative military arrangements with the Western Allies and the USSR to the declaration of the new republic after war's end. Documents pertaining specifically to the Belgrade-Moscow rupture are found in *The Soviet-Yugoslav Dispute: Text of the Published Correspondence* (1948) and Vaclav Benes et al., eds., *The Second Soviet-Yugoslav Dispute: Full Text of Main Documents, April–June 1958* (1959). *Bela knjiga o agresivnim postupcima vlada SSSR, Poljske, Cehoslovacke, Madjarske, Rumunije, Bugarske, i Albanije prema Jugoslaviji* (1951), also issued in English, publishes diplomatic notes on the Soviet-inspired bullying of heretical Yugoslavia at the outset of its separate road to socialism.

Several collections of Tito's pronouncements on specific topics have appeared in English. *Tito on Peace, Security, and Cooperation in Europe* (1977) gives Tito's vision of just and harmonious relations in Europe. Themes range from the independence struggle against fascism to détente to the successes of the Helsinki Accords; excerpts from sources such as *Skupstina* speeches and press interviews are fused together in one long narrative.

The National Question (1983) provides the ideological justification for equating the Yugoslav national liberation movement with social revolution. It also links the country's independence to a resolution of the interwar ethnic strife on the basis of workers' self-management. Other articles address Yugoslavia's peculiar position in the former socialist bloc as the most ethnically diverse of the people's democracies. Tito characterizes socialist patriotism as a positive development for international fraternalism, since it raises the general level of creative enthusiasm. Most important, Tito views Yugoslavia's internal community of nations and nationalities as the realization of Lenin's ideals of coexistence and respect for sovereignty.

Non-alignment: The Conscience and Future of Mankind (1979) includes Tito's addresses to his nonaligned partners and characterizes Yugoslavia's policy of active neutralism and peaceful coexistence as a contribution to the inevitable victory of progressive forces, which will benefit all peoples of the world.

Few specific treatments of Tito's personal role in foreign affairs exist. Thus a reader usually begins by consulting one of the better biographies, which do a good job of placing his diplomatic activity in a general context; a historical overview can then be used to fit Tito's diplomacy into the state's development. (Researchers may quickly note that it is difficult to separate Tito's views from those of the Yugoslav government. Likewise the Yugoslav state's foreign policy can for most purposes be attributed to Tito, so central was his role in the political and diplomatic development of the country.) Fitzroy Maclean, *Disputed Barricade: The Life and Times of Josip Broz Tito, Marshal of Yugoslavia* (1957), Phyllis Auty, *Tito: A Biography*, (1970), and Vladimir Dedijer, *Tito* (1953), are all very readable, wide-ranging, and somewhat sympathetic accounts of Tito's life, drawn to a fair extent from conversations with Tito himself. For historical perspective one may consult Fred Singleton, *A Short History of the Yugoslav Peoples* (1985), or Dennison Rusinow, *The Yugoslav Experiment, 1948–1974* (1977).

Tito was the subject of a large number of encomia published in Yugoslavia during his lifetime. Most have no value for scholarly research. An official biography, along with a sizable bibliography, may be found in "Josip Broz Tito," *Vojna Enciklopedija* (1959): 132–135; and in a later edition of the same work (1971: 80–86). See also "Josip Broz Tito," in *Enciklopedija Jugoslavije* (1956): 238–242. Tihomir Stanojevic, *Tito: His Life and Work* (1963), is a picture book with commentary. Tito's famous shuttle diplomacy— by plane and boat to all corners of the world—is the subject of Zvonko Staubringer's *Tito. Drzavljan sveta* (1974), while Mihailo Saranovic's *Svet o Titu* (1981), also available in English, is a collection of eulogies from world leaders.

Tito's leadership is sharply critiqued in Nora Beloff, *Tito's Flawed Legacy: Yugoslavia and the West since 1939* (1985), which points out that Tito used nonalignment as a prop for his repressive Marxist-Leninist regime. Other criticism of Tito's foreign policy is found in Nikolai Tolstoy, *The Minister and the Massacres* (1986), and Ivo Omrcanin, *Enigma Tito* (1984).

Contemporary observers published quite a few interim assessments of Tito's activities. One of the most detailed is Hamilton Fish Armstrong, *Tito and Goliath* (1951). Others, such as Slobodan M. Draskovitch, *Tito, Moscow's Trojan Horse* (1957), Alex Dragnich, *Tito's Promised Land* (1954), and R. H. Markham, *Tito's Imperial Communism* (1947), derogate his foreign policy.

Two other contemporary accounts present differing sides of the debate on the virtues of nonalignment. Wayne Vucinich, ed., *Contemporary Yugoslavia: Twenty Years of Socialist Experiment* (1969), emphasizes the benefits Tito accrued from the policy, such as experience, allies, publicity, and a platform palatable to most of his country; but George Hoffman and Frederick Warner Neal, *Yugoslavia and the New Communism* (1962), concentrates on Yugoslavia's increasingly close cooperation with the USSR.

Several surveys of Yugoslav diplomacy now exist. John C. Campbell's *Tito's Separate Road: America and Yugoslavia in World Politics* (1967) is one of the best. It examines Yugoslav policies toward the United States and the USSR, China, and Soviet-bloc and nonaligned states. *Jugoslawische Aussenpolitik, 1948–1968* by Irena Reuter-Hendrichs (1976) appraises favorably Yugoslavia's foreign policy, seeing its basis in long-standing principles of nonalignment. Ranko Petkovic, *Nesvrstana Jugoslavija i savremeni svet. Spoljna politika Jugoslavije, 1948–1985* (1985), offers an excellent discussion of Yugoslavia's relations with its neighbors; it is a valuable geopolitical study of small-state diplomacy during the Cold War.

From the wealth of memoirs bearing on Tito's diplomacy, one may begin with Edvard Kardelj, *Reminiscences* (1982), and Veljko Micunovic, *Moscow Diary* (1980). More detailed recollections include Arso Milatovic, *Pet diplomatskih misija*, 2 vols. (1985).

An interesting essay on Tito's legacy, with reference to nonalignment, Eurocommunism, and Yugoslavia's ambiguous relationship with the USSR, appears in Slobodan Stankovic, *The End of the Tito Era: Yugoslavia's Dilemmas* (1981). The author sees tension between Tito's long-held belief in an ideological kinship with the Soviet Union and a fierce resistance to Soviet hegemonism.

Researchers should be aware that there is a growing number of fine works on specific foreign policy topics. Adam Ulam's solid *Titoism and the Cominform* (1952) focuses on maintenance of personal power as opposed to nationalist or dogmatic struggles. Walter Roberts, *Tito, Mihailovic and the Allies, 1941–1945* (1987), discusses the controversial Partisan negotiations with the Nazis. John C. Campbell, ed., *Successful Negotiation: Trieste 1954. An Appraisal by the Five Participants* (1976), is one of the many good books on Tito's stand-off with the Western Allies over Slovene-inhabited territories in Italy. The Cominform rift provides the occasion for Darko Bekic's richly detailed and documented account of Yugoslavia's struggle to end its isolation. His *Jugoslavija u hladnom ratu. Odnosi s velikim silama, 1949–1955* (1988) is a good companion work to Wayne Vucinich, ed., *At the Brink of War and Peace: The Tito-Stalin Break in a Historic Perspective* (1982). Efforts at Balkan federation in the 1950s are lucidly discussed in John O. Iatrides, *Balkan Triangle: Birth and Decline of an Alliance Across Ideological Boundaries* (1968), while Stella Alexander brings to light Yugoslavia's relations with the Vatican (over the Stepinac case and Trieste) and with Bulgaria (over Macedonia) in *Church and State in Yugoslavia since 1945* (1979).

Tito's nonalignment is addressed by Alvin Rubinstein in *Yugoslavia and the Nonaligned World* (1970). Based on extensive interviews and press coverage, it is an excellent chronicle of diplomatic activity, incorporating a study of Yugoslavia's search for identity among the new states of the UN. Leo Mates and Lars Nord provide theoretical Marxist interpretations of nonalignment in their respective works, *Nonalignment: Theory and Current Policy* (1972) and *Nonalignment and Socialism: Yugoslav Foreign Policy in Theory and Practice* (1974). Bojana Tadic, *Istorijski razvoj politike nesvrstavanja, 1946–1966* (1968), is a brief but scholarly history of the movement's main meetings, with some documents reproduced.

Bibliography

Alexander, Stella. *Church and State in Yugoslavia since 1945*. Cambridge: Cambridge University Press, 1979.

Armstrong, Hamilton Fish. *Tito and Goliath*. New York: Macmillan, 1951.

Auty, Phyllis. *Tito: A Biography*. London: Longman, 1970.

Bekic, Darko. *Jugoslavija u hladnom ratu. Odnosi s velikim silama, 1949–1955*. Zagreb: Globus, 1988.

Bela knjiga o agresivnim postupcima vlada SSSR, Poljske, Cehoslovacke, Madjarske,

Rumunije, Bugarske, i Albanije prema Jugoslaviji. Belgrade: Ministarstvo inos-
tranih poslova, 1951.

Beloff, Nora. *Tito's Flawed Legacy: Yugoslavia and the West since 1939.* Boulder, Colo.:
Westview Press, 1985.

Benes, Vaclav, et al., eds. *The Second Soviet-Yugoslav Dispute: Full Text of Main
Documents, April–June 1958.* Bloomington: Indiana University Press, 1959.

Campbell, John C. *Tito's Separate Road: America and Yugoslavia in World Politics.*
New York: Council on Foreign Relations, 1967.

————, ed. *Successful Negotiation: Trieste 1954. An Appraisal by the Five Participants.*
Princeton, N.J.: Princeton University Press, 1976.

Christman, Henry, ed. *The Essential Tito.* New York: St. Martin's Press, 1970.

Dedijer, Vladimir. *Tito.* New York: Simon and Schuster, 1953.

Dragnich, Alex. *Tito's Promised Land.* New Brunswick, N.J.: Rutgers University Press,
1954.

Draskovitch, Slobodan M. *Tito, Moscow's Trojan Horse.* Chicago: Regnery, 1957.

Enciklopedija Jugoslavije. 1956 ed. S.v. "Josip Broz Tito," by Mose Pijade.

Hoffman, George, and Frederick Warner Neal. *Yugoslavia and the New Communism.*
New York: Twentieth Century Fund, 1962.

Horton, John J., ed. *Yugoslavia.* Rev. ed. Oxford: Clio, 1990.

Hunter, Brian. *Soviet-Yugoslav Relations, 1948–1972: A Bibliography of Soviet, Western,
and Yugoslav Comment and Analysis.* New York: Garland, 1976.

Iatrides, John O. *Balkan Triangle: Birth and Decline of an Alliance Across Ideological
Boundaries.* The Hague: Mouton, 1968.

Kardelj, Edvard. *Reminiscences.* London: Blond and Briggs, 1982.

Maclean, Fitzroy. *Disputed Barricade: The Life and Times of Josip Broz Tito, Marshal
of Yugoslavia.* London: Cape, 1957.

Markham, R. H. *Tito's Imperial Communism.* Chapel Hill: University of North Carolina
Press, 1947.

Mates, Leo. *Nonalignment: Theory and Current Policy.* Belgrade: IMPP, 1972.

Micunovic, Veljko. *Moscow Diary.* New York: Doubleday, 1980.

Milatovic, Arso. *Pet diplomatskih misija.* 2 vols. Ljubljana: Cankarjeva, 1985.

Nesovic, Slobodan, and Branko Petranovic, eds. *AVNOJ i revolucija. Tematska zbirka
dokumenata, 1941–1945.* Belgrade: Narodna knjiga, 1983.

Nord, Lars. *Nonalignment and Socialism: Yugoslav Foreign Policy in Theory and Practice.* Stockholm: Political Science Association in Uppsala, 1974.

Omrcanin, Ivo. *Enigma Tito.* Washington, D.C.: Samizdat, 1984.

Petkovic, Ranko. *Nesvrstana Jugoslavija i savremeni svet. Spoljna politika Jugoslavije,
1948–1985.* Zagreb: Skolska knjiga, 1985.

Petrovich, Michael Boro. *Yugoslavia: A Bibliographic Guide.* Washington, D.C.: Library
of Congress, 1974.

Reuter-Hendrichs, Irena. *Jugoslawische Aussenpolitik, 1948–1968.* Cologne: Heymann,
1976.

Roberts, Walter. *Tito, Mihailovic and the Allies, 1941–1945.* Durham, N.C.: Duke
University Press, 1987.

Rubinstein, Alvin. *Yugoslavia and the Nonaligned World.* Princeton, N.J.: Princeton
University Press, 1970.

Rusinow, Dennison. *The Yugoslav Experiment, 1948–1974.* Berkeley: University of California Press, 1977.

Saranovic, Mihailo, ed. *Svet o Titu*. Belgrade: Tanjug, 1981.

Sentic, Marija. *Josip Broz Tito, Bibliografije*. Zagreb: Spektar, 1984.

Singleton, Fred. *A Short History of the Yugoslav Peoples*. Cambridge: Cambridge University Press, 1985.

The Soviet-Yugoslav Dispute: Text of the Published Correspondence. London: Royal Institute of International Affairs, 1948.

Stankovic, Slobodan. *The End of the Tito Era: Yugoslavia's Dilemmas*. Stanford, Calif.: Hoover Institution Press, 1981.

Stanojevic, Tihomir. *Tito: His Life and Work*. Zagreb: Stvarnost, 1963.

Staubringer, Zvonko, comp. *Tito. Drzavljan sveta*. Ljubljana: Delsvska enotnost, 1974.

Stojanovic, Stanislav, ed. *Nezavisnost i savremeni svijet*. 2 vols. Belgrade: Komunist, 1982.

Tadic, Bojana. *Istorijski razvoj politike nesvrstavanja, 1946–1966*. Belgrade: IMPP, 1968.

Tito, Josip Broz. *Govori i clanci*. 21 vols. Zagreb: Naprijed, 1959–1972.

———. *The National Question*. Belgrade: STP, 1983.

———. *Non-alignment: The Conscience and Future of Mankind*. Belgrade: STP, 1979.

———. *Sabrana Djela*. 20 vols. Belgrade: Komunist, 1977–1984.

———. *Selected Speeches and Articles, 1941–1961*. Zagreb: Naprijed, 1963.

———. *Tito on Peace, Security, and Cooperation in Europe*. Belgrade: Jugoslovenska stvarnost, 1977.

Tolstoy, Nikolai. *The Minister and the Massacres*. London: Century and Hutchison, 1986.

Ulam, Adam. *Titoism and the Cominform*. Cambridge, Mass.: Harvard University Press, 1952.

Vojna Enciklopedija. 1959 ed. S.v. "Josip Broz Tito."

Vucinich, Wayne, ed. *At the Brink of War and Peace: The Tito-Stalin Break in a Historic Perspective*. Boulder, Colo.: East European Quarterly, 1982.

———, ed. *Contemporary Yugoslavia: Twenty Years of Socialist Experiment*. Berkeley: University of California Press, 1969.

Zidovec, Zdravko, comp. *Josip Broz Tito. Intervjui*. Zagreb: Cesarec, 1980.

JOHN K. COX

Carlos R. Tobar (1854–1920).   Carlos R. Tobar was born in Quito, Ecuador, in 1854. He graduated in 1878 from the Central University in Quito with doctoral degrees in medicine and natural science. Tobar began his professional career, however, teaching literature at the Central University. He assumed the position of dean of the university's School of Letters in 1880 and in 1891 became rector of the university. Tobar represented Ecuador at international medical conferences held in Lima, Peru, and Santiago, Chile, and was elected vice president of a scientific conference that convened in Buenos Aires. As a man of letters Tobar earned a widespread reputation as both a novelist and a linguist. His fictional work includes historical as well as *costumbrista* novels. Among his nonfiction works are several analyses of contemporary Spanish usage in Ecuador.

In addition to his scientific and literary endeavors, Tobar was active in Ecuadoran domestic politics, serving on various occasions as a deputy or senator in the national congress. In 1900 he held the position of vice president of the

Ecuadoran senate. Tobar also served as a counselor of state for the national government and as a municipal counselor for the city of Quito. In 1912, following a period of political upheaval in Ecuador, Tobar chose self-exile in Spain. He died in Barcelona on May 12, 1920.

Latin America has long prided itself on the occasional emergence of what can be termed the Renaissance man—a cosmopolitan individual whose interests and abilities span a broad range of endeavors. Successful emulation of such a model is not an easy task, and many individuals who aspire to multifaceted excellence succeed only in becoming dilettantes. Carlos R. Tobar did not suffer such a fate, for he received well-deserved acclaim from his peers not only for his contributions as an author, educator, and politician but also for his achievements as a diplomat and statesman.

Tobar's diplomatic career included positions as Ecuador's minister to Argentina, Brazil, Chile, and Spain. He also served as his nation's foreign minister in 1889 and again in 1911. The most publicized episode of Tobar's diplomatic career occurred during his 1904–1905 tenure as minister to Brazil. On May 6, 1904, Tobar signed the Tobar–Rio Branco Treaty, an agreement that not only defined the frontiers between the two nations but also, in a secret protocol, established a defensive alliance linking the two countries. Brazil, however, soon withdrew its support from the pact, an action that for all intents and purposes rendered it null and void.

There is no question, given the diplomatic activities described above, that Tobar was a significant figure in hemispheric circles. His reputation, however, is not based only on his diplomatic career. Indeed, Tobar the diplomat is relatively unimportant when contrasted with Tobar the statesman. A statesman can be defined as one who demonstrates the highest kind of ability in directing the affairs of a government or in dealing with important public issues. Tobar's impact on the world of international politics relates to this latter attribute, for it would be his development of a far-reaching international doctrine that secured his standing throughout the hemisphere and beyond.

The essence of what would become known as the Tobar Doctrine first appeared in a March 15, 1907, letter that Tobar wrote from Barcelona to the Bolivian consul in Brussels. The Bolivian diplomat had sent Tobar some literature that elaborated on Bolivia's recent success in establishing internal peace, a peace that promised to lay the foundation for that nation's future economic and political progress. Tobar effusively congratulated his correspondent for Bolivia's escape "from the infamous straitjacket of militarism." He then went on to observe that other Latin American nations such as Brazil, Argentina, Chile, Colombia, and Peru were also blessed with internal peace and prosperity. There were, however, in Tobar's view, some unfortunate areas in Latin America where despotism still reigned. Indeed, it was with considerable regret that Tobar acknowledged that his native Ecuador found itself "convulsed by the dismal affliction of revolution."

For Tobar the persistence of revolutionary turmoil in Latin America was a tragedy. Nothing, in Tobar's opinion, was worse than civil war, and nothing blackened Latin America's reputation more than this cruel phenomenon. As he reluctantly pointed out, when word of a specific Latin American revolutionary upheaval reached Europe, the continental press usually tarred the entire hemisphere with the same brush by employing such headlines as "Ungovernable America," "Savage America," and "Revolutionary America." Some nations, Tobar indicated, were offended at having their representatives at international conferences interact with Latin American delegates who came "stained with the blood of civil war." The Latin American nations thus had a responsibility to keep their internal affairs in order. He therefore proceeded to outline a strategy to help accomplish this objective.

Tobar felt that an appropriate forum for the elaboration of his projected policy would be a Pan American congress. Such congresses had already been held in the United States (1889), Mexico (1901), and Brazil (1906) and had dealt with matters relating to progress, civilization, and culture. As far as Tobar was concerned, however, these hemispheric fora had neglected a very important responsibility: the consideration of specific proposals that would serve to bring "an end to the lethal revolutions of the Hispanic-American Republics." Tobar had such a specific proposal at hand, and he lost little time in sharing it with his Bolivian colleague: "The American Republics, for their good name and credit—if not for other humanitarian and altruistic considerations—should intervene indirectly in the internal dissensions of the continent. Such intervention should involve, at least, the denial of recognition to de facto governments which spring from revolutions against the established constitutional order."

Tobar was quick to point out that such a policy was both nonviolent and collective. He felt that these criteria removed the sting from the term *intervention* and in effect legitimized collective nonrecognition as an instrument of international policy. Indeed, Tobar emphatically affirmed that "to proscribe such intervention" would be tantamount to opening international society up to anarchy. "Once the right of such intervention is suppressed," Tobar noted, "the only thing that remains is individualism with its inherent right of the strongest dominating the weakest. Then one could say in all truth that might does indeed make right."

Tobar's vision, as expressed in his letter to the Bolivian consul, was not necessarily limited to the Western Hemisphere. Indeed, he noted that the upcoming Hague and Pan American conferences would be well advised to include on their respective agendas discussion of measures that would serve to discourage civil war. While it was obviously Tobar's hope that a major international gathering would institutionalize his recognition policy, it was at the microcosmic rather than the macrocosmic level that the Tobar Doctrine first became incorporated into the fabric of international law. The Central American nations, meeting in Washington, D.C., from November 14 to December 20, 1907, first proclaimed their official adherence to Tobar's principles.

The persistence of isthmian revolutionary violence and the threat that this in turn would lead to the outbreak of international conflict prompted the United States and Mexico, two nations with substantial interests in Central America, to convene the 1907 Washington Conference. Once the conference began, however, the host powers effectively withdrew from the proceedings, thus allowing the Central Americans sufficient latitude to resolve their own outstanding international problems. The resultant Washington Treaties represented an effort on the part of the isthmian states to create an institutional basis for future peace and prosperity. Article I of the Additional Convention to the General Treaty of Peace and Amity explicitly incorporated the sentiments of Carlos Tobar into the formal treaty structure. The Central American delegates agreed that their respective governments "would not recognize any other government which may come into power in any of the five Republics as a consequence of a coup d'état, or of a revolution against a recognized government, so long as the freely elected representatives of the people thereof have not constitutionally reorganized the country."

Tobar's ideas had already appeared widely in the international press and thus were well known to the delegates who attended the Washington Conference. On December 16, 1907, during the fourteenth session of the conference, Policarpo Bonilla of Honduras placed the Tobar Doctrine before his isthmian colleagues. Tobar's original proscription of recognition of a revolutionary regime, however, was tempered a bit by Bonilla's suggestion that recognition of such a state could come in the wake of that state's constitutional reorganization, a formula that the assembled delegations eventually accepted. Although the United States and Mexico, the cosponsors of the conference, did not sign the 1907 treaties, they did pledge to respect the new recognition policy in their relations with the Central American nations.

Application of the Tobar Doctrine during the ten-year life span of the 1907 Washington Treaties was inconsistent at best. Mexico's violent internal crisis, beginning in 1910 and lasting the rest of the decade, effectively removed that nation from its role as a supporter of the 1907 Central American treaty structure. The United States was thus left virtually alone to influence the Central American nations as they endeavored to make the treaties work. U.S. interests on the isthmus, however, were sometimes at variance with de jure recognition policy; accordingly, the U.S. government often acted in isthmian recognition crises as if the Tobar Doctrine did not exist. In 1917, following a dispute over the Bryan-Chamorro Treaty, Nicaragua denounced the 1907 agreements and gave the required one year's notice regarding its intended withdrawal from the treaty system. This action in effect destroyed the Central American juridical structure created at Washington in 1907 and with it, at least temporarily, the region's adhesion to Tobar's recognition policy.

In December 1922, the United States, for reasons remarkably similar to those prevailing in 1907, hosted another conference for the Central American states in Washington, D.C. The subsequent 1923 Treaty of Peace and Amity contained an article that revived, in much more restrictive terms, the Tobar Doctrine of

1907. Costa Rica, a nation that from 1917 to 1919 had undergone a traumatic revolutionary experience, provided the impetus for the reestablishment of isthmian de jure recognition policy. After 1923, however, those isthmian revolutionary regimes that had constitutionally reorganized themselves would still be denied diplomatic recognition if the leaders of the new government had been leaders in the original coup or if they had a blood or marital relationship with such leaders. Furthermore, no diplomatic recognition would be tendered to an individual who had held a ministerial or high military command during the coup or subsequent constitutional reorganization process, or if this individual had held such office or command "within six months preceding the coup d'état, revolution, or the election."

A succession of subsequent isthmian recognition crises, rather than reinforcing the newly amended recognition doctrine, convinced many Central Americans that strict adherence to Tobar's principles was not in their best interests. In 1932 Costa Rica and El Salvador, dissatisfied with the strict de jure isthmian recognition policy, denounced the Central American Treaty of 1923. Efforts to resurrect the Tobar Doctrine at the 1934 Central American Conference held in Guatemala City were unsuccessful.

Central America's unsatisfactory experience with the Tobar Doctrine was reflected, at least in part, by a Mexican diplomatic initiative relating to the question of recognition. On September 27, 1930, Mexican Foreign Minister Genaro Estrada stated that Mexico "would not make any declarations regarding recognition because it considers that such a policy is an insulting practice which, in addition to offending the sovereignty of other nations, places them in a position of having their internal affairs judged by other governments." This was the essence of the so-called Estrada Doctrine, which developed out of Mexico's problems in obtaining recognition from the United States and other powers during its own recent revolutionary period. The Mexican initiative also derived from that nation's reluctance to respect the Tobar recognition principle as it applied to the Central American nations under the 1923 Washington Treaty.

Although called into question in Mexico and Central America during the early 1930s, the Tobar Doctrine would surface once again in Latin America. Rómulo Betancourt, the democratic leader of Venezuela in the late 1950s and early 1960s, gave new life to Tobar's principles when he called for the nonrecognition of dictatorial regimes in Latin America. Betancourt's policy, however, was not sustained. Venezuela's president, Rafael Caldera, renounced the Betancourt Doctrine in 1969 and proclaimed that the nation would return to a policy of recognizing all de facto governments.

In sum, Carlos R. Tobar's primary contribution to modern statesmanship is the doctrine bearing his name. There is no disputing the fact that Tobar's inspiration sprang from altruistic as well as humanitarian considerations. Deeply distressed by the persistence in Latin America of revolutionary violence and concomitant caudillo rule, Tobar endeavored to create a nonviolent and collective international instrument to combat such systemic malaise. The result was the Tobar Doctrine.

It was Tobar's fondest hope that the international community, and in particular the Latin American nations, would institutionalize his recognition policy. As things turned out, however, the only multilateral application of the Tobar Doctrine occurred in Central America, and even in this restricted arena the doctrine did not prevail. Inconsistent application, in combination with unforeseen consequences when the doctrine was actually implemented, served to undercut the policy over the years. Indeed, most authorities would ultimately agree that the Tobar Doctrine was a noble experiment that failed to make the frequently difficult transition from theory to successful practice.

Annotated Bibliography

Material relating to the diplomatic career of Carlos R. Tobar is available in the Foreign Relations Archive of Ecuador, located at 10 de Agosto in Quito. Scholars must obtain prior permission to review documents in the archive. The prospective researcher should write a letter of inquiry to the foreign minister outlining the type of documents to be consulted and the chronological limits of the projected study. The most relevant documentary materials on Tobar's diplomatic activities are the bound volumes containing correspondence exchanged between the foreign ministry and Ecuador's diplomatic missions. There are, however, many documents that the foreign ministry retains in a confidential category, and special permission is needed to gain access to this material.

Although a prolific author, Carlos Tobar produced relatively few works on international affairs. Indeed, two essays by Tobar, *Une Affaire digne d'être traitée au Congrès de la Paix à La Haye* (1907) and *Quand viendra la paix* (1918), are his only published works with an international focus. In these studies Tobar offers a reprise, in somewhat extended form, of the points he originally developed in his letter of March 15, 1907.

In both essays Tobar calls attention to the tragic consequences of civil strife and dictatorial rule in Latin America and suggests that the acceptance on the part of the international community of a de jure recognition policy would have a beneficial impact on democratic development in the hemisphere and beyond. In the 1907 study, Tobar indicates that the upcoming Hague Peace Conference would do well to give his proposal serious consideration. The Tobar Doctrine, however, did not appear on the Hague Conference agenda. Writing in the last months of World War I, Tobar, citing *David Lloyd George, *Woodrow Wilson, and others, once again asserted his faith in government by the consent of the governed. A necessary first step in achieving this ideal on the international level would involve the formation of a League of Nations which, in turn, through collective action, could help to encourage peace and popular rule throughout the world. Acceptance on the part of such an international organization of the principles elaborated in the Tobar Doctrine would bring to bear the powers of collective and nonviolent intervention within the international community. Such intervention was especially appropriate within Latin America where, according to Tobar, endemic revolutionary violence had long served to perpetuate the evils of militarism. Once again, however, Tobar would be disappointed, as neither the Versailles Peace Conference nor its creation, the League of Nations, acted to institutionalize his doctrine.

In December 1908, Santiago, Chile, hosted the First Pan American Scientific Congress. The Tobar Doctrine was included among the topics for discussion at the conference, and

Leonidas García, the official representative of the Juridic-Literary Society of Quito, presented to the assembled delegates an assessment of the doctrine. Garcia's study, "La doctrina Tobar," was published in 1913 in the *Revista de la Sociedad "Jurídico-Literaria."*

García noted in his presentation that the Central American nations had recently incorporated the Tobar Doctrine in the 1907 Washington Treaties. The passage of just one year, however, had not provided sufficient opportunity to evaluate the impact of Tobar's principles on isthmian affairs. García was nonetheless confident that such a collective and nonviolent intervention policy would have a salutary effect on the Central American states. Indeed, García believed that if this type of collective action were extended throughout the Americas, it would serve to diminish the frequency of revolutionary violence and lead to the establishment of a base for the formation of a true league of American states. He therefore proposed that the Scientific Congress recommend that "men of good will," and especially those who would participate in the next Pan American Congress, should make every effort to develop a formula that would not only "assure the internal peace of the nations of this continent," but also "constitute a base of unity among the American nations."

In *Quand viendra la paix* Tobar alludes to the work of the First Pan American Scientific Congress. Indeed, the congress had tendered Tobar a special invitation to address the delegates on the doctrine bearing his name. Tobar regretfully pointed out, however, that circumstances had prevented him from leaving Europe to attend the conference. Thus the architect of the recognition doctrine was not present to sustain his thesis before an important American audience. Tobar suggests in his essay that had he indeed been present in Santiago the delegates would have given his doctrine even greater support. Whether or not such support would have been sufficient to place the Tobar Doctrine on the agenda of the next Pan American Congress remains, however, very much an open question.

Two studies appeared in the mid–1920s dealing with the Tobar Doctrine from differing Latin American perspectives. Carlos J. Arangua Rivas, in his work *La intervención: Doctrinas de Monroe, Drago, y Tobar* (1924), was favorably impressed by the doctrine's potential. Luís Anderson Morúa, on the other hand, in his study *El gobierno de facto* (1925), was highly critical of Tobar's creation.

According to Arangua Rivas, the more politically advanced nations of Latin America had an obligation to help their less fortunate hemispheric brethren avoid the negative consequences of violent revolution. Application of the Tobar Doctrine through the collective and treaty-sanctioned action of the American states would be an indispensable element in resolving this problem. Arangua Rivas lamented in particular that the Pan American Congresses to date had failed to consider the Tobar Doctrine. If serious examination and discussion of Tobar's principles had taken place at the 1923 Pan American Conference held in Santiago, for example, Arangua Rivas was certain that a convention would have resulted that in turn would have brought an end to the Latin American political tradition of caudillos and revolutions.

Luís Anderson first presented his observations on de facto regimes and, by extension, his criticism of the Tobar Doctrine, to the subcommittee on public international law of the 1925 Scientific Congress held in Lima, Peru. As far as Anderson was concerned, recognition of a nation was simply an acknowledgment of "the real and effective fact of the existence of the new government." He was quick to point out that such recognition in no way implied approval of the means such a government employed to gain power. Moreover, the legal structure of a government was, in Anderson's view, a strictly internal question that concerned only the citizens of that particular nation and should not, therefore, serve as a criterion for the granting or denial of recognition on the part of other states.

Luís Anderson possessed impressive credentials within the hemispheric community as a diplomat and international jurist. The author of an impressive number of treatises on international topics, Anderson had served as Costa Rica's foreign minister as well as in a number of overseas diplomatic assignments. Indeed, Anderson represented Costa Rica at the 1907 Washington Conference and was elected its president. It was at Washington, as noted above, that the Tobar Doctrine received official isthmian sanction. What Anderson supported in 1907, however, had not, in his view, stood the test of time. While lauding Tobar's spirit of compassion and humanity, Anderson, from a 1925 perspective, asserted that "the painful memory of the bloody revolutions and coups that have occurred in a number of isthmian nations from 1907 to the present obliges us to recognize that Tobar's noble objective has not been realized."

Articles by two North American scholars have focused on the impact of the Tobar Doctrine in Central America. Charles L. Stansifer, in "Application of the Tobar Doctrine to Central America," *The Americas* 23, 3 (1967): 251–272, evaluates the doctrine from its promulgation in 1907 to its ultimate demise in 1934. Richard V. Salisbury, in "Domestic Politics and Foreign Policy: Costa Rica's Stand on Recognition, 1923–1934," *Hispanic American Historical Review* 54, 3 (1974), emphasizes the Costa Rican role in the evolution of the doctrine.

As Stansifer correctly points out, the Central American acceptance of the Tobar Doctrine meant a significant departure from normal international procedures. In effect, a de facto government was usually accorded recognition if it demonstrated that it was in control, if it agreed to meet its international obligations, and if it appeared to enjoy the general support of the people. Tobar's de jure recognition policy, however, was a direct challenge to this traditional, indeed, almost automatic, recognition process. The reasons for the Central American adoption of the Tobar principle were, according to Stansifer, very clear indeed. If the 1907 Washington Treaties were consistently and successfully applied, this "would have legitimized indefinitely the existing governments of the signatory powers by rendering revolution useless." Although altruistic considerations were certainly a factor in the deliberations at Washington, "the obvious objective," in Stansifer's view, "was the consolidation of existing governments in power." This, of course, was not exactly what Tobar originally had in mind.

The failure of the delegates at the Washington Conference to ponder the possible results of the new recognition policy eventually led to dissatisfaction with, and ultimately abandonment of, the Tobar Doctrine. Adhesion to the doctrine resulted, over the years, in an unanticipated degree of outside interference in the internal affairs of the isthmian states. Such interference came from the Central American nations themselves as well as from the United States. When a succession of isthmian recognition crises erupted in the 1920s and early 1930s, the Tobar Doctrine, in the eyes of many Central Americans, appeared to undermine rather than promote regional peace and stability. As Stansifer succinctly concludes, when the Central Americans finally abandoned the doctrine, few mourned its loss.

Salisbury's contribution to the study of the Tobar Doctrine resides in the discovery that it was a Costa Rican initiative that led to the tightening of the de jure recognition policy at the 1922–1923 Washington Conference. He then analyzes the pivotal role that

Costa Rica played as that nation first implemented, then questioned, and finally rejected the doctrine during the period from 1923 to 1934.

Bibliography

Anderson Morúa, Luís. *El gobierno de facto*. San José, Costa Rica: Lehmann, 1925.
Arangua Rivas, Carlos J. *La intervención: Doctrinas de Monroe, Drago, y Tobar*. Santiago, Chile: Imprenta "La Sud-América," 1924.
García, Leonidas. "La doctrina Tobar." *Revista de la Sociedad "Jurídico-Literaria"* (Quito) 1, 1 (January - February 1913): 25–71.
Salisbury, Richard V. "Domestic Politics and Foreign Policy: Costa Rica's Stand on Recognition, 1923–1934." *Hispanic American Historical Review* 54, 3 (August 1974): 453–478.
Stansifer, Charles L. "Application of the Tobar Doctrine to Central America." *The Americas* 23, 3 (January 1967): 251–272.
Tobar, Carlos R. *Une Affaire digne d'être traitée au Congrès de la Paix à la Haye*. Barcelona: J. Ruíz Romero, 1907.
———. *Quand viendra la paix*. Barcelona: J. Ruíz Romero, 1918.

RICHARD V. SALISBURY

William II (1859–1941).   The last and most controversial German emperor, William II, born in Berlin on January 27, 1859, was the eldest son of Prince Frederick William of Prussia and Princess Victoria, the daughter of Britain's Queen Victoria. William's childhood was marred by a severe injury, received during a difficult birth, which prevented his left arm from growing to its normal size and strength. The injury left him without normal balance, and his early life was characterized by difficulties in overcoming his handicap. In overcompensating for his near-useless arm, young William developed an obsession with physical activity and athletic accomplishment. During this period he was also subjected to strict Prussian military discipline.

As a German prince and eventual successor to the crown, William was expected to follow a Prussian military career. His earliest education was provided by his mother, from whom he mastered Greek, Latin, English, and French, and by Georg Hintzpeter, a strict Calvinist tutor. From an early age William cultivated an intense interest in military history; at age ten he was appointed colonel of a Prussian cavalry regiment. At age fifteen, at his mother's insistence, William attended public school in Kassel (much to the astonishment of the rest of his family) and later studied for two years at the University of Bonn.

By the time William reached early adulthood, he had lost most of the liberal ideals his mother and father had tried to instill in him, and instead readily adopted the Prussian-dominated militarist attitudes of the most conservative elements in German society, most especially the strongly monarchical feelings of his grandfather, the Emperor William I, and the emperor's principal advisor, *Otto von Bismarck. At the same time, his relationship with his mother and her family in England became increasingly hostile, eventually resulting in an acrimonious break.

In February 1881 William married Augusta Victoria of Schleswig-Holstein-Sonderburg-Augustenberg. Six sons and a daughter were born to the couple. The years following his marriage were filled with official state visits to most of the European courts, including Britain, Austria, and Russia. During his travels, William acquired a keen interest in politics and an obsession with extending German influence both inside and outside Europe. On March 9, 1888, William I died, and William's father ascended the throne as Frederick III. The reign was short-lived, however, as Frederick had been suffering from throat cancer for many months. After three months as emperor, Frederick III died and was succeeded by his twenty-nine-year-old son.

From 1888 until the end of his reign and the collapse of the German Empire in 1918, William II's policies were driven by his militaristic, imperialistic, and aggressive worldview. Upon his succession as emperor, he devoted himself to altering his grandfather's and father's sober, austere Germany. Obsessed with uniforms, he was seldom seen without his great, gold eagle-crowned helmet and Prussian military decorations. By the end of 1888 William had surrounded himself with splendor, including the renovation and expansion of his imperial residences. He also ignored the constitutional restraints on his imperial authority (especially in internal politics and administration) and appointed to high office those individuals most likely to follow his lead. Styling himself the "All-Highest," William demanded that he be consulted on important affairs of state, while simultaneously devoting more of his time to travel, sailing, and visiting his many country estates.

At times insufferably autocratic, William considered himself the apostle of a "New Germany" that would rival the accomplishments of past European empires, but most especially a Germany that would be a major political and economic force worldwide. He had long admired the British Empire, and, with the growing sentiment in German business circles, especially the *Kolonialverein*, for colonial expansion after the mid–1880s, his principal interest lay in adding German territories abroad that would rival British holdings. Long a lover of the sea, William intended also that Germany become a major naval power, an aspect of the German military establishment that had held little interest for his grandfather or Bismarck.

From the 1880s to 1914, William's personal influence was considered most important in the German parliament's passage of sweeping naval expenditure bills, including the construction of a fleet of battleships, which would place Germany in a commanding position in Europe. William's reasons for supporting such an unprecedented naval buildup included his desire for a fleet that would protect German colonies and trade abroad, and the idea that Germany would eventually lead the combined European states against the so-called Yellow Peril of Asiatic expansion.

Perhaps the most telling aspect of William's personality was his continuous, aggressive personal intervention in foreign policy. With his dismissal of the elderly Bismarck in 1890, German foreign affairs turned from a cautious policy of maintaining the balance of power in Europe to William's tactless attempts (abetted by pliant chancellors who had no wish to confront the emperor) to expand German influence at the expense of the rest of Europe.

Following his accession in 1888, William maintained relatively good relations with the old chancellor, Bismarck. Since 1871, Bismarck had followed a cautious foreign policy aimed at keeping Germany the dominant force in central Europe by isolating Germany's longtime adversary France, forging good relations between Germany and Russia, and, by not threatening British colonial interests, keeping Britain out of European affairs. By 1890, however, William had begun to assert his own views of Germany's role as a world power, with himself as the key player; Bismarck was forced to retire and his largely successful strategy was overturned.

By the mid–1890s the spirit of colonialism had resulted in extensive German colonial holdings in east Africa, southwest Africa, and the South Pacific. Germany's active imperialistic role spurred growing anti-German sentiment in Britain, which was aggravated by William's bombastic opinions on European and world affairs, all trumpeted in the press. Inevitably, the British government drew the inference that the increase in German naval expenditures and warship construction was directed toward eventual hostilities with Great Britain. Moreover, William on several occasions allowed his obnoxious nature to interfere in British imperial affairs. He repeatedly proffered unwelcome advice on the Anglo-Boer troubles in southern Africa, and on several occasions he publicly took anti-British positions during the Boer War of 1899–1902.

By 1900 William had already scuttled the formerly cordial relationship between Germany and Russia by failing to renew the German-Russian Reinsurance Treaty of 1887. Thereafter, Russia moved closer to an entente with France, culminating in the Franco-Russian alliance of 1894. The military applications of the Franco-Russian treaty virtually ensured that Germany would be bracketed by two hostile forces in the event of a European war. And William's push to extend German prestige and influence worldwide continued to heighten tensions in Europe.

With Chancellor Bernhard von Bülow, he moved in 1905 to improve Germany's deteriorating diplomatic position in Europe by provoking a confrontation in Morocco, where the French government was in the process of establishing a protectorate. The German government declared that it had interests in North Africa and spoke in support of Moroccan independence. By so doing, William hoped to fracture the entente between France and Russia, which was then occupied with a war against Japan in the Far East. He also gambled on weak British support for France. At the 1906 Algeciras conference on the Moroccan question Germany found itself virtually isolated, with only its unwieldy ally, Austria-Hungary, in support. With Russia, Britain, and Italy firmly backing France, the French government proceeded with its colonial claims in Morocco amid mounting anti-German feeling in most of Europe. The final result of William's ill-advised forays into foreign affairs was the Triple Entente of 1907, linking Britain, France, and Russia against Germany and its partners in the Triple Alliance (created in 1882), Austria-Hungary and Italy.

William II's role in World War I was less important than his influence during the preceding two decades. For much of the war, although he was nominally supreme commander, William allowed his generals to conduct strategy, and he certainly acquiesced in Germany's schemes for territorial expansion.

Far more important than his conduct during the war years, however, was the emperor's direction of events in the years immediately preceding the hostilities. Along with his authoritarian-minded chancellors and military advisors, William bears considerable responsibility for policies that by 1912 led the German government to consider a European war as beneficial to the nation. A related factor in the government's idea of a beneficial war was the internal political situation. The conservative-nationalist government was besieged by demands from the socialist left and moderate liberal parties that the German parliament (in which the Social Democratic party had the largest delegation) be given greater control over foreign and domestic policies. To William and his government, a European war would provide the necessary excuse to continue authoritarian rule, unify the nation, and effectively eliminate political opposition.

Due largely to Germany's international diplomatic meddling, Europe was seething with tension in 1914. Any limited European conflict was certain to escalate into a much wider war. The official German government documents show that William and the German military leaders believed that a war would solve internal political strife and also achieve foreign policy goals, especially the annexation of foreign territories to the east and west of Germany. In the midst of the Austro-Serbian crisis following the assassination of the Austrian archduke Franz Ferdinand, Germany used its influence over Austria-Hungary to promote hostilities. William personally was confident of German military superiority and deliberately risked conflict with Russia and France between June and August 1914. The German government only briefly backed away from its belligerent stance due to the likelihood of drawing Britain into the war. While the emperor's involvement in this crisis is unclear (William was on a sailing holiday in the Baltic while Europe lurched toward war), he bears ultimate responsibility for the outcome.

The German collapse in November 1918 found William and his generals unwilling to accept responsibility for defeat. On November 9, 1918, William abdicated his imperial authority and accepted exile in the Netherlands. For the next two decades William, the last member of the House of Hohenzollern to rule in Germany, lived in quiet country retirement in a secluded castle at Doorn, Holland. He spent most of his time attempting to explain his policies as emperor and polishing his public image. However, William was never able to justify his reign, and he remained a symbol of Prussian militarism and aggression. He died on June 4, 1941, and was buried at Doorn.

William's contribution to German foreign relations was, on the whole, disastrous. He was bombastic in his demands for German influence worldwide, incautious in his wrecking of Bismarck's carefully wrought system of German alliances prior to 1890, and, arguably, criminal in his helping push Europe into a war that led to the deaths of millions. William's personal role in the pursuit of diplomatic aims after 1890 will continue to be the subject of debate. Yet he allowed Germany's foreign policy to be based on such dubious policies as aggressive territorial annexations and the acquisition of an economically non-viable colonial empire, which led to the near-destruction of his nation.

Annotated Bibliography

The major primary documents for the life and reign of William II are housed at several archives. The Bismarck Papers, held in the German Federal Archives at Koblenz, contain documents of the chancellor and his family, many of which relate to Bismarck's relationship with William. Also relevant to William's early life are the Hohenzollern documents, including letters from and to William and members of his extended family. The Hohenzollern papers are located in the Secret State Archives in Berlin-Dahlem. For William's policies after his succession as emperor, the papers of Chancellor von Bulow, stored in the German Federal Archives, Koblenz, should be consulted. They include many personal and official accounts of William's reign. The most detailed and important holdings regarding William II are the Eulenburg Papers, also in the Federal Archives at Koblenz, an immense collection of Count Eulenburg, who was a leading diplomat and William's most intimate friend. Other important collections include the Federal Archive–Military Archive at Freiburg, and the British Royal Archives, Windsor Castle. Access to the archives and repositories in Germany is possible only after obtaining the permission in writing of the individual archive directors.

Like many of the statesmen responsible for the planning and prosecution of World War I, William in retirement wrote extensively on his reign and policies, especially in light of the controversy engendered by German acceptance of the "War Guilt Clause" in the 1919 Treaty of Versailles. In his principal memoir, translated into English as *The Kaiser's Memoirs* (1922), William omits many of his mistakes as German emperor. He attempts, unsuccessfully, to justify himself and Germany regarding the war guilt question, but virtually nothing is included on the overall planning and strategy of the German war effort. Only in a concluding chapter does William offer his opinion on the root causes for the war, and he concludes that neither he nor Germany was responsible for the events of August 1914. In William's incredible, self-serving version, Russia and France were entirely guilty for leading Europe into war. Overall, the former emperor portrays himself as victim—the innocent bystander and neglected peacemaker—a view of himself contradicted by the postwar publication of German state documents attesting to his responsibility. William's apologia reveals only his lack of moral depth, his personal arrogance, and his disregard for historical fact. In subsequent remembrances of his reign, published in the 1920s and 1930s, the former emperor follows the same discredited formula.

In the first biography of William II, Emil Ludwig's *Wilhelm Hohenzollern* (1927), the author does not provide an objective, scholarly history, but an impressionistic study of a man and an epoch. Most of Ludwig's sources are William's friends, associates, ministers, generals, and courtiers. Only in rare cases does the author resort to less-biased evidence. What emerges is a portrait of William as a talented young man, badly educated and ill-advised, who was elevated prematurely to supreme power. In this view, William was operating against forces he could not comprehend, and the ultimate collapse of the German Empire was largely the result of fate. While Ludwig does provide some useful insight into William II's character, he neglects the documentary evidence linking William to the aggressive policies in Europe that were the leading cause for the tragedy of 1914–1918.

Since the 1960s studies of William II have focused on the historical context in which the emperor and his era may be placed. In an ongoing historiographical debate, the question of the extent and importance of William's personal role in the governmental decisions leading to World War I has been addressed. The focus of the debate has been whether or not Germany, from the early nineteeth century to the end of the Third Reich in 1945, has been dominated by a manipulative class of wealthy elites, governing from above without any semblance of democratic institutions, resulting in a clear line of continuity from Bismarck to *Adolf Hitler.

John C.G. Rohl in *Germany Without Bismarck: The Crisis of Government in the Second Reich, 1890–1900* (1967), argues that the German constitution of 1871 was a confusing patchwork that only Bismarck could use effectively. Under this system of government some twenty important individuals in high positions determined the destiny of Germany. By divorcing the monarchy from any parliamentary control, the German constitution was inherently flawed, and provided the perfect working model of an authoritarian state. Rohl argues that, with the succession of a neurotic and obsessive William II, Germany's governmental flaws were magnified into calamity. Based on extensive archival research, the author demonstrates that politics and political parties had little role in Germany under William II. Instead, all major policies were decided by the secret conflicts inside the foreign ministry and the military leadership. With their support, by 1900 William's personal authority had become unassailable. Thus the entire direction of German foreign policy after Bismarck was William's responsibility, both directly and indirectly.

In *Kaiser Wilhelm II: New Interpretations* (1982), edited by Rohl and Nicolaus Sombart, additional evidence is provided for this thesis. Included in the collection of essays focusing on William's reign after 1897 are explorations of the emperor's personality and its influence on the Anglo-German crisis, reflections on William's personal role in foreign policy, and an evaluation of the emperor's standing with the German public.

A popular biography published in 1963, *The Kaiser*, by Virginia Cowles, traces in lavish detail the life of the German emperor from his birth to his long exile. Based almost entirely on the diaries and memoirs of his family and associates, Cowles's book places much emphasis on the tangled family relationships that influenced the young William, especially his unhappy boyhood and his mother's domination of his education. Cowles concludes that William, due largely to his contentious relationship with his parents, lacked the temperament, training, and discretion so important to his position as emperor. The author dismisses much of the argument that William personally decided on war in August 1914. Instead, she concludes that he did not want a European war but blundered into it, as did the other belligerent powers. Cowles places the blame for World War I on the failure of international diplomacy, but she also concedes that Germany failed miserably when it unconditionally backed Austria-Hungary against Serbia. William is also spared the blame for the prosecution of the war—he is described as having little interest in war planning or in the direction of internal affairs. William's abdication, Cowles concludes, was the inevitable result of his indifference to the responsibilities of his position.

Lamar Cecil's *Wilhelm II: Prince and Emperor, 1859–1900* (1989), the first of two volumes on the life of the German emperor, is certain to be the definitive biography. Based on exhaustive archival research, Cecil narrates William's early life in minute detail. Although Cecil adds little new to an understanding of the future monarch's troubled upbringing, the chapters on William's education, the role of his authoritarian tutor, the personality of William's father, and his turbulent life with his mother are rich with detail. The biography is most valuable when it addresses the historical debate relating to William's personal influence on German foreign policy. Cecil generally takes a middle position on the controversy, contending that German policies after 1888 were a blend of William's intrusive, belligerent personality and the government bureaucracy's failure to heed the voices of restraint. William was at the center of the decision making, but he was also greatly removed from the fabric of German politics and society, about which he knew little and cared even less. Cecil concludes that, whatever one's opinion of William II, he manages to confound and annoy those who study his role in history.

Bibliography

Balfour, Michael Leonard Graham. *The Kaiser and His Times*. Boston: Houghton Mifflin, 1964.

Berghahn, V. R. *Germany and the Approach of War in 1914*. New York: St. Martin's Press, 1973.

Burmeister, Hans Wilhelm. *Prince Philipp Eulenburg-Hertefeld (1847–1921): His Influence on Kaiser Wilhelm II and His Role in the German Government, 1888–1902*. Wiesbaden: Steiner, 1981.

Cecil, Lamar. *Wilhelm II: Prince and Emperor, 1859–1900*. Chapel Hill: University of North Carolina Press, 1989.

Cowles, Virginia. *The Kaiser*. New York: Harper and Row, 1963.

Craig, Gordon Alexander. *Germany, 1866–1945*. New York: Oxford University Press, 1978.

Eley, Geoff. *From Unification to Nazism: Reinterpreting the German Past*. Boston: Allen and Unwin, 1986.

Fenske, Hans, ed. *Unter Wilhelm II. 1890–1918*. Darmstadt: Wissenschaftliche Buchgesellschaft, 1982.

Fischer, Fritz. *Germany's Aims in the First World War*. New York: Norton, 1967.

Haffner, Sebastian. *The Ailing Empire: Germany from Bismarck to Hitler*. Translated by Jean Steinberg. New York: Fromm, 1989.

Hartau, Friedrich. *Wilhelm II. [i.e. der Zweite] in Selbstzeugnissen und Bilddokumenten*. Reinbek bei Hamburg: Rowohlt, 1978.

Hull, Isabel V. *The Entourage of Kaiser Wilhelm II, 1888–1918*. New York: Cambridge University Press, 1982.

Lerchenfeld-Kofering, Hugo, Graf. *Kaiser Wilhelm II. Als Persönlichkeit und Herrscher*. Kallmunz Opf.: Lassleben, 1985.

Ludwig, Emil. *Wilhelm Hohenzollern, the Last of the Kaisers*. Translated by Ethel Colburn Mayne. New York: Putnam's, 1927.

Muller, George Alexander von. *The Kaiser and His Court*. Edited by Walter Gorlitz. New York: Harcourt, Brace and World, 1964.

Nipperdey, Thomas. *Deutsche Geschichte 1866–1918*. Munich: Beck, 1990.

Palmer, Alan W. *The Kaiser: Warlord of the Second Reich*. New York: Scribner's, 1978.

Ponsonby, Frederick, ed. *Letters of the Empress Fredericke*. London: Macmillan, 1929.

Rohl, John C.G. *Germany Without Bismarck: The Crisis of Government in the Second Reich, 1890–1900*. Berkeley and Los Angeles: University of California Press, 1967.

Rohl, John C.G., and Nicholaus Sombart, eds. *Kaiser Wilhelm II: New Interpretations*. New York: Cambridge University Press, 1982.

Sontag, Raymond James. *Germany and England: Background of Conflict, 1848–1894.* New York: Appleton-Century, 1938.

Tyler-Whittle, Michael Sidney. *The Last Kaiser: A Biography of Wilhelm II, German Emperor and King of Prussia.* New York: Times Books, 1977.

Wehler, Hans Ulrich. *The German Empire, 1871–1918.* Translated by Kim Traynor. Dover, N.H.: Berg, 1985.

William II. *The Kaiser's Memoirs.* Translated by Thomas R. Ybarra. New York: Harper, 1922.

WILLIAM G. RATLIFF

Woodrow Wilson (1856–1924).   As the statesman responsible for guiding the United States through the pivotal events of World War I, Woodrow Wilson probably stands as the single most important figure in U.S. diplomatic history. He presided over U.S. foreign policy at a vital crossroads. On the one hand, largely because of the nation's economic growth, the United States had achieved status as a world power; on the other, Americans continued to see themselves as a special people, unsullied by the corrupt politics of the Old World. Wilson absorbed these competing directions and made himself the boldest Western statesman of his day by insisting that the United States would assume its role as a world power and would draw out of its liberal tradition new and democratic methods of diplomacy.

Thomas Woodrow Wilson was born on December 28, 1856, in Staunton, Virginia, where his father, Joseph, was a Presbyterian pastor. The family moved often while Joseph struggled up the ladder of the Southern Presbyterian Church, but the Wilsons remained in the South. His upbringing as the son of a southern minister had enduring influence on the younger Wilson. His embrace of racist presumptions, his revulsion against the tariff, and his allegiance to the Democratic party all show the southern influence. As a statesman, he often invoked divine will with a homiletic passion characteristic of a good minister.

His choice of colleges demonstrated these early influences, for Princeton was both Presbyterian and "southern." Wilson matriculated there in 1875, graduated in 1879, and proceeded to study law at the University of Virginia. Unhappy with law, he opted in 1883 to enter Johns Hopkins University, which had established the first American program for training professional social scientists. Earning his Ph.D. in 1886, he began an academic career that took him to Bryn Mawr, Wesleyan, and Hopkins before he returned to his alma mater, Princeton, in 1890. There he taught jurisprudence and political economy until 1902, when he was elected president of the university.

The Princeton presidency marked the beginning of Wilson's public career, not least because he gained a reputation as an educational reformer. A growing reputation brought him to the attention of conservative Democrats in the East who were interested in ridding the party of both agrarian populism and urban machines. For them, Wilson became a marketable, if exotic, candidate, and they guided him to success in the 1910 New Jersey gubernatorial race on a mildly reformist platform. Success in New Jersey propelled Wilson into the 1912 presidential race, which he won primarily because the Republicans had split between the conservative William Howard Taft and the Bull Moose Progressive *Theodore Roosevelt. As he had as New Jersey governor, President Wilson managed a highly successful legislative program composed of tepid reforms—tariff reductions, banking reform, and antitrust clarification—that obscured his conservative temperament.

Wilson was well aware that domestic matters interested him more than foreign affairs. He once quipped that it would be a terrific irony if international events were to define his presidency, but that was exactly what happened. Before 1912 he had never systematically thought about foreign affairs. He tended to view international events in terms of the same ideals, and as amenable to the same solutions, as domestic events. His foreign policy therefore must be understood as a product of his basic political beliefs. Essentially a liberal idealist, Wilson believed that the world was moving inexorably toward greater democracy, freer trade, deepened interdependence, and, ultimately, a ''new age'' of political harmony.

Wilson relied on his liberal instincts when he confronted the first of many crises in foreign affairs, the Mexican Revolution. The revolution, he believed, resulted from the legitimate aspirations of the Mexican people, who were fighting against both a reactionary government and the influence of self-interested European nations. Wilson first sent several emissaries to investigate the situation with an eye toward discovering who best represented Mexican liberalism. When he learned that the U.S. ambassador, Henry Lane Wilson, had actively conspired in favor of reactionary forces against Francisco Madero, he terminated the ambassador's appointment. After Madero's fall, Mexico devolved into a factional struggle that drew the competing Europeans into countless diplomatic intrigues. Intrigue Wilson expected; rampant disorder he did not. But by most measures, he pursued a policy of genuine propriety through 1913.

In April 1914, however, he contradicted his many assertions that the United States was ''disinterested'' by engineering a military intervention at Veracruz, designed to unseat the reactionary Victoriano Huerta and thereby aid the liberal Constitutionalist forces behind Venustiano Carranza. The Veracruz landing did deny Huerta a European arms shipment, but it drove a wedge between the Americans and Carranza, who logically had to denounce the intervention as a threat to Mexican sovereignty. Convinced of the propriety of his own motives, Wilson could not understand Carranza'a position, and he thereafter began to search for a more ''liberal'' leader, even considering the colorful bandit Pancho Villa before finally conceding in 1915 that Carranza deserved recognition. Even then, Wilson approved another intervention, the famous ''Pershing expedition,'' which sought to punish Villa for his March 1916 raid on Columbus, New Mexico. Mexican-American relations remained strained for the next twenty years, particularly after the 1917 constitution permitted expropriation of American-owned oil.

Had it not been for the larger distraction of World War I, Wilson conceivably might have launched a larger intervention into Mexico. There certainly were influential supporters of such a move, and Wilson demonstrated a penchant for intervention throughout the hemisphere, notably in Haiti and Nicaragua. His Caribbean and Latin American policies were punctuated by an essentially racist paternalism that assumed that these "backward" people were unfit for self-determination. Understood more broadly as part of his idealist reading of world events and his view that the other powers were avaricious imperialists, Wilson's interventions can be seen as preludes to his wartime policies. Particularly in Haiti, where fiscal mismanagement had made the nation vulnerable to European demands, Wilson believed his quarrels to be primarily with imperialists. His Mexican policy, guided by the optimistic presumption that liberals would prevail, and yet spoiled by a frustrated impatience with revolutionaries who rejected his idea of orderly political development, presaged Wilson's approach to the Bolshevik Revolution.

World War I, of course, defined Wilson's historic role. Like most Americans, he saw no reason to intervene in the war in 1914, and thus the neutrality policy that he established conformed both to contemporary public opinion and to traditional American isolationism. Yet Wilson was neither preoccupied with public approval nor an isolationist. In his hands, neutrality was an assertive doctrine that upheld accepted international law and neutral economic rights.

Because this neutrality never sought to diminish economic or diplomatic ties with Europe, it made Wilson's policy vulnerable to the strategies of the belligerents. The British naval blockade and German submarine warfare were bound to disrupt Wilson's policy. The British blockade interrupted American trade to the point where, especially during the so-called cotton crisis, it threatened to push the American economy into depression. The English avoided a serious diplomatic confrontation when they agreed to prop up world cotton prices. The German submarine posed a more difficult problem. This new weapon promised to equalize the naval war for the Germans, but it was ill-designed to obey international law, not least the distinction between assaults against combatants and civilians. Wilson never considered war against Britain over the blockade, but he was forced to consider war in defense of innocent civilians. To counter the English, however, the Germans addressed this possibility by agreeing, in spring 1916, to recognize search-and-seizure laws.

The Germans broke their "Sussex Pledge" and renewed unrestricted submarine warfare in February 1917, but this action did not impel Wilson to ask for an American declaration of war. Instead, Wilson had determined, as early as January 1916, that American interests were best served in the short term if he were to mediate an end to war. By May 1916, he had decided that national interests in the long term were best secured through U.S. involvement in some postwar international organization. He began to insist on American mediation in January 1916, when he sent his personal advisor, Col. Edward M. House, to Europe. In this complicated episode, House assured the French that the Americans were virtually certain to intervene as an ally in the war. In London, he agreed to U.S. intervention if the Germans refused to attend a peace conference. The House mission produced misunderstandings all around. House thought the Allies welcomed U.S. mediation; the French believed that the United States was poised to enter the war; the English looked upon U.S. mediation as a last resort; and Wilson, relying on House's rendition of the meetings, believed that mediation was at hand.

The Allies, however, would not risk a peace conference while the Germans held territory, and the Germans had no incentive to bargain away the territory they held. In this atmosphere, Wilson had come to see victory by either side as dangerous, and he doubtless decided that only through military intervention could he hope to influence the peace. Aligning with Germany was out of the question; siding with the Allies was more palatable, especially after the March revolution in Russia removed the tsar from power and made it possible to argue that the Allies best represented liberal aspirations.

His wartime policies bear out this explanation, for Wilson struggled from the first to define the war as a battle for "democracy" against Prussian "militarism." He was under no illusions about Allied motives, for he was well aware that each nation had its eyes on war spoils. Wilson believed he could compel a final peace conference and organize a postwar league of nations that would oversee the end of imperialism and, by definition, the culmination of liberal democracy's world-wide development. He propounded on these themes consistently throughout the war, but summed them up best in the Fourteen Points address of January 8, 1918. In this speech, Wilson beckoned the world toward a liberal interdependence based on free trade, disarmament, open diplomacy, and self-determination. In an effort to undercut the imperialistic designs of the Allies, Wilson also recommended specific territorial readjustments in the most troublesome areas of war-torn Europe.

The tragedy of Wilson's career was that his vision was simultaneously just and intolerant. He welcomed the revolutionary turn that the war took in 1918, when the vacuum of power in central and eastern Europe sent nations there careening into disorder. But he insisted, as in Mexico, that revolutionaries behave like good liberal gentlemen.

Events inevitably destroyed Wilson's hope for orderly political development, beginning with the November 1917 Bolshevik Revolution in Russia. Hardly the genteel revolutionaries that Wilson had expected, the Bolsheviks quickly antagonized the Allies when they concluded the Brest-Litovsk peace with the Germans, thereby removing the pressure of the eastern front and allowing the Germans to launch a final offensive toward Paris in spring 1918. Throughout the spring, the Allies brought heavy pressure to bear on Wilson to intervene in Russia, ostensibly to restore the eastern front. These far-fetched plans barely concealed the anti-Bolshevik intentions of some of the Allies, for the only possible ports of entry, Murmansk in the north and Vladivostok in the east, were of little strategic importance. Murmansk, at least, lay near various military stores, and after no less a revolutionary than Leon Trotsky agreed to a modest effort there, Wilson permitted symbolic U.S. participation in the Allied intervention of March 1918. Against its better instincts, the administration eventually sent 4,500 Americans to protect the Murmansk stores.

The more important intervention came in Vladivostok in summer 1918, which Wilson grudgingly approved for two reasons. First, the Japanese had established their territorial designs when they began sending troops into Siberia as early as January. Much as with his decision to go to war, Wilson concluded that the only way to control the Japanese was to participate with them. Meanwhile, the Siberian situation became more convoluted when a group of Czech soldiers, allegedly attempting to remove themselves east through Vladivostok so that they might resume fighting the Germans, ran afoul of various local Bolsheviks. By July, fighting had broken out along the length of the Trans-Siberian railway. The Czechs preoccupied themselves with fighting Russians instead of Germans, and civil disorder provided the perfect excuse for deeper Allied intervention.

In order to stem the Japanese and aid the Czechs, whom he considered good liberals, Wilson agreed to move into Vladivostok. Both the Japanese and the Americans were to limit themselves to 7,000 troops. But the administration failed to secure a hard and fast Japanese promise, and, encouraged by the French and Italians, the Japanese heedlessly spilled as many as 70,000 troops into Siberia. Compared to the cynical Allies and the aggressive Japanese, Wilson had followed a policy that recognized the legitimacy of the Bolshevik Revolution. Even when he had come to detest them as a "poison," he still saw them as an extreme swing of the revolutionary pendulum. If left alone, Russia would return to a democratic equilibrium. Because the Allies had no intention of leaving Russia alone, the Bolshevik problem wore on well past the German surrender of November 1918 and thereafter became one of many sources of continuing frustration for Wilson.

The Russian debacle was a prelude to the Versailles Peace Conference, for there too Wilson discovered that military participation did not translate into diplomatic leverage. The conference began with high hopes that Wilson could achieve the liberal peace he had promised in the Fourteen Points. Europe received him with stunning public outpourings; several million people reportedly turned out in Paris alone to hail the leader of the "new age." Responding to this initial note of idealism, the nations at Paris permitted Wilson to lay out the plan for the League of Nations. In these first weeks, Wilson dominated the conference.

After a brief recess, the conferees got down to the most serious of tasks. Usually meeting in the Council of Four, in which the heads of state from France, Britain, Italy, and the United States did business, the conferees dealt with the adjustments concerning basic national interests. The French insisted on control over the Saar basin and the Rhineland. Wilson agreed that the French should be recompensed for wartime damage by gaining control over Saar coal mines, but he resisted French demands for outright annexation. Wilson's determined opposition forced the French to settle for a fifteen-year occupation of the region, overseen by the new League of Nations, in exchange for an American promise to defend France against any future German attack.

He fought more vigorously against the Italian territorial demands for control over the eastern side of the Adriatic coast, which the Allies had promised as a reward for entering the war. Italy also sought control of the port of Fiume, which the Allies had not promised. Wilson believed it essential to put the port under the control of the new Yugoslav state, and he stood his ground.

Wilson's opposition to the Italian claims stands in contrast to his concessions to the Japanese. Like the Italians, the Japanese had secured Allied promises of territorial gains in the Chinese province of Shantung. Wilson was apprehensive about the these claims; he distrusted the Japanese, and he believed that the Chinese were "fit" for self-government. But the Japanese were entrenched in the area, and it was impractical to think of evicting them. Wilson also expressed a far-sighted concern over Asian security, warning that the next important conflict might emerge there. He conceded the Japanese claims to Shantung, though he expected them to forfeit the concession to China soon and join the League of Nations.

The final issue of great importance revolved around the treatment of a defeated Germany, though this issue was less contentious than confused. The victors agreed to blame Germany for the war, which conveniently allowed them to demand extensive reparations. The French—and initially the English—argued that war damage was so extensive that it was impossible to name a fixed sum. Leaning on his own experts, Wilson argued that reparations ought to be pegged to Germany's ability to pay and that the amount requested should be definitive. Along with the British prime minister, *David Lloyd George, Wilson worried that too harsh a treaty would destroy the reconstruction of Germany and invite the spread of Bolshevism. Together, the two worked for a last-minute softening of the treaty, but one that left the amount of the reparations to be decided by a future committee.

Any examination of Wilson at Versailles must conclude that he fought for his principles while yielding to those demands that threatened to undo the conference. Two ideas compelled him: that the basis of a long-term peace was individual national security, which in turn was based on sensible territorial arrangements, economic viability, and political coherence; and that the League of Nations provided the forum through which the inadequacies of the treaty itself would be worked out. Given these guiding principles, Wilson did not see fit to carry his devotion to self-determination so far as to call for Irish independence or even for the immediate dismantling of imperialism. On these issues, he expected the League to do the work. On the other hand, he demanded the immediate self-determination of the so-called new states of central Europe—Czechoslovakia, Poland, and Yugoslavia—where he believed that establishing order was immediately necessary.

Wilson failed to carry the day on those issues where his power to act was limited. Indeed, one can argue that Wilson's overall diplomatic position was weak. U.S. military aid had been crucial in 1918, but it was neither needed nor predominant in 1919. Though American economic aid was important, it proved a clumsy instrument that could not match the allure of immediate national aggrandizement. American political prestige was high at the outset of the conference, and Wilson had considerable faith in his ability to mobilize mass opinion on his behalf. But in the inner sanctum of high diplomacy, that weapon proved of little value.

Wilson came home with a treaty that was less than he had promised and that had generated considerable opposition before it had been formalized. Domestic opposition to the treaty came from three directions: isolationists, the so-called irreconcilables, who had opposed the war itself; liberals, many of whom had supported the war but felt that Wilson had betrayed his own principles; and conservative nationalists, who opposed the treaty for partisan reasons and because they believed that its provision of collective security violated U.S. sovereignty. It was a varied opposition, and Wilson could have pushed the treaty through the Senate had he been willing to accept the reservations of Henry Cabot Lodge, which were essentially designed to protect American freedom of action. It is clear now that Wilson was increasingly ill, and the serious stroke that crippled him in September 1919 had been encroaching on him since late spring. Given the extent to which he had compromised small issues for larger principles at Versailles, it is difficult to believe that he would not have done the same at home had he not been ill. Instead, beset by neurological disorder, Wilson refused to compromise. From his sickbed, he ordered Senate Democrats to kill the treaty so long as it carried the Lodge reservations, and thus he committed, in the still-wrenching phrase of Thomas Bailey, "the supreme infanticide." He never fully recovered from his stroke and died in Washington, D.C., on February 3, 1924.

This tragic ending hardly dims Wilson's historic importance. He continued to influence American statesmen directly for the next twenty years. Men like Henry Stimson, even if they had opposed specific Wilson policies, nevertheless shared his basic presuppositions about international relations. Others, such as Cordell Hull, were frank devotees of Wilson. Even the enigmatic *Franklin D. Roosevelt worked under the shadow of Wilsonian diplomacy during World War II, hoping to extract the good from what had failed. After World War II, American diplomats often renounced Wilson as a naive and idealistic dilettante, but the amount of time scholar-diplomats like *George Kennan and Hans Morgenthau spent attacking his record testifies to the sway Wilson continued to exercise even over those who renounced him. Today, those who speak of themselves as "Wilsonians" are few and far between.

Annotated Bibliography

Not only are the main primary sources for Wilsonian diplomacy readily available, but the bulk of them have been published by Arthur Link in *The Public Papers of Woodrow Wilson* (1967–   ), which at this writing numbers sixty volumes. All Wilson scholars owe Link an enormous debt of gratitude for his meticulous and even-handed editing of this large collection. It is fair to say that every important document that Wilson dealt with directly is included in the collection. The Papers are the last word on Wilson historiography, which is as it should be.

There are also, of course, many other manuscript collections with material relating to Wilsonian foreign policy. The Library of Congress Manuscript Division holds the papers of the following Wilson era diplomats, politicians, and bureaucrats, all of which contain material related to Wilson: Newton D. Baker, Tasker H. Bliss, George Creel, Josephus Daniels, Norman Davis, Robert Lansing, Joseph Tumulty, and Henry White. The original copy of the Fourteen Points Address is in the Francis B. Sayre Papers, also at the Library of Congress.

As president of Yale after World War I, Charles Seymour saw to it that the Sterling Library gathered considerable material from the war. Yale has the William C. Bullitt Papers, the Edward House Papers, the Walter Lippmann Papers, the Vance McCormick Papers, and the William Wiseman Papers. While Princeton houses the staff working on the *Papers of Woodrow Wilson*, the only helpful collection at Princeton is the Raymond B. Fosdick Papers.

Coming to terms with Wilson's historiographical legacy forces one to begin with works by contemporaries and finish by wading through each and every interpretive school of American foreign relations. Wilson himself never wrote on foreign affairs, but his academic writings, especially those works that show his preoccupation with liberal progress, such as *The State* (1889) and *Division and Reunion* (1894), demonstrate how consistent his thought was. Nor did Wilson write on major events. But the liberals surrounding him provided many firsthand accounts of Wilson and U.S. foreign policy. The most valuable, Ray Stannard Baker, *Woodrow Wilson and the World Settlement*, 3 vols. (1922), and David Hunter Miller, *My Diary at the Conference at Paris*, 21 vols. (1924) and *The Drafting of the Covenant*, 2 vols. (1928), are sympathetic and systematic accounts of the peace conference. Other firsthand accounts—*The Intimate Papers of Colonel House*, 4 vols., edited by Charles Seymour (1926–1928), Edward House and Charles Seymour, *What Really Happened at Paris* (1921), and Robert Lansing, *The Peace Negotiations* (1921)—are less sympathetic.

Wilson has had his share of biographers. The reader should start with Arthur S. Link, *Wilson*, 5 vols. (1947–1965), the judiciousness of which keeps the work fresh. Other general biographies of value are Kendrick Clements, *Woodrow Wilson: World Statesman* (1987), and Arthur Walworth, *Woodrow Wilson*, 2 vols. (1965). Wilson's early years are detailed in John M. Mulder, *Woodrow Wilson: The Years of Preparation* (1978), and Henry Bragdon, *Woodrow Wilson: The Academic Years* (1967). The work that best places Wilson within a contemporary political context is John Milton Cooper, Jr., *The Warrior and the Priest* (1983), a comparative biography of Wilson and Theodore Roosevelt. Dr. Edwin Weinstein's medical biography, *Woodrow Wilson: A Medical and Psychological Biography* (1981), is also valuable. In addition to the general biographies, overviews of Wilson's foreign policy are Lloyd Gardner, *Safe for Democracy* (1984), Arthur Link, *Woodrow Wilson: Revolution, War, and Peace* (1979), and Link, ed., *Woodrow Wilson and a Revolutionary World* (1982).

Wilson's policy in the Western Hemisphere has inspired many works that address theoretical considerations of how a powerful United States related to the weaker nations of the region. Wilson's paradoxical desire to welcome and yet control revolution forces scholars to handle such issues with subtlety and sophistication. Among such works are Mark T. Gilderhus, *Pan-American Visions* (1986), and Robert Freeman Smith, *The United States and Revolutionary Nationalism in Mexico* (1972). Works dealing with relations between the United States and Europe in Mexico include Peter Calvert, *The Mexican Revolution, 1910–1914: The Diplomacy of Anglo-American Conflict* (1968), Friedrich Katz, *The Secret War in Mexico* (1981), and Gardner, *Safe for Democracy*. Wilson's relations with one or another actor on the Mexican stage have inspired Clarence Clendenen, *The United States and Pancho Villa* (1961), Mark T. Gilderhus, *Diplomacy and Revolution: U.S.-Mexican Relations Under Wilson and Carranza* (1977), and Kenneth Grieb, *The United States and Huerta* (1969). Larry Hill, *Emissaries to a Revolution* (1973), shows that the unlikely characters whom Wilson sent to Mexico were poor judges of Mexican affairs. Robert Quirk, *An Affair of Honor* (1962), examines the occupation at Veracruz. There are fewer works on Caribbean policy. Dana Munro, *Intervention and Dollar Diplomacy* (1964), is badly dated. Of greater value are Hans Schmidt, *The United States Occupation of Haiti* (1971), and David Healy, *Gunboat Diplomacy in the Wilson Era* (1976).

The policy of neutrality from 1914 to 1917 is covered in Ernest May, *World War and American Isolation, 1914–1917* (1959), Daniel Smith, *The Great Departure* (1965), and Patrick Devlin, *Too Proud to Fight* (1974). Each of these works ventures ideas about the decision to intervene, but for a systematic overview of the various interpretations of the decision see Daniel Smith, "National Interests and American Intervention, 1917," *Journal of American History* 52 (1965). Arthur Link's explanation in *Woodrow Wilson: Revolution, War, and Peace* that "only by going to war could [Wilson] win . . . a reasonable peace settlement and the reconstruction of the world order" (p. 71) remains the most satisfying.

Overviews of wartime policy can be found in N. Gordon Levin, *Woodrow Wilson and World Politics* (1968), Robert Ferrell, *Woodrow Wilson and World War I* (1985), and Gardner, *Safe for Democracy*. Wilton B. Fowler details Anglo-American relations in his study of Sir William Wiseman, *British-American Relations, 1917–1918* (1969). Lawrence Gelfand, *The Inquiry* (1963), examines the Fourteen Points through the secret committee under House's direction that was charged with developing territorial adjustments.

The intervention in Russia understandably has brought about more intense debate than any other single issue. Regardless of the position, there is general agreement that Wilson acted with more circumspection than the Allies. The oldest works, George Kennan, *Soviet-American Relations, 1917–1920*, 2 vols. (1956), and Betty Miller Unterberger, *America's Siberian Expedition* (1956), thus have held up fairly well. New Left historians produced several important books on the issue, including Levin, *Woodrow Wilson and World Politics* (1968), Christopher Lasch, *American Liberals and the Russian Revolution* (1962), and Arno Mayer, *The Political Origins of the New Diplomacy* (1959), the gist of which was that Wilson badly misunderstood the nature of the revolution he expected to tame. The counter-revisionists shot back with John M. Thompson, *Russia, Bolshevism, and the Versailles Peace* (1966), and Robert Maddox, *The Unknown War with Russia* (1977). Predictably, the latest studies avoid the larger issues by focusing on specifics, as with Linda Killen, *The Russian Bureau: A Case Study in Wilsonian Diplomacy* (1983). But Betty Miller Unterberger, *The United States, Revolutionary Russia, and the Rise of Czechoslovakia* (1989), helps us see how Wilson expected Russia to follow the liberal path of Czechoslovakia.

For general studies on Wilson at Versailles, one should take up the challenge of Arno Mayer, *The Politics and Diplomacy of Peacemaking* (1967). Less contentious but still worthwhile is Arthur Walworth, *Wilson and His Peacemakers* (1986). Perhaps the best overall work on the conference, however, is Howard Elcock, *Portrait of a Decision*

(1972). Lloyd Ambrosius details important parts of the conference in his work on the development of the League of Nations covenant, *Woodrow Wilson and the American Diplomatic Tradition* (1987).

There are many books that concern specific issues or Wilson's relations with a particular nation. See Louis Gerson, *Woodrow Wilson and the Rebirth of Poland* (1953), Louis Yates, *The United States and French Security* (1957), Seth Tillman, *Anglo-American Relations at the Paris Peace Conference of 1919* (1961), A. Lentin, *Lloyd George, Woodrow Wilson, and the Guilt of Germany* (1984), and Klaus Schwabe, *Woodrow Wilson, Revolutionary Germany, and Peacemaking* (1985). Inga Floto, *Colonel House in Paris* (1973), views American policy through a critical look at the president's personal advisor.

War on the home front is covered thoroughly in David M. Kennedy, *Over Here* (1980). Robert Cuff details the important changes in political economy ushered in by wartime mobilization in *The War Industries Board* (1973), while Stephen Vaughn examines American propaganda in his book on the Committee of Public Information, *Holding Fast the Inner Lines* (1980). H. C. Peterson and Gilbert Fite, *Opponents of War* (1957), and Ralph Stone, *The Irreconcilables* (1970), examine the isolationists who resisted Wilson's call to arms on behalf of liberal ideals. Warren Kuehl, *Seeking World Order* (1969), and Sondra Herman, *Eleven Against War* (1969), meanwhile, deal with American internationalism before and during the war. For the Senate treaty fight, see Thomas Bailey, *Woodrow Wilson and the Great Betrayal* (1945), in which he describes the fight as the "supreme infanticide." William Widenor, *Henry Cabot Lodge and the Search for an American Foreign Policy* (1983), places the bulk of the blame on Wilson for the treaty's failure. Ambrosius, in *Woodrow Wilson and the American Diplomatic Tradition*, more recently has depicted Lodge's position and Wilson's idealism as competing ideas about how to organize America's response to the modern world.

In addition, Wilsonian diplomacy can be used to follow the main lines of scholarly debate on American foreign relations. Walter Millis, *Road to War* (1935), represents the isolationist attack against the influence of bankers and munitions makers on foreign policy. George Kennan laid out the basis of the realist critique of U.S. foreign policy when he mocked Wilson's penchant for moral abstractions in *American Diplomacy* (1951). William Appleman Williams pioneered in New Left historiography when he saw in Wilson the ultimate example of America's anticolonial imperialism in *The Tragedy of American Diplomacy* (1959). While some post-revisionists have not found much inspiration in Wilsonian diplomacy, both Lloyd Gardner, *A Covenant with Power* (1984), and Ambrosius, *Woodrow Wilson and the American Diplomatic Tradition*, have attempted to outline the persistence of Wilsonian ideals in American diplomacy while moving away from the materialism of the New Left.

Finally, Peter H. Buckingham has compiled a thorough bibliography of printed sources concerning Wilson, America in his day, and foreign policy during the Wilson era in *Woodrow Wilson: A Bibliography of His Times and His Presidency* (1990).

Bibliography

Published Memoirs, Diaries, and Contemporary Observations

Baker, Ray Stannard. *Woodrow Wilson and the World Settlement.* 3 vols. Garden City, N.Y.: Doubleday, 1922.

Baruch, Bernard. *The Making of the Reparation and Economic Sanctions of the Treaty*. New York: Harper, 1920.

Beer, George Louis. *African Questions at the Paris Peace Conference*. Edited by Louis Gray. New York: Macmillan, 1923.

Bernstorff, Johann H. von. *My Three Years in America*. New York: Scribner's, 1920.

Bonsal, Stephan. *Unfinished Business*. Garden City, N.Y.: Doubleday, 1944.

Creel, George. *Rebel at Large: Recollections after Fifty Crowded Years*. New York: Putnam's, 1947.

Daniel, Josephus. *The Wilson Era*. 2 vols. Chapel Hill: University of North Carolina Press, 1944–1946.

Dillon, E. J. *The Inside Story of the Peace Conference*. New York: Harper, 1920.

Francis, David R. *Russia from the American Embassy, April 1916–November 1918*. New York: Scribner's, 1921.

Grayson, Cary T. *Woodrow Wilson: A Personal Memoir*. 2nd ed. Washington, D.C.: Potomac, 1977.

Hendrick, Burton J., ed. *The Life and Letters of Walter Hines Page*. 3 vols. Garden City, N.Y.: Doubleday, 1924–1926.

House, Edward. *The Intimate Papers of Colonel House*. 4 vols. Edited by Charles Seymour. Boston: Houghton Mifflin, 1926–1928.

House, Edward, and Charles Seymour. *What Really Happened at Paris: The Story of the Paris Peace Conference, 1918–1919*. New York: Scribner's, 1921.

Lansing, Robert. *The Peace Negotiations: A Personal Narrative*. Boston: Houghton Mifflin, 1921.

Miller, David Hunter. *The Drafting of the Covenant*. 2 vols. New York: Putnam's, 1928.

———. *My Diary at the Peace Conference at Paris*. 21 vols. New York: Appeal, 1924.

Seymour, Charles. *Letters from the Paris Peace Conference*. New Haven, Conn.: Yale University Press, 1965.

Shotwell, James. *At the Paris Peace Conference*. New York: Macmillan, 1937.

General Works and Early Career

Blum, John Morton. *Woodrow Wilson and the Politics of Morality*. Boston: Little, Brown, 1956.

Bragdon, Henry W. *Woodrow Wilson: The Academic Years*. Cambridge, Mass.: Harvard University Press, 1967.

Buckingham, Peter H. *Woodrow Wilson: A Bibliography of His Times and His Presidency*. Wilmington, Del.: Scholarly Resources, 1990.

Clements, Kendrick A. *Woodrow Wilson: World Statesman*. Boston: Twayne, 1987.

Cooper, John Milton, Jr. *The Warrior and the Priest: Woodrow Wilson and Theodore Roosevelt*. Cambridge, Mass.: Harvard University Press, 1983.

Gardner, Lloyd. *A Covenant with Power: America and World Order from Wilson to Reagan*. New York: Oxford University Press, 1984.

———. *Safe for Democracy: The Anglo-American Response to Revolution, 1913–1923*. New York: Oxford University Press, 1984.

Link, Arthur S. *The Higher Realism of Woodrow Wilson and Other Essays*. Nashville: Vanderbilt University Press, 1971.

———. *Wilson*. 5 vols. Princeton, N.J.: Princeton University Press, 1947–1965.

———. *Woodrow Wilson: Revolution, War, and Peace*. Arlington Heights, Ill.: Harlan-Davidson, 1979.

————, ed. *The Public Papers of Woodrow Wilson.* 60 vols. to date. Princeton, N.J.: Princeton University Press, 1967- .

————, ed. *Woodrow Wilson and a Revolutionary World, 1913–1921.* Chapel Hill: University of North Carolina Press, 1982.

Mulder, John M. *Woodrow Wilson: The Years of Preparation.* Princeton, N.J.: Princeton University Press, 1978.

Walworth, Arthur. *Woodrow Wilson.* 2 vols. Boston: Houghton Mifflin, 1965.

Weinstein, Edwin. *Woodrow Wilson: A Medical and Psychological Biography.* Princeton, N.J.: Princeton University Press, 1981.

Latin America and the Caribbean

Calvert, Peter. *The Mexican Revolution, 1910–1914: The Diplomacy of Anglo-American Conflict.* Cambridge: Cambridge University Press, 1968.

Clendenen, Clarence. *The United States and Pancho Villa: A Study in Unconventional Diplomacy.* Ithaca, N.Y.: Cornell University Press, 1961.

Gilderhus, Mark T. *Diplomacy and Revolution: U.S.-Mexican Relations Under Wilson and Carranza.* Tucson: University of Arizona Press, 1977.

————. *Pan-American Visions: Woodrow Wilson in the Western Hemisphere, 1913–1921.* Tucson: University of Arizona Press, 1986.

Grieb, Kenneth. *The United States and Huerta.* Lincoln: University of Nebraska Press, 1969.

Haley, P. Edward. *Revolution and Intervention: The Diplomacy of Taft and Wilson in Mexico, 1910–1917.* Cambridge, Mass.: MIT Press, 1970.

Healy, David. *Gunboat Diplomacy in the Wilson Era: The U.S. Navy in Haiti, 1915–1916.* Madison: University of Wisconsin Press, 1976.

Hill, Larry D. *Emissaries to a Revolution: Woodrow Wilson's Executive Agents in Mexico, 1910–1917.* Baton Rouge: Louisiana State University Press, 1973.

Katz, Friedrich. "Pancho Villa and the Attack on Columbus, New Mexico." *American Historical Review* 83 (1978): 101–130.

————. *The Secret War in Mexico: Europe, the United States, and the Mexican Revolution.* Chicago: University of Chicago Press, 1981.

Meyer, Michael. "The Arms of the Ypiranga." *Hispanic American Historical Review* 50 (1970): 543–556.

Munro, Dana G. *Intervention and Dollar Diplomacy in the Caribbean, 1913–1917.* Princeton, N.J.: Princeton University Press, 1964.

Quirk, Robert. *An Affair of Honor: Woodrow Wilson and the Occupation of Veracruz.* Lexington: University of Kentucky Press, 1962.

Schmidt, Hans. *The United States Occupation of Haiti.* New Brunswick, N.J.: Rutgers University Press, 1971.

Smith, Robert Freeman. *The United States and Revolutionary Nationalism in Mexico, 1916–1932.* Chicago: University of Chicago Press, 1972.

Trow, Clifford. "Woodrow Wilson and the Mexican Interventionist Movement of 1919." *Journal of American History* 58 (1971): 46–72.

Neutrality and the Decision for War

Devlin, Patrick. *Too Proud to Fight.* New York: Oxford University Press, 1974.

Kennan, George. *American Diplomacy.* Chicago: University of Chicago Press, 1951.

Link, Arthur S. "That Cobb Interview." *Journal of American History* 72 (1985): 7–17.

May, Ernest. *World War and American Isolation, 1914–1917*. Cambridge, Mass.: Harvard University Press, 1959.

Millis, Walter. *Road to War: America, 1914–1917*. Boston: Houghton Mifflin, 1935.

Ross, Gregory. *The Origins of American Intervention in the First World War*. New York: Norton, 1971.

Smith, Daniel M. *The Great Departure: The United States and World War I*. New York: Wiley, 1965.

———. "National Interests and American Intervention, 1917: A Historiographical Appraisal." *Journal of American History* 52 (1965): 5–24.

Thompson, J. A. "Woodrow Wilson and World War I: A Reappraisal." *Journal of American Studies* 19 (1985): 325–348.

War and Peace

Ambrosius, Lloyd. *Woodrow Wilson and the American Diplomatic Tradition*. New York: Cambridge University Press, 1987.

Bailey, Thomas. *Woodrow Wilson and the Great Betrayal*. New York: Macmillan, 1945.

———. *Woodrow Wilson and the Lost Peace*. New York: Macmillan, 1944.

Cuff, Robert D. *The War Industries Board: Business-Government Relations During World War I*. Baltimore: Johns Hopkins University Press, 1973.

Elcock, Howard. *Portrait of a Decision: The Council of Four and the Treaty of Versailles*. London: Eyre Methuen, 1972.

Ferrell, Robert. *Woodrow Wilson and World War I, 1917–1921*. New York: Harper and Row, 1985.

Fleming, Dana. *The United States and the League of Nations, 1918–1920*. New York: Putnam's, 1932.

Floto, Inga. *Colonial House in Paris: A Study of American Policy at the Paris Peace Conference, 1919*. Aarhus: DBK, 1973.

Fowler, Wilton B. *British-American Relations, 1917–1918: The Role of Sir William Wiseman*. Princeton, N.J.: Princeton University Press, 1969.

Gelfand, Lawrence. *The Inquiry: American Preparations for Peace, 1917–1919*. New Haven, Conn.: Yale University Press, 1963.

Gerson, Louis. *Woodrow Wilson and the Rebirth of Poland, 1914–1920*. New Haven, Conn.: Yale University Press, 1953.

Herman, Sondra. *Eleven Against War*. Stanford, Calif.: Hoover Institute, 1969.

Kennan, George. *Soviet-American Relations, 1917–1920*. 2 vols. Princeton, N.J.: Princeton University Press, 1956.

Kennedy, David. *Over Here: The First World War and American Society*. New York: Oxford University Press, 1980.

Killen, Linda. *The Russian Bureau: A Case Study in Wilsonian Diplomacy*. Lexington: University of Kentucky Press, 1983.

Kuehl, Warren. *Seeking World Order*. Nashville: Vanderbilt University Press, 1969.

Lasch, Christopher. *American Liberals and the Russian Revolution*. New York: Columbia University Press, 1962.

Lentin, A. S. *Lloyd George, Woodrow Wilson, and the Guilt of Germany: An Essay in the Pre-history of Appeasement*. Baton Rouge: Louisiana State University Press, 1984.

Levin, N. Gordon. *Woodrow Wilson and World Politics: America's Response to War and Revolution*. New York: Oxford University Press, 1968.

Maddox, Robert. *The Unknown War with Russia: Wilson's Siberian Adventure*. San Rafael, Calif.: Presidio, 1977.

Mayer, Arno. *The Political Origins of the New Diplomacy, 1917–1918*. New Haven, Conn.: Yale University Press, 1959.

————. *The Politics and Diplomacy of Peacemaking: Containment and Counterrevolution at Versailles, 1918–1919*. New York: Knopf, 1967.

Peterson, H. C., and Gilbert Fite. *Opponents of War, 1917–1918*. Seattle: University of Washington Press, 1957.

Schwabe, Klaus. *Woodrow Wilson, Revolutionary Germany, and Peacemaking, 1918–1919*. Chapel Hill: University of North Carolina Press, 1985.

Stone, Ralph A. *The Irreconcilables: The Fight Against the League of Nations*. Lexington: University of Kentucky Press, 1970.

Thompson, John M. *Russia, Bolshevism, and the Versailles Peace*. Princeton, N.J.: Princeton University Press, 1966.

Tillman, Seth P. *Anglo-American Relations at the Paris Peace Conference of 1919*. Princeton, N.J.: Princeton University Press, 1961.

Unterberger, Betty Miller. *America's Siberian Expedition, 1918–1920*. Durham, N.C.: Duke University Press, 1956.

————. *The United States, Revolutionary Russia, and the Rise of Czechoslovakia*. Chapel Hill: University of North Carolina Press, 1989.

Vaughn, Stephen. *Holding Fast the Inner Lines: Democracy, Nationalism, and the Committee on Public Information*. Chapel Hill: University of North Carolina Press, 1980.

Walworth, Arthur. *Wilson and His Peacemakers: American Diplomacy at the Paris Peace Conference, 1919*. New York: Norton, 1986.

Widenor, William C. *Henry Cabot Lodge and the Search for an American Foreign Policy*. Berkeley: University of California Press, 1983

Williams, William A. *The Tragedy of American Diplomacy*. Cleveland: World Publishing, 1959.

Yates, Louis. *The United States and French Security, 1917–1921*. New York: Twayne, 1957.

DAVID STEIGERWALD

APPENDIX A

HISTORICAL FIGURES

ABERDEEN, LORD [GEORGE HAMILTON-GORDON] (1784–1860). Born in Edinburgh and educated at Cambridge, Lord Aberdeen took part in the negotiations ending the War of 1812, served as foreign secretary from 1828 to 1830 and from 1841 to 1846, and was prime minister from 1852 to 1855.

ALBERT, PRINCE (1819–1861). Queen Victoria's consort, the German-born prince, Albert of Saxe-Coburg-Gotha usually reinforced Victoria's conservative inclinations, although his moderating role during the initial months of the American Civil War helped to prevent the further deterioration of Anglo-American relations.

ALENÇON, FRANCIS, DUKE OF (1555–1584). The youngest son of Catherine de Medici, queen mother of France, the Duke of Alençon, who was to become the Duke of Anjou, was the last in a long line of suitors for *Elizabeth I's hand. Ultimately, the forty-nine-year-old Elizabeth rejected the twenty-six-year-old duke, causing a minor but temporary setback to Anglo-French relations.

ALEXANDER I (1888–1934). Born Alexander Karadjordjevic, the future king of Yugoslavia found himself in line to inherit a crown when his father, Peter, overthrew the Obrenovic dynasty and became king of Serbia in 1903. Acting as regent for his father from 1914 onward, Alexander was named "prince-regent of the Serbs, Croats, and Slovenes" in 1918. He became king of Yugoslavia in 1921, but was assassinated by disgruntled Croats at Marseille in 1934.

ANDROPOV, YURI (1914–1984). Named general secretary of the Communist Party of the Soviet Union after Leonid Brezhnev's death in 1982, Yuri Andropov himself was terminally ill at the time. His short tenure as leader of the Soviet Union was generally uneventful.

ASQUITH, HENRY H. (1852–1928). Asquith was an Oxford-educated British politician who for many years was the leader of the Liberal party. He was prime minister between 1908 and 1916 and was considered a master of parliamentary politics.

ATTLEE, CLEMENT (1883–1967). Leader of the British Labour party, Attlee served as prime minister from 1945 to 1951. With the Labour party's triumph in the 1945 election, Attlee replaced *Winston Churchill in the midst of the Potsdam Conference. During the early years of the Cold War he joined with U.S. president Harry S. Truman to oppose *Joseph Stalin's Soviet Union.

AUGUSTUS II (1670–1733). Both as king of Poland and elector of Saxony, Augustus II spent most of his adult life either at war, deeply involved in diplomatic intrigue, or living lavishly and lasciviously. He is credited with making his Saxon capital city, Dresden, one of the finest in Europe.

BALDWIN, STANLEY (1867–1947). The Cambridge-educated Baldwin was prime minister of Britain on three different occasions: 1923, 1924–1929, and 1935–1937. A Conservative, Baldwin was a shrewd politician behind an unimposing personal image.

BARUCH, BERNARD (1870–1965). A highly successful financier, Bernard Baruch held government posts from time to time. He was a member of the U.S. delegation to the Paris Peace Conference (1919) but was much better known for his service soon after World War II as U.S. representative on the UN Atomic Energy Commission, where he sought without success to formulate a plan for the international control of atomic energy.

BAYLE, PIERRE (1647–1706). A professor of philosophy at the University of Rotterdam, Bayle was one of the important early figures of the Enlightenment. He insisted that everything be examined critically and was especially effective in calling for religious toleration.

BEAUHARNAIS, JOSEPHINE DE (1763–1814). A woman of great charm, grace, and political sense, Josephine, who became empress of the French (1804–1810) as *Napoleon I's consort, married the young Corsican in 1796. The marriage was annulled in 1810 when Napoleon married the Austrian princess Marie-Louise.

BENTHAM, JEREMY (1748–1832). An English thinker of the late Enlightenment, Bentham insisted that all human behavior, including that of monarchs, be measured by its usefulness to mankind. By the early nineteenth century, Bentham and his followers, the Benthamites, were pressing for extensive reform in England on the basis of utilitarianism, or the concept of the greatest good for the greatest number.

BLUM, LÉON (1872–1950). Longtime leader of the French Socialist party, Léon Blum became premier in 1936 at the head of a Popular Front ministry. Blum pushed through several social welfare and economic reforms, but refused to help the hard-pressed forces of the Spanish republic before he was forced from office in 1937.

BOHLEN, CHARLES (1904–1974). A career diplomat who joined the State Department in 1928, Bohlen had a hand in much of the foreign policymaking during and after World War II. He was involved with the Marshall Plan and served as ambassador to the Soviet Union (1953–1957), the Philippines (1957–1959), and France (1962–1968).

BREZHNEV, LEONID (1906–1982). General secretary of the Communist Party of the Soviet Union, Brezhnev led the Soviet Union from Nikita Khrushchev's overthrow in 1964 until his death in 1982. Under Brezhnev the Soviet Union continued its grip on eastern Europe, played a more active role in Third World affairs, and experimented with but later abandoned a policy of improved relations with the United States.

BULLITT, WILLIAM C. (1891–1967). An early expert on the Soviet Union, Bullitt traveled to Moscow on behalf of President *Woodrow Wilson in 1919 and was instrumental in discussions leading up to the Roosevelt-Litvinov Agreements (1933) that established diplomatic relations between the United States and the Soviet Union. The first U.S. ambassador to the USSR (1933–1936), Bullitt grew disillusioned and was an outspoken anti-Communist the rest of his life.

BYRNES, JAMES F. (1879–1972). James F. Byrnes was secretary of state (1945–1947) under President Harry S. Truman and guided the nation's foreign policy during the development of the Cold War. Prior to that service, he had been in the U.S. Congress (1911–1941), on the U.S. Supreme Court (1941–1942), and head of vital wartime agencies in the administration of *Franklin D. Roosevelt.

BYRON, LORD [George Gordon] (1788–1824). One of England's most acclaimed Romantic poets, Lord Byron was also a bitter opponent of the reactionary tide sweeping across Europe after the Napoleonic Wars. He lent his powerful voice to the movement for Greek independence and died in camp at Missolonghi during the Greek revolution.

CAMPBELL-BANNERMAN, HENRY (1836–1908). Sir Henry Campbell-Bannerman was born and educated in Glasgow and entered Parliament in 1868. He held a number of cabinet posts in Liberal governments in the late nineteenth century and was prime minister from 1905 to 1908.

CHAMBERLAIN, AUSTEN (1863–1937). Austen Chamberlain was the brother of *Neville Chamberlain and was educated at Cambridge. Between 1918 and 1931 he held a number of posts in Conservative government cabinets, including the foreign secretaryship, 1924–1929.

CHARLEMAGNE (768–814). A Frankish king of substantial energy and intelligence, Charlemagne was crowned emperor of the West by the pope in 800. Although Charlemagne's empire fell apart soon after his death, numerous subsequent European rulers have tried to revive it under their authority.

CHERNENKO, KONSTANTIN (1911–1985). Appointed general secretary of the Communist Party of the Soviet Union upon Yuri Andropov's death in 1984, Chernenko proved to be little more than a transitional caretaker.

CHIANG KAI-SHEK (1887–1975). With the death of Sun Yat-sen in 1925, Chinese political figure Chiang Kai-shek became head of the Kuomintang, or Nationalist, party. Chaos reigned in China, and Chiang struggled—chiefly against Mao Tsetung's Communists—to assert his authority over the country. After Japan's conquest of and subsequent expulsion from China, Chiang was defeated by Mao in the Chinese civil war (1946–1949) and fled with his supporters to Taiwan, where he established a Kuomintang, or "Nationalist Chinese," government.

CHRZANOWSKI, WOJCIECH (1793–1861). Beginning a long military career as an officer in the army of the Duchy of Warsaw, Chrzanowski was chief of staff of the Polish army during the ill-fated Polish Revolution of 1830–1831. Subsequently he undertook fact-finding missions to Turkey for British foreign secretary *Palmerston, and in 1849 was de facto commander of the Piedmontese army at the Battle of Novara.

CLAY, HENRY (1777–1852). Clay served many years in the U.S. Senate and ran for president three times (1824, 1832, 1844). He served as secretary of state under President *John Quincy Adams (1825–1829).

CLAY, LUCIUS D. (1897–1978). A West Point graduate, Clay became commander in chief of U.S. forces in Europe and military governor of Germany in 1947. In that post, he did much to alleviate the suffering of the German people, directed the Berlin airlift (1948), and helped in the development of West Germany once the Cold War became a reality.

CONKLING, ROSCOE (1829–1888). A Republican politician from New York, Conkling served in Congress from 1859 to 1863 and from 1867 to 1881. His career was enmeshed in the intricacies of party politics, where he was an enemy of *James G. Blaine.

CONSTANTINE, GRAND DUKE. *See* Konstantin Pavlovich.

CORTÉZ, HERNANDO (1485–1547). A Spanish conquistador, Cortéz was responsible for the conquest of Mexico in 1519.

CURZON, GEORGE NATHANIEL (1859–1925). Lord Curzon was educated at Oxford and after service as viceroy of India, 1898–1905, became a member of the war cabinet, 1916–1918, and foreign secretary, 1919–1924. More than almost any other British leader, he epitomized the attitudes and lifestyle of the English aristocracy.

DAVID, JACQUES-LOUIS (1748–1825). A noted French painter who actively supported the revolution, David's canvasses tended to glorify both heroic figures such as *Napoleon I and the common man.

DE GASPERI, ALCIDE (1881–1954). Leader of the Christian Democratic party, De Gasperi dominated Italian politics from 1946 to 1953. He opposed the Communists, favored strong ties with the United States, and worked with *Robert Schuman of France and *Konrad Adenauer of Germany to bring about the first steps toward European economic unification.

DEANE, SILAS (1737–1789). A diplomatic representative of the United States in Europe during the war for independence, Deane worked with the French to secure aid for America. He was recalled because of allegations (by Arthur Lee) of corrupt activity but spent the rest of his life in exile in Britain.

DECEMBRISTS (1825). *See* Decembrist Revolt, Appendix C.

DEWEY, THOMAS (1902–1971). A Republican, Thomas Dewey was elected governor of New York in 1942 and won the presidential nomination of his party in 1944 and 1948, losing the elections to *Franklin D. Roosevelt and Harry S. Truman, respectively. An internationalist, he supported the United Nations and the Marshall Plan for European recovery.

DRAKE, SIR FRANCIS (c. 1540–1596). Commander of the English fleet that bested the Spanish Armada in 1588, Drake gained fame and fortune by raiding Spanish colonial outposts and capturing Spanish vessels laden with treasures from the New World.

EDEN, ANTHONY (1897–1977). From an aristocratic background, Eden served Great Britain as both foreign secretary (1935–1938; 1940–1945; 1951–1955) and prime minister (1955–1957). As foreign minister, Eden opposed *Neville Chamberlain's appeasement policy and later worked well with *Winston Churchill to resist first *Adolf Hitler's aggression and, later, Soviet expansion. Brought down by the 1956 Suez Crisis, Eden became a supporter of European cooperation.

EGMONT, LAMORAL (1522–1568). A Dutch aristocrat with ties to William of Orange, Egmont opposed *Philip II's close control over the Netherlands as well as his financial and religious policies. He was executed for his pains.

ERHARD, LUDWIG (1897–1977). After serving as *Konrad Adenauer's economics minister, where he received much of the credit for West Germany's post–World War II economic miracle, Erhard was a rather unsuccessful chancellor from 1963 to 1966.

EUGENE OF SAVOY (1663–1736). Leader of the forces that defeated the Turks at the end of the seventeenth century and brought Hungary under Habsburg control, Prince Eugene, a Frenchman by birth, also successfully commanded the Austrian forces during the War of the Spanish Succession. He is given credit for modernizing the Austrian state.

FERDINAND THE CATHOLIC (1452–1516). Ferdinand the Catholic is another name for King Ferdinand of Aragon who, along with his consort, Queen Isabella of Castile, is given credit for creating the modern Spanish monarchy.

FLEURY, ANDRÉ CARDINAL (1653–1743). Already seventy-three years old when he became chief minister to Louis XV in 1726, Fleury, who was elevated to cardinal in the same year, directed French affairs with an eye toward rebuilding the state's finances. Although cautious and inclined to prefer peace to war, Fleury was drawn into the War of the Polish Succession (1733–1735) and the War of the Austrian Succession (1740–1748).

FORRESTAL, JAMES V. (1892–1949). An advisor to the *Franklin D. Roosevelt administration during World War II on naval and defense matters, James Forrestal became secretary of the navy in 1944 and the first secretary of defense in 1947 following the passage of the National Security Act. He favored the maintenance of a strong postwar military to counter a perceived Soviet threat.

FOSTER, JOHN WATSON (1836–1917). Foster served as minister to Mexico (1873–1880) and to Spain (1883–1885) before becoming secretary of state (1892–1893) under President Benjamin Harrison. He also wrote extensively on American diplomatic history and was the grandfather of *John Foster Dulles.

FRANCIS FERDINAND, ARCHDUKE (1863–1914). Heir to the aged Francis Joseph, emperor of Austria-Hungary, Francis Ferdinand was assassinated at Sarajevo on June 28, 1914, by Bosnian terrorists with the complicity of important Serbian officials. His murder provoked a major crisis, which led to the outbreak of World War I several weeks later.

FRANCO, FRANCISCO (1892–1975). Military commander of Spanish forces stationed in Morocco, Franco launched the Spanish Civil War (1936–1939) when he led his troops against the Republican government. Victorious thanks to the help of *Mussolini's Italy and *Hitler's Germany, Franco established an authoritarian, fascist-type regime in Spain, which lasted until his death in 1975.

GALLATIN, ALBERT (1761–1849). The Swiss-born Gallatin served many years in the U.S. Congress and as secretary of the treasury. He helped negotiate the Treaty of Ghent, ending the War of 1812, and was minister to France (1815–1823) and Great Britain (1826–1831).

GENÊT, EDMUND CHARLES (1763–1834). The French-born Genêt came to the United States in 1793 as the representative of the forces then prevailing in the French Revolution. On his own authority, and contrary to the desires of George Washington's administration, he set about recruiting privateers to prey on British shipping. Washington demanded his recall, but Genêt stayed in the United States after his successor arrived and eventually became an American citizen.

GLADSTONE, WILLIAM E. (1809–1898). Prime Minister of Great Britain on four separate occasions, Gladstone reflected the sentiment of the "Little Englanders," who believed that Britain's empire was too costly to maintain.

GREY, EDWARD (1862–1933). Edward Grey, educated at Oxford, served as Britain's foreign secretary from 1905 to 1916, under Liberal and coalition governments. He was an early supporter of a postwar League of Nations.

GUSTAVUS ADOLPHUS II (1594–1632). Ruler of Sweden from 1611, Gustavus Adolphus was a popular king and an exceptionally able military leader. Entering into the Thirty Years War in part due to enticements from France's Cardinal *Richelieu, the staunchly Protestant Gustavus Adolphus administered several crushing defeats to the Catholic forces of the Holy Roman Emperor before he was killed at the Battle of Lützen.

HAIG, DOUGLAS (1861–1928). General Haig was Great Britain's highest-ranking military leader during most of World War I, serving as commander-in-chief of British troops in France from 1915 to 1919 and of Home Forces from 1919 to 1921.

HAMILTON, ALEXANDER (1755–1804). Born illegitimate in the British West Indies, Alexander Hamilton came to New York in 1773 and became George Washington's aide during the American Revolution. During Washington's presidency he was secretary of the treasury and influential in developing a foreign policy that favored Britain over France.

HARDENBERG, KARL (1750–1822). An important Prussian statesman of the early nineteenth century, Hardenberg served as foreign minister from 1804 to 1806 and again in 1807, before being named chancellor in 1810. He represented Prussia at the 1814–1815 Congress of Vienna, where he pressed Prussia's claims for additional territory.

HARRIMAN, W. AVERILL (1891–1986). Son of a famous railroad magnate, Averill Harriman became a successful banker and businessman in his own right before entering government service in 1940. He was ambassador to the Soviet Union (1943–1946) and chief administrator of the Marshall Plan (1948–1950). Later, as an ambassador-at-large, he held numerous other diplomatic posts. Harriman was also governor of New York during the 1950s.

HAWKINS, SIR JOHN (1532–1595). Like Sir Francis Drake, Hawkins was an English privateer who preyed on Spanish treasure ships. Hawkins, one of the first to engage in the slave trade before he became principal administrative officer of the royal navy, is credited with successfully redesigning the English fleet in order to meet the Spanish naval challenge.

HAY, JOHN (1838–1905). Secretary of state under Presidents William McKinley and *Theodore Roosevelt, John Hay formulated the Open Door policy, guaranteeing access to commerce in China, settled several outstanding Anglo-American problems, and negotiated the treaty with Panama that allowed the Panama Canal to be built.

HILFERDING, RUDOLF (1877–1941). The Austrian-born Hilferding, who later became a German citizen, played an active role in the German socialist movement. His principal work, *Das Finanz Kapital*, greatly influenced *Vladimir Lenin. Later Hilferding attacked Lenin and the Bolsheviks for their brutality, imperialism, and opportunism. Hilferding held several government posts during the Weimar Republic.

HIRSCH, ÉTIENNE (b. 1901). Teaming with *Jean Monnet and several other technocrats, Hirsch helped to create the European Economic Community. He also succeeded Monnet as director of France's post–World War II office for overall economic planning (1952–1959).

HISS, ALGER (b. 1904). Alger Hiss was a high-ranking State Department official during World War II, with particular responsibility for United Nations planning. In 1948 he was accused of having Communist ties; the subsequent investigation and trials drew much attention to the anti-Communist movement in the United States. Hiss eventually served nearly four years in jail for perjury.

HOBBES, THOMAS (1588–1679). Hobbes, an English philosopher, took a dim view of human nature and believed that men were incapable of governing themselves. His most important work was *Leviathan*.

HOBSON, JOHN (1858–1940). An English socialist, Hobson's 1902 book, *Imperialism*, argued that imperialism resulted from capitalism's desire for ever greater profits. *Vladimir Lenin essentially reiterated this claim in his *Imperialism as the Highest Stage of Capitalism* (1916).

HORN, PHILIP (1518–1568). A Dutch aristocrat, Horn, after first supporting *Philip II, joined with William of Orange to oppose the king's exercise of royal prerogative in the Netherlands. He also objected to Philip's religious and fiscal policies. With the arrival of the duke of Alba in the Netherlands, Horn was executed.

HOUSE, EDWARD M. (1858–1938). A Texas businessman and politician, Colonel House, as he was known, was for many years the closest foreign policy advisor of President *Woodrow Wilson. Between 1914 and 1916 House traveled in Europe seeking a negotiated settlement to the war. After American entry into the war, he served on the Allied Supreme War Council. In 1919 he broke with Wilson over the Treaty of Versailles.

HOWE, RICHARD, EARL (1726–1799). Born into a titled family, Howe became one of the most successful eighteenth-century British admirals. Undoubtedly his greatest triumph occurred at the Battle of the First of June (1794) when the British Channel fleet under his command caught and defeated the French Brest fleet under Villaret-Joyeuse.

HULL, CORDELL (1871–1955). Secretary of state during nearly the entire presidency of *Franklin D. Roosevelt, Hull was principally concerned with reciprocal trade relations and Latin American matters. During World War II he concentrated on United Nations planning, for which he received the Nobel Peace Prize in 1945.

JAY, JOHN (1745–1829). A member of the peace commission that negotiated the Treaty of Paris (1783), which gave the United States its independence, Jay was also secretary of foreign affairs (1784–1790) under the Articles of Confederation government and negotiated Jay's Treaty (1795), settling some outstanding differences with Great Britain.

KENNEDY, ROBERT (1925–1968). The brother of President John F. Kennedy, Robert Kennedy served as attorney general in his brother's administration and was elected to the U.S. Senate from New York in 1964. He became a critic of the Vietnam War and was contending for the Democratic party nomination for president when he was assassinated in 1968.

KHRUSHCHEV, NIKITA S. (1894–1971). Descended from peasants, in 1954 Nikita S. Khrushchev became first secretary of the Communist Party of the Soviet Union and, by virtue of this, leader of the USSR. Until his ouster ten years later, Khrushchev pursued a policy of peaceful coexistence with the capitalist world, patched up relations with *Tito's Yugoslavia, alienated Mao's China, and relaxed the rigid Stalinist system within the USSR.

KOCHUBEY, VICTOR (1768–1834). Count Kochubey first gained prominence as a member of Tsar *Alexander I's young kitchen cabinet, or "Unofficial Committee," where he proposed a number of reforms. Subsequently he held several government posts under both Alexander and his successor, Nicholas I, including diplomatic assignments to Sweden, Turkey, and Great Britain.

KONSTANTIN PAVLOVICH, GRAND DUKE (1779–1831). The brother of Russian tsar *Alexander I, Konstantin devoted his energies to military matters. Named commander in chief of the Polish army in 1815, he renounced his right to the Russian throne a few years later. Widely unpopular in Poland, Konstantin's brutal and incompetent ways contributed to the outbreak of the Polish Revolution of 1830–1831.

KRÜDENER, BARONESS JULIE DE (1764–1824). In her earlier years a very attractive and socially engaging Russian noblewoman, Julie Krüdener underwent a religious conversion in 1804. In her role as religious mystic she captivated Tsar *Alexander I and encouraged his romantic-pietistic tendencies.

LA HARPE, FRÉDÉRIC-CÉSAR DE (c. 1754–1838). *Catherine the Great selected La Harpe, a Swiss, to tutor her beloved grandson, the future Tsar *Alexander I. La Harpe's devotion to the ideals of liberalism left an indelible mark on his pupil, who nevertheless as ruler failed to transform these abstract concepts into a viable program.

LANSING, ROBERT (1864–1928). Secretary of state under President *Woodrow Wilson, Robert Lansing was a lawyer with much experience in various international arbitration proceedings and tribunals. As secretary of state, he negotiated the purchase of the Danish West Indies but broke with the president over the Treaty of Versailles, preferring to compromise with the Senate rather than have no treaty at all.

LAW, ANDREW BONAR (1858–1923). A Canadian-born Scot, Law was colonial secretary, 1915–1916, chancellor of the exchequer of the war cabinet, 1916–1918, lord of the privy seal, 1919–1921, and Conservative party prime minister, 1922–1923.

LEE, ARTHUR (1740–1792). Along with *Benjamin Franklin and Silas Deane, Lee sought to win European recognition and aid for the United States during its war for independence. His allegations that Deane was corrupt helped bring about the latter's recall.

LESSEPS, FERDINAND DE (1805–1894). Ferdinand de Lesseps was a French diplomat who interested himself in the Near East. Establishing an international company to build a canal connecting the Mediterranean and the Gulf of Suez, de Lesseps gained the support of *Napoleon III. The Suez Canal, begun in 1859, was opened ten years later.

LIPPMANN, WALTER (1889–1974). One of the most influential journalists in U.S. history, Walter Lippmann wrote for the *New Republic*, the *New York World* and *Herald Tribune* newspapers, and *Newsweek*. Over a fifty-year career, he espoused an internationalist foreign policy built around the notion of an Atlantic community. In the 1960s he was a leading critic of the war in Vietnam.

LOCKE, JOHN (1632–1704). An English philosophe, Locke endorsed the concepts of natural law, knowledge through experience and observation, and self-government. His most important works were *An Essay Concerning Human Understanding* and *Second Treatise on Civil Government*.

LODGE, HENRY CABOT, JR. (1902–1985). The grandson of Henry Cabot Lodge, Sr., Henry Cabot Lodge, Jr., served in the U.S. Senate (1936–1944, 1945–1953) and as ambassador to the United Nations (1953–1960). Later, he was ambassador to (South) Vietnam (1963–1964, 1965–1967), where he strongly defended U.S. policy. In 1969–1970 he was involved briefly in negotiations that sought to end the Vietnam War.

LODGE, HENRY CABOT, SR. (1850–1924). A longtime U.S. Senator and chairman of the Senate Foreign Relations Committee, Lodge is perhaps best known as the leading opponent of *Woodrow Wilson and the League of Nations. He was also a close friend and confidant of *Theodore Roosevelt.

LUDENDORFF, ERICH VON (1865–1937). As quartermaster general of the German army in World War I, Ludendorff, along with Paul von Hindenburg, chief of the General Staff, exercised virtual dictatorial power over Germany during the waning years of the war. After Germany's defeat, Ludendorff embarked upon an ultranationalistic course, going so far as to join former corporal *Adolf Hitler in Hitler's failed Beer Hall Putsch against the legitimate German government in November 1923.

MACARTHUR, DOUGLAS (1880–1964). A West Point graduate and military hero in the Pacific theater of World War II, Douglas MacArthur was supreme commander of the occupation of Japan (1945–1950). In that post, he ruled benignly but despotically and guided Japan toward democratic government and economic recovery. As commander of United Nations forces during the Korean War, he was relieved of duty by President Harry S. Truman because of insubordination after publicly questioning the administration's war policies.

MCCARTHY, JOSEPH (1908–1957). Elected to the U.S. Senate as a Republican from Wisconsin in 1946, Joseph McCarthy gained notoriety between 1950 and 1954 as the leading spokesman of a crusade against domestic communism, a movement that became known as McCarthyism.

MACDONALD, JAMES RAMSAY (1866–1937). Ramsay MacDonald was the most important leader of the British Labour party from 1911 until his break with the party in 1931. He served as prime minister in 1924 and from 1929 to 1931, and then headed a national government from 1931 to 1935. He opposed British entry into World War I and did much to shape Labour party foreign policy in the 1920s.

MCLANE, LOUIS (1786–1857). Louis McLane was minister to Great Britain (1829–1831) and secretary of the treasury under President Andrew Jackson (1831–1833) before becoming secretary of state in 1833. In a second stint as minister to Great Britain (1845–1846), he was involved in negotiations over Oregon.

MCNAMARA, ROBERT (b. 1919). After a business career, primarily with the Ford Motor Company, McNamara served as secretary of defense, 1961–1967, under Presidents Kennedy and Johnson. He resigned over policy differences with the Johnson administration concerning the Vietnam War.

MAGELLAN, FERDINAND (1480?–1521). A Spanish explorer, Magellan headed an expedition that circumnavigated the globe (1519–1522). Although Magellan died during the expedition, the voyage not only proved that the earth was round but also gave a fairly clear idea of how large it was.

MAO TSE-TUNG (1893–1976). One of the founders of the Chinese Communist party, Mao Tse-tung led his followers to victory over Chiang Kai-shek's Nationalists in the Chinese civil war (1946–1949). After his victory, Mao established a Communist regime in China with the support of the Soviet Union. Later he was to challenge the Soviets for leadership of the global Communist movement.

MARX, KARL (1818–1883). A German publicist, historian, philosopher, and sociologist, Karl Marx is generally regarded as the father of modern socialist theory. The most cogent synopsis of his ideas is his *Communist Manifesto* (1848).

MAZZINI, GIUSEPPE (1805–1872). One of the foremost theoreticians of modern nationalism, Mazzini believed that every national group possessed intrinsic value and should have the right to determine its own fate. He saw nationalism as the savior of Europe. Although he spent most of his life in exile, Mazzini played a major role in the drive for Italian unification, founding the Young Italy movement in 1831 and even briefly participating in the ill-fated, radical Roman Republic (1849).

MEDICI. One of the outstanding families of the Renaissance, the Medici, who were merchant princes, dominated Florence, using it as their power base in Italy. Important Medici included Cosimo (1389–1464), a major figure in Florentine politics; Lorenzo the Magnificent (1449–1492), who is as well known for his patronage of the arts as for his political exploits; Giovanni (1475–1521), who served as Pope Leo X; Giulio (1478–1534), who served as Pope Clement VII; Catherine (1519–1589), who as queen mother was a dominant force on the French scene in the latter half of the sixteenth century; and Marie (1573–1642), the wife of France's first Bourbon king, Henry IV.

MICHELS, ROBERT (1876–1936). A German-born political sociologist and economist who spent his adult life in Italy as an academic, Michels developed the "iron law of oligarchy," which states that voluntary organizations, particularly political parties, inevitably become oligarchic and authoritarian in their structure in order to meet organizational and societal demands such as quick decision making and a full-time commitment to the organization's cause. His elitist ideas helped to bolster ˙Mussolini's fascism.

MITTERAND, FRANÇOIS (b. 1916). An important figure in the French resistance during World War II, Mitterand emerged as leader of the Socialist party after the war. Mitterand, who is best described as a moderate socialist, was elected president of France in 1981 and reelected for a seven-year term in 1988.

MONTESQUIEU, CHARLES LOUIS BARON DE (1689–1755). An influential figure from the eighteenth-century Age of Reason, the French nobleman Montesquieu is probably most famous for his ideas about a system of checks and balances and the separation of powers as a way to limit governmental power. Both concepts eventually found their way into the American system of government.

MURAT, JOACHIM (1767–1815). An officer in ˙Napoleon I's cavalry who married the emperor's sister Caroline, Murat was placed on the throne of Naples in 1808 by Napoleon. He was forced to abdicate in 1815 when Napoleon fell.

NELSON, HORATIO (1758–1805). A famous English sailor, Nelson commanded the British naval force that destroyed the combined Spanish and French fleets off Cape Trafalgar on October 21, 1805.

NIETZSCHE, FRIEDRICH (1844–1900). An eccentric German philosopher, Nietzsche developed an antirational worldview that became popular after his death and greatly influenced the thinking of many twentieth-century figures. Condemning as a slave mentality such Christian ideals as faith, hope, and charity, Nietzsche endorsed courage, action, and will as model virtues. He glorified the "supreme" figure, who by sheer force of personality would lead and dominate the masses.

NORTH, FREDERICK, LORD (1732–1792). A British statesman who served as prime minister from 1770 to 1782, Lord North is perhaps best known for his failed policies in North America, which hastened the American Revolution.

NOVOSILTSEV, NIKOLAI (1761–1836). Illegitimate son of a Russian noblewoman, Novosiltsev first gained prominence as a friend of and advisor to the young Tsar *Alexander I. In 1804 Alexander sent him to Great Britain with a proposal for an alliance against *Napoleon I. After 1815, Novosiltsev represented the tsar in the newly created kingdom of Poland.

ORLOV, ALEKSEI (1737–1808). A Russian nobleman and brother of Gregory Orlov, Aleksei Orlov played a key role in the conspiracy that toppled Peter III and placed *Catherine the Great on the throne. Subsequently, he commanded the Russian fleet, which destroyed the Turkish fleet at the Battle of Chesme in 1770.

ORLOV, GREGORY (1734–1783). Teaming with other conspirators, including his brother Aleksei, Gregory Orlov helped to engineer the coup that overthrew Peter III and made *Catherine the Great ruler of Russia. Orlov, who for a number of years was Catherine's lover and closest advisor, urged an aggressive policy toward both Turkey and Poland.

PARETO, VILFREDO (1848–1923). An Italian economist and sociologist, Pareto, professor of political economy at the University of Lausanne in Switzerland, developed several complex theories endorsing the role of elites in society. Twentieth-century fascists such as *Benito Mussolini seized upon Pareto's ideas to justify their leadership positions and their actions.

PETER II (1923–1970). Upon the assassination of his father, King Alexander, in 1934, eleven-year-old Peter came to the throne of Yugoslavia. A regency under his uncle, Prince Paul, ruled in his stead until the eve of the German occupation of Yugoslavia. *Tito abolished the Yugoslav monarchy in 1945.

PLEVEN, RENÉ (1901–1993). Twice premier of France (1950–1951, 1951–1952), Pleven is perhaps best known for the Pleven Plan, which envisioned an integrated European army, the European Defense Community (EDC). When EDC failed to materialize, West German rearmament took place, and in 1955 West Germany joined NATO.

PORTER, HORACE (1837–1921). A West Point graduate and Civil War hero, Horace Porter served as ambassador to France (1897–1905), where he worked to get French compliance with the Open Door policy. He was a delegate to the Second Hague Peace Conference (1907) and successfully urged the acceptance of a variation of the Drago Doctrine.

PUGACHEV, EMILIAN (1726–1775). *See* Pugachev's Rebellion, Appendix C.

PYM, JOHN (1584–1643). Originally a gentleman farmer, Pym proved to be an effective leader of the parliamentary forces that challenged the absolutist inclinations of Charles I. By the time of his death, Pym had laid the groundwork for *Oliver Cromwell's successful struggle against the king.

ROBERTSON, SIR WILLIAM (1860–1933). General Robertson was a Scot who worked his way up through the ranks to become chief of staff for British forces in France in 1915 and then chief of the Imperial General Staff from 1915 to 1918, where he was a staunch supporter of Douglas Haig and a believer in the primacy of the western front.

ROCKEFELLER, NELSON A. (1908–1979). A grandson of the notable John D. Rockefeller, Nelson Rockefeller served in the State Department during World War II, specializing in Latin American policy. Later he was governor of New York (1958–1973) and U.S. vice-president (1974–1977).

RÖHM, ERNST (1887–1934). At one time a close personal friend of *Adolf Hitler, Röhm, head of the Nazi's SA or *Sturm Abteilungen*, was murdered on Hitler's orders during the "Night of the Long Knives" (June 30, 1934) when Hitler purged the ranks of the Nazis.

ROTHSCHILD, LIONEL DE (1808–1879). A leading member of the famous banking family, Rothschild came to prime minister *Benjamin Disraeli's rescue in 1875 when, on short notice, he floated a loan of £4 million to the British government in order for it to purchase the khedive's shares in the Suez Canal.

ROUSSEAU, JEAN JACQUES (1712–1778). A transitional figure from the late Enlightenment to the early stages of the Romantic era, Rousseau published extensively. His most important work was *The Social Contract*, which included elements of rudimentary democratic thought and embryonic nationalism. In his novels he tended to glorify the common man and the simple life.

RUSK, DEAN (b. 1909). Rusk, a career foreign policy maker who entered the State Department in 1947, climaxed his career as secretary of state, 1961–1969, under Presidents Kennedy and Johnson, where he was a strong supporter of the Vietnam War.

SALTER, SIR ARTHUR (1881–1975). During World War I, this British economist held a number of logistical command positions including director of ship requisitioning and secretary of the Allied Maritime Transport Council. Interrupting an academic career at Oxford University, Salter performed similar duties during World War II.

SAVONAROLA, GIROLAMO (1452–1498). A Dominican friar who came to Florence in 1481, Savonarola attracted many supporters and gained significant political influence after 1494 due to his attacks on worldliness. However, Savonarola overplayed his hand and was burned at the stake in 1498.

SFORZA. One of the outstanding families of the Italian Renaissance, the Sforza ruled as dukes of Milan. The death of the last Sforza in the early sixteenth century opened the way for renewed French and Spanish meddling in the Italian peninsula.

SLIDELL, JOHN (1793–1871). Minister to Mexico under President *James K. Polk, Slidell was unsuccessful in negotiating the purchase of New Mexico and California, later acquired through war. During the American Civil War, Slidell was the Confederate representative in France.

SMITH, ADAM (1723–1790). After studying at Glasgow and Oxford, Smith became a professor at Edinburgh, where he wrote *The Wealth of Nations* (1776). This seminal book promoted the concept of laissez faire, or the elimination of restrictions, especially governmental ones, on commerce and industry.

SOREL, GEORGES (1847–1922). A French intellectual, Georges Sorel was the father of revolutionary syndicalism, which envisioned rule by workers' unions following a successful general strike to paralyze society. Syndicalism, which by the early twentieth century embraced indiscriminate violence, a state of continued agitation, and disdain for the rational, gained a number of supporters in Spain, Italy, and France. Many of its ideas were subsequently borrowed by post–World War I fascist movements.

SPERANSKY, MICHAEL (1772–1839). Speransky was one of Tsar *Alexander I's closest advisors during the early years of the reign. His proposal for a Russian constitution came to naught, and he was dismissed in 1812 for his alleged pro-French attitude. Later, under Alexander's successor Nicholas I, Speransky was responsible for codifying Russian law.

STETTINIUS, EDWARD R., JR. (1900–1949). Secretary of state (1944–1945) at the end of World War II, Stettinius came to the office from a business career and had little foreign policy experience. He was, however, involved in the early activity of the United Nations and played an important role in conciliating major power differences.

STROGANOV, PAUL (1772–1817). Born into a rich and powerful family, Count Stroganov found favor with Tsar *Alexander I and joined the ruler's small, intimate circle of reforming friends called the "Unofficial Committee." Later he proved to be an effective commander of Russian military forces.

SULEIMAN THE MAGNIFICENT (1494–1566). Perhaps the most famous of all Turkish sultans, Suleiman came to the throne in 1520. A constant foe of first *Charles V and then *Philip II, Suleiman ruled over not only an Asian and African empire, but the Balkans and Hungary as well. Under his reign the Ottoman Empire reached its apex.

SULLY, MAXIMILIEN, DUC DE (1560–1641). Known chiefly for his exceptional work as King Henry IV of France's finance minister, Sully—in retirement—promoted the so-called Grand Design, which he attributed to his royal master. The Grand Design envisioned a confederation of Europe's Christian states, a concept that *Alexander I also promoted at the conclusion of the Napoleonic Wars.

TAFT, ROBERT A. (1889–1953). An Ohio Republican and son of President William Howard Taft, Robert Taft was elected to the U.S. Senate in 1938, where he voiced his opposition to the New Deal and U.S. involvement in the European war. After Pearl Harbor, however, he supported American entry into the war. Following World War II, he only reluctantly favored the Marshall Plan but was critical of NATO and Truman administration foreign policy generally.

THOMASIUS, CHRISTIAN (1655–1728). An important figure in the German Enlightenment, Thomasius wrote extensively about natural law, attacking religious prejudices in particular. He was a famous teacher as well and helped to found the University of Halle.

TRESCOT, WILLIAM H. (1822–1898). Trescot served briefly in a diplomatic role with the Confederacy during the American Civil War (1861–1865), but he saw more extensive diplomatic service in China and South America under Secretaries of State William M. Evarts and *James G. Blaine in the early 1880s.

TRIST, NICHOLAS (1800–1874). A career State Department official, Trist negotiated the Treaty of Guadalupe Hidalgo (1848), ending the U.S. war with Mexico.

TROTSKY, LEON (1879–1940). Born Lev Davidovich Bronstein, Leon Trotsky was active in the Russian social democratic movement from his youth. Something of a lone wolf in revolutionary circles, Trotsky teamed up with *Vladimir Lenin to engineer the successful Bolshevik Revolution in November 1917 and to sustain it during the civil war that followed. He was the Bolsheviks' first commissar for foreign affairs (1917–1918). After clashing with *Joseph Stalin, Trotsky went into exile, where he continued to play a major role in the international revolutionary movement until murdered in Mexico City by Stalin's agent.

TRUDEAU, PIERRE ELLIOTT (b. 1919). Leader of the Canadian Liberal party, Trudeau served as prime minister of Canada from 1969 to 1979 and from 1980 to 1984. During his time in office he beat back the Quebec separatist movement, which had been stimulated by intemperate remarks made by President *Charles de Gaulle of France during a state visit. Trudeau repaired Canada's relations with France after de Gaulle left office.

TURGENEV, IVAN (1818–1883). A Russian writer, Turgenev is most famous for his novel *Fathers and Sons*, which depicts generational tensions in nineteenth-century Russia.

ULBRICHT, WALTER (1893–1973). The Communist leader of East Germany, or the German Democratic Republic, Ulbricht faithfully followed the Soviet Union's international lead while erecting a rigid, uncompromising Stalinist regime at home that lasted until 1989. In 1971 he was replaced by the slightly more flexible Erich Honecker.

URI, PIERRE (1911–1991). Together with *Jean Monnet and several other experts, most of whom were French, Uri was instrumental in establishing the European Economic Community and promoting economic and social planning within Europe.

VOLTAIRE [Arouet, Francçis-Marie] (1694–1778). Perhaps the most important figure of the Enlightenment, Voltaire came to symbolize the eighteenth-century Age of Reason. His fame was universal throughout the Western world, and he maintained close relations not only with the leading intellectuals of the century but with major political figures as well, including *Catherine the Great and *Frederick the Great.

VORONTSOV, ALEXANDER (1741–1805). Tsar *Alexander I's chancellor during the early days of his reign, Count Vorontsov also served as minister of foreign affairs. As foreign minister, Vorontsov favored close ties with England and tried to distance Russia from *Napoleon I's France.

WELLES, BENJAMIN SUMNER (1892–1961). A career U.S. diplomat who figured prominently in Latin American and World War II policy making, Sumner Welles met with *Benito Mussolini, *Adolf Hitler, and *Neville Chamberlain during a swing through war-torn Europe in 1940.

WELLINGTON, DUKE OF [Arthur Wellesley] (1769–1852). Known primarily for his military exploits against *Napoleon I in Spain and at the Battle of Waterloo, the Duke of Wellington also served as Great Britain's prime minister (1828–1830). Wellington, who led the Tory party, was an arch-conservative whose views on liberalism and change in general matched those of *Metternich.

WILLIAM OF NASSAU, PRINCE OF ORANGE (1533–1584). Originally *Philip II's stadholder, or lieutenant, in Holland, William of Orange, also known as William the Silent, led the rebellious Dutch against Philip and his Spanish administrators. Although assassinated before the rebellion's outcome was determined, William was the driving force behind what was to be the Dutch victory and subsequent independence.

WILSON, HENRY LANE (1857–1932). A native of Indiana, Wilson served as minister or ambassador to several countries between 1897 and 1913. His most notable service was in Mexico, 1909–1913, where he earned criticism by siding with the coup that resulted in the assassination of the democratically inclined Francisco Madero.

WITT, JOHN DE (1625–1672). The chief minister of the United Provinces, John de Witt, aided by his brother Cornelius, guided Dutch policy from 1653 to 1672. Although he successfully opposed *Louis XIV when necessary, he preferred to placate the French king. Shortly after the election of William of Orange as stadholder, the de Witt brothers were murdered by a riotous crowd that blamed them for the French invasion of the United Provinces.

WOLFF, CHRISTIAN (1679–1754). A major figure of the German Enlightenment, Wolff advanced from the study of mathematics and physics to philosophy. His then controversial ideas on the supremacy of reason mired him in conflict with the religious and political authorities of the day, but his views appealed to many educated Germans including ˙Frederick the Great.

APPENDIX B

CONFERENCES AND TREATIES

ADAMS-ONÍS TREATY (1819). Also known as the Transcontinental Treaty, this agreement with Spain secured for the United States the territory of Florida and Spanish claims to the Oregon Territory, also claimed by Great Britain. It marked the first time the United States had legitimate claims to land on the Pacific coast.

AIX-LA-CHAPELLE, CONGRESS OF (1818). The first of the series of congresses following the end of the Napoleonic Wars, Aix-la-Chapelle provided for the end of the allied occupation of France on terms favorable to the Bourbons. The participants also discussed ways of restoring Spanish control over its newly independent American colonies. Great Britain opposed a Franco-Russian plan aimed at restoring the colonies through interventionist means short of direct military action.

ALASKA BOUNDARY TRIBUNAL (1903). Also known as the Alaska Arbitral Tribunal, this mixed commission included representatives from the United States and Great Britain and settled a long-standing dispute over the boundary between Alaska and Canada near the area of the Klondike gold discoveries of the 1890s.

ALGECIRAS CONFERENCE (1906). This international conference dealt with the Franco-German dispute over Morocco. *Theodore Roosevelt instigated the conference and worked behind the scenes to reconcile the points of controversy.

ALLIANCE FOR PROGRESS. Created during the administration of John F. Kennedy, the Alliance for Progress was an ambitious Latin American development and social reform program that was to be funded by a combination of U.S. government and private sources. Public funding for the Alliance fell far short of expectations, in part because of the demands of the Vietnam War, and after a decade the Alliance had generated very little development or reform.

AMIENS, TREATY OF (1802). This treaty brought about a truce in the Napoleonic Wars between France and Great Britain and enabled President *Thomas Jefferson to initiate the process that led to the purchase of the Louisiana Territory in 1803.

ANGLO-JAPANESE ALLIANCE (1902). This treaty was designed to isolate Russia and pledged Britain and Japan to the conditional defense of each other in the event of a Far Eastern war. It was superseded by the Four-Power Treaty in 1921, in which the United States, Britain, Japan, and France pledged to respect one another's interests in the Pacific.

ATLANTIC ALLIANCE. This is another name for the North Atlantic Treaty Organization, or NATO.

ATLANTIC CHARTER (1941). This statement, approved by *Franklin D. Roosevelt and *Winston Churchill at a conference in 1941, outlined the principles that should guide the Allies in World War II. It endorsed self-determination and access for all to raw materials and suggested a postwar organization to guarantee peace. The United States and Britain also abjured territorial gain as a result of the war.

BASEL, TREATY OF (1795). In the wake of the French republic's victories over the First Coalition, Prussia sued for peace at the Treaty of Basle. By the terms of the treaty French possession of the left bank of the Rhine was confirmed. Several months later Spain made a similar treaty with France at Basel, ceding Santo Domingo in the process.

BRETTON WOODS CONFERENCE (1944). Out of this conference came recommendations to establish the International Monetary Fund (IMF) and the International Bank for Reconstruction and Development (IBRD), also known as the World Bank. These two organizations were important in postwar reconstruction and continue to assist developing nations.

BRUSSELS CONFERENCE (1937). Sponsored by the League of Nations, this conference sought to deal with the crisis precipitated by Japan's invasion of China. The United States opposed any coercive measures, and the conference adjourned having done nothing more than verbally chastise the Japanese.

BRYAN-CHAMORRO TREATY (1916). Negotiated by Secretary of State William Jennings Bryan and Nicaraguan minister Emiliano Chamorro, this treaty granted the United States the right to build an isthmian canal across Nicaragua. The United States never exercised its right, and the treaty was abrogated in 1970.

BURLINGAME TREATY (1868). This treaty between the United States and China was negotiated by Anson Burlingame, a former U.S. minister to China. Among other things, the treaty guaranteed the right of Chinese to immigrate to the United States, a measure that provoked so much controversy that it was revoked and Chinese immigration was suspended.

CAIRO DECLARATION (1943). A statement issued at the close of a wartime conference among President *Franklin D. Roosevelt, Prime Minister *Winston Churchill, and Chinese Generalissimo Chiang Kai-shek. This avowed that Japan would be stripped of its conquests at the end of the war, that the Allies harbored no desire for territorial expansion, and that Korea would be restored as a free and independent nation.

CAMP DAVID AGREEMENT (1978). This agreement was negotiated between Israel and Egypt at Camp David, Maryland, with President Jimmy Carter as mediator. The agreement consisted of a framework for Israeli-Egyptian peace and a framework for a comprehensive Middle East settlement. The first was implemented in a 1979 Israeli-Egyptian treaty; the second never has been.

CLAYTON-BULWER TREATY (1850). This treaty between the United States and Great Britain provided that any Central American canal or other transportation means would be under joint control. It was superseded in 1901 by the Hay-Pauncefote Treaty, which granted the United States the exclusive right to build and operate an isthmian canal.

CONGRESS OF VIENNA (1814–1815). Meeting in the Austrian capital at the conclusion of the Napoleonic Wars, the Congress of Vienna redrew the map of Europe and defined European political orthodoxy according to the precepts of its major participants, including *Metternich, *Castlereagh, *Talleyrand, and *Alexander I. As a result of the Congress of Vienna, several displaced rulers were returned to their thrones, liberalism as a doctrine was condemned, and nationalism as a political force was ignored.

CONVENTION OF 1818. This treaty between the United States and Great Britain settled several issues left over from the War of 1812. Most important, it established 49° north latitude as the U.S.-Canadian boundary from the Lake of the Woods to the Rocky Mountains.

CSCE (CONFERENCE ON SECURITY AND COOPERATION IN EUROPE). Comprising the United States and nearly every European nation, the CSCE met between 1973 and 1975 and issued the Helsinki Declaration, which contained a number of principles related to European security matters as well as measures for cooperation in economic, scientific, and environmental areas.

EUROPEAN ADVISORY COMMISSION (1943). This was a body established by the Allied foreign ministers in World War II to consider issues pertaining to the terms of surrender that might arise at that time. It could make suggestions for common action but had no real authority.

FIVE-POWER TREATY (1922). *See* Washington Naval Treaty (1922).

GENEVA DISARMAMENT CONFERENCE (1932–1934). Also known as the World Disarmament Conference, this international meeting convened annually for three years but accomplished nothing of substance, especially after the German decision in 1933 to renounce the Treaty of Versailles and rearm.

GENOA CONFERENCE (1922). At this postwar conference, European leaders tried to settle problems left over from the war, including German reparations, the international status of Soviet Russia, and Allied war debts. The United States did not attend, and the conference failed to settle any of the major disputes.

GERMAN-SOVIET NON-AGGRESSION PACT. *See* Nazi-Soviet Non-Aggression Pact.

GHENT, TREATY OF (1814). This treaty between the United States and Great Britain ended the War of 1812 and led to subsequent agreements and a long period of amicable relations between the two nations.

GOOD NEIGHBOR POLICY. This U.S. policy of friendlier and more equitable relations with Latin America was largely implemented during the *Franklin D. Roosevelt administration. It involved the creation of reciprocal trade agreements and a renouncement by the United States of its policy of intervention.

GUADALUPE HIDALGO, TREATY OF (1848). This treaty brought an end to the war between the United States and Mexico. The United States acquired most of what is now the southwestern part of the country for a payment of $15 million plus the assumption of $3.25 million in American claims against Mexico.

HAGUE PEACE CONFERENCES (1899 and 1907). These two international conferences, held at The Hague, Netherlands, dealt principally with the question of arbitration. The 1899 conference established a Permanent Court of Arbitration, while the 1907 conference improved the procedures for voluntary arbitration.

HAY-HERRAN TREATY (1903). This proposed treaty between the United States and Colombia would have provided for the construction of an isthmian canal across the then Colombian province of Panama. When it was rejected by the Colombian senate, President *Theodore Roosevelt supported Panamanian independence and signed a canal treaty with Panama later the same year.

HELSINKI ACCORDS (1975). These were agreements emanating from a meeting of the Conference on Security and Cooperation in Europe (CSCE) and involved a wide variety of issues, some of which had the effect of formally ratifying the Soviet hegemony over Eastern Europe that had existed since the end of World War II.

HOLY ALLIANCE (1815). Following twenty-six years of revolution, war, and upheaval, the Great Powers met at Vienna in 1814–1815 to make peace for Europe. During the course of the Congress of Vienna, the Russian tsar, *Alexander I, proposed that traditional diplomacy, including the concept of the balance of power, be jettisoned in favor of a new world order based on Christian principles. This Holy Alliance was rejected by Viscount *Castlereagh, who called it "sublime nonsense," but Austria and Prussia endorsed the tsar's proposal. Subsequently, the Holy Alliance came to be seen as a vehicle by which the three conservative eastern monarchies could suppress liberalism and nationalism.

IMPERIAL ECONOMIC CONFERENCE (1932). At this conference, held in Ottawa, British leaders tried to develop a system of free trade within the empire. They failed, however, when depression-ridden dominions felt that they had to protect their own producers of raw materials and foodstuffs.

INF TREATY (1987). This treaty between the United States and the Soviet Union marked the first time that nuclear armaments were actually reduced in number, with each side destroying a certain number of medium-range offensive missiles. The treaty also featured asymmetrical missile reductions and an unprecedentedly intrusive verification procedure.

INTERMEDIATE NUCLEAR FORCE TREATY (1987). See INF Treaty.

JAY'S TREATY (1794). Named for U.S. diplomat John Jay, this treaty with Great Britain brought about British evacuation from forts in the Northwest Territory but did not achieve for the United States trading rights in the British West Indies. It was an unpopular treaty, but it did prevent a likely war between the two nations.

KISSINGER COMMISSION (1983). See National Bipartisan Commission on Central America.

LAIBACH, CONGRESS OF (1821). When Great Britain and France failed to endorse *Clemens Metternich's Troppau Protocol, the Austrian chancellor with his Prussian and Russian allies adjourned to Laibach, where they affirmed the right of the Great Powers to intervene against revolution wherever and whenever it surfaced. Bolstered by this support, Metternich sent Austrian forces to crush the Neapolitan revolution.

LONDON CONFERENCE (1831). Occasioned by the successful revolt of the Belgians against their Dutch masters, the London Conference saw *Palmerston and *Talleyrand work out an agreement whereby Belgian independence was recognized. According to the agreement, Belgium would be perpetually neutral. The Great Powers also pledged themselves to guarantee Belgium against invasion.

LONDON ECONOMIC CONFERENCE (1933). Also known as the World Economic Conference, this meeting brought together delegates from virtually every nation in the world to seek an end to the global depression. When the United States refused to stabilize the value of the dollar, which had been removed from the gold standard, the conference was stalemated and adjourned.

MOLOTOV-RIBBENTROP PACT. See Nazi-Soviet Non-Aggression Pact.

MONROE-PINCKNEY TREATY (1806). This proposed treaty, named for U.S. diplomats James Monroe and William Pinckney, would have liberalized British trade policy with respect to the United States. But because it was silent on the question of impressment of U.S. seamen, President *Thomas Jefferson refused to submit it to the U.S. Senate for ratification.

MUNICH CONFERENCE (1938). Desperate to maintain peace in Europe, Great Britain's *Neville Chamberlain, aided by France's Edouard Daladier, met with Germany's *Adolf Hitler at Munich in September 1938. Italy's *Benito Mussolini was also present. The ensuing Munich Conference endorsed Hitler's demands on Czechoslovakia, thereby destroying that state's independence. The Munich Conference represented the height of appeasement.

NATIONAL BIPARTISAN COMMISSION ON CENTRAL AMERICA (1983). This commission was appointed by the Ronald Reagan administration to make recommendations to the administration with respect to its policy in Central America. Headed by *Henry Kissinger, the commission generally supported what the administration was already doing in the region but also recommended a five-year, $8 billion economic aid program for Central America. The commission was also, and more popularly, known as the Kissinger Commission.

NAZI-SOVIET NON-AGGRESSION PACT (1939). Signed by *Joseph Stalin's Soviet Union and *Adolf Hitler's Nazi Germany on August 23, 1939, the Nazi-Soviet Non-Aggression Pact bound the signatories to refrain from attacking each other. An additional, secret protocol divided the Baltic states and Poland between Germany and the USSR.

NINE-POWER TREATY (1922). Negotiated and signed at the Washington Naval Conference, this treaty pledged its signatories to guarantee the territorial integrity of China and support equal commercial opportunity there. The treaty was a public international affirmation of the Open Door policy.

NUCLEAR NON-PROLIFERATION TREATY (1968). The Nuclear Non-Proliferation Treaty was an attempt by the superpowers to prevent the spread of nuclear weapons to nonnuclear countries. One of the more dramatic examples of superpower cooperation, the treaty was ratified by the United Nations and signed by most of the world's states. However, it lacked an effective enforcement mechanism and has been breached by a number of nations.

OLMÜTZ PUNCTATION (1850). Against a backdrop of rivalry for preeminence in the German-speaking lands, Austria and Prussia almost came to blows in 1850 over a complex but insignificant question concerning the German state of Hesse-Kassel. At the last instant Prussia backed down, signing the Olmütz Punctation, which acknowledged Austria's right to impose a settlement on Hesse-Kassel and which signaled a significant triumph for Austria in its struggle with Prussia.

PARIS, DECLARATION OF (1856). This was a multilateral agreement providing protection for enemy goods on neutral ships, except for contraband, and asserting that a blockade, to be recognized, must be effective.

PARIS, TREATY OF (1763). Concluding the hostilities between Great Britain and France at the end of the Seven Years War, the Treaty of Paris dealt very leniently with a defeated France, which surrendered to Britain only mainland Canada, several Caribbean islands, and the British conquests in India. The conciliatory nature of the treaty greatly angered *William Pitt the Elder, who had been the architect of Britain's victory.

PEACE OF WESTPHALIA (1648). Marking the end of the Thirty Years War, the Peace of Westphalia signaled the failure of the Habsburg bid for supremacy in Europe. The Peace of Westphalia also stopped the Counter-Reformation in Germany, although it did not roll it back. Germany was now divided into more than 300 states, each of which was virtually sovereign.

PINCKNEY'S TREATY (1795). This treaty, named for U.S. envoy Thomas Pinckney, settled various problems between the United States and Spain. Most important, the United States gained navigation rights on the Mississippi River. The pact is also known as the Treaty of San Lorenzo.

PORTSMOUTH, TREATY OF (1905). This treaty ended the Russo-Japanese War (1904–1905). Engineered by President *Theodore Roosevelt, who won the Nobel Peace Prize for his efforts, the treaty forced Russia out of Korea and parts of Manchuria but did not give the Japanese, the military victors, all they wanted.

POTSDAM CONFERENCE (1945). Held in a suburb of Berlin not long after the end of World War II in Europe, this conference included President Harry Truman, *Winston Churchill (replaced in mid-conference by Clement Attlee), and *Joseph Stalin. Issues under discussion included German occupation questions and reparations.

QUADRUPLE ALLIANCE (1814). Entered into by Austria, Great Britain, Prussia, and Russia in March 1814, the Quadruple Alliance sought to defeat *Napoleon I. After achieving its initial goal, it was renewed in November 1815, with the object being the preservation of European tranquility. To that end, the Quadruple Alliance aimed to prevent Napoleon and his family from ever coming to power in France again, and to keep France from falling into revolution. It also called for the four signatories to hold periodic meetings to consult with each other and to consider measures to keep the peace in Europe. In 1818 the alliance was expanded to include France under its restored Bourbon monarchs.

QUINTUPLE ALLIANCE (1818). See Quadruple Alliance.

RE-INSURANCE TREATY (1887). One of *Otto von Bismarck's greatest triumphs, the Re-insurance treaty allied Russia to the German Empire. When the treaty came up for renewal in 1890, *William II, who had dismissed Bismarck, refused to renew it, thus "breaking the line" between Berlin and St. Petersburg and virtually forcing a now isolated Russia to find an ally in Germany's enemy, France.

REPARATIONS COMMISSION (1919). Established at the Paris Peace Conference following World War I, this commission was empowered to fix the amount of reparations and to collect them from Germany. In 1921 the commission decided to include Allied pensions in the sum, raising the total owed to an unmanageable sum and contributing to economic chaos in postwar Germany.

RIO TREATY (1947). This inter-American mutual defense treaty provides for regional security and was the model for other such treaties, including the North Atlantic Treaty, that were signed by the United States and its allies in the early years of the Cold War.

RUSH-BAGOT AGREEMENT (1817). An agreement between the United States and Great Britain in the wake of the War of 1812, this pact largely demilitarized the Great Lakes, limiting the use of naval vessels to the enforcement of revenue laws.

RUSSO-GERMAN NON-AGGRESSION PACT. See Nazi-Soviet Non-Aggression Pact.

SALT I (1972). SALT is an acronym for Strategic Arms Limitation Talks. SALT I, the treaty that emerged from these talks between the United States and the Soviet Union, contained a number of agreements designed to limit the growth of nuclear weapons arsenals and thus ease global tensions. Included in SALT I were an antiballistic missile treaty and an interim agreement on strategic offensive weapons. SALT represented a major aspect of the policy known as détente.

SÈVRES, TREATY OF (1920). This was the treaty between the victorious Allies and Turkey ending World War I. It partitioned the Ottoman Empire of the Turks and in general was very vindictive. It was replaced by the more accommodating Treaty of Lausanne (1923).

START. This acronym stands for Strategic Arms Reduction Talks, a process begun in 1982, interrupted in 1983, and resumed in 1985. Still ongoing, START aims at the reduction of U.S. and Soviet strategic offensive weapons by 50 percent over a seven-year period. The dissolution of the Soviet Union in 1991 placed START in diplomatic limbo.

TESCHEN, TREATY OF (1779). The Treaty of Teschen, which ended the War of the Bavarian Succession, confirmed Austria's failure to expand at the expense of Bavaria. Mediated by ˚Catherine the Great's Russia, the treaty seemed to legitimize Russia's entry onto the German stage, but this proved to be illusory.

TIENTSIN, TREATY OF (1858). This treaty with China opened up several ports to U.S. commerce, granted Americans the right to travel freely in China, and legalized the opium trade. Great Britain, Russia, and France signed similar treaties with China at the same time.

TRANSCONTINENTAL TREATY (1819). *See* Adams-Onís Treaty.

TROPPAU, CONGRESS OF (1820). Fearing the consequences of a revolution in Naples, ˚Clemens Metternich invited the Great Powers to Troppau in order to condemn revolutionary behavior and to coordinate action against it. Metternich produced the Troppau Protocol, which rejected any changes brought about by revolution and reserved for the Great Powers the right to intervene at their pleasure to destroy such changes.

VERONA, CONGRESS OF (1822). The last of the congresses dating back to Aix-la-Chapelle (1818), the Congress of Verona foreshadowed the end of the Concert of Europe. Called to deal with the problems of rebellion in Spain's American colonies, revolution in Spain itself, and Alexander Ypsilanti's attempt to raise the Greeks in the Ottoman Empire, the congress encouraged France to intervene in Spain and left Ypsilanti to his fate. Britain, however, strongly opposed any suggestion that the congress restore Spain's colonies.

VIENNA ACCORDS. *See* Congress of Vienna.

WAR GUILT CLAUSE. Article 231 of the 1919 Treaty of Versailles, or the War Guilt Clause, laid responsibility for starting the disastrous World War I solely on the aggression of Germany and its allies. Designed to justify the imposition of reparations on Germany, the War Guilt Clause angered Germans from all walks of life and hardened their determination to destroy the Treaty of Versailles.

WARSAW PACT. This was a Soviet-East European alliance created in 1955 as a response to the North Atlantic Treaty Organization (NATO). Under its provisions, the Soviet Union maintained many thousands of troops and much equipment in Poland, Czechoslovakia, Hungary, East Germany, and other Eastern European states. The Warsaw Treaty Organization, as it was formally known, was dissolved in 1990.

WASHINGTON CONFERENCE (1907). This conference brought together delegates from the Central American nations to discuss their mutual problems under the aegis of the United States and Mexico. The most important accomplishment was the creation of a Central American Court of Justice to adjudicate future disputes.

WASHINGTON NAVAL TREATY (1922). Also known as the Five-Power Treaty, this pact established ratios of naval strength among the five largest naval powers in the post–World War I world. In it, the United States and Great Britain were granted parity in capital ship tonnage, while Japan, France, and Italy consented to lesser amounts.

YALTA CONFERENCE (1945). This was a World War II conference that brought *Franklin Roosevelt, *Winston Churchill, and *Joseph Stalin together at the Soviet resort of Yalta three months before the end of the war. Many important issues concerning the postwar world were discussed, including the future of Germany and eastern Europe, the United Nations, and Soviet entry into the Pacific war.

ZIMMERWALD CONFERENCE (1915). The first of several conferences (Kienthal, 1916; Stockholm, 1917) held by European socialists during World War I, the Zimmerwald Conference called for peace ''without annexations or indemnities.''

DIPLOMATIC, POLITICAL, AND MILITARY EVENTS

ACHESON-LILIENTHAL REPORT (1946). This report dealt with the ways in which atomic energy might be placed under international control through licensing and inspection procedures handled by the United Nations. Before it reached the United Nations, however, it was replaced by a plan devised by Bernard Baruch that later proved unacceptable to the Soviet Union.

ANSCHLUSS (1938). In March 1938, *Adolf Hitler marched into Austria and annexed it to his Third Reich. The European democracies greeted the annexation, or Anschluss, passively, thereby encouraging Hitler's aggressive, expansionist foreign policy.

ARMY OF ITALY. One of the armies raised by the French revolutionaries, the Army of Italy came under *Napoleon I's command in 1796. Sweeping into northern Italy, the Army of Italy defeated the Austrian forces stationed there. Napoleon's spectacular victories not only secured the Po valley for France, but also gave a tremendous boost to the general's career.

AUSTERLITZ, BATTLE OF (1805). *Napoleon I's most famous victory occurred on December 2, 1805, when he crushed a combined Austro-Russian army near the village of Austerlitz in Moravia. In the wake of this defeat, Austria was forced to seek peace while Russia withdrew its troops from central Europe.

BAD EMS DISPATCH (1870). Anxious to provide an excuse for war against France, *Otto von Bismarck seized upon a telegram sent to him by his sovereign, William I, from the resort of Bad Ems describing an interview between the king and French ambassador to Prussia Vincente Benedetti. Editing the telegram in a way that made the interview appear to be insulting to both the Prussians and the French, Bismarck released the dispatch to the press. Pandemonium ensued in both Berlin and Paris, and war followed shortly thereafter.

BALFOUR DECLARATION (1917). Named for Sir Arthur Balfour, this British declaration asserted that Palestine, then predominantly inhabited by Arabs, should become a national homeland for Jewish people.

BAY OF PIGS INVASION (1961). Undertaken by the Central Intelligence Agency for the purpose of overthrowing the government of *Fidel Castro in Cuba, the Bay of Pigs invasion was a military fiasco and a huge embarrassment for the John F. Kennedy administration, which had been in office less than three months.

BEER HALL PUTSCH (1923). Organized by *Adolf Hitler and staged in the streets of Munich, the Beer Hall Putsch was a failed attempt to overthrow the Weimar Republic. In his subsequent trial, Hitler gained national notoriety while receiving a five-year sentence, of which he served less than one year.

BELGIAN REVOLUTION (1830). Inspired by the July Revolution in France, the Belgians successfully rebelled against the Dutch monarchy, to which they had been joined by the Congress of Vienna. Belgium, a new state, was created. A constitutional monarchy that pledged to remain perpetually neutral, Belgium was guaranteed against invasion by the Great Powers.

BERLIN BLOCKADE (1948–1949). This important Cold War crisis involved the closing of land access to the Western occupation zones of Berlin, which lay well inside the Soviet zone of Germany. In response, the United States and its allies supplied their zones in Berlin with food, fuel, and medicines by air in the famous Berlin airlift. The Soviet Union lifted the blockade after eleven months.

BERLIN CRISIS (1958–1962). This Cold War crisis involved the fear that the USSR would sign a separate treaty with East Germany, turning over control of access to West Berlin to the East Germans, who were greatly troubled by an outflow of refugees to the West. The treaty was never signed, and the refugee problem was largely solved by the erection of the Berlin Wall in 1961, but tensions remained high for quite some time.

BERLIN WALL. Constructed in August 1961 to halt the exodus of people from East Germany, the Berlin Wall separated East Berlin from West Berlin. The wall came to represent the post–World War II division of Europe in general and Germany specifically. A continual source of irritation between East and West, the Berlin wall was destroyed in November 1989, thereby signaling the end of the Communist regime in East Germany and clearing the way for German reunification.

BOER WAR (1899–1902). This war pitted British troops against Afrikaaner, or Dutch, settlers in southern Africa and represented an effort to bring the Boer Republics of Transvaal and the Orange Free State into the British Empire. While the unpopular war did not bring any immediate results, the Boer Republics were incorporated into the Union of South Africa in 1912.

BOXER REBELLION (1900). The Boxers were a secret society in China which, with the support of the government, launched a terrorist campaign against foreigners in 1900. A multinational military force relieved the diplomatic community, under siege in Peking, and diplomatic pressure finally resulted in the suppression of the Boxers.

CAPORETTO ROUT (1917). Caporetto was a World War I battle in northeastern Italy in which German and Austro-Hungarian troops broke through Italian defenses and threatened Venice.

CARLSBAD DECREES (1819). Alarmed by signs of rising German nationalism, *Clemens Metternich seized on the murder of conservative playwright August Kotzebue to assemble the principal German states at Carlsbad, where he easily persuaded them to issue a set of decrees imposing harsh control over the German press and universities and dissolving the Burschenschaften, or German student societies. The Carlsbad Decrees retarded liberalism and nationalism in Germany for many years.

CONNALLY RESOLUTION (1943). This resolution, named for Texas senator Tom Connally and passed by the U.S. Senate in 1943, pledged that the United States would join a postwar international organization established to maintain peace.

CONTADORA PROCESS (1983–1985). This was a series of discussions at several separate meetings among delegates from Panama, Mexico, Venezuela, and Colombia seeking to find a peaceful resolution to the problems in Central America. The process received only limited support from the United States and never really succeeded in its objectives.

CORN LAWS. In 1815 Parliament passed the Corn Laws, or protective tariffs on imported grain, in order to protect Great Britain's landed interests. The tariffs were so high that importation of grain virtually ceased and the price of food rose accordingly. In turn, the Corn Laws provoked fierce opposition from the masses and from industrialists who had to pay their workers higher wages for subsistence. In 1846 Parliament repealed the Corn Laws, thereby ushering in an era of free trade.

CRIMEAN WAR (1853–1856). Ostensibly fought over the question of who was to control the Christian shrines in the Holy Land, the Crimean War was in fact an unintended struggle pitting Great Britain and France against Russia over the question of influence in the declining Ottoman Empire. After two years of generally inconclusive combat on Russia's Crimean peninsula, the Treaty of Paris (1856) was signed, which weakened Russia but failed to end either that state's ambitions in the Balkans or its desire to dominate the Ottoman Empire.

CUBAN MISSILE CRISIS (1962). When U.S. surveillance planes noted the installation by the Soviet Union of nuclear missiles in Cuba, the John F. Kennedy administration demanded that they be removed and instituted a naval quarantine around Cuba to prevent more missiles from getting to the island. After several days of high international tension, the Soviets agreed to remove the missiles in return for a U.S. pledge not to invade Cuba.

DECEMBRIST REVOLT (1825). Rising discontent with conditions in Russia and Tsar Alexander I's failure to fulfill his promises of reform prompted disgruntled army officers who had been exposed to western Europe following the Napoleonic Wars to form secret societies. In the confusion occasioned by Alexander's death, these malcontents, known as the Decembrists after the month in which they rose, staged an unsuccessful revolution, which was crushed with ferocity by the new tsar, Nicholas I. The example of the Decembrist Revolt inspired a number of future Russian revolutionaries.

DOMINICAN INTERVENTION (1965). Following the outbreak of a revolution in the Dominican Republic's capital, Santo Domingo, the Lyndon Johnson administration sent U.S. Marines to the scene, ostensibly to protect U.S. lives and property, but also to prevent the establishment of a Communist-oriented government.

ESSEX CASE (1805). This British admiralty court case resulted in a decision that essentially made it more difficult for American commercial interests to engage in legitimate re-export trade without harassment from British naval forces. It was one of the factors that contributed to the War of 1812 between the United States and Great Britain.

FALKLAND ISLANDS WAR (1982). This war was the result of a dispute between Argentina and Great Britain over the sovereignty of the Falkland, or Malvinas, Islands in the South Atlantic Ocean. After Argentina invaded and seized control of the islands, the British responded with military force and brought about Argentina's surrender after ten weeks of fighting.

FLIGHT TO VARENNES (1791). Having decided to abandon the new system imposed upon him by the French Revolution, Louis XVI and his family attempted to flee in order to rally loyal supporters and to seek help abroad to defeat the revolution. However, he was apprehended at Varennes in Lorraine and returned to Paris. Although Louis was permitted to rule as a constitutional monarch after his return, the flight to Varennes seriously damaged his credibility.

FREE FRENCH MOVEMENT. In the wake of Nazi Germany's stunning conquest of France in spring 1940, a number of French resistance groups came into existence. The most important of these was the Free French National Committee under the leadership of *Charles de Gaulle. The Free French consistently harassed the German occupiers and aided the Allies, thereby playing an important role in the liberation of France and establishing de Gaulle's legitimacy as a French leader.

GOVERNMENT OF INDIA ACT (1919). This act of the British Parliament rejected many liberal reforms recommended by a select committee, including more local self-government. Instead, it made only minor changes in the authority of colonial governors.

GREAT PATRIOTIC WAR (1941–1945). This term is commonly used by the citizens of the former Soviet Union to describe World War II. Attacked by Nazi Germany on the night of June 21/22, 1941, the Soviet Union suffered perhaps as many as 20 million casualties before Germany's surrender in May 1945.

GREAT WHITE FLEET. This was the name applied to the world cruise of the U.S. Navy, 1907–1909, authorized by President *Theodore Roosevelt as both a gesture of international goodwill and a frank display of U.S. naval power.

GREEK REVOLT (1821–1830). Symptomatic of the decline of the Ottoman Empire, the Greek revolt attracted the attention and later support of such Great Powers as France, Great Britain, and Russia. However, Austria under *Metternich opposed it as a threat to the European balance of power and as destructive of the principle of legitimacy. The London Protocol (1830) ratified the revolt's success by conferring independence upon Greece.

GULF OF TONKIN RESOLUTION (1964). The U.S. Congress passed this resolution in August 1964 following reports of two incidents in which North Vietnamese patrol boats had attacked U.S. naval vessels. The resolution gave President Lyndon Johnson a free hand to prosecute the war in Vietnam and cleared the way for the introduction of U.S. combat forces.

IRISH FREE STATE ACT (1922). This act of the British Parliament endorsed the constitution for the Irish Free State, which was composed of the twenty-six counties of southern Ireland. The act confirmed the independence of Ireland in virtually every respect, although the nation remained a dominion within the British Commonwealth.

IRISH REBELLION (1798). Disgusted with English rule and inspired by the example of the French Revolution, a handful of Irish radicals led by a young lawyer, Wolfe Tone, staged an unsuccessful rebellion in the summer of 1798. Effective French assistance failed to materialize, and the rebellion was quickly crushed. Viscount *Castlereagh played a major role in suppressing the rebellion, while the festering Irish problem, of which the rebellion was only the most spectacular manifestation, eventually brought down the government of *Pitt the Younger.

JERBA, BATTLE OF (1560). Contesting the Ottoman Turks in the Mediterranean, *Philip II established a garrison on the island of Jerba off the eastern coast of Tunisia. The Turks, however, besieged the island, destroyed a Spanish fleet sent to break the siege, and wiped out the garrison.

JULY REVOLUTION (1830). Frustrated by Charles X's reactionary policies, which threatened to strip it of any political power, the French bourgeoisie in July 1830 joined with other disaffected elements who sought either a republic or improved economic conditions to oust France's last Bourbon ruler. A constitutional monarchy with Charles's cousin, Louis Philippe of the house of Orleans, on the throne replaced the Bourbon monarchy.

JUNE UPRISING (1953). Chafing under a Stalinist dictatorship and enraged by increased work norms with no corresponding increase in the standard of living, workers in East Berlin spontaneously took to the streets on June 17, 1953. Within a few hours, demonstrations mushroomed into a full-scale uprising with political as well as economic overtones. The uprising was suppressed only when Soviet tanks intervened.

KULTURKAMPF (1872–1887). Initiated by the German chancellor, *Otto von Bismarck, who was suspicious of the Vatican's influence in German and European affairs, the Kulturkampf was an unsuccessful attempt to crush the power of the Roman Catholic Church in Germany.

LEND-LEASE (1941–1945). Lend-Lease, authorized by the U.S. Congress, sought to help countries friendly to the United States fight the war against *Hitler without directly involving the United States. Under the program, military equipment was provided to allies with the understanding that it would be returned after the war. Once the United States entered the war, however, Lend-Lease became an organization to facilitate the pooling of resources for a common goal.

LEPANTO, BATTLE OF (1571). Aroused by Turkish encroachments in the Mediterranean, *Philip II of Spain joined the papal-sponsored Holy League, which vowed to stop Ottoman expansion. A huge fleet led by Philip's half-brother, Don Juan, annihilated the Turks at Lepanto off the western coast of Greece; however, jealousy and inaction allowed the fruits of this victory to slip through the fingers of the Christian forces.

LEVÉE EN MASSE (1793). On August 23, 1793, the revolutionary National Convention ordered a levée en masse for France. This envisioned the total mobilization of France's human and material resources for the purpose of defending the revolution against its enemies. The example of a nation in arms provided by the levée en masse has gained popularity, especially in the twentieth century.

MARSHALL PLAN (1948–1952). Named for Secretary of State *George C. Marshall, the Marshall Plan was a massive economic aid program designed to stimulate European recovery after World War II and stave off a perceived Communist threat in western Europe during the early Cold War years. In four years, the United States provided nearly $14 billion in aid, mostly to Great Britain, France, and West Germany.

MONROE DOCTRINE (1823). The Monroe Doctrine was a unilateral pronouncement by the United States asserting that European (or other) nations should not create new colonies or attempt to regain former colonies in the Western Hemisphere. In return, the United States pledged to keep out of European affairs. In time, it became a hallmark of U.S. foreign policy, denoting that the United States considered the Western Hemisphere its sphere of influence.

MOSCOW TRIALS (1936–1938). Part of *Joseph Stalin's systematic campaign to eliminate all real or imaginary opposition to his iron rule, the Moscow trials featured prominent Communists confessing to fantastic transgressions such as a lifetime commitment to spying for capitalist states.

MUTUAL DEFENSE ASSISTANCE ACT (1949). This act was the first of many passed by Congress to provide military aid to Europe. It appropriated $1.5 billion for that purpose in 1949 and was the financial underpinning for the newly created NATO.

NEUTRALITY ACTS (1935–1937). A series of three acts passed by Congress, these were designed to keep the United States out of a future European war by removing the causes that many felt had pushed the United States unwisely into World War I. Most of their provisions were removed in a 1939 neutrality act.

NIXON DOCTRINE (1969). President *Richard Nixon revealed this change in U.S. foreign policy in 1969 as a response to criticism of the Vietnam War. The doctrine stated that while the United States would maintain its nuclear umbrella over the Far East and continue to provide military supplies to allies there, Asian troops rather than U.S. troops would have to fight any future land war in that part of the world.

NORMANDY INVASION (1944). Only after defeating the German army in North Africa and successfully invading Italy did the combined Anglo-American military force undertake a cross-channel invasion. Landing on the Normandy beaches on June 6, 1944, the British and the Americans soon established a foothold in France and moved on to liberate Paris in August.

NUREMBERG TRIALS (1945–1946). In an effort to discredit the Nazis in the eyes of the Germans, the victorious World War II allies (France, Great Britain, the United States, and the USSR) put the captured leaders of the Third Reich on trial at Nuremberg. Charging the defendants with crimes against humanity and world peace, the tribunal convicted and executed most of them. Some observers questioned the precedent of prosecuting leaders of a defeated state, while others worried about the appearance of ''victors' justice.''

NYE COMMITTEE (1934–1936). A U.S. Senate committee headed by Gerald Nye, a North Dakota Republican, the Nye Committee looked into the political influence of the banking and munitions industries in the years just before U.S. entrance into World War I. The committee's findings were influential in the passage of a series of Neutrality Acts by Congress between 1935 and 1937.

OPEN DOOR POLICY (1899–1900). Devised by John Hay, secretary of state under presidents William McKinley and *Theodore Roosevelt, the Open Door policy was designed to protect Chinese sovereignty and access to trade in China. In form, the policy was contained in a set of diplomatic notes circulated by Hay, to which no nation objected. The policy was formalized in the Nine-Power Treaty (1922).

ORDERS-IN-COUNCIL (1807). A British maritime regulation designed to deprive Britain's enemies of foreign supplies, the Orders-in-Council of 1807 set up a virtual blockade of all countries at war with Great Britain. The Orders-in-Council led to *Napoleon I's Milan Decree as well as to various U.S. measures designed to force an end to the commercial restrictions of Britain and France.

ORDERS-IN-COUNCIL (1809). This British order slightly relaxed the stipulations of the Orders-in-Council of 1807 by declaring a general blockade against *Napoleon I's France and its immediate satellites, but opening Germany and the Baltic area to American and other properly licensed neutral ships. The order also reduced the duties on goods transshipped through Britain to Europe.

PARIS COMMUNE (1871). In the wake of France's defeat in the Franco-Prussian War (1870–1871), left-wing radicals seized control of Paris with the purpose of bringing about social revolution. This Paris Commune was bloodily suppressed in the spring of 1871, and many of its supporters were executed or exiled.

PARTITION OF SILESIA (1921). With the reestablishment of a Polish state after World War I, attempts to define its boundaries proved difficult. One area of controversy was the former German holdings in Silesia. After a disputed referendum led to violent clashes between Poles and Germans, the League of Nations stepped in to partition Silesia. Poland received the southeastern portion, which contained many mines and factories.

PARTITIONS OF POLAND (1772, 1793, 1795). Seizing on the ingrained weakness of the dilapidated Polish state, its three neighbors (Austria, Prussia, and Russia) on three occasions at the end of the eighteenth century partitioned Poland. The third and final partition removed Poland from the map and simultaneously created the Polish Question, which plagued European diplomacy in the nineteenth century. By participating in the partitions, the three eastern monarchies created a community of interests that bound them together.

PASSCHENDAELE, BATTLE OF (1917). A notable three-month-long battle in Belgium during World War I, in which the British suffered some 250,000 casualties to gain control of the small village of Passchendaele, near Ypres. It was the climactic battle of trench warfare on the western front.

PAZZI CONSPIRACY (1479). The Pazzi were an old and wealthy Florentine family. Jealous of the power exercised by the Medici, the Pazzi planned to murder Giuliano and Lorenzo Medici during mass at the cathedral and then seize power for themselves. Although Giuliano was killed, Lorenzo escaped. The coup failed, and the Medici hold on Florence was strengthened.

PEASANTS' WAR (1524–1525). Excited by Martin Luther's words and deeds, peasants throughout the German-speaking lands, but especially Swabia, Thuringia, and Switzerland, rose in rebellion. Although stirred by the religious ferment of the time, the peasants were chiefly interested in socioeconomic reform at the expense of local lords. Luther condemned the peasants, and they were put down with great brutality.

PLATT AMENDMENT (1901). Named for Republican senator Orville Platt of Connecticut, this was a U.S.-imposed amendment to the Cuban constitution that provided for U.S. intervention in Cuba for a variety of reasons. It was implemented several times prior to World War I and eliminated in a 1934 U.S.-Cuban treaty.

POINT FOUR (1949–1953). Point Four was a technical assistance program launched by the administration of President Harry S Truman and directed mainly at Latin America. It was supposed to ensure peace by means other than military assistance but never reached its full potential before being phased out in the 1950s.

PROCLAMATION OF 1763. This act followed the British acquisition of French territory in North America and mandated that no settlement would be permitted west of a line drawn more or less along the ridge line of the Appalachian Mountains. This measure angered expansionist-minded colonists and was a cause of the American Revolution.

PUGACHEV'S REBELLION (1773–1774). Led by the charismatic peasant Emilian Pugachev, Russia's serfs staged a major insurrection that threatened to topple ˙Catherine the Great. Seeking the end of serfdom in Russia and redress of long-standing social and economic grievances, Pugachev's followers made considerable headway in the Ural region and the valley of the Volga River until defeated and dispersed by regular military units.

REIGN OF TERROR (1793–1794). At the height of the French Revolution, the most radical figures gained control of the state and introduced the Reign of Terror, which sought to crush all signs of opposition to the revolutionary government. During this period thousands of persons were executed.

RUSSIAN REVOLUTION (1905). In the wake of Russia's defeat in the Russo-Japanese War (1904–1905), revolution broke out in Russia. Sometimes called the "First Russian Revolution," the Russian Revolution of 1905 seemed to end the unlimited power of the tsar and establish a constitutional monarchy. However, in subsequent years the tsar withdrew many of the concessions made in 1905.

RUSSO-JAPANESE WAR (1904–1905). In 1904 two expanding powers, Russia and Japan, collided in the Far East. In the ensuing struggle for control of Korea and Manchuria, Japan defeated Russia, thereby exposing tsarist incompetence and setting the stage for the Russian Revolution of 1905.

RUSSO-TURKISH WAR (1768–1774). One of a series of wars fought between Russia and the Ottoman Empire from the seventeenth century through 1917, the Russo-Turkish War of 1768–1774 ended with the Treaty of Kuchuk Kainarji, which gave Russia control over the northern littoral of the Black Sea. In also giving to Russia the right to oversee Christian interests in Constantinople, Kuchuk Kainarji provided the tsars with a convenient excuse for constant meddling in Ottoman affairs.

SAAR SETTLEMENT (1919). Part of the Treaty of Versailles addressed the question of the Saar, Germany's coal-rich province situated on the Franco-German border. The treaty gave France the right to exploit the Saar economically for fifteen years while the province remained under international administration. At the end of this period (1935), Saarlanders voted almost unanimously to rejoin *Adolf Hitler's Germany.

SAINT BARTHOLOMEW'S DAY MASSACRE (1572). During the late sixteenth century, political ambitions and jealousies as well as religious animosities tore at the fabric of French life. A climax of sorts was reached in the Saint Bartholomew's Day Massacre when over 3,000 French Huguenots were murdered in Paris. The scene was subsequently repeated in the French countryside.

SEVEN YEARS WAR (1756–1763). A truly global conflict, the Seven Years War engaged virtually every European state and was fought in such venues as North America, the Caribbean, and India as well as Europe. Winners included Prussia, which retained Silesia, and Great Britain, which expelled France from the North American mainland east of the Mississippi River and gained a preponderance in India.

SINO-BRITISH WAR (1856–1858). Following the signing of the Treaty of Nanking (1842), which ended the Opium War between China and Great Britain, China continued to resist British economic penetration. When Great Britain insisted that China open itself to additional Western trade, war ensued. The Treaty of Tientsin (1858), which ended the Sino-British War, was a victory for Great Britain's free trade policy.

SIX ARTICLES (1832). Alarmed by the revolutions of 1830 and subsequent insignificant student demonstrations in a few German states, the German princes, led by the

Austrian chancellor °Clemens Metternich, pushed the Six Articles through the German Federal Diet. They outlawed political associations, forbade public meetings, and blamed the press for fomenting discontent.

SPANISH ARMADA (1588). Assembled by °Philip II in 1588, the armada was intended for an invasion of England. Commanded by the inexperienced duke of Medina Sidonia, the heavy, clumsy Spanish ships were soundly defeated in the English Channel by the smaller and more nimble English vessels.

SPANISH CIVIL WAR (1936–1939). Precipitated by fundamental disagreements over the nature of the Spanish state, the Spanish Civil War pitted a loose coalition of republicans, socialists, Communists, anarchists, and syndicalists against the forces of tradition—clericals, aristocrats, monarchists, big businessmen, army officers, and Falangists, or Spanish fascists. Aided by °Benito Mussolini and °Adolf Hitler, the traditionalists, or nationalists, under the leadership of General Francisco Franco, defeated the loyalists, or republicans, who were aided by °Joseph Stalin.

SPARTAKIST UPRISING (1919). The Spartakist Uprising was a muddled and ultimately disastrous attempt by German Communists to seize power during the tumultuous period following Germany's defeat in World War I.

SPIEGEL AFFAIR (1962). When the German newsmagazine *Der Spiegel* published confidential documents indicating a lack of preparedness on the part of certain West German military units, Chancellor °Konrad Adenauer responded rashly. He permitted his minister of defense to order the arrest of *Der Spiegel's* editors and to search the magazine's offices. The ensuing uproar badly damaged Adenauer's reputation and set the stage for his resignation less than a year later.

STAMP ACT (1765). This act of the British Parliament was designed to raise revenue by the imposition of a tax on newspapers, playing cards, and various kinds of legal documents. It was the first direct tax levied on the colonists by Parliament, and colonial outrage brought about its repeal in 1766.

STUART RESTORATION (1660). Following the death of °Oliver Cromwell and the enfeeblement of his Protectorate, the Stuart family was recalled to the throne of England. Charles II, the son of the executed Charles I, returned in 1660, but the male branch of the Stuart family was ousted once again in 1688 at the time of the Glorious Revolution.

SUEZ CRISIS (1956). This crisis began when Egypt nationalized the Suez Canal. Great Britain, France, and Israel conspired in a military action to take it out of Egyptian control, but the United Nations, with the United States and the Soviet Union in a rare alliance, intervened. Egypt maintained control of the canal, and Britain and France lost much influence in the region.

SUSSEX PLEDGE (1916). This was the name given to a statement by Germany that its navy would not sink ships without giving warning and without attempting to save lives. The statement was in response to a strong protest by President °Woodrow Wilson following the sinking of the British channel steamer *Sussex*.

TOWNSHEND DUTIES (1767). This was a British measure to raise tax revenues from colonists by means of import duties on a number of items, including glass, paper and lead products, and tea. It was received with hostility in the colonies, and the duties, except for that on tea, were repealed in 1770.

TRENT AFFAIR (1861). The United States precipitated this crisis with Great Britain by removing two Confederate diplomats from a British ship, the *Trent*. The British protested strongly, and Secretary of State °William Seward found a way to release the Confederates without appearing to submit to British demands.

TRIPARTITE DECLARATION (1950). Issued by U.S. Secretary of State ˚Dean Acheson, British Foreign Secretary Ernest Bevin, and French Foreign Minister ˚Robert Schuman, this asserted that all Middle Eastern nations ought to have sufficient military forces to protect their own security and that Western powers would provide military assistance to states that pledged to follow a policy of nonaggression.

TRUMAN DOCTRINE (1947). The Truman Doctrine was the name given to the call by President Harry Truman for $400 million in aid to Greece and Turkey to help those countries in their struggles against communism. Such aid was a departure for the United States in peacetime and represented a recognition of the reality of the Cold War.

TWENTIETH PARTY CONGRESS (1956). Held in Moscow in February 1956, the Twentieth Party Congress of the Communist Party of the Soviet Union featured a lengthy speech by Nikita S. Khrushchev, the party's first secretary, harshly criticizing the late Soviet dictator ˚Joseph Stalin. The unexpected speech signaled a relaxation of the rigid Stalinist regime within the Soviet Union.

U–2 INCIDENT (1960). For the United States, this was an embarrassing incident in which the Soviet Union shot down a U–2 surveillance plane and captured the pilot. The United States was forced to recant early denials of such surveillance flights, and the incident scuttled a planned summit conference between President Dwight D. Eisenhower and Soviet Premier Nikita Khrushchev.

ULM, BATTLE OF (1805). On October 15, 1805, ˚Napoleon I defeated an Austrian force of 50,000 at the small Bavarian town of Ulm. Napoleon's victory at the Battle of Ulm enabled him to capture Vienna without a fight.

VIENNA FINAL ACT (1820). Following on the heels of the repressive Carlsbad Decrees, the Vienna Final Act aimed yet another blow at the liberal movement in Germany. Under the guidance of the Austrian chancellor, ˚Clemens Metternich, the German Federal Diet imposed severe restrictions on the German press, purged German educational institutions, and dissolved the Burschenschaften.

WAR OF THE AUSTRIAN SUCCESSION (1740–1748). Occasioned by the death of Emperor Charles VI, the War of the Austrian Succession started with ˚Frederick the Great's seizure of Silesia from the new sovereign, Maria Theresa, but soon involved every major European state and spread to North America, the Caribbean, and India. Concluding with the Treaty of Aix-la-Chapelle, the War of the Austrian Succession revealed the weakness of both Austria and France and the strength of Prussia and Great Britain. After a short period of peace, war resumed in 1756.

WAR OF THE BAVARIAN SUCCESSION (1778–1779). When the Bavarian ruler Maximilian Joseph died in 1777, the Austrian emperor, Joseph II, advanced dubious claims to the Bavarian throne. This precipitated the War of the Bavarian Succession in which Prussia moved successfully to block the Austrians, thereby preventing an increase of Habsburg power within Germany.

WAR OF THE POLISH SUCCESSION (1733–1735). The ramshackle Polish state of the early eighteenth century did not have a hereditary monarch. Rather, the Polish king was elected by the Polish nobility, who in turn were frequently manipulated by foreign powers. In 1733 a dispute among France, Prussia, Austria, and Russia over whose client should be elected king of Poland led to the War of the Polish Succession, which ended with a significant increase in Austria's and Russia's influence over Poland at the expense of France.

WAR OF THE THIRD COALITION (1805–1807). One of the many phases of the Napoleonic Wars, the War of the Third Coalition featured Austria, Great Britain, Sweden, Russia, and later Prussia, against France. *Napoleon I defeated his opponents at Ulm, Austerlitz, Jena, Auerstadt, and Friedland, setting the stage for the Treaty of Tilsit, which confirmed the French emperor's domination of the Continent.

WAR POWERS RESOLUTION (1973). This joint congressional resolution reflected the desire of Congress to reassert control over foreign policymaking following the unhappy experience of the Vietnam War. The resolution limits the freedom of presidential action in utilizing U.S. military forces in hostile situations without the prior consent of Congress.

WATERGATE AFFAIR (1972–1974). This was the name given to a political scandal that undermined the administration of *Richard Nixon and led to the resignation of the president. The scandal involved a variety of politically motivated crimes and unethical behavior; the president was undone by purposefully concealing his knowledge of these crimes and lying to the American people about the extent of his knowledge and involvement in the cover-up.

WATERLOO, BATTLE OF (1815). After *Napoleon I escaped from Elba and returned to France on March 1, 1815, he managed to raise an army and threatened to plunge Europe into chaos once again. Napoleon's plans were thwarted when he was defeated at Waterloo, a small Belgian town, on June 18, by a combined force under the Duke of Wellington. Waterloo marked the end of Napoleon's career, as he was exiled to St. Helena shortly thereafter.

XYZ AFFAIR (1797–1798). This was a diplomatic incident between the United States and France in which three French agents (designated X, Y, and Z in a report to Congress) attempted to extort a bribe from U.S. diplomats as a condition for negotiations with France. The extortion attempt was rebuffed and led to a period of hostile relations between the two countries.

ZOLLVEREIN (1834). In 1818 Prussia established uniform customs duties throughout its scattered territories. The increased economic activity that followed encouraged other German states to follow Prussia's example. In 1834 the Zollverein, or Prussian Customs Union, was created. Including most of the German states with the notable exception of Austria, the Zollverein not only stimulated German trade and commerce, but also bolstered Prussia's claim to leadership in Germany.

APPENDIX D

ORGANIZATIONS AND TERMS

ACTION FRANÇAISE. A right-wing, antidemocratic, anti-Semitic, ultranationalist French political movement founded by Charles Maurras, the Action Française was active during the first half of the twentieth century. It sought the destruction of the French republic and the restoration of the monarchy as the only way to unite French society. Its strong support of the collaborationist Vichy regime (1940–1944) destroyed its influence.

AGE OF REACTION. A term occasionally applied to Europe in the period following the Napoleonic Wars, the Age of Reaction (1815–1848) saw the Austrian chancellor ˙Metternich's power at its height.

ANCIEN RÉGIME. The political and social system existing in France before the Revolution of 1789, ancien régime also refers to any defunct system.

APPARATCHIK. A term denoting an official of the Soviet bureaucracy, apparatchik is usually used in a pejorative sense to mean an unimaginative, rigid, frequently corrupt, opportunistic time-server.

APPEASEMENT. Originally defined as the act of placating or pacifying, since the Munich Conference (1938) appeasement has come to have the pejorative meaning of making territorial or other concessions to potential aggressors in order to maintain peace.

ARBITRATION. Arbitration is a method of peacefully resolving an international conflict by having the adversarial parties select an impartial agent—an arbiter—or court of arbitration to whom or which both sides of the case are presented. Both parties agree in advance to accept the decision that is rendered.

BALANCE OF POWER. One of the dominant concepts of international relations, the balance of power holds that preventing the dangerous growth of power in one nation or a combination of nations is desirable. An effective distribution of power among nations often can be accomplished through alliance and counteralliance.

BENELUX. This term is an acronym for Belgium, the Netherlands, and Luxembourg.

BLITZKRIEG. From the German, blitzkrieg means lightning war or a sudden, swift, overwhelming attack. Designed to avoid the debilitating trench warfare of World War I, this tactic was employed by the Nazi armies with great success during the initial years of World War II.

BOLSHEVIKS. Members of the Leninist wing of the Russian Social Democratic party, the Bolsheviks, who were committed to a radical interpretation of Marxism, seized control of Russia in November 1917 and subsequently created the USSR.

BRINKMANSHIP. Secretary of State *John Foster Dulles used this notion in his foreign policy. It referred to the willingness of the United States to carry a diplomatic crisis to the verge of war in order to win its objective, with the adversary presumably understanding the consequences of war with the United States and its nuclear arsenal.

BUNDESTAG. The lower house of the Federal Republic of Germany's parliament, the Bundestag consists of at least 496 representatives elected by universal adult suffrage.

CALVINISM. A form of Protestantism based on the radical teachings of the French lawyer and reformer John Calvin, Calvinism gained popularity during the sixteenth century and became a strong religious force in France, Scotland, Germany, the Netherlands, and England.

CAROLINGIAN. This term refers to the Frankish dynasty that reached its height at the time of Charlemagne (742–814). Its lands included present day France, western Germany, the Benelux countries, and the northern two-thirds of Italy.

CARTE BLANCHE. From the French, carte blanche, which literally means white card, signifies a condition in which a person, group, or institution has full authority to do as it pleases.

CASUS BELLI. From the Latin, casus belli is an event or events provoking war or used as a pretext for making war.

CATHOLIC EMANCIPATION. The term *Catholic emancipation* describes a series of proposals put forth by *William Pitt the Younger and supported by Viscount *Castlereagh in the early 1790s. In addition to extending the franchise to prosperous Irish Catholics and allowing them to serve on juries, bear arms, and hold minor offices, Catholic emancipation also called for Catholics in both England and Ireland to gain the right to sit in Parliament and hold major offices. Opposed by King George III and most of the English gentry, Catholic emancipation failed, bringing down Pitt's government.

CENTRAL AMERICAN COURT OF JUSTICE. This was a short-lived judicial body that was established in 1907 to settle disputes among Central American nations. It ceased to function after the United States and Nicaragua refused to accept its jurisdiction in a suit brought against the terms of the Bryan-Chamorro Treaty (1916).

CENTRAL COMMITTEE. The most important body of the Communist Party of the Soviet Union, the Central Committee directs party activity during the period between party congresses. During the early phases of Soviet rule, the Central Committee functioned as a kind of parliament with open debate. Under *Joseph Stalin, however, the Central Committee was turned into a rubber stamp.

CENTRAL POWERS. During World War I, this was the name given to the set of belligerents consisting of Germany, Austria-Hungary, Bulgaria, and Turkey.

CHANCELLOR OF THE EXCHEQUER. A member of the British cabinet, the chancellor of the exchequer is the minister of finance.

CHARTISM. Appearing in Great Britain between 1836 and 1848, Chartism was a popular movement for democratic social and political reform. Based on principles set forth in the People's Charter (1838), the Chartists demanded universal male suffrage, the secret ballot, equal electoral districts, annual election of the House of Commons, abolition of property requirements for membership in the House of Commons, and salaries for members of the House of Commons.

CHINA HANDS. This was the name given to a group of experts on U.S.-China relations after World War II. Many of them fell victim to McCarthyism because of their presumed sympathy toward the Chinese Communist revolution and were forced to leave the State Department.

CMEA. *See* COMECON.

COMECON. Also known as the Council for Mutual Economic Aid, or CMEA, CO-MECON was formed under Soviet leadership in 1949. The Soviet bloc's equivalent of the European Economic Community (EEC), COMECON attempted to integrate the economies of eastern Europe to meet the demands of the USSR. COMECON disbanded in 1991.

COMINFORM. Established in Poland in 1947, the Cominform, or Communist Information Bureau, was a Soviet attempt to revive the Comintern. Consisting of Communist parties from the USSR, eastern Europe, France, and Italy, the Cominform did the bidding of the Soviet Union. Shaken by "Tito's break with "Stalin in 1948, the Cominform disappeared in 1956.

COMINTERN. Officially known as the Third International or Communist International, the Comintern was formed in Moscow in 1919. Firmly under the control of the Bolsheviks, the Comintern attacked less radical socialists, promoted world revolution, and served the interests of the Soviet state. "Joseph Stalin abolished the Comintern in 1943 as a concession to his wartime allies, the United States and Great Britain.

COMMISSAR. Commissar was the title given to various high-ranking officials of the Soviet regime. First used extensively after the Russian revolution of 1917, the term *commissar* was discarded in 1946 in favor of the more conventional *minister*.

COMMON MARKET. *See* European Economic Community.

COMMUNIST INTERNATIONAL. *See* Comintern.

CONCERT OF EUROPE. Referring to nineteenth-century Europe, particularly the years immediately following the Congress of Vienna, the Concert of Europe featured the Great Powers acting as a continuing directorate, meeting whenever necessary to preserve the European peace based on the Vienna settlement. Sometimes the Concert of Europe is known as the Congress System because the directorate's meetings were frequently called congresses.

CONCIERGERIE. A prison of some renown in Paris, the Conciergerie hosted a number of famous inmates including Marie Antoinette and Louis Napoleon ("Napoleon III).

CONFEDERATION OF THE RHINE. Established by "Napoleon I in 1806, the Confederation of the Rhine, which included most of the German states, was a puppet state controlled from Paris. With Napoleon's defeat at the Battle of Leipzig in 1813, the confederation broke up and most of its members joined the coalition against Napoleon.

CONTAINMENT. A U.S. diplomatic policy devised by "George Kennan in 1947, containment became the cornerstone of Cold War policy for nearly twenty years. In essence, containment meant preventing the further expansion of the Communist empire while waiting for it to collapse from within or evolve into something more comfortable for the United States and its allies to live with.

CORTES. This is the name given to the Spanish consultative body that traced its roots back to the medieval period. Like other similar bodies in Europe at that time, the Cortes represented the "estates of the realm." Although the king conferred with it, it was the monarch and not the Cortes who made law.

COSSACKS. Descended from Tatars and escaped serfs, the Cossacks, who inhabited southern and southwestern Russia, formed independent communities and enjoyed a degree of autonomy in exchange for providing mounted military units. In the seventeenth and eighteenth centuries, the Cossacks were gradually brought under the control of the Russian tsar, but they continued to provide much-feared soldiers.

COUNCIL FOR MUTUAL ECONOMIC AID. *See* COMECON.

COUNCIL OF EUROPE. Established at Strasbourg in 1949, the Council of Europe works to promote the political integration of Europe.

COUNCIL ON FOREIGN RELATIONS. This is a U.S. internationalist organization, created in 1921, that includes several hundred prominent business, professional, and governmental leaders. The organization publishes the influential journal *Foreign Affairs* and over the years has developed a kind of semiofficial status because of the many links it has with the State Department.

COURT OF ST. JAMES. This is the name given to the theoretical place where the ambassadors to Great Britain serve.

DANUBIAN PRINCIPALITIES. Consisting of Moldavia and Wallachia, the Danubian Principalities were under Ottoman control from the sixteenth century. In 1774 the principalities were placed under Russia's protection, although they continued to be part of the Ottoman Empire. In the nineteenth century they formed the heart of the newly created Romanian state.

DÉTENTE. A French word meaning relaxation or easing of tensions, détente characterized U.S.-Soviet relations as they developed under *Richard M. Nixon and *Henry Kissinger. This policy stressed direct cooperative dealings in areas that were competitive, but avoided ideological accommodations. With the Soviet invasion of Afghanistan in late 1979, the cooperative spirit of détente collapsed and a period of heightened U.S.-Soviet tension ensued.

EASTERN QUESTION. Plaguing European statesmen from the Congress of Vienna until World War I, the Eastern Question concerned a declining Ottoman Empire. Beset by rising discontent among its national and religious minorities, the empire was frequently manipulated by various Great Powers. During the nineteenth century, the Ottoman Empire's growing weakness led to innumerable rebellions on the part of its unhappy subjects as well as several wars including the Russo-Turkish War of 1828–1829, the Crimean War of 1853–1856, and the Russo-Turkish War of 1877–1878.

ECSC. *See* European Coal and Steel Community.

EEC. *See* European Economic Community.

ENLIGHTENED ABSOLUTISM. *See* Enlightened despotism.

ENLIGHTENED DESPOTISM. Evolving from the medieval and early modern concept of monarchy, enlightened despotism tended to downplay the idea of divine right and instead justified itself in terms of reason and secular usefulness. With enlightened despotism the state came to be seen as an abstract but eternal entity of which the monarch was merely the first servant. Enlightened despots employed reason and logic to promote reforms designed to strengthen their state and—not coincidentally—themselves as well.

ENTENTE. A French term meaning a friendly understanding or agreement, entente also came to designate the cordial relationship among Great Britain, France, and Russia on the eve of World War I. At the outbreak of the war this relationship solidified into a formal alliance.

ENTREPÔT. From the French, an entrepôt is a trading or market center. During the eighteenth and especially the nineteenth centuries, British diplomacy often aimed at securing entrepôts.

ESCORIAL. Built during the reign of *Philip II, the Escorial, a gloomy stone palace, monastery, and church situated in the rough terrain of the Sierra de Guadarrama, became a royal residence for the Spanish monarchs.

ETON. A private preparatory school for boys, situated not far from London, Eton—along with Harrow—has traditionally been the school of choice for many of Great Britain's most important families.

EUROPEAN ATOMIC ENERGY COMMUNITY. Sometimes known by its acronym EURATOM, the European Atomic Energy Community, established in 1957, was one of the many post–World War II institutions promoting western European unification. The members of the European Atomic Energy Community pool their resources and their research on the atom.

EUROPEAN COAL AND STEEL COMMUNITY. Sometimes referred to as ECSC, the European Coal and Steel Community was established in 1951. It featured the pooling of coal and steel resources by France, West Germany, Italy, and the Benelux countries. The European Coal and Steel Community was a forerunner of the European Economic Community.

EUROPEAN ECONOMIC COMMUNITY. Known variously as the EEC or the Common Market, the European Economic Community grew from the 1957 Treaty of Rome. Beginning with France, West Germany, Italy, and the Benelux countries, the EEC, which has grown to include twelve countries with a total population of about 350 million, was designed to remove tariff barriers and expedite the unhindered movement of capital and labor. The founders of the European Economic Community also envisioned the eventual political unification of Europe.

FLQ. These initials stand for the Front de Libération du Québec, a terrorist organization in the Canadian province of Quebec that favors the independence of Quebec.

FMLN. These are the initials for the revolutionary party in El Salvador, the Frente Farabundo Martí para la Liberación Nacional. It was the principal group engaged in a civil war with the government of El Salvador from the late 1970s until 1992.

FOUR FREEDOMS. As stated by President *Franklin D. Roosevelt early in World War II, the Four Freedoms were freedom of speech and religion and freedom from want and fear.

FOUR POWERS. This term describes the victorious Allies (United States, USSR, Great Britain, and France) in their occupation of Germany (and its capital, Berlin) after World War II. Frequently the Four Powers disagreed over how to proceed with affairs in Germany. Most often Berlin became the focal point of their disagreements.

FOURTEEN POINTS. These represented *Woodrow Wilson's plan for a peaceful world after World War I. First outlined in a January 1918 speech, they were partially incorporated into the Treaty of Versailles that ended the war. The fourteenth point called for the creation of a League of Nations.

FREE CITY OF DANZIG. Following World War I, the representatives to the Paris Peace Conference (1919) detached Danzig from Germany and established it as a free city under the supervision of the League of Nations. While this step gave the newly revived Polish state unimpeded access to a Baltic port, Germany never reconciled itself to the loss. The return of Danzig to Germany was an important issue leading to the outbreak of World War II.

GATCHINA. The name of a village located not far from St. Petersburg, Gatchina became a favorite residence of the Russian royal family. This was especially true of *Catherine the Great's son, the future Tsar Paul, who virtually established his court at Gatchina.

GERMAN QUESTION. A term with two meanings, the German Question originally referred to the problem of German unification in the nineteenth century. Was there to be unification and, if so, on what terms and when? The second reference is to post–World War II Germany when the same questions reappeared in a different context.

GESTAPO. Organized in 1933 under the Nazis, the *Geheime Staatspolizei* or Gestapo, a secret political police, brutally eradicated all signs of opposition to *Hitler's regime in Germany.

GONFALONIER. A gonfalonier was a member of the gonfalonieri, a Florentine administrative body that advised the signoria on policy and endorsed its executive decrees. The gonfalonieri also played a role in selecting officials for minor administrative posts.

GRAND ARMÉE. The name given to the force assembled in 1812 by *Napoleon I for his invasion of Russia, the Grand Armée numbered about 600,000 men. It was the largest force ever assembled up to that time; however, it met disaster in Russia, suffering a loss of perhaps 500,000 men.

GREAT POWER. Used most frequently to describe several European states between 1815 and 1914, the Great Powers at that time included Great Britain, France, Austria, Prussia (Germany), and Russia. These five states largely controlled international relations in Europe.

GROSSDEUTSCH. From the German, grossdeutsch literally means "big German." Grossdeutsch was a solution to the problem of German unification calling for a unified Germany that would include Austria and its large but subservient non-German population.

GUNBOAT DIPLOMACY. This phrase describes a diplomatic policy employed by strong naval powers, especially the United States and Great Britain, during the nineteenth and early twentieth centuries. Under this policy, naval vessels were stationed near harbors of countries experiencing internal political instability. The display of naval power was presumed to be sufficient to ameliorate a bad situation and avert military intervention, although in practice there were numerous examples of direct intervention.

HARROW. A private preparatory school for boys, situated not far from London, Harrow—along with Eton—has traditionally been the school of choice for many of Great Britain's most important families.

HOLY ROMAN EMPIRE. A loosely governed state in central and western Europe, the Holy Roman Empire was formally established in 962 and dissolved by *Napoleon I in 1806. For much of its existence a member of the Habsburg family ruled the empire; however, real power rested with the empire's princes, who ruled over the state's component parts.

HUDSON'S BAY COMPANY. This British fur-trading company, established in 1670, was the principal British presence in the Oregon Territory in the early nineteenth century, building forts, engaging in a great deal of trade, and generally representing the British claim to the region.

HUGUENOT. Huguenot is a term applied to sixteenth- and seventeenth-century French Protestants, many of whom fled to Protestant countries such as England, Holland, or Prussia after ˚Louis XIV revoked the Edict of Nantes in 1685.

IMPRESSMENT. This term refers to the practice, employed by the British navy between 1790 and 1812, of stopping U.S. ships at sea and forcibly removing sailors deemed to be deserters from the British navy. Since many of those so impressed were native-born Americans, the practice was highly controversial and was a cause of the War of 1812.

INTERNATIONAL BANK FOR RECONSTRUCTION AND DEVELOPMENT (IBRD). More commonly known as the World Bank, this organization was created at the Bretton Woods Conference (1944) with the object of providing funds, in concert with private investment, for long-term capital development, particularly in developing nations. Along with the International Monetary Fund, the World Bank in recent years has been concerned with the international debt crisis.

INTERNATIONAL MONETARY FUND (IMF). The IMF was created at the Bretton Woods Conference (1944) as a lending organization to developing countries and as a facilitator of monetary reform programs. In the 1980s, the IMF was deeply involved in seeking solutions for the international debt crisis.

IRISH EMANCIPATION. *See* Catholic Emancipation.

IRREDENTA. From the Italian, irredenta means unredeemed. It is used to describe territory inhabited chiefly by the natives of a specified country which formerly held it and seeks to recover it. In the nineteenth and twentieth centuries the term *irredenta* has been used frequently to delineate lands populated by Italians but belonging to Austria-Hungary or, after 1918, Yugoslavia.

JACOBINS. A society of revolutionary democrats in France at the time of the revolution of 1789, the Jacobins, although drawn almost entirely from the bourgeoisie, espoused the most radical doctrines. Fragmenting during the course of the revolution, various Jacobin factions guided France until the fall of Maximilien Robespierre in July 1794. Jacobin is now a term applied to any political radical.

JUNTA. From the Spanish, a junta is a body of men gathered together for some secret purpose, usually political in nature.

KALMYK. A Kalmyk is a member of a tribe of Mongolian origin inhabiting an area extending from western China to the Volga River.

KGB. The abbreviation for Komitet Gosudarstvennoy Bezopastnosti, or Committee of State Security, the KGB was the Soviet Union's security service. Adopting its current name in 1953, the KGB was the successor to earlier Soviet security police such as the NKVD and Cheka, and to the imperial Russian secret police, the Okhrana.

KHEDIVE. This is the title given to the Turkish viceroys of Egypt from 1867 to 1914. The khedives were virtually independent of Constantinople's rule. By 1882 they had come under the control of Great Britain, which established a protectorate over Egypt.

KLEINDEUTSCH. From the German, kleindeutsch literally means "little German." Kleindeutsch was a solution to the problem of German unification calling for a unified Germany that would exclude Austria and its non-Germanic population.

KOLONIALVEREIN. Founded in 1882 at Frankfurt am Main, the Kolonialverein agitated for an active and aggressive German colonial policy. It had as its objective the creation of a large and expanding German colonial empire.

KOMSOMOL. The Komsomol, or All-Union Leninist Communist Union of Youth, was the Communist Party of the Soviet Union's youth organization. Aimed at Soviet youth from their mid-teens to their mid-twenties, the Komsomol served both to indoctrinate Soviet youth and to provide a pool of talent for the party. Komsomol members usually received special consideration in matters such as employment and education.

LAISSEZ FAIRE. In economics, the theory of laissez faire postulates that the economy will perform most effectively when the state refrains from interfering in economic life.

LANDTAG. The name given to Prussia's legislative assembly or parliament. After becoming chief minister of Prussia in 1862, *Otto von Bismarck was able to run roughshod over the Landtag thanks to his success in wars against Denmark (1864), Austria (1866), and France (1870).

LEBENSRAUM. From the German, *Lebensraum* literally means living space. Lebensraum became a rallying cry for *Adolf Hitler, who claimed that Germany needed additional territory for political and economic expansion. It was generally understood that such expansion would come at the expense of the Slavs (Poles, Ukrainians, and Russians) who lived to the east of Germany.

LOTHARINGIA. The name given to the kingdom assigned to Lothar (795–855), one of Charlemagne's three grandsons, when the Treaty of Verdun (843) split up the old Carolingian Empire. Sometimes called the ''middle kingdom,'' Lotharingia quickly fell apart due to a lack of defensible borders and no political or linguistic unity. In modern times the lands of Lotharingia have been a constant source of friction between Germany and France.

LOW COUNTRIES. A term commonly applied to that region of northwestern Europe consisting of Belgium, Luxembourg, and the Netherlands, the Low Countries have often been the scene of international conflict.

MANIFEST DESTINY. This popular phrase from the 1840s attempted to rationalize U.S. territorial expansion by asserting the existence of some kind of providential destiny for the United States to extend its hegemony across the North American continent.

MASSIVE RETALIATION. This diplomatic-military slogan refers to a policy adopted by the United States in the 1950s of relying on the deterrent effect of nuclear weapons rather than on large-scale conventional military forces. It was cheaper but greatly reduced the number of foreign policy options that could be utilized.

MEIN KAMPF. While imprisoned after the failed Beer Hall Putsch (1923), *Adolf Hitler wrote *Mein Kampf* (My Struggle) in 1924. *Mein Kampf* features Hitler's vision of the future for Germany, his virulent anti-Semitism, and the half-baked theories and ideas that became the foundation of his later Nazi regime.

MOGUL EMPIRE. In the sixteenth century a powerful Moslem warrior conquered the bulk of the Indian subcontinent and established a dynasty that lasted until 1707. The Mogul Empire resisted European penetration, especially into the interior of India. With the death of the last strong Mogul emperor, a scramble for power in India ensued, which Great Britain ultimately won.

MOST-FAVORED-NATION STATUS. A diplomatic arrangement, usually found in trade agreements, that specifies that one or both signatories will have the same rights and privileges accorded to any other treaty partner.

MPLA. These initials stand for the leftist party active in the Angolan civil war since the mid–1970s, the Popular Movement for the Liberation of Angola. It was supported by the Soviet Union and Cuba, and Cuban forces fought for it.

NATIONAL ASSEMBLY. At the time of the French Revolution, the National Assembly grew out of the Estates General, which gathered at Versailles in 1789. It was the vehicle by which moderate revolutionaries enacted their program between 1789 and 1791. Today, the National Assembly is the lower house of the French parliament. It consists of 577 representatives elected by universal adult suffrage.

NATIONAL SECURITY COUNCIL (NSC). This U.S. governmental organization was created in the National Security Act (1947) to advise the president on those policies related to national security. Over the years, the NSC has occasionally clashed with the State Department for primacy in the foreign policymaking arena and has also from time to time become involved in policymaking itself.

NATIONAL SOCIETY. Established in embryonic form in 1855, the National Society emerged as a force for Italian national independence and unification. For the most part it confined itself to disseminating propaganda, although it did rise in rebellion in the Papal States in 1860.

NEW STYLE. *See* Old Style.

NONALIGNED MOVEMENT. This was an organization that grew out of the Afro-Asian Conference, held in Bandung, Indonesia, in 1955. It included those countries that professed to be neutral in the Cold War then being waged between the United States and the Soviet Union.

NORTH ATLANTIC TREATY ORGANIZATION. An important step in the evolution of the policy of containment, NATO was created by the North Atlantic Treaty (1949) and came into existence in August 1949. NATO, a military alliance consisting of the United States, Canada, and fourteen European countries, was designed to serve as a deterrent to Soviet expansion. NATO features an integrated military force in Europe under the Supreme Allied Commander for Europe (SACEUR) and the Supreme Headquarters of the Allied Powers in Europe (SHAPE).

NORTH GERMAN CONFEDERATION. Organized by 'Otto von Bismarck in 1867, the North German Confederation consisted of Prussia, fresh from its recent victory over Austria, and twenty-one smaller states that it dominated. The confederation, which confirmed Prussian hegemony in northern Germany, disappeared in 1871 when Bismarck achieved German unification under Prussian auspices.

NORTHWEST TERRITORY. A term that refers to a part of the United States including the present-day states of Indiana, Illinois, Michigan, Wisconsin, and part of Minnesota. It was organized as a territory by an act of the Articles of Confederation government in 1787 and was for some years the site of disputes between the United States and Great Britain.

ODER-NEISSE LINE. Following the course of the Oder and Neisse rivers, the Oder-Neisse line became the temporary and then permanent border between Poland and the German state after World War II.

OLD REGIME. *See* Ancien régime.

OLD STYLE. A form of the calendar traceable to Julius Caesar, Old Style, or O.S., was superseded by the Gregorian calendar, or New Style (N.S.), in 1582. Most European countries gradually adopted New Style, although Russia continued to use Old Style until the Bolshevik Revolution. In the nineteenth century the Julian calendar was twelve days behind the Gregorian; in the twentieth century it is thirteen days behind.

OPEC. This acronym stands for the Organization of Petroleum Exporting Countries, a cartel created by oil-rich nations to regain control over their resources from the various oil companies that had received favorable concessions. In the 1970s, OPEC worked to raise prices and nationalize foreign-owned production facilities.

OREGON TERRITORY. This term refers to territory west of the Rocky Mountains, north of 42° north latitude, and south of 54° 40′ north latitude, that was jointly claimed by Great Britain and the United States until the signing of the Oregon Treaty (1846), which divided the territory at 49° north latitude.

ORGANIZATION OF AMERICAN STATES (OAS). This regional organization for hemispheric collective security was created in 1948 at a conference in Bogota, Colombia, and provides an organizational base for the Rio Treaty (1947).

PAN-AMERICANISM. This term, first used by Secretary of State ˙James G. Blaine in the 1880s, refers to the idea of hemispheric unity in the interests of peace and commercial advantage.

PAN-SLAVISM. Pan-Slavism is the idea of uniting all Slavic peoples, especially under the hegemony of Russia. In the latter half of the nineteenth century Pan-Slavic feelings ran high in Russia, and occasionally affected Russian foreign policy.

PAPAL STATES. Consisting of territory in central and north central Italy, the Papal States were governed by the pope as a secular ruler. In 1860, against the wishes of the pope, the Papal States were amalgamated into the new kingdom of Italy.

PARLEMENT. A type of court in France under the ancien régime, a parlement was the supreme court for a certain region of the country. Frequently parlements stood in the way of royal absolutism by refusing to enforce decrees that they deemed "unconstitutional," or by upholding certain "rights" supposedly beyond the reach of the king.

PAX BRITANNICA. A term used to describe Britain's global domination in the nineteenth century, the Pax Britannica rested on Great Britain's naval strength and its commercial and industrial wealth and power.

PENTAGON PAPERS. This was the name given to a collection of documents from the early years of the Vietnam War that were removed from Defense Department files and published in 1971 by the *New York Times* and others. Since the documents had been classified, the incident caused a great deal of controversy at the time.

PERMANENT COURT OF INTERNATIONAL JUSTICE. Also known as the World Court, this judicial body was originally established in 1921 by the League of Nations. It was incorporated into the United Nations Charter as an integral part of that body and still functions today, although without attracting much attention.

PHILOSOPHE. In its simplest form, philosophe is French for philosopher. In the context of the eighteenth century, however, philosophe took on a new meaning, describing one who wrote extensively and favorably about the Enlightenment. Not philosophers in the strictest sense, the philosophes did much to spread the ideas of the Enlightenment to the literate public.

POCKET BOROUGH. Prior to the Reform Bill of 1832, representation in the British House of Commons was drawn from counties and boroughs, or towns that had the right to send a representative to Parliament. When a borough was controlled by one person or family, it was called a pocket borough.

POLISH QUESTION. With the third and final partition of Poland in 1795, the Polish state disappeared from the map of Europe. However, the Polish Question, or what to do with Polish territory and the Poles themselves, repeatedly confronted the Great Powers during the nineteenth century. Although never leading to war among the Great Powers, the Polish Question at various times seriously strained Russia's relations with Austria and France, and, to a lesser extent, with Great Britain.

POLITBURO. An acronym for the Political Bureau of the Central Committee of the Bolshevik or Communist party, the Politburo was first organized in 1917. It directed the work of the party between plenary sessions of the Central Committee. With only a handful of members, the Politburo set policy for the party.

POOR LAWS. Providing for public relief and support of the poor, the poor laws—especially in Great Britain during the first decades of the nineteenth century—were the subject of much controversy. The 1834 Poor Law, seeking to end abuses inherent in earlier poor laws, aimed at eliminating poverty through devices such as the workhouse, which would make public relief much less attractive than any job.

POPULAR FRONT. Terrified by ˙Adolf Hitler's violent anti-Soviet rhetoric, ˙Joseph Stalin endorsed the Popular Front concept in 1935. According to this scheme, Communist parties throughout Europe were to abandon their revolutionary goals and cooperate with all antifascist groups to form a united opposition to fascism. In the wake of the Munich Agreement, Stalin abandoned the Popular Front strategy.

PORTE. This term is a synonym for the Ottoman Turkish government or its foreign office.

PRAGMATIC SANCTION. Defined as an imperial or royal edict or decree having the force of a fundamental law, the Habsburg Pragmatic Sanction played a major role in the diplomacy of the eighteenth century. During the seventeenth century the Austrian monarchy grew dramatically, but it remained a collection of separate territories held together by the person of the monarch. In order to ensure that the crowns of the separate territories would be inherited by the same person, Charles VI in 1713 issued the Pragmatic Sanction by which all the Habsburg territories and all the members of the Habsburg family pledged themselves to recognize a single, specific heir. The matter gained some urgency when it became clear that Charles would die without a male heir and that his daughter, Maria Theresa, would succeed him. Charles spent most of his life securing promises that all concerned—but especially foreign powers—would adhere to the Pragmatic Sanction. Upon his death in 1740, however, the Pragmatic Sanction failed and the War of the Austrian Succession began.

PROTECTORATE. A protectorate can be the relationship of a stronger country to a weaker country or region in which the former dominates the latter; or it can be the name given to the country or region being protected.

QUAI D'ORSAY. The offices of the French Foreign Ministry are located on the Quai d'Orsay in the heart of Paris. The term is frequently used as a synonym for the French Foreign Ministry or the French government.

RAJ. From the Hindu, raj is an Indian term meaning sovereignty or rule. Frequently raj refers to the British rule of India.

REALPOLITIK. From the German, the term *realpolitik* means the politics of reality. Frequently associated with German Chancellor °Otto von Bismarck, realpolitik came to mean the use of any means available, regardless of moral considerations, to achieve one's goals.

RECIPROCAL TRADE. Reciprocal trade, or reciprocity, refers to bilateral or multilateral trade arrangements in which each party agrees to give the same or similar commercial advantages to the other parties, often in the form of tariff reductions.

REGENCY. The period in English history between 1811 and 1820. With the onset of George III's final bout of insanity late in 1810, his son, the Prince of Wales and the future George IV, was named regent. The Regency style was dictated by the prince, a man of good taste who enjoyed a robust life.

REICHSTAG. The name formerly given to the German legislative assembly or parliament. Although °Otto von Bismarck permitted the establishment of the Reichstag when he created the German Empire, he made sure that it served a decorative purpose only and frequently ignored it during his tenure as chancellor.

RISORGIMENTO. Appearing in the latter part of the eighteenth century, the Risorgimento was a movement for the liberation, reform, and unification of the Italian peninsula. Greatly stimulated by the French Revolution and °Napoleon I, the Risorgimento gathered steam during the nineteenth century and finally achieved its objectives under the leadership of °Camillo di Cavour.

ROMAN QUESTION. After having aided °Camillo di Cavour in what turned out to be the unification of Italy, °Napoleon III found himself in a dilemma that became known as the Roman Question. Pope Pius IX, adamantly opposed to Italian unification and unreconciled to the loss of the Papal States, confined himself to Rome. To placate Catholic opinion in France, Napoleon III sent a French garrison to Rome to protect the pope. In doing so, however, he alienated his Italian friends. The issue was finally resolved in 1870 when Italy took advantage of France's involvement in the Franco-Prussian War to seize Rome and make it the Italian capital, while the pope retreated behind the walls of the Vatican.

ROYALIST. A royalist is an adherent of royalism. Royalists support a specific monarch or the concept of monarchy. This support is usually most obvious in times of revolution, civil war, or civil disturbance. The term is frequently applied to those who supported the Bourbons in France or Charles I in England.

SANDINISTAS. This is the popular name of the members of the Frente Sandinista de Liberación Nacional (FSLN), the movement that overthrew the Anastasio Somoza government in Nicaragua in 1979 and ruled the country until losing in national elections in 1990.

SECOND FRONT. During World War II, a long-standing objective of the Allies was to open a second theater of military operations against the Axis powers in western Europe. This second front was finally accomplished in June 1944 with the successful cross-channel landing of Allied troops at Normandy. The failure to open a second front at an earlier date and thereby relieve military pressure on Soviet Russia angered °Joseph Stalin and perhaps contributed to the subsequent onset of the Cold War.

SECOND INTERNATIONAL. Formed in 1889, the Second International was an international body of socialists who debated the theories, strategies, and tactics of socialism. It broke up in 1914 under the strains of World War I.

SECURITY COUNCIL. An integral part of the United Nations, the Security Council has as its primary responsibility the preservation of peace. The Security Council consists of five permanent members (China, France, Great Britain, Russia, and the United States) and ten rotating members elected by the United Nations General Assembly for two-year terms.

SHARIF. From the Arabic, sharif means noble or high-born. This Arabic title of respect has many applications including that of a Moroccan prince or ruler.

SIGNORIA. The signoria was the governing council of Renaissance Florence. Representing the oligarchy that dominated Florence, the signoria oversaw internal administration, conducted foreign affairs, and initiated legislation.

SLAVOPHILES. In the mid-nineteenth century, Russia witnessed fierce debate over the question of its relationship to Europe. The Slavophiles condemned attempts to westernize Russia, preferring to find Russia's strength in its traditions and its unique nonwestern origins and history. The Slavophiles were opposed by the Westernizers.

SOCIAL DARWINISM. Derived from Charles Darwin's pioneering nineteenth-century work on evolution, Social Darwinism concluded that the struggle for existence and survival of the fittest applied to man as well as plants and lesser animals. This concept served to justify a number of injustices including racism, belligerent nationalism, genocide, and monopoly capitalism.

SOCIALIST UNITY PARTY. Known by its initials, SED, the Socialist Unity Party came about in 1946 from the forced merger of the Social Democratic party into the Communist party in the Soviet zone of occupied Germany. Controlled entirely by the Communists, the Stalinist-minded SED ruled East Germany with an iron fist until its collapse in 1989–1990.

SOVIET. The Russian word for council, Soviet also refers to the USSR, the citizens of the USSR, and the revolutionary council that *Vladimir Lenin and the Bolsheviks controlled and used as a vehicle to seize power in November 1917. During the 1905 Russian revolution, Soviets were bodies of workers and radicals that organized and directed massive strikes.

SPLENDID ISOLATION. Beginning with *George Canning's term at the Foreign Office and extending through the balance of the nineteenth century, Great Britain consciously avoided permanent entanglements with any of the continental states. Dubbed splendid isolation, this policy seemed to be predicated on the belief that Great Britain was strong enough to go it alone. Certainly it bestowed upon Britain an unusual freedom of action. By the end of the century, as Britain became more vulnerable, its isolation became less than splendid. Eventually, splendid isolation was abandoned in favor of a closer relationship with France.

SULTAN. Derived from the Arabic, a sultan is a Moslem ruler. Most frequently the term refers to the ruler of the Ottoman Empire.

THIRD INTERNATIONAL. *See* Comintern.

THIRD REICH. This term was applied by *Adolf Hitler to the German state after he came to power. Hitler saw the Third Reich as the legitimate successor to the First

Reich, or Holy Roman Empire, and the Second Reich, or *Otto von Bismarck's German Empire. Intended to last for a thousand years, the Third Reich disappeared along with Hitler in 1945.

TORY. Tory is a nickname for an English political party that tended to support the prerogatives of the king and to promote the interests of the landed classes. Since about 1832 the Tory party has called itself the Conservative party, although its members are still known as Tories.

TRIDENTINE. This adjective refers to the Council of Trent (1545–1563) or the decisions of the Council of Trent, which reinvigorated the Roman Catholic Church in the wake of the Reformation. Policies decided upon at Trent remained virtually unchanged until the 1960s when the Second Vatican Council met.

UNESCO. This acronym stands for the United Nations Economic, Scientific, and Cultural Organization. Planned in the latter years of World War II, it began operations in 1946 with the purpose of fostering justice and human rights through educational, scientific, and cultural means.

UNION JACK. The Union Jack is the national flag of the United Kingdom. It is a combination of the flags of England, Scotland, and Ireland. Occasionally the term *Union Jack* is used as a synonym for Great Britain.

UNITA. An acronym for the National Union for the Total Independence of Angola, a U.S.- and South Africa-supported organization that fought against the MPLA in the Angolan civil war beginning in the mid–1970s.

UNITED NATIONS RELIEF AND REHABILITATION ADMINISTRATION (UNRRA). Created in late 1943, this agency provided relief for those people in liberated nations who had suffered from the effects of World War II as well as for displaced persons from Axis nations such as Italy, Austria, and Hungary. Most of UNRRA's work was terminated with the rise of the Cold War in 1947.

VERSAILLES. The name of a small village outside of Paris, Versailles was the site of a colossal palace of the same name built by *Louis XIV in the 1670s. The Versailles palace was widely imitated by European royalty and came to symbolize the power of absolutist monarchy.

VIETNAMIZATION. This term refers to the practice, introduced in *Richard Nixon's administration, of gradually withdrawing U.S. troops from Vietnam and replacing them on the front lines with South Vietnamese troops.

WELTANSCHAUUNG. From the German, weltanschauung means an ideology providing a comprehensive philosophy of life, nature, and history.

WESTERNIZERS. Participants in a major debate that absorbed the attention of Russia's educated classes in the middle of the nineteenth century, the Westernizers strongly supported the westernization of the Russian state, especially in the political, cultural, and social realms. The Westernizers were opposed by the Slavophiles.

WHIG. A Whig was a member of an English political party that tended to champion popular rights and change in the direction of democracy. Established in the late eighteenth century, the Whig party evolved into the Liberal party during the first half of the nineteenth century.

WHITEHALL. The offices of the British Foreign Office are located on Whitehall Street in the heart of London. The term is frequently used as a synonym for the British Foreign Office.

WORKERS' AND PEASANTS' INSPECTORATE. Established shortly after the Russian Revolution, the Workers' and Peasants' Inspectorate, or Rabkin, was assigned to identify and root out corruption and inefficiency in all branches of the government. In 1919 ˚Stalin was named commissar, or chief officer, of Rabkin.

YUCATAN. The Yucatan is a somewhat remote province in southeastern Mexico and the center of pre-Columbian Mayan civilization. From time to time in the nineteenth century, it was an object of interest to U.S. annexationists.

APPENDIX E

HEADS OF STATE

Austria

House of Habsburg

Albert V	1404-1439
Frederick V	1439-1493
Maximilian I	1493-1519
Charles V	1519-1556
Ferdinand I	1556-1564
Maximilian II	1564-1576
Rudolph II	1576-1612
Matthias	1612-1619
Ferdinand II	1619-1637
Ferdinand III	1637-1657
Leopold I	1657-1705
Joseph I	1705-1711
Charles VI	1711-1740
Maria Theresa	1740-1780
Joseph II	1780-1790
Leopold II	1790-1792
Francis II	1792-1835
Ferdinand I	1835-1848
Francis Joseph	1848-1916
Charles I	1916-1918

At the end of World War I, the Austrian Empire was dismembered.

British Isles

Kings of England and Ireland

House of Tudor

Henry VII	1485-1509
Henry VIII	1509-1547
Edward VI	1547-1553
Mary I	1553-1558
Elizabeth I	1558-1603

With the death of Elizabeth in 1603, the Tudor line became extinct and the crown passed to her nearest male relative, James Stuart, who already ruled as King James VI of Scotland. Although remaining separate, England and Scotland were ruled by the same king. In 1707, the Act of Union officially joined the two kingdoms. The monarch became king of Great Britain and, separately, king of Ireland.

House of Stuart

James I	1603-1625
Charles I	1625-1649

Interregnum

Oliver Cromwell	1653-1658
Richard Cromwell	1658-1660

House of Stuart-restored

Charles II	1660-1685
James II	1685-1688
William III	1689-1702
and Mary II	1689-1694
Anne	1702-1714

House of Hanover, later Windsor

George I	1714-1727
George II	1727-1760

In 1801, the kingdom of Great Britain which had been formed in 1707 was expanded to become the United Kingdom of Great Britain and Ireland.

George III	1760-1820
George IV	1820-1830
William IV	1830-1837
Victoria	1837-1901
Edward VII	1901-1910

In 1922, with Irish independence, the monarchy was retitled the United Kingdom of Great Britain and Northern Ireland.

George V	1910-1936
Edward VIII	1936
George VI	1936-1952
Elizabeth II	1952-

France

House of Valois

Louis XI	1461-1483
Charles VIII	1483-1498
Louis XII	1498-1515
Francis I	1515-1547
Henry II	1547-1559
Francis II	1559-1560
Charles IX	1560-1574
Henry III	1574-1589

House of Bourbon

Henry IV	1589–1610
Louis XIII	1610–1643
Louis XIV	1643–1715
Louis XV	1715–1774
Louis XVI	1774–1792

The First Republic

Convention	1792–1795
Directory	1795–1799
Consulate	1799–1804

The First Empire

Napoleon I	1804–1814

House of Bourbon-restored

Louis XVIII	1814–1824
Charles X	1824–1830

House of Orleans

Louis-Philippe	1830–1848

The Second Republic   **1848–1852**

The Second Empire

Napoleon III	1852–1870

The Third Republic   **1870–1940**

Vichy France   **1940–1944**

Provisional Government   **1944–1946**

The Fourth Republic   1946–1958

The Fifth Republic   1958–

Germany/Prussia

The House of Hohenzollern began its rule in 1417 as Electors of Brandenburg. In 1618 the Elector of Brandenburg added the Duchy of Prussia to his holdings and began to call himself the Duke of Prussia.

House of Hohenzollern

George William	1619–1640
Frederick William the "Great Elector"	1640–1688
Frederick III	1688–1713

As the price for entering the War of the Spanish Succession in 1701, the elector demanded and received from the Habsburg emperor the title of king. Henceforth the Hohenzollern electors would be known as Kings of Prussia.

Frederick I	1701–1713
Frederick William I	1713–1740
Frederick II the "Great"	1740–1786
Frederick William II	1786–1797
Frederick William III	1797–1840
Frederick William IV	1840–1861
William I	1861–1888

At the end of the Franco-Prussian War (1870–1871), the Prussian chancellor, Otto von Bismarck declared the German empire with the Prussian king as emperor

William I	1871–1888
Frederick III	1888
William II	1888–1918

The German Republic (**Weimar Republic**)	**1919–1933**
The Third Reich	**1933–1945**

After the defeat of Germany in World War II, the victorious Allies occupied the country and ruled it directly until 1949 when two distinct successor states were formed.

German Federal Republic (**West Germany**)	**1949–1990**
German Democratic Republic (**East Germany**)	**1949–1990**

In 1990, Germany was reunited.

German Federal Republic	**1990–**

Holy Roman Empire

House of Habsburg

Albert II	1438–1439
Frederick III	1452–1493
Maximilian I	1493–1519
Charles V	1519–1556
Ferdinand I	1556–1564
Maximilian II	1564–1576
Rudolph II	1576–1612
Matthias	1612–1619
Ferdinand II	1619–1637
Ferdinand III	1637–1657
Leopold I	1658–1705
Joseph I	1705–1711
Charles VI	1711–1740

House of Wittelsbach

Charles VII	1742–1745

House of Lorraine

Francis I	1745–1765

House of Habsburg-Lorraine

Joseph II	1765–1790
Leopold II	1790–1792
Francis II	1792–1806

In 1806, Napoleon Bonaparte terminated the Holy Roman Empire.

Italy

In 1720, the Duke of Savoy, Victor Amadeo II, acquired the island of Sardinia and claimed the title King of Sardinia.

House of Savoy

Victor Amadeo II	1720–1730
Charles Emmanuel III	1730–1773
Victor Amadeo III	1773–1796
Charles Emmanuel IV	1796–1802
Victor Emmanuel I	1802–1821
Charles Felix	1821–1831
Charles Albert	1831–1849

Italian unification under the leadership of the House of
Savoy was accomplished in 1861 when Victor Emmanuel II was
proclaimed King of Italy

Victor Emmanuel II	1849-1878
Humbert I	1878-1900
Victor Emmanuel III	1900-1946
Humbert II	1946

In 1946 a republic replaced the Kingdom of Italy.

The Italian Republic	**1946-**

Russia/USSR

As the Mongol grip loosened, the Grand Dukes of Moscow
emerged as the strongest political figures in Russia.

Grand Dukes of Moscow

Ivan III	
the "Great"	1462-1505
Basil III	1505-1533
Ivan IV	
the "Terrible"	1533-1584

In 1547, Ivan IV claimed the title Tsar of Russia.

Tsars of Russia

Ivan IV	
the "Terrible"	1547-1584
Feodor I	1584-1598
Boris Godunov	1598-1605

Time of Troubles	**1604-1613**

Following the anarchical Time of Troubles, Michael Romanov
was elected tsar.

House of Romanov

Michael	1613-1645
Alexis	1645-1676
Feodor II	1676-1682
Ivan V and	
Peter I	1682-1689
Peter I the "Great"	1689-1725
Catherine I	1725-1727
Peter II	1727-1730
Anna	1730-1740
Ivan VI	1740-1741
Elizabeth	1741-1762
Peter III	1762

```
           Catherine II
             the "Great"      1762-1796
           Paul              1796-1801
           Alexander I       1801-1825
           Nicholas I        1825-1855
           Alexander II      1855-1881
           Alexander III     1881-1894
           Nicholas II       1894-1917
```

In 1917, the rule of the tsars was overthrown.

Provisional Government   **1917**

Soviet Government   **1917-1922**

Union of Soviet   **1922-1991**
Socialist Republics

At the end of 1991, the Union of Soviet Socialist Republics
disintegrated and its component parts, including a Russian
state, reappeared.

Spain

The marriage of Ferdinand and Isabella brought together
Aragon and Castile, two of the largest states of the Iberian
peninsula. Their rule designates the start of modern Spain.

Ferdinand and Isabella   1479-1504/1516

House of Habsburg

```
           Charles I         1516-1556
           Philip II         1556-1598
           Philip III        1598-1621
           Philip IV         1621-1665
           Charles II        1665-1700
```

House of Bourbon

```
           Philip V          1700-1746
           Ferdinand VI      1746-1759
           Charles III       1759-1788
           Charles IV        1788-1808
```

House of Bonaparte

```
           Joseph            1808-1813
```

House of Bourbon-restored

```
           Ferdinand VII     1813-1833
           Isabella II       1833-1868
```

After the abdication of Isabella, the throne remained vacant until 1870.

House of Savoy

    Amadeo I   1870–1873

The First Republic   **1873–1874**

House of Bourbon-restored

    Alfonso XII   1874–1885
    Alfonso XIII   1885–1931

The Second Republic   **1931–1939**

Dictatorship of   **1939–1975**
  Francisco Franco

House of Bourbon-restored

    Juan Carlos I   1975–

UNITED STATES

PRESIDENT		SECRETARY OF STATE	
George Washington	1789-1797	Thomas Jefferson	1789-1793
		Edmund Randolph	1794-1795
		Timothy Pickering	1795-1797
John Adams	1797-1801	Timothy Pickering	1797-1800
		John Marshall	1800-1801
Thomas Jefferson	1801-1809	James Madison	1801-1809
		Robert Smith	1809-1811
James Madison	1809-1817	James Monroe	1811-1817
James Monroe	1817-1825	John Quincy Adams	1817-1825
John Quincy Adams	1825-1829	Henry Clay	1825-1829
Andrew Jackson	1829-1837	Martin Van Buren	1829-1831
		Edward Livingston	1831-1833
		Louis McLane	1833-1834
		John Forsyth	1834-1837
Martin Van Buren	1837-1841	John Forsyth	1837-1841
William Henry Harrison	1841	Daniel Webster	1841
John Tyler	1841-1845	Daniel Webster	1841-1843
		Abel P. Upshur	1843-1844
		John C. Calhoun	1844-1845
James K. Polk	1845-1849	James Buchanan	1845-1849
Zachary Taylor	1849-1850	John M. Clayton	1849-1850
Millard Fillmore	1850-1853	Daniel Webster	1850-1852
		Edward Everett	1852-1853
Franklin Pierce	1853-1857	William L. Marcy	1853-1857
James Buchanan	1857-1861	Lewis Cass	1857-1860
		Jeremiah S. Black	1860-1861
Abraham Lincoln	1861-1865	William H. Seward	1861-1865
Andrew Johnson	1865-1869	William H. Seward	1865-1869
Ulysses S. Grant	1869-1877	Elihu B. Washburne	1869
		Hamilton Fish	1869-1877
Rutherford B. Hayes	1877-1881	William M. Evarts	1877-1881
James A. Garfield	1881	James G. Blaine	1881
Chester A. Arthur	1881-1885	Frederick T. Frelinghuysen	1881-1885
Grover Cleveland	1885-1889	Thomas F. Bayard	1885-1889
Benjamin Harrison	1889-1893	James G. Blaine	1889-1892
		John W. Foster	1892-1893
Grover Cleveland	1893-1897	Walter Q. Gresham	1893-1895
		Richard Olney	1895-1897
William McKinley	1897-1901	John Sherman	1897-1898
		William R. Day	1898
		John Hay	1898-1901
Theodore Roosevelt	1901-1909	John Hay	1901-1905
		Elihu Root	1905-1909
		Robert Bacon	1909
William Howard Taft	1909-1913	Philander C. Knox	1909-1913

Woodrow Wilson	1913–1921	William Jennings Bryan	1913–1915
		Robert Lansing	1915–1920
		Bainbridge Colby	1920–1921
Warren G. Harding	1921–1923	Charles E. Hughes	1921–1923
Calvin Cooldige	1923–1929	Charles E. Hughes	1923–1925
		Frank B. Kellogg	1925–1929
Herbert Hoover	1929–1933	Henry L. Stimson	1929–1933
Franklin D. Roosevelt	1933–1945	Cordell Hull	1933–1944
		Edward R. Stettinius, Jr.	1944–1945
Harry S Truman	1945–1953	Edward R. Stettinius, Jr.	1945
		James F. Byrnes	1945–1947
		George C. Marshall	1947–1949
		Dean G. Acheson	1949–1953
Dwight D. Eisenhower	1953–1961	John Foster Dulles	1953–1959
		Christian A. Herter	1959–1961
John F. Kennedy	1961–1963	Dean Rusk	1961–1963
Lyndon B. Johnson	1963–1969	Dean Rusk	1963–1969
Richard M. Nixon	1969–1974	William P. Rogers	1969–1973
		Henry A. Kissinger	1973–1974
Gerald R. Ford	1974–1977	Henry A. Kissinger	1974–1977
James E. Carter	1977–1981	Cyrus A. Vance	1977–1980
		Edmund S. Muskie	1980–1981
Ronald Reagan	1981–1989	Alexander Haig	1981–1983
		George Shultz	1983–1989
George Bush	1989–1993	James Baker	1989–1992
		Lawrence Eagleburger	1992–1993
William J. Clinton	1993–	Warren Christopher	1993–

INDEX

Page numbers in *italic* indicate main entries.

ABOUT THE EDITORS AND CONTRIBUTORS

LAWRENCE P. ADAMCZYK is an assistant professor of history and political science at Parks College of St. Louis University, Cahokia, Illinois. He received his Ph.D. from the University of Maryland, and he has published "The Crimean War and Its Effects upon Perceptions of British Foreign Policy," *Potomac Review* 26–27 (1984–1985): 51–71. He is currently researching the role of Italy at the Congress of Berlin, 1878.

JOHN T. ALEXANDER teaches at the University of Kansas. He received his Ph.D. from Indiana University and is the author of several books on early modern Russia, including the award-winning *Catherine the Great: Life and Legend* (1989). He is currently working on a dual biography of Peter the Great and Catherine the Great.

FREDERICK J. AUGUSTYN, JR., works at the Library of Congress, Washington, D.C., and is also affiliated with the University of Maryland, from which he received M.A. and M.L.S. degrees. He has contributed articles to *Political Parties and Elections in the United States: An Encyclopedia* (1991).

DONALD H. BARRY is adjunct professor of history at Florida State University, from which he also received his Ph.D. He is the author of articles on France in the American Revolution and on the French Revolution, and has traveled widely and lived frequently in Europe and the Middle East during the past twenty years.

ROBERT A. BERRY teaches at Salisbury State University in Maryland. He received his Ph.D. from Indiana University and is the author of several articles on Czartoryski and his diplomacy.

ROBERT D. BILLINGER, JR., is professor of history at Wingate College in North Carolina. He received his Ph.D. from the University of North Carolina and is the author of *Metternich and the German Question* (1991). A former

Fulbright scholar in Vienna, he is a member of the Consortium on Revolutionary Europe and the German Studies Association.

GEORGE P. BLUM teaches in the department of history at the University of the Pacific. He received his Ph.D. from the University of Minnesota and has contributed articles to *Great Lives from History: Twentieth Century* (1990), *Research Guide to European Biography* (forthcoming), and *Encyclopedia of World War II in Europe* (forthcoming).

ARNOLD BLUMBERG is professor of history at Towson State University in Maryland. He received his Ph.D. from the University of Pennsylvania and is the author of *The Diplomacy of the Mexican Empire, 1863–1867* (1971; 1987); *A View from Jerusalem, 1849–1858* (1980); *Zion Before Zionism, 1838–1880* (1986); and *A Carefully Planned Accident: The Italian War of 1859* (1990). He has also published studies of Ottoman Turkish policy in nineteenth-century Jerusalem.

VERENA BOTZENHART-VIEHE is an assistant professor of history at Westminster College in Pennsylvania. She received her Ph.D. from the University of California at Santa Barbara and has published articles and reviews in various history journals in the area of American foreign policy and German-American relations.

NEWELL D. BOYD is professor of history at Houston Baptist University. He received his Ph.D. from Texas Tech University and is a contributor to *Victorian Britain, an Encyclopedia* and *Encyclopedia of Twentieth Century Britain*. He is the creator and director of Houston Baptist University's Master of Liberal Arts program.

RONALD CALINGER teaches at Catholic University of America in Washington, D.C. He received his Ph.D. from the University of Chicago and is the author of *Gottfried Wilhelm Leibniz* (1976) and *A History of Mathematics* (forthcoming) and the editor of *Classics of Mathematics* (1982). His recent research has focused on the life and times of Leonhard Euler, the foremost scientist during the European Enlightenment.

GEORG CAVALLAR received his Doktor der Philosophie from the University of Vienna in 1989. He is presently affiliated with the Gymnasium und Realgymnasium 4 in Vienna and has published several articles on the political philosophy of the Enlightenment and on Immanuel Kant.

FRANS COETZEE of Yale University is currently working at the Institute for Advanced Study at Princeton University. He received his Ph.D. from the University of Chicago and is the author of *For Party or Country: Nationalism and the Dilemmas of Popular Conservatism in Edwardian England* (1990) as well as articles on British conservatism in various journals.

MARILYN SHEVIN-COETZEE of Yale University is currently working at the Institute for Advanced Study at Princeton University. She received her Ph.D. from the University of Chicago and is the author of *The German Army League: Popular Nationalism in Wilhelmine Germany* (1990) and articles on German nationalism in various journals.

BERNARD A. COOK is professor of history at Loyola University in New Orleans. He received his Ph.D. from St. Louis University and is the coauthor of *German Americans* (1991). He has also contributed articles to *Great Events from History: Human Rights* (1992) and *Encyclopedia of World War II in Europe* (forthcoming). He is a former Fulbright scholar to the University of Marburg.

JOHN K. COX is a Ph.D. candidate at Indiana University. He has contributed reviews to various journals and is a former MacArthur Foundation fellow and current Fulbright scholar in Vienna, where he is researching post–World War II Yugoslavian foreign policy.

DON M. CREGIER is professor of history at the University of Prince Edward Island, Canada. He is the author of *The Decline of the British Liberal Party* (1966; 1985); *Bounder from Wales: Lloyd George's Career Before the First World War* (1976); *Novel Exposures* (1979); and *Chiefs Without Indians* (1982). His current research centers on Lloyd George during World War I, Irish nationalism, and Sir William Bull, a British politician.

MICHAEL J. DEVINE is the director of the American Heritage Center at the University of Wyoming. He received his Ph.D. from Ohio State University and is the author of *John W. Foster: Politics and Diplomacy in the Imperial Era* (1981) as well as various journal articles. He was a former Fulbright scholar in Argentina and the former state historian of Illinois.

BRIAN R. DUCHIN teaches history at Williams College in Massachusetts. He received his Ph.D. from the University of Texas at Austin and has published articles on Eisenhower era foreign policy in *Diplomatic History*.

THOMAS C. FIDDICK is professor of history at the University of Evansville. He received his Ph.D. from Indiana University and is the author of *Russia's Retreat from Poland, 1920* (1990). He is currently doing research in the area of psychohistory and is working on a comparative psychological study of Hitler and Stalin.

JOHN E. FINDLING is professor of history at Indiana University Southeast,

New Albany. He received his Ph.D. from the University of Texas and is the author of *Dictionary of American Diplomatic History* (1980; 1989) and *Close Neighbors, Distant Friends: United States-Central American Relations* (1987) and the editor of *Historical Dictionary of World's Fairs and Expositions, 1851–1988* (1990). His current research continues to focus on world's fairs.

BERTRAM M. GORDON is professor of history at Mills College in California. He received his Ph.D. from Rutgers University and is the author of *Collaborationism in France During the Second World War* (1980) and articles on Charles de Gaulle. He is currently researching the history of the political right in recent France and the history of gastronomy.

DANIEL P. O'C. GREENE teaches in the department of history at Williams College in Massachusetts. He received his Ph.D. from the University of Texas at Austin and has published articles on the foreign policy of the Eisenhower administration in *Diplomatic History*.

SURENDRA K. GUPTA is professor of history at Pittsburg State University in Kansas. He received his Ph.D. from Johns Hopkins University and is the author of *Stalin's Policy Towards India, 1946–1953* (1988). He has also contributed articles to *The Modern Encyclopedia of Russian and Soviet History* (1978) and *Great Lives in History: Renaissance to 1900* (1989).

SALLY E. HADDEN is in the Ph.D. program at Harvard University, where she received her M.A. and J.D. A legal historian, she is studying the public regulation of slavery from 1700 to 1865 in Virginia and the Carolinas.

DONALD E. HEIDENREICH, JR., teaches at the Kemper Military Junior College. He received his M.A. from the University of Arizona and has contributed articles to *St. James Guide to Biography* (1991) and *Research Guide to American Historical Biography*, vol. 4 (1990). He is currently a doctoral student at the University of Missouri, Columbia.

DANIEL W. HOLLIS III is professor of history at Jacksonville State University in Alabama. He received his Ph.D. from Vanderbilt University and is the coauthor of *Civilizations to 1715: A Study and Review Program* (1983). He has also contributed articles to *Biographical Dictionary of British Radicals* (1982–1984) and *Historical Dictionary of Tudor England, 1485–1603* (1991).

RICHARD A. LEIBY is an assistant professor of history at Rosemont College in Pennsylvania. He received his Ph.D. from the University of Delaware and has written numerous articles and papers dealing with the social history of Germany during the Nazi period and the postwar occupation years.

MICHAEL M. LUSTIG teaches history at Boston University. He received his Ph.D. from Brown University and is the author of *Trotsky and Djilas: Critics of Communist Bureaucracy* (1989) as well as papers on Gorbachev and post-Tito Yugoslavia.

GARRETT L. MCAINSH is professor of history at Hendrix College in Conway, Arkansas. He received his Ph.D. from Emory University.

ROBERT W. MACDONALD is a retired foreign service officer. He received his Ph.D. from Georgetown University and is the author of *Morocco: A Politico-Economic Analysis* (1962), *The League of Arab States* (1965), and numerous articles. He is currently working on a study of twentieth-century American writers in Italy.

DAVID MACGREGOR is currently Vice Admiral Edwin B. Hooper Scholar at the Naval Historical Center, Washington, D.C. He received his Ph.D. from the University of Rochester and has taught both there and at the State University of New York at Geneseo.

HENRY E. MATTOX is a retired foreign service officer. He received his Ph.D. from the University of North Carolina and has taught at North Carolina State University. He is the author of *The Twilight of Amateur Diplomacy: The American Foreign Service and Its Senior Officers in the 1890s* (1989).

ALLEN B. MAXWELL is an associate professor of political science at Indiana University at Kokomo. He received his Ph.D. from the Fletcher School of Law and Diplomacy at Tufts University and has for many years been active in the Model United Nations movement.

DAVID MAYERS is an associate professor of political science at Boston University. He received his Ph.D. from the University of Chicago and is the author of *George Kennan and the Dilemmas of U.S. Foreign Policy* (1988) and *Reporting from Moscow: U.S. Diplomats and Policy Toward the USSR* (forthcoming).

MICHAEL J. MULLIN is an assistant professor of history at Augustana College in Sioux Falls, South Dakota. He received his Ph.D. from the University of California at Santa Barbara and is the author of articles on colonial-Indian relations between 1738 and 1776. He is also interested in American policy toward non–English-speaking societies in the nineteenth century.

JONATHAN M. NIELSON teaches at Sonoma State University in California. He received his Ph.D. from the University of California at Santa Barbara and is the author of *Armed Forces on a Northern Frontier* (1988) and *In Peace and*

War: American Historians, Patriotism, and Diplomacy, Versailles 1919 (1992) as well as many articles on military and diplomatic history.

BARBARA BENNETT PETERSON is professor of history at the University of Hawaii. She received her Ph.D. from the University of Hawaii and is the author of *Notable Women of Hawaii* (1984) and the coauthor of *A Woman's Place is in the History Books: Her Story, 1620–1980* (1980). She is a former Fulbright scholar in Japan and China and is the founding president of the Fulbright Alumni Association in Hawaii.

WILLIAM B. PICKETT is professor of history at Rose-Hulman Institute of Technology, Terre Haute, Indiana. He received his Ph.D. from Indiana University and is the author of *Homer E. Capehart: A Senator's Life, 1897–1979* (1990). He is a former Fulbright lecturer in Japan and the president of the Indiana Association of Historians.

PETER PIERSON is professor of history and chairman of the department at Santa Clara University. He received his Ph.D. from the University of California at Los Angeles and is the author of *Philip II of Spain* (1975) and *Commander of the Armada: The Seventh Duke of Medina Sidonia* (1989). He is a former Fulbright scholar to Spain.

DAVID L. PORTER is Louis Tuttle Shangle Professor of History at William Penn College, Oskaloosa, Iowa. He received his Ph.D. from Pennsylvania State University and is the author of *The Seventy-Sixth Congress and World War II, 1939–1940* (1979) and *Congress and the Waning of the New Deal* (1980), and the editor of *Biographical Dictionary of American Sports* (1988–   ).

DONALD A. RAKESTRAW is an assistant professor of history at Georgia Southern University. He received his Ph.D. from the University of Alabama and is currently completing a manuscript on the Anglo-American controversy over the Oregon Territory in the 1840s.

WILLIAM G. RATLIFF is a lecturer in the department of history at Texas A&M University. He received his Ph.D. from Texas Tech University and is the author of *Faithful to the Fatherland: Julius Curtius and Weimar Foreign Policy* (1990) and the associate editor of *Historical Dictionary of European Imperialism* (1991).

JAMES J. SACK is an associate professor of history at the University of Illinois at Chicago. He received his Ph.D. from the University of Michigan and is the author of *The Grenvillites, 1801–1829: Party Politics and Factionalism in the Age of Pitt and Liverpool* (1979).

RICHARD V. SALISBURY is professor of history at Western Kentucky University. He received his Ph.D. from the University of Kansas and is the author of *Anti-Imperialism and International Competition in Central America, 1920–1929* (1988) and *Costa Rica y el Istmo* (1984).

MARIJAN SALOPEK teaches in the department of history at the University of British Columbia in Vancouver. He received his Ph.D. from Cambridge University and is the author of "Western Canadians and Civil Defence," *Prairie Forum* 14, 1 (1989). He is currently completing a book on the French ministry of colonies from 1894 to 1914.

LOWELL J. SATRE teaches in the department of history at Youngstown State University in Ohio. He received his Ph.D. from the University of South Carolina and is the author of several articles on late Victorian and Edwardian Britain.

STEVEN E. SIRY is an assistant professor of history at Baldwin-Wallace College in Ohio. He received his Ph.D. from the University of Cincinnati and has published articles on early nineteenth-century American politics.

JOHN D. STANLEY is affiliated with the Ontario Ministry of Education. He received his Ph.D. from the University of Toronto and has published articles on the Duchy of Warsaw in the early nineteenth century.

S. J. STEARNS teaches in the history department of the College of Staten Island, a part of the City University of New York. He received his Ph.D. from the University of California at Berkeley and is the author of articles on English military history in the sixteenth and seventeenth centuries. He is also a contributor to *The Biographical Dictionary of British Radicals in the Seventeenth Century* (1982).

DAVID STEIGERWALD is an assistant professor of history at the Marion campus of Ohio State University. He received his Ph.D. from the University of Rochester and is the author of articles on Woodrow Wilson and Wilsonianism.

TAYLOR STULTS is professor of history at Muskingum College in Ohio. He received his Ph.D. from the University of Missouri and is the author of numerous articles on modern Soviet history. He is currently completing an extensive revision of the late Melvin Wren's *The Course of Russian History*.

FRANZ A.J. SZABO teaches in the department of history at Carleton University in Ottawa, Canada. He received his Ph.D. from the University of Alberta and is the author of numerous articles on Kaunitz in Austrian, Italian, and North American journals. He is completing the first major biography of Kaunitz.

FRANK W. THACKERAY is professor of history at Indiana University Southeast in New Albany. He received his Ph.D. from Temple University and is the author of *Antecedents of Revolution: Alexander I and the Polish Congress Kingdom* (1980) as well as numerous articles on Russian-Polish relations in the nineteenth century and Polish-American relations in the twentieth century. He is a former Fulbright scholar in Poland.

WILLIAM N. TILCHIN teaches history at Rhode Island College in Providence, Rhode Island. He received his Ph.D. from Brown University and is the author of articles on Theodore Roosevelt and his foreign policy.

ANDREW P. TROUT is professor of history at Indiana University Southeast in New Albany. He received his Ph.D. from the University of Notre Dame and is the author of *Jean-Baptiste Colbert* (1978) as well as numerous articles on seventeenth-century France, the tontine, and the economic policies of Alexander Hamilton.

ELEANOR L. TURK is professor of history at Indiana University East in Richmond. She received her Ph.D. from the University of Wisconsin and has published numerous articles on German history in the Wilhelmian period. She is currently working on a book dealing with civil liberty in Wilhelmian Germany.

RICHARD A. VOELTZ is an associate professor of history at Cameron University in Lawton, Oklahoma. He received his Ph.D. from the University of California at Los Angeles and is the author of *German Colonialism and the South West Africa Company* (1988) as well as numerous articles and contributions to reference books.

PAUL R. WAIBEL is an associate professor of history at Liberty University in Virginia. He received his Ph.D. from West Virginia University and is a former Fulbright scholar in Germany. He is the author of *Politics of Accommodation: German Social Democracy and the Catholic Church* (1983).

A. MARTIN WAINWRIGHT teaches at the University of Akron in Ohio. He received his Ph.D. from the University of Wisconsin and is currently working on a book examining aspects of British policy toward India in the period just before decolonization.

FRANKLIN A. WALKER is professor emeritus at Loyola University of Chicago. He received his Ph.D. from Cornell University and has published articles on early nineteenth-century Russia and Russian-Polish relations at that time.

WILLIAM T. WALKER is the chair of the department of humanities and associate professor of history at the Philadelphia College of Pharmacy. He received his Ph.D. from the University of South Carolina and is the author of *Disraeli: An Annotated Bibliography* (forthcoming).

WILLIAM EARL WEEKS teaches at San Diego State University. He received his Ph.D. from the University of California at San Diego and is the author of *John Quincy Adams and American Global Empire* (1992).

W. MICHAEL WEIS teaches at Illinois Wesleyan University. He received his Ph.D. from Ohio State University and is the author of *The Demise of the Brazilian-American Alliance, 1945–1964* (1992) as well as articles on aspects of U.S.–Latin American relations.

WILLIAM WEISBERGER is professor of history at Butler County Community College in Pennsylvania. He received his Ph.D. from the University of Pittsburgh and is the author of several articles and contributions to reference works on Masonry and on Benjamin Franklin.

THOMAS PHILLIP WOLF is professor of political science at Indiana University Southeast in New Albany. He received his Ph.D. from Stanford University. He has contributed to *Great Lives from History: Twentieth Century* (1990) and has published other articles and reviews on politics in Great Britain and the state of New Mexico.